YEARBOOK OF AMERICAN & CANADIAN CHURCHES 2002

Previous Issues

Year of Publication/Title		*Editor*
1916	Federal Council Year Book	H. K. Carroll
1917	Federal Council Year Book	H. K. Carroll
1918	Yearbook of the Churches	C. F. Armitage
1919	Yearbook of the Churches	C. F. Armitage
1920	Yearbook of the Churches	S. R. Warburton
1922	Yearbook of the Churches	E. O. Watson
1923	Yearbook of the Churches	E. O. Watson
1925	Yearbook of the Churches	E. O. Watson
1927	The Handbook of the Churches	B. S. Winchester
1931	The New Handbook of the Churches	Charles Steizle
1933	Yearbook of American Churches	H. C. Weber
1935	Yearbook of American Churches	H. C. Weber
1937	Yearbook of American Churches	H. C. Weber
1939	Yearbook of American Churches	H. C. Weber
1941	Yearbook of American Churches	B. Y. Landis
1943	Yearbook of American Churches	B. Y. Landis
1945	Yearbook of American Churches	B. Y. Landis
1947	Yearbook of American Churches	B. Y. Landis, G. F. Ketcham
1949	Yearbook of American Churches	G. F. Ketcham
1951	Yearbook of American Churches	G. F. Ketcham
1952	Yearbook of American Churches	B. Y. Landis
1953	Yearbook of American Churches	B. Y. Landis
1954	Yearbook of American Churches	B. Y. Landis
1955	Yearbook of American Churches	B. Y. Landis
1956	Yearbook of American Churches	B. Y. Landis
1957	Yearbook of American Churches	B. Y. Landis
1958	Yearbook of American Churches	B. Y. Landis
1959	Yearbook of American Churches	B. Y. Landis
1960	Yearbook of American Churches	B. Y. Landis
1961	Yearbook of American Churches	B. Y. Landis
1962	Yearbook of American Churches	B. Y. Landis
1963	Yearbook of American Churches	B. Y. Landis
1964	Yearbook of American Churches	B. Y. Landis
1965	Yearbook of American Churches	B. Y. Landis
1966	Yearbook of American Churches	C. H. Jacquet
1967	Yearbook of American Churches	L. B. Whitman
1968	Yearbook of American Churches	L. B. Whitman
1969	Yearbook of American Churches	C. H. Jacquet
1970	Yearbook of American Churches	C. H. Jacquet
1971	Yearbook of American Churches	C. H. Jacquet
1972	Yearbook of American Churches	C. H. Jacquet
1973	Yearbook of American & Canadian Churches	C. H. Jacquet
1974	Yearbook of American & Canadian Churches	C. H. Jacquet
1975	Yearbook of American & Canadian Churches	C. H. Jacquet
1976	Yearbook of American & Canadian Churches	C. H. Jacquet
1977	Yearbook of American & Canadian Churches	C. H. Jacquet
1978	Yearbook of American & Canadian Churches	C. H. Jacquet
1979	Yearbook of American & Canadian Churches	C. H. Jacquet
1980	Yearbook of American & Canadian Churches	C. H. Jacquet
1981	Yearbook of American & Canadian Churches	C. H. Jacquet
1982	Yearbook of American & Canadian Churches	C. H. Jacquet
1983	Yearbook of American & Canadian Churches	C. H. Jacquet
1984	Yearbook of American & Canadian Churches	C. H. Jacquet
1985	Yearbook of American & Canadian Churches	C. H. Jacquet
1986	Yearbook of American & Canadian Churches	C. H. Jacquet
1987	Yearbook of American & Canadian Churches	C. H. Jacquet
1988	Yearbook of American & Canadian Churches	C. H. Jacquet
1989	Yearbook of American & Canadian Churches	C. H. Jacquet
1990	Yearbook of American & Canadian Churches	C. H. Jacquet
1991	Yearbook of American & Canadian Churches	C. H. Jacquet, Alice M. Jones
1992	Yearbook of American & Canadian Churches	Kenneth B. Bedell, Alice M. Jones
1993	Yearbook of American & Canadian Churches	Kenneth B. Bedell
1994	Yearbook of American & Canadian Churches	Kenneth B. Bedell
1995	Yearbook of American & Canadian Churches	Kenneth B. Bedell
1996	Yearbook of American & Canadian Churches	Kenneth B. Bedell
1997	Yearbook of American & Canadian Churches	Kenneth B. Bedell
1998	Yearbook of American & Canadian Churches	Eileen W. Lindner
1999	Yearbook of American & Canadian Churches	Eileen W. Lindner
2000	Yearbook of American & Canadian Churches	Eileen W. Lindner
2001	Yearbook of American & Canadian Churches	Eileen W. Lindner

Seventieth Issue Annual

YEARBOOK OF AMERICAN & CANADIAN CHURCHES 2002

Edited by Eileen W. Lindner

Prepared and edited for the
National Council of the Churches of Christ in the U.S.A.
475 Riverside Drive, New York, NY 10115-0050

Published and Distributed
by Abingdon Press
Nashville

YEARBOOK OF AMERICAN & CANADIAN CHURCHES
2002

Telephone: (212) 870-2031

Fax: (212) 870-2817

E-mail: yearbook@ncccusa.org

Printed in the United States of America
ISBN 0-687-06435-X
ISSN 0195-9034
Library of Congress catalog card number
16-5726

Preparation of this *Yearbook* is an annual project of the National Council of the Churches of Christ in the United States of America.

This is the seventieth edition of a yearbook that was first published in 1916. Previous editions have been entitled: *Federal Council Yearbook* (1916-1917), *Yearbook of the Churches* (1918-1925), The *Handbook of the Churches* (1927), *The New Handbook of the Churches* (1928), *Yearbook of American Churches* (1933-1972), and *Yearbook of American & Canadian Churches* (1973-2001).

Eileen W. Lindner — *Editor*
Marcel A. Welty — *Redevelopment & Technical Director*

Nathan Hanson — *Assistant Editor*

Contents

Editor's Preface

It has become axiomatic to note the ways in which the events of September 11, 2001 have wrought change in nearly every aspect of American culture. The area of religious research is not immune to this effect. As we go to press at the beginning of Advent 2001, church attendance data, which is collected by other researchers, continue to show an increase in post-September 11th church attendance. While this rise in church attendance is likely to be transitory, it will be some time before the full impact of these tragic events upon religious faith and practice can be measured.

The editorial office of the *Yearbook of American & Canadian Churches* is located in New York City, and we too have been affected by the attack on the World Trade Centers and its dire consequences. The events of September 11th followed by the anthrax deaths and continued fears make 2001 a year like no other. In the pages that follow we have striven to place on record our annual accounting of membership, financial records, personnel assignments, church changes, and myriad details that help shape the American religious landscape at this strained moment in time.

As is annually the case, our work is dependent on the efforts of thousands of others some of whom are known to us and many of whom are not. We are grateful again, as we are each year, for the efforts of all who take the time and care to furnish us with statistical information, church information updates, and other annual reports that are essential to the timeliness and accuracy of the *Yearbook*. All deserve our thanks and respect for a difficult task done with great dedication and, in most instances, with good cheer. Further, all deserve our assurance that neither the *Yearbook* editorial staff nor Abingdon Press uses the information gathered to prepare and distribute lists for commercial solicitation, except in those limited circumstances related to the publication and distribution of the *Yearbook* itself.

New Electronic Format

We are delighted on this 70th anniversary of the *Yearbook of American & Canadian Churches* to announce the first electronic edition of the *Yearbook*. The print and electronic editions of the *Yearbook* are bundled together, so that purchasers of the print edition also have access to the electronic edition. The electronic edition will allow us to update the Yearbook throughout the year, providing even better information service to our readers. We will continue to print a hardcopy of the *Yearbook* once a year.

24/7 online access to the electronic edition is included with your purchase of this print edition of the *Yearbook*. Whether looking for the name, address, or phone number of a a particular person or searching for information about a particular religious body, you will be able to take advantage of look-up queries that are offered with the online edition of the *Yearbook*. The queries will enable you to search the full text of the *Yearbook*.

A unique serial number is printed inside the back cover of this print copy of the *Yearbook*. This serial number will authorize the buyer's online subscription to the *Yearbook* database for a period of up to 12 months, depending on the date of purchase. Detailed instructions on accessing the electronic edition are also to be found inside the back cover of this volume.

We also wish to announce the availability of the *Yearbook of American & Canadian Churches* Historic Archive CD. This disk contains all financial and membership data from 1916 to 2000 for more than fifty denominations. The archive may be previewed at www.ElectronicChurch.org/index-CD.html. It may be ordered toll-free at (888) 870-3325.

2002 Yearbook Highlights

- Last year's theme chapter "Considering Charitable Choice" was published precisely at the moment President Bush was announcing his related initiative on faith-based organizations. The chapter was frequently reprinted and was published electronically on Beliefnet. In the course of the year the *Yearbook* editor has been actively engaged in a number of the discussions and arenas in which the outlines of a national consensus concerning faith-based initiatives have begun to emerge. The theme section of this edition of the *Yearbook* offers an overview of where we have been, where we are now, and where we might go as the national debate around faith-based initiatives takes on legislative form and programmatic reality.
- The rankings by membership represented in **Table 2** in the "Perspectives on America's Religious Landscape" measures the relative numerical strength of one church in relation to others. For most of the twentieth century the positions of the nation's largest churches remained stable. In the last thirty years there have been highly noted displacements of "old line" or mainline churches. For instance, according to the figures reported by the *Yearbook* in 1970, while the Catholic Church and the Southern Baptist Convention were ranked first and second respectively, they were followed in order by The United Methodist Church, the Episcopal Church, and the Lutheran Church in America. The top five ranked churches today are more diverse theologically and racially, with only The United Methodist Church remaining to represent mainline churches within the top five. The Church of Jesus Christ of Latter-day Saints is, for the first time, ranked among the top five churches.
- In addition to membership data the *Yearbook* is noted for its annual report of financial contributions. The number of national churches reporting full financial data has risen from 62 in the 2001 edition to 65 in the 2002 edition. Of greater interest and importance is that all giving rose by $2.4 billion to a nearly $30 billion. Benevolent giving, that is, giving for those in most dire need, rose from 16% to 17% of revenue.
- Some interesting trends in seminary enrollment are noted in the data reported by the Association of Theological Schools. Between 1990-2000 the enrollment figures increased from approximately 59,000 to 73,000. Further, diversity among students enrolled in theological schools continues to broaden. In 1990 women accounted for 30% of total enrollment; in 2000, 35%.

It is our hope that you find both the printed and electronic versions of the *Yearbook of American & Canadian Churches* to be valuable resources in your work.

Eileen W. Lindner
Editor

I

PERSPECTIVES ON AMERICA'S RELIGIOUS LANDSCAPE

Trends & Developments, 2002

The longevity represented by this 70th edition of the *Yearbook of American & Canadian Churches* provides a unique perspective from which to view the demographic changes in the American religious landscape. The churches on which we report are often exceedingly large, some with membership in the tens of millions. Data collection practices vary widely from church to church; and even within a given church, collection procedures and practices are rarely uniform. Added to these realities are a number of other factors that affect data collection, including widely disparate levels of sophistication in research personnel and in computer technology, differences in reporting timeframes, and variations regarding the precise definition of membership. Given these factors and the sheer size of the samples being measured, the difficulty of identifying trends and patterns would be insurmountable for an effort spanning only a few years or even a decade. However, the now seven decades of effort represented by the *Yearbook of American & Canadian Churches* (compiled in a comprehensive historic archive available on CD-ROM) provide a longitudinal backdrop for the analysis that follows. Only through such a decades-long study of growth and decline in membership are we able to capture and analyze the emerging patterns. Our annual analysis of trends and developments should be regarded as a snapshot taken at a precise moment in history. The meaning of the figures within that snapshot will best be given definition by the larger and longer context of which they are a part.

With this understanding of the inherent limitations of analyzing year to year changes, we offer the following analysis of the data reported for the year 2000. (N.B. Data reports run a full two years behind the "edition" year of the *Yearbook*).

Longitudinal Membership

Table 1 represents a longitudinal view of composite membership growth for all churches reporting to the *Yearbook*. The current figures are consistent with the slow pattern of increase in membership over the years. Other researchers may wish to make comparative studies of these membership figures in relation to new census data and analogous data for prior years. Note that these figures do not reflect the entirety of national church membership, since some churches do not report to the *Yearbook*. With over 152 million adherents, the churches collectively continue to maintain a substantial organizational and institutional presence within the United States.

Table 1
INCLUSIVE MEMBERSHIP 1890–2000

Year	Membership	Source	Year	Membership	Source
1890	41,699,342	CRB	1965	124,682,422	YBAC
1906	35,068,058	CRB	1966	125,778,656	YBAC
1916	41,926,852	CRB	1967	126,445,110	YBAC
1926	54,576,346	CRB	1968	128,469,636	YBAC
1931	59,268,764	CH	1969	128,505,084	YBAC
1932	60,157,392	CH	1970	131,045,053	YBAC
1933	60,812,624	CH	1971	131,389,642	YBAC
1934	62,007,376	CH	1972	131,424,564	YBAC
1935	62,678,177	CH	1973	131,245,139	YBAC
1936	55,807,366	CRB	1974	131,871,743	YBACC
1936	63,221,996	CH	1975	131,012,953	YBACC
1937	63,848,094	CH	1976	131,897,539	YBACC
1938	64,156,895	YBAC	1977	131,812,470	YBACC
1940	64,501,594	YBAC	1978	133,388,776	YBACC
1942	68,501,186	YBAC	1979	133,469,690	YBACC
1944	72,492,699	YBAC	1980	134,816,943	YBACC
1945	71,700,142	CH	1981	138,452,614	YBACC
1946	73,673,182	CH	1982	139,603,059	YBACC
1947	77,386,188	CH	1983	140,816,385	YBACC
1948	79,435,605	CH	1984	142,172,138	YBACC
1949	81,862,328	CH	1985	142,926,363	YBACC
1950	86,830,490	YBAC	1986	142,799,662	YBACC
1951	88,673,005	YBAC	1987	143,830,806	YBACC
1952	92,277,129	YBAC	1988	145,383,739	YBACC
1953	94,842,845	YBAC	1989	147,607,394	YBACC
1954	97,482,611	YBAC	1990	156,331,704	YBACC
1955	100,162,529	YBAC	1991	156,629,918	YBACC
1956	103,224,954	YBAC	1992	156,557,746	YBACC
1957	104,189,678	YBAC	1993	153,127,045	YBACC
1958	109,557,741	YBAC	1994	158,218,427	YBACC
1959	112,226,905	YBAC	1995	157,984,194	YBACC
1960	114,449,217	YBAC	1996	159,471,758	YBACC
1961	116,109,929	YBAC	1997	157,503,033	YBACC
1962	117,946,002	YBAC	1998*	150,105,525	YBACC
1963	120,965,238	YBAC	1999*	151,161,906	YBACC
1964	123,307,499	YBAC	2000*	152,145,344	YBACC

*Note: The total membership figure for this year excludes the membership of the National Baptist Convention, U.S.A., Inc., which has been included in the total membership figure of earlier years.

CRB—Census of Religious Bodies, Bureau of the Census, Washington
CH—*The Christian Herald*, New York
YBAC—*Yearbook of American Churches*, New York
YBACC—*Yearbook of American and Canadian Churches*, New York

Church Membership Ranking

Table 2 enables us to look at the present size of churches relative to one another. Again, caution is advised in analyzing the data, lest one draw a greater inference from such a table than is warranted. Some denominations exercise influence out of proportion to their numbers when measured by other indices. One thinks, for example, of the number of Episcopalians serving in Congress; such representation would be disproportional to the size of the denomination. The social influence or prominence of a church is not solely a function of its ranking by membership.

Nevertheless, several interesting features emerge in this year's ranking. For the first time The Church of Jesus Christ of Latter-Day Saints is reported within the five largest churches. This ranking represents a very brisk

Table 2
US MEMBERSHIP DENOMINATIONAL RANKING: Largest 25 Churches*

Denomination Name	Inclusive Membership	Percent of Total Reported	Cumulative Percentage
The Catholic Church	63,683,030	41.86%	41.86%
Southern Baptist Convention	15,960,308	10.49%	52.35%
The United Methodist Church	8,340,954	5.48%	57.83%
The Church of God in Christ	5,499,875	3.61%	61.44%
The Church of Jesus Christ of Latter-day Saints	5,208,827	3.42%	64.87%
Evangelical Lutheran Church in America	5,125,919	3.37%	68.24%
National Baptist Convention of America, Inc.	3,500,000	2.30%	70.54%
Presbyterian Church (U.S.A.)	3,485,332	2.29%	72.83%
Assemblies of God	2,577,560	1.69%	74.52%
The Lutheran Church—Missouri Synod (LCMS)	2,554,088	1.68%	76.20%
Progressive National Baptist Convention, Inc.	2,500,000	1.64%	77.84%
African Methodist Episcopal Church	2,500,000	1.64%	79.49%
National Missionary Baptist Convention of America	2,500,000	1.64%	81.13%
Episcopal Church	2,311,398	1.52%	82.65%
Greek Orthodox Archdiocese of America	1,500,000	0.99%	83.64%
Pentecostal Assemblies of the World, Inc.	1,500,000	0.99%	84.62%
Churches of Christ	1,500,000	0.99%	85.61%
American Baptist Churches in the U.S.A.	1,436,909	0.94%	86.55%
United Church of Christ	1,377,320	0.91%	87.46%
African Methodist Episcopal Zion Church	1,296,662	0.85%	88.31%
Baptist Bible Fellowship International	1,200,000	0.79%	89.10%
Christian Churches and Churches of Christ	1,071,616	0.70%	89.80%
The Orthodox Church in America	1,000,000	0.66%	90.46%
Jehovah's Witnesses	998,166	0.66%	91.12%
Church of God (Cleveland, Tennessee)	895,536	0.58%	91.70%

*The National Baptist Convention U.S.A., Inc., one of the ten largest churches in the U.S., is currently at work producing an actual count to be available in subsequent editions.

increase in membership for a church with a relatively brief history (founded in 1830). The distinctive theological position of the LDS and its history of persecution make such rapid growth all the more remarkable; however, the church's strong emphasis in outreach through both mission personnel and electronic and print advertising makes it unique among contemporary North American churches. While the international growth of the LDS is beyond the scope of this *Yearbook*, it too is remarkable and unprecedented for an American- born church.

The Evangelical Lutheran Church in America moved out of the top five ranking. As a result, The United Methodist Church is the sole remaining "mainline Protestant" church in the top five. The five largest Christian bodies in the U.S. are far more diverse theologically, racially, and socially than the protestant cultural hegemony of an earlier age would have suggested. The Southern Baptist Convention, although still regionally based, is the nation's largest Protestant body. The Church of God in Christ, long the largest Black Pentecostal church, is now among the five largest denominations, indicative of the growth of Pentecostal churches. (Another instance of this phenomenon can be seen in the advancement in the rankings of Assemblies of God, moving from tenth to ninth.) The Catholic Church retains its primacy of place as the largest church.

Table 3
PATTERNS OF US MEMBERSHIP CHANGE OF SELECTED LARGE CHURCHES 1997–2000

Denomination	1997 Membership Change	Percentage Change	1998 Membership Change	Percentage Change	1999 Membership Change	Percentage Change	2000 Membership Change	Percentage Change
The Catholic Church	355,855	0.58	810,522	1.30	373,048	0.60	1,291,546	2.07
Southern Baptist Convention	199,550	1.25	-162,158	-1.03	122,400	0.77	108,522	0.68
The United Methodist Church	-44,005	-0.52	-40,539	-0.48	-33,841	-0.40	-36,708	-0.44
Evangelical Lutheran Church in America	4,145	0.08	-6,830	-0.13	-28,557	-0.55	-23,749	-0.46
The Church of Jesus Christ of Latter-Day Saints	123,100	2.50	99,951	1.99	90,358	1.78	95,418	1.87
Presbyterian Church (U.S.A.)	-26,622	-0.74	-35,794	-0.99	-13,775	-0.39	-75,852	-2.13
The Lutheran Church—Missouri Synod	1,892	0.07	-8,632	-0.33	-11,964	-0.46	-28,352	-1.1
Assemblies of God	26,986	1.08	31,238	1.25	48,719	1.90	3,029	0.12
American Baptist Churches in the U.S.A.	2,066	0.14	2,067	0.14	-53,012	-3.64	-17,479	-1.2

Table 4
US FINANCIAL SUMMARIES 1993-2000

Year	Number Reporting	Full or Confirmed Members	Inclusive Members	Total Contributions	Per Capita Full or Confirmed Members	Per Capita Inclusive Members	Total Congregational Contributions
1993	52	41,842,642	46,667,687	$19,631,560,798	$469.18	$420.67	$16,152,245,431
1994	47	40,997,058	44,886,207	$15,308,625,032	$373.41	$341.05	$15,308,625,032
1995	55	43,104,555	48,115,704	$21,433,517,908	$497.24	$445.46	$17,743,597,668
1996	55	43,321,039	50,047,599	$24,970,133,464	$576.40	$498.93	$20,422,403,297
1997	58	44,804,383	49,936,836	$25,181,416,276	$562.03	$504.27	$21,212,711,615
1998	62	44,574,101	49,679,497	$26,242,626,313	$588.74	$528.24	$22,202,379,038
1999	62	44,288,906	49,196,965	$26,997,610,588	$609.58	$548.77	$22,801,548,715
2000	65	44,401,451	49,178,675	$29,464,889,024	$663.60	$559.14	$24,475,897,453

Year	Per Capita Full or Confirmed Members	Per Capita Inclusive Members	Total Benevolences	Per Capita Full or Confirmed Members	Per Capita Inclusive Members	Benevolences as a Percentage of Total Contributions
1993	$386.02	$346.11	$3,481,455,047	$83.20	$74.60	18%
1994	$373.41	$341.05	$3,259,090,326	$79.50	$72.61	21%
1995	$411.64	$368.77	$3,689,920,239	$85.60	$76.69	17%
1996	$471.42	$408.06	$3,739,584,874	$86.32	$74.72	15%
1997	$473.45	$424.79	$3,968,704,661	$88.58	$79.47	16%
1998	$498.10	$446.91	$4,040,247,275	$90.64	$81.33	15%
1999	$514.84	$463.47	$4,197,087,981	$94.77	$85.31	16%
2000	$551.24	$497.69	$4,988,352,266	$112.35	$101.43	17%

Patterns of Membership Gains and Losses

Table 3 provides a comparative longitudinal study of nine large churches. While shifts in patterns for one year ought not to be considered a "trend," consistency in ***direction*** and/or ***rate*** of growth or decline over several years may be predictive of an emerging pattern; thus readers should attend to both the raw numbers and the percentages of change.

The Catholic Church shows an acceleration in the rate of growth. This acceleration may be attributed to a combination of factors, including: a high replacement rate secondary to a relatively high birth rate, the Catholic affiliation of nearly 45% of all new immigrant populations, changes in reporting practices, and observance of a special "Jubilee" emphasis on evangelism.

For most churches, both the direction and the rate of change have remained largely consistent when compared with figures reported in recent editions of the *Yearbook*. However, some slowing of the rate of growth for the Southern Baptist Convention and the Assemblies of God will bear closer observation in the years ahead.

Constancy in the direction of change was recorded by the Lutheran Church Missouri Synod and the American Baptist Churches, both of which reported declines in membership. With respect to the rate of change, however, the Lutheran Church Missouri Synod recorded an accelerated rate of decline while the American Baptist Churches reported a reduced rate.

The Presbyterian Church (U.S.A.) figures report what appears to be a rather accelerated rate of decline at 2.13%. This accelerated rate may be attributable to reporting practices that call for "cleaning" church rolls every three years.

Financial Trends

Table 4 reports on U.S. financial data for 2000. The annual report of contributions demonstrates that local congregations continue to collect and disburse substantial monies, now totaling nearly $30 billion. In any given year the list of churches that elect to report on finances may differ somewhat from that of previous years; hence, caution is advised when drawing conclusions from these data. Sixty-five churches, an all-time high, reported on finances for the 2002 edition of the *Yearbook.*

Many church leaders will find the reported increase of contributions in all categories to be heartening, as they indicate greater resources available to fund ministries and missions. Indeed, the increase reported this year is the largest in a decade, in terms of both the total dollars contributed per capita of inclusive membership (up $50.37) and the contributions for benevolence per capita of inclusive membership (up $16.12). While the three additional reporting churches would account for some of this increase, the strength of the U.S. economy during the reporting period offers a more satisfying explanation, since an observable increase remains present when figures for the newly reporting churches are excluded. Overall, the increase in reported giving totals $2,467,278,436. There has been a marked increase in benevolence giving as a percentage of total contributions, from 16% to 17%. These financial figures provide an important baseline for comparison as the U.S. economy enters a period of uncertainty.

The Fevered Frenzy Over Faith-Based Initiatives

Eileen W. Lindner, Editor

Just as the *Yearbook of American & Canadian Churches 2001* was published last February, the Washington press corps and much of the nation were briefly consumed by a debate over the relative roles of religious organizations and the government in addressing the most profound social needs among the poor, the elderly, the destitute, and the very young. What led to the fevered frenzy was not a sudden outpouring of compassion for those in need. Nor was the debate occasioned by an overpowering national compulsion to address with finality an array of social ills such as unemployment, substance abuse, homelessness, or juvenile delinquency. The origins of the rigorous and sometimes heated debate about the capacity of faith-based institutions to provide social service with public funds derived from at least two very different impulses. One of the driving forces was a rather clear and simple idea that religious organizations can provide cost-effective social services, thus reducing the burden on (and perhaps the inefficiencies of) the federal government. This theme, initiated with Charitable Choice, seemed to build on the philosophic approach of other earlier Republican ideas, such as the "Points of Light." Enthusiasts saw in the administration's initiative the possibility of a small governmental structure built on high moral ground. The White House Office of Faith-Based Initiatives was created in the document "Rallying the Armies of Compassion." The very title suggested the kind of broad and bold hopes being bandied about. A second source of energy infused the debate. This energy arose from a more cautious, even wary, sense of vigilance emanating from the quarters of those concerned about church/state issues and the dangers of a government far too comfortable in partnership with churches.

Surveying the scene a year ago the *Yearbook of American & Canadian Churches* argued that too little empirical social science research had been done to measure the claims to either cost-effectiveness or success in a way that could inform the national debate. Now, a year later; the first director of the White House Office has come and gone, the departments of government have dutifully produced a catalog of "obstacles" to be overcome if religious and community groups are to compete on a level playing field, and the whole issue of faith-based initiatives has been supplanted by the attacks of September 11th and the pursuit of an overseas war. Yet, an economic slowdown and the persistent commitment of the religious community to the poor cause us to return to this theme and once again document the significant advances in framing the national debate that must inevitably accompany any legislation that would extend the concepts of Charitable Choice to broader areas of social service provision by faith-based organizations.

Religious leaders and civil libertarians are quick to point out the long history of religiously-based efforts to alleviate human suffering. Yet the very same groups have sounded a warning note that important American traditions of church/state separation could be imperiled by the rush to find the kind of cost-effective delivery of social services that would enable politically popular tax cuts. Moreover, faith-based organizations, over time, could grow dependent upon public monies and shrink from social criticism, thereby forsaking the prophetic witness they sought to offer. Only by engagement of persons from varying points of view could an approach be envisioned to enable partnerships at the community level that utilized the most trusted local resources fueled with public dollars to promote individual and community development.

During the course of 2001 several outstanding initiatives were taken to produce documents and reports that will do much to further the national dialogue and which will help frame that discussion so that progress is attained in both social welfare and constitutional understanding. While many other resources and publications exist and can easily be located through conventional or Internet research, the *Yearbook* would identify the following as particularly promising in fostering a new consensus:

1) In May the First Amendment Center published "Partnership or Peril" which recognized areas of agreement and disagreement and concluded that, "At present, there seems to be little chance of finding common ground.... Ultimately the issue will be decided by the Supreme Court."
2) In May the Urban Institute's Center on Nonprofits and Philanthropy and Harvard University's Hauser Center for Nonprofit Organizations held a seminar and later published a report entitled "Faith-Based Initiatives: Sacred Deeds and Secular Dollars". This report called for additional research to establish the potential gains of such an approach while recognizing the reality that the issue of faith-based partnership has been placed irretrievably on the national agenda.
3) In July the Aspen Institute's Nonprofit Sector Strategy Group convened a week-long seminar that brought together both Strategy Group members and a number of persons with expertise in religious social service provision and church/state issues. The report of this collegium entitled, "Religious Organizations and Government" enumerated guiding principles, which will need to be observed in any legislation that seeks to maintain appropriate church/state relationships while enabling social service provision. The report comes to some cautious conclusions about ways in which the potential for religious organizations to be involved in social problem solving can be realized while preserving important church/state distance.
4) A series of Brookings Institution conferences culminated in the December release of a book entitled "Sacred Places, Civic Purposes: Should Government Help Faith-Based Charity?" Released at New York's Abyssinian Baptist Church (a site for much publicly-funded social service), this volume offers a host of case studies of social service provision and reinforces both the disparate need for partnerships and the potential for the unacceptable loss of religious capacity for social criticism.

I. TYPOLOGY: FAITH CHARACTERISTICS OF SOCIAL SERVICE AND EDUCATIONAL ORGANIZATIONS

	Faith-Saturated	Faith-Centered	Faith-Related	Faith Background	Faith-Secular Partnership	Secular
1. Mission Statement	Explicitly religious	Explicitly religious	May be either explicit or implicit	Implicit (e.g. general reference to "promoting values")	No reference to religion in mission of the partnership or the secular partner	No spiritual content, but implicit or explicit references to values often present
2. Founding	By religious group or for religious purpose	By religious group or for religious purpose	By religious group or for religious purpose	May or may not be founded by religious group	No reference to spiritual views of founder	No reference to spiritual views of founders
3. Controlling Board	Explicitly religious. May be a) self-perpetuating board with explicit religious criteria; b) board elected by a religious body	Explicitly religious. May be a) self-perpetuating board with explicit religious criteria; b) board elected by a religious body.	Some board members may be required or expected to have a particular faith or ecclesiastical commitment but not all	Board might have been explicitly religious at one time, but is now inter-faith; very little concern for faith commitment of board	Program controlled by secular partners, with heavy input from faith partners.	No discussion of faith commitment of board members
4. Selection of Senior Management	Faith commitment an explicit prerequisite	Faith commitment understood to be a prerequisite	Normally (perhaps by unwritten expectation) share the founders' faith	Not relevant whether they share the faith commitment of founders.	Required to have respect for, but not to share partners' faith	To consider faith commitment considered improper
5. Selection of other staff	Religious faith is very important at all levels, and most staff share organization's faith commitments	Religious faith is very important for faith-centered projects, but is sometimes less important in other projects. Most staff share founders' faith commitments.	Project staff expected to have knowledge, sensitivity to faith commitment of founders; religious beliefs motivate some staff/volunteers	Almost no attention to whether any staff share a faith commitment; religious beliefs may motivate some staff/volunteers	Staff expected to understand, and respect faith of partners; program relies significantly on volunteers from faith-based organizations.	No consideration of faith commitment of any staff
6. If affiliated with an external agency, is that agency religious?	Yes	Yes	Often	Sometimes	Sometimes	No
7. Financial Support	Overwhelming if not all from private (often) religious sources	Substantially private; explicit policy of refusing funds that would undermine above policies (1-5.)	Funding is a mix of religious and secular sources (private and/or government)	Majority of funding is from secular sources (private and/or government)	Major funding from secular sources; in-kind contributions of space and time from faith-partners.	No attention to religious commitments of donors; virtually all funding is from secular sources.
8. Receives reimbursement for entitlement benefits (e.g., food stamps, Medicaid/ Medicare, child care)	Often, but encounter different conditions among different programs, levels of government, and administrators	Often, but not automatic; may encounter rejection or resistance based on program content.	Usually	Always	Always	Always
9. Would requiring a separate 501(c)3 be considered problematic?	Yes for some, no for others	Usually not	Almost never	Almost never	Not for secular partner, yes if faith-based partners were required to do so	Never

II. TYPOLOGY: FAITH CHARACTERISTICS OF PROGRAMS/PROJECTS

	Faith-Saturated	Faith-Centered	Faith-Related	Faith Background	Faith-Secular Partnership	Secular
1. Religious Content of Program	Explicit, extensive mandatory religious content integrated throughout the program; staff and clients are expected to engage in religious activities.	Explicit religious content that is usually integrated with social service provision, but not to the degree that clients cannot opt out of explicitly religious activities. May be segregated into separate components (e.g., when mandated by government funding.) Staff are explicit about their faith commitments but respect the option of nonparticipation.	Very little religious program content and entirely optional; clients may be invited to participate in religious activities outside program parameters, or hold informal conversations with staff. The religious component is seen primarily in the act of caring for the needy rather than in involving clients in religious activities.	No explicit religious content in program. Religious materials or resources may be available to clients who seek it out. The religious component is seen primarily in the act of caring for the needy rather than in involving clients in religious activities.	No explicit reference to religious content	No reference to religious content; exclusive use of medical and social sciences
2. Main Form of Integration of Religious Content with Other Program Components *See Addendum A	Integrated /Mandatory	Integrated/Optional or Invitational	Invitational or Relational	Passive	Relational or Passive, depending on volunteers/staff	None
3. Expected Connection Between Religious Content and Outcome	Expectation of religious change and belief that such change is essential to desired outcome (e.g., drug rehab)	Strong hope for religious change and belief that such change significantly contributes to desired outcome	Little expectation that religious change or activity is necessary for desired outcome, though it may be valued for its own sake	No expectation that religious change is needed for desired outcome	Religious change is not necessary for outcomes, but it is expected that the faith of volunteers from religious partners will add value to the program	No expectation of religious change
4. Religious Environment (building, name, religious symbols)	Usually	Usually	Often	Sometimes	Sometimes (program may take place in secular or religious environment)	No

Adapted from a typology originally developed by Ronald J. Sider and Heidi Rolland Unruh, based in part on the research of the Congregations, Communities and Leadership Development Project, which they direct.

5) Finally, in June, the Search for Common Ground formed a broadly bipartisan Working Group, including civil liberties and religious groups, led by former U.S. Senator Harris Wofford (D-PA) at the request of U.S. Senator Rick Santorum (R-PA). This select group was composed of persons participating in one or more of the above venues. Working intensively from June through December, this report goes further perhaps than others in framing and surveying the topographical features of the common ground that must be occupied if the needs of America's poor and the demands of the constitutionally mandated separation of church and state are both to be addressed. Among the very promising contents of this report is a typology that was produced by Ronald J. Sider and Heidi Rolland Unruh and adapted in the course of the Working Group's discussion. (The typology on pages 16-17 is adapted from a typology originally developed by Sider and Unruh, based in part on the research of the Congregations, Communities and Leadership Development Project, which they direct.) This typology does much to advance the conversation since it enables a far better nuanced understanding of the variety of faith-based organizations that may provide services. Each type of faith-based organization raises different needs and challenges when a partnership utilizing public monies is envisioned.

This Yearbook has been privileged to participate in each of the above attempts to clarify the issues endemic to a government partnership with religiously based organizations. As we go to press legislation is anticipated that will seek to make a larger percentage of government funds for social services available to faith-based organizations under the proper circumstances. What constitutes those "proper circumstances" will never be easily defined and will require ongoing review if the best in both the free exercise clause and the non-establishment clause of the First Amendment are to be maintained. Nor will even the most universal accord on faith-based initiatives enable religious organizations to shoulder the burden of providing for the general welfare that is the duty of government. Yet, the strivings of the individuals and agencies outlined above have set a high standard of vigilance and thoughtfulness that should aid us in the near term to build upon the best of our national and cultural traditions on behalf of those in need.

- Free copies of "Partnership or Peril" (Freedom Forum Publication O. 01-F06) are available by calling (800) 830-3733 or download by visiting *http://www.freedomforum.org/templates/document.asp?documentID-13903.*
- Free copies of "Faith-Based Initiatives: Sacred Deeds and Secular Dollars" (Urban Institute) are available by calling (202) 261-2687 or (877) 847-7377.
- Free Copies of "Religious Organizations and Government" (Aspen Institute Publication No. 01-033) are available by contacting: Giulia Companaro, Nonprofit Sector Strategy Group, The Aspen Institute, One Dupont Circle, NW, Suite 700, Washington DC 20036, Tel. (202) 736-5811.
- "Sacred Places, Civic Purposes: Should Government Help Faith-Based Charity?" is available for $20.95 by calling (800) 275-1447 or (202) 797-6258 or by visiting *www.brookings.edu.*
- Search for Common Ground's Working Group report can be obtained by calling (202) 265-4300.

II

DIRECTORIES

1. United States Cooperative Organizations, National

The organizations listed in this section are cooperative religious organizations that are national in scope. Regional cooperative organizations in the United States are listed in Directory 7, "United States Regional and Local Ecumenical Bodies."

The Alban Institute, Inc.

Founded in 1974, the Alban Institute, Inc. (www.alban.org) is a non-profit, non-denominational membership organization which provides resources for vital congregations. Through its book publishing, Congregations magazine, education programs, consulting and training services, and research, the Alban Institute provides resources and services including www.congregationalresources.org, its online resource database, to congregations and judicatories of all denominations and their lay and ordained leaders.

The Institute has long been a pioneer in identifying, researching, and publishing information about key issues in the religious world such as conflict management, clergy transition, leadership, worship, and congregation size transitions. The Institute's resources include over 100 book titles, over 40 courses offered nationally each year, and a staff of senior and regional consultants located across the country ready to assist local congregations. Individuals, congregations, and institutions support Alban's work and maintain their cutting-edge skills for ministry through membership in the Institute or as constituants and consumers of Alban's products and services.

Headquarters

7315 Wisconsin Ave., Ste. 1250 W., Bethesda, MD 20814-3211 Tel. (800)486-1318

Media Contact, Marketing Director, Holly Hemphill

Officers

Pres., The Rev. James P. Wind, Ph.D.

American Bible Society

In 1816, pastors and laymen representing a variety of Christian denominations gathered in New York City to establish an organization "to disseminate the Gospel of Christ throughout the habitable world." Since that time the American Bible Society (ABS) has continued to provide God's Word, without doctrinal note or comment, wherever it is needed and in the language and format the reader can most easily use and understand. The ABS is the servant of the denominations and local churches. It provides Scriptures at exceptionally low costs in various attractive formats for their use in outreach ministries here in the United States and all across the world.

Today the ABS serves more than 100 denominations and agencies, and its board of trustees is composed of distinguished laity and clergy drawn from these Christian groups.

Fifty years ago the American Bible Society played a leading role in the founding of the United Bible Societies, a federation of 138 national Bible Societies around the world that enables global cooperation in Scripture translation, publication, and distribution in more than 200 countries and territories. The ABS contributes approximately 45 percent of the support provided by the UBS to those national Bible Societies which request support to meet the total Scripture needs of people in their countries.

The work of the ABS is supported through gifts from individuals, local churches, denominations, and cooperating agencies. Their generosity helped make the distribution of 287.2 million copies of the Scriptures during 1994, out of a total of 608 millon copies of the Scriptures distributed by all member societies of the UBS.

Headquarters

National Service Center, 1865 Broadway, New York, NY 10023 Tel. (212)408-1200

Media Contact, Dir. Communications, Mike Maus, Tel. (212)408-1419, Fax (212)408-1456

Officers

Chpsn., Sally Shoemaker Robinson

Vice-Chpsn., Harold Bennett

Pres., Dr. Eugene B. Habecker

Exec. Vice-Pres., Peter Bradley

Vice-Pres. for Scripture Publications, Maria I. Martinez

Vice-Pres. for Development and Communications, Arthur Caccese

Vice-Pres. for Finance and Administration, Patrick English
Acting Vice-Pres. for Marketing, John Cruz
Department Heads, Church Relations, Rev. Fred A. Allen; Scripture Publications, Assoc. Vice-Pres., Rev. Dr. David G. Burke; Volunteer Activities & Field Services, Dir., Frank Gomez; Catholic Ministries, Dir., Jeanette Russo; Human Resources, Dir., Steven King; Communications, Dir., Mike Maus; Scripture Production Services, Dir., Alain Sasson; Publications, Dir., David Singer; Development and Communications, Assoc. Vice-Pres., Jeffrey Towers; Finance and Administration, Assoc. Vice-Pres. and Controller, Donald Cavanaugh

American Council of Christian Churches

The American Council of Christian Churches is a Fundamentalist multidenominational organization whose purposes are to provide information, encouragement, and assistance to Bible-believing churches, fellowships, and individuals; to preserve our Christian heritage through exposure of, opposition to, and separation from doctrinal impurity and compromise in current religious trends and movements; to protect churches from religious and political restrictions, subtle or obvious, that would hinder their ministries for Christ; and to promote obedience to the inerrant Word of God.

Founded in 1941, The American Council of Christian Churches (ACCC) is a multi-denominational agency for fellowship and cooperation among Bible-believing churches in various denominations/fellowships: Bible Presbyterian Church, Evangelical Methodist Church, Fellowship of Fundamental Bible Churches (formerly Bible Protestant), Free Presbyterian Church of North America, Fundamental Methodist Church, General Association of Regular Baptist Churches, Independent Baptist Fellowship of North America, Independent Churches Affiliated, along with hundreds of independent churches. The total membership nears 2 million. Each denomination retains its identity and full autonomy, but cannot be associated with the World Council of Churches, National Council of Churches or National Association of Evangelicals.

Headquarters

P.O. Box 5455, Bethlehem, PA 18015 Tel. (610)865-3009, Fax (610)865-3033
Media Contact, Exec. Dir., Dr. Ralph Colas

Officers

Pres., Dr. Richard A. Harris
Vice-Pres., Dr. John McKnight
Exec. Sec., Dr. Ralph Colas
Sec., Rev. Craig Griffith
Treas., William H. Worrilow, Jr.
Commissions: Chaplaincy; Education; Laymen; Literature; Missions; Radio & Audio Visual; Relief; Youth

American Friends Service Committee

Founded: 1917, Regional Groups: 9. Founded by and related to the Religious Society of Friends (Quakers) but supported and staffed by individuals sharing basic values regardless of religious affiliation. Attempts to relieve human suffering and find new approaches to world peace and social justice through nonviolence. Work in 22 countries includes development and refugee relief, peace education, and community organizing. Sponsors off-the-record seminars around the world to build better international understanding. Conducts programs with U.S. communities on the problems of minority groups in areas such as housing, employment, and denial of legal rights. Maintains Washington, D.C. office to present AFSC experience and perspectives to policy-makers. Seeks to build informed public resistance to militarism and the military-industrial complex. A co-recipient of the Noble Peace Prize. Programs are multiracial, non-denominational, and international.

Divisions: Community Relations Unit, International Programs, Peacebuilding Unit

Headquarters

1501 Cherry St., Philadelphia, PA 19102 Tel. (215)241-7000, Fax (215)864-0104
Dir. of Media Relations

Officers

Presiding Clerk., Donald Gann
Treas., Kate Nicklin
General Secretary, Mary Ellen McNish

The American Theological Library Association

The American Theological Library Association (ATLA) is a library association that works to improve theological and religious libraries and librarianship by providing continuing education, developing standards, promoting research and experimental projects, encouraging cooperative programs and publishing, and disseminating research tools and aids. Founded in 1946, ATLA currently has a membership of over 245 institutions and 550 individuals.

Headquarters

250 S. Wacker Dr., Suite 1600, Chicago, IL, 60606-5834, Tel. (312)454-5100, Fax (312)454-5505
Media Contact, Jonathan West, Web Editor

Officers

Pres., Sharon A. Taylor, Andover Newton Theological School, 169 Herrick Road, Newton Centre, MA 02459
Vice Pres., Eileen K. Saner, Associated Mennonite Biblical Seminary, 3003 Benham Ave., Elkhart, IN 46517-1999

Sec., Paul F. Stuehrenberg, Yale University Divinity School, 409 Prospect St., New Haven, CT 06510
Exec. Dir., Dennis A. Norlin, ATLA, 250 S. Wacker Dr., Suite 1600, Chicago, IL 60606-5834

American Tract Society

The American Tract Society is a nonprofit, interdenominational organization, instituted in 1825 through the merger of most of the then-existing tract societies. As one of the earliest religious publishing bodies in the United States, ATS has pioneered in the publishing of Christian books, booklets, and leaflets. The volume of distribution has risen to over 35 million pieces of literature annually. For free samples or a free catalog, contact 1-800-54-TRACT.

Headquarters

P.O. Box 462008, Garland, TX 75046 Tel. (972)276-9408, Fax (972)272-9642
Media Contact, Director of Marketing, Mark A. Brown

Officers

Chpsn., John A. Mawhinney

The American Waldensian Society

The American Waldensian Society (AWS) promotes ministry linkages, broadly ecumenical, between U.S. churches and Waldensian (Reformed)-Methodist constituencies in Italy and Waldensian constituencies in Argentina-Uruguay. Founded in 1906, AWS aims to enlarge mission discovery and partnership among overseas Waldensian-Methodist forces and denominational forces in the U.S.

AWS is governed by a national ecumenical board, although it consults and collaborates closely with the three overseas Waldensian-Methodist boards.

The Waldensian experience is the earliest continuing Protestant experience.

Headquarters

475 Riverside Dr., Rm. 1850, New York, NY 10115 Tel. (212)870-2671, Fax (212)870-2499
Media Contact, Exec. Dir., Rev. Frank G. Gibson, Jr.

Officers

Pres., Rev. Laura R. Jervis
Vice-Pres., Rev. James O'Dell
Sec., Rev. Kent Jackson
Treas., Lon Haines
Exec. Dir., Rev. Frank G. Gibson, Jr.

Appalachian Ministries Educational Resource Center (AMERC)

The mission of AMERC is to promote contextual, cross-cultural education for theological students, faculties, ministers, and other Christian leaders. Working primarily through an ecumenical consortium of theological schools, AMERC supports experiential learning about the theological, spiritual, social, economic and environmental aspects of Appalachian culture, especially for rural and small town settings for ministry.

Since 1985 AMERC, a consortium of nearly 40 seminaries has provided quality educational programs and learning experiences for seminaries and other religious leaders interested in ministry in Appalachia and other rural areas. The centerpiece of these programs has been in-depth, contextually based dialogue with local people engaged in creative ministries, exploring with them social, economic, political, ecological, cultural, and religious issues. Intense theological reflection is used to understand these issues through the eyes of faith, equipping students and other leaders for ministry in the Appalachian context.

In the new millennium AMERC's form of ministry has changed. AMERC is now supporting its consortium of members by providing program grants, technical and library support, and leadership consultation. The consortium seminaries and other groups, in turn, design and offer an even wider variety of experiential programs in rural and small town ministry in the context of Appalachia. In 2000 AMERC launched its Grants Program for members of the consortium and funded five 2001 January Travel Seminars and one Seminary Faculty Immersion experience with grants of up to $10,000.

Headquarters

300 Harrison Rd., Berea, KY 40403 Tel. (859) 986-8789, Fax (859)986-2576
Media Contact, Rev. Dr. Bennett D. Poage, Executive Director
Executive Assistant, Norma Collins

Officers

Chair, Rev. Dr. Leon Carroll, Columbia Theological Seminary
Vice Chair, Rev. Dr. Bill J. Leonard, Wake Forest University Divinity School
Secretary, Ms. Tena Willemsma, Commission on Religion in Appalachia
Treasurer, Mr. Jim Strand, Berea College

The Associated Church Press

The Associated Church Press was organized in 1916. Its member publications include major Protestant, Catholic, and Orthodox groups in the U.S. and Canada. Some major ecumenical journals are also members. It is a professional Christian journalistic association seeking to promote excellence among editors and writers, recognize achievements, and represent the interests of the religious press. It sponsors seminars, conventions, awards programs, and workshops for editors, staff people, and business managers. It is active in postal rates and regulations on behalf of the religious press.

Headquarters

Media Contact, Exec. Dir., Mary Lynn Stapert, P.O. Box 30379, Chicago, IL 60630-0379, Tel. (773)283-9323, Fax (773)283-9483

Officers

Exec. Dir., Mary Lynn Stapert, P.O. Box 30379, Chicago, IL 60630-0379, Tel. (773)283-9323, Fax (773)283-9483, acpoffice@earthlink.net

Pres., Bob Terry, The Alabama Baptist, 3310 Independence Dr., Birmingham. AL 35209-5602, Tel. (205)870-4720, Fax (205)870-8957, bterry@alabapnews.org

Vice Pres., Marguerite Rourk, Southern Bulletin, 4201 N. Main St., Columbia, SC 29203-5898, Tel. (803)786-5150 ext. 256, Fax (803)786-6499, mrourk@ltss.edu

Treas., Tim Postuma, The Banner, 2850 Kalamazoo Ave. SE, Grand Rapids, MI 49560-0001, Tel. (616)224-0793, Fax (616)224-0834, posturmat@crcpublications.org

The Associated Gospel Churches

Organized in 1939, The Associated Gospel Churches (AGC) endorses chaplains primarily for Fundamental Independent Baptist and Bible Churches to the U.S. Armed Forces. The AGC has been recognized by the U.S. Department of Defense for 61 years as an Endorsing Agency, and it supports a strong national defense. The AGC also endorses VA chaplains, police, correctional system, and civil air patrol chaplains.

The AGC provides support for its associated constituent churches, (Fundamental Independent Churches), seminaries, Bible colleges, and missionaries.

The AGC believes in the sovereignty of the local church, the historic doctrines of the Christian faith, and the infallibility of the Bible.

The AGC is a member of the National Conference on Ministry to the Armed Forces (NCMAF) and the Endorsers Conference for Veterans Affairs Chaplaincy (ECVAC).

Headquarters

Media Contact, Pres., George W. Baugham, D.D., National Hdqt., P.O. Box 733, Taylors, SC 29687 Tel. (864)268-9617, Fax (864)268-0166

Officers

Commission on Chaplains, Pres. and Chmn., Billy Baugham, D.D.

Vice-Pres., Rev. Chuck Flesher

Sec.-Treas., Eva Baugham

Executive Committee, Chaplain (Captain) James Poe, USN Member

ADRIS-Association for the Development of Religious Information Services

The Association for the Development of Religious Information Services was established in 1971 to facilitate coordination and cooperation among information services that pertain to religion. Its goal is a worldwide network that is interdisciplinary, inter-faith and interdenominational to serve both administrative and research applications. ADRIS publishes an ezine and provides internet consulting services toward these goals.

Headquarters

ADRIS Newsletter Office, P.O. Box 210735, Nashville, TN 37221-0735 Tel. (615)429-8744, Fax (508)632-0370

Media Contact, Ezine Ed., Edward W. Dodds, P.O. Box 210735, Nashville, TN 37221-0735 Tel. (615)429-8744, Fax (508)632-0370

Association of Gospel Rescue Missions

The Association of Gospel Rescue Missions (AGRM), formerly the International Union of Gospel Missions, is an association of 290 rescue missions and other ministries that serve more than 7 million homeless and needy people in the inner cities of the U.S., Canada, and overseas each year. Since 1913, AGRM member ministries have offered emergency food and shelter, evangelical outreach, Christian counsel, youth and family services, prison and jail outreach, rehabilitation, and specialized programs for the mentally ill, the elderly, the urban poor, and street youth. The AGRM operates RESCUE College, an Internet-based distance education program to prepare and train rescue mission workers. The AGRM sponsors Alcoholics Victorious, a network of Christian support groups.

Headquarters

1045 Swift, N. Kansas City, MO 64116-4127 Tel. (816)471-8020, Fax (816)471-3718

Media Contact, Exec. Dir., Rev. Stephen E. Burger or Phil Rydman

Officers

Exec. Dir., Rev. Stephen E. Burger

Pres., Dr. Malcolm C. Lee, P.O. Box 1112, Richmond, CA 94802 Tel. (510)215-4888, Fax (510)215-0178

Vice-pres., Mr. Rick Alvis, Box 817, Indianapolis, IN 46206 Tel. (317)635-3575, Fax (317)687-3629

Sec.-Treas., Mr. Tom Zobel, Box 461, Salem, OR 97308, Tel. (503)362-3983, Fax (503)399-8673

NATIONAL PROGRAM UNITS AND STAFF

Education, Rev. Michael Liimatta

Membership Services, Tammy Sharp

Newsletter and Magazine, Stephen E. Burger; Philip Rydman

Convention, Stephen E. Burger

Business Admn., Len Conner

Historian, Delores Burger

Exec. Sec., Madeleine Wooley

Communications & Development, Phillip Rydman

Expansion, Gary Meek

US COOPERATIVE ORGANIZATIONS

Association of Catholic Diocesan Archivists

The Association of Catholic Diocesan Archivists, which began in 1979, has been committed to the active promotion of professionalism in the management of diocesan archives. The Association meets annually: in the even years it has its own summer conference, in the odd years it meets in conjunction with the Society of American Archivists. Publications include Standards for Diocesan Archives, Access Policy for Diocesan Archives and the quarterly Bulletin.

Headquarters

Archives & Records Center, 711 West Monroe, Chicago, IL 60661 Tel. (312)831-0711, Fax (312)736-0488

Media Contact, Ms. Nancy Sandlebac

Officers

Episcopal Mod., —

Pres., Msgr. Francis J. Weber, 15151 San Fernando Mission Blvd., Mission Hills, CA 91345 Tel. (818)365-1501

Vice-Pres., Dr. Charles Nolan, 1100 Chartres St., New Orleans, LA 70116 Tel. (504)529-2651, Fax (504)529-2001

Sec.-Treas., Sr. Catherine Louise LaCoste, C.S.J., 1029 1/2 Hayes Ave., San Diego, CA 92103 Tel. (619)298-6608

Bd. Members, Kinga Perzynska, P.O. Box 13124, Capital Station, Austin, TX 78711 Tel. (512)476-6296, Fax (512)476-3715; Timothy Cary, P.O. Box 07912, Milwaukee, WI 19807 Tel. (414)769-3407, Fax (414)769-3408; Lisa May, P.O. Box 907, 1700 San Jacinto, Houston, TX 77001 Tel. (713)659-5461, Fax (713)759-9151; John J. Treanor, 711 W. Monroe, Chicago, IL 60661 Tel. (312)736-5150, Fax (312)736-0488; Bernice Mooney, 27 C St., Salt Lake City, UT 84103-2397 Tel. (801)328-8641, Fax (801)328-9680

Newsletter Editor, Nancy Sandleback

Association of Statisticians of American Religious Bodies

This Association was organized in 1934 and grew out of personal consultations held by representatives from The Yearbook of American Churches, The National (now Official) Catholic Directory, the Jewish Statistical Bureau, The Methodist (now The United Methodist), the Lutheran, and the Presbyterian churches.

ASARB has a variety of purposes: to bring together those officially and professionally responsible for gathering, compiling, and publishing denominational statistics; to provide a forum for the exchange of ideas and sharing of problems in statistical methods and procedure; and to seek such standardization as may be possible in religious statistical data.

Headquarters

c/o John P. Marcum, Presbyterian Church (U.S.A.), 100 Witherspoon St., Rm. 2623, Louisville, KY 40202-1396 Tel. (502)569-5161, Fax (502)569-5501

Media Contact, Sec.-Treas., John P. Marcum

Officers

Pres., Cliff Tharp, Southern Baptist Convention, 127 Ninth Ave. N., Nashville, TN 37220 Tel. (615)251-2517, Fax (615)251-5636, cliff.tharp@lifeway.com

1st Vice-Pres., Rich Houseal, Church of the Nazarene, 6401 The Paseo, Kansas City, MO 64131 Tel. (816)333-7000, Fax (816)361-5202, rhouseal@nazarene.org

2nd Vice Pres., Sherri Doty, Assemblies of God, 1445 N. Boonville Ave., Springfield, MO 65802-1894, Tel. (417)862-2781 ext. 3230, Fax (417)863-6614, sdoty@ag.org

Sec.-Treas., John P. Marcum, Presbyterian Church (U.S.A.), 100 Witherspoon St., Rm. 2623, Louisville, KY 40202-1396 Tel. (502)569-5161, Fax (502)569-5501, jackm@ctr.pcusa.org

MEMBERS-AT-LARGE

Clifford Grammich, 3166 South Bentley Ave., Los Angeles, CA 90034-3008 Tel. (310)444-1826

James Schwartz, UJA Federations of N.A., 111 Eighth Ave., Suite 11E, New York, NY 10011-5201 Tel. (212)284-6729, Fax (212)284-6805, jim_schwartz@cjfny.org

The Association of Theological Schools in the United States and Canada

The Association of Theological Schools is the accrediting and program agency for graduate theological education in North America. Its member schools offer graduate professional and academic degrees for church-related professions.

Headquarters

10 Summit Park Drive, Pittsburgh, PA 15275-1103 Tel. (412)788-6505, Fax (412)788-6510

Media Contact, Dir. Of Comm., Nancy Merrill, Tel. (412)788-6505

Officers

Pres., Martha J. Horne, Protestant Episcopal Theological Seminary in Virginia, Alexandria, VA

Vice-Pres., David L. Tiede, Luther Seminary, St. Paul, MN

Secretary, Clarence G. Newsome, Howard University School of Divinity, Washington, DC

Treasurer, Thomas E. Fahey, Ernst & Young, New York, NY

Staff

Executive Director, Daniel O. Aleshire

Blanton-Peale Institute

Blanton-Peale Institute is dedicated to helping people overcome emotional obstacles by joining mental health expertise with religious faith and values. The Blanton-Peale Graduate Institute provides advanced training in marriage and family therapy, psychotherapy and pastoral care for ministers, rabbis, sisters, priests, and other counselors. The Blanton-Peale Counseling Centers provide counseling for individuals, couples, families, and groups. Blanton-Peale also offers a nationwide telephone support service for clergy, social service agencies, and other employers and promotes interdisciplinary communication among theology, medicine, and the behavioral sciences. Blanton-Peale was founded in 1937 by Dr. Norman Vincent Peale and psychiatrist Smiley Blanton, M.D.

Headquarters

3 W. 29th St., New York, NY 10001 Tel. (212)725-7850, Fax (212)689-3212

Officers

Chpsn., John Allen
Vice-Chpsn., Arthur Caliandro
Sec., Janet E. Hunt
Treas., Mary McNamara
Pres. & CEO, Dr. Holly Johnson

Bread For The World

Bread for the World is a non-profit, nondenominational Christian citizen's movement of 45,000 members that advocates specific hunger policy changes and seeks justice for hungry people at home and abroad. Founded in 1974, Bread for the World is supported by more than 45 Protestant, Catholic, and Evangelical denominations and church agencies. Rooted in the gospel of God's love in Jesus Christ, its 45,000 members write, call, and visit their members of Congress to win specific legislative changes that help hungry people, and place the issue of hunger on the nation's policy agenda.

Bread for the World works closely with Bread for the World Institute. The Institute seeks to inform, educate, nurture, and motivate concerned citizens for action on policies that affect hungry people.

Headquarters

50 F St., NW, Ste. 500, Washington, DC 20001 Tel. (202)639-9400, Fax (202)639-9401
Media Contact, Aimee Moiso

Officers

Pres., Rev. David Beckmann
Bd. Chpsn., Christine Vladimiroff, O.S.B.
Bd. Vice-Chpsn., Pablo Sanchez

Campus Crusade for Christ International

Campus Crusade for Christ International is an interdenominational, evangelistic, and discipleship ministry dedicated to helping fulfill the Great Commission through the multiplication strategy of "win-build-send." Formed in 1951 on the campus of UCLA, the organization now includes 68 plus separate ministries and special projects reaching out to almost every segment of society. There are more than 20,500 staff members and 663,000 trained volunteers in 181 countries.

Headquarters

100 Lake Hart Dr., Orlando, FL 32832 Tel. (407) 826-2000, Fax (407)826-2120
Media Contact, Sid Wright

Officers

Pres., William R. Bright
Exec. Vice-Pres., Stephen B. Douglass
Vice-Pres. of Admn. & Chief Fin. Officer, Kenneth P. Heckman
Vice-Pres. of Intl. Ministries, Bailey E. Marks

CARA-Center for Applied Research in the Apostolate

CARA-the Center for Applied Research in the Apostolate is a not-for-profit research organization of the Roman Catholic Church. It operates on the premise that not only theological principles but also findings of the social sciences must be the basis for pastoral care.

CARA's mission since its founding in 1964 has been "To discover, promote, and apply modern techniques and scientific informational resources for practical use in a coordinated and effective approach to the Church's social and religious mission in the modern world, at home and overseas."

CARA performs a wide range of research studies and consulting services. Since its roots are Roman Catholic, many of its studies are done for dioceses, religious orders, parishes, and the National Conference of Catholic Bishops. Interdenominational studies are also performed. Publishes The CARA Report, a research newsletter on Catholic Church related topics, four times a year, and The Catholic Ministry Formation Directory, a guide and statistical compilation of enrollments for Catholic seminaries, diaconate formation programs, and lay ministry formation programs.

Headquarters

Georgetown University, Washington, DC 20057-1203 Tel. (202)687-8080, Fax (202)687-8083
Media Contact, Executive Director, Dr. Bryan Froehle

Officers

Bishop William B. Friend, Chair, CARA Board of Directors

Center for Parish Development

The Center for Parish Development is an ecumenical, non-profit research and development agency whose mission is to help church bodies learn to become faithful expressions of God's mission in today's post-modern, post-Christendom world. Founded in 1968, the Center brings to its client-partners a strong theological orientation, a missional ecclesial paradigm with a focus on faithful Christian communities as the locus of mission, research-based theory and practice of major change, a systems approach, and years of experience working with national, regional, and local church bodies.

The Center staff provides research, consulting and training support for church organizations engaging in major change. The Center is governed by a 12-member Board of Directors.

Headquarters

1525 East 55th St., Suite 201, Chicago, IL 60615, Tel. (773)752-1596, Fax (773)752-5093

Media Contact, Office Manager, Beatrice Vansen

Officers

Chpsn., Eugene L. Delves, 9142 S. Winchester Ave., Chicago, IL 60620

Vice-Chpsn., Pastor Gordon Nusz, First United Methodist Church, 777 West Eight Mile Road, Northville, MI 48167

Sec., Delton Krueger, 10616 Penn Ave. South, Bloomington, MN 55431

Exec. Dir., Paul M. Dietterich

Center on Conscience & War (NISBCO)

CCW(NISBCO), formed in 1940, is a nonprofit service organization supported by individual contributions and related to more than thirty religious organizations. Its purpose is to defend and extend the rights of conscientious objectors to war and organized violence. CCW provides information on how to register for the draft and to document one's convictions and qualify as a conscientious objector, how to cope with penalties if one does not cooperate, and how to qualify as a conscientious objector while in the Armed Forces. It also provides information for counselors and the public about conscientious objection, military service, and the operation of the draft. It provides information to and support for conscientious objectors in other countries.

As a national resource center it assists research in its area of interest including the peace witness of religious bodies. Its staff provides referral to local counselors and attorneys and professional support for them. Through publications and speaking, CCW-NISBCO encourages people to decide for themselves what they believe about participation in war and to act on the basis of the dictates of their own informed consciences.

Headquarters

1830 Connecticut Ave. NW, Washington, DC 20009-5732 Tel. (202)483-2220, Fax (202) 483-1246

Media Contact, Exec. Dir., J.E. McNeil

Officers

Exec. Dir., J.E. McNeil

Chpsn., Jonathan Ogle

Sec., Titus Peachy

Treas., Frank Massey

Chaplaincy of Full Gospel Churches

The Chaplaincy of Full Gospel Churches (CFGC) is a unique coalition of 138 nondenominational churches and networks of churches united for the purpose of being represented in military and civilian chaplaincies. Since its inception in 1984, CFGC has grown rapidly-recently representing over 7.5 million American Christians.

Churches, fellowships, and networks of churches which affirm the CFGC statement of faith that "Jesus is Savior, Lord and Baptizer in the Holy Spirit today, with signs, wonders and gifts following" may join the endorsing agency. CFGC represents its 138 member-networks of churches (consisting of over 60,000 churches nation wide) before the Pentagon's Armed Forces Chaplains Board, the National Conference of Ministry to the Armed Forces, Endorsers Conference for Veterans Affairs Chaplaincy, Federal Bureau of Prisons, Association of Professional Chaplains, and other groups requiring professional chaplaincy endorsement. The organization also ecclesiastically credentials professional counselors.

Headquarters

2715 Whitewood Dr., Dallas, TX 75233 Tel. (214)331-4373, Fax (214)333-4401

Media Contact, Rev. Dr. E. H. Jim Ammerman

Officers

Pres. & Dir., Rev. Dr. E. H. Jim Ammerman

Deputy Dir., Rev. Dr. Charlene Ammerman

Vice-Pres., Ed Leach

Christian Endeavor International

Christian Endeavor International is a Christ-centered, youth-oriented ministry which assists local churches in reaching young people with the gospel of Jesus Christ, discipling them in the Christian faith, and equipping them for Christian ministry and service in their local church, community and world. It trains youth leaders for effective ministry and provides opportunities for Christian inspiration, spiritual growth, fellowship, and service. Christian Endeavor International reaches across denominational, cultural, racial, and geographical boundaries.

Headquarters

309 South Main St., Mount Vernon, OH 43050, Tel. (800)260-3234, Fax (740)397-0198

Media Contact, Exec. Dir., Rev. David G. Jackson

Officers

Pres., Jonathan Stewart

Exec. Dir., Carl A. Blunt

Christian Management Association

Christian Management Association provides management training and leadership resources for Christian organizations and larger churches. Its membership represents CEOs-executive directors, pastors, church administrators, finance officers, and other managers from more than 1,500 organizations in the United States. CMA publishes a bimonthly magazine, Christian Management Report, a monthly newsletter, an annual Who's Who in Christian Management membership directory, and other resources. CMA also provides comprehensive training and strategic networking opportunities through CMA's annual leadership and management conference for Christian organizations (the next conference is CMA California, 2002), CEO Dialogues one-day roundtables, School of Management (multiple sites), local chapter meetings, management books, and audiotapes. Annual membership is open to Christian Organizations and individuals. Companies that provide products or services to Christian organizations and churches may apply for Business Membership. Contact CMA for a FREE membership information packet and sample publications.

Headquarters

P.O. Box 4090, San Clemente, CA 92674, Tel. (800)727-4CMA, Fax (949)487-0927

John Pearson, CEO

Media Contact, Director of Membership Development, Jackie Tsujimoto

Officers

Chairman, James A. Gwinn, President, CRISTA Ministries

Vice-Chairman, Molly Davis Scott, President, The Molly Davis Scott Company

Sec.-Treas., James A. Canning, Chief Financial Officer, World Vision International

CEO, John Pearson

A Christian Ministry in the National Parks

This ministry is recognized by over 40 Christian denominations and extends the ministry of Christ to the millions of people who live, work, and vacation in our National Parks. Ministry Staff Members conduct services of worship in the parks on Sundays. The staff are employed by park concessionaires and have full-time jobs in which their actions, attitudes, and commitment to Christ serve as witness. Room and board are provided at a minimal cost; minimum commitment of 90 days needed.

Headquarters

45 School Street, Boston, MA 02108 Tel. (617)720-5655, Fax (617)720-7899

Media Contact, The Rev. Richard P. Camp, Jr.

Officers

Dir., The Rev. Richard P. Camp, Jr.

Deputy Director, Gordon Compton

Church Growth Center: Home of the Church Doctor Ministries

The Church Growth Center is an interfaith, nonprofit, professional organization which exists to bring transformational change of the Christian church toward the effective implementation of the Lord's Great Commission, to make disciples of all people. This effort is done through consultations, resources, and educational events.

Founded in 1978 by Kent R. Hunter, president and chairman of the board, the Church Growth Center offers several services including church consultations by experienced consultants under the Creative Consultation Services arm, cutting edge resources through our bookstore, The Church Doctor™ Resource Center, and by providing educational events at churches and organizations in the way of providing speakers and resources at seminars, workshops, and conferences.

Other ministries under the arm of the Church Growth Center include Mission Teams International (taking teams overseas to train pastors to be more effective in their churches), The Church Doctor™ daily radio program (which is practical direction and helps for the lay person in the church), Nehemiah Guest Missionary House (where short-term missionaries may stay while learning church growth and working at the Center), and Strategies for Today's Leader (a quarterly magazine with timely thematic issues geared for pastors and leaders). The quarterly newsletter is the Church Doctor Report

Headquarters

1230 U. S. Highway Six, P.O. Box 145, Corunna, IN 46730 Tel. (219)281-2452, Fax (219)281-2167

Media Contact, Assistant to Pres., Michelle Jones

Officers

Pres., Dr. Kent R. Hunter, D.Min, Ph.D.

Vice-Pres., Rev. Paul Griebel, 312 S. Oak St., Kendallville, IN 46755

Sec.-Treas., Roger Miller, 1060 Park Dr., Turkey Lake, LaGrange, IN 46761

Church Women United in the U.S.A.

Church Women United in the U.S.A. is a grassroots ecumenical movement of one-half million Protestant, Orthodox, Roman Catholic, and other Christian women, organized into more than 1,200 local and state units throughout the United States and Puerto Rico. Founded in 1941, CWU works in coalition with religious and secular groups on issues of peace and justice. A major program emphasis in the 2000-2004 quadrennium is "Strengthening Families Worldwide in the 21st Century".

Headquarters

NATIONAL OFFICE

475 Riverside Dr., Ste. 500, New York, NY 10115 Tel. (800)CWU-5551 OR (212)870-2347, Fax (212)870-2338

Media Contact, Anne Llamoso-Songco, Tel. (212)870-3339, Email: allamoso@church-women.org
LEGISLATIVE OFFICE
CWU Washington Ofc., 100 Maryland Ave. NE, Rm. 100, Washington, DC 20002 Tel. (202)544-8747, Fax (202)544-9133
Legislative Dir., Wash. Ofc., Tiffany L. Heath, Email: tlheath@churchwomen.org
UNITED NATIONS OFFICE
475 Riverside Dr., Ste. 500, New York, NY 10115 Tel. (212)661-3856
UN Ofc., Staff Liaison, Tiffany L. Heath, Email: tlheath@churchwomen.org
ADMINISTRATION
Controller/Administrative Manager, Roberto Vazquez, Email: rvazquez@churchwomen.org
Office Manager, Venus Jones, Email: vjones@churchwomen.org

Officers

Pres., Jerrye Champion, Scottsdale, AZ
Vice-Pres., Jane Erdahl, Salt Lake City, UT
Secretary, Joan Regal, Maplewood, MN
Treasurer, Doris Roberts Hughes, Martinsburg, WV
Regional Coordinators, Central, Helen Traudt, Lincoln, NE; East Central, Gladys Kapenga, Wyoming, MI; Mid-Atlantic, Blanche Crim, Dover, DE; Northeast, Marilyn Lariviere, Hyannis, MA; Northwest, Edna Best, Billings, MT; South Central, Mickey Simpson, Tulsa, OK; Southeast, Mona Hayes, Nashville, TN; Southwest, Martha DeWarf, Tucson, AZ

Consultation on Church Union

Officially constituted in 1962, the Consultation on Church Union is a venture in reconciliation of nine American communions. It has been authorized to explore the formation of a uniting church, truly catholic, truly evangelical, and truly reformed. In 1992 the participating bodies were African Methodist Episcopal Church, African Methodist Episcopal Zion Church, Christian Church (Disciples of Christ), Christian Methodist Episcopal Church, The Episcopal Church, International Council of Community Churches, Presbyterian Church (U.S.A.), United Church of Christ and The United Methodist Church. These churches are to enter a relationship of covenanted communion, to be called "Churches Uniting in Christ" and is scheduled for inauguration in January 2002. At the January, 1999 Plenary, at St. Louis, Missouri, the Assembly affirmed the Visible Marks of Churches Uniting in Christ and the marks of the fuller unity sought by "entering into a new level of visible commitment" by openly inviting participating churches to enter into this new relationship in 2002 or "to be partners in continuing relationship to realize fully that unity for which Christ prayed." This 18th Plenary dared to hope that other American Christian bodies may enter this dialogue, commending "to the churches the actions recommended in 'A call to Christian Commitment and Action to Combat Racism' approved by the 18th Plenary."

The Consultation on Church Union will no longer exist with the Inauguration of Churches Uniting in Christ at the Mount Olive Cathedral of the Christian Methodist Episcopal Church, Memphis, TN, January 20, 2002. The national ecumenical office of each of the Communions which have been members of COCU are expected to take on that responsibility of seeing to it that its counterpart at the local level is implementing the goals of Churches Uniting in Christ. Neighboring congregations of these Christan traditions will be encouraged to celebrate the Eucharist together, to study Scripture together and to discover ways in which they might witness together, especially in combatting racism as well as other social injustices. In conjunction with this, on Martin Luther King, Jr. Day, January 21, 2002, the Heads of Communion will sign An Appeal to the Churches to work together for the eradication of racism and encourage the signing of the Appeal by members of congregations throughout the nation. Those signatures will be sent back to the national social justice office of each Communion. The future of Churches Uniting in Christ will depend on congregations in every possible locality witnessing as the One Body of Christ.

Headquarters

260 Gorham Street, Lowell, MA 01851
Mailing Address, Highland Station, P.O. Box 2143, Lowell, MA 01851
Tel (978)453-2842, Fax (978)441-0692
Media Contact, Associate General Secretary, The Rev. K. Gordon White

Officers

General Sec., The Rev. Dr. Michael Kinnamon
Associate General Sec., The Rev., K. Gordon White
Pres., The Rev. Dr. Jeffrey R. Newhall, 25 Francis St., P.O. Box 60074, Worcester, MA 01606-0074
Vice Pres., Bishop McKinley Young, 700 Martin Luther King Jr., Dr., SW, ITC P.O. Box 456, Atlanta, GA 30314-4143
Vice Pres., The Rev. Diane Kessler, Massachusetts Council of Churches, 14 Beacon St., Room 416, Boston, MA 02108
Sec., The Rev. Kathy Bannister, 204 W. First St., P.O. Box 327, Bison, KS 67502
REP. FROM PARTICIPATING CHURCHES
African Methodist Episcopal Church, Bishop Vinton R. Anderson, 4144 Lindell Blvd., Ste. 222, St. Louis, MO 63108; Bishop McKinley Young, 700 Martin Luther King Jr., Dr., SW, ITC P.O. Box 456, Atlanta, GA 30314-4143
African Methodist Episcopal Zion Church, Bishop Marshall H. Strickland, 2000 Cedar Circle Dr., Baltimore, MD 21228; Bishop

Cecil Bishop, 2663 Oakmeade Dr., Charlotte, NC 28270

Christian Church (Disciples of Christ), Rev. Dr. Robert K. Welsh., P.O. Box 1986, Indianapolis, IN 46206; Rev. Dr. Suzanne Webb, 7018 Putney Road, Arcadia, MI 49613-9600

Christian Methodist Episcopal Church, Bishop Charles Helton, 6524 16th St, NW, Washington, DC 20012; Dr. Vivian U. Robinson, 8th Episcopal Dist. Hdqt., 1256 Hernlen St., Augusta, GA 30901

The Episcopal Church, Rev. Lucinda Laird, St. Matthew's Episcopal Church, 330 N. Hubbards Lane, Louisville, KY 40207; Rt. Rev. Edwin F. Gulick, Jr., 425 S. Second Street, Louisville, KY 40202

Intl. Council of Community Churches, Mr. Abraham Wright, 1912-3 Rosemary Hills Drive, Silver Springs, MD 20910; The Rev. Dr. Jeffrey R. Newhall, 25 Francis St., P.O. Box 60074, Worcester, MA 01606-0074

Presbyterian Church (U.S.A.), Ms. Georgette Huie, McCormick Seminary, Presbyterian Church (USA) 5555 Woodlawn Ave., Chicago, IL 60737

United Church of Christ, Rev. Dr. Thomas E. Dipko, 319 Parkway Dr., Berea, OH 44017; Rev. Diane C. Kessler, Mass. Council of Churches, 14 Beacon St., Boston, MA 02108

The United Methodist Church, Bishop William B. Grove, 109 McDavid Lane, Charleston, W. Virginia 25311; Rev. Kathy Bannister, 204 W. First Street, P.O. Box 327, Bison, Kansas 67520

Evangelical Council for Financial Accountability

Founded in 1979, the Evangelical Council for Financial Accountability has the purpose of helping Christ-centered, evangelical, nonprofit organizations earn the public's trust through their ethical practices and financial accountability. ECFA assists its over 1000 member organizations in making appropriate public disclosure of their financial practices and accomplishments, thus materially enhancing their credibility and support potential among present and prospective donors.

Headquarters

440 W. Jubal Early Drive, Winchester, VA 22601 Tel. (540)535-0103 Fax (540)535-0533

Media Contact, Pres., Paul D. Nelson

Officers

Pres., Paul D. Nelson

Vice-Pres., Donor & Member Services, Daniel D. Busby

Dir. of Member Review & Compliance, Lucinda Repass

V.P. Member Review & Compliance, Bill Altman

Evangelical Press Association

The Evangelical Press Association is an organization of editors and publishers of Christian periodicals which seeks to promote the cause of Evangelical Christianity and enhance the influence of Christian journalism.

Headquarters

314 Dover Rd., Charlottesville, VA 22901 Tel. (804)973-5941, Fax (804)973-2710

Media Contact, Exec. Dir., Ronald Wilson

Officers

Pres., David Neff, Christianity Today, 465 Gundersen Dr., Carol Stream, IL, 60188

Pres. Elect, Terry White, Inside Journal, P.O. Box 17429, Washington, DC 20041-0429

Treas., Lamar Keener, Christian Times, P.O. Box 2606, El Cajon, CA 92021

Sec., Jeanette Thomason, Aspire, 107 Kenner Ave., Nashville, TN 37205

Advisor, Dean Ridings, Christian Camp & Conference Journal, P.O. Box 62189, Colorado Springs, CO 80962-2189

Advisor, Brian Peterson, New Man, 600 Rinehart Rd., Lake Mary, FL 32746

Exec. Dir., Ronald Wilson

Faith & Values Media

Faith & Values Media is a service of the National Interfaith Cable Coalition, Inc. (NICC), whose 30 members represent 70 faith groups with 200,000 congregations and 120 million members. It is the nation's largest coalition of Jewish and Christian faith groups dedicated to media production, distribution, and promotion. Faith & Values Medias programming is available on Hallmark Channel U.S. (formerly Odyssey Network) and on www.faithandvalues.com. NICC is the founding partner of Odyssey Network. Today, Hallmark Channel U.S. is owned and operated by Crown Media Holdings, Inc. VISN Management Corp., a for-profit subsidiary of NICC, is among the strategic investors in Crown Media.

Headquarters

74 Trinity Place, Suite 1550, New York, NY 10006, Tel. (212)406-4121, Fax (212)406-4105

Media Contact, Melissa Gonzalez, melissagonzalez@faithandvalues.com

Officers

Chair, Dr. Daniel Paul Matthews

Vice Chair, Elder Ralph Hardy Jr.

Secretary, Rabbi Paul J. Menitoff

Treasurer, Betty Elam

Staff

President and CEO, Edward J. Murray

Vice President, Beverly Judge

Friends World Committee for Consultation (Section of the Americas)

The Friends World Committee for Consultation (FWCC) was formed in 1937. There has been an American Section as well as a

European Section from the early days and an African Section was organized in 1971. In 1974 the name, Section of the Americas, was adopted by that part of the FWCC with constituency in North, Central, and South America and in the Caribbean area. In 1985 the Asia-West Pacific Section was organized. The purposes of FWCC are summarized as follows, To facilitate loving understanding of diversities among Friends while discovering together, with God's help, a common spiritual ground; and to facilitate full expression of Friends' testimonies in the world.

Headquarters

Section of the Americas Headquarters

1506 Race St., Philadelphia, PA 19102 Tel. (215)241-7250, Fax (215)241-7285

Media Contact, Exec. Sec., Cilde Grover

Latin American Office, Guerrero 223 Pte., Zona Centro, Cd. Mante, TAM 89800 Mexico

The Fund for Theological Education, Inc.

Begun in 1954 with the goal of supporting excellence in the profession of ministry, the Fund for Theological Education has enjoyed a long and rich history, providing gifted women and men with nearly 5000 fellowships and generation innovative new programs for theological and ministerial support. Supported by individuals and grants from a group of U.S. Foundations, FTE envisions new and imaginatve programs to encourage diversity and excellence in the churches and seminaries of North America.

Headquarters

825 Houston Mill Rd., Suite 250, Atlanta, GA 30329, Tel. (404)727-1450, Fax (404)727-1490

Website: www.thefund.org

Email: fte@thefund.org

Officers

Pres., Dr. James L. Waits

Vice Pres. for Advancement, Jack Gilbert

Dir., Expanding Horizons Partnership, Dr. Sharon Watson Fluker

Dir., Partnership for Excellence, Melissa Wiginton

Glenmary Research Center

The Research Center is a department of the Glenmary Home Missioners, a Catholic society of priests and brothers. The Center was established in 1966 to serve the rural research needs of the Catholic Church in the United States. Its research has led it to serve ecumenically a wide variety of church bodies. Local case studies as well as quantitative research is done to understand better the diversity of contexts in the rural sections of the country. The Center's statistical profiles of the nation's counties cover both urban and rural counties.

Headquarters

1312 Fifth Ave. North, Nashville, TN 37208 Tel. (615)256-1905, Fax (615)251-1472

Media Contact, —

Officers

Pres., Rev. Gerald Dorn, P.O. Box 465618, Cincinnati, OH 45246-5618

1st Vice-Pres., Rev. Daniel Dorsey, P.O. Box 465618, Cincinnati, OH 45246-5618

2nd Vice-Pres., Bro. Jack Henn, P.O. Box 465618, Cincinnati, OH 45246-5618

Treas., Robert Knueven, P.O. Box 465618, Cincinnati, OH 45246-5618

Dir., Kenneth M. Sanchagrin, Ph.D., ksanchagrin @glenmary.org

Graymoor Ecumenical & Interreligious Institute (GEII)

Graymoor Ecumenical & Interreligious Institute has its roots in the Graymoor Ecumenical Institute which was founded in 1967 by the Franciscan Friars of the Atonement, to respond to the Friars' historical concern for Christian Unity in light of the theological and ecumenical developments arising from the Second Vatican Council.

In 1991, in response to developments in both the Institute and the wider ecumenical scene, the Graymoor Ecumenical Institute was expanded into an information and service organization with a mission of Christian Unity and interreligious dialogue. Today, the Graymoor Ecumenical & Interreligious Institute employs several means to acomplish this goal. Among these are specialization desks for African-American Churches; Evangelical and Free Churches; Lutheran, Anglican, Roman Catholic Affairs; Interreligious Dialogue; and Social Ecumenism. Another is the annual Week of Prayer of Christian Unity, "a world-wide observance initiated in 1908 by the Rev. Paul Wattson, co-founder of the Society of the Atonement," the theme and text of which are now chosen and prepared by the Pontifical Council for Promoting Christian Unity and representatives of the World Council of Churches. The Institute publishes the monthly journal Ecumenical Trends—to keep clergy and laity abreast of developments in the ecumenical and interreligious movements; provides membership in, and collaboration with, national and local ecumenical and interreligious organizations and agencies; and cooperates with individuals engaged in ecumenical and interreligious work.

Over the years, the Graymoor Ecumenical & Interreligious Institute has sponsored and co-sponsored meetings, colloquia, and workshops in areas of ecumenical and interreligious dialogue. These have been as diverse as colloquia between African-American and Hispanic Pentecostal scholars; Christians, Muslims, and Jews; state Councils of Churches; and interfaith training workshops for Christian leaders.

Headquarters

475 Riverside Dr., Rm. 1960, New York, NY 10115-1999 Tel. (212)870-2330, Fax (212) 870-2001

Staff

General Ecumenical and Interreligious Affairs Desk, Dir., Rev. James Loughran, SA, Tel. (212)870-2342

Lutheran, Anglican, Roman Catholic Research Desk, Assoc. Dir., Lorelei F. Fuchs, SA, MA, STL; Tel. (212)870-2331, 100772.372@ compu serve.com

Ecumenical Trends, Editor, Assoc. Dir., Kevin McMorrow, SA; Graymoor, Route 9, P.O. Box 300, Garrison, NY 10524-0300 Tel. (845)424-3671 ext. 3120, Kmcmorrow@atonementfriars.org

Business Office/Week of Prayer for Christian Unity, Graymoor, Rt. 9, P.O. Box 300, Garrison, NY 10524-0300, Tel. (845)424-3671 ext. 2109, Fax (845)424-2163, rsullivan@ atonementfriars.org

Inter-Varsity Christian Fellowship of the U.S.A.

Inter-Varsity Christian Fellowship is a non-profit, interdenominational student movement that ministers to college and university students and faculty in the United States. Inter-Varsity began in the United States when students at the University of Michigan invited C. Stacey Woods, then General Secretary of the Canadian movement, to help establish an Inter-Varsity chapter on their campus. Inter-Varsity Christian Fellowship-USA was incorporated two years later, in 1941.

Inter-Varsity's uniqueness as a campus ministry lies in the fact that it is student-initiated and student-led. Inter-Varsity strives to build collegiate fellowships that engage their campus with the gospel of Jesus Christ and develop disciples who live out biblical values. Inter-Varsity students and faculty are encouraged in evangelism, spiritual discipleship, serving the church, human relationships, righteousness, vocational stewardship, and world evangelization. A triennial missions conference held in Urbana, Illinois, jointly sponsored with Inter-Varsity-Canada, has long been a launching point for missionary service.

Headquarters

6400 Schroeder Rd., P.O. Box 7895, Madison, WI 53707 Tel. (608)274-9001, Fax (608)274-7882

Media Contact, Dir. of Development Services, Carole Sharkey, P.O. Box 7895, Madison, WI 53707 Tel. (608)274-9001, Fax (608)274-7882

Officers

Pres. & CEO, Stephen A. Hayner

Vice-Pres., C. Barney Ford; Robert A. Fryling; Samuel Barkat; Ralph Thomas; Jim Malliet

Bd. Chpsn., Virginia Viola

Bd. Vice-Chpsn., E. Kenneth Nielson

Interfaith Impact for Justice and Peace

Interfaith Impact for Justice and Peace is the religious community's united voice in Washington. It helps Protestant, Jewish, Muslim and Catholic national organizations have clout on Capitol Hill and brings grassroots groups and individual and congregational members to Washington and shows them how to turn their values into votes for justice and peace.

Interfaith Impact for Justice and Peace has established the following Advocacy Networks to advance the cause of justice and peace, Justice for Women; Health Care; Hunger and Poverty; International Justice and Peace; Civil and Human Rights. The Interfaith Impact Foundation provides an annual Legislative Briefing for their members.

Members receive the periodic Action alerts on initiatives, voting records, etc., and a free subscription to the Advocacy Networks of their choice.

Headquarters

100 Maryland Ave. N.E., Ste. 200, Washington, DC 20002 Tel. (202)543-2800, Fax (202)547-8107

Media Contact, Jane Hull Harvey

Officers

Chpsn. of Bd., Jane Hull Harvey, United Methodist Church

MEMBERS

African Methodist Episcopal Church
African Methodist Episcopal Zion Church
Alliance of Baptists
American Baptist Churches, USA, Washington Office; World Relief Office
American Ethical Union
American Muslim Council
Center of Concern
Christian Methodist Episcopal (CME) Church
Christian Church (Disciples of Christ)
Church of the Brethren
Church Women United
Commission on Religion in Appalachia
Episcopal Church
Episcopal Urban Caucus
Evangelical Lutheran Church in America
Federation of Southern Cooperatives-LAF
Federation for Rural Empowerment
Graymoor Ecumenical and Interreligious Institute
Jesuit Social Ministries
Maryknoll Fathers and Brothers
Moravian Church in America
National Council of Churches of Christ, Church World Service; Washington Office
National Council of Jewish Women

NETWORK

Peoria Citizens Committee
Presbyterian Church (USA)
Progressive National Baptist Convention

Presbyterian Hunger Fund
Reformed Church in America
Rural Advancement Fund
Society of African Missions
Southwest Organizing Project
Southwest Voter Registration-Education Project
Toledo Metropolitan Ministries
Union of American Hebrew Congregations
Unitarian Universalist Association
Unitarian Universalist Service Committee
United Church of Christ, Bd. for Homeland Ministries; Bd. for World Ministries; Hunger Action Ofc.; Ofc. of Church in Society
United Methodist Church, Gen. Bd. of Church & Society; Gen. Bd. of Global Ministries Natl. Div.; Gen. Bd. of Global Ministries Women's Div.; Gen. Bd. of Global Ministries World Div.
Virginia Council of Churches
Western Organization of Resource Councils

Interreligious Foundation for Community Organization (IFCO)

IFCO is a national ecumenical agency created in 1966 by several Protestant, Roman Catholic, and Jewish organizations, to be an interreligious, interracial agency for support of community organization and education in pursuit of social justice. Through IFCO, national and regional religious bodies collaborate in development of social justice strategies and provide financial support and technical assistance to local, national, and international social-justice projects.

IFCO serves as a bridge between the churches and communities and acts as a resource for ministers and congregations wishing to better understand and do more to advance the struggles of the poor and oppressed. IFCO conducts workshops for community organizers and uses its national and international network of organizers, clergy and other professionals to act in the interest of justice.

Churches, foundations, and individual donors use IFCO services as a fiscal agent to make donations to community organizing projects.

IFCO's global outreach includes humanitarian aid shipments through its Pastors for Peace program to Cuba, Haiti, Nicaragua, Honduras, and Chiapas, Mexico.

Headquarters

402 W. 145th St., New York, NY 10031 Tel. (212)926-5757, Fax (212)926-5842
Media Contact, Dir. of Communications, Gail Walker

Officers

Pres., Rev. Schuyler Rhodes
Vice President & Treasurer, Marilyn Clement

The Kairos Institute, Inc.

The Kairos Institute provides quality support, consultation, and in-depth educational opportunities to the professional, medical, mental health, and religious communities and promotes assistance, consultation, education, and care to families of exceptional children.

Headquarters

107 Green Ave., Madison, NJ 07940, Tel. (973) 966-9099, Fax (973)377-8509

Officers

Rev. Robert Clark, Executive Director

The Liturgical Conference

Founded in 1940 by a group of Benedictines, the Liturgical Conference is an independent, ecumenical, international association of persons concerned about liturgical renewal and meaningful worship. The Liturgical Conference is known chiefly for its periodicals, books, materials, and sponsorship of regional and local workshops on worship-related concerns in cooperation with various church groups.

Headquarters

8750 Georgia Ave., Ste. 123, Silver Spring, MD 20910-3621 Tel. (301)495-0885
Media Contact, Exec. Dir., Robert Brancatelli

Officers

Pres., Eleanor Bernstein
Vice-Pres., Samuel Torvend
Sec., Robert Rimbo
Treas., Victor Cinson

Lombard Mennonite Peace Center

The Lombard Mennonite Peace Center (LMPC) is a nonprofit organization with the mission "to proclaim Christ's good news, the gospel of peace and justice—and to be active in the sacred ministry of reconciliation." With an emphasis on equipping clergy and churches to function in healthy ways, LMPC offers training in conflict transformation and in a family systems approach to church leaders' management of themselves and their congregations.

One- and two-day educational workshops and a five-day Mediation Skills Training Institute for Church Leaders are offered throughout the U.S. Ongoing clergy clinics provide church leaders with regular opportunities to reflect on their won functioning. LMPC also provides educational events, consultation, and mediation services for congregations and judicatories of all denominations, as well as consultation for individual clergy.

Founded in 1983 as a ministry of a local congregation, LMPC became an independent, 501(c)3 corporation in 1997.

Headquarters

1263 South Highland Avenue, Suite 1N, Lombard, IL 60148 Tel. (630)627-0507, Fax. (630)627-0519

Officers

Executive Director, Richard G. Blackburn

The Lord's Day Alliance of the United States

The Lord's Day Alliance of the United States, founded in 1888 in Washington, D.C., is the only national organization whose sole purpose is the preservation and cultivation of Sunday, the Lord's Day, as a day of rest and worship. The Alliance also seeks to safeguard a Day of Common Rest for all people regardless of their faith. Its Board of Managers is composed of representatives from 25 denominations. It serves as an information bureau, publishes a magazine, Sunday, and furnishes speakers and a variety of materials such as pamphlets, videos, posters, radio spot announcements, cassettes, news releases, articles for magazines, and television programs.

Headquarters

2930 Flowers Rd. S., Atlanta, GA 30341 Tel. (770)936-5376, Fax (770)936-5385

Media Contact, Exec. Dir. & Ed., Rev. Timothy A. Norton

Officers

Exec. Dir. & Ed., Timothy A. Norton

Pres., Dr. Paul Craven, Jr.

Vice-Pres., Charles Holland; Roger A. Kvam; Timothy E. Bird; Wendell J.Schaal; William B. Shea; W. David Sapp

Sec., Rev. Donald Pepper

Treas., E. Larry Eidson

Lutheran World Relief

Lutheran World Relief (LWR) is an overseas development and relief agency based in Baltimore which responds quickly to natural and man-made disasters and supports more than 160 long-range development projects in countries throughout Africa, Asia, the Middle East, and Latin America.

Founded in 1945 to act on behalf of Lutherans in the United States, LWR has as its mission "to support the poor and oppressed overseas in their efforts to meet basic human needs and participate with dignity and equity in the life of their communities; and to alleviate human suffering resulting from natural disaster, war, social conflict or poverty."

Headquarters

700 Light Street, Baltimore, MD 21230-3850, Tel. (410)230-2700, Fax (410)230-2882

Media Contact, Jonathan C. Frerichs

Officers

Pres., Kathryn F. Wolford

The Mennonite Central Committee

The Mennonite Central Committee is the relief and service agency of North American Mennonite and Brethren in Christ Churches. Representatives from Mennonite and Brethren in Christ groups make up the MCC, which meets annually in June to review its program and to approve policies and budget. Founded in 1920, MCC administers and participates in programs of agricultural and economic development, education, health, self-help, relief, peace, and disaster service. MCC has about 900 workers serving in 60 countries in Africa, Asia, Europe, Middle East, and South, Central, and North America.

MCC has service programs in North America that focus both on urban and rural poverty areas. There are also North American programs focusing on such diverse matters as community conciliation, employment creation and criminal justice issues. These programs are administered by two national bodies—MCC U.S. and MCC Canada.

Contributions from North American Mennonite and Brethren in Christ churches provide the largest part of MCC's support. Other sources of financial support include the contributed earnings of volunteers, grants from private and government agencies, and contributions from Mennonite churches abroad. The total income in FYE2001, including material aid contributions, amounted to $63.2 million.

MCC tries to strengthen local communities by working in cooperation with local churches or other community groups. Many personnel are placed with other agencies, including missions. Programs are planned with sensitivity to locally felt needs.

Headquarters

21 S. 12th St., P.O. Box 500, Akron, PA 17501-0500 Tel. (717)859-1151, Fax (717)859-2171

Canadian Office, 134 Plaza Dr., Winnipeg, MB R3T 5K9 Tel. (204)261-6381, Fax (204)269-9875

Media Contact, Exec. Dir., Ronald J.R. Mathies, P.O. Box 500, Akron, PA 17501 Tel. (717)859-1151, Fax (717)859-2171

Officers

Exec. Directors., Intl., Ronald J.R. Mathies; Canada, Donald Peters; U.S.A., Jose Ortiz

National Association of Ecumenical and Interreligious Staff

NAEIS is an association of professional staff in ecumenical and interreligious work. Founded as the Association of Council Secretaries in 1940, the Association was widened to include program staff in 1971, and renamed the National Association of Ecumenical Staff. It has included staff of any faith engaged in interreligious work since 1994. NAEIS provides means for personal and professional growth, and for mutual support, through national and regional conferences, a newsletter and exchange among its membership.

NAEIS was established to provide creative relationships among them and to encourage mutual support and personal and professional growth. This is accomplished through training programs, through exchange and discussion of common concerns at conferences, and through the publication of the Corletter, in collaboration with NCCC Ecumenical Networks.

Headquarters

Currently best reached through Janet E. Leng, Membership Officer, P.O. Box 7093, Tacoma, WA 98406-0093. Tel. (253)759-0141

Media contact, Dr. Jay T. Rock, Interfaith Relations Commission, NCCC USA, 475 Riverside Dr., Rm. 870, New York, NY 10115 Tel (212)870-2560, Fax (212)870-2158

Officers

Pres., Dr. Jay T. Rock, Interfaith Relations Commission, NCCC USA, 475 Riverside Dr., Rm. 870, New York, NY 10115 Tel. (212)870-2560, Fax (212)870-2158

Vice-Pres., Julia Sibley Juras, South Carolina Christian Action Council, P.O. Box 3248, Columbia, SC 29230-3248 Tel. (803)786-7115, Fax (803)786-7116

Imm. Past-Pres., Arthur Lee, Emergency Feeding Program, Church Council of Greater Seattle, P.O. Box 18145, Seattle, WA 98118-0145 Tel. (206)723-0647

Sec., Sister Paul Teresa Hennessee, Graymoor Ecumenical and Interreligious Institute, 475 Riverside Dr., Room 1960, New York, NY 10115, Tel. (212)870-2968, Fax (212)870-2001

Tres., James W. Robinson, Tulsa Metropolitan Ministry, 221 South Nogales Ave., Tulsa, OK 74127-8721 Tel. (918)582-3147, Fax (918) 582-3159

The National Association of Evangelicals

The National Association of Evangelicals (NAE) is a voluntary fellowship of evangelical denominations, churches, organizations, and individuals demonstrating unity in the body of Christ by standing for biblical truth, speaking with a representative voice, and serving the evangelical community through united action, cooperative ministry, and strategic planning.

The association is comprised of approximately 43,000 congregations nationwide from 50 member denominations and fellowships, as well as several hundred independent churches. The membership of the association includes over 250 parachurch ministries and educational institutions. Through the cooperative ministry of these members, NAE directly and indirectly benefits over 27 million people. These ministries represent a broad range of theological traditions, but all subscribe to the distinctly evangelical NAE Statement of Faith. The association is a nationally recognized entity by the public sector with a reputation for integrity and effective service.

The cooperative ministries of the National Association of Evangelicals demonstrate the association's intentional desire to promote cooperation without compromise.

Headquarters

P.O. Box 1325, Azusa, CA 91702 Tel. (626)963-5966

NAE-Washington, 718 Capitol Square SW, Washington, DC 20024 Tel. (202)789-1011, Fax (202)842-0392

Media Contact, Rev. John Mendez, Tel. (626)963-5966

Staff

Vice President of Ministry Develpoment, Rev. John N. Mendez

Vice President of Governmental Affairs, Rev. Rich Cizik

MEMBER DENOMINATIONS

Advent Christian General Conference
Assemblies of God
Association of Vineyard Churches
Baptist General Conference
The Brethren Church
Brethren in Christ Church
Christian & Missionary Alliance
Christ Community Church
Christian Church of North America
Christian Reformed Church in North America
Christian Union
Church of God, Cleveland, TN
Church of God, Mountain Assembly
Church of the Nazarene
United Brethren in Christ Church
Churches of Christ in Christian Union
Congregational Holiness Church
Conservative Baptist Assoc. of America
Conservative Congregational Christian Conf.
Conservative Lutheran Association
Elim Fellowship
Evangelical Church of North America
Evangelical Congregational Church
Evangelical Free Church of America
Evangelical Friends Intl.—North America
Evangelical Mennonite Church
Evangelical Methodist Church
Evangelical Presbyterian Church
Evangelistic Missionary Fellowship
Fellowship of Evangelical Bible Churches
Fire-Baptized Holiness Church of God of the Americas
Free Methodist Church of North America
General Association of General Baptists
Intl. Church of the Foursquare Gospel
Intl. Pentecostal Church of Christ
Intl. Pentecostal Holiness Church
Mennonite Brethren Churches, USA
Missionary Church, Inc.
Open Bible Standard Churches
Pentecostal Church of God
Pentecostal Free Will Baptist Church
Presbyterian Church in America
Primitive Methodist Church, USA
Reformed Episcopal Church
Reformed Presbyterian Church of N.A.
Salvation Army
Regional Synod of Mid-America (Reformed Church in America)

Wesleyan Church
Worldwide Church of God

National Bible Association

The National Bible Association is an autonomous, interfaith organization of lay people who advocate regular Bible reading and sponsors National Bible Week (Thanksgiving week) each November. Program activities include public service advertising, distribution of nonsectarian literature, and thousands of local Bible Week observances by secular and religious organizations. The Association also urges constitutionally acceptable use of the Bible in public school classrooms, i.e.the study of the Bible in literature. All support comes from individuals, corporations, and foundations.

Founded in 1940 by a group of business and professional people, the Association offers daily Bible readings in several English and Spanish translations on its website and has the IRS nonprofit status of a 501(c)(3) educational association.

Headquarters

1865 Broadway, New York, NY 10023 Tel. (212)408-1390, Fax (212)408-1448
Media Contact, Pres., Thomas R. May

Officers

Chpsn., Stewart S. Furlong
Vice-Chpsn., Philip J. Clements
Pres., Thomas R. May
Treas., Paul Werner
Sec., J. Marshall Gage

The National Conference for Community and Justice

The National Conference for Community and Justice, founded in 1927 as the National Conference of Christians and Jews, is a human relations organization dedicated to fighting bias, bigotry, and racism in America. The NCCJ promotes understanding and respect among all races, religions, and cultures through advocacy, conflict resolution, and education.

Programmatic strategies include interfaith and interracial dialogue, youth leadership workshops, workplace training, human relations research, and the building of community coalitions. NCCJ has 65 regional offices staffed by approximately 350 people. Nearly 200 members comprise the National Board of Advisors and members from that group form the 27-member National Board of Directors. Each regional office has its own Regional Board of Directors with a total of about 2,800. The National Board of Advisors meets once annually, the National Board of Directors at least three times annually.

Headquarters

475 Park Ave. South, New York, NY 10016 Tel. (212)545-1300, Fax (212)545-8053
Media Contact, Dir. of Communications, Diane Powers

Officers

Pres. & CEO, Sanford Cloud, Jr.

National Conference on Ministry to the Armed Forces

The Conference is an incorporated civilian agency. Representation in the Conference with all privileges of the same is open to all endorsing or certifying agencies or groups authorized to provide chaplains for any branch of the Armed Forces.

The purpose of this organization is to provide a means of dialogue to discuss concerns and objectives and, when agreed upon, to take action with the appropriate authority to support the spiritual ministry to and the moral welfare of Armed Forces personnel.

Headquarters

4141 N. Henderson Rd., Ste. 13, Arlington, VA 22203 Tel. (703)276-7905, Fax (703)276-7906
Media Contact, Jack Williamson

Staff

Coord., Jack Williamson
Admn. Asst., Maureen Francis

Officers

Chpsn., David Peterson
Chpsn.-elect, Robert Jemerson
Sec., Lemuel Boyles
Treas., John Murdoch

National Council of the Churches of Christ in the U.S.A.

The National Council of the Churches of Christ in the U.S.A. is the preeminent expression in the United States of the movement toward Christian unity. The NCC's 36 member communions, including Protestant, Orthodox and Anglican church bodies, work together on a wide range of activities that further Christian unity, that witness to the faith, that promote peace and justice and that serve people throughout the world. Over 50 million U.S. Christians belong to churches that hold Council membership. The Council was formed in 1950 in Cleveland, Ohio, by the action of representatives of the member churches and by the merger of 12 previously existing ecumenical agencies, each of which had a different program focus. The roots of some of these agencies go back to the nineteenth century.

Headquarters

475 Riverside Dr., New York, NY 10115. Tel. (212)870-2141
Media Contact, Dir. of News Services, Ms. Carol J. Fouke, Tel. (212)870-2252

Officers

GENERAL OFFICERS
Pres., Ms. Elenie K. Huszagh, Esq.
Gen. Sec., Rev. Dr. Robert W. Edgar

Pres.-Elect, Bishop Thomas L. Hoyt
Immediate Past Pres., The Honorable Andrew J. Young
Sec., Rev. Roberto Delgado
Treas., Mr. Philip Young
Vice-Pres., Church World Service and Witness, Rev. Patrick Mauney
Vice-Pres., National Ministries, Dr. Audrey Miller
Vice Pres. at Large, Bishop Jon S. Enslin, Rev. Dr. Bertrice Wood, Ms. Barbara Ricks Thompson

THE GENERAL SECRETARIAT
Tel. (212)870-2141, Fax (212)870-2817
Gen. Sec., Rev. Dr. Robert W. Edgar
Dir. of Development, Mr. John A. Briscoe
Deputy General Secretary for Research and Planning, Rev. Dr. Eileen W. Lindner, Tel. (212) 870-2333

YEARBOOK OF AMERICAN AND CANADIAN CHURCHES
Editor, Rev. Dr. Eileen W. Lindner, Tel. (212)870-2031
Redevelopment Technical Dir., Rev. Marcel A. Welty Tel. (212)870-2379
Assistant Editor, Mr. Nathan Hanson, Tel. (212)870-2031, Fax (212)870-2817

WASHINGTON OFFICE
110 Maryland Ave. NE Washington, D.C. 20002. Tel. (202)544-2350,. Fax (202)543-1297.
Dir., Ms. Brenda Girton-Mitchell, Esq.

COMMUNICATIONS COMMISSION
Tel. (212)870-2574, Fax (212)870-2030
Associate General Secretary for Communication and Interpretation, Mr. Wesley M. Pattillo
Dir., News Services, Ms. Carol J. Fouke
Dir., Electronic Media, Rev. David W. Pomeroy
Dir., Interpretation Resources, Ms. Sarah Vilankulu

UNITY, EDUCATION, AND JUSTICE PROGRAM MINISTRIES
Faith and Order, Interim Dir., Sr. Paul Teresa Hennessee, Tel. (212)870-2569
Interfaith Relations, Dr. Jay T. Rock, Tel. (212)870-2560
Orthodox Liaison, Mr. Gabriel Habib Tel. (202) 544-2350
Dir., Ministries in Christian Education, Rev. Patrice Rosner Tel. (212)870-2738
Ministries in Christian Education, Dr. Joe Leonard Tel. (212)870-2673
Economic and Environmental Justice, Rev. Richard Killmer Tel. (212)870-2385
Justice for Women, Prog. Cood., Ms. Karen M. Hessel, Tel. (212)870-2421
Interfaith Center for Corporate Responsibility, Interim Dir., Tel. (212)870-2293
Natl. Farm Worker Ministry, Executive Director, Ms. Virginia Nesmith, 438 N. Skinner Blvd., St. Louis, MO 63130, Tel. (314)726-6470

ADMINISTRATION AND FINANCE
Tel. (212)870-2088, Fax (212)870-3112
Interim Associate General Secretary for Administration and Finance, Mr. Spencer B. Bates
Dept. of Business Services, Tel. (212)870-2181
Dir. of Administration., Ms. Melrose B. Corley Tel. (212)870-2267, Fax (212)890-3112

CHURCH WORLD SERVICE AND WITNESS
Tel. (212)870-2061, Fax (212)870-3523
Exec. Dir., Rev. John L. McCullough, Tel. (212)870-2175
Deputy Dir., Operations and CFO, Ms. Joanne Rendall, Tel. (219)264-3102 x. 332
Deputy Dir., Programs, Ms. Kirsten M. Laursen, Tel. (212)870-2798
Chief Development Officer, Mr. Rhonnie Hemphill, Tel. (219)264-3102 x. 454
Dir., Human Resources, Mr. Bernard Kirchoff, Tel. (219)264-3102 x. 346
Dir., Mission Relationships & Witness Program, Mr. David Weaver, Tel. (212)870-2818
Dir., Education & Advocacy for International Justice & Human Rights, Mr. Susanne Riveles, Tel. (212)870-2377
Dir., Social and Economic Development, Dr. Stephen Mbandi, Tel. (212)870-2074
Dir., Emergency Response, Mr. Rick Augsburger, Tel. (212)870-3154
Dir., Immigration & Refugee Program, Rev. Joseph Roberson, Tel. (212)870-2167

CONSTITUENT BODIES OF THE NATIONAL COUNCIL (with membership dates)
African Methodist Episcopal Church (1950)
African Methodist Episcopal Zion Church (1950)
The Alliance of Baptists in the U.S.A. (2000)
American Baptist Churches in the U.S.A. (1950)
The Antiochian Orthodox Christian Archdiocese of North America (1966)
Armenian Apostolic Church, Diocese of the (1957)
Christian Church (Disciples of Christ) (1950)
Christian Methodist Episcopal Church (1950)
Church of the Brethren (1950)
Coptic Orthodox Church (1978)
The Episcopal Church (1950)
Evangelical Lutheran Church in America (1950)
Friends United Meeting (1950)
Greek Orthodox Archdiocese of America (1952)
Hungarian Reformed Church in America (1957)
Intl. Council of Community Churches (1977)
Korean Presbyterian Church in America, Gen. Assembly of the (1986)
Malankara Orthodox Syrian Church, Diocese of America (1998)
Mar Thoma Church (1997)
Moravian Church in America, Northern Province, Southern Province (1950)
National Baptist Convention of America, Inc. (1950)
National Baptist Convention, U.S.A., Inc. (1950)
National Missionary Baptist Convention of America (1995)
Orthodox Church in America (1950)

Philadelphia Yearly Meeting of the Religious Society of Friends (1950)
Polish Natl. Catholic Church of America (1957)
Presbyterian Church (U.S.A.) (1950)
Progressive Natl. Baptist Convention, Inc. (1966)
Reformed Church in America (1950)
Russian Orthodox Church in the U.S.A., Patriarchal Parishes of the (1966)
Serbian Orthodox Church in the U.S.A. & Canada (1957)
The Swedenborgian Church (1966)
Syrian Orthodox Church of Antioch (Archdiocese of the U.S. and Canada) (1960)
Ukrainian Orthodox Church of the U.S.A. (1950)
United Church of Christ (1950)
The United Methodist Church (1950)

National Institute of Business and Industrial Chaplains

NIBIC is the professional organization for workplace chaplains, that includes members from a wide variety of denominations and work settings, including corporations, manufacturing plants, air and sea ports, labor unions and pastoral counseling centers. NIBIC has six membership categories, including Clinical, Professional, Affiliates, and Organizational.

NIBIC works to establish professional standards for education and practice; promotes and conducts training programs; provides mentoring, networking, and chaplaincy information; encourages research and public information dissemination; communicates with business leaders and conducts professional meetings. NIBIC publishes a quarterly newsletter and co-sponsors The Journal of Pastoral Care. A public membership meeting and training conference is held annually.

Headquarters

7100 Regency Square Blvd., Ste. 210, Houston, TX 77036-3202 Tel. (713)266-2456, Fax (713) 266-0845
Media Contact, Rev. Diana C. Dale, 7100 Regency Square Blvd., Ste. 210, Houston, TX 77036-3202 Tel. (713)266-2456, Fax (713) 266-0845

Officers

Executive Dir., Rev. Diana C. Dale, D.Min.
Vice-Pres., Rev. Stephen Holden
President, Rev. Timothy Bancroft, D.Min.
Treas., Rev. Gregory Edwards

National Interfaith Cable Coalition, Inc. (NICC)

The National Interfaith Cable Coalition, Inc. (NICC) was formed as a not-for-profit 501(c)3 corporation, in December, 1987, and is currently comprised of nearly 70 associated faith groups from the Jewish and Christian traditions.

In September 1988, NICC launched a religious cable network called VISN (Vision Interfaith Satellite Network), now known as Odyssey Network. Today, Odyssey is owned and operated by Crown Media Holdings, Inc., in which NICC is a strategic investor. Odyssey provides a mix of high-quality family entertainment and faith-based programming. NICC provides 30 hours a week of programming on the network.

In 2000, NICC adopted Faith & Values Media as its service mark and expanded its mission to include a significant Web presence (FaithandValues.com) and plans for a full-time digital channel.

Headquarters

74 Trinity Place, Ste. 1550, New York, NY 10006 Tel. (212)406-4121, Fax (212)406-4105
Media Contact, Melissa Gonzalez

Officers

Chair, Dr. Daniel Paul Matthews
Vice Chair, Elder Ralph Hardy Jr.
Secretary, Rabbi Paul J. Menitoff
Treasurer, Betty Elam

Staff

President and CEO, Edward J. Murray
Vice President, Beverly Judge

National Interfaith Coalition on Aging

The National Interfaith Coalition on Aging (NICA), a constituent unit of the National Council on Aging, is composed of Protestant, Roman Catholic, Jewish, and Orthodox national and regional organizations and individuals concerned about the needs of older people and the religious community's response to problems facing the aging population in the United States. NICA was organized in 1972 to address spiritual concerns of older adults through religious sector action.

Mission Statement: The National Interfaith Coalition on Aging (NICA), affiliated with the National Council on the Aging (NCOA), is a diverse network of religious and other related organizations and individual members which promotes the spiritual well being of older adults and the preparation of persons of all ages for the spiritual tasks of aging. NICA serves as a catalyst for new and effective research, networking opportunities, resource development, service provision, and dissemination of information.

Headquarters

c/o NCOA, 409 Third St., SW, 2nd Floor, Washington, DC 20024 Tel. (202)479-6655, Fax (202)479-0735
Media Contact, Rita Chow, Ph.D.

Officers

Chpsn., Rev. Dr. Richard H. Gentzler, Jr.
Chpsn.-Elect, Rev. Dr. Robert W. Carlson
Past Chpsn., Josselyn Bennett
Sec., Rev. Dr. James W. Ellor
Vol. Dir., Dr. Rita K. Chow

National Interfaith Committee for Worker Justice

The National Interfaith Committee for Worker Justice (NICWJ) is a network of fifty-six interfaith groups and people of faith who educate and mobilize the U.S. religious community on issues and campaigns to improve wages, benefits and working conditions for workers, especially low-wage workers. The organization rebuilds relationships between the religious community and organized labor.

The organization supports and organizes local interfaith worker justice groups around the country, publishes Faith Works six times a year providing congregations resources and updates on religion-labor work, coordinates the Poultry Justice project to improve conditions for poultry workers, and promotes healthy dialogue between management and unions in religious owned or sponsored health care facilities.

Headquarters

1020 West Bryn Mawr, 4th floor, Chicago, IL 60660-4627. Tel. (773)728-8400, Fax (773) 728-8409

Media Contact, Mr. Toure Muhammed

Officers

President, Rabbi Robert Marx, Congregation Hakafa

Vice-President, Rev. Nelson Johnson, Faith Community Church

Secretary-Treasurer, Rev. Dr. Paul Sherry, Recent Past President, United Church of Christ

Issues and Action Committee Chair, Ms. Tiffany Heath, Acting Director, Washington Office, Church Women United

Education Committee Chair, Mr. Tom Chabolla, Director of Justice & Peace Commission, Archdiocese of Los Angeles

Development Committee Chair, Rev. Clete Kiley, Executive Director, Secretariat for Priestly Life, U.S. Catholic Conference

Board Development Chair, Ms. Karen McLean Hessel, Director, Justice for Women, National Council of Churches

Staff

Executive Director, Kim Bobo, kim@nicwj.org

General Information, Bridget Harris, bridget@nicwj.org

EDUCATION AND OUTREACH

Regina Botterill, Education Outreach Coordinator and Faith Works Editor, regina@nicwj.org

Toure Muhammad, Public Relations and Network Coordinator, toure@nicwj.org

Jana Winch, Graphic and Web Designer, jana@nicwj.org

ISSUES AND ACTION

Miltoria Bey, Caregivers Justice Project Coordinator, miltoria@nicwj.org

Leone Bicchieri, National Poultry Justice Campaign Coordinator, leone@nicwj.org

Joan Malone, Labor Management Relations Project Coordinator, pruejo@aol.com

Barbara Pfarr, SSND, Labor Management Relations Project Coordinator, bpfarr@nicwj.org

Mary Priniski, OP, Health Care Workers' Advocate, mary@nicwj.org

Denise Starkey, OP, Religious Employers Project Coordinator, denise@nicwj.org

Deborah Young, NC Interfaith Alliance for Worker Justice, debyoungnc@aol.com

DEVELOPMENT

Tom Levinson, Development Director, tom@nicwj.org

Liz Stake, Bookkeeper, liz@nicwj.org

INTERNS

Rebekah Jordan, Garrett Evangelical Theological Seminary, rebekah@nicwj.org

Teresa Mithen, Episcopal Church, tkmithen@yahoo.com

Warren Wilcox, United Methodist Mission Program, warren@nicwj.org

Steven Wilson, Unitarian Universalist, steve@nicwj.org

ARIZONA

SAAEJ—Interfaith Committee, 931 North Fifth Ave., Tucson, AZ 85705, Tel. (520)670-1515, Lupita Calderon

ARKANSAS

Arkansas Interfaith Committee for Worker Justice, P.O. Box 2441, Little Rock, AR 72203, Tel. (870)548-2574, Rev. Steve Copley

CALIFORNIA

Martinez—

Contra Costa Faith Works!, 1333 Pine Street, Ste. E, Martinez, CA 94553, Tel. (925)228-0161, Fax (925)228-0224, John Dalrymple

Los Angeles—

Clergy and Laity United for Economic Justice, 548 S. Spring St., Suite 630, Los Angeles, CA 90013-2313, Tel. (213)239-6771, Fax (486) 6572, Rev. William Johnson

Monterey Bay—

Interfaith Council on Social & Economic Justice, 2560 Garden Rd., Suite 210, Monterey, CA 93940, Tel. (831)333-9016, Karen Osmundson

Oakland—

East Bay Interfaith Committee for Worker Justice, 548 20th St., Oakland, CA 94612, Tel. (510)893-7106, Fax (510)893-5362, Kirsten Cross

San Diego—

Interfaith Committee for Worker Justice of San Diego, 3727 Camino Del Rio South, Ste. 100, San Diego, CA 92108, Tel. (619)584-5740, Fax (619)584-5748, Mike Daniels, www.onlinecpi.org-interfaith

San Jose—

Interfaith Council on Race, Religion, Economic & Social Justice, 2102 Almaden Rd., #107, Santa Clara, CA 95125, Tel. (408)266-3790, Fax (508)266-2653, Rudy Gonzalves, www.atwork.org tic

CONNECTICUT

New Haven Community and Labor Coalition, 425 College St., New Haven, CT 06511, Tel. (203)624-5161, Fax (203)776-6438, Andrea Cole

Waterbury—Good Jobs! Partnership, P.O. Box 2662, Hartford, CT 06146, Tel. (860)232-8844, Hannah Roditi, www.goodjobsCT.com

DELAWARE

Delmarva Poultry Justice Alliance, 257 Oyster Shell Cove, Bethany Beach, DE 19930, Tel. (302)537-5314, Fax (302)537-5318, Rev. Jim Lewis, www.dpja.org

FLORIDA

Central Florida Interfaith Committee for Economic Justice and Dignity, 924 N. Magnolia Ave., Ste. 304, Orlando, FL 32803, Tel. (407)839-3454, Fred Morris

Interfaith Action of Southwest Florida, 1107 Newmarket Rd., Immokalee, FL 34142, Tel. (941)867-9160, Demara Luce, www.interfaithaction.org

South Florida Interfaith Committee for Worker Justice, 10840 NW 46th Dr., Coral Springs, FL 33076, Tel. (954)575-0950, Bruce Jay

GEORGIA

Georgia Poultry Justice Alliance, c/o Epworth Methodist Church, 1561 McLendon Ave. NE, Atlanta, GA 30307, Tel. (770) 330-8338, Ernie Curtis, www.geocities.com/gpja2000/index2.html

Metro Atlanta Religion-Labor Roundtable, (404) 522-0604, Bo Chagnon

HAWAII

Hawai'i Interfaith Committee for Worker Justice, P.O. Box 61212, Honolulu, HI 96839, Tel. (808)988-3673, Fax (808)988-3673, Nancy Aleck

ILLINOIS

Chicago Interfaith Committee on Worker Issues, 1020 W. Bryn Mawr, 4th Fl., Chicago, IL 60660, Tel. (773)728-8400, Fax (773)728-8409, Kristi Sanford, www.chicagointerfaith.org

INDIANA

Northwest Indiana—Calumet Project, 7128 Arizona Ave., Hammond, IN 46323-2223 (219)845-5008, Fax (219)845-5032, David Klein

Central Indiana—St. Joseph Valley Project, 2015 W. Western, #209, South Bend, IN 46629, Tel. (219)287-3834, Fax (219)233-5543, Kevin Hunter

Indianapolis—Interfaith Committee of Jobs with Justice, c/o Speedway United Methodist Church, 5065 W. 16th St., Indianapolis, IN 46224, Tel. (317)241-1563, Fax (219)241-2075, Rev. Darren Cushman-Wood

Interfaith Committee on Work & Community, 1401 Prairie Dr., Bloomington, IN 47408, Tel. (812)332-1710, Fax (812)332-1720, Rev. C.J. Hawking

IOWA

Des Moines—Faith Labor Network, 4211 Grand Ave., Des Moines, IA 50312, Tel. (515)274-6027, Fax (515)274-2003, Josh Crandall

KENTUCKY

Worker Rights Outreach & Kentucky Jobs with Justice, 7902 Old Minors Lane, Louisville, KY 40219, Tel. (502)582-3508 x 124, Amanda LaDuke

LOUSIANA

Interfaith Committee for Worker Justice, 40 Killdeer St., New Orleans, LA 70124, Tel. (504)288-1216, Jerry Siefken

MASSACHUSETTS

Massachusetts Interfaith Committee for Worker Justice, 33 Harrison Ave., 4th floor, Boston, MA 02111, Tel. (617)574-9296, Fax (617) 426-7684; Dr. Jonathan Fine

Religion & Labor Committee, c/o Labor Guild of Boston, 883 Hancock St., Quincy, MA 02170, Tel. (617)786-1822, Fax (617)472-2486, Father Edward Boyle

Holy Cross Student Labor Action Committee, c/o Justin Holmes, College of the Holy Cross, Box 1191, Worcester, MA 01610, jcholmes@holycross.edu

MICHIGAN

Detroit Interfaith Committee on Worker Issues, 1641 Webb, Detroit, MI 48206, Tel. (313) 869-1632, Fax (313)869-8266, Vivian Gladden

MINNESOTA

Duluth Labor and Religion Network, 2830 E. 4th St., Duluth, MN 55812, Tel. (218)724-9111, Fax (218)724-1056, Patrice Critchley-Menor

Twin Cities Religion and Labor Network, 328 W. Kellogg Blvd. St. Paul, MN 55102, Tel. (612) 501-9186, Bob Hulteen

MISSOURI

Labor & Religion Committee of the Human Rights Commission, 3519 N. 14th St., St. Louis, MO 63107, Tel. (314)241-9165, Fax (314)436-9291, Rev. Rich Creason

MONTANA

Montana Community-Labor Alliance, 2416 Teakwood Ln., Helena, MT 59601, Tel. (406) 443-7023, Tom Huddleston

NEVADA

Las Vegas Interfaith Council for Worker Justice, 2100 S. Maryland, Suite 9, Las Vegas, NV 89104, Tel. (702)866-6008, Fax (702)866-6012, Mike Slater, www.lvinterfaith.org

NEW HAMPSHIRE

Interfaith Committee for Worker Justice, P.O. Box 292, Goffstown, NH 03045, Tel. (603) 497-5167, Fred Robinson

NEW YORK

Albany—Capitol District Labor Religion Coalition, 159 Wolf Rd., Albany, NY 12205, Tel. (518)459-5400, Fax (518)454-6412, Bill Peltz

Buffalo—Coalition for Economic Justice, 2123 Bailey Ave., Buffalo, NY 14211, Tel. (716) 892-5877, Maria Whyte

Long Island—Long Island Labor Religion

Coalition, P.O. Box 1147, Central Islip, NY 11722, Tel. (631) 435-1658, Ryland Gaines

New York City—Labor-Religion Coalition, 40 Fulton St., 22nd Fl., New York, NY 10038, Tel. (212)406-2156 x 4637, Fax (212)406-2296, labrelig@aol.com, Rabbi Michael Feinberg

New York State—Labor-Religion Coalition, 159 Wolf Rd., Albany, NY 12205, Tel. (518)459-5400, Fax (518)454-6412; Brian O'Shaughnessy, www.labor-religion.org

Rochester—Labor-Religion Coalition, 42 Hickory St., Rochester, NY 14620, Tel. (716) 454-3295, Gale Lynch

Southern Tier—Labor-Religion Coalition, c/o Catholic Charities, 215 E. Church St.,

Elmira, NY 14901, (607)734-9784 x134, Ruth Elliott

Syracuse—Central New York Labor-Religion Coalition, 4983 Britton Field Pkwy., P.O. Box 247, East Syracuse, NY 13057, Tel. (315)431-4040 x40; Bonnie Pierce

NORTH CAROLINA

NC Interfaith Alliance for Worker Justice, 1556 Lamont Norwood Rd., Pittsboro, NC 27312, Tel./Fax, (919)929 6104, Deborah Young

Pulpit Forum, 1310 MLK Dr., Greensboro, NC 27406, Tel. (336)272-8441, Fax (336)378-1164, Rev. W.F. Wright

OHIO

Cincinnati—Interfaith Committee on Worker Justice, 745 Derby Ave., Cincinnati, OH 45232, Tel. (513)591-1100, Sarah Namaste

Cleveland—Cleveland Jobs with Justice, 20525 Center Ridge Rd., Rocky River, OH 44116, Tel. (440)333-6363, Fax (440)333-1491, Steve Cagan

Dayton—Interfaith Committee for Worker Justice, 1512 Cory Dr. Dayton, OH 45406 (937) 277-7102, Dick Righter

OKLAHOMA

Eastern Oklahoma Labor Religion Council, P.O. Box 471313, Tulsa, OK 74147, Tel. (918)50-5496, Jim Cook

Oklahoma City—Central Oklahoma Community Forum, 5315 S. Shartel, Oklahoma City, OK 73109, Tel. (405)634-4030, Tim O'Connor

OREGON

Eugene—Springfield Solidarity Network, P.O. Box 10272; Eugene, OR 97440, Tel. (541) 736-9041, essn@efn.org, Sarah Jacobson

PENNSYLVANIA

Pittsburgh—Religion-Labor Committee, c/o Allegheny Labor Council, Arrott Bldg.,

401 Wood St., Ste. 501, Pittsburgh, PA 15222, Tel. (412)281-7450, Fr. Jack O'Malley

TENNESSEE

Nashville—Middle Tennessee Jobs with Justice, 2001 Elm Hill Pike, Nashville, TN 37210, Tel. (615)872-8792, Fax (615)874-1253, Dillard Tabor

Knoxville—Religious Outreach Committee, Central Labor Council, 311 Morgan St., Knoxville, TN 37917, Tel. (865)523-9752; Fax (865)523-9478, Harold & Sylvia Woods

TEXAS

Brazor Valley—Interfaith Alliance for Worker Justice, St. Mary's Catholic Church

603 Church St., College Station, TX 77840, Tel. (409)846-5717, Fax (409)846-4493, Maureen Murray

Dallas—Dallas Jobs with Justice, c/o Camp Wisdom UMC, 1300 W. Camp Wisdom Rd., Dallas, TX 75232, Tel. (972)224-4556, Fax (972)228-9434, Rev. Charles Stovall

Houston—Houston Interfaith Committee for Worker Justice, c/o Worklife Ministries

7100 Regency Sq., Suite 210, Houston, TX 77036, Tel. (713)266-2456; Fax (713)266-0845; Rev. Diana Dale

VERMONT

Vermont Faith Communities for a Just Economy, 21 Church St., Burlington, VT 05401, Tel. (802)863-2345 x 1, Ellen Kahler

WASHINGTON

Washington Religious Labor Partnership, c/o WA Association of Churches, 419 Occidental Ave., South, #201, Seattle, WA 98104, Tel. (206)625-9790, Fax (206)625-9791, Rev. John Boonstra

WISCONSIN

Faith Community for Worker Justice, 2128 N. 73rd St., Wauwatosa, WI 53213, Tel. (414) 771- 7250, Fax (414)771-0509, Bill Lange

South Central, WI—Interfaith Coalition for Worker Justice of South Central Wisconsin, P.O. Box 1104, Madison, WI 53701, Tel. (608) 246-4355, Fax (608)246-4349, Ann McNeary, www.workerjustice.org

National Religious Broadcasters

National Religious Broadcasters is an association of 1,300 organizations which produce religious programs for radio and television and other forms of electronic mass media or operate stations carrying predominately religious programs. NRB member organizations are responsible for more than 75 percent of all religious radio and television in the United States, reaching an average weekly audience of millions by radio, television, and other broadcast media.

Dedicated to the communication of the Gospel, NRB was founded in 1944 to safeguard free and complete access to the broadcast media. By encouraging the development of Christian programs and stations, NRB helps make it possible for millions to hear the good news of Jesus Christ through the electronic media.

Headquarters

7839 Ashton Ave., Manassas, VA 20109 Tel. (703)330-7000, Fax (703)330-7100

Media Contact, Pres., Brandt Gustavson; Vice-Pres., Michael Glenn

Officers

Chmn., Wayne A. Pederson, Northwestern College Radio, St. Paul, MN

1st Vice Chmn., Glenn R. Plummer, Christian Television Network, Detroit, MI
2nd Vice Chmn., Michael D. Little, Christian Broadcasting Network, Virginia Beach, VA
Sec., William Skelton, Love Worth Finding Ministries, Memphis, TN
Treas., James A. Gwinn, CRISTA Ministries, Seattle, WA

National Woman's Christian Temperance Union

The National WCTU is a not-for-profit, non-partisan, interdenominational organization dedicated to the education of our nation's citizens, especially children and teens, on the harmful effects of alcoholic beverages, other drugs, and tobacco on the human body and the society in which we live. The WCTU believes in a strong family unit and, through legislation, education, and prayer, works to strengthen the home and family.

WCTU, which began in 1874 with the motto, "For God and Home and Every Land," is organized in 58 countries.

Headquarters

1730 Chicago Ave., Evanston, IL 60201 Tel. (708)864-1396
Media Contact, Sarah F. Ward, Tel. (765)345-7600

Officers

Pres., Sarah F. Ward, 33 N. Franklin, Knightstown, IN 46148, sarah@wctu.org
Vice-Pres., Rita Wert, 2250 Creek Hill Rd., Lancaster, PA 17601
Promotion Dir., Nancy Zabel, 1730 Chicago Ave., Evanston, IL 60201-4585
Treas., Faye Pohl, P.O. Box 739, Meade, KS 67864
Rec. Sec., Dorothy Russell, 18900 Nestueca Dr., Cloverdale, OR 97112

MEMBER ORGANIZATIONS

Loyal Temperance Legion (LTL), for boys and girls ages 6-12
Youth Temperance Council (YTC), for teens through college age

North American Baptist Fellowship

Organized in 1964, the North American Baptist Fellowship is a voluntary organization of Baptist Conventions in Canada and the United States, functioning as a regional body within the Baptist World Alliance. Its objectives are, (a) to promote fellowship and cooperation among Baptists in North America and (b) to further the aims and objectives of the Baptist World Alliance so far as these affect the life of the Baptist churches in North America. Its membership, however, is not identical with the North American membership of the Baptist World Alliance.

Church membership of the Fellowship bodies is more than 28 million.

The NABF assembles representatives of the member bodies once a year for exchange of information and views in such fields as evangelism and education, missions, stewardship promotion, lay activities and theological education. It conducts occasional consultations for denominational leaders on such subjects as church extension. It encourages cooperation at the city and county level where churches of more than one member group are located.

Headquarters

Baptist World Alliance Bldg., 405 North Washington St, Falls Church VA 22046
Media Contact, Dr. Denton Lotz

Officers

Pres., Dr. Robert Ricker, 2002 S. Arlington Heights Rd., Arlington Heights, IL 60005, rricker@baptistgeneral.org
Vice-Pres., Dr. David Emmanuel Goatley, 300 I St., NE, Suite 104, Washington, DC 20002, degoatley@aol.com
Vice-Pres., Dr. Phillip Wise, 300 West Main St., Box 2025, Dothan, AL 36301, philip@fbc-dothan.org
Vice-Pres., Dr. Gary Nelson, 7185 Millcreek Dr. Mississauga, ON 15N 5R4, Canada, nelsong@cbmin.org

MEMBER BODIES

American Baptist Churches in the USA
Baptist General Conference
Canadian Baptist Federation
General Association of General Baptists
National Baptist Convention of America
National Baptist Convention, USA, Inc.
Progressive National Baptist Convention, Inc.
Seventh Day Baptist General Conference
North American Baptist Conference
Southern Baptist Convention

Oikocredit: Ecumenical Development Cooperative Society

Based in the Netherlands, EDCS is often called "the churches' bank for the poor." EDCS borrows funds from churches, religious communities, and concerned individuals and re-lends the funds to enterprises operated by low-income communities. Launched in 1975 through an initiative of the World Council of Churches, EDCS is organized as a cooperative of religious institutions and is governed by annual membership meetings and an elected board of religious leaders and development and financial professionals.

An international network of 15 EDCS Regional Managers is responsible for lending funds to cooperative enterprises and microcredit institutions. At the present time over $50 million is at work in coffee shops, fishing enterprises, handicraft production, truck farming, and many other commercial ventures owned and operated by poor people.

EDCS is represented in the United States by the Ecumenical Development Corporation- USA (EDC-USA), a 501(c)3 non-profit corporation. American individuals and congregations can invest in EDCS by purchasing one, three, and five year notes paying 0-2% interest that are issued by EDC-USA.

U. S. Headquarters

475 Riverside Dr., 16th Floor, New York, NY 10115 Tel. (212)870-2725, Fax (212)870-2722

Media Contact, Regional Manager for North America, The Rev. Louis L. Knowles

Officers, EDC-USA

Chpsn., The Rev. Dr. Darell Weist
Vice-Chpsn., Thomas Dowdell
Treas., Bruce Foresman
Sec., Suzanne Sattler, IHM

Parish Resource Center, Inc.

Parish Resource Center, Inc. promotes, establishes, nurtures, and accredits local Affiliate Parish Resource Centers. Affiliate centers educate, equip, and strengthen subscribing congregations of all faiths by providing professional consultants, resource materials, and workshops. The Parish Resource Center was founded in 1976. In 2001, there were six free-standing affiliates located in Lancaster, PA; Long Island, NY; South Bend, IN.; Denver, CO.; Dayton, OH and New York City. These centers serve congregations from 49 faith traditions.

Headquarters

633 Community Way, Lancaster, PA 17603 Tel. (717)299-2223, Fax (717)299-7229

Media Contact, Pres., Dr. D. Douglas Whiting

Officers

Chair, Richard J. Ashby, Jr.
Vice-Chair, Margaret M. Obrecht
Sec., Dr. Robert Webber
Treas., Stephen C. Eyre
Pres., Dr. D. Douglas Whiting

Pentecostal-Charismatic Churches of North America

The Pentecostal-Charismatic Churches of North America (PCCNA) was organized October 19, 1994, in Memphis, TN. This organizational meeting came the day after the Pentecostal Fellowship of North America (PFNA) voted itself out of existence in order to make way for the new fellowship.

The PFNA had been formed in October 1948 in Des Moines, IA. It was composed of white-led Pentecostal denominations. The move to develop a multiracial fellowship began when the PFNA Board of Administration initiated a series of discussions with African-American Pentecostal leaders. The first meeting was held July 10-11, 1992, in Dallas, TX. A second meeting convened in Phoenix, AZ, January 4-5, 1993. On January 10-11, 1994, 20 representatives from each of the two groups met in Memphis to make final plans for a Dialogue which was held in Memphis, October 1994.

This racial reconciliation meeting has been called "The Memphis Miracle." During this meeting the PFNA was disbanded, and the PCCNA was organized. The new organization quickly adopted the "Racial Reconciliation Manifesto." Subsequent meetings were held in Memphis, TN (1996), Washington, DC (1997), Tulsa, OK (1998), and Hampton, VA (1999)

In an effort to further increase the spirit of reconciliation, the PCCNA meeting of 2000 was held during the North American Renewal Service committee (NARSC) Conference in St. Louis, Missouri. Furthermore, the PCCNA acted as host for the 19th Pentecostal World Conference held in Los Angeles, California, May 2001.

Headquarters

1910 W. Sunset Blvd. Ste. 200, Los Angeles, CA 90026-0176 Tel. (213)484-2400, ext. 309, Fax (213)413-3824

Media Contact, Dr. Ronald Williams

Officers

PCCNA EXECUTIVE BOARD

Co-Chairperson, Bishop James D. Leggett, International Pentecostal Holiness Church, P.O. Box 12609, Oklahoma City, OK 73157-2609, Tel. (405)787-7110 ext. 3302, Fax (405) 787-3650, jdl@iphc.org

Co-Chairperson, Bishop George D. McKinney, St. Stephen's Church of God in Christ, 5825 Imperial Ave., San Diego, CA 92114, Tel. (619)262-2671, Fax (619)262-8335, ststephens@pcsinter.net

First Vice-Chairperson, Bishop Oswill Williams, Church of God of Prophecy, P.O. Box 2910, Cleveland, TN 37320-2910, Tel. (423)559-5218, Fax (423)559-5219, ossie@wingnet.net

Second Vice-Chairperson, Rev. Jeff Farmer, Open Bible Standard Churches, 2020 Bell Ave., Des Moines, IA 50315, Tel. (515)288-6761, Fax (515)288-2510

Secretary, Dr. Lamar Vest, Church of God, P.O. Box 2430, Cleveland, TN 37320-2430, Tel. (423)478-7137, Fax (423)478-7443

Treasurer, Dr. Ronald Williams, Int'l Church of the Foursquare Gospel, P.O. Box 26902, Los Angeles, CA 90026, Tel. 213-989-4221, Fax (213)989-4544, ron@foursquare.org

ADVISORS

Rev. Billy Joe Daugherty, Victory Christian Center, 7700 South Lewis Ave., Tulsa, OK 74136-7700, Tel. (918)493-1700, Fax (918) 491-7795

Rev. Thomas Trask, Assemblies of God, 1445 Boonville Ave., Springfield, MO 65802, Tel. 417-862-2781 ext. 3000, Fax 417-862-8558

Bishop Barbara Amos, Mt. Sinai Holy Church of America, 1010 East 26th St., Norfolk, VA 23504, Tel. (757)-624-1950, Fax (757)625-6648

Project Equality, Inc.

Project Equality is a non-profit national interfaith program for affirmative action and equal employment opportunity.

Project Equality serves as a central agency to receive and validate the equal employment commitment of suppliers of goods and services to sponsoring organizations and participating institutions, congregations and individuals. Employers filing an accepted Annual Participation Report are included in the Project Equality "Buyer's Guide."

Workshops, training events, and consultant services in affirmative action, diversity, and equal employment practices in recruitment, selection, placement, transfer, promotion, discipline, and discharge are also available to sponsors and participants.

Headquarters

Pres., 7132 Main St., Kansas City, MO 64114-1406 Tel. (816)361-9222 or toll free 1877-PE-IS-EEO, Fax (816)361-8997

Media Contact, Pres., Rev. Kirk P. Perucca

Officers

Chpsn., Donald Hayashi
Vice-Chpsn., Gloria Foldsl
Sec., Barbara George
Treas., Joan Green
Pres., Rev. Kirk P. Perucca

SPONSORS-ENDORSING ORGANIZATIONS

American Baptist Churches in the U.S.A.
American Friends Service Committee
American Jewish Committee
Assoc. Of Junior Leagues, Intl.
Central Conference of American Rabbis
Church of the Brethren
The Episcopal Church
Evangelical Lutheran Church in America
National Council of Churches of Christ in the U.S.A.
National Education Association
Presbyterian Church (USA)
Reorganized Church of Jesus Christ of Latter-Day Saints
The United Methodist Church
Unitarian Universalist Association
United Church of Christ
United Methodist Assoc. of Health & Welfare Ministries
YWCA of the USA

The Protestant Hour, Inc.

The Protestant Hour, Inc. is an interdenominational organization dedicated to the purpose of creating, producing, marketing and distributing media resources. The "Flagship" production is the weekly radio show "The Protestant Hour."

Affiliate members include the Episcopal Media Center, Evangelical Lutheran Church in America, Presbyterian Church (U.S.A.), United Methodist Communications, Agnes Scott College, Candler School of Theology, Emory University and Columbia Theological Seminary.

Headquarters

644 West Peachtree St., Suite 300, Atlanta, GA 30308-1925 Tel. (404)815-9110, Fax (404) 815-0258

Media Contact, Nan Ross

Officers

Bd. Chpsn., Ms. Harriet Tumlin Jobson
Vice-Chpsn., Bishop L. Bevel Jones, III
Pres., Peter M. Wallace
Treas., Edward Stoners, Jr.
Sec., Ann Gillies

The Religion Communicators Council, Inc.

RCC is an international, interfaith, interdisciplinary association of professional communicators who work for religious groups and causes. It was founded in 1929 and is the oldest non-profit professional public relations organization in the world. RCC's more than 600 members include those who work in communications and related fields for church-related institutions, denominational agencies, non-and interdenominational organizations and communications firms who primarily serve religious organizations.

Members represent a wide range of faiths, including Presbyterian, Baptist, Methodist, Lutheran, Episcopalian, Mennonite, Roman Catholic, Seventh-day Adventist, Jewish, Salvation Army, Brethren, Bahá'i, Disciples, Latter-Day Saints, and others.

On the national level, RCC sponsors an annual three-day convention, and has published six editions of a Religious Public Relations Handbook for churches and church organizations, and a videostrip, The Church at Jackrabbit Junction. Members receive a quarterly newsletter (Counselor). There are 11 regional chapters.

RCC administers the annual Wilbur Awards competition to recognize high quality coverage of religious values and issues in the public media. Wilbur winners include producers, reporters, editors, and broadcasters nationwide. To recognize communications excellence within church communities, RCC also sponsors the annual DeRose-Hinkhouse Awards for its own members.

In 1970, 1980, 1990, and 2000, RCC initiated a global Religious Communications Congress bringing together thousands of persons from western, eastern, and third-world nations who are involved in communicating religious faith.

Headquarters

475 Riverside Dr., Rm. 1948A, New York, NY 10115-1948 Tel. (212)870-2985, Fax (212) 870-3578

Officers

Pres., Jeanean D. Merkel, Paulist Media Works, 3055 Fourth St., NE, Washington, DC 20017, Tel. 202-269-6064, jmerkel@paulist.org

Vice-Pres., Rev. Eric Shafer, Evangelical Lutheran Church in America, 8765 West Higgins Road, Chicago, IL 60631 Tel. (773) 380-2960, eshafer@elca.org

Religion In American Life, Inc.

Religion In American Life (RIAL) is a unique cooperative program of some 50 major national religious groups (Catholic, Eastern Orthodox, Jewish, Protestant, Muslim, etc.). It provides services for denominationally-supported, congregation-based outreach and growth projects such as the current Invite a Friend program. These projects are promoted through national advertising campaigns reaching the American public by the use of all media. The ad campaigns are produced by a volunteer agency with production-distribution and administration costs funded by denominations and business groups, as well as by individuals.

Since 1949, RIAL ad campaign projects have been among the much coveted major campaigns of The Advertising Council. This results in as much as $35 million worth of time and space in a single year, contributed by media as a public service. Through RIAL, religious groups demonstrate respect for other traditions and the value of religious freedom. The RIAL program also includes seminars and symposia, research and leadership awards, and produces a weekly syndicated radio broadcast, "SpiriTalk".

Headquarters

2001 West Main St., Suite 120, Stamford, CT 06902, Tel. (203)355-1220, Fax (203)355-1221

Media Contact, Exec. Admin., Randy M. Bucknoff, Tel. (203)355-1220

Executive Committee

Natl. Chpsn., Thomas S. Johnson, Chairman & CEO, Greenpoint Bank, NY

Chpsn. of Bd., Robert A. Wilson

Vice-Chpsns., Bishop Khajag Barsamian, Primate (Armenian Church of America); The Rev. Dr. M. William Howard, (President, New York Theological Seminary); Most Rev. William Cardinal Keeler, (Archbishop of Baltimore); Rabbi Ronald B. Sobel, (Cong. Emanu-El of the City of N.Y.)

Sec., Timothy A. Hultquist (Morgan Stanley Dean Witter)

Treas., Robertson H. Bennett (Smith Barney)

Staff

Pres. & CEO, Robert B. Lennick, Rabbi, D.Min.

Exec. Admin., Randy M. Bucknoff

Religion News Service

Religion News Service (RNS) has provided news and information to the media for almost 70 years. Owned by the Newhouse News Service, it is staffed by veteran journalists who cover stories on all of the world religions as well as trends in ethics, morality, and spirituality.

RNS provides a daily news service, a weekly news report, and photo and graphic services. The daily service is available via the AP Data Features wire, fax, Ecunet, or e-mail. The weekly report is available by wire or email. Photos and graphics are supplied online.

Headquarters

1101 Connecticut Ave. NW, Ste. 350, Washington, DC 20036, Tel. (202)463-8777, Fax (202) 463-0033

Media Contact, David Anderson

Officers

Editor, David Anderson

Religion Newswriters Association

Founded in 1949, the RNA is a professional association of religion news editors and reporters on secular daily and weekly newspapers, news services, news magazines, radio, and television stations. It sponsors five annual contests for excellence in religion news coverage in the secular press. Annual meetings are held in the fall.

Headquarters

P.O. Box 2037, Westerville, OH 43086 Tel. (614)891-9001, Fax (614) 891-9774

Media Contact, Exec. Dir., Debra Mason

Religious Conference Management Association, Inc.

The Religious Conference Management Association, Inc. (RCMA) is an interfaith, non-profit, professional organization of men and women who have responsibility for planning and/or managing meetings, seminars, conferences, conventions, assemblies, or other gatherings for religious organizations.

Founded in 1972, RCMA is dedicated to promoting the highest professional performance by its members and associate members through the mutual exchange of ideas, techniques, and methods.

Today RCMA has more than 3,000 members and associate members.

The association conducts an annual conference and exposition which provides a forum for its membership to gain increased knowledge in the arts and sciences of religious meeting planning and management.

Headquarters

One RCA Dome, Ste. 120, Indianapolis, IN 46225 Tel. (317)632-1888, Fax (317)632-7909

Media Contact, Exec. Dir., Dr. DeWayne S. Woodring

Officers

Pres., Dr. Jack Stone, Church of the Nazarene, 6401 The Paseo, Kansas City, MO 64131-1213

Vice-Pres., Ms. Linda M. de Leon, General Conference Seventh-Day Adventist Church, 12501 Old Columbia Pike, Silver Spring, MD 20904

Sec.-Treas., Dr. Melvin Worthington, Natl. Assoc. of Free Will Baptists, P.O. Box 5002, Antioch, TN 37011-5002
Exec. Dir., Dr. DeWayne S. Woodring

The Seminary Consortium for Urban Pastoral Education (SCUPE)

Founded in 1976, SCUPE is an interdenominational agency committed to the development of individuals, congregations, and organizations for leadership in urban ministry. For individuals, we offer three accredited graduate-level academic programs, the semester- and/or summer-term Graduate Theological Urban Studies program for seminary students; an M.A. in Community Development degree developed in partnership with North Park University; and Nurturing the Call, a year-long sequence of graduate courses in theology and ministry for urban pastors who have not previously attended seminary.

SCUPE also consults to other ministries and urban institutions, providing specially-designed training programs around issues including diversity, strategic planning, leadership development, and human resource mobilization. We operate an urban ministry resource center and publish the Resource Review, as well as other occasional materials, as a service to the urban church. Every two years, SCUPE also organizes the Congress on Urban Ministry as a training and networking event for those in urban ministry.

Headquarters

200 N. Michigan Ave., Suite 502, Chicago, IL 60601 Tel. (312)726-1200, Fax (312)726-0425
Media Contact, President, Dr. David Frenchak; Dir. Marketing & Development, Mark Walden

Officers

Chair, Rev. Donald Sharp
Vice Chair, Ms. Cheryl Hammock
Treasurer, Mr. Case Hoogendoorn
Secretary, Dr. Bill VanWyngaarden
Lead Program Staff
President, Dr. David Frenchak
Co-Directors, M.A. in Community Development, Rev. Carol Ann McGibbon & Dr. Arthur Lyons
Director, Graduate Theological Urban Studies, Rev. Bill Wylie-Kellermann
Coordinator, Special Events, Ms. Angela Janssen
Director, Nurturing the Call, Rev. Kazi Joshua

United Ministries in Higher Education

United Ministries in Higher Education is a cooperative effort to provide religious programs and services to those engaged in higher education ministries.

Headquarters

7407 Steele Creek Rd., Charlotte, NC 28217 Tel. (704)588-2182, Fax (704)588-3652
Media Contact, Res. Sec., Linda Danby Freeman

Officers

Treas., Linda Danby Freeman
Personnel Service, Kathy Carson, 11720 Borman Dr., Ste. 240, St. Louis, MO 63146 Tel. (314)991-3000, Fax (314)991-2957
Resource Center, Linda Danby Freeman
PARTICIPATING DENOMINATIONS
Christian Church (Disciples of Christ)
Presbyterian Church (U.S.A.)
United Church of Christ

United Religions Initiative

The purpose of the United Religions Initiative is to promote enduring, daily interfaith cooperation, to end religiously motivated violence, and to create cultures of peace, justice, and healing for the Earth and all living beings.

The United Religions initiative is a growing, global community of over 130 Cooperation Circles, involving thousands of people around the world. The URI is inspired by the leadership potential inherent in every individual, leadership that is discovered and deepened through dialogue with others when dreams are shared and cooperative destinies are realized. The individuals who make up the URI network are committed to interfaith peacebuilding, recognizing that for peace to prevail on earth, "peace must begin with me." They believe that by talking with others who come from different faiths, cultures, or spiritual traditions, all involved can begin to better understand their own beliefs and recognize their common bonds.

The URI seeks to create safe spaces throughout the world where these interfaith partnerships can be seeded, and the ideas and initiative that they spark can be practically applied. With the mandate in the URI Charter that each Cooperation Circle represent at least three different faith traditions, the very act of coming together builds peace by creating interfaith cooperation among neighbors and within communities where it may never before have been possible. The Charter "Guidelines for Action" affirm the "essentially self-organizing nature" of the Cooperation Circles and empower CC participants to "choose what they want to do" while providing guidance for community-building. The Guidelines assure that all URI activities and actions demonstrate the following heartfelt considerations: (a) sharing the wisdom and cultures of different faith traditions; (b) nurturing cultures of healing and peace; (c) upholding human rights; (d) supporting the health of the entire Earth; (e) integrating spirituality in issues of economic justice; and (f) providing grassroot support for all URI activities.

The initial vision for the United Religions Initiative began in 1993 with a dream by its founder, Bishop William Swing. He writes that it came with "a sudden realization that religions, together, have a vocation to be a force for good in the world." In just seven years, tens of thousands of people in more than sixty countries around the world have responded to this vision with a resounding, "Yes!" Their affirmations have taken on a myriad of forms. For example, during the 72 Hours Project at the turn of the Millennium, over a million people in 40 countries participated in 200 projects for peace. Highlights included a 12-day interfaith pilgrimage across Pakistan and the celebration of 1 million signature on a petition to ban handguns in Rio de Janeiro.

Headquarters

P.O. Box 29242, San Francisco, CA 94129-0242 Tel. (415)561-2300, Fax (415)562-2313

Media Contact, Barbara H. Hartford, Operations Manager

Staff

Executive Director, Charles Gibbs
Office Coordination, Victor Gresser
Peacebuilding, Barbara H. Hartford
Global Fundraising, Philanthropy, Jennifer Kirk
Membership and Organizational Development, Sally Mahe
Communications and Technology, Kristin Swenson
Annual Giving and Knowledge Management, Sarah Talcott
Financial Manager, Ray Signer
INTERIM GLOBAL COUNCIL
President and Founding Trustee, Bishop William Swing
Chair, Ms. Rita R. Semel
Vice-Chair, Rev. Dr. Jack Lundin
Treasurer, Mr. Rick Murray
Secretary, Rev. Paul Chaffee

The United States Conference of Religions for Peace (USCRP)

The United States Conference of Religions for Peace (USCRP) provides a forum for the nation's religious bodies based upon respect for religious differences. In today's world, cooperation among religions offers an important opportunity to mobilize and coordinate the great moral and sociological capacities for constructive action inherent in religious communities.

USCRP provides American religious bodies with opportunities for the following: to identify shared commitments to constructive social development, justice, and peace; to coordinate their efforts with other religious groups on behalf of widely-shared concerns; and to design, undertake, and evaluate joint action projects.

Headquarters

USCRP, 777 United Nations Plaza, New York, NY 10017 Tel. (212)338-9140, (212)983-0566

Officers

Sec. Gen./Executive Dir., Mr. Antonios Kireopoulos
Moderator, V. Rev. Leonid Kishkovsky

Vellore Christian Medical College Board (USA), Inc.

The Vellore Christian Medical College Board (USA) has been linked since 1900 to the vision of a young American medical doctor, Dr. Ida S. Scudder, who founded Christian Medical College and Hospital in Vellore, India. Dr. Ida's vision was to train women in all the healing arts so that they could treat women and their families. Today after 100 years of teaching and service, the College and Hospital is directed by an Indian woman, Dr. Joyce Ponnaiya. The Vellore Christian Medical College Board (USA) supports the work of Christian Medical College and Hospital in Vellore through exchange personnel programs including volunteers to Vellore and senior CMC staff receiving fellowships to study and work in the United States over 3 month periods. The Vellore Board also assists CMC&H with Capital Campaigns and high tech medical equipment.

Headquarters

475 Riverside Dr., Rm. 243, New York, NY 10115 Tel. (212)870-2640, Fax (212)870-2173

Media Contact, President, Rev. William Salmond

E-mail: wsalmond@vellorecmc.org

Officers

Chair., Dr. Mani M. Mani, 5137 West 60th Terrace, Mission, KS 66205
Vice-Chair., Miriam Ballert, 7104 Olde Oak Ct., Prospect, KY 40059
Sec., Mrs. Edwina Youth, 211 Blue Ridge Dr., Levittown, PA 19057
Treas., Michael Holt, 352 Pines Lake Dr. East, Wayne, NJ 07470

World Council of Churches, United States Office

The United States Conference of the World Council of Churches was formed in 1938 when the WCC itself was still in the "Process of Formation." Henry Smith Leiper, an American with many national and international connections, was given the title of "Associate General Secretary" of the WCC and asked to carry out WCC work in the U.S. After the World Council of Churches was officially born in 1948 in Amsterdam, Netherlands, Leiper raised millions of dollars for WCC programs.

Today the U.S. Conference of the WCC is composed of representatives of U.S. member churches of the worldwide body. The U.S. Office of the WCC works to develop relationships among the churches, advance the work of WCC and interpret the council in the United States.

Headquarters

475 Riverside Dr., Rm. 915, New York, NY 10115 Tel. (212)870-2533, Fax (212)870-2528

Media Contact, Philip E. Jenks

Officers

WCC President from North America and

Moderator, Rev. Kathryn Bannister, United Methodist Church
Vice-Moderator, Bishop McKinley Young, African Methodist Episcopal Church
Vice-Moderator and Treasurer, The Rev. Leonid Kishkovsky, Orthodox Church in America

Staff

Exec. Dir., Jean S. Stromberg, Tel. (212)870-2522
Communications Officer, Philip E. Jenks, Tel. (212)870-3193
Office Admn., Sonia P. Omulepu, Tel. (212)870-2470

World Day of Prayer

World Day of Prayer is an ecumenical movement initiated and carried out by Christian women in 170 countries who conduct a common day of prayer on the first Friday of March to which all people are welcome. There is an annual theme for the worship service that has been prepared by women in a different country each year. For 2001 the women of Samoa have prepared a worship service on the theme, "Informed Prayer, Prayerful Action" which is also the WDP motto. The offering at this service is gathered by each WDP National or Regional Committee and given to help people who are in need.

Headquarters

World Day of Prayer International Comm., 475 Riverside Dr., Rm. 560, New York, NY 10115 Tel. (212)870-3049, Fax (212)864-8648
Media Contact, Exec. Dir., Eileen King

Officers

Chairperson, Yvonne Harrison
Treasurer, Karen Prudente
North America, Susan Shank Mix (USA); Sylvia Lisk Vanhaverbeke (Canada)
Africa, Sarie Jansen; Karen Ngigi
Asia, Shunila Ruth; Jong Ok Lee
Caribbean, Waveney Benjamin; Neva Edwards
Europe, Inge Lise Lollike; Alena Naimanova
Latin America, Renee Carter; Inez Proverbs
Middle East, Aida Haddad; Nadia Menes
Pacific, Margaret Kenna; Gwen Tulo
Member at Large, Maria Gabriela Trimbitas

World Methodist Council-North American Section

The World Methodist Council, one of the 30 or so "Christian World Communions," shares a general tradition which is common to all Christians. The world organization of Methodists and related United Churches is comprised of 74 churches with roots in the Methodist tradition. These churches found in 130 countries have a membership of more than 34 million.

The Council's North American Section, comprised of ten Methodist and United Church denominations, provides a regional focus for the Council in Canada, the United States and Mexico. The North American Section meets at the time of the quinquennial World Conference and Council, and separately as Section between world meetings. The Section met in Rio de Janeiro, Brazil in August 1996 during the 17th World Methodist Conference to elect its officers for the 1997-2001 quinquennium. 2001-2006 officers will be elected in Brighton, England, July 2001.

North American Churches related to the World Methodist Council have a membership of approximately 16 million and a church community of more than 30 million.

Headquarters

P.O. Box 518, Lake Junaluska, NC 28745 Tel. (828)456-9432, Fax (828)456-9433
Media Contact, Gen. Sec., Joe Hale

Officers

Section Pres., Bishop Neil L. Irons, 900 S. Arlington Ave., Rm. 214, Harrisburg, PA 17109-5097 Tel. (717)652-6705, Fax (717) 652-5109
First Vice-Pres., Bishop Thomas L. Hoyt, CME Church
Vice-Pres., Bishop John R. Bryant, AME Church; Bishop Cecil Bishop, AMEZ Church; Bishop Richard D. Snyder, Free Methodist Church; Bishop Gracela Alverez, Methodist Church in Mexico; Bishop Keith Elford, Free Methodist Church of Canada; Rev. Carol Hancock, United Church of Canada; Dr. Jack Stone, Church of the Nazarene; Dr. Earle L. Wilson, The Wesleyan Church; Chairman, Finance Committee, Dr. Donald V. Fites
Treas., Dr. James W. Holsinger, Jr.
Asst. Treas., Edna Alsdurf
General Sec., Dr. Joe Hale
World Officers from North America, Dr. Frances M. Alguire; Dr. Maxie D. Dunnam; Bishop Donald Ming

World Vision

World Vision is an international, Christian relief and development organization working to promote the well being of all people—especially that of children. Established in 1950 to care for Asian orphans, World Vision has grown to embrace the larger issues of community development and advocacy for the poor in its mission to help children and their families build sustainable futures. Working on six continents, World Vision is one of the largest Christian relief and development organizations in the world. World Vision U.S., one of the members of this international partnership also works in the U.S. to alleviate poverty and its effects, focusing on key metro areas. Programs that are geared to the church include the 30 Hour Famine and Love Loaf. The Church Relations department faciliates partnerships between churches and local or international projects.

Headquarters

P.O. Box 9716, Federal Way, WA 98063-9716, Tel. (253)815-1000
Media Contact, Dean Owen, Tel. (253)815-2158

Officers

President, Richard Stearns
Vice Presidents, Scott Jackson, Atul Tandon, Bruce Wilkinson, John Reid, Julie Regnier

YMCA of the USA

The YMCA is one of the largest private voluntary organizations in the world, serving about 30 million people in more than 100 countries. In the United States, more than 2,000 local branches, units, camps, and centers annually serve more than 14 million people of all ages, races, and abilities. About half of those served are female. No one is turned away because of an inability to pay.

The Y teaches youngsters to swim, organizes youth basketball games and offers adult aerobics. But the Y represents more than fitness—it works to strengthen families and help people develop values and behavior that are consistent with Christian principles.

The Y offers hundreds of programs including day camp for children, child care, exercise for people with disabilities, teen clubs, environmental programs, substance abuse prevention, family nights, job training, and many more programs from infant mortality prevention to overnight camping for seniors.

The kind of programs offered at a YMCA will vary; each is controlled by volunteer board members who make their own program, policy, and financial decisions based on the special needs of their community. In its own way, every Y works to build strong kids, strong families, and strong communities.

The YMCA was founded in London, England, in 1844 by George Williams and friends who lived and worked together as clerks. Their goal was to save other live-in clerks from the wicked life of the London streets. The first members were evangelical Protestants who prayed and studied the Bible as an alternative to vice. The Y has always been nonsectarian and today accepts those of all faiths at all levels of the organization.

Headquarters

101 N. Wacker Dr., Chicago, IL 60606 Tel. (312)977-0031, Fax (312)977-9063
Media Contact, Media Relations Manager, Arnie Collins

Officers

Board Chpsn., Daniel E. Emerson
Exec. Dir., David R. Mercer
(Int.) Public Relations Assoc., Mary Pyke Gover

YWCA of the U.S.A.

The YWCA of the U.S.A. is comprised of 313 affiliates in communities and on college campuses across the United States. It serves one million members and program participants. It seeks to empower women and girls to enable them, coming together across lines of age, race, religious belief, and economic and occupational status to make a significant contribution to the elimination of racism and the achievement of peace, justice, freedom, and dignity for all people.

Headquarters

Empire State Building, 350 Fifth Ave., Ste. 301 New York, NY 10118 Tel. (212)273-7800, Fax (212)465-2281
Media Contact, Khristina Lew

Officers

National Pres., Leticia Paez
Sec., Carol O. Markus
Chief Exec. Officer, Margaret Tyndall

Youth for Christ-USA

Founded in 1944, as part of the body of Christ, our vision is to see every young person in every people group in every nation have the opportunity to make an informed decision to be a follower of Jesus Christ and become a part of a local church.

There are 220 locally controlled YFC programs serving in cities and metropolitan areas of the United States.

YFC's Campus Life Club program involves teens who attend approximately 58,236 high schools in the United States. YFC's staff now numbers approximately 1,000. In addition, nearly 10,000 part-time and volunteer staff supplement the full-time staff. Youth Guidance, a ministry for nonschool-oriented youth includes group homes, court referrals, institutional services and neighborhood ministries. The year-round conference and camping program involves approximately 200,000 young people each year. Other ministries include DC Ministries, World Outreach, Project Serve, and Teen Moms. Independent, indigenous YFC organizations also work in 127 countries overseas.

Headquarters

U.S. Headquarters, P.O. Box 228822, Denver, CO 80222 Tel. (303)843-9000, Fax (303)843-9002
Canadian Organization, 1212-31 Avenue NE, #540, Calgary, AB T2E 7S8
Media Contact, Pres., Roger Cross

Officers

United States, President, Roger Cross
Canada, Pres., Gary D. Helland
Intl. Organization, Pres., Jean-Jacques Weiler

2. Canadian Cooperative Organizations, National

In most cases, the organizations listed here work on a national level and cooperate across denominational lines. Regional cooperative organizations in Canada are listed in Directory 8, "Canadian Regional and Local Ecumenical Bodies."

Aboriginal Rights Coalition (ARC)

ARC works towards the transformation of the relationship between Canadian society and Aboriginal peoples. Through education, research, advocacy, and action, this coalition of national churches, faith bodies, and regional groups works in solidarity with Aboriginal peoples. ARC seeks to embody true partnership by building authentic alliances in the global struggle for Aboriginal justice.

Headquarters

153 Laurier Ave. East, 2nd Floor, Ottawa, ON K1N 6N8 Tel. (613)235-9956, Fax (613)235-1302

E-mail: arc@istar.ca

Media Contact, Natl. Coord., Ed Bianchi

Officers

Co-Chairs., Richard Renshaw, Mildred Poplar

Natl. Coord., Ed Bianchi

MEMBER ORGANIZATIONS

Anglican Church of Canada

Canadian Conference of Catholic Bishops

Canadian Religious Conference

Council of Christian Reformed Churches in Canada

Evangelical Lutheran Church in Canada

Mennonite Central Committee

Oblate Conference in Canada

Presbyterian Church of Canada

Religious Society of Friends (Quakers)

Society of Jesus (Jesuits)

Canadian Unitarian Council

United Church of Canada

Alcohol and Drug Concerns Inc.

Alcohol and Drug Concerns is a registered, non-profit, charitable organization that has a long association with the Christian Church. The organization's mission is to empower youth to make positive lifestyle choices relating to alcohol, tobacco, and other drugs.

The organization was granted a national charter in 1987, moving from an Ontario charter dating back to 1934. Among its services are: Choices F.I.T. (Fostering Independent Thinking)—a substance abuse prevention resource for grade 4 to 8 teachers; an Institute on Addiction Studies; Making the Leap—a substance abuse prevention resource for grade 7 to 8 teachers created by high school students; Drug and Alcohol Game Show for grades 6 to 9—a classroom activity; education and awareness courses for clients of the Ontario Ministry of Corrections.

Headquarters

4500 Sheppard Ave. E, Ste. 112, Toronto, ON M1S 3R6 Tel. (416)293-3400, Fax (416)293-1142

Media Contact, Robert Walsh, CEO

Officers

Pres., Jean Desgagne, Toronto

Treas., Peter Varley, Toronto

Vice-Pres., Nanci Harris, Toronto

Vice-Pres., Valerie Petroff, Oak Ridges

Vice-Pres., Heidi Stanley, Orillia

Past Pres., Larry Gillians, Napanee

CEO, Robert Walsh

Association of Canadian Bible Colleges

The Association brings into cooperative association Bible colleges in Canada that are evangelical in doctrine and whose objectives are similar. Services are provided to improve the quality of Bible college education in Canada and to further the interests of the Association by means of conferences, seminars, cooperative undertakings, information services, research, publications, and other projects.

Headquarters

Box 4000, Three Hills, AB T0M 2N0 Tel. (403) 443-3051 Fax (403)443-5540

Media Contact, Sec.-Treas., Peter Doell, peter.doell@pbi.ab.ca

Officers

Pres., Larry J. McKinney, Tel. (204)433-7488, Fax (204)433-7158

Vice-Pres., Dr. Arthur Maxwell, Tel. (506)432-4400, Fax (506)432-4425

Sec.-Treas., Peter Doell, Tel. (403)443-3051, Fax (403)443-5540

Members-at-Large, Nil Lavallee Tel. (705)748-9111, Fax (705)748-3931; Wendy Thomas Tel. (306)545-1515, Fax (306)545-0201; Earl Marshall Tel. (519)651-2869, Fax (519)651-2820

Canadian Bible Society

As early as 1804, the British and Foreign Bible Society was at work in Canada. The oldest Bible Society branch is at Truro, Nova Scotia, and has been functioning continually since 1810. In

1904, the various auxiliaries of the British and Foreign Bible Society joined to form the Canadian Bible Society.

The Canadian Bible Society has 16 district offices across Canada, each managed by a District Secretary. The Society holds an annual meeting consisting of one representative from each district, plus an Executive Committee whose members are appointed by the General Board.

Each year contributions, bequests and annuity income of $11 million come from Canadian supporters. Through the Canadian Bible Society's membership in the United Bible Societies' fellowship, over 74 million Bibles, Testaments, and Portions were distributed globally in 1994. At least one book of the Bible is now available in over 2090 languages.

The Canadian Bible Society is nondenominational and interconfessional. Its mandate is to translate, publish, distribute and encourage the use of the Scriptures, without doctrinal note or comment, in languages that can be easily read and understood.

Headquarters

National Support Office, 10 Carnforth Rd., Toronto, ON M4A 2S4 Tel. (416)757-4171, Fax (416)757-3376

Media Contact, Communications Officer, Bruce Allen

Officers

National Director, The Rev. Fr. Greg Bailey, 10 Canforth Rd., Toronto, ON M4A 2S4, Tel. (416)757-4171, Fax (416)757-1292

Canadian Centre for Ecumenism

The Centre has facilitated understanding and cooperation among believers of various Christian traditions and world religions since 1963. An active interdenominational Board of Directors meets annually.

Outreach:

ECUMENISM, a quarterly publication, develops central themes such as Rites of Passage, Sacred Space, Interfaith Marriages, Care of the Earth, etc. through contributions from writers of various churches and religions in addition to its regular ecumenical news summaries, book reviews and resources.

A specialized LIBRARY is open to the public for consultation in the areas of religion, dialogue, evangelism, ethics, spirituality, etc.

CONFERENCES and SESSIONS are offered on themes such as Ecumenism and Pastoral Work, Pluralism, World Religions, Prayer and Unity.

Headquarters

2065 Sherbrooke St. W. Montreal, QC H3H 1G6 Tel. (514)937-9176, Fax (514)937-4986

Email: ccocce@total.net

Website: www.total.net/~ccocce

Officers

Media Contact, Bernice Baranowski

Associate Directors, Emmanuel Lapierre, O.P.

Director, Gilles Bourdeau, O.F.M.

Assistant Director, Angelika Piché

Canadian Evangelical Theological Association

In May 1990, about 60 scholars, pastors, and other interested persons met together in Toronto to form a new theological society. Arising out of the Canadian chapter of the Evangelical Theological Society, the new association established itself as a distinctly Canadian group with a new name. It sponsored its first conference as CETA in Kingston, Ontario, in May 1991.

CETA provides a forum for scholarly contributions to the renewal of theology and church in Canada. CETA seeks to promote theological work which is loyal to Christ and his Gospel, faithful to the primacy and authority of Scripture and responsive to the guiding force of the historic creeds and Protestant confessions of the Christian Church. In its newsletters and conferences, CETA seeks presentations that will speak to a general theologically-educated audience, rather than to specialists.

CETA has special interest in evangelical points of view upon and contributions to the wider conversations regarding religious studies and church life. Members therefore include pastors, students, and other interested persons as well as professional academicians. CETA currently includes about 100 members, many of whom attend its annual conference in the early summer. It publishes the Canadian Evangelical Review and supports an active internet discussion group, which may be accessed by emailing ceta-l@egroups.com.

Headquarters

Dr. Douglas Harink, The King's University College, 9125-50 Street, Edmonton, AB T6B 2H3

Media Contact, Dr. Douglas Harink

Officers

Pres., Dr. Douglas Harink

Sec.-Treas., Dr. Tony Cummins

Editor, Canadian Evengelical Review, Dr. Archie Pell

Executive Member, Mr. John Franklin

Canadian Tract Society

The Canadian Tract Society was organized in 1970 as an independent distributor of Gospel leaflets to provide Canadian churches and individual Christians with quality materials proclaiming the Gospel through the printed page. It is affiliated with the American Tract Society, which encouraged its formation and assisted in its founding, and for whom it serves as an exclusive Canadian distributor. The CTS is a nonprofit international service ministry.

Headquarters

26 Hale Rd., P.O. Box 2156, Brampton, ON L6T 3S4 Tel. (905)457-4559, Fax (905)457-0529

Media Contact, Mgr., Donna Croft

Officers

Director/Sec., Robert J. Burns
Director, John Neufeld
Director, Patricia Burns

The Canadian Council of Churches

The Canadian Council of Churches was organized in 1944. Its basic purpose is to provide the churches with an agency for conference and consultation and for such common planning and common action as they desire to undertake. It encourages ecumenical understanding and action throughout Canada through local councils of churches. It also relates to the World Council of Churches and other agencies serving the worldwide ecumenical movement.

The Council has a Governing Board which meets semiannually and an Executive Committee. Program is administered through two commissions—Faith and Witness, Justice and Peace.

Headquarters

3250 Bloor St. West, 2nd Floor, Toronto, ON M8X 2Y4 Tel. (416)232-6070, Fax (416)236-4532
Media Contact, General Secretary, Ms. Janet Somerville
E-mail: ccchurch@web.net
Website: www.web.net/~ccchurch

Officers

Pres., Bishop Andre Vallee
Vice-Presidents., Rev. Michael Winnowski, Fr. Shenork Sovin, Ms. Karen MacKay Llewellyn
Treas., Nancy Bell
Treas. Emeritus, Mr. Jack Hart
Gen. Secretary., Ms. Janet Somerville

MEMBER CHURCHES:

The Anglican Church of Canada
The Armenian Orthodox Church-Diocese of Canada
Baptist Convention of Ontario and Quebec
British Methodist Episcopal Church*
Canadian Conference of Catholic Bishops
Christian Church (Disciples of Christ)
Coptic Orthodox Church of Canada
Christian Reformed Church in North America—Canadian Ministries
Ethiopian Orthodox Church in Canada
Evangelical Lutheran Church in Canada
Greek Orthodox Metropolis of Toronto, Canada
Orthodox Church in America, Diocese of Canada
Polish National Catholic Church
Presbyterian Church in Canada
Reformed Church in Canada
Religious Society of Friends-Canada Yearly Meeting
Salvation Army-Canada and Bermuda
The Ukrainian Orthodox Church
The United Church of Canada
*Associate Member

Canadian Society of Biblical Studies-Société Canadienne des Études Bibliques

The object of the Society shall be to stimulate the critical investigation of the classical biblical literatures, together with other related literature, by the exchange of scholarly research both in published form and in public forum.

Headquarters

Dept. of Religion and Culture, Wilfrid Laurier University, Waterloo, ON N2L 3C5 Tel. (519)884-0710, ext.3323, Fax (519)884-9387
Media Contact, Exec. Sec., Dr. Michel Desjardins

Officers

President (2000-01), John S. Kloppenborg Verbin, Faculty of Theology, St. Michael's College, 81 St. Mary Street, Toronto, ON M5S 1J4 Tel. (416)926-7267, Fax (416)926-7294, kloppen@chass.utoronto.ca
Vice-Pres. (2000-01), Ehud Ben Zvi, Department of Comparative Literature, Religion and Film-Media Studies, University of Alberta, 347 Old Arts Building, Emonton, AB T6G 2E6, Tel. (780)492-7183, Fax (780)492-2715, ehud.ben.zvi @ualberta.ca
Exec. Secretary. (1997-02), Dr. Michel Desjardins, Dept. of Religion and Culture, Wilfrid Laurier University, Waterloo, ON N2L 3C5 Tel. (519)884-0710, ext. 3323, mdesjard @mach1.wlu.ca
Treas. (2000-03), Dietmar Neufeld, Department of Classical, Near Eastern and Religious Studies, University of British Columbia, Vancouver, BC V6T 1Z1, Tel. (604)822-4065, Fax (604)8229431, dneufeld@interchange.ubc.ca
Programme Coord. (1998-01), Edith Humphrey, 42 Belmont, Aylmer, QC J9H 2M7 Tel. (819)682-9257, ehumphre@ccs.carleton.ca
Communications Officer (1999-02), John McLaughlin, Department of Theology and Religious Studies, Wheeling Jesuit University, Wheeling, WV 26003, Tel. (304)243-2310, Fax (304)243-2243, mclaugh@wju.edu
Student Member-at-Large (1999-01), David A. Bergen, 7101 Huntercrest Rd., N.W., Calgary, AB T2K 4J9, Tel. (403)275-5369, bergend@ cadvision.com

The Church Army in Canada

The Church Army in Canada has been involved in evangelism and Christian social service since 1929.

Headquarters

50 Gervais Dr, Suite 301, Don Mills, ON M3C 1Z3 Tel. (416)385-9686 or 1-(888)316-8169, Fax (416)385-9689
Media Contact, National Dir., Capt. R. Bruce Smith

Officers

National Dir., Capt. R. Bruce Smith
Bd. Chmn., John B. Cameron

The Churches' Council on Theological Education in Canada, An Ecumenical Foundation

The Churches' Council (CCTE,EF) maintains an overview of theological education in Canada on behalf of its constituent churches and functions as a bridge between the schools of theology and the churches which they serve.

Founded in 1970 with a national and ecumenical mandate, the CCTE,EF provides resources for research into matters pertaining to theological education, opportunities for consultation and cooperation, and a limited amount of funding in the form of grants for the furtherance of ecumenical initiatives in theological education.

Headquarters

60 St. Clair Avenue E., Ste. 302, Toronto, ON M4T 1N5 Tel. (416)928-3223, Fax (416)928-3563
Media Contact, Exec. Dir., Dr. Stewart Gillan
Email: ccte@web.ca
Website: www.web.net/~ccte

Officers

Bd. of Dir., Chpsn., Dr. Richard C. Crossman, Waterloo Lutheran Seminary, 75 University Ave. W., Waterloo, ON N2L 3C5
Bd. of Dir., Vice-Chpsn., Sr. Ellen Leonard, CSJ, Univ. of St. Michaels's College, 81 St. Mary St., Toronto, ON M5S 1J4
Treas., Mr. Ralph Kendall, 9 Sari Cres., Toronto, ON M1E 4W3, ralph.sheila@home.com
Exec. Dir., Dr. Stewart Gillan

MEMBER ORGANIZATIONS

The General Synod of the Anglican Church of Canada
Canadian Baptist Ministries
The Evangelical Lutheran Church in Canada
The Presbyterian Church in Canada
The Canadian Conference of Catholic Bishops
The United Church of Canada

Ecumenical Coalition for Economic Justice (ECEJ)

The Ecumenical Coalition for Economic Justice (ECEJ) enables member churches to have a more effective public voice in advocating for a just, moral, and sustainable economy. ECEJ undertakes research, education, and advocacy to promote economic policy alternatives that are grounded in a Christian perspective. Sponsoring denominations include: the Anglican Church of Canada, the Canadian Catholic Bishops Conference, the Evangelical Lutheran Church in Canada, the Presbyterian Church in Canada, and the United Church of Canada. ECEJ also acts as a link to social movements and coalitions to bring a collective church presence to them and to inform our own analysis.

The program focus of the next three years will be to advance alternative economic policies which support our vision of an "economy of hope". This includes proposing different ways to assess economic prosperity, challenging the growth model, envisioning a new model for social programs in global economy, and presenting alternative fiscal and monetary policies.

ECEJ publishes a quarterly briefing paper on current issues, the Economic Justice Report, as well as education and action resources.

An Administrative Committee oversees ECEJ and is made up of representatives from the sponsoring denominations as well as participating members which currently include, the School Sisters of Notre Dame, the Scarboro Foreign Mission, and the Religious Society of Friends (Quaker).

Headquarters

77 Charles St. W, Ste. 402, Toronto, ON M5S 1K5 Tel. (416)921-4615, Fax (416)922-1419
Media Contact, Educ. & Communications, Jennifer Henry

Officers

Co-Chpsn., Doryne Kirby
Co-Chpsn., Jim Marshall

Staff

Research, John Dillon
Women & Economic Justice Programme, Kathryn Robertson
Education-Communication, Jennifer Henry
Administration-Finance, Diana Gibbs

Evangelical Fellowship of Canada

The Fellowship was formed in 1964. There are 31 denominations, 124 organizations, 1,200 local churches and 11,000 individual members.

Its purposes are, "Fellowship in the gospel" (Phil. 1:5), "the defence and confirmation of the gospel" (Phil. 1:7) and "the furtherance of the gospel" (Phil. 1:12). The Fellowship believes the Holy Scriptures, as originally given, are infallible and that salvation through the Lord Jesus Christ is by faith apart from works.

In national and regional conventions the Fellowship urges Christians to live exemplary lives and to openly challenge the evils and injustices of society. It encourages cooperation with various agencies in Canada and overseas that are sensitive to social and spiritual needs.

Headquarters

Office, 600 Alden Rd., Ste. 300, Markham, ON L3R 0E7 Tel. (905)479-5885, Fax (905)479-4742
Mailing Address, M.I.P. Box 3745, Markham, ON L3R 0Y4
Media Contact, Pres., Dr. Gary Walsh, 600 Alden Rd., Ste. 300, Markham, ON L3R 0E7 Tel. (905)479-5885, Fax (905)479-4742

Officers

Pres., Dr. Gary Walsh
Chair, Dr. Paul Magnus

Vice-Chair, Dr. Rick Penner
Treas., Lt. Col. David Luginbuhl
Past Pres., Dr. Brian Stiller

EXECUTIVE COMMITTEE

Rev. Scott Campbell; Rev. Carson Pue; Ms. Ruth Andrews; Rev. Stewart Hunter; Ms. Jacqueline Dugas; Dr. Rick Penner; Lt. Col. David Luginbuhl; Dr. Ralph Richardson; Rev. Abe Funk; Rev. Gillis Killam; Dr. Paul Magnus; Rev. Winston Thurton

Task Force on Evangelism-(Vision Canada), Interim Chair, Gary Walsh

Social Action Commission, Chpsn., Dr. James Read

Education Commission, Chpsn., Dr. Glenn Smith

Women in Ministry Task Force, Chpsn., Rev. Eileen Stewart-Rhude

Aboriginal Task Force, Co-Chairs, Ray Aldred; Wendy Peterson

Religious Liberties Commission, Chpsn., Dr. Paul Marshall

Task Force on Global Mission, Chpsn., Dr. Geoff Tunnicliffe

Inter-Varsity Christian Fellowship of Canada

Inter-Varsity Christian Fellowship is a non-profit, interdenominational student movement centering on the witness to Jesus Christ in campus communities, universities, colleges, and high schools and through a Canada-wide Pioneer Camping program. It also ministers to professionals and teachers through Nurses and Teacher Christian Fellowship.

IVCF was officially formed in 1928-29 by the late Dr. Howard Guinness, whose arrival from Britain challenged students to follow the example of the British Inter-Varsity Fellowship by organizing themselves into prayer and Bible study fellowship groups. Inter-Varsity has always been a student-initiated movement emphasizing and developing leadership in the campus to call Christians to outreach, challenging other students to a personal faith in Jesus Christ and studying the Bible as God's revealed truth within a fellowship of believers. A strong stress has been placed on missionary activity, and the triennial conference held at Urbana, IL. (jointly sponsored by U.S. and Canadian IVCF) has been a means of challenging many young people to service in Christian vocations. Inter-Varsity works closely with and is a strong believer in the work of local and national churches.

Headquarters

Unit 17, 40 Vogell Rd., Richmond Hill, ON L4B 3N6 Tel. (905)884-6880, Fax (905)884-6550

Media Contact, Gen. Dir., Rob Regier

Officers

Gen. Dir., Rob Regier

Interchurch Communications

Interchurch Communications is made up of the communication units of the Anglican Church of Canada, the Evangelical Lutheran Church in Canada, the Presbyterian Church in Canada, the Canadian Conference of Catholic Bishops (English Sector), and the United Church of Canada. ICC members collaborate on occasional video or print coproductions and on addressing public policy issues affecting religious communications.

Headquarters

3250 Bloor St. W., Etobicoke, ON M8X 2Y4

Media Contact, Chpsn., Douglas Tindal, Anglican Church of Canada, 600 Jarvis St., Toronto, ON M4Y 2J6 Tel. (416)924-9199 x. 286, Fax (416)968-7983

Email: doug.tindal@national.anglican.ca

MEMBERS

Mr. Douglas Tindal, Anglican Church of Canada, 600 Jarvis St., Toronto, ON M4Y 2J6 Tel. (416)924-9199 ext.286, Fax (416)968-7983, dtindal@national.anglican.ca

Mr. William Kokesch, Canadian Conference of Catholic Bishops, 90 Parent Ave., Ottawa, ON K1N 7B1 Tel. (613)241-9461, Fax (613)241-8117, kokesch@cccb.ca

Mr. Merv Campone, Evangelical Lutheran Church in Canada, 305-896 Cambie St. Vancouver, BC V6B 2P6 Tel. (604)888-4562 Fax (604)687-6593, mcampone@spiritscall.com

Rev. Keith Knight, Presbyterian Church in Canada, 50 Wynford Dr., Don Mills, ON M3C 1J7 Tel. (416)441-1111, Fax (416)441-2825, kknight@presbyterian.ca

Mr. Gordon How, United Church of Canada, 3250 Bloor St. W., Etobicoke, ON M8X 2Y4 Tel. (416)231-7680, Fax (416)231-3103, ghow@uccan.org

Religious Television Associates, 3250 Bloor St. W., Etobicoke, ON M8X 2Y4 Tel. (416)231-7680, Fax (416)232-6004

John Howard Society of Ontario

The John Howard Society of Ontario is a registered non-profit charitable organization providing services to individuals, families, and groups at all stages in the youth and criminal justice system. The Society also provides community education on critical issues in the justice system and advocacy for reform of the justice system. The mandate of the Society is the prevention of crime through service, community education, advocacy, and reform.

Founded in 1929, the Society has grown from a one-office service in Toronto to 17 local branches providing direct services in the major cities of Ontario and a provincial office providing justice policy analysis, advocacy for reform, and support to branches.

Headquarters

6 Jackson Pl., Toronto, ON M6P 1T6 Tel. (416) 604-8412, Fax (416)604-8948

Media Contact, Exec. Dir., William Sparks

Officers

Pres., Susan Reid-MacNevin, Dept. of Sociology, Univ. Of Guelph, Guelph, ON N1G 2W1

Vice-Pres., Richard Beaupe, 4165 Fernand St., Hamner, ON B3A 1X4

Treas., Jack Battler, Waterloo, ON

Sec., Peter Angeline, OISE, 252 Bloor St. W., Toronto, ON

Exec. Dir., William Sparks

LOCAL SOCIETIES

Collins Bay; Hamilton; Kingston; Lindsay; London; Niagara; Oshawa; Ottawa; Peel; Peterborough; Sarnia; Sault Ste. Marie; Sudbury; Thunder Bay; Toronto; Waterloo; Windsor

John Milton Society for the Blind in Canada

The John Milton Society for the Blind in Canada is an interdenominational Christian charity whose mandate is producing Christian publications for Canadian adults or young people who are blind, deafblind, or visually impaired. As such, it produces Insight, a large-print magazine, Insound, a cassette magazine and In Touch, a braille magazine. The John Milton Society also features an audio cassette library called the Library in Sound, which contains Christian music, sermons, seasonal materials, and workshops.

Founded in 1970, the Society is committed to seeing that visually-impaired people receive accessible Christian materials by mail.

Headquarters

40 St. Clair Ave. E., Ste. 202, Toronto, ON M4T 1M9 Tel. (416)960-3953, Fax (416)960-3570

Media Contact, Ex. Dir., The Rev. Barry R. Brown

Officers

Exec. Dir., The Rev. Barry R. Brown

Pres., The Rev. Ian Nichols

Lutheran Council in Canada

The Lutheran Council in Canada was organized in 1967 and is a cooperative agency of the Evangelical Lutheran Church in Canada and Lutheran Church-Canada.

The Council's activities include communications, coordinative service, and national liaison in social ministry, chaplaincy, and scout activity.

Headquarters

302-393 Portage Ave., Winnipeg, MB R3B 3H6 Tel. (204)984-9150, Fax (204)984-9185

Media Contact, Pres., Rev. Ralph Mayan, 3074 Portage Ave., Winnipeg, MB R3K 0Y2 Tel. (204)895-3433, Fax (204)897-4319

Officers

Pres., Rev. Ralph Mayan

Treas., -vacant-

Sec., Rev. Leon C. Gilbertson

Vice Pres., Bishop Telmore Sartison

Mennonite Central Committee Canada (MCCC)

Mennonite Central Committee Canada was organized in 1964 to continue the work which several regional Canadian inter-Mennonite agencies had been doing in relief, service, immigration, and peace. All but a few of the smaller Mennonite groups in Canada belong to MCC Canada.

MCCC is part of the Mennonite Central Committee (MCC) International which has its headquarters in Akron, Pa. from where most of the overseas development and relief projects are administered. In 1999-2000 MCCC's income was $25 million, about 33 percent of the total MCC income. There were 390 Canadians out of a total of 930 MCC workers serving in North America and abroad during the same time period.

The MCC office in Winnipeg administers projects located in Canada. Domestic programs of Voluntary Service, Native Concerns, Peace and Social Concerns, Food Program, Employment Concerns, Ottawa Office, Victim-Offender Ministries, Mental Health, and Immigration are all part of MCC's Canadian ministry. Whenever it undertakes a project, MCCC attempts to relate to the church or churches in the area.

Headquarters

134 Plaza Dr., Winnipeg, MB R3T 5K9 Tel. (204)261-6381, Fax (204)269-9875

Communications, Rick Fast, 134 Plaza Dr., Winnipeg, MT R3T 5K9 Tel. (204)261-6381, Fax (204)269-9875

Officers

Exec. Dir., Dave Dyck

Project Ploughshares

The founding of Project Ploughshares in 1976 was premised on the biblical vision of transforming the material and human wealth consumed by military preparations into resources for human development. An internationally recognized Canadian peace and justice organization, the Project undertakes research, education, and advocacy programs on common security, demilitarization, security alternatives, arms transfer controls, demobilization, and peace building. Project Ploughshares is a project of the Canadian Council of Churches and is supported by national churches, civic agencies, affiliated community groups and more than 10,000 individuals.

Publications: the Ploughshares Monitor (quarterly), the Armed Conflicts Report(annual), Briefings and Working Papers(occasional).

Headquarters

Institute of Peace and Conflict Studies, Conrad Grebel College, Waterloo, ON N2L 3G6 Tel. (519)888-6541, Fax (519)885-0806

Media Contact, Director, Ernie Regehr

Officers

Chair, Walter Pitman
Treasurer, Philip Creighton

SPONSORING ORGANIZATIONS

Anglican Church of Canada
Canadian Catholic Organization for Development & Peace
Canadian Unitarian Council
Canadian Voice of Women for Peace
Canadian Yearly Meeting, Religious Society of Friends
Conrad Grebel College
Evangelical Lutheran Church in Canada
Mennonite Central Committee Canada
Presbyterian Church in Canada
United Church of Canada

Religious Television Associates

Religious Television Associates was formed in the early 1960s for the production units of the Anglican, Baptist, Presbyterian, Roman Catholic Churches, and the United Church of Canada. In the intervening years, the Baptists have withdrawn and the Lutherans have come in. RTA provides an ecumenical umbrella for joint productions in broadcasting and development education. The directors are the heads of the Communications Departments participating in Interchurch Communications.

Headquarters

3250 Bloor St. W., Etobicoke, ON M8X 2Y4 Tel. (416)231-7680 ext. 4051, Fax (416)232-6004
Media Contact, Exec. Dir., Rod Booth

Officers

The Anglican Church of Canada
Canadian Conference of Catholic Bishops
The Canadian Council of Churches
The Evangelical Lutheran Church in Canada
The Presbyterian Church in Canada
The United Church of Canada

Scripture Union

Scripture Union is an international interdenominational missionary movement working in 130 countries.

Scripture Union aims to work with the churches to make God's Good News known to children, young people, and families, and to encourage people of all ages to meet God daily through the Bible and prayer.

In Canada, a range of daily Bible guides are offered to individuals, churches, and bookstores from age four through adult. Sunday School curriculum and various evangelism and discipling materials are also offered for sale.

A program of youth and family evangelism, including beach missions and community-based evangelistic holiday clubs, is also undertaken.

Headquarters

1885 Clements Rd., Unit 226, Pickering, ON L1W 3V4 Tel. (905)427-4947, Fax (905)427-0334
Media Contact, Gen. Dir., John W. Irwin, Email: john_w_irwin@compuserve.com

Officers

Chair of the Board, Harold Murray, 216 McKinnon Pl. NE, Calgary, AB T2E 7B9, Tel. (403)276-4716, hjmurray@home.com
General Director, John W. Irwin, 1885 Clements Rd., Unit 226, Pickering, ON L1W 3V4, john_w_irwin@compuserve.com

Student Christian Movement of Canada

The Student Christian Movement of Canada was formed in 1921 from the student arm of the YMCA. It has its roots in the Social Gospel movements of the late nineteenth and early twentieth centuries. Throughout its intellectual history, the SCM in Canada has sought to relate the Christian faith to the living realities of the social and political context of each student generation.

The present priorities are built around the need to form more and stronger critical Christian communities on Canadian campuses within which individuals may develop their social and political analyses, experience spiritual growth and fellowship and bring Christian ecumenical witness to the university.

The Student Christian Movement of Canada is affiliated with the World Student Christian Federation.

Headquarters

310 Danforth Ave., Toronto, ON M4K 1N6 Tel. (416)463-4312, Fax (416)466-6854
Media Contact, Natl. Coord., Susannah Schmidt

Officers

Natl. Coord., Susannah Schmidt

Taskforce on the Churches and Corporate Responsibility

The Taskforce on the Churches and Corporate Responsibility is a national ecumenical coalition of the major churches in Canada. Official representatives from the General Synod of the Anglican Church of Canada, the Canadian Conference of Catholic Bishops, the Evangelical Lutheran Church in Canada, the Presbyterian Church in Canada, the Religious Society of Friends (Quakers), the United Church of Canada, CUSO, the YWCA, and a number of religious orders of women and men, serve as links between the Taskforce and the decision-making structures of the members. The Taskforce assists the members in implementing policies adopted by the churches in the areas of corporate responsibility. Among the policies and issues placed on the agenda of the Taskforce by the participating churches are: principles for global corporate responsibility and bench marks for measuring business performance; corporate operating practices and codes of operation conduct; environmental reporting; human rights and Aboriginal land rights in relation to corporate conduct; social and environmental issues relative to corporate global citizenship; corporate governance issues; and responsible investing issues.

Headquarters

129 St. Clair Ave. W., Toronto, ON M4V 1N5 Tel. (416)923-1758, Fax (416)927-7554

Media Contact, Coord., Daniel Gennarelli, Tel. (416)923-1758, Fax (416)927-7554

Officers

Coord., Daniel Gennarelli
Bd. Co-Chpsns., Tim Ryan, David Hallman
Treas., Doug Peter
Chpsn., Corp. Governance Comm., Richard Soo
Co-Chpsns. Inter-Church Comm. on Ecology, Joy Kennedy, Jim Profit

MEMBERS

Anglican Church of Canada
Basilian Fathers
Baptist Convention Ontario-Quebec
Canadian Conference of Catholic Bishops
Canadian Religious Conference
Christian Reformed Church in Canada
Conference religieuse canadiene- Quebec
Congregation of Notre Dame
Evangelical Lutheran Church in Canada
Grey Sisters of the Immaculate Conception
Jesuit Fathers of Upper Canada
Les Soeurs de Sainte-Anne
Oblate Conference of Canada
Presbyterian Church in Canada
Redemptorist Fathers
Religious Hospitallers of St. Joseph
Religious Society of Friends (Quakers)
School Sisters of Notre Dame
Scarboro Foreign Mission Society
Sisterhood of St. John the Divine
Sisters of Charity-Mount St. Vincent
Sisters of Charity of the Immaculate Conception
Sisters of Mercy Generalate
Sisters of St. Ann, Victoria
Sisters of St. Joseph of Hamilton
Sisters of St. Joseph-Diocese of London
Sisters of Service of Canada
Sisters of St. Joseph-Sault Ste. Marie
Sisters of St. Joseph-Toronto
Sisters of the Holy Names of Jesus & Mary Windsor, ON
Sisters of Holy Names of Jesus and Mary, Longueil, P.Q.
Sisters of Providence of St. Vincent dePaul
Sisters of St. Martha
Toronto United Church Council
United Church of Canada
Ursulines of Chatham Union
Young Women's Christian Association

Ten Days for Global Justice

Supported by five of Canada's major Christian denominations, Ten Days is dedicated to helping people discover, examine, and reflect on the ways global and domestic structures and policies promote and perpetuate poverty and injustice for the majority of the world's people. Ten Days is an education and action program that attempts to influence the policies and practice of Canadian churches, government, business, labour, education, and the media.

Headquarters

77 Charles St. W. Ste. 401, Toronto, ON M5S 1K5 Tel. (416)922-0591, Fax (416)922-1419
Email: tendays@web.net
Website: www.web.net/~tendays
Media Contact, Natl. Coord., Dennis Howlett

Staff

Natl. Coord., Dennis Howlett
Coord. for Leadership Dev. & Regional Communication, David Reid
Resource Coord., Julie Graham
Admn. Asst., Ramya Hemachandra

MEMBER ORGANIZATIONS

Anglican Church of Canada
Canadian Cath. Orgn. for Dev. & Peace
Evangelical Lutheran Church in Canada
Presbyterian Church in Canada
United Church of Canada

Women's InterChurch Council of Canada

Women's Inter-Church Council of Canada is a national Christian women's council that encourages women to grow in ecumenism, to strengthen ecumenical community, to share their spirituality and prayer, to engage in dialogue about women's concerns, and to stand in solidarity with one another. The Council calls women to respond to national and international issues affecting women and to take action together for justice. WICC sponsors the World Day of Prayer and Fellowship of the Least Coin in Canada. Human rights projects for women are supported and a quarterly magazine "Making Waves" distributed.

Headquarters

Suite 201, 394 Bloor St. W, Toronto, ON M5S 1X4 Tel. (416)929-5184, Fax (416)929-4064
Media Contact, Communications Coordinator, Gillian Barfoot

Officers

Pres., Joyce Christie
Exec. Dir., Rev. Karen Hincke

CHURCH MEMBER BODIES

African Methodist Episcopal, Anglican Church of Canada, Baptist Convention of Ontario & Quebec, Christian Church (Disciples of Christ), Evangelical Lutheran Church in Canada, Mennonite Central Committee, Presbyterian Church in Canada, Religious Society of Friends, Roman Catholic Church, Salvation Army in Canada, United Church of Canada

World Vision Canada

World Vision Canada is a Christian humanitarian relief and development organization. Although its main international commitment is to translate child sponsorship into holistic, sustainable community development, World Vision also allocates resources to help Canada's poor and complement the mission of the church.

World Vision's Reception Centre assists government-sponsored refugees entering Canada. The NeighbourLink program mobilizes church volunteers to respond locally to people's needs. A quarterly publication, Context, provides data on the Canadian family to help churches effectively reach their communities. The development education program provides resources on development issues. During the annual 30-Hour Famine, people fast for 30 hours while discussing poverty and raising funds to support aid programs.

Headquarters

6630 Turner Valley Rd., Mississauga, ON L5N 2S4 Tel. (905)821-3030, Fax (905)821-1356

Media Contact, Philip Maher, Tel. (905)567-2726

Officers

Pres., Dave Toycen

Vice-Pres., Intl. & Govt. Relations, Linda Tripp; Natl. Programs, Don Posterski; Fin. & Admin., Charlie Fluit; Donor Development Group, Brian Tizzard

Young Men's Christian Association in Canada

The YMCA began as a Christian association to help young men find healthy recreation and meditation, as well as opportunities for education, in the industrial slums of nineteenth century England. It came to Canada in 1851 with the same mission in mind for young men working in camps and on the railways.

Today, the YMCA maintains its original mission, helping individuals to grow and develop in spirit, mind and body, but attends to those needs for men and women of all ages and religious beliefs. The YMCA registers 1.5 million participants in 250 communities that are served by 64 autonomous associations across Canada.

The program of each association differs according to the needs of the community, but most offer one or more programs in each of the following categories: health and fitness, child care, employment councelling and training, recreation, camping, community support and outreach, international development, and short-term accommodation.

The YMCA encourages people of all ages, races, abilities, income, and beliefs to come together in an environment which promotes balance in life, breaking down barriers, and helping to create healthier communities.

Headquarters

42 Charles St. E., 6th Floor., Toronto, ON M4Y 1T4 Tel. (416)967-9622, Fax (416)967-9618

Media Contact, Sol Kasimer

Officers

Chpsn., Ray Mantha

CEO, Sol Kasimer

Young Women's Christian Association of/du Canada

The YWCA of/du Canada is a national voluntary organization serving 44 YWCAs and YM-YWCAs across Canada. Dedicated to the development and improved status of women and their families, the YWCA is committed to service delivery and to being a source of public education on women's issues and an advocate of social change. Services provided by YWCAs and YM-YWCAs include adult education programs, residences and shelters, child care, fitness activities, wellness programs, and international development education. As a member of the World YWCA, the YWCA of/du Canada is part of the largest women's organization in the world.

Headquarters

80 Gerrard St. E., Toronto, ON M5B 1G6 Tel. (416)593-9886, Fax (416)971-8084

Media Contact, Int. CEO, Margaret MacKenzie

Officers

Pres., Ann Mowatt

Youth for Christ/Canada

Youth For Christ is an interdenominational organization founded in 1944 by Torrey Johnson. Under the leadership of YFC's 11 national board of directors, Youth For Christ/Canada cooperates with churches and serves as a mission agency reaching out to young people and their families through a variety of ministries.

YFC seeks to have maximum influence in a world of youth through high-interest activities and personal involvement. Individual attention is given to each teenager through small group involvement and counselling. These activities and relationships become vehicles for communicating the message of the Gospel.

Headquarters

822-167 Lombard Ave., Winnipeg, MB R3B 0V3 Tel. (204)989-0056, Fax (204)989-0067

Officers

Natl. Dir., Randy L. Steinwand

3. Religious Bodies in the United States

The United States, with its staunch constitutional stance on religious freedom and successive waves of immigrants over the last three centuries, has proved to be a fertile soil for the development of varied Christian traditions. In the directory which follows, some 215 distinct church traditions are represented. Many of these groups represent the processes of dividing and re-uniting that are a hallmark of American religious life. Many churches listed here represent those with a long tradition in Europe, Africa, or Asia predating their American tenure. Others are American-born churches. The researcher may be helped by consulting the churches grouped by tradition at the end of this directory in the section entitled, "Religious Bodies in the United States Arranged by Families." In this section, all the Baptists bodies are listed together, all the Lutheran bodies, Methodists, etc.

The following directory information is supplied by the national headquarters of each church. Each listing contains a brief description of the church, followed by the national headquarters contact information, which includes a mailing address, telephone and fax numbers, email and website addresses (when available), and the name of the media contact. After the headquarters, there are data regarding the church officers or leaders, including names, titles, and contact information (when contact information differs from the headquarters). There is a staggering array of churches, each with its own form of organization; not all of them refer to their leaders as "officers." In some places, the reader will find the term "Bishops," "Board Members," or "Executives" in place of "Officers." Finally, when applicable, each entry contains a list of the names of church publications.

The churches are printed in alphabetical order by the official name of the organization. There are a few instances in which certain churches are more commonly known by another name. In such cases, the reader is referred incidentally within the text to the appropriate official name. Churches that are member communions of the National Council of Churches of Christ in the U.S.A. are marked with an asterisk (*).

Other useful information about the churches listed here can be found in other chapters or directories within the book: Statistical information for these churches can be found in the tables toward the end of this book in Chapter III. Further, more extensive information about the publications listed in this directory can be found in Directory 11, "Religious Periodicals in the United States". For a list of church websites, see Directory 5, "The Emerging Electronic Church."

The organizations listed here represent the denominations to which the vast majority of church members in the United States belong. It does not include all religious bodies functioning in the United States. The Encyclopedia of American Religions (Gale Research Inc., P.O. Box 33477, Detroit MI 48232-5477) contains names and addresses of additional religious bodies.

Advent Christian Church

The Advent Christian Church is a conservative, evangelical denomination which grew out of the Millerite movement of the 1830s and 1840s. The members stress the authority of Scripture, justification by faith in Jesus Christ alone, the importance of evangelism and world missions and the soon visible return of Jesus Christ.

Organized in 1860, the Advent Christian Church maintains headquarters in Charlotte, N.C., with regional offices in Rochester, N. H., Princeton, N.C., Ellisville, MO., Lewiston, Idaho, and Lenoir, N.C. Missions are maintained in India, Nigeria, Ghana, Japan, Liberia, Croatia, New Zealand, Malaysia, the Philippines, Mexico, South Africa, Namibia, Honduras, and Memphis, Tenn.

The Advent Christian Church maintains doctrinal distinctives in three areas: conditional immortality, the sleep of the dead until the return of Christ, and belief that the kingdom of God will be established on earth made new by Jesus Christ.

Headquarters

P.O. Box 23152, Charlotte, NC 28227 Tel. (704) 545-6161, Fax (704)573-0712

Media Contact, Exec. Director, David E. Ross

Email: acpub@adventchristian.org

Website: www.adventchristian.org

Officers

Pres., Rev. James Crouse, 326 9th St., Baraboo, WI 53913

Exec. Dir., David E. Ross

Sec., Rev. Thomas S. Warren II, 8912 Snow Hill Ln., Jacksonville, FL 32221

Appalachian Vice-Pres., Rev. James Lee, 1338 Delwood Dr. SW, Lenoir, NC 28645

Central Vice-Pres., Mr. Homer Easley, 1529 Southlawn Pl., Aurora, IL 60506

Eastern Vice-Pres., Rev. Glenn Rice, 130 Leighton St., Bangor, ME 04401

Southern Vice-Pres., Rev. Brent Ross, 3635 Andrea Lee Ct., Snellville, GA 30278-4941

Western Vice-Pres., Brad Neil, 4035 S. 275th Pl., Auburn, WA 98001

The Woman's Home & Foreign Mission Soc., Pres., Hazel Blackstone, 2141 Broadway, Bangor, ME 04901

Periodicals

Advent Christian News; The Advent Christian Witness; Insight; Maranatha; Henceforth . . . ; Coast to Coast on Campus; Leadership Letter; Prayer and Praise

African Methodist Episcopal Church*

This church began in 1787 in Philadelphia when persons in St. George's Methodist Episcopal Church withdrew as a protest against color segregation. In 1816 the denomination was started, led by Rev. Richard Allen who had been ordained deacon by Bishop Francis Asbury and was subsequently ordained elder and elected and consecrated bishop.

Headquarters

3801 Market St., Suite 300, Philadelphia, PA 29204 Tel. 215-662-0506

Email: Administrator@amecnet.org

Website: www.amecnet.org

Officers

Senior Bishop, Bishop John Hurst Adams, Presiding Bishop, Eleventh Episcopal District, African Methodist Episcopal Church, 101 East Union St., Suite 301, Jacksonville, FL 32202 Tel. (904)355-4310, Fax (904)356-1617

Chief Ecumenical & Urban Affairs Officer, Bishop Theodore Larry Kirkland, African Methodist Episcopal Church, 4519 Admiralty Way, Marina delRey, CA 90292 Tel. (310)577-8530, Fax (310)577-8540, bishoptkirkland @aol.com

President, General Board, Bishop Henry Allen Belin, Jr., Presiding Bishop, Seventh Episcopal District, African Methodist Episcopal Church, 110 Pisgah Church Rd., Columbia, SC 29203 Tel. (803)935-0500, Fax (803)935-0830

President, Council of Bishops 2001-2002, Bishop Theodore Larry Kirkland, African Methodist Episcopal Church, 4519 Admiralty Way, Marina delRey, CA 90292 Tel. (310)577-8530, Fax (310)577-8540, bishoptkirkland@ aol.com

President, Council of Bishops 2002-2003, Bishop Adam Jefferson Richardson, Presiding Bishop, Nineteenth Episcopal District, African Methodist Episcopal Church, 3715 Forsythe Way, P.O. Box 13146, Tallahassee, FL 32317 Tel. (850)893-1939, Fax (850)893-1959

General Secretary-Chief Information Officer, Dr. Clement W. Fugh, 500 Eighth Ave., Suite 211-213, Nashville, TN 37203 Tel. (615)254-0911, Fax (615)254-0912, cioamec@bellsouth.net

Treasurer-Chief Financial Officer, Mr. Richard A. Lewis, 1134 11th St., NW, Washington, DC 20001 Tel. (202)371-8700, Fax (202)371-8735

President, Connectional Lay Organization, Mr. Arthur D. Brown, 5300 E. Main St., Columbus, OH 43213 Tel. (614)235-3270

Publisher-Secretary-Treasurer, Sunday School Union, Dr. Johnny Barbour, Jr., 500 Eighth Avenue, S., Suite 200, Nashville, TN 37203 Tel. (615)256-5882, Fax (613)244-7604, amecinfo@edge.net

President, Women's Missionary Society, Dr. Dorothy Adams Peck, 1134 11th St., NW, Washington, DC 20001 Tel. (202)371-8886, Fax (202)371-8820

Director, Young People's Division, Ms. Adrienne A. Morris, Women's Missionary Society, 327 Washington Ave., Wyoming, OH 45115 Tel. (513)821-1481, Fax (513)821-3073

Periodicals

The Christian Recorder; A.M.E. Review; Journal of Christian Education; Secret Chamber; Women's Missionary Magazine, Voice of Mission, YPD Newsletter

African Methodist Episcopal Zion Church*

The A.M.E. Zion Church is an independent body, having withdrawn from the John Street Methodist Church of New York City in 1796. The first bishop was James Varick.

Headquarters

Dept. of Records & Research, 3225 West Sugar Creek Rd., Charlotte, NC 28269 Tel. (704)599-4630, Fax (704)688-2549, j1gsa@aol.com

Media Contact, Gen. Sec.-Aud., Dr. W. Robert Johnson, III

Email: info@amezion.org

Website: www.amezion.org

BOARD OF BISHOPS

Officers

*President, Joseph Johnson, 1408 Jack White Dr., Rock Hill, SC 29732, Tel. 704-849-0521, Fax 704-849-0571

*NOTE—Presidency rotates every six months according to seniority.

Secretary, Bishop Marshall H. Strickland I, 2000 Cedar Circle Dr., Baltimore, MD 21215 Tel. (410)744-7330, Fax 410-788-5510

Asst. Sec., Bishop Clarence Carr, 2600 Normandy Dr., Greendale, MO 63121, Tel. (314)727-2931, Fax (314)727-0663

Treas., Bishop George Washington Carver Walker, Sr., 137 Talcott Notch Rd., Farmington, CT 06032 Tel.(860)676-8414, Fax (860)676-8424

MEMBERS

ACTIVE

Battle, Jr. George Edward, 8403 Dembridge Ln., Davidson, NC 28036 Tel. (704)895-2236, Office Tel. (704)332-7600, Fax (704)343-3745

Bishop, Cecil, 2663 Oakmeade Dr., Charlotte, NC 28270 Tel. (704)846-9370, Fax (704)846-9371

Brown, Warren Matthew, 22 Crowley Dr., Randolph, MA 02368 Tel. (781)961-2434, Fax (781)961-2939

Carr, Clarence, 2600 Normandy Dr., Greendale, MO 63121, Tel. (314)727-2931, Fax (314) 727-0663

Ekeman, Sr., Samuel Chuka, 98 Okigwe Rd., P.O. Box 1149, Owerri, Nigeria West Africa, Tel. (011)234-83-232271

Jarrett, Jr., Nathaniel, 7322 South Clyde Ave., Chicago, IL 60649 Tel. (773)684-8098, Fax (773)684-0810

Johnson, Joseph, 320 Walnut Point Dr., P.O. Box 608 Matthews, NC 28106 Tel. (704)849-0521, Fax (704)849-0571

Rochester, Enoch Benjamin, Office: Hwy. 130 South, Suite 2A, Cinnaminson, NJ 08077 Tel. (609)786-2555, Fax (609)786-8568; Home: 129 Sagebush Dr., Belleville, IL 62221 Tel. (618)257-8481

Strickland I, Marshall Hayward, 2000 Cedar Circle Dr., Baltimore, MD 21215 Tel. (410)744-7330, Fax (410)788-5510

Thompson, Richard Keith, 1420 Missouri Ave., N.W., Washington, DC 20011, Mailing Address-PO Box 55458, Washington, DC, 20040 Tel. (202)723-8993, Fax (202)722-1840

Walker, Sr., George Washington Carver, 137 Talcott Notch Rd., Farmington, CT 06032 Tel.(860)676-8414, Fax (860)676-8424

Williams, Milton Alexander, 12904 Canoe Court, Fort Washington, MD 20744 Tel. (301)292-0002, Fax (301)292-6655; Office: 2001 Ninth St., N.W., Suite 306, Box 322, Washington, DC 20001 Tel. (202)265-9590, Fax (202)265-9593

RETIRED

Hilliard , William Alexander, 690 Chicago Blvd., Detroit, MI 48202

Hoggard, James Clinton, 4515 Willard Ave., Apt, 2203, South Chevy Chase, MD 20815 Tel. (301)652-9010; Office: Howard University School of Divinity, 1400 Shepherd St., N.E., Suite 189-191, Washington, DC 20017 Tel. (202)635-6201

Miller, Sr., John Henry, Springdale Estates, 8605 Caswell Ct., Raleigh, NC 27612 Tel. (919) 848-6915

EPISCOPAL ASSIGNMENTS

Piedmont Episcopal District: Blue Ridge, West Central North Carolina, Western North Carolina, and Jamaica Conferences: Bishop Cecil Bishop

North Eastern Episcopal District: New England, New York, Western New York, and Bahamas Islands Conferences: Bishop George W. Walker, Sr.

Mid-Atlantic II Episcopal District: East Tennessee-Virginia, India, London-Birmingham, Manchester-Midland, Philadelphia- Baltimore, and Virginia Conferences: Bishop Milton A. Williams

Eastern West Africa Episcopal District: Central Nigeria, Lagos- West Nigeria, Nigeria, Northern Nigeria, and Rivers Conferences: Bishop S. Chuka Ekemam, Sr.

Eastern North Carolina Episcopal District: Albemarle, Cape Fear, Central North Carolina, North Carolina, and Virgin Islands Conferences: Bishop George E. Battle, Jr.

South Atlantic Episcopal District: Georgia, Palmetto, Pee Dee, South Carolina, and South Georgia Conferences: Bishop Joseph Johnson

Alabama-Florida Episcopal District: Alabama, Cahaba, Central Alabama, North Alabama, South Alabama, West Alabama, Florida, and South Florida Conferences: Bishop Richard K. Thompson

Mid-West Episcopal District: Indiana, Kentucky, Michigan, Missouri, Tennessee, and South Africa Conferences: Bishop Enoch B. Rochester

Mid-Atlantic I Episcopal District: Allegheny, New Jersey, Ohio, Guyana, Trinidad-Tobago, and Barbados Conferences: Bishop Marshall Haywood Strickland I

Western Episcopal District: Alaska, Arizona, California, Oregon-Washington, Southwest Rocky Mountain, and Colorado Conferences: Bishop Clarence Carr

Southwestern Delta: Arkansas, Louisiana, Oklahoma, South Mississippi, West Tennessee-Mississippi, and Texas Conferences: Bishop Nathaniel Jarrett

Western West Africa: Cote D'Ivore, East Ghana, Liberia, Mid-Ghana, and West Ghana Conferences: Bishop Warren Matthew Brown

General Officers and Departments

Dept. of Records & Research: Gen. Sec.-Aud., Dr. W. Robert Johnson, III, 401 E. Second St., Ste. 108, Charlotte, NC 28202 Tel. (704)332-3851 Fax (704)333-1769; Mailing Address, P.O. Box 32843, Charlotte, NC 28232; j1gsa@aol.com

Dept. of Finance: CFO, Shirley Welch, 401 E. Second St., Ste. 101, Charlotte, NC 28202 Tel. (704)333-4847, Fax (704)333-6517; Mailing Address, P.O. Box 31005, Charlotte, NC 28231

Star of Zion: Michael Libsy, Editor, 401 E. Second St., Suite 106, Charlotte, NC 28202 Tel. (704)377-4329, Fax (704)377-4329, Fax (704)377-2809; starozion@juno.com
Mailing Address, P.O. Box 31005, Charlotte, NC 28231

A.M.E. Zion Quarterly Review and Historical Society: James D. Armstong, Sec.-Ed., 401 E. Second St., Suite 103, Charlotte, NC 28202 Tel. (704)334-0728, Fax (704)333-1769 Mailing Address, P.O. Box 33247, Charlotte, NC 28231

Dept. of Overseas Missions and Missionary Seer: Sec.-Ed., Dr. Kermit J. DeGraffenreidt, 475 Riverside Dr., Rm. 1935, New York, NY 10115 Tel. (212)870-2952, Fax (212)870-2808

Dept. Brotherhood Pensions & Min. Relief: Sec.-Treas., Dr. David Miller, 401 E. Second St., Suite 209, Charlotte, NC 28202 Tel. (704)333-3779 or 1-800-762-5106, Fax (704)333-3867, P.O. Box 34454, Charlotte, NC 28234-4454

Christian Education Dept.: Gen. Sec., Rev. Raymon Hunt, 401 E. Second St., Suite 207, Charlotte, NC 28202 Tel. (704)332-9323, Fax (704)332-9332, ced1amez@juno.com Mailing Address, P.O. Box 32305, Charlotte, NC 28232-2305

Dept. of Church School Literature: Ed., Dr. Mary A. Love, 401 E. Second St., Suite 208, Charlotte, NC 28202 Tel. (704)332-1034, Fax (704)333-1769, Mailing Address, P.O. Box 31005, Charlotte, NC 28231

Dept. of Church Extension & Home Mission: Sec-Treas., Dr. Lem Long, Jr., 401 E. Second St., Suite 104, Charlotte, NC 28202 Tel. (704)334-2519, Fax (704)334-3806, Mailing Address, P.O. Box 31005, Charlotte, NC 28231

Bureau of Evangelism: Dir., Rev. Darryl B. Starnes, Sr., 401 E. Second St., Suite 111, Charlotte, NC 28202 Tel. (704)342-3070, Fax (704)342-2389, Mailing Address, P.O. Box 33623, Charlotte, NC 28233-3623

Public Affairs and Convention Manager: Dir., Rev. George E. McKain, II, 943 West First North St., Summerville, SC 29483 Tel. (803)873-2475

Dept. of Health & Social Concerns: Dir., Dr. Bernard H. Sullivan, P.O. Box 972, Gastonia, NC 28053 Tel. (704)866-0325 or (704)864-1791, Fax (704)864-7641

A.M.E. Zion Publishing House, Interim Gen. Mgr., Dr. David Miller, 401 E. Second St., Suite 106, Charlotte, NC 28202 Tel. (704)334-9596, Fax (704)334-9592; 1-800-343-9835 Mailing Address, P.O. Box 30714, Charlotte, NC 28230

Periodicals

Star of Zion; Quarterly Review; Church School Herald, Missionary Seer, and Vision Focus

Albanian Orthodox Archdiocese in America

The Albanian Orthodox Church in America traces its origins to the groups of Albanian immigrants which first arrived in the United States in 1886, seeking religious, cultural, and economic freedoms denied them in the homeland.

In 1908 in Boston, the Rev. Fan Stylian Noli (later Archbishop) served the first liturgy in the Albanian language in 500 years, to which Orthodox Albanians rallied, forming their own diocese in 1919. Parishes began to spring up throughout New England and the Mid-Atlantic and Great Lakes states. In 1922, clergy from the United States traveled to Albania to proclaim the self-governance of the Orthodox Church in the homeland at the Congress of Berat.

In 1971 the Albanian Archdiocese sought and gained union with the Orthodox Church in America, expressing the desire to expand the Orthodox witness to America at large, giving it an indigenous character. The Albanian Archdiocese remains vigilant for its brothers and sisters in the homeland and serves as an important resource for human rights issues and Albanian affairs, in addition to its programs for youth, theological education, vocational interest programs, and retreats for young adults and women.

Headquarters

523 E. Broadway, S. Boston, MA 02127

Media Contact, Sec., Dorothy Adams, Tel. (617) 268-1275, Fax (617)268-3184

Website: www.oca.org/OCA/AL/

Officers

Metropolitan Theodosius, Tel. (617)268-1275

Chancellor, V. Rev. Arthur E. Liolin, 60 Antwerp St., East Milton, MA 02186 Tel. (617)698-3366

Lay Chpsn., William Poist, 40 Forge Village Rd., Westford, MA 01885 Tel. (978)392-0759

Treas., Cynthia Vasil Brown, 471 Capt. Eames Circle, Ashland, MA 01721 Tel. (508)881-0072

Albanian Orthodox Diocese of America

This Diocese was organized in 1950 as a canonical body administering to the Albanian faithful. It is under the ecclesiastical jurisdiction of the Ecumenical Patriarchate of Constantinople (Istanbul).

Headquarters

6455 Silver Dawn Lane, Las Vegas, NV 89118 Tel. (702)221-8245, Fax (702)221-9167

Media Contact, Rev. Ik. Ilia Katre

Officers

Vicar General, Rev. Ik. Ilia Katre

The Allegheny Wesleyan Methodist Connection (Original Allegheny Conference)

This body was formed in 1968 by members of the Allegheny Conference (located in eastern Ohio and western Pennsylvania) of the Wesleyan Methodist Church, which merged in 1966 with the Pilgrim Holiness Church to form The Wesleyan Church.

The Allegheny Wesleyan Methodist Connection is composed of persons "having the form and seeking the power of godliness, united in order to pray together, to receive the word of exhortation, and to watch over one another in love, that they may help each other to work out their salvation." There is a strong commitment to congregational government and to holiness of heart and life. There is a strong thrust in church extension within the United States and in missions worldwide.

Headquarters

P.O. Box 357, Salem, OH 44460 Tel. (330)337-9376

Media Contact, Pres., Rev. Michael Marshall

Email: awmc@juno.com

Website: c1web.com/local_info/churches/aw.html

Officers

Pres., Rev. Michael Marshall, P.O. Box 357, Salem, OH 44460

Vice-Pres., Rev. William Cope, 1827 Allen Drive, Salem, OH 44460

Sec., Rev. Ray Satterfield, Rt. 4, Box 300, Salem, WV 26426

Treas., James Kunselman, 1022 Newgarden Ave., Salem, OH 44460

Periodicals

The Allegheny Wesleyan Methodist

The Alliance of Baptists in the U.S.A.*

The Alliance of Baptists is an alliance of individuals and churches dedicated to the preservation of historic Baptist principles, freedoms, and traditions, and to the expression of our ministry and mission through cooperative relationships with other Baptist bodies and the larger Christian community.

From its inception in early 1987, the Alliance has stood for those values that have distinguished the Baptist movement from its beginnings nearly four centuries ago "the freedom and accountability of every individual in matters of faith; the freedom of each congregation under the authority of Jesus Christ to determine its own ministry and mission; and religious freedom for all in relationship to the state."

Headquarters

1328 16th St. N.W., Washington, DC 20036 Tel. (202)745-7609, Fax (202)745-0023

Media Contact, Exec. Dir., Rev. Dr. Stan Hastey

Website: www.allianceofbaptists.org

Officers

Exec. Dir., Rev. Dr. Stan Hastey

Assoc. Dir., Jeanette Holt

Pres., The Rev. Paula Clayton Dempsey, Mars Hill, NC, Tel. (828)689-1128

Vice-Pres., Craig Henry, Monroe, LA, Tel. (318) 388-4400

Sec., Relma Hargus, Baton Rouge, LA, Tel. (225) 291-6516

Periodicals

connections

The American Association of Lutheran Churches

This church body was constituted on November 7, 1987. The AALC was formed by laity and pastors of the former American Lutheran Church in America who held to a high view of Scripture (inerrancy and infallibility). This church body also emphasizes the primacy of evangelism and world missions and the authority and autonomy of the local congregation.

Congregations of the AALC are distributed throughout the continental United States from Long Island, N.Y., to Los Angeles, CA. The primary decision-making body is the General Convention, to which each congregation has proportionate representation.

Headquarters

The AALC National Office, 10800 Lyndale Ave. S., Ste. 210, Minneapolis, MN 55420-5614 Tel. (612)884-7784, Fax (612)884-7894,

The AALC Regional Office, 2211 Maynard St., Waterloo, IA 50701 Tel. (319)232-3971, Fax (319)232-1523

Media Contact, Admn. Coord., Rev. Charles D. Eidum, 10800 Lyndale Ave. So., #210 Minneapolis, MN 55420-5614 Tel. (612)884-7784, Fax (612)884-7894

Email: aa2taalc@aol.com

Website: www.taalc.com

Officers

Presiding Pastor, Rev. Thomas V. Addland, 10800, Lyndale Ave., So., #210, Minneapolis, MN 55420-5614, Tel. (612)884-7784, Fax (612)884-7894, aadland@aol.com

Asst. Presiding Pastor, Rev. John A. Anderson, 310 Seventh St., Ames, IA 50010 Tel. (515)232-3815

Sec., Rev. Dick Hueter, N9945 Highway 180, Wausaukee, WI 54177 Tel. (715)732-0327

Treas., Rev. Dale Zastrow, 700 Second Ave. NE, Minot, ND 58703 Tel. (701)839-7474

Periodicals

The Evangel

The American Baptist Association

The American Baptist Association (ABA) is an international fellowship of independent Baptist churches voluntarily cooperating in missionary, evangelistic, benevolent, and Christian education activities throughout the world. Its beginnings can be traced to the landmark movement of the 1850s. Led by James R. Graves and J.M. Pendleton, a significant number of Baptist churches in the South, claiming a New Testament heritage, rejected as extrascriptural the policies of the newly formed Southern Baptist Convention (SBC). Because they strongly advocated church equality, many of these churches continued doing mission and benevolent work apart from the SBC, electing to work through local associations. Meeting in Texarkana, TX, in 1924, messengers from the various churches effectively merged two of these major associations, the Baptist Missionary Association of Texas and the General Association, forming the American Baptist Association.

Since 1924, mission efforts have been supported in Australia, Africa, Asia, Canada, Central America, Europe, India, Israel, Japan, Korea, Mexico, New Zealand, South America, and the South Pacific. An even more successful domestic mission effort has changed the ABA from a predominantly rural southern organization to one with churches in 48 states.

Through its publishing arm in Texarkana, the ABA publishes literature and books numbering into the thousands. Major seminaries include the Missionary Baptist Seminary, founded by Dr. Ben M. Bogard in Little Rock, AR; Texas Baptist Seminary, Henderson, TX; Oxford Baptist

Institute, Oxford, MS; and Florida Baptist Schools in Lakeland, FL.

While no person may speak for the churches of the ABA, all accept the Bible as the inerrant Word of God. They believe Christ was the virgin-born Son of God, that God is a triune God, that the only church is the local congregation of scripturally baptized believers, and that the work of the church is to spread the gospel.

Headquarters

4605 N State Line Ave. Texarkana, TX 75503 Tel. (903) 792-2783

Media Contact, Steve Reeves, Public Relations Director

Email: bssc@abaptist.org

Website: www.abaptist.org

Officers

President, George Raley, 9890 Hwy 15, Rison, AR 71665

Vice Presidents, Neal Clark, Rt. 1, Box 48A, Daingerfield, TX 75638; John Owen, P.O. Box 142, Bryant, AR 72089; David Butimore Sr., 1602 Winters Rd., Brementon, WA 98311

Recording Clerks, Larry Clements, 270 Tracy Dr., Monticello, AR 71655; Lonnie Wiggins, 1114 Occidental St., Redlands, CA 92374

Publications, Editor in Chief, Bill Johnson; Bus. Mgr., Wayne Sewell, 4605 N. State Line Ave., Texarkana, TX 75503

Meeting Arrangements Director, Edgar N. Sutton, P.O. Box 240, Alexander, AR 72002

Sec.-Treas. of Missions, Randy Cloud, P.O. Box 1050 Texarkana, TX 75504

American Baptist Churches in the U.S.A.*

Originally known as the Northern Baptist Convention, this body of Baptist churches changed the name to American Baptist Convention in 1950 with a commitment to "hold the name in trust for all Christians of like faith and mind who desire to bear witness to the historical Baptist convictions in a framework of cooperative Protestantism."

In 1972 American Baptist Churches in the U.S.A. was adopted as the new name. Although national missionary organizational developments began in 1814 with the establishment of the American Baptist Foreign Mission Society and continued with the organization of the American Baptist Publication Society in 1824 and the American Baptist Home Mission Society in 1832, the general denominational body was not formed until 1907. American Baptist work at the local level dates back to the organization by Roger Williams of the First Baptist Church in Providence, R. I. in 1638.

Headquarters

American Baptist Churches Mission Center

P.O. Box 851, Valley Forge, PA 19482-0851 Tel. (610)768-2000, Fax (610)768-2320

Media Contact, Dir., Office of Comm., Richard W. Schramm, Tel. (610)768-2077, Fax (610) 768-2320

Email: richard.schramm@abc-usa.org

Website: www.abc-usa.org

Officers

Pres., David Hunt

Vice-Pres., Yosh Nakagawa

Budget Review Officer, Melva Gray

Gen. Sec., Rev. A. Roy Medley

Assoc. Gen. Sec.-Treas., Cheryl H. Wade

REGIONAL ORGANIZATIONS

Central Region, ABC of, Fred A. Ansell, 5833 S.W. 29th St., Topeka, KS 66614-2499

Chicago, ABC of Metro, William R. Nelson (Interim), 28 E. Jackson Blvd., Ste. 210, Chicago, IL 60604-2207

Cleveland Baptist Assoc., Dennis E. Norris, 1836 Euclid Ave., Ste. 603, Cleveland, OH 44115-2234

Connecticut, ABC of, Lowell H. Fewster, 100 Bloomfield Ave., Hartford, CT 06105-1097

Dakotas, ABC of, Riley H. Walker, 1524 S. Summit Ave., Sioux Falls, SD 57105-1697

District of Columbia Bapt. Conv., Jeffrey Haggray, 1628 16th St., NW, Washington, DC 20009-3099

ABC of the Great Rivers Region, J. Dwight Stinnett, P.O. Box 3786, Springfield, IL 62708-3786

Indiana, ABC of, Larry D. Mason, 1350 N. Delaware St., Indianapolis, IN 46202-2493

Indianapolis, ABC of Greater, Larry D. Sayre, 1350 N. Delaware St., Indianapolis, IN 46202-2493

Los Angeles, ABC of, Samuel S. Chetti, 605 W. Olympic Blvd., Ste. 700, Los Angeles, CA 90015-1426

Maine, ABC of, Alfred Fletcher, 107 Winthrop St., P.O. Box 617, Augusta, ME 04332-0617

Massachusetts, ABC of, Linda Spoolstra, 20 Milton St., Dedham, MA 02026-2967

Metropolitan New York, ABC of, James O. Stallings, 475 Riverside Dr., Rm. 432, New York, NY 10115-0432

Michigan, ABC of, Michael A. Williams, 4578 S. Hagadorn Rd., East Lansing, MI 48823-5396

Mid-American Baptist Churches, interim, Ste. 15, 2400 86th St., Des Moines, IA 50322-4380

Nebraska, ABC of, Susan E. Gillies, 6404 Maple St., Omaha, NE 68104-4079

New Jersey, ABC of, A. Roy Medley, 3752 Nottingham Way, Ste. 101, Trenton, NJ 08690-3802

New York State, ABC of, William A. Carlsen, 5842 Heritage Landing Dr., East Syracuse, NY 13057-9359

Northwest, ABC of, Lucy Brand, interim, 409 Third Ave. South, Suite A, Kent, WA 98032-5843

Ohio, ABC of, C. Jeff Woods, 136 N. Galway Dr., P.O. Box 376, Granville, OH 43023-0376

Oregon, ABC of, W. Wayne Brown, 0245 SW Bancroft St., Ste. G, Portland, OR 97201-4270

Pacific Southwest, ABC of the, Dale V. Salico, 970 Village Oaks Dr., Ste. 101, Covina, CA 91724-3679

Pennsylvania & Delaware, ABC of, Clayton R. Woodbury, 106 Revere Lane, Coatesville, PA 19320

Philadelphia Baptist Assoc., Roy Thompson, interim, 100 N. 17th St., Philadelphia, PA 19103-2736

Pittsburgh Baptist Assoc., Lawrence O. Swain, 429 Forbes Ave., #1620, Pittsburgh, PA 15219-1604

Puerto Rico, Baptist Churches of, Miladys Oliveras (Interim) #21, San Juan, PR 00917

Rhode Island, ABC of, Donald R. Rasmussen, P.O. Box 330, Exeter, RI 02822

Rochester-Genesee Region, ABC of, Lisa Drysdale, interim, 151 Brooks Ave., Rochester, NY 14619-2454

Rocky Mountains, ABC of, Louise B. Barger, 3900 Wadsworth Blvd. Suite 365, Lakewood, CO 80235-2220

South, ABC of the, Walter L. Parrish, II, 5124 Greenwich Ave., Baltimore, MD 21229-2393

Vermont-New Hampshire, ABC of, George Daniels, Interim, Wheeler Professional Park, One Oak Ridge Rd., Bldg. 3, Suite 4A, West Lebanon, NH 03784-3121

West, ABC of the, Paul D. Borden, 2420 Camino Ramon, Ste. 140, San Ramon, CA 94583-4207

West Virginia Baptist Convention, Lloyd D. Hamblin, Jr., P.O. Box 1019, Parkersburg, WV 26102-1019

Wisconsin, ABC of, Arlo R. Reichter, 15330 W. Watertown Plank Rd., Elm Grove, WI 53122-2391

BOARDS

Bd. of Educational Ministries, Exec. Dir., Jean B. Kim; Pres., William D. Apel

American Baptist Assembly, Green Lake, WI 54941; Pres., Kenneth P. Giacoletto; Chpsn., Hector Gonzalez

American Baptist Historical Society, 1106 S. Goodman St., Rochester, NY 14620; or P.O. Box 851, Valley Forge, PA 19482-0851; Admn. Archivist, Deborah B. VanBroekhoven; Pres., Beverly Davison

American Baptist Men, Dir., Z. Allen Abbott, Jr.; Pres., Cody Pollington

American Baptist Women's Ministries, Exec. Dir., Virginia Holmstrom; Pres., Karen Selig

Ministerial Leadership Commission, Exec. Dir., Ivan George

Bd. of Intl. Ministries, Exec. Dir., John A. Sundquist; Pres., Stephen Hasper

Bd. of Natl. Ministries, Exec. Dir., Aidsand F. Wright-Riggins; Pres., Vernell C. Neely

Ministers & Missionaries Benefit Bd., Exec. Dir., Sumner M. Grant; Pres., Mary H. Purcell, 475 Riverside Dr., New York, NY 10115

Minister Council, Dir., Carole (Kate) H. Harvey; Pres., Sara Day Cheesman

Periodicals

Tomorrow Magazine; The Secret Place; American Baptist Quarterly; American Baptists In Mission

The American Carpatho-Russian Orthodox Greek Catholic Church

The American Carpatho-Russian Orthodox Greek Catholic Church is a self-governing diocese that is in communion with the Ecumenical Patriarchate of Constantinople. The late Patriarch Benjamin I, in an official Patriarchal Document dated Sept. 19, 1938, canonized the Diocese in the name of the Orthodox Church of Christ.

Headquarters

312 Garfield St., Johnstown, PA 15906 Tel. (814)539-4207, Fax (814)536-4699

Media Contact, Chancellor, V. Rev. Protopresbyter Frank P. Miloro, Tel. (814)539-8086, Fax (814)536-4699

Email: archdiocese@goarch.org

Website: www.goarch.org

Officers

Bishop, Metropolitan Nicholas Smisko, 312 Garfield St., Johnstown, PA 15906 Tel. (814)539-4207, Fax (814)536-4699

Chancellor, V. Rev. Protopresbyter Frank P. Miloro, 127 Chandler Ave., Johnstown, PA 15906 Tel. (814)539-9143, Fax (814)536-4699, acrod@helicon.net

Treas., V. Rev. Protopresbyter Ronald A. Hazuda, 115 East Ave., Erie, PA 16503 Tel. (814)453-4902

Periodicals

The Church Messenger

American Catholic Church—please see Reformed Catholic Church.

American Evangelical Christian Churches

Founded in 1944, the AECC is composed of individual ministers and churches who are united in accepting "Seven Articles of Faith." These seven articles are: the Bible as the written word of God; the Virgin birth; the deity of Jesus Christ; Salvation through the atonement; guidance of our life through prayer; the return of the Saviour; the establishment of the Millennial Kingdom.

The American Evangelical Christian Churches offers the following credentials: Certified Christian Worker, Commission to Preach, Licensed Minister, and Ordained Minister to those who accept the Seven Articles of Faith, who put unity in Christ first, and are approved by AECC.

A.E.C.C. seeks to promote the gospel through its ministers, churches and missionary activities. Churches operate independently with all decisions concerning local government left to the individual churches.

The organization also has ministers in Canada, England, Bolivia, Philippines Thailand, Brazil and South America.

Headquarters

P.O. Box 47312, Indianapolis, IN 46227 Tel. (863)314-9370, Fax (863)314-9570

Media Contact, International Mod., Dr. Otis O. Osborne, 1421 Roseland Ave., Sebring, FL 33870 Tel. (863)314-9370

Email: alpha@strato.net

Website: www.aeccministries.com

Officers

INTERNATIONAL OFFICERS

Mod., Dr. Charles Wasielewski, Box 51, Wells Rd., Barton, NY 13734 Tel. (607)565-4074

Sec., Dr. Gene McClain, 520 Blooming Pike, Morgantown, IN 46160 Tel. (812)597-5021

Treas., Dr. Michael Ward, Sr., 4802 Chervil Ct., Indianapolis, IN 46237 Tel. (317)888-2095

Bd. Member, Dr. S. Omar Overly, 2481 Red Rock Blvd., Grove City, OH 43123-1154 Tel. (614)871-0710

Bd. Member, Dr. David Burgess, 5420 Caribbean Pl., Jonesboro, AR 72404 Tel. (870)802-1010

REGIONAL MODERATORS

Northwest Region, Rev. Alvin House, P.O. Box 393, Darby MT 59829 Tel. (406)821-3141

Central-West Region, Rev. Charles Clark, Box 314, Rockport, IL 62370 Tel. (217)437-2507

Far West Region, Pastor Richard Cuthbert, 1195 Via Serville, Cathedral City, CA 92234 Tel. (706)321-6682

Central Region, Dr. S. Omar Overly, 2481 Red Rock Blvd., Grove City, OH 43123-1154 Tel. (614)871-0710

Northeast Region, Rev. John Merrill, P.O. Box 183, East Smithfield, PA 18817 Tel. (717)596-4598

East Region, Rev. Larry Walker, P.O. Box 1165, Lillington, NC 27546 Tel. (919)893-9529

Southeast Region, Rev. James Fullwood, 207 Fifth Avenue, NE, Lutz, FL 33549

STATE MODERATORS

Rev. James Brown, Maryland

Rev. John W. Coats, Delaware

Brenda Osborne, New York

Dr. Berton G. Heleine, Illinois

Rev. R. Eugene Hill, New Jersey

Rev. Kenneth Pope, Washington

Rev. Art Mirek, Michigan

Rev. Charles Jennings, Pennsylvania

Rev. Jerry Myers, Indiana

FOREIGN OUTREACH MINISTRIES

American Evangelical Christian Churches- Canada

Regional Moderator, Dr. Stephen K. Massey, 730 Ontario street, Suite 709, Toronto, Ontario M4X 1N3, Canada Tel. (416)323-9076

Philippine Evangelical Christian Churches

Director, Rev. Alan A. Olubalang, P.O. Box 540, Cotabato City, Philippines 9600

American Evangelical Christian Churches-Philippines

Regional Moderator, Rev. Oseas Andres, P.O. Box 2695, Central Post Office, 1166 Q.C. Metro Manila, Philippines 430-6549

Periodicals

The American Evangelical Christian Churches Newsletter- Monthly

American Rescue Workers

Major Thomas E. Moore was National Commander of Booth's Salvation Army when a dispute flared between Booth and Moore. Moore resigned from Booth's Army, and due to the fact that Booth's Army was not incorporated at the time, Moore was able to incorporate under said name. The name was changed in 1890 to American Salvation Army. In 1913 the current name American Rescue Workers was adopted.

It is a national religious social service agency which operates on a quasimilitary basis. Membership includes officers (clergy), soldiers-adherents (laity), members of various activity groups, and volunteers who serve as advisors, associates, and committed participants in ARW service functions.

The motivation of the organization is the love of God. Its message is based on the Bible. This is expressed by its spiritual Ministry, the purposes of which are to preach the gospel of Jesus Christ and to meet human needs in his name without discrimination. It is a branch of the Christian Church . . . A Church with a Mission.

Headquarters

Operational Headquarters, 25 Ross Street, Williamsport, PA 17701 Tel. (570)323-8693, Fax (570)323-8694

National Field Office, 1209 Hamilton Blvd., Hagerstown, MD 21742 Tel. (301)797-0061

Media Contact, Natl. Communication Sec., Col. Robert N. Coles, Rev., Natl. Field Ofc., Fax (301)797-1480

Email: amerscwk@pcspower.net

Website: www.arwus.com/

Officers

Commander-In-Chief & Pres. Of Corp., General Claude S. Astin, Jr. Rev.

Chief of Staff, Col. Larry D. Martin

Natl. Bd. Pres., Col. George B. Gossett, Rev.

Ordination Committee, Chpsn., Gen. Paul E. Martin, (Emeritus) Rev.

Natl. Chief Sec., Major Dawn R. Astin, NQ-643 Elmira St., Williamsport, PA 17701

Periodicals

The Rescue Herald

Amish—please see Old Order Amish Church.

The Anglican Orthodox Church—please see The Episcopal Orthodox Church.

The Antiochian Orthodox Christian Archdiocese of North America*

The spiritual needs of Antiochian faithful in North America were first served through the Syro-Arabian Mission of the Russian Orthodox Church in 1895. In 1895, the Syrian Orthodox Benevolent Society was organized by Antiochian immigrants in New York City. Raphael Hawaweeny, a young Damascene clergyman serving as professor of Arabic language at the Orthodox theological academy in Kazan, Russia, came to New York to organize the first Arabic-language parish in North America in 1895, after being canonically received under the omophorion of the head of the Russian Church in North America. Saint Nicholas Cathedral, now located at 355 State St. in Brooklyn, is considered the "mother parish" of the Archdiocese.

On March 12, 1904, Hawaweeny became the first Orthodox bishop to be consecrated in North America. He traveled throughout the continent and established new parishes. The unity of Orthodoxy in the New World, including the Syrian Greek Orthodox community, was ruptured after the death of Bishop Raphael in 1915 and by the Bolshevik revolution in Russia and the First World War. Unity returned in 1975 when Metropolitan Philip Saliba, of the Antiochian Archdiocese of New York, and Metropolitan Michael Shaheen of the Antiochian Archdiocese of Toledo, Ohio, signed the Articles of Reunification, ratified by the Holy Synod of the Patriarchate. Saliba was recognized as the Metropolitan Primate and Shaheen as Auxiliary Archbishop. A second auxiliary to the Metropolitan, Bishop Antoun Khouri, was consecrated at Brooklyn's Saint Nicholas Cathedral, in 1983. A third auxiliary, Bishop Basil Essey was consecrated at Wichita's St. George Cathedral in 1992. Two additional bishops were added in 1994, Bishop Joseph Zehlaoui and Bishop Demetri Khoury.

The Archdiocesan Board of Trustees (consisting of 60 elected and appointed clergy and lay members) and the Metropolitan's Advisory Council (consisting of clergy and lay representatives from each parish and mission) meet regularly to assist the Primate in the administration of the Archdiocese. Currently, there are 227 parishes and missions in the Archdiocese.

Headquarters

358 Mountain Rd., Englewood, NJ 07631 Tel. (201)871-1355, Fax (201)871-7954

Media Contact, Father Thomas Zain, 52 78th St., Brooklyn, NY 11209 Tel. (718)748-7940, Fax (718)855-3608

Email: FrJoseph@antiochian.org

Website: www.antiochian.org/

Officers

Primate, Metropolitan Philip Saliba
Auxiliary, Bishop Antoun Khouri
Auxiliary, Bishop Joseph Zehlaoui
Auxiliary, Bishop Basil Essey
Auxiliary, Bishop Demetri Khoury

Periodicals

The Word; Credo; Again Magazine

Apostolic Catholic Assyrian Church of the East, North American Dioceses

The Holy Apostolic Catholic Assyrian Church of the East is the ancient Christian church that developed within the Persian Empire from the day of Pentecost. The Apostolic traditions testify that the Church of the East was established by Sts. Peter, Thomas, Thaddaeus, and Bartholomew from among the Twelve and by the labors of Mar Mari and Aggai of the Seventy. The Church grew and developed carrying the Christian gospel into the whole of Asia and islands of the Pacific. Prior to the Great Persecution at the hands of Tamer'leng the Mongol, it is said to have been the largest Christian church in the world.

The doctrinal identity of the church is that of the Apostles. The church stresses two natures and two Qnume in the One person, Perfect God-Perfect man. The church gives witness to the original Nicene Creed, the Ecumenical Councils of Nicea and Constantinople and the church fathers of that era. Since God is revealed as Trinity, the appellation "Mother of God" is rejected for the "Ever Virgin Blessed Mary Mother of Christ," we declare that she is Mother of Emmanuel, God with us!

The church has maintained a line of Catholicos Patriarchs from the time of the Holy Apostles until this present time. Today the present occupant of the Apostolic Throne is His Holiness Mar Dinkha IV, 120th successor to the See of Selucia Ctestiphon.

Headquarters

Catholicos Patriarch, His Holiness Mar Dinkha, IV, Metropolitanate Residence, The Assyrian Church of the East, Baghdad, Iraq

Media Contact, Rev. Chancellor C. H. Klutz, 7201 N. Ashland, Chicago, IL 60626 Tel. (773)465-4777, Fax (773)465-0776

Email: ABSoro@aol.com

Website: www.cired.org/ace.html

Officers

BISHOPS- NORTH AMERICA

Diocese Eastern USA, His Grace Bishop Mar Aprim Khamis, 8908 Birch Ave., Morton Grove, IL 60053 Tel. (847)966-0617, Fax (847) 966-0012; Chancellor to the Bishop, Rev. Chancellor C. H. Klutz, 7201 N. Ashland, Chicago, IL 60626 Tel. (773)465-4777, Fax (773)465-0776

Diocese Western USA, ———, St. Joseph Cathedral, 680 Minnesota Ave., San Jose, CA 95125 Tel. (408)286-7377, Fax (408)286-1236

Diocese of Canada, His Grace Bishop Mar Emmanuel Joseph, St. Mary Cathedral, 57

Apted Ave., Weston, ON M9L 2P2 Tel. (416)744-9311

Comm. on Inter-Church & Religious Ed., His Grace Bishop Mar Bawai, Diocese of Seattle in WA, 165 NW 65th, Seattle, WA 98117 Tel. (206)789-1843

Periodicals

Qala min M'Dinkha (Voice from the East)

Apostolic Christian Church (Nazarene)

This body was formed in America by an immigration from various European nations, from a movement begun by Rev. S. H. Froehlich, a Swiss pastor, whose followers are still found in Switzerland and Central Europe.

Headquarters

Apostolic Christian Church Foundation, 1135 Sholey Rd., Richmond, VA 23231 Tel. (804) 222-1943, Fax (804)236-0642

Media Contact, Exec. Dir., James Hodges

Officers

Exec. Dir., James Hodges

Apostolic Christian Churches of America

The Apostolic Christian Church of America was founded in the early 1830s in Switzerland by Samuel Froehlich, a young divinity student who had experienced a religious conversion based on the pattern found in the New Testament. The church, known then as Evangelical Baptist, spread to surrounding countries. A Froehlich associate, Elder Benedict Weyeneth, established the church's first American congregation in 1847 in upstate New York. In America, where the highest concentration today is in the Midwest farm belt, the church became known as Apostolic Christian.

Church doctrine is based on a literal interpretation of the Bible, the infallible Word of God. The church believes that a true faith in Christ's redemptive work at Calvary is manifested by a sincere repentance and conversion. Members strive for sanctification and separation from worldliness as a consequence of salvation, not as a means to obtain it. Security in Christ is believed to be conditional based on faithfulness. Uniform observance of scriptural standards of holiness are stressed. Holy Communion is confined to members of the church. Male members are willing to serve in the military, but do not bear arms. The holy kiss is practiced and women wear head coverings during prayer and worship. Doctrinal authority rests with a council of elders, each of whom serves as a local elder (bishop). Both elders and ministers are chosen from local congregations, do not attend seminary and serve without compensation. Sermons are delivered extemporaneously as led by the Holy Spirit, using the Bible as a text.

Headquarters

3420 N. Sheridan Rd., Peoria, IL 61604

Media Contact, Secretary., William R. Schlatter, 14834 Campbell Rd., Defiance, OH 43512 Tel. (419)393-2621, Fax (419)393-2144

Email: Questions@ApostolicChristian.org

Website: www.apostolicchristian.org/

Officers

Sec., Elder (Bishop) William R. Schlatter, 14834 Campbell Rd., Defiance, OH 43512 Tel. 419-393-2621, Fax 419-393-2144

Periodicals

The Silver Lining

Apostolic Episcopal Church

The Apostolic Episcopal Church on Sept. 23-24, 2000 in New York City signed Concordats of Intercommunion with the following Christian Churches—The Anglican Independent Communion, The Ethiopian Orthodox Coptic Archdiocese of North and South America, The Uniate Western Orthodox Catholic Church, and the Byelorussian Orthodox national Church in Exile under the administration of His Beatitude Yury I.

In effect, the Apostolic Episcopal Church thus became a Uniate Western Rite of the Orthodox Church of the East, using the 1928 Book of Common Prayer. In 1905, under the guidance of Archbishop Tikhon Bellavin (later Patriarch of Moscow), the Holy Synod in St. Petersburg approved the use of the Anglican Liturgy for Western Rite Orthodox Christians. Today this usage is calld the Rite of St. Tikhon and is in use among many Orthodox Western Rite Jurisdictions.

This Pilgrimage to Orthodoxy among Anglicans began in 1712 with the Non-Jurors Anglican Hierarchy and faithful. These Non-Jurors were Anglican Clergy who in 1689 refused allegiance to King William III and Queen Mary, the usurpers who had overthrown King James II. In 1712 Metropolitan-Bishop Arsenios of the Alexandrine Patriarchate visited England and received many of these "British Katholicks" into the Orthodox Church.

Headquarters

The Province of the Eastern USA and the Editorial Office of the Tover of St. Cassian, 80-46 234th St., Jamaica, NY 11427-2116, Attn Editor, the Rt. Rev. Francis C. Spataro DD, Tel. (718)740-4134.

The Province of Guyana and the Caribbean, c/o The Rev. Lloyd U. Samuel OCR, P.O. Box 10844, Georgetown, Guyana, South America, Tel. 630875.

Belgium Mission, St. Michael's, Domein Fort 3, Frans Beirenlaan 2A, 2150 Borsbeek, Belgium

Media Contact, The Rt. Rev. Paget E.J. Mack OSBM, P.O. Box 170234, Brooklyn, NY 11217-0234 Tel. (718)622-0072

Email: osbm_ny@yahoo.com

Website: www.cinemaparallel.com/AECSynod.html

Officers

President, The Rt. Rev. Francis C. Spataro, DD
Coadjutor Bishop, The Rt. Rev. Paget E. J. Mack, OSBM
OCR Provost, The Rt. Rev. Peter P. Brennan, OCR
Vicar for Guyana & the Caribbean, Rev. Lloyd U. Samuel, OCR
International Primate for the OCR, The M. Rev. Bertil Persson, THD
Belgium Mission, The Rt. Rev. Walter M. C. Walgraeve

Periodicals

The Tover of St. Cassian

Apostolic Faith Mission Church of God

The Apostolic Faith Mission Church of God was founded and organized July 10, 1906, by Bishop F. W. Williams in Mobile, Alabama.

Bishop Williams was saved and filled with the Holy Ghost at a revival in Los Angeles under Elder W. J. Seymour of The Divine Apostolic Faith Movement. After being called into the ministry, Bishop Williams went out to preach the gospel in Mississippi, then moved on to Mobile.

On Oct. 9, 1915, the Apostolic Faith Mission Church of God was incorporated in Mobile under Bishop Williams, who was also the general overseer of this church.

Headquarters

Ward's Temple, 806 Muscogee Rd., Cantonment, FL 32533
Media Contact, Natl. Sunday School Supt., Elder Thomas Brooks, 3298 Toney Dr., Decatur, GA 30032 Tel. (404)284-7596

Officers

BOARD OF BISHOPS

Presiding Bishop, Donice Brown, 2265 Welcome Cir., Cantonement, FL 32535 Tel. (904)968-5225
Bishop T.C. Tolbert Sr., 226 Elston Ave., Anniston, AL, 36201; Bishop John Crum, 4236 Jackson St., Birmingham, AL, 35217; Bishop Samuel Darden, 25 Taunton Ave., Hyde Park, MA 02136; Bishop James Truss, P.O. Box 495, Lincoln, AL, 35096; Bishop T.C. Tolbert, Jr., 768 Grayton Rd., Ohatchee, AL 36271; Bishop T. L. Frye, 223 Carver, Atmore, AL 36502

NATIONAL DEPARTMENTS

Missionary Dept., Pres., Sarah Ward, Cantonment, FL
Youth Dept., Pres., Johnny Kennedy, Birmingham, AL
Sunday School Dept., Supt., Thomas Brooks, Decatur, GA
Mother Dept., Pres., Mother Bessie Davis, 1003 Northeast St., Pensacola, FL 32501

INTERNATIONAL DEPARTMENTS

Morobia, Liberia, Bishop Beter T. Nelson, Box 3646, Bush Rhode Islane, Morobia, Liberia

Apostolic Faith Mission of Portland, Oregon

The Apostolic Faith Mission of Portland, Oregon, was founded in 1907. It had its beginning in the Latter Rain outpouring on Azusa Street in Los Angeles in 1906.

Some of the main doctrines are justification by faith which is a spiritual new birth, as Jesus told Nicodemus and as Martin Luther proclaimed in the Great Reformation; sanctification, a second definite work of grace; the Wesleyan teaching of holiness; the baptism of the Holy Ghost as experienced on the Day of Pentecost and again poured out at the beginning of the Latter Rain revival in Los Angeles.

Mrs. Florence L. Crawford, who had received the baptism of the Holy Ghost in Los Angeles, brought this Latter Rain message to Portland on Christmas Day 1906. It has spread to the world by means of literature which is still published and mailed everywhere without a subscription price. Collections are never taken in the meetings and the public is not asked for money.

Camp meetings have been held annually in Portland, Oregon since 1907, with delegations coming from around the world.

Missionaries from the Portland headquarters have established churches in Korea, Japan, the Philippines, and many countries in Africa.

Headquarters

6615 S.E. 52nd Ave., Portland, OR 97206 Tel. (503)777-1741, Fax (503)777-1743
Media Contact, Superintendent, Darrel D. Lee
Website: www.apostolicfaith.org

Officers

President, Rev. Darrel D. Lee

Periodicals

Higher Way

Apostolic Lutheran Church of America

Organized in 1872 as the Solomon Korteniemi Lutheran Society, this Finnish body was incorporated in 1929 as the Finnish Apostolic Lutheran Church in America and changed its name to Apostolic Lutheran Church of America in 1962.

This body stresses preaching the Word of God. There is an absence of liturgy and formalism in worship. A seminary education is not required of pastors. Being called by God to preach the Word is the chief requirement for clergy and laity. The church stresses personal absolution and forgiveness of sins, as practiced by Martin Luther, and the importance of bringing converts into God's kingdom.

Headquarters

P.O. Box 2948, Battle Ground, WA 98604-2948
Media Contact, Secretary, Ivan M. Seppala
Website: www.apostolic-lutheran.org/

Officers

Chairman, Richard C. Juuti, RRI, Bentley, AB T0C 0J0, Canada

Treas., Ben Johnson, 98920 Keller Rd., Astoria, OR 97103

Secretary, Ivan M. Seppala, 332 Mt. Washington Way, Clayton, CA 94517

Periodicals

Christian Monthly

Apostolic Orthodox Catholic Church of North America

The Christian Church was established by the Lord Jesus Christ and His Holy Apostles in Jerusalem in 29 A.D. From Jerusalem, the Church spread to other centers of the known world, including Constantinople and Kiev, founded in 37 A.D. by St. Andrew the First-Called Holy Apostle. In 864, the Church of Constantinople expanded the Orthodox Christian Faith in present-day Russia. In 988, Rus' Prince Vladimir converted and declared Orthodoxy the State religion, while hundreds of thousands were baptized at Kiev. The resulting Russian Orthodox Church became the greatest safe-guard and body of Orthodox Christians in the world.

The history of American Orthodox Catholic Christianity began in 1794 when Russian Orthodox Church missionaries established the first Orthodox mission on North American soil at present-day Alaska. Their missionary efforts continued down the Pacific coast in 1824, then across the whole continent. Being the canonical founder of Orthodox Christianity in North America, the Russian Orthodox Church maintained and presided over all Orthodox missions, churches, and Christians throughout North America without question or challenge for over 100 years. However, the 1917 Bolshevik Revolution which resulted in severe persecution and imprisonment of the Russian Orthodox Mother Church also resulted in the unrestrained rise of old-country nationalism and great ethnic turbulence between Orthodox Catholic Christians and their churches in North America. They seperated and divided, often violently, along ethnic and nationalist lines with each creating their own old-world ethnic administrations. The once long-held unity and single Orthodox Church canonical administration in North America was destroyed.

The Apostolic Orthodox Catholic Church (AOCC) is canonically independent and indigenous to North America and comprised of bishops, clergy, and faithful possessing unbroken Apostolic Succession since the time of Jesus Christ's appointment of His Twelve Holy Apostles to the present day through American Orthodoxy's Luminary and Defender, Russian Orthodox Prelate-Archbishop Aftimios Ofiesh of Blessed Memory.

The AOCC has unquestionable Apostolic Succession passed on to its bishops through the Russian Orthodox Church by Archbishop Aftimios Ofiesh, his succeeding Bishops Sophronios Beshara and Christopher Contogeorge, and through consecrating support of such memorable Orthodox leaders as Albanian Orthodox Church Metropolitan Theophan Noli. The Apostolic Succession and Canonicity of these bishops and their successors was recognized as valid, authentic and independent by the Orthodox Church Ecumenical Patriarchate of Constantinople in 1945, and re-affirmed in 1951. English-speaking and non-ethnic restrictive, the AOCC's further validity is evidenced by its life, mind, discourse, and teaching all being governed and directed in accordance with the Sacred Canons of the Most Ancient Holy Orthodox Catholic Church. The AOCC embraces the ideals and theology of Orthodoxy and freedom which Archbishop Aftimios Ofiesh stood for, taught, and passed on by selfless devotion and love for Christ and His Church, and by his personal example.

Headquarters

AOCC Chancery, P.O. Box 1834, Glendora, CA 91740-1834 Tel. (626)335-7369

Media Contact, Rt. Rev. Fr. Bartimaeus, Archpriest, Ecumenical Relations Officer, 2324 9th St., South, Great Falls, MT 59405 Tel/Fax (406) 452-0674, aoccna.relations@usa.com

Email: aoccna.relations@usa.com

Website: American Bible Society, fordenominations

Officers

Presiding Bishop, Most Rev. Gorazd

Second-Presiding Bishop, Most Rev. Aftimios II

Bishop Secretary, Most Rev. Angelo

Synod of Bishops & Dioceses,

Most Rev. Gorazd, Bishop of the Diocese of Los Angeles & Greater Pacific, P.O. Box 1834, Glendora, CA 91740-1834 Tel. (626)335-7369

Most Rev. Aftimios II, Bishop of the Diocese of the Rocky Mountains & Midwest, 4696 S.E. Horseshoe Ct., Salem, OR 97301 Tel. (503)375-6175, BaftimII@aol.com,

Most Rev. Richard, Bishop of the Diocese of Indiana, 3615 Arizona Street #C, Lake Station, IN 46405

Most Rev. John, Bishop of the Diocese of New York, 4-20 Green Way Ave., Manorville, NY 11949 Tel. (516)878-4172

Most Rev. Angelo, Bishop of the Diocese of the Eastern States, 37 Shippee School House Rd., Foster, RI 02825 Tel. (401)647-2867

Most Rev. Alexei, Bishop of Monte Cristo Skete, P.O. Box 16591, Colorado Springs, CO 80935-6591

SEMINARY

Holy Trinity Apostolic Orthodox Catholic Seminary, P.O. Box 1834, Glendora, CA 91740-1834

Periodicals

Carpenter's Workshop

Apostolic Overcoming Holy Church of God, Inc.

The Right Reverend William Thomas Phillips (1893-1973) was thoroughly convinced in 1912 that Holiness was a system through which God wanted him to serve. In 1916 he was led to Mobile, Alabama, where he organized the Ethiopian Overcoming Holy Church of God. In April 1941 the church was incorporated in Alabama under its present title.

Each congregation manages its own affairs, united under districts governed by overseers and diocesan bishops and assisted by an executive board comprised of bishops, ministers, laymen and the National Secretary. The General Assembly convenes annually.

The church's chief objective is to enlighten people of God's holy Word and to be a blessing to every nation. The main purpose of this church is to ordain elders, appoint pastors, and send out divinely called missionaries and teachers. This church enforces all ordinances enacted by Jesus Christ. The church believes in water baptism (Acts Ch.2 v.38, Ch.8 v.12, and Ch.10 v.47), administers the Lord's Supper, observes the washing of feet (John Ch.13 vs.4-7), believes that Jesus Christ shed his blood to sanctify the people and cleanse them from all sin and believes in the resurrection of the dead and the second coming of Christ.

Headquarters

1120 N. 24th St., Birmingham, AL 35234

Media Contact, Dr. Juanita R. Arrington, Business Manager, A.O.H. Church of God Public Relations Department

Email: traydoc@mindspring.com

Officers

Presiding Senior Bishop & Exec. Head, Rt. Rev. Jasper Roby

Assistant Presider for the Year 2000-2001, Bishop Joe Bennett

Periodicals

The People's Mouthpiece

Armenian Apostolic Church of America

Widespread movement of the Armenian people over the centuries caused the development of two seats of religious jurisdiction of the Armenian Apostolic Church in the World-the See of Etchmiadzin, in Armenia, and the See of Cilicia, in Lebanon.

In America, the Armenian Church functioned under the jurisdiction of the Etchmiadzin See from 1887 to 1933, when a division occurred within the American diocese over the condition of the church in Soviet Armenia. One group chose to remain independent until 1957, when the Holy See of Cilicia agreed to accept them under its jurisdiction.

Despite the existence of two dioceses in North America, the Armenian Church has always functioned as one church in dogma and liturgy.

Headquarters

Eastern Prelacy, 138 E. 39th St., New York, NY 10016 Tel. (212)689-7810, Fax (212)689-7168

Western Prelacy, 4401 Russel Ave., Los Angeles, CA 90027 Tel. (323)663-8273, Fax (323)663-0438

Media Contact, Vazken Ghougassian

Email: prelacy@gis.net

Website: www.armprelacy.org/

Officers

Eastern Prelacy, Prelate, Archbishop Oshagan Choloyan

Eastern Prelacy, Chpsn., Jack Mardoian, Esq.

Western Prelacy, Prelate, Bishop Moushegh Mardirossian

Western Prelacy, Chpsn., Arsen Danielian, Esq.

DEPARTMENTS

Eastern Prelacy Offices, Executive Director, Vazken Ghougassian

AREC, Armenian Religious Educ. Council, Exec. Coord., Deacon Shant Kazanjian

ANEC, Armenian Natl. Educ. Council, Exec. Coord., Gilda Kupelian

Periodicals

Outreach

Armenian Apostolic Church, Diocese of America*

The Armenian Apostolic Church was founded at the foot of the biblical mountain of Ararat in the ancient land of Armenia, where two of Christ's Holy Apostles, Saints Thaddeus and Bartholomew, preached Christianity. In A.D. 303 the historic Mother Church of Etchmiadzin was founded by Saint Gregory the Illuminator, the first Catholicos of All Armenians. This cathedral still stands and serves as the center of the Armenian Church. A branch of this Church was established in North America in 1889. The first church building was consecrated in 1891 in Worcester, MA. The first Armenian Diocese was set up in 1898 by the then-Catholicos of All Armenians, Mgrditch Khrimian (Hairig). Armenian immigrants built the first Armenian church in the new world in Worcester, MA, under the jurisdiction of Holy Etchmiadzin.

In 1927, the churches and the parishes in California were formed into a Western Diocese and the parishes in Canada formed their own diocese in 1984. Other centers of major significance of the Armenian Apostolic Church are the Catholicate of Cilicia, now located in Lebanon, the Armenian Patriarchate of Jerusalem, and the Armenian Patriarchate of Constantinople.

Headquarters

Eastern Diocese, 630 Second Ave., New York, NY 10016-4885 Tel. (212)686-0710, Fax (212) 779-3558

Western Diocese, 3325 North Glenoaks Blvd., Burbank, CA 91504 Tel. (818) 558-7474, Fax (818)558-6333

Canadian Diocese, 615 Stuart Ave., Outremont, QC H2V 3H2 Tel. (514)276-9479, Fax (514)276-9960

Media Contact, Dir., Zohrab Information Ctr., V. Rev. Fr. Krikor Maksoudian, Eastern Diocese

Officers

Eastern Diocese

Primate, Archbishop Khajag Barsamian, Eastern Diocese Ofc.

Chancellor, Rev. Fr. Garabed Kochakian

Diocesan Council, Chpsn., Haig Dadourian, 415 Madison Ave., 7th Fl., New York, NY 10017

Western Diocese

Primate, His Em. Archbishop Vatche Hovsepian, Western Diocese Ofc.

Diocesan Council, Chpsn., Dn. Dr. Varouj Altebarmakian, 7290 North San Pedro, Fresno, CA 93011

Diocesan Council, Sec., Mr. John Yaldezian, 23221 Aetna St., Woodland Hills, CA 91367 Tel. (B) (818)346-6163

Canadian Diocese

Primate, His Em. Archbishop Hovnan Derderian

Diocesan Council Chpsn, Mr. Takvor Hopyan, 20 Pineway Blvd., Willowdale, ON M2H 1A1, Canada Tel. (B) (416)222-2639

Diocesan Council secretary., Mr. Vahe Ketli, 750 Montpellier, # 909, St. Laurens, QC H4L 5A7, Canada Tel. (R) (514)747-1347

Periodicals

The Armenian Church; The Mother Church

Assemblies of God

From a few hundred delegates at its founding convention in 1914 at Hot Springs, Ark., the Assemblies of God has become one of the largest church groups in the modern Pentecostal movement with over 38 million adherents worldwide. Throughout its existence it has emphasized the power of the Holy Spirit to change lives and the participation of all members in the work of the church.

The revival that led to the formation of the Assemblies of God and numerous other church groups early in the 20th century began during times of intense prayer and Bible study. Believers in the United States and around the world received spiritual experiences like those described in the Book of Acts. Accompanied by baptism in the Holy Spirit and its initial physical evidence of "speaking in tongues," or a language unknown to the person, their experiences were associated with the coming of the Holy Spirit at Pentecost (Acts 2), so participants were called Pentecostals.

The church also believes that the Bible is God's infallible Word to man, that salvation is available only through Jesus Christ, that divine healing is made possible through Christ's suffering and that Christ will return again for those who love him. In recent years, this Pentecostal revival has spilled over into almost every denomination in a wave of revival sometimes called the charismatic renewal.

Assemblies of God leaders credit their church's rapid and continuing growth to its acceptance of the New Testament as a model for the present-day church. Aggressive evangelism and missionary zeal at home and abroad characterize the denomination.

Assemblies of God believers observe two ordinances-water baptism by immersion and the Lord's Supper, or Holy Communion. The church is trinitarian, holding that God exists in three persons—Father, Son, and Holy Spirit.

Headquarters

1445 Boonville Ave., Springfield, MO 65802 Tel. (417)862-2781, Fax (417)862-8558

Media Contact, Dir. of Public Relations, Juleen Turnage, Fax (417)862-5554

Email: info@ag.org

Website: www.ag.org/top/

Officers

EXECUTIVE PRESBYTERY

Gen. Supt., Thomas E. Trask

Asst. Supt., Charles T. Crabtree

Gen. Sec., George O. Wood

Gen. Treas., James E. Bridges

Foreign Missions, Exec. Dir., John Bueno

Home Missions, Exec. Dir., Charles Hackett

Great Lakes, Charles Crank, 8750 Purdue Rd., Indianapolis, IN 46268 Tel. (317)872-9812

Gulf, L. Alton Garrison, P.O. Box 191670, Little Rock, AR 72219 Tel. (501)568-2194

North Central, David Argue, 1111 Old Cheney Rd., Lincoln, NE 68512 Tel. (402)421-1111

Northeast, H. Robert Rhoden, P.O. Box 1045, Fairfax, VA 22030 Tel. (703)273-7805

Northwest, Warren Bullock, Suite Y150, 9930 Evergreen Way, Everett, WA 98204 Tel. (425)423-0222

South Central,

Southeast, Dan Betzer, 4701 Summerlin Rd., Ft. Myers, FL 33919 Tel. (941)936-6277

Southwest, Richard Dresselhaus, 8404 Phyllis Pl., San Diego, CA 92123 Tel. (858)560-1870

Language Area Spanish, Jesse Miranda, 3257 Thaxton, Hacienda Heights, CA 91745 Tel. (714)668-6196

Language Area Other, Nam Soo Kim, 130-30 31st Ave., 4th Fl, Flushing, NY 11354 Tel. (718)321-7800

Ethnic Fellowship, Spencer Jones, 7724 S. Racine Ave., Chicago, IL 60620 Tel. (773)488-3443

INTERNATIONAL HEADQUARTERS

Division of the Treasury, Gen. Treas., James E. Bridges

Division of Christian Education, Natl. Dir., LeRoy Bartel
Division of Church Ministries, Executive Liaison, Charles Crabtree
Division of Foreign Missions, Exec Dir., John Bueno
Division of Home Missions, Exec. Dir., Charles Hackett
Division of Publication, Gospel Publishing House, Natl. Dir., Arlyn Pember

Periodicals

Enrichment: A Journal for Pentecostal Ministry; At Ease; Caring; High Adventure; Club Connection; Pentecostal Evangel; Woman's Touch; Heritage; On Course

Assemblies of God International Fellowship (Independent/Not affiliated)

April 9, 1906 is the date commonly accepted by Pentecostals as the twentieth-century outpouring of God's spirit in America, which began in a humble gospel mission at 312 Azusa Street in Los Angeles. This spirit movement spread across the United States and gave birth to the Independent Assemblies of God (Scandinavian). Early pioneers instrumental in guiding and shaping the fellowship of ministers and churches into a nucleus of independent churches included: Pastor B. M. Johnson, founder of Lakeview Gospel Church in 1911; Rev. A. A. Holmgren, a Baptist minister who received his baptism of the Holy Spirit in the early Chicago outpourings, was publisher of Sanningens Vittne, a voice of the Scandinavian Independent Assemblies of God, and also served as secretary of the fellowship for many years; Gunnar Wingren, missionary pioneer in Brazil; and Arthur F. Johnson, who served for many years as chairman of the Scandinavian Assemblies.

In 1935, the Scandinavian group dissolved its incorporation and united with the Independent Assemblies of God of the U.S. and Canada, which by majority vote of members formed a new corporation in 1986, Assemblies of God International Fellowship (Independent/Not Affiliated).

Headquarters

6325 Marindustry Dr. , San Diego, CA 92121 Tel. (858)677-9701, Fax (858)677-0038
Media Contact, Exec. Dir. & Ed., Rev. T. A. Lanes
Email: agifellowship.org
Website: www.agifellowship.org/

Officers

Exec. Dir., Rev. T. A. Lanes
Sec., Rev. George E. Ekeroth
Treas., M. J. Ekeroth
Canada, Sec., Harry Nunn, Sr., 15 White Crest Ct., St. Catherines, ON 62N 6Y1

Periodicals

The Fellowship Magazine

Associate Reformed Presbyterian Church (General Synod)

The origin of the Associate Reformed Presbyterian Church began in Scotland with the Covenanters of the seventeenth century and Seceder movement of the eighteenth. The Covenanters broke from the established Church of Scotland to eventually form separate "praying societies", which led to the Reformed Presbyterian Church of Scotland. The Seceders, about a hundred years later, became the Associate Church of Scotland.

The Associate Reformed Presbyterian Church stems form the 1782 merger of these two groups in America. in 1822 the "Synod of the South" was granted independent status from the national body. It continued to hold to the 1799 Constitution of the church with no changes, and probably consisted of around 2,000 members. The present Associate Reformed Presbyterian Church, (General Synod), is the ongoing denomination resulting from that action, the original "General Synod" of the denomination having become a part of the United Presbyterian Church.

The government is by a three-layered court system, the local "Session", the regional "Presbytery" and the national "General Synod", each of which is composed of both ruling and teaching elders. The Standards of the denomination include the Westminster Confession of Faith, the Catechisms, and the Forms of Government, Worship, and Discipline.

Headquarters

Associate Reformed Presbyterian Center, One Cleveland St., Greenville, SC 29601-3696 Tel. (864)232-8297, Fax (864)271-3729
Media Contact, Principal Clk., Rev. C. Ronald Beard, D.D., 3132 Grace Hill Rd., Columbia, SC 29204 Tel. (803)787-6370
The Rev. H. Neely Gaston, 741 Cleveland St. Greenville, SC 29601
Moderator, Rev. Dwight L. Pearson, D.D., P.O. Box 174, Chester, SC 29706-0174 Tel.(864) 385-2228
Email: dragondraw@aol.com
Website: www.arpsynod.org/

AGENCIES AND INSTITUTIONS (In the A.R. Presbyterian Center in Greenville)

Admn. Ser. Dir., Ed Hogan
Christian Education, Dir., Dr. David Vickery
Church Extension, Dir., Rev. James T. Corbitt, D.D.
Publications, Editor, E. Benton Johnston
Treasurer, Guy H. Smith, III
World Witness, Bd. of Foreign Missions, Exec. Sec., John E. Mariner

OTHER INSTITUTIONS

Bonclarken Assembly, Dir., James T. Brice, 500 Pine St., Flat Rock, NC 28731 Tel. (704)692-2223

Erskine College, Pres., Rev. John L. Carson, Ph.D., Due West, SC 29639 Tel. (864)379-8759
Erskine Theological Seminary, Dean, Ralph J. Gore, Jr., Ph.D., Due West, SC 26939 Tel. (864)379-8885

Periodicals

The Associate Reformed Presbyterian; The Adult Quarterly

The Association of Free Lutheran Congregations

The Association of Free Lutheran Congregations, rooted in the Scandinavian revival movements, was organized in 1962 by a Lutheran Free Church remnant which rejected merger with The American Lutheran Church. The original 42 congregations were joined by other like-minded conservative Lutherans, and there has been almost a sixfold increase in the number of congregations. Members subscribe to the Apostles', Nicene, and Athanasian creeds; Luther's Small Catechism; and the Unaltered Augsburg Confession. The Fundamental Principles and Rules for Work (1897) declare that the local congregation is the right form of the kingdom of God on earth, subject to no authority but the Word and the Spirit of God.

Distinctive emphases are (1) the infallibility and inerrancy of Holy Scriptures as the Word of God; (2) congregational polity; (3) the spiritual unity of all believers, resulting in fellowship and cooperation transcending denominational lines; (4) evangelical outreach, calling all to enter a personal relationship with Jesus Christ; (5) a wholesome Lutheran pietism that proclaims the Lordship of Jesus Christ in all areas of life and results in believers becoming the salt and light in their communities; (6) a conservative stance on current social issues.

A two-year Bible school and a theological seminary are in suburban Minneapolis. Mission support is channeled to churches in Brazil, Mexico, Canada, India, and Portugal.

Headquarters

3110 E. Medicine Lake Blvd., Minneapolis, MN 55441 Tel. (763)545-5631, Fax (763)545-0079
Media Contact, Pres., Rev. Robert L. Lee
Email: www.aflc.org
Website: webmaster@aflc.org

Officers

Pres., Rev. Robert L. Lee
Vice-Pres., Rev. Elden K. Nelson, 1633 Co. Rd. 8 SE, Kandiyohi, MN 56251
Sec., Rev. Brian Davidson, 3110 E. Medicine Lake Blvd., Minneapolis, MN 55441

Periodicals

The Lutheran Ambassador

Baptist Bible Fellowship International

Organized on May 24, 1950 in Fort Worth, Texas, the Baptist Bible Fellowship was founded by about 100 pastors and lay people who had grown disenchanted with the policies and leadership of the World Fundamental Baptist Missionary Fellowship, an outgrowth of the Baptist Bible Union formed in Kansas City in 1923 by fundamentalist leaders from the Southern Baptist, Northern Baptist, and Canadian Baptist Conventions. The BBF elected W. E. Dowell as its first president and established offices and a three-year (now four-year with a graduate school) Baptist Bible College.

The BBF statement of faith was essentially that of the Baptist Bible Union, adopted in 1923, a variation of the New Hampshire Confession of Faith. It presents an infallible Bible, belief in the substitutionary death of Christ, his physical resurrection, and his premillennial return to earth. It advocates local church autonomy and strong pastoral leadership and maintains that the fundamental basis of fellowship is a missionary outreach. The BBF vigorously stresses evangelism and the international missions office reports 901 adult missionaries working on 110 fields throughout the world.

There are BBF-related churches in every state of the United States, with special strength in the upper South, the Great Lakes region, southern states west of the Mississippi, Kansas and California. There are seven related colleges and one graduate school or seminary.

A Committee of forty-five, elected by pastors and churches within the states, sits as a representative body, meeting in three subcommittees, each chaired by one of the principal officers: an administration committee chaired by the president, a missions committee chaired by a vice-president, and an education committee chaired by a vice-president.

Headquarters

World Mission Service Center
Baptist Bible Fellowship Missions Bldg., 720 E. Kearney St., Springfield, MO 65803 Tel. (417) 862-5001, Fax (417)865-0794
Mailing Address, P.O. Box 191, Springfield, MO 65801
Media Contact, Mission Dir., Dr. Bob Baird, P.O. Box 191, Springfield, MO 65801
Email: www.bbfi.org/
Website: csbc@cherrystreet.org

Officers

Pres., Ken Gillming Sr., Cherry Street Baptist Church, 1201 S. Oak Grove Ave., Springfield, MO 65804
First Vice-Pres., Rev. Bill Monroe, Florence Baptist Temple, 2308 S. Irby Street, Florence, SC 29505-0809
Second Vice-Pres., Bill Dougherty, First Coast Baptist Church, 7587 Blanding Blvd., Jacksonville, FL 32244-5155
Sec., K. B. Murray, Millington Street Baptist Church, 1304 Millington St., Winfield, KS 67156

Treas., Wayne Guinn, Bethany Baptist Church, 1100 Dorchester Ave., Melborne, FL

Mission Dir., Dr. Bob Baird, P.O. Box 191, Springfield, MO 65801

Periodicals

The Baptist Bible Tribune; The Preacher; Global Partners

Baptist General Conference

The Baptist General Conference, rooted in the pietistic movement of Sweden during the 19th century, traces its history to Aug. 13, 1852. On that day a small group of believers at Rock Island, Illinois, under the leadership of Gustaf Palmquist, organized the first Swedish Baptist Church in America. Swedish Baptist churches flourished in the upper Midwest and Northeast, and by 1879, when the first annual meeting was held in Village Creek, Iowa, 65 churches had been organized, stretching from Maine to the Dakotas and south to Kansas and Missouri.

By 1871, John Alexis Edgren, an immigrant sea captain and pastor in Chicago, had begun the first publication and a theological seminary. The Conference grew to 324 churches and nearly 26,000 members by 1902. There were 40,000 members in 1945 and 135,000 in 1993.

Many churches began as Sunday schools. The seminary evolved into Bethel, a four-year liberal arts college with 1,800 students, and theological seminaries in Arden Hills, Minnesota, and San Diego, California. Missions and the planting of churches have been main objectives both in America and overseas. Today churches have been established in the United States, Canada, and Mexico, as well as twenty countries overseas. In 1985 the churches of Canada founded an autonomous denomination, The Baptist General Conference of Canada.

The Baptist General Conference is a member of the Baptist World Alliance, the Baptist Joint Committee on Public Affairs and the National Association of Evangelicals. It is characterized by the balancing of a conservative doctrine with an irenic and cooperative spirit. Its basic objective is to seek the fulfillment of the Great Commission and the Great Commandment.

Headquarters

2002 S. Arlington Heights Rd., Arlington Heights, IL 60005 Tel. (847)228-0200, Fax (847)228-5376

Media Contact, Pres., Dr. Robert S. Ricker

Email: gmarsh@baptist

Website: www.bgc.bethel.edu

Officers

Pres. & Chief Exec. Officer, Dr. Robert Ricker

Exec, Vice-Pres., Ray Swatkowski

Vice-Pres. Of Ministry Partner Services, Dr. Lou Petrie

Vice-Pres. of Finance, Stephen R. Schultz

Vice Pres. of Church Enrichment, Dr. Jerry Sheveland

Vice-Pres. of Church Planting, Dr. Ronald Larson

OTHER ORGANIZATIONS

Bd. of Trustees, Bethel College & Seminary, Pres., Dr. George K. Brushaber, 3900 Bethel Dr., St. Paul, MN 55112

Periodicals

The Standard

Baptist Missionary Association of America

A group of regular Baptist churches organized in associational capacity in May, 1950, in Little Rock, Ark., as the North American Baptist Association. The name changed in 1969 to Baptist Missionary Association of America. There are several state and numerous local associations of cooperating churches. In theology, these churches are evangelical, missionary, fundamental and for the most part premillennial.

Headquarters

9219 Sibly Hole Rd., Little Rock, AR Tel. (501) 455-4977, Fax (501)455-3636

Mailing Address, P.O. Box 193920, Little Rock, AR 72219-3920

Media Contact, Dir. of Baptist News Service, Kenneth W. Vanderslice, P.O. Box 97, Jacksonville, TX 75766 Tel. (903)586-2501, Fax (903)586-0378

Officers

Pres., Ronald Morgan, 208 N. Arkansas St., Springhill, LA 71075-2704

Vice-Pres., Leon J. Carmical, 85 Midway Church Rd., Sumrall, MS 39428; David T. Watkins, 1 Pineridge St., Magnolia, AR 71753

Rec. Sec., Rev. Ralph Cottrell, P.O. Box 1203, Van, TX 75790; Don J. Brown, P.O. Box 8181, Laruel, MS 39441; James Ray Raines, 5609 N. Locust, N. Little Rock, AR 72116

DEPARTMENTS

Missions, Gen. Sec., Rev. F. Donald Collins, P.O. Box 193920, Little Rock, AR 72219-3920

Publications, Ed.-in-Chief, Rev. James L. Silvey, 311 Main St., P.O. Box 7270, Texarkana, TX 75505

Christian Education, Bapt. Missionary Assoc. Theological Sem., Pres., Dr. Charley Holmes, Seminary Heights, 1530 E. Pine St., Jacksonville, TX 75766

Baptist News Service, Dir., Rev. Kenneth W. Vanderslice, P.O. Box 97, Jacksonville, TX 75766

Life Word Broadcast Ministries, Dir., Rev. George Reddin, P.O. Box 6, Conway, AR 72032

Armed Forces Chaplaincy, Exec. Dir., Bobby C. Thornton, P.O. Box 240, Flint, TX 75762

BMAA Dept. of Church Ministries, Donny Parish, P.O. Box 10356, Conway, AR 72033

Daniel Springs Encampment, James Speer, P.O. Box 310, Gary, TX 75643

Ministers Resource Services, Craig Branham, 4001 Jefferson St., Texarkana, TX 75501

OTHER ORGANIZATIONS

Baptist Missionary Assoc. Brotherhood, Pres., Bill Looney, 107 Bearskin Dr., Sherwood, AR 72120

National Women's Missionary Auxiliary, Pres., Mrs. Bill Skinner, RR1 Box 213 B, Mineola, TX 75773-9742 Tel. 903-365-2465

Periodicals

The Gleaner

Beachy Amish Mennonite Churches

The Beachy Amish Mennonite Church was established in 1927 in Somerset County, PA following a division in the Amish Mennonite Church in that area. As congregations in other locations joined the movement, they were identified by the same name. There are currently 97 churches in the United States, 9 in Canada and 34 in other countries. Membership in the United States is 7,059, according to the 1996 Mennonite Yearbook.

Beachy Churches believe in one God eternally existent in three persons (Father, Son, and Holy Spirit); that Jesus Christ is the one and only way to salvation; that the Bible is God's infallible Word to us, by which all will be judged; that heaven is the eternal abode of the redeemed in Christ; and that the wicked and unbelieving will endure hell eternally.

Evangelical mission boards sponsor missions in Central and South America, Belgium, Ireland, and in Kenya, Africa.

The Mission Interests Committee, founded in 1953 for evangelism and other Christian services, sponsors homes for handicapped youth and elderly people, mission outreaches among the North American Indians in Canada, and a mission outreach in Europe.

Headquarters

Media Contact, Paul L. Miller, 7809 S. Herren Rd. Partridge, KS 67566 Tel. (620)567-2286

Officers

Amish Mennonite Aid, Sec.-Treas., Vernon Miller, 2675 U.S. 42 NE, London, OH 43140 Tel. (614)879-8616

Mission Interests Committee, Sec.-Treas., Melvin Gingerich, 42555 900W, Topeka, IN 46571 Tel. (219)593-9090

Choice Books of Northern Virginia, Supervisor, Simon Schrock, 4614 Holly Ave., Fairfax, VA 22030 Tel. (703)830-2800

Calvary Bible School, HC 61, Box 202, Calico Rock, AR 72519 Tel. (501)297-8658; Sec.-Treas., Elmer Gingerich, HC 74, Box 282, Mountain View, AR 72560 Tel. (501)296-8764

Penn Valley Christian Retreat, Bd. Chmn., Wayne Schrock, RR 2, Box 165, McVeytown, PA 17015 Tel. (717)529-2935

Periodicals

The Calvary Messenger

Berean Fundamental Church

Founded 1932 in North Platte, Nebraska, this body emphasizes conservative Protestant doctrines.

Headquarters

Box 6103, Lincoln, NE 68506 Tel. (402)489-8056, Fax (402)489-8056

Media Contact, Pres., Pastor Doug Shada

Email: office@bereanfellowship.org

Website: www.bereanfellowship.org

Officers

Pres., Doug Shada

Vice-Pres., Richard Crocker, 419 Lafayette Blvd., Cheyenne, WY 82009 Tel. (307)635-5914

Sec., Roger Daum, 1510 O Street, Cozad, NE 69130 Tel. (308)784-3675

Treas., Virgil Wiebe, P.O. Box 6103, Lincoln, NE 68506

Exec. Advisor, Curt Lehman, Tel. (402)483-4840

The Bible Church of Christ, Inc.

The Bible Church of Christ was founded on March 1, 1961 by Bishop Roy Bryant, Sr. Since that time, the Church has grown to include congregations in the United States, Africa, and India. The church is trinitarian and accepts the Bible as the divinely inspired Word of God. Its doctrine includes miracles of healing, deliverance, and the baptism of the Holy Ghost.

Headquarters

1358 Morris Ave., Bronx, NY 10456 Tel. (718) 588-2284, Fax (718) 992-5597

Media Contact, Pres., Bishop Roy Bryant, Sr

Email: bccbookstore@earthlink.net

Website: www.thebiblechurchofchrist.org

Officers

Pres., Bishop Roy Bryant, Sr.

V. Pres., Asst. Bishop Derek G. Owens

Sec., Sissieretta Bryant, Treas., Elder Artie Burney

EXECUTIVE TRUSTEE BOARD

Chpsns., Elder Alberto L. Hope, 1358 Morris Ave., Bronx, NY 10456, Tel. (718)588-2284; Bishop Derek G. Owens, 100 W. 2nd St., Mount Vernon, NY 10550 Tel. (914)664-4602

Exec. Admn., Sr. Hermenia Benjamin

OTHER ORGANIZATIONS

Bookstore, Mgr., Evangelist Beryl C. Foster, Tel. (718)293-1928

Evangelism, Intl. Pres., Evangelist Gloria Gray

Foreign Missions, Pres., Sr. Autholene Smith

Food Pantry, Dir., Evangelist Susie Jones

Home Missions, Pres., Evangelist Mary Jackson

Minister of Music, Ray Brown

Prison Ministry Team, Pres., Evangelist Marvin Lowe

Public Relations, Deacon Abraham Jones

Publications, Dir., Deaconess Betty Hamilton

Sunday Schools, Gen. Supt., Elder A. M. Jones
Theological Institute, Pres., Dr. Roy Bryant, Sr.; Dean, Elder A. M. Jones
Vessels Unto Honor Deliverance Ministries, Pres., Evangelist Antoinette Cannaday
Women's Committee, Natl. Chpsn., Sissieretta Bryant
Youth, Pres100 W. 2nd St., Mount Vernon, NY 10550; Bronx, Elder Anita Robinson, 1358 Morris Ave., Bronx, NY 10456, Tel. (718)588-2284; Annex, Elder Reginald Gullette, 1069 Morris Ave., Bronx, NY 10456 Tel. (718)992-4653; Bishop Derek Owens, Pastor, Minister Monica Hope, Assistant, 1140 Congress St., Schenetady, NY 12303; India, Dr. B. Veeraswamy, 46-7-34, Danavaya Peta, Rajahmunry, India, 533103; Haiti, Antoine Polycarpe, P.O. Box 197, Port-au-Prince, Haiti; St. Croix, Elder Floyd Thomas, 1-J Diamond Ruby, P.O. Box 5183, Sunny Isles, Christiansted, St. Croix Tel. (809)778-1002

Periodicals

The Voice; The Gospel Light; The Challenge

Bible Fellowship Church

The Bible Fellowship Church grew out of divisions in the Mennonite community in Pennsylvania in the 1850s. Traditional church leadership resisted the freedom of expression and prayer meetings initiated by several preachers and church leaders. These evangelical Mennonites formed the Evangelical Mennonite Society. Over the next two decades various like minded groups in Canada, Ohio, and Pennsylvania joined the Society.

In 1959 the Conference became the Bible Fellowship Church and new articles of faith were ratified. They now hold a unique combination of Reformed doctrines with insistence on "Believer Baptism" and Premillennialism.

Headquarters

Bible Fellowship Church, 3000 Fellowship Dr., Whitehall, PA 18052
Media Contact, David J. Watkins, Bible Fellowship Church, 2270 Little Rd., Perkiomenville, PA 18704 Tel. (610)754-7463
Email: bfc@bfc.org
Website: www.bfc.org/

Officers

Chmn., Randall A. Grossman
Vice-Chmn., William G. Schlonecker
Sec., David A. Thomann
Asst. Sec., Robert W. Smock
BOARDS AND COMMITTEES
Bd. of Dir., Bible Fellowship Church
Bd. of Christian Education
Board of Extension
Bible Fellowship Church Homes, Inc.
Board of Pensions
Board of Pinebrook Bible Conference
Board of Missions
Board of Publication and Printing
Bd. of Victory Valley Camp
Board of Higher Education

Periodicals

Fellowship News

Bible Holiness Church

This church came into being about 1890 as the result of definite preaching on the doctrine of holiness in some Methodist churches in southeastern Kansas. It became known as The Southeast Kansas Fire Baptized Holiness Association. The name was changed in 1945 to The Fire Baptized Holiness Church and in 1995 to Bible Holiness Church. It is entirely Wesleyan in doctrine, episcopal in church organization, and intensive in evangelistic zeal.

Headquarters

600 College Ave., Independence, KS 67301 Tel. (316)331-3049
Media Contact, Gen. Supt., Leroy Newport

Officers

Gen. Supt., Leroy Newport
Gen. Sec., Wayne Knipmeyer, Box 457, South Pekin, IL 61564
Gen. Treas., Robert Davolt, 1323 Laura, Wichita, KS 67211

Periodicals

The Flaming Sword; John Three Sixteen

Bible Way Church of Our Lord Jesus Christ World Wide, Inc.

This body was organized in 1957 in the Pentecostal tradition for the purpose of accelerating evangelistic and foreign missionary commitment and to effect a greater degree of collective leadership than leaders found in the body in which they had previously participated.

The doctrine is the same as that of the Church of Our Lord Jesus Christ of the Apostolic Faith, Inc., of which some of the churches and clergy were formerly members.

This organization has churches and missions in Africa, England, Guyana, Trinidad, and Jamaica, and churches in 25 states in America. The Bible Way Church is involved in humanitarian as well as evangelical outreach with concerns for urban housing, education, and economic development.

Headquarters

4949 Two-Notch Rd., Columbia, SC 29204 Tel. (800)432-5612, Fax (803)691-0583
Media Contact, Chief Apostle, Presiding Bishop Huie Rogers
Email: mr.ed5strings@worldnet.att.net
Website: www.biblewaychurch.org/

Officers

Presiding Bishop, Bishop Huie Rogers, 4949 Two Notch Rd., Columbia, SC 29204 Tel. (800)432-5612, Fax (803)691-0583

Gen. Sec., Bishop Edward Williams, 5118 Clarendon Rd., Brooklyn, NY 11226 Tel. (718)451-1238

Brethren in Christ Church

The Brethren in Christ Church was founded in Lancaster County, PA in about the year 1778 and was an outgrowth of the religious awakening which occurred in that area during the latter part of the eighteenth century. This group became known as "River Brethren" because of their original location near the Susquehanna River. The name "Brethren in Christ" was officially adopted in 1863. In theology they have accents of the Pietist, Anabaptist, Wesleyan, and Evangelical movements.

Headquarters

General Church Office, P.O. Box A, Grantham, PA 17027 Tel. (717)697-2634, Fax (717)697-7714

Media Contact, Mod., Dr. Warren L. Hoffman, Tel. (717)697-2634, Fax (717)697-7714

Email: RRoss@BIC-church.org

Website: www.bic-church.org/index.htm

Officers

Mod., Dr. Warren L. Hoffman, P.O. Box A, Grantham, PA 17027 Tel. (717)697-2634, Fax (717)697-7714

Gen. Sec., Dr. Kenneth O. Hoke

Tresurer, Elizabeth Brown

OTHER ORGANIZATIONS

General Conference Board, Chpsn., Mark Garis, 504 Swartley Rd., Hatfield, PA 19440

Bd. for Media Ministries, Chpsn., Harold Chubb, 540 Douglas Rd., Hummelstown, PA 17036-9453

Bd. for World Missions, Chpsn., Marti Byers, 116 Slover Rd., Mechanicsburg, PA 17055; Exec. Dir., Rev. John Brubaker, P.O. Box 390, Grantham, PA 17027-0390

Brethren in Christ Foundation CEO, Julie Stout, CPA

Pension Fund Trustees, Chpsn., Eric Mann

Bd. for Stewardship Services, Chpsn., Donald J. Winters, 2404 Willow Glen Dr., Lancaster, PA 17602; Exec. Dir., Rev. Phil Keefer, Box A, Grantham, PA 17027

Publishing House, Exec. Dir., Roger Williams, Evangel Press, P.O. Box 189, Nappanee, IN 46550

Periodicals

The Visitor; Yes!

Brethren Church (Ashland, Ohio)

The Brethren Church (Ashland, Ohio) was organized by progressive-minded German Baptist Brethren in 1883. They reaffirmed the teaching of the original founder of the Brethren movement, Alexander Mack, and returned to limited congregational government.

Headquarters

524 College Ave., Ashland, OH 44805 Tel. (419) 289-1708, Fax (419)281-0450

Media Contact, Editor of Publications, Richard C. Winfield

Email: brethren@brethrenchurch.org

Website: www.brethrenchurch.org

Officers

Executive Dir., Dr. Emanuel W. Sandberg

Dir. of Missionary Ministries, Rev. Reilly Smith

Dir. of Congregational Ministries, Dr. Dan Lawson

Dir. of Pastoral Ministries, Rev. David Cooksey

Dir. of Administrative Services, Mr. Stanley Gentle

Director of Publications, Rev. Richard C. Winfield

Periodicals

The Brethren Evangelist

The Catholic Church

The largest single body of Christians in the United States, The Catholic Church is under the spiritual leadership of His Holiness the Pope. Its establishment in America dates back to the priests who accompanied Columbus on his second voyage to the New World. A settlement, later discontinued, was made in 1565 at St. Augustine, Florida. The continuous history of this Church in the Colonies began at St. Mary's in Maryland, in 1634.

Headquarters

INTERNATIONAL ORGANIZATION

His Holiness the Pope, Bishop of Rome, Vicar of Jesus Christ, Supreme Pontiff of the Catholic Church.

Pope John Paul II, Karol Wojtyla (born May 18, 1920; installed Oct. 22, 1978)

APOSTOLIC NUNCIO TO THE UNITED STATES

Archbishop Gabriel Montalvo, 3339 Massachusetts Ave., N.W., Washington, DC 20008 Tel. (202)333-7121, Fax (202)337-4036

U.S. ORGANIZATION

United States Conference of Catholic Bishops, 3211 Fourth St., Washington, DC 20017-1194. Tel. (202)541-3000

The United States Conference of Catholic Bishops (USCCB) is an assembly of the hierarchy of the United States and the U.S. Virgin Islands who jointly exercise certain pastoral functions on behalf of the Christian faithful of the United States. The purpose of the Conference is to promote the greater good which the Church offers humankind, especially through forms and programs of the apostolate fittingly adapted to the circumstances of time and place. This purpose is drawn from the universal law of the Church and applies to the episcopal conferences which are established all over the world for the same purpose.

The bishops themselves constitute the membership of the Conference and are served by a staff of over 350 people, priests, and religious located at the Conference headquarters in Washington, DC. There is also a small Office of Film and Broadcasting in New York City and a branch office of Migration and Refugee Services in Miami.

The Conference is organized as a corporation in the District of Columbia. Its purposes under civil law are, "To unify, coordiante, encourage, promote and carry on Catholic activities in the United States; to organize and conduct religious, charitable and social welfare work at home and abroad; to aid in education; to care for immigrants; and generally to enter into and pormote by education, publication and direction the objects of its being."

On July 1, 2001 the NCCB and the USCC were combined to form the United states Conference of Catholic Bishops (USCCB). The USCCB continues all of the work formerly done by the NCCB and the USCC with the same staff. The bishops themselves form apporximately 50 committees, each with its own particular responsibility.

Website: www.usccb.org

Officers

UNITED STATES CONFERENCE OF CATHOLIC BISHOPS (USCCB)

GENERAL SECRETARIAT

General Sec., Msgr. WillIam P. Fay

Assoc. Gen. Sec., Mr. Bruce E. Egnew, Msgr. David Malloy, Sr. Lourdes Sheehan, RSM

Officers

Pres., Bishop Joseph A. Fiorenza

Vice-Pres., Bishop Wilton D. Gregory

Treas., Bishop Henry J. Mansell

Sec., Archbishop Harry J. Flynn

USCCB STANDING COMMITTEES

Administrative Committee, Chmn., Bishop Joseph A. Fiorenza

Executive Committee, Chmn., Bishop Joseph A. Fiorenza

Committee on Budget and Finance, Chmn., Bishop Henry J. Mansell

Committee on Personnel, Bishop Wilton D. Gregory

Committee on Priorities and Plans, Chmn., Bishop Joseph A. Fiorenza

African American Catholics, Chmn., Bishop J. Terry Steib, SVD

American Bishops' Overseas Appeal, Chmn., Bishop Joseph A. Fiorenza

American College Louvain, Chmn., Bishop Edward K. Braxton

Boundaries of Dioceses and Provinces, Chmn., Bishop Joseph A. Fiorenza

Canonical Affairs, Chmn., Bishop A. James Quinn

Church in Latin America, Chmn., Bishop Edmond Carmody

Consecrated Life, Chmn., Bishop Sean P. O'Malley, OFM

Diaconate, Chmn., Bishop Gerald F. Kicanas

Doctrine, Chmn., Bishop Donald W. Troutman

Ecumenical and Interreligious Affairs, Chmn., Bishop Tod D. Brown

Subcommittee on Interreligious Dialogue, Chmn., Bishop Joseph J. Gerry, OSB

Evangelization, Chmn., Bishop Michael W. Warfel

Hispanic Affairs, Chmn., Bishop Arthur N. Tafoya

Home Missions, Chmn., Bishop Paul A. Zipfel

Laity, Chmn., Bishop John J. McRaith

Subcommittee on Lay Ministry, Chmn., Bishop Joseph P. Delaney

Subcommittee on Youth and Young Adults, Chmn., Bishop Kevin M. Britt

Liturgy, Chmn., Archbishop Oscar H. Lipscomb

Marriage and Family Life, Chmn., Bishop Anthony J. O'Connell

Migration, Chmn., Bishop Nicholas A. DiMarzio

North American College Rome, Chmn., Archbishop Daniel A. Cronin

Pastoral Practices, Chmn., Bishop Stephen E. Blaire

Priestly Formation, Chmn., Bishop John R. Graydos

Priestly Life and Ministry, Chmn., Bishop Richard C. Hanifen

Pro-Life Activities, Chmn., William Cardinal Keeler

Relationship Between Eastern and Latin Catholic Churches, Chmn., Bishop Basil H. Losten

Science and Human Values, Chmn., Bishop John S. Cummins

Selection of Bishops, Chmn., Bishop Joseph A. Fiorenza

Vocations, Chmn., Archbishop Roger L. Schwietz, OMI

Woman in Society and in the Church, Chmn., Archbishop John G. Vlazny

World Mission, Chmn., Bishop Curtis J. Guillory, SVD

USCCB AD HOC COMMITTEES

Agricultural Issues, Chmn., Bishop William S. Skylstad

Aid to the Church in Central and Eastern Europe, Chmn., Adam Cardinal Maida

Bishops' Life and Ministry, Chmn., Bishop William S. Skylstad

Catholic Charismatic Renewal, Chmn., Bishop Sam G. Jacobs

Catholic Health Care Issues and the Church, Chmn., Bishop Joseph L. Charron, CPPS

Diocesan Audits, Chmn., Bishop Joseph P. Delaney

Economic Concerns of the Holy See, Chmn., Archbishop James P. Keleher

Mandatum, Chmn., Archbishop Daniel E. Pilarczyk

Native American Catholics, Chmn., Bishop Donald E. Pelotte, SSS
Nomination of Conference Officers, Chmn., Archbishop Jerome G. Hanos, OSB
Oversee the Use of the Catechism, Chmn., Archbishop Daniel M. Buechlein, OSB
Publishing and Promotion Services, Chmn., Bishop James A. Griffin
Review of Scripture Translations, Chmn., Bishop Richard J. Sklba
Sexual Abuse, Chmn., Bishop John B. McCormick
Shrines, Chmn., Archbishop James P. Keleher
Stewardship, Chmn., Bishop Sylvester D. Ryan

USCCB EXECUTIVE COMMITTEES

Administrative Board, Chmn., Bishop Joseph A. Fiorenza
Executive Committee, Chmn., Bishop Joseph A. Fiorenza
Committee on Budget and Finance, Chmn. Bishop Henry J. Mansell
Committee on Personnel, Chmn., Bishop Wilton D. Gregory
Committee on Priorities and Plans, Chmn., Bishop Joseph A. Fiorenza

USCCB DEPARTMENTAL COMMITTEES

Catholic Campaign for Human Development, Chmn., Bishop John J. Leibrecht
Communications, Chmn., Bishop Joseph A. Galante
Domestic Policy, Chmn., Roger Cardinal Mahony
International Policy, Chmn., Bernard Cardinal Law
Education, Chmn., Bishop Donald W. Wuerl
Advisory Committee on Public Policy and Catholic Schools, Chmn., Bishop Donald W. Wuerl
Bishops and Catholic College and University Presidents, Chmn., Bishop Donald W. Wuerl
Catechesis, Chmn., Bishop Donald W. Wuerl
Sapientia Christiana, Chmn., Bishop John P. Boles
For information on related organizations and individual dioceses, consult the Official Catholic Directory (published annually by P.J. Kenedy and Sons) and the USCCB website (www.usccb.org).

Periodicals

Catholic News Service, L'Osservatore Romano, The Living Light, Origins, Lay Ministry Update, Bishops Committee on the Liturgy Newsletter, life Insight, SEIA Newsletter on the Eastern Churches and Ecumenism, Law Briefs, Catholic Trends

Christ Catholic Church

The church is a catholic communion established in 1968 to minister to the growing number of people who seek an experiential relationship with God and who desire to make a total commitment of their lives to God. The church is catholic in faith and tradition. Participating cathedrals, churches, and missions are located in several states.

Headquarters

405 Kentling Rd., Highlandville, MO 65669 Tel. (417)443-3951
Media Contact, Archbishop, Most Rev. Karl Pruter
Email: ergoegosum@aol.com
Website: christcatholicchurch.freeyellow.com/

Officers

Archbishop, Most Rev. Karl Pruter, P.O. Box 98, Highlandville, MO 65669 Tel. (417)443-3951

Periodicals

St. Willibrord Journal

Christ Community Church (Evangelical-Protestant)

This church was founded by the Rev. John Alexander Dowie on Feb. 22, 1896 at Chicago, IL. In 1901 the church founded the city of Zion, IL, and moved their headquarters there. Theologically, the church is rooted in evangelical orthodoxy. The Scriptures are accepted as the rule of faith and practice. Other doctrines call for belief in the necessity of repentance for sin and personal trust in Christ for salvation.

The Christ Community Church is a denominational member of The National Association of Evangelicals. It has work in six other nations in addition to the United States. Branch ministries are found in Tonalea, Arizona; Lindenhurst, Illinois; and Toronto, Canada.

Headquarters

2500 Dowie Memorial Dr., Zion, IL 60099 Tel. (847)746-1411, Fax (847)746-1452

Officers

Senior Pastor, Ken Langley

Christadelphians

The Christadelphians are a body of people who believe the Bible to be the divinely inspired word of God, written by "Holy men who spoke as they were moved by the Holy Spirit" (2 Peter Ch. 1 vs. 21). They believe that the Old Testament presents God's plan to establish His Kingdom on earth in accord with the promises He made to Abraham and David; and that the New Testament declares how that plan works out in Jesus Christ, who died a sacrificial death to redeem sinners. They believe in the personal return of Jesus Christ as King, to establish "all that God spoke by the mouth of his holy prophets from of old" (Acts Ch.3 vs.21). They believe that at Christ's return many of the dead will be raised by the power of God to be judged. Those whom God deems worthy will be welcomed into eternal life in the Kingdom on earth. Christadelphians believe in the mortality of man; in spiritual rebirth requiring belief and immersion in the name of Jesus; and in a godly walk in this life. They have no ordained clergy, and are organized in a loose confederation of autonomous congregations (ecclesias) in approximately 100 countries. They are conscientiously apposed to participation in war. They endeavor to be enthusiastic in work, loyal in marriage, generous in giving, dedicated in preaching, and cheerful in living.

The denomination was organized in 1844 by a medical doctor, John Thomas, who came to the United States from England in 1832, having survived a near shipwreck in a violent storm. This experience affected him profoundly, and he vowed to devote his life to a search for the truth of God and a future hope from the Bible.

Headquarters

Media Contact, Trustee, Norman D. Zilmer, Christadelphian Action Society, 1000 Mohawk Dr., Elgin, IL 60120-3148 Tel. (847)741-5253, Fax (847)888-3334

Email: Nzilmer@aol.com

Website: www.christadelphia.org

Leaders

(Co-Ministers) Norman Fadelle, 815 Chippewa Dr., Elgin, IL 60120; Norman D. Zilmer, 1000 Mohawk Dr., Elgin, IL 60120

Periodicals

Christadelphian Tidings; Christadelphian Advocate

Christian Brethren (also known as Plymouth Brethren)

The Christian Brethren began in the 1820s as an orthodox and evangelical movement in the British Isles and is now worldwide. The name Plymouth Brethren was given by others because the group in Plymouth, England, was a large and influential congregation. In recent years the term Christian Brethren has replaced Plymouth Brethren for the "open" branch of the movement in Canada and British Commonwealth countries and to some extent in the United States.

The unwillingness to establish a denominational structure makes the autonomy of local congregations an important feature of the movement. Other features are weekly observance of the Lord's Supper and adherence to the doctrinal position of conservative, evangelical Christianity.

In the 1840s the movement divided. The "exclusive" branch, led by John Nelson Darby, stressed the interdependency of congregations. Since disciplinary decisions were held to be binding on all assemblies, exclusives had subdivided into seven or eight main groups by the end of the century. Since 1925 a trend toward reunification has reduced that number to three or four.

The "open" branch of the movement was led by George Müller of orphanage fame. It stressed evangelism and foreign missions. Now the larger of the two branches, it has never experienced world-wide division.

CORRESPONDENT

James A. Stahr, 327 W. Prairie Ave., Wheaton, Il 60187-3408 Tel. (630)665-3757

RELATED ORGANIZATIONS

Interest Ministries, 2060 Stonington Ave., Suite 101, Hoffman Estates, IL 60195

Christian Missions in Many Lands, P.O. Box 13, Spring Lake, NJ 07762-0013

Stewards Foundation, 14285 Midway Rd., Ste. 330, Addison, TX 75001-3622

International Teams, 411 W. River Rd., Elgin, IL 60123

Emmaus Bible College, 2570 Asbury Rd., Dubuque, IA 52001-3044

Stewards Ministries, 18-3 E. Dundee Rd., Ste. 100, Barrington, IL 60010

Christian Church (Disciples of Christ) in the United States and Canada*

Born on the American frontier in the early 1800s as a movement to unify Christians, this body drew its major inspiration from Thomas and Alexander Campbell in western Pennsylvania and Barton W. Stone in Kentucky. Developing separately, the "Disciples, under Alexander Campbell, and the "Christians," led by Stone, united in 1832 in Lexington, KY.

The Christian Church (Disciples of Christ) is marked by informality, openness, individualism, and diversity. The Disciples claim no official doctrine or dogma. Membership is granted after a simple statement of belief in Jesus Christ and baptism by immersion— although most congregations accept transfers baptized by other forms in other denominations. The Lord's Supper—generally called Communion—is open to Christians of all persuasions. The practice is weekly Communion, although no church law insists upon it.

Thoroughly ecumenical, the Disciples helped organize the National and World Councils of Churches. The church is a member of the Consultation on Church Union. The Disciples and the United Church of Christ have declared themselves to be in "full communion" through the General Assembly and General Synod of the two churches. Official theological conversations have been going on since 1967 directly with the Roman Catholic Church, and since 1987 with the Russian Orthodox Church.

Disciples have vigorously supported world and national programs of education, agricultural assistance, urban reconciliation, care of persons with retardation, family planning and aid to victims of war and calamity. Operating ecumenically, Disciples' personnel or funds work in more than 100 countries outside North America.

Three manifestations or expressions of the church (general, regional, and congregational) operate as equals, with strong but voluntary covenantal ties to one another. Entities in each manifestation manage their own finances, own their own property, and conduct their own programs. A General Assembly meets every two years and has voting representation from each congregation.

Headquarters

Disciples Center, 130 E. Washington St., P.O. Box 1986, Indianapolis, IN 46206-1986 Tel. (317)635-3100, Fax (317)635-3700

Media Contact, Dir. of News & Information, Curtis M. Miller

Email: cmiller@oc.disciples.org

Website: www.disciples.org

Officers

Gen. Minister & Pres., Richard L. Hamm, dhamm@ogmp.disciples.org

Mod., Alvin O. Jackson, National City Christian Church, Five Thomas Circle, Washington, DC 20005-4153 Tel. (202)232-0323, Fax (202) 797-0111, ajackson@nationalcitycc.org

1st Vice-Mod., Patricia Payuyo, 1098 W Kensington Rd, Los Angeles, CA 90026-4379, Tel. (213)250-4817, cisa@tsenet.com

2nd Vice-Mod., Ted Waggoner, 3406 Gregory Farm Rd, Rochester, IN 46975 Tel. (219)223-4292, Fax (219)223-4701, waggfam@rtcol.com

General Officers

Gen. Minister & Pres., Richard L. Hamm, dhamm@ogmp.disciples.org

Assoc. Gen. Minister & Vice Pres., William H. Edwards, bedwards@ogmp.disciples.org

Assoc. Gen. Min. for Admn., Donald B. Manworren, dmanworren@ogmp.disciples.org

Assoc. Gen Min. & Admin. Sec. Of the National Convention, John R. Foulkes, Sr., jfoulkes@ogmp.disciples.org

ADMINISTRATIVE UNITS

Bd. of Church Extension, dba Church Extension, Pres., James L. Powell, 130 E. Washington St., P.O. Box 7030, Indianapolis, IN 46207-7030 Tel. (317)635-6500, Fax (317)635-6534, bce@ churchextension.org

Christian Bd. of Publ. (Chalice Press), Pres., Cyrus N. White, 1316 Convention Plaza Dr., P.O. Box 179, St. Louis, MO 63166-0179 Tel. (314)231-8500 or (800)668-8016, Fax (314) 231-8524, customerservice@cbp21.com

Christian Church Foundation, Inc., Pres., James P. Johnson, Tel. (317)635-3100 or 800-668-8016, Fax (317)635-1991, jcullumb@ccf.disciples.org

Church Finance Council, Inc., Pres., Lois Artis, drussell@cfc.disciples.org

Council on Christian Unity, Inc., Pres., Robert K. Welsh, Tel. (317)713-2586, Fax (317)713-2588, robert.welsh@ecunet.org

Disciples of Christ Historical Society, Pres., Peter M. Morgan, 1101 19th Ave. S., Nashville, TN 37212-2196 Tel. (615)327-1444, Fax (615)327-1445, dishistsoc@aol.com

Division of Higher Education, Pres., Dennis L. Landon, 11720 Borman Dr., Ste. 104, St. Louis, MO 63146-4187 Tel. (314)991-3000, Fax (314)991-2957, dhe@dhedisciples.org

Division of Homeland Ministries, Interim Pres., Raymond E. Brown, Tel. (317)635-3100 or (888)346-2631, Fax (317)635-4426, homelandministries@dhm.disciples.org

Division of Overseas Ministries, Pres., Patricia Tucker Spier, Fax (317)635-4323, dom@disciples.org

National Benevolent Association, Pres., Cindy Dougherty, 11780 Borman Dr., St. Louis, MO 63146-4157 Tel. (314)993-9000, Fax (314) 993-9018, nba@nbacares.org

Pension Fund, Pres., Arthur A. Hanna, 130 E. Washington St., Indianapolis, IN 46204-3645 Tel. (317)634-4504, Fax (317)634-4071, pfcc1@pension.disciples.org

REGIONAL UNITS OF THE CHURCH

Alabama-Northwest Florida, Regional Minister, John P. Mobley, 1336 Montgomery Hwy., Birmingham, AL 35216-2799 Tel. (205)823-5647, Fax (205)823-5673, alnwfl@aol.com

Arizona, Regional Minister, Dennis L. Williams, 4423 N. 24th St., Ste 700, Phoenix, AZ 85016-5544 Tel. (602)468-3815, Fax (602)468-3816, azregion@worldnet.att.net

Arkansas, Regional Min., Pres., Barbara E. Jones, 9302 Geyer Springs Rd., P.O. Box 191057, Little Rock, AR 72219-1057 Tel. (501)562-6053, Fax (501)562-7089, ccark@swbell.net

California, Northern-Nevada, Regional Min., Pres., Charles R. Blaisdell, 9260 Alcosta Blvd., C-18, San Ramon, CA 94583-4143 Tel. (925)556-9900, Fax (925)556-9904, info@ ccncn.org

Canada, Exec. Regional Minister, F. Thomas Rutherford, P.O. Box 23030, 417 Wellington St., St. Thomas, ON N5R 6A3, Tel. (519)633-9083, Fax (519)637-6407, ccic@netrover.com

Capital Area, Regional Minister, Wm. Chris Hobgood, 11501 Georgia Ave., Ste. 400, Wheaton, MD 20902-1955 Tel. (301)942-8266, Fax (301)942-8366, chris.hobgood@ecunet.org

Central Rocky Mountain Region, Exec. Regional Minister, Ronald L. Parker, 2950 Tennyson #300, P.O. Box 12186, Denver, CO 80212-0186 Tel. (303)561-1790, Fax (303)561-1795, info@crmrdoc.org

Florida, Regional Minister, William C. Morrison, Jr., 924 N. Magnolia Ave., Ste. 200, Orlando, FL 32803-3845 Tel. (407)843-4652, Fax (407) 843-0272, regionaloffice@floridadisciples.org

Georgia, Regional Minister, Tom W. Neal, 2370 Vineville Ave., Macon, GA 31204-3163 Tel. (478)743-8649 or (800)755-0485, Fax (478) 741-1508, ccinga@bellsouth.net

Idaho, South, Regional Minister, Larry Crist, 6465 Sunrise Ave., Nampa, ID 83686-9461 Tel. (208)468-8976, Fax (208)468-8973, ccsi@micron.net

Illinois and Wisconsin, Regional Minister, Pres., Herbert L. Knudsen, 1011 N. Main St.,

Bloomington, IL 61701-1753 Tel. (309)828-6293, Fax (309)829-4612, cciwrmp@aol.com

Indiana, Regional Minister, Richard L. Spleth, 1100 W. 42nd St., Indianapolis, IN 46208-3375 Tel. (317)926-6051, Fax (317)931-2034, cci@ccindiana.org

Kansas, Regional Minister, Pres., Patsie Sweeden, 2914 S.W. MacVicar Ave., Topeka, KS 66611-1787 Tel. (785)266-2914, Fax (785)266-0174, ccks@ksmessenger.org

Kansas City, Greater, Regional Min., Pres., Paul J. Diehl, Jr., 5700 Broadmoor, Ste. 702, Mission, KS 66202-2405 Tel. (913)432-1414, Fax (913)432-3598, ksdisciple@aol.com

Kentucky, Gen. Minister, A. Guy Waldrop, 1125 Red Mile Rd., Lexington, KY 40504-2660 Tel. (859)233-1391, Fax 859-233-2079, cck@ccinky.net

Louisiana, Transitional Regional Minister, Zena S. McAdams, 3524 Holloway Prairie Rd., Pineville, LA 71360-5816 Tel. (318)443-0304, Fax (318)449-1367, mac4722@aol.com

Michigan, Regional Minister, Morris Finch, Jr., 2820 Covington Ct., Lansing, MI 48912-4830 Tel. (517)372-3220, Fax (517)372-2705, ccmr@michigandisciples.org

Mid-America Region, Int. Regional Minister, David L. Webb, Hwy. 54 W., P.O. Box 104298, Jefferson City, MO 65110-4298 Tel. (573)636-8149, Fax (573)636-2889, david-ccma@socket.net

Mississippi, Regional Minister, William E. McKnight, 1619 N. West St., P.O. Box 4832, Jackson, MS 39296-4832 Tel. (601)352-6774, Fax (601)355-1221, ccdcmsbill@aol.com

Montana, Regional Minister, Karen Frank-Plumlee, 1019 Central Ave., Great Falls, MT 59401-3784 Tel. (406)452-7404, Fax (406) 452-7404, ccm@imt.net

Nebraska, Regional Ministers, Kenneth W. Moore, 1268 S. 20th St., Lincoln, NE 68502-1612 Tel. (402)476-0359 or (800)580-8851, Fax (402)476-0350, ccnebraska@earthlink.net

North Carolina, Regional Minister, Rexford L. Horne, 509 N.E. Lee St., P.O. Box 1568, Wilson, NC 27894-1568 Tel. (252)291-4047, Fax (252)291-3338, ccnc@simflex.com

Northeastern Region, Co-Assoc. Regional Ministers, Lonnie F. Oates, & Allyson D. Platt, 475 Riverside Dr., Rm. 1950, New York, NY 10115-1999 Tel. (212)870-2734, Fax (212) 2735, n.christian.church@worldnet.att.net

Northwest Region, Regional Minister, Pres., Jack Sullivan, Jr., 6558-35th Ave. SW, Seattle, WA 98126-2899 Tel. (206)938-1008, Fax (206)933-1163, nwrcc@disciplesnw.org

Ohio, Regional Pastor, Pres., Howard M. Ratcliff, 38007 Butternut Ridge Rd., P.O. Box 299, Elyria, OH 44036-0299 Tel. (440)458-5112, Fax (440)458-5114, ccio@christian churchinohio.org

Oklahoma, Regional Pastor, Thomas R. Jewell, 301 N.W. 36th St., Oklahoma City, OK 73118-8661 Tel. (405)528-3577, Fax (405)528-3584, okdiscip@telepath.com

Oregon, Co-Regional Ministers, Douglas Wirt & Cathy Myers-Wirt, 0245 S.W. Bancroft St., Ste. F, Portland, OR 97201-4267 Tel. (503)226-7648, Fax (503)226-0598, mail@oregondisciples.org

Pacific Southwest Region, Regional Minister, Pres., Don W. Shelton, 2401 N. Lake Ave., Altadena, CA 91001-2418 Tel. (626)296-0385, Fax (626)296-1280, pswr@jps.net

Pennsylvania, Regional Minister, W. Darwin Collins, 670 Rodi Rd., Pittsburgh, PA 15235-4524 Tel. (412)731-7000, Fax (412)731-4515, wdar@padisciples.org

South Carolina, Regional Minister, Arnold Nelson, Jr., 5103 Rhett Ave., P.O. Box 5135, North Charleston, SC 29405-1001 Tel. (843)744-5786, Fax (843)744-5787, ccsc@lowcountry.com

Southwest Region, Regional Minister, Ralph E. Glenn, 3209 S. University Dr., Fort Worth, TX 76109-2239 Tel. (817)926-4687, Fax (817) 926-5121, ccsw@ccsw.org

Tennessee, Regional Minister, Pres., Glen J. Stewart, 50 Vantage Way, Ste. 251, Nashville, TN 37228-1523 Tel. (615)251-3400, Fax (615)251-3415, ccdtn@yahoo.com

Upper Midwest Region, Regional Minister, Pres., Richard L. Guentert, 3300 University Ave., P.O. Box 41217, Des Moines, IA 50311-0504 Tel. (515)255-3168, Fax (515)255-2625, rg@uppermidwestcc.org

Virginia, Regional Minister, George Lee Parker, 518 Brevard St., Lynchburg, VA 24501 Tel. (804)846-3400, Fax (804)528-4919, ccinva@aol.com

West Virginia, Regional Minister, William B. Allen, 1400 Washington Ave., P.O. Box 264, Parkersburg, WV 26102-0264 Tel. (304)428-1681, Fax (304)428-1684, wvdisciples@juno.com

Periodicals

The Disciple; Mid-Stream, An Ecumenical Journal

Christian Church of North America, General Council

Originally known as the Italian Christian Church, its first General Council was held in 1927 at Niagara Falls, NY. This body was incorporated in 1948 at Pittsburgh, PA, and is described as Pentecostal but does not engage in the "the excesses tolerated or practiced among some churches using the same name."

The movement recognizes two ordinances—baptism and the Lord's Supper. Its moral code is conservative and its teaching is orthodox. Members are exhorted to pursue a life of personal holiness, setting an example to others. A conservative position is held in regard to marriage and divorce. The governmental form is, by and large, congregational. District and National officiaries, however, are referred to as Presbyteries led by Overseers.

The group functions in cooperative fellowship with the Italian Pentecostal Church of Canada and the Evangelical Christian Churches-Assemblies of God in Italy. It is an affiliate member of the Pentecostal Fellowship of North America and of the National Association of Evangelicals.

Headquarters

1294 Rutledge Rd., Transfer, PA 16154-2299 Tel. (724)962-3501, Fax (724)962-1766

Exec. Sec., Terri Metcalfe; Admin. Asst., Chris Marini

Email: cnna@nauticom.net

Website: www.ccna.org/

Officers

Executive Bd., Gen. Overseer, Rev. John DelTurco, P.O. Box 1198, Hermitage, PA 16148

Exec. Vice-Pres., Rev. Charles Gay, 26 Delafield Dr., Albany, NY 12205

Asst. Gen. Overseers, Rev. Joseph Shipley 44-19 Francis Lewis Blvd., Bayside, NY 11361; Rev. Vincent Prestigiacomo, 21 Tyler Hill Rd., Jaffrey, NH 03452; Rev. Charles Gay, 26 Delafield Dr., Albany, NY 12205; Rev. Michael Trotta, 224 W. Winter Ave., New Castle, PA 16101; Rev. Douglas Bedgood, Sr., 442 Trinidad Ln., Teakwood Village, Largo, FL 33770

DEPARTMENTS

Benevolence, Rev. John Del Turco, P.O. Box 1198, Hermitage, PA 16148

Home Missions, Rev. John Ferguson

Faith, Order & Credentials, Rev. Rev. Charles Gay, 26 Delafield Dr., Albany, NY 12205

Missions, Rev. David Verzilli, 4875 Shadow Oak, Youngstown, OH 44515

Publications Relations, Rev. John Tedesco, 1188 Heron Rd., Cherry Hill, NJ 08003

Lay Ministries, Rev. Eugene De Marco, 155 Scott St., New Brighton, PA 15066

Education, Rev. Lucian Gandolfo, 1030 Fairfield Circle, Clarks Summit, PA 18411

Periodicals

Vista

Christian Churches and Churches of Christ

The fellowship, whose churches were always strictly congregational in polity, has its origin in the American movement to "restore the New Testament church in doctrine, ordinances and life" initiated by Thomas and Alexander Campbell, Walter Scott and Barton W. Stone in the early nineteenth century.

Headquarters

Media Contact, No. American Christian Convention Dir., Rod Huron, 4210 Bridgetown Rd., Box 11326, Cincinnati, OH 45211 Tel. (513) 598-6222, Fax (513)598-6471

Email: Jowston@cwv.edu

Website: www.cwv.net/christ'n/

CONVENTIONS

North American Christian Convention, Dir., Rod Huron, 4210 Bridgetown Rd., Box 11326, Cincinnati, OH 45211 Tel. (513)598-6222, NACC Mailing Address: Box 39456, Cincinnati, OH 45239

National Missionary Convention, Coord., Walter Birney, Box 11, Copeland, KS 67837 Tel. (316)668-5250

Eastern Christian Convention, Kenneth Meade, 5300 Norbeck Rd., Rockville, MD 20853 Tel. (301)460-3550

Periodicals

Christian Standard; Restoration Herald; Horizons; The Lookout

The Christian Congregation, Inc.

The Christian Congregation is a denominational evangelistic association that originated in 1787 and was active on the frontier in areas adjacent to the Ohio River. The church was an unincorporated organization until 1887. At that time a group of ministers who desired closer cooperation formally constituted the church. The charter was revised in 1898 and again in 1970.

Governmental polity basically is congregational. Local units are semi-autonomous. Doctrinal positions, strongly biblical, are essentially universalist in the sense that ethical principles, which motivate us to creative activism, transcend national boundaries and racial barriers. A central tenet, John 13 vs.34-35, translates to such respect for sanctity of life that abortions on demand, capital punishment, and all warfare are vigorously opposed. All wars are considered unjust and obsolete as a means of resolving disputes.

Early leaders were John Chapman, John L. Puckett and Isaac V. Smith. Bishop O. J. Read was chief administrative and ecclesiastic officer for 40 years until 1961. Rev. Dr. Ora Wilbert Eads has been general Superintendent since 1961. Ministerial affiliation for independent clergymen is provided.

Headquarters

812 W. Hemlock St., LaFollette, TN 37766

Media Contact, Gen. Supt., Rev. Ora W. Eads, D.D., Tel. (423)562-6330

Email: Revalnas@aol.com

Website: netministries.org/see/churches.exe/ch10619

Officers

Gen. Supt., Rev. Ora W. Eads, D.D.

Christian Methodist Episcopal Church*

The Christian Methodist Episcopal Church (CME) is a historically African-American denomination that was established in Jackson, Tennessee in 1870 when a group of former slaves, representing eight annual conferences of the Methodist Episcopal Church South, organized the

Colored Methodist Episcopal Church in America. In 1954 at its General Conference in Memphis, Tennessee it was overwhelmingly voted to change the term "Colored" to "Christian". On January 3, 1956 the official name became Christian Methodist Episcopal Church. Its boundaries reach from the continental United States, Alaska, Haiti, Jamaica, and the West African countries of Nigeria, Ghana, and Liberia. One of its most significant witnessing arenas has been the education of African Americans. Today the CME Church supports Paine College, August, GA; Lane College, Jackson, TN; Miles College, Birmingham, AL; Texas College, Tyler, TX; and the Phillips School of Theology in Atlanta, GA.

Headquarters

First Memphis Plaza, 4466 Elvis Presley Blvd., Memphis, TN 38116

Media Contact, Exec. Sec., Attorney Juanita Bryant, 3675 Runnymede Blvd., Cleveland Hts., OH 44121 Tel. (216)382-3559, Fax (216)382-3516, Email, juanbr4law@aol.com

Email: juanbr4law@aol.com

Website: www.c-m-e.org/

Officers

Exec. Sec., Attorney Juanita Bryant, 3675 Runnymede Blvd., Cleveland Hts., OH 44121 Tel. (216)382-3559, Fax (216)382-3516, Email, juanbr4law@aol.com

Sec. Gen. Conf., Rev. John Gilmore, 111 S. Highland, Suite 334, Memphis, TN 38111 Tel. (901)323-3514

OTHER ORGANIZATIONS

Christian Education, Gen. Sec., Dr. Ronald M. Cunningham, 4466 Elvis Presley Blvd., Ste. 214, Box 193, Memphis, TN 38116-7100 Tel. (901)345-0580, Fax (901)345-4118

Lay Ministry, Gen. Sec., Dr. Victor Taylor, 9560 Drake Ave., Evanston, IL 60203, Tel. (800) 782-4335 x. 6029, Fax (312)345-6056, victav@idt.net

Evangelism & Missions, Gen. Sec., Dr. Willie C. Champion, 102 Pearly Top Dr., Glen Heights, TX 75154 Tel. (214)372-9505

Finance, Sec., Dr. Joseph C. Neal, Jr., P.O. Box 75085, Los Angeles, CA 90075 Tel. (323)233-5050

Editor, The Christian Index, Dr. Kenneth E. Jones, P.O. Box 431, Fairfield, AL 35064, Tel. (205)929-1640, Fax (205)791-1910, Goodoc@aol.com

Publication Services, Gen. Sec., Rev. William George, 4466 Elvis Presley Blvd., Memphis, TN 38116 Tel. (901)345-0580, Fax (901)767-8514

Personnel Services, Gen. Sec., Dr. N. Charles Thomas, P.O. Box 9, Memphis, TN 38101-0074 Tel. (901)345-4120

Women's Missionary Council, Pres., Dr. Judith E. Grant, 723 E. Upsal St., Philadelphia, PA 19119 Tel. (215)843-7742

BISHOPS

First District, Bishop William H. Graves, Sr., 4466 Elvis Presley Blvd., Ste. 222, Memphis, TN 38116 Tel. (901)345-0580

Second District, Bishop Nathaniel L. Linsey, 5115 Rollman Estate Dr., Cincinnati, OH 45236 Tel. (513)772-8622

Third District, Bishop Dotcy I. Isom, Jr., 5925 W. Florissant Ave., St. Louis, MO 63136 Tel. (314)381-3111

Fourth District, Bishop Thomas L. Hoyt, Jr., 109 Holcomb Dr., Shreveport, LA 71103 Tel. (318) 222-6284

Fifth District, Bishop Paul A.G. Stewart, Sr., 310 18th St. N., Ste. 400D, Birmingham, AL 35203 Tel. (205)655-0346

Sixth District, Bishop Othal H. Lakey, 2001 M.L. King, Jr. Dr. SW, Ste. 423, Atlanta, GA 30310 Tel. (404)752-7800

Seventh District, Bishop Charles L. Helton 6524 16th St., NW, Washington, DC 20012 and 5337 Ruth Dr., Charlotte, NC 28215 Tel. (704)536-8067

Eighth District, Bishop Marshall Gilmore, Sr., 1616 E. Illinois, Dallas, TX 75216 Tel. (214) 372-9073

Ninth District, Bishop E. Lynn Brown, 3844 W. Slauson Ave., Ste. 1, Los Angeles, CA 90043 Tel. (213)294-3830

Tenth District, Bishop Lawrence L. Reddick III, P.O. Box 27147, Memphis, TN 38167, Tel. (901)274-1070

Retired, Bishop Caesar D. Coleman, 1000 Longmeadow Ln., DeSoto, TX 75115, Bishop Richard O. Bass, Sr., 1556 Delton Pl., Midfield, AL 35228; Bishop Oree Broomfield, Sr., 3505 Springrun Dr., Decatur, GA 30032

Periodicals

The Christian Index; The Missionary Messenger

The Christian and Missionary Alliance

The Christian and Missionary Alliance was formed in 1897 by the merger of two organizations begun in 1887 by Dr. Albert B. Simpson, The Christian Alliance and the Evangelical Missionary Alliance. The Christian and Missionary Alliance is an evangelical church which stresses the sufficiency of Jesus as Savior, Sanctifier, Healer, and Coming King and has earned a worldwide reputation for its missionary accomplishments. The Canadian districts became autonomous in 1981 and formed The Christian and Missionary Alliance in Canada.

NATIONAL OFFICE

P.O. Box 35000, Colorado Springs, CO 80935-3500 Tel. (719)599-5999, Fax (719)593-8692

Media Contact, Peter Burgo, director for Media Development

Email: www.gospelcom.net/cmalliance/

Website: info@cmalliance.org

Officers

Pres., Rev. Peter N. Nanfelt, D.D.
Corp. Vice Pres., Rev. Abraham H. Poon, D. Min
Corp. Sec., Rev. David L. Goodin
Vice Pres. for Administration, Rev. Randall B. Corbin, D. Min.
Vice Pres., for Advancement, Rev. John P. Stumbo
Vice Pres. for International Ministries, Rev. Robert L. Fetherlin, D. Min.
Vice Pres. For National Church Ministries, Rev. Donald A. Wiggins, D. Min.
Vice Pres. For Operations/Finance, Mr. Duane A. Wheeland, CPA

Board of Managers

Chpsn., Dr. James A. Davey
Vice-Chpsn., Rev. Rockwell L. Dillaman

DISTRICTS

Cambodian, Rev. Nareth May, 1616 S. Palmetto Ave., Ontario, CA 91762, Tel. (909)988-9434
Central, Dr. Gordon F. Meier, 1218 High St., Wadsworth, OH 44281, Tel. (303)336-2911
Central Pacific, Rev. Edward (Ted) A. Cline, 715 Lincoln Ave., Woodland, CA 95695 Tel. (530) 662-2500
E. Pennsylvania, Rev. Francis L. Leonard, 1200 Spring Garden Dr., Middletown, PA 17057, Tel. (717)985-9240
Great Lakes, Dr. Donald A Wiggins, 2250 Huron Parkway, Ann Arbor, MI 48104 Tel. (734)677-8555
Haitian North, Rev. Sainvilus Point Du Jour, P.O. Box 791, Nyack, NY 10960, Tel. (914)578-1804
Haitian South, Rev. Brave L. Laverdure, 2922 Oak Vista Way SW, Lawrenceville, GA 30044, Tel. (770)931-0456
Hmong, Rev. Chong-Neng Thao, 12287 Pennsylvania St., Thornton, CO 80241, Tel. (303)252-1793
Korean, Rev. P. Gil Kim, 713 W. Commonwealth Ave., Ste. C, Fullerton, CA 92832, Tel. (714)879-5201
Laotian, Rev. Bouathong Vangsoulatda, 715 Lincoln Ave., Woodland, CA 95695, Tel. (530)406-1189
Metropolitan, Rev. John F. Soper, 349 Watchung Ave., North Plainfield, NJ 07060, Tel. (908) 668-8421
Mid-America, Rev. Douglas L. Grogan, 1301 S. 119th St., Omaha, NE 68144, Tel. (402)330-1888
Mid-Atlantic, Rev. John E. Zuch, Jr., P.O. Box 1217, Frederick, MD 21702, Tel. (301)620-9934
Midwest, Dr. M. Fred Polding, 260 Glen Ellyn Road, Bloomingdale, IL 60108, Tel. (630)893-1355
Native American, Rev. Craig S. Smith, 19019 N. 74th Dr., Glendale, AZ 85308, Tel. (623)561-8134
New England, Dr. Richard E. Bush, P.O. Box 288, South Easton, MA 02375 Tel. (508)238-3820
Northeastern, Rev. David J. Phillips, 6275 Pillmore Dr., Rome, NY 13440 Tel. (315)336-4720
Northwestern, Rev. Craig L. Strawser, 1813 Lexington Ave., N., Roseville, MN 55113 Tel. (651)489-1391
Ohio Valley, Dr. David F. Presher, 4050 Executive Park Dr., #402, Cincinnati, OH 45241 Tel. (513)733-4833
Pacific Northwest, Rev. Kelvin J. Gardiner, P.O. Box 1030, Canby, OR 97013 Tel. (503)266-2238
Puerto Rico, Rev. Luis Felipa, P.O. Box 191794, San Juan, PR 00919-1794, Tel. (787)281-0101
Rocky Mountain, Rev. Delbert McKenzie, 2545 St. Johns Ave., Billings, MT 59102 Tel. (406)656-4233
South Atlantic, Rev. L. Ferrell Towns, 10801 Johnston Rd., Ste. 125, Charlotte, NC 28226 Tel. (704)543-0470
South Pacific, Rev. Bill J. Vaughn, 4130 Adams St., Ste. A, Riverside, CA 92504 Tel. (909)351-0111
Southeastern, Dr. Mark T. O' Farrell, P.O. Box 720430, Orlando, FL 32872-0430 Tel. (407) 823-9662
Southern, Rev. A. Eugene Hall, 5998 Deerfoot Parkway, Trussville, AL 35173 Tel. (205)661-9585
Southwestern, Rev. Daniel R. Wetzel, 5600 E. Loop 820 South Ste. 100, Fort Worth, TX 76119 Tel. (817)561-0879
Spanish Central, Rev. Jose Bruno, 260 Glen Ellyn Rd., Bloomingdale, IL 60108 Tel. (630) 924-7171
Spanish Eastern, Rev. Marcelo Realpe, 3133 Central Ave. Suite 202, Union City, NJ 07087 Tel. (201)866-6676
Spanish Western, Rev. Douglas M. Domier, P.O. Box 3805, Dana Point, CA 92629 Tel. (949) 489-3816
Vietnamese, Rev. Quang B. Nguyen, 2275 W. Lincoln Ave., Anaheim, CA 92801 Tel. (714) 491-8007
W. Great Lakes, Rev. Gary E. Russell, W6107 Aerotech Dr., Appleton, WI 54914 Tel. (920) 734-1123
W. Pennsyylvania, Rev. Palmer L. Zerbe, 600 Chestnut & Sutton Streets, Punxsutawney, PA 15767 Tel. (814)938-6920

NATIONAL ETHNIC ASSOCIATIONS

African-American, Exec. Sec., Rev. Gus H. Brown, 688 Diagonal Rd., Akron, OH 44320 Tel. (330)376-4654
Chinese, Exec. Sec., Rev. Peter Chu, 14209 Secluded Ln., N. Potomac, MD 20878 Tel. (301)294-8067
Filipino, Exec. Sec., Rev. Abednego Ferrer, 166 W. Harder Rd., Hayward, CA 94544 Tel. (510) 887-6261

ETHNIC/CULTURAL MINISTRIES

Arab & South Asian, Rev. Joseph S. Kong, P.O. Box 35000, Colorado Springs, CO 80935 Tel. (719)599-5999 x. 2052

Dega, Mr. Glik Rahlan, 713 Highgate Pl., Raleigh, NC 27610 Tel. (919)821-2351
Alliance Jewish Ministries Association, Rev. Abraham Sandler, 9820 Woodfern Rd., Philadelphia, PA 19115 Tel. (215)676-5122

Periodicals

Alliance Life

Christian Reformed Church in North America

The Christian Reformed Church represents the historic faith of Protestantism. Founded in the United States in 1857 and active in Canada since 1908, it asserts its belief in the Bible as the inspired Word of God, and is creedally united in the Belgic Confession (1561), the Heidelberg Catechism (1563), and the Canons of Dort (1618-19).

Headquarters

2850 Kalamazoo Ave., SE, Grand Rapids, MI 49560 Tel. (616)224-0744, Fax (616)224-5895
Media Contact, Gen. Sec., Dr. David H. Engelhard
Email: btgh@crcna.org
Website: www.crcna.org

Officers

Gen. Sec., Dr. David H. Engelhard
Exec. Dir. of Ministries, Dr. Peter Borgdorff
Canadian Ministries Director, Rev. William Veenstra, 3475 Mainway, P.O. Box 5070 STN LCR 1, Burlington, ON L7R 3Y8
Director of Finance and Administration, Kenneth Horjus

OTHER ORGANIZATIONS

The Back to God Hour, Dir. of Ministries, Dr. Calvin L. Bremer, International Headquarters, 6555 W. College Dr., Palos Heights, IL 60463
Christian Reformed Home Missions, Dir., Rev. John A. Rozeboom
Christian Reformed World Missions, US, Dir., Dr. Gary Bekker
Christian Ref. World Missions, Canada, Dir., Albert Karsten, 3475 Mainway, P.O. Box 5070 STN LCR 1, Burlington, ON L7R 3Y8
Christian Reformed World Relief, US, Dir., Andrew Ryskamp
Christian Reformed World Relief, Canada, Dir., H. Wayne deJong, 3475 Mainway, P.O. Box 5070 STN LCR 1, Burlington, ON L7R 3Y8
CRC Publications, Dir., Gary Mulder
Ministers' Pension Fund, Admn., Kenneth Horjus

Periodicals

The Banner

Christian Union

Organized in 1864 in Columbus, Ohio, the Christian Union stresses the oneness of the Church with Christ as its only head. The Bible is the only rule of faith and practice and good fruits the only condition of fellowship. Each local church governs itself.

Headquarters

316 Rexford Dr., Fort Wayne, IN 46816-1085 Tel. (800)357-8670, Fax (740)773-6259
Media Contact, Rev. Phil Harris, Pres.
Website: www.christianunion.com

Officers

Pres., Rev. Phil Harris, 316 Rexford Dr., Fort Wayne, IN 46816-1085, Tel. (219)744-7001
Vice-Pres., Rev. John Edwards, Rt. 1 Box 231, Ringwook, OK 73768-9790, Tel. (580)753-4488
Sec., Joseph Cunningham, 1005 N. 5th St., Greenfield, OH 45123 Tel. (937)981-3476
Asst. Sec., Wayne Haines, 8335 Blain Highway, Chillicothe, OH 45601-9046, Tel. (740)775-8132
Treas., Jim Eschenbrenner, 30055 130th Ave., Hedrick, IA 52563-8539 Tel. (515)653-4945

Church of the Brethren*

Eight German Pietists-Anabaptists, including their leader, Alexander Mack, founded the Brethren movement in 1708 in Schwarzenau, Germany. Begun in reaction to spiritual stagnation in state churches, the Brethren formed their own movement, modeled on the first-century church. They practice church discipline, believer baptism, anointing, and the love feast. They have no other creed than the new Testament, hold to principles of nonviolence, no force in religion, Christian service, and simplicity. They migrated to the colonies beginning in 1710 and settled at Germantown, Pennsylvania, moving westward and southward over the next 200 years. Emphasis on religion in daily life led to the formation of Brethren Volunteer Service in 1948, which continues today.

Headquarters

Church of the Brethren General Offices, 1451 Dundee Ave., Elgin, IL 60120 Tel. (847)742-5100, Fax (847)742-6103
Brethren Service Center, 500 Main Street, P.O. Box 188, New Windsor, MD 21776-0188 Tel. (410)635-8710, Fax (410)635-8789
Washington Office, 337 North Carolina Ave. SE, Washington, DC 20003 Tel. (202)546-3202, Fax (202)544-5852
Media Contact, Staff for Interpretation, Howard Royer, Elgin Ofc.
Email: cobweb@brethren.org
Website: www.brethren.org/

Officers

Moderator, Paul E. Grout, 728 W. Hill Rd., Putney, VT 05346-8983, Tel. (802)387-4177, Fax (802)387-4689
Moderator-elect, Harriet W. Finney, 604 N. Mill St., North Manchester, IN 46962-1865, Tel. (219)982-8805, Fax (219)982-7181, hfinney_ds@brethren.org
Secretary, Cathy S. Huffman, 2363 Brick Church

Rd., Rocky Mount, VA 24151-4017, Tel. (540) 334-57587, pashuffy@roanoke.infi.net

GENERAL BOARD STAFF

General Secretary, Judy Mills Reimer, 1451 Dundee Ave., Elgin, IL 60120-1694 Tel. (847) 742-5100 x201, Fax (847)742-8212, jreimer_gb @brethren.org

Manager of Office Operations, Jon Kobel, 1451 Dundee Ave., Elgin, IL 60120-1694 Tel. (847) 742-5100 x202, Fax (847)742-8212, jkobel_gb@ brethren.org

Coordinator of Human Resources, -vacant

LEADERSHIP TEAM

General Secretary, Judy Mills Reimer, 1451 Dundee Ave., Elgin, IL 60120-1694 Tel. (847) 742-5100 x201, Fax (847)742-8212, jreimer_gb @brethren.org

Treasurer and Director of Centralized Resources, Judy E. Keyser, 1451 Dundee Ave., Elgin, IL 60120-1694 Tel. (847)742-5100 x270, Fax (847)742-6103, jkeyser_gb@brethren.org

Director and Publisher of Brethren Press, Wendy McFadden, 1451 Dundee Ave., Elgin, IL 60120-1694 Tel. (847)742-5100 x278, Fax (847)742-1407, wmcfadden_gb@brethren.org

Director of Congregational Life Ministries, Glenn F. Timmons, 1451 Dundee Ave., Elgin, IL 60120-1694 Tel. (847)742-5100 x282, Fax (847)742-6103, gtimmons_gb@brethren.org

Director of Global Mission Partnerships, Mervin B. Keeney, 1451 Dundee Ave., Elgin, IL 60120-1694 Tel. (847)742-5100 x226, Fax (847)742-6103, mission_gb@brethren.org

Director of Brethren Service Center, Stanley J. Noffsinger, PO Box 1898, New Windsor, MD 21776-0188 Tel.(410)635-8731, Fax (410) 635-8739, snoffsinger_gb@brethren.org

Periodicals

Messenger

Church of Christ

Joseph Smith and five others organized the Church of Christ on April 6, 1830 at Fayette, New York. In 1864 this body was directed by revelation through Granville Hedrick to return in 1867 to Independence, Missouri to the "consecrated land" dedicated by Joseph Smith. They did so and purchased the temple lot dedicated in 1831.

Headquarters

Temple Lot, 200 S. River St., P.O. Box 472, Independence, MO 64051 Tel. (816)833-3995

Media Contact, Gen. Church Rep., William A. Sheldon, P.O. Box 472, Independence, MO 64051 Tel. (816)833-3995

Website: church-of-christ.com/

Officers

Council of Apostles, Secy., Apostle Smith N. Brickhouse, P.O. Box 472, Independence, MO 64051

Gen. Bus. Mgr., Bishop Alvin Harris, P.O. Box 472, Independence, MO 64051

Periodicals

Zion's Advocate

The Church of Christ (Holiness) U.S.A.

The Church of Christ (Holiness) U.S.A. has a Divine commission to propagate the gospel throughout the world, to seek the conversion of sinners, to reclaim backsliders, to encourage the sanctification of believers, to support divine healing, and to advance the truth for the return of our Lord and Savior Jesus Christ. This must be done through proper organization.

The fundamental principles of Christ's Church have remained the same. The laws founded upon these principles are to remain unchanged. The Church of Christ (Holiness) U.S.A. is representative in form of government; therefore, the final authority in defining the organizational responsibilities rests with the national convention. The bishops of the church are delegated special powers to act in behalf of or speak for the church. The pastors are ordained ministers, who under the call of God and His people, have divine oversight of local churches. However, the representative form of government gives ministry and laity equal authority in all deliberate bodies. With the leadership of the Holy Spirit, Respect, Loyalty and Love will greatly increase.

Headquarters

329 East Monument Street, P.O. Box 3622, Jackson, MS 39207 Tel. (601)353-0222, Fax (601)353-4002

Media Contact, Maurice D. Bingham, Ed. D., Senior Bishop

Email: Everything@cochusa.com

Website: www.cochusa.com/main.htm

BOARD OF BISHOPS

Senior Bishop, Maurice D. Bingham, Ed. D.
Eastern Diocese, Bishop Lindsay E. Jones
North Central Diocese, Elder Bennett Wolfe
Northern Diocese, Bishop Emery Lindsay
Pacific Northwest Diocese, Bishop Robert Winn
South Central Diocese, Bishop Joseph Campbell
Southeastern Diocese, Bishop Victor P. Smith
Southwestern Diocese, Bishop Vernon Kennebrew
Western Diocese, Bishop Robert Winn
Board Member, Bishop James K. Mitchell

Church of Christ, Scientist

The Church of Christ, Scientist, was founded in 1879 by Mary Baker Eddy "to commemorate the word and works of our Master [Christ Jesus], which should reinstate primitive Christianity and its lost element of healing" (Church Manual, p. 17). Central to the Church's mission is making available worldwide Mrs. Eddy's definitive work on health and Bible-based Christian healing, Science and Health with key to the scriptures, as well as its publications, Internet sites, and broadcast programs, all of which respond to humanity's search for spiritual answers to today's pressing needs.

The Church also maintains an international speakers' bureau to introduce the public to Christian Science and Mrs. Eddy. Christian Science practitioners, living in hundreds of communities worldwide, are available full-time, to pray with anyone seeking comfort and healing. And Christian Science teachers hold yearly classes for those interested in a more specific understanding of how to practice the Christian Science system of healing.

The worldwide activities and business of the Church are transacted by a five-member Board of Directors in Boston. About 2000 congregations, each democratically organized and governed, are located in approximately 75 countries. The church has no clergy. Worship services are conducted by lay persons elected to serve as Readers. Each church maintains a Reading Room—a bookstore open to the community for spiritual inquiry and research; and a Sunday School where young people discuss the contemporary relevance of ideas from the Bible and Science and Health.

Headquarters

The First Church of Christ, Scientist, 175 Huntington Ave., Boston, MA 02115

Media Contact, Mgr., Comm. on Publication, Gary A. Jones, Tel. (617)450-3301, Fax (617) 450-3325

Website: www.tfccs.com

Officers

Bd. of Directors, Virginia S. Harris; Walter D. Jones; John Lewis Selover; Mary Ridgeway; Mary Metzner Trammell

President, Christiane West Little

Treas., Walter D. Jones

Clk., Mary Ridgeway

First Reader, Candace duMars

Second Reader, William E. Moody

Periodicals

The Christian Science Monitor (website, www.csmonitor.com); The Christian Science Journal; Christian Science Sentinel; The Herald of Christian Science (13 languages); Christian Science Quarterly Bible Lessons in 16 languages and English Braille

Church of God (Anderson, Indiana)

The Church of God (Anderson, Indiana) began in 1881 when Daniel S. Warner and several associates felt constrained to forsake all denominational hierarchies and formal creeds, trusting solely in the Holy Spirit as their overseer and the Bible as their statement of belief. These people saw themselves at the forefront of a movement to restore unity and holiness to the church, not to establish another denomination, but to promote primary allegiance to Jesus Christ so as to transcend denominational loyalties.

Deeply influenced by Wesleyan theology and Pietism, the Church of God has emphasized conversion, holiness, and attention to the Bible. Worship services tend to be informal, accentuating expository preaching and robust singing.

There is no formal membership. Persons are assumed to be members on the basis of witness to a conversion experience and evidence that supports such witness. The absence of formal membership is also consistent with the church's understanding of how Christian unity is to be achieved—that is, by preferring the label Christian before all others.

The Church of God is congregational in its government. Each local congregation is autonomous and may call any recognized Church of God minister to be its pastor and may retain him or her as long as is mutually pleasing. Ministers are ordained and disciplined by state or provincial assemblies made up predominantly of ministers. National program boards serve the church through coordinated ministries and resource materials.

There are Church of God congregations in 89 foreign countries, most of which are resourced by one or more missionaries. There are slightly more Church of God adherents overseas than in North America. The heaviest concentration is in the nation of Kenya.

General Offices

Box 2420, Anderson, IN 46018-2420 Tel. (765)642-0256, Fax (765)642-5652

Media Contact, Communications Coordinator, Church of God Ministries, Don Taylor

CHURCH OF MINISTRIES

Includes Congregational Ministries, Resource & Linking Ministries and Outreach Ministries

Email: dtaylor@chog.org

Website: www.chog.org

OTHER ORGANIZATIONS

Bd. of Church Extension, Pres., J. Perry Grubbs, Box 2069, Anderson, IN 46018

Women of the Church of God, Natl. Coord., Linda J. Mason, Box 2328, Anderson, IN 46018

Bd. of Pensions, Exec. Sec.-Treas., Jeffrey A. Jenness, Box 2299, Anderson, IN 46018

Periodicals

Inform; Church of God Missions; The Shining Light; Metro Voice

The Church Of God In Christ

The Church of God in Christ was founded in 1907 in Memphis, Tennessee, and was organized by Bishop Charles Harrison Mason, a former Baptist minister who pioneered the embryonic stages of the Holiness movement beginning in 1895 in Mississippi.

Its founder organized four major departments between 1910-1916, the Women's Department, the Sunday School, Young Peoples Willing Workers, and Home and Foreign Mission.

The Church is trinitarian and teaches the infallibility of scripture, the need for regeneration, and subsequent baptism of the Holy Ghost. It emphasizes holiness as God's standard for Christian conduct. It recognizes as ordinances Holy Communion, Water Baptism, and Feet Washing. Its governmental structure is basically episcopal with the General Assembly being the Legislative body.

Headquarters

Mason Temple, 938 Mason St., Memphis, TN 38126 Tel. (901)947-9300

Mailing Address, P.O. Box 320, Memphis, TN 38101

Temple Church Of God In Christ, 672 S. Lauderdale St., Memphis, TN 38126 Tel. (901)527-9202

Email: EJOHNCOGIC@aol.com

Website: netministries.org/see/churches/ch00833

GENERAL OFFICES

Office of the Presiding Bishop, Presiding Bishop, Bishop Chandler D. Owens, Tel. (901)947-9338

Office of the General Secretary, Gen. Sec., Bishop W. W. Hamilton, Tel. (901)947-9358

Office of the Financial Secretary, Sec., Bishop Frank O. White, Tel. (901)947-9310

Office of the Treasurer, Treasurer, Bishop Samuel L. Lowe, Tel. (901)947-9381

Office of the Board of Trustees, Chmn., Elder Dwight Green, Tel. (901)947-9326

Office of the Chief Operating Officer at World Headquarters, Elder A.Z. Hall, Jr., 930 Mason Street, Memphis, TN Tel. (901)947-9358

Office of the Clergy Bureau, Dir., Bishop W. W. Hamilton, Tel. (901)974-9358

Office of Supt. of National Properties, Supt., Elder Marles Flowers, Tel. (901)947-9330

Office of Accounting, Chief Financial Officer, Ms. Sylvia H. Law, Tel. (901)947-9361

Department of Evangelism, Pres., Elder Richard White, Atlanta, GA, Tel. (404)361-7020

Department of Missions, Pres. Bishop Carlis L. Moody, Tel. (901)947-9316; Vice Pres., Elder Jesse W. Denny

Dept. of Music, Pres., Ms. LuVoinia Whittley, 20205 Augusta Dr., Olympia Fields, IL 60461 Tel. (312)626-1970

Dept. of Sunday Schools, Gen. Supt., Bishop Jerry Macklin, 1027 W. Tennyson Rd., Hayward, CA 94544 Tel. (510)783-9377

Dept. of Women, Pres.-Gen. Supervisor, Mother Willie Mae Rivers, P.O. Box 1052, Memphis, TN 38101, Tel. (901)775-0600

Dept. of Youth (Youth Congress), Pres., Elder J. Drew Sheard, 7045 Curtis Dr., Detroit, MI 48235, Tel. (313)864-7170

Church of God in Christ Book Store, Mgr., Geraldine Miller, 285 S. Main St., Memphis, TN 38103 Tel. (901)947-9304

Church of God in Christ Publishing House, CEO, Dr. David A. Hall, Sr., Tel. (901)947-9342

Board of Publications, Chmn., Bishop R.L.H. Winbush, Tel. (901)947-9342

Periodicals

The Whole Truth; The Voice of Missions

Church of God in Christ, International

The Church of God in Christ, International was organized in 1969 in Kansas City, Mo., by 14 bishops of the Church of God in Christ of Memphis, Tenn. The doctrine is the same, but the separation came because of disagreement over polity and governmental authority. The Church is Wesleyan in theology (two works of grace) but stresses the experience of full baptism of the Holy Ghost with the initial evidence of speaking with other tongues as the Spirit gives utterance.

Headquarters

170 Adelphi St., Brooklyn, NY 11205 Tel. (718) 625-9175

Media Contact, Natl. Sec., Rev. Sis. Sharon R. Dunn

Email: laity@cogic.org

Website: www.cogic.org/main.htm

Officers

Presiding Bishop, Most Rev. Carl E. Williams, Sr.

Vice-Presiding Bishop, Rt. Rev. J. P. Lucas, 90 Holland St., Newark, NJ 07103

Sec.-Gen., Deacon Dennis Duke, 360 Colorado Ave., Bridgeport, CT 06605

Exec. Admn., Horace K. Williams, Word of God Center, Newark, NJ

Women's Dept., Natl. Supervisor, Evangelist Elvonia Williams

Youth Dept., Pres., Dr. Joyce Taylor, 137-17 135th Ave., S., Ozone Park, NY 11420

Music Dept., Pres., Isaiah Heyward

Bd. of Bishops, Chpsn., Bishop J. C. White, 360 Colorado Ave., Bridgeport, CT 06605

Church of God in Christ, Mennonite

The Church of God in Christ, Mennonite was organized in Ohio in 1859 by the evangelist-reformer John Holdeman. The church unites with the faith of the Waldenses, Anabaptists, and other such groups. Emphasis is placed on obedience to the teachings of the Bible, including the doctrine of the new birth and spiritual life, noninvolvement in government or the military, head-coverings for the women, beards for the men and separation from the world shown by simplicity in clothing, homes, possessions, and life-style. The church has a worldwide membership of about 18,900, most of them in the United States and Canada.

Headquarters

P.O. Box 313, 420 N. Wedel Ave., Moundridge, KS 67107 Tel. (620)345-2532, Fax (620)345-2582

Media Contact, Dale Koehn, P.O. Box 230, Moundridge, KS 67107 Tel. (620)345-2532, Fax (620)345-2582

Periodicals

Messenger of Truth

Church of God (Cleveland, Tennessee)

It is one of America's oldest Pentecostal churches founded in 1886 as an outgrowth of the holiness revival under the name Christian Union. In 1907 the church adopted the organizational name Church of God. It has its foundation upon the principles of Christ as revealed in the Bible. The Church of God is Christian, Protestant, foundational in its doctrine, evangelical in practice, and distinctively Pentecostal. It maintains a centralized form of government and a commitment to world evangelization.

Headquarters

P.O. Box 2430, Cleveland, TN 37320 Tel. (423) 472-3361, Fax (423)478-7066

Media Contact, Dir. of Communications, Michael L. Baker, Tel. (423)478-7112, Fax (423)478-7066

Website: www.churchofgod.cc/default_nav40.asp

EXECUTIVES

Gen. Overseer, R. Lamar Vest

Asst. Gen. Overseers, G. Dennis McGuire; T. L. Lowery; Bill F. Sheeks

Secretary General, Gene D. Rice

DEPARTMENTS

Benefits Board, CEO, Arthur Rhodes

Business & Records, Dir., Julian B. Robinson

Care Ministries, Dir., John D. Nichols

Chaplains Commission, Dir., Robert D. Crick

Communications, Media Ministries, Director, Michael L. Baker

Education—European Bible Seminary, Dir., John Sims

Education—Hispanic Institute of Ministry, Dir., Jose D. Montanez

Education—International Bible College, Pres., Cheryl Busse

Education—Lee University, Pres., C. Paul Conn

Education—Patten College, Chancellor, Bebe Patten

Education—Puerto Rico Bible School, Pres., Ildefonso Caraballo

Education—School of Ministry, Chancellor, Paul L. Walker

Education—Theological Seminary, President, Donald M. Walker

Evangelism & Home Missions, Dir., Orville Hagan

Evangelism—Black Ministries, Dir., Asbury R. Sellers

Evangelism—Cross-Cultural Min., Dir., Wallace J. Sibley

Evangelism—Hispanic Ministry, Dir., Esdras Betancourt

Evangelism—Native American Ministries, Dir., Douglas M. Cline

Lay Ministries, Dir., Leonard Albert

Legal Services, Dir., Dennis W. Watkins

Men/Women of Action, Dir., Hugh Carver

Ministerial Development, Dir., Larry G. Hess

Ministry to Israel, Dir., J. Michael Utterback

Ministry to the Military, Dir., Robert A. Moore

Music Ministries, Dir., Delton Alford

Pentecostal Resource Center, Director, Frances Arrington

Publications, Dir., Daniel F. Boling

Stewardship, Dir., Al Taylor

Women's Ministries, Director, Rebecca J. Jenkins

World Missions, Dir., Lovell R. Cary

Youth & Christian Education, Dir., John D. Childers

Periodicals

Church of God Evangel; Church of God Evangelica; Save Our World; Ministry Now Profiles

Church of God by Faith, Inc.

Founded 1914, in Jacksonville Heights, Florida, by Elder John Bright, this church believes the word of God as interpreted by Jesus Christ to be the only hope of salvation and Jesus Christ the only mediator for people.

Headquarters

1315 Lane Ave. S., Suite 6, Jacksonville, FL 32205 Tel. (904)783-8500, Fax (904)783-9911

Media Contact, Ofc. Mgr., Sarah E. Lundy

Email: natl-hq@cogbf.org

Website: www.cogbf.org/

Officers

Presiding Bishop, James E. McKnight, P.O. Box 121, Gainesville, FL 32601

Treas., Elder Theodore Brown, 93 Girard Pl., Newark, NJ 07108

Ruling Elders, Elder John Robinson, 300 Essex Dr., Ft. Pierce, FL 33450; Elder D. C. Rourk, 207 Chestnut Hill Dr., Rochester, NY 14617

Exec. Sec., Elder George Matthews, 8834 Camphor Dr., Jacksonville, FL 32208

Church of God General Conference (Oregon, IL and Morrow, GA)

This church is the outgrowth of several independent local groups of similar faith. Some were in existence as early as 1800, and others date their beginnings to the arrival of British immigrants around 1847. Many local churches carried the name Church of God of the Abrahamic Faith.

State and district conferences of these groups were formed as an expression of mutual cooperation. A national organization was instituted at Philadelphia in 1888. Because of strong convictions on the questions of congregational rights and authority, however, it ceased to function until

1921, when the present General Conference was formed at Waterloo, Iowa.

The Bible is accepted as the supreme standard of faith. Adventist in viewpoint, the second (premillenial) coming of Christ is strongly emphasized. The church teaches that the kingdom of God will be literal, beginning in Jerusalem at the time of the return of Christ and extending to all nations. Emphasis is placed on the oneness of God and the Sonship of Christ, that Jesus did not pre-exist prior to his birth in Bethlehem and that the Holy Spirit is the power and influence of God. Membership is dependent on faith, repentance, and baptism by immersion.

The work of the General Conference is carried out under the direction of the board of directors. With a congregational church government, the General Conference exists primarily as a means of mutual cooperation and for the development of yearly projects and enterprises.

The headquarters and Bible College were moved to Morrow, Ga. in 1991.

Headquarters

P.O. Box 100,000, Morrow, GA 30260 Tel. (404)362-0052, Fax (404)362-9307
Media Contact, David Krogh
Email: info@abc-coggc.org
Website: www.abc-coggc.org

Officers

Chpsn., Charles Bottolfs, 43137 Happywoods Rd., Hammond, LA 70403
Vice-Chpsn., Pastor Greg Demmitt, 825 E. Drake Dr., Tempe, AZ 85283
Sec., Keith Williams, 3250 Vermont Ave SW, Grandville, MI 49418
Treas., Paul Duncan, 1044 Cottrell Hill, Lenoir, NC 28645

OTHER ORGANIZATIONS

Bus. Admn., Operations Manager, Gary Burnham, Georgia Ofc.
Atlanta Bible College, Acting Academic Dean, Dr. Joe Martin, Georgia Ofc.

Periodicals

The Restitution Herald; A Journal From the Radical Reformation; Church of God Progress Journal

Church of God, Mountain Assembly, Inc.

The church was formed in 1895 and organized in 1906 by J. H. Parks, S. N. Bryant, Tom Moses and William Douglas.

Headquarters

164 N. Florence Ave., P.O. Box 157, Jellico, TN 37762 Tel. (423)784-8260, Fax (423)784-3258
Media Contact, Gen. Sec.-Treas., Rev. Alfred Newton, Jr.
Email: cgmahdq@jellico.com
Website: www.cgmahdq.org

Officers

Gen. Overseer, Rev. Cecil Johnson
Asst. Gen. Overseer, World Missions Dir., Rev. Lonnie Lyke
Gen. Sec.-Treas., Rev. Alfred Newton, Jr.
Youth Ministries & Camp Dir., Rev. Ken Ellis

Periodicals

The Gospel Herald

Church of God of Prophecy

The Church of God of Prophecy is one of the churches that grew out of the work of A. J. Tomlinson in the first half of the twentieth century. Historically it shares a common heritage with the Church of God (Cleveland Tennessee) and is in the mainstream of the classical Pentecostal-holiness tradition.

At the death of A.J. Tomlinson in 1943, M.A. Tomlinson was named General Overseer and served until his retirement in 1990. He emphasized unity and fellowship unlimited by racial, social, or political differences. The next General Overseer, Billy D. Murray, Sr., who served from 1990 until his retirement in 2000, emphasized a commitment to the promotion of Christian unity and world evangelization. In July 2000, Fred S. Fisher, Sr. Was duly selected to serve as the fourth General Overseer of the Church of God of Prophecy.

From its beginnings, the Church has based its beliefs on "the whole Bible, rightly divided," and has accepted the Bible as God's Holy Word, inspired, inerrant, and infallible. The church is firm in its commitment to orthodox Christian belief. The Church affirms that there is one God, eternally existing in three persons, Father, Son, and Holy Spirit. It believes in the deity of Christ, His virgin birth, His sinless life, the physical miracles He performed, His atoning death on the cross, His bodily resurrection, His ascension to the right hand of the Father, and his Second coming. The church professes that salvation results from grace alone through faith in Christ, that regeneration by the Holy Spirit is essential for the salvation of sinful men, and that sanctification by the blood of Christ makes possible personal holiness. It affirms the present ministry of the Holy Spirit by Whose indwelling believers are able to live godly lives and have power for service. The church believes in, and promotes, the ultimate unity of believers as prayed for by Christ in John 17. The church stresses the sanctity of human life and is committed to the sanctity of the marriage bond and the importance of strong, loving Christian families. Other official teachings include Holy Spirit baptism with tongues as initial evidence; manifestation of the spiritual gifts; divine healing; premillenial second-coming of Christ; total abstinence from the use of tobacco, alcohol, and narcotics; water baptism by immersion; the Lord's supper and washing of the saints' feet; and a concern for moderation and holiness in all dimensions of lifestyle.

The Church is racially integrated on all levels, including top leadership. Women play a prominent role in church affairs, serving in pastoral roles and other leadership positions. The church presbytery has recently adopted plurality of leadership in the selection of a General Oversight Group. This group consists of eight bishops located around the world who, along with the General Overseer, are responsible for inspirational leadership and vision casting for the church body.

The Church has local congregations in all 50 states and more than 100 nations worldwide. Organizationally there is a strong emphasis on international missions, evangelism, youth and children's ministries, women's and men's ministries, stewardship, communications, publishing, leadership development, and discipleship.

CHURCH OF GOD OF PROPHECY INTERNATIONAL OFFICES

P.O. Box 2910, Cleveland, TN 37320-2910
Media Contact, Betty J. Fisher, Tel. (423)559-5100, Fax (423)559-5108
Email: betty@cogop.org
Website: www.cogop.org

Officers

Gen. Overseer, Bishop Fred S. Fisher, Sr.; General Presbyters, Sherman Allen, Sam Clements, Daniel Corbett, Clayton Endecott, Miguel Mojica, José Reyes, Sr., Felix Santiago, Brice Thompson

International Offices Ministries Dirs., Finance, Communications, and Publishing, Oswill Williams; Global Outreach and Administrative Asst. to the General Presbyters, Randy Howard; Leadership Development and Discipleship Ministries, Larry Duncan.

Periodicals

White Wing Messenger; Victory (Youth Magazine/ Sunday School Curriculum); The Happy Harvester

The Church of God (Seventh Day), Denver, Colorado

The Church of God (Seventh Day) began in southwestern Michigan in 1858, when a group of Sabbath-keepers led by Gilbert Cranmer refused to give endorsement to the visions and writings of Ellen G. White, a principal in the formation of the Seventh-Day Adventist Church. Another branch of Sabbath-keepers, which developed near Cedar Rapids, Iowa, in 1860, joined the Michigan church in 1863 to publish a paper called The Hope of Israel, the predecessor to the Bible Advocate, the church's present publication. As membership grew and spread into Missouri and Nebraska, it organized the General Conference of the Church of God in 1884. The words "Seventh Day" were added to its name in 1923. The headquarters of the church was in Stanberry, Missouri, from 1888 until 1950, when it moved to Denver.

The Church teaches salvation is a gift of God's grace, and is available solely by faith in Jesus Christ, the Savior; that saving faith is more than mental assent, it involves active trust and repentance from sin. Out of gratitude, Christians will give evidence of saving faith by a lifestyle that conforms to God's commandments, including the seventh-day Sabbath, which members observe as a tangible expression of their faith and rest in God as their Creator and Redeemer. The church believes in the imminent, personal, and visible return of Christ; that the dead are in an unconscious state awaiting to be resurrected, the wicked to be destroyed, and the righteous to be rewarded to eternal life in the presence of God on a restored earth. The church observes two ordinances, baptism by immersion and an annual Communion service accompanied by foot washing.

Headquarters

330 W. 152nd Ave., P.O. Box 33677, Denver, CO 80233 Tel. (303)452-7973, Fax (303)452-0657
Media Contact, Pres., Whaid Rose
Email: offices@cog7.org
Website: www.cog7.org

MINISTRIES

Missions Ministries, Dr., William Hicks, Church Planting Dir., Mike Vlad; Home Missions Dir., Ralph Diaz; Missions Abroad, Dir., Victor Burford
Publications/Bible of Advocate Press, Dir., John Crisp
Summit School of Theology, Dir., Jerry Griffin
Young Adult Ministry, Dir., Becky Riggs
Youth Ministry, Dirs., Kurt & Kristi Lang
Women's Ministry, Dir., Mary Ling
Spring Vale Academy (Para Church Ministry) Dir., John Tivald

Periodicals

The Bible Advocate

The Church of Illumination

The Church of Illumination was organized in 1908 for the express purpose of establishing congregations at large, offering a spiritual, esoteric, philosophic interpretation of the vital biblical teachings, thereby satisfying the inner spiritual needs of those seeking spiritual truth, yet permitting them to remain in, or return to, their former church membership.

Headquarters

Beverly Hall, 5966 Clymer Rd., Quakertown, PA 18951 Tel. (800)779-3796
Media Contact, Dir. General, Gerald E. Poesnecker, P.O. Box 220, Quakertown, PA 18951 Tel. (215)536-7048, Fax (215) 536-7058
Email: bevhall@comcat.com
Website: www.soul.org

Officers

Dir.-General, Gerald E. Poesnecker, P.O. Box 220, Quakertown, PA 18951

The Church of Jesus Christ (Bickertonites)

This church was organized in 1862 at Green Oak, Pa., by William Bickerton, who obeyed the Restored Gospel under Sidney Rigdon's following in 1845.

Headquarters

Sixth & Lincoln Sts., Monongahela, PA 15063 Tel. (412)258-3066

Media Contact, Exec. Sec., John Manes, 2007 Cutter Dr., McKees Rocks, PA 15136 Tel. (412)771-4513

Officers

Pres., Dominic Thomas, 6010 Barrie, Dearborn, MI 48126

First Counselor, Paul Palmieri, 319 Pine Dr., Aliquippa, PA 15001 Tel. (412)378-4264

Second Counselor, Robert Watson, Star Rt. 5, Box 36, Gallup, NM 87301

Exec. Sec., John Manes, 2007 Cutter Dr., McKees Rocks, PA 15136 Tel. (412)771-4513

Periodicals

The Gospel News

The Church of Jesus Christ of Latter-day Saints

This church was organized April 6, 1830, at Fayette, N.Y., by Joseph Smith. Members believe Joseph Smith was divinely directed to restore the gospel to the earth, and that through him the keys to the Aaronic and Melchizedek priesthoods and temple work also were restored. Members believe that both the Bible and the Book of Mormon (a record of the Lord's dealings with His people on the American continent 600 B.C.–421 A.D.) are scripture. Membership is over eleven million.

In addition to the First Presidency, the governing bodies of the church include the Quorum of the Twelve Apostles, the Presidency of the Seventy, the Quorums of the Seventy and the Presiding Bishopric.

Headquarters

47 East South Temple St., Salt Lake City, UT 84150 Tel. (801)240-1000, Fax (801)240-1167

Media Contact, Dir., Media Relations, Michael Otterson, Tel. (801)240-1111 Fax (801)240-1167

Website: www.lds.org

Officers

Pres., Gordon B. Hinckley

1st Counselor, Thomas S. Monson

2nd Counselor, James E. Faust

Quorum of the Twelve Apostles, Pres., Boyd K. Packer; L. Tom Perry; David B. Haight; Neal A. Maxwell; Russell M. Nelson; Dallin H. Oaks; M. Russell Ballard; Joseph B. Wirthlin; Richard G. Scott; Robert D. Hales; Jeffrey R. Holland; Henry B. Eyring

AUXILIARY ORGANIZATIONS

Sunday Schools, Gen. Pres., Cecil O. Samuelson, Jr.

Relief Society, Gen. Pres., Mary Ellen Smoot

Young Women, Gen. Pres.,Margaret Nadauld

Young Men, Gen. Pres., F. Melvin Hammond

Primary, Gen. Pres., Coleen K. Menlove

Periodicals

The Ensign; Liahona; The New Era; Friend Magazine

Church of the Living God (Motto, Christian Workers for Fellowship)

The Church of the Living God was founded by William Christian in April 1889 at Caine Creek, AR. It was the first black church in America without Anglo-Saxon roots and not begun by white missionaries.

Christian was born a slave in Mississippi on Nov. 10, 1856 and grew up uneducated. In 1875 he united with the Missionary Baptist Church and began to preach. In 1888 he left the Baptist Church and began what was known as Christian Friendship Work. Believing himself to have been inspired by the Spirit of God through divine revelation and close study of the Scriptures, he was led to the truth that the Bible refers to the church as The Church of the Living God (I Tim. Ch.3 vs.15).

The church believes in the infallibility of the Scriptures, is Trinitarian, and believes there are three sacraments ordained by Christ, baptism (by immersion), the Lord's Supper (unleavened bread and water), and foot washing.

The Church of the Living God, C.W.F.F., believes in holiness as a gift of God subsequent to the New Birth and manifested only by a changed life acceptable to the Lord.

Headquarters

430 Forest Ave., Cincinnati, OH 45229 Tel. (513)569-5660

Media Contact, Chief Bishop, W. E. Crumes

EXECUTIVE BOARD

Chief Bishop, W. E. Crumes

Vice-Chief Bishop, Robert D. Tyler, 3802 Bedford, Omaha, NE 68110

Exec. Sec., Bishop C. A. Lewis, 1360 N. Boston, Tulsa, OK 73111

Gen. Sec., Gwendolyn Robinson, 8611 S. University, Chicago, IL 60619

Gen. Treas., Elder Harry Hendricks, 11935 Cimarron Ave., Hawthorne, CA 90250

Bishop E. L. Bowie, 2037 N.E. 18th St., Oklahoma City, OK 73111

Chaplain, Bishop E. A. Morgan, 735 S. Oakland Dr., Decatur, IL 65525;

Bishop Luke C. Nichols, Louisville, KY

Bishop Jeff Ruffin, Phoenix, AZ

Bishop R. S. Morgan, 12100 Greystone,Terr., Oklahoma City, OK 73120

Bishop S. E. Shannon, 1034 S. King Hwy., St. Louis, MO 63110

Bishop J. C. Hawkins, 3804 N. Temple, Indianapolis, IN 46205

Overseer, Elbert Jones, 4522 Melwood, Memphis, TN 38109

NATIONAL DEPARTMENTS

Convention Planning Committee
Young People's Progressive Union
Christian Education Dept.
Sunday School Dept.
Natl. Evangelist Bd.
Natl. Nurses Guild
Natl. Women's Work Dept.
Natl. Music Dept.
Gen. Sec. Ofc.
Natl. Usher Board

Periodicals

The Gospel Truth

Church of the Lutheran Brethren of America

The Church of the Lutheran Brethren of America was organized in December 1900. Five independent Lutheran congregations met together in Milwaukee, Wisconsin, and adopted a constitution patterned very closely on that of the Lutheran Free Church of Norway.

The spiritual awakening in the Midwest during the 1890s crystallized into convictions that led to the formation of a new church body. Chief among the concerns were church membership practices, observance of Holy Communion, confirmation practices and local church government.

The Church of the Lutheran Brethren practices a simple order of worship with the sermon as the primary part of the worship service. It believes that personal profession of faith is the primary criterion for membership in the congregation. The Communion service is reserved for those who profess faith in Christ as savior. Each congregation is autonomous and the synod serves the congregations in advisory and cooperative capacities.

The synod supports a world mission program in Cameroon, Chad, Japan, and Taiwan. Approximately 40 percent of the synodical budget is earmarked for world missions. A growing home mission ministry is planting new congregations in the United States and Canada. Affiliate organizations operate several retirement, nursing homes, conference, and retreat centers.

Headquarters

1020 Alcott Ave., W., Box 655, Fergus Falls, MN 56538 Tel. (218)739-3336, Fax (218)739-5514

Media Contact, Pres., Rev. Joel Egge

Email: clba@clba.org

Website: www.clba.org/

Officers

Pres., Rev. Joel Egge

Vice-Pres., Rev. David Rinden

Sec., Rev. Richard Vettrus, 707 Crestview Dr., West Union, IA 52175

Exec. Dir. of Finance, Bradley Martinson

Lutheran Brethren Schools Representative, Dr. Eugene Boe

World Missions, Exec. Dir., Rev. Matthew Rogness

Home Missions, Exec. Dir., Rev. Armin Jahr

Church Services, Exec. Dir., Rev. Brent Juliot

Youth Ministries, Exec. Dir., Nathan Lee

Periodicals

Faith & Fellowship

Church of the Lutheran Confession

The Church of the Lutheran Confession held its constituting convention in Watertown, S.D., in August of 1960. The Church of the Lutheran Confession was begun by people and congregations who withdrew from church bodies that made up what was then known as the Synodical Conference over the issue of unionism. Following such passages as I Corinthians 1 vs.10 and Romans 16 vs.17-18, the Church of the Lutheran Confession holds the conviction that mutual agreement with the doctrines of Scripture is essential and necessary before exercise of church fellowship is appropriate.

Members of the Church of the Lutheran Confession uncompromisingly believe the Holy Scriptures to be divinely inspired and therefore inerrant. They subscribe to the historic Lutheran Confessions as found in the Book of Concord of 1580 because they are a correct exposition of Scripture.

The Church of the Lutheran Confession exists to proclaim, preserve, and spread the saving truth of the gospel of Jesus Christ, so that the redeemed of God may learn to know Jesus Christ as their Lord and Savior and follow him through this life to the life to come.

Headquarters

501 Grover Rd., Eau Claire, WI 54701 Tel. (715)836-6622

Media Contact, Pres., Daniel Fleischer Tel. (361)241-5147

Email: JohnHLau@juno.com

Website: www.clclutheran.org

Officers

Pres., Rev. Daniel Fleischer, 201 Princess Dr., Corpus Christi, TX 78410-1615

Vice-Pres., Rev. John Schierenbeck, 3015 Ave. K NW, Winter Haven, FL 33881

Mod., Prof. Ronald Roehl, 515 Ingram Dr. W., Eau Claire, WI 54701

Sec., Rev. James Albrecht, 102 Market St., P.O. Box 98 Okebena, MN 55432-2408

Treas., Lowell Moen, 3455 Jill Ave., Eau Claire, WI 54701

Archivist, Prof. David Lau, 507 Ingram Dr., Eau Claire, WI 54701

Statistician, Dr. James Sydow, 7863 Alden Way, Fridley, MN 55432-2408

Periodicals

The Lutheran Spokesman; Journal of Theology

Church of the Nazarene

The Church of the Nazarene resulted from the merger of three independent holiness groups. The Association of Pentecostal Churches in America, located principally in New York and New England, joined at Chicago in 1907 with a largely West Coast body called the Church of the Nazarene and formed the Pentecostal Church of the Nazarene. A southern group, the Holiness Church of Christ, united with the Pentecostal Church of the Nazarene at Pilot Point, Texas, in 1908. In 1919 the word "Pentecostal" was dropped from the name. Principal leaders in the organization were Phineas Bresee, William Howard Hoople, H. F. Reynolds and C. B. Jernigan. The first congregation in Canada was organized in November 1902 by Dr. H. F. Reynolds in Oxford, Nova Scotia.

The Church of the Nazarene emphasizes the doctrine of entire sanctification or Christian Holiness. It stresses the importance of a devout and holy life and a positive witness before the world by the power of the Holy Spirit. Nazarenes express their faith through evangelism, compassionate ministries, and education.

Nazarene government is representative, a studied compromise between episcopacy and congregationalism. Quadrennially, the various districts elect delegates to a general assembly at which six general superintendents are elected.

The international denomination has 9 liberal arts colleges, two graduate seminaries, 43 Bible colleges, two schools of nursing, and a junior college. The church maintains over 600 missionaries in 119 world areas. World services include medical, educational, and religious ministries. Books, periodicals, and other Christian literature are published at the Nazarene Publishing House.

The church is a member of the Christian Holiness Partnership and the National Association of Evangelicals.

Headquarters

6401 The Paseo, Kansas City, MO 64131 Tel. (816)333-7000, Fax (816)822-9071

Media Contact, Gen. Sec./Headquarters Operations Officer (HOO), Dr. Jack Stone, Tel. (816)333-7000, Ext. 2517

Website: www.nazarene.org

Officers

Gen. Supts., James H. Diehl; Paul G. Cunningham; Jerry D. Porter; Jim L. Bond; U. Talmadge Johnson; Jesse C. Middendorf;

Gen. Sec. (HOO), Jack Stone

Gen. Treas. (HFO), Robert Foster

OTHER ORGANIZATIONS

General Bd., Sec., Jack Stone; Treas., Robert Foster

USA-Canada Mission, Evangelism, Dir., Bill Sullivan

Clergy Services, Dir., Ron Blake

Communications, Dir., Michael Estep

NCN Productions, Dir., David Anderson

World Literature Ministries, Dir., Ray Hendrix

Int. Bd. of Educ., Ed. Commissioner, Jerry Lambert

Pensions & Benefits Services USA & Intl., Don Walter

Adult Min., Dir., David Felter

Children's Min., Dir., Lynda Boardman

Curriculum Dir., Randy Cloud

NYI Min., Dir., Gary Hartke

World Mission Div., Dir., Louie Bustle

Nazarene Mission International, Dir., Nina Gunter

Mission Strategy, Dir., Tom Nees

Information Technology and Research, Dir., Dale Jones

Periodicals

Holiness Today; Preacher's Magazine; Cross Walk; Grow Magazine

Church of Our Lord Jesus Christ of the Apostolic Faith, Inc.

This church body was founded by Bishop R.C. Lawson in Columbus, Ohio, and moved to New York City in 1919. It is founded upon the teachings of the apostles and prophets, Jesus Christ being its chief cornerstone.

Headquarters

2081 Adam Clayton Powell Jr. Blvd., New York, NY 10027 Tel. (212)866-1700

Media Contact, Exec. Sec., Bishop T. E. Woolfolk, P.O. Box 119, Oxford, NC 27565 Tel. (919)693-9449, Fax (919)693-6115

Email: tewmsw@gloryroad.net

Website: www.apostolic-faith.org/

Officers

Board of Apostles, Chief Apostle, Bishop William L. Bonner;

Presiding Apostle, Bishop Gentle L. Groover; Bishop Frank S. Solomon;

Vice-Presider, Bishop Matthew A. Norwood; Bishop James I. Clark, Jr.; Bishop Wilbur L. Jones; Bishop J. P. Steadman; Bishop Robert L. Sanders

Bd. of Bishops, Chmn., Bishop Henry A. Moultrie II

Bd. of Presbyters, Pres., Elder Michael A. Dixon

Exec. Sec., Bishop T. E. Woolfolk

Natl. Rec. Sec., Bishop Fred Rubin, Sr.

Natl. Fin. Sec., Bishop Clarence Groover

Natl. Corr. Sec., Bishop Raymond J. Keith, Jr.

Natl Treas., Elder Richard D. Williams

Periodicals

Contender for the Faith; Minute Book

Church of the United Brethren in Christ

The Church of the United Brethren in Christ had its beginning with Philip William Otterbein and Martin Boehm, who were leaders in the revival movement in Pennsylvania and Maryland from the late 1760s into the early 1800s.

On Sept. 25, 1800, they and others associated with them formed a society under the name of United Brethren in Christ. Subsequent conferences adopted a Confession of Faith in 1815 and a constitution in 1841. The Church of the United Brethren in Christ adheres to the original constitution as amended in 1957, 1961, and 1977.

Headquarters

302 Lake St., Huntington, IN 46750 Tel. (219) 356-2312, Fax (219)356-4730

Media Contact, Communications Dir., Steve Dennie

Email: sdennie@ub.org

Website: www.ub.org

Officers

Bishop, Dr. Ray A. Seilhamer

Gen. Treas., Office Mgr., Marda J. Hoffman

Dept. of Education, Dir., Dr. G. Blair Dowden

Dept. of Church Services, Dir., Rev. Paul Hirschy

Dept. of Missions, Dir., Rev. Kyle McQuillen

Churches of Christ

Churches of Christ are autonomous congregations whose members appeal to the Bible alone to determine matters of faith and practice. There are no central offices or officers. Publications and institutions related to the churches are either under local congregational control or independent of any one congregation.

Churches of Christ shared a common fellowship in the nineteenth century with the Christian Churches/Churches of Christ and the Christian Church (Disciples of Christ). Fellowship was gradually estranged following the Civil War due to theistic evolution, higher critical theories, centralization of church-wide activities through a missionary society, and addition of musical instruments.

Members of Churches of Christ believe in one God, one Lord and Savior, Jesus Christ, one Holy Spirit, one body or church of God, one baptism by immersion into Christ, one faith revealed in the Holy, inspired, inerrant scriptures, and one hope of eternal life based on the grace of God in Christ and a response by each individual of faith and obedience to God's gracious instructions in scripture. The New Testament pattern is followed for salvation and church membership, church organization and standards of Christian living.

Headquarters

Media Contact, Ed., Gospel Advocate, Mr. Neil Anderson, P.O. Box 150 Nashville, TN 37202 Tel. (800)251-8446, Fax (615)254-7411

Periodicals

Action; Christian Woman; Christian Bible Teacher; The Christian Chronicle; Firm Foundation; Gospel Advocate; Guardian of Truth; Restoration Quarterly; 21st Century Christian; Upreach; Rocky Mountain Christian; The Spiritual Sword; Word and Work

Churches of Christ in Christian Union

Organized in 1909 at Washington Court House, Ohio, as the Churches of Christ in Christian Union, this body believes in the new birth and the baptism of the Holy Spirit for believers. It is Wesleyan, with an evangelistic and missionary emphasis.

The Reformed Methodist Church merged with the Churches of Christ in Christian Union in 1952.

Headquarters

1426 Lancaster Pike, Box 30, Circleville, OH 43113 Tel. (614)474-8856, Fax (614)477-7766

Media Contact, Dir. of Comm., Rev. Ralph Hux

Email: devans@bright.net

Website: www.bright.net/~cccudoc/index.html

Officers

Gen. Supt., Dr. Daniel Tipton

Asst. Gen. Supt., Rev. Ron Reese

Gen. Treas.,

Gen. Bd. of Trustees, Chpsn., Dr. Daniel Tipton; Vice-Chpsn., Rev. Ron Reese

District Superintendents, West Central District, Rev. Ron Reese; South Central District, Rev. Don Spurgeon; Northeast District, Rev. Don Seymour; West Indies District, Rev. Stafford Prosper

Periodicals

The Evangelical Advocate

Churches of God, General Conference

The Churches of God, General Conference (CGGC) had its beginnings in Harrisburg, Pa., in 1825.

John Winebrenner, recognized founder of the Church of God movement, was an ordained minister of the German Reformed Church. His experience-centered form of Christianity, particularly the "new measures" he used to promote it, his close connection with the local Methodists, his "experience and conference meetings" in the church and his "social prayer meetings" in parishioners' homes resulted in differences of opinion and the establishment of new congregations. Extensive revivals, camp meetings, and mission endeavors led to the organization of additional congregations across central Pennsylvania and westward through Ohio, Indiana, Illinois, and Iowa.

In 1830 the first system of cooperation between local churches was initiated as an "eldership" in eastern Pennsylvania. The organization of other elderships followed. General Eldership was organized in 1845, and in 1974 the official name of the denomination was changed from General Eldership of the Churches of God in North America to its present name.

The Churches of God, General Conference, is composed of 16 conferences in the United States and 1 conference in Haiti. The polity of the church is presbyterial in form. The church has mission ministries in the southwest among native Americans and is extensively involved in church planting and whole life ministries in Bangladesh, Brazil, Haiti, and India.

The General Conference convenes in business session triennially. An Administrative Council composed of 16 regional representatives is responsible for the administration and ministries of the church between sessions of the General Conference.

Headquarters

Legal Headquarters, United Church Center, Rm. 213, 900 S. Arlington Ave., Harrisburg, PA 17109 Tel. (717)652-0255

Administrative Offices, General Conf. Exec. Dir., Pastor Wayne W. Boyer, 700 E. Melrose Ave., P.O. Box 926, Findlay, OH 45839 Tel. (419)424-1961, Fax (419)424-3343

Media Contact, Editor, Rachel L. Foreman, P.O. Box 926, Findlay, OH 45839 Tel. (419) 424-1961, Fax (419)424-3343

Email: director@cggc.org

Website: www.cggc.org

Officers

Pres., Pastor Robert L. Eatherton, 716 N SR 109, Columbia City, IN 46725, Tel. (210)248-8517, Fax (219)244-9663, director@midwestcggc.org

Sec., Pastor E. David Green, 700 E. Melrose Ave., P.O. Box 1132, Findlay, OH 45839 Tel. (419)423-3869, green.occg@juno.com

Treas., Robert E. Stephenson, 700 E. Melrose Ave., P.O. Box 926, Findlay, OH 45839 Tel. (419)424-1961

DEPARTMENTS

Cross-Cultural Ministries, Pastor Don Dennison

Pensions, Mr. James P. Thomas

Denominational Communications, Rachel L. Foreman

Church Renewal, Pastor Keith L. Raderstorf

Church Planting, Pastor Charles A. Hirschy

Youth & Family Life Ministries, Susan L. Callaway

Periodicals

The Church Advocate; The Gem; The Missionary Signal

Community of Christ

Community of Christ's mission is to proclaim Jesus Christ and promote communities of joy, hope, love, and peace. Founded on April 6, 1830, this Christian denomination is present in nearly 50 nations with approximately 250,000 members worldwide. The church's Temple, located in the international headquarters complex, is dedicated to peace, reconciliation, and healing of the Spirit. Priesthood includes both men and women.

Headquarters

International Headquarters, 1001 W. Walnut, Independence, MO 54050-3562 Tel. (816) 833-1000, Fax (816)521-3096

Media Contact; Kendra Friend, kfriend@cofchrist.org; or Jennifer Killpack, jkillpack@cofchrist. org

Website: www.cofchrist.org

Officers

First Presidency

President, W. Grant McMurray, gmcmurray@cofchrist.org

Counselor, Kenneth N. Robinson, krobinson@cofchrist.org

Counselor, Peter A. Judd, pjudd@cofchrist.org

Council of Twelve Apostles

President, A. Alex Kahtava, akahtava@cofchrist.org

Presiding Bishopric

Presiding Bishop, Larry R. Norris, lnorris@cofchrist.org

Counselor, Orval G. Fisher, ofisher@cofchrist.org

Counselor, Stephen M. Jones, sjones@cofchrist.org

Presiding Evangelist

Danny A. Belrose, dbelrose@cofchrist.org

World Church Secretary

A. Bruce Lindgren, blindgren@cofchrist.org

Public Relations, Fax (816)521-3043

Kendra Friend, kfriend@cofchrist.org

Jennifer Killpack, jkillpack@cofchrist.org

Periodicals

Herald; Restoration Witness

Congregational Holiness Church

This body was organized in 1921 and embraces the doctrine of Holiness and Pentecost. It carries on mission work in Mexico, Honduras, Costa Rica, Cuba, Brazil, Guatemala, India, Nicaragua, El Salvador, Venezula, Panama, and Chile.

Headquarters

3888 Fayetteville Hwy., Griffin, GA 30223 Tel. (404)228-4833, Fax (404)228-1177

Media Contact, Gen. Supt., Bishop Chet Smith

Email: chchurch@bellsouth.net

Website: www.ch.church.com

EXECUTIVE BOARD

Gen. Supt., Bishop Chet Smith

1st Asst. Gen. Supt., Rev. William L. Lewis

2nd Asst. Gen. Supt., Rev. Wayne Hicks

Gen. Sec., Rev. Leslee Bailey

Gen. Treas., Rev. Stephen Phillips

Periodicals

The Gospel Messenger

Conservative Baptist Association of America (CBAmerica)

The Conservative Baptist Association of America (now known as CBAmerica) was organized May 17, 1947 at Atlantic City, N.J. The Old and New Testaments are regarded as the divinely inspired Word of God and are therefore infallible and of supreme authority. Each local church is independent, autonomous, and free from ecclesiastical or political authority.

CBAmerica provides wide-ranging support to its affiliate churches and individuals through nine regional associations. CBA offers personnel to assist churches in areas such as growth and health conflict resolution and financial analysis. The association supports its clergy with retirement planning, referrals for new places of ministry, and spiritual counseling. The Conservative Baptist Women's Ministries assists women in the church to be effective in their personal growth and leadership.

Each June or July there is a National Conference giving members an opportunity for fellowship, inspiration, and motivation.

Headquarters

1501 W. Mineral Ave., Suite B, Littleton, CO 80120-5612 Tel. (888)627-1995 or (720)283-3030, Fax (720)283-3333

Media Contact, Executive Director, Dr. Dennis L. Gorton

Email: cba@cbamerica.org

Website: www.cbamerica.org

OTHER ORGANIZATIONS

CBInternational, Exec. Dir., Dr. Hans Finzel, 1501 W. Mineral Ave., Littleton, CO 80120-5612

Mission to the Americas, Exec. Dir., Rev. Rick Miller, Box 828, Wheaton, IL 60189

Conservative Baptist Higher Ed. Council, Dr. Bert Downs, Western Seminary, 5511 S. E. Hawthorne Blvd., Portland, OR 97215

Periodicals

Spectrum; Front Line

Conservative Congregational Christian Conference

In the 1930s, evangelicals within the Congregational Christian Churches felt a definite need for fellowship and service. By 1945, this loose association crystallized into the Conservative Congregational Christian Fellowship, committed to maintaining a faithful, biblical witness.

In 1948 in Chicago, the Conservative Congregational Christian Conference was established to provide a continuing fellowship for evangelical churches and ministers on the national level. In recent years, many churches have joined the Conference from backgrounds other than Congregational. These churches include Community or Bible Churches and churches from the Evangelical and Reformed background that are truly congregational in polity and thoroughly evangelical in conviction. The CCCC welcomes all evangelical churches that are, in fact, congregational. The CCCC believes in the necessity of a regenerate membership, the authority of the Holy Scriptures, the Lordship of Jesus Christ, the autonomy of the local church, and the universal fellowship of all Christians.

The Conservative Congregational Christian Conference is a member of the World Evangelical Congregational Fellowship (formed in 1986 in London, England) and the National Association of Evangelicals.

Headquarters

7582 Currell Blvd., Ste. #108, St. Paul, MN 55125 Tel. (651)739-1474, Fax (651)739-0750

Media Contact, Conf. Min., Rev. Clifford R. Christensen

Email: CCCC4@juno.com

Website: www.ccccusa.org/

Officers

Pres., Rev. Edward Whitman, 59 Province Rd., Barrington, NH 03825

Vice-Pres., Rev. Larry Scovil, 317 W. 40th Street, Scottsbluff, NE 69361

Conf. Min., Rev. Clifford R. Christensen, 457 S. Mary St., Maplewood, MN 55119

Controller, Mr. Orrin Bailey, 4260 East Lake Rd., Muskegon, MI 49444

Treas., Rev. Tay Kersey, 8450 Eastwood Rd., Moundsview, MN 55112

Sec., Rev. Peter Murdy, 4 Plympton St., Middleboro, MA 02346

Editor, Mr. Bill Nygren, P.O. Box 423, La Pointe, WI 54850

Historian, Rev. Milton Reimer, 507 Central Ave., New Rockford, ND 58356

Periodicals

Foresee

Conservative Lutheran Association

The Conservative Lutheran Association (CLA) was originally named Lutheran's Alert National (LAN) when it was founded in 1965 by 10 conservative Lutheran pastors and laymen meeting in Cedar Rapids, Iowa. Its purpose was to help preserve from erosion the basic doctrines of Christian theology, including the inerrancy of Holy Scripture. The group grew to a worldwide constituency, similarly concerned with maintaining the doctrinal integrity of the Bible and the Lutheran Confessions.

Headquarters

Trinity Lutheran Church, 4101 E. Nohl Ranch Rd., Anaheim, CA 92807 Tel. (714)637-8370

Media Contact, Pres., Rev. P. J. Moore

Email: PastorPJ@ix.netcom.com

Website: www.tlcanaheim.com/CLA/

fficers

Pres., Rev. P. J. Moore, 4101 E. Nohl Ranch Rd., Anaheim, CA 92807 Tel. (714)637-8370

Vice-Pres., Rev. Dr. R. H. Redal, 409 Tacoma Ave. N., Tacoma, WA 98403 Tel. (206)383-5528

Faith Seminary, Dean, Rev. Dr. Michael J. Adams, 3504 N. Pearl St., P.O. Box 7186, Tacoma, WA 98407 Tel. (888)777-7675, Fax (206)759-1790

Coptic Orthodox Church*

This body is part of the ancient Coptic Orthodox Church of Alexandria, Egypt which is currently headed by His Holiness Pope Shenouda III, 116th Successor to St. Mark the Apostle.

Egyptian immigrants have organized many parishes in the United States. Copts exist outside Egypt in Africa, Europe, Asia, Australia, Canada, and the United States. The total world Coptic community is estimated at 27 million. The church is in full communion with the other members of The Oriental Orthodox Church Family, The Syrian Orthodox Church, Armenian Orthodox Church, Ethiopian Orthodox Church, the Syrian Orthodox Church in India, and the Eritrean Orthodox Church.

Headquarters

5 Woodstone Dr., Cedar Grove, NJ 07009
4909 Cleland Ave., Los Angeles, CA 90042 Tel. (323)254-3333, Fax (323)254-2340
Media Contact, Fr. Abraam D. Sleman
Email: www.coptic.org/
Website: Webmaster@coptic.org

Officers

Bishop of Los Angeles, Bishop Serapion, 4909 Serapion Ave., Los Angeles, CA 90042 Tel. (323)254-3333, Fax (323)254-2340, bishopserapion@lacoptic.org

Periodicals

Agapg Magazine, El Karaza

Cumberland Presbyterian Church

The Cumberland Presbyterian Church was organized in Dickson County, Tennessee, on Feb. 4, 1810. It was an outgrowth of the Great Revival of 1800 on the Kentucky and Tennessee frontier. The founders were Finis Ewing, Samuel King, and Samuel McAdow, ministers in the Presbyterian Church who rejected the doctrine of election and reprobation as taught in the Westminster Confession of Faith.

By 1813, the Cumberland Presbytery had grown to encompass three presbyteries, which constituted a synod. This synod met at the Beech Church in Sumner County, Tenn., and formulated a "Brief Statement" which set forth the points in which Cumberland Presbyterians dissented from the Westminster Confession. These points are:

1. That there are no eternal reprobates;
2. That Christ died not for some, but for all people;
3. That all those dying in infancy are saved through Christ and the sanctification of the Spirit;
4. That the Spirit of God operates on the world, or as coextensively as Christ has made atonement, in such a manner as to leave everyone inexcusable.

From its birth in 1810, the Cumberland Presbyterian Church grew to a membership of 200,000 at the turn of the century. In 1906 the church voted to merge with the then-Presbyterian Church. Those who dissented from the merger became the nucleus of the continuing Cumberland Presbyterian Church.

Headquarters

1978 Union Ave., Memphis, TN 38104 Tel. (901)276-4572, Fax (901)272-3913
Media Contact, Stated Clk., Rev. Robert D. Rush, Fax (901)276-4578
Email: assembly@cumberland.org
Website: www.cumberland.org

Officers

Mod., Randy Jacob, P.O. Box 158, Broken Bow, OK 74728 Tel. (580)584-2099
Stated Clk., Rev. Robert D. Rush, Tel.(901)276-4572 Fax (901) 276-4578
General Assembly Council, Exec. Dir., Davis Gray, Tel.(901)276-4572 x. 3316, Fax (901) 272-3913

INSTITUTIONS

Cumberland Presbyterian Children's Home, Exec. Dir., Rev. Dr. Judy Keith, Drawer G, Denton, TX 76202 Tel. (940)382-5112, Fax (940)387-0821, cpch@gte.net
Cumberland Presbyterian Center, Tel.(901)276-4572, Fax (901)272-3913
Memphis Theological Seminary, 168 E. Parkway S., Memphis, TN 38104 Tel. (901)458-8232, Fax (901)452-4051
Bethel College, Pres., Dr. Robert Prosser, 325 Cherry St., McKenzie, TN 38201 Tel. (901)352-4004, Fax (901)352-4069, rprosser @bethel-college.edu
Historical Foundation, Archivist, Susan K. Gore, 1978 Union Avenue, Memphis, TN 38104 Tel. (901)276-8602, Fax (901)272-3913

BOARDS

Bd. of Christian Education, Exec. Dir., Claudette Pickle
Bd. of Missions, Exec. Dir., Rev. Michael Sharpe
Bd. of Stewardship, Exec. Sec., Rev. Richard Magrill
Bd. Of the Cumberland Presbyterian, Editor, Mrs. Pat Pottorrff Richards

Periodicals

The Cumberland Presbyterian; The Missionary Messenger

Cumberland Presbyterian Church in America

This church, originally known as the Colored Cumberland Presbyterian Church, was formed in May 1874. In May 1869, at the General Assembly meeting in Murfreesboro, Tennessee, Moses Weir of the Black delegation sucessfully appealed for help in organizing a separate African church so that: Blacks could learn self-reliance and independence; they could have more financial assistance; they could minister more effectively among Blacks; and they could worship close to the altar, not in the balconies. He requested that the Cumberland Presbyterian Church organize Blacks into presbyteries and synods, develop schools to train black clergy, grant loans to assist Blacks to secure hymnbooks, Bibles, and church buildings, and establish a separate General Assembly.

In 1874 the first General Assembly of the

Colored Cumberland Presbyterian Church met in Nashville. The moderator was Rev. P. Price and the stated clerk was Elder John Humphrey.

The denomination's General Assembly, the national governing body, is organized around its three program boards and agencies: Finance, Publication and Christian Education, and Missions and Evangelism. Other agencies of the General Assembly are under these three program boards.

The church has four synods (Alabama, Kentucky, Tennessee, and Texas), 15 presbyteries and 153 congregations. The CPC extends as far north as Cleveland, Ohio, and Chicago, as far west as Marshalltown, Iowa, and Dallas, Tex., and as far south as Selma, Ala.

Headquarters

Media Contact, Stated Clk., Rev. Dr. Robert. Stanley Wood, 226 Church St., Huntsville, AL 35801 Tel. (205)536-7481, Fax (205)536-7482
Email: mleslie598@aol.com
Website: www.cumberland.org/cpca/

Officers

Mod., Rev. Endia Scruggs, 1627 Carroll Rd., Harvest, AL 35749
Stated Clk., Rev. Dr. Rorbert. Stanley Wood, 226 Church St., Huntsville, AL 35801 Tel. (205) 536-7481

SYNODS

Alabama, Stated Clk., Arthur Hinton, 511 10th Ave. N.W., Aliceville, AL 35442
Kentucky, Stated Clk., Mary Martha Daniels, 8548 Rhodes Ave., Chicago, IL 60619
Tennessee, Stated Clk., Elder Clarence Norman, 145 Jones St., Huntington, TN 38334
Texas, Stated Clk., Arthur King, 2435 Kristen, Dallas, TX 75216

Periodicals

The Cumberland Flag

Disciples of Christ—please see Christian Church (Disciples of Christ) in the United States and Canada.

Elim Fellowship

The Elim Fellowship, a Pentecostal Body established in 1947, is an outgrowth of the Elim Missionary Assemblies formed in 1933.

It is an association of churches, ministers and missionaries seeking to serve the whole Body of Christ. It is of Pentecostal conviction and charismatic orientation, providing ministerial credentials and counsel and encouraging fellowship among local churches. Elim Fellowship sponsors leadership seminars at home and abroad and serves as a transdenominational agency sending long-term, short-term, and tent-making missionaries to work with national movements.

Headquarters

1703 Dalton Rd., Lima, NY 14485 Tel. (716)582-2790, Fax (716)624-1229
Media Contact, Gen. Sec., Paul Anderson
Email: 75551.743@compuserve.com
Website: www.ElimFellowship.org

Officers

Gen. Chairman, Bernard J. Evans
Asst. Gen. Chairman, Ron Burgio
Gen. Treas., Michael McDonald

Periodicals

Elim Herald

Episcopal Church*

The Episcopal Church entered the colonies with the earliest settlers at Jamestown, Va., in 1607 as the Church of England. After the American Revolution, it became autonomous in 1789 as The Protestant Episcopal Church in the United States of America. (The Episcopal Church became the official alternate name in 1967.) Samuel Seabury of Connecticut was elected the first bishop and consecrated in Aberdeen by bishops of the Scottish Episcopal Church in 1784.

In organizing as an independent body, the Episcopal Church created a bicameral legislature, the General Convention, modeled after the new U.S. Congress. It comprises a House of Bishops and a House of Deputies and meets every three years. A 38-member Executive Council, which meets three times a year, is the interim governing body. An elected presiding bishop serves as Primate and Chief Pastor.

After severe setbacks in the years immediately following the Revolution because of its association with the British Crown and the fact that a number of its clergy and members were Loyalists, the church soon established its own identity and sense of mission. It sent missionaries into the newly settled territories of the United States, establishing dioceses from coast to coast, and also undertook substantial missionary work in Africa, Latin America, and the Far East. Today, the overseas dioceses are developing into independent provinces of the Anglican Communion, the worldwide fellowship of 36 churches in communion with the Church of England and the Archbishop of Canterbury.

The beliefs and practices of The Episcopal Church, like those of other Anglican churches, are both Catholic and Reformed, with bishops in the apostolic succession and the historic creeds of Christendom regarded as essential elements of faith and order, along with the primary authority of Holy Scripture and the two chief sacraments of Baptism and Eucharist.

EPISCOPAL CHURCH CENTER

815 Second Ave., New York, NY 10017 Tel. (212)716-6240 or (800)334-7626, Fax (212) 867-0395 or (212)490-3298
Media Contact, Dir. of News & Info., James Solheim, Tel. (212)922-5385
Email: jrollins@ecusa.anglican.org
Website: www.ecusa.anglican.org

Officers

Presiding Bishop & Primate, Most Rev. Frank Tracy Griswold III

Vice Pres. Assist. to the Presiding Bishop for Administration, Patricia C. Mordecai

Assistant to the Presiding Bishop for Communication, Barbara L. Braver

Assistant to the Presiding Bishop for Program, Ms. Sonia Francis

Treas., Stephen C. Duggan

Canon to the Primate and Presiding Bishop, The Rev. Canon Carlson Gerdau

House of Deputies, Pres., The Very Rev. George L. Werner

Exec. Officer of the General Convention, Sec. Of the House of Deputies, Sec. Of the Domestic and Foreign Missionary Society, and Sec. Of the Executive Council, The Rev. Rosemari Sullivan

OFFICE OF THE PRESIDING BISHOP

Presiding Bishop, Most Rev. Frank Tracy Griswold III, Tel. (212)9229-5322

Vice Pres. Assistant to the Presiding Bishop for Administration, Patricia Mordecai, Tel. (212) 922-5313

Canon to the Presiding Bishop, Rev. Canon Carl Gerdau, Tel. (212)922-5282

Exec. Dir., Church Deployment Office, The Rev. James G. Wilson, Tel. (212)922-5251

Coordinator for Ministry Development, The Rev. Dr. Melford E. Holland, Jr., Tel. (212)922-5246

Exec. Dir., Office of Pastoral Dev., Rt. Rev. F. Clayton Mathews, Tel. (212)716-6163

Exec. Sec., General Board of Examining Chaplains, The Rev. Locke E. Bowman Jr., Tel. (919)489-1422

Suffragan Bishop for the Armed Services, Healthcare and Prison Ministries, Rt. Rev., George Packard, Tel. (212)922-5240

Suffragan Bishop for American Churches in Europe, Rt. Rev. Pierre W. Whalon, Tel. (011)33-1-472-01792

Dir., Ecumenical and Interfaith Relations, The Rt. Rev. Canon C. Christopher Epting, Tel. (212)716-6220

ADMINISTRATION AND FINANCE

Treasurer of the Domestic and Foreign Missionary Society and of the General Convention, Stephen C. Duggan, Tel. (212) 922-5296

Controller, Thomas Hershkowitz, Tel. (212)922-5366

Archivist, Mark Duffy, Tel. (800)525-9329

Human Resources, John Colon, Tel. (212)922-5158

SERVICE, EDUCATION AND WITNESS

Asst. to the Presiding Bishop for Program, Sonia Francis, Tel. (212)922-5198

Dir., Anglican and Global Relations, The Rev. Canon Patrick Mauney, Tel. (212)716-6223

Editor, Episcopal Life, Jerry Hames, Tel. (212) 716-6009

Interim Dir., Media Services, The Rev. Clement Lee, Tel. (212)922-5386

Dir., News & Information, James Solheim, Tel. (212)922-5385

Dir., Migration Ministries, Richard Parkins, Tel. (212)716-6252

Dir., Peace & Justice Ministries, The Rev. Brian Grieves, Tel. (212)922-5207

Dir., Ministries to the Young & Young Adult Ministries Staff Officer, Thomas Chu, Tel. (212)922-5267

Exec Dir., Episcopal Relief and Development, Sandra Swan, Tel. (212)716-6020

BISHOPS IN THE U.S.A.

(C)= Coadjutor; (S)= Suffragan; (A)= Assistant

Address: Right Reverend

Presiding Bishop & Primate, Most Rev. Frank Tracy Griswold III; Pastoral Dev., The Rt. Rev. F. Clayton Matthews

Alabama: Henry N. Parsley, Jr., 521 N. 20th St., Birmingham, AL 35203, (205)715-2066

Alaska: Mark MacDonald, David Elsensohn, 1205 Denali Way, Fairbanks, AK 99701-4137 Tel. (907)452-3040

Albany: Daniel W. Herzog, 68 S. Swan St., Albany, NY 12210-2301 Tel. (518)465-4737

Arizona: Robert Shahan, 114 W.Roosevelt, Phoenix, AZ 85003-1406 Tel. (602)254-0976

Arkansas: Larry E. Maze, P.O. Box 162668, Little Rock, AR 72216-4668 Tel. (501)372-2168

Atlanta: John Neil Alexander, 2744 Peachtree Rd. N.W., Atlanta, GA 30363 Tel. (404)365-1010

Bethlehem: Paul Marshall, 333 Wyandotte St., Bethlehem, PA 18015 Tel. (610)691-5655

California: William E. Swing, 1055 Taylor St., San Francisco, CA 94115 Tel. (415)288-9712

Central Florida: John H. Howe, 1017 E. Robinson St., Orlando, FL 32801 Tel. (407) 423-3567

Central Gulf Coast: Philip M. Duncan II, P.O. Box 13330, Pensacola, FL 32591-3330 Tel. (904)434-7337

Central New York: Gladstone B. Adams III, 310 Montgomery St., Ste. 200, Syracuse, NY 13202 Tel. (315)474-6596

Central Pennsylvania: Michael Creighton, P.O. Box 11937, Harrisburg, PA 17108 Tel. (717) 236-5959

Chicago: William D. Persell, 65 E. Huron St., Chicago, IL 60611 Tel. (312)751-4200

Colorado: William J. Winterrowd, 1300 Washington St., Denver, CO 802^3 Tel. (303) 837-1173

Connecticut: Andrew D. Smith, 1335 Asylum Ave., Hartford, CT 06105 Tel. (203)233-4481

Dallas: James M. Stanton, 1630 Garrett St., Dallas, TX 75206 Tel. (214)826-8310

Delaware: Wayne P. Wright, 2020 Tatnall St., Wilmington, DE 19802 Tel. (302)656-5441

East Carolina: Clifton Daniel III, P.O. Box 1336, Kinston, NC 28501 Tel. (919)522-0885

East Tennessee: Charles Von Rosenberg, 401 Cumberland Ave., Knoxville, TN 37902-2302 Tel. (615)521-2900

Eastern Michigan: Edward Leidel, 4611 Swede Ave., Midland, MI 48642 Tel. (517)752-6020

Eastern Oregon: William O. Gregg, P.O. Box 620, The Dalles, OR 97058 Tel. (541)298-4477

Easton: Martin G. Townsend, P.O. Box 1027, Easton, MD 21601 Tel. (410)822-1919

Eau Claire: Keith B. Whitmore, 510 S. Farwell St., Eau Claire, WI 54701 Tel. (715)835-3331

El Camino Real: Richard Shimpfky, P.O. Box 1903, Monterey, CA 93940 Tel. (408)394-4465

Florida: Stephen H. Jecko, 325 Market St., Jacksonville, FL 32202 Tel. (904)356-1328

Fond du Lac: Russell E. Jacobus, P.O. Box 149, Fond du Lac, WI 54936 Tel. (414)921-8866

Fort Worth: Jack Iker, 6300 Ridgelea Pl., Ste. 1100, Fort Worth, TX 76116 Tel. (817)738-9952

Georgia: Henry Louttit, Jr., 611 East Bay St., Savannah, GA 31401 Tel. (912)236-4279

Hawaii: Richard Chang, 229 Queen Emma Square, Honolulu, HI 96813 Tel. (808)536-7776

Idaho: Harry B. Bainbridge, P.O. Box 936, Boise, ID 83701 Tel. (208)345-4440

Indianapolis: Catherine M. Waynick,1100 W. 42nd St., Indianapolis, IN 46208 Tel. (317)926-5454

Iowa: -vacant, 225 37th St., Des Moines, IA 50312 Tel. (515)277-6165

Kansas: William E. Smalley, 833-35 Polk St., Topeka, KS 66612 Tel. (913)235-9255

Kentucky: Edwin F. Gulick, 600 E. Maine, Louisville, KY 40202 Tel. (502)584-7148

Lexington: Stacy F. Sauls, P.O. Box 610, Lexington, KY 40586 Tel. (606)252-6527

Long Island: Orris G. Walker, 36 Cathedral Ave., Garden City, NY 11530 Tel. (516)248-4800

Los Angeles: J. Jon Bruno; Chester Talton, (S), P.O. Box 2164, Los Angeles, CA 90051 Tel. (213)482-2040

Louisiana: Charles E. Jenkins, 1623 7th St., New Orleans, LA 70115-4411 Tel. (504)895-6634

Maine: Chilton Knudsen, 143 State St., Portland, ME 04101 Tel. (207)772-1953

Maryland: Bob Ihloff, 4 East University Pkwy., Baltimore, MD 21218-2437 Tel. (410)467-1399

Massachusetts: M. Thomas Shaw, SSJE; Barbara Harris, (S), 138 Tremont St., Boston, MA 02111 Tel. (617)482-5800

Michigan: Wendell N. Gibbs, 4800 Woodward Ave., Detroit, MI 48201 Tel. (313)832-4400

Milwaukee: Roger J. White, 804 E. Juneau Ave., Milwaukee, WI 53202 Tel. (414)272-3028

Minnesota: James L. Jelinek; 430 Oak Grove St., #306, Minneapolis, MN 55403 Tel. (612)871-5311

Mississippi: Alfred C. Marble, P.O. Box 23107, Jackson, MS 39225-3107 Tel. (601)948-5954

Missouri: Hays Rockwell, 1210 Locust St., St. Louis, MO 63103 Tel. (314)231-1220

Montana: -vacant, 515 North Park Ave., Helena, MT 59601 Tel. (406)442-2230

Nebraska: James E. Krotz, 200 N. 62nd St., Omaha, NE 68132 Tel. (402)341-5373

Nevada: Katharin Jefferts Schori, P.O. Box 6357, Reno, NV 89513 Tel. (702)737-9190

New Hampshire: Douglas E. Theuner, 63 Green St., Concord, NH 03301 Tel. (603)224-1914

New Jersey: -vacant, 808 W. State St., Trenton, NJ 08618

New York: Mark Sisk, 1047 Amsterdam Ave., New York, NY 10025 Tel. (212)316-7413

Newark: Jack Croneberger; Jack McKelvey, (S), 24 Rector St., Newark, NJ 07102 Tel. (201) 622-4306

North Carolin: Michael B. Curry, 201 St. Albans Dr., Raleigh, NC 27619 Tel. (919)787-6313

North Dakota: Andrew H. Fairfield, P.O. Box 10337, Fargo, ND 58106-0337 Tel. (701)235-6688

Northern California: Jerry A. Lamb, P.O. Box 161268, Sacramento, CA 95816 Tel. (916) 442-6918

Northern Indiana: Eduard S. Little, 117 N. Lafayette Blvd., South Bend, IN 46601 Tel. (219)233-6489

Northern Michigan: James Kelsey, 131 E. Ridge St., Marquette, MI 49855 Tel. (906)228-7160

Northwest Texas: C. Wallis Ohl, Jr., P.O. Box 1067, Lubbock, TX 79408 Tel. (806)763-1370

Northwestern Pennsylvania: Robert D. Rowley, 145 W. 6th St., Erie, PA 16501 Tel. (814)456-4203

Ohio: J. Clark Grew; Arthur B. Williams, (S), 2230 Euclid Ave., Cleveland, OH 44115 Tel. (216)771-4815

Oklahoma: Robert M. Moody; William J. Cox, (A), 924 N. Robinson, Oklahoma City, OK 73102 Tel. (405)232-4820

Olympia: Vincent W. Warner, P.O. Box 12126, Seattle, WA 98102 Tel. (206)325-4200

Oregon: Robert Louis Ladehoff, P.O. Box 467, Portland, OR 97034 Tel. (503)636-5613

Pennsylvania: Charles Bennison, 240 S. 4th St., Philadelphia, PA 19106 Tel. (215)627-6434

Pittsburgh: Robert W. Duncan, Jr., 325 Oliver Ave., Pittsburgh, PA 15222 Tel. (412)281-6131

Quincy: Keith L. Ackerman, 3601 N. North St., Peoria: IL 61604 Tel. (309)688-8221

Rhode Island: Geralyn Wolf, 275 N. Main St., Providence, RI 02903 Tel. (401)274-4500

Rio Grande: Terence Kelshaw, 4304 Carlisle St. NE, Albuquerque, NM 87107 Tel. (505)881-0636

Rochester: William G. Burrill, 935 East Ave., Rochester, NY 14607 Tel. (716)473-2977

San Diego: Gethin B. Hughes, St. Paul's Church, 2728 6th Ave., San Diego, CA 92103 Tel. (619)291-5947

San Joaquin: John-David Schofield, 4159 East Dakota Ave., Fresno, CA 93726 Tel. (209)244-4828

South Carolina: Edward L. Salmon, P.O. Box 20127, Charleston, SC 29413-0127 Tel. (843) 722-4075

South Dakota: Creighton Robertson, 500 S. Main St., Sioux Falls, SD 57102-0914 Tel. (605) 338-9751

Southeast Florida: Leopold Frade, 525 N.E. 15th St., Miami, FL 33132 Tel. (305)373-0881

Southern Ohio: Herbert Thompson, Jr.; Kenneth Price, (S), 412 Sycamore St., Cincinnati, OH 45202 Tel. (513)421-0311

Southern Virginia: David C. Bane, Jr., 600 Talbot Hall Rd., Norfolk, VA 23505 Tel. (804)423-8287

Southwest Florida: Rogers S. Harris, P.O. Box 491, St. Petersburg, FL 33731 Tel. (941)776-1018

Southwestern Virginia: John B. Lipscomb, P.O. Box 2279, Roanoke, VA 24009 Tel. (703)342-6797

Spokane: James E. Waggoner 245 E. 13th Ave., Spokane, WA 99202 Tel. (509)624-3191

Springfield, Peter H. Beckwith, 821 S. Second St., Springfield, IL 62704 Tel. (217)525-1876

Tennessee, Bertram M. Herlong, One LaFleur Bldg., Ste. 100, 50 Vantage Way, Nashville, TN 37228 Tel. (615)251-3322

Texas, Claude E. Payne, 3203 W. Alabama St., Houston, TX 77098 Tel. (713)520-6444

Upper South Carolina, Dorsey F. Henderson, Jr., P.O. Box 1789, Columbia, SC 29202 Tel. (803)771-7800

Utah, Carolyn Irish, 231 E. First St. S., Salt Lake City, UT 84111 Tel. (801)322-4131

Vermont, Thomas C. Ely, Rock Point, Burlington, VT 05401 Tel. (802)863-3431

Virginia, Peter J. Lee, (S), 110 W. Franklin St., Richmond, VA 23220 Tel. (804)643-8451

Washington, Jane H. Dixon, Bp Pro. Tem. (S), Episc. Church House, Mt. St. Alban, Washington, DC 20016 Tel. (202)537-6555

West Missouri, John Buchanan, P.O. Box 413216, Kansas City, MO 64141 Tel. (816)471-6161

West Tennessee: James M. Coleman, 692 Poplar Ave., Memphis, TN 38105 Tel. (901)526-0023

West Texas: James E. Folts; Earl N. MacArthur, (S), P.O. Box 6885, San Antonio, TX 78209 Tel. (210)824-5387

West Virginia: William M. Klusmeyer, P.O. Box 5400, Charleston, WV 25361-0400 Tel. (304) 344-3597

Western Kansas: Vernon Strickland, P.O. Box 2507, Salina, KS 67402 Tel. (913)825-1626

Western Louisiana: Robert J. Hargrove, Jr., P.O. Box 2031, Alexandria, LA 71309-2031 Tel. (318)442-1304

Western Massachusetts: Gordon P. Scruton, 37 Chestnut St., Springfield, MA 01103 Tel. (413)737-4786

Western Michigan: Edward L. Lee, 2600 Vincent Ave., Kalamazoo, MI 49008 Tel. (616)381-2710

Western New York: J. Michael Garrison, 1114 Delaware Ave., Buffalo, NY 14209 Tel. (716) 881-0660

Western North Carolina: Robert H. Johnson, P.O. Box 369, Black Mountain, NC 28711 Tel. (704)669-2921

Wyoming: Bruce Caldwell, 104 S. Fourth St., Laramie, WY 82070 Tel. (307)742-6606

Am. Churches in Europe-Jurisdiction: Pierre W. Whalon, The American Cathedral, 23 Avenue Georges V, 75008, Paris, France

Navajoland Area Mission: Steven Plummer, P.O. Box 40, Bluff, UT 84512 Tel. (505)327-7549

Periodicals

Episcopal Life

The Episcopal Orthodox Church

This Church was established in 1963 as a self-governing Anglican Body, known then as the Anglican Orthodox Church. It has been described as the "much more conservative cousin" of the Episcopal Church USA in NBC News anchor, Tom Brokaw's best seller, The Greatest Generation. The Church upholds orthodox theology and traditional liturgical practice, using the 1928 Book of Common Prayer and the Authorized Version of the Bible for public worship. The Church holds to the Thirty-Nine Artlicles of Religion and confesses the fundamental doctrines of the historic Christian Faith: the Virgin Birth, the Atonement, the Resurrection, the Trinity, and salvation by faith in Christ alone. In 1967, the Church authorized the creation of the worldwide Orthodox Anglican Communion, a global fellowship of traditionalist Anglican Bishops and clergy, with ministries in Europe, Africa, Asia, and South America. In 1971 the Church established Cranmer Seminary to train Godly men for Holy Orders. The seminary became the first of its kind to offer distance-delivered and internet-based learning opportunities for students around the world. In 1999 the name of the Church was changed to the Episcopal Orthodox Christian Archdiocese of America (The Episcopal Orthodox Church), to reflect the strong growth experienced by this body in the 1990's. On April 30, 2000, the Most Reverend Dr. Scott E. McLaughlin became the fourth Presiding Bishop of the Church and Metropolitan of the Orthodox Anglican Communion.

Headquarters

901 English Rd., High Point, NC 27262 Tel. (336)885-6020, Fax (336)885-6021

Email: eoc@orthodoxanglican.net

Website: orthodoxanglican.net

Officers

Presiding Bishop, The Most Rev. Dr. Scott E. McLaughlin, The Chancery of the Archdiocese, 901 English Rd., High Point, NC 27262 Tel.(336)885-6020, Fax (336)885-6021

Periodicals

The Episcopal Orthodox Encounter; The Cranmer Theological Review

The Estonian Evangelical Lutheran Church

For information on the Estonian Evangelical Lutheran Church (EELC), please see the listing in Chapter 4, "Religious Bodies in Canada."

Headquarters

383 Jarvis St., Toronto, ON M5B 2C7
Email: konsistoorium@eelk.ee
Website: www.eelk.ee/

The Evangelical Church

The Evangelical Church was born June 4, 1968 in Portland, Oregon, when 46 congregations and about 80 ministers, under the leadership of V. A. Ballantyne and George Millen, met in an organizing session. Within two weeks a group of about 20 churches and 30 ministers from the Evangelical United Brethren and Methodist churches in Montana and North Dakota became a part of the new church. Richard Kienitz and Robert Strutz were the superintendents.

Under the leadership of Superintendent Robert Trosen, the former Holiness Methodist Church became a part of the Evangelical Church in 1969, bringing its membership and a flourishing mission field in Bolivia. The Wesleyan Covenant Church joined in 1977, with its missionary work in Mexico, in Brownsville, Texas and among the Navajos in New Mexico.

The Evangelical Church in Canada, where T. J. Jesske was superintendent, became an autonomous organization on June 5, 1970. In 1982, after years of discussions with the Evangelical Church of North America, a founding General Convention was held at Billings, Montana, where the two churches united. In 1993 the Canadian conference merged with the Canadian portion of the Missionary Church to form the Evangelical Missionary Church. The new group maintains close ties with their American counterparts. Currently there are nearly 150 U.S. congregations of the Evangelical Church. The headquarters is located in Minneapolis, Minnesota.

The following guide the life, program, and devotion of this church: faithful, biblical and sensible preaching and teaching of those truths proclaimed by scholars of the Wesleyan-Arminian viewpoint; an itinerant system which reckons with the rights of individuals and the desires of the congregation; local ownership of all church properties and assets.

The church is officially affiliated with the Christian Holiness Partnership, the National Association of Evangelicals, Wycliffe Bible Translators, World Gospel Mission and OMS International. The denomination has nearly 150 missionaries.

Headquarters

Denominational Office, 7733 West River Rd., Minneapolis, MN 55444 Tel. (763)561-0886, Fax 763-561-0774, kjsditzel@juno.com
Missions Department, 9421 West River Rd., Minneapolis, MN 55444 Tel. (763)424-2589, Fax 763-424-9230, ecm@rnc.net
Media Contact, Gen. Supt., John F. Sills
Email: jsditzel@juno.com
Website: quakertownecna.com/conferences.html

Officers

Gen. Supt., Dr. John F. Sills, 7733 West River Rd., Minneapolis, MN 55444
Denominational Secretary, Dr. Bruce Moyer, P.O. Box 29, University Park, IA 52595 Tel. (641)673-8391
Exectuive Director, Evangelical Church Mission, Rev. Duane Erickson, 9421 West River Rd., Minneapolis, MN 55444

Periodicals

HeatBeat; The Evangelical Challenge

The Evangelical Church Alliance

What is known today as the Evangelical Church Alliance began in 1887 under the name "World's Faith Missionary Association." Years later, on March 28, 1928, a nonprofit organization was incorporated in the state of Missouri under the same name. In October, 1931, the name "Fundamental Ministerial Association" was chosen to reflect the organization's basis of unity.

On July 21, 1958, during the annual convention at Trinity Seminary and Bible College in Chicago, Illinois, a more comprehensive constitution was created and the name was changed to "The Evangelical Church Alliance."

The ECA licenses and ordains ministers who are qualified providing them with credentials from a recognized ecclesiastical body; provides training courses through the Bible Extension Institute for those who have not had the opportunity to attend Seminary or Bible School; provides Associate Membership for churches and Christian organizations giving opportunity for fellowship and networking with other evangelical ministers and organizations who share the same goals and mission, while remaining autonomous; provides endorsement for military, prison, hospital & other institutional chaplains; provides Regional Conferences and an Annual International Conference where members can find fellowship, encouragement and training; cooperates with churches in finding new pastors when they have openings.

ECA is an international, nonsectarian, Evangelical organization.

Headquarters

205 W. Broadway St., P.O. Box 9, Bradley, IL 60915 Tel. (815)937-0720, Fax (815)937-0001
Media Contact, Pres./CEO, Dr. George L. Miller
Email: info@ecainternational.org
Website: www.ecainternational.org/

Officers

Pres./CEO, Dr. George L. Miller

Periodicals

The Evangel

The Evangelical Congregational Church

This denomination had its beginning in the movement known as the Evangelical Association, organized by Jacob Albright in 1796. A division which occurred in 1891 in the Evangelical Association resulted in the organization of the United Evangelical Church in 1894. An attempt to heal this division was made in 1922, but a portion of the United Evangelical Church was not satisfied with the plan of merger and remained apart, taking the above name in 1928. This denomination is Wesleyan-Arminian in doctrine, evangelistic in spirit, and Methodist in church government, with congregational ownership of local church property.

Congregations are located from New Jersey to Illinois. A denominational center, two retirement villages, and a seminary are located in Myerstown, Pennsylvania. Three summer youth camps and four camp meetings continue evangelistic outreach. A worldwide missions movement includes conferences in North East India, Liberia, Mexico, Costa Rica, and Japan. The denomination is a member of National Association of Evangelicals.

Headquarters

Evangelical Congregational Church Center, 100 W. Park Ave., Myerstown, PA 17067 Tel. (800)866-7581, Fax (717)866-7383

Media Contact, Bishop, Rev. Michael W. Sigman, Tel. (717)866-7581

Email: eccenter@eccenter.com

Website: www.eccenter.com/church/

Officers

Presiding Bishop, Rev. Michael W. Sigman

1st Vice-Chpsn., Rev. Keith R. Miller

Sec., Dr. John Ragsdale

Asst. Sec., Rev. Robert Stahl, Lancaster, PA; Rev. Bruce Ray, Chicago, IL

Treas., Norma Minnich, Reedsville, PA

E.C.C. Retirement Village, Exec. Dir., Rev. Bruce Hill, Fax (717)866-6448

Evangelical School of Theology, Pres., Dr. Kirby N. Keller, Fax (717)866-4667

OTHER ORGANIZATIONS

Administrative Council, Chpsn., Bishop Michael W. Sigman; Vice-Chpsn., Rev. Keith R. Miller; Treas., Norma Minnich

Div. of Evangelism & Spiritual Care, Chpsn., Bishop Michael W. Sigman

Div. of Church Ministries & Services, Chpsn., Rev. Keith R. Miller

Div. of Missions, Chpsn., Rev. John Ragsdale

Bd. of Pensions, Pres., William Kautz, New Cumberland, PA; Business Mgr., Rev. Keith R. Miller, Myerstown, PA 17067

Periodicals

Window on the World (EC Missions)

The Evangelical Covenant Church

The Evangelical Covenant Church has its roots in historic Christianity as it emerged during the Protestant Reformation, in the biblical instruction of the Lutheran State Church of Sweden and in the great spiritual awakenings of the nineteenth century.

The Covenant Church adheres to the affirmations of the Protestant Reformation regarding the Holy Scriptures, believing that the Old and the New Testament are the Word of God and the only perfect rule for faith, doctrine, and conduct. It has traditionally valued the historic confessions of the Christian church, particularly the Apostles' Creed, while at the same time emphasizing the sovereignty of the Word over all creedal interpretations. It has especially cherished the pietistic restatement of the doctrine of justification by faith as basic to its dual task of evangelism and Christian nurture. It recognizes the New Testament emphasis upon personal faith in Jesus Christ as Savior and Lord, the reality of a fellowship of believers which acknowledges but transcends theological differences, and the belief in baptism and the Lord's Supper as divinely ordained sacraments of the church.

While the denomination has traditionally practiced the baptism of infants, in conformity with its principle of freedom it has also recognized the practice of believer baptism. The principle of personal freedom, so highly esteemed by the Covenant, is to be distinguished from the individualism that disregards the centrality of the Word of God and the mutual responsibilities and disciplines of the spiritual community.

Headquarters

5101 N. Francisco Ave., Chicago, IL 60625 Tel. (773)784-3000, Fax (773)784-4366

Media Contact, Sally A. Johnson sjohnson@covoffice.org

Email: president@covoffice.org

Website: www.covchurch.org/

Officers

Pres., Dr. Glenn R. Palmberg

Vice-Pres., Rev. Donn Engebretson

Administrative V.P., Rev. Mary C. Miller

Financial V.P., Dean A. Lundgren

ADMINISTRATIVE BOARDS

Bd. of Christian Educ. & Discipleship, Exec. Dir., Rev. Doreen L. Olson

Bd. of Church Growth & Evangelism, Exec. Dir., Rev. Gary B. Walter

Bd. of Covenant Women Ministries, Exec. Dir., Rev. Ruth Y. Hill

Bd. of Human Resources, Advisory Member, Rev. Mary C. Miller

Bd. of the Ministry, Exec. Dir., Rev. Dr. David Kersten

Bd. of Pensions, Dir. of Pensions, Rev. Mary C. Miller

Bd. of Communication, Exec. Dir., Donald L. Meyer

Bd. of World Mission, Exec. Dir., Rev. James W. Gustafson

Bd. of Benevolence, Pres. of Covenant Ministries of Benevolence, Paul V. Peterson, 5145 N. California Ave., Chicago, IL 60625

North Park University, Pres., Dr. David G.

Horner, 3225 W. Foster Ave., Chicago, IL 60625; North Park Theological Seminary, Pres. And Dean, Dr. John E. Phelan Jr.

SERVICE ORGANIZATIONS

National Covenant Properties: Pres., David W. Johnson, 5101 N. Francisco, Chicago, IL 60625 Tel. (773)784-3000

Covenant Trust Company: Pres., Gilman G. Robinson, 5101 N. Francisco, Chicago, IL 60625 Tel. (773)784-9911

REGIONAL CONFERENCES OF THE E.C.C.

Central Conference: Supt., Rev. Herbert M. Freedholm, 3319 W. Foster Ave., Chicago, IL 60625 Tel. (773)267-3060

East Coast Conferenc: Supt., Rev. Robert C. Dvorak, 52 Missionary Rd., Cromwell, CT 06416 Tel. (860)635-2691

Great Lakes Conference: Supt., Rev. David S. Dahlberg, 70 W. Streetsboro St., P.O. Box 728, Hudson, OH 44236 Tel. (330)655-9345

Midwest Conference: Supt., Rev. Kenneth P. Carlson, 13304 W. Center Rd. #229, Omaha, NE 68144 Tel. (402)334-3060

North Pacific Conference: Supt., Rev. Mark A. Novak, 9311 S.E. 36th St., Ste 120, Mercer Island, WA 98040 Tel. (206)275-3903

Northwest Conference: Supt., Rev. Paul Erickson, 4721 E. 31st St., Minneapolis, MN 55406 Tel. (612)721-4893

Pacific Southwest Conference: Supt., Rev. Evelyn M. R. Johnson, 1333 Willow Pass Rd., Ste 212, Concord, CA 94502 Tel. (925)677-2140

Southeast Conference: Supt., Rev. Kurt A. Miericke, 1759 W. Broadway St., #7, Oviedo, FL 32765 Tel. (407)977-8009

E.C.C. of Canada: Supt., Rev. Jeffrey Anderson, 2791 Pembina Hwy, Winnipeg, MN R3T 2H5 Tel. (204) 269-3437

Midsouth Conference: Conference Supt., Rev. Garth T Bolinder, 8411 Greenwood Circle, Lenexa, KS 66215 Tel. (785)888-1825

E.C.C. of Alaska: Field Dir., Rev. Paul W. Wilson, P.O. Box 770749, Eagle River, AK 99577 Tel. (907)694-6348

Periodicals

Covenant Companion; Covenant Quarterly; Covenant Home Altar

The Evangelical Free Church of America

In October 1884, 27 representatives from Swedish churches met in Boone, Iowa, to establish the Swedish Evangelical Free Church. In the fall of that same year, two Norwegian-Danish groups began worship and fellowship (in Boston and in Tacoma) and by 1912 had established the Norwegian-Danish Evangelical Free Church Association. These two denominations, representing 275 congregations, came together at a merger conference in 1950.

The Evangelical Free Church of America is an association of local, autonomous churches across the United States and Canada, blended together by common principles, policies, and practices. A 12-point statement addresses the major doctrines but also provides for differences of understanding on minor issues of faith and practice.

Overseas outreach includes 500 missionaries serving in 31 countries.

Headquarters

901 East 78th St., Minneapolis, MN 55420-1300 Tel. (612)854-1300, Fax (612)853-8488

Media Contact, Exec. Dir. of Ministry Advancement, Timothy Addington

Email: president@efca.org

Website: www.efca.org/

Officers

Acting Pres./Exec. Vice-Pres., Rev. William Hamel

Moderator, Ronald Aucutt, 3417 Silver Maple Pl., Falls Church, VA 22042

Vice-Moderator, Rev. Mark J. Wold, 41827 Higgins Way, Fremont, CA 94539

Sec., Dr. Roland Peterson, 235 Craigbrook Way, NE, Fridley, MN 55432

Vice-Sec., Rev. William S. Wick, 92 South Main, Northfield, VT 05663

Chief Fin. Ofc., Robert Peterson

Exec. Dir., Evangelical Free Church Mission, Dr. Ben Swatsky

Assoc. Dir. of Mission USA, Rev. Steve Hudson

Periodicals

Evangelical Beacon; Pursuit

Evangelical Friends International —North American Region

The organization restructured from Evangelical Friends Alliance in 1990 to become internationalized for the benefit of its world-wide contacts. The North America Region continues to function within the United States as EFA formerly did. The organization represents one corporate step of denominational unity, brought about as a result of several movements of spiritual renewal within the Society of Friends. These movements are: (1) the general evangelical renewal within Christianity, (2) the new scholarly recognition of the evangelical nature of seventeenth-century Quakerism, and (3) EFA, which was formed in 1965.

The EFA is conservative in theology and makes use of local pastors. Sunday morning worship includes singing, Scripture reading, a period of open worship, and a sermon by the pastor.

Headquarters

5350 Broadmoor Cir. NW, Canton, OH 44709 Tel. (330)493-1660, Fax (330)493-0852

Media Contact, Gen. Supt., Dr. John P. Williams, Jr.

Email: efcer@aol.com

Website: www.evangelical-friends.org

YEARLY MEETINGS

Evangelical Friends Church, Eastern Region, Wayne Ickes, 5350 Broadmoor Cir., N.W., Canton, OH 44709 Tel. (330)493-1660, Fax (330)493-0852

Rocky Mountain YM, John Brawner, 3350 Reed St., Wheat Ridge, CO 80033 Tel. (303)238-5200 Fax (303)238-5200

Mid-America YM, Duane Hansen, 2018 Maple, Wichita, KS 67213 Tel. (316)267-0391, Fax (316)267-0681

Northwest YM, Mark Ankeny, 200 N. Meridian St., Newberg, OR 97132 Tel. (503)538-9419, Fax (503)538-9410

Alaska YM, Sam Williams, P.O. Box 687, Kotzebue, AK 99752 Tel. (907)442-3906

Friends Church Southwest, YM, Linda Coop, P.O. Box 1607, Whittier, CA 90609-1607 Tel. (562)947-2883, Fax (562)947-9385

Periodicals

The Friends Voice

Evangelical Lutheran Church in America*

The Evangelical Lutheran Church in America (ELCA) was organized April 30-May 3, 1987, in Columbus, Ohio, bringing together the 2.25 million-member American Lutheran Church, the 2.85 million-member Lutheran Church in America, and the 100,000-member Association of Evangelical Lutheran Churches.

The ELCA is, through its predecessors, the oldest of the major U.S. Lutheran churches. In the mid-seventeenth century, a Dutch Lutheran congregation was formed in New Amsterdam (now New York). Other early congregations were begun by German and Scandinavian immigrants to Delaware, Pennsylvania, New York, and the Carolinas.

The first Lutheran association of congregations, the Pennsylvania Ministerium, was organized in 1748 under Henry Melchior Muhlenberg. Numerous Lutheran organizations were formed as immigration continued and the United States grew.

In 1960, the American Lutheran Church (ALC) was created through a merger of an earlier American Lutheran Church, formed in 1930, the Evangelical Lutheran Church, begun in 1917, and the United Evangelical Lutheran Church in America started in 1896. In 1963 the Lutheran Free Church, formed in 1897, merged with the ALC.

In 1962, the Lutheran Church in America (LCA) was formed by a merger of the United Lutheran Church, formed in 1918, with the Augustana Lutheran Church, begun in 1860, the American Evangelical Lutheran Church, founded in 1872, and the Finnish Lutheran Church or Suomi Synod, founded in 1891.

The Association of Evangelical Lutheran Churches arose in 1976 from a doctrinal split with the Lutheran Church-Missouri Synod.

The ELCA, through its predecessor church bodies, was a founding member of the Lutheran World Federation, the World Council of Churches, and the National Council of the Churches of Christ in the USA.

The church is divided into 65 geographical areas or synods. These 65 synods are grouped into nine regions for mission, joint programs, and service.

Headquarters

8765 W. Higgins Rd., Chicago, IL 60631 Tel. (773)380-2700, Fax (773)380-1465

Media Contact, Dir. for News, John Brooks, Tel. (773)380-2958, Fax (773)380-2406

Email: info@elca.org

Website: www.elca.org

Officers

Presiding Bishop, Rev. Mark Hanson

Sec., Rev. Dr. Lowell G. Almen

Treas., Richard L. McAuliffe

Vice-Pres., Dr. Addie J. Butler

Exec. for Admn.,

Office of the Bishop, Exec. Assts. for Federal Chaplaincies, Rev. Lloyd W. Lyngdal; Exec. Asst., Ms. Myrna J. Sheie

DIVISIONS

Div. for Congregational Min., Co-Exec. Dir., Rev. Mark R. Moller-Gunderson; Co-Exec. Dir., Rev. M. Wyvetta Bullock; Bd. Chpsn., Mr. Ronald C. Bruggeman; Lutheran Youth Organization, Pres., Leota Thomas-Breitfeld

Div. for Higher Educ. & Schools, Exec. Dir., Rev. Dr. Leonard G. Schultze; Bd. Chpsn., Rev. John G. Andreasen

Div. for Global Mission, Exec. Dir., Rev. Bonnie L. Jensen; Bd. Chpsn., Ms. Shai Celeste

Div. for Ministry, Exec. Dir., Rev. Dr. Joseph M. Wagner; Bd. Chpsn., Mr. Kevin J. Boatright

Div. for Outreach, Exec. Dir., Rev. Dr. Richard A. Magnus, Jr.; Bd. Chpsn., Ms. Dorothy Baumgartner

Div. for Church in Society, Exec. Dir., Rev. Charles S. Miller, Jr.; Chpsn., Rev. Denver W. Bitner

COMMISSIONS

Comm. for Multicultural Ministries, Exec. Dir., Rev. Frederick E.N. Rajan; Chpsn., Rev. Grace G. El-Yateem

Comm. for Women, Exec. Dir., Joanne Chadwick; Chpsn., Rev. Janet M. Corpus

CHURCHWIDE UNITS

Conference of Bishops, Asst. to the Bishop, Rev. Kathie Bender Schwich; Chpsn., Rev. Donald J. McCoid

ELCA Foundation, Exec. Dir., The Rev. Donald M. Hallberg, Chpsn., Mr. David D. Swartling

ELCA Publishing House, Exec. Dir., Rev. Marvin L. Roloff; Bd. Chpsn.,Mr. Timothy I. Maudlin

ELCA Bd. of Pensions, Exec. Dir., John G. Kapanke; Bd. Chpsn, Mr. Kenneth G. Bash

Women of the ELCA, Exec. Dir., Catherine I. H. Braasch; Bd. Chpsn., Ms. Linda Chinnia

DEPARTMENTS

Dept. for Communication, Dir., Rev. Eric C. Shafer

Dept. for Ecumenical Affairs, Interim Dir., Rev. Jon Enslin; Committee Chpsn., Ms. Kristen E. Kvam

Dept. for Human Resources, Dir., Ms. Else Thompson

Dept. for Research & Evaluation, Dir., Dr. Kenneth W. Inskeep

Dept. for Synodical Relations, Dir., Rev. Kathie Bender Schwich

SYNODICAL BISHOPS

Region 1

Alaska, Rev. Ronald D. Martinson, 1847 W. Northern Lights Blvd., #2, Anchorage, AK 99517-3343 Tel. (907)272-8899, Fax (907) 274-3141

Northwest Washington, Rev. William Chris Boerger, 5519 Pinney Ave. N., Seattle, WA 98103-5899 Tel. (206)783-9292, Fax (206) 783-9833

Southwestern Washington, Rev. Robert D. Hofstad, 420 121st St., S., Tacoma, WA 98444-5218 Tel. (253)535-8300, Fax (253) 535-8315

Eastern Washington-Idaho, Rev. Martin D. Wells, 314 South Spruce St., Ste. A, Spokane, WA 99204-1098 Tel. (509)838-9871, Fax (509) 838-0941

Oregon, Rev. Paul R. Swanson, 2800 N. Vancouver Ave., Ste. 101, Portland, OR 97227-1643 Tel. (503) 413-4191, Fax (503) 413-2407

Montana, Rev. Dr. Richard R. Omland, 2415 13th Ave. S., Great Falls, MT 59405-5199 Tel. (406)453-1461, Fax (406)761-4632

Regional Coord., Mr. Steven H. Lansing, Region 1, 766-B John St., Seattle, WA 98109-5186 Tel. (206)624-0093, Fax (206)626-0987

Region 2

Sierra Pacific, Rev. Robert W. Mattheis, 401 Roland Way, #215, Oakland, CA 94621-2011 Tel. (510)430-0500, Fax (510)430-8730

Southern California (West), Bishop, Rev. Dean W. Nelson, 1300 E. Colorado St., Glendale, CA 91205-1406 Tel. (818)507-9591, Fax (818) 507-9627

Pacifica, Rev. Murray D. Finck, 23655 Via Del Rio, Ste. B, Yorba Linda, CA 92887-2738 Tel. (714)692-2791, Fax (714)692-9317

Grand Canyon, Rev. Michael J. Neils, Interchurch Center 4423 N. 24th St., Ste. 400, Phoenix, AZ 85016-5544 Tel. (602)957-3223, Fax (602)956-8104

Rocky Mountain, Rev. Allan C. Bjornberg, 455 Sherman St., Ste. 160, Denver, CO 80203 Tel. (303)777-6700, Fax (303)733-0750

Region 2, Ms. Margaret Schmitt Ajer, Region 2, 3755 Avocado Blvd., PMB 411, La Mesa, CA 91941 Tel. (619)460-9312, Fax (619) 460-9314

Region 3

Western North Dakota, Rev. Duane C. Danielson, 1614 Capitol Way, P.O. Box 370, Bismarck, ND 58502-0370 Tel. (701)223-5312, Fax (701)223-1435

Eastern North Dakota, Rev. Richard J. Foss, 1703 32nd Ave., S., Fargo, ND 58103-5936 Tel. (701)232-3381, Fax (701)232-3180

South Dakota, Rev. Andrea F. DeGroot-Nesdahl, Augustana College, 29th & S. Summit, Sioux Falls, SD 57197-0001 Tel. (605)247-4011, Fax (605)274-4028

Northwestern Minnesota, Rev. Rolf P. Wangberg, Concordia College, 901 Eighth St. S., Moorhead, MN 56562-0001 Tel. (218)299-3019, Fax (218)299-3363

Northeastern Minnesota, Rev. E. Peter Strommen, 1105 E. Superior St., Upper Suite, Duluth, MN 55802-2085 Tel. (218)724-4424, Fax (218)724-4393

Southwestern Minnesota, Rev. Stanley N. Olson, 175 E. Bridge St., P.O. Box 499, Redwood Falls, MN 56283-0499 Tel. (507)637-3904, Fax (507)637-2809

Minneapolis Area, Rev. Craig E. Johnson, 122 W. Franklin Ave., Ste. 600, Minneapolis, MN 55404-2474 Tel. (612)870-3610, Fax (612)870-0170

Saint Paul Area, Interim, Rev. Paul M. Werger, 105 W. University Ave., St. Paul, MN 55103-2094 Tel. (651)224-4313, Fax (651)224-5646

Southeastern Minnesota, Rev. Harold L. Usgaard, Assisi Heights, 1001 14th St. NW, Ste. 300, Rochester, MN 55901-2511 Tel. (507)280-9457, Fax (507)280-8824

Regional Coord., Rev. Craig A. Boehlke, Region 3, Luther Seminary, 2481 Como Ave., St. Paul, MN 55108-1445 Tel. (651)649-0454 ext. 232, Fax (651)649-0468

Region 4

Nebraska, Rev. David L. deFreese, 4980 S. 118th St., Ste. D, Omaha, NE 68137-2220 Tel. (402)896-5311, Fax (402)896-5354

Central States, Rev. Dr. Gerald L. Mansholt, 6400 Glenwood St., Shawnee Mission, KS 66202-4021 Tel. (913)362-0733, Fax (913) 362-0317 (M-F)

Arkansas-Oklahoma, Rev. Floyd M. Schoenhals, 6911 S. 66th E. Ave., Ste. 200, Tulsa, OK 74133-1748 Tel. (918)492-4288, Fax (918) 491-6275

Northern Texas-Northern Louisiana, Rev. Kevin S. Kanouse, 1230 Riverbend Dr., Ste. 105, P.O. Box 560587, Dallas, TX 75356-0587 Tel. (214)637-6865, Fax (214)637-4805

Southwestern Texas, Rev. Ray Tiemann, 8919 Tesoro Dr., Ste. 109, P.O. Box 171270, San Antonio, TX 78217-8270 Tel. (210)824-0068, Fax (210)824-7009

Texas-Louisiana Gulf Coast, Rev. Paul J. Blom,

12707 N. Freeway, #580, Houston, TX 77060-1239 Tel. (281)873-5665, Fax (281)875-4716

Regional Coord., Region 4, 6400 Glenwood St., Ste. 210, Shawnee Mission, KS 66202-4021, Tel. (913)362-0733, Fax (913)362-0317

Region 5

Metropolitan Chicago, Rev. Paul R. Lansdahl, 1420 West Dickens Ave., Chicago, IL 60614-3004 Tel. (773)248-0021, Fax (773)248-8455

Northern Illinois, Rev. Gary M. Wollersheim, 103 W. State St., Rockford, IL 61101-1105 Tel. (815) 964-9934, Fax (815)964-2295

Central-Southern Illinois, Rev. Warren D. Freiheit, 524 S. Fifth St., Springfield, IL 62701-1822 Tel. (217)753-7915, Fax (217) 753-7976

Southeastern Iowa, Rev. Philip L. Hougen, 2635 Northgate Dr., P.O. Box 3167, Iowa City, IA 52244-3167 Tel. (319)338-1273, Fax (319) 351-8677

Western Iowa, Rev. Michael A. Last, 318 E. Fifth St., P.O. Box 577, Storm Lake, IA 50588-0577 Tel. (712)732-4968, Fax (712)732-6540

Northeastern Iowa, Rev. Steven L. Ullestad, 201-20th St. SW, P.O. Box 804, Waverly, IA 50677-0804 Tel. (319)352-1414, Fax (319) 352-1416

Northern Great Lakes, Rev. Thomas A. Shrenes, 1029 N. Third St., Marquette, MI 49855-3588 Tel. (906)228-2300, Fax (906)228-2527

Northwest Synod of Wisconsin, Rev. Robert D. Berg, 12 W. Marshall St., P.O. Box 730, Rice Lake, WI 54868-0730 Tel. (715)234-3373, Fax (715)234-4183

East-Central Synod of Wisconsin, Rev. James A. Justman, 16 Tri-Park Way, Appleton, WI 54914-1658 Tel. (920)734-5381, Fax (920) 734-5074

Greater Milwaukee, Rev. Peter Rogness, 1212 S. Layton Blvd., Milwaukee, WI 53215-1653 Tel. (414)671-1212, Fax (414)671-1756

South-Central Synod of Wisconsin, Rev. George G. Carlson, 2909 Landmark Pl., Ste. 202, Madison, WI 53713-4237 Tel. (608)270-0201, Fax (608)270-0202

La Crosse Area, Rev. April Ulring Larson, 3462 Losey Blvd. S., La Crosse, WI 54601-7217 Tel. (608)788-5000 Fax (608)788-4916

Regional Coord., Rev. Carl R. Evenson, Region 5, 675 Deerwood Dr., Ste. 4., Neenah, WI 54956-1629 Tel. (920)720-9880, Fax (920) 720-9881

Region 6

Southeast Michigan, Rev. Robert A. Rimbo, 218 Fisher Bldg., 3011 W. Grand Ave., Detroit, MI 48202-3011 Tel. (313)875-1881, Fax (313) 875-1889

North, West Lower Michigan, Rev. Gary L. Hansen, 801 S. Waverly Rd., Ste. 201, Lansing, MI 48917-4254 Tel. (517)321-5066, Fax (517)321-2612

Indiana-Kentucky, Rev. James R. Stuck, 911 E. 86th St., Ste. 200, Indianapolis, IN 46240-1840 Tel. (317)253-3522, Fax (317)254-5666

Northwestern Ohio, Rev. Marcus C. Lohrmann, 621 Bright Rd., Findlay, OH 45840-6987 Tel. (419) 423-3664, Fax (419)423-8801

Northeastern Ohio, Rev. Marcus J. Miller, 1890 Bailey Rd., Cuyahoga Falls, OH 44221-5259 Tel. (330)929-9022, Fax (330)929-9018

Southern Ohio, Rev. Dr. Callon W. Holloway, Jr., 300 S. 2nd St., Columbus, OH 43215-5001 Tel. (614)464-3532, Fax (614)464-3422

Regional Coord., Marilyn McCann Smith, Region 6, P.O. Box 91, 119 1/2 N. Main St. Bluffton, OH 45817 Tel. (419)369-4006 Fax (419)369-4007

Region 7

New Jersey, Rev. E. Roy Riley, Jr., 1930 State Hwy. 33, Hamilton Square, Trenton, NJ 08690-1799 Tel. (609)586-6800, Fax (609) 586-1597

New England, Rev. Margaret G. Payne, 20 Upland St., Worcester, MA 01607-1624 Tel. (508)791-1530, Fax (508)797-9295

Metropolitan New York, Rev. Stephen P. Bouman, Interchurch Center, 475 Riverside Dr., 16th Floor, New York, NY 10115 Tel. (212)665-0732, Fax (212)665-8640

Upstate New York, Rev. Dr. Lee M. Miller, 3049 E. Genesee St., Syracuse, NY 13224-1699 Tel. (315)446-2502, Fax (315)446-4642

Northeastern Pennsylvania, Rev. Dr. David R. Strobel, 4865 Hamilton Blvd., Wescosville, PA 18106-9705 Tel. (610)395-6891, Fax (610) 398-7083

Southeastern Pennsylvania, Rev. Roy G. Almquist, 506 Haws Ave., Norristown, PA 19401-4543 Tel. (610)278-7342, Fax (610) 696-2782

Slovak Zion, Rev. Juan Cobrda, 8340 N. Oleander Ave., Niles, IL 60714 Tel. (847)965-2475, Fax (847)583-8015

Regional Coord., Lutheran Theol. Seminary at Philadelphia, Hagan Hall, 7301 Germantown Ave., Philadelphia, PA 19119-1794 Tel. (215)248-6319, Fax (215)248-7377

Region 8

Northwestern Pennsylvania, Rev. Ralph E. Jones, Rte. 257, Salina Rd., P.O. Box 338, Seneca, PA 16346-0338 Tel. (814)677-5706, Fax (814)676-8591

Southwestern Pennsylvania, Rev. Donald J. McCoid, 9625 Perry Hwy., Pittsburgh, PA 15237-5590 Tel. (412)367-8222, Fax (412) 369-8840

Allegheny, Rev. Gregory R. Pile, 701 Quail Ave., Altoona, PA 16602-3010 Tel. (814)942-1042, Fax (814)941-9259

Lower Susquehanna, Rev. Carol S. Hendrix, 900 S. Arlington Ave., Ste. 208, Harrisburg, PA 17109-5031 Tel. (717)652-1852, Fax (717) 652-2504

Upper Susquehanna, Rev. Dr. A. Donald Main,

Rt. 192 & Reitz Blvd., P.O. Box 36, Lewisburg, PA 17837-0036 Tel. (570)524-9778, Fax (570)524-9757

Delaware-Maryland, Rev. Dr. H. Gerard Knoche, 700 Light St., Baltimore, MD 21230-3850 Tel. (410)230-2860, Fax (410)230-2871

Metropolitan Washington, D.C., Rev. Theodore F. Schneider, 1030-15th St., NW, Ste 1010, Washington, DC 20005-1503 Tel. (202)408-8110, Fax (202)408-8114

West Virginia-Western Maryland, Rev. Ralph W. Dunkin, The Atrium, 503 Morgantown Avenue, Ste. 100, Fairmont, WV 26554-4374 Tel. (304)363-4030, Fax (304)366-9846

Regional Coord., Rev. James E. Miley, Lutheran Theological Sem. at Gettysburg, 61 Seminary Ridge, Gettysburg, PA 17325-1795 Tel. (717)334-6286 ext. 2133, Fax (717)334-0323

Region 9

Virginia, Rev. James F. Mauney, Roanoke College, 221 College Ln., Bittle Hall, P.O. Drawer 70, Salem, VA 24153-0070 Tel. (540)389-1000, Fax (540)389-5962

North Carolina, Rev. Leonard H. Bolick, 1988 Lutheran Synod Dr., Salisbury, NC 28144-4480 Tel. (704)633-4861, Fax (704)638-0508

South Carolina, Rev. David A. Donges, 1003 Richland St., P.O. Box 43, Columbia, SC 29202-0043 Tel. (803)765-0590, Fax (803) 252-5558

Southeastern, Rev. Ronald B. Warren, 100 Edgewood Ave., NE, Ste. 1600, Atlanta, GA 30303 Tel. (404)589-1977, Fax (404)521-1980

Florida-Bahamas, Rev. Edward R. Benoway, 3838 W. Cypress St., Tampa, FL 33607-4897 Tel. (813)876-7660, Fax (813)870-0826

Caribbean, Rev. Margarita Martinez, PMB Num 359, 425 Carr 693, Ste. 1, Dorado, PR 00646-4802 Tel. (787) 273-8300, Fax (787)796-3365

Regional Coord., Rev. Harvey Huntley, Region 9, Lutheran Theological Southern Seminary, 4201 N. Main St., Columbia, SC 29203 Tel. (803)461-3263, Fax (803)461-3380

Periodicals

The Lutheran; Lutheran Partners; Lutheran Woman Today; Seeds for the Parish

Evangelical Lutheran Synod

The Evangelical Lutheran Synod had its beginning among the Norwegian settlers who brought with them their Lutheran heritage. The Synod was organized in 1853. It was reorganized in 1918 by those who desired to adhere to the synod's principles not only in word but also in deed.

The Synod owns and operates Bethany Lutheran College and Bethany Lutheran Theological Seminary. It has congregations in 20 states and maintains foreign missions in Peru, Chile, the Czech Republic, and Ukraine. It operates a seminary in Lima, Peru and in Ternopil, Ukraine.

Headquarters

6 Browns Court, Mankato, MN 56001 Tel. (507) 344-7356, Fax (507)344-7426

Media Contact, Pres., Rev. George Orvick

Email: gorvick@blc.edu

Website: www.EvLuthSyn.org

Officers

Pres., Rev. George Orvick, 6 Browns Ct., Mankato, MN 56082

Sec., Rev. Craig Ferkenstad, Rt. 3, Box 40, St. Peter, MN 56082

Treas., Keith Wiederhoeft, 6 Browns Ct., Mankato, MN 56001

OTHER ORGANIZATIONS

Lutheran Synod Book Co., Bethany Lutheran College, 700 Luther Dr., Mankato, MN 56001

Bethany Lutheran Theological Seminary, 6 Browns Court, Mankato, MN 56001

Periodicals

Lutheran Sentinel; Lutheran Synod Quarterly; Young Branches; ELS Educator; Oak Leaves; Mission News

Evangelical Mennonite Church

The Evangelical Mennonite Church is an American denomination in the European free church tradition, tracing its heritage to the Reformation period of the sixteenth century. The Swiss Brethren of that time believed that salvation could come only by repentance for sins and faith in Jesus Christ; that baptism was only for believers; and that the church should be separate from controls of the state. Their enemies called them Anabaptists, since they insisted on rebaptizing believers who had been baptized as infants. As the Anabaptist movement spread to other countries, Menno Simons became its principal leader. In time his followers were called Mennonites.

In 1693 a Mennonite minister, Jacob Amman, insisted that the church should adopt a more conservative position on dress and style of living and should more rigidly enforce the "ban" - the church's method of disciplining disobedient members. Amman's insistence finally resulted in a division within the South German Mennonite groups; his followers became known as the Amish.

Migrations to America, involving both Mennonites and Amish, took place in the 1700s and 1800s, for both religious and economic reasons.

The Evangelical Mennonite Church was formed in 1866 out of a spiritual awakening among the Amish in Indiana. It was first known as the Egly Amish, after its founder Bishop Henry Egly. Bishop Egly emphasized regeneration, separation and nonconformity to the world. His willingness to rebaptize anyone who had been baptized without repentance created a split in his church, prompting him to gather a new congregation in 1866. The conference, which has met annually since 1895, united a number of other congregations of like mind. This group became The Defenseless Mennonite Church in 1898 and has been known as the Evangelical Mennonite Church since 1948.

Headquarters

1420 Kerrway Ct., Fort Wayne, IN 46805 Tel. (219)423-3649, Fax (219)420-1905

Media Contact, Admn. Asst., Lynette Augsburger

Email: emcintlmin@aol.com

Officers

Pres., Rev. Ronald J. Habegger

Chpsn.., Rev. Doug Habegger, 1050 S. Fourth St., Morton, IL 61550

Vice-Chpsn., Rev. Bryce Winteregg, 11331 Coldwater Rd., Ft. Wayne, IN 46845

Sec., Gene Rupp, c/o Taylor University, 236 W. Reade Ave., Upland, IN 46989

Treas., Elmer Lengacher, 11507 Bull Rapids Rd., Harlan, IN 46743

Periodicals

EMC Today

Evangelical Methodist Church

The Evangelical Methodist Church was organized in 1946 at Memphis, Tenn., largely as a movement of people who opposed modern liberalism and wished for a return to the historic Wesleyan position. In 1960, it merged with the Evangel Church (formerly Evangelistic Tabernacles) and with the People's Methodist Church in 1962.

Headquarters

P.O. Box 17070, Indianapolis, IN 46217 Tel. (317)780-8017, Fax (317)780-8078

Media Contact, Gen. Conf. Sec.-Treas., Rev. James A. Coulston

Email: headquarters@emchurch.org

Website: www.emchurch.org/

Officers

Gen. Supt., Dr. Edward W. Williamson

Gen. Conf. Sec.-Treas., Rev. James A. Coulston

Evangelical Presbyterian Church

The Evangelical Presbyterian Church (EPC), established in March 1981, is a conservative denomination of 9 geographic presbyteries: 8 in the United States and one in Argentina. From its inception with 12 churches, the EPC has grown to 197 churches with a membership of over 63,000.

Planted firmly within the historic, Reformed tradition, evangelical in spirit, the EPC places high priority on church planting and development along with world missions. Sixty-one missionaries serve the church's mission.

Based on the truth of Scripture and adhering to the Westminster Confession of Faith plus its Book of Order, the denomination is committed to the "essentials of the faith." The historic motto "In essentials, unity; in nonessentials, liberty; in all things charity" catches the irenic spirit of the EPC, along with the Ephesians theme, "truth in love."

The Evangelical Presbyterian Church is a member of the World Alliance of Reformed Churches, National Association of Evangelicals, World Evangelical Fellowship and the Evangelical Council for Financial Accountability.

Headquarters

Office of the General Assembly, 29140 Buckingham Ave., Ste. 5, Livonia, MI 48154 Tel. (734)261-2001, Fax (734)261-3282

Media Contact, Stated Clk., Rev. Michael Glodo, 29140 Buckingham Ave., Ste. 5, Livonia, MI 48154 Tel. (734)261-2001, Fax (734)261-3282

Email: EPCHURCH@epc.org

Website: www.epc.org

Officers

Mod., Mr. John Graham, III, 11 Huntington Rd., SW, Rome, GA 30165

Administration Committee, Chmn., Dr. James McGuire, Ward Presbyterian Church, 40000 Six Mile Rd., Northville, MI 48167

Stated Clk., Rev. Michael Glodo

PERMANENT COMMITTEES

Board of Pension & Benefits, Chmn., Dr. Orin Littlejohn, 100 Azelea Way, Marshall, TX 75672

Committee on Admn., Chmn., Mr. John Graham, III; Smith, Shaw & Maddox, LLP, Suntrust Bank Bldg., 4th Fl., 100 East Second Ave., P.O. Box 29, Rome, GA 30162-0029

Committee on Fraternal Relations, Chmn., Dr. Paul Heidebrecht, Immanuel Pres. Church, 29W260 Batavia Rd., Warrenville, IL 62217

Committee on National Outreach, Chmn., Mr. Charles Overstreet, Forest Hill EPC, 7224 Park Rd., Charlotte, NC 28210

Committee on Presbytery Review, Chmn., Rev. George Woodcock, 27665 Yvette, Warren, MI 48167

Committee on World Outreach, Chmn., Dr. Bern Draper, 8103 Saguaro Ridge Rd., Parker, CO 80134

Committee on Ministerial Vocation, Chmn., Rev. Art Hunt, Christ Pres. Church, 3037 Lexington Ave, Cape Girardeau, MO 63701

Comm. on Christian Educ. & Publ., Chmn., Mr. Dan Tidwell, 3310 Oyster Cove Drive, Missouri City, TX 77459

Committee on Women's Ministries, Chmn., Mrs. Susie McQueen, 2280 Ellis Ct., Lakewood, CO 80228

Committee on Theology, Chmn., Mr. Charles Haden, 10709 Old Coach Rd., Houston, TX 77024

Committee on Student and Young Adult Ministries, Chmn., Rev. James Byrne, Fourth Presbyterian Church, 5500 River Rd., Bethesda, MD 20816

PRESBYTERIES

Central South, Stated Clk., Rev. Dennis Flach, New Covenant Evangelical Presbyterian Church, P.O. Box 842, Natchez, MS 39121

East, Stated Clk., Dr. Frank Johnson, 136 Chaucer Pl., Cherry Hills, NJ 08003
Florida, Stated Clk., Rev. Robert Garment, Trinity EPC, 5150 Oleander, Ft. Pierce, FL 34982
Mid-America, Stated Clk., Mr. Dexter Kuhlman, 1926 Prospector Ridge, Ballwin, MO 63011
Mid-Atlantic, Stated Clk., Dr. Howard Shockley, 58 Bear Trail, Fairview, NC 28730
Midwest, Stated Clk., Mr. John C. Manon, PO Box 6047, Auburn, IN 46706-6047
Southeast, Stated Clk., Rev. Bill Sharp, 1222 Village Green Dr., Chattanooga, TN 39343
West, Stated Clk., Mr. Cecil Matthews, 6137 E. Hinsdale Ct., Englewwod, CO 80111
St. Andrews, Stated Clk., Rev. Jorge Lumsden, Temperley Church, Gral Paz 191, (1834) Temperley PCIA Buenos Aires, Argentina

Periodicals

Reflections Magazine (3/year)

Fellowship of Evangelical Bible Churches

Formerly known as Evangelical Mennonite Brethren, this body emanates from the Russian immigration of Mennonites into the United States, 1873-74. Established with the emphasis on true repentance, conversion and a committed life to Jesus as Savior and Lord, the conference was founded in 1889 under the leadership of Isaac Peters and Aaron Wall. The founding churches were located in Mountain Lake, Minnesota, and in Henderson and Janzen, Nebraska. The conference has since grown to a fellowship of 44 churches with approximately 4,500 members in Argentina, Canada, Paraguay and the United States.

Foreign missions have been a vital ingredient of the total ministry. Today missions constitute about 35 percent of the total annual budget, with one missionary for every 30 members in the home churches. The conference does not develop and administer foreign mission fields of its own, but actively participates with existing evangelical "faith" mission societies. The conference has representation on several mission boards and has missionaries serving under approximately 40 different agencies around the world.

The church is holding fast to the inerrancy of Scripture, the deity of Christ, and the need for spiritual regeneration of man from his sinful natural state by faith in the death, burial, and resurrection of Jesus Christ as payment for sin. Members look forward to the imminent return of Jesus Christ and retain a sense of urgency to share the gospel with those who have never heard of God's redeeming love.

Headquarters

3339 N. 109th Plz., Omaha, NE 68164 Tel. (402)965-3860, Fax 402-965-3871
Admn., Paul Boeker, 3339 N 109th Plz., Omaha, NE 68164 Tel. 402-965-3860, Fax (402)965-3871
Email: febcoma@aol.com
Website: members.aol.com/febcoma/index.html

Officers

Pres., Mr.. Gerald Epp, P.O. Box 86, Waldheim, SK S0K 4R0 Tel. (306)945-2023, ggepp@sk.sympatico.ca
Vice-President, Rev. Charles Tschetter, 9001 Q St., Omaha, NE 68127-3548, cbcomaha@aol.com
Rec. Sec., Stan Seifert, 35351 Munroe Ave., Abbotsford, BC V3G 1L4 Tel. (604)852-3253, Fax (604)852-7887
Admn., Paul Boeker, 3339 N. 109th Plz., Omaha, NE 68164 Tel. 402-965-3860, Fax (402)965-3871, febcoma@aol.com
Ministries Coordinator, Harvey Schultz, 3011 3rd Ave. East, P.O. Box 8, Waldheim, SK S0K 4R0, Tel. (306)945-2220, Fax (306)945-2088, hesals@aol.com
Commission on Churches, Chpsn., Rev. Paul Carpenter, 401 Nebraska St., Box 141, Jansen, NE 68377-0141 Tel. (402)424-2645, jb95208@alltel.net
Commission on Education, Chpsn., Rev. Harvey Gilbert, 5112 N. 86th St., Omaha, NE 68134-2814, Tel. (402)571-3541, hgilbert@radiks.net
Commission on Missions, Chpsn., Martin Fast, SR 266, Box 9, Frazer, MT 59225 Tel. (406)392-5722, mkfast@juno.com
Commission of Trustees, Chpsn., William Janzen, 6212 Country Club Rd., Omaha, NE 68152-2057 Tel. [O] (402)397-7812, [H] (402)571-2352, Fax (204)397-2113
Commission on Church Planting, Chpsn., Rev. Randy Smart, Box 111, Stuartburn, MB R0A 2B0 Tel. [O](204)425-3383 [H](204)425-3990, smartr@mb.sympatico.ca
Comm. on Women's Ministries, Chpsn., Ruth Epp, Box 86, Waldheim, SK S0K 4R0 Tel. (306)945-2023, ggepp@sk.sympatico.ca

Periodicals

Fellowship Focus

Fellowship of Fundamental Bible Churches

The churches in this body represent the 1939 separation from the Methodist Protestant Church, when some 50 delegates and pastors (approximately one-third of the Eastern Conference) withdrew to protest the union of the Methodist Protestant Church with the Methodist Episcopal Church and the Methodist Episcopal Church South, and what they considered the liberal tendencies of those churches. These churches subsequently changed their name to the Bible Protestant Church. In 1985, this group again changed its name to the Fellowship of Fundamental Bible Churches to more accurately define their position.

As fundamentalists, this group strongly

adheres to the historic fundamentals of the faith, including the doctrine of separation. This group accepts a literal view of the Bible and, consequently, accepts premillennial theology and a pre-tribulational rapture.

The churches are currently located in New Jersey, New York, Pennsylvania, Virginia, Michigan, and California. It is a fellowship of independent Bible and Baptist churches. Baptism, by immersion, and the Lord's Supper, as a memorial, are recognized as ordinances. There are currently 21 churches representing 1500 members. This constituent body is a member of the American Council of Christian Churches.

The Fellowship of Fundamental Bible Churches owns and operates Tri-State Bible Camp and Conference Center in Montague, New Jersey, oversees a mission board called Fundamental Bible Missions, and conducts a Bible Institute called Fundamental Bible Institute.

Headquarters

P.O. Box 206, Penns Grove, NJ 08069

Media Contact, Sec., Rev. Edmund G. Cotton, 80 Hudson St., Port Jervis, NY 12771 Tel. (914)856-7695

Email: FFBC-USA@juno.com

Website: www.churches-ffbc.org/

Officers

Pres., Rev. Mark Franklin, 284 Whig Lane, Monroeville, NJ 08343 Tel. (609)881-0057

Vice-Pres., Rev. Gary Myers, P.O. Box 191, Meshoppen, PA 18630 Tel. (717)833-4898

Sec., Rev. Edmund G. Cotton, 80 Hudson St., Port Jervis, NY 12771 Tel. (914)856-7695

Treas., Ken Thompson, 501 N. Main Street, Elmer, NJ 08318 (865)358-0515

Fellowship of Grace Brethren Churches

A division occurred in the Church of the Brethren in 1882 on the question of the legislative authority of the annual meeting. It resulted in the establishment of the Brethren Church under a legal charter requiring congregational government. This body divided in 1939 with the Grace Brethren establishing headquarters at Winona Lake, Ind., and the Brethren Church at Ashland, Ohio.

Headquarters

Media Contact, Fellowship Coord., Rev. Thomas Avey, P.O. Box 386, Winona Lake, IN 46590 Tel. (219)269-1269, Fax (219)269-4066

Email: fgbc@fgbc.org

Website: www.fgbc.org

Officers

Mod., Dr. Galen Wiley, 22713 Ellsworth Ave., Minerva, OH 44657

1st Mod.-Elect, Dr. James Custer, 2515 Carriage Rd., Powell, OH 43065

2nd Mod.-Elect, Dr. Ron Manahan, 2316 E. Kemo Ave., Warsaw, IN 46580

Fellowship Coord., Rev. Thomas Avey, P.O. Box 386, Winona Lake, IN 46590 Tel. (219)269-1269, Fax (219)269-4066

Sec., Fellowship Coord., Rev. Thomas Avey, P.O. Box 386, Winona Lake, IN 46590

Treas., Thomas Staller, 2311 S. Cost-a-Plenty Drive, Warsaw, IN 46580

OTHER BOARDS

Grace Brethren International Missions, Exec. Dir., Rev. Tom Julien, P.O. Box 588, Winona Lake, IN 46590

Grace Brethren Home Missions, Exec. Dir., Larry Chamberlain, P.O. Box 587, Winona Lake, IN 46590

Grace College & Seminary, Pres., Ronald E. Manahan, 200 Seminary Dr., Winona Lake, IN 46590 Tel. (210)372-5100

Brethren Missionary Herald Co., Pub. & Gen. Mgr., James Bustram, P.O. Box 544, Winona Lake, IN 46590

CE National, Exec. Dir., Rev. Ed Lewis, P.O. Box 365, Winona Lake, IN 46590

Grace Brethren Navajo Ministries, Dir., Steve Galegor, Counselor, NM 87018

Grace Village Retirement Community, Admn., Jeff Carroll, P.O. Box 337, Winona Lake, IN 46590

Natl. Fellowship of Grace Brethren Ministries, Pres., Dr. Steve Taylor, 132 Summerall Ct., Aiken, SC 29801 Women's Missionary Council, Pres., Janet Minnix, 3314 Kenwick Tr., S.W., Roanoke, VA, 24015

Grace Brethren Men International, Pres., Morgan Burgess, 163 N. Franklin St., Delaware, OH 43015

Free Christian Zion Church of Christ

This church was organized in 1905 at Redemption, Ark., by a company of African-American ministers associated with various denominations. Its polity is in general accord with that of Methodist bodies.

Headquarters

1315 S. Hutchinson St., Nashville, AR 71852 Tel. (501)845-4933

Media Contact, Gen. Sec., Shirlie Cheatham

Officers

Chief Pastor, Willie Benson, Jr.

Free Methodist Church of North America

The Free Methodist Church was organized in 1860 in Western New York by ministers and laymen who had called the Methodist Episcopal Church to return to what they considered the original doctrines and lifestyle of Methodism. The issues included human freedom (anti-slavery), freedom and simplicity in worship, free seats so that the poor would not be discriminated against, and freedom from secret oaths (societies) so the truth might be spoken freely at all times. The founders emphasized the teaching of the entire sanctification of life by means of grace through faith.

The denomination continues to be true to its founding principles. It communicates the gospel and its power to all people without discrimination through strong missionary, evangelistic and educational programs. Six colleges, a Bible college and numerous overseas schools train the youth of the church to serve in lay and ministerial roles.

Its members covenant to maintain simplicity in life, worship, daily devotion to Christ, responsible stewardship of time, talent, and finance.

Headquarters

World Ministries Center, 770 N. High School Rd., Indianapolis, IN 46214 Tel. (317)244-3660, Fax (317)244-1247

Mailing Address, P.O. Box 535002, Indianapolis, IN 46253 Tel. (800)342-5531

Media Contact, Yearbook Ed., P.O. Box 535002, Indianapolis, IN 46253

Email: info@fmcna.org

Website: www.freemethodistchurch.org

Officers

Bishops, Bishop Roger W. Haskins, Jr.; Bishop Joseph F. James; Bishop Leslie L. Krober; Bishop Richard D. Snyder; Bishop Jim Tuan; Bishop Abner Chauke

General Conference Secretary, Miss Carol Bartlett

Dir. of Administraion and Finance, Mr. Gary Kilgore

Free Methodist Communications, Rev. Douglas Newton

Free Methodist World Missions, Dr. Arthur Brown

Men's Ministries International, Director, Rev. Jeffrey Johnson

Women's Ministries International, President, Mrs. Beth Webb

Periodicals

Light and Life Magazine; Free Methodist World Mission People

Evangelical Friends International—North American Region is listed under "E".

Philadelphia Yearly Meeting of the Religious Society of Friends is listed under "P".

Religious Society of Friends (Conservative) is listed under "R".

Religious Society of Friends (Unaffiliated Meetings) is listed under "R".

Friends General Conference

Friends General Conference (FGC) is an association of fourteen yearly meetings open to all Friends meetings which wish to be actively associated with FGC's programs and services. Friends General Conference includes Baltimore, Canadian, Illinois, Lake Erie, New England, New York, Northern, Ohio Valley, Philadelphia, South Central, and Southeastern Yearly Meetings; Alaska Friends Conference, Southern Appalachian Yearly Meeting and Association, and Piedmont Friends Fellowship; plus seven independently affiliated monthly meetings. Friends General Conference is primarily a service organization with the stated purpose of nurturing the spiritual life within its constituency of predominantly unprogrammed Friends. FGC offers services to all Friends, but has no authority over constituent meetings. A Central Committee, to which constituent Yearly Meetings name appointees (in proportion to membership), and its Executive Committee, are responsible for the direction of FGC's programs and services which include a bookstore, conferences, and traveling ministires program. The 1995 Central Committee approved the following Minute of Purpose,

Friends General Conference is a Quaker organization in the unprogrammed tradition of the Religious Society of Friends which primarily serves affiliated yearly and monthly meetings. It is our experience that,

**Faith is based on direct experience of God.

**Our lives witness this experience individually and corporately.

**By answering that experience of God in everyone, we build and sustain inclusive community.

Friends General Conference provides resources and opportunities that educate and invite members and attenders to experience, individually and corporately, God's living presence, and to discern and follow God's leadings. Friends General Conference reaches out to seekers and to other religious bodies inside and outside the Religious Society of Friends.

Headquarters

1216 Arch St., 2B, Philadelphia, PA 19107 Tel. (215)561-1700, Fax (215)561-0759

Media Contact, Gen. Sec., Bruce Birchard

Email: friends@fgcquaker.org

Website: www.fgcquaker.org

Officers

Gen. Sec., Bruce Birchard

Presiding Clerk, Janice Domanik

Treas., Mike Hubbart

YEARLY MEETINGS

Alaska Friends Conference, Clerk, Bill Schoder-Ehri, 480 Grubstake Ave., Homer, AK, Tel. (907)479-5257, lovenest@ptialaska.net

*Baltimore, Clerk, Lamar Matthew, 17100 Quaker Ln., Sandy Spring, MD 20860 Tel. (301)774-7663, dianajbym@igc.org

*Canadian, Clerk, John Calder, 91A Fourth Ave., Ottawa, ON K1S 2L1 Tel. (613)235-8553, cym@web.net

Illinois, Clerk, Margaret Katranides, 620 Fairview Ave., St. Louis, MO 63119-1809

Lake Erie, Clerk, Don Nagler, 1360 Tomah Dr., Mt. Pleasant, MI 48858

*New England, Clerk, Anne Kriebel, 901 Pleasant St., Worcester, MA 01602-1908 Tel. (508) 754-6760, neym@ultranet.com

*New York, Clerk, Linda Chidsey, 15 Rutherford Pl., New York, NY 10003 Tel. (212)673-5750, nyym@compuserve. com

Northern, Clerk, Christopher Sammond, 1718 10th St., Menomonie, WI 54751

Ohio Valley, Clerk, Cindi Goslee, 215 Woolper, Cincinnati, OH 45220

Philadelphia, Clerk, Arlene Kelly, 1515 Cherry St., Philadelphia, PA 19102 Tel. (215)241-7210, joanb@pym.org; Thomas Jeavons, staff, thomj@pym.org

Piedmont Friends Fellowship, Clerk, David Bailey, 1712 Lakemont Dr., Greensboro, NC 27410 Tel. (336)854-1225, DLLOYDBAI@aol.com

South Central, Clerk, Jan Michael, 1422 S. Western Stillwater, OK 74074-6832 Tel. (405)624-0778

*Southeastern, Clerk, Lyn Cope-Robinson, staff, P.O. Box 510975, Melbourne Beach, FL 32951, seym@bv.net

Southern Appalachian, Clerk, Sharon Annis, P.O. Box 2191, Abinton, VA 24212-2191

*also affiliated with Friends United Meeting

Periodicals

Friends Journal

Friends United Meeting*

Friends United Meeting was organized in 1902 (the name was changed in 1963 from the Five Years Meeting of Friends) as a loose confederation of North American yearly meetings to facilitate a united Quaker witness in missions, peace work, and Christian education.

Today Friends United Meeting is comprised of 20 full-member and 10 assoc. member yearly meetings representing about half the Friends in the world. FUM's current work includes programs of mission and service and congregational renewal. FUM publishes Christian education curriculum, books of Quaker history and religious thought and a magazine, Quaker Life.

Headquarters

101 Quaker Hill Dr., Richmond, IN 47374-1980 Tel. (765)962-7573, Fax (765)966-1293

Media Contact, General Secretary, Retha McCutchen

Email: info@fum.org

Website: www.fum.org

Officers

Presiding Clk., Stan Bauer

Treas., John Bell

Gen. Sec., Retha McCutchen

DEPARTMENTS

World Missions, Director, Retha McCutchen

North American Ministries, Director, Ben Richmond

Quaker Hill Bookstore, Mgr., Sue Gongwer

Friends United Press, Ed., Barbara Mays

YEARLY MEETINGS

Baltimore Yearly Meeting, 17100 Quaker Ln., Sandy Spring, MD 20860 Tel. (301)774-7663, (800)962-4766, Fax (301)774-7084, Lamar Matthew, clerk; Frank Massey, Gen. Sec.

Bware Yearly Meeting, P.O. Box 179, Suna, Kenya; Epainitus Adego, Gen Supt.

Canadian Yearly Meeting, 91-A Fourth Ave., Ottawa ON K1S 2L1, Canada; Tel. and Fax (613)235-8553; Gordon McClure, clerk; Website: www.quaker.ca

Chavakali Yearly Meeting, P.O. Box 102, Chavakali, Kenya, East Africa; Andrew Mukulu, Gen. Sec., Wilson Andenya, Clerk

Cuba Yearly Meeting, Ave. Libertad #110, Puerto Padre, Las Tunas, Cuba; Maria Renya Yi, President

East Africa Yearly Meeting of Friends, (Kaimosi) P.O. Box 35, Tiriki, Kenya, East Africa; Matthew Tsimbaki, Clerk, Thomas Ilote, Gen. Sec., Erastus Kesohole, Gen Supt.

East Africa Yearly Meeting of Friends (North), P.O. Box 544, Kitale, Kenya, East Africa; Geoffrey M. Wamocha, Gen. Sec., Titus Adira, Gen. Supt., H. M Mukwanja. Clerk

East Africa Yearly Meeting of Friends (South), P.O. Box 160, Vihiga, Kenya, East Africa; Joseph Kisia, Clerk; Lam Kisanya Osodo, Gen. Sec., Gilbert Akenga Oyando, Gen. Supt.

Elgon East Yearly Meeting, P.O. Box 2322, Kitale, Kenya, East Africa; Maurice Simiyu, Gen. Supt, Philip Musungu, Gen. Sec., John Kitui, Clerk.

Elgon Religious Society of Friends, P.O. Box 4, Wibuye, Kenya, East Africa, Tom Isiye, General Sec., John Ngoya, Gen. Supt., Charles Mbachi, Presiding Clerk

Evangelical Friends Church Uganda, P.O. Box 129, Mbali, Kenya, East Africa; George Welumoli, Simon Tsapwe

Indiana Yearly Meeting, 4715 N. Wheeling Ave., Muncie, IN 47304-1222; Tel. (765)284-6900, Fax (765)284-8925; Susan Kirkpatrick, Clerk; Alan Weinacht, Gen. Supt.

Iowa Yearly Meeting, Box 657, Oskaloosa, IA 52577; Tel. (515)673-9717, Fax (515)673-9718; Margaret Stoltzfus, Clerk, Kevin Mortimer, Gen. Superintendent

Jamaica Yearly Meeting, 4 Worthington Ave., Kingston 5, Jamaica WI; Tel. (809)926-7371, Isaiah Campbell, Pres. Clerk

Kakamega Yearly Meeting, P.O. Box 465, Kakamega, Kenya, East Africa; Jonathan Shisanya, Gen. Sec., Blastus Wawire, Clerk, Meschack Musindi, Gen. Supt.

Lugari Yearly Meeting, P.O. Box 483, Turbo, Kenya, East Africa; David A. Mulama, Gen.

Sec., Noah Inziria, Clerk, Japheth Vidoro, Gen. Supt.
Malava Yearly Meeting, P.O. Box 26, Malava, Kenya, East Africa; Andrew Namasaka Mulongo, Gen. Sec., Samson Marani, Clerk, Enoch Shinachi, Gen. Supt.
Nairobi Yearly Meeting, P.O. Box 8321, Nairobi, Kenya, East Africa; Stanley Ndezwa, Clerk, Aggrey Mukilima, Gen. Supt., Zablon Isaac Malenge, Gen. Sec.
Nandi Yearly Meeting, P.O. Box 102, Kapsabet, Kenya, East Africa; Joseph chemai Biama, Presiding clk., Solomon Mwanzi, Gen. Supt., Hezron Kigali, Gen. Sec.
Nebraska Yearly Meeting, 423 S. Tinker St., Hominy, OK 74035; Tel. (918)885-2714; David Nagle, Clerk
New England Yearly Meeting, 901 Pleasant St., Worcester, MA 01602 Tel. (508)754-6760; Elizabeth Muench, Clerk; Jonathan Vogel-Borne, Field Secretary
New York Yearly Meeting, 15 Rutherford Pl., New York, NY 10003 Tel. (212)673-5750; Victoria B. Cooley, Clerk; Helen Garay Toppins, Admin. Sec.
North Carolina Yearly Meeting, 5506 W. Friendly Ave., Greensboro, NC 27410; Tel. (336)292-6957; Brent McKinney, Clerk; John Porter, Gen. Superintendent
Southeastern Yearly Meeting, P.O. Box 510795, Melbourne Beach, FL 32951, Tel. (321)724-1162; Lyn Cope-Robinson, Gen. Sec.
Tanzania Yearly Meeting, P.O. Box 151, Mugumu, Serengeti, Tanzania; Joseph Lavuna Oguma, Gen. Supt. & Clerk
Uganda Yearly Meeting, P.O. Box 605, Kampala, Uganda, East Africa; Samuel Wefwafwa, Gen. Sec., Andrew H.S. Kurima, Gen. Supt., Christopher Wabuula Kakala, Clerk
Vokoli Yearly Meetings, P.O. Box 266, Wodanga, Kenya, 0331 45033; Javan Mirembe, Gen. Sec., Hannington Mbato, Presiding Clerk, TimonaKita, Gen Supt.
Western Yearly Meeting, P.O. Box 70, Plainfield, IN 46168; Tel. (317)839-2789 and 839-2849, Fax (317)839-2616; Curt Shaw, Gen. Superintendent
Wilmington Yearly Meeting, Pyle Center Box 1194, Wilmington, OH 45177; Tel. (937)382-2491, Fax (937)382-7077; Gary Farlow, Clerk; Marvin Hall, Ex. Sec.

Periodicals

Quaker Life

Full Gospel Assemblies International

The Full Gospel Assemblies International was founded in 1962 under the leadership of Dr. Charles Elwood Strauser. The roots of Full Gospel Assemblies may be traced to 1947 with the beginning of the Full Gospel Church of Coatesville, Pennsylvania. As an Assemblies of God Pentecostal church, the Full Gospel Church of Coatesville was active in evangelization and educational ministries to the community. In service to the ministers and students of the Full Gospel Church ministries, the Full Gospel Trinity Ministerial Fellowship was formed in 1962, later changing its name to Full Gospel Assemblies International.

Retaining its original doctrine and faith, Full Gospel Assemblies is Trinitarian and believes in the Bible as God's infallible Word to all people, in baptism in the Holy Spirit according to Acts 2, in divine healing made possible by the sufferings of our Lord Jesus Christ, and in the imminent return of Christ for those who love him.

The body of Full Gospel Assemblies is an evangelical missionary fellowship sponsoring ministry at home and abroad, composed of self governing ministries and churches. Congregations, affiliate ministries, and clerical bodies are located throughout the United States and over 31 countries of the world.

Headquarters

3170 Lincoln Hwy, Parkesburg, PA
Mailing Address, P.O. Box 1230, Coatesville, PA 19320 Tel. (610)857-2357, Fax (610)857-3109
Media Contact, Simeon Strauser

Officers

Gen. Supt., Dr. AnnaMae Strauser
Exec. Dir. of Ministry, J. Victor Fisk
Exec. Dir of Admn., Simeon Strauser
Exec. Dir. of Communications, Archie Neale
Exec. Sec., Betty Stewart
Trustee, Carol Strauser
Trustee, Edward Popovich

Periodicals

Full Gospel Ministries Outreach Report

Full Gospel Fellowship of Churches and Ministers International

In the early 1960s a conviction grew in the hearts of many ministers that there should be closer fellowship between the people of God who believed in the apostolic ministry. At the same time, many independent churches were experiencing serious difficulties in receiving authority from the IRS to give governmentally accepted tax-exempt receipts for donations.

In September 1962 a group of ministers met in Dallas, Texas, to form a Fellowship to give expression to the essential unity of the Body of Christ under the leadership of the Holy Spirit" a unity that goes beyond individuals, churches or organizations. This was not a movement to build another denomination, but rather an effort to join ministers, churches, and ministry organizations of like mind across denominational lines.

To provide opportunities for fellowship and to support the objectives and goals of local and national ministries, regional conventions and an annual international convention are held.

Headquarters

100 N. Belt Line Rd., Irving, TX 75061 Tel. (214)492-1254
Media Contact, Sec., Dr. Harry Schmidt
Email: FGFCMI@aol.com
Website: www.fgfcmi.org/

Officers

Pres., Dr. Don Arnold, P.O. Box 324, Gadsden, AL 35901
1st Vice-Pres., Dr. Ray Chamberlain
Sec., Dr. Harry Schmidt
Treas., Rev. Gene Evans P.O. Box 813 Douglasville, GA 30133
CFO, Dr. S.K. Biffle, 1000 N. Belt Line Rd., Irving, TX 75061
Ofc. Sec., Ms. Lanita Isbell & Nita Biffle
Vice-Pres. at Large, Rev. Maurice Hart, P.O. Box 4316, Omaha, NE 68104; Rev. Don Westbrook, 3518 Rose of Sharon Rd., Durham, NC 27705
Chmn. of Evangelism, David Ellis
Past Pres., Dr. James Helton

REGIONAL VICE-PRESIDENTS

Southeast, Rev. Gene Evans, P.O. Box 813, Douglasville, GA 30133
South Central, Rev. Robert J. Miller, P.O. Box 10621, Killeen, TX 76547
Southwest, Rev. Arlie Branson, 12504 4th St., Yucaipa, CA 92399
Northeast, Rev. David Ellis, 3636 Winchester Rd., Allertown, PA 18104
North Central, Rev. Raymond Rothwell, P.O. Box 367, Eaton, OH 45320
Northwest, Rev. Ralph Trask, 3212 Hyacinth NE, Salem, OR 97303

Periodicals

Fellowship Tidings

Fundamental Methodist Church, Inc.

This group traces its origin through the Methodist Protestant Church. It withdrew from The Methodist Church and organized on August 27, 1942.

Headquarters

1034 N. Broadway, Springfield, MO 65802
Media Contact, Dist. Supt., Rev. Ronnie Howerton, 1952 Highway H, Monett, MO 65708 Tel. (417)235-3849

Officers

Treas., Wayne Blades, Rt. 1, Crane, MO 65633 Tel. (417)723-8123
Sec., Betty Nicholson, Rt. 2, Box 397, Ash Grove, MO 65604 Tel. (417)672-2268
Dist. Supt., Rev. Ronnie Howerton, 1952 Highway H, Monett, MO 65708 Tel. (417)235-3849

General Assembly of the Korean Presbyterian Church in America—please see Korean Presbyterian Church in America, General Assembly of the.

General Association of General Baptists

Similar in doctrine to those General Baptists organized in England in the seventeenth century, the first General Baptist churches were organized on the Midwest frontier following the Second Great Awakening. The first church was established by the Rev. Benoni Stinson in 1823 at Evansville, Ind.

Stinson's major theological emphasis was general atonement - "Christ tasted death for every man." The group also allows for the possibility of apostasy. It practices open Communion and believer's baptism by immersion.

Called "liberal" Baptists because of their emphasis on the freedom of man, General Baptists organized a General Association in 1870 and invited other "liberal" Baptists (e.g., "Free Will" and Separate Baptists) to participate.

The policy-setting body is composed of delegates from local General Baptist churches and associations. Each local church is autonomous but belongs to an association. The group currently consists of more than 60 associations in 16 states, as well as several associations in the Philippines, Guam, Saipan, Jamaica and India. Ministers and deacons are ordained by a presbytery.

A number of boards continue a variety of missions, schools and other support ministries. General Baptists belong to the Baptist World Alliance, the North American Baptist Fellowship and the National Association of Evangelicals.

Headquarters

100 Stinson Dr., Poplar Bluff, MO 63901 Tel. (573)785-7746, Fax (573)785-0564
Media Contact, Exec. Dir., Dr. Ron Black

Officers

Mod., Dr. James Murray
Clk., Rev. Tommy Roberts
Exec. Dir., Dr. Ron Black

OTHER ORGANIZATIONS

International Missions, Dir., Rev. Jack Eberhardt
National Missions, Dir., Rev. Ron Byrd
Women's Ministries, Dir.,
Nursing Home Admn., Jack Cole, Rt. #2, Box 650, Campbell, MO 63933
University Bd., Pres., Dr. James Murray, Oakland City University, 143 N. Lucretia, Oakland City, IN 47660
Congregational Ministries, Dir., Rev. Mike Warren, 100 Stinson Dr., Poplar Bluff, MO 63901
Pastoral Ministries, Dir., Rev. Fred Brittain, 100 Stinson Dr., Poplar Bluff, MO 63901
Admin., Financial Services, Financial Officer, Linda McDonough, 100 Stinson Dr., Poplar Bluff, MO 63901
Stinson Press, Inc., Pres., Rev. Dale Bates, 400 Stinson Dr., Poplar Bluff, MO 63901

Oakview Heights Continuous Care & Rehab Center, Administrator, Scott Cole, 1320 West 9th St., Mt. Carmel, IL 62863

Compassionate Care Adoption Agency, Dir., Dr. John Clanton, Rt. 3, Box 12B, Oakland City, IN 47660

Periodicals

The General Baptist Messenger; Capsule; Voice; Church Talk; Pastor Talk;

General Association of Regular Baptist Churches

This association was founded in May, 1932, in Chicago by a group of churches which had withdrawn from the Northern Baptist Convention (now the American Baptist Churches in the U.S.A.) because of doctrinal differences. Its Confession of Faith, which it requires all churches to subscribe to, is essentially the old, historic New Hampshire Confession of Faith with a premillennial ending applied to the last article.

The churches of the General Association of Regular Baptist Churches voluntarily join together to accomplish four goals. (1) Champion Biblical truth—committed to communication with the whole counsel of God in its timeless relevance. (2) Impact the world for Christ—obeying the Lord's Great Commission to take the life-changing gospel to the entire world. (3) Perpetuate Its Baptist heritage—faithfully promoting its Scriptural legacy and identity. (4) Advancing GARBC churches—strengthening existing churches and planting new churches for the purposes of evangelism and edification.

Headquarters

1300 N. Meacham Rd., Schaumburg, IL 60173 Tel. (847)843-1600, Fax (847)843-3757

Media Contact, Natl. Rep., Dr. John Greening

Email: garbc@garbc.org

Website: www.garbc.org

Officers

Chpsn., Rev. Bryce Augsburger

Vice-Chpsn., Rev. W. David Warren

Treas.,Dr. David Gower

Sec., Rev. David Strope

Natl. Rep., Dr. John Greening

Periodicals

Baptist Bulletin

General Church of the New Jerusalem

The General Church of the New Jerusalem, also called the New Church, was founded in 1897. It is based on the teachings of the eighteenth Century scientist Emanuel Swedenborg, and stresses the oneness of God, who is the Lord Jesus Christ, a life of faith and love in service to others, in true married love, and in life after death.

Headquarters

P.O. Box 711, Bryn Athyn, PA 19009 Tel. (215) 938-2620

Media Contact, Ed., Church Journal, Donald L. Rose, Box 277, Bryn Athyn, PA 19009 Tel. (215)947-6225, Fax (215)947-3078

Email: svsimpso@newchurch.edu

Website: www.newchurch.org

Officers

Presiding Bishop, Rt. Rev. P. M. Buss

Sec., Susan V. Simpson

Treas., Daniel T. Allen

Periodicals

New Church Life

General Conference of Mennonite Brethren Churches

A small group, requesting that closer attention be given to prayer, Bible study, and a consistent lifestyle, withdrew from the larger Mennonite Church in the Ukraine in 1860. Anabaptist in origin, the group was influenced by Lutheran pietists and Baptist teachings and adopted a quasi-congregational form of church government. In 1874 and years following, small groups of these German-speaking Mennonites left Russia, settled in Kansas and then spread to the Midwest west of the Mississippi and into Canada. Some years later the movement spread to California and the West Coast. In 1960, the Krimmer Mennonite Brethren Conference merged with this body.

Today the General Conference of Mennonite Brethren Churches conducts services in many European languages as well as in Vietnamese, Mandarin, and Hindi. It works with other denominations in missionary and development projects in 25 countries outside North America.

Headquarters

4812 E. Butler Ave., Fresno, CA 93727 Tel. (209)452-1713, Fax (209)452-1752

Media Contact, Exec. Sec., Marvin Hein

Officers

Mod., Ed Boschman, 12630 N. 103rd Ave., Suite 215, Sun City, AZ 85351

Asst. Mod., Herb Kopp, 200 McIvor Ave., Winnipeg, NB R20 028

Sec., Valerie Rempel

Exec. Sec., Marvin Hein

Periodicals

Christian Leader; Mennotite Bretheren Herald

Grace Gospel Fellowship

The Grace Gospel Fellowship was organized in 1944 by a group of pastors who held to a dispensational interpretation of Scripture. Most had ministries in the Midwest. Two prominent leaders were J. C. O'Hair of Chicago and Charles Baker of Milwaukee. Subsequent to 1945, a Bible Institute was founded (now Grace Bible

College of Grand Rapids, Mich.), and a previously organized foreign mission (now Grace Ministries International of Grand Rapids) was affiliated with the group. Churches have now been established in most sections of the country. The body has remained a fellowship, each church being autonomous in polity. All support for its college, mission, and headquarters is on a contributory basis.

The binding force of the Fellowship has been the members' doctrinal position. They believe in the Deity and Saviorship of Jesus Christ and subscribe to the inerrant authority of Scripture. Their method of biblical interpretation is dispensational, with emphasis on the distinctive revelation to and the ministry of the apostle Paul.

Headquarters

Media Contact, Pres., Ken Parker, 2125 Martindale SW, P.O. Box 9432, Grand Rapids, MI 49509 Tel. (616)245-0100, Fax (616)241-2542

Email: ggfinc@aol.com

Website: www.ggfusa.org/

Officers

Pres., Roger G. Anderson

OTHER ORGANIZATIONS

Grace Bible College, Pres., Rev. Bruce Kemper, 1011 Aldon St. SW, Grand Rapids, MI 49509

Grace Ministries Intl., Exec. Dir., Dr. Samuel Vinton, 2125 Martindale Ave. SW, Grand Rapids, MI 49509

Prison Mission Association, Gen. Dir., Nathan Whitham, P.O. Box 1587, Port Orchard, WA 98366-0140

Grace Publications Inc., Exec. Dir., Roger G. Anderson, 2125 Martindale Ave. SW, Grand Rapids, MI 49509

Bible Doctrines to Live By, Exec. Dir., Lee Homoki, P.O. Box 2351, Grand Rapids, MI 49501

Periodicals

Truth

Greek Orthodox Archdiocese of America*

THE ORTHODOX CHURCH

The Orthodox Church today, numbering over 250 million worldwide, is a communion of self-governing Churches, each administratively independent of the other, but united by a common faith and spirituality. Their underlying unity is based on identity of doctrines, sacramental life, and worship, which distinguishes Orthodox Christianity. All recognize the spiritual preeminence of the Ecumenical Patriarch of Constantinople who is acknowledged as primus inter pares, first among equals. All share full communion with one another. The living tradition of the Church and the principles of concord and harmony are expressed through the common mind of the universal episcopate as the need arises. In all other matters, the internal life of each independent Church is administered by the bishops of that particular Church. Following the ancient priciple of the one people of God in each place and the universal priesthood of all believers, the laity share equally in the responsibility for the preservation and propagation of the Christian faith and Church.

THE GREEK ORTHODOX ARCHDIOCESE OF AMERICA

Before the establishment of an Archdiocese in the Western Hemisphere there were numerous communities of Greek Orthodox Christians. The first Greek Orthodox community in the Americas was founded in New Orleans, LA by a small colony of Greek merchants. History also records that on June 26,1768 the first Greek colonists landed at St. Augustine, FL, the oldest city in America. The first permanent community was founded in New York City in 1892, today's Archdiocesan Cathedral of the Holy Trinity and the See of the Archbishop of America. The Greek Orthodox Archdiocese of North and South America was incorporated in 1921 and officially recognized by the State of New York in 1922.

The Greek Orthodox Archdiocese of America is under the jurisdiction of the Ecumenical Patriarchate of Constantinople and is composed of an Archdiocesan District — New York and eight dioceses — New Jersey, Chicago, Atlanta, Detroit, San Francisco, Pittsburgh, Boston and Denver. It is governed by the Archbishop and the Synod of Bishops. The Synod of Bishops is headed by the Archbishop and comprised of the Bishops who are in charge of a diocese. It has all the authority and responsibility which the Church canons provide for a provincial synod.

Headquarters

8-10 E. 79th St., New York, NY 10021 Tel. (212)570-3500, Fax (212)570-3569

Media Contact, Nikki Stephanopoulos, Director, News and Information/Public Affairs Tel. (212) 570-3530 Fax. (212)774-0215, nikki@goarch.org

Email: archdiocese@goarch.org

Website: www.goarch.org

HOLY EPARCHIAL SYNOD OF BISHOPS

His Eminence Archbishop Demetrios

Primate of the Greek Orthodox Archdiocese of America

Exarch of the Atlantic and Pacific Oceans

Chairman of the Holy Synod of Bishops

Greek Orthodox Church in America, 8-10 East 79th Street, New York, NY 10021 (212) 570-3500, Fax. (212) 570-3592

DIOCESES

His Eminence Metropolitan Iakovos of Krinis

Presiding Hierarch of the Diocese of Chicago

40 East Burton Place, Chicago, IL 60610 (312) 337-4130, Fax (312) 337-9391

His Eminence Metropolitan Anthony of Dardanelles

Presiding Hierarch of the Diocese of San Francisco
372 Santa Clara Avenue, San Francisco, CA 94127 Tel. (415)753-3075, Fax. (415)753-1165
His Eminence Metropolitan Maximos of Aenos
Presiding Hierarch of the Diocese of Pittsburgh
5201 Ellsworth Avenue, Pittsburgh, PA 15232 Tel. (412)621-5529, Fax. (412)621-1522
His Eminence Metropolitan Methodios of Aneon
Presiding Hierarch of the Diocese of Boston
162 Goddard Avenue, Brookline, MA 02146 Tel. (617)277-4742 Fax. (617)739-9229
His Eminence Metropolitan Isaiah of Proikonisou
Presiding Hierarch of the Diocese of Denver
4610 East Alameda Avenue, Suite D1, Denver, CO 80222 Tel. (303)333-7794, Fax. (303)333-7796
His Grace Bishop Alexios of Atlanta
Diocese of Atlanta
2480 Clairmont Road NE, Atlanta, GA 30329 Tel. (404)634-9345, Fax. (404)634-2471
His Grace Bishop Nicholas of Detroit
Diocese of Detroit
19405 Renfrew Road, Detroit, MI 48221 Tel. (313)664-5433 Fax. (313)864-5543
Diocese of New Jersey
Locum Tenens
His Eminence Archbishop Demetrios
1811 Springfield Avenue, New Providence, NJ 07094 Tel. (908) 233-3070, Fax.(908)898-0980
Episcopal Assistant
His Grace Bishop Dimitrios of Xanthos

CLERGY-LAITY CONGRESS

The Clergy-Laity Congress, the highest legislative body of the Archdiocese, is convened biennially and presided over by the Archbishop. It is concerned with all matters, other than doctrinal or canonical, affecting the life, growth and unity of the Church, the institutions, finances, administration, educational, and philanthropic concerns and its increasing growing role in the life of the nations of the Western Hemisphere. The delegates are the pastors and elected lay representatives.

There are 540 parishes, 800 priests and approximately 1.5 million faithful in the Greek Orthodox Archdiocese of America

THE ARCHDIOCESAN COUNCIL

The Archdiocesan Council is the deliberative body of the Greek Orthodox Archdiocese which meets in the interim period between Clergy-Laity Congresses, held every two years.

Executive Committee,

His Eminence Archbishop Demetrios Chairman
The Holy Synod of Bishops
Vice Chairman, Michael Jaharis; Treasurer, Peter Dion; Secretary, Nicholas Bouras; George Behrakis, Dr. John Collis, John Pappajohn,John Payiavlas, Georgia Skeadas, Anthony Stefanis, Emanuel G. Demos, Legal Counselor to the Archdiocese.

INSTITUTIONS

Archdiocesan Cathedral of the Holy Trinity
The Rev. Dr. Robert G. Stephanopoulos, Dean
319-337 East 74th Street, New York, NY 10021 Tel. (212)288-3215,Fax (212)288-5876
Web: www.thecathedral.goarch.org
Hellenic College/Holy Cross School of Theology
The Rev. Nicholas Triantafilou, President
50 Goddard Avenue, Brookline,MA 02445 Tel. (617)731-3500, Fax (617)850-1460
Email: admission@hchc.edu
Saint Basil Academy
The Rev. Constantine L. Sitaras,Director
79 Saint Basil Road, Garrison, NY 10524 Tel. (845)424-3500, Fax (845)424-4172
Email: stbasil@bestweb.net
Web:www.stbasil.goarch.org

ST. MICHAEL'S HOME

The Very Rev. Andonios Paropoulos, Director
3 Lehman Terrace, Yonkers, NY 10705 Tel. (914) 476-3374, Fax (914)476-1744
Email: Stmichaelshome@msn.com
Web: stmichael.goarch.org

ARCHDIOCESE OF NEW YORK

Office of the Archbishop, Alice Keurian; Director; Office of the Chancellor, Very Rev. Savas Zembillas, Chancellor; Office of Administration, Jerry Dimitriou, Executive Director.

ARCHDIOCESAN DEPARTMENTS

Registry, Finance, Stewardship & LOGOS, Religious Education, Greek Education, Communications, Internet Ministries, Information Technologies, Youth and Young Adults, Camping Ministry, Ionian Village Ecumenical, Interfaith/Interchurch Marriages, Archives, Benefits

RELATED ORGANIZATIONS, AUXILIARIES

Ladies Philoptochos Society, Presbyters Council, Sisterhood of Presvyteres, Retired Clergy of America, National Forum of Greek Orthodox Musicians, Hellenic Cultural Center, Archons of the Ecumenical Patriarchate, Archbishop Iakovos Leadership 100 Endowment Fund, St. Photios National Shrine, International Orthodox Christian Charities(IOCC), Orthodox Christian Mission Center, Trinity Children & Family Services.

OTHER JURISDICTIONS OF THE ECUMENICAL PATRIARCHATE IN THE USA

Albanian Orthodox Diocese in America; Belarusian Council of Orthodox Churches in North America; American Carpatho-Russian Orthodox Greek Catholic Diocese of the USA; Ukrainian Orthodox Church of the USA

The Holy Eastern Orthodox Catholic and Apostolic Church in North America, Inc.

This Church was canonically established by the Russian Orthodox Synod of Bishops in North America on Feb. 2, 1927 with the approval of the

Russian Patriarch. Archbishop Aftimios Ofiesh was appointed first Archbishop of this church and headed this Church until his repose in 1966. The Church was incorporated on Feb. 1, 1928 and continues today. We recently registered our name and logo as our service mark since some in the independent movement claimed to be us, and would use our name, and occasionally our logo, to attempt to "prove" to the public that they are us. They go so far as to claim they changed our name, and all mention our 1927 Charter as if it was issued to them and the general public. We continue today as the same Church and same corporation and not a reincorporated group using this name. Today we are a western rite jurisdiction but do include eastern rite clergy and liturgies.

Prior to the death of Abp. Aftimios, the Church had only one bishop after the deaths of Dr. Joseph Zuk (Ukrainian) and Bp. Sophronios leaving only Abp. Aftimios. On the death of Abp. Aftimios the Church continues in locum tenens prior to his election in 1997 as Metropolitan President of the Church. According to an October 1932 NY Times newspaper article with photograph Abp. Aftimios, B. Zuk and B. Sophronios were the only Members of the North American Holy Synod. Bp. Ignastius was mentioned but not as a synod member.

This Church name, over the years, has been used by members of the independent movement who like to claim they are this Church. These people for the most part are not orthodox but use the name as a status symbol.

Headquarters

Orthodox Catholic Archdiocese of Arkansas, 733 Tick Rd., Mountain View, AR 72569, Tel. (870)269-6071
Primate, Metropolitan Victor
Email: theocacna@webtv.net
Website: www.theocacna.org

Officers

President, Primate, Metropolitan Victor
Archbishop Peter Mar Kepha
Bishop Gerald
Archbishop Lawrence, retired
Archbishop Joseph, retired
Bishop Robert

SYNOD ADVISORS

Archbishop James
Bishop Donald

Holy Ukrainian Autocephalic Orthodox Church in Exile

This church was organized in a parish in New York in 1951 by Ukrainian laymen and clergy who settled in the Western Hemisphere after World War II. In 1954 two bishops, immigrants from Europe, met with clergy and laymen and formally organized the religious body.

Headquarters

103 Evergreen St., W. Babylon, NY 11704

Officers

Admn., Rt. Rev. Serhij K. Pastukhiv, Tel. (516) 669-7402

House of God, Which is the Church of the Living God, the Pillar and Ground of the Truth, Inc.

This body, founded by Mary L. Tate in 1919, is episcopally organized.

Headquarters

1301 N. 58th St., Philadelphia, PA 19131
Media Contact, Sec., Rose Canon, 515 S. 57th St., Philadelphia, PA 19143 Tel. (215)474-8913

Officers

Bishop, Raymond W. White, 6107 Cobbs Creek Pkwy., Philadelphia, PA 19143 Tel. (215)748-6338

Hungarian Reformed Church in America*

A Hungarian Reformed Church was organized in New York in 1904 in connection with the Reformed Church of Hungary. In 1922, the Church in Hungary transferred most of its congregations in the United States to the Reformed Church in the U.S. Some, however, preferred to continue as an autonomous, self-supporting American denomination, and these formed the Free Magyar Reformed Church in America. This group changed its name in 1958 to Hungarian Reformed Church in America.

This church is a member of the World Alliance of Reformed Churches, Presbyterian and Congregational, the World Council of Churches and the National Council of Churches of Christ.

Headquarters

Bishop's Office, 13 Grove St., Poughkeepsie, NY 12601 Tel. (914)454-5735

Officers

Bishop, Rt. Rev. Alexander Forro
Chief Lay-Curator, Prof. Stephen Szabo, 464 Forest Ave., Paramus, NJ 07652
Gen. Sec. (Clergy), Rt. Rev. Stefan M. Torok, 331 Kirkland Pl., Perth Amboy, NJ 08861 Tel. (908)442-7799
Gen Sec. (Lay), Zoltan Ambrus, 3358 Maple Dr., Melvindale, MI 48122
Eastern Classes, Dean (Senior of the Deans, Chair in Bishop's absence), Very Rev. Imre Bertalan, 10401 Grosvenor Pl., #1521, Rockville, MD 20852 Tel. (301)493-5036, Fax (301)571-5111; Lay-Curator, Balint Balogh, 519 N. Muhlenberg St., Allentown, PA 18104
New York Classes, Supervisor, Rt. Rev. Alexander Forro; Lay-Curator, Laszlo B. Vanyi, 229 E. 82nd St., New York, NY 10028
Western Classes, Dean, V. Rev. Andor Demeter, 3921 W. Christy Dr., Phoenix, AZ 85029; Lay-Curator, Zolton Kun, 2604 Saybrook Dr., Pittsburgh, PA 15235

Periodicals

Magyar Egyhaz

Hutterian Brethren

Small groups of Hutterites derive their names from Jacob Hutter, a sixteenth-century Anabaptist who taught true discipleship after accepting Jesus as Saviour, advocated communal ownership of property and was burned as a heretic in Austria in 1536.

Many believers are of German descent and still use their native tongue at home and in church. Much of the denominational literature is produced in German and English. "Colonies" share property, practice non-resistance, dress plainly, do not participate in politics, and operate their own schools. There are 428 colonies with 42,000 members in North America. Each congregation conducts its own youth work through Sunday school. Until age 15, children attend German and English school which is operated by each colony. All youth ages 15 to 20 attend Sunday school. They are baptized as adults upon confession of faith, around age 20.

Headquarters

Media Contact, Philip J. Gross, 3610 N. Wood Rd., Reardon, WA 99029 Tel. (509)299-5400 Fax (509)299-3099

Email: philsjg@juno.com

Officers

Smiedleut Chmn., No. 1, Jacob Waldner, Blumengard Colony, Box 13 Plum Coulee, MB R0G 1R0 Tel. (204)829-3527

Smiedleut Chmn., No. 2, Jacob Wipf, Spring Creek Colony, 36562 102 Street, Forbes, ND 58439 Tel. (701)358-8621

Dariusleut, Chmn., No. 1, Martin Walter, Springpoint Colony, Box 249, Pincher Creek, AB T0K 1W0 Tel. (403)553-4368

Lehrerleut, Chmn., Rev. John Wipf, Rosetown Colony, Box 1509, Rosetown, SK S0L 2V0 Tel. (306)882-3344

IFCA International, Inc.

This group of churches was organized in 1930 at Cicero, Illinois, by representatives of the American Council of Undenominational Churches and representatives of various independent churches. The founding churches and members had separated themselves from various denominational affiliations.

The IFCA provides a way for independent churches and ministers to unite in close fellowship and cooperation, in defense of the fundamental teachings of Scripture and in the proclamation of the gospel of God's grace.

Headquarters

3520 Fairlanes, Grandville, MI 49418 Tel. (616) 531-1840, Fax (616)531-1814

Mailing Address, P.O. Box 810, Grandville, MI 49468-0810

Media Contact, Exec. Dir., Rev. Les C. Lofquist

Email: office@ifca.org

Website: www.ifca.org

Officers

Exec. Dir., Rev. Les C. Lofquist

Pres., Dr. Robert Graves, Santa Rosa, CA

Periodicals

The Voice

International Church of the Foursquare Gospel

Founded by Aimee Semple McPherson in 1927, the International Church of the Foursquare Gospel proclaims the message of Jesus Christ the Savior, Healer, Baptizer with the Holy Spirit, and Soon-coming King. Headquartered in Los Angeles, this evangelistic missionary body of believers consists of nearly 1,907 churches in the United States and Canada.

The International Church of the Foursquare Gospel is incorporated in the state of California and governed by a Board of Directors who direct its corporate affairs. A Foursquare Cabinet, consisting of the Corporate Officers, Board of Directors and District Supervisors of the various districts of the Foursquare Church in the United States and other elected or appointed members, serves in an advisory capacity to the President and the Board of Directors.

Each local Foursquare Church is a subordinate unit of the International Church of the Foursquare Gospel. The pastor of the church is appointed by the Board of Directors and is responsible for the spiritual and physical welfare of the church. To assist and advise the pastor, a church council is elected by the local church members.

Foursquare Churches seek to build strong believers through Christian education, Christian day schools, youth camping and ministry, Foursquare Women International who support and encourage Foursquare missionaries abroad, radio and television ministries, the Foursquare World Advance Magazine, and 276 Bible Colleges worldwide.

Worldwide missions remains the focus of the Foursquare Gospel Church with 27,222 churches and meeting places, 44,457 national Foursquare pastors, leaders and 3,402,307 members and adherents in 114 countries around the globe. The Church is affiliated with the Pentecostal/ Charismatic Churches of North America, National Association of Evangelicals and the World Pentecostal Fellowship.

Headquarters

1910 W. Sunset Blvd., Ste. 200, P.O. Box 26902, Los Angeles, CA 90026-0176 Tel. (213)989-4234, Fax (213)989-4590

Media Contact, Editor, Dr. Ron Williams

Email: comm@foursquare.org

Website: www.foursquare.org

CORPORATE OFFICERS

Pres., Dr. Paul C. Risser
Vice-Pres., Dr. Clifford Hanes
Gen. Supvr., Dr. Jared Roth
Dir. of Missions Intl., Rev. Michael Larkin
Sec., Rev. Herbert Schneidau
Treas., Mr. Brent Morgan
Bd. of Directors, Dr. Paul C. Risser; Rev. Jeff Kolodziej; Rev. Arthur Gray; Mark Simon; Rev. Alan Eastland; Rev. Lolita Frederick; Rev. Steve Overman; Rev. James Cecil; Rev. Ron Pinkston; Rev. Ivy Stanton
District Supervisors, Eastern, Dr. Cliff Hanes; Great Lakes, Dr. Fred Parker; Midwest, Rev. Larry Spousta; Northwest, Dr. Tom Ferguson; South Central, Rev. Dennis Easter; Southeast, Rev. Glenn Burris, Jr.; Southern California, Rev. James C. Scott, Jr.; Southwest, Rev. Don Long; Western, Rev. Robert Booth
Foursquare Cabinet, Composed of Corp. Officers; Board of Directors; District Supervisors, Cabinet, Thomas A. Baker, Cosette M. Conaway; James P. Freund; Mark T. Harris; Eric D. Hulet; Parnell M. Lovelace, Jr.; Mary L. Phillips; David W. Wing; Enrique Zone; Richard E. Scott; Jack W. Hayford; Ron D. Mehl; Jesus De Paz; Roger Al Whitlow; Wayne Cordeiro; Ralph E. Moore; Eddie Rodriguez; Charles Williams, Joe Wittwer

SUPPORT MINISTRIES

Natl. Dept. of Youth, Natl. Youth Minister, Walter R. Hoefflin
Natl. Dept. of Chr. Educ., Dir., Rev. Rick Wulfestieg

Periodicals

Foursquare World Advance

International Council of Community Churches*

This body is a fellowship of locally autonomous, ecumenically minded, congregationally governed, non-creedal Churches. The Council came into being in 1950 as the union of two former councils of community churches, one formed of black churches known as the Biennial Council of Community Churches in the United States and elsewhere and the other of white churches known as the National Council of Community Churches.

Headquarters

21116 Washington Pky., Frankfort, IL 60423-3112 Tel. (815)464-5690, Fax (815)464-5692
Media Contact, Exec. Dir., Rev. Michael E. Livingston

Officers

Pres., Rev. Albert Wright
Vice-Pres., Grace O'Neal
Vice-Pres., Rev. Herbert Freitag
Sec., Rev. Gary Batey
Treas., Rev. Martin Singley, III

OTHER ORGANIZATIONS

Commission on Laity and Church Relations, Erlene O'Brien
Commission on Ecumenical Relations, Rev. Herman Harmelink, III
Commission on Clergy Relations, Rev. Dr. Martin Bolton
Commission on Faith, Justice & Mission, Rev. Eric Biehl
Women's Christian Fellowship, Pres., Anetta Duarte
Samaritans (Men's Fellowship), Pres., Don Fair
Young Adult Fellowship, Pres., Corwin Mason
Youth Fellowship, Pres., Amanda Schlegel

Periodicals

The Christian Community; The Inclusive Pulpit

The International Pentecostal Church of Christ

At a General Conference held at London, Ohio, Aug. 10, 1976, the International Pentecostal Assemblies and the Pentecostal Church of Christ consolidated into one body, taking the name International Pentecostal Church of Christ.

The International Pentecostal Assemblies was the successor of the Association of Pentecostal Assemblies and the International Pentecostal Missionary Union. The Pentecostal Church of Christ was founded by John Stroup of Flatwoods, Ketucky, on May 10, 1917 and was incorporated at Portsmouth, Ohio, in 1927. The International Pentecostal Church of Christ is an active member of the Pentecostal/Charismatic Churches of North America, as well as a member of the National Association of Evangelicals.

The priorities of the International Pentecostal Church of Christ are to be an agency of God for evangelizing the world, to be a corporate body in which people may worship God and to be a channel of God's purpose to build a body of saints being perfected in the image of His Son.

The Annual Conference is held each year during the first full week of August in London, Ohio.

Headquarters

2245 St. Rt. 42 SW, P.O. Box 439, London, OH 43140 Tel. (740)852-4722, Fax (740)852-0348
Media Contact, Gen. Overseer, Clyde M. Hughes
Email: hqipcc@aol.com
Website: members.aol.com/hqipcc/

EXECUTIVE COMMITTEE

Gen. Overseer, Clyde M. Hughes, P.O. Box 439, London, OH 43140 Tel. (740)852-4722, Fax (740)852-0348
Asst. Gen. Overseer, B.G. Turner, RR5, Box 1286, Harpers Ferry, WV 25425 Tel. (304)535-221, Fax (304)535-1357
Gen. Sec., Asa Lowe, 513 Johnstown Rd., Chesapeake, VA 23322 Tel. (757)547-4329
Gen. Treas., Ervin Hargrave, P.O. Box 439, London, OH 43140 Tel. (740)852-4722, Fax (740)852-0348

Dir. of Global Missions, Dr. James B. Keiller, P.O. Box 18145, Atlanta, GA 30316 Tel. (404) 627-2681, Fax (404)627-0702

DISTRICT OVERSEERS

Central District, Lindsey Hayes, 609 Lansing Rd., Akron, OH 44312, Tel. (330)784-3453

Mid-Eastern District, H. Gene Boyce, 705 W. Grubb St., Hertford, NC 27944 Tel. (252)426-5403

Mountain District, Terry Lykins, P.O. Box 131, Staffordsville, KY 41256 Tel. (606)297-3282

New River District, Calvin Weikel, RR. 2, Box 300, Ronceverte, WV 24970 Tel. (304)647-4301

North Central District, Edgar Kent, P.O. Box 275, Hartford, MI 49057 Tel. (616)621-3326

North Eastern District, Wayne Taylor, 806 Eighth St., Shenandoah, VA 22849 Tel. (540)652-8090

South Eastern District, Frank Angie, 2507 Old Peachtree Rd., Duluth, GA 30097 Tel. (770) 476-5196

Tri-State District, Cline McCallister, 5210 Wilson St., Portsmouth, OH 45662 Tel. and Fax (740)776-6357

Portugese District, Pedro Messias, 34 Woodside Ave., Danbury, CT 06810 Tel. (203)790-9628

OTHER ORGANIZATIONS

Beulah Heights Bible College, Pres., Samuel R. Chand, P.O. Box 18145, Atlanta, GA 30316 Tel. (404)627-2681, Fax (404)627-0702

Women's Ministries, Gen. Pres., Janice Boyce, 121 W. Hunters Tr., Elizabeth City, NC 27909 Tel. and Fax (252)338-3003

Pentecostal Ambassadors, Dustin Hughes, National Youth Dir., P.O Box 439, London, OH 43140 Tel. (740)852-0448, Fax (740)852-0348

National Christian Education Dept., Dir., Dustin Hughes, P.O. Box 439, London, OH 43140 Tel. (740)852-0448, Fax (740)852-0348

Periodicals

The Bridegroom's Messenger; The Pentecostal Leader

International Pentecostal Holiness Church

This body grew out of the National Holiness Association movement of the last century, with roots in Methodism. Beginning in the South and Midwest, the church represents the merger of the Fire-Baptized Holiness Church founded by B. H. Irwin in Iowa in 1895; the Pentecostal Holiness Church founded by A. B. Crumpler in Goldsboro, North Carolina, in 1898; and the Tabernacle Pentecostal Church founded by N. J. Holmes in 1898.

All three bodies joined the ranks of the pentecostal movement as a result of the Azusa Street revival in Los Angeles in 1906 and a 1907 pentecostal revival in Dunn, N.C., conducted by G. B. Cashwell, who had visited Azusa Street. In 1911 the Fire-Baptized and Pentecostal Holiness bodies merged in Falcon, N.C., to form the present church; the Tabernacle Pentecostal Church was added in 1915 in Canon, Georgia.

The church stresses the new birth, the Wesleyan experience of sanctification, the pentecostal baptism in the Holy Spirit, evidenced by speaking in tongues, divine healing, and the premillennial second coming of Christ.

Headquarters

P.O. Box 12609, Oklahoma City, OK 73157-2609 Tel. (405)787-7110, Fax (405)789-3957

Media Contact, Admn. Asst.

Officers

Email: jdl@iphc.org (for Bishop Leggett)

Website: www.iphc.org

Gen. Supt., Bishop James D. Leggett

Vice Chpsn., Rev. M. Donald Duncan

Executive Director of Evangelism USA, Dr. Ronald Carpenter, Sr.

Executive Director of Church Education Ministries, Dr. A.D. Beacham, Jr.

Executive Director of Stewardship Ministries/ General Secretary-Treasurer, Rev. Edward Wood

OTHER ORGANIZATIONS

The Publishing House (LifeSprings), CEO, Greg Hearn, Franklin Springs, GA 30639

Women's Ministries, Exec. Dir., Mrs. Jewell Stewart

Men's Ministries, General. Dir., Col. Jack Kelley, P.O. Box 53307, Fayetteville, NC 28305-3307

Periodicals

IssacharFile; Helping Hand; Evangelism USA; Worldorama; CEM Connection

Jehovah's Witnesses

Modern-day Jehovah's Witnesses began in the early 1870s when Charles Taze Russell was the leader of a Bible study group in Allegheny City, Pennsylvania. In July 1879, the first issue of Zion's Watch Tower and Herald of Christ's Presence (now called The Watchtower) appeared. In 1884 Zion's Watch Tower Tract Society was incorporated, later changed to Watch Tower Bible and Tract Society. Congregations spread into other states and followers witnessed from house to house.

By 1913, printed sermons were in four languages in 3,000 newspapers in the United States, Canada and Europe. Hundreds of millions of books, booklets and tracts were distributed. Publication of the magazine now known as Awake! began in 1919. Today, it is published in more than 80 languages and has a circulation of upwards of 20,000,000. In 1931 the name Jehovah's Witnesses, based on Isaiah 43 vs.10-12, was adopted.

During the 1930s and 1940s Jehovah's Witnesses fought many court cases in the interest of preserving freedom of speech, press, assembly, and worship. They have won a total of 43 cases before the United States Supreme Court. A missionary training school was established in 1943, and it has been a major factor in the international expansion of the Witnesses. There are now 6 million Witnesses in 235 lands.

Jehovah's Witnesses believe in one almighty God, Jehovah, who is the Creator of all things. They believe in Jesus Christ as God's Son, the first of His creations. While Jesus is now an immortal spirit in heaven, ruling as King of God's Kingdom, he is still subject to his heavenly Father, Jehovah God. Christ's human life was sacrificed as a ransom to open up for obedient mankind the opportunity of eternal life. With Christ in heaven, 144,000 individuals chosen from among mankind will rule in righteousness over an unnumbered great crowd who will survive the destruction of wickedness and receive salvation into an earth cleansed of evil. (Rev. Ch.7 vs.9, 10; Ch.14 vs.1-5). These, along with the resurrected dead, will transform the earth into a global earthly paradise and will have the prospect of living forever on it.

Headquarters

25 Columbia Heights, Brooklyn, NY 11201-2483 Tel. (718)560-5600
Media Contact, Office of Public Information, J. R. Brown
Editorial Contact, Writing Department, James N. Pellechia
Website: www.watchtower.org

Officers

Pres. Watch Tower Bible and Tract Society of Pennsylvania, Don Adams

Periodicals

Awake!, The Watchtower

Korean Presbyterian Church in America, General Assembly of the*

This body came into official existence in the United States in 1976 and is currently an ethnic church, using the Korean and English language.

Headquarters

General Assembly of the Korean Presbyterian Church in America, 17200 Clark Ave., Bellflower, CA 90706 Tel. (714)816-1100, Fax (714)816-1120

Officers

Moderator, Rev. In Chul Kim, 44 Holsworthy Cres., Thornhill, ON L5T 4C6, Tel. (905)764-7905, Fax (416)250-1305
General Secretary, Rev. Seung Koo Choi, 3146 W. Ball Rd., #31, Anaheim, CA 92804 Tel. (714)816-1100

The Latvian Evangelical Lutheran Church in America

This body was organized into a denomination on Aug. 22, 1975 after having existed as the Federation of Latvian Evangelical Lutheran Churches in America since 1955. This church is a regional constituent part of the Lutheran Church of Latvia Abroad, a member of the Lutheran World Federation and the World Council of Churches.

The Latvian Evangelical Lutheran Church in America works to foster religious life, traditions and customs in its congregations in harmony with the Holy Scriptures, the Apostles', Nicean and Athanasian Creeds, the unaltered Augsburg Confession, Martin Luther's Small and Large Catechisms and other documents of the Book of Concord.

The LELCA is ordered by its Synod (General Assembly), executive board, auditing committee and district conferences.

Headquarters

2140 Orkla Dr., Golden Valley, MN 55427 Tel. (612)722-0174 Email: ucepure@aol.com
Media Contact, Juris Pulins, 9531 Knoll Top Rd., Union, IL 60180 Tel. (815)923-5919
Email: pulins@flash.net

Officers

Pres., Rev. Uldis Cepure, Tel. (612)546-3712
Vice-Pres., Rev. Anita Varsbergs, 9908 Shelburne Terr., 312, Gathersburg, MD 20878 Tel. (301)251-4151
Sec.,Girts Kugars, 5209 Douglas Ave., Kalamazoo, MI 49004 Tel. (616)381-3798
Treas., Vilmars Beinikis, 17 John Dr., Old Bethpage, NY 11804 Tel. (516)293-8432

Periodicals

Cela Biedrs; Lelba Zinas

The Liberal Catholic Church—Province of the United States of America

The Liberal Catholic Church was founded Feb. 13, 1916 as a reorganization of the Old Catholic Church in Great Britain with the Rt. Rev. James I. Wedgwood as the first Presiding Bishop. The first ordination of a priest in the United States was Fr. Charles Hampton, later a Bishop. The first Regionary Bishop for the American Province was the Rt. Rev. Irving S. Cooper (1919-1935).

Headquarters

Pres., The Rt. Rev. William S.H. Downey, 1206 Ayers Ave., Ojai, CA 93023 Tel. (805)646-2573, Fax (805)646-2575
Media Contact, Regionary Bishop, The Rt. Rev. William S.H. Downey
Email: bshp052497@aol.com
Website: www.thelcc.org

Officers

Pres. & Regionary Bishop, The Rt. Rev. William S.H. Downey
Vice-Pres., Rev. L. Marshall Heminway, P.O. Box 19957 Hampden Sta., Baltimore, MD 21211-0957

Sec. (Provincial), Rev. Lloyd Worley, 1232 24th Avenue Ct., Greeley, CO 80631 Tel. (303)356-3002
Provost, Rev. Lloyd Worley
Treas., Rev. Milton Shaw

BISHOPS

Regionary Bishop for the American Province, The Rt. Rev. William S.H. Downey
Aux. Bishops of the American Province, Rt. Rev. Dr. Robert S. McGinnis, Jr., 3612 N. Labarre Rd., Metaire, LA 70002; Rt. Rev. Joseph L. Tisch, P.O. Box 1117, Melbourne, FL 32901; Rt. Rev. Dr. Hein VanBeusekom, 12 Krotona Hill, Ojai, CA 93023; Rt. Rev. Ruben Cabigting, P.O. Box 270, Wheaton, IL 60189; The Rt. Rev. Lawrence Smith 9740 S. Avers Ave., Evergreen Park, IL.

Periodicals

Ubique

The American Association of Lutheran Churches is listed under "A".

Apostolic Lutheran Church of America is listed under "A".

Conservative Lutheran Association is listed under "C".

Evangelical Lutheran Church in America is listed under "E".

Evangelical Lutheran Synod is listed under "E".

The Lutheran Church—Missouri Synod (LCMS)

The Lutheran Church-Missouri Synod, which was founded in 1847, has more than 6,000 congregations in the United States and works in 69 other countries. It has 2.6 million members and is the second-largest Lutheran denomination in North America.

Christian education is offered for all ages. The North American congregations operate the largest elementary and secondary school systems of any Protestant denomination in the nation, and 15,689 students are enrolled in 12 LCMS institutions of higher learning.

Traditional beliefs concerning the authority and interpretation of Scripture are important. The synod is known for mass-media outreach through "The Lutheran Hour" on radio, "This Is The Life" dramas on television, and the products of Concordia Publishing House, the third-largest Protestant publisher, whose Arch Books children's series has sold more than 60 million copies.

An extensive network of more than 1,000 volunteers in 58 work centers produces Braille, large-type, and audiocassette materials for the blind and visually impaired. Fifty-nine of the Eighty-five deaf congregations affiliated with U.S. Lutheran denominations are LCMS; and many denominations use the Bible lessons prepared for developmentally disabled persons.

The involvement of women is high, although they do not occupy clergy positions. Serving as teachers, deaconesses, and social workers, women comprise approximately half of total professional workers.

The members' responsibility for congregational leadership is a distinctive characteristic of the synod. Power is vested in voters' assemblies, generally comprised of adults of voting age. Synod decision making is given to the delegates at triennial national and district conventions, where the franchise is equally divided between lay and pastoral representatives.

Headquarters

The Lutheran Church-Missouri Synod, International Center, 1333 S. Kirkwood Rd., St. Louis, MO 63122-7295
Media Contact, Dir., News & Information, Rev. David Mahsman, Tel. (314)996-1227; Director, Public Affairs, Mr. David Strand, (314)996-1229; Manager, News Bureau, Mr. Joe Isenhower, Tel. (314)996-1231, Fax (314) 996-1126
Email: infocenter@lcms.org
Website: www.lcms.org

Officers

Pres., Dr. Gerald B. Kieschnick
1st Vice-Pres., Dr. Daniel Preus
2nd Vice-Pres., Dr. Wallace R. Schulz
3rd Vice-Pres., Dr. Robert H. King
4th Vice-Pres., Dr. Paul L. Maier
5th Vice-Pres., Dr. William C. Weinrich
Sec., Dr. Raymond L. Hartwig
Treas., Mr. Thomas Kuchta
Admn. Officer of Bd. of Dir., Dr. Bradford L. Hewitt
Exec. Dir., Human Resources, Barb Ryan
Bd. of Directors, Dr. Karl L. Barth, Milwaukee, WI; Rev. Roosevelt Gray, Detroit, MI; Dr. Betty Duda, Oviedo, FL; Ernest E. Garbe, Dieterich, IL; Dr. Jean Garton, Benton, AR; Oscar H. Hanson, Lafayette, CA; Ted Kober, Billings, MT; Christian Preus, Plymouth, MN; Rev. James E. Fandrey, Omaha, NE; Dave Hook, Fort Wayne, IN; Elizabeth A. Fluegel, Alexandria, VA; Dr. Robert T. Kuhn, Oviedo, FL; Dr. Edwin Trapp, Jr., Dallas, TX

BOARDS AND COMMISSIONS

Communication Services, Exec. Dir., Rev. J. Thomas Lapacka
Mission Services, Exec. Dir., -vacant
Higher Education Services, Exec. Dir., Dr. William F. Meyer
Human Care Ministries, Exec. Dir., Rev. Matthew Harrison
Worker Benefit Plans, Exec. Dir., Dan A. Leeman

Lutheran Church-Missouri Synod Foundation, Pres., Mark Stuenkel

Lutheran Church Ext. Fund-Missouri Synod, Pres., Merle Freitag

District and Congregational Services, Exec. Dir., Dr. Le Roy Wilke

Black Ministries Services, Exec. Dir., -vacant

ORGANIZATIONS

Concordia Publishing House, Pres./CEO, Dr. Stephen Carter, 3558 S. Jefferson Ave., St. Louis, MO 63118-3968

Concordia Historical Institute, Interim Dir., Rev. Paul McCain, Concordia Seminary, 801 De Mun Ave., St. Louis, MO 63105

Intl. Lutheran Laymen's League, Exec. Dir., Rodger W. Hebermehl, 2185 Hampton Ave., St. Louis, MO 63139-2983

KFUO Radio, Dir., Rev. Dennis Stortz

Intl. Lutheran Women's Missionary League, Pres., Virginia Von Seggern, 3558 S. Jefferson Ave., St. Louis, MO 63118-3910

Periodicals

The Lutheran Witness; Reporter

Malankara Orthodox Syrian Church, Diocese of America*

The American Diocese of the Malankara Orthodox Syrian Church is in full accord with the Mother Church- Malankara Orthodox Syrian Church, also known as the Indian Orthodox Church. The diocese is a national or missionary entity of the Indian Orthodox Church. The Malankara Orthodox Syrian Church established an American diocese in 1978 to serve her immigrant members in America. This diocese is a new phenomenon with great challenges and potentials, composed of immigrant Indian Orthodox members and their American born children. Now that some years have passed, the immigrant church is entering into an indigenous era with the second generation Indian Orthodox members. Currently there are 60 parishes, 68 clergy and about 12,000 members of this church in the United States. The diocese is still growing with immigrants and native-born members.

The Malankara Orthodox Syrian Church has claimed its roots in the Apostolic ministry of Apostle St. Thomas, who was martyred in India, since 52 AD. Although there is not much available about the early history of the Indian Church, it is known that later it was influenced by Roman Catholicism and then Protestant missionaries of the post Reformation period. During the sixteenth century, there arose an increased relationship with the Oriental churches with the arrival of Syrian Bishops. Although different segments of Christianity have been flourishing in India, the Church maintained a close faith in the Non-Chalcedonian councils.

The Malankara Orthodox Syrian Church has got its name "Malankara" from Maliankara, a nearby town of Dodungalloor where St. Thomas is believed to have arrived in 52 AD; "Orthodox" comes from the faith of the fathers-non Chalcedonian faith; "Syrian" comes from its connection with the Syrian Orthodox Church's traditions, practices, liturgy, language, and liturgical calendar.

Headquarters

80-34 Commonwealth Boulevard, Bellerose, NY 11426 Tel. (718)470-9844 Fax (718)470-9219

Media Contact, His Grace Mathews Mar Barnabas, Diocesan Metropolitan

Email: Malankara@malankara.org

Website: www.malankara.org/american.htm

Officers

Diocesan Metropolitan, His Grace Mathews Mar Barnabas

Mar Thoma Syrian Church of India*

According to tradition, the Mar Thoma Church was established as a result of the apostolic mission of St. Thomas, the apostle in 52 AD. Church history attests to the continuity of the community of faithful, throughout the long centuries in India. The liturgy and faith practices of the Church were based on the relationship between the Church in Kerala, India, which St. Thomas founded, with the East-Syrian and Persian Churches. This started in the third century and continued up to the sixteenth century. In the seventeenth century, the Malabar Church of St. Thomas (as the Church in Kerala was known) renewed her relationship with the Orthodox Patriarchate of Antioch as part of the resistance to forced Latinization by the Portuguese. This process also led to the development of the Kerala Episcopacy, whereby the first Indian Bishop Mar Thoma I was consecrated in Kerala.

The Mar Thoma Church retains her Eastern Orthodoxy. She follows an Orthodox (true) worship form and liturgy, believes in the catholicity of grace, is missionary and evangelistic in approach. She derives Episcopal succession from the Syrian Orthodox Church of Antioch and follows Eastern Reformed Theology. She is independent, autonomous, and indigenous, constitutionally combining democratic values and Episcopal authority. She has been in full communion with the Anglican Church since 1954.

The Diocese of North America was organized in 1988 in order to serve the needs of the immigrant community. It has a membership of around six thousand families in sixty-eight parishes.

Headquarters

Sinai Mar Thoma Center, 2320 S. Merrick Avenue, Merrick, New York 11566 Tel. (516)377-3311, Fax (516)377-3322

Email: webmaster@marthomachurch.org

Website: www.marthomachurch.org/

Officers

Diocesan Bishop, The Rt. Rev. Dr. Zacharias Mar Theophilus Episcopa

Diocesan/Bishop's Sec., Rev. Dr. John Joseph
Diocesan Treasurer, Mr. Abraham Thomas

Periodicals

Mar Thoma Messenger

Church of God in Christ, Mennonite is listed under "C".

Evangelical Mennonite Church is listed under "E".

General Conference of Mennonite Brethren Churches is listed under "G".

Mennonite Church USA

Mennonite Church USA was formed in July 2001 when the two largest Mennonite bodies in the United States—the General Conference Mennonite Church (established in 1860) and the Mennonite Church (formally established in 1898, but with roots that go back much further)—voted to merge into one denomination.

Mennonite Church USA, with 116,000 members, is one of several denominations that traces its beginnings to the Protestant Reformation in the early 1500s. Mennonites hold many common core beliefs with other Christian denominations, but they live out God's call is some ways that make them distinct. Mennonites believe in giving ultimate loyalty to God rather than to the nations in which they live, or to the military. They believe that Jesus revealed a way for people to live peacefully and nonviolently, and they seek to be peacemakers in everyday life.

Mennonite church USA exists as a community of believers in local congregations, as a community of congregations in area conferences, and as a churchwide body in the USA. It joins with the Mennonite church in other countries as part of the worldwide Mennonite community of faith.

The vision statement of Mennonite Church USA reads, "God calls us to be follower of Jesus Christ and, by the power of the Holy Spirit, to grow as communities of grace, joy, and peace, so that God's healing and hope flow through us to the world."

Mennonite church USA lists as its strengths a high level of integrity recognized in both society and the religious community; high church attendance (90% of members attend church regularly); expanded global awareness through exposure to other world cultures; strong commitment to nonviolence and use of conflict resolution skills; above average giving to the work of the church; a natural communitarian impulse demonstrated by an emphasis on congregational relationships and mutual accountabilities; strong support of volunteer efforts, relief and service activities; and a holistic theology that holds word and deed together.

Mennonite Church USA is committed to sharing its faith and passion for Jesus with others and is open to anyone who confesses Jesus Christ as Lord and Savior and wants to live as Jesus taught.

Headquarters

722 Main St., P.O. Box 347, Newton, KS 67114 Tel. (316)283-5100, Fax (316)283-0454
421 S. Second St., Suite 600, Elkhart, IN 46516 Tel. (219)294-7131, Fax (219)293-3977
Media contact, Cindy Snider, Director of Communication, Tel. (316)283-5100, csnider@mennoniteusa.org
Email: info@MennoniteUSA.org
Website: www.MennoniteChurchUSA.org

Officers

Moderator, Ervin Stutzman, 1200 Park Rd., Harrison, VA 22802, Tel. (540)432-4261, stutzerv@emu.edu
Moderator Elect, Duane Oswald, 1111 E. Herndon Ave., Suite 308, Fresno, CA 93720-3100, Tel. (559)261-9070, doswald@avante-health.com
Executive Director, James M. Schrag, 722 Main St., P.O. Box 347, Newton, KS 67114 Tel. (316)283-5100, jschrag@menonniteusa.org
Associate Executive Director, J. Ron Byler, 421 S. Second St., Suite 600, Elkhart, IN 46516 Tel. (219)294-7131, byler@mennoniteusa.org
Mennonite Mutual Aid, President, Howard Brenneman, P.O. Box 486, Goshen, IN 46527 Tel. (219)533-9511, howard.brenneman@mma-online.org
Mennonite Mission Network, Executive Director, Stanley Green, 421 S. Second St., Suite 600, Elkhart, IN 46516 Tel. (219)294-7131, stanleygreen@mennonitemission.net
Mennonite Publishing House, Publisher, Dennis Good, 616 Walnut Ave., Scottdale, PA 15683 Tel. (724)887-8500, dennisg@mph.org
Mennonite Education Agency, Executive Director (to be named)

Periodicals

The Mennonite; Builder; Christian Living; Rejoice!; Mennonite Historical Bulletin; Mennonite Quarterly Review; On the Line; Purpose; Story Friends; With

Fundamental Methodist Church, Inc. is listed under "F".

The United Methodist Church is listed under "U".

The Metropolitan Church Association, Inc.

Organized after a revival movement in Chicago in 1894 as the Metropolitan Holiness Church, this organization was chartered as the Metropolitan Church Association in 1899. It has Wesleyan theology.

Headquarters

415 Broad St., Suite 2, Lake Geneva, WI 53147 Tel. (414)248-6786
Media Contact, Pres., Rev. Warren W. Bitzer

Officers

Pres., Rev. Warren W. Bitzer
Vice-Pres. & Sec., Elbert L. Ison
Treas., Gertrude J. Puckhaber

Periodicals

The Burning Bush

The Missionary Church

The Missionary Church was formed in 1969 through a merger of the United Missionary Church (organized in 1883) and the Missionary Church Association (founded in 1898). It is evangelical and conservative with a strong emphasis on missionary work and church planting.

There are three levels of church government with local, district, and general conferences. There are 11 church districts in the United States. The general conference meets every two years. The denomination operates one college in the United States.

Headquarters

3811 Vanguard Dr., P.O. Box 9127, Ft. Wayne, IN 46899-9127 Tel. (219)747-2027, Fax (219) 747-5331
Media Contact, Pres., Dr. John Moran
Email: mcdenomusa@aol.com
Website: www.mcusa.org

Officers

Pres., Rev. William Hossler
Vice-Pres., Rev. Joel DeSelm
Sec., Rev. Dave Engbrecht
Treas., Darrel Schlabach
Director of Church Planting, Rev. Robert Ransom
Director of World PartnersUSA, Rev. David Mann
Director of Discipling Ministries, Rev. Tom Swank
Dir. of Ad. Services, David Von Gunten
Director of Financial Services, Neil Rinehart
Youth Dir., Eric Liechty
Children's Dir., Mrs. Pam Merillat
Resource & Curriculum, Dr. Duane Beals
Sunday School
Senior Adult Ministry Dir., Dr. Charles Cureton
Missionary Men Liaison, Rev. Ron Phipps
Missionary Women Intl., Pres., Barbara Reffey
Missionary Church Investment Foundation, Mr. Eric Smith

Periodicals

Emphasis on Faith and Living; Priority

Moravian Church in America (Unitas Fratrum)*

In 1735 German Moravian missionaries of the pre-Reformation faith of Jan Hus came to Georgia, in 1740 to Pennsylvania, and in 1753 to North Carolina. They established the American Moravian Church, which is broadly evangelical, ecumenical, liturgical, "conferential" in form of government, and has an episcopacy as a spiritual office. The Northern and Southern Provinces of the church operate on a semi-autonomous basis.

Headquarters

Denominational offices or headquarters are called the Provincial Elders' Conference.
See addresses for Northern and Southern Provinces:

NORTHERN PROVINCE HEADQUARTERS

1021 Center St., P.O. Box 1245, Bethlehem, PA 18016-1245 Tel. (610)867-7566, Fax (610) 866-9223
Media Contact, Ms. Deanna Hollenbach

PROVINCIAL ELDERS' CONFERENCE

Pres., Rev. R. Burke Johnson, burke@mcnp.org
Vice-Pres./Sec. (Eastern Dist.), Rev. David L. Wickmann, dave@mcnp.org
Vice-Pres. (Western Dist.), Rev. Lawrence Christianson, christlr@aol.com
Comptroller, Theresa E. Kunda, 1021 Center St., P.O. Box 1245, Bethlehem, PA 18016-1245, theresa@mcnp.org

NORTHERN PROVINCE

1021 Center St., P.O. Box 1245, Bethlehem, PA 18016-1245 Tel. (610)867-7566, Fax (610) 866-9223
Eastern District Pres., Rev. David L. Wickmann, P.O. Box 1245, Bethlehem, PA 18016-1245
Western District Pres., Rev. Lawrence Christianson, P.O. Box 386, Sun Prairie, WI 53590
Canadian District Pres., Mr. Graham Kerslake, 10910 Harvest Lake Way, NE, Calgary, AB T3K 4L1

SOUTHERN PROVINCE HEADQUARTERS

459 S. Church St., Winston-Salem, NC 27101 or Mailing address, Drawer O, Winston-Salem, NC 27108 Tel. (336)725-5811, Fax (336)723-1029
Email: rsawyer@mcsp.org
Website: www.moravian.org (for Moravian Church, Northern and Southern Province)

PROVINCIAL ELDERS' CONFERENCE

Pres., Rev. Dr. Robert E. Sawyer
Vice President, Rev. Lane A. Sapp
Sec. Mr. George Johnson
Treas., Mr. Richard Cartner, Drawer M, Salem Station, Winston-Salem, NC 27108
Other Members, Mrs. Betsy R. Bombick, Rev. Tom Shelton
Asst. to Pres., Robert Hunter

ALASKA PROVINCE

P.O. Box 545, Bethel, AK 99559

PROVINCIAL ELDERS' CONFERENCE

Pres., Rev. Isaac Amik
Vice-Pres., Rev. Peter Green
Sec., Sarah Owens
Treas., Juanita Asicksik
Dir. of Theological Education, Rev. Will Updegrove

Email: burke@mcnp.org
Website: www.moravian.org

Periodicals

The Moravian

Mormons—please see The Church of Jesus Christ of Latter-Day Saints.

National Association of Congregational Christian Churches

This association was organized in 1955 in Detroit, Michigan, by delegates from Congregational Christian Churches committed to continuing the Congregational way of faith and order in church life. Participation by member churches is voluntary.

Headquarters

P.O. Box 1620, Oak Creek, WI 53154 Tel. (414)764-1620, Fax (414)764-0319
Media Contact, Assoc. Exec. Sec., Rev. Dr. Donald P. Olsen, 8473 S. Howell Ave., Oak Creek, WI 53154 Tel. (414)764-1620, Fax (414)764-0319
Email: naccc@naccc.org
Website: www.naccc.org

Officers

Exec. Sec., Rev. Dr. Thomas M. Richard, 8473 South Howell Ave., Oak Creek, WI 53154
Assoc. Exec. Secs., Rev. Phil Jackson and Rev. Dr. Donald P. Olsen

Periodicals

The Congregationalist

National Association of Free Will Baptists

This evangelical group of Arminian Baptists was organized by Paul Palmer in 1727 at Chowan, North Carolina. Another movement (teaching the same doctrines of free grace, free salvation, and free will) was organized June 30, 1780, in New Durham, N.H., but there was no connection with the southern organization except for a fraternal relationship.

The northern line expanded more rapidly and extended into the West and Southwest. This body merged with the Northern Baptist Convention Oct. 5, 1911, but a remnant of churches reorganized into the Cooperative General Association of Free Will Baptists Dec. 28, 1916, at Pattonsburg, Mo.

Churches in the southern line were organized into various conferences from the beginning and finally united in one General Conference in 1921.

Representatives of the Cooperative General Association and the General Conference joined Nov. 5, 1935 to form the National Association of Free Will Baptists.

Headquarters

5233 Mt. View Rd., Antioch, TN 37013-2306 Tel. (615)731-6812, Fax (615)731-0771
Mailing Address, P.O. Box 5002, Antioch, TN 37011-5002
Media Contact, Exec. Sec., Melvin Worthington
Email: webmaster@nafwb.org
Website: www.nafwb.org/

Officers

Exec. Sec., Dr. Melvin Worthington
Mod., Rev. Carl Cheshier, P.O. Box 7208, Moore, OK 73153

DENOMINATIONAL AGENCIES

Free Will Baptist Foundation, Exec. Dir., William Evans
Free Will Baptist Bible College, Pres., Dr. Tom Malone
Foreign Missions Dept., Dir., Rev. James Forlines
Home Missions Dept., Dir., Rev. Larry Powell
Bd. of Retirement, Dir., Rev. William Evans
Historical Commission, Chpsn., Dr. Thomas Marberry
Comm. for Theological Integrity, Chpsn., Rev. Leroy Forlines, P.O. Box 50117, Nashville, TN 37205
Music Commission, Chpsn., Rev. Randy Sawyer, 2316 Union Rd., Gastonia, NC 28054
Media Comm., Chpsn., Rev. Steve Faison, P.O. Box 295, Cedar Springs, GA 31732
Sunday School & Church Training Dept., Dir., Dr. Alton Loveless
Women Nationally Active for Christ, Exec. Sec., Majorie Workman
Master's Men Dept., Dir., Rev. Tom Dooley

Periodicals

Attack, A Magazine for Christian Men; Contact; Free Will Bible College Bulletin; Co-Laborer; Free Will Baptist Gem; Heartbeat; AIM

National Baptist Convention of America, Inc.*

The National Baptist Convention of America, Inc., was organized in 1880. Its mission is articulated through its history, constitution, articles of incorporation, and by-laws. The Convention (corporate churches) has a mission statement with fourteen (14) objectives including fostering unity throughout its membership and the world Christian community by proclaiming the gospel of Jesus Christ; validating and propagating the Baptist doctrine of faith and practice, and its distinctive principles throughout the world; and harnessing and encouraging the scholarly and Christian creative skills of its membership for Christian writing and publications.

Headquarters

Media Contact, Liaison Officer, Dr. Richard A. Rollins, 777 S. R.L. Thornton Fwy., Ste. 205, Dallas, TX 75203 Tel. (214)946-8913, Fax (214)946-9619

Officers

Pres., Dr. E. Edward Jones, 1327 Pierre Ave.,

Shreveport, LA 71103 Tel. (318)221-3701, Fax (318)222-7512
Gen. Rec. Sec., Dr. Clarence C. Pennywell, 2016 Russell Rd., Shreveport, LA 71107
Corres. Sec., Rev. E. E. Stafford, 6614 South Western Ave., Los Angeles, CA 90047
Liaison Officer, Dr. Richard A. Rollins, 777 So. R.L. Thornton Frwy., Ste. 205, Dallas, TX 75203 Tel. (214)946-8913, Fax (214)946-9619

Periodicals

The Lantern

National Baptist Convention, U.S.A., Inc.*

The older and parent convention of black Baptists, this body is to be distinguished from the National Baptist Convention of America.

Headquarters

1700 Baptist World Center Dr., Nashville, TN 37207 Tel. (615)228-6292, Fax (615)226-5935

Officers

Pres., Dr. William J. Shaw, 1700 Baptist World Center Dr., Nashville, TN 37207 Tel. (615)228-6292, Fax (615)226-5935
Gen. Sec., Dr. Harry Blake, Mt. Canaan Baptist Church, 1666 Alston St., Shreveport, LA 71101 Tel. (318)227-9993

Periodicals

Mission Herald

National Missionary Baptist Convention of America*

The National Missionary Baptist Convention of America was organized in 1988 as a separate entity from the National Baptist Convention of America, Inc., after a dispute over control of the convention's publishing efforts. The new organization intended to remain committed to the National Baptist Sunday Church School and Baptist Training Union Congress and the National Baptist Publishing Board.

The purpose of the National Missionary Baptist Convention of America is to serve as an agency of Christian education, church extension, and missionary efforts. It seeks to maintain and safeguard full religious liberty and engage in social and economic development.

Headquarters

1404 E. Firestone, Los Angeles, CA 90001 Tel. (213)582-0090
Media Contact, Dr. W. T. Snead, Sr.

Officers

Pres., Dr. W. T. Snead, Sr.
Vice-Pres., At-large, Dr. Harvey E. Leggett, 866 Monroe St., Ypsilanti, MI 48197
Vice-Pres., Ecumenical Affairs, Dr. F. Benjamin Davis, 1535 Dr. A.J. Brown Blvd. N., Indianapolis, IN 46202
Vice-Pres., Auxiliaries, T. J. Prince, 2219 Sea Island Dr., Dallas, TX 75232
Vice-Pres., Boards, Dr. O. E. Piper, 4220 W. 18th St., Chicago, IL 60623
Vice-Pres., Financial Affairs, J. A. Boles, 2001 South J St., Tacoma, WA 98405
Pres., National Baptist Publishing Bd., Dr. T. B. Boyd, III, 6717 Centennial Blvd., Nashville, TN 37209
Gen. Sec., Dr. Melvin V. Wade, 4269 S. Figueroa, Los Angeles, CA 90037
Corres. Sec., Dr. H. J. Johnson, 2429 South Blvd., Dallas, TX 75215
Treas., Dr. W. N. Daniel, 415 W. Englewood Ave., Chicago, IL 60612
Rec. Sec., Dr. Lonnie Franks, Crocker, TX

National Organization of the New Apostolic Church of North America

This body is a variant of the Catholic Apostolic Church which began in England in 1830. The New Apostolic Church distinguished itself from the parent body in 1863 by recognizing a succession of Apostles.

Headquarters

3753 N. Troy St., Chicago, IL 60618
Media Contact, Sec. & Treas., Ellen E. Eckhardt, Tel. (773)539-3652, Fax (773)478-6691
Email: info@nak.org
Website: www.nak.org

Officers

Pres., Rev. Erwin Wagner, 330 Arlene Pl., Waterloo, ON N2J 2G6
First Vice-Pres., Rev. Richard C. Freund, 1 Mikel Ln., Glen Head, NY 11545-1591
Second Vice-Pres., Rev. Leonard E Kolb, 4522 Wood St., Erie, PA 16509-1639
Treas. & Sec., Ellen E. Eckhardt, 6380 N. Indian Rd., Chicago, IL 60646
Asst. Sec., Rev. John E. Doderer, 58 15th Ave., Sea Cliff, NY 11579

National Primitive Baptist Convention, Inc.

Throughout the years of slavery and the Civil War, the Negro population of the South worshipped with the white population in their various churches. At the time of emancipation, their white brethren helped them establish their own churches, granting them letters of fellowship, ordaining their deacons and ministers, and helping them in other ways.

The doctrine and polity of this body are quite similar to that of white Primitive Baptists, yet there are local associations and a national convention, organized in 1907.

Each church is independent and receives and controls its own membership. This body was formerly known as Colored Primitive Baptists.

Headquarters

6433 Hidden Forest Dr., Charlotte, NC 28213 Tel. (704)596-1508
Media Contact, Elder T. W. Samuels

Officers

Natl. Convention, Pres., Elder T. W. Samuels, Tel. (704)596-3153

Natl. Convention, Vice-Pres., Elder Ernest Ferrell, Tallahassee, FL

Natl. Convention, Chmn. Bd. of Dirs., Elder Ernest Ferrell, Tallahassee, FL

Natl. Church School Training Union, Pres., Jonathan Yates, Mobile, AL

Natl. Ushers Congress, Pres., Bro. Carl Batts, 21213 Garden View Dr., Maple Heights, OH 44137

Publishing Bd., Chpsn., Elder E. W. Wallace, Creamridge, NJ

Women's Congress, Pres., Betty Brown, Cocoa Beach, FL

Natl. Laymen's Council, Pres., Densimore Robinson, Huntsville, AL

Natl. Youth Congress, Pres., Robert White, Trenton, NJ

National Spiritualist Association of Churches

This organization is made up of believers that Spiritualism is a science, philosophy, and religion based upon the demonstrated facts of communication between this world and the next.

Headquarters

NSAC General Offices, Rev. Sharon L. Snowman, Secretary, P.O. Box 217, Lily Dale, NY 14752-0217

Media Contact, Mr. Robert Egby, 720 Almonesson, Westville, NJ 08093

Email: nsac@nsac.org

Website: www.nsac.org

Officers

Pres., Rev. Barbara Thurman, 200 Marina Vista Rd., Larkspur, CA 94939-2144

Vice-Pres., Rev. Pamla Ashlay, 11811 Watertown Plank Rd., Milwaukee, WI 53226

Sec., Rev. Sharon L. Snowman, P.O. Box 217, Lily Dale, NY 14752 Tel. (716)595-2000, Fax (716)595-2020

Treas., Rev. Lelia Cutler, 7310 Medfield St. #1, Norfolk, VA 23505

OTHER ORGANIZATIONS

Bureau of Educ., Supt., Rev. Catherine Snell, 17 Ann Court, Kings Park, NY 11754

Bureau of Public Relations, Mr. Robert Egby, 720 Almonesson, Westville, NJ 08093

The Stow Memorial Foundation, Sec., Rev. Sharon L. Snowman, P.O. Box 217, Lily Dale, NY 14752 Tel. (716)595-2000, Fax (716)595-2020

Spiritualist Benevolent Society, Inc., P.O. Box 217, Lily Dale, NY 14752

Periodicals

The National Spiritualist Summit; Spotlight

Netherlands Reformed Congregations

The Netherlands Reformed Congregations organized denominationally in 1907. In the Netherlands, the so-called Churches Under the Cross (established in 1839, after breaking away from the 1834 Secession congregations) and the so-called Ledeboerian churches (established in 1841 under the leadership of the Rev. Ledeboer, who seceded from the Reformed State Church), united in 1907 under the leadership of the then 25-year-old Rev. G. H. Kersten, to form the Netherlands Reformed Congregations. Many of the North American congregations left the Christian Reformed Church to join the Netherlands Reformed Congregations after the Kuyperian presupposed regeneration doctrine began making inroads.

All Netherlands Reformed Congregations, office-bearers, and members subscribe to three Reformed Forms of Unity: The Belgic Confession of Faith (by DeBres), the Heidelberg Catechism (by Ursinus and Olevianus), and the Canons of Dort. Both the Belgic Confession and the Canons of Dort are read regularly at worship services, and the Heidelberg Catechism is preached weekly, except on church feast days.

Headquarters

Media Contact, Synodical Clk., Rev. C. Vogelaar, 2339 Deer Trail Dr. NE, Grand Rapids, MI 49505 Tel. (616)364-9889, Fax (616)364-9979

OTHER ORGANIZATIONS

Netherlands Reformed Book and Publishing, 1233 Leffingwell NE, Grand Rapids, MI 49505

Periodicals

The Banner of Truth; Paul (mission magazine); *Insight Into* (for young people); *Learning and Living* (for school and home)

The New Church—please see General Church of the New Jerusalem.

North American Baptist Conference

The North American Baptist Conference was begun by immigrants from Germany. The first church was organized by the Rev. Konrad Fleischmann in Philadelphia in 1843. In 1865 delegates of the churches met in Wilmot, Ontario, and organized the North American Baptist Conference. Today only a few churches still use the German language, mostly in a bilingual setting.

The Conference meets in general session once every three years for fellowship, inspiration, and to conduct the business of the Conference through elected delegates from the local churches. The General Council, composed of representatives of the various Associations and Conference organizations and departments, meets annually to determine the annual budget and programs for the Conference and its departments and agencies. The General Council also makes recommendations to the Triennial Conference on policies, long-range plans, and election of certain personnel, boards and committees.

Approximately 65 missionaries serve in Brazil, Cameroon, Japan, Mexico, Nigeria, Philippines, and Russia.

Ten homes for the aged are affiliated with the Conference and 12 camps are operated on the association level.

Headquarters

1 S. 210 Summit Ave., Oakbrook Terrace, IL 60181 Tel. (630)495-2000, Fax (630)495-3301
Media Contact, Marilyn Schaer

Officers

Mod., Rev. Harvey R. Wilkie
Vice-Mod., Gordon Unger
Exec. Dir., Dr. Philip Yntema
Treas., Jackie Loewer

OTHER ORGANIZATIONS

Intl. Missions Dept., Dir., Ron Salzman
Home Missions Dept., Dir., Rev. Bob Walther
Church Extension Investors Fund, Dir., Les D. Collins

Periodicals

NABtoday

North American Old Roman Catholic Church (Archdiocese of New York)

This body is identical with the Roman Catholic Church in faith but differs from it in discipline and worship. The Mass is offered with the appropriate rite either in Latin or in the vernacular. All other sacraments are taken from the Roman Pontifical. This jurisdiction allows for married clergy.

PRIMATIAL HEADQUARTERS

Box 021647 GPO, Brooklyn, NY 11202-0036 Tel. (718)855-0600
Media Contact, Chancellor, Most Rev. Albert J. Berube

Officers

Primate, The Most Rev. Herve L. Quessy
Chancellor, Most Rev. Albert J. Berube
Diocese of New York, Ordinary, Most Rev. Albert J. Berube
Diocese of Montreal & French Canada, Ordinary, Most Rev. Herve L. Quessy

Old German Baptist Brethren Church

This group separated from the Church of the Brethren (formerly German Baptist Brethren) in 1881 in order to preserve and maintain historic Brethren Doctrine.

Headquarters

Vindicator Ofc. Ed., Steven L. Bayer, 6952 N. Montgomery County Line Rd., Englewood, OH 45322-9748 Tel. (937)884-7531

Periodicals

The Vindicator

Old Order Amish Church

The congregations of this Old Order Amish group have no annual conference. They worship in private homes. They adhere to the older forms of worship and attire. This body has bishops, ministers, and deacons.

INFORMATION

Der Neue Amerikanische Calendar, c/o Raber's Book Store, 2467 C R 600, Baltic, OH 43804
Telephone Contact, LeRoy Beachy, Beachy Amish Mennonite Church, 4324 SR 39, Millersburg, OH 44654 Tel. (216)893-2883

Old Order (Wisler) Mennonite Church

This body arose from a separation of Mennonites dated 1872, under Jacob Wisler, in opposition to what were thought to be innovations.

The group is in the Eastern United States and Canada. Each state, or district, has its own organization and holds semi-annual conferences.

Headquarters

Media Contact, Amos B. Hoover, 376 N. Muddy Creek Rd., Denver, PA 17517 Tel. (717)484-4849, Fax (717)484-104

Open Bible Standard Churches

Open Bible Standard Churches originated from two revival movements, Bible Standard Conference, founded in Eugene, Oregon, under the leadership of Fred L. Hornshuh in 1919, and Open Bible Evangelistic Association, founded in Des Moines, Iowa, under the leadership of John R. Richey in 1932.

Similar in doctrine and government, the two groups amalgamated on July 26, 1935 as "Open Bible Standard Churches, Inc." with headquarters in Des Moines, Iowa.

The original group of 210 ministers has enlarged to incorporate over 2,479 ministers and 1,397 churches in 36 countries. The first missionary left for India in 1926. The church now ministers in Asia, Africa, South America, Europe, Canada, Mexico, Central America, and the Caribbean Islands.

Historical roots of the parent groups reach back to the outpouring of the Holy Spirit in 1906 at Azusa Street Mission in Los Angeles and to the full gospel movement in the Midwest. Both groups were organized under the impetus of pentecostal revival. Simple faith, freedom from fanaticism, emphasis on evangelism and missions and free fellowship with other groups were characteristics of the growing organizations.

The highest governing body of Open Bible Standard Churches meets biennially and is composed of all ministers and one voting delegate per 100 members from each church. A National Board of Directors, elected by the national and regional conferences, conducts the business of the organization. Official Bible College is Eugene Bible College in Oregon.

Open Bible Standard Churches is a charter member of the National Association of Evangelicals and of the Pentecostal/Charismatic Churches of North America. It is a member of the Pentecostal World Conference.

NATIONAL OFFICE

2020 Bell Ave., Des Moines, IA 50315 Tel. (515)288-6761, Fax (515)288-2510

Media Contact, Exec. Dir., Communications & Resources, Jeff Farmer, Tel. (515)288-6761, Fax (515)288-2510

Email: info@openbible.org

Website: www. openbible.org

Officers

Pres., Jeffrey E. Farmer

Sec.-Treas., Teresa A. Beyer

Dir. of Intl. Min., Paul V. Canfield

Periodicals

Message of the Open Bible

The (Original) Church of God, Inc.

This body was organized in 1886 as the first church in the United States to take the name "The Church of God." In 1917 a difference of opinion led this particular group to include the word (Original) in its name. It is a holiness body and believes in the whole Bible, rightly divided, using the New Testament as its rule and government.

Headquarters

P.O. Box 592, Wytheville, VA 24382

Media Contact, Gen. Overseer, Rev. William Dale, Tel. (800)827-9234

Officers

Gen. Overseer, Rev. William Dale

Asst. Gen. Overseer, Rev. Alton Evans

Periodicals

The Messenger

The Orthodox Church in America*

The Orthodox Church of America entered Alaska in 1794 before its purchase by the United States in 1867. Its canonical status of independence (autocephaly) was granted by its Mother Church, the Russian Orthodox Church, on April 10, 1970, and it is now known as The Orthodox Church in America.

Headquarters

P.O. Box 675, Syosset, NY 11791-0675 Tel. (516)922-0550, Fax (516)922-0954

Media Contact, Dir. of Communications, V. Rev. John Matusiak, 7900 W. 120 St., Palos Park, IL 60464 Tel. (708)361-1684, Fax (708)923-1706, jjm@oca.org

Email: jjm@oca.org

Website: www.oca.org

Officers

Primate, Archbishop of Washington, Metropolitan of All America & Canada, Most Blessed Theodosius

Chancellor, V. Rev. Robert S. Kondratick, P.O. Box 675, Syosset, NY 11791 Tel. (516)922-0550, Fax (516)922-0954

SYNOD

Chpsn., His Beatitude Theodosius, P.O. Box 675, Syosset, NY 11791

Archbishop of New York, Most Rev. Peter, 33 Hewitt Ave., Bronxville, NY 10708

Archbishop of Pittsburgh & Western PA, Most Rev. Kyrill, P.O. Box R, Wexford, PA 15090

Archbishop of Dallas, Archbishop Dmitri, 4112 Throckmorton, Dallas, TX 75219

Archbishop of Philadelphia, Archbishop Herman, St. Tikhon's Monastery, South Canaan, PA 18459

Aux. Bishop of Baltimore, Rt. Rev. Nikolai, P.O. Box 240805, Anchorage, AK 99524-0805

Archbishop of Detroit, Rt. Rev. Nathaniel, P.O. Box 309, Grass Lake, MI 49240-0309

Bishop of Midwest, Rt. Rev. Job, 927 N. LaSalle, Chicago, IL 60610

Bishop of San Francisco, Rt. Rev. Tikhon, 649 North Robinson St., Los Angeles, CA 90026

Bishop of Ottawa and Canada, Rt. Rev. Seraphim, P.O. Box 179, Spencerville, ON K0E 1X0 Tel. (613)925-5226

Retired Bishop, Rt. Rev. Mark, 9511 Sun Pointe Dr., Boynton Beach, FL 33437

Titular Bishop of Hagerstown, Rt. Rev. Innocent, 513 E. 24th St., Ste. #3, Anchorage, AK 99503 Tel. (907)279-0025

Periodicals

The Orthodox Church

The Orthodox Presbyterian Church

On June 11, 1936, certain ministers, elders, and lay members of the Presbyterian Church in the U.S.A. withdrew from that body to form a new denomination. Under the leadership of the late Rev. J. Gresham Machen, noted conservative New Testament scholar, the new church determined to continue to uphold the Westminster Confession of Faith as traditionally understood by Presbyterians and to engage in proclamation of the gospel at home and abroad.

The church has grown modestly over the years and suffered early defections, most notably one in 1937 that resulted in the formation of the Bible Presbyterian Church under the leadership of Dr. Carl McIntire. It now has congregations throughout the states of the continental United States.

The denomination is a member of the North American Presbyterian and Reformed Council and the International Council of Reformed Churches.

Headquarters

607 N. Easton Rd., Bldg. E, Box P, Willlow Grove, PA 19090-0920 Tel. (215)830-0900, Fax (215)830-0350
Media Contact, Stated Clerk, Rev. Donald J. Duff
E-mail: duff.1@opc.org
Website: www.opc.org

Officers

Moderator of General Assembly, The Rev. David J. O'Leary, 344 Spring St., Reading, PA 19601-2131
Stated Clk., Rev. Donald J. Duff

Periodicals

New Horizons in the Orthodox Presbyterian Church

Patriarchal Parishes of the Russian Orthodox Church in the U.S.A.*

This group of parishes is under the direct jurisdiction of the Patriarch of Moscow and All Russia, His Holiness Aleksy II, in the person of a Vicar Bishop, His Grace Mercurius, Bishop of Zaraisk.

Headquarters

St. Nicholas Cathedral, 15 E. 97th St., New York, NY 10029 Tel. (212)831-6294, Fax (212)427-5003
Media Contact, Sec. to the Bishop, Boris Komaishko, Tel. (212)996-6638
Email: bmercurius@ruscon.com
Website: www.orthodox.net

Officers

Secretary to the Bishop, Boris Komaishko

Pentecostal Assemblies of the World, Inc.

This organization is an interracial Pentecostal holiness of the Apostolic Faith, believing in repentance, baptism in Jesus's name, and being filled with the Holy Ghost, with the evidence of speaking in tongues. It originated in the early part of the century in the Middle West and has spread throughout the country.

Headquarters

3939 Meadows Dr., Indianapolis, IN 46205 Tel. (317)547-9541
Media Contact, Admin., John E. Hampton, Fax (317)543-0512

Officers

Presiding Bishop, Norman L. Wagner
Asst. Presiding Bishop, James E. Tyson
Bishops, Arthus Brazier; George Brooks; Ramsey Butler; Morris Golder; Francis L. Smith, Francis L.; Brooker T. Jones; C. R. Lee; Robert McMurray; Philip L. Scott; William L. Smith; Samuel A. Layne; Freeman M. Thomas; James E. Tyson; Charles Davis; Willie Burrell; Harry Herman; Jeremiah Reed; Jeron Johnson; Clifton Jones; Robert Wauls; Ronald L. Young; Henry L. Johnson; Leodis Warren; Thomas J. Weeks; Eugene Redd; Thomas W. Weeks, Sr.; Willard Saunders; Davis L. Ellis; Earl Parchia; Vanuel C. Little; Norman Wagner; George Austin; Benjamin A. Pitt; Markose Thopil; John K. Cole; Peter Warkie; Norman Walters; Alphonso Scott; David Dawkins
Gen. Sec, Dr. Aletha Cushinberry
Assist. Gen Sec., Suffragan Bishop Noel Jones
Gen. Treas., Elder James Loving
Asst. Treas., Dist. Eld. Charles Ellis III

Periodicals

Christian Outlook

Pentecostal Church of God

Growing out of the pentecostal revival at the turn of the century, the Pentecostal Church of God was organized in Chicago on Dec. 30, 1919, as the Pentecostal Assemblies of the U.S.A. The name was changed to Pentecostal Church of God in 1922; in 1934 it was changed again to The Pentecostal Church of God of America, Inc.; and finally the name became the Pentecostal Church of God (Inc.) in 1979.

The International Headquarters was moved from Chicago, Illinois to Ottumwa, Iowa, in 1927, then to Kansas City, Missoui, in 1933 and finally to Joplin, Missouri, in 1951.

The denomination is evangelical and pentecostal in doctrine and practice. Active membership in the National Association of Evangelicals and the Pentecostal/Charismatic Churches North America is maintained.

The church is Trinitarian in doctrine and teaches the absolute inerrancy of the Scripture from Genesis to Revelation. Among its cardinal beliefs are the doctrines of salvation, which includes regeneration; divine healing, as provided for in the atonement; the baptism in the Holy Ghost, with the initial physical evidence of speaking in tongues; and the premillennial second coming of Christ.

Headquarters

4901 Pennsylvania, P.O. Box 850, Joplin, MO 64802 Tel. (417)624-7050, Fax (417)624-7102
Media Contact, Gen. Sec., Dr. Ronald R. Minor
Email: pcg@pcg.org
Website: www.pcg.org

Officers

Gen. Supt., Dr. Phil L. Redding
Gen. Sec., Dr. Ronald R. Minor

OTHER GENERAL EXECUTIVES

Dir. of World Missions, Rev. John K. Norvell
Dir. of Indian Missions, Dr. C. Don Burke
Dir. of Youth Ministries, Rev. Reggie O. Powers
Dir. of Home Missions/Evangelism, Rev. Stephen E. Oates

ASSISTANT GENERAL SUPERINTENDENTS

Northwestern Division, Rev. Jamie J. Joiner
Southwestern Division, Rev. Lloyd L. Naten

North Central Division, Rev. Donald R. Dennis
South Central Division, Rev. Leon A. McDowell
Northeastern Division, Rev. Charles R. Mosier
Southeastern Division, Rev. C.W. Goforth

OTHER DEPARTMENTAL OFFICERS

Bus. Mgr., Rev. Alan Greagrey
Director of Women's Ministry, Sharon K. Redding
Christian Educ., Dir., Mrs. Billie Palumbo

Periodicals

The Pentecostal Messenger; Spirit

Pentecostal Fire-Baptized Holiness Church

Organized in 1918, this group consolidated with the Pentecostal Free Will Baptists in 1919. It maintains rigid discipline over members.

Headquarters

P.O. Box 261, La Grange, GA 30241-0261 Tel. (706)884-7742
Media Contact, Gen. Mod., Wallace B. Pittman, Jr.

Officers

Gen. Treas., K. N. (Bill) Johnson, P.O. Box 1528, Laurinburg, NC 28352 Tel. (919)276-1295
Gen. Sec., W. H. Preskitt, Sr., Rt. 1, Box 169, Wetumpka, AL 36092 Tel. (205)567-6565
Gen. Mod., Wallace B. Pittman, Jr.
Gen. Supt. Mission Bd., Jerry Powell, Rt. 1, Box 384, Chadourn, NC 28431

Periodicals

Faith and Truth

The Pentecostal Free Will Baptist Church, Inc.

The Cape Fear Conference of Free Will Baptists, organized in 1855, merged in 1959 with The Wilmington Conference and The New River Conference of Free Will Baptists and was renamed the Pentecostal Free Will Baptist Church, Inc. The doctrines include regeneration, sanctification, the Pentecostal baptism of the Holy Ghost, the Second Coming of Christ, and divine healing.

Headquarters

P.O. Box 1568, Dunn, NC 28335 Tel. (910)892-4161, Fax (910)892-6876
Media Contact, Gen. Supt., Preston Heath
Email: pheath@intrstar.net
Website: www.pfwb.org/

Officers

Gen. Supt., Rev. Preston Heath
Asst. Gen. Supt., Rev. Reynolds Smith
Gen. Sec., Rev. Horace Johnson
Gen. Treas., Dr. W. L. Ellis
Christian Ed. Dir., Rev. Murray King
World Witness Dir., Rev. Dock Hobbs
Gen. Services Dir., Danny Blackman
Ministerial Council Dir., —
Ladies' Auxiliary Dir., Dollie Davis
Heritage Bible College, Pres., Dr. W. L. Ellis
Crusader Youth Camp, Dir., Rev. Murray King

OTHER ORGANIZATIONS

Heritage Bible College
Crusader Youth Camp
Blessings Bookstore, 1006 W. Cumberland St., Dunn, NC 28334 Tel. (910)892-2401
Cape Fear Christian Academy, Rt 1 Box 139, Erwin, NC 28339 Tel. (910)897-5423

Periodicals

The Messenger

Philadelphia Yearly Meeting of the Religious Society of Friends*

PYM traces its roots to the yearly meeting of 1681 in Burlington, New Jersey. For more than three centuries, PYM has served Monthly Meetings and Quarterly Meetings throughout eastern Pennsylvania, southern New Jersey, northern Maryland and Delaware. In general, the activities of PYM are organized under five Standing Committees: Standing Committee on Worship and Care; Standing Committee on Education; Standing Committee on Peace and Concerns; Standing Committee on Support and Outreach; and Standing Committee on General Services.

Headquarters

Philadelphia Yearly Meeting, 1515 Cherry Street, Philadelphia, PA 19102-1479 Tel. (215)241-7000, Fax (215)567-2096
Website: www.pym.org

Officers

Gen. Sec., Thomas Jeavons
Clerk, Standing Committee on Worship and Care, Edward Breadfires & James Morrissey, Email: worship@pym.org
Clerk, Standing Committee on Education, Deborah Lyons, Email: education@pym.org
Clerk, Standing Committee on Peace and Concerns, Elizabeth R. Marsh, Email: peace@pym.org
Clerk, Standing Committee on Support and Outreach, Frances Dreisbach & Pamela Carter, Email: outreach@pym.org
Clerk, Standing Committee on General Services, Anne Meore, Email: services@pym.org

Pillar of Fire

The Pillar of Fire was founded by Alma Bridwell White in Denver on Dec. 29, 1901 as the Pentecostal Union. In 1917, the name was changed to Pillar of Fire. Alma White was born in Kentucky in 1862 and taught school in Montana where she met her husband, Kent White, a Methodist minister, who was a University student in Denver.

Because of Alma White's evangelistic endeavors, she was frowned upon by her superiors, which eventually necessitated her withdrawing from Methodist Church supervision. She was ordained as Bishop and her work spread to many states, to England, and since her death to Liberia, West Africa, Malawi, East Africa, Yugoslavia, Spain, India, and the Philippines.

The Pillar of Fire organization has a college and two seminaries stressing Biblical studies. It operates eight separate schools for young people. The church continues to keep in mind the founder's goals and purposes.

Headquarters

P.O. Box 9159, Zarephath, NJ 08890 Tel. (732) 356-0102

Western Headquarters, 1302 Sherman St., Denver, CO 80203 Tel. (303)427-5462

Media Contact, 1st Vice Pres., Robert B. Dallenbach, 3455 W. 83 Ave., Westminster, CO 80031 Tel. (303)427-5462, Fax (303)429-0910

Email: info@zarephath.edu

Website: www.gospelcom.net/pof/

Officers

Pres. & Gen. Supt., Dr. Robert B. Dallenbach

1st Vice-Pres. & Asst. Supt., Rev. Joseph Gross

2nd Vice-Pres./Sec.-Treas., Lois R. Stewart

Trustees, Kenneth Cope; S. Rea Crawford; Lois Stewart; Dr. Donald J. Wolfram; Robert B. Dallenbach; Rob W. Cruver; Joseph Gross

Periodicals

The Pillar Monthly

Plymouth Brethren—please see Christian Brethren.

Polish National Catholic Church of America*

After a number of attempts to resolve differences regarding the role of the laity in parish administration in the Roman Catholic Church in Scranton, Pennsylvania, this Church was organized in 1897. With the consecration to the episcopacy of the Most Rev. F. Hodur, this Church became a member of the Old Catholic Union of Utrecht in 1907.

Headquarters

Office of the Prime Bishop, 1004 Pittston Ave., Scranton, PA 18505 Tel. (570)346-9131

Media Contact, Prime Bishop, Most Rev. John F. Swantek, 1002 Pittston Ave., Scranton, PA 18505 Tel. (570)346-9131 Fax (570)346-2188

Email: ads22244@aol.com

Website: www.PNCC.org/

Officers

Prime Bishop, Most Rev. John F. Swantek, 115 Lake Scranton Rd., Scranton, PA 18505

Central Diocese, Bishop, Rt. Rev. Casimir Grotnik, 529 E. Locust St., Scranton, PA 18505

Eastern Diocese, Bishop, Rt. Rev. Thomas J. Gnat, 166 Pearl St., Manchester, NH 03104

Buffalo-Pittsburgh Diocese, Bishop, Rt. Rev. Thaddeus S. Peplowski, 5776 Broadway, Lancaster, NY 14086

Western Diocese, Rt. Rev. Robert M. Nemkovich, 920 N. Northwest Hwy., Park Ridge, IL 60068; Rt. Rev. Jan Dawidziuk (Auxilliery Bp.) 1901 Wexford Ave., Parma, OH 44134

Canadian Diocese, Bishop, Sede Vacante, 186 Cowan Ave., Toronto, ON M6K 2N6

Ecumenical Officer, V. Rev. Marcell Pytlarz

Periodicals

God's Field; Polka

Presbyterian Church in America

The Presbyterian Church in America is an Evangelical, Reformed covenant community of churches in the United States and Canada committed to a common doctrinal standard (The Westminster Standards), mutual accountability (representative church government), and cooperative ministry. The PCA traces its historical roots to the First General Assembly of the Church of Scotland of 1560, the establishment of the Presbytery of Philadelphia, 1789, and the General Assembly of the Southern Presbyterian Church, Augusta in 1861. Organized in 1973 by conservative churches formerly associated with the Presbyterian Church in the United States, the Church was first known as the National Presbyterian Church but changed its name in 1974 to the Presbyterian Church in America. The PCA seeks to be "Faithful to the Scriptures, True to the Reformed Faith, and Obedient to the Great Commission." In 1982 the Reformed Presbyterian Church, Evangelical Synod joined the PCA bringing with it a rich tradition that had antecedents in colonial America.

The PCA holds to the ancient creeds of the Church such as the Apostles' Creed and the Nicene Creed and has a firm commitment to its doctrinal standards, The Westminster Confession of Faith, Larger and Shorter Catechisms, that have been significant in Presbyterianism since 1645, These doctrinal standards reflect the distinctives of the Reformed tradition, Calvinism, and Covenant Theology. Ministers, ruling elders, and deacons are required to subscribe to the Westminster Standards in good faith. Individuals are received by a Session as communing members of the Church upon their profession of faith in Jesus Christ as Lord and Saviour, their promise to live a Christian lifestyle, and their commitment to worship and service in the Church.

The PCA is a connectional Church, led by ruling elders (lay leaders) and teaching elders (ministers). The Session governs a local congregation; the Diaconate carries out mercy ministries. The Presbytery is responsible for regional matters and the General Assembly is responsible for national matters in the USA and Canada.

Cooperative ministry is carried out through over sixty Presbyteries and ten General Assembly Ministries.

The educational institutions of the Church are Covenant College of Lookout Mountain, CA and Covenant Theological Seminary of St. Louis, MO. The PCA and the Orthodox Presbyterian Church participate in a joint publication venture, Great Commission Publications, for the publication of Christian Education materials.

In its ecumenical relations the PCA is a member of the North American Presbyterian and Reformed Council, the National Association of Evangelicals, and the World Reformed Fellowship.

The General Assembly approved a statement of purpose, "It is the purpose of the PCA to bring glory to God as a worshipping and serving community until the nations in which we live are filled with churches that make Jesus Christ and His word their chief joy, and the nations of the world, hearing the Word, are discipled in obedience to the Great Commission."

The Church has grown beyond its origin in the southeastern states to have congregations in forty-nine states in the USA and in several provinces of Canada. Growth is due to the PCA's ministry in evangelism, discipleship, church planting, church renewal, and campus ministry. Indicative of her concern for cross-cultural ministry, the PCA has the largest international missionary force in Presbyterian Church history.

Headquarters

1700 N. Brown Rd., Lawrenceville, GA 30043-8122, Tel. (678)825-1000

Email: ac@pcanet.org

Website: www.pcanet.org

Officers

Moderator—Mr. Steve Fox, P.O. Box 11425, Montgomery, AL 36111 Tel. (334)832-4975, Fax (334)265-2408, stevefox@walkerprinting.com

Stated Clerk/Coordinator of Administration—Dr. L. Roy Taylor, 1700 N. Brown Rd., Suite 105, Lawrenceville, GA 30043-8122 Tel. (678) 825-1100, ac@pcanet.org

Christian Education & Publications Coordinator—Dr. Charles Dunahoo, 1700 N. Brown Rd., Suite 102, Lawrenceville, GA 30043-8122 Tel. (678)825-1100, cep@pacnet.org

Mission to the World Coordinator—Dr. Paul D. Kooistra, 1600 N. Brown Rd., Lawrenceville, GA 30043-8141 Tel. (678)823-0004, mtw@mtw.org

Mission to North America Coordinator—Dr. James C. Bland, 1700 N. Brown Rd., Suite 101, Lawrenceville, GA 30043-8122 Tel. (678)825-1200, mna@pcanet.org

Reformed University Ministries Coordinator—Dr. Rod Mays, 1700 N. Brown Rd., Suite 104, Lawrenceville, GA 30043-8122 Tel. (678) 825-1070, rum@pcanet.org

PCA Foundation President—Mr. James L. Hughes, 1700 N. Brown Rd., Suite 103, Lawrenceville, GA 30043-8122 Tel. (678) 825-1040, pcaf@pcanet.org

Insurance-Annuities President—Mr. James L. Hughes, 1700 N. Brown Rd., Suite 106, Lawrenceville, GA 30043-8122 Tel. (678) 825-1260, iar@pcanet.org

Ridge Haven Conference Director—Rev. Morse Up De Graff, P.O. Box 969, Rosman, NC 28772, Tel. (828)862-3916, Fax (828)884-6988, ridgehaven@citcom.net

Covenant College President—Dr. Frank A. Brock, 14049 Scenic Highway, Lookout Mountain, GA 30750 Tel. (706)820-1560, Fax (706)820-2165, webmaster@covenant. edu

Covenant Theological Seminary President—Dr. Bryan Chapell, 12330 Conway Rd., St. Louis, MO 63141-8697 Tel. (314)434-4044, Fax (314)434-4819, webmaster@covenantseminary.edu

Periodicals

Equip, Covenant, Multiply, The View, Network, PCANews.com

Presbyterian Church (U.S.A.)*

The Presbyterian Church (U.S.A.) was organized June 10, 1983, when the Presbyterian Church in the United States and the United Presbyterian Church in the United States of America united in Atlanta. The union healed a major division which began with the Civil War when Presbyterians in the South withdrew from the Presbyterian Church in the United States of America to form the Presbyterian Church in the Confederate States.

The United Presbyterian Church in the United States of America had been created by the 1958 union of the Presbyterian Church in the United States of America and the United Presbyterian Church of North America. Of those two uniting bodies, the Presbyterian Church in the U.S.A. dated from the first Presbytery organized in Philadelphia, about 1706. The United Presbyterian Church of North America was formed in 1858, when the Associate Reformed Presbyterian Church and the Associate Presbyterian Church united.

Strongly ecumenical in outlook, the Presbyterian Church (U.S.A.) is the result of at least 10 different denominational mergers over the last 250 years. A restructure, adopted by the General Assembly meeting in June 1993, has been implemented. The Presbyterian Church (U.S.A.) dedicated its new national offices in Louisville, Kentucky in 1988.

Headquarters

100 Witherspoon St., Louisville, KY 40202 Tel. (888)728-7228, Fax (502)569-5018

Media Contact, Assoc. Dir. for Communications, Gary W. Luhr, Tel. (502)569-5515, Fax (502) 569-8073

Email: presytel@pcusa.org
Website: www.pcusa.org

Officers

Mod., Jack Rogers
Vice-Mod., Janet Arbesman
Stated Clk., Clifton Kirkpatrick

THE OFFICE OF THE GENERAL ASSEMBLY

Tel. (888)728-7228 x. 5424, Fax (502)569-8005
Stated Clk., Clifton Kirkpatrick
Strategic Operations, Dir., Gradye Parsons
Middle Governing Body Relations, Coord., Gary Torrens
Dept. of the Stated Clerk, Dir., Loyda Aja
Dept. of Constitutional Services, Dir., Mark Tammen
Ecumenical & Agency Relations, Dir., Robina Winbush
Dept. of Communication& Technology, Dir., Kerry Clements
Dept. of Hist., Philadelphia, 425 Lombard St., Philadelphia, PA 19147 Tel. (215)627-1852, Fax (215)627-0509; Dir., Frederick J. Heuser, Jr.; Deputy Dir., Margery Sly; Deputy Dir., Vacant, P.O. Box 849, Montreat, NC 28757

GENERAL ASSEMBLY COUNCIL

Exec. Dir., John J. Detterick
Deputy Exec. Dir., Kathy Luekert
Worldwide Ministries Division, Dir., Marian McClure
Congregational Ministries Division, Dir., Donald G. Campbell
National Ministries Division, Dir., Curtis A. Kearns, Jr.
Mission Support Services Dir., Joey Bailey

BOARD OF PENSIONS

200 Market St., Philadelphia, PA 19103-3298, Tel. (800)773-7752, Fax (215)587-6215
Chpsn. of the Bd., Earldean V. S. Robbins
Pres., & CEO, Robert W. Maggs, Jr.

PRESBYTERIAN CHURCH (U.S.A.) FOUNDATION

200 E. Twelfth St., Jeffersonville, IN 47130 Tel. (812)288-8841, Fax (502)569-5980
Chpsn. of the Bd., James Henderson
Pres. & CEO, Robert E. Leech

PRESBYTERIAN CHURCH (U.S.A.) INVESTMENT & LOAN PROGRAM, INC.

Tel. (800)903-7457, Fax (502)569-8868
Chpsn. of the Board, Ben McAnally
Pres. & CEO, Kenneth G.Y. Grant

PRESBYTERIAN PUBLISHING CORPORATION

Chpsn. of the Bd., Robert Bohl
Pres. & CEO, Davis Perkins

SYNOD EXECUTIVES

Alaska-Northwest, Rev.Kittie Carland, 217 Sixth Ave. N., Seattle, WA 98109 Tel. (206)448-6403
Boriquen in Puerto Rico, Rev. Harry Fred Del Valle, Ave. Hostos Edificio 740, Cond. Medical Center Plaza, Ste. 216, Mayaguez, PR 00680 Tel. (787)832-8375
Covenant, Elder Edith Patton, Interim, 6172 Busch Blvd., Ste. 3000, Columbus, OH 43229-2564 Tel. (614)436-3310
Lakes & Prairies, Rev. Grant Lowe, Interim, 8012 Cedar Ave. S., Bloomington, MN 55425-1210 Tel. (612)854-0144
Lincoln Trails, Rev. Jay Hudson, 1100 W. 42nd St., Indianapolis, IN 46208-3381 Tel. (317) 923-3681
Living Waters, Rev. P. David Snellgrove, 318 Seaboard Ln., Ste. 205, Franklin, TN 37067, Tel. (615)261-4008
Mid-America, Rev. John L. Williams, 6400 Glenwood, Ste. 111, Overland Park, KS 66202-4072 Tel. (913)384-3020
Mid-Atlantic, Rev. Barry Van DeVenter, Interim, P.O. Box 27026, Richmond, VA 23261-7026 Tel. (804)342-0016
Northeast, Rev. Robert Howell White, Jr., 5811 Heritage Landing Dr., East Syracuse, NY 13057-9360 Tel. (315)446-5990
Pacific, Rev. Robert Brinks, 8 Fourth St., Petaluma, CA 94952-3004 Tel. (707)765-1772
Rocky Mountains, Vacant, 3025 West 37th Ave., Ste. 206, Denver, CO 80211-2799 Tel. (303) 477-9070
South Atlantic, Rev. Floyd N. Rhodes, 118 E. Monroe St., Ste. 3, Jacksonville, FL 32202 Tel. (904)356-6070
Southern California & Hawaii, Rev. John N. Langfitt, 1501 Wilshire Blvd., Los Angeles, CA 90017-2293 Tel. (213)483-3840
Southwest, Rev. Janet DeVries, 4423 N. 24th St., Ste. 800, Phoenix, AZ 85016 Tel. (602)468-3800
The Sun, Rev. Judy R. Fletcher, 920 S. I 35 E, Denton, TX 76205-7898 Tel. (940)382-9656
The Trinity, Rev. Jim Cushman, 3040 Market St., Camp Hill, PA 17011-4599 Tel. (717)737-0421

Periodicals

American Presbyterians, Journal of Presbyterian History; Presbyterian News Service "News Briefs"; Church & Society Magazine; Horizons; Monday Morning; Presbyterians Today; Interpretation; Presbyterian Outlook

Primitive Advent Christian Church

This body split from the Advent Christian Church. All its churches are in West Virginia. The Primitive Advent Christian Church believes that the Bible is the only rule of faith and practice and that Christian character is the only test of fellowship and communion. The church agrees with Christian fidelity and meekness; exercises mutual watch and care; counsels, admonishes, or reproves as duty may require, and receives the same from each other as becomes the household of faith. Primitive Advent Christians do not believe in taking up arms.

The church believes that three ordinances are set forth by the Bible to be observed by the Christian church: (1) baptism by immersion; (2) the Lord's Supper, by partaking of unleavened bread and wine; (3) feet washing, to be observed by the saints' washing of one another's feet.

Headquarters

Media Contact, Sec.-Treas., Roger Wines, 1971 Grapevine Rd., Sissonville, WV 25320 Tel. (304)988-2668

Officers

Pres., Herbert Newhouse, 7632 Hughart Dr., Sissonville, WV 25320 Tel. (304)984-9277

Vice-Pres., Roger Hammons, 273 Frame Rd., Elkview, WV 25071 Tel. (304)965-6247

Sec. & Treas., Roger Wines, 1971 Grapevine Rd., Sissonville, WV 25320 Tel. (304)988-2668

Primitive Baptists

This large group of Baptists, located throughout the United States, opposes all centralization and modern missionary societies. They preach salvation by grace alone.

Headquarters

P.O. Box 38, Thornton, AR 71766 Tel. (501)352-3694

Media Contact, Elder W. Hartsel Cayce

Officers

Elder W. Hartsel Cayce

Elder Lasserre Bradley, Jr., Box 17037, Cincinnati, OH 45217 Tel. (513)821-7289

Elder S. T. Tolley, P.O. Box 68, Atwood, TN 38220 Tel. (901)662-7417

Periodicals

Baptist Witness; The Christian Baptist; The Primitive Baptist; For the Poor

Primitive Methodist Church in the U.S.A.

Hugh Bourne and William Clowes, local preachers in the Wesleyan Church in England, organized a daylong meeting at Mow Cop in Staffordshire on May 31, 1807, after Lorenzo Dow, an evangelist from America, told them of American camp meetings. Thousands attended and many were converted but the Methodist church, founded by the open-air preacher John Wesley, refused to accept the converts and reprimanded the preachers.

After waiting for two years for a favorable action by the Wesleyan Society, Bourne and Clowes established The Society of the Primitive Methodists. This was not a schism, Bourne said, for "we did not take one from them ... it now appeared to be the will of God that we ... should form classes and take upon us the care of churches in the fear of God." Primitive Methodist missionaries were sent to New York in 1829. An American conference was established in 1840. Missionary efforts reach into Guatemala, Spain, and other countries. The denomination joins in federation with the Evangelical Congregational Church, the United Brethren in Christ Church and the Southern Methodist Church and is a member of the National Association of Evangelicals.

The church believes the Bible is the only true rule of faith and practice, the inspired Word of God. It believes in one Triune God, the Deity of Jesus Christ, the Deity and personality of the Holy Spirit, the innocence of Adam and Eve, the Fall of the human race, the necessity of repentance, justification by faith of all who believe, regeneration witnessed by the Holy Spirit, sanctification by the Holy Spirit, the second coming of the Lord Jesus Christ, the resurrection of the dead and conscious future existence of all people, and future judgments with eternal rewards and punishments.

Headquarters

Media Contact, Pres., Rev. Wayne Yarnall, 1045 Laurel Run Rd., Wilkes-Barre, PA 18702 Tel. (570)472-3436, Fax (570)472-9283

Email: pmconf@juno.com

Website: www.primitivemethodistchurch.org

Officers

Pres., Rev. Wayne Yarnall, 1045 Laurel Run Rd., Wilkes-Barre, PA 18702 Tel. (570)472-3436 Fax (570)472-9283

Vice-Pres., Rev. Kerry R. Ritts, 723 Preston Ln., Hatboro, PA 19040

General. Secretary., Rev. David Allen, Jr., 1199 Lawrence St., Lowell, MA 01852-5526 Tel. (978) 453-2052

E-mail, pahson@banet.net

Treas., Mr. Raymond C. Baldwin, 18409 Mill Run Ct., Leesburg, VA 20176-4583

E-mail: Rbaldwin32@aol.com

Progressive National Baptist Convention, Inc.*

This body held its organizational meeting in Cincinnati in November, 1961. Subsequent regional sessions were followed by the first annual session in Philadelphia in 1962.

Headquarters

601 50th Street, NE, Washington, DC 20019 Tel. (202)396-0558, Fax (202)398-4998

Media Contact, Gen. Sec., Dr. Tyrone S. Pitts

Officers

Pres., Dr. Bennett W. Smith, Sr., St. John Baptist Church, 184 Goodell St., Buffalo, NY 14204

Gen. Sec., Dr. Tyrone S. Pitts

OTHER ORGANIZATIONS

Dept. of Christian Education, Exec. Dir., Dr. C. B. Lucas, Emmanuel Baptist Church, 3815 W. Broadway, Louisville, KY 40211

Women's Dept., Mildred Wormley, 218 Spring St., Trenton, NJ 08618

Home Mission Bd., Exec. Dir., Rev. Archie LeMone, Jr.

Congress of Christian Education, Pres., Rev. Harold S. Diggs, Mayfield Memorial Baptist Church, 700 Sugar Creek Rd. W., Charlotte, NC 28213
Baptist Global Mission Bureau, Dr. Ronald K. Hill, 161-163 60th St., Philadelphia, PA 19139
Nannie Helen Burroughs School, Tel. (202)398-5266

Periodicals

Baptist Progress

Protestant Reformed Churches in America

The Protestant Reformed Churches (PRC) have their roots in the sixteenth century Reformation of Martin Luther and John Calvin, as it developed in the Dutch Reformed churches. The denomination originated as a result of a controversy in the Christian Reformed Church in 1924 involving the adoption of the "Three Points of Common Grace." Three ministers in the Christian Reformed Church, the Reverends Herman Hoeksema, George Ophoff, and Henry Danhof, and their consistories (Eastern Avenue, Hope, and Kalamazoo, respectively) rejected the doctrine. Eventually these men were deposed, and their consistories were either deposed or set outside the Christian Reformed Church. The denomination was formed in 1926 with three congregations. Today the denomination is comprised of some twenty-seven churches (more than 6,000 members) in the USA and Canada.

The presbyterian form of church government as determined by the Church Order of Dordt is followed by the PRC. The doctrinal standards of the PRC are the Reformed confessions " the Heidelberg Catechism, Belgic Confession of Faith, and Canons of Dordrecht. The doctrine of the covenant is a cornerstone of their teaching. They maintain an unconditional, particular covenant of grace that God establishes with His elect.

Headquarters

16511 South Park Ave., South Holland, IL 60473 Tel. (708)333-1314
Media Contact, Stat. Clk., Don Doezema, 4949 Ivanrest Ave., Grandville, MI 49418 Tel. (616) 531-1490
Email: doezema@prca.org
Website: www.prca.org

Officers

Stat. Clk., Don Doezema, 4949 Ivanrest Ave., Grandville, MI 49418 Tel. (616)531-1490, Fax (616)531-3033, doezema@prca.org

Periodicals

The Standard Bearer

Quakers—please see Friends.

Reformed Catholic Church

The Reformed Catholic Church was founded in 1988, and incorporated in 1989, as an alternative to the structures and strictures of the Roman Catholic Church, yet without denying basic catholic beliefs of faith and love, spirituality and community, prayer and sacramentality. The Reformed Catholic Church is a federation of independent churches offering a progressive alternative in the Catholic tradition. It is a newly formed rite, as in the tradition of the Orthodox churches of the Catholic tradition and the Old Catholic Church of Utrecht. It remains a Catholic Church, and its priests are considered Catholic priests.

Headquarters

Good Shepherd Rectory, P.O. Box 725, Hampton Bays, NY 11946 Tel. (516)723-2012
Media Contact, Archbishop, Most Rev. Robert J. Allmen, D.D.
Email: berzol@apollo3.com
Website: www.geocities.com/WestHollywood/4136/

Officers

Archbishop, Most Rev. Robert J. Allmen, D.D.

Reformed Church in America*

The Reformed Church in America was established in 1628 by the earliest settlers of New York. It is the oldest Protestant denomination with a continuous ministry in North America. Until 1867 it was known as the Reformed Protestant Dutch Church.

The first ordained minister, Domine Jonas Michaelius, arrived in New Amsterdam from The Netherlands in 1628. Throughout the colonial period, the Reformed Church lived under the authority of the Classis of Amsterdam. Its churches were clustered in New York and New Jersey. Under the leadership of Rev. John Livingston, it became a denomination independent of the authority of the Classis of Amsterdam in 1776. Its geographical base was broadened in the nineteenth century by the immigration of Reformed Dutch and German settlers in the midwestern United States. The Reformed Church now spans the United States and Canada.

The Reformed Church in America accepts as its standards of faith the Heidelberg Catechism, Belgic Confession and Canons of Dort. It has a rich heritage of world mission activity. It claims to be loyal to reformed tradition which emphasizes obedience to God in all aspects of life.

Although the Reformed Church in America has worked in close cooperation with other churches, it has never entered into merger with any other denomination. It is a member of the World Alliance of Reformed Churches, the World Council of Churches and the National Council of the Churches of Christ in the United States of America. In 1998 it also entered into a relationship of full communion with the Evangelical Lutheran Church in America, Presbyterian Church (U.S.A.), and the United Church of Christ by way of the Formula of Agreement.

Headquarters

475 Riverside Dr., New York, NY 10115 Tel. (212)870-2841, Fax (212)870-2499
Media Contact, Dir., Communication and Production Services, Kim Nathan Baker, 4500 60th St. SE, Grand Rapids, MI 49512, Tel. (616)698-7071, Fax (616)698-6606
Email: kbaker@rca.org
Website: www.rca.org

OFFICERS AND STAFF OF GENERAL SYNOD

President, The Rev. Steven Brooks, 475 Riverside Dr., 18th Floor, New York, NY 10115
General Snod Council; Moderator, Ms. Carol Mutch, 475 Riverside Dr., 18th Floor, New York, NY 10115
General Secretary, The Rev. Wesley Granberg-Michaelson, 475 Riverside Dr., 18th Floor, New York, NY 10115
Policy, Planning & Administrative Services, Director & Assistant Secretary, The Rev. Kenneth Bradsell
Ministry & Personnel Services, Director, The Rev. Dr. Vernon Hoffs
Congregational Services/Evangelism & Church Development Services, Director, The Rev. Richard Welscott
Finance Services, Treasurer, Ms. Susan Converse
Mission Services, Director, The Rev. Bruce Menning
African-American Council, Executive Director, The Rev. Dr. Glen Missick
Council for Hispanic Ministries, Executive Secretary, The Rev. Luis Perez
Native American Indian Ministries Council, Vacant
Council for Pacific/Asian-American Ministries, Executive Secretary, Ms. Ella Campbell

OTHER ORGANIZATIONS

Board of Benefits Services, Director, Mr. Jack Dalenberg, 8765 W. Higgins Rd., Suite 410, Chicago, IL 60631; President, The Rev. Robert White; Secretary, The Rev. Kenneth Bradsell
RCA Foundation, Director, Mr. Larryl Humme, 8765 W. Higgins Rd., Suite 410, Chicago, IL 60631
RCA Building and Extension Fund, Fund Executive, Mr. Paul Karssen, 612 Eighth St. SE, Orange City, IA 51014
Reformed Church Women's Ministries, Executive Director, Ms. Arlene Waldorf, 4500 60th St. SE, Grand Rapids, MI 49512

Periodicals

Perspectives; The Church Herald

Reformed Church in the United States

Lacking pastors, early German Reformed immigrants to the American colonies were led in worship by "readers." One reader, schoolmaster John Philip Boehm, organized the first congregations near Philadelphia in 1725. A Swiss pastor, Michael Schlatter, was sent by the Dutch Reformed Church in 1746. Strong ties with the Netherlands existed until the formation of the Synod of the German Reformed Church in 1793.

The Eureka Classis, organized in North and South Dakota in 1910 and strongly influenced by the writings of H. Kohlbruegge, P. Geyser and J. Stark, refused to become part of the 1934 merger of the Reformed Church with the Evangelical Synod of North America, holding that it sacrificed the Reformed heritage. (The merged Evangelical and Reformed Church became part of the United Church of Christ in 1957.) Under the leadership of pastors W. Grossmann and W. J. Krieger, the Eureka Classis in 1942 incorporated as the continuing Reformed Church in the United States.

The growing Eureka Classis dissolved in 1986 to form a Synod with four regional classes. An heir to the Reformation theology of Zwingli and Calvin, the Heidelberg Catechism, the Belgic Confession and the Canons of Dort are used as the confessional standards of the church. The Bible is strictly held to be the inerrant, infallible Word of God.

The RCUS supports Dordt College, Mid-America Reformed Seminary, New Geneva Theological Seminary, West Minster Theological Seminary in California, and Hope Haven. The RCUS is the official sponsor to the Reformed Confessing Church of Zaire.

Headquarters

Media Contact, Rev. Frank Walker Th.M., 6121 Pine Vista Way, Elk Grove City, CA 95758-4205, Tel. (661)827-9885
Email: fhw@iname.com
Website: www.rcus.org

Officers

Pres., Rev. Vernon Pollema, 235 James Street, Shafter, CA 93263 Tel. (661)746-6907
Vice-Pres., Rev. Robert Grossmann, Th.M., 1905 200th St., Garner, IA 50438 Tel. (515)923-3060
Stated Clk., Rev. Frank Walker Th.M., 5601 Spring Blossom St., Bakersfield, CA 93313-6025 Tel. (661)827-9885
Treas., Clayton Greiman, 2115 Hwy. 69, Garner, IA 50438 Tel. (515)923-2950

Periodicals

Reformed Herald

Reformed Episcopal Church

The Reformed Episcopal Church was founded December 2, 1873 in New York City by Bishop George D. Cummins, an assistant bishop in the Protestant Episcopal Church from 1866 until 1873. Cummins and other evangelical Episcopalians viewed with alarm the influence of the Oxford Movement in the Protestant Episcopal

Church, for the interest it stimulated in Roman Catholic ritual and doctrine and for intolerance it bred toward evangelical Protestant doctrine.

Throughout the late 1860s, evangelicals and ritualists clashed over ceremonies and vestments, exchanges of pulpits with clergy of other denominations, the meaning of critical passages in the Book of Common Prayer, interpretation of the sacraments and validity of the Apostolic Succession.

In October, 1873, other bishops publicly attacked Cummins in the church newspapers for participating in an ecumenical Communion service sponsored by the Evangelical Alliance. Cummins resigned and drafted a call to Episcopalians to organize a new Episcopal Church for the "purpose of restoring the old paths of their fathers." On Dec. 2, 1873, a Declaration of Principles was adopted and Dr. Charles E. Cheney was elected bishop to serve with Cummins. The Second General Council, meeting in May 1874 in New York City, approved a Constitution and Canons and a slightly amended version of the Book of Common Prayer. In 1875, the Third General Council adopted a set of Thirty-Five Articles.

Cummins died in 1876. The church had grown to nine jurisdictions in the United States and Canada at that time. The Reformed Episcopal Church is a member of the National Association of Evangelicals.

Headquarters

7372 Henry Ave., Philadelphia, PA 19128-1401 Tel. (215)483-1196, Fax (215)483-5235

Media Contact, Rt. Rev. Leonard Riches

Media Contact, Rt. Rev. Royal U. Grote, Jr., Church Growth Office, 211 Byrne Ave., Houston, TX 77009 Tel. (713)862-4929

Email: wycliffe@jps.net

Website: recus.org

Officers

Pres. & Presiding Bishop, Rt. Rev. Leonard W. Riches

Vice-Pres., Rt. Rev. Royal U. Grote, Jr.

Sec., Rev. Walter Banek

Treas., Rev. Jon W. Abboud

OTHER ORGANIZATIONS

Bd. of Foreign Missions, Pres., Dr. Barbara J. West, 316 Hunters Rd., Swedesboro, NJ 08085 Tel. (609) 467-1641

Bd. of Natl. Church Extension, Pres., Rt. Rev. Royal U. Grote, Jr., 211 Byrne Ave., Houston, TX 77009 Tel. (713)862-4929

Publication Society, Pres., Rt. Rev. Gregory K. Hotchkiss, 318 Main St., Somerville, NJ 08876 Tel. (908)725-2678, Fax (908)725-4641; Orders, Rev. Jonathan S. Riches, 7372 Henry Ave., Philadelphia, PA 19128 25-956-0655

The Reapers, Pres., Susan Higham, 472 Leedom St., Jenkintown, PA 19046

Committee on Women's Work, Pres., Joan Workowski, 1162 Beverly Rd., Rydal, PA 19046

BISHOPS

William H.S. Jerdan, Jr., 414 W. Second South St., Summerville, SC 29483

Sanco K. Rembert, P.O. Box 20068, Charleston, SC 29413

Franklin H. Sellers, Sr., 81 Buttercup Ct., Marco Island, FL 33937-3480

Leonard W. Riches, Sr., 85 Smithtown Rd., Pipersville, PA 18947 Tel. (215)483-1196, Fax (215)294-8009

Royal U. Grote, Jr., 211 Byrne Ave., Houston, TX 77009

James C. West, Sr., 408 Red Fox Run, Summerville, SC 29485

Robert H. Booth, 1611 Park Ave., #212, Quakertown, PA 18951

Gregory K. Hotchkiss, 318 E. Main St., Somerville, NJ 08876

George B. Fincke, 155 Woodstock Circle, Vacaville, CA 95687-3381

Daniel R. Morse, 11259 Wexford Dr., Eads, TN 38025

Michael Fedechko, Box 2532, New Liskeard, ON P0J 1P0

Charles W. Dorrington, 626 Blanshard St., Victoria, BC V8W 3G6

Ted Follows, 626 Blanshard St., Victoria, BC V8W 3G6

Daniel G. Cox, 9 Hilltop Pl., Baltimore, MD 21228

Ray R. Sutton, 3421 Madison Park Blvd., Shreveport, LA 71104

Periodicals

Reformed Episcopalians

Reformed Mennonite Church

This is a small group of believers in Pennsylvania, Ohio, Michigan, Illinois, and Ontario, Canada who believe in non-resistance of evil, and non-conformity to the world and who practice separation from unfaithful worship. They believe that Christian unity is the effect of brotherly love and are of one mind and spirit. Their church was established in 1812 by John Herr who agreed with the teachings of Menno Simon as well as those of Jesus Christ.

Headquarters

Lancaster County only, Reformed Mennonite Church, 602 Strasburg Pike, Lancaster, PA 17602

Media Contact, Bishop, Glenn M. Gross, Tel. (717)697-4623

Officers

Bishop Glenn M. Gross, 906 Grantham Rd., Mechanicsburg, PA 17055

Reformed Methodist Union Episcopal Church

The Reformed Methodist Union Episcopal church was formed after a group of ministers withdrew from the African Methodist Episcopal Church following a dispute over the election of ministerial delegates to the General Conference.

These ministers organized the Reformed Methodist Union church during a four-day meeting beginning on January 22, 1885 at Hills Chapel (now known as Mt. Hermon RMUE church), in Charleston, South Carolina. The Rev. William E. Johnson was elected president of the new church. Following the death of Rev. Johnson in 1896, it was decided that the church would conform to regular American Methodism (the Episcopacy). The first Bishop, Edward Russell Middleton, was elected, and "Episcopal" was added to the name of the church. Bishop Middleton was consecrated on Dec. 5, 1896, by Bishop P. F. Stephens of the Reformed Episcopal Church.

Headquarters

1136 Brody Ave., Charleston, SC 29407

Media Contact, Gen. Secretary, Brother Willie B. Oliver, P.O. Box 1995, Orangeburg, SC 29116 Tel. (803)536-3293

Officers

Bishop, Rt. Rev. Leroy Gethers, Tel. (803)766-3534

Asst. Bishop, Rt. Rev. Jerry M. DeVoe, Jr.

Gen. Sec., Brother Willie B. Oliver

Treas., Rev. Daniel Green

Sec. of Education, Rev. William Polite

Sec. of Books Concerns, Sister Ann Blanding

Sec. of Pension Fund, Rev. Joseph Powell

Sec. of Church Extension, Brother William Parker

Sec. of Sunday School Union, Sister Wine

Sec. of Mission, Rev. Warren Hatcher

Reformed Presbyterian Church of North America

Also known as the Church of the Covenanters, this church's origin dates back to the Reformation days of Scotland when the Covenanters signed their "Covenants" in resistance to the king and the Roman Church in the enforcement of state church practices. The Church in America has signed two "Covenants" in particular, those of 1871 and 1954.

Headquarters

Media Contact, Stated Clk., Louis D. Hutmire, 7408 Penn Ave., Pittsburgh, PA 15208 Tel. (412)731-1177, Fax (412)731-8861

Email: RPTrustees@aol.com

Website: www.reformedpresbyterian.org/

Officers

Mod., Rev. William J. Edgar, 25 Lawrence Rd., Broomall, PA 19008 Tel. (610)353-1371

Clk., J. Bruce Martin, 310 Main St., Ridgefield Park, NJ 07660 Tel. (201)440-5993

Asst. Clk., Raymond E. Morton, 411 N. Vine St., Sparta, IL 62286 Tel. (618)443-3419

Stated Clk., Louis D. Hutmire, 7408 Penn Ave., Pittsburgh, PA 15208 Tel. (412)731-1177

Periodicals

The Covenanter Witness

Reformed Zion Union Apostolic Church

This group was organized in 1869 at Boydton, Va., by Elder James R. Howell of New York, a minister of the A.M.E. Zion Church, with doctrines of the Methodist Episcopal Church.

Headquarters

Rt. 1, Box 64D, Dundas, VA 23938 Tel. (804) 676-8509

Media Contact, Bishop G. W. Studivant

Officers

Exec. Brd., Chair, Rev. Hilman Wright, Tel. (804)447-3988

Sec., Joseph Russell, Tel. (804)634-4520

Religious Society of Friends (Conservative)

These Friends mark their present identity from separations occurring by regions at different times from 1845 to 1904. They hold to a minimum of organizational structure. Their meetings for worship, which are unprogrammed and based on silent, expectant waiting upon the Lord, demonstrate the belief that all individuals may commune directly with God and may share equally in vocal ministry.

They continue to stress the importance of the Living Christ and the experience of the Holy Spirit working with power in the lives of individuals who obey it.

YEARLY MEETINGS

North Carolina YM, Robert Gosner, P.O. Box 489, Woodland, NC 27897 Tel. (252)587-2571

Iowa YM, Deborah Frisch, Clerk, 916 41st Street, Des Moines, Iowa 50312-2612

Ohio YM, S. S. Smith, Clerk, 61830 Sandy Ridge Road, Barnesville, OH 43713

Religious Society of Friends (Unaffiliated Meetings)

Though all groups of Friends acknowledge the same historical roots, nineteenth-century divisions in theology and experience led to some of the current organizational groupings. Many newer yearly meetings, often marked by spontaneity, variety and experimentation and hoping for renewed Quaker unity, have chosen not to identify with past divisions by affiliating in traditional ways with the larger organizations within the Society. Some of these unaffiliated groups have begun within the past 25 years.

YEARLY MEETINGS

Central Yearly Meeting (I), Supt., Jonathan Edwards, 5597 West County Rd., 700 N., Ridgeville, IN 47380

Intermountain Yearly Meeting(I), Clerk, Ted Church, 4 Arco, N.W., Albuquerque, NM 87120 Tel. (505)898-5305

North Pacific Yearly Meeting (I), Contact,, Helen Dart, 3311 NW Polk, Corvallis, OR 97330 Tel. (206)633-4860

Pacific Yearly Meeting (I), Clerk, Margaret Mossman, 2151 Vine St., Berkeley, CA 94709

Periodicals

Friends Bulletin

Reorganized Church of Jesus Christ of Latter-Day Saints—please see Community of Christ.

The Roman Catholic Church—please see The Catholic Church.

The Romanian Orthodox Church in America

The Romanian Orthodox Church in America is an autonomous Archdiocese chartered under the name of "Romanian Orthodox Archdiocese in America."

The diocese was founded in 1929 and approved by the Holy Synod of the Romanian Orthodox Church in Romania in 1934. The Holy Synod of the Romanian Orthodox Church of July 12, 1950, granted it ecclesiastical autonomy in America, continuing to hold only dogmatical and canonical ties with the Holy Synod and the Romanian Orthodox Patriarchate of Romania.

In 1951, approximately 40 parishes with their clergy from the United States and Canada separated from this church. In 1960, they joined the Russian Orthodox Greek Catholic Metropolia, now called the Orthodox Church in America, which reordained for these parishes a bishop with the title "Bishop of Detroit and Michigan."

The Holy Synod of the Romanian Orthodox Church, on June 11, 1973, elevated the Bishop of Romanian Orthodox Missionary Episcopate in America to the rank of Archbishop.

Headquarters

19959 Riopelle St., Detroit, MI 48203 Tel. (313) 893-8390

Media Contact, Archdiocesan Dean & Secretary, V. Rev. Fr. Nicholas Apostola, 44 Midland St., Worcester, MA 01602-4217 Tel. (508)799-0040, Fax (508)756-9866

Officers

Archbishop, His Eminence Victorin Ursache

Vicar, V. Rev. Archim. Dr. Vasile Vasilachi, 45-03 48th Ave., Woodside, Queens, NY 11377 Tel. (718)784-4453

Inter-Church Relations, Dir., Rev. Fr. Nicholas Apostola, 14 Hammond St., Worcester, MA 01610 Tel. (617)799-0040

Sec., V. Rev. Fr. Nicholas Apostola, 44 Midland St., Worchester, MA 01602 Tel. (508)756-9866, Fax (508)799-0040

Periodicals

Credinta-The Faith

The Romanian Orthodox Episcopate of America

This body of Eastern Orthodox Christians of Romanian descent was organized in 1929 as an autonomous Diocese under the jurisdiction of the Romanian Patriarchate. In 1951 it severed all relations with the Orthodox Church of Romania. Under the canonical jurisdiction of the autocephalous Orthodox Church in America since 1970, it enjoys full administrative autonomy and is headed by its own Bishop.

Headquarters

P.O. Box 309, Grass Lake, MI 49240-0309 Tel. (517)522-4800, Fax (517)522-5907

Media Contact, Ed./Sec., Dept. of Publications, Rev. Protodeacon David Oancea, P.O. Box 185, Grass Lake, MI 49240-0185 Tel. (517) 522-3656, Fax (517)522-5907

Email: roeasolia@aol.com

Website: www.roea.org

Officers

Ruling Bishop, His Eminence Archbishop Nathaniel Popp

Dean-Michigan, The V. Rev. Fr. Laurence Lazar, 18430 W 9 Mile Rd., Southfield, MI 48075-4032 Tel. (248)356-4144

Dean-Pacific Coast, The V. Rev. Fr. Constantin Alesce, P.O. Box 65853, Los Angeles, CA 90065-0853 Tel. (818)361-2750

Dean-Atlantic Seaboard, -vacant

Dean-Midwest, The V. Rev. Fr. Simion Pavel, 5825 N Mozart St., Chicago, IL 60659-3801 Tel. (773)878-0873

Dean-Ohio & Western Pennsylvania, The V. Rev. Fr. Panteleimon Stanciu, 1427 33rd St. NE, Canton, OH 44717-1547 Tel. (330)452-1940

Dean-South, The V. Rev. Fr. Dumitru Viorel Sasu, 6055 SW 19th St., Miramar, FL 33023-2906 Tel. (954)986-9866

OTHER ORGANIZATIONS

The American Romanian Orthodox Youth, Pres., Jonathan Groza, 968 Kertesz Rd., Clinton, OH 44216

Assoc. of Romanian Orthodox Ladies' Aux., Pres., Louise Gibb, 837 Lynita Dr, Brookfield, OH 4403

Orthodox Brotherhood U.S.A., Pres., Eugenia Peru, 16732 Merriman Rd., Livonia, MI 48154-3162 Tel. (734)525-3558

Orthodox Brotherhood of Canada, Pres., Gloria Buchanan, 26 Mill Bay, Regina, SK S4N 1L6, Canada

Periodicals

Solia-The Herald; Calendarul Solia (annual); *Good News- Buna Vestire* (quarterly)

The Russian Orthodox Church Outside of Russia

This group was organized in 1920 to unite in one body of dioceses the missions and parishes of the Russian Orthodox Church outside of Russia. The governing body, set up in Constantinople, was sponsored by the Ecumenical Patriarchate. In November 1950, it came to the United States. The Russian Orthodox Church Outside of Russia emphasizes being true to the old traditions of the Russian Church. It is not in communion with the Moscow Patriarchate.

Headquarters

75 E. 93rd St., New York, NY 10128 Tel. (212) 534-1601, Fax (212)426-1086

Media Contact, Dep. Sec., Bishop Gabriel

SYNOD OF BISHOPS

Pres., His Eminence Metropolitan Vitaly

Sec., Archbishop of Syracuse and Trinity, Laurus

Dep. Sec., Bishop of Manhattan, Gabriel, Tel. (212)722-6577

Periodicals

Living Orthodoxy; Orthodox Family; Orthodox Russia (Russian); Orthodox Voices; Pravoslavnaya Rus; Pravoslavnaya Zhisn; Orthodox America

The Salvation Army

The Salvation Army, founded in 1865 by William Booth (1829-1912) in London, England, and introduced into America in 1880, is an international religious and charitable movement organized and operated on a paramilitary pattern and is a branch of the Christian church. To carry out its purposes, The Salvation Army has established a widely diversified program of religious and social welfare services which are designed to meet the needs of children, youth and adults in all age groups.

Headquarters

615 Slaters Ln., Alexandria, VA 22313 Tel. (703)684-5500, Fax (703)684-5538

Media Contact, Community Relations & Devel., Lt. Colonel Tom Jones, Tel. (703)684-5521, Fax (703)684-5538

Officers

Natl. Commander, Commissioner John A. Busby

Natl. Chief Sec., Col. Tom Lewis

Natl. Community Relations, Dir., Lt. Colonel Tom Jones

TERRITORIAL ORGANIZATIONS

Central Territory, 10 W. Algonquin Rd., Des Plaines, IL 60016 Tel. (847)294-2000, Fax (847)294-2299; Territorial Commander, Commissioner Lawrence Moretz

Eastern Territory, 440 W. Nyack Rd., P.O. Box C-635, West Nyack, NY 10994 Tel. (914)620-7200, Fax (914)620-7766; Territorial Commander, Commissioner Joe Noland

Southern Territory, 1424 Northeast Expressway, Atlanta, GA 30329 Tel. (404)728-1300, Fax (404)728-1331; Territorial Commander, Commissioner Raymond A. Cooper

Western Territory, 180 E. Ocean Blvd., Long Beach, CA Tel. (562)436-7000, Fax (562)491-8792; Territorial Commander, Commissioner David Edwards

Periodicals

The War Cry

The Schwenkfelder Church

The Schwenkfelders are the spiritual descendants of the Silesian nobleman Caspar Schwenkfeld von Ossig (1489-1561), a scholar, reformer, preacher, and prolific writer who endeavored to aid in the cause of the Protestant Reformation. A contemporary of Martin Luther, John Calvin, Ulrich Zwingli and Phillip Melanchthon, Schwenkfeld sought no following, formulated no creed and did not attempt to organize a church based on his beliefs. He labored for liberty of religious belief, for a fellowship of all believers and for one united Christian church.

He and his cobelievers supported a movement known as the Reformation by the Middle Way. Persecuted by state churches, ultimately 180 Schwenkfelders exiled from Silesia emigrated to Pennsylvania. They landed at Philadelphia Sept. 22, 1734. In 1782, the Society of Schwenkfelders, the forerunner of the present Schwenkfelder Church, was formed. The church was incorporated in 1909.

The General Conference of the Schwenkfelder Church is a voluntary association for the Schwenkfelder Churches at Palm, Worcester, Lansdale, Norristown and Philadelphia, Pennsylvania.

They practice adult baptism and dedication of children, and observe the Lord's Supper regularly with open Communion. In theology, they are Christo-centric; in polity, congregational; in missions, world-minded; in ecclesiastical organization, ecumenical.

The ministry is recruited from graduates of colleges, universities, and accredited theological seminaries. The churches take leadership in ecumenical concerns through ministerial associations, community service and action groups, councils of Christian education and other agencies.

Headquarters

105 Seminary St., Pennsburg, PA 18073 Tel. (215)679-3103

Media Contact, Dennis Moyer

Officers

Mod., John Graham, Collegeville, PA 19426

Sec., Frances Witte, Central Schwenkfelder Church, Worcester, PA 19490

Treas., Syl Rittenhouse, 1614 Kriebel Rd., Lansdale, PA 19446

Periodicals

The Schwenkfeldian

Separate Baptists in Christ

The Separate Baptists in Christ are a group of Baptists found in Indiana, Ohio, Kentucky, Tennessee, Virginia, West Virginia, Florida, and North Carolina dating back to an association formed in 1758 in North Carolina and Virginia.

Today this group consists of approximately 100 churches. They believe in the infallibility of the Bible, the divine ordinances of the Lord's

Supper, feetwashing, baptism, and that those who endureth to the end shall be saved.

The Separate Baptists are Arminian in doctrine, rejecting both the doctrines of predestination and eternal security of the believer.

At the 1991 General Association, an additional article of doctrine was adopted. "We believe that at Christ's return in the clouds of heaven all Christians will meet the Lord in the air, and time shall be no more," thus leaving no time for a literal one thousand year reign. Seven associations comprise the General Association of Separate Baptists.

Headquarters

Media Contact, Clk., Greg Erdman, 10102 N. Hickory Ln., Columbus, IN 47203 812-526-2540

Email: mail@separatebaptist.org

Website: www.separatebaptist.org

Officers

Mod., Rev. Jim Goff, 1020 Gagel Ave., Louisville, KY 40216

Asst. Mod., Rev. Jimmy Polston, 785 Kitchen Rd., Mooresville, IN 46158 Tel. (317)831-6745

Clk., Greg Erdman, 10102 N. Hickory Ln., Columbus, IN 47203 Tel. (812)526-2540

Asst. Clk., Rev. Mattew Cowan, 174 Oak Hill School Rd., Lot 30, Smiths Grove, KY 42171 Tel. (270)678-5599

Serbian Orthodox Church in the U.S.A. and Canada*

The Serbian Orthodox Church is an organic part of the Eastern Orthodox Church. As a local church it received its autocephaly from Constantinople in 1219 A.D.

In 1921, a Serbian Orthodox Diocese in the United States of America and Canada was organized. In 1963, it was reorganized into three dioceses, and in 1983 a fourth diocese was created for the Canadian part of the church. The Serbian Orthodox Church in the USA and Canada received its administrative autonomy in 1928. However, it remains canonically an integral part of the Serbian Orthodox Patriarchate with its see in Belgrade. The Serbian Orthodox Church is in absolute doctrinal unity with all other local Orthodox Churches.

Headquarters

St. Sava Monastery, P.O. Box 519, Libertyville, IL 60048 Tel. (847)367-0698

Email: oea@oea.serbian-church.net

Website: oea.serbian-church.net/

BISHOPS

Metropolitan of Midwestern America, Most Rev. Metropolitan Christopher

Bishop of Canada, Georgije, 5A Stockbridge Ave., Toronto, ON M8Z 4M6 Tel. (416)231-4009

Bishop of Eastern America, Rt. Rev. Bishop Mitrophan, P.O. Box 368, Sewickley, PA 15143 Tel. (412)741-5686

Diocese of Western America, Bishop Jovan, 2541 Crestline Terr., Alhambra, CA 91803 Tel. (818)264-6825

OTHER ORGANIZATIONS

Brotherhood of Serbian Orth. Clergy in U.S.A. & Canada, Pres., V. Rev. Nedeljko Lunich, Joliet, IL, Merrilville, IN

Federation of Circles of Serbian Sisters

Serbian Singing Federation

Periodicals

The Path of Orthodoxy

Seventh-day Adventist Church

The Seventh-day Adventist Church grew out of a worldwide religious revival in the mid-nineteenth century. People of many religious persuasions believed Bible prophecies indicated that the second coming or advent of Christ was imminent.

When Christ did not come in the 1840s, a group of these disappointed Adventists in the United States continued their Bible studies and concluded they had misinterpreted prophetic events and that the second coming of Christ was still in the future. This same group of Adventists later accepted the teaching of the seventh-day Sabbath and became known as Seventh-day Adventists. The denomination organized formally in 1863.

The church was largely confined to North America until 1874, when its first missionary was sent to Europe. Today, over 48,900 congregations meet in 204 countries. Membership exceeds 11 million and increases between five and six percent each year.

In addition to a mission program, the church has the largest worldwide Protestant parochial school system with approximately 6,064 schools with more than 1,065,000 students on elementary through college and university levels.

The Adventist Development and Relief Agency (ADRA) helps victims of war and natural disasters, and many local congregations have community service facilities to help those in need close to home.

The church also has a worldwide publishing ministry with 56 printing facilities producing magazines and other publications in over 300 languages and dialects. In the United States and Canada, the church sponsors a variety of radio and television programs, including Christian Lifestyle Magazine, It Is Written, Breath of Life, Ayer, Hoy, y Mañana, Voice of Prophecy, and La Voz de la Esperanza.

The North American Division of Seventh-day Adventist includes 58 Conferences which are grouped together into 9 organized Union Conferences. The various Conferences work under the general direction of these Union Conferences.

Headquarters

12501 Old Columbia Pike, Silver Spring, MD 20904-6600 Tel. (301)680-6000

Media Contact, Dir., Archives & Statistics, Bert Haloviak

WORLD-WIDE OFFICERS

Pres., Jan Paulsen
Sec., Matthew A. Bediako
Treas., Robert L. Rawson

WORLD-WIDE DEPARTMENTS

Adventist Chaplaincy Ministries, Dir., Richard O. Stenbakken
Children's Ministries, Dir., Virginia L. Smith
Education, Dir., Humberto M. Rasi
Communication, Dir., Rajmund Dabrowski
Family Ministries, Dir., Ronald M. Flowers
Health Ministries, Dir., Allan R. Handysides
Ministerial Assoc., Dir., James A. Cress
Public Affairs & Religious Liberty, Dir., John Graz
Publishing, Dir., Jose Luis Campos
Sabbath School & Personal Ministries, James W. Zackrison
Stewardship, Dir., Benjamin C. Maxson
Trust Services, Jeffrey K. Wilson
Women's Ministries, Ardis D. Stenbakken
Youth, Baraka G. Muganda

NORTH AMERICAN OFFICERS

Pres., Don C. Schneider
Vice-Pres., Debra Brill; Clarence E. Hodges; James W. Gilley; Don Hevener; Alvin M. Kibble; Manuel Vasquez
Sec., Harold W. Baptiste
Assoc. Sec., Rosa T. Banks
Treas., Juan R. Prestol
Assoc. Treas., Marshall Chase; Del L. Johnson; Kenneth W. Osborn

NORTH AMERICAN ORGANIZATIONS

Atlantic Union Conf., P.O. Box 1189, South Lancaster, MA 01561-1189; Pres., Benjamin D. Schoun
Canada, Seventh-day Adventist Church in Canada (see Ch. 4)
Columbia Union Conf., 5427 Twin Knolls Rd., Columbia, MD 21045; Pres., Harold L. Lee
Lake Union Conf., P.O. Box C, Berrien Springs, MI 49103; Pres., Gordon L. Retzer
Mid-America Union Conf., P.O. Box 6128, Lincoln, NE 68506; Pres., Charles Sandefur
North Pacific Union Conf., Pres., Jere D. Patzer, P.O. Box 16677, Portland, OR 97216;
Pacific Union Conf., P.O. Box 5005, Westlake Village, CA 91359; Pres., Thomas J. Mostert, Jr
Southern Union Conf., P.O. Box 849, Decatur, GA 30031; Pres., Malcolm D. Gordon
Southwestern Union Conf., P.O. Box 4000, Burleson, TX 76097; Pres., Max A. Trevino

Periodicals

ADRA Works; Advent View; The Adventist Chaplain; Adventist Review; ASI Magazine; ASI Update; Audit Trails; AWR Transmissions; AWR Current; AWRecorder; AWResource; Children's Friend; Christian Record; Client Connection; College and University Dialogue; Collegiate Quarterly; Cornerstone Youth Resource Magazine; Cornerstone Connections; Elder's Digest; Encounter; For God and Country; Geoscience Reports; Guide; Insight; It is Written Channels; The Journal of Adventist Education; Kid's Ministry Ideas; Liberty; Lifeglow; Listen; Literature Evangelist; Message; Ministry; Mission—children, youth, adult; Origins; Our Little Friend; Primary Treasure; Publishing Mirror; Sabbath School Teaching Aids; Sabbath School Program Helps; Sabbath School Leadership; Shabbat Shalom; Shepherdess International Journal; Signs of the Times; The Student; Telenotes; Vibrant Life; Voice of Prophecy News; The Window; Winner; Women of Spirit; Young and Alive; Youth Ministry ACCENT

Seventh Day Baptist General Conference, USA and Canada

Seventh Day Baptists emerged during the English Reformation, organizing their first churches in the mid-1600s. The first Seventh Day Baptists of record in America were Stephen and Ann Mumford, who emigrated from England in 1664. Beginning in 1665 several members of the First Baptist Church at Newport, R.I. began observing the seventh day Sabbath, or Saturday. In 1671, five members, together with the Mumfords, formed the first Seventh Day Baptist Church in America at Newport.

Beginning about 1700, other Seventh Day Baptist churches were established in New Jersey and Pennsylvania. From these three centers, the denomination grew and expanded westward. They founded the Seventh Day Baptist General Conference in 1802.

The organization of the denomination reflects an interest in home and foreign missions, publications and education. Women have been encouraged to participate. From the earliest years religious freedom has been championed for all and the separation of church and state, advocated.

Seventh Day Baptists are members of the Baptist World Alliance and Baptist Joint Committee. The Seventh Day Baptist World Federation has 17 member conferences on six continents.

Headquarters

Seventh Day Baptist Center, 3120 Kennedy Rd., P.O. Box 1678, Janesville, WI 53547-1678 Tel. (608)752-5055, Fax (608)752-7711
Media Contact, Ex. Sec., Calvin Babcock
Email: sdbgen@inwave.com
Website: www.seventhdaybaptist.org

OTHER ORGANIZATIONS

Seventh Day Baptist Missionary Society, Exec. Dir., Kirk Looper, 119 Main St., Westerly, RI 02891
Seventh Day Bapt. Bd. of Christian Ed., Exec. Dir., Dr. Ernest K. Bee, Jr., Box 115, Alfred Station, NY 14803

Women's Soc. of the Gen. Conference, Pres., Mrs. Ruth Probasco, 858 Barrett Run Rd., Bridgeton, NJ 08302

American Sabbath Tract & Comm. Council, Dir. of Communications, Rev. Kevin J. Butler, 3120 Kennedy Rd., P.O. Box 1678, Janesville, WI 53547

Seventh Day Baptist Historical Society, Historian, Don A. Sanford, 3120 Kennedy Rd., P.O. Box 1678, Janesville, WI 53547

Seventh Day Baptist Center on Ministry, Dir. of Pastoral Services, Rev. Rodney Henry, 3120 Kennedy Rd., P.O. Box 1678, Janesville, WI 53547

Periodicals

Sabbath Recorder

Southern Baptist Convention

The Southern Baptist Convention was organized on May 10, 1845, in Augusta, Georgia. Cooperating Baptist churches are located in all 50 states, the District of Columbia, Puerto Rico, American Samoa, and the Virgin Islands. The members of the churches work together through 1,219 district associations and 41 state conventions or fellowships. The Southern Baptist Convention has an Executive Committee and 12 national agencies - four boards, six seminaries, one commission, and one auxiliary organization.

The purpose of the Southern Baptist Convention is "to provide a general organization for Baptists in the United States and its territories for the promotion of Christian missions at home and abroad and any other objects such as Christian education, benevolent enterprises, and social services which it may deem proper and advisable for the furtherance of the Kingdom of God". (Constitution, Article II)

The Convention exists in order to help the churches lead people to God through Jesus Christ.

From the beginning, there has been a mission desire to share the Gospel with the peoples of the world. The Cooperative Program is the basic channel of mission support. In addition, the Lottie Moon Christmas Offering for Foreign Missions and the Annie Armstrong Easter Offering for Home Missions support Southern Baptists' world mission programs.

In 2000, there were more than 4,900 foreign missionaries serving in 153 foreign countries and more than 5,000 home missionaries serving in North America.

Headquarters

901 Commerce St., Nashville, TN 37203 Tel. (615)244-2355

Media Contact, Vice-Pres. for Convention Relations, A. William Merrell, Tel. (615)244-2355, Fax (615)782-8684

Email: bmerrell@sbc.net

Website: www.sbc.net

Officers

Recording Sec., John Yeats, P.O. Box 12130, Oklahoma City, OK 73112

Executive Committee, Pres., Morris H. Chapman; Vice-Pres., Business & Finance, Jack Wilkerson; Vice-Pres., Convention News, Will Hall; Vice-Pres., Convention Relations, A. William Merrell; Vice-Pres., Convention Policy, Augie Boto; Vice-Pres., Cooperative Program, David E. Hankins

GENERAL BOARDS AND COMMISSION

International Mission Board, Pres., Jerry A. Rankin, 3806 Monument Ave, Richmond, VA 23230 Tel. (804)353-6655

North American Mission Board, Pres., Robert E. Reccord, 4200 No. Point Pkwy., Alpharetta, GA 30002 Tel. (770) 410-6519

Annuity Board, Pres., O. S. Hawkins, 2401 Cedar Springs Rd, Dallas, TX 75201 Tel. (214)720-4700

LifeWay Christian Resources, Pres., James T. Draper, Jr. 127 Ninth Ave. N., Nashville, TN 37234 Tel. (615)251-2605

Ethics and Religious Liberty Commission, Pres., Richard D. Land, 901 Commerce St., Suite 550, Nashville, TN 37202 Tel. (615)782-8404

STATE CONVENTIONS

Alabama, Rick Lance, 2001 E. South Blvd., Montgomery, AL 36116 Tel. (334)288-2460

Alaska, David N. Baldwin, 1750 O'Malley Rd., Anchorage, AK 99516 Tel. (907)344-9627

Arizona, Steve Bass, 3031 W. Northern Ave., Ste. 131, Phoenix, AZ 85052 Tel. (602)864-0337

Arkansas, Emil Turner, 525 West Capitol, Little Rock, AR 72201 Tel. (501)376-4791

California, Fermin A. Whittaker, 678 E. Shaw Ave., Fresno, CA 93710 Tel. (529)229-9533

Colorado, Mark Edlund, 7393 So. Alton Way, Englewood, CO 80112 Tel. (303)771-2480

District of Columbia, Rev. Jeffrey Haggray, 1628 16th St. NW, Washington, DC 20009 Tel. (202)265-1526

Florida, John Sullivan, 1230 Hendricks Ave., Jacksonville, FL 32207 Tel. (904)396-2351

Georgia, Dr. J. Robert White, 2930 Flowers Rd., S, Atlanta, GA 30341 Tel. (770)936-5200

Hawaii, O. W. Efurd, 2042 Vancouver Dr., Honolulu, HI 96822 Tel. (808)946-9581

Illinois, Bob Wiley, 3085 Stevenson Dr, Springfield, IL 62794 Tel. (217)786-2600

Indiana, Charles W. Sullivan, 900 N. High School Rd., Indianapolis, IN 46224 Tel. (317)241-9317

Baptist Convention of Iowa, Jimmy Barrentine, Suite #27, 2400 86th St., Des Moines, IA 50322 Tel. (515)278-4369

Kansas-Nebraska, R. Rex Lindsay, 5410 W. Seventh St., Topeka, KS 66606 Tel. (785)273-4880

Kentucky, Bill Mackey, 10701 Shelbyville Rd., Middletown, KY 40243 Tel. (502)245-4101

Louisiana, Dean Doster, 1250 Macarthur Dr., Alexandria, LA 71303 Tel. (318)448-3402

Maryland-Delaware, David Lee, 10255 Old Columbia Rd., Columbia, MD 21046 Tel. (410)290-5290

Michigan, Michael Collins, 15635 W. 12 Mile Rd., Southfield, MI 48076 Tel. (248)557-4200

Minnesota-Wisconsin, William C. Tinsley, 519 16th St. SE, Rochester, MN 55904 Tel. (507)282-3636

Mississippi, James R. Futral, 515 Mississippi St., Jackson, MS 39201 Tel. (601)968-3800

Missouri, James L. Hill, 400 E. High Street, Jefferson City, MO 65101 Tel. (573)635-7931

Nevada, David F. Meacham, 406 California Ave., Reno, NV 89509 Tel. (775)786-0406

New England, James Wideman, 87 Lincoln St., Northborough, MA 01532 Tel. (508)393-6013

New Mexico, Claude W. Cone, 616 Central SE, Albuquerque, NM 87102 Tel. (505)924-2300

New York, J. B. Graham, 6538 Collamer Rd., East Syracuse, NY 13057 Tel. (315)433-1001

North Carolina, James H. Royston, 205 Convention Dr., Cary, NC 27511 Tel. (919)467-5100

Northwest, Jeff Iorg, 3200 NE 109th Ave., Vancouver, WA 98682 Tel. (360)882-2100 x. 121

Ohio, Exec. Dir., Jack P. Kwok, 1680 E. Broad St., Columbus, OH 43203 Tel. (614)258-8491

Oklahoma, Anthony L. Jordan, 3800 N. May Ave., Oklahoma City, OK 73112 Tel. (405)942-3800

Pennsylvania-South Jersey, David C. Waltz, 4620 Fritchey St., Harrisburg, PA 17109 Tel. (717)652-5856

South Carolina, B. Carlisle Driggers, 190 Stoneridge Dr., Columbia, SC 29210 Tel. (803)765-0030

Tennessee, James M. Porch, 5001 Maryland Way, Brentwood, TN 37027 Tel. (615)371-2090

Texas, Charles Wade, 333 N. Washington, Dallas, TX 75246 Tel. (214)828-5300

Southern Baptists of Texas, James W. Richards, 1304 W. Walnut Hill Ln., Suite 220, Irving, TX 75038 Tel. (972)953-0878

Utah-Idaho, Tim Clark, 12401 S. 450 East, #G-1, Draper, UT 84020 Tel. (801)572-5350

Baptist General Association of Virginia, Reginald M. McDonough, 2828 Emerywood Pkwy, Richmond, VA 23226 Tel. (804)915-2430

Southern Baptist Conservatives of Virginia, H. Doyle Chauncey, 4101 Cox Rd., Suite 100, Glen Allen, VA 23060 Tel. (804)270-1848

West Virginia, David Jicka, Number One Missions Way, Scott Depot, WV 25560 Tel. (304)757-0944

Wyoming, John W. Thomason, 3925 Casper Mountain Rd., Casper, WY 82601 Tel. (307)472-4087

FELLOWSHIPS

Dakota Southern Baptist Fellowship, W.D. "Doc" Lindsey, Interim,, 2020 Lovett Ave., Bismarck, ND 58506 Tel. (701)255-3765

Montana Southern Baptist Fellowship, 1130 Cerise Rd., Billings, MT 59103 Tel. (406)252-7537

Canadian Convention of Southern Baptists, Gerry Taillon, Postal Bag 300, Cochrane, Alberta T0L 0W0 Tel. (403)932-5688

Periodicals

The Commission; SBC Life; On Mission

Southern Methodist Church

Organized in 1939, this body is composed of congregations desirous of continuing in true Biblical Methodism and preserving the fundamental doctrines and beliefs of the Methodist Episcopal Church, South. These congregations declined to be a party to the merger of the Methodist Episcopal Church, The Methodist Episcopal Church, South and the Methodist Protestant Church into The Methodist Church.

Headquarters

P.O. Box 39, Orangeburg, SC 29116-0039 Tel. (803)536-1378, Fax (803)535-3881

Media Contact, Pres., Rev. Bedford F. Landers

Email: smchq@juno.com

Officers

Pres., Rev. Bedford F. Landers

Admn. Asst. to Pres., Philip A. Rorabaugh

Director of Foreign Missions, Rev. Franklin D. McLellan, P.O. Box 39, Orangeburg, SC 29116-0039

Southern Methodist College Pres., Rev. Daniel H. Shapley, P.O. Box 1027, Orangeburg, SC 29116-1027

The Eastern Conf., Vice-Pres., Rev. John T. Hucks, Jr., 221 Pinewood Dr., Rowesville, SC 29133

Alabama-Florida-Georgia Conf., Vice-Pres., Rev. Glenn A Blank, 2275 Scenic Highway, Apt. 109, Pensacola, FL 32502

Mid-South Conf., Vice-Pres., Rev. Dr. Ronald R. Carrier, 5030 Hillsboro Rd., Nashville, TN 37215

South-Western Conf., Vice-Pres., Rev. Ira Schilling, 106 Albert Dr., Haughton, LA 71037

Gen. Conf., Treas., Rev. Philip A. Rorabaugh, P.O. Drawer A, Orangeburg, SC 29116-0039

Periodicals

The Southern Methodist

Sovereign Grace Believers

The Sovereign Grace Believers are a contemporary movement which began its stirrings in the mid-1950s when some pastors in traditional Baptist churches returned to a Calvinist-theological perspective.

The first "Sovereign Grace" conference was

held in Ashland, Kentucky, in 1954 and since then, conferences of this sort have been sponsored by various local churches on the West Coast, Southern and Northern states and Canada. This movement is a spontaneous phenomenon concerning reformation at the local church level. Consequently, there is no interest in establishing a Sovereign Grace Baptist "Convention" or "Denomination." Each local church is to administer the keys to the kingdom.

Most Sovereign Grace Believers formally or informally relate to the "First London" (1646), "Second London" (1689) or "Philadelphia" (1742) Confessions.

There is a wide variety of local church government in this movement. Many Calvinist Baptists have a plurality of elders in each assembly. Other Sovereign Grace Believers, however, prefer to function with one pastor and several deacons.

Membership procedures vary from church to church but all require a credible profession of faith in Christ, and proper baptism as a basis for membership.

Calvinistic Baptists financially support gospel efforts (missionaries, pastors of small churches at home and abroad, literature publication and distribution, radio programs, etc.) in various parts of the world.

Headquarters

Media Contact, Corres., Jon Zens, P.O. Box 548, St. Croix Falls, WI 54024 Tel. (651)465-6516, Fax (651)465-5101
Email: jon@searchingtogether.org
Website: www.searchingtogether.org

Periodicals

Searching Together, Sound of Grace

The Swedenborgian Church*

Founded in North America in 1792 as the Church of the New Jerusalem, the Swedenborgian Church was organized as a national body in 1817 and incorporated in Illinois in 1861. Its biblically-based theology is derived from the spiritual, or mystical, experiences and exhaustive biblical studies of the Swedish scientist and philosopher Emanuel Swedenborg (1688-1772).

The church centers its worship and teachings on the historical life and the risen and glorified present reality of the Lord Jesus Christ. It looks with an ecumenical vision toward the establishment of the kingdom of God in the form of a universal Church, active in the lives of all people of good will who desire and strive for freedom, peace and justice for all. It is a member of the NCCC and active in many local councils of churches.

With churches and groups throughout the United States and Canada, the denomination's central administrative offices and its seminary—Swedenborg House of Studies— are located in Newton, Massachusetts and Berkeley, California. Affiliated churches are found in Africa, Asia, Australia, Canada, Europe, the United Kingdom, Japan, South Korea, and South America. Many philosophers and writers have acknowledged their appreciation of Swedenborg's teachings.

Headquarters

11 Highland Ave., Newtonville, MA 02460 Tel. (617)969-4240, Fax (617)964-3258
Media Contact, Central Ofc. Mgr., Martha Bauer
Email: manager@swedenborg.org
Website: www.swedenborg.org

Officers

Pres., Rev. Ronald P. Brugler, 489 Franklin St., N., Kitchener, ON, Canada N2A 1Z2
Vice-Pres., Christine Laitner, 10 Hannah Court, Midland, MI 48642
Rec. Sec., Gloria Toot, 10280 Gentlewind Dr., Montgomery, OH 45242
Treas., Lawrence Conant, 52 Wales St., Apt. 2R, Taunton, MA 02780
Ofc. Mgr., Martha Bauer

Periodicals

The Messenger; Our Daily Bread

Syrian (Syriac) Orthodox Church of Antioch*

The Syrian Orthodox Church of Antioch traces its origin to the Patriarchate established in Antioch by St. Peter the Apostle. It is under the supreme ecclesiastical jurisdiction of His Holiness the Syrian Orthodox Patriarch of Antioch and All the East, now residing in Damascus, Syria. The Syrian Orthodox Church—composed of several archdioceses, numerous parishes, schools and seminaries—professes the faith of the first three Ecumenical Councils of Nicaea, Constantinople and Ephesus, and numbers faithful in the Middle East, India, the Americas, Europe and Australia.

The first Syrian Orthodox faithful came to North America during the late 1800s, and by 1907 the first Syrian Orthodox priest was ordained to tend to the community's spiritual needs. In 1949, His Eminence Archbishop Mor Athanasius Y. Samuel came to America and was soon appointed Patriarchal Vicar. The Archdiocese was officially established in 1957. In 1995, the Archdiocese of North America was divided into three separate Patriarchal Vicariates (Eastern United States, Western United States and Canada), each under a hierarch of the Church.

There are 19 official archdiocesan parishes and three mission congregations in the United States, located in California, District of Columbia, Florida, Illinois, Massachusetts, Michigan, New Jersey, New York, Oregon, Rhode Island and Texas. In Canada, there are five official parishes: three in the Province of

Ontario and two in the Province of Quebec and a mission congregation in the Province of Alberta.

Headquarters

Archdiocese for the Eastern U.S., 260 Elm Avenue, Teaneck, NJ 07666 Tel. (201)801-0660, Fax (201)801-0603

Archdiocese of Los Angeles and Environs, 417 E. Fairmont Rd., Burbank, CA 91501 Tel. (818)845-5089, Fax (818)845-5436

Media Contact, Archdiocesan Gen. Sec., V. Rev. Chorepiscopus John Meno, 260 Elm Ave., Teaneck, NJ 07666 Tel. (201)907-0122, Fax (201)907-0551

Email: syrianoc@syrianorthodoxchurch.org

Website: www.syrianorthodoxchurch.org

Officers

Archdiocese for Eastern U.S., Archbishop, Mor Cyril Aphrem Karim

Archdiocese of Los Angeles and Environs, Archbishop, Mor Clemis Eugene Kaplan

The Syro-Russian Orthodox Catholic Church, Romano Byzantine Synod

The Syro-Russion Orthodox Catholic Church was originally established in May of 1892 as the American Orthodox Catholic Archdiocese of America, and this was canonized by His Holiness Ignatius Peter III, Patriarch of Antioch. It was this same Patriarch that issued the Bull for the consecration of its first Archbishop Metropolitan, Timotheos Vilathi, as named by Patriarch Ignatius. Because the jurisdiction also has some Western Rite parishes, the Synod has been named "Romano Byzantine Synod of Bishops." First parishes of this jurisdiction were established in Wisconsin among Belgians, Italians, Slavs, and other ethnic groups. After Archbishop Timotheos' consecration, parishes were later formed in Ohio, Illinois, and New York, and some missionary work begun in Canada.

After much disagreement with the Patriarchate concerning administration and the Council of Chalcedon, which the Patriarchate did not accept concerning the two natures of Christ, on January 1, 1910 a Consistory was held concerning the future of the Archdiocese of America. The Bishops agreed upon and decided that, "Our reality as a branch, a part of the true Catholic and Orthodox Church of God, is not dependent upon the recognition of any ecclesiastical authority outside the Councils of our own American Ecclesiastical Consistory and National Synod of Bishops and Clergy." Archbishop Timotheos believed strongly in the truths of the Council of Chalcedon, and the rights of the American Church to name its own bishops, and from here the Church was known as Autocephalous and severed from the Patriarchate of Antioch. However, after this time several schisms occurred that gave way to some heretical newly established "churches" that caused the Church to eventually be renamed "Syro-Russian Orthodox Catholic." In the 1970's, after the retirement for health reasons of Archbishop John, Archbishop Joseph of Blessed Memory became the newly enthroned Metropolitan Hierarch of the Church. He possessed Apostolic Succession from both the Syrian and Russian Orthodox Churches later giving the Synod the name of Syro-Russian Orthodox Catholic Church. In 1987, before his death, a meeting was held at St. Paul's Monastery in LaPorte, Indiana and Very Right Reverend Archimandrite Stephen (Thomas) was duly elected metropolitan Hierarch. He was consecrated Bishop on October 18th, 1987, by Archbishop Joseph assisted by Archbishop George and Bishop Norman at St. Mary's Chapel, LaPorte, Indiana, and the following year enthroned as metropolitan Archbishop Hierarch. Archbishop Stephen has caused the Church to grow throughout the world. In 1994-96, he endured many sufferings as the result of some clergy who went astray and since deposed of their faculties and offices. Since that time, the Church has experienced peace, growth, and new viability. The official liturgy of the Church is the Divine Liturgy of Saint James, the oldest liturgy of the Christian Church authored by St. James the Brother of our Lord. In addition, as with all other Orthodox Churches, the Liturgy of Saint Basil is used ten times a year, and the Presanctified Liturgy as prescribed. The Traditions of Holy Orthodoxy are observed in the administration of the Holy Mysteries (Sacraments) and, as is practice in the Russian Orthodox Church, Holy Myron (Chrism) is consecrated by the Metropolitan Hierarch on Holy Thursday and distributed to the clergy of the Church.

Some western customs exist within the Church. Hyperveneration is given to icons that memorialize the saints and events in the life of Jesus Christ and the Holy Theotokos Mary. It follows the Gregorian Calendar and the Orthodox date of Pascha (Easter). The Romano Byzantine Synod of Bishops, and the Syro-Russian Orthodox Catholic Church, strongly believes in the separation of Church and State, and in the administration of healing by licensed practitioners, and by the clergy in the Mystery of Holy Unction. The Synodal Metropolinate has received official recognition from the Hellenic (Greek) Orthodox Church of Athens, and has been involved in ecumenical dialogue with the Orthodox Patriarchate of Jerusalem, the Russian Orthodox Patriarchate, and more recently has opened dialogue with the Ukrainian Autocephalous Orthodox Church. There is one monastic order, The Monastic Community of Saint Basil, open to men and women that is headquartered in England. The canonical diocese of the Church, and their Bishops, are Archbishop

Stephen (United States), Bishop Andreas (Guatemala), Bishop Benjamin (Bangladesh), Bishop Cristobal (Spain), Bishop John (India), Bishop Joseph (Africa), Bishop Pedro (Cuba), and retired Chorbishop John (United States). The Diocese of Pakistan currently is served by a Vicar General as the result of an episcopal vacancy there. Vicars serve the mission territories of Belgium, Kenya, Tanzania, and soon a Bishop (George) will be consecrated for the United Kingdom. The Church of Bangladesh recently united with the Syro-Russian Orthodox Catholic Church, and the independent Diocese of Bogota is now in dialogue with Metropolitan Stephen concerning union. Clergy are trained for the Church through Holy Family Collegiate Seminary of Tacoma, Washington; St. Basil's Seminary of Havana, Cuba; or St. Efrem's Seminary of Cordoba, Spain. A distance education program for mature candidates is offered through Romano Byzantine College (Virginia). The national headquarters at this time is at St. Mary the Theotokos Pro-Cathedral in Duluth, Minnesota.

Headquarters

St. Mary the Theotokos Pro-Cathedral, 5907 Grand Ave, Duluth, MN 55087 Tel. 218-624-0202

Email: rbsocc@juno.com

Periodicals

Orthodox Christian Herald

Triumph the Church and Kingdom of God in Christ Inc. (International)

This church was given through the wisdom and knowledge of God to the Late Apostle Elias Dempsey Smith on Oct. 20, 1897, in Issaquena County, Mississippi, while he was pastor of a Methodist church.

The Triumph Church, as this body is more commonly known, was founded in 1902. Its doors opened in 1904 and it was confirmed in Birmingham, Alabama, with 225 members in 1915. It was incorporated in Washington, D.C. in 1918 and currently operates in 31 states and overseas. The General Church is divided into 13 districts, including the Africa District.

Triumphant doctrine and philosophy are based on the principles of life, truth and knowledge; the understanding that God is in man and expressed through man; the belief in manifested wisdom and the hope for constant new revelations. Its concepts and methods of teaching the second coming of Christ are based on these and all other attributes of goodness.

Triumphians emphasize that God is the God of the living, not the God of the dead.

Headquarters

213 Farrington Ave. S.E., Atlanta, GA 30315

Media Contact, Bishop C. W. Drummond, 7114 Idlewild, Pittsburg, PA 15208 Tel. (412)731-2286

Officers

Chief Bishop, Bishop C. W. Drummond, 7114 Idlewild, Pittsburgh, PA 15208 Tel. (412)731-2286

Gen. Bd of Trustees, Chmn., Bishop Leon Simon, 1028 59th St., Oakland, CA 94608 Tel. (415)652-9576

Gen. Treas., Bishop Hosea Lewis, 1713 Needlewood Ln., Orlando, FL 32818 Tel. (407)295-5488

Gen. Rec. Sec., Bishop Zephaniah Swindle, Box 1927, Shelbyville, TX 75973 Tel. (409)598-3082

True Orthodox Church of Greece (Synod of Metropolitan Cyprian), American Exarchate

The American Exarchate of the True (Old Calendar) Orthodox Church of Greece adheres to the tenets of the Eastern Orthodox Church, which considers itself the legitimate heir of the historical Apostolic Church.

When the Orthodox Church of Greece adopted the New, or Gregorian, Calendar in 1924, many felt that this breach with tradition compromised the Church's festal calendar, based on the Old, or Julian, Calendar, and its unity with world Orthodoxy. In 1935, three State Church Bishops returned to the Old Calendar and established a Synod in Resistance, the True Orthodox Church of Greece. When the last of these Bishops died, the Russian Orthodox Church Abroad consecrated a new Hierarchy for the Greek Old Calendarists and, in 1969, declared them a Sister Church.

In the face of persecution by the State Church, some Old Calendarists denied the validity of the Mother Church of Greece and formed two synods, now under the direction of Archbishop Chrysostomos of Athens and Archbishop Andreas of Athens. A moderate faction under Metropolitan Cyprian of Oropos and Fili does not maintain communion with the Mother Church of Greece, but recognizes its validity and seeks a restoration of unity by a return to the Julian Calendar and traditional ecclesiastical polity by the State Church. About 1.5 million Orthodox Greeks belong to the Old Calendar Church.

The first Old Calendarist communities in the United States were formed in the 1930s. The Exarchate under Metropolitan Cyprian was established in 1986. Placing emphasis on clergy education, youth programs, and recognition of the Old Calendarist minority in American Orthodoxy, the Exarchate has encouraged the establishment of monastic communities and missions. Cordial contacts with the New Calendarist and other Orthodox communities are encouraged. A center for theological training and

Patristic studies has been established at the Exarchate headquarters in Etna, California.

In July 1994, the True Orthodox Church of Greece (Synod of Metropolitan Cyprian), the True Orthodox Church of Romania, the True Orthodox Church of Bulgaria, and the Russian Orthodox Church Abroad entered into liturgical union, forming a coalition of traditionalist Orthodox bodies several million strong.

Headquarters

St. Gregory Palamas Monastery, P.O. Box 398, Etna, CA 96027-0398 Tel. (530)467-3228 Fax (530)467-5828

Media Contact, Exarch in America, His Eminence, Archbishop Chrysostomos

Officers

Acting Synodal Exarch in America, His Grace Bishop Auxentios

Chancellor of the Exarchate, The Very Rev. Raphael Abraham, 3635 Cottage Grove Ave. S.E., Cedar Rapids, IA 52403-1612

Periodicals

Orthodox Tradition (quarterly theological journal)

Ukrainian Orthodox Church of the U.S.A.*

The Ukrainian Orthodox Church of the USA has its origin in the ancient lands of Rus-Ukraine (present day Ukraine). It was to the inhabitants of these lands that the Apostle Andrew first preached the Gospel. Christianization began early in the history of Rus-Ukraine by missionaries from the Orthodox Christian See of Constantinople. In 988 AD, the Saintly Prince Volodymyr, crowned a process of Christian Evangelization begun in the 4th century, by personally accepting Orthodox Christianity and inspiring his subjects to do the same. The baptism of Volodymyr, his household and the inhabitants of Kyiv, altered the face of Kyivan Rus-Ukraine and Slavic history for all time. Kyiv became the spiritual heart of Orthodox Christians in Rus-Ukraine. It was from this See that missionaries were sent into every corner of St. Volodymyr's realm. Through their efforts the Gospel was preached and new communities were established. The Mother Church of Kyiv and its See of Saint Sophia, modeled after Constantinople's See of the same name, gave birth to many Orthodox Christian centers and communities in the west, east and north of the Dnipro river, among them the Orthodox Christian See of Moscow, Russia (Rosia).

The Ukrainian Orthodox Church of USA ministers to the needs of the faithful whose ancestral roots are in Ukraine. The Church found haven in America in the early 1920's. Its first bishop, Metropolitan Ioan (John) Teodorovych, arrived from Ukraine in 1924 and shepherded the Church as Metropolitan until his death in 1971. His successor, Archbishop Mstyslav, arrived in the USA in 1950, and shepherded the Church as Metropolitan from 1971 until his death in 1993. It was Metropolitan Mstyslav who, as a consequence of Ukraine's independence, was named Patriarch of Kyiv and All Ukraine, in 1990. Previous to 1996 there were two Ukrainian Orthodox jurisdictions in the USA. Formal unification of the Ukrainian Orthodox Church of the USA, shepherded by His Beatitude Metropolitan Constantine, and the Ukrainian Orthodox Church of America, shepherded by His Grace Bishop Vsevolod, was concluded in November 1996.

Headquarters

P.O. Box 495, South Bound Brook, NJ 08880 Tel. (732)356-0090, Fax (732)356-5556

Media Contact, His Eminence Antony, Archbishop of New York, Consistory President

Email: uocofusa@aol.com

Website: www.uocofusa.org

Officers

Metropolitan, His Beatitude Constantine, 1803 Sidney Street, Pittsburgh, PA 15203

CENTRAL EPARCHY:

Eparchial Bishop : Metropolitan Constantine

Eparchial Seat: St. Volodymyr Cathedral, Parma, Ohio. 5913 State Road, Parma, OH 44134 Tel. (216)885 1509 States embraced: Florida, Georgia, Ohio, Western Pennsylvania

EASTERN EPARCHY: Eparchial Bishop: Archbishop Antony.

Eparchial Seat: St. Volodymyr Cathedral, New York, NY. 160 West 82nd St. New York, NY 10024 Tel. (212)873 8550 States embraced: Connecticut, Deleware, Massachusetts, Maryland, New Jersey, New York, Pennsylvania and Rhode Island

WESTERN EPARCHY: Eparchial Bishop: Archbishop Vsevolod

Eparchial Seat: St. Volodymyr Cathedral, Chicago, Illinois. 2230-50 West Cortez St. Chicago, IL 60622 Tel. (312)278 2827 States embraced: Arizona, California, Colorado, Illinois, Indiana, Michigan, Minnesota, North Dakota, Nebraska, Oregon, Washington, Wisconsin, Ontario Province

COUNCIL OF THE METROPOLIA

Metropolitan Constantine - Chairman

Archbishop Antony

Archbishop Vsevolod

METROPOLITAN COUNCIL MEMBERS

Archimandrite Andrij - Vice-chairman

Protopresbyter William Diakiw

Protopresbyter Frank Estocin

Protopresbyter Nestor Kowal

Protopresbyter Taras Chubenko

Protopriest John Nakonachny

Rev. Fr. Michael Kochis

Eng. Emil Skocypec

Dr. Gayle Woloschak - Secretary

Dr. George Krywolap- Secretary

Dr. Anatole Lysyj

Ms. Olga Liskiwsky-Morgan
Dr. Paul Micevych
LTC (Ret.) Stephen Hallick-Holutiak
Ms. Helen Greenleaf - UOL President
Mrs. Nadia Mirchuk - United Sisterhood President
Eng. Michael Heretz - St. Andrew Society Pres.
CONSISTORY
Consistory President, His Eminence Antony, Archbishop of New York, P.O. Box 495, South Bound Brook, NJ 08880 Tel. (732)356-0090, Fax (732)356-5556, uocofusa@aol. com
Vice Pres., V. Rev. Willam Diakiw
Sec., V. Rev. Frank Estocin
Treas., Mr. Emil Skocypec
Member, V. Rev. John Nakonachny
Member, V. Rev. Myron Oryhon
Member, Dr. George Krywolap

Unitarian Universalist Association of Congregations

The Unitarian Universalist Association (UUA), created in 1961 through a consolidation of the Universalist Church of America with the American Unitarian Association, combines two liberal religious traditions. The religion traces its roots back to Europe where in 1569, the Transylvanian king, John Sigismund (1540-1571), issued an edict of religious freedom. The religious philosophy led to the organization of the Universalists in this country in 1793, and the Unitarians (organized here in 1825).

Founders of Universalism believed in universal salvation, while founders of Unitarianism believed in the unity of God (as opposed to the Trinity). Today, Unitarian Universalism is a liberal, creedless religion with Judeo-Christian roots. It draws also from Eastern, humanist, and other religious traditions, and encourages its members to seek religious truth out of their own reflection and experience. The denomination teaches tolerance and respect for other religious viewpoints, and affirms the worth and dignity of every person.

The Unitarian Universalist Association consists of over 1,055 congregations located principally in the United States and Canada, with over 220,000 members, and is served by more than 1,400 ministers. The Association is the fastest-growing liberal religion in North America, and this year completed its eighteenth consecutive year of growth. Each member congregation within the UUA is governed independently. The Association is made up of 22 Districts (served by a District Executive who is a member of the UUA staff) in North America, with each congregation having district affiliation. The Association is governed by an elected Board of Trustees, chaired by an elected Moderator. An elected President, three vice presidents, and directors of five departments form the Executive Staff which administers the daily activities of the Association.

The General Assembly, held each June in a different UUA District, serves as the Association's annual business meeting. The UUA includes Departments of Ministry; Religious Education; Congregational, District and Extension Services; Communications; Development; and Faith in Action. The "UU World", published bi-monthly, is the denominational journal. Beacon Press, an internationally honored publishing house, is wholly owned by the Unitarian Universalist Association.

Headquarters

25 Beacon Street, Boston, MA 02108, Tel. (617) 742-2100, Fax (617)367-323
Media Contact, John Hurley, Director of Information, Tel. (617)742-2100 x. 131
Email: jhurley@uua.org
Website: www.uua.org

Officers

President, The Rev. William Sinkford
Moderator, Diane Olson
Executive Vice President, Kathleen C. Montgomery

Periodicals

UU World; InterConnections

United Christian Church

The United Christian Church originated about 1864. There were some ministers and laymen in the United Brethren in Christ Church who disagreed with the position and practice of the church on infant baptism, voluntary bearing of arms and belonging to oath-bound secret combinations. This group developed into United Christian Church, organized at a conference held in Campbelltown, Pennsylvania, on May 9, 1877. The principal founders of the denomination were George Hoffman, John Stamn and Thomas Lesher. Before they were organized, they were called Hoffmanites.

The United Christian Church has district conferences, a yearly general conference, a general board of trustees, a mission board, a board of directors of the United Christian Church Home, a camp meeting board, a young peoples' board and local organized congregations.

It believes in the Holy Trinity and the inspired Holy Scriptures with the doctrines they teach. The church practices the ordinances of Baptism, Holy Communion and Foot Washing.

It welcomes all into its fold who are born again, believe in Jesus Christ as Savior and Lord and have received the Holy Spirit.

Headquarters

c/o John P. Ludwig, Jr., 523 W. Walnut St., Cleona, PA 17042 Tel. (717)273-9629
Media Contact, Presiding Elder, John P. Ludwig, Jr.

Officers

Presiding Elder, Elder John P. Ludwig, Jr.
Conf. Sec., Mr. Lee Wenger, 1625 Thompson Ave., Annville, PA 17003

Conf. Moderator, Elder Gerald Brinser, 2360 Horseshoe Pike, Annville, PA 17003

OTHER ORGANIZATIONS

Mission Board, Pres., Elder John P. Ludwig, Jr.; Sec., Elder David Heagy, 4129 Oak St., Lebanon, PA 17042; Treas., LeRoy Bomgardner, 1252 Royal Rd., Annville, PA 17003

United Church of Christ*

The United Church of Christ was constituted on June 25, 1957 by representatives of the Congregational Christian Churches and of the Evangelical and Reformed Church, in Cleveland, Ohio.

The Preamble to the Constitution states, "The United Church of Christ acknowledges as its sole head, Jesus Christ... It acknowledges as kindred in Christ all who share in this confession. It looks to the Word of God in the Scriptures, and to the presence and power of the Holy Spirit... It claims... the faith of the historic Church expressed in the ancient creeds and reclaimed in the basic insights of the Protestant Reformers. It affirms the responsibility of the Church in each generation to make this faith its own in... worship, in honesty of thought and expression, and in purity of heart before God.... it recognizes two sacraments, Baptism and the Lord's Supper." The creation of the United Church of Christ brought together four unique traditions:

(1) Groundwork for the Congregational Way was laid by Calvinist Puritans and Separatists during the late 16th-early 17th centuries, then achieved prominence among English Protestants during the civil war of the 1640s. Opposition to state control prompted followers to emigrate to the United States, where they helped colonize New England in the 17th century. Congregationalists have been self-consciously a denomination from the mid-19th century.

(2) The Christian Churches, an 18th-century American restorationist movement emphasized Christ as the only head of the church, the New Testament as their only rule of faith, and "Christian" as their sole name. This loosely organized denomination found in the Congregational Churches a like disposition. In 1931, the two bodies formally united as the Congregational Christian Churches.

(3) The German Reformed Church comprised an irenic aspect of the Protestant Reformation, as a second generation of Reformers drew on the insights of Zwingli, Luther and Calvin to formulate the Heidelberg Catechism of 1563. People of the German Reformed Church began immigrating to the New World early in the 18th century, the heaviest concentration in Pennsylvania. Formal organization of the American denomination was completed in 1793. The church spread across the country. In the Mercersburg Movement, a strong emphasis on evangelical catholicity and Christian unity was developed.

(4) In 19th-century Germany, Enlightenment criticism and Pietist inwardness decreased long-standing conflicts between religious groups. In Prussia, a royal proclamation merged Lutheran and Reformed people into one United Evangelical Church (1817). Members of this new church way migrated to America. The Evangelicals settled in large numbers in Missouri and Illinois, emphasizing pietistic devotion and unionism; in 1840 they formed the German Evangelical Church Society in the West. After union with other Evangelical church associations, in 1877 it took the name of the German Evangelical Synod of North America.

On June 25, 1934, this Synod and the Reformed Church in the U.S. (formerly the German Reformed Church) united to form the Evangelical and Reformed Church. They blended the Reformed tradition's passion for the unity of the church and the Evangelical tradition's commitment to the liberty of conscience inherent in the gospel.

Headquarters

700 Prospect Avenue, Cleveland, OH 44115 Tel. (216)736-2100, Fax (216)736-2103

Media Contact, Rev. Robert Chase, 700 Prospect Ave., Cleveland, OH 44115 Tel. (216)736-2173, Fax (216)736-2223

Email: langa @ucc.org

Website: www.ucc.org

Officers

Exec. Minister, Wider Church Ministries, Mr. Dale L. Bishop

Exec. Minister, Justice and Witness Ministries , Ms. Bernice Powell Jackson

Exec. Minister, Local Church Ministries , Rev. Jose A. Malayang

Chair, Executive Council, Ms. Olga Sandman

Vice Chair, Executive Council, Rev. Robert Lee

Mod., General Synod , Mr. Nate Lewis

Asst. Mod., General Synod, Rev. Christine Smith

Asst. Mod., General Synod, Ms. Carol Wassmuth

ORGANIZATIONS

Office of General Ministries, National Office, 700 Prospect Avenue, Cleveland, Ohio 44115. Tel. (216)736-2100, Fax (216)736-2103, Associate General Minister, Ms. Edith A. Guffey; General Minister and President, Rev. John H. Thomas; Executive Associate and Team Leader, Covenantal Relations Ministry, Rev. C. Nozomi Ikuta

Justice and Witness Ministries, National Offices (as above), Tel. (216)736-3700, Fax (216)736-3703, Franklinton Center at Bricks, PO Box 220, Whitakers, NC Tel. (252)437-1723, Fax (252)437-1278, Washington Office, 110 Maryland Avenue, NE, Washington, DC Tel. (202)543-1517, Fax (202)543-5994, Executive Minister, Ms. Bernice Powell Jackson; Executive Associate, Rev. F. Allison Phillips

Local Church Ministries, Tel. (216)736-3800, Fax (216)736-3803. Executive Minister, Rev. Jose A. Malayang

Wider Church Ministries, National Offices (as above), Tel. (216)736-3200, Fax (216)736-3203, 475 Riverside Drive, New York, NY 10115, Disciples of Christ Division of Overseas Ministries, PO Box 1986, Indianapolis, IN 46206 Tel. (317)635-3100, Fax (317)635-4323, Executive Minister, Mr. Dale L. Bishop; Executive Associate to the Executive Minister, Rev. Joan Ishibashi

Pension Boards, Main Office, 475 Riverside Drive, New York, NY 10115 Tel. (212)870-2777, Fax (212)870-2877; National Office, 700 Prospect Avenue, Cleveland, OH 44115 Tel. (216)736-2271, Fax (216)736-2274, Executive Vice President, Mrs. Joan F. Brannick

United Church Foundation, Inc., 475 Riverside Drive, New York, NY 10115 Tel. (212)870-2582, Fax (212)870-2366, Executive Vice President, Mr. Donald G. Hart

Council for American Indian Ministry, 471 3rd Street, Box 412, Excelsior, MN 55331 Tel. (612)474-3532, Executive Director, Rev. Armin L. Schmidt

Council for Health and Human Services Ministries, National Office (as above). Tel. (216)736-2250, Fax (216)736-2251, Executive Director, Rev. Bryan W. Sickbert

CONFERENCES

Western Region

California, Nevada, Northern, Rev. Mary Susan Gast, 9260 Alcosta Blvd.,#C18, San Ramon, CA 94583-4143

California, Southern, Rev. Daniel F. Romero, 2401 N. Lake Ave., Altadena, CA 91001

Hawaii, Rev. David P. Hansen, 15 Craigside Pl., Honolulu, HI 96817

Montana-Northern Wyoming, Rev. John M. Schaeffer, 2016 Alderson Ave., Billings, MT 59102

Central Pacific, Rev. Hector Lopez, 0245 SW Bancroft St., Ste. E, Portland, OR 97201

Rocky Mountain, Rev. Lynne E. Simxcox Fitch, 7000 Broadway, Ste. 420, ABS Bldg., Denver, CO 80221

Southwest, Rev. Ann C. Rogers-Witte, 4423 N. 24th St., Ste. 600, Phoenix, AZ 85016

Washington-North Idaho, 720 14th Ave. E., Seattle, WA 98102; Rev. Randall Hyvonen, S. 412 Bernard St., Spokane, WA 99204

West Central Region

Iowa, Rev. Susan J. Ingham, 600 42nd St., Des Moines, IA 50312

Kansas-Oklahoma, Rev. John H. Krueger, 1248 Fabrique, Wichita, KS 67218

Minnesota, Rev. William Kaseman, 122 W. Franklin Ave., Rm. 323, Minneapolis, MN 55404

Missouri, Rev. A. Gayle Engel, 461 E. Lockwood Ave., St. Louis, MO 63119

Nebraska, Rev. George S. Worcester, 825 M St., Lincoln, NE 68508

North Dakota, Rev. Jack J. Seville, Jr., 227 W. Broadway, Bismarck, ND 58501

South Dakota, Rev. Gene E. Miller, 3500 S. Phillips Ave., #121, Sioux Falls, SD 57105-6864

Great Lakes Region

Illinois, Rev. Charlene Burch, 1840 Westchester Blvd., Westchester, IL 60154

Illinois South, Rev. Ronald L. Eslinger, Box 325, 1312 Broadway, Highland, IL 62249

Indiana-Kentucky, Rev. Stephen C. Gray, 1100 W. 42nd St., Indianapolis, IN 46208

Michigan, Rev. Kent J. Ulery, P.O. Box 1006, East Lansing, MI 48826

Ohio, Rev. Ralph C. Quellhorst, 6161 Busch Blvd.,#95, Columbus, OH 43229

Wisconsin, Rev. Frederick R. Trost, 4459 Gray Rd., Box 495, De Forest, WI 53532-0495

Southern Region

Florida, Rev. M. Douglas Borko, 222 E. Welbourne Ave., Winter Park, FL 32789

South Central, Rev. Mark H. Miller, 6633 E. Hwy. 290, #200, Austin, TX 78723-1157

Southeast, Rev. Timothy C. Downs, 756 W. Peachtree St., NW, Atlanta, GA 30308

Southern, Rev. Herman Haller, 217 N. Main St., Box 658, Graham, NC 27253

Middle Atlantic Region

Central Atlantic, Rev. John R. Deckenback, 916 S. Rolling Rd., Baltimore, MD 21228

New York, Rev. C. Jack Richards, The Church Center, Rm. 202, 3049 E. Genesee St., Syracuse, NY 13224

Pennsylvania Central, Rev. Lyle J. Weible, The United Church Center, Rm. 126, 900 S. Arlington Ave., Harrisburg, PA 17109

Pennsylvania Northeast, Rev. Daniel A. Vander Ploeg, 431 Delaware Ave., P.O. Box 177, Palmerton, PA 18071

Pennsylvania Southeast, Rev. Franklin R. Mittman, Jr., 505 Second Ave., P.O. Box 400, Collegeville, PA 19426

Pennsylvania West, Rev. Kenneth G. Leishner, 320 South Maple Ave., Greensburg, PA 15601

Puerto Rico, Rev. Luis Rosario, Box 8609, Caguas, PR 00762

New England Region

Connecticut, Rev. Davida Foy Crabtree, 125 Sherman St., Hartford, CT 06105

Maine, Rev. Jean M. Alexander, Rev. David R. Gaewski, 68 Main St., P.O. Box 966, Yarmouth, ME 04096

Massachusetts, Rev. Erwin R. Bode, Jr., P.O. Box 2246, 1 Badger Rd., Framingham, MA 01701

New Hampshire, Rev. Carole C. Carlson; Rev. Benjamin C. L. Crosby; Rev. John W. Lynes, 314 S. Main, P.O. Box 465, Concord, NH 03302

Rhode Island, Rev. H. Dahler Hayes, 56 Walcott St., Pawtucket, RI 02860

Vermont, Rev. Arnold I. Thomas, 285 Maple St., Burlington, VT 05401

Nongeographic

Calvin Synod, Rev. Louis Medgyesi, 607 Plum St., Fairport Harbor, OH 44077

Periodicals

United Church News; Common Lot; Courage in the Struggle for Justice and Peace

United Holy Church of America, Inc.

The United Holy Church of America, Inc. is an outgrowth of the great revival that began with the outpouring of the Holy Ghost on the Day of Pentecost. The church is built upon the foundation of the Apostles and Prophets, Jesus Christ being the cornerstone.

During a revival of repentence, regeneration and holiness of heart and life that swept through the South and West, the United Holy Church was born. The founding fathers had no desire to establish a denomination but were pushed out of organized churches because of this experience of holiness and testimony of the Spirit-filled life. On the first Sunday in May 1886, in Method, North Carolina, what is today known as the United Holy Church of America, Inc. was born. The church was incorporated on Sept. 25, 1918.

Baptism by immersion, the Lord's Supper and feet washing are observed. The premillennial teaching of the Second Coming of Christ, Divine healing, justification by faith, sanctification as a second work of grace and Spirit baptism are accepted.

Headquarters

5104 Dunstan Rd., Greensboro, NC 27405 Tel. (336)621-0669

Media Contact, Gen. Statistician, Ms. Jacquelyn B. McCain, 1210 N. Euclid Ave., Apt. A, St. Louis, MO 63113-2012, Tel. (314)367-8351, Fax (314)367-1835

Email: books@mohistory.org

GENERAL ADMINISTRATION

Gen. Pres., The Rt. Rev. Odell McCollum, 707 Woodmark Run, Gahanna, OH 43230, Tel. (614)475-4713, Fax (614)475-4713

Gen. Vice Pres., Bishop Elijah Williams, 901 Briarwood St., Reidsville, NC 27320 Tel. (919)349-7275

Gen. 2nd Vice-Pres., The Rt. Rev. Kenneth O. Robinson, Sr., 33 Springbrook Road, Nanuet, NY 10954-4423, Tel. (914)425-8311, Fax (914)352-2686

Gen. Rec. Sec., Rev. Mrs. Elsie Harris, 2304 Eighth Street, Portsmouth, VA 23704, Tel. (757)399-0926

Asst. Rec. Sec., Mrs. Cassandra Jones, 3869 JoAnn Drive, Cleveland, OH 44122, Tel. (216)921-0097

Gen. Fin. Sec., Vera Perkins-Hughes, P.O. Box 6194, Cleveland, OH Tel. (216)851-7448

Asst. Fin. Sec., Bertha Williams, 4749 Shaw Dr., Wilmington, NC 28405 Tel. (919)395-4462

Gen. Corres. Sec., Ms. Gwendolyn Lane, 3069 Hudson Street, Columbus, OH 43219

Gen. Treas., Louis Bagley, 8779 Wales Dr., Cincinnati, OH 45249 Tel. (513)247-0588

GENERAL OFFICERS

Gen Pres. Missionary Dept., Rev. Ardelia M. Corbett, 519 Madera Dr., Youngstown, OH 44504 Tel. (216)744-3284

Gen. Evangelism & Extension Dept., Pres., Elder Clifford R. Pitts, 3563 North 14th St., Milwaukee, WI 53206, Tel. (414)244-1319

Gen. Bible Church School Dept., Superintendent, Robert L. Rollins, 1628 Avondale Ave., Toledo, OH 43607 Tel. (419)246-4046

Gen. Y.P.H.A., Pres., Elder James W. Brooks, Rt. 3 Box 105, Pittsboro, NC 27312 Tel. (919)542-5357

Gen. Ushers Department, Pres., Ms. Sherly M. Hughes, 1491 East 191st Street, #H-604, Euclid, OH 44117, Tel. (216)383-0038

Gen. Educ. Dept., Elder Roosevelt Alston, 168 Willow Creek Run, Henderson, NC 27636, Tel. (919)438-5854

Gen. Music Dept., Chair, Rosie Johnson, 2009 Forest Dale Dr., Silver Spring, MD 20932

Gen. Historian, Dr. Chester Gregory, Sr., 1302 Lincoln Woods Dr., Baltimore, MD 21228, Tel. (410)788-5144

Gen. Counsel, Mr. Joe L. Webster, Esquire, Attorney-At-Law, P.O. Box 2301, Chapel Hill, NC 27515-2301, Tel. (919)542-5150

UHCA Academy, Dir., Ms. Stephanie Davis, The United Holy Church of America, Inc., 5104 Dunstan Road, Greensboro, NC 27405, Tel. (336)621-0069

Gen. Statistician, Ms. Jacquelyn B. McCain, 1210 N. Euclid Ave., Apt. A, St. Louis, MO 63113-2012, Tel. (314)367-8351, Fax (314) 367-1835

PRESIDENTS OF CONVOCATIONAL DISTRICTS

Barbados District; The Rt. Rev. Jestina Gentles, 5 West Ridge St., Britton's Hill, St. Michael, BH2 Barbados, West Indies, Tel. (246)427-7185

Bermuda Dist., The Rt. Rev. Calvin Armstrong, P.O. Box 234, Paget, Bermuda, Tel. (441)296-0828 or 441-292-8383

Central Western Dist., Bishop Bose Bradford, 6279 Natural Bridge, Pine Lawn, MO 63121 Tel. (314)355-1598

Ghana, West Africa Dist., The Rt. Rev. Robert Blount, 231 Arlington Av., Jersey City, NJ 07035, Tel. (201)433-5672

New England Dist., The Rt. Rev. Lowell Edney, 85 Woodhaven St., Mattapan, MA 02126, Tel. (617)296-5366

Northern Dist., The Rt. Rev. Kenneth O. Robinson, Sr., 33 Springbrook Rd., Nanuet, NY 10954, Tel. (914)425-8311

Northwestern Dist., The Rt. Rev. M. Daniel Borden, 8655 North Melody Lane, Macedonia, OH 44056, Tel. (330)468-0270

Pacific Coast Dist., The Rt. Rev. Irvin Evans, 235 Harvard Rd., Linden, NJ 07036, Tel. (908)925-6138

Southeastern Dist., The Rt. Rev. James C. Bellamy, 1825 Rockland Dr., SE, Atlanta, GA 30316, Tel. (404)241-1821

Southern Dist.- Goldsboro, The Rt. Rev. Ralph E. Love, Sr., 200 Barrington Rd., Greenville, NC 27834, Tel. (252)353-0495

Southern Dist.- Henderson, The Rt. Rev. Jesse Jones, 608 Cecil Street, Durham, NC 27707, Tel. (919)682-8249

St. Lucia Dist., The Rt. Rev. Carlisle Collymore, P.O. Box 51, Castries, St. Lucia, West Indies, Tel. (758)452-5835

Virginia Dist., The Rt. Rev. Albert Augson, 1406 Melton Ave., Richmond, VA 23223, Tel. (804)222-0463

West Virginia Dist., The Rt. Rev. Alvester McConnell, Route 3, Box 263, Bluefield, WV 24701, Tel. (304)248-8046

Western North Carolina Dist., The Rt. Rev. Elijah Williams, 901 Briarwood St., Reidsville, NC 27320-7020, Tel. (336)349-7275

Periodicals

The Holiness Union; The United Holy Church General Church Organ

United House of Prayer

The United House of Prayer was founded and organized as a hierarchical church in the 1920s by the late Bishop C. M. Grace, who had built the first House of Prayer in 1919 in West Wareham, MA, with his own hands. The purpose of the organization is to establish, maintain and perpetuate the doctrine of Christianity and the Apostolic Faith throughout the world among all people; to erect and maintain houses of prayer and worship where all people may gather for prayer and to worship the almighty God in spirit and in truth, irrespective of denomination or creed, and to maintain the Apostolic faith of the Lord and Savior, Jesus Christ.

Headquarters

1117 7th St. NW, Washington, DC 20001 Tel. (202)289-0238, Fax (202)289-8058

Media Contact, Apostle S. Green

Officers

CEO, Bishop S. C. Madison, 1665 N. Portal Dr. NW, Washington, DC 20012 Tel. (202)882-3956, Fax (202)829-4717

NATIONAL PROGRAM STAFF

The General Assembly, Presiding Officer, Bishop S. C. Madison, 1665 N. Portal Dr. NW, Washington, DC 20012 Tel. (202)882-3956, Fax (202)829-4717

General Council Ecclesiastical Court, Clerk, Apostle R. Price, 1665 N. Portal Dr. NW, Washington, DC 20012 Tel. (202)882-3956, Fax (202)829-4717

Annual Truth & Facts Publication, Exec. Editor, Bishop S. C. Madison, 1665 N. Portal Dr. NW, Washington, DC 20012 Tel. (202)882-3956, Fax (202)829-4717

Nationwide Building Program, General Builder, Bishop S. C. Madison, 1665 N. Portal Dr. NW, Washington, DC 20012 Tel. (202)882-3956, Fax (202)829-4717

Special Projects, Dir., Apostle S. Green

The United Methodist Church*

The United Methodist Church was formed April 23, 1968, in Dallas by the union of The Methodist Church and The Evangelical United Brethren Church. The two churches shared a common historical and spiritual heritage. The Methodist Church resulted in 1939 from the unification of three branches of Methodism - the Methodist Episcopal Church, the Methodist Episcopal Church, South, and the Methodist Protestant Church.

The Methodist movement began in 18th-century England under the preaching of John Wesley, but the Christmas Conference of 1784 in Baltimore is regarded as the date on which the organized Methodist Church was founded as an ecclesiastical organization. It was there that Francis Asbury was elected the first bishop in this country.

The Evangelical United Brethren Church was formed in 1946 with the merger of the Evangelical Church and the Church of the United Brethren in Christ, both of which had their beginnings in Pennsylvania in the evangelistic movement of the 18th and early 19th centuries. Philip William Otterbein and Jacob Albright were early leaders of this movement among the German-speaking settlers of the Middle Colonies.

Headquarters

Information, InfoServ, United Methodist Information Service, Dir., Mary Lynn Holly, Tel. 1-800-251-8140, Fax (615)742-5423 infoserv@umcom.umc.org

Media Contact, Dir., United Methodist News Service, Thomas S. McAnally, newsdesk@umcom.umc.org Tel. (615)742-5470, Fax (615)742-5469

Email: infoserv@umcom.umc.org

Website: www.umc.org

Officers

Gen. Conference, Sec., Carolyn M. Marshall, 204 N. Newlin St., Veedersburg, IN 47987

Council of Bishops, Pres., Bishop Elias G. Galvan, 2112 3rd Ave., Suite 301, Seattle, WA 98121-2333, Tel. (206)728-7674, Fax (206)728-8442, pnwbishop@aol.com; Sec., Bishop Sharon Zimmerman Rader, 750 Windsor St., Ste 303, Sun Prairie, WI 53590, Toll Free Tel. (800)240-7328 Tel. (608)837-8526, Fax (608)837-0281, Email, EpiscopalOffice@WisconsinUMC.org

BISHOPS

North Central Jurisdiction

Chicago Episcopal Area, Bishop C. Joseph Sprague, 77 West Washington St., Suite 1820, Chicago, IL 60602-1603, Tel. (312)346-9766 x321, Fax (312)214-9031, jsprague@umc-nic.org

Dakotas Episcopal Area, Bishop Michael J. Coyner, 3910 25th St. S., Fargo, ND 58104-6880, Tel. (701)232-2241, Fax (701)232-2615, bishopcoyner@juno.com

Illinois Episcopal Area, Bishop Sharon Brown Christopher, 400 Chatham Rd., Suite 100, Springfield, IL 62704-1468, Tel. (217)726-8071, Fax (217)726-8074, ilareaumc@aol.com

Indiana Episcopal Area, Bishop Woodie W. White, 1100 West 42nd St., Suite 210, Indianapolis, IN 46208, Tel. (317)924-1321, Fax (317)924-1380, kjulian@inareaumc.org

Iowa Episcopal Area, Bishop Gregory V. Palmer, 500 East Court Ave., Suite C, Des Moines, IA 50309-2019, Tel. (515)283-1996, Fax (515) 283-8672, bishop.palmer@iaumc.org

Michigan Episcopal Area, Bishop Linda Lee, PO Box 25068, Lansing, MI 48909-5068, Tel. (517)347-4030, Fax (517)347-4003, mareaumc @tir.com

Minnesota Episcopal Area, Bishop John L. Hopkins, 122 West Franklin Ave., Room 200, Minneapolis, MN 55404-2472, Tel. (612)870-4007, Fax (612)870-3587, jhopkins@msn.com

Ohio East Episcopal Area, Bishop Jonathan D. Keaton, PO Box 2800, North Canton, OH 44720-0800, Tel. (800)831-3972 or (330)499-3972, Fax (330)497-4911, jonathan@eocumc.com

Ohio West Episcopal Area, Bishop Bruce R. Ough, 32 Wesley Blvd., Worthington, OH 43085-3585, Tel. (800)437-0028, or (614)844-6200, Fax (614)781-2625, bishop@wocumc.org

Wisconsin Episcopal Area, Bishop Sharon Zimmerman Rader, 750 Windsor St., Suite 303, Sun Prairie, WI 53590-2100, Tel. (888)240-7328 or (608)837-8526, Fax (608) 837-0281, episcopaloffice@wisconsinumc.org

Northeastern Jurisdiction

Albany Episcopal Area, Bishop Susan Murch Morrison, 215 Lancaster St., Albany, NY 12210-1131, Tel. (518)426-0386, Fax (518) 426-0347, albepisarea@worldnet.att.net

Boston Episcopal Area, Bishop Susan Wolfe Hassinger, PO Box 249, Lawrence, MA 01842-0449, Tel. (978)682-7555 x30, Fax (978)682-9555, bishopsoffice@neumc.org

Harrisburg Episcopal Area, Bishop Neil Irons, 303 Mulberry Dr., Suite 100, Mechanicsburg, PA 17050-3141, Tel. (800)874-8474 or (717) 766-7871 x3100, Fax (717)766-3210, bishop @cpcumc.org

New Jersey Episcopal Area, Bishop Alfred Johnson, Pennington School, 112 West Delaware Ave., Pennington, NJ 08534-1616, Tel. (609)737-3940 or (609)737-3941, Fax (609)737-6962, bishop@gnjumc.org

New York Episcopal Area, Bishop Ernest Shaw Lyght, 252 Bryant Ave., White Plains, NY 10605-2198, Tel. (888)696-6922 or (914)684-6922, Fax (914)997-1628, bishopnyac@aol.com

New York West Episcopal Area, Bishop Violet Lucinda Fisher, 1010 East Ave, Rochester, NY 14607-2220, Tel. (716)271-3400, Fax (716) 271-3404, nywestarea@aol.com

Philadelphia Episcopal Area, Bishop Peter D. Weaver, PO Box 820, Valley Forge, PA 19482-0820, Tel. (610)666-9090 x233, Fax (610)666-9181, bishop@epaumc.org

Pittsburgh Episcopal Area, Bishop Hae-Jong Kim, PO Box 5002, Cranberry Township, PA 16066-4914, Tel. (724)776-1499 or (724)776-1599, Fax (776)1683, umbishop@umchurch.org

Washington DC Episcopal Area, Bishop Felton Edwin May, 100 Maryland Ave NE, Suite 510, Washington, DC 20002-5611, (Tel) 202-546-3110, Fax (202)546-8330, bishopmay@bwcumc.org

West Virginia Episcopal Area, Bishop S. Clifton Ives, 900 Washington St. E., Room 300F, Charleston, WV 25301, Tel. (304)344-8330, Fax (304)344-8330, wvarea@aol.com

South Central Jurisdiction

Arkansas Episcopal Area, Bishop Janice Riggle Huie, 723 Center St., Little Rock, AR 72201-4399, Tel. (877)646-1816 or (501)324-8019, Fax (501)324-8021, bishophuie@aristotle.net

Dallas Episcopal Area, Bishop William B. Oden, PO Box 6600127, Dallas, TX 75360-0127, Tel. (214)522-6741, Fax (214)528-4435, bishop_dallas@mail.smu.edu

Fort Worth Episcopal Area, Bishop Ben R. Chamness, 464 Bailey, Ft. Worth, TX 76107-2153, Tel. (800)460-8622 or (817)877-5222, Fax (817)332-4609, bishopsoffice@prodigy. net

Houston Episcopal Area, Bishop Alfred L. Norris, 5215 Main St. Houston, TX 77002-9792, Tel. (713)528-6881, Fax (713)529-7736, ijarratt@methodists.net

Kansas Episcopal Area, Bishop Albert Frederick Mutti, PO Box 4187, Topeka, KS 66604-0187, Tel. (785)272-0587, Fax (785)272-9135, ksbishumc@mindspring.com

Louisiana Episcopal Area, Bishop William Wayne Hutchinson, 527 North Blvd., Baton Rouge, LA 70802-5720, Tel. (888)239-5286 or (225)346-1646, Fax (225)387-3662, lcumc@bellsouth.net

Missouri Episcopal Area, Bishop Ann Brookshire Shere, 4800 Santana Circle, Suite 100, Columbia, MO 65203-7138, Tel. (877) 736-1806 or (573)441-1770, Fax (573)441-0765, mo.bishop.office.ume@ecunet.org

Nebraska Episcopal Area, Bishop Rhymes H. Moncure, Jr., 2641 N. 49th St., Lincoln, NE 68504-2899, Tel. (402)466-4955, Fax (402) 466-7931, bishop@umcneb.org

Northwest Texas/New Mexico Episcopal Area, Bishop D. Max Whitfield, 7920 Mountain Rd. NE, Albuquerque, NM 87110-7805, Tel. (800) 678-8786 or (505)255-9361, Fax (505)255-8738, mbelu@nmconfum.com

Oklahoma Episcopal Area, Bishop Bruce P. Blake, 2420 N. Blackwelder Ave., Oklahoma City, OK 73106-1499, Tel. (405)525-2252 x201, Fax (405)525-2216, buptegraft@okumc.org

San Antonio Episcopal Area, Bishop Joel N. Martinez, PO Box 781688, San Antonio, TX 78278-1688, Tel. (888)349-4191 or (210)408-4500, Fax (210)408-4501, bishop@umc-swtx.org

Southwestern Jurisdiction

Alabama-West Florida Episcopal Area, Bishop Larry M. Goodpaster, 424 Interstate Park Dr., Montgomery, AL 36109, Tel. (334)277-1787, Fax (334)277-0109, bishop.awf@knology.net

Birmingham Episcopal Area, Bishop Robert E. Fannin, 898 Arkadelphia Rd., Birmingham, AL 35204-5011, Tel. (205)322-8665, Fax (205)322-8938, rfannin@umcna.bsc.edu

Charlotte Episcopal Area, Bishop Charlene Kammerer, PO Box 18005, Charlotte, NC 28218-0750, Tel. (704)535-2260, Fax (704) 535-9160, jclark@wnccumc.org

Columbia Episcopal Area, Bishop J. Lawrence McCleskey, 4908 Colonial Dr., Suite 108, Columbia, SC 29203-6000, Tel. (803)786-9486, Fax (803)754-9327, bishop@umcsc.org

Florida Episcopal Area, Bishop Timothy Wayne Whitaker, PO Box 1747, Lakeland, FL 33802-1747, Tel. (863)688-4427, Fax (863)687-0568, bishop@flumc.org

Holston Episcopal Area, Bishop Ray W. Chamberlain, Jr., PO Box 32929, Knoxville, TN 37930-2939, Tel. (865)690-4080, Fax (865)690-7112, bishop@holston.org

Louisville Episcopal Area, Bishop James R. King, Jr., 2000 Warrington Way, Suite 280, Louisville, KY 40222-3407, Tel. (800)530-7236 or (502)425-4240, Fax (502)426-5181, bishop@kyumc.org

Mississippi Episcopal Area, Bishop Kenneth L. Carder, PO Box 931, Jackson, MS 39205-0931, Tel. (601)948-4561, Fax (601)948-5981, bishop@mississippi-umc.org

Nashville Episcopal Area, Bishop William W. Morris, 520 Commerce St., Suite 201, Nashville, TN 37203-3714, Tel. (615)742-8834, Fax (615)742-3726, umcoffice@aol.com

North Georgia Episcopal Area, Bishop G. Lindsey Davis, 159 Ralph McGill Blvd NE, Suite 208, Atlanta, GA 30308-3391, Tel. (404) 659-0002 x3226, Fax (404)577-0068, bishop@ngumc.org

Raleigh Episcopal Area, Bishop Marion M. Edwards, 1307 Glenwood Ave, PO Box 10955, Raleigh, NC 27605-0955, Tel. (800) 849-4433 or (919)832-9560 x243, Fax (919) 832-4721, bishopmme@nccumc.org

Richmond Episcopal Area, Bishop Joe E. Pennel, Jr., PO Box 11367, Richmond, VA 23230-1367, Tel. (800)768-6040 or (804)359-9451, Fax (804)358-7736, estellepruden@vaumc.org

South Georgia Episcopal Area, Bishop B. Michael Watson, PO Box 13616, Macon, GA 31208-3616, Tel. (912)738-0048, Fax (912) 738-9033, bishopsga@aol.com

Western Jurisdiction

Denver Episcopal Area, Bishop Warner H. Brown, Jr., 2200 South University Blvd., Denver, CO 80210-4797, Tel. (800)536-3736 or (303)733-3736, Fax (303)733-5047, bishop@rmcumc.com

Los Angeles Episcopal Area, Bishop Mary Ann Swenson, PO Box 6006, Pasadena, CA 91102-6006, Tel. (626)568-7312, Fax (626)568-7377, calpacbishop@earthlink.net

Phoenix Episcopal Area, Bishop William W. Dew, 1550 East Meadowbrook Ave., Suite 200, Phoenix, AZ 85014-4040, Tel. (602)266-6956, Fax (602)279-1355, bishop@desertsw.org

Portland Episcopal Area, Bishop Edward W. Paup, 1505 SW 18th Ave., Portland, OR 97201-2599, Tel. (800)593-7539 or (503)226-1530, Fax (503)228-3189, bishop@umoi.org

San Francisco Episcopal Area, Bishop Beverly J. Shamana, PO Box 980250, West Sacramento, CA 95798-0250, Tel. (916)374-1510, Fax (916)372-9062, bishop@calnevumc.org

Seattle Episcopal Area, Bishop Elias G. Galvan, 2112 3rd Ave, Suite 301, Seattle, WA 98121-2333, Tel. (206)728-7674, Fax (206)728-8442, pnwbishop@aol.com

Periodicals

Mature Years; El Interprete; New World Outlook; Newscope; Interpreter; Methodist History; Christian Social Action; Pockets; Response; Social Questions Bulletin; United Methodist Reporter; United Methodist Review; Quarterly Review; Alive Now; Circuit Rider; El Aposento Alto; Weavings-A Journal of the Christian Spiritual Life; The Upper Room

United Pentecostal Church International

The United Pentecostal Church International came into being through the merger of two oneness Pentecostal organizations—the Pentecostal Church, Inc., and the Pentecostal Assemblies of Jesus Christ. The first of these was known as the Pentecostal Ministerial Alliance from its inception in 1925 until 1932. The second was formed in 1931 by a merger of the Apostolic Church of Jesus Christ with the Pentecostal Assemblies of the World.

The church contends that the Bible teaches that there is one God who manifested himself as the Father in creation, in the Son in redemption and as the Holy Spirit in regeneration; that Jesus is the name of this absolute deity and that water baptism should be administered in his name, not in the titles Father, Son and Holy Ghost (Acts Ch.2 vs.38, Ch.8 vs.16, and Ch.19 vs.6).

The Fundamental Doctrine of the United Pentecostal Church International, as stated in its Articles of Faith, is "the Bible standard of full salvation, which is repentance, baptism in water by immersion in the name of the Lord Jesus Christ for the remission of sins, and the baptism of the Holy Ghost with the initial sign of speaking with other tongues as the Spirit gives utterance."

Further doctrinal teachings concern a life of holiness and separation, the operation of the gifts of the Spirit within the church, the second coming of the Lord and the church's obligation to take the gospel to the whole world.

Headquarters

8855 Dunn Rd., Hazelwood, MO 63042 Tel. (314)837-7300, Fax (314)837-4503

Media Contact, Gen. Sec.-Treas., Rev. C. M. Becton

Officers

Gen. Supt., Rev. Nathaniel A. Urshan

Asst. Gen. Supts., Rev. Kenneth Haney, 7149 E. 8 Mile Rd., Stockton, CA 95212; Jesse Williams, P.O. Box 64277, Fayetteville, NC 28306

Gen. Sec.-Treas., Rev. C. M. Becton

Dir. of Foreign Missions, Rev. Harry Scism

Gen. Dir. of Home Missions, Rev. Jack Cunningham

Editor-in-Chief, Rev. J. L. Hall

Gen. Sunday School Dir., Rev. E. J. McClintock

OTHER ORGANIZATIONS

Pentecostal Publishing House, Mgr., Rev. Marvin Curry

Youth Division (Pentecostal Conquerors), Pres., Brian Kinsey, Hazelwood, MO 63042

Ladies Auxiliary, Pres., Gwyn Oakes, P.O. Box 247, Bald Knob, AR 72010

Harvestime Radio Broadcast, Dir., Rev. J. Hugh Rose, 698 Kerr Ave., Cadiz, OH 43907

Stewardship Dept., Contact Church Division, Hazelwood, MO 63042

Education Division, Supt., Rev. Arless Glass, 4502 Aztec, Pasadena, TX 77504

Public Relations Division, Contact Church Division, Hazelwood, MO 63042

Historical Society & Archives

Periodicals

World Harvest Today; The North American Challenge; Homelife; Conqueror; Reflections; Forward

The United Pentecostal Churches of Christ

In a time when the Church of Jesus Christ is challenged to send the "Evening Light Message" to the uppermost part of the Earth, a group of men and women came together on May 29, 1992 at the Pentecostal Church of Christ in Cleveland, Ohio to form what is now called The United Pentecostal Churches of Christ.

Organized and established by Bishop Jesse Delano Ellis, II, the United Pentecostal Churches of Christ is about the business of preparing people to see the Lord of Glory. The traditional barriers of yesteryear must not keep saints or like faith apart ever again and this fellowship of Pentecostal, Apostolic Independent Churches have discovered the truth of Our Lord's Prayer in the seventeenth chapter of Saint John, "that they may all be One."

The United Pentecostal Churches of Christ is a fellowship of holiness assemblies which has membership in the universal Body of Christ. As such, we preserve the message of Christ's redeeming love through His atonement and declare holiness of life to be His requirement for all men who would enter into the Kingdom of God. We preach repentence from sin, baptism in the Name of Jesus Christ, a personal indwelling of the Holy Spirit, a daily walk with the Lord and life after death. Coupled with the cardinal truths of the Church are the age old customs of ceremony and celebration.

Headquarters

10515 Chester Ave., (at University Circle), Cleveland, OH 44106 Tel. (216)721-5935, Fax (216)721-6938

Contact Person, Public Relations, Rev. W. Michelle James Williams

REGIONAL OFFICE

493-5 Monroe St., Brooklyn, New York 11221 Tel. (718)574-4100, Fax (718)574-8504

Contact Person, Secretary General., Rev. Rodney McNeil Johnson

Officers

Presiding Bishop and Gen. Overseer, Bishop J. Delano Ellis, II, Cleveland, OH

Asst. Presiding Bishop, Bishop Carl Halloway Montgomery, II, Baltimore, MD

Secretary General, Bishop James R. Chambers, Brookyn, NY

Pres. Of Pentacostal Youth Congress, Overseer Darryl D. Woodson, Memphis, TN

Periodicals

The Pentecostal Flame

United Zion Church

A branch of the Brethren in Christ which settled in Lancaster County, Pennsylvania, the United Zion Church was organized under the leadership of Matthias Brinser in 1855.

Headquarters

United Zion Retirement Community, 722 Furnace Hills Pk., Lititz, PA 17543

Media Contact, Bishop, Carl Eberly, 270 Clay School Rd., Ephrata, PA 17522 Tel. (717)733-3932

Officers

Gen. Conf. Mod., Bishop Carl Eberly, 270 Clay School Rd., Ephrata, PA 17522 Tel. (717)733-3932

Asst. Mod., Rev. John Leisey

Gen. Conf. Sec., Rev. Clyde Martin

Gen. Conf. Treas., Kenneth Kleinfelter, 919 Sycamore Lane, Lebanon, PA 17042

Periodicals

Zion's Herald

Unity of the Brethren

Czech and Moravian immigrants in Texas (beginning about 1855) established congregations which grew into an Evangelical Union in 1903, and with the accession of other Brethren in Texas, into the Evangelical Unity of the Czech-Moravian Brethren in North America. In 1959, it shortened the name to the original name used in 1457, the Unity of the Brethren (Unitas Fratrum, or Jednota Bratrska).

Headquarters

4009 Hunter Creek, College Station, TX 77845

Media Contact, Sec. of Exec. Committee, Ginger McKay, 148 N. Burnett, Baytown, TX 77520

Officers

Pres., Kent Laza, 4009 Hunter Creek, College Station, TX 77845

1st Vice Pres., Rev. Michael Groseclose, 902 Church St., Belleville, TX 77418 Tel. (512)365-6890

Sec. of Exec. Committee, Ginger McKay, 148 N. Burnett, Baytown, TX 77520

Fin. Sec., Rev. Joseph Polasek, 4241 Blue Heron, Bryan, TX 77807

Treas., Arranna Jakubik, P.O. Box 408, Snook, TX 77878

OTHER ORGANIZATIONS

Bd. of Christian Educ., Dr., Donald Ketcham, 900 N. Harrison, West, TX 76691

Brethren Youth Fellowship, Pres., Jamie Brooke Bryan, 1231 Four Corners, West, TX 76691

Friends of the Hus Encampment, Jim Baletka, 727 San Benito, College Station, TX 77845

Christian Sisters Union, Pres., Janet Pomykal, P.O. Box 560, Brenham, TX 77834

Sunday School Union, Pres., Dorothy Kocian, 107 S. Barbara Dr., Waco, TX 76705

Youth Director, Kimberly Stewart, 1500 Lawnmont Dr., Apt. 208, Round Rock, TX 78664

Periodicals

Brethren Journal, Editor, Rev.Milton Maly, 6703 FM 2502, Brenham, TX 77833; Bus Mngr., Jean Maly, 6703 FM 2502, Brenham, TX 77833

Universal Fellowship of Metropolitan Community Churches

The Universal Fellowship of Metropolitan Community Churches was founded Oct. 6, 1968 by the Rev. Troy D. Perry in Los Angeles, with a particular but not exclusive outreach to the gay community. Since that time, the Fellowship has grown to include congregations throughout the world.

The group is Trinitarian and accepts the Bible as the divinely inspired Word of God. The Fellowship has two sacraments, baptism and holy communion, as well as a number of traditionally recognized rites such as ordination.

This Fellowship acknowledges "the Holy Scriptures interpreted by the Holy Spirit in conscience and faith, as its guide in faith, discipline, and government." The government of this Fellowship is vested in its General Council (consisting of Elders and District Coordinators), clergy and church delegates, who exert the right of control in all of its affairs, subject to the provisions of its Articles of Incorporation and By-Laws.

Headquarters

8704 Santa Monica Blvd. 2nd Floor, West Hollywood, CA 90069-4548 Tel. (310)360-8640 x. 226, Fax (310)360-8680

Media Contact, Dir. of Communications, Jim Birkett

Email: communications@ufmcchq.com

Website: www.ufmcchq.com

Officers

Mod., Rev. Elder Troy D. Perry

Vice-Mod., Rev. Elder Nancy L. Wilson

Treas., Rev. Elder Donald Eastman

Clk., Rev. Elder Darlene Garner

Elder Mel Johnson, PMB #63, 2261 Market St., San Francisco, CA 94114-1600

Rev. Elder Nori Rost, 214 S. Prospect St., Colorado Springs, CO 80903

Rev. Elder Hong Kia Tan, 72 Fleet Rd., Hampstead, London, NW3 2QT England

Deputy Chief Executive Officer, Jane Wagner, 8704 Santa Monica Blvd., 2nd Floor, West Holywood, CA 90069-4548

Dir., Communications, Jim Birkett, 8704 Santa Monica Blvd., 2nd Floor, West Hollywood, CA 90069-4548

Chief Officer, Office of Ecumenical and Interreligious Concerns, Rev. Gwynne Guibord, 4311 Wilshire Blvd., Ste. 308, Los Angeles, CA 90010 Tel. (213)932-1516

OTHER COMMISSIONS & COMMITTEES

Min. of Global Outreach, Field Dir., Rev. Judy Dahl

Commission on the Laity, Chpsn., Stan Kimer

Clergy Credentials & Concerns, Admn., Rev. Justin Tanis

UFMCC AIDS Ministry, AIDS Liaison., Rev. Robert Griffin

Chief Financial Officer, Margaret Mahlman, 8704 Santa Monica Blvd., 2nd Floor, West Hollywood, CA 90069-4548

Periodicals

Keeping in Touch; UFMCC E-Mail News Service (Free)

Volunteers of America

Volunteers of America is a national, nonprofit, spiritually based organization providing local human service programs and opportunities for individual and community involovement. Founded in 1896 by Christian social reformers Ballington and Maud Booth, Volunteers of America provides about 100 different types of programs and services in more than 300 communities nationwide for abused and neglected children, youth at risk, the elderly, people with disabilities, homeless individuals and families, and many others.

Headquarters

1660 Duke St., Alexandria, VA 22314-3427 Tel. (800)899-0089

Email: voa@voa.org

Website: www.voa.org/

Officers

Chpsn., Walter C. Patterson

Pres., Charles W. Gould

Periodicals

Spirit

The Wesleyan Church

The Wesleyan Church was formed on June 26, 1968, through the union of the Wesleyan Methodist Church of America (1843) and the Pilgrim Holiness Church (1897). The headquarters was established at Marion, Ind., and relocated to Indianapolis in 1987.

The Wesleyan movement centers around the beliefs, based on Scripture, that the atonement in Christ provides for the regeneration of sinners and the entire sanctification of believers. John Wesley led a revival of these beliefs in the 18th century.

When a group of New England Methodist ministers led by Orange Scott began to crusade for the abolition of slavery, the bishops and others sought to silence them. This led to a series of withdrawals from the Methodist Episcopal Church. In 1843, the Wesleyan Methodist Connection of America was organized and led by Scott, Jotham Horton, LaRoy Sunderland, Luther Lee and Lucius C. Matlack.

During the holiness revival in the last half of the 19th century, holiness replaced social reform as the major tenet of the Connection. In 1947 the name was changed from Connection to Church and a central supervisory authority was set up.

The Pilgrim Holiness Church was one of many independent holiness churches which came into existence as a result of the holiness revival. Led by Martin Wells Knapp and Seth C. Rees, the International Holiness Union and Prayer League was inaugurated in 1897 in Cincinnati. Its purpose was to promote worldwide holiness evangelism and the Union had a strong missionary emphasis from the beginning. It developed into a church by 1913.

The Wesleyan Church is now spread across most of the United States and Canada and 68 other countries. The Wesleyan World Fellowship was organized in 1972 to unite Wesleyan mission bodies developing into mature churches. The Wesleyan Church is a member of the Christian Holiness Partnership, the National Association of Evangelicals and the World Methodist Council.

Headquarters

P.O. Box 50434, Indianapolis, IN 46250 Tel. (317)570-5100

Media Contact, Gen. Sec., Dr. Ronald D. Kelly, Tel. (317)570-5154, Fax (317)570-5280, kellyr@wesleyan.org

Email: gensupts@wesleyan.org

Website: www.wesleyan.org

Officers

General Superintendents:

Dr. Earle L. Wilson, Tel. (317)570-5146, Fax (317)570-5255, wilsone@wesleyan.org;

Dr. Thomas E. Armiger, Tel. (317)570-5147, Fax (317)570-5255, armigert@wesleyan.org; Dr. David W. Holdren, Tel. (317)570-5148, Fax (317)570-5255, holdrend@wesleyan.org;

General Officers

Gen. Sec., Dr. Ronald D. Kelly, Tel. (317)570-5154, Fax (317)570-5280, kellyr@wesleyan.org

Gen. Treas., Donald M. Frase, Tel. (317)570-5150, Fax (317)570-5285, frased@wesleyan.org

Gen. Publisher, Mr. Donald D. Cady, Tel. (317) 570-5317, Fax (317)570-5370, cadyd@wesleyan.org

Gen. Director of Communications, Dr. Norman G. Wilson, Tel. (317)570-5156, Fax (317)570-5260, wilsonn@wesleyan.org

Gen. Dir. of Sunday School & Discipleship, Dr. Ray E. Barnwell, Sr., Tel. (317)570-5180, Fax (317)570-5290, barnwelr@wesleyan.org

Gen. Dir. of Evangelism & Church Growth, Dr. Jerry Pence, Tel. (317)570-5125, Fax (317) 570-5265, pencej@wesleyan.org

Gen. Dir. of Education & the Ministry, Rev. Kerry D. Kind, Tel. (317)570-5130, Fax (317) 570-5270, kindk@wesleyan.org

Gen. Dir. of World Missions, Dr. Donald L. Bray, Tel. (317)570-5160, Fax (317)570-5256, brayd@wesleyan.org

Gen. Dir. of Youth, Rev. Ross A. DeMerchant, Tel. (317)570-5140, Fax (317)570-5257, demerchr@ wesleyan.org

Auxiliaries/Subsidiary Agencies

Estate Planning, Gen. Dir., Rev. Howard B. Castle, Tel. (317)570-5162, Fax (317)570-5273, castleh@wesleyan.org

Wesleyan Investment Foundation, Gen. Dir., Dr. Craig A. Dunn, Tel. (317)570-5136, Fax (317) 570-6190, wif@wesleyan.org

Wesleyan Pension Fund, Gen. Dir., Mr. Robert L. (Bobby) Temple, Tel. (317)570-5131, Fax (317)570-5253, templer@wesleyan.org

Wesleyan Women, Mrs. Nancy Heer, Tel. (317) 570-5164, heern@wesleyan.org

Wesleyan Kids for Mission, Mrs. Peggy Camp, Tel. (317)570-5164, Fax (317)570-5254, heern@wesleyan.org or wwi@wesleyan.org

Wesleyan Men, Dr. Jerry Pence, Tel. (317)570-5125, Fax (317)570-5265, pencej@wesleyan.org

Address Service, Tel. (317)570-5200

Archives & Historical Library, Tel. (317)570-5145

Computer Information Services, Tel. (317)570-5121

Wesleyan Publishing House, Tel. (317)570-5300

Periodicals

Wesleyan Woman; The Wesleyan Advocate; Wesleyan World

Wesleyan Holiness Association of Churches

This body was founded Aug. 4, 1959 near Muncie, Indiana by a group of ministers and laymen who were drawn together for the purpose of spreading and conserving sweet, radical, scriptural holiness. These men came from various church bodies. This group is Wesleyan in doctrine and standards.

Headquarters

1141 North US Hwy 27, Fountain City, IN 47341-9757 Tel. (765)584-3199

Media Contact, Gen. Sec.-Treas., Rev. Robert W. Wilson, RR3 Box 218, Selinsgrove, PA 17870

Officers

Gen. Supt., Rev. John Brewer

Asst. Gen. Supt., Rev. Jack W. Dulin, 3 Crescent Dr., Wabash, IN

Gen. Sec.-Treas., Rev. Robert W. Wilson, RR3 Box 218, Selinsgrove, PA 17870 Tel. (717)966-4147

Gen. Youth Pres., Rev. Nathan Shockley, 504 W. Tyrell St., St. Louis, MI 48880 Tel. (517)681-2591

Periodicals

Eleventh Hour Messenger

Wisconsin Evangelical Lutheran Synod

Organized in 1850 at Milwaukee, Wisconsin, by three pastors sent to America by a German mission society, the Wisconsin Evangelical Lutheran Synod still reflects its origins, although it now has congregations in 50 states and three Canadian provinces. It supports missions in 26 countries.

The Wisconsin Synod federated with the Michigan and Minnesota Synods in 1892 in order to more effectively carry on education and mission enterprises. A merger of these three Synods followed in 1917 to give the Wisconsin Evangelical Lutheran Synod its present form.

Although at its organization in 1850 WELS turned away from conservative Lutheran theology, today it is ranked as one of the most conservative Lutheran bodies in the United States. WELS confesses that the Bible is the verbally inspired, infallible Word of God and subscribes without reservation to the confessional writings of the Lutheran Church. Its interchurch relations are determined by a firm commitment to the principle that unity of doctrine and practice are the prerequisites of pulpit and altar fellowship and ecclesiastical cooperation. It does not hold membership in ecumenical organizations.

Headquarters

2929 N. Mayfair Rd., Milwaukee, WI 53222 Tel. (414)256-3888, Fax (414)256-3899

Dir. of Communications, Rev. Gary Baumler

Email: webbin@sab.wels.net

Website: www.wels.net

Officers

Pres., Rev. Karl R. Gurgel

1st Vice-Pres., Rev. Richard E. Lauersdorf

2nd Vice-Pres., Rev. Jon Mahnke, 5828 Santa Teresa Blvd., San Jose CA 95123

Sec., Rev. Douglas L. Bode, Box 423, Aurora, CO 80040

OTHER ORGANIZATIONS

Bd. for Ministerial Education, Admn., Rev. Peter Kruschel

Bd. for Parish Services, Admn., Rev. Wayne Mueller

Bd. for Home Missions, Admn., Rev. Harold J. Hagedorn

Bd. for World Missions, Admn., Rev. Daniel Koelpin

Periodicals

Wisconsin Lutheran Quarterly; Forward in Christ; Lutheran Leader; The Lutheran Educator; Mission Connection

Religious Bodies in the United States Arranged by Families

The following list of religious bodies appearing in the Directory Section of the *Yearbook* shows the "families," or related clusters into which American religious bodies can be grouped. For example, there are many communions that can be grouped under the heading "Baptist" for historical and theological reasons. It should not be assumed, however, that all denominations under one family heading are necessarily consistent in belief or practice. The family clusters tend to represent historical factors more often than theological or practical ones. These family categories provide one of the major pitfalls when compiling church statistics because there is often a tendency to combine the statistics by "families" for analytical and comparative purposes. Such combined totals are deeply flawed, even though they are often used as variables for sociological analysis. The arrangement by families offered here is intended only as a general guide for conceptual organization when viewing the broad sweep of American religious culture.

Religious bodies that can not be categorized under family headings appear alphabetically and are not indented in the following list.

Adventist Bodies

Advent Christian Church
Church of God General Conference (Oregon, IL and Morrow, GA)
Primitive Advent Christian Church
Seventh-day Adventist Church

American Evangelical Christian Churches
American Rescue Workers

Anglican Bodies

Episcopal Church
The Episcopal Orthodox Church
Reformed Episcopal Church

Apostolic Christian Church (Nazarene)
Apostolic Christian Churches of America
Apostolic Episcopal Church

Baptist Bodies

The Alliance of Baptists in the U.S.A.
The American Baptist Association
American Baptist Churches in the U.S.A.
Baptist Bible Fellowship International
Baptist General Conference
Baptist Missionary Association of America
Conservative Baptist Association of America
General Association of General Baptists
General Association of Regular Baptist Churches
National Association of Free Will Baptists
National Baptist Convention of America, Inc.
National Baptist Convention, U.S.A., Inc.
National Missionary Baptist Convention of America
National Primitive Baptist Convention, Inc.
North American Baptist Conference
Primitive Baptists
Progressive National Baptist Convention, Inc.
Separate Baptists in Christ
Seventh Day Baptist General Conference, USA and Canada
Southern Baptist Convention
Sovereign Grace Believers

Berean Fundamental Church

Brethren (German Baptists)

Brethren Church (Ashland, Ohio)
Church of the Brethren
Fellowship of Grace Brethren Churches
Old German Baptist Brethren

Brethren, River

Brethren in Christ Church
United Zion Church

The Catholic Church
Christ Community Church (Evangelical-Protestant)
Christadelphians
Christian Brethren (also known as Plymouth Brethren)
The Christian Congregation, Inc.
The Christian and Missionary Alliance
Christian Union
The Church of Christ (Holiness) U.S.A.
Church of Christ, Scientist
The Church of Illumination
Church of the Living God
Church of the Nazarene

Churches of Christ—Christian Churches

Christian Church (Disciples of Christ)
Christian Churches and Churches of Christ
Churches of Christ
Churches of Christ in Christian Union

Churches of God

Church of God (Anderson, Indiana)
The Church of God (Seventh Day), Denver, Colorado

Church of God by Faith, Inc.
Churches of God, General Conference

Churches of the New Jerusalem

General Church of the New Jerusalem
The Swedenborgian Church

Conservative Congregational Christian Conference

Eastern Orthodox Churches

Albanian Orthodox Archdiocese in America
Albanian Orthodox Diocese of America
The American Carpatho-Russian Orthodox Greek Catholic Church
The Antiochian Orthodox Christian Archdiocese of North America
Apostolic Catholic Assyrian Church of the East, North American Dioceses
Apostolic Orthodox Catholic Church
Greek Orthodox Archdiocese of America
The Holy Eastern Orthodox Catholic and Apostolic Church in North America, Inc.
Holy Ukrainian Autocephalic Orthodox Church in Exile
The Orthodox Church in America
Patriarchal Parishes of the Russian Orthodox Church in the U.S.A.
The Romanian Orthodox Church in America
The Romanian Orthodox Episcopate of America
The Russian Orthodox Church Outside of Russia
Serbian Orthodox Church in the U.S.A. and Canada
The Syro-Russian Orthodox Catholic Church, Romano-Byzantine Synod
True Orthodox Church of Greece (Synod of Metropolitan Cyprian), American Exarchate
Ukrainian Orthodox Church of the U.S.A.

The Evangelical Church
The Evangelical Church Alliance
The Evangelical Congregational Church
The Evangelical Covenant Church
The Evangelical Free Church of America
Fellowship of Fundamental Bible Churches
Free Christian Zion Church of Christ

Friends

Evangelical Friends International—North American Region
Friends General Conference
Friends United Meeting
Philadelphia Yearly Meeting of the Religious Society of Friends
Religious Society of Friends (Conservative)
Religious Society of Friends (Unaffiliated Meetings)

Grace Gospel Fellowship
House of God, Which is the Church of the Living God, the Pillar and Ground of the Truth, Inc.
Independent Fundamental Churches of America/IFCA International, Inc.
International Council of Community Churches
Jehovah's Witnesses

Latter Day Saints (Mormons)

Church of Christ
The Church of Jesus Christ of Latter-day Saints
The Church of Jesus Christ (Bickertonites)
Community of Christ

The Liberal Catholic Church—Province of the United States of America

Lutheran Bodies

The American Association of Lutheran Churches
Apostolic Lutheran Church of America
The Association of Free Lutheran Congregations
Church of the Lutheran Brethren of America
Church of the Lutheran Confession
Conservative Lutheran Association
The Estonian Evangelical Lutheran Church
Evangelical Lutheran Church in America
Evangelical Lutheran Synod
The Latvian Evangelical Lutheran Church in America
The Lutheran Church—Missouri Synod
Wisconsin Evangelical Lutheran Synod

Mennonite Bodies

Beachy Amish Mennonite Churches
Bible Fellowship Church
Church of God in Christ, Mennonite
Evangelical Mennonite Church
Fellowship of Evangelical Bible Churches
General Conference of Mennonite Brethren Churches
Hutterian Brethren
Mennonite Church, USA
Old Order (Wisler) Mennonite Church
Old Order Amish Church
Reformed Mennonite Church

Methodist Bodies

African Methodist Episcopal Church
African Methodist Episcopal Zion Church
Allegheny Wesleyan Methodist Connection (Original Allegheny Conference)
Bible Holiness Church
Christian Methodist Episcopal Church
Evangelical Methodist Church
Free Methodist Church of North America
Fundamental Methodist Church, Inc.
Primitive Methodist Church in the U.S.A.
Reformed Methodist Union Episcopal Church
Reformed Zion Union Apostolic Church
Southern Methodist Church
The United Methodist Church
The Wesleyan Church

The Metropolitan Church Association, Inc.
The Missionary Church

Moravian Bodies

Moravian Church in America (Unitas Fratrum)
Unity of the Brethren

National Association of Congregational Christian Churches
National Organization of the New Apostolic Church of North America
National Spiritualist Association of Churches
North American Old Roman Catholic Church (Archdiocese of New York)

Old Catholic Churches

Christ Catholic Church

Oriental Orthodox Churches

Armenian Apostolic Church of America
Armenian Apostolic Church, Diocese of America
Coptic Orthodox Church
Syrian (Syriac) Orthodox Church of Antioch

Pentecostal Bodies

Apostolic Faith Mission of Portland, Oregon
Apostolic Faith Mission Church of God
Apostolic Overcoming Holy Church of God, Inc
Assemblies of God
Assemblies of God International Fellowship (Independent/Not affiliated)
The Bible Church of Christ, Inc.
Bible Way Church of Our Lord Jesus Christ World Wide, Inc.
Christian Church of North America, General Council
Church of God of Prophecy
Church of God (Cleveland, Tennessee)
Church of God in Christ, International
The Church Of God In Christ
The (Original) Church of God, Inc.
Church of God, Mountain Assembly, Inc.
Church of Our Lord Jesus Christ of the Apostolic Faith, Inc.
Congregational Holiness Church
Elim Fellowship
Full Gospel Assemblies International
Full Gospel Fellowship of Churches and Ministers International
International Church of the Foursquare Gospe
The International Pentecostal Church of Christ
International Pentecostal Holiness Church
Open Bible Standard Churches
Pentecostal Assemblies of the World, Inc.
Pentecostal Church of God
Pentecostal Fire-Baptized Holiness Church
The Pentecostal Free Will Baptist Church, Inc.
Pillar of Fire
United Holy Church of America, Inc.
United Pentecostal Church International
The United Pentecostal Churches of Christ

Polish National Catholic Church of America

Presbyterian Bodies

Associate Reformed Presbyterian Church (General Synod)
Cumberland Presbyterian Church
Cumberland Presbyterian Church in America
Evangelical Presbyterian Church
Korean Presbyterian Church in America, General Assembly of the
The Orthodox Presbyterian Church
Presbyterian Church (U.S.A.)
Presbyterian Church in America
Reformed Presbyterian Church of North America

Reformed Bodies

Christian Reformed Church in North America
Hungarian Reformed Church in America
Netherlands Reformed Congregations
Protestant Reformed Churches in America
Reformed Church in America
Reformed Church in the United States
United Church of Christ

Reformed Catholic Church
The Salvation Army
The Schwenkfelder Church

Thomist Churches

Malankara Orthodox Syrian Church, Diocese of America
Mar Thoma Syrian Church of India

Triumph the Church and Kingdom of God in Christ Inc. (International)
Unitarian Universalist Association of Congregations

United Brethren Bodies

Church of the United Brethren in Christ
United Christian Church

United House of Prayer
Universal Fellowship of Metropolitan Community Churches
Volunteers of America
Wesleyan Holiness Association of Churches

4. Religious Bodies in Canada

A large number of Canadian religious bodies were organized by immigrants from Europe and elsewhere, and a smaller number sprang up originally on Canadian soil. In the case of Canada, moreover, many denominations that transcend the U.S.-Canada border have headquarters in the United States.

A final section in this directory lists churches according to denominational families. This can be a helpful tool in finding a particular church if you don't know the official name. Complete statistics for Canadian churches are found in the statistical section in Chapter 3: Table 1 contains memberhsip figures, and Table 4 contains giving figures. Addresses for periodicals are found in the directory entitled, "Religious Periodicals in Canada."

The Anglican Church of Canada

Anglicanism came to Canada with the early explorers such as Martin Frobisher and Henry Hudson. Continuous services began in Newfoundland about 1700 and in Nova Scotia in 1710. The first Bishop, Charles Inglis, was appointed to Nova Scotia in 1787. The numerical strength of Anglicanism was increased by the coming of American Loyalists and by massive immigration both after the Napoleonic wars and in the later 19th and early 20th centuries.

The Anglican Church of Canada has enjoyed self-government for over a century and is an autonomous member of the worldwide Anglican Communion. The General Synod, which normally meets triennially, consists of the Archbishops, Bishops and elected clerical and lay representatives of the 30 dioceses. Each of the Ecclesiastical Provinces—Canada, Ontario, Rupert's Land and British Columbia—is organized under a Metropolitan and has its own Provincial Synod and Executive Council. Each diocese has its own Diocesan Synod.

Headquarters

Church House, 600 Jarvis St., Toronto, ON M4Y 2J6 Tel. (416)924-9192, Fax (416)968-7983, Website, www.anglican.ca

Media Contact, Dir. of Information Resources

General Email: info@national.anglican.ca

Officers

GENERAL SYNOD OFFICERS

Primate of the Anglican Church of Canada, Most Rev. Michael G. Peers

Prolocutor, Ms. Dorothy Davies-Flindall

Gen. Sec., Ven. James B. Boyles

Treas., Gen. Synod, Mr. James Cullen

DEPARTMENTS AND DIVISIONS

Faith, Worship & Ministry, Dir., Rev. Canon Alyson Barnett-Cowan

Financial Management and Dev., Dir., Mr. James Cullen

Inform. Resources Dir., -vacant

Partnerships, Dir., Dr. Eleanor Johnson

Pensions, Dir., Mrs. Jenny Mason

Primate's World Relief and Dev. Fund, Dir., Mr. Andrew Ignatieff

METROPOLITANS (ARCHBISHOPS)

Ecclesiastical Province of: Canada, -vacant; Rupert's Land, The Most Rev. Thomas O. Morgan, Box 1965, Saskatoon, SK S7K 3S5 Tel. (306)244-5651, Fax (306)933-4606, E-mail: diocese.stoon@sk.sympatico.ca; British Columbia, The Most Rev. David P. Crawley, 1876 Richter St., Kelowna, BC V1Y 2M9 Tel. (250)762-3306, Fax (250)762-4150; Ontario, The Most Rev. Terence E. Finlay, 135 Adelaide St. East, Toronto, ON M5C 1L8, Tel. (416)363-6021, Fax (416)363-3683, tfinlay@toronto.anglican.ca

DIOCESAN BISHOPS

Algoma, The Rt. Rev. Ronald Ferris, Box 1168, Sault Ste. Marie, ON P6A 5N7 Tel. (705)256-5061, Fax (705)946-1860, dioceseofalgoma@on.aibn.com

Arctic, The Rt. Rev. Christopher Williams, 4910 51st St., Box 1454, Yellowknife, NT X1A 2P1 Tel. (867)873-5432, Fax (867)873-8478, cwill@internorth.com

Athabasca, The Right Rev. John R. Clarke, Box 6868, Peace River, AB T8S 1S6 Tel. (780)624-2767, Fax (780)624-2365, bpath@ telusplanet.net

Brandon, -vacant-, Box 21009 WEPO, Brandon, MB R7B 3W8 Tel. (204)727-7550, Fax (204)727-4135, bishopbdn@escape.ca

British Columbia, The Rt. Rev. Barry Jenks, 900 Vancouver St., Victoria, BC V8V 3V7 Tel. (250)386-7781, Fax (250)386-4013, bishop @acts.bc.ca

Caledonia, -vacant-, Box 278, Prince Rupert, BC V8J 3P6 Tel. (250)624-6013, Fax (250)624-4299, synodofc@citytel.net

Calgary, Archbishop, The Rt. Rev. Barry C.B. Hollowell, #560, 1207 11th Ave., SW, Salgary, AB T3C 0M5, Tel. (403)243-3673, Fax (403)243-2182, Diocesan Email: synod@calgary.anglican.ca

Cariboo, The Right Rev. James D. Cruickshank, 5-618 Tranquille Rd., Kamloops, BC V2B 3H6 Tel. (250)376-0112 Fax (250)376-1984, cariboo@sageserve.com

Central Newfoundland, The Rt. Rev. Donald A. Young, 34 Fraser Rd., Gander, NF A1V 2E8,

Tel. 709-256-2372, Fax 709-256-2396, bishop central@nfld.net

Eastern Newfoundland and Labrador, The Rt. Rev. Donald F. Harvey, 19 King's Bridge Rd., St. John's, NF A1C 3K4 Tel. (709)576-6697, Fax (709)576-7122, dharvey@anglicanenl.nf.net

Edmonton, The Rt. Rev. Victoria Matthews, 10035 - 103 St., Edmonton, AB T5J 0X5 Tel. (780)439-7344, Fax (780)439-6549, bishopv @telusplanet.net

Fredericton, The Rt. Rev. William J. Hockin, 115 Church St., Fredericton, NB E3B 4C8 Tel. (506)459-1801, Fax (506)459-8475, bishfton @nbnet.nb.ca

Huron, The Rt. Rev. Bruce H. W. Howe, One London Place, 903-255 Queens Ave., London, ON N6A 5R8 Tel. (519)434-6893, Fax (519) 673-4151, bishops@huron.anglican.ca

Keewatin, -vacant-, 915 Ottawa St., Keewatin, ON P0X 1C0 Tel. (807)547-3353, Fax (807) 547-3356, keewatin@kenora.com

Kootenay, Archbishop, The Most Rev. David P. Crawley, 1876 Richter St., Kelowna, BC V1Y 2M9 Tel. (250)762-3306, Fax (250)762-4150, diocese_of_kootenay@telus.net

Montreal, The Rt. Rev. Andrew S. Hutchison, 1444 Union Ave., Montreal, QC H3A 2B8 Tel. (514)843-6577, Fax (514)843-3221, bishops.office@montreal.anglican.ca

Moosonee, The Rt. Rev. Caleb J. Lawrence, Box 841, Schumacher, ON P0N 1G0 Tel. (705)360-1129, Fax (705)360-1120, lawrence @ntl.sympatico.ca

New Westminster, The Rt. Rev. Michael C. Ingham, 580-401 W. Georgia St., Vancouver, BC V6B 5A1 Tel. (604)684-6306, Fax (604)684-7017, michael_ingham@ ecunet.org

Niagara, The Rt. Rev. Ralph Spence, 252 James St. N., Hamilton, ON L8R 2L3 Tel. (905)527-1278, Fax (905)527-1281, adatri@niagara.anglican.ca

Nova Scotia, -vacant-, 5732 College St., Halifax, NS B3H 1X3 Tel. (902)420-0717, Fax (902)425-0717, diocese@fox.nstn.ca

Ontario, The Rt. Rev. Peter Mason, 90 Johnson St., Kingston, ON K7L 1X7 Tel. (613)544-4774, Fax (613)547-3745, pmason@ ontario.anglican.ca

Ottawa, The Rt. Rev. Peter R. Coffin, 71 Bronson Ave., Ottawa, ON K1R 6G6 Tel. (613)232-7124, Fax (613)232-7088, ann-day@ottawa.anglican.ca

Qu'Appelle, The Rt. Rev. Duncan D. Wallace, 1501 College Ave., Regina, SK S4P 1B8 Tel. (306)522-1608, Fax (306)352-6808, quappelle @sk.sympatico.ca

Quebec, The Rt. Rev. Bruce Stavert, 31 rue des Jardins, Quebec, QC G1R 4L6 Tel. (418)692-3858, Fax (418)692-3876, diocese_of_ quebec @sympatico.ca

Rupert's Land, Rt. Rev. Donald D. Phillips, 935 Nesbitt Bay, Winnipeg, MB R3T 1W6 Tel. (204)453-6130, Fax (204)452-3915, bishop@ rupertsland.anglican.ca

Saskatchewan, The Rt. Rev. Anthony Burton, 1308 5th Ave. East, Prince Albert, SK S6V 2H7 Tel. (306)763-2455, Fax (306)764-5172, burton@sk.sympatico.ca

Saskatoon, The Archbishop, Most Rev. Thomas O. Morgan, Box 1965, Saskatoon, SK S7K 3S5 Tel. (306)244-5651, Fax (306)933-4606, diocese.stoon@sk.sympatico.ca

Toronto, The Most Rev. Terence E. Finlay, 135 Adelaide St. East, Toronto, ON M5C 1L8 Tel. (416)363-6021, Fax (416)363-3683, tfinlay@ toronto.anglican.ca

Western Newfoundland, The Rt. Rev. Leonard Whitten, 25 Main St., Corner Brook, NF A2H 1C2 Tel. (709)639-8712, Fax (709)639-1636, dsownc@nf.aibn.com

Yukon, The Rt. Rev. Terry Buckle, Box 4247, Whitehorse, YT Y1A 3T3 Tel. (867)667-7746, Fax (867)667-6125, dioyuk@internorth.com

Periodicals

Anglican Journal (National Newspaper); Ministry Matters

The Antiochian Orthodox Christian Archdiocese of North America

The approximately 100,000 members of the Antiochian Orthodox community in Canada are under the jurisdiction of the Antiochian Orthodox Christian Archdiocese of North America with headquarters in Englewood, N.J. There are churches in Edmonton, Winnipeg, Halifax, London, Ottawa, Toronto, Windsor, Montreal, Saskatoon, Hamilton, Vancouver, Charlottestown, PEI.

Headquarters

Metropolitan Philip Saliba, 358 Mountain Rd., Englewood, NJ 07631 Tel. (201)871-1355, Fax (201)871-7954

Website: www.antiochian.com

Media Contact, Rev. Fr. Thomas Zain, 52 78th St., Brooklyn, NY 11209 Tel. (718)748-7940, Fax (718)855-3608

Periodicals

The Word; Again; Handmaiden

Apostolic Christian Church (Nazarene)

This church was formed in Canada as a result of immigration from various European countries. The body began as a movement originated by the Rev. S. H. Froehlich, a Swiss pastor, whose followers are still found in Switzerland and Central Europe.

Headquarters

Apostolic Christian Church Foundation, 1135 Sholey Rd., Richmond, VA 23231 Tel. (804)222-1943

Media Contact, James Hodges

Officers

Exec. Dir., James Hodges

The Apostolic Church in Canada

The Apostolic Church in Canada is affiliated with the worldwide organization of the Apostolic Church with headquarters in Great Britain. A product of the Welsh Revival (1904 to 1908), its Canadian beginnings originated in Nova Scotia in 1927. Today its main centers are in Nova Scotia, Ontario and Quebec. This church is evangelical, fundamental and Pentecostal, with special emphasis on the ministry gifts listed in Ephesians 4:11-12.

Headquarters

27 Castlefield Ave., Toronto, ON M4R 1G3

Media Contact, Pres., Rev. John Kristensen, 685 Park St. S., Peterborough, ON K9J 3S9 Tel. (705)742-1618

Website: www.apostolic.ca

Officers

Pres., Rev. John Kristensen, 685 Park St. S., Peterborough, ON K9J 3S9 Tel. (705)742-1618

Natl. Sec., Rev. J. Karl Thomas, 22 Malamute Cres., Scarborough, ON M1T 2C7 Tel. (416)298-0977

Periodicals

Canadian News Up-Date; The News Magazine of the Apostolic Church in Canada

Apostolic Church of Pentecost of Canada Inc.

This body was founded in 1921 at Winnipeg, Manitoba, by Pastor Frank Small. Doctrines include belief in eternal salvation by the grace of God, baptism of the Holy Spirit with the evidence of speaking in tongues, water baptism by immersion in the name of the Lord Jesus Christ.

Headquarters

#119-2340 Pegasus Way NE, Calgary, AB T2E 8M5

Email: acop@acop.ca

Website: www.acop.ca

Media Contact, Admn., Rev. Wes Mills, Tel. (403)273-5777, Fax (403)273-8102

Officers

Mod., Rev. G. Killam

Admin., Rev. Wes Mills

Mission Director, Rev. Brian Cooper

Periodicals

Fellowship Focus; Harvest Time

Armenian Evangelical Church

Founded in 1960 by immigrant Armenian evangelical families from the Middle East, this body is conservative doctrinally, with an evangelical, biblical emphasis. The polity of churches within the group differ with congregationalism being dominant, but there are presbyterian Armenian Evangelical churches as well. Most of the local churches have joined main-line denominations. All of the remaining Armenian Evangelical (congregational or presbyterian) local churches in the United States and Canada have joined with the Armenian Evangelical Union of North America.

Headquarters

Armenian Evangelical Church of Toronto, 2851 John St., P.O. Box 42015, Markham, ON L3R 5R0 Tel. (905)305-8144

Media Contact, Chief Editor, Rev. Yessayi Sarmazian

A.E.U.N.A. Officers

Min. to the Union, Rev. Karl Avakian, 1789 E. Frederick Ave., Fresno, CA 93720

Mod., Rev. Bernard Geulsgeugian

Officers

Min., Rev. Yessayi Sarmazian

Periodicals

Armenian Evangelical Church

Armenian Holy Apostolic Church—Canadian Diocese

The Canadian branch of the ancient Church of Armenia founded in A.D. 301 by St. Gregory the Illuminator was established in Canada at St. Catharines, Ontario, in 1930. The diocesan organization is under the jurisdiction of the Holy See of Etchmiadzin, Armenia. The Diocese has churches in St. Catharines, Hamilton, Toronto, Ottawa, Vancouver, Mississauga, Montreal, Laval, Windsor, Halifax, Winnipeg, Edmonton and Calgary.

Headquarters

Diocesan Offices, Primate, Canadian Diocese, Archbishop Hovnan Derderian, 615 Stuart Ave., Outremont, QC H2V 3H2 Tel. (514)276-9479, Fax (514)276-9960

Email: adiocese@ aol.com

Website: www.canarmdiocese.org

Media Contact, Exec. Dir., Arminé Keuchgerian; Silva Mangassarian, Secretary

Officers

Exec. Dir, Armine Keuchgerian

Sec., Silva Mangassarian

Webmaster, Garen Migirditzian

Associated Gospel Churches

The Associated Gospel Churches (AGC) traces its historical roots to the 1890s. To counteract the growth of liberal theology evident in many established denominations at this time, individuals and whole congregations seeking to uphold the final authority of the Scriptures in all matters of faith and conduct withdrew from those denominations and established churches with an evangelical ministry. These churches defended the belief that "all Scripture is given by inspiration of God" and also declared that the Holy Spirit gave the identical word of sacred writings of holy men of old, chosen by Him to be the channel of His revelation to man.

At first this growing group of independent churches was known as the Christian Workers' Churches of Canada, and by 1922 there was desire for forming an association for fellowship, counsel and cooperation. Several churches in southern Ontario banded together under the leadership of Dr. P. W. Philpott of Hamilton and Rev. H. E. Irwin, K. C. of Toronto.

When a new Dominion Charter was obtained on March 18, 1925, the name was changed to Associated Gospel Churches. Since that time the AGC has steadily grown, spreading across Canada by invitation to other independent churches of like faith and by actively beginning new churches.

Headquarters

3228 South Service Rd., Burlington, ON L7N 3H8 Tel. (905)634-8184, Fax (905)634-6283

Email: admin@agcofcanada.com

Website: www.agcofcanada.com

Media Contact, Rev. Tim Davis, c-o 3228 South Service Rd., Burlington, ON L7N 3H8 Tel. (905)634-8184, Fax (905)634-6283

Officers

Pres., Rev. A.F. (Bud) Penner, 3228 South Service Rd., Burlington, ON L7N 3H8 Tel. (905)634-8184 Fax (905)634-6283

Mod., Mrs. Debra Teakle, 2589 Noella Cres., Niagara Falls, ON L2J 3H7 Tel. (905)356-4767, Fax (same)

Sec.-Treas., Rev. Don Ralph, Box 3203, Stn. C, Hamilton, ON L8H 7K6 Tel. (905)549-4516

Association of Regular Baptist Churches (Canada)

The Association of Regular Baptist Churches was organized in 1957 by a group of churches for the purpose of mutual cooperation in missionary activities. The Association believes the Bible to be God's word, stands for historic Baptist principles, and opposes modern ecumenism.

Headquarters

17 Laverock St., Tottenham, ON L0G 1W0, Tel. 905-936-3786

Officers

Chmn., Rev. S. Kring, 67 Sovereen St., Delhi, ON N4B 1L7

Baptist Convention of Ontario and Quebec

The Baptist Convention of Ontario and Quebec is a family of 386 churches in Ontario and Quebec, united for mutual support and encouragement and united in missions in Canada and the world.

The Convention was formally organized in 1888. It has two educational institutions—McMaster Divinty College founded in 1887, and the Baptist Leadership Education Centre at Whitby. The Convention works through the all-Canada missionary agency, Canadian Baptist Ministries. The churches also support the Sharing Way, its relief and development arm of Canadian Baptist Ministries.

Headquarters

195 The West Mall, Ste. 414, Etobicoke, ON M9C 5K1 Tel. (416)622-8600, Fax (416)622-2308

Media Contact, Exec. Min., Dr. Ken Bellous

Officers

Pres., Rev. Ian Dixon

1st Vice-Pres., Mrs. Brenda Mann

2nd Vice-Pres., Mr. Roger Harris

Treas.-Bus. Admn., Nancy Bell

Exec. Min., Dr. Ken Bellous

Past Pres., Rev. Don Crisp

Periodicals

The Canadian Baptist

Baptist General Conference of Canada

The Baptist General Conference was founded in Canada by missionaries from the United States. Originally a Swedish body, BGC Canada now includes people of many nationalities and is conservative and evangelical in doctrine and practice.

Headquarters

4306-97 St. NW, Edmonton, AB T6E 5R9 Tel. (780)438-9127, Fax (780)435-2478

Media Contact, Exec. Dir., Rev. Abe Funk

Officers

Exec. Dir., Rev. Abe Funk, 4306-97 St. NW, Edmonton, AB T6E 5R9 Tel. (780)438-9127, Fax (780)435-2478

Exec. Dir., Gordon Sorensen, BGC Stewardship Foundation

DISTRICTS

Baptist Gen. Conf.- Central Canada,

Baptist General Conference in Alberta, Exec. Min., Dr. Cal Netterfield, 5011 122nd A St., Edmonton, AB T6H 3S8 Tel. (780)438-9126, Fax (780)438-5258

British Columbia Baptist Conference, Exec. Min., Rev. Walter W. Wieser, 7600 Glover Rd., Langley, BC V2Y 1Y1 Tel. (604)888-2246, Fax (604)888-0046

Baptist General Conf. in Saskatchewan,

Periodicals

BGC Conference Corner

Baptist Union of Western Canada

Headquarters

302,902-11 Ave., SW, Calgary, AB T2R 0E7

Media Contact, Exec. Min., Dr. Gerald Fisher

Officers

Pres., Mr. Bill Mains, 4576 Rainer Crescent, Prince George, BC V2K 1X4

Exec. Minister, Dr. Gerald Fisher, 302, 902-11 Ave SW, Calgary, AB T2R 0E7

Alberta Area Minister, Rev. Ed Dyck, 302, 902-11 Ave SW, Calgary, AB T2R 0E7

BC Area Minister, Dr. Paul Pearce, 201, 20349-88th Ave., Langely, BC V1M 2K5

SK-MB Area Minister, Dr. Robert Krahn, 414 Cowley Place, Saskatoon, SK S7N 3X2

Carey Theological College, Principal, Dr. Brian Stelck, 5920 Iona Dr., Vancouver, BC V6T 1J6

Baptist Resources Centre, 302, 902-11 Ave SW, Calgary, AB T2R 0E7

The Bible Holiness Movement

The Bible Holiness Movement, organized in 1949 as an outgrowth of the city mission work of the late Pastor William James Elijah Wakefield, an early-day Salvation Army officer, has been headed since its inception by his son, Evangelist Wesley H. Wakefield, its bishop-general.

It derives its emphasis on the original Methodist faith of salvation and scriptural holiness from the late Bishop R. C. Horner. It adheres to the common evangelical faith in the Bible, the Deity and the atonement of Christ. It stresses a personal experience of salvation for the repentant sinner, of being wholly sanctified for the believer and of the fullness of the Holy Spirit for effective witness.

Membership involves a life of Christian love and evangelistic and social activism. Members are required to totally abstain from liquor and tobacco. They may not attend popular amusements or join secret societies. Divorce and remarriage are forbidden. Similar to Wesley's Methodism, members are, under some circumstances, allowed to retain membership in other evangelical church fellowships. Interchurch affiliations are maintained with a number of Wesleyan-Arminian Holiness denominations.

Year-round evangelistic outreach is maintained through open-air meetings, visitation, literature and other media. Noninstitutional welfare work, including addiction counseling, is conducted among minorities. There is direct overseas famine relief, civil rights action, environment protection and antinuclearism. The movement sponsors a permanent committee on religious freedom and an active promotion of Christian racial equality.

The movement has a world outreach with branches in the United States, India, Nigeria, Philippines, Ghana, Liberia, Cameroon, Kenya, Zambia, South Korea, Mulawi, and Tanzania. It also ministers to 89 countries in 42 languages through literature, radio and audiocassettes.

Headquarters

Box 223, Postal Stn. A, Vancouver, BC V6C 2M3 Tel. (250)492-3376

Media Contact, Bishop-General, Evangelist Wesley H. Wakefield, P.O. Box 223, Postal Station A, Vancouver, BC V6C 2M3 Tel. (250)492-3376

DIRECTORS

Bishop-General, Evangelist Wesley H. Wakefield, (Intl. Leader)

Evangelist M. J. Wakefield, Penticton, BC

Pastor Vincente & Mirasal Hernando, Phillipines

Pastor & Mrs. Daniel Stinnett, 1425 Mountain View W., Phoenix, AZ 85021

Evangelist I. S. Udoh, Abak, Akwalbom, Nigeria, West Africa

Pastor Richard & Laura Wesley, Protem, Monrovia, Liberia

Pastor Choe Chong Dee, Cha Pa Puk, S. Korea

Pastor S. A. Samuel, Andra, India

Pastors Heinz and Catherine Speitelsbach, Sardis, BC V2R 3W2

Pastor and Mrs. Daniel Vandee, Ghana, W. Africa

Periodicals

Hallelujah!

Brethren in Christ Church, Canadian Conference

The Brethren in Christ, formerly known as Tunkers in Canada, arose out of a religious awakening in Lancaster County, Pennsylvania late in the 18th century. Representatives of the new denomination reached Ontario in 1788 and established the church in the southern part of the present province. Presently the conference has congregations in Ontario, Alberta, Quebec and Saskatchewan. In theology they have accents of the Pietist, Anabaptist, Wesleyan and Evangelical movements.

Headquarters

Brethren in Christ Church, Gen. Ofc., P.O. Box A, Grantham, PA 17027-0901 Tel. (717)697-2634, Fax (717)697-7714

Canadian Headquarters, Bishop's Ofc., 2619 Niagara Pkwy., Ft. Erie, ON L2A 5M4 Tel. (905)871-9991

Media Contact, Mod., Dr. Warren L. Hoffman, Brethren in Christ Church Gen. Ofc.

Officers

Mod., Bishop Darrell S. Winger, 2619 Niagara Pkwy., Ft. Erie, ON L2A 5M4 Tel. (905)871-9991

Sec., Betty Albrecht, RR 2, Petersburg, ON N0B 2H0

Periodicals

Evangelical Visitor; "Yes", Shalom

British Methodist Episcopal Church of Canada

The British Methodist Episcopal Church was organized in 1856 in Chatham, Ontario and incorporated in 1913. It has congregations across the Province of Ontario.

Headquarters

430 Grey Street, London, ON N6B 1H3 Tel.
Media Contact, Gen. Sec., Rev. Jacqueline Collins, 47 Connolly St., Toronto, ON M6N 4Y5 Tel. (416)653-6339

Officers

Gen. Supt., Rt. Rev. Dr. Douglas Birse, R.R. #5, Thamesville, ON N0P 2K0, Tel. (519)692-3628
Asst. Gen. Supt., Maurice M. Hicks, 3 Boxdene Ave., Scarborough, ON M1V 3C9 Tel. (416)298-5715
Gen. Sec., Rev. Jacqueline Collins, 47 Connolly St., Toronto, ON M6N 4Y5 Tel. (416)653-6339
Gen. Treas., Ms. Hazel Small, 7 Wood Fernway, North York, ON M2J 4P6, Tel. (416)491-0313

Periodicals

B.M.E. Church Newsletter

Canadian and American Reformed Churches

The Canadian and American Reformed Churches accept the Bible as the infallible Word of God, as summarized in The Belgic Confession of Faith (1561), The Heidelberg Cathechism (1563) and The Canons of Dordt (1618-1619). The federation was founded in Canada in 1950 and in the United States in 1955.

Headquarters

Synod, 607 Dynes Rd., Burlington, ON L7N 2V4
Canadian Reformed Churches, Ebenezer Canadian Reformed Church, 607 Dynes Rd., Burlington, ON L7N 2V4
Theological College, Dr. N. H. Gootjes, 110 W. 27th St., Hamilton, ON L9C 5A1 Tel. (905)575-3688, Fax (905)575-0799
Media Contact, Rev. G. Nederveen, 3089 Woodward Ave., Burlington, ON L7N 2M3 Tel. (905)681-7055, Fax (905)681-7055

Periodicals

Reformed Perspective, A Magazine for the Christian Family; Evangel, The Good News of Jesus Christ; Clarion, The Canadian Reformed Magazine; Diakonia-A Magazine of Office-Bearers; Book of Praise; Koinonia, A periodical of the Ministers of the CARC; Horizon, A quarterly magazine published by the League of CARC Women Societies; A Gift from Heaven, A Reformed Bible course.

Canadian Baptist Ministries

The Canadian Baptist Ministries has four federated member bodies, (1) Baptist Convention of Ontario and Quebec, (2) Baptist Union of Western Canada, (3) the United Baptist Convention of the Atlantic Provinces, (4) Union d'Églises Baptistes Françaises au Canada (French Baptist Union). Its main purpose is to act as a coordinating agency for the four groups for mission in all five continents.

Headquarters

7185 Millcreek Dr., Mississauga, ON L5N 5R4 Tel. (905)821-3533, Fax (905)826-3441
Website: www.cbmin.org
Media Contact, Communications, David Rogelstad
Email: daver@cbmin.org

Officers

Pres., Doug Coomas
Gen. Sec., Rev. Gart Nelson
Email: NelsonG@cbmin.org

Canadian Conference of Mennonite Brethren Churches

The conference was incorporated November 22, 1945.

Headquarters

3-169 Riverton Ave., Winnipeg, MB R2L 2E5 Tel. (204)669-6575, Fax (204)654-1865
Media Contact, Exec. Dir., Dave Wiebe

Officers

Mod., Jascha Boge, 261 Bonner Ave., Winnipeg, MB R2G 1B3 Tel. (204)663-1414
Asst. Mod., Ralph Gliege, Box 67, Hepburn, SK S0K 1Z0 Tel. (306)947-2030
Sec., Gerald Janzen, 32145 Austin Ave., Abbotsford, BC V2T 4P4

Periodicals

Mennonite Brethren Herald; Mennonitische Rundschau; IdeaBank; Le Lien; Expression; Chinese Herald

Canadian Convention of Southern Baptists

The Canadian Convention of Southern Baptists was formed at the Annual Meeting, May 7-9, 1985, in Kelowna, British Columbia. It was formerly known as the Canadian Baptist Conference, founded in Kamloops, British Columbia, in 1959 by pastors of existing churches.

Headquarters

Postal Box 300, Cochrane, AB T0L 0W0 Tel. (403)932-5688, Fax (403)932-4937
Email: office@ccsb.ca
Media Contact, Exec. Dir.-Treas., Rev.Gerald Taillon

Officers

Exec. Dir.-Treas., Gerald Taillon, 17 Riverview Close, Cochrane, AB T0L 0W4
Pres., Alan Braun, 334 Norton St., Penticton, BC V2A 4H7

Periodicals

The Baptist Horizon

Canadian District of the Moravian Church in America, Northern Province

The work in Canada is under the general oversight and rules of the Moravian Church, Northern

Province, general offices for which are located in Bethlehem, Pennsylvania. For complete information, see "Religious Bodies in the United States" section of the Yearbook.

Headquarters

1021 Center St., P.O. Box 1245, Bethlehem, PA 18016-1245

Media Contact, Rev. R. Burke Johnson

Officers

Pres., Mr. Graham Kerslake, 10910 Harvest Lake Way NE, Calgary, AB T3K 4L1 Tel (403)508-7765, Fax (403)226-2467

Periodicals

The Moravian

Canadian Evangelical Christian Churches

The Canadian Evangelical Christian Church is an international, full-gospel new apostolic denomination, emphasizing the New Testament apostolic paradigm pattern which recognizes the ministry gifts beyond the apostle, prophet, evangelist, pastor and teacher to spread the Gospel, according to Ephesians 4:11,12. The congregations are associated through full-gospel doctrine that is in combination with Calvinistic and Arminian beliefs. Each and every congregation is connected with CECC as congregational and ordination is supervised by National Office.

Headquarters

General Superintendent, Rev. David P. Lavigne, 410-125 Lincoln Rd., Waterloo, ON N2J 2N9, Tel. (519)725-5578 , Toll free (888)981-8881, Fax (519)725-5578

Email: cecc@globalserve.net

Website: www.cecconline.org & cetsonline.com

Officers

Gen. Supt., Rev. David P. Lavigne, 410-125 Lincoln Rd., Waterloo, ON N2J 2N9, Tel. (519)725-5578 , Toll free (888)981-8881, Fax (519)725-5578, cecc@globalserve.net

Exec. Dir., Rev. Otto Ferber, 139 Ste. Ann Ave., Box 237, St. Agatha, ON N0B 2L0, Tel. (519) 886-8809

Gen. Sec., Rev. Bill St. Pierre, Box 7, Oro, ON N3P 1B9, Tel. 888-297-5551

Canadian Yearly Meeting of the Religious Society of Friends

Canadian Yearly Meeting of the Religious Society of Friends was founded in Canada as an offshoot of the Quaker movement in Great Britain and colonial America. Genesee Yearly Meeting, founded 1834, Canada Yearly Meeting (Orthodox), founded in 1867, and Canada Yearly Meeting, founded in 1881, united in 1955 to form the Canadian Yearly Meeting. Canadian Yearly Meeting is affiliated with Friends United Meeting and Friends General Conference. It is also a member of Friends World Committee for Consultation.

Headquarters

91A Fourth Ave., Ottawa, ON K1S 2L1 Tel. (613)235-8553 or (613)296-3222, Fax (613) 235-1753

Email: cym@web.net

Media Contact, Gen. Sec.-Treas., —

Officers

Gen. Sec.-Treas., —

Clerk, Gale Wills

Archivist, Jane Zavitz Bond

Archives, Arthur G. Dorland, Pickering College, 389 Bayview St., Newmarket, ON L3Y 4X2 Tel. (416)895-1700

Periodicals

The Canadian Friend; Quaker Concern

Christ Catholic Church International

Christ Catholic Church International now has churches and/or missions in 17 countries spread over four continents. They are located in the United States, Canada, Norway, Sweden, Bolivia, Poland, England, Portugal, Bahamas, Belgium, Trinidad-Tobago, Germany, Viet Nam, Colombia, Paraguay, Australia and Croatia. Some countries have active churches and missions; some just missions and/or prayer groups. CCCI is an Orthodox-Catholic Communion tracing Apostolic Succession through the Old Catholic and Orthodox Catholic Churches.

The church ministers to a growing number of people seeking an experiential relationship with their Lord and Savior Jesus Christ in a Sacramental and Scripture based church. As one of the three founding members of FOCUS, Federation of Orthodox Catholic Churches United Sacramentally, CCCI is working to bring together Old and Orthodox Catholicism into one united church under the headship of Jesus Christ.

Headquarters

5165 Palmer Ave., P.O. Box 73, Niagara Falls, ON L2E 6S8 Tel. (905)354-2329, Fax (905)354-9934

Email: dwmullan@sympatico.ca

Website: www3.sympatico.ca/dwmullan

Media Contact, The Rt. Rev. John W. Brown, 1504-75 Queen St., Hamilton, ON L8R 3J3 Tel. (905)527-9089, Fax (905)354-9934, bishopjohn@primus.ca

Officers

PRESIDING ARCHBISHOP

The Most Rev. Donald Wm. Mullan, 6190 Barker St., Niagara Falls, ON L2G 1Y4, Tel. (905)354-2329, Fax (905)357-9934, dmullan1@home.com

ARCHBISHOPS

The Most Rev. Kyrillos Markskog, Skoldgatan 3 C, S-212 29 Malmo, Sweden, Tel. +040-930088, cyril@mbox301.swipnet.se

The Most Rev. Jose Ruben Garcia Matiz, Calle 52 Sur #24A-35-Bq. #1, Ap. 301, Santa Fe de

Bogota, D.C., Colombia, South America, Tel. 57-71447 87, jorugama@col1.telecom.com.co

BISHOPS

The Rt. Rev. Richard Blalack, 220 Cold Indian Springs Rd., Wayside, NJ 07712, Tel. (732) 542-1370, Fax (732)922-6430, rblalack@monmouth.com

The Rt. Rev. Curtis Bradley, 5567 E 97th Pl., Thornton, CO 80209, Tel. (303)451-0683, cbrad99@aol.com

The Rt. Rev. John Wm. Brown, 1504-75 Queen St., N. Hamilton, ON L8R 3J3, Tel. (905)522-6240, bishopjohn@primus.ca

The Rt. Rev. James Judd, 1624 Luella St. N., St. Paul, MN 55119-3017, Tel. (651)776-3172, jrjudd@aol.com

The Rt. Rev. Trond Hans Farner Kverno, Jarhaug, N-2750 Gran, Norway, Tel. 47-61-32-75-37, tkverno@online.no

The Rt. Rev. Gerard La Plante, 715 E 51st Ave., Vancouver, BC V5X 1E2 Tel. (604)327-1066, Fax (604)327-1066, oldcatholic@telus.ca

The Rt. Rev. Luis Fernando Hoyos Maldonado, A.A. 24378 Santa Fe de Bogota, D.C., Colombia, South America Tel. 57-276-68-16, jourgama@col1.telecom.com.co

The Rt. Rev. L.M. (Mac) McFerran, #206-6020 East Boulevard, Vancouver, BC, Tel. 604-261-2494

The Rt. Rev. Jose Moises Moncada Quevedo, A.A. 24378 Santa Fe de Bogota, D.C., Colombia, South America, Tel. 57-276-68-16, jourgama@col1.telecom.com.co

The Rt. Rev. Jerome Robben, PO Box 566, Chesterfield, MO 63006-0566, Tel. (314)205-8422, abbajn17@aol.com

The Rt. Rev. Andrzej J. Sarwa, ul. Krucza 16 27-600 Sandomierz, Poland, Tel.-Fax 084-(0-15) 833-21-41, andrzej-san@poczta.wp.pl

The Rt. Rev. Robert Smith, 824 Royal Oak Dr., Orlando, FL 32809, Tel (407)240-7833, yshwa@webtv.net

SEMINARY

St. Mary's Seminary, The Very Rev. Del Baier, 8287 Lamont, Niagara Falls, ON L2G 7L4 (offering on-site and correspondence programs)

The New Order of St. Francis, (Priests, Brothers and Sisters), Sec. General, Rev. Bro. Sean Ross, 5768 Summer St., Niagara Falls, ON L2G 1M2

Periodicals

St. Luke Magazine, The Franciscan

Christian Brethren (also known as Plymouth Brethren)

The Christian Brethren are a loose grouping of autonomous local churches, often called "assemblies." They are firmly committed to the inerrancy of Scripture and to evangelical doctrine of salvation by faith alone apart from works or sacrament. Characteristics and common elements are a weekly Breaking of Bread and freedom of ministry without a requirement of ordination. For their history, see "Religious Bodies in the United States" in the Directories section of this Yearbook.

CORRESPONDENT

Patrick Long, MSC Canada, 509-3950 14th Avenue, Markham, ON L3R 0A9, Tel (905)947-0468, Fax (905)947-0352

RELATED ORGANIZATIONS

Christian Brethren Church in the Province of Quebec, Exec. Sec., Marj Robbins, P.O. Box 1054, Sherbrooke, QC J1H 5L3 Tel. (819)820-1693 Fax (819)821-9287

MSC Canada, Administrator, William Yuille, 509-3950 14th Ave., Markham, ON L3R 0A9 Tel. (905)947-0468 Fax (905)947-0352

Vision Ministries Canada, Dir., Gord Martin, P.O. Box 28032, Waterloo, ON N2L 6J8 Tel. (519)725-1212 Fax (519)725-9421

Periodicals

News of Quebec

Christian Church (Disciples of Christ) in Canada

Disciples have been in Canada since 1810, and were organized nationally in 1922. This church served the Canadian context as a region of the whole Christian Church (Disciples of Christ) in the United States and Canada.

Headquarters

Christian Church in Canada, PO Box 23030, 417 Wellington St., St. Thomas, ON N5R 6A3, Tel. (519)633-9083, Fax (519)637-6407, ccic@ netrover.com

Media Contact, Reg. Min., F. Thomas Rutherford

Officers

Mod., Peter Fountain, PO Box 344, Milton, NS B0T 1P0, Tel. (902)354-5988, pjfountain@auracom.com

Reg. Min., F. Thomas Rutherford, PO Box 23030, 417 Wellington St., St. Thomas, ON N5R 6A3, Tel. (519)633-9083, Fax (519)637-6407, ccic@netrover.com

Periodicals

Canadian Disciple

Christian and Missionary Alliance in Canada

A Canadian movement, dedicated to the teaching of Jesus Christ the Saviour, Sanctifier, Healer and Coming King, commenced in Toronto in 1887 under the leadership of the Rev. John Salmon. Two years later, the movement united with The Christian Alliance of New York, founded by Rev. A. B. Simpson, becoming the Dominion Auxiliary of the Christian Alliance, Toronto, under the presidency of the Hon. William H. Howland. Its four founding branches were Toronto, Hamilton, Montreal, and Quebec. In 1980, the Christian and Missionary Alliance in Canada became autonomous. Its General Assembly is held every two years.

NATIONAL OFFICE

30 Carrier Dr, Suite 100, Toronto, ON M9W 5T7, Tel. (416)674-7878, Fax (416)674-0808
Email: nationaloffice@cmacan.org
Media Contact, Vice-Pres.-Advancement, David Freeman

Officers

Pres., Dr. Franklin Pyles, pyles@cmacan.org
Vice-Pres.-Personnel & Missions, Rev. Wallace C.E. Albrecht, albrechtw@cmacan.org
Vice-Pres.-Fin., Paul D. Lorimer, lorimer@cmacan.org
Vice-Pres.-Canadian Ministries, Rev. C. Stuart Lightbody, lightbodys@cmacan.org
Vice-Pres.-Advancement, Rev. David Freeman, freemand@cmacan.org
Chairman of the Board, Mr. Jake Bueckert
Secretary of the Board, Dr. T.V. Thomas

Periodicals

Alliance Life

Christian Reformed Church in North America

Canadian congregations of the Christian Reformed Church in North America have been formed since 1908. For detailed information about this denomination, please refer to the listing for the Christian Reformed Church in North America in Chapter 3, "Religious Bodies in the United States."

Headquarters

United States Office, 2850 Kalamazoo Ave., S.E., Grand Rapids, MI 49560 Tel. (616)224-0744, Fax (616)224-5895
Canadian Office, 3475 Mainway, P.O. Box 5070 STN LCR 1, Burlington, ON L7R 3Y8 Tel. (905)336-2920, Fax (905)336-8344
Website: www.crcna.org
Media Contact, Gen. Sec., Dr. David H. Engelhard, U.S. Office; Director of Communication, Mr. Henry Hess, Canadian Office

Officers

Gen. Sec., Dr. David H. Engelhard, U.S. Office
Exec. Dir.-Ministries, Dr. Peter Borgdorff, U.S.Office
Dir. of Fin.& Administration, Kenneth Horjus, U.S. Office

Periodicals

The Banner

Church of God (Anderson, Ind.)

This body is one of the largest of the groups which have taken the name "Church of God." Its headquarters are at Anderson, Indiana. It originated about 1880 and emphasizes Christian unity.

Headquarters

Western Canada Assembly, Chpsn., Hilda Nauenburg, 4717 56th St., Camrose, AB T4V 2C4 Tel. (780)672-0772, Fax (780)672-6888
Eastern Canada Assembly, Chpsn., Jim Wiebe, 38 James St., Dundas, ON L9H 2J6
Email: wcdncog@cable-lynx.net
Website: www.cable-lynx.net/~wcdncog
Media Contact for Western Canada, Church Service/Mission Coordinator, John D. Campbell, 4717 56th St., Camrose, AB T4V 2C4 Tel. (780)672-0772, Fax (780)672-6888

Periodicals

College News & Updates; The Gospel Contact; The Messenger

Church of God in Christ (Mennonite)

The Church of God in Christ, Mennonite was organized by the evangelist-reformer John Holdeman in Ohio. The church unites with the faith of the Waldenses, Anabaptists and other such groups throughout history. Emphasis is placed on obedience to the teachings of the Bible, including the doctrine of the new birth and spiritual life, noninvolvement in government or the military, a head-covering for women, beards for men and separation from the world shown by simplicity in clothing, homes, possessions and lifestyle. The church has a worldwide membership of about 18,300, largely concentrated in the United States and Canada.

Headquarters

P.O. Box 313, 420 N. Wedel Ave., Moundridge, KS 67107 Tel. (316)345-2532, Fax (316)345-2582
Media Contact, Dale Koehn, P.O.Box 230, Moundridge, KS 67107 Tel. (316)345-2532, Fax (316)345-2582

Periodicals

Messenger of Truth

Church of God (Cleveland, Tenn.)

It is one of America's oldest Pentecostal churches founded in 1886 as an outgrowth of the holiness revival under the name Christian Union. In 1907 the church adopted the organizational name Church of God. It has its foundation upon the principles of Christ as revealed in the Bible. The Church of God is Christian, Protestant, foundational in its doctrine, evangelical in practice and distinctively Pentecostal. It maintains a centralized form of government and a commitment to world evangelization.

The first church in Canada was extablished in 1919 in Scotland Farm, Manitoba. Paul H. Walker became the first overseer of Canada in 1931.

Headquarters

Intl. Offices, 2490 Keith St., NW, Cleveland, TN 37320 Tel. (423)472-3361, Fax (423)478-7066

Media Contact, Dir. of Communications, Michael L. Baker, P.O. Box 2430, Cleveland, TN 37320-2430 Tel. (423)478-7112, Fax (423)478-7066

EXECUTIVES

Genearl Overseer, Paul L. Walker

Assistant Genearl Overseers, R. Lamar Vest, G. Dennis McGuire, T.L. Lowery

Genearl Secretary-Treasurer, Bill F. Sheeks

Canada-Eastern, Rev. Canute Blake, P.O. Box 2036, Brampton, ON L6T 3TO Tel. (905)793-2213, Fax (905)793-9173

Canada-Western, Rev. Raymond W. Wall, Box 54055, 2640 52 St. NE, Calgary, AB T1Y 6S6 Tel. (403)293-8817, Fax (403)293-8832

Canada-Quebec-Maritimes, Rev. Jacques Houle, 19 Orly, Granby, QC J2H 1Y4 Tel. (514)378-4442, Fax (514)378-8646

Periodicals

Church of God Evangel, Editorial Evangelica

The Church of God of Prophecy in Canada

In the late 19th century, people seeking God's eternal plan as they followed the Reformation spirit began to delve further for scriptural light concerning Christ and his church. A small group of people emerged which dedicated and covenanted themselves to God and one another to be the Church of God. On June 13, 1903, A.J. Tomlinson joined them during a period of intense prayer and Bible study. Under Tomlinson's dynamic leadership, the church enjoyed tremendous growth.

In 1923 two churches emerged. Those that opposed Tomlinson's leadership are known today in Canada as the New Testament Church of God. Tomlinson's followers are called the Church of God of Prophecy.

In Canada, the first Church of God of Prophecy congregation was organized in Swan River, Manitoba, in 1937. Churches are now established in British Columbia, Manitoba, Alberta, Saskatchewan, Ontario, Quebec and all 50 states.

The church accepts the whole Bible rightly divided, with the New Testament as the rule of faith and practice, government and discipline. The membership upholds the Bible as the inspired Word of God and believes that its truths are known by the illumination of the Holy Spirit. The Trinity is recognized as one supreme God in three persons—Father, Son and Holy Ghost. It is believed that Jesus Christ, the virgin-born Son of God, lived a sinless life, fulfilled his ministry on earth, was crucified, resurrected and later ascended to the right hand of God. Believers now await Christ's return to earth and the establishment of the millenial kingdom.

Headquarters

World Headquarters, Bible Place, P.O. Box 2910, Cleveland, TN 37320-2910

National Office, Bishop Adrian L. Varlack, P.O. Box 457, Brampton, ON L6V 2L4 Tel. (905)843-2379, Fax (905)843-3990

Media Contact, Bishop Mirriam Bailey, P.O. Box 457, Brampton, ON L6V 2L4 Tel. (905)843-2379, Fax (905)843-3990

Officers

Pres., Bishop Adrian L. Varlack

V. Pres & Sec., Aston R. Morrison

Asst. Sec. & Treas., Mirriam Bailey

Periodicals

Canada Update

The Church of Jesus Christ of Latter-day Saints in Canada

The Church has had a presence in Canada since the early 1830's. Joseph Smith and Brigham Young both came to Eastern Canada as missionaries. There are now 157,000 members in Canada in more than 400 congregations.

Leading the Church in Canada are the presidents of over 40 stakes (equivalent to a diocese). World headquarters is in Salt Lake City, UT (See U.S. Religious Bodies chapter of the Directories section of this Yearbook).

Headquarters

50 East North Temple St., Salt Lake City, UT 84150

Media Contact, Public Affairs Dir., Bruce Smith, 1185 Eglinton Ave., Box 116, North York, ON M3C 3C6 Tel. (416)431-7891, Fax (416)438-2723

Church of the Lutheran Brethren

The Church of the Lutheran Brethren of America was organized in December 1900. Five independent Lutheran congregations met together in Milwaukee, Wisconsin, and adopted a constitution patterned very closely to that of the Lutheran Free Church of Norway.

The spiritual awakening in the Midwest during the 1890s crystallized into convictions that led to the formation of a new church body. Chief among the concerns were church membership practices, observance of Holy Communion, confirmation practices and local church government. The Church of the Lutheran Brethren practices a simple order of worship with the sermon as the primary part of the worship service. It believes that personal profession of faith is the primary criterion for membership in the congregation. The Communion service is reserved for those who profess faith in Christ as savior. Each congregation is autonomous and the synod serves the congregations in advisory and cooperative capacities.

The synod supports a world mission program in Cameroon, Chad, Japan and Taiwan. Approximately 40 percent of the synodical budget is earmarked for world missions. A growing home mission ministry is planting new congregations in the United States and Canada. Affiliate organizations operate several retirement-nursing homes, conference and retreat centers.

Headquarters

1020 Alcott Ave., W., P.O. Box 655, Fergus Falls, MN 56538 Tel. (218)739-3336, Fax (218)739-5514

Email: rmo@clba.org

Website: www.clba.org

Media Contact, Rev. Brent Juliot

Officers

Pres., Rev. Arthur Berge, 72 Midridge Close SE, Calgary, AB T2X 1G1

Vice-Pres., Rev. Luther Stenberg, PO Box 75, Hagen, SK S0J 1B0

Sec., Mr. Alvin Herman, 3105 Taylor Street E., Saskatoon, SK S7H 1H5

Treas., Edwin Rundbraaten, Box 739, Birch Hills, SK S0J 0G0

Youth Coord., Rev. Harold Rust, 2617 Preston Ave. S., Saskatoon, SK S7J 2G3

Periodicals

Faith and Fellowship

Church of the Nazarene in Canada

The first Church of the Nazarene in Canada was organized in November, 1902, by Dr. H. F. Reynolds. It was in Oxford, Nova Scotia. The Church of the Nazarene is Wesleyan Arminian in theology, representative in church government and warmly evangelistic.

Headquarters

20 Regan Rd., Unit 9, Brampton, ON L7A 1C3 Tel. (905)846-4220, Fax (905)846-1775

Email: nazerene@interlog.com

Website:web.1-888.com.nazarene/national/

Media Contact, Gen. Sec., Dr. Jack Stone, 6401 The Paseo, Kansas City, MO 64131 Tel. (816) 333-7000, Fax (816)822-9071

Officers

Natl. Dir., Dr. William E. Stewart, 20 Regan Rd. Unit 9, Brampton, ON L7A 1C3 Tel. (905) 846-4220, Fax (905)846-1775

Exec. Asst., John T. Martin, 20 Regan Rd. Unit 9, Brampton, ON L7A 1C3 Tel. (905)846-4220, Fax (905)846-1775

Chmn., Rev. Wesley G. Campbell, #205, 1255 56th St., Delta, BC V4L 2B9

Vice-Chmn., Rev. Ronald G. Fry, 1280 Finch Ave. W. Ste. 416, North York, ON M3J 3K6

Sec., Rev. Larry Dahl, 14320 94th St., Edmonton, AL T5E 3W2

Churches of Christ in Canada

Churches of Christ are autonomous congregations, whose members appeal to the Bible alone to determine matters of faith and practice. There are no central offices or officers. Publications and institutions related to the churches are either under local congregational control or independent of any one congregation.

Churches of Christ shared a common fellowship in the 19th century with the Christian Churches-Churches of Christ and the Christian Church (Disciples of Christ). Fellowship was broken after the introduction of instrumental music in worship and centralization of church-wide activities through a missionary society. Churches of Christ began in Canada soon after 1800, largely in the middle provinces. The few pioneer congregations were greatly strengthened in the mid-1800s, growing in size and number.

Members of Churches of Christ believe in the inspiration of the Scriptures, the divinity of Jesus Christ, and immersion into Christ for the remission of sins. The New Testament pattern is followed in worship and church organization.

Headquarters

Media Contact, Man. Ed., Gospel Herald, Eugene C. Perry, 4904 King St., Beansville, ON L0R 1B6 Tel. (905)563-7503, Fax (905) 563-7503

Email: eperry9953@aol.com

Periodicals

Gospel Herald; Sister Triangle

Congregational Christian Churches in Canada

This body originated in the early 18th century when devout Christians within several denominations in the northern and eastern United States, dissatisfied with sectarian controversy, broke away from their own denominations and took the simple title "Christians." First organized in 1821 at Keswick, Ontario, the Congregational Christian Churches in Canada was incorporated on Dec. 4, 1989, as a national organization. In doctrine the body is evangelical, being governed by the Bible as the final authority in faith and practice. It believes that Christian character must be expressed in daily living; it aims at the unity of all true believers in Christ that others may believe in Him and be saved. In church polity, the body is democratic and autonomous. It is also a member of The World Evangelical Congregational Fellowship.

Headquarters

241 Dunsdon St. Ste. 405, Brantford, ON N3R 7C3 Tel. (519)751-0606, Fax (519)751-0852

Media Contact, Past Pres., Jim Potter, 8 Church St., Waldemar, ON L0N 1G0 Tel. (519)928-5561

Officers

Pres., Rev. Michael Shute

Exec. Dir., Rev. Bruce Robertson

Sec., Rev. Ron Holden

The Coptic Orthodox Church in Canada

The Coptic Orthodox Church in North America was begun in Canada in 1964 and was registered in the province of Ontario in 1965. The Coptic Orthodox Church has spread rapidly since then. The total number of local churches in both Canada and the USA exceeded one hundred. Two dioceses, a monastery with a bishop, monks and novices, and two theological seminaries were established in the USA.

The Coptic Orthodox Church is the church of Alexandria founded in Egypt by St. Mark the Apostle in the first century A.D. She is a hierarchical church and the administrative governing body of each local church is an elected Board of Deacons approved by the Bishop. The current patriarch of the church is H. H. Pope Shenouda III, Pope of Alexandria and Patriach of the see of St. Mark. The Coptic Orthodox Church is a member of the Canadian Council of Churches.

Headquarters

St. Mark's Coptic Orthodox Church, 41 Glendinning Ave., Scarborough, ON M1W 3E2 Tel. (416)494-4449, Fax (416)494-2631, Email: mail@coptorthodox.ca, Website www.stmark. toronto.on.coptorthodox.ca

Media Contact, Fr. Ammonius Guirguis, Tel. (416)494-4449, Fax (416)494-2631, frammonius@coptorthodox.ca

Elim Fellowship of Evangelical Churches and Ministers

The Elim Fellowship of Evangelical Churches and Ministers, a Pentecostal body, was established in 1984 as a sister organization of Elim Fellowship in the United States.

This is an association of churches, ministers and missionaries seeking to serve the whole body of Christ. It is Pentecostal and has a charismatic orientation.

Headquarters

379 Golf Road, RR#6, Brantford, ON N3T 5L8, Tel. (519)753-7266, Fax (519)753-5887

Email: elim@bfree.on.ca

Website: Bfree.ON.ca/comdir/churchs/elim

Ofc. Mgr., Larry Jones

Officers

Pres., Errol Alchin

Vice-Pres., John Woods, 3G Crestlea Cres. Nepean, ON N2G 4N1

Sec., Howard Ellis, 102 Ripley Cres., Kitchener, ON N2N 1V4

Treas., Aubrey Phillips, P.O. Box 208, Blairsville, GA 30512

President Emeritus, Carlton Spencer

COUNCIL OF ELDERS

Errol Alchin, Tel. (519)753-7266

Howard Ellis, Tel. (519)579-9844

Claude Favreau (819)477-7421

Aubrey Phillips, Tel. (706)745-2473

John Woods, Tel. (613)228-1796

Bernard Evans, Tel. (716)528-2790

Howard Ellis

The Estonian Evangelical Lutheran Church Abroad

The Estonian Evangelical Lutheran Church (EELC) was founded in 1917 in Estonia and reorganized in Sweden in 1944. The teachings of the EELC are based on the Old and New Testaments, explained through the Apostolic, Nicean and Athanasian confessions, the unaltered Confession of Augsburg and other teachings found in the Book of Concord.

Headquarters

383 Jarvis St., Toronto, ON M5B 2C7 Tel. (416)925-5465, Fax (416)925-5688

Media Contact, Archbishop, Rev. Udo Petersoo

Email: udo.petersoo@eelk.ee

Website: www.eelk.ee/~e.e.l.k./

Officers

Archbishop, The Rev. Udo Petersoo

Gen. Sec., Mr. Ivar Nippak

Periodicals

Eesti Kirik

The Evangelical Covenant Church of Canada

A Canadian denomination organized in Canada at Winnipeg in 1904 which is affiliated with the Evangelical Covenant Church of America and with the International Federation of Free Evangelical Churches, which includes 31 federations in 26 countries.

This body believes in the one triune God as confessed in the Apostles' Creed, that salvation is received through faith in Christ as Saviour, that the Bible is the authoritative guide in all matters of faith and practice. Christian Baptism and the Lord's Supper are accepted as divinely ordained sacraments of the church. As descendants of the 19th century northern European pietistic awakening, the group believes in the need of a personal experience of commitment to Christ, the development of a virtuous life and the urgency of spreading the gospel to the "ends of the world."

Headquarters

2791 Pembina Highway, Winnipeg, MB R3T 2H5

Media Contact, Supt., Jeff Anderson

Officers

Supt., Rev. Jerome W. Johnson

Chpsn., Les Doell, RR 2, Wetaskiwin, AB T9A 1W9

Sec., Lori Koop, 6568 Claytonwood Pl., Surrey, BC V3S 7T5

Treas., Rod Johnson, Box 196, Norquay, SK S0A 2V0

Periodicals

The Covenant Messenger

Evangelical Free Church of Canada

The Evangelical Free Church of Canada traces its beginning back to 1917 when the church in

Enchant, Alberta opened its doors. Today the denomination has 151 churches from the West Coast to Quebec. Approximately 58 missionaries are sponsored by the EFCC in 10 countries. The Evangelical Free Church is the founding denomination of Trinity Western University in Langley, British Columbia. Church membership is 7,690, average attendance is 17,823.

Headquarters

Mailing Address, P.O. Box 850 LCD1, Langley, BC V3A 8S6 Tel. (604)888-8668, Fax (604)888-3108

Location, 7600 Glover Rd., Langley, BC

Email: efcc@twu.ca

Website: www.twu.ca/efcc/efcc.htm

Media Contact, Exec. Sec., Carol Jones, P.O. Box 850 LCD1, Langley, BC V3A 8S6 Tel. (604)888-8668, Fax (604)888-3108

Officers

Board Chairman, Rev. William Dyck, Box 170, Fosston, SK, S0E 0V0, efcc@twu.ca

Periodicals

The Pulse

Evangelical Lutheran Church in Canada

The Evangelical Lutheran Church in Canada was organized in 1985 through a merger of The Evangelical Lutheran Church of Canada (ELCC) and the Lutheran Church in America-Canada Section.

The merger is a result of an invitation issued in 1972 by the ELCC to the Lutheran Church in America-Canada Section and the Lutheran Church-Canada. Three-way merger discussions took place until 1978 when it was decided that only a two-way merger was possible. The ELCC was the Canada District of the ALC until autonomy in 1967.

The Lutheran Church in Canada traces its history back more than 200 years. Congregations were organized by German Lutherans in Halifax and Lunenburg County in Nova Scotia in 1749. German Lutherans, including many United Empire Loyalists, also settled in large numbers along the St. Lawrence and in Upper Canada. In the late 19th century, immigrants arrived from Scandinavia, Germany and central European countries, many via the United States. The Lutheran synods in the United States have provided the pastoral support and help for the Canadian church.

Headquarters

302-393 Portage Avenue, Winnipeg, MB R3B 3H6 Tel. (204)984-9150, Fax (204)984-9185

Media Contact, Bishop, Rev. Telmor G. Sartison

Officers

Bishop, Rev. Telmor G. Sartison

Vice-Pres., Janet Morley

Sec., Mr. Robert H. Granke

Treas., Doreen Lecuyer

ASSISTANTS TO THE BISHOPS

Rev. Cynthia Halmarson

Rev. Richard Stetson

DIVISIONS AND OFFICES

Evangelical Lutheran Women, Pres., Lindy Wozniak

Exec. Dir., Ruth Vince

SYNODS

Alberta and the Territories, Bishop, Rev. Stephen P. Kristenson, 10014-81 Ave., Edmonton, AB T6E 1W8 Tel. (403)439-2636, Fax (403)433-6623

Eastern, Bishop, Rev. Michael J. Pryse, 50 Queen St. N., Kitchener, ON N2H 6P4 Tel. (519)743-1461, Fax (519)743-4291

British Columbia, Bishop, Rev. Raymond L. Schultz, 80-10th Ave., E., New Westminster, BC V3L 4R5 Tel. (604)524-1318, Fax (604)524-9255

Manitoba-Northwestern Ontario, Bishop, Rev. Richard M. Smith, 201-3657 Roblin Blvd., Winnipeg, MB R3G 0E2 Tel. (204)889-3760, Fax (204)869-0272

Saskatchewan, Bishop, Rev. Allan A. Grundahl, 601 Spadina Cres. E., Saskatoon, SK S7K 3G8 Tel. (306)244-2474, Fax (306)664-8677

Periodicals

Canada Lutheran; Esprit

The Evangelical Mennonite Conference

The Evangelical Mennonite Conference is a modern church of historic Christian convictions, tracing its indebtedness to the Radical Reformation, which, in turn, is rooted in the Protestant Reformation of the 16th century. The center of faith, and of Scripture, is found in Jesus Christ as Saviour and Lord.

The church's name was chosen in 1959. It's original name, Kleine Gemeinde, which means "small church", reflected its origins as a renewal movement among Mennonites in southern Russia. Klaas Reimer, a minister, was concerned about a decline of spiritual life and discipline in the church, and inappropriate involvement in the Napoleanic War. About 1812, Reimer and others began separate worship services, and two years later were organized as a small group.

Facing increasing government pressure, particularly about military service, the group migrated to North America in 1874 to 1875. Fifty families settled in Manitoba and 36 in Nebraska. Ties between the groups weakened and eventually the U.S. group gave up its KG identity. The KG survived several schisms and migrations, dating from its years in Russia through the 1940s.

As an evangelical church, The Evangelical Mennonite Conference holds that Scripture has final authority in faith and practice, a belief in Christ's finished work, and that assurance of salvation is possible. As Mennonite, the denomination has a commitment to discipleship, baptism upon confession of faith, community, social concern, non-violence and the Great Commission. As a conference, it seeks to encourage local churches, to work together on evangelism and matters of social concern, and relates increasingly well to other denominations.

In the year 2000 its membership surpassed 7000, with many more people as treasured adherents and a wider circle of ministry influence. Membership is for people baptized on confession of faith (usually in adolescence or older). Children are considered safe in Christ until they reach an age where they are accountable for their own spiritual decision and opt out; they are considered part of the church, while full inclusion occurs upon personal choice.

The Conference has 53 churches from British Columbia to Ontario (33 in Manitoba) and roughly 135 mission workers in 25 countries. The cultural make-up of the Conference is increasingly diverse, though its Dutch-German background remains dominant nationally. Ten churches have pastors or leaders who are of non-Dutch-German background.

Some churches have a multiple leadership pattern (ministers and deacons can be selected from within the congregation); others have new patterns. Most churches support their leading minister full time. Its church governance moved from a bishop system to greater local congregational autonomy. It currently functions as a conference of churches with national boards, a conference council, and a moderator.

Woman can serve on most national boards, as conference council delegates, as missionaries, and within a wide range of local church activities; while they can be selected locally, they cannot currently serve as nationally recognized or commissioned ministers.

It is a supporting member of Mennonite Central Committee and the Evangelical Fellowship of Canada. About 80 percent of its national budget goes toward mission work in Canada and other countries.

Headquarters

Box 1268, 440 Main St., Steinbach, MB R0A 2A0 Tel. (204)326-6401, Fax (204)326-1613

Email: emconf@mts.net

Media Contact, Conf. Pastor, John Koop

Officers

Acting Conf. Mod., Harvey Plett

General Sec., Len Barkman

Conference Pastor, David Thiessen

Bd. of Missions, Exec. Sec., Henry Klassen

Bd. of Missions, Foreign Sec., Lester Olfert

Bd. of Church Ministries, Exec. Sec.-Editor, Terry M. Smith

Canadian Sec., Conf. Pastor, John Koop

Conference Youth Minister, Gerald Reimer

Periodicals

The Messenger

Evangelical Mennonite Mission Conference

This group was founded in 1936 as the Rudnerweider Mennonite Church in Southern Manitoba and organized as the Evangelical Mennonite Mission Conference in 1959. It was incorporated in 1962. The Annual Conference meeting is held in July.

Headquarters

Box 52059, Niakwa P.O., Winnipeg, MB R2M 5P9 Tel. (204)253-7929, Fax (204)256-7384

Email: emmc@mb.sympatico.ca

Media Contact, John Bergman, Box 206, Niverville, MB R0A 1E0 Tel. (204)388-4775, Fax (204)388-4775

Email: jbergman@mb.sympatico.ca

Officers

Mod., David Penner, 906-300 Sherk St., Leamington, ON N8H 4N7

Vice-Mod., Carl Zacharias, R.R. 1, Box 205, Winkler, MB R6W 4A1

Sec., Darrell Dyck, R.R. 1, Box 186, Winkler, MB R6W 4A1

Dir. of Conference Ministries, Jack Heppner

Dir. of Missions, Rev. Leonard Sawatzky

Business Admin., Henry Thiessen

OTHER ORGANIZATIONS

The Gospel Message, Box 1622, Saskatoon, SK S7K 3R8 Tel. (306)242-5001, Fax (306)242-6115; 210-401-33rd St. W., Saskatoon, SK S7L 0V5 Tel. (306)242-5001

Radio Pastor, Rev. Ed Martens

Periodicals

EMMC Recorder

The Evangelical Missionary Church of Canada

This denomination was formed in 1993 with the merger of The Evangelical Church of Canada and The Missionary Church of Canada. The Evangelical Missionary Church of Canada maintains fraternal relations with the worldwide body of the Missionary Church, Inc. and with the Evangelical Church of North America.The Evangelical Church of Canada was among those North American Evangelical United Brethern Conferences which did not join the EUB in merging with the Methodist Church in 1968. The Missionary Church of Canada is Anabaptist in heritage. Its practices and theology were shaped by the Holiness Revivals of the late 1800s. The Evangelical Missionary Church consists of 135 churches in two conferences in Canada.

Headquarters

4031 Brentwood Rd., NW, Calgary, AB T2L 1L1 Tel. (403)250-2759, Fax (403)291-4720

Media Contact, Exec. Dir., Missions and Administration, G. Keith Elliott

Email: evanmiss@emcc.ca

Officers

Pres., Rev. Mark Bolender, 1280 Ottawa St. S., Kitchener, ON N2E 1M1 Tel. (519)578-7275, Fax (519)578-7472

Canada East District, Dist. Supt., Rev. Phil Delsaut, 130 Fergus Ave., Kitchener, ON N2A 2H2 Tel. (519)894-9800

Canada West District, Dist. Supt., Rev. Walter Erion, 4031 Brentwood Rd., NW, Calgary, AB T2L 1L1 Tel. (403)250-2759, Fax (403)291-4720

The Fellowship of Evangelical Baptist Churches in Canada

This organization was founded in 1953 by the merging of the Union of Regular Baptist Churches of Ontario and Quebec with the Fellowship of Independent Baptist Churches of Canada.

Headquarters

679 Southgate Dr., Guelph, ON N1G 4S2 Tel. (519)821-4830, Fax (519)821-9829

Media Contact, Pres., Rev. Terry D. Cuthbert

Email: president@fellowship.ca

Officers

Pres., Rev. Terry D. Cuthbert

Chmn., Rev. James A. Reese

Periodicals

B.C. Fellowship Baptist; The Evangelical Baptist; Intercom

Foursquare Gospel Church of Canada

The Western Canada District was formed in 1964 with the Rev. Roy Hicks as supervisor. Prior to 1964 it had been a part of the Northwest District of the International Church of the Foursquare Gospel with headquarters in Los Angeles, California.

A Provincial Society, the Church of the Foursquare Gospel of Western Canada, was formed in 1976; a Federal corporation, the Foursquare Gospel Church of Canada, was incorporated in 1981 and a national church formed. The provincial society was closed in 1994.

Headquarters

#100 8459 160th St., Surrey, BC V3S 3T9

Email: fgcc@canada.com

Media Contact, Pres. & Gen. Supervisor, Timothy J. Peterson, #100-8459 160th St., Surrey, BC V4N 1B4 Tel. (604)543-8414, Fax (604)543-8417

Officers

Pres. & Gen. Supervisor, Timothy J. Peterson

Periodicals

VIP Communique

Free Methodist Church in Canada

The Free Methodist Church was founded in New York in 1860 and expanded in 1880. It is Methodist in doctrine, evangelical in ministry and emphasizes the teaching of holiness of life through faith in Jesus Christ.

The Free Methodist Church in Canada was incorporated in 1927 after the establishment of a Canadian Executive Board. In 1959 the Holiness Movement Church merged with the Free Methodist Church. Full autonomy for the Canadian church was realized in 1990 with the formation of a Canadian General Conference. Mississauga, Ontario, continues to be the location of the Canadian Headquarters.

The Free Methodist Church ministers in 50 countries through its World Ministries Center in Indianapolis, Indiana.

Headquarters

4315 Village Centre Ct., Mississauga, ON L4Z 1S2 Tel. (905)848-2600, Fax (905)848-2603

Email: ministrycentre@fmc-canada.org

Website: www.fmc-canada.org

Media Contact, Mary-Elsie Wolfe

Officers

Bishop, Rev. Keith Elford

Dir. of Admn. Ser., Norman Bull

Dir. of Ministry Advancement, Rev. Mary-Elsie Wolfe

Supt., Personnel, Rev. Alan Retzman

Supt., Growth Ministries, Rev. Dr. Ron Bonar

Periodicals

The Free Methodist Herald

Free Will Baptists

As revival fires burned throughout New England in the mid- and late 1700s, Benjamin Randall proclaimed his doctrine of Free Will to large crowds of seekers. In due time, a number of Randall's converts moved to Nova Scotia. One such believer was Asa McGray, who was to become instrumental in the establishment of several Free Baptist churches. Local congregations were organized in New Brunswick. After several years of numerical and geographic gains, disagreements surfaced over the question of music, Sunday school, church offerings, salaried clergy and other issues. Adherents of the more progressive element decided to form their own fellowship. Led by George Orser, they became known as Free Christian Baptists.

The new group faithfully adhered to the truths and doctrines which embodied the theological basis of Free Will Baptists. Largely through Archibald Hatfield, contact was made with Free Will Baptists in the United States in the 1960s. The association was officially welcomed into the Free Will Baptist family in July 1981, by the National Association.

Headquarters

5233 Mt. View Rd., Antioch, TN 37013-2306 Tel. (615)731-6812, Fax (615)731-0771

Media Contact, Mod., Dwayne Broad, RR 3, Bath, NB E0J 1E0 Tel. (506)278-3771

Officers

Mod., Dwayne Broad
Promotional Officer, Dwayne Broad

General Church of the New Jerusalem

The Church of the New Jerusalem, also called The New Church, is a Christian Church founded on the Bible and the Writings of Emanuel Swedenborg (1688-1772). These Writings were first brought to Ontario in 1835 by Christian Enslin.

Headquarters

c/o Olivet Church, 279 Burnhamthorpe Rd., Etobicoke, ON M9B 1Z6 Tel. (416)239-3054, Fax (416)239-4935
Email: Mgladish@interlog.com
Website: www.newchurch.org
Media Contact, Exec. Vice-Pres., Rev. Michael D. Gladish

Officers

Pres., Rt. Rev. P. M. Buss, Bryn Athyn, PA 19009
Exec. Vice-Pres., Rev. Michael D. Gladish
Sec., Carolyn Bellinger, 110 Chapel Hill Dr., Kitchener, ON N2G 3W5
Treas., James Bellinger, 2 Shaver Court, Etobicoke, ON M9B 4P5

Periodicals

New Church Canadian

Greek Orthodox Metropolis of Toronto (Canada)

Greek Orthodox Christians in Canada are under the jurisdiction of the Ecumenical Patriarchate of Constantinople (Istanbul).

Headquarters

86 Overlea Blvd., Toronto, ON M4H 1C6 Tel. (416)429-5757, Fax (416)429-4588
Email: gocanada@total.net
Media Contact, Orthodox Way Committee

Officers

Metropolitan Archbishop of the Metropolis of Toronto (Canada), His Eminence Metropolitan Archbishop Sotirios

Periodicals

Orthodox Way

Independent Assemblies of God International (Canada)

This fellowship of churches has been operating in Canada for over 52 years. It is a branch of the Pentecostal Church in Sweden. Each church within the fellowship is completely independent.

Headquarters

1211 Lancaster St., London, ON N5V 2L4 Tel. (519)451-1751, Fax (519)453-3258
Media Contact, Gen. Sec., Rev. Harry Wuerch
Email: jwuerch@odyssey.on.ca

Officers

Gen. Sec., Rev. Harry Wuerch
Treas., Rev. David Ellyatt, 1795 Parkhurst Ave., London, ON N5V 2C4
Email: david.ellyatt@odyssey.on.ca

Periodicals

The Mantle

Independent Holiness Church

The former Holiness Movement of Canada merged with the Free Methodist Church in 1958. Some churches remained independent of this merger and they formed the Independent Holiness Church in 1960, in Kingston, Ontario. The doctrines are Methodist and Wesleyan. The General Conference is every three years, next meeting in 2004.

Headquarters

Rev. R. E. Votary, 1564 John Quinn Rd., R.R.1, Greely, ON K4P 1J9 Tel. (613)821-2237
Media Contact, Gen. Sec., Dwayne Reaney, 5025 River Rd. RR #1, Manotick, ON K4M 1B2 Tel. (613)692-3237

Officers

Gen. Supt., Rev. R. E. Votary, 1564 John Quinn Rd., Greeley, ON K4P 1J9
Gen. Sec., Dwayne Reaney
Additional Officers, E. Brown, 104-610 Pesehudoff Cresc., Saskatoon, SK S7N 4H5; D. Wallace, 1456 John Quinn Rd., R#1, Greely, ON K4P 1J9

Periodicals

Gospel Tidings

The Italian Pentecostal Church of Canada

This body had its beginnings in Hamilton, Ontario, in 1912 when a few people of an Italian Presbyterian Church banded themselves together for prayer and received a Pentecostal experience of the baptism in the Holy Spirit. Since 1912, there has been a close association with the teachings and practices of the Pentecostal Assemblies of Canada.

The work spread to Toronto, then to Montreal, where it also flourished. In 1959, the church was incorporated in the province of Quebec. The early leaders of this body were the Rev. Luigi Ippolito and the Rev. Ferdinand Zaffuto. The churches carry on their ministry in both the English and Italian languages.

Headquarters

6724 Fabre St., Montreal, QC H2G 2Z6 Tel. (514)593-1944, Fax (514)593-1835
Media Contact, Gen. Sec., Rev. John DellaForesta, 12216 Pierre Baillargeon, Montreal, QC H1E 6K1 Tel. (514)494-6969

Officers

Gen. Supt., Rev. Daniel Ippolito, 46 George Anderson Dr., Toronto, ON M6M 2Y8 Tel. (416)244-4005, Fax (416)244-0381

Gen. Sec., Rev. John DellaForesta, 12216 Pierre Baillargeon, Montreal, QC H1E 6K1
Tel. (514)494-6969
Gen. Treas., Rev. David Mortelliti, 6724 Fabre St., Montreal, QC H2G 2Z6 Tel. (514)593-1944, Fax (514)593-1835
Overseer, Rev. Mario Spiridigliozzi, 23 Wildwood Dr., Port Moody, BC V3H 4M4 Tel. (604)469-0788
Overseer, Rev. Tom Ciccarella, 1235 Minto Ave., LaSalle, ON N9J 3H0 Tel. (519)734-1340

Periodicals

Voce Evangelica-Evangel Voice

Jehovah's Witnesses

For details on Jehovah's Witnesses see "Religious Bodies in United States" in this edition of the Yearbook.

Headquarters

25 Columbia Heights, Brooklyn, NY 11201-2483 Tel. (718)560-5600, Fax (718)560-5619
Canadian Branch Office, Box 4100, Halton Hills, ON L7G 4Y4
Media Contact, Director, Public Affairs Office, James N. Pellechia
Media Contact, Public Affairs Office in Canada, Dennis Charland

Lutheran Church-Canada

Lutheran Church-Canada was established in 1959 at Edmonton, Alberta, as a federation of Canadian districts of the Lutheran Church - Missouri Synod; it was constituted in 1988 at Winnipeg, Manitoba, as an autonomous church.

The church confesses the Bible as both inspired and infallible, the only source and norm of doctrine and life and subscribes without reservation to the Lutheran Confessions as contained in the Book of Concord of 1580.

Headquarters

3074 Portage Ave., Winnipeg, MB R3K 0Y2 Tel. (204)895-3433, Fax (204)897-4319, info@lutheranchurch.ca
Media Contact, Dir. of Comm., Ian Adnams, communications@lutheranchurch.ca

Officers

Pres., Rev. Ralph Mayan, 3074 Portage Ave., Winnipeg, MB R3K 0Y2, president@lutheranchurch.ca
Vice-Pres., Rev. Dennis Putzman, 24 Valencia Dr., St. Catharines, ON L2T 3X8
2nd Vice-Pres., Rev. Daniel Rinderknecht, Box 1 Site 11 R.R. 4, Stony Plain, AB T7Z 1X4
3rd Vice-Pres., Rev. James Fritsche, 30 Dayton Dr., Winnipeg, MB R2J 3N1
Sec., Rev. William Ney, 4906 55th Ave., Stony Plain, AB T7Z 1B5
Treas., Allan Webster, C.A., 3074 Portage Ave., Winnipeg, MB R3K 0Y2

DISTRICT OFFICES

Alberta-British Columbia, Pres., Rev. D. Schiemann, 7100 Ada Blvd., Edmonton, AB T5B 4E4 Tel. (403)474-0063, Fax (403)477-9829, info@lccabc.ca
Central, Pres., Rev. T. Prachar, 1927 Grant Dr., Regina, SK S4S 4V6 Tel. (306)586-4434, Fax (306)586-0656, tprachar@accesscomm.ca
East, Pres., Rev. A. Maleske, 275 Lawrence Ave., Kitchener, ON N2M 1Y3 Tel. (519)578-6500, Fax (519)578-3369, lcced@aol.com

Periodicals

The Canadian Lutheran

Mennonite Church Canada

This body has its origins in Europe in 1525 as an outgrowth of the Anabaptist movement. It was organized in North America in 1898. Mennonite Church Canada began in 1902 as an organized fellowship of Mennonite immigrants from Russia clustered in southern Manitoba and around Rosthern, Saskatchewan. The first annual sessions were held in July, 1903. Its members hold to traditional Christian beliefs, believer's baptism and congregational polity. They emphasize practical Christianity, opposition to war, service to others and personal ethics. Further immigration from Russia in the 1920s and 1940s increased the group which is now located in all provinces from New Brunswick to British Columbia. In recent years a variety of other ethnic groups, including native Canadians, have joined the conference. This conference is affiliated with Mennonite Church USA whose offices are at Newton, Kansas. (See Mennonite Church USA description in the section "Religious Bodies in the United States")

Headquarters

600 Shaftesbury Blvd., Winnipeg, MB R3P 0M4 Tel. (204)888-6781, Fax (204)831-5675
Media Contact, Dan Dyck
Email: office@mennonitechurch.ca
Website: www.mennonitechurch.ca

Officers

Chpsn., Ron Sawatsky
Gen. Sec., Dan Nighswander

Periodicals

Canadian Mennonite

North American Baptist Conference

Churches belonging to this conference emanated from German Baptist immigrants of more than a century ago. Although scattered across Canada and the U.S., they are bound together by a common heritage, a strong spiritual unity, a Bible-centered faith and a deep interest in missions.

Note, the details of general organization, officers, and periodicals of this body will be found in the North American Baptist Conference directory in the "Religious Bodies in the United States" section of this Yearbook.

Headquarters

1 S. 210 Summit Ave., Oakbrook Terrace, IL 60181 Tel. (630)495-2000, Fax (630)495-3301

Media Contact, Marilyn Schaer

Officers

Exec. Dir., Dr. Philip Yntema

Periodicals

N.A.B. Today

The Old Catholic Church of Canada

The church was founded in 1948 in Hamilton, Ontario. The first bishop was the Rt. Rev. George Davis. The Old Catholic Church of Canada accepts all the doctrines of the Eastern Orthodox Churches and, therefore, not Papal Infallibility or the Immaculate Conception. The ritual is Western (Latin Rite) and is in the vernacular language. Celibacy is optional.

Headquarters

RR #1, Midland, ON L4R 4K3 Tel. (705)835-6940

Media Contact, Bishop, The Most Rev. David Thomson

Officers

Vicar General and Auxiliary Bishop, The Rt. Rev. A.C. Keating, PhD., 5066 Forest Grove Crest, Burlington, ON L7L GG6 Tel. (905)331-1113

Old Order Amish Church

This is the most conservative branch of the Mennonite Church and direct descendants of Swiss Brethren (Anabaptists) who emerged from the Reformation in Switzerland in 1525. The Amish, followers of Bishop Jacob Ammann, became a distinct group in 1693. They began migrating to North America about 1720; all of them still reside in the United States or Canada. They first migrated to Ontario in 1824 directly from Bavaria, Germany and also from Pennsylvania and Alsace-Lorraine. Since 1953 some Amish have migrated to Ontario from Ohio, Indiana and Iowa.

In 2001 there were 24 congregations in Ontario, each being autonomous. No membership figures are kept by this group, and there is no central headquarters. Each congregation is served by a bishop, two ministers and a deacon, all of whom are chosen from among the male members by lot for life.

CORRESPONDENT

Pathway Publishers, David Luthy, Rt. 4, Aylmer, ON N5H 2R3

Periodicals

Blackboard Bulletin; Herold der Wahreit; The Budget; The Diary; Die Botschaft; Family Life; Young Companion

Open Bible Faith Fellowship of Canada

This is an Evangelical, Full Gospel Fellowship of Churches and Ministries emphasizing evangelism, missions and the local church for success in the present harvest of souls. OBFF was chartered January 7, 1982.

Headquarters

Word of Life Church, P.O. Box 968, St. Catharines, ON L2R 6Z4 Tel. (905)646-0970

Media Contact, Exec. Dir., Randy Neilson

Officers

Pres., Peter Youngren
V-Pres., Peter Morgan
Exec. Dir., Randy Neilson
Sec., George Woodward
Treas., Ron Cosby

Orthodox Church in America (Canada Section)

The Archdiocese of Canada of the Orthodox Church in America was established in 1916. First organized by St. Tikhon, martyr Patriarch of Moscow, previously Archbishop of North America, it is part of the Russian Metropolia and its successor, the autocephalous Orthodox Church in America.

The Archdiocesan Council meets twice yearly, the General Assembly of the Archdiocese takes place every three years. The Archdiocese is also known as "Orthodox Church in Canada."

Headquarters

P.O. Box 179, Spencerville, ON K0E 1X0 Tel. (613)925-5226 (Office) (613)925-3004 (Home), Fax (613)925-1521

Email: zoe@recorder.ca

Officers

Bishop of Ottawa & Canada, The Rt. Rev. Seraphim; Chancellor, V. Rev. Dennis Pinach, 17319

Treas., Nikita Lopoukhine, 55 Clarey Ave., Ottawa, ON K1S 2R6

Eastern Sec., Olga Jurgens, P.O. Box 179, Spencerville, ON K0E 1X0

ARCHDIOCESAN COUNCIL

Clergy Members, Rev. Lawrence Farley; Rev. R.S. Kennaugh; Rev. Larry Reinheimer; Igumen Irenee Rochon; Rev. James Griggs; Rev. Rodion Luciuk

Lay Members, David Grier; John Hadjinicolaou; Denis Lessard; Mother Sophia (Zion); David Rystephanuk; Rod Tkachuk; Geoff Korz

Ex Officio, Chancellor; Treas.; Eastern Sec.; Western Sec.

Periodicals

Canadian Orthodox Messenger

Patriarchal Parishes of the Russian Orthodox Church in Canada

This is the diocese of Canada of the former Exarchate of North and South America of the Russian Orthodox Church. It was originally founded in 1897 by the Russian Orthodox Archdiocese in North America.

Headquarters

St. Barbara's Russian Orthodox Cathedral, 10105 96th St., Edmonton, AB T5H 2G3

Media Contact, Sec.-Treas., Victor Lopushinsky, #303 9566-101 Ave., Edmonton, AB T5H 0B4 Tel. (780)455-9071

Officers

Admn., Archbishop of Kashira, Most Rev. Mark, 10812-108 St., Edmonton, AB T5H 3A6 Tel. (780)420-9945

The Pentecostal Assemblies of Canada

This body is incorporated under the Dominion Charter of 1919 and is also recognized in the Province of Quebec as an ecclesiastical corporation. Its beginnings are to be found in the revivals at the turn of the century, and most of the first Canadian Pentecostal leaders came from a religious background rooted in the Holiness movements.

The original incorporation of 1919 was implemented among churches of eastern Canada only. In the same year, a conference was called in Moose Jaw, Saskatchewan, to which the late Rev. J. M. Welch, general superintendent of the then-organized Assemblies of God in the U.S., was invited. The churches of Manitoba and Saskatchewan were organized as the Western District Council of the Assemblies of God. They were joined later by Alberta and British Columbia. In 1921, a conference was held in Montreal, to which the general chairman of the Assemblies of God was invited. Eastern Canada also became a district of the Assemblies of God, joining Eastern and Western Canada as two districts in a single organizational union.

In 1920, at Kitchener, Ontario, eastern and western churches agreed to dissolve the Canadian District of the Assemblies of God and unite under the name The Pentecostal Assemblies of Canada.

Today the Pentecostal Assemblies of Canada operates throughout the nation and in about 30 countries around the world. Religious services are conducted in more than 25 different languages in the 1,100 local churches in Canada. Members and adherents number about 230,000. The number of local churches includes approximately 100 Native congregations.

Headquarters

6745 Century Ave., Mississauga, ON L5N 6P7 Tel. (905)542-7400, Fax (905)542-7313

Media Contact, Public Relations, Rev. W. A. Griffin Email: wgriffin@paoc.org

Officers

Gen. Supt., Rev. William D. Morrow

Asst. Gen. Supt., Rev. E. Stewart Hunter

Gen. Sec.-Treas., Rev. David Ball

DISTRICT SUPERINTENDENTS

British Columbia, Rev. William R. Gibson, 5641 176 A St., Surrey, BC V3S 4G8 Tel. (604)576-9421, Fax (604)576-1499

Alberta, Rev. Lorne D. McAlister, 10585-111 St., #101, Edmonton, AB T5H 3E8 Tel. (403)426-0084, Fax (403)420-1318

Saskatchewan, Rev. Samuel O. Biro, 3488 Fairlight Dr., Saskatoon, SK S7M 3Z4 Tel. (306)652-6088, Fax (306)652-0199

Manitoba, Rev. Gordon V. Peters, 187 Henlow Bay, Winnipeg, MB R3Y 1G4 Tel. (204)488-6800, Fax (204)489-0499

Western Ontario, Rev. David Shepherd, 3214 S. Service Rd., Burlington, ON L7M 3J2 Tel. (905)637-5566, Fax (905)637-7558

Eastern Ontario and Quebec, Rev. Richard Hilsden, Box 13250, Kanata, ON K2K 1X4 Tel. (613)599-3422, Fax (613)599-7284

Maritime Provinces, Rev. David C. Slauenwhite, Box 1184, Truro, NS B2N 5H1 Tel. (902)895-4212, Fax (902)897-0705

BRANCH CONFERENCES

German Conference, Rev. Philip F. Kniesel, #310, 684 Belmont Ave., W, Kitchener, ON N2M 1N6

Slavic Conferences, Eastern District, Rev. A. Muravski, 44 Glenabbey Dr. Courtice, ON L1E 1B7; Western District, Rev. Michael Brandebura, 4108-134 Ave., Edmonton, AB T5A 3M2

Finnish Conference, Rev. E. Ahonen, 1920 Argyle Dr., Vancouver, BC V5P 2A8

Periodicals

Pentecostal Testimony; Resource, The National Leadership Magazine

The Pentecostal Assemblies of Newfoundland

This body began in 1911 and held its first meetings at Bethesda Mission at St. John's. It was incorporated in 1925 as The Bethesda Pentecostal Assemblies of Newfoundland and changed its name in 1930 to The Pentecostal Assemblies of Newfoundland.

Headquarters

57 Thorburn Rd., Box 8895, Stn. "A", St. John's, NF A1B 3T2 Tel. (709)753-6314, Fax (709)753-4945

Email: paon@paon.nf.ca

Media Contact, Gen. Sup't., A. Earl Batstone, 57 Thorburn Rd., Box 8895, Stn. "A", St. John's, NF A1B 3T2

GENERAL EXECUTIVE OFFICERS

Gen. Sup't. A. Earl Batstone, 57 Thorburn Rd., Box 8895, Stn. "A", St. John's, NF A1B 3T2

Gen. Sec.-Treas., Clarence Buckle, 57 Thorburn Rd., Box 8895, Stn. "A", St. John's, NF A1B 3T2
Ex. Dir. of Home Missions, Barry Q. Grimes, 57 Thorburn Rd., Box 8895, Stn. "A", St. John's, NF A1B 3T2
Ex. Dir. of Ch. Ministries, Robert H. Dewling, 57 Thorburn Rd., Box 8895, Stn. "A", St. John's, NF A1B 3T2

PROVINCIAL DIRECTORS

Sunday school Ministries, Alvin F. Peddle, Box 40, Baytona, NF A0G 2J0
Children's Ministries, Lorinda R. Moulton, Box 56, New Harbour, NF A0B 2P0
Women's Ministries, Nancy L. Hunter, 12 Harp Place, Paradise, NF A1L 1G9
Men's Ministries, Norman C. Joy, 2 Firgreen Ave., Mount Pearl, NF A1N 1T7
Youth Ministries, B. Dean Brenton, Box 21100, St. John's, NF A1B 3L5
Mature Adult Ministries, Clayton Rice, 29 Diana Rd., St. John's, NF A1B 1H7
Family Ministries, Eva M. Winsor, 26 Ireland Dr., Grand Falls-Windsor, NF A2A 2S6

AUXILIARY SERVICES

Chaplain for Institutions, Roy A. Burden, 293 Frecker Dr., St. John's, NF A1E 5T8
Pentecostal Senior Citizens Home Administrator, Beverley Bellefleur, Box 130, Clarke's Beach, NF A0A 1W0
Evergreen Manor, Summerford, NF A0G 4E0
Pastoral Enrichment Ministries, Gary D. & Eva M. Winsor, 26 Ireland Dr., Grand Falls-Windsor, NF A2A 2S6
Chaplain, Memorial University of Newfound land, Gregory R. Dewling, Memorial University of Newfoundland, Box 102, St. John's, NF A1C 5S7
Emmanuel Convention Centre Administrator, Ronald M. Dicks, Box 1558, Lewisporte, NF A0G 3A0
World Missions Promotions, A. Scott Hunter, 12 Harp Place, Paradise, NF A1L 1G9
Managing Editor, Good Tidings, Burton K. Janes, 57 Thornburn Rd., Box 8895, Stn. "A", St. John's, NF A1B 3T2

Periodicals

Good Tidings

Presbyterian Church in America (Canadian Section)

Canadian congregations of the Reformed Presbyterian Church, Evangelical Synod, became a part of the Presbyterian Church in America when the RPCES joined PCA in June 1982. Some of the churches were in predecessor bodies of the RPCES, which was the product of a 1965 merger of the Reformed Presbyterian Church in North America, General Synod and the Evangelical Presbyterian Church. Others came into existence later as a part of the home missions work of RPCES. Congregations are located in seven provinces, and the PCA is continuing church extension work in Canada. The denomination is committed to world evangelization and to a continuation of historic Presbyterianism. Its officers are required to subscribe to the Reformed faith as set forth in the Westminster Confession of Faith and Catechisms.

Headquarters

Media Contact, Correspondent, Doug Codling, Faith Reformed Presbyterian Church, 2581 E. 45th St., Vancouver, BC V5R 3B9 Tel. (604) 438-8755

Periodicals

Equip for Ministry; Multiply; Network

Presbyterian Church in Canada

This is the nonconcurring portion of the Presbyterian Church in Canada that did not become a part of The United Church of Canada in 1925.

Headquarters

50 Wynford Dr., Toronto, ON M3C 1J7 Tel. (416)441-1111, Fax (416)441-2825
Website, www.presbyterian.ca
Media Contact, Principal Clk., Rev. Stephen Kendall

Officers

Principal Clk., Rev. Stephen Kendall

Periodicals

Channels; The Presbyterian Message; Presbyterian Record; Glad Tidings; La Vie Chrétienne

Reformed Church in Canada

The Canadian region of the Reformed Church in America was organized under the General Synod of the Reformed Church in America. The RCA in Canada has 41 churches which includes three classes (lower assemblies). The reformed churches in Canada are member congregations of the Reformed Church in America and the Regional Synod of Canada (one of eight RCA regional synods established by it General Synod) and three classes, Ontario, Canadian Prairies and British Columbia.

The first ordained minister, Domine Jonas Micahelius, arrive in New Amsterdam from The Netherlands in 1628. Throughout the colonial period, the Reformed Church lived under the authority of the Classis of Amsterdam. Its churches were clustered in New York and New Jersey. Under the leadership of Rev. John Livingston, it became a denomination independent of the authority of the Classis of Amsterdam in 1776. Its geographical base was broadened in the 19th century by the immigration of Reformed Dutch and German settlers in the midwestern United States. The Reformed Church now spans the United States and Canada. The Reformed

Church in America accepts as its standards of faith the Heidelberg Catechism, Belgic Confession and Canons of Dort. It has a rich heritage of world mission activity. It claims to be loyal to reformed tradition which emphasizes obedience to god in all aspects of life.

Although the Reformed Church in America has worked in close cooperation with other churches, it has never entered into merger with any other denomination. It is a member of the World Alliance of Reformed Churches, the World Council of Churches and the National Council of the Churches of Christ in the United States of America. In 1998 it also entered into a relationship of full communion with the Evangelical Lutheran Church in America, Presbyterian Church (U.S.A.), and the United Church of Christ by way of the Formula of Agreement.

Headquarters

475 Riverside Dr., Rm. 1812, New York, NY 10115 Tel. (212)870-2841, Fax (212)870-2499

Media Contact, Dir., Communication and Production Services, Kim Nathan Baker, 4500 60th St., SE, Grand Rapids, MI 49512 Tel. (616)698-7071, Fax (616)698-6606

Website: www.rca.org

OFFICERS AND STAFF OF GENERAL SYNOD

Regional Synod of Canada, Executive Secretary, Vacant

President, The Rev. Steven Brooks, 475 Riverside Dr., 18th Floor, New York, NY 10115

General Synod Council; Moderator, Ms. Carol Mutch, 475 Riverside Dr., 18th Floor, New York, NY 10115

General Secretary, The Rev. Wesley Granberg-Michaelson, 475 Riverside Dr., 18th Floor, New York, NY 10115

Policy, Planning & Administrative Services, Director & Assistant Secretary, The Rev. Kenneth Bradsell

Ministry & Personnel Services, Director, The Rev. Dr. Vernon Hoffs

Congregational Servcies-Evangelism & Church Development Services, Director, The Rev. Richard Welscott

Finance Services, Treasurer, Ms. Susan Converse

The Reformed Episcopal Church of Canada

The Reformed Episcopal Church is a separate entity. It was established in Canada by an act of incorporation given royal assent on June 2, 1886. It maintains the founding principles of episcopacy (in historic succession from the apostles), Anglican liturgy and Reformed doctrine and evangelical zeal. In practice it continues to recognize the validity of certain nonepiscopal orders of evangelical ministry. The Church has reunited with the Reformed Episcopal Church and is now composed of two Dioceses in this body - the Diocese of Central and Eastern Canada and the Diocese of Western Canada and Alaska. The current Presiding Bishop is Bishop Leonard Riches in Philadelphia.

Headquarters

Box 2532, New Liskeard, ON P0J 1P0 Tel. (705)647-4565, Fax (705)647-4565

Email: fed@nt.net

Website, www.forministry.com/REC-Canada

Media Contact, Pres., Rt. Rev. Michael Fedechko, M.Div., D.D.

Officers

Pres., Rt. Rev. Michael Fedechko, 320 Armstrong St., New Liskeard, ON P0J 1P0

Sec., Janet Dividson, 224 Haliburton,New Liskeard, ON P0J 1P0

BISHOPS

Diocese of Central & Eastern Canada, Rt. Rev. Michael Fedechko, 320 Armstrong St., New Liskeard, ON P0J 1P0 Tel. (705)647-4565, Fax (705)647-4565

Diocese of Western Canada & Alaska, Rt. Rev. Charles W. Dorrington, 54 Blanchard St., Victoria, BC V8X 4R1 Tel. (604)744-5014, Fax (604)388-5891

Periodicals

The Messenger

Reinland Mennonite Church

This group was founded in 1958 when 10 ministers and approximately 600 members separated from the Sommerfelder Mennonite Church. In 1968, four ministers and about 200 members migrated to Bolivia. The church has work in five communities in Manitoba and one in Ontario

Headquarters

Bishop William H. Friesen, P.O. Box 96, Rosenfeld, MB R0G 1X0 Tel. (204)324-6339

Media Contact, Deacon, Henry Wiebe, Box 2587, Winkler, MB R6W 4C3 Tel. (204)325-8487

Reorganized Church of Jesus Christ of Latter Day Saints

Founded April 6, 1830, by Joseph Smith, Jr., the church was reorganized under the leadership of the founder's son, Joseph Smith III, in 1860. The Church is established in 38 countries including the United States and Canada, with nearly a quarter of a million members. A biennial world conference is held in Independence, Missouri. The current president is W. Grant McMurray.

Headquarters

World Headquarters Complex, P.O. Box 1059, Independence, MO 64051 Tel. (816)833-1000, Fax (816)521-3095

Ontario Regional Ofc., 390 Speedvale Ave. E., Guelph, ON N1E 1N5

Media Contact, Public Relations Coordinator, Susan Naylor

Officers

CANADIAN REGIONS AND DISTRICTS

North Plains & Prairie Provinces Region, Regional Admn., Kenneth Barrows, 84 Hidden Park NW, Calgary, AB T3A 5K5; Alberta District, R.A.(Ryan) Levitt, #325, 51369 Range Rd., Sherwood Park, AB T8C 1H3; Saskatchewan District, Robert G. Klombies, 202 Saskatchewan Crescent W., Saskatoon, SK S7M 0A4

Pacific Northwest Region, Regional Admn., Raymond Peter, P.O. Box 18469, 4820 Morgan, Seattle, WA 98118; British Columbia District, E. Carl Bolger, 410-1005 McKenzie Ave., Victoria, BC V8X 4A9

Ontario Region, Regional Admn., Larry D. Windland, 390 Speedvale Ave. E., Guelph, ON N1E 1N5; Chatham District, David R. Wood, 127 Mount Pleasant Crescent, Wallaceburg, ON N8A 5A3; Grand River District, C. Allen Taylor, R R 2, Orangeville, ON L9W 2Y9; London District, William T. Leney, Jr., 18 Glendon Road, Stratford, ON N5A 5B3; Niagara District, Willis L. Hopkin, 765 Rymal Rd. E., Hamilton, ON L8W 1B6; Northern Ontario District, Douglas G. Bolger, 482 Timmins St., North Bay, ON P1B 4K7; Ottawa District, Marion Smith, 70 Mayburry St., Hull, QC J9A 2E9; Owen Sound District, Robin M. Duff, P.O. Box 52, Owen Sound, ON N1K 5P1; Toronto Metropole, Kerry J. Richards, 74 Parkside Dr., Brampton, ON L6Y 2G9

Periodicals

Saints Herald

The Roman Catholic Church in Canada

The largest single body of Christians in Canada, the Roman Catholic Church is under the spiritual leadership of His Holiness the Pope. Catholicism in Canada dates back to 1534, when the first Mass was celebrated on the Gaspé Peninsula on July 7, by a priest accompanying Jacques Cartier. Catholicism had been implanted earlier by fishermen and sailors from Europe. Priests came to Acadia as early as 1604. Traces of a regular colony go back to 1608 when Champlain settled in Quebec City. The Recollets (1615), followed by the Jesuits (1625) and the Sulpicians (1657), began the missions among the native population. The first official Roman document relative to the Canadian missions dates from March 20, 1618. Bishop François de Montmorency-Laval, the first bishop, arrived in Quebec in 1659. The church developed in the East, but not until 1818 did systematic missionary work begin in western Canada.

In the latter 1700s, English-speaking Roman Catholics, mainly from Ireland and Scotland, began to arrive in Canada's Atlantic provinces. After 1815 Irish Catholics settled in large numbers in what is now Ontario. The Irish potato famine of 1847 greatly increased that population in all parts of eastern Canada.

By the 1850s the Catholic Church in both English- and French-speaking Canada had begun to erect new dioceses and found many religious communities. These communities did educational, medical and charitable work among their own people as well as among Canada's native peoples. By the 1890s large numbers of non-English and non-French-speaking Catholics had settled in Canada, especially in the Western provinces. In the 20th century the pastoral horizons have continued to expand to meet the needs of what has now become a very multicultural church.

The Canadian Conference of Catholic Bishops is the national association of the Latin and Eastern Catholic Bishops of Canada. Its main offices are in Ottawa, Ontario.

Headquarters

Media Contact, Communications Service Dir., Rev. Mr. William Kokesch, Email: kokesch@ccb.ca

Dir. Service des Communications, Sylvain Salvas, Email: salvas@cccb.ca

Officers

General Secretariat of the Canadian Conference of Catholic Bishops

General Secretary, Msgr. Peter Schonenbach

Associate General Secretary (English Sector), Bede Martin Hubbard

Secrétaire général adjoint (French Sector), M. Benoit Bariteau

CANADIAN ORGANIZATION

Canadian Conference of Catholic Bishops-Conférence des évêques catholiques du Canada, 90 Parent Ave., Ottawa, ON K1N 7B1 Tel. (613)241-9461, Fax (613)241-8117, Email: cecc@cccb.ca, Website, www.cccb.ca

EXECUTIVE COMMITTEE

National Level

Pres., Most Rev. Gerald Wiesner, OMI

Vice-Pres., Mgr. Jacques Berthlete, c.s.v.

Co-Treas., Mgr. Andre Gaumond, Most Rev. Brendan O'Brien

EPISCOPAL COMMISSIONS

National Level

Social Affairs, Most Rev. James Weisgerber

Canon Law, Mgr. Joseph Khoury

Relations with Assoc. of Clergy, Consecrated Life & Laity, Mgr. Clement Fecteau

Evangelization of Peoples, Most Rev. Colin Campbell

Ecumenism, Mgr. Jean-Louis Plouffe

Theology, Most Rev. Thomas Collins

Sector Level

Comm. Sociales; Mgr. Andre Vallee

Social Comm.; Most Rev. J. Faber MacDonald
Éducation chrétienne; Mgr. Paul Marchand
Christian Education; Most Rev. Eugene Cooney
Liturgie; Mgr. Bertrand Blanchet
Liturgy; Most Rev. Douglas Crosby, OMI

OFFICES

Affaires sociales-Social Affairs, Mr. Joe Gunn, Dir.

Communications, Rev. Mr. William Kokesch, Dir. (English Sector); M. Sylvain Salvas, Dir. (French Sector)

Droit canonique'inter-rites-Canon Law—Inter-rite, Msgr. Peter Schonenbach, Secr.

Editions-Publications, Mme Johanne Gnassi, Dir.

Education chretienne, Mme Adele Bolduc, Secr.

Evangelisation des peuples-Evangelization of Peoples, Mme Adele Bolduc, Dir.

Liturgie-Liturgy, M. Paul Boily, Dir. (French Sector); Sr. Donna Kelly (English Sector)

National Office of Religious Education, Ms Joanne Chafe, Dir.

Occumenisme-Ecumenism, Sr. Donna Geernaert, SC, Dir.

Relations avec les associations du clerge, de la vie conseacree et du laicat-Relations with Association of Clergy, Consecrated Life and Laity, Ms. Jennifer Leddy, Secr.

Theologie-Theology, P. Richard Cote, o.m.i., Dir.

Tribunal d'appel du Canada-The Canadian Appeal Tribunal, P. Pierre Allard, s.m., Vicaire judiciaire-Judicial Vicar

REGIONAL EPISCOPAL ASSEMBLIES

Atlantic Episcopal Assembly (AEA)-Assemblee des eveques de l'Atlantique (AEA), Pres., Mgr Raymond Lahey; Vice Pres., Most Rev. Terrence Prendergast, SJ and Mgr Francois Thibodeau, c.j.m; Secretary-Treasurer, P. Daniel Deveau, c.s.c.; Tel. (506)653-6859, Fax (506)653-6859

Assemblee des eveques du Quebec (AEQ), Pres., Mgr Pierre Morissette; Vice-pres., Mgr Raymond Saint-Gelais; Secretaire general, M. Guy St-Onge, s.g; Tel. (514)274-4323, Fax (514)274-4383

Ontario Conference of Catholic Bishops (OCCB)-Conference des eveques catholiques de l'Ontario (CECO), Pres., Mgr Jean-Louis Plouffe, Vice Pres., Most Rev. Matthew F.Ustrzycki; Secretary-Treasurer, Right Rev. Peter Novecosky, OSB; Tel. (306)682-1788, Fax (306)682-1766

MILITARY ORDINARIATE-ORDINARIAT MILITAIRE

Bishop, Most Rev. Donald J. Theriault, Military Ordinariate of Canada, Canadian Forces Support Unit (Ottawa), Uplands Site Building 469, Ottawa, ON K1A 0K2, Tel. (613)998-8747, Fax (613)991-1056

Canadian Religious Conference, Sec. Gen., Sr. Jocelyne Fallu, FDLS., 219 Argyle St., Ottawa, ON K2P 2H4 Tel. (613)236-0824, Fax (613)236-0825
Email: crcn@web.net
Website: www.crcn.ca

Periodicals

Cahiers de Spiritualité Ignatienne; The Catholic Register; The Catholic Times (Montreal); Companion Magazine; Global Village Voice; Discover the Bible; L'êglise Canadienne; The Monitor; National Bulletin on Liturgy; The New Freeman; Messenger (of the Sacred Heart); Foi et Culture (Bulletin natl. de liturgie) Liturgie; Prairie Messenger; Vie Liturgique; La Vie des Communautés religieuses; Relations; Présence; The Communicator; Scarboro Missions; Missions Today

Romanian Orthodox Church in America (Canadian Parishes)

The first Romanian Orthodox immigrants in Canada called for Orthodox priests from their native country of Romania. Between 1902 and 1914, they organized the first Romanian parish communities and built Orthodox churches in different cities and farming regions of western Canada (Alberta, Saskatchewan, Manitoba) as well as in the eastern part (Ontario and Quebec).

In 1929, the Romanian Orthodox parishes from Canada joined with those of the United States in a Congress held in Detroit, Michigan, and asked the Holy Synod of the Romanian Orthodox Church of Romania to establish a Romanian Orthodox Missionary Episcopate in America. The first Bishop, Policarp (Morushca), was elected and consecrated by the Holy Synod of the Romanian Orthodox Church and came to the United States in 1935. He established his headquarters in Detroit with jurisdiction over all the Romanian Orthodox parishes in the United States and Canada.

In 1950, the Romanian Orthodox Church in America (i.e. the Romanian Orthodox Missionary Episcopate in America) was granted administrative autonomy by the Holy Synod of the Romanian Orthodox Church of Romania, and only doctrinal and canonical ties remain with this latter body.

In 1974 the Holy Synod of the Romanian Orthodox Church of Romania recognized and approved the elevation of the Episcopate to the rank of the Romanian Orthodox Archdiocese in America and Canada.

Headquarters

Canadian Office, Descent of the Holy Ghost, Romanian Orthodox Church, 2895 Seminole St., Windsor, ON N8Y 1Y1

Media Contact, Most Rev. Archbishop Victorin, 19959 Riopelle St., Detroit, MI 48203 Tel. (313)893-8390

Officers

Archbishop, Most Rev. Archbishop Victorin,

19959 Riopelle St., Detroit, MI 48203 Tel. (313)893-8390

Vicar, V. Rev. Archim., Dr. Vasile Vasilachi, 45-03 48th Ave., Woodside, Queens, NY 11377 Tel. (718)784-4453

Cultural Councilor, Very Rev. Fr. Nicolae Ciurea, 19 Murray St. W., Hamilton, ON L8L 1B1 Tel. (416)523-8268

Admn. Councilor, V. Rev. Fr. Mircea Panciuk, 11024-165th Ave., Edmonton, AB T5X 1X9

Sec., Rev. Fr. Simion John Catau, 31227 Roan Dr., Warren, MI 48093 Tel. (810)264-1924

The Romanian Orthodox Episcopate of America (Jackson, MI)

This body of Eastern Orthodox Christians of Romanian descent is part of the Autocephalous Orthodox Church in America. For complete description and listing of officers, please see chapter 3, "Religious Bodies in the United States."

Headquarters

2535 Grey Tower Rd., Jackson, MI 49201 Tel. (517)522-4800, Fax (517)522-5907

Email: roeasolia@aol.com

Website: www.roea.org

Mailing Address, P.O. Box 309, Grass Lake, MI 49240-0309

Media Contact, Ed.-Sec., Rev. Protodeacon David Oancea, P.O. Box 185, Grass Lake, MI 49240-0185 Tel. (517)522-3656, Fax (517) 522-5907

Officers

Ruling Hierarch, Most. Rev. Archbishop Nathaniel Popp

Dean for All Canada and the Western Provinces, Very Rev. Daniel Nenson, 2855 Helmsing St., Regina, SK S4V 0W7 Tel. (306)761-2379

Periodicals

Solia—The Herald; Good News- Buna Vestire (in Canada only)

The Salvation Army in Canada

The Salvation Army, an evangelical branch of the Christian Church, is an international movement founded in 1865 in London, England. The ministry of Salvationists, consisting of clergy (officers) and laity, comes from a commitment to Jesus Christ and is revealed in practical service, regardless of race, color, creed, sex or age.

The goals of The Salvation Army are to preach the gospel, disseminate Christian truths, instill Christian values, enrich family life and improve the quality of all life.

To attain these goals, The Salvation Army operates local congregations, provides counseling, supplies basic human needs and undertakes spiritual and moral rehabilitation of any needy people who come within its influence.

A quasi-military system of government was set up in 1878, by General William Booth, founder (1829-1912). Converts from England started Salvation Army work in London, Ontario, in 1882. Two years later, Canada was recognized as a Territorial Command, and since 1933 it has included Bermuda. An act to incorporate the Governing Council of The Salvation Army in Canada received royal assent on May 19, 1909.

Headquarters

2 Overlea Blvd., Toronto, ON M4H 1P4 Tel. (416)425-2111

Media Contact, Major Robert MacKenzie, Tel. (416)425-6153, Fax (416)425-6157

Email: bob.mackenzie@sallynet.org

Website: www.sallynet.org

Officers

Territorial Commander, Commissioner Norman Howe

Territorial Pres., Women's Organizations, Commissioner Marian Howe

Chief Sec., Col. Clyde Moore

Sec. for Personnel, Lt. Col. Merv Leach

Bus. Adm. Sec., Lt. Col. Peter Wood

Fin. Sec., Major Susan McMillan

Program Sec., Lt. Col. David Luginbuhl

Community Rel. and Communications Secretary, Major Robert Mac Kenzie

Property Sec., Col. Donald Copple

Periodicals

The War Cry; Faith & Friends; En Avant!; The Young Soldier; The Edge; Catherine; Horizons

Serbian Orthodox Church in the U.S.A. and Canada, Diocese of Canada

The Serbian Orthodox Church is an organic part of the Eastern Orthodox Church. As a local church it received its autocephaly from Constantinople in A.D. 1219. The Patriarchal seat of the church today is in Belgrade, Yugoslavia. In 1921, a Serbian Orthodox Diocese in the United States of America and Canada was organized. In 1963, it was reorganized into three dioceses, and in 1983 a fourth diocese was created for the Canadian part of the church. The Serbian Orthodox Church is in absolute doctrinal unity with all other local Orthodox Churches.

Headquarters

7470 McNiven Rd., RR 3, Campbellville, ON L0P 1B0 Tel. (905)878-0043, Fax (905)878-1909

Email: vladika@istocnik.com

Website: www. istocnik.com

Media Contact, Rt. Rev. Georgije

Officers

Serbian Orthodox Bishop of Canada, Rt. Rev. Georgije

Dean of Western Deanery, V. Rev. Mirko Malinovic, 924 12th Ave., Regina, SK S4N 0K7 Tel. (306)352-2917

Dean of Eastern Deanery, V. Rev. Zivorad Subotic, 351 Mellville Ave., Westmount, QC H3Z 2Y7 Tel. + Fax (514)931-6664

Periodicals

Istocnik, Herald of the Serbian Orthodox Church— Canadian Diocese

Seventh-day Adventist Church in Canada

The Seventh-day Adventist Church in Canada is part of the worldwide Seventh-day Adventist Church with headquarters in Washington, D.C. (See "Religious Bodies in the United States" section of this Yearbook for a fuller description.) The Seventh-day Adventist Church in Canada was organized in 1901 and reorganized in 1932.

Headquarters

1148 King St., E., Oshawa, ON L1H 1H8 Tel. (905)433-0011, Fax (905)433-0982

Media Contact, Orville Parchment

Officers

Pres., Orville Parchment

Sec., Claude Sabot

Treas., Donald Upson

DEPARTMENTS

Under Treas., Brian Christenson

Asst. Treas., Clareleen Ivany

Computer Services, Brian Ford

Coord. of Ministries, John Howard

Education, Mike Lekic

Public Affairs-Religious Liberty Trust, Karnik Doukmetzian

Periodicals

Canadian Adventist Messenger

Syriac Orthodox Church of Antioch

The Syriac Orthodox Church professes the faith of the first three ecumenical councils of Nicaea, Constantinople and Ephesus and numbers faithful in the Middle East, India, the Americas, Europe and Australia. It traces its origin to the Patriarchate established in Antioch by St. Peter the Apostle and is under the supreme ecclesiastical jurisdiction of His Holiness the Syrian Orthodox Patriarch of Antioch and All the East, now residing in Damascus, Syria.

The Archdiocese of the Syrian Orthodox Church in the U.S. and Canada was formally established in 1957. In 1995, the Archdiocese of North America was divided into three separate Patriarchal Vicariates, including one for Canada. The first Syrian Orthodox faithful came to Canada in the 1890s and formed the first Canadian parish in Sherbrooke, Quebec. Today five official parishes of the Archdiocese exist in Canada—two in Quebec and three in Ontario. There is also an official mission congregation in Calgary, Alberta and Ottawa, Ontario.

Headquarters

Archdiocese of Canada, The New Archdiocesan Centre, 4375 Henri-Bourassa Ouest, St.-Laurent, Quebec H4L 1A5, Canada Tel. (514)334-6993, Fax (514)334-8233

Officers

Archbishop Mor Timotheos Aphrem Aboodi

Ukrainian Orthodox Church of Canada

Toward the end of the 19th century many Ukrainian immigrants settled in Canada. In 1918, a group of these pioneers established the Ukrainian Orthodox Church of Canada (UOCC), today the largest Ukrainian Orthodox Church beyond the borders of Ukraine. In 1990, the UOCC entered into a eucharistic union with the Ecumenical Patriarchate at Constantinople (Istanbul).

Headquarters

Ukrainian Orthodox Church of Canada, Office of the Consistory, 9 St. Johns Ave., Winnipeg, MB R2W 1G8 Tel. (204)586-3093, Fax (204)582-5241

Email: consistory@uocc.ca

Website: www. uocc.ca

Media Contacts, Rev. Fr. Andrew Jarmus, 9st. John's Ave., Winnipeg, MB R2W 1G8, Tel. (204)586-3093 Fax (204)582-5241; Ms. M. Zurek, 9 St. Johns Ave., Winnipeg, MB R2W 1G8 Tel. (204)586-3093, Fax (204)582-5241

Officers

Primate, Most Rev. Metropolitan Wasyly Fedak, 9 St. Johns Ave., Winnipeg, MB R2W 1G8 Tel. (204)586-3093, Fax (204)582-5241

Chancellor, Rt. Rev. Dr. Oleg Krawchenko

Periodicals

Visnyk-The Herald-Le Messager (newspaper)

Ridna Nyva (almanac-annual)

Union d'Eglises Baptistes Françaises au Canada

Baptist churches in French Canada first came into being through the labors of two missionaries from Switzerland, Rev. Louis Roussy and Mme. Henriette Feller, who arrived in Canada in 1835. The earliest church was organized in Grande Ligne (now St.-Blaise), Quebec in 1838.

By 1900 there were 7 churches in the province of Quebec and 13 French-language Baptist churches in the New England states. The leadership was totally French Canadian.

By 1960, the process of Americanization had caused the disappearance of the French Baptist churches. During the 1960s, Quebec as a society, began rapidly changing in all its facets, education, politics, social values and structures. Mission, evangelism and church growth once again flourished. In 1969, in response to the new conditions, the Grande Ligne Mission passed control of its work to the newly formed Union of French Baptist Churches in Canada, which then included 8 churches. By 1990 the French Canadian Baptist movement had grown to include 25 congregations.

The Union d'êglises Baptistes Françaises au Canada is a member body of the Canadian Baptist Ministries and thus is affiliated with the Baptist World Alliance.

Headquarters

2285 avenue Papineau, Montreal, QC H2K 4J5 Tel. (514)526-6643, Fax (514)526-9269

Media Contact, Gen. Sec., Rev. David Affleck

Officers

Sec. Gen., Rev. Roland Grimard

Periodicals

www.UnionBaptiste.com (Internet)

Union of Spiritual Communities of Christ (Orthodox Doukhobors in Canada)

The Doukhobors are groups of Canadians of Russian origin living in the western provinces of Canada, but their beginnings in Russia are unknown. The name "Doukhobors," or "Spirit Wrestlers," was given in derision by the Russian Orthodox clergy in Russia as far back as 1785. Victims of decades of persecution in Russia, about 7,500 Doukhobors arrived in Canada in 1899.

The teaching of the Doukhobors is penetrated with the Gospel spirit of love. Worshiping God in the spirit, they affirm that the outward church and all that is performed in it and concerns it has no importance for them; the church is where two or three are gathered together, united in the name of Christ. Their teaching is founded on tradition, which they call the "Book of Life," because it lives in their memory and hearts. In this book are sacred songs or chants, partly composed independently, partly formed out of the contents of the Bible, and these are committed to memory by each succeeding generation. Doukhobors observe complete pacifism and non-violence.

The Doukhobors were reorganized in 1938 by their leader, Peter P. Verigin, shortly before his death, into the Union of Spiritual Communities of Christ, commonly called Orthodox Doukhobors. It is headed by a democratically elected Executive Committee which executes the will and protects the interests of the people.

At least 99 percent of the Doukhobors are law-abiding, pay taxes, and "do not burn or bomb or parade in the nude" as they say a fanatical offshoot called the "Sons of Freedom" does.

Headquarters

USCC Central Office, Box 760, Grand Forks, BC V0H 1H0 Tel. (250)442-8252, Fax (250) 442-3433

Media Contact, John J. Verigin, Sr.

Officers

Hon. Chmn. of the Exec. Comm., John J. Verigin, Sr.

Chpsn., Andrew Evin

Periodicals

ISKRA

United Baptist Convention of the Atlantic Provinces

The United Baptist Convention of the Atlantic Provinces is the largest Baptist Convention in Canada. Through the Canadian Baptist Ministries, it is a member of the Baptist World Alliance.

In 1763 two Baptist churches were organized in Atlantic Canada, one in Sackville, New Brunswick and the other in Wolfville, Nova Scotia. Although both these churches experienced crises and lost continuity, they recovered and stand today as the beginning of organized Baptist work in Canada.

Nine Baptist churches met in Lower Granville, Nova Scotia in 1800 and formed the first Baptist Association in Canada. By 1846 the Maritime Baptist Convention was organized, consisting of 169 churches. Two streams of Baptist life merged in 1905 to form the United Baptist Convention. This is how the term "United Baptist" was derived. Today there are 554 churches within 21 associations across the Convention.

The Convention has two educational institutions, Atlantic Baptist University in Moncton, New Brunswick, a Christian Liberal Arts University, and Acadia Divinity College in Wolfville, Nova Scotia, a Graduate School of Theology. The Convention engages in world mission through Canadian Baptist Ministries, the all-Canada mission agency. In addition to an active program of home mission, evangelism, training, social action and stewardship, the Convention operates ten senior citizen complexes and a Christian bookstore.

Headquarters

1655 Manawagonish Rd., Saint John, NB E2M 3Y2 Tel. (506)635-1922, Fax (506)635-0366

Email: ubcap@fundy.net

Media Contact, Executive Minister, Dr. Harry G. Gardner

Officers

Pres., Rev. Gordon Sutherland

Vice-Pres., Mr. Sterling Gosman

Exec. Min., Dr. Harry G. Gardner

Dir. of Operations., Daryl MacKenzie

Dir. of Atlantic Baptist Mission, Dr. Malcolm Beckett

Dir. of Youth and Family, Rev. Bruce Fawcett

United Brethren Church in Canada

Founded in 1767 in Lancaster County, Pennsylvania, missionaries came to Canada about 1850. The first class was held in Kitchener in

1855, and the first building was erected in Port Elgin in 1867.

The Church of the United Brethren in Christ had its beginning with Philip William Otterbein and Martin Boehm, who were leaders in the revivalistic movement in Pennsylvania and Maryland during the late 1760s.

Headquarters

302 Lake St., Huntington, IN 46750 Tel. (219)356-2312, Fax (219)356-4730

GENERAL OFFICERS

Pres., Rev. Brian Magnus, 120 Fife Rd., Guelph, ON N1H 6Y2 Tel. (519)836-0180

Treas., Brian Winger, 2233 Hurontario St., Apt. 916, Mississauga, ON L5A 2E9 Tel. (905)275-8140

The United Church of Canada

The United Church of Canada was formed on June 10, 1925, through the union of the Methodist Church, Canada, the Congregational Union of Canada, the Council of Local Union Churches and 70 percent of the Presbyterian Church in Canada. The union culminated years of negotiation between the churches, all of which had integral associations with the development and history of the nation.

In fulfillment of its mandate to be a uniting as well as a United Church, the denomination has been enriched by other unions during its history. The Wesleyan Methodist Church of Bermuda joined in 1930. On January 1, 1968, the Canada Conference of the Evangelical United Brethren became part of The United Church of Canada. At various times, congregations of other Christian communions have also become congregations of the United Church.

The United Church of Canada is a full member of the World Methodist Council, the World Alliance of Reformed Churches (Presbyterian and Congregational), and the Canadian and World Councils of Churches.

The United Church is the largest Protestant denomination in Canada.

NATIONAL OFFICES

The United Church House, 3250 Bloor St. W., Ste. 300, Etobicoke, ON M8X 2Y4 Tel. (416) 231-5931, Fax (416)231-3103

Email: info@uccan.org

Website: www.uccan.org

Media Contact, Manager Public Relations & Info. Unit, Mary-Frances Denis

GENERAL COUNCIL

Mod., Marion Pardy

Gen. Sec., K. Virginia Coleman

Human Resources, Sec., Anne Shirley Sutherland

Theology, Faith & Ecumenism, Sec., Rev. S. Peter Wyatt

Archivist, Sharon Larade, 73 Queen's Park Cr., E., Toronto, ON M5C 1K7 Tel. (416)585-4563, Fax (416)585-4584

Email: uccvu.archives@utoronto.ca

Website: www. vicu.utoronto.ca/archives/archives.htm

ADMINISTRATIVE DIVISIONS

Communication, Gen. Sec., Gordon How

Finance, Gen. Sec., Steven Adams

Ministry Personnel & Education, Gen. Sec., Rev. Steven Chambers

Mission in Canada, Gen. Sec., Rev. David Iverson

World Outreach, Gen. Sec., Rev. Christopher Ferguson

CONFERENCE EXECUTIVE SECRETARIES

Alberta and Northwest, Rev. George H. Rodgers, 9911-48 Ave., NW, Edmonton, AB T6E 5V6 Tel. (780)435-3995, Fax (780)438-3317

Email: coffice@anwconf.com

All Native Circle, Speaker, Dianne Cooper (interim), 367 Selkirk Ave., Winnipeg, MB R2W 2N3 Tel. (204)582-5518, Fax (204)582-6649

Email: allnat@mb.aibn.com

Bay of Quinte, Rev. Wendy Bulloch, P.O. Box 700, 67 Mill St., Frankford, ON K0K 2C0 Tel. (613)398-1051, Fax (613)398-8894

Email: bayq.conference@sympatico.ca

British Columbia, Rev. Debra A. Bowman, 4383 Rumble St., Burnaby, BC V5J 2A2 Tel. (604)431-0434, Fax (604)431-0439

Email: bcconf@infoserve.net

Hamilton, Rev. Roslyn A. Campbell, Box 100, Carlisle, ON L0R 1H0 Tel. (905)659-3343, Fax (905)659-7766

Email: office@hamconf.org

London, W. Peter Scott, 359 Windermere Rd., London, ON N6G 2K3 Tel. (519)672-1930, Fax (519)439-2800

Email: lonconf@execulink.com

Manitoba and Northwestern Ontario, Rev. Roger A. Coll, 170 Saint Mary's Rd., Winnipeg, MB R2H 1H9 Tel. (204)233-8911 Fax (204)233-3289

Email: office@confmnwo.mb.ca

Manitou, Rev. Rev. Jim Sinclair, 319 McKenzie Ave., North Bay, ON P1B 7E3 Tel. (705)474-3350, Fax (705)497-3597

Email: manitou@efni.com

Maritime, Rev. Catherine H. Gaw, 32 York St., Sackville, NB E4L 4R4 Tel. (506)536-1334 Fax (506)536-2900

Email: marconf@nbnet.nb,ca

Montreal and Ottawa, Rev. Rev. David C. Estey, 225-50 Ave., Lachine, QC H8T 2T7 Tel. (514)634-7015, Fax (514)634-2489

Email: lachine@istar.ca

Newfoundland and Labrador, Rev. Clarence R. Sellers, 320 Elizabeth Ave., St. John's, NF A1B 1T9 Tel. (709)754-0386, Fax (709)754-8336

Email: newlab@seascape.com

Saskatchewan, Rev. Bruce G. Faurschou (inter-

im), 418 A. McDonald St., Regina, SK S4N 6E1 Tel. (306)721-3311, Fax (306)721-3171
Email: ucskco@sk.sympatico.ca
Toronto, Rev. David W. Allen, 65 Mayall Ave., Downsview, ON M3L 1E7 Tel. (416)241-2677, Fax (416)241-2689
Email: torconf@web.net

Periodicals

Fellowship Magazine; United Church Observer; Mandate; Aujourd'hui Credo

United Pentecostal Church in Canada

This body, which is affiliated with the United Pentecostal Church, International, with headquarters in Hazelwood, Missouri, accepts the Bible standard of full salvation, which is repentance, baptism by immersion in the name of the Lord Jesus Christ for the remission of sins and the baptism of the Holy Ghost, with the initial signs of speaking in tongues as the Spirit gives utterance. Other tenets of faith include the Oneness of God in Christ, holiness, divine healing and the second coming of Jesus Christ.

Headquarters

United Pentecostal Church Intl., 8855 Dunn Rd., Hazelwood, MO 63042 Tel. (314)837-7300, Fax (314)837-4503
Media Contact, Gen. Sec.-Treas., Rev. C. M. Becton

DISTRICT SUPERINTENDENTS

Atlantic, Rev. Harry Lewis, P.O. Box 1046, Perth Andover, NB E0J 1V0
British Columbia, Rev. Paul V. Reynolds, 13447-112th Ave., Surrey, BC V3R 2E7
Canadian Plains, Rev. Johnny King, 615 Northmount Dr., NW, Calgary, AB T2K 3J6
Central Canadian, Rev. Clifford Heaslip, 4215 Roblin Blvd., Winnipeg, MB R3R 0E8
Newfoundland, Jack Cunningham
Nova Scotia, Superintendent, Rev. John D. Mean, P.O. Box 2183, D.E.P.S., Dartmouth, NS B2W 3Y2
Ontario, Rev. Carl H. Stephenson, 63 Castlegrove Blvd., Don Mills, ON M3A 1L3

Universal Fellowship of Metropolitan Community Churches

The Universal Fellowship of Metropolitan Community Churches is a Christian church which directs a special ministry within, and on behalf of, the gay and lesbian community. Involvement, however, is not exclusively limited to gays and lesbians; U.F.M.C.C. tries to stress its openness to all people and does not call itself a "gay church."

Founded in 1968 in Los Angeles by the Rev. Troy Perry, the U.F.M.C.C. has over 300 member congregations worldwide. Congregations are in Vancouver, Edmonton, Windsor, London, Toronto, Ottawa (2), Guelph, Fredericton, Winnipeg, Halifax, Barrie and Belleville.

Theologically, the Metropolitan Community Churches stand within the mainstream of Christian doctrine, being "ecumenical" or "interdenominational" in stance (albeit a "denomination" in their own right).

The Metropolitan Community Churches are characterized by their belief that the love of God is a gift, freely offered to all people, regardless of sexual orientation and that no incompatibility exists between human sexuality and the Christian faith.

The Metropolitan Community Churches in Canada were founded in Toronto in 1973 by the Rev. Robert Wolfe.

Headquarters

Media Contact, Marcie Wexler, 33 Holly St., #1117, Toronto, ON M4S 2G8 Tel. (416)487-8429, Fax (416)932-1836

Officers

Eastern Canadian District, Rev. Marcie Wexler, 33 Holly St., #1117, Toronto, ON M4S 2G8 Tel. (416)487-8429

The Wesleyan Church of Canada

This group is the Canadian portion of The Wesleyan Church which consists of the Atlantic and Central Canada districts. The Central Canada District of the former Wesleyan Methodist Church of America was organized at Winchester, Ontario, in 1889 and the Atlantic District was founded in 1888 as the Alliance of the Reformed Baptist Church, which merged with the Wesleyan Methodist Church in July, 1966.

The Wesleyan Methodist Church and the Pilgrim Holiness Church merged in June, 1968, to become The Wesleyan Church. The doctrine is evangelical and Wesleyan Arminian and stresses holiness beliefs. For more details, consult the U.S. listing under The Wesleyan Church.

Headquarters

The Wesleyan Church Intl. Center, P.O. Box 50434, Indianapolis, IN 46250-0434
Media Contact, Dist. Supt., Central Canada, Rev. Donald E. Hodgins, 3 Applewood Dr., Ste. 101, Belleville, ON K8P 4E3 Tel. (613)966-7527, Fax (613)968-6190

DISTRICT SUPERINTENDENTS

Central Canada, Rev. Donald E. Hodgins, 3 Applewood Dr., Ste.101, Belleville, ON K8P 4E3
Email: ccd@on.aibn.com
Atlantic, Rev. Dr. H. C. Wilson, 1600 Main st., Ste. 216, Moncton, NB E1E 1G5
Email: ncwilson@nbnet.nb.ca

Periodicals

Central Canada; The Clarion

Religious Bodies in Canada Arranged by Families

The following list of religious bodies appearing in the Directory Section of the *Yearbook* shows the "families," or related clusters into which Canadian religious bodies can be grouped. For example, there are many communions that can be grouped under the heading "Baptist" for historical and theological reasons. It should not be assumed, however, that all denominations under one family heading are necessarily consistent in belief or practice. The family clusters tend to represent historical factors more often than theological or practical ones. These family categories provide one of the major pitfalls when compiling church statistics because there is often a tendency to combine the statistics by "families" for analytical and comparative purposes. Such combined totals are deeply flawed, even though they are often used as variables for sociological analysis. The arrangement by families offered here is intended only as a general guide for conceptual organization when viewing the broad sweep of Canadian religious culture.

Religious bodies that can not be categorized under family headings appear alphabetically and are not indented in the following list.

The Anglican Church of Canada
Apostolic Christian Church (Nazarene)
Armenian Evangelical Church
Associated Gospel Churches

Baptist Bodies

Association of Regular Baptist Churches (Canada)
Baptist Convention of Ontario and Quebec
Baptist General Conference of Canada
Baptist Union of Western Canada
Canadian Baptist Ministries
Canadian Convention of Southern Baptists
The Fellowship of Evangelical Baptist Churches in Canada
Free Will Baptists
North American Baptist Conference
Union d'Eglises Baptistes Françaises au Canada
United Baptist Convention of the Atlantic Provinces

Brethren in Christ Church, Canadian Conference
Canadian District of the Moravian Church in America, Northern Province
Canadian Evangelical Christian Churches
Canadian Yearly Meeting of the Religious Society of Friends
Christ Catholic Church International
Christian Brethren (also known as Plymouth Brethren)
Christian and Missionary Alliance in Canada
Church of God (Anderson, Ind.)
Church of the Nazarene in Canada

Churches of Christ—Christian Churches

Christian Church (Disciples of Christ) in Canada
Churches of Christ in Canada

Congregational Christian Churches in Canada

Eastern Orthodox Churches

The Antiochian Orthodox Christian Archdiocese of North America
Greek Orthodox Metropolis of Toronto (Canada)
Orthodox Church in America (Canada Section)
Patriarchal Parishes of the Russian Orthodox Church in Canada
Romanian Orthodox Church in America (Canadian Parishes)
The Romanian Orthodox Episcopate of America (Jackson, MI)
Serbian Orthodox Church in the U.S.A. and Canada, Diocese of Canada
Ukrainian Orthodox Church of Canada

The Evangelical Covenant Church of Canada
Evangelical Free Church of Canada
The Evangelical Missionary Church of Canada
General Church of the New Jerusalem
Jehovah's Witnesses

Latter-Day Saints (Mormons)

The Church of Jesus Christ of Latter-Day Saints in Canada
Community of Christ

Lutheran Bodies

Church of the Lutheran Brethren
The Estonian Evangelical Lutheran Church
Evangelical Lutheran Church in Canada
Lutheran Church—Canada

Mennonite Bodies

Canadian Conference of Mennonite Brethren Churches
Church of God in Christ (Mennonite)
The Evangelical Mennonite Conference

Evangelical Mennonite Mission Conference
Mennonite Church (Canada)
Old Order Amish Church
Reinland Mennonite Church

Methodist Bodies

British Methodist Episcopal Church of Canada
Free Methodist Church in Canada
Independent Holiness Church
The Wesleyan Church of Canada

The Old Catholic Church of Canada
Open Bible Faith Fellowship of Canada

Oriental Orthodox Churches

Armenian Holy Apostolic Church—Canadian Diocese
The Coptic Orthodox Church in Canada
Syriac Orthodox Church of Antioch

Pentecostal Bodies

The Apostolic Church in Canada
Apostolic Church of Pentecost of Canada Inc.
The Bible Holiness Movement
Church of God (Cleveland, Tenn.)
The Church of God of Prophecy in Canada
Elim Fellowship of Evangelical Churches and Ministers
Foursquare Gospel Church of Canada
Independent Assemblies of God International (Canada)
The Italian Pentecostal Church of Canada
The Pentecostal Assemblies of Canada
Pentecostal Assemblies of Newfoundland
United Pentecostal Church in Canada

Presbyterian Bodies

Presbyterian Church in America (Canadian Section)
Presbyterian Church in Canada

Reformed Bodies

Canadian and American Reformed Churches
Christian Reformed Church in North America
Reformed Church in Canada

The Reformed Episcopal Church of Canada
The Roman Catholic Church in Canada
The Salvation Army in Canada
Seventh-day Adventist Church in Canada
Union of Spiritual Communities of Christ (Orthodox Doukhobors in Canada)
United Brethren Church in Canada
The United Church of Canada
Universal Fellowship of Metropolitan Community Churches

5. The Emerging Electronic Church

Information of all types by and about religious bodies in Canada and the United States is available "on line" in electronic form: religious discussion, news, music, graphic images (including video), disaster reports, speeches, pastoral letters and sermons, exegetical material, primary and historical texts, historic and biographical data, program information, bulletin notes, and contact information for staff members of local churches, or of regional, national or international bodies.

During the current year, church-related organizations continued to explore the potential of the new, evolving media in highly effective and creative ways. Many church bodies and related organizations dramatically enhanced their electronic offerings, and increasingly list web and email addresses; 134 of our listed US religious bodies use registered Internet domains suggestive of their names.

Sites sponsored by well-established, non-profit religious organizations such as those listed in the Yearbook dramatically improved in quality and sophistication, and in some cases took their place among the most innovative on the Internet. Many of the for-profit Internet companies catering to the religious market were hurt by declines in the capital markets doubtful about online companies' future profitability and by reductions in advertising revenues. Some large commercial church-oriented Web sites announced plans to fold or merged with retail establishments, while well-established companies that survived the shakeout improved their content's breadth and scope and have emerged in a stronger position within their markets.

Despite some negative trends, religious content continued to be one of the most popular online categories. Particularly in the aftermath of the World Trade Towers and Pentagon terrorist attacks, religious sites saw significant increases in traffic and interest, especially where information and discussion related to Islam.

The World Wide Web (www) addresses listed below are merely beginning points for exploring the vast interlinked "web" of church-related material.

Expanded and updated email and website information pertaining to U.S. and Canadian religious organizations, and an expanded church body listing is provided for *Yearbook* readers at: www.ElectronicChurch.org.

Helpful Databases and Search Engines for Local Churches and Denominations

THE EMERGING ELECTRONIC CHURCH

About.com - http://christianity.about.com

Academic Info - www.academicinfo.net/Christian.html

Adherents - www.adherents.com

All-in-one Christian Index - http://allinone.crossdaily.com

American Religion Data Archive - www.thearda.com

BeliefNet - www.beliefnet.org

Christian Century - www.christiancentury.org

Christianity Today - www.christianitytoday.com

Crosssearch.com - www.crosssearch.com

Ecunet - www.ecunet.org

ForMinistry - www.forministry.com

Hartford Institute for Religion Research - http://hirr.hartsem.edu

National Center for Charitable Statistics - www.nccs.urban.org

The Text This Week - www.textweek.com

Resources for American Christianity - www.resourcingchristianity.org

Virtual Religion Index - www.rci.rutgers.edu/~religion/vri

Yahoo Society and Culture Directory -
http://dir.yahoo.com/Society_and_Culture/Religion_and_Spirituality/Faiths_and_Practices/Christianity

Index of Electronic Addresses of Denominations listed in the US Religious Bodies Chapter of this *Yearbook*

Advent Christian Church—Email: acpub@adventchristian.org
Web: www.adventchristian.org

African Methodist Episcopal Church—Email: Administrator@amecnet.org
Web: www.amecnet.org

African Methodist Episcopal Zion Church—Email: info@amezion.org
Web: www.amezion.org

Albanian Orthodox Archdiocese in America—Web: www.oca.org

The Allegheny Wesleyan Methodist Connection (Original Allegheny Conference)
Email: awmc@juno.com
Web: c1web.com/local_info/churches/aw.html

The Alliance of Baptists in the U.S.A.—Web: www.allianceofbaptists.org

The American Association of Lutheran Churches—Email: aa2taalc@aol.com
Web: www.taalc.com

The American Baptist Association—Email: bssc@abaptist.org
Web: www.abaptist.org

American Baptist Churches in the U.S.A.—Email: richard.schramm@abc-usa.org
Web: www.abc-usa.org

The American Carpatho-Russian Orthodox Greek Catholic Church—Email: archdiocese@goarch.org
Web: www.goarch.org

American Evangelical Christian Churches—Email: alpha@strato.net
Web: www.aeccministries.com

American Rescue Workers—Email: amerscwk@pcspower.net
Web: www.arwus.com

The Antiochian Orthodox Christian Archdiocese of North America—Email: FrJoseph@antiochian.org
Web: www.antiochian.org

Apostolic Catholic Assyrian Church of the East, North American Dioceses—Email: ABSoro@aol.com
Web: www.cired.org/ace.html

Apostolic Christian Churches of America—Email: Questions@ApostolicChristian.org
Web: www.apostolicchristian.org

Apostolic Episcopal Church—Email: osbm_ny@yahoo.com
Web: www.cinemaparallel.com/AECSynod.html

Apostolic Faith Mission of Portland, Oregon—Web: www.apostolicfaith.org

Apostolic Lutheran Church of America—Web: www.apostolic-lutheran.org

Apostolic Orthodox Catholic Church of North America—Email: aoccna.relations@usa.com

Apostolic Overcoming Holy Church of God, Inc.—Email: traydoc@mindspring.com

Armenian Apostolic Church of America—Email: prelacy@gis.net
Web: www.armprelacy.org

Assemblies of God—Email: info@ag.org
Web: www.ag.org

Assemblies of God International Fellowship (Independent/Not affiliated)—Email: admin@agifellowship.org
Web: www.agifellowship.org

Associate Reformed Presbyterian Church (General Synod)—Email: dragondraw@aol.com
Web: www.arpsynod.org

The Association of Free Lutheran Congregations—Email: webmaster@aflc.org
Web: www.aflc.org

Baptist Bible Fellowship International—Email: csbc@cherrystreet.org
Web: www.bbfi.org

Baptist General Conference—Email: gmarsh@baptistgeneral.org.
Web: www.bgcworld.org

Berean Fundamental Church—Email: office@bereanfellowship.org
Web: www.bereanfellowship.org

The Bible Church of Christ, Inc.—Email: bccbookstore@earthlink.net
Web: www.thebiblechurchofchrist.org

Bible Fellowship Church—Email: bfc@bfc.org
Web: www.bfc.org

Bible Way Church of Our Lord Jesus Christ World Wide, Inc.—Email: BWC@biblewaychurch.org
Web: www.biblewaychurch.org

Brethren in Christ Church—Email: RRoss@BIC-church.org
Web: www.bic-church.org/index.htm

Brethren Church (Ashland, Ohio)—Email: brethren@brethrenchurch.org
Web: www.brethrenchurch.org

The Catholic Church—Web: www.usccb.org

Christ Catholic Church—Email: ergoegosum@aol.com
Web: christcatholicchurch.freeyellow.com

Christadelphians—Email: Nzilmer@aol.com
Web: www.christadelphia.org

Christian Church (Disciples of Christ) in the United States and Canada
Email: cmiller@cm.disciples.org
Web: www.disciples.org

Christian Church of North America, General Council—Email: cnna@nauticom.net
Web: www.ccna.org

Christian Churches and Churches of Christ—Email: Jowston@cwv.edu
Web: www.cwv.net/christ'n (Unofficial)

The Christian Congregation, Inc.—Email: Revalnas@aol.com
Web: netministries.org/see/churches.exe/ch10619

Christian Methodist Episcopal Church—Email: juanbr4law@aol.com
Web: www.c-m-e.org

The Christian and Missionary Alliance—Email: info@cmalliance.org
Web: www.cmalliance.org

Christian Reformed Church in North America—Email: btgh@crcna.org
Web: www.crcna.org

Christian Union—Web: www.christianunion.com

Church of the Brethren—Email: cobweb@brethren.org
Web: www.brethren.org

Church of Christ—Web: church-of-christ.com

The Church of Christ (Holiness) U.S.A.—Email: Everything@cochusa.com
Web: www.cochusa.com/main.htm

Church of Christ, Scientist—Web: www.tfccs.com

Church of God (Anderson, Indiana)—Email: JMartin@chog.org
Web: www.chog.org

The Church Of God In Christ—Email: EJOHNCOGIC@aol.com
Web: netministries.org/see/churches/ch00833

Church of God in Christ, International—Email: laity@cogic.org
Web: www.cogic.org/main.htm

Church of God (Cleveland, Tennessee)—Email: info@cogtn.org
Web: www.chofgod.org

Church of God by Faith, Inc.—Email: natl-hq@cogbf.org
Web: www.cogbf.org

Church of God General Conference (Oregon, IL and Morrow, GA)—Email: info@abc-coggc.org
Web: www.abc-coggc.org

Church of God, Mountain Assembly, Inc.—Email: cgmahdq@jellico.com
Web: www.cgmahdq.org

Church of God of Prophecy—Email: betty@cogop.org
Web: www.cogop.org

The Church of God (Seventh Day), Denver, Colorado—Email: offices@cog7.org
Web: www.cog7.org

The Church of Illumination—Email: bevhall@comcat.com
Web: www.soul.org

The Church of Jesus Christ of Latter-day Saints—Web: www.lds.org

Church of the Lutheran Brethren of America—Email: clba@clba.org
Web: www.clba.org

Church of the Lutheran Confession—Email: JohnHLau@juno.com
Web: www.clclutheran.org

Church of the Nazarene—Email: ssm@nazarene.org
Web: www.nazarene.org

Church of Our Lord Jesus Christ of the Apostolic Faith, Inc.—Email: tewmsw@gloryroad.net
Web: www.apostolic-faith.org

Church of the United Brethren in Christ—Email: sdennie@ub.org
Web: www.ub.org

Churches of God, General Conference—Email: director@cggc.org
Web: www.cggc.org

Community of Christ—Email: snaylor@CofChrist.org
Web: www.CofChrist.org

Congregational Holiness Church—Email: chchurch@bellsouth.net
Web: www.chchurch.com

Conservative Baptist Association of America (CBAmerica)—Email: cba@cbamerica.org
Web: www.cbamerica.org

Conservative Congregational Christian Conference—Email: CCCC4@juno.com
Web: www.ccccusa.org

Conservative Lutheran Association—Email: PastorPJ@ix.netcom.com
Web: www.tlcanaheim.com/CLA

Coptic Orthodox Church—Web: www.coptic.org

Cumberland Presbyterian Church—Email: assembly@cumberland.org
Web: www.cumberland.org

Cumberland Presbyterian Church in America—Email: mleslie598@aol.com
Web: www.cumberland.org/cpca

Elim Fellowship—Email: 75551.743@compuserve.com
Web: www.ElimFellowship.org

Episcopal Church—Email: jrollins@ecusa.anglican.org
Web: www.ecusa.anglican.org

The Episcopal Orthodox Church—Email: eoc@orthodoxanglican.net
Web: orthodoxanglican.net

The Estonian Evangelical Lutheran Church—Email: konsistoorium@eelk.ee
Web: www.eelk.ee

The Evangelical Church—Email: jsditzel@juno.com
Web: quakertownecna.com/conferences.html

The Evangelical Church Alliance—Email: info@ecainternational.org
Web: www.ecainternational.org

The Evangelical Congregational Church—Email: eccenter@eccenter.com
Web: www.eccenter.com/church

The Evangelical Covenant Church—Email: president@covoffice.org
Web: www.covchurch.org

The Evangelical Free Church of America—Email: president@efca.org
Web: www.efca.org

Evangelical Friends International - North American Region—Email: efcer@aol.com
Web: www.evangelical-friends.org

Evangelical Lutheran Church in America—Email: info@elca.org
Web: www.elca.org

Evangelical Lutheran Synod—Email: gorvick@blc.edu
Web: www.EvLuthSyn.org

Evangelical Mennonite Church—Email: emcintlmin@aol.com

Evangelical Methodist Church—Email: headquarters@emchurch.org
Web: www.emchurch.org

Evangelical Presbyterian Church—Email: EPCHURCH@epc.org
Web: www.epc.org

Fellowship of Evangelical Bible Churches—Email: febcoma@aol.com
Web: members.aol.com/febcoma/index.html

Fellowship of Fundamental Bible Churches—Email: FFBC-USA@juno.com
Web: www.churches-ffbc.org

Fellowship of Grace Brethren Churches—Email: fgbc@fgbc.org
Web: www.fgbc.org

Free Methodist Church of North America—Email: info@fmcna.org
Web: www.freemethodistchurch.org

Friends General Conference—Email: friends@fgcquaker.org
Web: www.fgcquaker.org

Friends United Meeting—Email: info@fum.org
Web: www.fum.org

Full Gospel Fellowship of Churches and Ministers International—Email: FGFCMI@aol.com
Web: www.fgfcmi.org

General Association of Regular Baptist Churches—Email: garbc@garbc.org
Web: www.garbc.org

General Church of the New Jerusalem—Email: svsimpso@newchurch.edu
Web: www.newchurch.org

Grace Gospel Fellowship—Email: ggfinc@aol.com
Web: www.ggfusa.org

Greek Orthodox Archdiocese of America—Email: archdiocese@goarch.org
Web: www.goarch.org

The Holy Eastern Orthodox Catholic and Apostolic Church in North America, Inc.
Email: theocacna@webtv.net
Web: www.theocacna.org

Hutterian Brethren—Email: philsjg@juno.com

IFCA International, Inc.—Email: office@ifca.org
Web: www.ifca.org

International Church of the Foursquare Gospel—Email: comm@foursquare.org
Web: www.foursquare.org

The International Pentecostal Church of Christ—Email: hqipcc@aol.com
Web: members.aol.com/hqipcc

Jehovah's Witnesses—Web: www.watchtower.org

The Latvian Evangelical Lutheran Church in America—Email: pulins@flash.net

The Liberal Catholic Church–Province of the United States of America—Email: bshp052497@aol.com
Web: www.thelcc.org

The Lutheran Church—Missouri Synod (LCMS)—Email: infocenter@lcms.org
Web: www.lcms.org

Malankara Orthodox Syrian Church, Diocese of America—Email: Malankara@malankara.org
Web: www.malankara.org/american.htm

Mar Thoma Syrian Church of India—Email: webmaster@marthomachurch.org
Web: www.marthomachurch.org

Mennonite Church USA—Email: info@MennoniteUSA.org
Web: www.MennoniteChurchUSA.org

The Missionary Church—Email: mcdenomusa@aol.com
Web: www.mcusa.org

Moravian Church in America (Unitas Fratrum)—Email: burke@mcnp.org
Web: www.moravian.org

National Association of Congregational Christian Churches—Email: naccc@naccc.org
Web: www.naccc.org

National Association of Free Will Baptists—Email: webmaster@nafwb.org
Web: www.nafwb.org

National Organization of the New Apostolic Church of North America—Email: info@nak.org
Web: www.nak.org

National Spiritualist Association of Churches—Email: nsac@nsac.org
Web: www.nsac.org

Open Bible Standard Churches—Email: info@openbible.org
Web: www.openbible.org

The Orthodox Church in America—Email: jjm@oca.org
Web: www.oca.org

Patriarchal Parishes of the Russian Orthodox Church in the U.S.A.—Email: bmercurius@ruscon.com
Web: www.orthodox.net

Pentecostal Church of God—Email: pcg@pcg.org
Web: www.pcg.org

The Pentecostal Free Will Baptist Church, Inc.—Email: pheath@intrstar.net
Web: www.pfwb.org

Philadelphia Yearly Meeting of the Religious Society of Friends—Web: www.pym.org

Pillar of Fire—Email: info@zarephath.edu
Web: www.gospelcom.net/pof

Polish National Catholic Church of America—Email: ads22244@aol.com
Web: www.PNCC.org

Presbyterian Church in America—Email: ac@pcanet.org
Web: www.pcanet.org

Presbyterian Church (U.S.A.)—Email: presytel@pcusa.org
Web: www.pcusa.org

Primitive Methodist Church in the U.S.A.—Email: pmconf@juno.com
Web: www.primitivemethodistchurch.org

Protestant Reformed Churches in America—Email: doezema@prca.org
Web: www.prca.org

Reformed Catholic Church—Email: berzol@apollo3.com
Web: www.geocities.com/WestHollywood/4136

Reformed Church in America—Email: kbaker@rca.org
Web: www.rca.org

Reformed Church in the United States—Email: fhw@iname.com
Web: www.rcus.org

Reformed Episcopal Church—Email: wycliffe@jps.net
Web: recus.org

Reformed Presbyterian Church of North America—Email: RPTrustees@aol.com
Web: www.reformedpresbyterian.org

The Romanian Orthodox Episcopate of America—Email: roeasolia@aol.com
Web: www.roea.org

Separate Baptists in Christ—Email: mail@separatebaptist.org
Web: www.separatebaptist.org

Serbian Orthodox Church in the U.S.A. and Canada—Email: oea@oea.serbian-church.net
Web: oea.serbian-church.net

Seventh Day Baptist General Conference, USA and Canada—Email: sdbgen@inwave.com
Web: www.seventhdaybaptist.org

Southern Baptist Convention—Email: bmerrell@sbc.net
Web: www.sbc.net

Southern Methodist Church—Email: smchq@juno.com

Sovereign Grace Believers—Email: jon@searchingtogether.org
Web: www.searchingtogether.org

The Swedenborgian Church—Email: manager@swedenborg.org
Web: www.swedenborg.org

Syrian (Syriac) Orthodox Church of Antioch—Email: syrianoc@syrianorthodoxchurch.org
Web: www.syrianorthodoxchurch.org

The Syro-Russian Orthodox Catholic Church, Romano Byzantine Synod—Email: rbsocc@juno.com

Ukrainian Orthodox Church of the U.S.A.—Email: uocofusa@aol.com
Web: www.uocofusa.org

Unitarian Universalist Association of Congregations—Email: jhurley@uua.org
Web: www.uua.org

United Church of Christ—Email: langa@ucc.org
Web: www.ucc.org

United Holy Church of America, Inc.—Email: books@mohistory.org

The United Methodist Church—Email: infoserv@umcom.umc.org
Web: www.umc.org

Universal Fellowship of Metropolitan Community Churches
Email: communications@ufmcchq.com
Web: www.ufmcchq.com

Volunteers of America—Email: voa@voa.org
Web: www.voa.org

The Wesleyan Church—Email: gensupts@wesleyan.org
Web: www.wesleyan.org

Wisconsin Evangelical Lutheran Synod—Email: webbin@sab.wels.net
Web: www.wels.net

6. Sources of Religion-Related Research

I. Directory of Selected Research Organizations

The editorial office of the *Yearbook of American & Canadian Churches* receives innumerable requests for data about churches, religious organizations, attendance patterns, and comparative religion concerns. Sometimes we are able to furnish the requested data, but more often we refer the inquirer to other research colleagues in the field. We are always interested in and aided by such requests, and we find ourselves informed by each question.

In response to such inquiries, the "Sources in Religion-Related Research" directory was initiated in the 1999 edition of the *Yearbook* In addition to asking each organization to provide a brief overall description, each was also asked to indicate any special research foci (i.e. denominational, congregational, interfaith, gender, etc.). Further, each organization was asked to identify the sociological, methodological, or theological approaches that serve to guide their research, and to describe any current or recent research projects. Lastly, we asked for a list of recurrent publications. Below the organizations' responses to these questions are reported as clearly and completely as is possible. Contact information appears just beneath the title of each organization. In most cases, the organization's website provides very detailed information about current research projects.

Numerous other research centers in the area of American religious life, each with specific areas of concern, conduct timely and significant research. We hope that readers will find utility in this directory and we invite them to identify additional sources by email: yearbook@ncccusa.org or by Fax: (212) 870-2817.

American Academy of Religion (AAR)

AAR Executive Office
825 Houston Mill Rd., Ste. 300
Atlanta, GA 30329
Tel. (404)727-7920
Email: aar@emory.edu
Website: www.aar-site.org
President: Dr. Lawrence E. Sullivan
Exec. Dir.: Dr. Barbara DeConcini

The AAR is the major learned society and professional association for scholars whose object of study is religion. Its mission—in a world where religion plays so central a role in social, political and economic events, as well as in the lives of communities and individuals—is to meet a critical need for ongoing reflection upon and understanding of religious traditions, issues, questions and values. As a learned society and professional association of teachers and research scholars, the American Academy of Religion has over 8000 members who teach in some 1,500 colleges, universities, seminaries, and schools in North America and abroad. The Academy is dedicated to furthering knowledge of religion and religious institutions in all their forms and manifestations. This is accomplished through Academy-wide and regional conferences and meetings, publications, programs, and membership services. Within a context of free inquiry and critical examination, the Academy welcomes all disciplined reflection on religion—both from within and outside of communities of belief and practice—and seeks to enhance its broad public understanding.

The AAR's annual meeting, over 7,500 scholars gather to share research and collaborate on scholarly projects. The annual meeting sessions are grouped into over 70 program units, each representing an ongoing community of scholars who are collectively engaged in pursuing knowledge about a specific religious tradition or a specific aspect of religion. In addition, the AAR's ten regional organizations sponsor smaller annual meetings that are similar in structure to the Academy-wide meeting. All of the world's major religious traditions, as well as indigenous and historical religions, are explored in the work of AAR members.

Current or Recent Research

Currently, for example, the AAR offers Teaching Workshops for both junior and senior scholars. It is organizing efforts to gather data on the field to facilitate departmental planning and funding. A full explanation of the many current research projects is available on the AAR website, which is listed above.

Periodicals

The *Journal of the American Academy of Religion* is the scholarly periodical of the AAR. In addition, the AAR publishes a semi-annual periodical titled "Spotlight on Teaching" in the society's newsletter, *Religious Studies News*

American Religion Data Archive (ARDA)

Department of Sociology / Anthropology
Purdue University
1365 Stone Hall
West Lafayette, IN 47907-1476
Tel. (765) 494-0081
Fax (765) 496-1476
Email: archive@sri.soc.purdue.edu
Website: www.TheARDA.com
Director: Dr. Roger Finke

The American Religion Data Archive (ARDA) is an Internet-based data archive that stores and distributes quantitative data sets from the leading studies on American religion—free of charge. Supported by the Lilly Endowment and housed at Purdue University, ARDA strives to *preserve* data files for future use, *prepare* the data files for immediate public use, and make the data files easily *accessible* to all. Data files can be downloaded from the Internet site or they can be analyzed online.

The ARDA includes national surveys on American and Canadian religion, regional surveys, surveys sampling the membership of specific denominations, and surveys of religions professionals. The 1952, 1971, 1980, and 1990 Church and Church Membership surveys for counties and states are also included in the ARDA.

Association of Theological Schools (ATS)

10 Summit Park Dr.
Pittsburgh, PA 15275-1103
Tel. (412) 788-6505
Fax (412) 788-6510
Email: ats@ats.edu
Website: www.ats.edu
Exec. Dir.: Daniel O. Aleshire
Contact: Nancy Merrill, Dir. of Communications and Membership Services

The Association of Theological Schools (ATS) is the accrediting and program agency for graduate theological education in North America. Its 237 member institutions represent the broad spectrum of denominational, ecclesiastical, and theological perspectives evident in North America today, making it the most broad-based religious organization of its kind. The Association comprises Protestant, Roman Catholic, and Orthodox schools of theology, both university-related divinity schools and freestanding seminaries. A full list of members is available on the above website.

The primary purpose of the Association is the improvement of theological schools, which ATS seeks to attain by accrediting schools and by providing programs and service to its membership, such as, among others, a data center of statistical information on the member schools; leadership education for seminary presidents, academic deans, trustees, and development officers; grants for faculty scholarship and research; faculty development programs sponsored by the Faculty Resource Center; student information resources; a program of globalization in theological education; efforts to enhance the participation of under-represented constituencies in theological education; and various publications. In addition, the Association provides a venue for addressing the critical and emerging issues in North American theological education.

Current or Recent Research

The current discussion focuses on identifying the nature, characteristics, and related issues related to the "Public Character of Theological Education." The major activities of the project include convening five study groups to explore the issue from varying ecclesial and institutional contexts; a regranting program to provide the stimulus for schools to experiment with programs to establish a greater civic presence in their communities; and opportunities to focus though and conversation about the public character of theological education broadly among faculties and administrative leaders of ATS schools. The discussion will explore how more rigorous theological thinking about the public issues that face democratic cultures can contribute not only to the intellectual life of the theological school but to the broader society as well.

Periodicals

Fact Book on Theological Education is published annually and provides statistical data on theological education in the U.S. and Canada. Also, the Association publishes a journal, *Theological Education* bi-annually, a newsletter bimonthly called *Colloquy*, and the formal institutional documents of the Association entitled the *Bulletin*. The Bulletin also contains an ATS directory and a membership list.

Auburn Theological Seminary

3041 Broadway
New York, NY 10027
Tel. (212) 662-4315
Fax (212) 663-5214
Email: mnw@auburn.org
Website: www.auburnsem.org
Director: Dr. Barbara G. Wheeler
Contact: Ms. Sharon Miller

Auburn Theological Seminary's mission is to strengthen religious leadership. It carries out its mission through programs of non-degree theological education for clergy and laity; through programs for Presbyterian students enrolled at its partner institution, Union Seminary in New York City; and by conducting research on theological education at its Center for the Study of Theological Education. Auburn was founded in 1818 in Auburn, New York; it is currently located on Union Seminary's campus.

Auburn Seminary is related by covenant agreement with Presbyterian Church (U.S.A.), but most of its programs are ecumenical, and many have a multi-faith focus. The Center for the Study of Theological Education includes rabbinical schools and Protestant and Roman Catholic seminaries and divinity schools in its studies.

Research is conducted using a variety of methods, including survey and ethnographic research, structured interview and documentary research, research reports on surveys and case studies. Reports of findings are frequently published with accompanying information on the history of the issue being studied and with theological commentaries written from a variety of perspectives.

Current or Recent Research

Currently, the Center is completing studies of seminary students, of public perceptions of theological education and church leadership, and of history of religion and urban America. The Center is about to begin a study of seminary trustees and senior administrators.

Periodicals

Auburn Studies, an occasional bulletin in which the Center publishes its research results. Research reports are also available on Auburn's website (listed above).

Barna Research Group, Ltd.

5528 Everglades
Ventura, CA 93003
Tel. (805) 658-8885
Fax (805) 658-7298
Website: www.barna.org
President: George Barna
Contact: David Kinnaman, Vice President

Barna Research Group works with Christian churches and parachurch ministries throughout the nation by providing primary research data related to cultural change, people's lifestyles, values, attitudes, beliefs and religious practices. Its vision is to provide current accurate and reliable information, in bite-sized pieces and at reasonable costs, to ministries who will use the information to make better strategic decisions. They conduct primary research for ministries that commission such research, studying their community, their church or special population. Barna also produces many research-based books, reports, and ministry tools to help churches understand the national context of ministry. Barna Research conducts seminars in many markets across the nation to inform church leaders of its findings, and to train church leaders in the application of that information. The organization works with churches from all Christian denominations.

Barna Research has no special research focus. It conducts projects based upon existing needs in the Church at-large, or for its clients specifically, and analyzes all of its findings in relation to a minimum of three dozen population subgroups involved in the survey interviews. Methodologically, Barna Research uses both qualitative approaches (focus groups, depth interviews) and quantitative approaches (cross-sectional surveys, longitudinal studies, panel research). Data collection methods include telephone surveys, mail surveys, in-person interviews, on-line surveys, self-administered surveys, focus groups.

Current or Recent Research

Barna Research conducts more than 50 studies each year, covering a broad range of topics. Some of the recent non-proprietary studies completed are focused on understanding the state of the Church; the habits of highly effective churches; worship efficacy; the unchurched; strategies and techniques for developing lay leaders; understanding effective discipleship processes; pastoral profiles; beliefs and core attitudes of religious donors; Biblical knowledge, and many others.

Periodicals

Barna Research offers a bi-weekly update on current information related to faith matters from its national non-proprietary research. This information is free to those who register for it at the website (listed above).

Center for the Study of Religion and American Culture

Indiana University
Purdue University at Indianapolis
425 University Blvd, Room 341
Indianapolis, IN 46202-5140
Tel. (317) 274-8409
Fax (317) 278-3354
Email: Ccherry@iupui.edu
Website: www.iupui.edu/it/raac
Director: Dr. Conrad Cherry

The Center for the Study of Religion and American Culture is a research and public outreach institute devoted to the promotion of the understanding of the relation between religion and other features of American culture. Research methods are both inter-disciplinary and multi-disciplinary. Established in 1989, the Center is based in the School of Liberal Arts and Indiana University-Purdue University at Indianapolis. Center activities include national conferences and symposia, commissioned books, essays, bibliographies, and research projects, fellowships for younger scholars, data based communication about developments in the field of American religion, a newsletter devoted to the promotion of Center activities, and the semi-annual scholarly periodical, *Religion and American Culture: A Journal of Interpretation.*

Current or Recent Research

The Center is currently conducting research on the "public dimensions of American Religion," and on "Religion in Higher Education."

Periodicals

Religion and American Culture: A Journal of Interpretation. Center books include the series, "The Public Expressions of Religion in America."

empty tomb, inc.

301 North Fourth Street
P.O. Box 2404
Champaign, IL 61825-2404
Tel. (217)356-9519
Fax (217)356-2344
Website: www.emptytomb.org
CEO: John L. Ronsvalle
Exec.Vice-Pres.: Sylvia Ronsvalle

empty tomb, inc. is a Christian research and service organization. On a local level, it coordinates direct services to people in need in cooperation with area congregations. On a national level, it studies church member giving patterns of historically Christian churches, including Roman Catholic, mainline and evangelical Protestant, Anabaptist, Pentecostal, Orthodox, and fundamentalist communions. empty tomb publishes the annual *State of Church Giving* series. Staff also work with a select number of congregations, discovering ways to reverse the negative giving trends indicated by national data, through its project, The National Money for Mission Program.

Current or Recent Research

Current research monitors and analyzes church member giving patters, and is published in *The State of Church Giving* series produced by empty tomb, inc. The description of dynamics affecting current giving patterns is presented in *Behind The Stained Glass Windows: Money Dynamics in The Church* (Grand Rapids, MI: Baker Books, 1996).

Periodicals

The State of Church Giving series is an annual publication. It considers denominational giving data, analysis of giving and membership trends, and other estimates of charitable giving. Each edition has featured a special focus chapter, which discusses giving issues relevant to a broad audience. Selected data tables are posted on the empty tomb website (listed above).

The Hartford Institute for Religious Research of Hartford Seminary

Hartford Seminary
77 Sherman Street
Hartford, CT 06105
Tel. (860)509-9543
Fax (860)509-9559
Email: hirr@hartsem.edu Website: www.hartsem.edu/csrr/

The Hartford Institute for Religion Research of Hartford Seminary was established in 1981, formalizing a research program initiated by the Seminary in 1974. Until recently it was known as The Center for Social and Religious Research. The Institute's work is guided by a disciplined understanding of the interrelationship between (a) the inner life and resources of American religious institutions and (b) the possibilities and limits placed on those institutions by the social and cultural context into which God has called them.

Its twenty-year record of rigorous, policy-relevant research, anticipation of emerging issues, commitment to the creative dissemination of learning, and strong connections to both theological education and the church has earned the Institute an international reputation as an important bridge between the scholarly community and the practice of ministry.

Current or Resent Research

Some of the titles of current projects at the Institute are: "Organizing Religious Work for the 21st Century: Exploring `Denominationalism;'" "Cooperative Congregational Studies Project;" "Congregational Consulting Services;" "New England Religion Discussion Society (NERDS);" "Congregational Studies Team." Descriptions of these programs are available on the Institute's website, listed above.

Periodicals

Praxis is Hartford Seminary's magazine, which focuses on the activities and faculty of the Institute.

Institute for Ecumenical and Cultural Research

P.O. Box 6188
Collegeville, MN 56321-6188
Tel. (320) 363-3366
Fax (320) 363-3313
Email: iecr@csbsju.edu
Website: www.csbsju.edu/iecr
Exec. Dir.: Dr. Patrick Henry

The Institute for Ecumenical and Cultural Research brings together well-trained, creative, articulate men and women for careful thought and dialogue in a place of inquiry and prayer. The Resident scholars Program welcomes researchers and their families for either individual semesters or for an entire academic year. Resident scholars work on their own projects but meet once a week for seminars, and have other occasions for conversation. Each scholar presents a public lecture. Ecumenism happens at the Institute as people come to know one another in community. The Institute is an independent corporation, but shares in the Benedictine and academic life of Saint John's Abbey and University, and of nearby Saint Benedict's Monastery and the College of Saint Benedict. In the summer the Institute uses its facilities for invitational consultations on subjects considered by the Board of Directors to be of special ecumenical interest.

In the Resident Scholars Program, the subjects of research are determined by the interests of the applicants who are invited to come by the Admissions Committee. While most of the work tends to be in traditional theological areas, we encourage people in all fields to consider applying, both because ecumenism is of concern across the spectrum of disciplines, and because the term "cultural" in our title extends our reach beyond theology and religious studies. In particular cases, work done here may have a denominational, congregational, or interfaith focus, but the Institute does not prescribe or delimit, in any narrow way, what is appropriate.

Current or Recent Research

Recent summer consultations have had the following titles: "Prayer in the Ecumenical Movement"; "Virtues for an Ecumenical Heart"; "The Price of Disunity"; "Living Faithfully in North America Today." Among subjects dealt with in earlier years are "Orthodoxy at Home in North America"; "transmitting Tradition to Children and Young People"; "The Nature of Christian Hope"; "Women and the Church"; Jewish and Christian Relatedness to Scripture"; "Confessing Christian Faith in a Pluralistic Society."

Periodicals

Ecumenical People, Programs, Papers is an bi-annual newsletter containing brief sketches of resident scholars, reports on Institute programs, and, in nearly every issue, an "An Occasional Paper" on a subject of ecumenical interest. The newsletter is free.

Institute for the Study of American Evangelicals (ISAE)

Wheaton College
Wheaton, IL 60187
Tel. (630) 752-5437
Fax (630) 752-5516
Email: isae@wheaton.edu
Website: www.wheaton.edu/isae
Director: Dr. Edith Blumhofer

Founded in 1982, the Institute for the Study of American Evangelicals is a center for research and functions as a program of Wheaton College. The purpose of the ISAE is to encourage and support research on evangelical Christianity in the United States and Canada. The institute seeks to help evangelicals develop a mature understanding of their own heritage and to inform others about evangelicals' historical significance and contemporary role. For the most part, the ISAE focuses on historical research, with occasional sociological or economic researchers participating in the projects.

Current or Recent Research

One recent project entitled, "Hymnody in American Protestantism" is a research project focusing on the history of hymnology in American religious life.

Periodicals

Evangelical Studies Bulletin (ESB) is designed to aid both the scholar and the layman in his or her education and research of evangelicalism. Issued quarterly, the bulletin contains articles, book reviews, notices, a calendar of events, and bibliographic information on the latest dissertations, articles and books related to the study of evangelicalism.

Institute for the Study of American Religion

P.O. Box 90709
Santa Barbara, CA 93190-0709
Tel. (805)967-7721
Fax (805)961-0141
Website: www.americanreligion.org

The Institute for the Study of American Religion was founded in 1969 in Evanston, Illinois as a religious studies research facility with a particular focus upon the smaller religions of the United States. Those groups which it has concentrated upon have been known under a variety of labels including sect, cult, minority religion, alternative religion, non-conventional religion, spiritual movement, and new religious movement. It quickly extended its attention to Canada developed a worldwide focus in the 1990's. In 1985, the institute moved to its present location in Santa Barbara, California.

Over the years the institute built a large collection of both primary and secondary materials on the religious groups and movements it studied. In 1985 this collection of more than 40,000 volumes and thousands of periodicals and archival materials was deposited to the Davidson Library at the University of California in Santa Barbara. The reference material exists today as the *American Religious Collection* and is open to scholars and the interested public. The institute continues to support the collection with donations of additional materials.

Current or Recent Research

Today the institute has two main foci. It monitors all of the religious denominations, organizations, and movements functioning in North America and regularly publishes reports drawing from that activity in a series of reference books. The most important of these reference books is the *Encyclopedia of American Religions* (Detroit: Gale research, 5th edition, 1996). Among the most called for information is factual data on the many new and more controversial religious movements, which are popularly labeled as "cults." The institute's second focus developed out of its more recent refocusing on the international scene, provoked by the international life of most of the religious groups which it has studied in previous decades. With support from the Institute of World Spirituality in Chicago, Illinois, the institute launched the International Religions Directory Project in 1996, a massive five year project that aims to create a full directory of religious bodies, interfaith organizations, and other religious groups world-wide. Please see the above website for more information.

J.W. Dawson Institute of Church-State Studies at Baylor University

P.O. Box 97308
Waco, TX 76798-7308
Tel. (254) 710-1510
Fax (254) 710-1571
Email: dere_davis@baylor.edu
Website: www.baylor.edu/~Church_State
Director: Dr. Derek Davis

Baylor University established the J.M. Dawson Institute of Church-State Studies in 1957, so named in honor of an outstanding alumnus, an ardent advocate of religious liberty, and a distinguished author of publications on church and state. The Institute is the oldest and most well-established facility of its kind located in a university setting. It is exclusively devoted to research in the broad field of church and state and the advancement of religious liberty around the world.

From its inception in 1957, the stated purpose of the Institute has been to stimulate academic interest and encourage research and publication in the broad area of church-state relations. In carrying out its statement of purpose, the Institute has sought to honor a threefold commitment: to be interfaith, interdisciplinary, and international.

Current or Recent Research

Some current research includes: Government persecution of minority religions in Europe; original intent of Founding Fathers regarding religion and public life; Christian Right views on political activism; conservative versus moderate Baptist views on church-state relations; role of civil religion in America; international treaties and religious liberty.

Periodicals

Journal of Church and State is the only scholarly journal expressly devoted to church-state relations.

The Louisville Institute

1044 Alta Vista Road
Louisville, KY 40205-1798
Tel. (502) 895-3411 ext. 487
Fax (502) 894-2286
Email: info@louisville-institute.org
Website: www.louisville-institute.org
Exec. Dir.: Dr. James W. Lewis

The Louisville Institute is a Lilly Endowment program for the study of American religion based at the Louisville Presbyterian Seminary. As a program of Lilly Endowment, the Louisville Institute builds upon the Endowment's long-standing support of both leadership education and scholarly research on American religion, focusing on American Protestantism, American Catholicism, the historic African-American churches, and the Hispanic religious experience. The distinctive mission of the Louisville Institute is to enrich the religious life of American Christians and to encourage the revitalization of their institutions by bringing together those who lead religious institutions with those who study them, so that the work of each might stimulate and inform the other. The Louisville Institute seeks to fulfil its mission through a program of grantmaking and conferences.

The work of the Louisville Institute focuses on religion in North America, with particular attention to three issues. The first, Christian faith and life, concerns the character and role of the theology and spirituality that are effectively at work in the lives of American Christians. The second, religious institutions, asks how America's religious institutions might respond most constructively in the midst of the bewildering institutional reconfiguration occurring in American society. The third, pastoral leadership, explores various strategies for improving the quality of religious leadership in North America. The various research projects employ a variety of disciplinary perspectives, including but not limited to, theology, history, ethics, and the social sciences. They may also be interdisciplinary in nature.

Current or Recent Research

Please see the Louisville Institute website (listed above) for lists of recent grants made by the Louisville Institute.

The Pluralism Project

Harvard University
201 Vanserg Hall
25 Francis Avenue
Cambridge, MA 02138
Tel. (617)496-2481
Fax (617)496-2428
Email: pluralsm@fas.harvard.edu
Website: www.fas.harvard.edu/~pluralsm
Director: Dr. Diana L. Eck
Project Manager: Ellie J. Pierce

The Pluralism Project was developed by Dr. Diana L. Eck at Harvard University to study and document the growing religious diversity of the United States, with a special view to its new immigrant religious communities. The religious landscape of the U.S. has radically changed in the past 30 years; in light of these changes, how Americans of all faiths begin to engage with one another in shaping a positive pluralism is one of the most important questions American society faces in the years ahead. In addressing these phenomena, the Project has three goals: 1) to document some further changes taking place in America's cities and towns by beginning to map their new religious demography with old and new mosques and Islamic centers, Sikh gurdwaras, Hindu and Jain temples, Buddhist temples and meditation centers, Zoroastrian and Taoist religious centers. 2) To begin to study how these religious traditions are changing as they take root in American soil and develop in a new context. How are they beginning to recreate their community life, religious institutions, rites and rituals, and forms of transmission in the cultural environment of the United States? 3) To explore how the United States is changing as we begin to appropriate this new religious diversity in our public life and institutions, and in emerging forms of interfaith relationships.

The Pluralism Project has the most comprehensive archive anywhere of the print materials of America's new immigrant religious communities: newsletters, serial publications, anniversary programs, handbooks, prayer books, calendars, and educational materials. The Project files also include research papers as well as a variety of materials donated directly by centers.

The Pluralism Project On-Line Directory maintains an extensive directory of religious centers in the United States. At present, this directory exists in a sortable database, with listings of nearly 3,000 centers across the U.S.

Current or Recent Research

The Pluralism Project produced a CD-ROM, *On Common Ground: World Religions in America*, to present some of the wide range of work that had emerged from three years of research. A further grant from the Ford Foundation has enabled the Project to extend its research on the American religious landscape.

Princeton Religion Research Center (PRRC)

47 Hulfish Street
P.O. Box 389
Princeton, NJ 08542
Tel. (609) 279-2255
Fax (609) 924-0228
Email: marie_swirsky@gallup.com
Website: www.prrc.com
Exec. Dir.: George Gallup, Jr.
Contact: Marie Swirsky

The Princeton Religion Research Center is a venerable interfaith, non-denominational organization founded by George Gallup, Jr. and Dr. Miriam Murphy in 1977. The PRRC specializes in creative, practical research, utilizing the worldwide Gallup survey facilities. The purpose of the PRRC is to gain a better understanding of the nature and depth of religious commitment, and to explore the factors behind spiritual growth and decline. The research employs qualitative and quantitative Gallup survey research using scientifically-selected samples of people.

Current or Recent Research

The Princeton Religion Research Center, the Gallup Organization, the Gallup Poll, and the Gallup Youth Survey have conducted surveys for more than 100 denominations or religious groups.

Periodicals

Emerging Trends, published since 1979, provides up-to-date Gallup survey information on religion and society. The six-page monthly keeps readers abreast of national issues facing church and society, as well as the latest findings on religious belief, practice, and knowledge. *Religion in America* is a bi-annual report.

The Public Religion Project

919 North Michigan Ave.
Suite 540
Chicago, IL 60611-1681
Tel. (312)397-6400
Email: prp-info@publicreligionproj.org
Website: www.publicreligionproj.org
Director: Dr. Martin E. Marty

Building on the strength of personal and private expressions of religious faith, the Public Religion Project addresses the issue of public expressions of faith in a diverse civil society. The Chicago-based directors, staff, and advisors of the Project cooperate internationally with the many agencies, academies, and individuals who would bridge the gap between public and private articulations and actions. It is through this cooperation that the Public Religion Project seeks to contribute to the improved quality of life in the republic. The Public Religion Project has no particular ideological bias, and its only agenda is to help assure that the role of religion is given a representative hearing. The Project's leadership listens carefully for expressions by people of profound conviction and institutions that represent the ever-growing variety of religious impulses in America. It seeks to promote that expression in public life. The role of The Public Religion Project is to provide public access to experts; it does not do original research.

Current or Recent Research

The Public Religion Project maintains a comprehensive database of contact information about individuals who can address questions about religion and about the role it plays in public life. The database consists of internationally recognized scholars, experts, spokespersons and authorities who have agreed to be listed as resources. The database serves a great variety of researchers, including academics, politicians, religious leaders, and many others.

II. Directory of Selected Faith Traditions in America

Compiling a directory of faith groups is an arduous but rewarding task in religiously plural America. In part, because the very self understanding and definition of community varies so greatly from faith group to faith group. In order to present a reasonably parallel and well balanced listing of organizations for each faith, care must be taken not to impose categories or terms from one's own universe of understanding upon other contexts. The very terms, "church," "membership," "denomination, " "hierarchy" which are essential constructs of certain Christian universes of understanding, are rendered meaningless when applied to other faith groups.

Further, it is important to remember that many religious traditions lack a centralized organization which speaks for the whole of the community. Often, this lack of centralization speaks to the existence of several distinct forms or branches of the religion. In some instances, different ethnic groups immigrating to the U.S., bring with them a distinctive form of their religion, which is particular to their culture of origin. In other cases, plural forms of a faith exist resulting from theological, political, or economic differences. Still other faith groups may be more tightly organized, but the religious center which provides guidance in matters of faith and, perhaps, even organizational discipline may not be in the United States. Hence, the organizations before us are not necessarily religious hierarchical organizations, but are often groups assembled for other purposes that are associated with a particular faith group, or subdivision of that faith group. Caution is advised in regarding these entries as one might regard a "church headquarters."

The compilation of any directory relies upon the existence of a some common organizational structure within all the entities listed. Yet, when compiling a directory of faith groups, it cannot be assumed such organizational parallels exist. Oblique ways must be found to adequately represent individual faith groups. The many religious communities in the United States are associated with myriad organizations of all different types. Some of these are primarily places of worship; others are organizations seeking to represent either the religious community as a whole or some particular constituency within it. Others are community centers; some are educational groups; some are organizations particularly for women or youths; and some are political action groups. Still others are peace organizations or relief organizations. That said, a directory of this sort cannot include an exhaustive list of organizations for each faith group nationwide. The omission of any particular organization or branch of any of the major faith groups listed does not reflect a deliberate attempt to homogenize the rich pluralities that exist within faith groups. Instead, the listings which follow are intended to provide the interested reader with a few initial contacts within each religious community.

Despite the above cautions, this directory provides a rich resource for readers and researchers who wish to learn more about other faith groups. The churches listed here consist of organizations of importance within the communities they represent, and serve as excellent introductory points of contact with those communities.

In some cases, these religious communities are in a state of flux; those with access to the Internet will often find it an excellent way to keep contact with changing religious organizations. There is a plethora of information available about nearly all religious traditions on the Internet with varying degrees of accuracy. Some sites provide extensive links to information and to organizations on the web. For an extensive listing of religious search engines, please see Directory 5, "The Electronic Church."

For directory information about national Inter-faith organizations in the United States, please see Directory 1, "U.S. Cooperative Organizations". For directory information on local Inter-faith organizations, please see Directory 7, "U.S. Regional and Local Ecumenical Bodies".

BAHA'ISM

Baha'ism was founded in Persia during the late 19th century by Mirza Hussein Ali Nuri, also known as Baha'ullah, which means "Glory of God" in Arabic. Baha'i is an outgrowth of an earlier Persian religious movement called Babism, which was initiated by Mirza Ali Muhammad, who was referred to as the "Bab". In 1844, the Bab prophesied that in nineteen years, a divine manifestation of God would appear. Shortly afterward, the Babis endured a massive period of persecution in which the Bab was martyred. In 1863, Baha'ullah, a close follower of the Bab, claimed that he, himself was this divine manifestation of God. Further, he claimed that he was the last in a line of such divine figures, which included Zoroaster, the Buddha, Christ, and Muhammad. Along these lines, Baha'ullah's teachings called for a religious universalism in which moral truths could be gleaned from all faiths. His son, Abd al-Baha, spread his father's teachings to the Western world, insisting on certain social principles such as universal equality of the sexes, or races, and of religious adherence.

The Baha'i National Center of the U.S.A.
536 Sheridan Road
Wilmette, IL 60091
Tel: (708) 869-9039
Website: www.bahai.org

This center can provide information about the Baha'i faith and provide contacts with Baha'i organizations throughout the country and the world. There are over 1,400 Baha'i local spiritual assemblies in the United States. The community is very concerned about issues involving peace, justice, racial unity, economic development, and education (among others) and has available resources on a number of these issues as well as on Baha'i scriptures and theology. The website listed above is the official Baha'i website on the Internet.

BUDDHISM

Buddhism began in northern India between the 6th–5th centuries B.C.E. with the teachings of Siddhartha Gautama, who is called the Buddha, which means "The One Who is Enlightened."

Buddhism grew out of the Hindu tradition of the time, but it rejected certain fundamental philosophical, cosmological, social, hierarchical, and scriptural aspects of that tradition, which set the two deeply apart from each other. Most Buddhists believe that suffering is the central predicament of life, and that desires are the source of this suffering. One need only remove desires and it follows that suffering disappears as well. Buddhism has grown in different directions over the centuries among many different cultures, and its traditions have varied widely. All are usually characterized by an emphasis on meditation and compassion. Buddhism is divided into three major branches: *Theravada*, "the way of the Elders," *Mahayana* "the Great Vehicle," and *Vajrayana*, "the indestructible vehicle" or path of devotion. Buddhism spread through parts of South Asia, the Himalayan region, all over China, Japan, and Korea, and deeply into South East Asia. Although its origins are Indian, Buddhism is almost entirely absent from that country. In the past hundred and fifty years, Buddhism has spread to the Western world. In this religious tradition, with few national bodies and great variation among particular branches and cultural expressions, organization is more localized than in some other faith groups.

American Buddhist Congress
4267 West Third Street
Los Angeles, CA 20020
Tel: 213-386-8139
An association of leaders from a variety of Buddhist traditions in the U.S.

Buddhist Churches of America
1710 Octavia Street
San Francisco, CA 94109
Tel: 415-776-5600
Fax: 415-771-6293
Bishop, Ven. Hakubun Watanabe
The national body of Japanese Shin tradition was founded in 1899. It provides programmatic resources for local temples around the U.S.

Buddhist Council of the Midwest
2400 Prairie
Evanston, IL 60201
Tel: 847-869-4975
A regional organization active in coordinating activities among the Buddhist communities in the mid-west.

Buddhist Sangha Council of Southern California
933 South New Hampshire Ave.
Los Angeles, CA 90006
Tel: 213-739-1270
FAX: 213-386-6643
The umbrella organization of Buddhist communities in Southern California.

Texas Buddhist Council
8727 Radio Road
Houston, TX 77075
Tel: 713-744-1334
The regional coordinating body for Buddhists in Texas.

The Buddhist Peace Fellowship
P. O. Box 4650
Berkeley, CA 94704
Tel: 510-655-6169
FAX: 510-655-1369
Email: bpf@bpf.org
Director, Alan Senauke
A national organization through which Buddhists of many traditions work for peace and justice.

HINDUISM

Hinduism has been evolving since roughly 1500 B.C.E. and has its origins in India. Most of the inhabitants of India are still Hindus, but many have emigrated to Europe, North America, East Africa, South and South East Asia. The beliefs and practices of Hinduism vary so deeply and widely throughout India, and are so diffused throughout every aspect of life, that one may describe Hinduism not so much as a tradition, but more accurately as the collection of many traditions, encompassed by the great history and geography of India. Throughout its history, Hinduism has had an enormous propensity for the absorption of new elements into its practices and its understanding of deity. There is no central authority or priestly hierarchy that regulates the evolution of Hinduism, very few traditions are shared by all Hindus; adaptations and evolutions can and do occur, but usually at the regional level. Simultaneously, ancient practices and beliefs persist in some places, where elsewhere, they have been long since replaced or never occurred. Nevertheless, all Hindus believe in the authority of the *Vedas*, the ancient scriptural tradition of India. All accept the *dharma*, or "way," of the four *varnas*, or social classes, which constitute the complex caste system, which is interwoven in the practice of the religion. Further, most Hindus worship Shiva or Vishnu or Devi, in addition to individual devotions to other deities or divine manifestations. Most Hindus are vegetarians.

The International Society for Krishna Consciousness
North American Communications
10310 Oaklyn Drive

Potomac, MD 20854
Tel: 301-299-9707
FAX: 301-299-5025
Email: anuttama.acbsp@com.bbt.se
Communications Director, Anuttama Dasa

Council of Hindu Temples of North America
45-57 Bowne Street
Flushing, NY 11355
Tel: 1-800-99HINDU

One of a number of Hindu organizations, which connect Hindus in certain regions of the U.S.

American Hindus Against Defamation
8914 Rotherdam Avenue
San Diego, CA 92129
Tel: 619-484-4564
Email: ajay@hindunet.org
Director, Mr. Ajay Shah

A new organization devoted to defending Hindus from stereotyping and discriminatory or defamatory acts/speech.

ISLAM

Islam began in 7th century Arabia under the leadership of the Prophet Muhammad, to whom God (*Allah* in Arabic) revealed a collection of verses known as the *Holy Qur'an*. The word *islam* means "making peace through submission" and in the context of religion, it means "submission to the will of God". A person who practices Islam is a Muslim, meaning, "one who is submitting to the will of God." A Muslim follows the teachings of the *Holy Qur'an*, which was presented to human kind by Muhammad, but which is the very word of the one and only God, and is therefore perfect and complete. Integral to the Muslim Tradition are the "Five Pillars of Islam," which are the five obligations each Muslim must uphold. The first of these is the *shahadah*, or profession of faith, which states, "There is no God but God, and Muhammad is his prophet." The second obligation is that a Muslim prays five times each day at prescribed times. Thirdly, a Muslim must pay the *zakat*, which is a form of mandatory almsgiving. Fourth, a Muslim is required to fast from dawn until sunset during the month of *Ramadan*, the ninth month of the Muslim year. And finally, if able, once in his/her lifetime, every Muslim is required to make a pilgrimage called the *Hajj* to the holy city of Mekkah, where the *ka'bah* is housed, a stone structure, built by Abraham and Ishmael. Early in the history of the Islam, the religion split into two distinct branches, known as the Sunni and the Shiah, both of which contain subbranches. Muslims worldwide constitute an enormous community which is rapidly spreading throughout North America as a result of recent immigration as well as conversion.

The Islamic Society of North America (ISNA)
P.O. Box 38
Plainfield, IN 46168
Tel: (317) 839-8157
Website: www.isna.net
Dr. Sayyid M. Syeed, General Secretary

The Islamic Society of North America grew out of the Muslim Students Association and is one of the oldest national Muslim organizations in the United States. It has a varied program primarily serving the Muslim community, but also seeks to promote friendly relations between Muslims and non-Muslims. It has a speakers' bureau, film loans, library assistance program, and several other services. It has also has a number of publications. Since ISNA is well represented throughout much of the United States, it is a good initial contact. It has been very active in the area of interfaith relations.

The Islamic Circle of North America (ICNA)
166-22 89th Ave.
Jamaica, NY 11432
Tel: (718) 658-1199
Web site: www.icna.org

The Islamic Circle of North America is a smaller national organization than ISNA, but is involved in many of the same activities. They also have a presence in many different parts of the country and provide a number of resources both to Muslims and non-Muslims. ICNA also has been very active in the world of interfaith relations.

The Muslim American Society
The Ministry of W. Deen Mohammed
P.O. Box 1944
Calumet City, IL 60409

This is the community of Imam W. Deen Mohammed and represents the largest single grouping of orthodox African-American Muslims in the United States. It is important to distinguish this group from the Nation of Islam (Black Muslims). African Americans constitute probably the largest single group of Muslims in the United States. Given the loose structure of the organization, it is often both possible and helpful to make contact with a local mosque in your area.

The American Muslim Council
1212 New York Ave., NW
Washington, DC 20005
Tel: (202) 789-22 62
Web sight: www.amermuslim.org
Dr. Aly R. Abuzaakouk, Executive Director

An organization which exists, in part, to represent the political and social interests of American Muslims and to defend their rights. It often has information about Muslim reaction to national and international events and also publishes informative booklets and brochures which include basic information on Islam and a journalistic style sheet.

JAINISM

Jainism was founded in the 6th century B.C.E. in India by Vardhamana Jnatiputra (also known as Nataputta Mahavira, whom the Jains call Jina, which means "Spiritual Conqueror." Mahavira was a contemporary of the Buddha, and to some extent, Buddhism was an important rival to Jainism at the time. Both grew out of the Hindu tradition but rejected certain of its aspects. Jains honor a number of saints, or prophets from remote history called *tirthankaras,* who had liberated themselves from the bondage of *karma,* and hence from the cycle of reincarnation. Mahavira is the 24th of these *tirthankaras*. Emulating these saints, one may free the soul from the shackles of *karma* and rebirth, by observing the "three jewels" of "right faith," "right knowledge," "and right conduct." There is a strong emphasis in Jainism on peacefulness, moderation, and the refusal to injure animals in any way. There are religious orders, called *yatis,* which observe strict vows. The laity hold a pious respect for the *yatis.* There are two main branches of Jainism, the *Digambara* ("sky-clad" or "naked") and the *Svetambara* ("white-clad"). Despite the fact that the Jains constitute a relatively small proportion of the Indian population, they have a great influence on the Hindu community. The essential philosophy of non-violence had a great effect on the teachings of Gandhi in this century.

Federation of Jain Associations in North America
66 Viscount
Williamsville, NY 14221
Tel: 716-688-3030

Siddhachalam/International Mahavira Jain Mission
65 Mud Pond Road
Blairstown, NJ 07285
Tel: 908-362-9793

A residential center for the teaching of the Jain way of life in the United States.

JUDAISM

Judaism is one of the world's oldest religions, encompassing a rich and complex tradition that has evolved over centuries and has given rise to, or influenced, other major world traditions. Numerous expressions of Judaism have always coexisted with one another, as they do today. The central concern shared by all is to live in relation to God and to follow God's will. Jews understand themselves to be in covenant with God, who is the one transcendent God, Creator of the Universe. God revealed the Torah to the people of Israel as his way of life. History brought the Jewish people into contact with many cultures and civilizations, contacts that continuously transformed the nature of their worship, the understanding of God's law, and even their conceptualization of peoplehood. At the time of the second Diaspora, or great migration of Jews throughout the Middle East, North Africa, and Europe at the beginning of the common era, was the rise of the Rabbinical Tradition, with its emphasis on the study of scripture. Today's Judaism has grown out of these roots. In the 19th century, Reform Judaism arose in Europe and the United States as one Jewish response to modernity. Conservative Judaism and Reconstructionism are branches of Jewish practice that first developed in America. Orthodox Judaism also has a number of modern forms.

American Jewish Committee
165 East 56th Street,
New York, NY 10022
Tel: 212-751-4000
FAX: 212-750-0326
Executive Director, David A. Harris

Founded in 1906, The AJC protects the rights and freedoms of Jews world-wide; combats bigotry and anti-Semitism and promotes democracy and human rights for all. It is an independent community-relations organization, with strong interest in interreligious relations and public-policy advocacy. The AJC publishes the *American Jewish Yearbook*, and *Commentary magazine*.

The Anti-Defamation League of B'nai B'rith
823 United Nations Plaza
New York, NY 10017
Tel: 212-885-7700
FAX: 212-867-0779
Website: www.adl.org
Director, Abraham H. Foxman

Since 1913, the Anti-Defamation League has been involved in combating and documenting anti-Semitism. It also works to secure fair treatment for all citizens through law, education and community relations.

Jewish Council for Public Affairs
443 Park Avenue South, 11th Floor
New York, NY 10016
Tel: 212-684-6950
FAX: 212-686-1353
Website: www.thejcpa.org
Executive Vice Chairman, Lawrence Rubin

This national coordinating body for the field of Jewish community relations comprises 13 national and 122 local Jewish communal agencies. Through the Council's work, and in its collaboration with other religious groups, its constituent agencies work on public policy issues, both international and domestic.

Jewish Reconstructionist Federation
7804 Montgomery Ave., Suite 9
Elkins Park, PA 19027
Tel: 212-782-8500
Email: jfrnatl@aol.com
Executive Director, Rabbi Mordechai Liebling

Fosters the establishment and ongoing life of Reconstructionist congregations and fellowship groups. Publishes *The Reconstructionist* and other materials. Rabbis who relate to this branch of Judaism are often members of the Reconstructionist Rabbinical Association.

Union of American Hebrew Congregations
633 Third Avenue
New York, NY 10017
Tel: 212-650-4000
FAX: 212-650-4169
Website: www.uahc.org
President: Rabbi Eric H. Yoffie

The central congregational body of Reform Judaism, founded in 1873. It serves approx. 875 affiliated temples and its members through religious, educational, cultural and administrative programs. Women's Men's and Youth organizations. *Reform Judaism* is one of its publications. The Central Conference of American Rabbis is the affiliated rabbinical body.

The Union of Orthodox Jewish Congregations of America
333 Seventh Avenue
New York, NY 10001

Tel: 212-563-4000
FAX: 212-564-9058
Website: www.ou.org
Executive Vice-President, Rabbi Raphael Butler

The national central body of Orthodox synagogues since 1898, providing kashrut supervision, women's and youth organizations, and a variety of educational, religious and public policy programs and activities. Publishers of *Jewish Action* magazine and other materials. The Rabbinical Council of America is the related organization for Orthodox Rabbis.

The United Synagogue of Conservative Judaism
155 Fifth Avenue
New York, NY 10010-6802
Tel: 212-533-7800
FAX: 212-353-9439
Executive Vice-President, Rabbi Jerome M. Epstein

The International organization of 800 congregations, founded in 1913. Provides religious, educational, youth, community and administrative programming. Publishes *United Synagogue Review* and other materials. The Rabbinical Assembly is the association of Conservative Rabbis.

NATIVE AMERICAN TRADITIONAL SPIRITUALITY

Native American spirituality is difficult to define or categorize because it varies so greatly across the continent. Further, it is deeply entwined with elements of nature which are associated with different geographical regions. For example, while Plains Indians possess a spiritual relationship with the buffalo, Indigenous Peoples from the Northwest share a similar relationship with salmon. Hence, the character of Native American spirituality is dependent, to some extent, on the surrounding geography and its incumbent ecosystems. Despite this great variety, there are some similarities which allow us to consider the many Native American forms of spirituality together: Contrary to popular belief, Native American peoples are monotheistic; they do not worship the sun or buffalo or salmon, but rather understand that these elements of nature are gifts from the "Great Mystery," and are parts of it. Today, while still working toward religious freedom in the United States, Native Americans are also struggling to protect sacred sites, which they consider to be comparable to "churches." But since these sites are actually part of the land, not man-made structures, many are constantly under attack for the natural resources they contain. Such exploitation of these resources is an offense to the Native American sense of spirituality, which views resources like timber, oil, and gold, as gifts from the Great Mystery. The struggle to protect and respect these sacred sites is a universal and essential part of Native American spirituality.

National Congress of American Indians (NCAI)
1301 Connecticut Ave., NW
Suite 200
Washington, DC 20036
Tel: (202) 466-7767
Fax: (202) 466-7797
Email: jdossett@erols.com
Website: www.ncai.org
Exec. Dir., JoAnn K. Chase

The National Congress of American Indians (NCAI), founded in 1944, is the oldest, largest and most representative national Indian organization serving the needs of a broad membership of American Indian and Alaska Native governments. NCAI stresses the need for unity and cooperation among tribal governments and people for the security and protection of treaty and sovereign rights. As the preeminent national Indian organization, NCAI is organized as a representative congress aiming for consensus on national priority issues.

The NCAI website contains links for a directory of Indian nations in the continental U.S. and Alaska as well as a directory of tribal governments. There are also links to other Native American websites.

Native American Rights Fund (NARF)
1506 Broadway
Boulder, CO 80302
Tel: (303) 447-8760
Fax: (303) 433-7776

Email: pereira@narf.org
Website: www.narf.org
Exec. Dir., Walter Echohawk

The Native American Rights Fund is the non-profit legal organization devoted to defending and promoting the legal rights of the Indian people. NARF attorneys, most of whom are Native Americans, defend tribes who otherwise cannot bear the financial burden of obtaining justice in the courts of the United States. The NARF mission statement outlines five areas of concentration: 1) Preservation of tribal existence; 2) Protection of tribal natural resources; 3) Promotion of human rights; 4) Accountability of government; 5) Development of Indian law.

SIKHISM

Sikhism was founded by Guru Nanak during the 15th and 16th centuries C.E. in the state of Punjab in northwestern India. Nanak was greatly influenced by the teachings of Kabir, a Muslim who became deeply inspired by Hindu philosophies. Kabir's poems called for a synthesis between Islam and Hinduism. In the footsteps of Kabir's wisdom, Nanak drew upon elements of Bhakti Hinduism and Sufi Islam: He stressed the existence of a universal, single God, who transcends religious distinctions. Union with God is accomplished through meditation and surrender to the divine will. Nanak also called for the belief in reincarnation, karma, and also the cyclical destruction and recreation of the universe. However, he rejected the caste system, the devotion to divine incarnations, priesthood, idol worship, all of which were elements of the Hindu tradition. Nanak was the first of ten *gurus*, or teachers. The fourth guru, built the Golden Temple in Amritsar, the Sikh religious center. The fifth guru compiled the *Adi Granth*, a sort of hymn-book of spiritual authority. All male sikhs are initiated into the religious brotherhood called the *Khalsa*. Members of this order vow never to cut their beard or hair, to wear special pants, to wear an iron bangle as an amulet against evil, to carry a steel dagger, and a comb.

The Sikh Center of Orange County
2514 West Warner Ave.
Santa Ana, CA 92704
Tel: (714) 979-9328
Website: www.sikhcenter.org

The Sikh Center of Orange County describes itself as follows: "Our mission, in following the tradition and teaching of our honorable Guru Nanak, is to provide accurate, reliable and complete religious, social and cultural teachings and understanding of Sikhism and the people who practice it."

7. United States Regional and Local Ecumenical Bodies

One of the many ways Christians and Christian churches relate to one another locally and regionally is through ecumenical bodies. The membership in these ecumenical organizations is diverse. Historically, councils of churches were formed primarily by Protestants, but many local and regional organizations now include Orthodox and Roman Catholics. Many are made up of congregations or judicatory units of churches. Some have a membership base of individuals. Others foster cooperation between ministerial groups, community ministries, coalitions, or church agencies. While "council of churches" is a term still commonly used to describe this form of cooperation, other terms such as "conference of churches," "ecumenical councils," "churches united," "metropolitan ministries," are coming into use. Ecumenical organizations that are national in scope are listed in Director 1, "United States Cooperative Organizations."

An increasing number of ecumenical bodies have been exploring ways to strengthen the interreligious aspect of life in the context of religious pluralism in the U.S. today. Some organizations in this listing are fully interfaith agencies primarily through the inclusion of Jewish congregations in their membership. Other organizations nurture partnerships with a broader base of religious groups in their communities, especially in the areas of public policy and interreligious dialogue.

This list does not include all local and regional ecumenical and interfaith organizations in existence today. The terms regional and local are relative, making identification somewhat ambiguous. Regional councils may cover sections of large states or cross-state borders. Local councils may be made up of several counties, towns, or clusters of congregations. State councils or state-level ecumenical contacts exist in 43 of the 50 states. These state-level or multi-state organizations are marked with an asterisk (*). The organizations are listed alphabetically by state.

ALABAMA

Greater Birmingham Ministries

2304 12th Ave. N, Birmingham, AL 35234-3111 Tel. (205)326-6821, Fax (205)252-8458
Media Contact, Scott Douglas
Exec. Dir., Scott Douglas
Economic Justice, Co-Chpsn., Helen Holdefer; Karnie Smith
Direct Services, Chpsn., Benjamin Greene
Finance & Fund-Raising, Chpsn., Dick Sales
Pres., Richard Ambrose
Sec., Lois Martin
Treas., Chris Hamlin
Major Activities: Direct Service Ministries (Food, Utilities, Rent and Nutrition Education, Shelter); Alabama Arise (Statewide legislative network focusing on low income issues); Economic Justice Issues (Low Income Housing and Advocacy, Health Care, Community Development, Jobs Creation, Public Transportation); Faith in Community Ministries (Interchurch Forum, Interpreting and Organizing, Bible Study)

Interfaith Mission Service

411-B Holmes Ave. NE, Huntsville, AL 35801 Tel. (256)536-2401, Fax (256)536-2284
Email: ims@hiwaay.net
Exec. Dir., Susan J. Smith
Pres., Richard C. Titus
Major Activities: Foodline & Food Pantry; Local FEMA Committee; Ministry Development; Clergy Luncheon; Workshops; Response to Community Needs; Information and Referral; Interfaith Understanding; Christian Unity; Homeless Needs; School Readiness Screenings

ALASKA

Alaska Christian Conference

Episcopal Diocese of Alaska, 1205 Denali Way, Fairbanks, AK 99701-4178 Tel. (907)452-3040
Email: mmcdonald@gci.net
Media Contact, Rt. Rev. Mark MacDonald
Pres., Rt. Rev. Mark MacDonald
Vice-Pres., Rev. David I. Blanchett, 1100 Pullman Drive, Wasilla, AK 99654 Tel. (907)352-2517
Treas., Carolyn M. Winters, 2133 Bridgewater Drive, Fairbanks, AK 99709-4101 Tel. (907) 456-8555
Major Activities: Legislative & Social Concerns; Resources and Continuing Education; New Ecumenical Ministries; Communication; Alcoholism (Education & Prevention); Family Violence (Education & Prevention); Native Issues; Ecumenical-Theological Dialogue; HIV-AIDS Education and Ministry; Criminal Justice

ARIZONA

Arizona Ecumenical Council*

4423 N. 24th St., Ste. 750, Phoenix, AZ 85016 Tel. (602)468-3818, Fax (602)468-3839
Media Contact, Exec. Dir., Dr. Paul Eppinger, Tel. (602)967-6040, Fax (602)468-3839

Exec. Dir., Dr. Paul Eppinger

Pres., Rev. Gail Davis, 4423 N. 24th St. Ste. 700, Phoenix, AZ 85016

Major Activities: Donohoe Ecumenical Forum Series; Political Action Team; Legislative Workshop; Arizona Ecumenical Indian Concerns Committee; Mexican-American Border Issues; ISN-TV; Disaster Relief; Break Violence-Build Community; Truckin' for Kids; "Souper Bowl"; Gun Information and Safety Program

ARKANSAS

Arkansas Interfaith Conference*

P.O. Box 151, Scott, AR 72142 Tel. (501)961-2626 Email: aicark@aol.com

Media Contact, Conf. Exec., Mimi Dortch

Conf. Exec., Mimi Dortch

Pres., Rabbi Eugene Levy, 3700 Rodney Park Ave., Little Rock, AR 72212

Sec., Rev. Thurston Lamb, Bethel AME Church, Little Rock, AR 72202

Treas., Jim Davis, Box 7239, Little Rock, AR 72217

Major Activities: Institutional Ministry; Interfaith Executives' Advisory Council; Interfaith Relations; Church Women United; AIDS Task Force; Our House-Shelter; Legislative Liaison; Ecumenical Choir Camp; Tornado Disaster Relief; Camp for Jonesboro School Children Massacre; Welfare Reform Work; Med Center Chaplaincy

CALIFORNIA

California Council of Churches-California Church Impact*

2700 L Street, Sacramento, CA 95816 Tel. (916) 442-5447, Fax (916)442-3036

Email: cccinfo@calchurches.org

Website: www.calchurches.org

Media Contact, Exec. Dir., Scott D. Anderson

Exec. Dir., Scott D. Anderson

Major Activities: Monitoring State Legislation; California IMPACT Network; Legislative Principles; Food Policy Advocacy; Family Welfare Issues; Health; Church-State Issues; Violence Prevention; Child Care Program-Capacity Coordinator to Increase Quality Child Care within California for the Working Poor, etc.

The Council of Churches of Santa Clara County

1710 Moorpark Avenue, San Jose, CA 95128 Tel. (408)297-2660, Fax (408)297-2661

Media Contact, Interim Ex. Dir., Rev. R. Richard Roe

Interim Exec. Dir., Rev. R. Richard Roe

Pres., Rev. Dr. Kristin Sundquist

Major Activities: Social Education-Action; Ecumenical and Interfaith Witness; Affordable Housing; Environmental Ministry; Family-Children; Convalescent Hospital Ministries; Gay Ministry

The Ecumenical Council of Pasadena Area Churches

P.O. Box 41125, 444 E. Washington Blvd., Pasadena, CA 91114-8125 Tel. (626)797-2402, Fax (626)797-7353

Email: ecpac@prodigy.net

Exec. Dir., Rev. Frank B. Clark

Major Activities: Christian Education; Community Worship; Community Concerns; Christian Unity; Ethnic Ministries; Hunger; Peace; Food, Clothing Assistance for the Poor; Emergency Shelter

Ecumenical Council of San Diego County

1880 Third Ave., San Diego, CA 92101 Tel. (619)238-0649

Website: home.earthlink.net/~searay1/

Exec. Dir., Rev. Glenn S. Allison

Admn., Patricia R. Munley

Pres., George Mitrovich

Treas., Joseph Ramsey

Major Activities: Interfaith Shelter Network-El Nido Transitional Living Program; Emerging Issues; Faith Order & Witness; Worship & Celebration; Ecumenical Tribute Dinner; Advent Prayer Breakfast; AIDS Chaplaincy Program; Third World Opportunities; Seminars and Workshops; Called to Dance Assn.; S.D. Names Project Quilt; Children's Sabbath Workshops and events; Edgemoor Chaplaincy; Stand for Children events; Continuing Education for clergy and laypersons

Fresno Metro Ministry

1055 N. Van Ness, Ste. H, Fresno, CA 93728 Tel. (559)485-1416, Fax (559)485-9109

Email: metromin@qnis.net

Website: www.fresnometmin.org

Media Contact, Exec. Dir., Rev. Walter P. Parry

Exec. Dir., Rev. Walter P. Parry

Pres., Claudia Martinez

Major Activities: Hunger Relief Advocacy; Human Relations and Anti-Racism; Health Care Advocacy; Public Education Concerns; Children's Needs; Biblical and Theological Education For Laity; Ecumenical & Interfaith Celebrations & Cooperation; Youth Needs; Community Network Building; Human Services Facilitation; Anti-Poverty Efforts; Hate Crime Prevention and Response

Interfaith Council of Contra Costa County

1543 Sunnyvale Ave., Walnut Creek, CA 94596 Tel. (925)933-6030, Fax (925)952-4554

Chaplains, Rev. Charles Tinsley; Rev. Duane Woida; Rev. Harold Wright; Laurie Maxwell

Pres., Rev. Steve Harms

Treas., Robert Bender
Major Activities: Institutional Chaplaincies, Community Education, Interfaith Cooperation; Social Justice

Interfaith Service Bureau

3720 Folsom Blvd., Sacramento, CA 95816 Tel. (916)456-3815, Fax (916)456-3816
Email: isbdexter@aol.com
Media Contact, Executive Dir., Dexter McNamara
Executive Dir., Dexter McNamara
Pres., Richard Montgomery
Vice-Pres., Lloyd Hanson
Major Activities: Religious and Racial Cooperation and Understanding; Welfare Reform Concerns; Refugee Resettlement & Support; Religious Cable Television; Violence Prevention; Graffiti Abatement

Marin Interfaith Council

845 Olive Ave., Suite 110, Novato, CA 94945 Tel. (415)209-6278, Fax (415)209-6527
Email: faiths@peacenet.org
Media Contact, Exec. Dir., Rev. Kevin F. Tripp
Exec. Dir., Rev. Kevin F. Tripp
Major Activities: Interfaith Dialogue; Education; Advocacy; Convening; Interfaith Worship Services & Commemorations

Northern California Interreligious Conference*

534 22nd St., Oakland, CA 94612 Tel. (510)433-0822, Fax (510)433-0813
Email: NCIC@igc.org
Website: ncic.home.igc.org
Media Contact, Pres., Rev. Phil Lawson
Exec. Dir., Catherine Coleman
Pres., Rev. Phil Lawson
Vice-Pres., Nancy Nielsen
Sec., Robert Forsberg
Major Activities: Peace with Justice Commission; Interreligious Relationships Commission; Public Policy Advocacy; Welfare Reform, Founding member of California Interfaith Power and Light; Soul of Justice, a spiritual and leadership concepts interactive performance troupe of teens and young adults; death penalty moratorium; video produced for sale for congregations-organizations to study legal, theological and social implications of marriage and same gender marriage.

Pacific and Asian American Center for Theology and Strategies (PACTS)

Graduate Theological Union, 2400 Ridge Rd., Berkeley, CA 94709 Tel. (510)849-0653 Email: pacts@igc.org
Media Contact, Dir., Kyle Minura
Dir., Kyle Minura
Pres., Ronald Nakasone
Major Activities: Collect and Disseminate Resource Materials; Training Conferences; Public Seminars; Women in Ministry; Racial and Ethnic Minority Concerns; Journal and Newsletter; Hawaii & Greater Pacific Programme; Sale of Sadao Watanabe Calendars; Informational Forums on Peace & Social Justice in Asian Pacific American Community and Asia-Pacific Internationally; Forums & Conferences for Seminarians Asian Pacific Heritage; holistic health and healing ministries; affirming support groups for gay, lesbian, transgender, and questioning Asian and Pacific Islanders.

Pomona Inland Valley Council of Churches

1753 N. Park Ave., Pomona, CA 91768 Tel. (909)622-3806, Fax (909)622-0484
Media Contact, Dir. of Development, Mary Kashmar
Pres., The Rev. Henry Rush
Acting Exec. Dir., The Rev. La Quetta Bush-Simmons
Sec., Ken Coates
Treas., Anne Ashford
Major Activities: Advocacy and Education for Social Justice; Ecumenical Celebrations; Hunger Advocacy; Emergency Food and Shelter Assistance; Farmer's Market; Affordable Housing; Transitional Housing

San Fernando Valley Interfaith Council

10824 Topanga Canyon Blvd., No. 7, Chatsworth, CA 91311 Tel. (818)718-6460, Fax (818)718-0734
Email: sfvic@earthlink.net
Website: www.sfvic.org
Media Contact, Communications Coord., Eileen Killoren, ext. 3002
Exec. Dir., Barry Smedberg; Ext. 3011
Pres., Ms. Katherine Rousseau
Major Activities: Seniors Multi-Purpose Centers; Nutrition & Services; Meals to Homebound; Meals on Wheels; Interfaith Reporter; Interfaith Relations; Social Adult Day Care; Hunger-Homelessness; Volunteer Care-Givers; Clergy Gatherings; Food Pantries and Outreach; Social Concerns; Aging; Hunger; Human Relations; Child Abuse Program; Medical Service; Homeless Program; Disaster Response Preparedness; Immigration Services; Self-Sufficiency Program for Section 8 Families

South Coast Ecumenical Council

3300 Magnolia Ave., Long Beach, CA 90806 Tel. (562)595-0268, Fax (562)490-9920
Email: SCEC2@earthlink.net
Website: www.southcoastecumenical.org
Media Contact, Exec. Dir., Rev. Ginny Wagener
Exec. Dir., Rev. Ginny Wagener

Farmers' Markets, Rev. Dale Whitney
Pres., Elder Rob Robbins
Centro Shalom, Amelia Nieto
New Communion, David Satchwell
Major Activities: Homeless Support Services; Farmers' Markets; CROP Hunger Walks; Church Athletic Leagues; Community Action; Easter Sunrise Worships; Interreligious Dialogue; Justice Advocacy; Martin Luther King, Jr. Celebration; Violence Prevention; Long Beach Church Women United; Long Beach Interfaith Clergy; Publishing Area Religious Directories; South Bay-Long Beach Million Mom March Chapter

Southern California Ecumenical Council*

54 N. Oakland Ave., Pasadena, CA 91101-2086 Tel. (626)578-6371, Fax (626)578-6358
Email: scec@loop.com
Media Contact, Exec. Dir., Rev. Albert G. Cohen
Exec. Dir., Rev. Albert G. Cohen
Pres., Rev. Donald Smith
Treas., Fr. Arshag Khatchadourian
Sec., Ms. Laura Ramirez
V.P. Faith & Tradition, Rev. Wil Tyrrell, S.A.
V.P. Special Events, Dr. Gwynne Guibord
Member at Large, Rev. Dr. Efstathios Mylonas
Faith and Order Chair, Rev. Dr. Rod Parrott
Past Pres., Rev. Sally Welch
Major Activities: Consultation with the regional religious sector concerning the well being and spiritual vitality of this most diverse and challenging area

Westside Interfaith Council

P.O. Box 1402, Santa Monica, CA 90406 Tel. (310)394-1518, Fax (310)576-1895
Media Contact, Rev. Janet A. Bregar
Exec. Dir., Rev. Janet A. Bregar
Major Activities: Meals on Wheels; Community Religious Services; Convalescent Hospital Chaplaincy; Homeless Partnership; Hunger & Shelter Coalition

COLORADO

Colorado Council of Churches*

3690 Cherry Creek S. Dr., Denver, CO 80209 Tel. (303)825-4910, Fax (303)744-8605
Email: jryan@americanisp.net
Media Contact, Council Executive, Rev. Dr. James R. Ryan
Pres., Beth Robey Hyde
Staff Assoc, Taylor Morgan Chapin
Coordinator Climate Change Campaign, Rev. Robert Weiss.
Major Activities: Addressing issues of Christian Unity, Justice, and Environment

Interfaith Council of Boulder

3700 Baseline Rd., Boulder, CO 80303 Tel. (303)494-8094 Media Contact, Pres., Stan Grotegut, 810 Kalma Ave., Boulder, CO 80304 Tel. (303)443-2291
Pres., Stan Grotegut
Major Activities: Interfaith Dialogue and Programs; Thanksgiving Worship Services; Food for the Hungry; Share-A-Gift; Monthly Newsletter

CONNECTICUT

Association of Religious Communities

325 Main St., Danbury, CT 06810 Tel. (203)792-9450, Fax (203)792-9452
Email: arc325@aol.com
Media Contact, Exec. Dir., Samuel E. Deibler, Jr.
Exec. Dir., Samuel E. Deibler, Jr.
Pres., The Rev. Mark Lingle
Major Activities: Refugee Resettlement; Family Counseling; Family Violence Prevention; Affordable Housing

The Capitol Region Conference of Churches

30 Arbor St., Hartford, CT 06106 Tel. (860)236-1295, Fax (860)236-8071
Email: crcc@conferenceofchurches.org
Website: www.conferenceofchurches.org
Media Contact, Exec. Dir., Rev. Shelley Copeland
Exec. Dir., Rev. Shelley Copeland
Pastoral Care & Training, Dir., Rev. Kathleen Davis
Aging Project, Dir., Barbara Malcolm
Community Organizer, Joseph Wasserman
Broadcast Ministry Consultant, Ivor T. Hugh
Pres., Mr. David O. White
Major Activities: Organizing for Peace and Justice; Aging; Legislative Action; Cooperative Broadcast Ministry; Ecumenical Cooperation; Interfaith Reconciliation; Chaplaincies; Low-Income Senior Empowerment; Anti-Racism Education

Center City Churches

100 Constitution Plaza, Suite 721, Hartford, CT 06103-1721 Tel. (860)728-3201, Fax (860) 549-8550
Media Contact, Exec. Dir., Paul C. Christie
Exec. Dir., Paul C. Christie
Pres., Ann E. Thomas
Sec., Jane Wunder
Treas., Holly Billings
Major Activities: Senior Services; Family Resource Center; Energy Bank; Food Pantry; Assistance & Advocacy; After School Tutoring and Arts Enrichment; Summer Day Camp and Youth Employment; Housing for persons with AIDS; Community Soup Kitchen

Christian Community Action

98 S. Main St., South Norwalk, CT 06854 Tel. (203)899-2487, Fax (203)854-1870

Dir., Jacquelyn P. Miller
Major Activities: Emergency Food Program; Used Furniture; Loans for Emergencies; Loans for Rent, Security

Christian Community Action

168 Davenport Ave., New Haven, CT 06519 Tel. (203)777-7848, Fax (203)777-7923
Email: cca168@aol.com
Media Contact, Exec. Dir., The Rev. Bonita Grubbs
Exec. Dir., The Rev. Bonita Grubbs
Major Activities: Emergency Food Program; Used Furniture & Clothing; Security and Fuel; Emergency Housing for Families; Advocacy; Transitional Housing for Families

Christian Conference of Connecticut*

60 Lorraine St., Hartford, CT 06105 Tel. (860)236-4281, Fax (860)236-9977
Email: ssidorak@aol.com
Website: www.christconn.org
Media Contact, Exec. Dir., Rev. Stephen J. Sidorak, Jr.
Exec. Dir., Rev. Stephen J. Sidorak, Jr.
Pres., The Most Rev. Daniel A. Cronin
Vice-Pres., The Rev. Erica Wimber Avena
Sec., The Most Rev. Daniel A. Hart
Treas., Thomas F. Sarubbi
Major Activities: Communications; Institutional Ministries; Connecticut Ecumenical Council on Addiction; Ecumenical Forum; Faith & Order; Social Concerns; Public Policy; Peace and Justice Convocation; Restorative Justice & Death Penalty; Interreligious Dialogue & Interreligious Action on Economic Justice; Housing and Human Services Ministry

Council of Churches of Greater Bridgeport, Inc.

180 Fairfield Ave., Bridgeport, CT 06604 Tel. (203)334-1121, Fax (203)367-8113
Email: ccgb@ccgb.org
Website: www.ccgb.org
Media Contact, Exec. Dir., Rev. John S. Kidd
Exec. Dir., Rev. John S. Kidd
Pres., Rev. Collin Vice
Sec., Sharon Dobbins Albertson
Treas., Roger Perry
Major Activities: Youth in Crisis; Safe Places; Youth Shelter; Criminal Justice; Nursing Home and Jail Ministries; Local Hunger; Ecumenical Relations, Prayer and Celebration; Covenantal Ministries; Home-work Help; Summer Programs; Race Relations-Bridge Building;

Council of Churches and Synagogues of Southwestern Connecticut

461 Glenbrook Rd, Stamford, CT 06901 Tel. (203)348-2800, Fax (203)358-0627
Email: council@flvax.ferg.lib.ct.us
Website: www.interfaithcouncil.org
Media Contact, Communications Ofc., Lois Alcosser
Exec. Dir., Jack Penfield, Interim Director
Major Activities: Partnership Against Hunger; The Food Bank of Lower Fairfield County; Friendly Visitors and Friendly Shoppers; Senior Neighborhood Support Services; Christmas in April; Interfaith Programming; Prison Visitation; Friendship House; Help a Neighbor; Operation Fuel; Teaching Place

Greater Waterbury Interfaith Ministries, Inc.

84 Crown St., Waterbury, CT 06704 Tel. (203)756-7831, Fax (203)419-0024
Media Contact, Exec. Dir., Carroll E. Brown
Exec. Dir., Carroll E. Brown
Pres., The Rev. Dr. James G. Bradley
Major Activities: Emergency Food Program; Emergency Fuel Program; Soup Kitchen; Ecumenical Worship; Christmas Toy Sale; Annual Hunger Walk

Manchester Area Conference of Churches

P.O. Box 773, Manchester, CT 06045-0773 Tel. (860)647-8003
Media Contact, Exec. Dir., Denise Cabana
Exec. Dir., Denise Cabana
Dir. of Community Ministries, Joseph Piescik
Dept.of Ministry Development, Dir., Karen Bergin
Pres., Rev. Charles Ericson
Vice-Pres., Theresa Ghabrial
Sec., Jean Richert
Treas., Clive Perrin
Major Activities: Provision of Basic Needs (Food, Fuel, Clothing, Furniture); Emergency Aid Assistance; Emergency Shelter; Soup Kitchen; Reentry Assistance to Sex-Offenders; Pastoral Care in Local Institutions; Interfaith Day Camp; Advocacy for the Poor; Ecumenical Education and Worship

New Britain Area Conference of Churches (NEWBRACC)

830 Corbin Ave., New Britain, CT 06052 Tel. (860)229-3751, Fax (860)223-3445
Media Contact, Exec. Dir., Michael Gorzoch
Exec. Dir., Michael Gorzoch
Pastoral Care-Chaplaincy, Rev. Ron Smith; Rev. Will Baumgartner; Rev. Rod Rinnel
Pres., Alton Brooks
Treas., Joyce Chmura
Major Activities: Worship; Social Concerns; Emergency Food Bank Support; Communications-Mass Media; Hospital; Elderly Programming; Homelessness and Hunger Programs; Telephone Ministry

DISTRICT OF COLUMBIA

The Council of Churches of Greater Washington

5 Thomas Circle N.W., Washington, DC 20005 Tel. (202)722-9240, Fax (202)722-9241

Media Contact, Exec. Dir., The Rev. Rodger Hall Reed, Sr.

Pres., The Rev. Lewis Anthony

Exec. Dir., The Rev. Rodger Hall Reed, Sr.

Program Officer, Daniel M. Thompson

Major Activities: Promotion of Christian Unity-Ecumenical Prayer & Worship; Coordination of Community Ministries; Summer Youth Employment; Summer Camping-Inner City Youth; Supports wide variety of social justice concerns

InterFaith Conference of Metropolitan Washington

1419 V St. NW, Washington, DC 20009 Tel. (202)234-6300, Fax (202)234-6303

Email: ifc@interfaith-metrodc.org

Website: www.interfaith-metrodc.org

Media Contact, Exec. Dir., Rev. Dr. Clark Lobenstine

Exec. Dir., Rev. Dr. Clark Lobenstine

Admn. Sec., Najla Robinson

Pres., Rev. Elizabeth Orens

1st Vice-Pres., Ms. Amrit Kaur

Chpsn., Mr. Jack Serber

Sec., Janice Sadeghian, Ph.D.

Treas., Ms. Frances B. Albers

Major Activities: Interfaith Dialogue; Interfaith Concert; Racial and Ethnic Polarization; Youth Leadership Training; Hunger; Homelessness; Church-State Zoning Issues

FLORIDA

Christian Service Center for Central Florida, Inc.

808 W. Central Blvd., Orlando, FL 32805-1809 Tel. (407)425-2523, Fax (407)425-9513

Media Contact, Exec. Dir., Robert F. Stuart

Exec. Dir., Robert F. Stuart

Family Emergency Services, Dir., LaVerne Sainten

Alzheimers Respite, Dir., Mary Ellen Ort-Marvin

Fresh Start, Dir., Rev. Haggeo Gautier

Dir. of Mktg., Margaret Ruffier-Farris

Pres., Dr. Charles Horton

Treas., Rick Crandall

Sec., Annie Harris

Major Activities: Provision of Basic Needs (food, clothing, shelter); Emergency Assistance; Noontime Meals; Sunday Church Services at Walt Disney World; Collection and Distribution of Used Clothing; Shelter & Training for Homeless; Respite for Caregivers of Alzheimers

Florida Council of Churches*

924 N. Magnolia Ave., Ste. 304, Orlando, FL 32803 Tel. (407)839-3454, Fax (407)246-0019

Email: fced@aol.com

Website: www.floridachurches.org

Media Contact, Exec. Dir., Rev. Fred Morris

Exec. Dir., Rev. Fred Morris

Associate Dir., H. Basil Nichols,

Project Director, Cherishing the Creation, Russell Gebet

Major Activities: Justice and Peace; Disaster Response; Legislation & Public Policy; Local Ecumenism; Farmworker Ministry; Cherishing the Creation (Environmental Stewardship)

GEORGIA

Christian Council of Metropolitan Atlanta

465 Boulevard, S.E., Atlanta, GA 30312 Tel. (404)622-2235, Fax (404)627-6626

Email: dojccma@aol.com

Media Contact, Dir. of Development & Communication, Jane Hopson Enniss

Exec. Dir., Rev. Dr. David O. Jenkins

Assoc. Dir., -vacant-

Pres., Rev. Elizabeth Rechter

Major Activities: Refugee Services; Commission on Children and Youth, Supervised Ministry; Homeless; Ecumenical and Interreligious Events; persons with Handicapping Conditions; Women's Concerns; Task Force on Prison Ministry; Quarterly Forums on Ecumenical Issues; Faith and Order Concerns; Interracial & Intercultural Emphasis

Georgia Christian Council*

P.O. Box 7193, Macon, GA 31209-7193 Tel. (478)743-2085, Fax (478)743-2085

Email: lccollins@juno.com

Website: georgiachurches.org

Media Contact, Exec. Dir., Rev. Leland C. Collins

Exec. Dir., Rev. Leland C. Collins

Pres., Rev. Dr. Tom Neal, 2370 Vineville Ave., Macon, GA 31204

Sec., Rev. Scudder Edwards, 6865 Turner Ct., Cumming, GA 30131

Major Activities: Local Ecumenical Support and Resourcing; Legislation; Rural Development; Racial Justice; Networking for Migrant Coalition; Aging Coalition; GA To GA With Love; Medical Care; Prison Chaplaincy; Training for Church Development; Souper Bowl; Disaster Relief; Clustering; Development of Local Ecumenism

ILLINOIS

Churches United of the Quad City Area

630 9th St., Rock Island, IL 61201 Tel. (309)786-6494, Fax (309)786-5916

Email: clandon@churchesunited.net

Media Contact, Exec. Dir., Rev. Charles R. Landon, Jr.

Exec. Dir., Rev. Charles R. Landon, Jr.
Program Manager, Anne E. Wachal
Pres., Ms. K. Krewer
Pres. Elect, Rev. Richard Wereley
Treas., Mr. Joseph Lindsay
Major Activities: Jail Ministry; Hunger Projects; Minority Enablement; Criminal Justice; Radio-TV; Peace; Local Church Development; Living Wage

Contact Ministries of Springfield

1100 E. Adams, Springfield, IL 62703 Tel. (217)753-3939, Fax (217)753-8643
Media Contact, Exec. Dir., Ethel Butchek
Exec. Dir., Ethel Butchek
Major Activities: Information; Referral and Advocacy; Ecumenical Coordination; Low Income Housing Referral; Food Pantry Coordination; Prescription & Travel Emergency; Low Income Budget Counseling; 24 hours on call; Emergency On-site Family Shelter

Evanston Ecumenical Action Council

P.O. Box 1414, Evanston, IL 60204 Tel. (847)475-1150, Fax (847)475-2526
Website: members.aol.com/eeachome/eeac.html
Media Contact, Comm. Chpsn., Ken Wylie
Dir. Hospitality Cntr. for the Homeless, Sue Murphy
Co-Pres., Rev. Ted Miller; Rev. Hardist Lane
Treas., Caroline Frowe
Major Activities: Interchurch Communication and Education; Peace and Justice Ministries; Coordinated Social Action; Soup Kitchens; Multi-Purpose Hospitality Center for the Homeless; Worship and Renewal, Racial Reconciliation, Youthwork

Greater Chicago Broadcast Ministries

112 E. Chestnut St., Chicago, IL 60611-2014 Tel. (312)988-9001, Fax (312)988-9004
Media Contact, Exec. Dir., Lydia Talbot
Pres., Bd. of Dir., Eugene H. Winkler
Exec. Dir., Lydia Talbot
Admn. Asst., Margaret Early
Major Activities: Television, Cable, Inter-faith-Ecumenical Development; Social-Justice Concerns

The Hyde Park & Kenwood Interfaith Council

5745 S. Blackstone Ave., Chicago, IL 60637 Tel. (773)752-1911, Fax (773)752-2676
Media Contact, Exec. Dir., Lesley M. Radius
Exec. Dir., Lesley M. Radius
Pres., Rev. David Grainger
Sec., Barbara Krell
Major Activities: Interfaith Work; Hunger Projects; Community Development

Illinois Conference of Churches*

2211 Wabash Ave., Springfield, IL 62704 Tel. (217)698-3440, Fax (217)698-3445
Email: ilcoch@juno.com
Media Contact, Exec. Dir., Rev. David A. Anderson
Exec. Dir., Rev. David A. Anderson
Assoc. Dir.
Pres., Rev. C. Bruce Naylor
Major Activities: Unity and Relationships Commission, Annual Clergy Ecumenical Forum; Triennial Ecumenical Assembly; Church and Society Commission, Public Policy Ecumenical Network; Universal Health Care; Racism; Economic Justice

Oak Park-River Forest Community of Congregations

P.O. Box 3365, Oak Park, IL 60303-3365 Tel. (708)386-8802, Fax (708)386-1399
Website: www.lgrossman.com/comcong.htm
Media Contact, Patricia C. Koko
Admn. Sec., Patricia C. Koko
Pres., Mr. Leonard Grossman
Treas., Rev. Mark Reshan
Major Activities: Community Affairs; Ecumenical-Interfaith Affairs; Youth Education; Food Pantry; Senior Citizens Worship Services; Interfaith Thanksgiving Services; Good Friday Services; UNICEF Children's Fund Drive; Blood Drive; Literacy Training; CROP-CWS Hunger Walkathon; Work with Homeless Through PADS (Public Action to Deliver Shelter); Senior Resource Coordinator Program; Diversity Education; Social Justice Workshops

Peoria Friendship House of Christian Service

800 N.E. Madison Ave., Peoria, IL 61603 Tel. (309)671-5200, Fax (309)671-5206
Media Contact, Exec. Dir., Beverly Isom
Pres. of Bd., David Dadds
Major Activities: Children's After-School; Teen Programs; Recreational Leagues; Senior Citizens Activities; Emergency Food-Clothing Distribution; Emergency Payments for Prescriptions, Rent, Utilities; Community Outreach; Economic Development; Neighborhood Empowerment; GED Classes; Family Literacy; Mother's Group; Welfare to Work Programs

INDIANA

The Associated Churches of Fort Wayne & Allen County, Inc.

602 E. Wayne St., Fort Wayne, IN 46802 Tel. (219)422-3528, Fax (219)422-6721
Email: Vernchurch@aol.com
Media Contact, Exec. Dir., Rev. Vernon R. Graham

Exec. Dir., Rev. Vernon R. Graham
Sec., Elaine Williamson
Foodbank- Ellen Graham; John Kaiser; Bob James; Jenny Varecha
Prog. Development, Ellen Graham
WRE Coord., Kathy Rolf
Pres., Rev. Dennis Roberts, 6600 Trier Rd., Ft. Wayne, IN 46815
Treas., Ann Frellick, 170 Curdes Avenue, Ft. Wayne, IN 46805
Major Activities: Weekday Religious Ed.; Church Clusters; Church and Society Commission; Overcoming Racism; A Baby's Closet; Widowed-to-Widowed; CROP; Campus Ministry; Feeding the Babies; Food Bank System; Peace & Justice Commission; Welfare Reform; Endowment Development; Child Care Advocacy; Advocates Inc.; Ecumenical Dialogue; Feeding Children; Vincent House (Homeless); A Learning Journey (Literacy); Reaching Out in Love; The Jail Ministry; Curbing Youth Access to Handguns

Christian Ministries of Delaware County

401 E. Main St., Muncie, IN 47305 Tel. (317)288-0601, Fax (317)282-4522
Email: christianministries@netzero.net
Website: www.christianministries.ws
Media Contact, Exec. Dir., Marie Evans
Exec. Dir., Marie Evans
Pres., Dr. J. B. Black, Jr.
Treas., Joan McKee
Major Activities: Baby Care Program; Youth Ministry at Detention Center; Community Church Festivals; Food Pantry; Emergency Assistance; CROP Walk; Social Justice; Family Life Education; Homeless Shelter (sleeping room only); Clothing and household items available free; workshops for low income clients; homeless apartments available, short stays only at no cost; provide programs and workshops for pastors and churches in community; work with schools sponsoring programs.

Church Community Services

629 S. 3rd Street, Elkhart, IN 46516-3241 Tel. 219-295-3673, Fax 219-523-1551
Media Contact, Rev. Jeni Hiett Umble
Exec. Dir., Rev. Jeni Hiett Umble
Major Activities: Financial Assistance for Emergencies; Food Pantry; Information and Referral; Clothing Referral; Laundry Vouchers; Medication Vouchers; Transportation Vouchers; Job and Life Skills Training Program for Women

The Church Federation of Greater Indianapolis, Inc.

1100 W. 42nd St., Ste. 345, Indianapolis, IN 46208 Tel. (317)926-5371, Fax (317)926-5373
Email: churches@churchfederationindy.org
Website: www.churchfederationindy.org
Media Contact, Comm. Consultant, Julie Foster
Exec. Dir., Rev. Dr. Angelique Walker-Smith
Pres., Rev. Richard Clough
Treas., Hugh Moore
Major Activities: "Sacred Spaces" (A Christian Partnership of Neighborhood Action) Reclaiming Our Neighborhoods through Community Formation, Community Resourcing, Community Education, and Communications; The Sanctuary Church Movement; "Loving Our Children"- An Educational Partnership Between Church and Public Schools for "at risk" Children; Greater Indianapolis Prayer Network to Stop the Violence; Racial Reconciliation; Clearinghouse Ministry; Ecumenical Project for Reconciliation and Healing; Faaith and Fathers Ministry (Family Congregation and Mentoring Program); Benevolence Fund Ministry; TV Broadcasts; Indiana Faith-Based Climate Change Campaign; FaithFest!

Evansville Area Community of Churches, Inc.

414 N.W. Sixth St., Evansville, IN 47708-1332 Tel. (812)425-3524, Fax (812)425-3525
Media Contact, Dir. of Programs & Church Relations, Barbara G. Gaisser
Dir. of Programs, Ofc. Mgr., Barbara G. Gaisser
Exec. Dir., Rev. William F. Bower
Weekday Dir., Linda M. Schenk
Pres., Rev. Steve Lintzench
V. Pres., John Musgrove
Sec., Rev. Shane O'Neill
Treas., Ms. Julia Wood
Major Activities: Christian Education; Community Responsibility & Service; Public Relations; Interpretation; Church Women United; Institutional Ministries; Interfaith Dialogue; Earth Care Ethics; Public Education Support; Disaster Preparedness; Job Loss Networking Support Group; Interfaith TV Program; Women in Ministry Support Group; International Women's Day Celebration Events

Indiana Partners for Christian Unity and Mission

P.O. Box 88790, Indianapolis, IN 46208-0790 Tel. (800)746-2310, Fax 815-377-8228
Email: indunity@aol.com
Website: www.IPCUM.org
Media Contact, James Dougans
Pres., Rev. Robert Kirk
Treas., Rev. Thomas Bridges
Major Activities: Initiating dialogue on issues of social concern by organizing conferences on the death penalty, racism, welfare reform and violence; facilitating communication through an electronic newsletter and web site; promot-

ing the National Day of Prayer and the Week of Prayer for Christian Uity; and advancing Churches Uniting in Christ in Indiana

Interfaith Community Council, Inc.

702 E. Market St., New Albany, IN 47150 Tel. (812)948-9248, Fax (812)948-9249
Email: icc@digicove.com
Media Contact, Exec. Dir., Houston Thompson
Exec. Dir., Houston Thompson
Programs-Emergency Assistance, Denise Lochner
RSVP, Dir., Ceil Sperzel
Major Activities: Emergency Assistance; Retired Senior Volunteer Program; New Clothing and Toy Drives; Convalescent Sitter & Mother's Aides; Senior Day College; Emergency Food Distribution; Homeless Prevention; Kids' Café; Youth Employment Scholastic Program

Lafayette Urban Ministry

525 N. 4th St., Lafayette, IN 47901 Tel. (317)423-2691, Fax (317)423-2693
Media Contact, Exec. Dir., Joseph Micon
Exec. Dir., Joseph Micon
Advocate Coord., Rebecca Smith
Public Policy Coord., Harry Brown
Pres., John Wilson
Major Activities: Social Justice Ministries with and among the Poor

United Religious Community of St. Joseph County

2015 Western Ave., Suite 336, South Bend, IN 46629 Tel. (219)282-2397, Fax (219)282-8014
Email: sfisko@sbcsc.k12.in.us
Media Contact, Exec. Dir., Dr. Carol L. Mayernick
Exec. Dir., Dr. Carol L. Mayernick
Pres., Marilyn Gardner
Victim Offender Reconciliation Prog., Victim Impact Panel Coord., Martha Sallows
Volunteer Advocacy Project, Coord., Sara Goetz; Coord., Linda Jung-Zimmerman
Major Activities: Religious Understanding; Interfaith-Ecumenical Education; CROP Walk; Hunger Education; Housing and Homelessness Issues; Clergy Education and Support; Refugee Resettlement; Victim Assistance; Advocacy for the Needy

West Central Neighborhood Ministry, Inc.

1316 Broadway, Fort Wayne, IN 46802-3304 Tel. (219)422-6618, Fax (219)422-9319
Media Contact, Exec. Dir., Andrea S. Thomas
Exec. Dir., Andrea S. Thomas
Ofc. Mgr., J. R. Stopperich
Neighborhood Services Dir., Carol Salge
Senior Citizens Dir., Gayle Mann
Youth Director, Laura Watt
Major Activities: After-school Programs; Teen Drop-In Center; Summer Day Camp; Summer Overnight Camp; Information and Referral Services; Food Pantry; Nutrition Program for Senior Citizens; Senior Citizens Activities; Tutoring; Developmental Services for Families & Senior Citizens; Parent Club

IOWA

Churches United, Inc.

1035 3rd Ave., Suite 202, Cedar Rapids, IA 52403 Tel. (319)366-7163 Media Contact, Admn. Sec., Marcey Luxa
Admn. Sec., Marcey Luxa
Pres., Rev. Matt Noffke
Treas., Joseph Luxa, 450 19th St. NW, Cedar Rapids, IA 52405
Major Activities: Communication-resource center for member churches; Community Information and Referral; Community Food Bank; L.E.A.F. (Local Emergency Assistance Fund; Ecumenical City-wide Celebrations; CROP-World Hunger; Jail Chaplaincy Ministry

Des Moines Area Religious Council

3816 - 36th St., Des Moines, IA 50310 Tel. (515) 277-6969, Fax (515)274-8389
Email: dmreligious@mcleodusa.net
Website: dmreligious.org
Media Contact, Exec. Dir., Forrest Harms
Exec. Dir., Forrest Harms
Pres., Bobbretta M. Brewton
Pres. Elect, Jim Kratz
Treas., Louise Patrick
Major Activities: Outreach and Nurture; Education; Social Concerns; Mission; Emergency Food Pantry; Ministry to Widowed; Child Care Assistance

Ecumenical Ministries of Iowa (EMI)*

3816-36th St., Ste. 202, Des Moines, IA 50310-4722 Tel. (515)255-5905, Fax (515)255-1421
Email: emofiowa@aol.com
Media Contact, Exec. Dir., Rev. Sarai Schnucker Beck
Exec. Dir., Rev. Sarai Schnucker Beck
Program Cood., Martha E. Hedberg
Major Activities: Facilitating the denominations—cooperative agenda of resourcing local expression of the church; Assess needs & develop responses through Justice and Unity Commissions

Iowa Religious Media Services*

3816 36th St., Des Moines, IA 50310 Tel. (515) 277-2920, Fax (515)277-0842
Email: orderirms@aol.com
Website: www.irms.org
Media Contact, Director
Exec. Dir., Sharon E. Strohmaier
Educ. Consultant, Paulette M. Chapman

Major Activities: Media Library for Churches in 7 Denominations in Iowa; Provide Video Production Services for Churches, Non-profit & Educational organizations; will rent media to all churches in the continental U.S. (details on the website)

IDAHO

The Regional Council for Christian Ministry, Inc.

237 N. Water, Idaho Falls, ID 83403 Tel. (208)524-9935 Exec. Sec., Wendy Schoonmaker

Major Activities: Island Park Ministry; Community Food Bank; Community Observances; Community Information and Referral Service; F.I.S.H.

KANSAS

Cross-Lines Cooperative Council

736 Shawnee Ave., Kansas City, KS 66105 Tel. (913)281-3388, Fax (913)281-2344
Email: rhea@cross-lines.org
Website: www.cross-lines.org
Media Contact, Dir. of Dev., Bill Scholl
Exec. Dir., Marilynn Rudell
Dir. of Programs, Rev. Robert L. Moore
Major Activities: Emergency Assistance; Family Support Advocacy; Crisis Heating-Plumbing Repair; Thrift Store; Workcamp Experiences; Adult Education (GED and Basic English Literacy Skills); School Supplies; Christmas Store; Institute for Poverty and Empowerment Studies (Education on poverty for the non-poor)

Inter-Faith Ministries-Wichita

829 N. Market, Wichita, KS 67214-3519 Tel. (316)264-9303, Fax (316)264-2233
Email: smuyskens@juno.com
Media Contact, Exec. Dir., Sam Muyskens
Exec. Dir., Rev. Sam Muyskens
Adm. Asst., Kathy Freed
Inter-Faith Inn (Homeless Shelter), Dir., Sandy Swank
Operation Holiday, Dir., Ashley Davis
Dev.-Communications, Dir., -vacant-
Campaign to End Childhood Hunger, Connie Pace
Community Ministry, Cammie Funston
Racial Justice, Coord., Cammie Funston
Major Activities: Communications; Urban Education; Inter-religious Understanding; Community Needs and Issues; Theology and Worship; Hunger; Family Life; Multi-Cultural Concerns

Kansas Ecumenical Ministries*

5833 SW 29th St., Topeka, KS 66614-2499 Tel. (785)272-9531, Fax (785)272-9533
Email: kemstaff@terraworld.net
Website: kemontheweb.org
Media Contact, Exec. Dir., Dr. Joe M. Hendrixson
Email: joe_hendrixson@ecunet.org
Exec. Dir., Dr. Joe M. Hendrixson
Pres., Rev. Sally Fahrenthold
Vice-Pres., Winnie Crapson
Sec., Rev. Anne Rosebrock
Major Activities: State Council of Churches; Legislative Activities; Program Facilitation and Coordination; Education; Mother-to-Mother Program; Rural Concerns; Health Care; Hate group monitoring; Children & Families; AIDS-HIV Programs; Domestic Violence; Faith and Order

KENTUCKY

Eastern Area Community Ministries

P.O. Box 43049, Louisville, KY 40253-0049 Tel. (502)244-6141, Fax (502)254-5141
Email: easternacm@cs.com
Website: ourworld.cs.com/eacministry
Media Contact, Acting Exec. Dir., Sharon Eckler
Acting Exec. Dir., Sharon Eckler
Board Pres., Rev. Dee Wade
Board Sec., Betty Wilborn
Board Treas., Homer Lacy, Jr.
Youth and Family Services, Prog. Dir., Ken Evans
Older Adult Services, Associate Program Dir., Sharon Eckler
Neighborhood Visitor Program, Prog. Dir., Nancy Moudy
Major Activities: Food Pantry; Clothes Closet; Meals on Wheels; Community Worship Services; Good Start for Kids; Juvenile Court Diversion; Community Development; Transient Fund; Ministerial Association

Fern Creek-Highview United Ministries

7502 Tangelo Dr., Louisvlle, KY 40228 Tel. (502)239-7407, Fax (502)239-7454
Email: FernCreek.Ministries@crnky.org
Media Contact, Exec. Dir., Kay Sanders, 7502 Tangelo Dr., Louisville, KY 40228 Tel. (502)239-7407
Exec. Dir., Kay Sanders
Pres., David Pooler
Major Activities: Ecumenically supported social service agency providing services to the community, including Emergency Financial Assistance, Food-Clothing, Health Aid Equipment Loans, Information-Referral, Advocacy, Monthly Blood-Pressure Checks; Holiday Programs, Life Skills Training; Mentoring; Case Management; Adult Day-Care Program

Hazard-Perry County Community Ministries, Inc.

P.O. Box 1506, Hazard, KY 41702-1506 Tel. (606)436-0051, Fax (606)436-0071

Media Contact, Gerry Feamster-Roll
Exec. Dir., Gerry Feamster-Roll
Chpsn., Sarah Hughes
V. Chpsn., Susan Duff
Sec., Virginia Campbell
Treas., Margaret Adams
Major Activities: Food Pantry-Crisis Aid Program; Day Care; Summer Day Camp; After-school Program; Christmas Tree; Family Support Center; Adult Day Care; Transitional Housing

Highlands Community Ministries

1140 Cherokee Rd., Louisville, KY 40204 Tel. (502)451-3695
Email: hcmexecu@hotmail.com
Media Contact, Exec. Dir., Stan Esterle
Exec. Dir., Stan Esterle
Major Activities: Welfare Assistance; Day Care; Counseling with Youth, Parents and Adults; Adult Day Care; Social Services for Elderly; Housing for Elderly and Handicapped; Ecumenical Programs; Community Classes; Activities for Children; Neighborhood and Business organization

Kentuckiana Interfaith Community

1113 South 4th St., Suite 200, Louisville, KY 40203 Tel. (502)587-6265, Fax (502)540-5017
Email: interfaith@bellsouth.net
Media Contact, Interim Executive Director, Ronald Higdon
Pres., Sara Wagner
Vice-Pres., Geoffrey Ellis
Treas., Larry Crossland
Interim Executive Dir., Ronald Higdon
Major Activities: Christian-Jewish Ministries in KY, Southern IN; Consensus Advocacy; Interfaith Dialogue; Community Hunger Walk; Racial Justice Forums; Network for Neighborhood-based Ministries; Hunger & Racial Justice Commission; Faith Channel-Cable TV Station, Horizon News Paper; Police-Comm. Relations Task Force; Ecumenical Strategic Planning; Networking with Seminaries & Religious-Affiliated Institutions

Kentucky Council of Churches*

2549 Richmond Road, Suite 302, Lexington, KY 40509 Tel. (859)269-7715, Fax (859)269-1240
Email: kcc@kycouncilofchurches.org
Website: www.kycouncilofchurches.org
Media Contact, Exec. Dir., Nancy Jo Kemper
Exec. Dir., Rev. Dr. Nancy Jo Kemper
Pres., The Rev. Dr. C.K. Henry
Kentucky Interchurch Disaster Recovery Program Coodinator., Rev. Dr. John Kays
Program Associate for Local Ecumenism, Rev. W. Chris Benham Skidmore
Major Activities: Christian Unity; Public Policy; Justice; Disaster Response; Peace Issues; Anti-Racism; Health Care Issues; Local Ecumenism; Rural Land-Farm Issues; Gambling; Capital Punishment

Ministries United South Central Louisville (M.U.S.C.L., Inc.)

1207 Hart Avenue, Louisville, KY 42013 Tel. (502)363-9087, Fax (502)363-9087
Media Contact, Ex. Dir., Rev. Antonio (Tony) Aja, M.Div. Tel. (502)363-2383
Email: Tony_Aja@pcusa.org
Ex. Dir., Rev. Antonio (Tony) Aja, M.Div.
Airport Relocation Ombudsman, Rev. Phillip Garrett, M.Div. Tel. (502)361-2706
Email: philombud@aol.com
Senior Adults Programs, Dir., Mrs. Jeannine Blakeman, BSSW
Emergency Assistance, Dir., Mr. Michael Hundley
Low-Income Coord., Ms. Wanda Irvio
Youth Services, Dir., Rev. Bill Sanders, M.Div.
Volunteers Coord., Mrs. Carol Stemmle

Northern Kentucky Interfaith Commission, Inc.

901 York St., PO Box 72296, Newport, KY 41072 Tel. (859)581-2237, Fax (859)261-6041
Email: wneuroth@hotmail.com
Media Contact, Exec. Dir., Rev. William C. Neuroth
Pres., Ms. Wanda Trinkle
Sec., Ms. Cordelia Koplow
Treas., Ms. Peggy McEntee
Admin. Asst., Pat McDermott
Major Activities: Understanding Faiths; Meeting Spiritual and Human Needs; Enabling Churches to Greater Ministry

Paducah Cooperative Ministry

1359 S. 6th St., Paducah, KY 42003 Tel. (270)442-6795, Fax (270)442-6812
Media Contact, Dir., Heidi Suhrheinrich
Dir., Heidi Suhrheinrich
Chpsn., Rev. Larry Walker
Vice-Chpsn., Rev. Larry McBride
Major Activities: Programs for Hungry, Elderly, Poor, Homeless, Handicapped, Undereducated

St. Matthews Area Ministries

201 Biltmore Rd., Louisville, KY 40207 Tel. (502)893-0205, Fax (502)893-0206
Media Contact, Exec. Dir., Dan G. Lane
Exec. Dir., Dan G. Lane
Child Care, Dir., Janet Hennessey
Dir. Assoc., Eileen Bartlett
Major Activities: Child Care; Emergency Assistance; Youth Services; Interchurch Worship and Education; Housing Development; Counseling; Information & Referral; Mentor Program; Developmentally Disabled

South East Associated Ministries (SEAM)

6500 Six Mile Ln., Ste. A, Louisville, KY 40218 Tel. (502)499-9350

Media Contact, Mary Beth Helton

Exec. Dir., Mary Beth Helton

Life Skills Center, Dir., Robert Davis

Youth Services, Dir., Bill Jewel

Pres., David Ehresman

Treas., Bill Trusty

Major Activities: Emergency Food, Clothing and Financial Assistance; Life Skills Center (Programs of Prevention and Case Management and Self-Sufficiency Through Education, Empowerment, Support Groups, etc.); Bloodmobile; Ecumenical Education and Worship; Juvenile Court Diversion; TEEN Court; Teen Crime & the Community

South Louisville Community Ministries

Peterson Social Services Center, 204 Seneca Trail, Louisville, KY 40214 Tel. (502)367-6445, Fax (502)361-4668

Email: slcm@crnky.org

Website: www.slcm.org

Media Contact, Exec. Dir., J. Michael Jupin

Bd. Chair., Greg Greenwood

Bd. Vice-Chair., Virginia Woodward

Bd. Treas., Jane Davis

Exec. Dir., Rev. J. Michael Jupin

Major Activities: Food, Clothing & Financial Assistance; Home Delivered Meals; Transportation; Ecumenical Worship; Juvenile Ct. Diversion Program; Affordable Housing; Adult Day Care; Truancy Prevention; Case Management, Prenatal Education

LOUISIANA

Greater Baton Rouge Federation of Churches and Synagogues

P.O. Box 626, Baton Rouge, LA 70821 Tel. (225) 925-3414, Fax (225)925-3065

Media Contact, Exec. Dir., Rev. Jeff Day

Exec. Dir., Rev. Jeff Day

Admn. Asst., Marion Zachary

Pres., Bette Lavine

Pres.-Elect, Tom Sylvest

Treas., Randy Trahan

Major Activities: Combating Hunger; Housing (Helpers for Housing); Interfaith Relations; Interfaith Concert; Race Relations

Greater New Orleans Federation of Churches

4640 S. Carrollton Ave, Suite 2B, New Orleans, LA 70119-6077 Tel. (504)488-8788, Fax (504)488-8823

Exec. Dir., Rev. J. Richard Randels

Major Activities: Information and Referral; Food Distribution(FEMA); Forward Together TV Program; Sponsors seminars for pastors (e.g. church growth, clergy taxes, etc.); Police Chaplaincy; Fire Chaplaincy

Louisiana Interchurch Conference*

660 N. Foster Dr., Ste. A-225, Baton Rouge, LA 70806 Tel. (225)924-0213, Fax (225)927-7860

Email: lainterchurch@aol.com

Media Contact, Exec. Dir., Rev. C. Dana Krutz

Exec. Dir., Rev. C. Dana Krutz

Pres., The Rev. Richard Hardy

Major Activities: Ministries to Aging; Prison Reform; Liaison with State Agencies; Ecumenical Dialogue; Institutional Chaplains; Racism; Environmental

MAINE

Maine Council of Churches*

15 Pleasant Ave., Portland, ME 04103 Tel. (207)772-1918, Fax (207)772-2947

Email: mecchurches@aol.com

Website: www.mainecouncilofchurches.org

Media Contact, Communications Director, Karen Caouette

Exec. Dir., Thomas C. Ewell

Assoc. Dir., Douglas Cruger

Admin. Asst., Sandra Buzzell

Pres., Rev. Margrethe Brown

Sec., —

Treas., Rev. Thomas Merrill

Major Activities: Criminal Justice Reform and Restorative Justice; Legislative Work and Coalition Work in Health, Homelessness, and Children; Advocacy

MARYLAND

Central Maryland Ecumenical Council*

Cathedral House, 4 E. University Pkwy., Baltimore, MD 21218 Tel. (410)467-6194, Fax (410)554-6387

Email: cmec@bcpl.net

Media Contact, Exec. Dir., Martha Young

Pres., Rev. Iris Farabee-Lewis

Major Activities: Interchurch Communications and Collaboration; Information Systems; Ecumenical Relations; Urban Mission and Advocacy; Staff for Judicatory Leadership Council; Commission on Dialogue; Commission on Church & Society; Commission on Admin. & Dev.; Ecumenical Choral Concerts; Ecumenical Worship Services

The Christian Council of Delaware and Maryland's Eastern Shore*

The Lutheran Center, 700 Light St., Baltimore, MD 21213 Tel. (410)230-2860, Fax (410)230-2817

Website: www.DeMdSynod.org

Media Contact, Pres., Bishop Wayne P. Wright,

Diocese of Delaware, 2020 N. Tatnall Street, Wilmington, DE 19802

Pres., Bishop Wayne P. Wright, Diocese of Delaware, 2020 N. Tatnall Street, Wilmington, DE 19802

Moderator, The Rev. Patricia McClurg, Presbyterian Church (USA), E-62 Omega Drive, Newark, DE 19713

Major Activities: Exploring Common Theological, Ecclesiastical and Community Concerns; Racism; Prisons

Community Ministries of Rockville

114 West Montgomery Ave., Rockville, MD 20850 Tel. (301)762-8682, Fax (301)762-2939

Email: cmr114cmr@aol.com

Media Contact, Managing Dir., Agnes Saenz

Exec. Dir. & Comm. Min., Mansfield M. Kaseman

Managing Dir., Agnes Aaenz

Major Activities: Shelter Care; Emergency Assistance; Elderly Home Care; Affordable Housing; Political Advocacy; Community Education; Education to Recent Immigrants

Community Ministry of Montgomery County

114 West Montgomery Ave., Rockville, MD 20850 Tel. (301)762-8682, Fax (301)762-2939

Media Contact, Exec. Dir., Rebecca Wagner

Exec. Dir., Rebecca Wagner

Major Activities: Interfaith Clothing Center; Emergency Assistance Coalition; The Advocacy Function; Information and Referral Services; Friends in Action; The Thanksgiving Hunger Drive; Thanksgiving in February; Community Based Shelter

MASSACHUSETTS

Attleboro Area Council of Churches, Inc.

505 N. Main St., Attleboro, MA 02703 Tel. (508)222-2933, Fax (508)222-2008

Email: aacc@naisp.net

Media Contact, Interim Executive Director, Rev. Janet Long

Exec. Dir., Rev. Janet Long

Office Manager- Kathleen Trowbridge

Staff Asst., Emergency Food Program, Dorothy Embree

Hosp. Chplns., Rev. Dr. William B. Udall, Rev. Lynn MacLagen

Pres., Rev. David Hill, 52 Glendale Rd., Attleboro, MA 02703

Treas., Ray Larson, 33 Watson Ave., Attleboro, MA 02703

Major Activities: Hospital Chaplaincy; personal Growth-Skill Workshops; Ecumenical Worship; Media Resource Center; Referral Center; Communications-Publications; Community Social Action; Food'n Friends Kitchens; Nursing Home Volunteer Visitation Program; Lay School of Christian Theology; Clergy Fellowship-Learning Events

The Cape Cod Council of Churches, Inc.

320 Main St., P.O. Box 758, Hyannis, MA 02601 Tel. (508)775-5073

Media Contact, Exec. Dir., Rev. Susan Royce Scribner

Exec. Dir., Rev. Susan Royce Scribner

Pres., Mr. Barry Jones-Henry, Sr.

Chaplain, Cape Cod Hospital, Rev. William Wilcox

Chaplain, Falmouth Hospital, Rev. Allen Page

Chaplain, House of Correction & Jail, Rev. Thomas Shepherd

Chaplain, Rehabilitation Hospital of the Cape and Islands, Mrs. Elizabeth Stommel

Service Center & Thrift Shop, P.O. Box 125, Dennisport, MA 02639 Tel. (508)394-6361

Major Activities: Pastoral Care; Social Concerns; Religious Education; Emergency Distribution of Food, Clothing, Furniture; Referral and Information; Church World Service; Interfaith Relations; Media Presence; Hospital & Jail Chaplaincy; Arts & Religion

Cooperative Metropolitan Ministries

474 Centre St., Newton, MA 02158 Tel. (617)244-3650, Fax (617)244-0569

Email: coopmet@aol.com

Website: cmm.50megs.com

Media Contact, Exec. Dir., Claire Kashuck

Exec. Dir., Claire Kashuck

Bd. Pres., Francis Grady

Treas., Karen Gunn

Clk., Anna Lee Court

Major Activities: Low Income; Suburban-Urban Bridges; Racial and Economic Justice

Council of Churches of Greater Springfield

39 Oakland St., Springfield, MA 01108 Tel. (413)733-2149, Fax (413)733-9817

Media Contact, Asst. to Dir., Sr. John Bridgid

Interim Exec. Dir., Rev. Karen L. Rucks

Community Min., Dir.

Pres., The Rev. Dr. David Hunter

Treas., John Pearson, Esq

Major Activities: Advocacy; Emergency Fuel Fund; Peace and Justice Division; Community Ministry; Task Force on Racism; Hospital and Jail Chaplaincies; Pastoral Service; Crisis Counseling; Christian Social Relations; Relief Collections; Ecumenical and Interfaith Relations; Ecumenical Dialogue with Roman Catholic Diocese; Mass Media; Church-Community Projects and Community Dialogues; Publication, "Knowing My Neighbor- Religious Beliefs and Traditions at Times of Death"

Greater Lawrence Council of Churches

117A S. Broadway, Lawrence, MA 01843 Tel. (978)686-4012
Email: pointer53a@aol.com
Media Contact, Exec. Dir., David Edwards
Exec. Dir., David Edwards
Pres., Carol Rabs
Vice-Pres., Rev. Michael Graham
Admn. Asst., Linda Sullivan
Major Activities: Ecumenical Worship; Radio Ministry; Hospital and Nursing Home Chaplaincy; Church Women United; Afterschool Children's Program; Vacation Bible School

Inter-Church Council of Greater New Bedford

412 County St., New Bedford, MA 02740-5096 Tel. (508)993-6242, Fax (508)991-3158
Email: administration@inter-churchcouncil.org
Website: www.inter-churchcouncil.org
Media Contact, Min., Rev. Edward R. Dufresne, Ph.D.
Exec. Min., Rev. Edward R. Dufresne, Ph.D.
Pres., Pamela Pollock
Treas., George Mock
Major Activities: Pastoral Counseling; Spiritual Direction; Chaplaincy; Housing for Elderly; Urban Affairs; Community Spiritual Leadership; Parish Nurse Ministry; Accounting and Spiritual Care for the Developmentally Challenged; Ecumenical and Interfaith Ministries

Massachusetts Commission on Christian Unity

32 Luce St, Lowell, MA 01852 Tel. 978-453-5423, Fax 978-453-5423
Email: kgordonwhite@msn.com
Media Contact, Exec. Dir., Rev. K. Gordon White
Exec. Sec., Rev. K. Gordon White
Pres., Rev. Fr. Edward O'Flaherty, Ecumenical Officer, Roman Catholic Boston Archdiocese
Major Activities: Faith and Order Dialogue with Church Judicatories; Guidelines & Pastoral Directives for Inter-Church Marriages; Guidelines for Celebrating Baptism in an Ecumenical Context

Massachusetts Council of Churches*

14 Beacon St., Rm. 416, Boston, MA 02108 Tel. (617)523-2771, Fax (617)523-1483
Email: council@masscouncilofchurches.org
Website: www.council@masscouncilofchurches.org
Media Contact, Dir., Rev. Dr. Diane C. Kessler
Exec. Dir., Rev. Dr. Diane C. Kessler
Assoc. Dir., Rev. Jill Wiley
Adjunct Assoc., Rev. Betsy Sowers, Mr. Stanley Rossier
Pres., Rev. Canon Edward Rodman
Vice-Pres., Rev. John Stendahl
Sec., Ms. Eden Grace
Treas., Mr. Robert Sarly
Major Activities: Christian Unity; Education and Evangelism; Defend Social Justice & Individual Rights; Ecumenical Worship; Services and Resources for Individuals and Churches

Worcester County Ecumenical Council

4 Caroline St., Worcester, MA 01604 Tel. (508)757-8385, Fax (508)795-7704
Email: worcecumen@aol.com
Media Contact, Sec., Rev. Steven Alspach
Dir., Rev. Steven Alspach
Pres., Rev. Rrances Langille
Major Activities: Ecumenical worship and dialogue networking congregations together in partnerships of mission, education and spiritual renewal. Clusters of Churches; Ecumenical Worship and Dialogue; Interfaith Activities; Resource Connection for Churches; Group Purchasing Consortium

MICHIGAN

Bay Area Ecumenical Forum

103 E. Midland St., Bay City, MI 48706 Tel. (517)686-1360 Media Contact, Rev. Karen Banaszak
Major Activities: Ecumenical Worship; Community Issues; Christian Unity; Education; CROP Walk

Berrien County Association of Churches

275 Pipestone, P.O. Box 1042, Benton Harbor, MI 49023-1042 Tel. (616)926-0030
Media Contact, Sec., Mary Ann Hinz
Pres., Rev. Robert Gouwens
Dir., Street Ministry, Rev. James Atterberry
Major Activities: Street Ministry; CROP Walk; Community Issues; Fellowship; Christian Unity; Hospital Chaplaincy Program; Publish Annual County Church Directory and Monthly Newsletter; Resource Guide for Helping Needy; Distribution of Worship Opportunity— Brochure for Tourists

Grand Rapids Area Center for Ecumenism (GRACE)

38 Fulton West, Grand Rapids, MI 49503-2628 Tel. (616)774-2042, Fax (616)774-2883
Email: dbaak@graceoffice.org
Website: www.graceoffice.org
Media Contact, Exec. Dir., Rev. David P. Baak
Exec. Dir., Rev. David P. Baak
Prog. Dir., Lisa H. Mitchell
Major Activities: AIDS Care Network (Client Services Education/Volunteer Services);

Hunger Walk ; Education-Relationships; (Ecumenical Lecture, Christian Unity Worship-Events, Interfaith Dialogue Conference); (Affiliates, ACCESS-All County Churches Emergency Support System, FISH for My People-transportation); Publications (Religious Community Directory, Grace Notes); Racial Justice Institute; Mentoring Partners (Welfare Reform Response); West Michigan Call to Renewal (Response to Poverty Advocacy)

Greater Flint Council of Churches

310 E. Third St., Suite 600, Flint, MI 48502 Tel. (810)238-3691, Fax (810)238-4463

Email: gfcc1929@aol.com

Media Contact, Mrs. Constance D. Neely

President, Rev. Annie R. Duncan

Major Activities: Christian Education; Christian Unity; Christian Missions; Nursing Home Visitors; Church in Society; American Bible Society Materials; Interfaith Dialogue; Church Teacher Exchange Sunday; Directory of Area Faiths and Clergy; Thanksgiving & Easter Sunrise Services; CROP Walks

In One Accord

157 Capital Ave., NE, Battle Creek, MI 49017 Tel. (616)966-2500, Fax (616)660-6665

Email: inoneaccord@aol.com

Website: www.skywebsite.com/In-One-Accord

Media Contact, Executive Director, Rev. Ron L. Keller

Pres., Mrs. Carolyn Christ

Vice-Pres., Rev. Craig Tatum

Exec. Dir., Rev. Ron L. Keller

Secretary, Mrs. Carla Dearing

Major Activities: CROP Walk; Food Closet; Week of Prayer for Christian Unity; Ecumenical Worship; Faith Health Network; Martin Luther King Jr. Community Service, Church Softball & Volleyball Leagues; Clergy support groups; Burmese Refugee Resettlement; Neighborhood Poverty Action Group; Racism Action Group; Building Spirituality In the Schools

The Jackson County Interfaith Council

425 Oakwood, P.O. Box 156, Clarklake, MI 49234-0156 Tel. (517)529-9721 Media Contact, Exec. Dir., Rev. Loyal H. Wiemer

Exec. Dir., Rev. Loyal H. Wiemer

Major Activities: Chaplaincy at Institutions and Senior Citizens Residences; Martin L. King, Jr. Day Celebrations; Ecumenical Council Representation; Radio and TV Programs; Food Pantry; Interreligious Events; Clergy Directory

The Metropolitan Christian Council: Detroit-Windsor

1300 Mutual Building, 28 W. Adams, Detroit, MI 48226 Tel. (313)962-0340, Fax (313)962-9044

Email: councilweb@aol.com

Website: users.aol.com/councilweb/index.htm

Media Contact, Rev. Richard Singleton

Exec. Dir., Rev. Richard Singleton

Meals for Shut-ins, Prog. Dir., John Simpson; Add. Asst., Mrs. Elaine Kisner

Web Calendar Supervisor, Mr. Gerald Morgan

Major Activities: Theological and Social Concerns; Ecumenical Worship; Educational Services; Electronic Media; Print Media; Meals for Shut-Ins; Summer Feeding Program

Michigan Ecumenical Forum*

809 Center St., Ste. 5, Lansing, MI 48906 Tel. (517)485-4395, Fax (517)482-8751

Email: ecumenicalforum@aol.com

Media Contact, Exec. Dir., Candyce Williams

Coord.-Exec. Dir., Candyce Williams

Major Activities: Communication and Coordination; Support and Development of Regional Ecumenical Fora; Ecumenical Studies; Fellowship and Celebration; Church and Society Issues; Continuing Education

Muskegon County Cooperating Churches

2525 Hall Road, Muskegon, MI 49442-1520 Tel. 231-777-2888, Fax 231-773-4007

Media Contact, Program Coordinator, Delphine Hogston

President, Rev. Tim Vander Haar

Major Activities: Racial Reconciliation, Dialogue, & Healing; Ecumenical Worship; Faith News TV Ministry; CROP Walk; Community Issues; Prison Ministry; Jewish-Christian Dialogue; Tutoring; Senior Issues

SUBSIDIARY ORGANIZATION

Institute for Healing Racism— Muskegon

2525 Hall Road, Muskegon, MI 49442-1520, Tel. 231-777-7883, Fax. 231-773-4007

Media Contact, Gordon Rinard, Dir.

Major Activities, Racial Reconciliation, Dialogue, & Healing

MINNESOTA

Arrowhead Interfaith Council*

230 E. Skyline Pkwy., Duluth, MN 55811 Tel. (218)727-5020, Fax (218)727-5022

Media Contact, Pres., Alan Cutter

Pres., Alan Cutter

Vice-Pres., Amy Berstein

Sec., John H. Kemp

Major Activities: InterFaith Dialogue; Joint Religious Legislative Coalition; Corrections Chaplaincy; Human Justice and Community Concerns; Community Seminars; Children's Concerns

Community Emergency Assistance Program (CEAP)

6840 78th Ave N, Brooklyn Park, MN 55445 Tel. (763)566-9600, Fax (763)566-9604

Email: smklein@isd.net
Website: www.ceap.homestead.com
Media Contact, Exec. Dir., Stephen Klein
Exec. Dir., Stephen Klein
Major Activities: Provision of Basic Needs (Food, Clothing); Emergency Financial Assistance for Shelter; Home Delivered Meals; Chore Services and Homemaking Assistance; Family Loan Program; Volunteer Services

Greater Minneapolis Council of Churches

1001 E. Lake St., P.O. Box 7509, Minneapolis, MN 55407-0509 Tel. (612)721-8687, Fax (612)722-8669
Email: info@gmcc.org
Website: www.gmcc.org
Media Contact, Dir. of Communications, Darcy Hanzlik
President and CEO, Rev. Dr. Gary B. Reierson, reierson@gmcc.org
Chair, Michael McCarthy
Treas., Kent Eklund
Division Indian Work, Vice President & Exec. Dir., Noya Woodrich; Dir. Of Programs, Denise Estey
Programs, Vice President., Edward L. Duren, Jr.
Russ Ewald Center for Urban Service, Dir., Bruce Bjork
Minnesota FoodShare, Dir., Barbara Thell
Handyworks, Dir., Katherine Panasuk
Correctional Chaplains, Rev. Susan Allers Hatlie; Rev. Thomas Van Leer; Rev. Anne Waters
Discover Learning Centers, Coord., Rev. Janet Larson
Div. of Indian Work, Director, Youth Services, Andrea Keezer; Director, Adult Services, Janice Donnelly.Finance & Admin., Vice President and CFO., Dennis Anderson
Advancement, Sr. Vice President., Don R. Riggs
Urban Immersion Service Retreats, Assoc. Dir., Mike Manhard
Metro Paint-A-Thon, Dir., Sara Holmdahl
Discover Support Groups, Coordinator, Paris Gatlin
Minnesota Churches Anti-Racism Initiative, Dir., James Addington
Congregations Concerned for Children Child Advocacy Network, Coord., Norma Bourland
Project Restoration, Coordinator, William Schoonover
Church and Community Initiatives, Coords., Briana Franzmeier and Bridget Ryan
Major Activities: Indian Work (Emergency Assistance, Youth Leadership, Self-Sufficiency, Jobs Program, Teen Indian Parents Program, and Family Violence Program); Minnesota FoodShare; Metro Paint-A-Thon; Correctional Chaplaincy Program; HandyWorks; Anti-racism Initiative; Child Advocacy; Social Justice Advocacy; Home Renovation; Affordable Housing; Urban Immersion Service Retreats; Welfare Reform; Economic Self-Sufficiency; Discover Support Groups; Job Readiness; Discover Learning Centers; Church and Community Initiatives

The Joint Religious Legislative Coalition

122 W. Franklin Ave., Rm. 315, Minneapolis, MN 55404 Tel. (612)870-3670, Fax (612)870-3671
Email: info@jrlc.org
Website: www.jrlc.org
Media Contact, Exec. Dir., Brian A. Rusche
Exec. Dir., Brian A. Rusche
Research Dir., Dr. James Casebolt
Congregational Organizer, Rev. Becky Myrick
Major Activities: Lobbying at State Legislature; Researching Social Justice Issues and Preparing Position Statements; Organizing Grassroots Citizen's Lobby

Metropolitan Interfaith Council on Affordable Housing (MICAH)

122 W. Franklin Ave., #310, Minneapolis, MN 55404 Tel. (612)871-8980, Fax (612)813-4501
Email: info@micah.org
Website: www.micah.org
Media Contact, Ex. Dir., Joy Sorensen Navarre
Ex. Dir., Joy Sorensen Navarre
Assoc. Dir., JosÇ Trejo
Congregational Organizer, Jodi Nelson, Jean Pearson, Rev. John Buzza, Gloria Little
Pres., Sue Watlov Phillips
Sec., Rev. Paul Robinson
Vice Pres., Dick Little
Treas., Joseph Holmberg
Pres. Elect, Kristine Gentilini
Major Activities: MICAH is a regional advocacy organization made up of over 100 Catholic, Islamic, Jewish, and Protestant congregations dedicated to ensuring decent, safe, and affordable housing for everyone in our community. Its central organizing motto is, "To think regionally, act locally, and live faithfully." In partnership with its members and other groups, MICAH has created community support for 200 new apartment homes in the past two years. In addition it has preserved over 1,000 structurally sound apartments at risk of demolition.

Minnesota Council of Churches*

122 W. Franklin Ave., Rm. 100, Minneapolis, MN 55404 Tel. (612)870-3600, Fax (612)870-3622
Email: mcc@mnchurches.org
Website: www.mnchurches.org
Media Contact, Exec. Dir., Rev. Peg Chemberlin, pegchemberlin@mnchurches.org
Officers and Staff
Exec. Dir., Rev. Peg Chemberlin, pegchemberlin@mn.churches.org

Refugee Services, Dir., Joel Luedtke, refserv@mnchurches.org
Indian Ministry, Field Organizer, Sandy Berlin
Communications, Dir., Christopher Dart
Facilities, Dir., James Cotten
Tri-Council Coordinating Commission, Co-Dirs., James and Nadine Addington
Research Dir. & Admn. Asst., James Casebolt
Joint Religious Legislative Coalition, Exec., Brian A. Rusche
Pres., Rev. Judith Kolwicz
Major Activities: Minnesota Church Center; Local Ecumenism; Life & Work, Rural Life-Ag Crisis; Racial Reconciliation; Indian Ministry; Legislative Advocacy; Refugee Services; Service to Newly Legalized-Undocumented Persons; Unity & Relationships, Sexual Exploitation within the Religious Community; Clergy Support; Consultation on Church Union; Ecumenical Study & Dialogue; Jewish-Christian Relations; Muslim-Christian Relations; State Fair Ministry; Tri-Council Coordinating Commission (Minnesota Churches Anti-Racism Initiative)

St. Paul Area Council of Churches

1671 Summit Ave, St. Paul, MN 55105 Tel. (651)646-8805, Fax (651)646-6866
Email: rwalz@spacc.com
Website: www.spacc.com
Media Contact, Mary Kane
Exec. Dir., Rev. Thomas A. Duke
Dir. of Development, Kristi Anderson
Congregations in Community, Bob Walz
Congregations Concerned for Children, Peg Wangensteen
Project Spirit, Talaya Tolefree
Project Home, Sara Liegl
Dept. of Indian Work, Sheila WhiteEagle
Criminal Justice Care Services, Rev. Kathleen Gatson
Pres. of the Board, Diane E. Follmer
Treas., James Verlautz
Sec., Art Sidner
Major Activities: Chaplaincy at Detention and Corrections Authority Institutions; Police Chaplaincy; Education and Advocacy Regarding Children and Poverty; Assistance to Churches Developing Children's Parenting Care Services; Ecumenical Encounters and Activities; Indian Ministries; Leadership in Forming Cooperative Ministries for Children and Youth; After School Tutoring; Assistance to Congregations; Training Programs in Anti-racism; Shelters for Homeless

Tri-Council Coordinating Commission

122 W. Franklin, Rm. 100, Minneapolis, MN 55404 Tel. (612)871-0229, Fax (612)870-3622
Email: naja@gmcc.org
Website: www.amcc.org/tcc.html
Media Contact, Dir., R. James Addington
Assoc. Dir., Rev. Carmen Valenzuela
Dir., R. James Addington
Assoc. Dir., Rev. Carmen Valenzuela
Pres., Rev. Thomas Duke, 1671 Summit Ave., St. Paul, MN 55105
Major Activities: Anti-Racism training and organizational consultation; Institutional anti-racism team development and coaching; training and coaching of anti-racism trainers and organizers (in cooperation with corss roads ministry)

MISSISSIPPI

Mississippi Religious Leadership Conference*

P.O. Box 68123, Jackson, MS 39286-8123 Tel. (601)948-5954, Fax (601)354-3401
Media Contact, Exec. Dir., Rev. Canon Thomas E. Tiller, Jr.
Exec. Dir., Rev. Canon Thomas E. Tiller, Jr.
Chair, Bishop Marshall Meadors
Treas., Rev. Tom Clark
Major Activities: Cooperation among Religious Leaders; Lay-Clergy Retreats; Social Concerns Seminars; Disaster Task Force; Advocacy for Disadvantaged

MISSOURI

Council of Churches of the Ozarks

P.O. Box 3947, Springfield, MO 65808-3947 Tel. (417)862-3586 Fax (417)862-2129
Email: ccozarks@ccozarks.org
Website: www.ccozarks.org
Media Contact, Comm. Dir., Susan Jackson
Interim Dir., Noel D. Chase
Major Activities: Ministerial Alliance; Retired Sr. Volunteer Prog.; Treatment Center for Alcohol and Drug Abuse; Helping Elderly Live More Productively; Daybreak Adult Day Care Services; Ombudsman for Nursing Homes; Family Day Care Homes; USDA Food Program; Youth Ministry; Disaster Aid and Counseling; Homebound Shoppers; Food and Clothing Pantry; Ozarks Food Harvest; Families for Children; Therapeutic Riding of the Ozarks

Ecumenical Ministries

#2 St. Louis Ave., Fulton, MO 65251 Tel. (573)642-6065
Email: em_fulton@ecunet.org
Website: www.coin.missouri.edu/region/callaway/em.html
Media Contact, Admin Asst., Karen Luebbert
Chair, Bd. Of Dir.; William Jessop

Major Activities: Kingdom Hospice; CROP Hunger Walk; Little Brother and Sister; Unity Service; Senior Center Bible Study; County Jail Ministry; Fulton High School Baccalaureate Service, HAVEN House; Missouri Youth Treatment Center Ministry

Interfaith Community Services
200 Cherokee St., P.O. Box 4038, St. Joseph, MO 64504-0038 Tel. (816)238-4511, Fax (816) 238-3274
Email: DaveB@PonyExpress.net
Website: www.inter-serv.org
Media Contact, Exec. Dir., David G. Berger
Exec. Dir., David G. Berger
Major Activities: Child Development; Neighborhood Family Services; Group Home for Girls; Retired Senior Volunteer Program; Nutrition Program; Mobile Meals; Southside Youth Program; Church and Community; Housing Development; Homemaker Services to Elderly; Emergency Food, Rent, Utilities; AIDS Assistance; Family Respite; Family and Individual Casework

Interfaith Partnership of Metropolitan St. Louis

418 E. Adams Ave., Kirkwood, MO 63122 Tel. (314)821-3808
Email: ipstlouis@mindspring.com
Director, Barbara Russell
President, Tim Carson

MONTANA

Montana Association of Churches*

180 24th St. W., Ste. G, Billings, MT 59102 Tel. (406)656-9779, Fax (406)656-2156
Email: montanachurches@earthlink.net
Website: www.montana-churches.org
Media Contact, Exec. Dir., Margaret MacDonald
Exec. Dir., Margaret E. MacDonald
Admn. Asst., Hung Vu
Pres., Rev. Jessica Crist, 401 4th Ave. N., Great Falls, MT 59401-2310
Treas., Rev. Barbara Archer, 802 W. Galena, Butte, MT 59701
Sec., Paul Kaiser, Diocese of Great Falls-Billings, Box 1399, Great Falls, MT 59403
Christian Advocates Network, Betty Whiting
Major Activities: Montana Christian Advocates Network; Christian Unity; Junior Citizen Camp; Public Information; Ministries Development; Social Ministry; Faith Responses to Extremism and Racism; Renewing the Public Church

NEBRASKA

Interchurch Ministries of Nebraska*

215 Centennial Mall S., Rm. 411, Lincoln, NE 68508-1888 Tel. (402)476-3391, Fax (402) 476-9310
Email: im50427@alltel.net
Media Contact, Exec., Mrs. Marilyn P. Mecham
Pres., Rev. Dr. Bart Brenner
Treas., Rev. Dr. Kenneth W. Moore
Exec., Mrs. Marilyn Mecham
Health Ministry Coordinator, Ronnette L. Sailors
Admin. Asst., Sharon K. Kalcik
Major Activities: Interchurch Planning and Development; Comity; Indian Ministry; Rural Church Strategy; United Ministries in Higher Education; Disaster Response; Rural Response Hotline; Health Ministry; Community Organizing Initiative Planning; Peace with Justice; Angel Connection

Lincoln Interfaith Council

140 S. 27th St., Ste. B, Lincoln, NE 68510-1301 Tel. (402)474-3017, Fax (402)475-3262
Email: mail@lincolninterfaith.org
Website: www.lincolninterfaith.org
Media Contact, Doug Boyd
Exec. Dir., Rev. Dr. Norman E. Leach
Pres., Mrs. Gail Linderholm
Vice-Pres., Mrs. Amriza Mahapatra
Sec., Ms. Barb Dewey
Treas., Mr. Steve Clements
Media Specialist, Mr. Doug Boyd
Urban Ministries, Rev. Dr. Norman E. Leach
Chief Prog. Coord., Jean Scali
Fiscal Mgr., Jean Scali
Lion Dance Instructors; Tom Dao, Todd Burnham
Migrant Child Education Outreach; Marina Wray, Bich Tang
Faces of the Middle East; Mohammed Al-Bezerji, Zainab Al-Baaj
Families First and Foremost; Zainab Al-Baaj, Zainab Al-Batat
Major Activities: Emergency Food Pantries System; MLK, Jr. Observance; Interfaith Passover Seder; Week of Prayer Christian Unity; Festival of Faith & Culture; Holocaust Memorial Observance; Citizens Against Racism & Discrimination; HIV-AIDS; Community Organization; Anti-Drug & Anti-Alcohol Abuse Projects; Youth Gang & Violence Prevention; Domestic Abuse Prevention; Migrant Child Education; American Citizenship Classes; Survival English for Pre-literate AmerAsians and Elderly Refugees; Ecumenical Deaf Ministry; Multi-Faith & Multi-Cultural Training; Faces of the Middle East Project; Crop Walk for Hunger; Unicef Drive; New Clergy Orientation; Directory of Clergy, Congregations & Religious Resources; Multi-Faith Planning Calendar Publication; "Faith Report"; "Lincoln Faith & Culture" on Cable TV-13; African Multicultural Community Center

NEW HAMPSHIRE

New Hampshire Council of Churches*

316 S. Main St., P.O. Box 1087, Concord, NH 03302-1087 Tel. (603)224-1352, Fax (603) 224-9161

Email: churchesnh@aol.com
Media Contact, Exec. Dir., David Lamarre-Vincent
Email: davidlv@aol.com
Exec. Dir., David Lamarre-Vincent
Pres., Rev. Janet Smith-Rushton, 19 Norwich St., Concord, NH 03301
Treas., Mr. Alvah Chisholm
Major Activities: Statewide Ecumenical Work For Christian Unity, Interfaith Understanding, and Social Justice

NEW JERSEY

Bergen County Council of Churches

58 James Street, Bergenfield, NJ 07621 Tel. (201)384-7505 Fax (201)384-2585
Email: smcgiordano@compuserve.com
Website: www.njcommunity.com/sites/BCCC
Media Contact, Pres., Rev. Dr. Stephen T. Giordano, Clinton Avenue Reformed Church, Clinton Ave. & James St., Bergenfield, NJ 07621 Tel. (201)384-2454, Fax (201)384-2585
Exec. Sec., Anne Annunziato
Major Activities: Ecumenical and Religious Institute; Brotherhood-Sisterhood Breakfast; Center for Food Action; Homeless Aid; Operation Santa Claus; Aging Services; Boy & Girl Scouts; Easter Dawn Services; Music; Youth; Ecumenical Representation; Support of Chaplains in Jails & Hospitals; Faith & Values Online project www.njfaithandvalues.org; Welfare into Workplace

Ecclesia

1001 Pennington Rd., Trenton, NJ 08618-2629 Tel. (609)882-5942, Media Contact, Exec. Dir., Rev. Dr. T.L. Steele
Exec. Dir., Rev. Dr. T.L. Steele
Pres., Rev. Joseph P. Ravenell
Campus Chaplains- Rev. Nancy Schulter; Rev. Joanne B. Bullock
Major Activities: Racial Justice; Children & Youth Ministries; Advocacy; CROP Walk; Ecumenical Worship; Hospital Chaplaincy; Church Women United; Campus Chaplaincy; Congregational Empowerment; Prison Chaplaincy; Substance Abuse Ministry Training

Metropolitan Ecumenical Ministry

525 Orange St., Newark, NJ 07107 Tel. 973-485-8100, Fax 973-485-1165
Media Contact, Consultant, Rev. M. L. Emory
Exec. Dir., C. Stephen Jones
Major Activities: Community Advocacy (education, housing, environment); Church Mission Assistance; Community and Clergy Leadership Development; Economic Development; Affordable Housing

Metropolitan Ecumenical Ministry Community Development Corp.

525 Orange St., Newark, NJ 07107 Tel. (973) 481-3100, Fax (201)481-7883
Email: memcdc@juno.com
Exec. Dir., Jacqueline Jones
Major Activities: Housing Development; Neighborhood Revitalization; Commercial-Small Business Development; Economic Development; Community Development; Credit Union; Home Ownership Counseling; Credit Repair; Mortgage Approval; Technical Assitance To Congregations

New Jersey Council of Churches*

176 W. State St., Trenton, NJ 08608 Tel. (609) 396-9546, Fax (609)396-7646
Media Contact, Public Policy Dir., Joan Diefenbach, Esq.
Pres., Rev. Jack Johnson
Vice-Pres., —
Sec., Beverly McNally
Treas., Marge Christie
Major Activities: Racial Justice; Children's Issues; Theological Unity; Ethics Public Forums; Advocacy; Economic Justice

NEW MEXICO

Faith Community Assistance Center

PO Box 15517, Santa Fe, NM 87592 Tel. (505) 438-4782, Fax (505)473-5637
Media Contact, Barbara A. Robinson
Major Activities: Faith Community Assistance Center; Providing Emergency Assistance to the Poor; Interfaith Dialogues-Celebrations-Visitations; Peace Projects; Understanding Hispanic Heritage; Newsletter

New Mexico Conference of Churches*

124 Hermosa Dr. SE, Albuquerque, NM 87108-2610 Tel. (505)255-1509, Fax (505)256-0071
Email: nmcc@nmchurches.org
Website: www.nmchurches.org
Media Contact, Exec. Dir.., Rev. Barbara E Dua
Pres., Rev. James E. Large
Treas., Daniel Borrego
Exec. Dir., Rev. Barbara E. Dua
Major Activities: Ecumenical Institute for Ministry; Affordable Housing; Social Justice Coalitions; Spiritual Life & Ministries

NEW YORK

Brooklyn Council of Churches

125 Ft. Greene Pl., Brooklyn, NY 11217 Tel. (718)625-5851, Fax 718-522-1231
Media Contact, Dir., Charles Henze
Program Dir., Charles Henze
Pres., Rev. John L. Pratt., Sr.
Treas., Rev. Charles H. Straut , Jr.
Major Activities: Education Workshops; Food Pantries; Welfare Advocacy; Hospital and Nursing Home Chaplaincy; Church Women United; Legislative Concerns

Broome County Council of Churches, Inc.

William H. Stanton Center, 3 Otseningo St., Binghamton, NY 13904 Tel. (607)724-9130, Fax (607)724-9148
Email: bgeorge@broomecouncil.org
Website: www.broomecouncil.org
Media Contact, Barbara J. George
Exec. Dir., Barbara J. George (Interim)
Exec. Asst., Brigitte Stella
Hospital Chaplains, Betty Pomeroy; Rev. Nadine Ridley
Jail Chaplain, Rev. Cris Mogenson
Aging Ministry Coord., Linda McColgin
CHOW Prog. Coord.,
Pres., Betty Krech
Treas.,
Caregiver Program Coord., Joanne Kays
Community and Donor Relations, Dir., Eric Shafer
Major Activities: Hospital and Jail Chaplains; Youth and Aging Ministries; Broome Bounty (Food Rescue Program); Emergency Hunger & Advocacy Program; Faith & Family Values; Ecumenical Worship and Fellowship; Media; Community Affairs; Peace with Justice; Day by Day Marriage Prep Program; Interfaith Coalition; Interfaith Volunteer Caregiver Program

Capital Area Council of Churches, Inc.

646 State St., Albany, NY 12203-3815 Tel. (518)462-5450, Fax (518)462-5450
Email: capareacc@aol.com
Media Contact, Admn. Asst.,Kitt Jackson
Exec. Dir., Rev. John U. Miller
Admn. Asst.,Kitt Jackson
Pres., Harold Howes
Treas.,David Wood
Major Activities: Hospital Chaplaincy; Food Pantries; CROP Walk; Jail and Nursing Home Ministries; Martin Luther King Memorial Service and Scholarship Fund; Emergency Shelter for the Homeless; Campus Ministry; Ecumenical Dialogue; Forums on Social Concerns; Peace and Justice Education; Inter-Faith Programs; Legislative Concerns; Comm. Thanksgiving Day and Good Friday Services; Annual Ecumenical Musical Celebration

CAPITAL Region Ecumenical Organization (CREO)

Box 2199, Scotia, NY 12302 Tel. (518)382-7505, Fax (518)382-7505
Email: TishMurph@aol.com
Media Contact, Coord., Jim Murphy
Coord., Jim Murphy
Major Activities: Promote Cooperation-Coordination Among Member Judicatories and Ecumenical Organizations in the Capital Region in Urban Ministries, Social Action

Chautaugua County Rural Ministry

127 Central Ave., P.O. Box 362, Dunkirk, NY 14048 Tel. (716)366-1787
Media Contact, Exec. Dir., Kathleen Peterson
Exec. Dir., Kathleen Peterson
Major Activities: Chautaugua County Food Bank; Collection-Distribution of Furniture, Clothing, & Appliances; Homeless Services; Advocacy for the Poor; Soup Kitchen; Emergency Food Pantry; Thrift Store

Concerned Ecumenical Ministry to the Upper West Side

286 LaFayette Ave., Buffalo, NY 14213 Tel. (716)882-2442, Fax (716)882-2477
Email: catrg@juno.com
Media Contact, Exec. Dir., Betty Gamble
Pres., The Rev. Robert Grimm
Major Activities: Community Center Serving Youth, Refugee Families, Seniors and the Hungry

Cortland County Council of Churches, Inc.

7 Calvert St., Cortland, NY 13045 Tel. (607)753-1002
Media Contact, Office Mgr., Joy Niswender
Exec. Dir., Rev. Donald M. Wilcox
Major Activities: College Campus Ministry; Hospital Chaplaincy; Nursing Home Ministry; Newspaper Column; Interfaith Relationships; Hunger Relief; CWS; Crop Walk; Leadership Education; Community Issues; Mental Health Chaplaincy; Grief Support; Jail Ministry

Council of Churches of Chemung County, Inc.

330 W. Church St., Elmira, NY 14901 Tel. (607)734-2294
Email: ecumenic@exotrope.net
Media Contact, Exec. Dir., Joan Geldmacher, Tel. (607)734-7622
Exec. Dir., Joan Geldmacher
Pres., Rev. Fred Kelsey, Christ's U.M., (607)734-2293
Major Activities: CWS Collection; CROP Walk; UNICEF; Institutional Chaplaincies; Radio, Easter Dawn Service; Communications Network; Produce & Distribute Complete Church Directories; Representation on Community Boards and Agencies; Ecumenical Services; Interfaith Coalition; Taskforce on Children & Families; Compeer; Interfaith Hospitality Center

Council of Churches of the City of New York

475 Riverside Dr., Rm. 720, New York, NY 10115 Tel. (212)367-4222, Fax (212)367-4280
Email: JEHiemstra@aol.com
Media Contact, Exec. Dir., Dr. John E. Hiemstra

Exec. Dir., Dr. John E. Hiemstra
Pres., Rev. Calvin O. Butts
1st Vice-Pres., Friend Carol Holmes
2nd Vice-Pres., Rev. Carolyn Holloway
3rd Vice-Pres., Ven. Michael Kendall
4th Vice-Pres., Morris Gurley
Sec., Rev.N.J. L'Heureux
Treas., Dr. John Cole
Major Activities: Radio & TV; Pastoral Care; Christ for the World Chapel, Kennedy International Airport; Coordination and Strategic Planning; Interfaith Coordinator, Religious Conferences; Referral & Advocacy; Youth Development; Directory of Churches and Database Available

Dutchess Interfaith Council, Inc.

9 Vassar St., Poughkeepsie, NY 12601 Tel. (914)471-7333
Media Contact, Exec. Dir., Rev. Gail A. Burger
Exec. Dir., Rev. Gail A. Burger
Pres.,Rev. Dr. Brian E. McWeeney
Treas., Edward Koziol
Major Activities: CROP Hunger Walk; Interfaith Music Festival; Public Worship Events; Interfaith Dialogue; Christian Unity; Interfaith Youth Evening; Oil Purchase Group; HIV-AIDS Work; Weekly Radio Program; Racial Unity Work; Poverty Forums

Genesee County Churches United, Inc.

P.O. Box 547, Batavia, NY 14021 Tel. (716)343-6763
Media Contact, Pres.,Captain Leonard Boynton, Salvation Army, 529 East Main St., Batavia, NY 14020 Tel. (716)343-6284
Pres., James Woodruff
Exec. Sec., Cheryl Talone
Chaplain, Rev. Peter Miller
Major Activities: Jail Ministry; Food Pantries; Serve Needy Families; Radio Ministry; Pulpit Exchange; Community Thanksgiving; Ecumenical Services at County Fair

Genesee-Orleans Ministry of Concern

Arnold Gregory Memorial Complex, Suite 271
243 South Main St., Albion, NY 14411 Tel. (716)589-9210, Fax (716)589-9617
Media Contact, Exec. Dir., Marian M. Adrian, GNSH
Exec. Dir., Marian M. Adrian, GNSH
Advocates, JoAnn McCowan; Heather Cook
Pres., John W. Cebula, Esq.
Chaplains, Orleans County Jail, Rev. Wilford Moss; Orleans Albion Correctional Facility, Sr. Dolores O'Dowd, GNSH
Major Activities: Advocacy Services for the Disadvantaged, Homeless, Ill, Incarcerated and Victims of Family Violence; Emergency Food, Shelter, Utilities, Medicines

Graymoor Ecumenical & Interreligious Institute

475 Riverside Dr., Rm. 1960, New York, NY 10115-1999 Tel. (212)870-2330, Fax (212) 870-2001
Email: lmnygeii@aol.com
Website: www.atonementfriars.org
Media Contact, Ms. Elizabeth Matos
Major Activities: (See Listing in US Cooperative Directory)

Greater Rochester Community of Churches

2 Riverside St., Rochester, NY 14613-1222 Tel. (716)254-2570, Fax (716)254-6551
Email: grcc@juno.com
Media Contact, Coord., Elder Marie E. Gibson
Major Activities: Ecumenical Worship; Chaplaincy Services; Christian Unity; Interfaith Health Care Coalition; Interfaith Cooperation; Community Economic Development; Annual Faith in Action Celebration; Rochester's Religious Community Directory; Religious Information-Resources; Justice Issues; Children & Poverty

InterReligious Council of Central New York

3049 E. Genesee St., Syracuse, NY 13224 Tel. (315)449-3552, Fax (315)449-3103
Email: IRCCNY@aol.com
Media Contact, Dir. for Resource Development, Chrissie Rizzo
Executive Dir., The Rev. Robert E. Hanson
Pres., The Rev. Emily S. Gibson
Bus. Mgr., Joseph Sarno
Director for Resource Development, Chrissie Rizzo
Pastoral Care Prog., Dir., The Rev. Terry Culbertson
Refugee Resettlement Prog., Dir., Nona Stewart
Senior Companion Prog., Dir., Virginia Frey
Long Term Ombudsman Prog., Dir., Linda Kashdin
Covenant Housing Prog., Dir., Kimberlee Dupcak
Southeast Asia Center, Dir., Mai Lan Putnam
Community Wide Dialogue on Racism, Race Relations and Racial Healing, Co-Dirs., Milady Andrews, Morgan and Van Leary-Hammerstedt
InterReligious Council News, Ed., Ed Griffin-Nolan
Major Activities: Pastoral Ministries; Community Ministries; Interreligious and Ecumenical Relations; Diversity Education; Worship; Community Advocacy and Planning

The Long Island Council of Churches

1644 Denton Green, Hempstead, NY 11550 Tel. 516-565-0290, Fax 516-565-0291

Email: licc@netzero.com
Website: www.ncccusa.org/ecmin/licc
Media Contact, Exec. Dir., Thomas W. Goodhue
Exec. Dir., Rev. Thomas W. Goodhue
Pastoral Care, Dir., Rev. Richard Lehman
Social Services, Dir., Anne Vaughn, Tel. (516)565-0390
Nassau County Ofc., Social Services Sec., LaToya Walker
Suffolk County Ofc., Food Program & Family Support, Carolyn Gumbs
Major Activities: Pastoral Care in Jails; Emergency Food; Family Support & Advocacy; Advocacy for Domestic and International Peace & Justice; Blood Donor Coordination; Church World Service; Multifaith Education; Clergy-Laity Training; Newsletter; Church Directory; AIDS Interfaith of Long Island

Network of Religious Communities

1272 Delaware Ave., Buffalo, NY 14209-2496 Tel. (716)882-4793, Fax (716)882-3797
Email: ReligiousNet@aol.com
Website: ReligiousNet.org
Media Contact, Co-Exec. Dir., Rev. Dr. G. Stanford Bratton
Co-Exec. Dir. & COO, Rev. Dr. G. Stanford Bratton
Co-Exec. Dir., Rev. Francis X. Mazur
Pres.,Rev. Jeff Carter (Church of God in Christ)
Vice-Pres. For Program, The Rev. Dr. David McKee (General Presbyter, Presbytery of WNY)
Vice-Pres. For Administration, Ms. Marlene Glickman (Dir., American Jewish Committee)
Secretary, Ms. Sheila Nickson (Episcopal Church)
Treasurer, The Rev. Amos Acree (Disciples of Christ)
Chpsn., Interreligious Concerns, Rabbi Michael Feshbach, President Board of Rabbis
Chpsn., Personnel, The Rev. James Croglio (Diocese of Buffalo- Roman Catholic)
Chpsn., Membership, The Rev. Robert Grimm (United Church of Christ)
Chpsn., Riefler Enablement Fund, Mrs. Thelma Lanier (African Methodist Episcopal Church)
Chpsn., Public Issues, Rev. Merle Showers (United Methodist Church)
Chpsn., Religious Leaders Forum, Rev. Paul Litwin (Diocese of Buffalo-Roman Catholic)
Chpsn., Church Women United, Ms. Alma Arnold (United Church of Christ)
STAFF (Other than Executive Directors)
Program Coordinator, Ms. Maureen Gensler
Office Coordinator, Ms. Sally Giordano
Director of Food For All, Patricia Griffin
Nutrition Outreach and Education Coordinator, Ms. Carolyn Williams
Staff Assistant, Mr. Lamont Gist
Major Activities: Regionwide Interreligious Conversation, Hunger Advocacy, Food Distribution, Roll Call Against Racism, Buffalo Coalition for Common Ground, Ecumenical and Interreligious Relations and Celebrations, Radio-TV Broadcast and Production, Church Women United, Lay-Religious Leaders Education, Community Development, Chaplaincy, Yom Hashoah Commemoration Service, Aids Memorial Service, Police-Community Relations, CROP Walks

New York State Community of Churches, Inc.*

362 State St, Albany, NY 12210-1202 Tel. (518)436-9319, Fax (518)427-6705
Email: nyscoc@aol.com
Website: www.nyscommunityofchurches.org
Media Contact, Mr. Thomas McPheeters
Executive Dir., Ms. Mary Lu Bowen
Pres., Bishop Susan M. Morrison
Corp. Sec., The Rev. Dr. Jon Norton
Treas., The Rev. Dr. Robert White
Convener, Bishop Lee M. Miller
Coordinator of Chaplaincy Services, Ms. Damaris McGuire
Public Policy Advocate, The Rev. Daniel Hahn
Communications Coord, Mr. Thomas McPheeters
Admin. Asst., Sylvenia F. Cochran
Major Activities: Faith & Order; Interfaith Dialogue; State Chaplaincy and Public Policy Advocacy in the following areas, Anti-Racism; Campaign Reform; Criminal Justice System Reform; Disability; Ecomomic-Social Justice; Environmental; Health Care; Homelessness-Shelter; Hunger-Food Programs; Immigrant Issues; Public Education; Rural Issues; Substance Abuse; Violence; Women's Issues

The Niagara Council of Churches Inc.

St. Paul UMC, 723 Seventh St., Niagara Falls, NY 14301 Tel. (716)285-7505
Media Contact, Pres., Nessie S. Bloomquist, 7120 Laur Rd., Niagara Falls, NY 14304 Tel. (716)297-0698, Fax (716)298-1193
Exec. Dir., Ruby Babb
Pres., Nessie S. Bloomquist
Treas., Shirley Bathurst
Trustees Chpsn., Rev. Vincent Mattoni, 834 19th St., Niagara Falls, NY 14304
Major Activities: Ecumenical Worship; Bible Study; Christian Ed. & Social Concerns; Church Women United; Evangelism & Mission; Institutional Min. Youth Activities; Hymn Festival; Week of Prayer for Christian Unity; CWS Projects; Audio-Visual Library; UNICEF; Food Pantries and Kitchens; Community Missions, Inc.; Political Refugees; Eco-Justice Task Force; Migrant-Rural Ministries; Interfaith Coalition on Energy

Niagara County Migrant Rural Ministry

6507 Wheeler Rd., Lockport, NY 14094 Tel. (716)434-4405
Media Contact, Exec. Dir., Grayce M. Dietz
Chpsn., Lois Farley
Vice-Chpsn., Beverly Farnham
Sec., Anne Eifert
Treas., Rev. Patricia Ludwig
Major Activities: Migrant Farm Worker Program; Assist with Immigration Problems and Application Process for Social Services; Monitor Housing Conditions; Assist Rural Poor; Referrals to Appropriate Service Agencies; Children's Daily Enrichment Program

Queens Federation of Churches

86-17 105th St., Richmond Hill, NY 11418-1597 Tel. (718)847-6764, Fax (718)847-7392
Email: qfc@ecunet.org
Website: queenschurches.org
Media Contact, Rev. N. J. L'Heureux, Jr.
Exec. Dir., Rev. N. J. L'Heureux, Jr.
York College Chaplain, Rev. Dr. Hortense Merritt
Pres., Paule Alexander
Treas., Annie Lee Phillips
Major Activities: Emergency Food Service; York College Campus Ministry; Blood Bank; Scouting; Christian Education Workshops; Planning and Strategy; Church Women United; Community Consultations; Seminars for Church Leaders; Directory of Churches and Synagogues; Christian Relations (Prot-RC); Chaplaincies; Public Policy Issues; N.Y.S. Interfaith Commission on Land-marking of Religious Property; Queens Interfaith Hunger Network; "The Nexus of Queens" (tri-weekly newspaper)

Rural Migrant Ministry

P.O. Box 4757, Poughkeepsie, NY 12602 Tel. (845)485-8627, Fax (845)485-1963
Email: rmmhope@earthlink.net
Website: ruralmigrantministry.org
Media Contact, Exec. Dir., Rev. Richard Witt
Exec. Dir., Rev. Richard Witt
Pres., Melinda Trotti
Major Activities: Serving the Rural Poor and Migrants Through a Ministry of Advocacy & Empowerment; Youth Program; Latino Committee; Organization and Advocacy with and for Rural Poor and Migrant Farm Workers

Schenectady Inner City Ministry

930 Albany St., Schenectady, NY 12307-1514 Tel. (518)374-2683, Fax (518)382-1871
Email: sicm@knick.net
Website: www. crisny.org/not-for-profit/sicm
Media Contact, Marianne Comfort
Urban Agent, Rev. Phillip N. Grigsby
Off. Mgr., Vjuana Anderson
Fiscal Officer, Joan LaMonica
Emergency Food Liaison, Patricia Obrecht
Church-Community Worker, Rev. Jim Murphy
Pres., Starr and Tom DiCiuvcio
Save and Share, Cindy Hofer
Damien Center, Glenn Read
Youth Improvisational Teen Theatre, Laurie Bacheldor
Jobs, Etc., David Coplon
Summer Food
Housing Task Force, Eric Dahl
Major Activities: Food Security; Advocacy; Housing; Neighborhood and Economic Issues; Ecumenical Worship and Fellowship; Community Research; Education in Churches on Faith Responses to Social Concerns; Legislative Advocacy; Food Buying Coop; Homelessness Prevention; CROP Walk; HIV-AIDS Ministry; Teen Theatre; Job Training and Placement Center; Summer Lunch for Youth; Study Circles Initiative on Embracing Diversity; EPRUS-Americorps; Community Crisis Nework; Housing Services and Advocacy

Southeast Ecumenical Ministry

25 Westminster Rd., Rochester, NY 14607 Tel. (716)271-5350, Fax (716)271-8526
Email: sem@frontiernet.net
Media Contact, Laurie Jenkins
Dir., Laurie Jenkins
Pres., Alistair Lewis, C
Major Activities: Transportation of Elderly & Disabled; Emergency Food Cupboard; Supplemental Nutrition Program

Staten Island Council of Churches

2187 Victory Blvd., Staten Island, NY 10314 Tel. (718)761-6782
Media Contact, Exec. Sec., Mildred J. Saderholm, 94 Russell St., Staten Island, NY 10308 Tel. (718)761-6782
Pres., Rev. Gard Rowe
Exec. Sec., Mildred J. Saderholm
Major Activities: Support; Christian Education; Pastoral Care; Congregational Concerns; Urban Affairs

Troy Area United Ministries

17 First St., #2, Troy, NY 12180 Tel. (518)274-5920 Fax (518)271-1909
Email: TAUM@knick.net
Media Contact, Exec. Dir., Rev. Donna Elia
Pres., Michael L. Desantels, Esq.
Chaplain, R.P.I. And Russel Sage, Rev. Beth Illingworth
Damien Center, Dir., Glenn Read
Furniture Program, Dir., Michael Barrett
Major Activities: College Ministry; Nursing Home Ministry; CROP Walk; Homeless and Housing Concerns; Weekend Meals Program at

Homeless Shelter; Community Worship Celebrations; Racial Relations; Furniture Program; Damien Center of Troy Hospitality for persons with HIV-AIDS; Computer Ministries

Wainwright House

260 Stuyvesant Ave., Rye, NY 10580 Tel. (914)967-6080, Fax (914)967-6114
Media Contact, Exec. Dir., Judith W. Milinowski
Exec. Dir., Judith W. Milinowski
Pres., Dr. Robert A. Rothman
Exec. Vice-Pres., Beth Adams Smith
Major Activities: Educational Program and Conference Center; Intellectual, Psychological, Physical and Spiritual Growth; Healing and Health

NORTH CAROLINA

Asheville-Buncombe Community Christian Ministry (ABCCM)

30 Cumberland Ave., Asheville, NC 28801 Tel. (704)259-5300, Fax (704)259-5923
Media Contact, Exec. Dir., Rev. Scott Rogers, Fax (704)259-5323
Exec. Dir., Rev. Scott Rogers
Pres., Dr. Rev. Mark Nieting
Major Activities: Crisis Ministry; Jail-Prison Ministry; Shelter Ministry; Medical Ministry; Home Repair Ministry

Greensboro Urban Ministry

305 West Lee St., Greensboro, NC 27406 Tel. (910)271-5959, Fax (910)271-5920
Email: Guministry@aol.com
Website: www.greensboro.com/gum
Media Contact, Exec. Dir., Rev. Mike Aiken
Exec. Dir., Rev. Mike Aiken
Major Activities: Emergency Financial Assistance; Emergency Housing; Hunger Relief; Inter-Faith and Inter-Racial Understanding; Justice Ministry; Chaplaincy with the Poor

North Carolina Council of Churches*

Methodist Bldg., 1307 Glenwood Ave., Ste. 162, Raleigh, NC 27605-3258 Tel. (919)828-6501, Fax (919)828-9697
Email: nccofc@nccouncilofchurches.org
Website: www.nccouncilofchurches.org
Media Contact, Communications Associate, Aleta Payne
Exec. Dir., Rev. J. George Reed
Program Associate, Sr. Evelyn Mattern
Communications Associate, Aleta Payne
Pres., Rev. Joseph C. Brown, Jr., 709 Church St., Wilmington, NC 28409
Treas., Dr. James W. Ferree, 5108 Huntcliff Tr., Winston-Salem, NC 27104
Major Activities: Children and Families; Health Care Justice; Christian Unity; Women's Issues; Legislative Program; Criminal Justice; Farmworker Ministry; Rural Crisis; Racial Justice; Death Penalty; Poverty and Response to Welfare Changes; Climate Change; Public Education

NORTH DAKOTA

North Dakota Conference of Churches*

411 N 4th St Ste 8, Bismarck, ND 58501-4078 Tel. (701)255-0604, Fax (701)223-6075
Media Contact, Executive Sec., Renee Gopal
Pres., Bishop Andrew Fairfield
Vice Pres., Bishop Michael Coyner
Treas., Christopher Dodson
Secretary, Rev. Arabella Meadows-Rogers
Executive Sec., Renee Gopal
Major Activities: Prison Chaplaincy; Rural Life Ministry; Faith and Order; North Dakota 101; Current Ecumenical Proposals

OHIO

Akron Area Association of Churches

350 S. Portage Path, Akron, OH 44320 Tel. (330)535-3112, Fax (330)374-5041
Email: aaac1@juno.com
Website: www.triple-ac.org
Media Contact, Exec. Dir., Rev. Jon A. Dainty
Admin. Asst., Chloe Ann Kriska
Bd. of Trustees, Pres., Rev. Dr. J. Wayman Butts
Vice-Pres., Rev. Mark Frey
Sec., Dale Kline
Treas., Dr. Stephen Laning
Christian Ed., Dir., Chloe Ann Kriska
Major Activities: Messiah Sing; Interfaith Council; Newsletters; Resource Center; Community Worship; Training of Local Church Leadership; Radio Programs; Clergy and Lay Fellowship Luncheons; Cable TV; Neighborhood Development; Community Outreach; Church Interracial Partnerships

Alliance of Churches

470 E. Broadway, Alliance, OH 44601 Tel. (330)821-6648
Media Contact, Dir., Lisa A. Oyster
Dir., Lisa A. Oyster
Pres., Rev. Bud Hoffman
Treas., Betty Rush
Major Activities: Christian Education; Community Relations & Service; Ecumenical Worship; Community Ministry; Peacemaking; Medical Transportation for Anyone Needing It; Emergency Financial Assistance

Churchpeople for Change and Reconciliation

Box 488, Lima, OH 45802 Tel. 419-224-2086, Fax 419-224-2086
Media Contact, Exec. Dir., Sharron Thirkill
Exec. Dir., Sharron Thirkill

Major Activities: Developing Agencies for Minorities, Poor, Alienated and Despairing; Our Daily Bread Soup Kitchen

Council of Christian Communions of Greater Cincinnati

42 Calhoun St., Cincinnati, OH 45219-1525 Tel. (513)559-3151
Media Contact, Exec. Dir., Joellen W. Grady
Exec. Dir., Joellen W. Grady
Justice Chaplaincy, Assoc. Dir., Rev. Jack Marsh
Educ., Assoc., Lillie D. Bibb
Pres., Rev. Damon Lynch III
Major Activities: Christian Unity & Interfaith Cooperation; Justice Chaplaincies; Police-Clergy Team; Adult and Juvenile Jail Chaplains; Religious Education

Greater Dayton Christian Connections

601 W. Riverview Ave., Dayton, OH 45406 Tel. 937-227-9485, Fax 937-227-9407
Email: gdcc@donet.com
Media Contact, Exec. Dir., James S. Burton
Exec. Dir., James S. Burton
Pres., Rev. Burton Wolf
Major Activities: Communications, Service to Churches and Community; Reconciliation Ministry; CROP Walk; Martin Luther King Activities; Micah 6 Churches; Supportive Housing Project

Mahoning Valley Association of Churches

30 W. Front St., Youngstown, OH 44503 Tel. (330)744-8946, Fax (330)774-0018
Email: mvac@onecom.com
Media Contact, Exec. Dir., Elsie L. Dursi
Exec. Dir., Elsie L. Dursi
Pres., Jack Ritter
Treas., Ray Hurd
Major Activities: Communications; Christian Education; Ecumenism; Social Action; Advocacy

Metropolitan Area Church Council

760 E. Broad St., Columbus, OH 43205 Tel. (614)461-7103
Media Contact, Exec. Dir., Rev. Burton Cantrell
Exec. Dir., Rev. Burton Cantrell
Chpsn. of Bd., Alvin Hadley
Sec.,Treas., Lily Schlichter
Major Activities: Newspaper; Liaison with Community organizations; Assembly; Week of Prayer for Christian Unity; Support for Ministerial Associations and Church Councils; Seminars for Church Leaders; Prayer Groups; CROP Walk; Social Concerns Hearings

Metropolitan Area Religious Coalition of Cincinnati

Ste. 1035, 617 Vine St., Cincinnati, OH 45202-2423 Tel. (513)721-4843, Fax (513)721-4891
Email: marcc@fuse.net
Media Contact, Dir., Rev. Duane Holm
Dir., Rev. Duane Holm
Pres., Taylor T. Thompson
Major Activities: Local Social Policy Decisions Chosen Annually.
2001, Community-Police Relations, Welfare Reform.

Ohio Council of Churches*

6877 N. High St., Ste. 206, Columbus, OH 43085-2516 Tel. (614)885-9590, Fax (614) 885-6097
Email: mail@ohcouncilchs.org
Website: www.ohcouncilchs.org
Exec. Dir., Rev. Rebecca J. Tollefson
Public Policy, Dir., Tom Smith
Pres., Jack B. Davis
Vice Pres., Rev. Joseph Witmer
Treas., Rev. Clifford W. Atkinson
Major Activities: Agricultural Issues; Economic & Social Justice; Ecumenical Relations; Health Care Reform; Public Policy Issues; Theological Dialogue; Racial Relations; Education-Funding; Childcare-Children Issues; Poverty-Welfare; Rural Life-Farm Crisis and Environment, Casino Gambling, Global Warming

Pike County Outreach Council

122 E. North St., Waverly, OH 45690-1146 Tel. (740)947-7151 Dir., Judy Dixon
Major Activities: Emergency Service Program; Self Help Groups; Homeless Shelter

Toledo Ecumenical Area Ministries

444 Floyd St., Toledo, OH 43620 Tel. (419)242-7401, Fax (419)242-7404
Media Contact, Admn., Nancy Lee Atkins
Metro-Toledo Churches United, Admn., Nancy Lee Atkins
Toledo Metropolitan Mission, Exec. Dir., Nancy Lee Atkins
Major Activities: Ecumenical Relations; Interfaith Relations; Food Program; Housing Program; Social Action-Public Education; Health Care; Urban Ministry; Employment; Welfare Rights; Housing; Mental Retardation; Voter Registration-Education; Substance Abuse Treatment; Youth Leadership; Children At-risk; Elimination of Discrimination

Tuscarawas County Council for Church and Community

107 West High, Ste. B, New Philadelphia, OH 44663 Tel. (330)343-6012, Fax (330)343-9845
Media Contact, Barbara E. Lauer
Exec. Dir., Barbara E. Lauer
Pres., Zoe Ann Kelley, 201 E. 12th St., Dover, OH 44622
Treas., James Barnhouse, 120 N. Broadway, New Philadelphia, OH 44663

Major Activities: Human Services; Health; Family Life; Child Abuse; Housing; Educational Programs; Emergency Assistance; Legislative Concerns; Juvenile Prevention Program; Character Formation; Prevention Program for High Risk Children; Bimonthly newsletter The Pilot

West Side Ecumenical Ministry

5209 Detroit Ave, Cleveland, OH 44102 Tel. (216)651-2037, Fax (216)651-4145

Email: Eotero@wsem.org

Website: www.wsem.org

Media Contact, Director of Marketing and Public Relations, Kami L. Marquardt

Pres., & CEO, Elving F. Otero

Chief Operation Officer, Adam Roth

Major Activities: WSEM is dedicated to serving urban low-income families by providing programs that encourage self-sufficiency. Three food pantries and outreach centers, a job-training program, early childhood, preschool, and schol-age child care, crisis intervention, counseling, youth services, a theatre education program and a senior nutrition program are among the services available. WSEM serves more than 56,000 children, families, and individuals annually with a staffing of more than 300 employees and 3,200 volunteers.

OKLAHOMA

Oklahoma Conference of Churches*

301 Northwest 36th St., Oklahoma City, OK 73118 Tel. (405)525-2928, Fax (405)525-2636

Email: okconfch@flash.net

Website: www.flash.net/~okconfch

Media Contact, Deborah Canary-Marshall

Exec. Dir., The Rev. Dr. Rita K. Newton

Pres., Ms. Carolyn Stephens

Major Activities: Christian Unity Issues; Community Building Among Members; Rural Community Care; Ecumenical Decade with Women; Children's Advocacy; Day at the Legislature; Impact; Criminal Justice; Hunger & Poverty; Legislative Advocacy; Aging; Women's Issues

Tulsa Metropolitan Ministry

221 S. Nogales, Tulsa, OK 74127 Tel. (918)582-3147, Fax (918)582-3159

Email: TMM@ionet.net

Website: www.TUMM.org

Media Contact, Operation-Associate Dir., James W. Robinson

Exec. Dir., The Rev. Dr. Stephen V. Cranford

Operations Dir., James Robinson

Pres., Rev. Barney McLaughlin

Vice-Pres., Sara Jo Waggoner

Treas., Kelly Kirby

Major Activities: Religious Understanding; Legislative Issues; Interfaith Dialogue TV Series; Christian Issues; Justice Issues; Against Racism; Disability Awareness; Directory of Metro. Religious Community

OREGON

Ecumenical Ministries of Oregon*

0245 S.W. Bancroft St., Ste. B, Portland, OR 97201 Tel. (503)221-1054, Fax (503)223-7007

Email: emo@emoregon.org

Website: www.emoregon.org

Media Contact, Stephanie Howell, EMO Communications Manager

Exec. Dir., David A. Leslie

Associate Dir., Rick Stoller

Compassionate Care and Education, Dir., Melinda Smith

Finance and Administrative Services, Dir., Gary B. Logsdon

Developments Dir., Gordon Dickey

Refugees & Immigration Ministries Division, Dir., Ann Stephani

Russian Oregon Social Services, Yelena Sergeva

Portland International Community School, Ellen Irish

Public Policy Dir., Enid Edwards

Interfaith Network for Earth Concerns, Jenny Holmes

Parent Mentor Program, Sylvia Hart-Landsberg

HIV Day Center, Lowen Berman

Shared Housing, Verlin Byers

Northeast Emergency Food Program, Jennifer Core

President, Virginia Robertson

Public Relations Manager, Stephanie Howell

Major Activities: Theological Education and Dialogue; Public Policy Advocacy; Community Ministries including "Basic Human Needs" (HIV Day Center, NE Emergency Food, Parent Mentor, Shared Housing); "Refugee and Immigration Ministries" (Portland International Community School, Russian Oregon Social Services, Sponsors Organized to Assist Refugees); and "Compassionate Care & Education" (Hopewell House Hospice Center).

PENNSYLVANIA

Allegheny Valley Association of Churches

1333 Freeport Rd., P.O. Box 236, Natrona Heights, PA 15065 Tel. (724)226-0606, Fax (724)226-3197

Email: avac@salsgiver.com

Website: www.avaoc.org

Media Contact, Exec. Dir., Karen Snair

Exec. Dir., Karen Snair

Pres., Rev. Dr. W. James Legge, 232 Tarentum-Culmerville Rd., Tarentum, PA 15084

Treas., Libby Grimm, 312 Butternut Ln., Tarentum, PA 15084

Major Activities: Ecumenical Services; Dial-a-Devotion; Walk for Hunger; Food Bank; Emergency Aid; Cross-on-the-Hill; AVAC Hospitality Network for Homeless Families; AVAC Volunteer Caregivers; Senior Citizen Housing-Pine Ridge Heights Senior Complex, AVAC Chaplaincy Program; Summer Camp for Children

Christian Associates of Southwest Pennsylvania

204 37th St., Suite 201, Pittsburgh, PA 15201 Tel. (412)688-9070, Fax (412)688-9091
Email: casp1817@aol.com
Website: www.casp.org
Media Contact, Dir. of Communications, Bruce J. Randolph
Pres., Board of Delegates, Fr. Roger Statnick
Television Studio Director, Earl C. Hartman, Jr.
Executive Administrative Asst., Tracie Richie
Director of Jail Chaplaincy Services, Rev. Ulli Klemm
Protestant Chaplain, Rev. Dallas Brown
Protestant Chaplain- Shuman Youth Detention Center, Rev. Floyd Palmer
Jail Administrative Assistant, Karen Mack
Executive Director, Fr. Gregory C. Wingenbach
Director of Communications, Bruce J. Randolph
Exec. Admin. Assistant, Nancy Raymond
Major Activities: Christian Associates Television (CATV); Christian Associates Radio (the Witness); Media Ministries; Special-Cooperative-Volunteer Ministries; Jail-Youth-Incarceration Chaplaincies; Church & Community; Social Service Ministries; Theological Dialogue-Religious Education; Racism-Interracial Understanding

Christian Churches United of the Tri-County Area

413 South 19th St., Harrisburg, PA 17106-0750 Tel. (717)230-9550 Fax (717)230-9554
Email: ccuhbg@aol.com
Media Contact, Exec. Dir., Jaqueline P. Rucker
Exec. Dir., Jaqueline P. Rucker
Pres., Ken Wise, Esq.
Treas., James Smeltzer
Vice-Pres., Peter Pennington
Sec., Lenore Cameron, Esq.
HELP & LaCasa Ministries, Dir., Tonya Mitchell-Weston, P.O. Box 60750, Harrisburg, PA 17106-0750 Tel. (717)238-2851, Fax (717)238-1916
Major Activities: Volunteer Ministries to Prisons; HELP (Housing, Rent, Food, Medication, Transportation, Home Heating, Clothing); La Casa de Amistad (The House of Friendship) Social Services; AIDS Outreach; Prison Chaplaincy; Lend-A-Hand (Disaster Rebuilding)

Christians United in Beaver County

1098 Third St., Beaver, PA 15009 Tel. (724)774-1446, Fax (724)774-1446
Media Contact, Exec. Sec., Lois L. Smith
Exec. Sec., Lois L. Smith
Chaplains: Rev. Dennis Ugoletti; Rev. Anthony Massey; Rev. Kathleen Schoeneck; John Pusateri
Pres., Rev. Bernard Tench, 2322 10th Street, Beaver Falls, PA 15010
Treas., Ima Moldovan, 302 Lynn Dr., New Brighton, PA 15066
Major Activities: Christian Education; Evangelism; Social Action; Church Women United; United Church Men; Ecumenism; Hospital, Detention Home and Jail Ministry

East End Cooperative Ministry

250 N. Highland Ave., Pittsburgh, PA 15206 Tel. (412)361-5549, Fax (412)361-0151
Email: eecm@usaor.net
Media Contact, Michele Griffiths, Community Development Director
Exec. Dir., Myrna Zelenitz
Ass. Dir., Rev. Darnell Leonard
Major Activities: Food Pantry; Soup Kitchen; Men's Emergency Shelter; Drop-In Shelter for Homeless; Meals on Wheels; Casework and Supportive Services for Elderly; Information and Referral; Programs for Children and Youth; Bridge Housing Program for Men and PennFree for Women in Recovery and Their Children

Ecumenical Conference of Greater Altoona

PO Box 372, Duncansville, PA 16635 Tel. (814)942-0512
Email: eilbeck@aol.com
Media Contact, Exec. Dir., Eileen Becker
Exec. Dir., Eileen Becker
Major Activities: Religious Education; Workshops; Ecumenical Activities; Religious Christmas Parade; Campus Ministry; Community Concerns; Peace Forum; Religious Education for Mentally Challenged; Inter-faith Committee; Prison Ministry

Greater Bethlehem Area Council of Churches

1021 Center St., P.O. Box 1245, Bethlehem, PA 18016-1245 Tel. (610)867-8671, Fax (610) 866-9223
Exec. Dir., Rev. Dr. Helen Baily Cochrane
Pres., Robert D. Romeril
Treas., Robert Gerst, 900 Wedgewood Rd., Bethlehem, PA 18017
Major Activities: World-local Hunger Projects; Ecumenical Worship-Cooperation; Prison Ministry Programs; Support for Homeless and Welfare to Work Programs; Emergency Food Pantry; Support for Hospice and Share Care Programs; Regional Grave Bank; Support Summer Youth Camps and Church Sports League

Hanover Area Council of Churches

136 Carlisle St., Hanover, PA 17331-2406 Tel. (717)633-6353, Fax (717)633-1992
Email: cathy@sun-link.com
Website: www. netrax.net/~bouchard/hacc.htm
Exec. Dir., Cathy Ferree
Major Activities: Meals on Wheels, Provide a Lunch Program, Fresh Air Program, Clothing Bank, Hospital Chaplaincy Services; Congregational & Interfaith Relations, Public Ecumenical Programs and Services, State Park Chaplaincy Services & Children's Program; Compeer; Faith at Work; CROP Walk; Stolte Scholarship Fund; Community Needs

Inter-Church Ministries of Erie County

2216 Peach St., Erie, PA 16502 Tel. (814)454-2411
Pres., Msgr. William E. Biebel, 230 10th St., Erie, PA 16501
Treas., Ms. Margaret Lorei
Major Activities: Local Ecumenism; Ministry with Aging; Social Ministry; Continuing Education; North West Pennsylvania Conference of Bishops and Judicatory Execs.; Theological Dialogue; Coats for Kids; Voucher Program for Emergency Assistance, Voucher Program, Jeremy Stewart

Lancaster County Council of Churches

134 E. King St., Lancaster, PA 17602 Tel. (717)291-2261, Fax (717)291-6403
Email: lccc134@lancnews.infi.net
Media Contact, Executive Dir., Rev. John Smaligo
Pres., Armon Snowden
Prescott House, Dir., John Stoudt
Asst. Admn., Kim Y. Wittel
Encounter, Dir., Louise Schiraldi
CONTACT, Dir., Lois Gascho
Service Ministry, Dir., Adela Dohner
Major Activities: Social Ministry; Residential Ministry to Youthful Offenders; CONTACT; Advocacy; Child Abuse Prevention

Lebanon County Christian Ministries

818 Water St., P.O. Box 654, Lebanon, PA 17046 Tel. (717)274-2601
Media Contact, Exec. Dir., Lillian Morales
Exec. Dir., Lillian Morales
Noon Meals Coord., Wenda Dinatale
Major Activities: H.O.P.E. (Helping Our People in Emergencies); Food & Clothing Bank; Free Meal Program; Commodity Distribution Program; Ecumenical Events

Lehigh County Conference of Churches

534 Chew St., Allentown, PA 18102 Tel. (610)433-6421, Fax (610)439-8039
Email: lcc@lcconfchurch.org
Website: www.lcconfchurch.org
Media Contact, Develpoment, Dr. Sandra Gaspar
Exec. Dir., The Rev. Dr. Christine L. Nelson
Assoc. Dir., Marlene Merz
Pres., Mr. Anthony Muir
1st Vice-Pres., Mr. Charles Ehninger
Sec., The Rev. Dr. David Charles Smith
Treas., Mr. Nelson Rubenold
Major Activities: Prison Chaplaincy Program; Social Concerns and Action; Clergy Dialogues; Daybreak Drop-In-Center for De-Institutionalized Adults; Ecumenical Soup Kitchen; Housing Advocacy Program; Pathways (Referral to Social Services); Street Contact; Linkage; Guardianship; Community Exchange; Homelessness Prevention; Pharmaceutical Assistance; Campbell Ecumenism-Unity lecture; Clothing Distribution; Aspires Mentoring Program

Lewisburg Council of Churches

RR2 Box75, Winfield, PA 17889 Tel. 570-524-4726
Email: larryconfer@hotmail.com
Media Contact, Rev. Alton Motter
5 S. Aspen Pl.
Lewisburg, PA 17837
(570) 523-7749
President, Janet Betzer
Treasurer, Larry Confer, RR2 Winfield, PA 17889 tel. (570) 524-4726
Major Activities: Supplementary and Emergency Food Pantries; Clothing Bank; CROP Walk; Week of Prayer for Christian Unity; Soup & Scripture Lenten Series; 3-hour Good Friday Service; Social Services Directory; Transient-Homeless Aid

Metropolitan Christian Council of Philadelphia

1501 Cherry St., Philadelphia, PA 19102-1429 Tel. (215)563-7854, Fax (215)563-6849
Email: geiger@mccp.org
Website: www.mccp.org
Media Contact, Assoc. Communications, Nancy L. Nolde
Exec. Dir., Rev. C. Edward Geiger
Assoc. Communications, Nancy L. Nolde
Office Mgr., Joan G. Shipman
Pres., Rev. Steven B. Laurence
First Vice-Pres., Rev. G. Daniel Jones
Treas., A. Louis Denton, Esq.
Major Activities: Congregational Clusters; Public Policy Advocacy; Communication; Theological Dialogue (Christian & Interfaith); Women's Issues

North Hills Youth Ministry Counseling Center

802 McKnight Park Dr., Pittsburgh, PA 15237 Tel. (412)366-1300
Email: NHYM@SGI. NET

Media Contact, Exec. Dir., Rev. Ronald B. Barnes
Exec. Dir., Ronald B. Barnes
Major Activities: Elementary, Junior and Senior High School Individual and Family Counseling; Elementary Age Youth Early Intervention Counseling; Educational Programming for Churches and Schools; Youth Advocacy; Parent Education; Marital Counseling

Northside Common Ministries

P.O. Box 99861, Pittsburgh, PA 15233 Tel. (412)323-1163, Fax (412)323-1749
Email: NCM@city-net.com
Media Contact, Exec. Dir., Janet E. Holtz
Exec. Dir., Janet E. Holtz
Major Activities: Pleasant Valley Shelter for Homeless Men; Advocacy around Hunger, Housing, Poverty, and Racial Issues; Community Food Pantry and Service Center; Supportive Housing

Northwest Interfaith Movement

6757 Greene St., Philadelphia, PA 19119 Tel. (215)843-5600, Fax (215)843-2755
Email: rrf@dca.net
Website: www.nim-phila.org
Media Contact, Exec. Dir., Rev. Richard R. Fernandez
Exec. Dir., Rev. Richard R. Fernandez
Chpsn., Marion S. Taylor
Long Term Care Program, Dir., Donald Carlin
Neighborhood Child Care Resource Prog., Dir., Leslie S. Eslinger
School Age Ministry, Dir., Brenda Rochester
Major Activities: Resources amd Technical Assistance for Child Care Programs; Conflict Mediation and Support for Nursing and Boarding Home Residents; Development of After-School Programs

Pennsylvania Conference on Interchurch Cooperation*

P.O. Box 2835, 223 North St., Harrisburg, PA 17105 Tel. (717)238-9613, Fax (717)238-1473
Email: staff@pacatholic.org
Website: www.pacatholic.org/about/pcic.htm
Media Contact, Carolyn Astfalk
Co-Staff, Dr. Robert J. O'Hara, Jr., Rev. Gary Harke
Co-Chpsns., Bishop Joseph Martino; Bishop Paull Spring.
Major Activities: Theological Consultation; Social Concerns; Public Policy; Conferences and Seminars

The Pennsylvania Council of Churches*

900 S. Arlington Ave., Ste. 100, Harrisburg, PA 17109-5089 Tel. (717)545-4761, Fax (717) 545-4765
Email: pcc@pachurches.org
Website: www.pachurches.org
Media Contact, Exec. Dir., Rev. Gary L. Harke
Exec. Dir., Rev. Gary L. Harke
Public Policy, Dir., Rev. K. Joy Kaufmann
Coord. for Contract Chaplaincy, Rev. Robert A. Meschke
Coord. for Leisure Ministries, Rev. Robert W. Brown
Coord. For Direct Ministries, Rev. Douglas Hodges
Pres., Rev. Dr. Lyle J. Weible
Vice-Pres., Rev. Clarice L. Chambers
Sec., Mrs. Nancy S. Ritter
Treas., David B. Hoffman, CPA
Bus. Mgr., Janet A. Gulick
Major Activities: Racial-ethic empowerment; inter-church dialogue; trade association activities; faith and order; seasonal farmworker ministry; trucker-traveler ministry; institutional chaplaincy; public policy advocacy and education; leisure ministry; conferences and continuing education events; disaster response; church education; global warming project; public education initiative

Project of Easton, Inc.

330 Ferry St., Easton, PA 18042 Tel. (215)258-4361 Pres., Dr. John H. Updegrove
Vice-Pres. Public Relations, Rev. Charles E. Staples
Vice-Pres. Operations, Don Follett
Sec., Rosemary Reese
Treas., Steve Barsony
Exec. Dir., Maryellen Shuman
Major Activities: Food Bank; Adult Literacy Program; English as a Second Language; Children's Programs; Parents as Student Support; CROP Walk; Interfaith Council; Family Literacy; Emergency Assistance; Even Start Family Literacy

Reading Berks Conference of Churches

54 N. 8th St., Reading, PA 19601 Tel. (610)375-6108, Fax (610)375-6205
Email: rdgbrkscc@aol.com
Media Contact, Exec. Dir., Rev. Calvin Kurtz
Exec. Dir., Rev. Calvin Kurtz
Pres., James Elliker
Treas., William Maslo
Major Activities: Institutional Ministry; Social Action; Migrant Ministry; CWS; CROP Walk for Hunger; Emergency Assistance; Prison Chaplaincy; AIDS Hospice Development; Hospital Chaplaincy; Interchurch-Intercultural Services; Children & Youth Ministry

Reading Urban Ministry

150 North 11th St, Reading, PA 19601 Tel. (610)374-6917, Fax (610)371-9791
Media Contact, Susan Sentz

Exec. Dir., Susan Sentz
Pres., David Hunsberger
Vice-Pres., Darrin Love
Sec., Eleanor Hay
Treas., Sally Waters
Major Activities: Youth Ministry Program; Family Action Support Team (Parent Education & Child Abuse Prevention); Heal Thyself (offers a love-based reality)

South Hills Interfaith Ministries

1900 Sleepy Hollow Rd., Library, PA 15129 Tel. (412)854-9120, Fax (412)854-9123
Media Contact, Exec. Dir., Donald Guinn
Prog. Dir., Susan Simons
Psychological Services, Don Zandier
Family Assistance Coordinator, Sherry Kotz
Business Mgr., Jeff Walley
Volunteer Coordinator, Kristin Snodgrass
Major Activities: Basic Human Needs; Community Organization and Development; Inter-Faith Cooperation; Personal Growth; At-Risk Youth Development; Women in Transition; Elderly Support

United Churches of Lycoming County

202 E. Third St., Williamsport, PA 17701 Tel. (570)322-1110, Fax (570)326-4572
Email: uclc@sunlink.net
Website: www.uclc.org
Media Contact, Exec. Dir., Gwen Nelson Bernstine
Exec. Dir., Gwen Nelson Bernstine
Ofc. Sec., Linda Winter
Pres., Mrs. Mikey Kamienski, 515 Vallamont Dr., Williamsport, PA 17701
Treas., Raymond Fisher, 145 Linden St., S. Williamsport, PA 17701
Shepherd of the Streets, Rev. J. Morris Smith, 130 E. 3rd St., Williamsport, PA 17701
Ecumenism, Dir., Rev. George Doran, 122 S. Main St., Hughesville, PA 107737
Educ. Ministries, Dir., Rev. Jeffrey Letto, 369 Broad St., Montoursville, PA 17701
Institutional Ministry, Dir., Linda Leonard, 12 E. Water St., Hughesville, PA 17737, Rev. Darlene Little, 266 Wagner Rd., Williamsport, PA 17701
Radio-TV, Dir., Rev. David Reinwald, 201 Market St., South Williamsport, PA 17702
Prison Ministry, Dir., Rev. Donald Visseher, 1063 Cemetary St., Williamsport, PA 17701
Christian Social Concerns, Dir., Dr. Dan Doyle, 301 South Main St., Muney, PA 17756
Major Activities: Ecumenism; Educational Ministries; Church Women United; Church World Service and CROP; Prison Ministry; Radio-TV; Nursing Homes; Fuel Bank; Food Pantry; Family Life; Shepherd of the Streets Urban Ministry; Peace Concerns; Housing Initiative; Interfaith Dialogue

Wilkinsburg Community Ministry

710 Mulberry St., Pittsburgh, PA 15221 Tel. (412)241-8072, Fax (412)241-8315
Email: wcm15221@juno.com
Website: trfn.clpgh.org/wcm
Media Contact, Dir., Rev. Vivian Lovingood
Dir., Rev. Vivian Lovingood
Pres. of Bd., Cathy Newport
Major Activities: Hunger Ministry; After School Children's Programs; Summer Reading Camp; Teen-Moms Infant Care; Meals on Wheels; Church Camp Scholarships; Utility Assistance; Clothing-Furniture Assistance; Case Management for Elderly Homebound Persons and Families

Wyoming Valley Council of Churches

70 Lockhart St., Wilkes-Barre, PA 18702 Tel. (570)825-8543
Media Contact, Exec. Dir., Susan Grine Harper
Exec. Dir., Susan Grine Harper
Ofc. Sec., Sandra Karrott
Pres., Dn. Sergei Kapral
Treas., H. Merritt Hughes
Major Activities: Nursing Home Chaplaincy; Martin Luther King, Jr. Fuel Drive in Association with Local Agencies; Hospital Referral Service; Choral Festival of Faith; Migrant Ministry; Ecumenical Pulpit Exchange, Int.; CROP Hunger Walk; Pastoral Care Ministries; Clergy Retreats and Seminars

York County Council of Churches

P.O. Box 1865, York, PA 17405-1865 Tel. (717)854-9504, Fax (717)843-5295
Email: yccc@juno.com
Media Contact, Exec. Dir., Rev. Patrick B. Walker
Pres., Rev. Donald Zobler
Past Pres., Rev. Stephany Sechrist
Exec. Dir., Rev. Patrick B. Walker
Major Activities: Educational Development; Spiritual Growth and Renewal; Worship and Witness; Congregational Resourcing; Outreach and Mission

RHODE ISLAND

The Rhode Island State Council of Churches*

734 Hope St., Providence, RI 02906 Tel. (401)861-1700, Fax (401)331-3080
Email: ricouncil@aol.com
Media Contact, Interim Exec. Min., Rev. Sharon Key
Exec. Min., Rev. James C. Miller
Admn. Asst., Peggy MacNie
Pres., Rev. Carl H. Balark, Jr.
Treas., George Weavill
Major Activities: Urban Ministries; TV; Institutional Chaplaincy; Advocacy-Justice & Service, Legislative Liaison; Faith & Order; Leadership Development; Campus Ministries

SOUTH CAROLINA

South Carolina Christian Action Council, Inc.*

P.O. Drawer 3248, Columbia, SC 29230 Tel. (803)786-7115, Fax (803)786-7116
Email: sccouncil@sccouncil.net
Website: www.sccouncil.net
Media Contact, Exec. Minister, Rev. Brenda Kneece
Exec. Minister, Rev. Brenda Kneece
Pres., Rev. Dr. Richard Dozier
Major Activities: Advocacy and Ecumenism; Continuing Education; Interfaith Dialogue; Citizenship and Public Affairs; Publications; Race Relations; Child Advocacy; Faith and Health; Climate Change

United Ministries

606 Pendleton St., Greenville, SC 29601 Tel. (864)232-6463, Fax (864)370-3518
Email: info@united-ministries.org
Website: www.united-ministries.org
Media Contact, Exec. Dir., Rev. Beth Templeton
Exec. Dir., Rev. Beth Templeton
Pres., The Rev. David Chandler
Vice-Pres., Dr. Lynne Shackelford
Sec., Rufus E. Perry
Treas., Gordon Gibson
Major Activities: Survival Programs (Emergency Assistance, Place of Hope, a Day Shelter for Homeless, Travelers Aid); Stabilization Program (Transitions); Barrier Removal Programs (Employment Readiness); Magdalene Project (Women in Crisis); Life Skills (Educational Classes, Living Skills)

SOUTH DAKOTA

Association of Christian Churches of South Dakota*

100 S. Spring Ave., Suite 106, Sioux Falls, SD 57104-3626 Tel. (605)334-1980
Email: accsd@dtgnet.com
Media Contact, Rev. Christian Franklin, First Christian Church, 524 W. 13th St., Sioux Falls, SD 57104-4309 Tel. (605)338-9474
Pres., Bd. Of Directors, Rev. Christian Franklin
Ofc. Mgr., Pat Willard
Major Activities: Ecumenical Forums; Continuing Education for Clergy; Legislative Information; Resourcing Local Ecumenism; Native American Issues; Ecumenical Fields Ministries; Rural Economic Development; Children at Risk; 2002 Ecumenical Assembly —"Together in Christ—A Dakotas Celebration"

TENNESSEE

Metropolitan Inter Faith Association (MIFA)

P.O. Box 3130, Memphis, TN 38173-0130 Tel. (901)527-0208, Fax (901)527-3202
Media Contact, Dir., Media Relations, Caroline Vonicessler
Exec. Dir., Margaret Craddock
Major Activities: Emergency Services (Rent, Utility, Food, Clothing Assistance); Home-Delivered Meals and Senior Support Services; Youth Services; Homeless Programs

Tennessee Association of Churches*

103 Oak St., Ashland City, TN 37015 Tel. (615) 792-4631
Ecumenical Admn., —
Pres., Rev. Steve Mosley
Treas., Paul Milliken
Major Activities: Faith and Order; Christian Unity; Social Concern Ministries; Governmental Concerns; Governor's Prayer Breakfast

Volunteer Ministry Center

103 South Gay St., Knoxville, TN 37902 Tel. (423)524-3926, Fax (423)524-7065
Media Contact, Exec. Dir., Angelia Moon
Exec. Dir., Angelia Moon
Pres., David Leech
Vice-Pres., John Moxham
Treas., Doug Thompson
Major Activities: Homeless Program; Food Line; Crisis Referral Program; Subsidized Apartment Program; Counselling Program; Parenting Education for Single Parents

TEXAS

Austin Area Interreligious Ministries

2026 Guadalupe, Ste. 226, Austin, TX 78705 Tel. (512)472-7627
Fax (512)472-5274
Email: aaim@ammaustin.org
Website: www.ammaustin.org
Media Contact, Exec. Dir., Susan Wills
Exec. Dir., Susan Wills
Pres., Rev. James Mayfield
Treas., Camille Miller
Program Director, Patty Harris
Admn., Carole Hatfield
Major Activities: Youth at Risk Mentoring; Housing Rehabilitation; Refugee Resettlement; Broadcast Ministry; Interfaith Dialogues; Family Issues; Homeless Issues; Hunger Issues; Racial Reconciliation

Border Association for Refugees from Central America (BARCA), Inc.

P.O. Box 1725, Edinburg, TX 78540 Tel. (956)631-7447, Fax (956)687-9266
Email: barcainc@aol.com
Media Contact, Exec. Dir., Ninfa Ochoa-Krueger
Exec. Dir, Ninfa Ochoa-Krueger

Outreach Services, Dir., Juanita Ledesma
Major Activities: Food, Shelter, Clothing to Newly Arrived Indigent Immigrants & Refugees; Medical and Other Emergency Aid; Special Services to Children; Speakers on Refugee and Immigrant Concerns for Church Groups; Orientation, Advocacy and Legal Services for Immigrants and Refugees

Corpus Christi Metro Ministries

1919 Leopard St., P.O. Box 4899, Corpus Christi, TX 78469-4899 Tel. (361)887-0151, Fax (361)887-7900
Email: edseeger@electrotex.com
Media Contact, Exec. Dir., Rev. Edward B. Seeger
Exec. Dir., Rev. Edward B. Seeger
Admn. Dir., Ginger Flewelling-Leeds
Volunteer Dir., Ann Cox
Fin. Coord., Sue McCown
Loaves & Fishes Dir., Ray Gomez
Emergency Services Mgr., Elsa Haecker
Employment Dir., Larry Curtis
Health and Human Services, Dir., Ann Cox
Major Activities: Free Cafeteria; Transitional Shelters; Job Readiness; Job Placement; Primary Health Care; Community Service Restitution; Emergency Clothing; Information and Referral; Case Management

East Dallas Cooperative Parish

P.O. Box 720305, Dallas, TX 75372-0305 Tel. (214)823-9149, Fax (214)823-2015
Email: edcp@swbell.net
Media Contact, Nancy Jellinek, Exec. Dir.
Pres., Debbie Thorpe
Major Activities: Emergency Food, Clothing, Job Bank; Medical Clinic; Legal Clinic, Tutorial Education; Home Companion Service; Pre-School Education; Hispanic Ministry; Activity Center for Low Income Older Adults; Pastoral Counseling; English Language Ministry, Pre-GED program

Greater Dallas Community of Churches

624 N. Good-Latimer #100, Dallas, TX 75204-5818 Tel. (214)824-8680, Fax (214)824-8726
Email: greaterdallascc@aol.com
Media Contact, Exec. Dir., Ray Flachmeier
Exec. Dir., Ray Flachmeier
Assoc. Dirs., The Rev. Holsey Hickman; John Stoesz
AmeriCorps-Building Blocks Dir., Wendy Hodges-Kent
Development Dir., Mary Sue Foster
Pres., Rev. George Mason, Ph.D.
Treas., Jerry McNabb
Major Activities: Interdenominational, Interfaith and Interracial Understanding and Joint Work; AmeriCorps-Building Blocks (Direct Service to Develop Inner City Children, Youth & Families); Summer Food & Reading; Hunger; Peacemaking; Public Policy; Social Justice; Faith & Life; Children's Health Outreach; Child Advocacy; Dismantaling Racism

Interfaith Ministries for Greater Houston

3217 Montrose Blvd., Houston, TX 77006 Tel. (713)522-3955, Fax (713)520-4663
Media Contact, Exec. Dir., Betty P. Taylor
Exec. Dir., Betty P. Taylor
Pres., Charles R. Erickson
Development, Dir., Sharon Ervine
Assoc. Exec. Dir., Larry Norton
Treas., Fort D. Flowers, Jr.
Sec., Darlene Alexander
Major Activities: Community Concerns, Hunger; Older Adults; Families; Youth; Child Abuse; Refugee Services; Congregational Relations and Development; Social Service Programs, Refugee Services; Hunger Coalition; Youth Victim Witness; Family Connection; Meals on Wheels; Senior Health; RSVP; Foster Grandparents

North Dallas Shared Ministries

2530 Glenda Ln., #500, Dallas, TX 75229 Tel. (214)620-8696, Fax (214)620-0433
Media Contact, Exec. Dir., J. Dwayne Martin
Exec. Dir., J. Dwayne Martin
Pres., —
Major Activities: Emergency Assistance; Job Counseling; ESL

Northside Inter-Church Agency (NICA)

1600 Circle Park Blvd., Fort Worth, TX 76106-8943 Tel. (817)626-1102, Fax (817)626-9043
Email: nicaagency@earthlink.net
Media Contact, Exec. Dir., Judy Gutierrez
Exec. Dir., Judy Gutierrez
Major Activities: Food; Clothing; Counseling; Information and Referral; Furniture and Household Items; Nutrition Education and Teen Program; Employment Services; Thanksgiving Basket Program; "Last Resort" Christmas Program; Community Networking; Ecumenical Worship Services; Volunteer Training; Newsletter

San Antonio Community of Churches

1101 W. Woodlawn, San Antonio, TX 78201 Tel. (210)733-9159, Fax (210)733-5780
Media Contact, Exec. Dir., Dr. Kenneth Thompson
Exec. Dir., Dr. Kenneth Thompson
Pres., Fr. Jose De La Rosa
Major Activities: Christian Education; Missions; Infant Formula and Medical Prescriptions for Children of Indigent Families; Continuing Education For Clergy and Laity; Media Resource Center; Social Issues; Aging Concerns; Youth Concerns; Family Concerns;

Sponsor annual CROP Walk for Hunger; Peace and Anti-Violence Initiatives

San Antonio Urban Ministries

535 Bandera Rd., San Antonio, TX 78228 Tel.
Media Contact, Sue Kelly
Exec. Dir., Sue Kelly
Pres., Rev. Leslie Ellison
Major Activities: Homes for Discharged Mental Patients; After School Care for Latch Key Children; Christian Based Community Ministry

Southeast Area Churches (SEARCH)

P.O. Box 51256, Fort Worth, TX 76105 Tel. (817)531-2211
Exec. Dir., Dorothy Anderson-Develrow
Major Activities: Emergency Assistance; Advocacy; Information and Referral; Community Worship; School Supplies; Direct Aid to Low Income and Elderly

Tarrant Area Community of Churches

P.O. Box 11471, Fort Worth, TX 76110-0471 Tel. (817)534-1790, Fax (817)534-1995
Email: revkm@flash.net
Pres., Regina Taylor
Treas., Don Hoak
Exec. Dir., Dr. Kenneth W. McIntosh
Major Activities: Eldercare Program; Children's Sabbath Sponsorship; Week of Prayer for Christian Unity; CROP Walk for Hunger Relief; Community Issues Forums; Family Pathfinders

Texas Conference of Churches*

1033 La Posada, Ste. 225, Austin, TX 78752 Tel. (512)451-0991, Fax (512)451-5348
Email: tcc@txconfchurches.org
Website: www.txconfchurches.org
Media Contact, Communications and Web Services, Liz Yeats
Exec. Dir., Dr. Carol M. Worthing
Office Manager, Caryn Wontor
Pres., Byrd Bonner
Major Activities: Faith & Order; Related Ecumenism; Christian-Jewish Relations; Church and Society Issues

United Board of Missions

1701 Bluebonnet Ave., P.O. Box 3856, Port Arthur, TX 77643-3856 Tel. (409)982-9412, Fax (409)985-3668
Media Contact, Admn. Asst., Carolyn Schwarr
Exec. Dir., Clark Moore
Pres., Glenda McCoy
Major Activities: Emergency Assistance (Food and Clothing, Rent and Utility, Medical, Dental, Transportation); Share a Toy at Christmas; Counseling; Back to School Clothing Assistance; Information and Referral; Hearing Aid Bank; Meals on Wheels; Super Pantry; Energy Conservation Programs; Job Bank Assistance to Local Residents Only

VIRGINIA

Virginia Council of Churches, Inc.*

1214 W. Graham Rd., Richmond, VA 23220-1409 Tel. (804)321-3300, Fax (804)329-5066
Email: Barton@vcc-net.org
Website: www.vcc-net.org
Media Contact, Gen. Min., Rev. Jonathan Barton
Gen. Min., Rev. Jonathan Barton
Migrant Head Start, Dir., Richard D. Cagan
Refugee Resettlement, Dir., Rev. Richard D. Cline
Weekday Rel. Educ., Coord., Faye Drewry, 2699 Lanier Lane, McGaheysville, VA 22840
Campus Ministry Forum, Coord., Rev. Steve Darr, c-o Community College Ministries, 305 Washington St., N.W., Blacksburg, VA 24060-4745
Major Activities: Faith and Order; Network Building & Coordination; Ecumenical Communications; Justice and Legislative Concerns; Educational Development; Rural Concerns; Refugee Resettlement; Migrant Ministries and Migrant Head Start; Disaster Coordination; Infant Mortality Prevention

VERMONT

Vermont Ecumenical Council and Bible Society*

285 Maple St., Burlington, VT 05401 Tel. (802)864-7723
Email: vecumen@together.net
Media Contact, Admn. Asst., Betsy Wackernagel
Exec. Sec., Mr. Philip C. Kimball
Pres., Rev. Arnold I. Thomas
Vice-Pres., Rev. Frederick K. Neu
Treas., Rev. E. Lon Schneider
Major Activities: Christian Unity; Bible Distribution; Social Justice; Committee on Faith and Order; Committee on Peace, Justice and the Integrity of Creation

WASHINGTON

Associated Ministries of Tacoma-Pierce County

1224 South I St., Tacoma, WA 98405-5021 Tel. (253)383-3056, Fax (253)383-2672
Email: info@associatedministries.org
Website: www. associatedministries.org
Media Contact, Exec. Dir., Rev. David T. Alger
Exec. Dir., Rev. David T. Alger
Deputy Dir., Maureen Fife
Dir. of Mental Health Chaplaincy, Rev. Eric Renz
Dir. of Project Interdependence, Valorie Crout
Dir. of Paint Tacoma-Pierce Beautiful, Sallie Shawl
Dir. Of Development, Tandi Rogers

Dir. of Hilltop Action Coalition, Jeannie Peterson
Director of Communication and Education, Judy Jones
Pres., Rev. Julia Price
Vice Pres., Justine Ostlund
Sec., Karen Davey
Treas., Eric Paige
Major Activities: County-wide Hunger Walk; Hunger Awareness; Economic Justice; Religious Education; Social Service Program Advocacy; Communication and Networking of Churches; Housing; Paint Tacoma-Pierce Beautiful; Anti-Poverty Resource Center; Mental Health Chaplaincy; Theological Dialogue; Welfare to Work Mentoring; Hilltop Action Coalition; ComPeer; Homelessness; Youth Ministry; Ecumenical Formation

Associated Ministries of Thurston County

P.O. Box 895, Olympia, WA 98507 Tel. (360)357-7224
Email: theamtc@aol.com
Media Contact, Exec. Dir., Cheri Gonyaw
Exec. Dir., Cheri Gonyaw
Pres., George Hinkel
Treas., Bob McCoy
Major Activities: Church Information and Referral; Interfaith Relations; Social and Health Concerns; Community Action; Social Justice

Center for the Prevention of Sexual and Domestic Violence

2400 N. 45th St, Suite 10, Seattle, WA 98103 Tel. (206)634-1903, Fax (206)634-0115
Email: cpsdv@cpsdv.org
Website: www.cpsdv.org
Media Contact, Rev. Dr. Marie M. Fortune
Executive Director, Rev. Kathryn J. Johnson, kjohnson@cpsdv.org
Founder & Senior Analyst, Rev. Dr. Marie M. Fortune, mfortune@cpsdv.org
Director of Training & Education, Rev. Thelma Burgonio-Watson, burgonio@cpsdv.org
Director of the Jewish Program, Rabbi Cindy Enger, cenger@cpsdv.org
Clearinghouse Coordinator, Dinah Hall, dhall@cpsdv.org
Finance Director, Marion J. Ward
Major Activities: Prevention and Response Education; Clergy and Lay Training; Video and Print Resources; Bi-national Educational Ministry

Church Council of Greater Seattle

4759 15th Ave. NE, Seattle, WA 98105-4404 Tel. (206)525-1213, Fax (206)525-1218
Email: CCGSea@churchcouncilseattle.org
Website: www.churchcouncilseattle.org
Media Contact, Acting Executive Dir., Alice Woldt
Acting Executive Dir., Alice Woldt
Associate Dir. for Development & Communications, Cal Kinnear
Emergency Feeding Prog., Dir., Arthur Lee
Friend to Friend, Dir., Marilyn Soderquist
Youth Chaplaincy Program, Dir. Chaplain, Rev. Benny Wright
The Sharehouse, Dir., Young Kim
The Homelessness Project, Dir., Nancy Dorman
Mission for Music & Healing, Dir., Susan Gallaher & Esther "Little Dove" John
Sound Youth-AmeriCorps, Dir., -vacant
Interfaith Relations, Prog. Assoc., Rev. Joyce Manson
Academy of Religious Broadcasting, Dir., Rev. J. Graley Taylor
Board Chair, The Rev. Ellis Casson
Board Treas., Steve Faust
Editor, The Source, and website, Leanne Skooglund Hofford
Seattle Youth Garden Works, Dir., Nancy Neal
SW King County Mental Health Ministry, Dir., Rev. Richard Lutz
JOY Initiative, Prog. Dir., Rick Jump
Global Economy Working Group Chair, Allen Paulson
St. Petersburg- Seattle Sister Churches Program Chair, Hal Hunt
Asia Pacific Task Force, Chair Bill Cafe
Commission on Racial Justice Chair, Paula Harris-White
Commission on Public Witness Staff, Alice Woldt
Self-Managed Housing Programs, Dir., Misti Uptain
Commission on Children, Youth & Families, Chair, Rev. Steve Baber
Pastors for Peace-Cuba Friendshipment, Chair, Doug Barnes
Palestinain Concerns Task Force, Chair, Rev. Ashlee Weist-Laird
Interfaith Network of Concern for the People of Iraq, Chair, Rev. Randall Mullins
Major Activities: Children; Youth & Families; Hunger Relief; Global Peace and Justice; Housing and Homelessness; Pastoral Care; Services for the Aging; Public Witness; Interfaith and Ecumenical Relations; Publisher of the Source, Monthly Ecumenical Newspaper

The Interfaith Association of Snohomish County

2301 Hoyt, P.O. Box 12824, Everett, WA 98206 Tel. (206)252-6672
Email: admin.tiasc@verizon.net
Media Contact, Exec. Dir., Janet Pope
Exec. Dir., Janet Pope
Pres., Dr. Tom Paulson
Major Activities: Housing and Shelter; Economic Justice; Hunger; Interfaith Worship and Collaboration

Northwest Harvest-E. M. M.

P.O. Box 12272, Seattle, WA 98102 Tel. (206) 625-0755, Fax (206)625-7518
Email: nharvest@blarg.net

Website: www. northwestharvest.org
Media Contact, Comm. Affairs Dir., Ellen Hansen
Exec. Dir., Ruth M. Velozo
Chpsn., Patricia Barcott
Major Activities: Northwest Harvest (Statewide Hunger Response); Cherry Street Food Bank (Community Hunger Response); Northwest Infants Corner (Special Nutritional Products for Infants and Babies)

Spokane Council of Ecumenical Ministries

1620 N. Monroe, Spokane, WA 99205 Tel. (509)329-1410, Fax (509)329-1409
Email: scem1620@aol.com
Media Contact, Marylin Ferguson, Admin. Asst.
Interim Director, Rev. Ron Greene
Chair, Fr. William Pugliese
Treas., Rev. Mark Randall
Sec., Linda Schearin
Major Activities: Camp PEACE, Multi-Cultural Human Relations- High School Youth Camp; Night Walk Ministry; Dir. of Churches & Community Agencies; Interfaith Thanksgiving Worship; Easter Sunrise Service; Friend to Friend Visitation with Nursing Home Patients; CROP Walk; Eastern Washington Legislative Conference; Inland Northwest Disaster Response; Ecumenical Sunday; Churches Against Racism; Family Friend Project; Living Wage Movement

Washington Association of Churches*

419 Occidental Ave. S., Ste. 201, Seattle, WA 98104-2886 Tel. (206)625-9790, Fax (206)625-9791
Email: wac@thewac.org
Website: www.thewac.org
Media Contact, John C. Boonstra
Email: boonstra@thewac.org
Exec. Min., Rev. John C. Boonstra
Public Policy Associate, Sara Fleming-Merten, merten@thewac.org
Economic Justice Associate, Michael Ramos, ramos@thewac.org
Communications Assoc., Bette Schneider, schneider@thewac.org
Racial & Environmental Justice Associate, Shelley Means, means@thewac.org
Major Activities: Faith and Order; Justice Advocacy; Confronting Poverty; Hunger Action; Legislation; Denominational Ecumenical Coordination; Theological Formation; Leadership Development; Refugee Advocacy; Racial Justice Advocacy; International Solidarity; Environmental Justice Advocacy

WISCONSIN

Center for Community Concerns

1501 Villa St., Racine, WI 53403 Tel. (414)637-9176, Fax (414)637-9265
Email: ccc1501@miliserv.net
Media Contact, Exec. Dir., Sr. Michelle Olley
Exec. Dir., Sr. Michelle Olley
Skillbank Coord., Eleanor Sorenson
RSVP (Retired Senior Volunteer Program), Chris Udell-Solberg, Cathy Townsend
Volunteer Today (55 and under), Janet LeSuer
Major Activities: Advocacy; Direct Services; Research; Community Consultant; Criminal Justice; Volunteerism; Senior Citizen Services; CROP Walk, Referral

Christian Youth Council

1715-52nd St., Kenosha, WI 53140 Tel. (414)652-9543 Fax (414)652-4461
Media Contact, Exec. Dir., Steven L. Nelson
Exec. Dir., Steven L. Nelson
Sports Dir., Jerry Tappen
Outreach Dir., Linda Osborne
Accountant, Debbie Cutts
Class Director, Jill Cox
Pres. & Chmn. of Board, Lon Knoedler
Gang Prevention Dir., Sam Sauceda
Major Activities: Leisure Time Ministry; Institutional Ministries; Ecumenical Committee; Social Concerns; Outreach Sports(with a Christian Philosophy)

Interfaith Conference of Greater Milwaukee

1442 N. Farwell Ave., Ste. 200, Milwaukee, WI 53202 Tel. (414)276-9050, Fax (414)276-8442
Email: IFCGM@aol.com
Media Contact, Exec. Dir., Marcus White
Chpsn., Rev. Velma Smith
First Vice-Chair, Archbishop Rembert G. Weakland
Second Vice-Chair, Rev. Charles Graves
Sec., Paula Simon
Treas., Rev. Mary Ann Neevel
Exec. Dir., Marcus White
Consultant in Communications, Rev. Robert P. Seater
Major Activities: Economic Issues; Racism; CROP Walk; Public Policy; Suburban and Urban Partnerships; TV Programming; Peace and International Issues Committee; Annual Membership Luncheon; Religion Diversity; Restorative Justice

Madison Urban Ministry

2300 S. Park St., Madison, WI 53713 Tel. (608)256-0906, Fax (608)256-4387
Exec. Dir., Mary K. Baum
Program Mgr., Judy Collison & Richard Wildermuth
Major Activities: Community Projects; Dialogue-Forums; Social & Economic Justice

Wisconsin Council of Churches*

750 Windsor St. Ste. 301, Sun Prairie, WI 53590-2149 Tel. (608)837-3108, Fax (608)837-3038

Email: wcoc@wichurches.org
Website: www.wichurches.org
Media Contact, Comm. Coord., Jeanette Johnson
Exec. Dir., Rev. Jerry Folk
Assoc. Dir., Rev. Gretchen Lord Anderson
Ofc. Mgr., Jeanette Johnson
Coordinator for Local Ecumenism, Rev. Kenneth Pennings
Corrdinator, Chaplaincy Commission, Dr. Barbara Jo Sorenson
Pres., Bishop April Ulring Larson
Treas., Dr. Robert Book
Accountant, Ms. Jann Brockmann
Receptionist, Mr. Christopher Marceil
Major Activities: Social Witness; Migrant Ministry; Aging; Wisconsin Interfaith IMPACT; Institutional Chaplaincy; Peace and Justice; Faith and Order; Rural Concerns; American Indian Ministries Council; Park Ministry; Women's RoundTable; Wisconsin Housing Partnership; Nonviolence, economic justice, corporate responsibility

WEST VIRGINIA

Greater Fairmont Council of Churches

P.O. Box 108, Fairmont, WV 26554 Tel. (304)367-0962
Media Contact, President, Rev. Jeremiah Jasper
President, Rev. Jeremiah Jasper
Major Activities: Community Ecumenical Services; Youth and Adult Sports Leagues; CROP Walk Sponsor; Weekly Radio Broadcasts

The Greater Wheeling Council of Churches

1060 Chapline St., 110 Methodist Building, Wheeling, WV 26003 Tel. (304)232-5315
Media Contact, Exec. Dir., Kathy J. Burley
Exec. Dir., Kathy J. Burley
Hospital Notification Sec., Anna Lou Lenz
Pres., Martha J. Morris
Finance Chpn., Rev. Robert P. Johnson- Doug Clatterbuck
Major Activities: Christian Education; Evangelism; Christian Heritage Week Celebration; Institutional Ministry; Regional Jail Chaplaincy; Church Women United; Volunteer Chaplaincy Care at OVMC Hospital; School of Religion; Hospital Notification; Hymn Sing in the Park; Anti-Gambling Crusade; Pentecost Celebration; Clergy Council; Easter Sunrise Service; Community Seder; Church Secretaries Fellowship; National Day of Prayer Service; Videotape Library-Audiotape Library; Flood Relief Network of the Upper Ohio Valley

West Virginia Council of Churches*

2207 Washington St. E., Charleston, WV 25311-2218 Tel. (304)344-3141, Fax (304)342-1506
Website: www.wvcc.org
Media Contact, Exec. Dir., The Rev. Nathan D. Wilson
Email: nathanwilson@wvcc.org
Pres., Dr. William B. Allen, CC (DOC)
Vice-Pres., Bishop S. Clifton Ives, UMC
Sec., The Rev. Peggy Scharff, UMC
Treas., The Very Rev. Frederick P. Annie, RC
Major Activities: Leisure Ministry; Disaster Response; Faith and Order; Family Concerns; Inter-Faith Relations; Peace and Justice; Government Concerns; Support Services Network

WYOMING

Wyoming Church Coalition*

P.O. Box 20812, Cheyenne, WY 82003-7017 Tel. (307)635-4251, Fax (307)778-9060
Email: wychco@aol.com
Media Contact, Mary Richey, Wyoming Church Coalition, PO Box 20812, Cheyenne, WY 82003
Chair, Joe Keys
Chaplain, Rev. Lynn Schumacher
Bookkeeper, Mary Richey
Office Manager, Peg Edwards
Major Activities: Alternatives to Violence; Prison Ministry; Beyond Tolerance; Malicious Harrasment; Domestic Violence; Empowering the Poor and Oppressed; Peace and Justice; Public Health Issues; Welfare Reform; Death Penalty

Index of Select Programs for U.S. Regional and Local Ecumenical Bodies

For many years the *Yearbook of American & Canadian Churches* has published the previous chapter, the "Directory of U.S. Regional and Local Ecumenical Bodies." Each entry of that directory contains a brief description of the diverse programs offered by each agency. However, researchers, pastors, service organizations and theological seminaries often inquire about specific programs and about which agencies carry out such programs. In response we have created this chapter, which indexes the various regional and local ecumenical agencies by twenty-five different program areas. These program areas are the twenty-five that have been the most frequent subjects of inquiry in our office. We have collected this program information directly from these organizations by means of a simple response form. There is an enormous diversity of ministries and missions conducted by these diverse organizations. Most organizations pursue several kinds of programs at once. However, some of these may focus their efforts most especially on only one of their programs; their other programs may be less well developed than their specialty. Consequently, the extent to which any of these ministries is a priority for any particular organization cannot be inferred from this list. For detailed information about the nature and extent of any particular ministry, the reader is urged to contact the organization directly using the directory of "U.S. Regional and Local Ecumenical Bodies," which is found in the pages just prior to this index.

AIDS/HIV Programs

Asheville-Buncombe Community Christian Ministry (ABCCM)—Asheville, NC
Center City Churches—Hartford, CT
Christian Churches United of the Tri-County Area—Harrisburg, PA
Dutchess Interfaith Council, Inc.—Poughkeepsie, NY
East End Cooperative Ministry—Pittsburgh, PA
Ecumenical Ministries—Fulton, MO
Ecumenical Ministries of Oregon—Portland, OR
Grand Rapids Area Center for Ecumenism (GRACE)—Grand Rapids, MI
Graymoor Ecumenical & Interreligious Institute—New York, NY
Greater Chicago Broadcast Ministries—Chicago, IL
Interfaith Community Services—St. Joseph, MO
Kansas Ecumenical Ministries—Topeka, KS
Lincoln Interfaith Council—Lincoln, NE
The Long Island Council of Churches—Hempstead, NY
Marin Interfaith Council—Novato, CA
New Britain Area Conference of Churches (NEWBRACC)—New Britain, CT
New Hampshire Council of Churches—Concord, NH
New Mexico Conference of Churches—Albuquerque, NM
Northern California Interreligious Conference—Oakland, CA
Reading Berks Conference of Churches—Reading, PA
The Rhode Island State Council of Churches—Providence, RI
Schenectady Inner City Ministry—Schenectady, NY
South Carolina Christian Action Council, Inc.—Columbia, SC
Southeast Ecumenical Ministry—Rochester, NY
Toledo Ecumenical Area Ministries—Toledo, OH
Troy Area United Ministries—Troy, NY
Wisconsin Council of Churches—Sun Prairie, WI
York County Council of Churches—York, PA

Anti-racism Programs

Akron Area Association of Churches—Akron, OH
Arkansas Interfaith Conference—Scott, AR
The Associated Churches of Fort Wayne & Allen County, Inc.—Fort Wayne, IN
Associated Ministries of Tacoma-Pierce County—Tacoma, WA
Association of Christian Churches—Sioux Falls, SD
Association of Religious Communities—Danbury, CT
Austin Metropolitan Ministries—Austin, TX
Bergen County Council of Churches—Bergenfield, NJ
Brooklyn Council of Churches—Brooklyn, NY
Capital Area Council of Churches, Inc.—Albany, NY
The Capitol Region Conference of Churches—Hartford, CT
Christian Associates of Southwest Pennsylvania—Pittsburgh, PA
Christian Conference of Connecticut—Hartford, CT
Christian Council of Metropolitan Atlanta—Atlanta, GA
Church Council of Greater Seattle—Seattle, WA

The Church Federation of Greater Indianapolis, Inc.—Indianapolis, IN
Churches United of the Quad City Area—Rock Island, IL
Cooperative Metropolitan Ministries—Newton, MA
Council of Churches of Chemung County, Inc.—Elmira, NY
Council of Churches of the City of New York—New York, NY
Council of Churches of Greater Bridgeport, Inc.—Bridgeport, CT
Council of Churches of Greater Springfield—Springfield, MA
The Council of Churches of Santa Clara County—San Jose, CA
Council of Churches and Synagogues of Southwestern Connecticut—Stamford, CT
Des Moines Area Religious Council—Des Moines, IA
Dutchess Interfaith Council, Inc.—Poughkeepsie, NY
East End Cooperative Ministry—Pittsburgh, PA
Eastern Area Community Ministries—Louisville, KY
Ecclesia—Trenton, NJ
Ecumenical Conference of Greater Altoona—Altoona, PA
The Ecumenical Council of Pasadena Area Churches—Pasadena, CA
Ecumenical Ministries—Fulton, MO
Ecumenical Ministries of Iowa (EMI)—Des Moines, IA
Ecumenical Ministries of Oregon—Portland, OR
Evanston Ecumenical Action Council—Evanston, IL
Florida Council of Churches—Orlando, FL
Georgia Christian Council—Macon, GA
Grand Rapids Area Center for Ecumenism (GRACE)—Grand Rapids, MI
Greater Chicago Broadcast Ministries—Chicago, IL
Greater Dallas Community of Churches—Dallas, TX
Greater Dayton Christian Connections—Dayton, OH
Greater Flint Council of Churches—Flint, MI
Greater Minneapolis Council of Churches—Minneapolis, MN
Greater Rochester Community of Churches—Rochester, NY
The Greater Wheeling Council of Churches—Wheeling, WV
Greensboro Urban Ministry—Greensboro, NC
Illinois Conference of Churches—Springfield, IL
In One Accord—Battle Creek, MI
Indiana Partners for Christian Unity and Mission—Indianapolis, IN
Inter-Church Council of Greater New Bedford—New Bedford, MA
Inter-Church Ministries of Erie County—Erie, PA
Interfaith Conference of Greater Milwaukee—Milwaukee, WI
Interfaith Council of Contra Costa County—Walnut Creek, CA
Inter-Faith Council of Santa Fe, New Mexico—Santa Fe, NM
Inter-Faith Ministries-Wichita—Wichita, KS
Interfaith Mission Service—Huntsville, AL
Interfaith Service Bureau—Sacramento, CA
InterReligious Council of Central New York—Syracuse, NY
The Joint Religious Legislative Coalition—Minneapolis, MN
Kansas Ecumenical Ministries—Topeka, KS
Kentuckiana Interfaith Community—Louisville, KY
Kentucky Council of Churches—Lexington, KY
Lincoln Interfaith Council—Lincoln, NE
The Long Island Council of Churches—Hempstead, NY
Louisiana Interchurch Conference—Baton Rouge, LA
Madison Urban Ministry—Madison, WI
Mahoning Valley Association of Churches—Youngstown, OH
Marin Interfaith Council—Novato, CA
Massachusetts Council of Churches—Boston, MA
Metropolitan Christian Council of Philadelphia—Philadelphia, PA
The Metropolitan Christian Council: Detroit-Windsor—Detroit, MI
Metropolitan Interfaith Council on Affordable Housing (MICAH)—Minneapolis, MN
Minnesota Council of Churches—Minneapolis, MN
Mississippi Religious Leadership Conference—Jackson, MS
Montana Association of Churches—Billings, MT
Muskegon County Cooperating Churches—Muskegon, MI
Network of Religious Communities—Buffalo, NY
New Britain Area Conference of Churches (NEWBRACC)—New Britain, CT
New Hampshire Council of Churches—Concord, NH
New Mexico Conference of Churches—Albuquerque, NM
New York State Community of Churches, Inc.—Albany, NY
North Carolina Council of Churches—Raleigh, NC
Northern California Interreligious Conference—Oakland, CA
Northern Kentucky Interfaith Commission, Inc.—Newport, KY
Northside Common Ministries—Pittsburgh, PA

Ohio Council of Churches—Columbus, OH
Oklahoma Conference of Churches—Oklahoma City, OK
The Pennsylvania Council of Churches—Harrisburg, PA
Reading Berks Conference of Churches—Reading, PA
The Rhode Island State Council of Churches—Providence, RI
St. Paul Area Council of Churches—St. Paul, MN
San Fernando Valley Interfaith Council—Chatsworth, CA
Schenectady Inner City Ministry—Schenectady, NY
South Carolina Christian Action Council, Inc.—Columbia, SC
South Coast Ecumenical Council—Long Beach, CA
South Hills Interfaith Ministries—Library, PA
Southern California Ecumenical Council—Pasadena, CA
Southside Area Ministries, Inc. (SAM)—Fort Worth, TX
Spokane Council of Ecumenical Ministries—Spokane, WA
Staten Island Council of Churches—Staten Island, NY
Tarrant Area Community of Churches—Fort Worth, TX
Texas Conference of Churches—Austin, TX
Toledo Ecumenical Area Ministries—Toledo, OH
Tri-Council Coordinating Commission—Minneapolis, MN
Tulsa Metropolitan Ministry—Tulsa, OK
United Churches of Lycoming County—Williamsport, PA
United Religious Community of St. Joseph County—South Bend, IN
Virginia Council of Churches, Inc.—Richmond, VA
Washington Association of Churches—Seattle, WA
West Virginia Council of Churches—Charleston, WV
York County Council of Churches—York, PA

Christian Education Programs

Akron Area Association of Churches—Akron, OH
The Associated Churches of Fort Wayne & Allen County, Inc.—Fort Wayne, IN
Associated Ministries of Tacoma-Pierce County—Tacoma, WA
Association of Christian Churches—Sioux Falls, SD
Attleboro Area Council of Churches, Inc.—Attleboro, MA
Bergen County Council of Churches—Bergenfield, NJ
Berrien County Association of Churches—Benton Harbor, MI
Brooklyn Council of Churches—Brooklyn, NY
Broome County Council of Churches, Inc.—Binghamton, NY
California Council of Churches/California Church Impact—Sacramento, CA
Christian Associates of Southwest Pennsylvania—Pittsburgh, PA
Christian Conference of Connecticut—Hartford, CT
Churches United of the Quad City Area—Rock Island, IL
Council of Christian Communions of Greater Cincinnati—Cincinnati, OH
Council of Churches of Greater Springfield—Springfield, MA
Council of Churches and Synagogues of Southwestern Connecticut—Stamford, CT
East End Cooperative Ministry—Pittsburgh, PA
Ecclesia—Trenton, NJ
Ecumenical Ministries of Oregon—Portland, OR
Georgia Christian Council—Macon, GA
Greater Chicago Broadcast Ministries—Chicago, IL
Greater Fairmont Council of Churches—Fairmont, WV
Greater New Orleans Federation of Churches—New Orleans, LA
The Greater Wheeling Council of Churches—Wheeling, WV
Greensboro Urban Ministry—Greensboro, NC
Inter-Church Council of Greater New Bedford—New Bedford, MA
Interchurch Ministries of Nebraska—Lincoln, NE
Iowa Religious Media Services—Des Moines, IA
Lincoln Interfaith Council—Lincoln, NE
The Long Island Council of Churches—Hempstead, NY
Louisiana Interchurch Conference—Baton Rouge, LA
Mahoning Valley Association of Churches—Youngstown, OH
Metropolitan Christian Council of Philadelphia—Philadelphia, PA
The Metropolitan Christian Council: Detroit-Windsor—Detroit, MI
Network of Religious Communities—Buffalo, NY
New Hampshire Council of Churches—Concord, NH
Oklahoma Conference of Churches—Oklahoma City, OK
The Pennsylvania Council of Churches—Harrisburg, PA
Peoria Friendship House of Christian Service—Peoria, IL
Reading Berks Conference of Churches—Reading, PA
The Rhode Island State Council of Churches—Providence, RI

Staten Island Council of Churches—Staten Island, NY
Tarrant Area Community of Churches—Fort Worth, TX
Toledo Ecumenical Area Ministries—Toledo, OH
United Churches of Lycoming County—Williamsport, PA
Vermont Ecumenical Council and Bible Society—Burlington, VT
Washington Association of Churches—Seattle, WA
West Virginia Council of Churches—Charleston, WV
York County Council of Churches—York, PA

Clothing Distribution Programs

Allegheny Valley Association of Churches—Natrona Heights, PA
Asheville-Buncombe Community Christian Ministry (ABCCM)—Asheville, NC
Christian Churches United of the Tri-County Area—Harrisburg, PA
Community Ministry of Montgomery County—Rockville, MD
Concerned Ecumenical Ministry to the Upper West Side—Buffalo, NY
Cooperative Metropolitan Ministries—Newton, MA
Corpus Christi Metro Ministries—Corpus Christi, TX
Council of Churches of the Ozarks—Springfield, MO
East End Cooperative Ministry—Pittsburgh, PA
Eastern Area Community Ministries—Louisville, KY
Ecumenical Conference of Greater Altoona—Altoona, PA
The Ecumenical Council of Pasadena Area Churches—Pasadena, CA
Evanston Ecumenical Action Council—Evanston, IL
Fern Creek/Highview United Ministries—Louisvlle, KY
Greater Fairmont Council of Churches—Fairmont, WV
Greensboro Urban Ministry—Greensboro, NC
Inter-Church Ministries of Erie County—Erie, PA
Interfaith Community Council, Inc.—New Albany, IN
Interfaith Community Services—St. Joseph, MO
Inter-Faith Ministries-Wichita—Wichita, KS
Lancaster County Council of Churches—Lancaster, PA
Lebanon County Christian Ministries—Lebanon, PA
Lehigh County Conference of Churches—Allentown, PA
The Long Island Council of Churches—Hempstead, NY
Northside Common Ministries—Pittsburgh, PA
Northside Inter-Church Agency (NICA)—Fort Worth, TX
Peoria Friendship House of Christian Service—Peoria, IL
Reading Berks Conference of Churches—Reading, PA
The Rhode Island State Council of Churches—Providence, RI
St. Paul Area Council of Churches—St. Paul, MN
South Coast Ecumenical Council—Long Beach, CA
South East Associated Ministries (SEAM)—Louisville, KY
South Hills Interfaith Ministries—Library, PA
South Louisville Community Ministries—Louisville, KY
Southside Area Ministries, Inc. (SAM)—Fort Worth, TX
West Side Ecumenical Ministry—Cleveland, OH
Wilkinsburg Community Ministry—Pittsburgh, PA

CROP Walks

Allegheny Valley Association of Churches—Natrona Heights, PA
Asheville-Buncombe Community Christian Ministry (ABCCM)—Asheville, NC
The Associated Churches of Fort Wayne & Allen County, Inc.—Fort Wayne, IN
Associated Ministries of Tacoma-Pierce County—Tacoma, WA
Associated Ministries of Thurston County—Olympia, WA
Attleboro Area Council of Churches, Inc.—Attleboro, MA
Austin Metropolitan Ministries—Austin, TX
Bergen County Council of Churches—Bergenfield, NJ
Berrien County Association of Churches—Benton Harbor, MI
Broome County Council of Churches, Inc.—Binghamton, NY
Capital Area Council of Churches, Inc.—Albany, NY
Center for Community Concerns—Racine, WI
Christians United in Beaver County—Beaver, PA
The Church Federation of Greater Indianapolis, Inc.—Indianapolis, IN
Churches United of the Quad City Area—Rock Island, IL
Corpus Christi Metro Ministries—Corpus Christi, TX
Council of Churches of Chemung County, Inc.—Elmira, NY
Council of Churches of the City of New York—New York, NY
Council of Churches of Greater Bridgeport, Inc.—Bridgeport, CT

Council of Churches of the Ozarks—Springfield, MO
The Council of Churches of Santa Clara County—San Jose, CA
Dutchess Interfaith Council, Inc.—Poughkeepsie, NY
East End Cooperative Ministry—Pittsburgh, PA
Eastern Area Community Ministries—Louisville, KY
Ecclesia—Trenton, NJ
Ecumenical Conference of Greater Altoona—Altoona, PA
The Ecumenical Council of Pasadena Area Churches—Pasadena, CA
Ecumenical Ministries—Fulton, MO
Evanston Ecumenical Action Council—Evanston, IL
Grand Rapids Area Center for Ecumenism (GRACE)—Grand Rapids, MI
Greater Bethlehem Area Council of Churches—Bethlehem, PA
Greater Dallas Community of Churches—Dallas, TX
Greater Dayton Christian Connections—Dayton, OH
Greater Fairmont Council of Churches—Fairmont, WV
Greater Flint Council of Churches—Flint, MI
Greater Waterbury Interfaith Ministries, Inc.—Waterbury, CT
Greensboro Urban Ministry—Greensboro, NC
Hanover Area Council of Churches—Hanover, PA
In One Accord—Battle Creek, MI
Inter-Church Ministries of Erie County—Erie, PA
Interfaith Community Services—St. Joseph, MO
Interfaith Conference of Greater Milwaukee—Milwaukee, WI
Inter-Faith Ministries-Wichita—Wichita, KS
Lancaster County Council of Churches—Lancaster, PA
Lehigh County Conference of Churches—Allentown, PA
Lincoln Interfaith Council—Lincoln, NE
The Long Island Council of Churches—Hempstead, NY
Mahoning Valley Association of Churches—Youngstown, OH
The Metropolitan Christian Council: Detroit-Windsor—Detroit, MI
Muskegon County Cooperating Churches—Muskegon, MI
Network of Religious Communities—Buffalo, NY
New Britain Area Conference of Churches (NEWBRACC)—New Britain, CT
Northside Inter-Church Agency (NICA)—Fort Worth, TX
Oak Park-River Forest Community of Congregations—Oak Park, IL
Peoria Friendship House of Christian Service—Peoria, IL
Reading Berks Conference of Churches—Reading, PA
The Rhode Island State Council of Churches—Providence, RI
St. Paul Area Council of Churches—St. Paul, MN
San Fernando Valley Interfaith Council—Chatsworth, CA
Schenectady Inner City Ministry—Schenectady, NY
South Coast Ecumenical Council—Long Beach, CA
Southeast Ecumenical Ministry—Rochester, NY
Spokane Council of Ecumenical Ministries—Spokane, WA
Staten Island Council of Churches—Staten Island, NY
Tarrant Area Community of Churches—Fort Worth, TX
Texas Conference of Churches—Austin, TX
Toledo Ecumenical Area Ministries—Toledo, OH
Troy Area United Ministries—Troy, NY
United Churches of Lycoming County—Williamsport, PA
United Religious Community of St. Joseph County—South Bend, IN
West Virginia Council of Churches—Charleston, WV
Wilkinsburg Community Ministry—Pittsburgh, PA
Worcester County Ecumenical Council—Worcester, MA
York County Council of Churches—York, PA

Programs with/for Persons with Disabilities

Asheville-Buncombe Community Christian Ministry (ABCCM)—Asheville, NC
The Associated Churches of Fort Wayne & Allen County, Inc.—Fort Wayne, IN
Bergen County Council of Churches—Bergenfield, NJ
Broome County Council of Churches, Inc.—Binghamton, NY
Capital Area Council of Churches, Inc.—Albany, NY
Christian Conference of Connecticut—Hartford, CT
Christian Council of Metropolitan Atlanta—Atlanta, GA
Churches United of the Quad City Area—Rock Island, IL
Des Moines Area Religious Council—Des Moines, IA
Eastern Area Community Ministries—Louisville, KY
Greater Chicago Broadcast Ministries—Chicago, IL

Inter-Church Council of Greater New Bedford —New Bedford, MA
Interfaith Service Bureau—Sacramento, CA
The Joint Religious Legislative Coalition—Minneapolis, MN
Lincoln Interfaith Council—Lincoln, NE
Massachusetts Council of Churches—Boston, MA
New York State Community of Churches, Inc. —Albany, NY
Reading Berks Conference of Churches—Reading, PA
The Rhode Island State Council of Churches —Providence, RI
Toledo Ecumenical Area Ministries—Toledo, OH
Tulsa Metropolitan Ministry—Tulsa, OK

Domestic Violence Programs

Asheville-Buncombe Community Christian Ministry (ABCCM)—Asheville, NC
Association of Christian Churches—Sioux Falls, SD
Association of Religious Communities—Danbury, CT
Austin Metropolitan Ministries—Austin, TX
Center for the Prevention of Sexual and Domestic Violence—Seattle, WA
The Church Federation of Greater Indianapolis, Inc.—Indianapolis, IN
Churches United of the Quad City Area—Rock Island, IL
Corpus Christi Metro Ministries—Corpus Christi, TX
Eastern Area Community Ministries—Louisville, KY
Ecumenical Ministries of Oregon—Portland, OR
Greater Bethlehem Area Council of Churches —Bethlehem, PA
Greater Chicago Broadcast Ministries—Chicago, IL
Greater Minneapolis Council of Churches—Minneapolis, MN
Indiana Partners for Christian Unity and Mission—Indianapolis, IN
Inter-Church Council of Greater New Bedford —New Bedford, MA
Kansas Ecumenical Ministries—Topeka, KS
Lancaster County Council of Churches—Lancaster, PA
Lincoln Interfaith Council—Lincoln, NE
The Long Island Council of Churches—Hempstead, NY
Madison Urban Ministry—Madison, WI
Peoria Friendship House of Christian Service —Peoria, IL
The Rhode Island State Council of Churches —Providence, RI
St. Paul Area Council of Churches—St. Paul, MN
Toledo Ecumenical Area Ministries—Toledo, OH
West Side Ecumenical Ministry—Cleveland, OH
West Virginia Council of Churches—Charleston, WV
York County Council of Churches—York, PA

Economic/Social Justice Programs

Akron Area Association of Churches—Akron, OH
Arkansas Interfaith Conference—Scott, AR
Asheville-Buncombe Community Christian Ministry (ABCCM)—Asheville, NC
The Associated Churches of Fort Wayne & Allen County, Inc.—Fort Wayne, IN
Associated Ministries of Tacoma-Pierce County—Tacoma, WA
Associated Ministries of Thurston County—Olympia, WA
Association of Christian Churches—Sioux Falls, SD
Association of Religious Communities—Danbury, CT
Berrien County Association of Churches—Benton Harbor, MI
Brooklyn Council of Churches—Brooklyn, NY
Broome County Council of Churches, Inc.—Binghamton, NY
California Council of Churches/California Church Impact—Sacramento, CA
Capital Area Council of Churches, Inc.—Albany, NY
The Capitol Region Conference of Churches—Hartford, CT
Christian Community Action~—New Haven, CT
Christian Conference of Connecticut—Hartford, CT
Christian Council of Metropolitan Atlanta—Atlanta, GA
Church Council of Greater Seattle—Seattle, WA
The Church Federation of Greater Indianapolis, Inc.—Indianapolis, IN
Churches United of the Quad City Area—Rock Island, IL
Community Ministry of Montgomery County—Rockville, MD
Concerned Ecumenical Ministry to the Upper West Side—Buffalo, NY
Cooperative Metropolitan Ministries—Newton, MA
Council of Churches of Chemung County, Inc.—Elmira, NY
Council of Churches of the City of New York—New York, NY
Council of Churches of Greater Bridgeport, Inc.—Bridgeport, CT
Council of Churches of Greater Springfield—Springfield, MA
The Council of Churches of Santa Clara County—San Jose, CA

South Coast Ecumenical Council—Long Beach, CA
South East Associated Ministries (SEAM)—Louisville, KY
South Louisville Community Ministries—Louisville, KY
Southern California Ecumenical Council—Pasadena, CA
Spokane Council of Ecumenical Ministries—Spokane, WA
Staten Island Council of Churches—Staten Island, NY
Tarrant Area Community of Churches—Fort Worth, TX
Texas Conference of Churches—Austin, TX
Toledo Ecumenical Area Ministries—Toledo, OH
Troy Area United Ministries—Troy, NY
Tulsa Metropolitan Ministry—Tulsa, OK
United Churches of Lycoming County—Williamsport, PA
Vermont Ecumenical Council and Bible Society—Burlington, VT
Virginia Council of Churches, Inc.—Richmond, VA
Washington Association of Churches—Seattle, WA
West Side Ecumenical Ministry—Cleveland, OH
West Virginia Council of Churches—Charleston, WV
Wisconsin Council of Churches—Sun Prairie, WI
Worcester County Ecumenical Council—Worcester, MA
York County Council of Churches—York, PA

Employment Assistance Programs

Asheville-Buncombe Community Christian Ministry (ABCCM)—Asheville, NC
The Associated Churches of Fort Wayne & Allen County, Inc.—Fort Wayne, IN
Associated Ministries of Tacoma-Pierce County—Tacoma, WA
Association of Religious Communities—Danbury, CT
Bergen County Council of Churches—Bergenfield, NJ
Corpus Christi Metro Ministries—Corpus Christi, TX
Council of Churches of Greater Bridgeport, Inc.—Bridgeport, CT
East End Cooperative Ministry—Pittsburgh, PA
Evanston Ecumenical Action Council—Evanston, IL
Genesee-Orleans Ministry of Concern—Albion, NY
Grand Rapids Area Center for Ecumenism (GRACE)—Grand Rapids, MI
Greater Chicago Broadcast Ministries—Chicago, IL
Greater Minneapolis Council of Churches—Minneapolis, MN
Greensboro Urban Ministry—Greensboro, NC
Interfaith Community Council, Inc.—New Albany, IN
The Joint Religious Legislative Coalition—Minneapolis, MN
Lehigh County Conference of Churches—Allentown, PA
Lincoln Interfaith Council—Lincoln, NE
Network of Religious Communities—Buffalo, NY
Northern California Interreligious Conference—Oakland, CA
Northside Common Ministries—Pittsburgh, PA
Northside Inter-Church Agency (NICA)—Fort Worth, TX
Peoria Friendship House of Christian Service—Peoria, IL
The Rhode Island State Council of Churches—Providence, RI
Schenectady Inner City Ministry—Schenectady, NY
South East Associated Ministries (SEAM)—Louisville, KY
Toledo Ecumenical Area Ministries—Toledo, OH
United Churches of Lycoming County—Williamsport, PA
United Ministries—Greenville, SC
United Religious Community of St. Joseph County—South Bend, IN
West Side Ecumenical Ministry—Cleveland, OH
York County Council of Churches—York, PA

Environmental Programs

The Church Federation of Greater Indianapolis, Inc.—Indianapolis, IN
Churches United of the Quad City Area—Rock Island, IL
Council of Churches of Chemung County, Inc.—Elmira, NY
The Council of Churches of Santa Clara County—San Jose, CA
Ecumenical Ministries of Iowa (EMI)—Des Moines, IA
Ecumenical Ministries of Oregon—Portland, OR
Florida Council of Churches—Orlando, FL
Georgia Christian Council—Macon, GA
Greater Chicago Broadcast Ministries—Chicago, IL
Greater Dayton Christian Connections—Dayton, OH
The Greater Wheeling Council of Churches—Wheeling, WV
Inter-Church Council of Greater New Bedford—New Bedford, MA
Interfaith Conference of Greater Milwaukee—Milwaukee, WI

Interfaith Mission Service—Huntsville, AL
The Joint Religious Legislative Coalition—Minneapolis, MN
Kansas Ecumenical Ministries—Topeka, KS
Lincoln Interfaith Council—Lincoln, NE
Louisiana Interchurch Conference—Baton Rouge, LA
Mahoning Valley Association of Churches—Youngstown, OH
Maine Council of Churches—Portland, ME
Marin Interfaith Council—Novato, CA
Metropolitan Christian Council of Philadelphia—Philadelphia, PA
The Metropolitan Christian Council: Detroit-Windsor—Detroit, MI
Michigan Ecumenical Forum—Lansing, MI
Mississippi Religious Leadership Conference—Jackson, MS
Montana Association of Churches—Billings, MT
Muskegon County Cooperating Churches—Muskegon, MI
Network of Religious Communities—Buffalo, NY
New Hampshire Council of Churches—Concord, NH
New York State Community of Churches, Inc.—Albany, NY
North Carolina Council of Churches—Raleigh, NC
Northern California Interreligious Conference—Oakland, CA
Ohio Council of Churches—Columbus, OH
The Pennsylvania Council of Churches—Harrisburg, PA
The Rhode Island State Council of Churches—Providence, RI
South Carolina Christian Action Council, Inc.—Columbia, SC
South Coast Ecumenical Council—Long Beach, CA
Southern California Ecumenical Council—Pasadena, CA
Toledo Ecumenical Area Ministries—Toledo, OH
United Churches of Lycoming County—Williamsport, PA
Vermont Ecumenical Council and Bible Society—Burlington, VT
Washington Association of Churches—Seattle, WA
West Virginia Council of Churches—Charleston, WV

Faith and Order Programs

Akron Area Association of Churches—Akron, OH
Allegheny Valley Association of Churches—Natrona Heights, PA
The Associated Churches of Fort Wayne & Allen County, Inc.—Fort Wayne, IN
Associated Ministries of Tacoma-Pierce County—Tacoma, WA
Associated Ministries of Thurston County—Olympia, WA
Association of Christian Churches—Sioux Falls, SD
Broome County Council of Churches, Inc.—Binghamton, NY
Capital Area Council of Churches, Inc.—Albany, NY
The Capitol Region Conference of Churches—Hartford, CT
Christian Conference of Connecticut—Hartford, CT
The Christian Council of Delaware and Maryland's Eastern Shore—Baltimore, MD
Christian Council of Metropolitan Atlanta—Atlanta, GA
The Church Federation of Greater Indianapolis, Inc.—Indianapolis, IN
Churches United of the Quad City Area—Rock Island, IL
Council of Churches of the City of New York—New York, NY
The Council of Churches of Santa Clara County—San Jose, CA
Council of Churches and Synagogues of Southwestern Connecticut—Stamford, CT
East End Cooperative Ministry—Pittsburgh, PA
Eastern Area Community Ministries—Louisville, KY
Ecclesia—Trenton, NJ
The Ecumenical Council of Pasadena Area Churches—Pasadena, CA
Ecumenical Ministries of Iowa (EMI)—Des Moines, IA
Ecumenical Ministries of Oregon—Portland, OR
Florida Council of Churches—Orlando, FL
Georgia Christian Council—Macon, GA
Grand Rapids Area Center for Ecumenism (GRACE)—Grand Rapids, MI
Graymoor Ecumenical & Interreligious Institute—New York, NY
Greater Chicago Broadcast Ministries—Chicago, IL
Greater Dayton Christian Connections—Dayton, OH
Greater New Orleans Federation of Churches—New Orleans, LA
Greater Rochester Community of Churches—Rochester, NY
Greater Waterbury Interfaith Ministries, Inc.—Waterbury, CT
The Greater Wheeling Council of Churches—Wheeling, WV
Illinois Conference of Churches—Springfield, IL
In One Accord—Battle Creek, MI
Indiana Partners for Christian Unity and Mission—Indianapolis, IN
Inter-Church Council of Greater New Bedford—New Bedford, MA
Interchurch Ministries of Nebraska—Lincoln, NE

Healthcare Issues

The Joint Religious Legislative Coalition—Minneapolis, MN
Lehigh County Conference of Churches—Allentown, PA
Lincoln Interfaith Council—Lincoln, NE
Marin Interfaith Council—Novato, CA
Massachusetts Council of Churches—Boston, MA
Metropolitan Ecumenical Ministry Community Development Corp.—Newark, NJ
Network of Religious Communities—Buffalo, NY
New York State Community of Churches, Inc.—Albany, NY
Northern California Interreligious Conference—Oakland, CA
Northside Common Ministries—Pittsburgh, PA
Ohio Council of Churches—Columbus, OH
Peoria Friendship House of Christian Service—Peoria, IL
The Rhode Island State Council of Churches—Providence, RI
South Louisville Community Ministries—Louisville, KY
Tarrant Area Community of Churches—Fort Worth, TX
Toledo Ecumenical Area Ministries—Toledo, OH
Vermont Ecumenical Council and Bible Society—Burlington, VT
Washington Association of Churches—Seattle, WA
West Virginia Council of Churches—Charleston, WV

Homelessness/Shelter Programs

Allegheny Valley Association of Churches—Natrona Heights, PA
Arkansas Interfaith Conference—Scott, AR
Asheville-Buncombe Community Christian Ministry (ABCCM)—Asheville, NC
The Associated Churches of Fort Wayne & Allen County, Inc.—Fort Wayne, IN
Associated Ministries of Tacoma-Pierce County—Tacoma, WA
Associated Ministries of Thurston County—Olympia, WA
Association of Religious Communities—Danbury, CT
Austin Metropolitan Ministries—Austin, TX
Bergen County Council of Churches—Bergenfield, NJ
California Council of Churches/California Church Impact—Sacramento, CA
Capital Area Council of Churches, Inc.—Albany, NY
The Capitol Region Conference of Churches—Hartford, CT
Center City Churches—Hartford, CT
Christian Churches United of the Tri-County Area—Harrisburg, PA
Christian Community Action—New Haven, CT
Christian Council of Metropolitan Atlanta—Atlanta, GA
Church Council of Greater Seattle—Seattle, WA
Community Ministries of Rockville—Rockville, MD
Community Ministry of Montgomery County—Rockville, MD
Corpus Christi Metro Ministries—Corpus Christi, TX
Council of Churches of Chemung County, Inc.—Elmira, NY
Council of Churches of Greater Bridgeport, Inc.—Bridgeport, CT
Council of Churches of Greater Springfield—Springfield, MA
The Council of Churches of Santa Clara County—San Jose, CA
East End Cooperative Ministry—Pittsburgh, PA
Eastern Area Community Ministries—Louisville, KY
Ecumenical Conference of Greater Altoona—Altoona, PA
The Ecumenical Council of Pasadena Area Churches—Pasadena, CA
Ecumenical Ministries—Fulton, MO
Ecumenical Ministries of Oregon—Portland, OR
Evanston Ecumenical Action Council—Evanston, IL
Grand Rapids Area Center for Ecumenism (GRACE)—Grand Rapids, MI
Greater Bethlehem Area Council of Churches—Bethlehem, PA
Greater Chicago Broadcast Ministries—Chicago, IL
Greater Minneapolis Council of Churches—Minneapolis, MN
Greensboro Urban Ministry—Greensboro, NC
Inter-Church Ministries of Erie County—Erie, PA
Interfaith Community Council, Inc.—New Albany, IN
Interfaith Community Services—St. Joseph, MO
Interfaith Conference of Greater Milwaukee—Milwaukee, WI
InterFaith Conference of Metropolitan Washington—Washington, DC
Inter-Faith Council of Santa Fe, New Mexico—Santa Fe, NM
Inter-Faith Ministries-Wichita—Wichita, KS
Interfaith Mission Service—Huntsville, AL
The Joint Religious Legislative Coalition—Minneapolis, MN
Lehigh County Conference of Churches—Allentown, PA
Lincoln Interfaith Council—Lincoln, NE
The Long Island Council of Churches—Hempstead, NY

Metropolitan Interfaith Council on Affordable Housing (MICAH)—Minneapolis, MN
Network of Religious Communities—Buffalo, NY
New Britain Area Conference of Churches (NEWBRACC)—New Britain, CT
New York State Community of Churches, Inc.—Albany, NY
Northern California Interreligious Conference—Oakland, CA
Northern Kentucky Interfaith Commission, Inc.—Newport, KY
Northside Common Ministries—Pittsburgh, PA
Oak Park-River Forest Community of Congregations—Oak Park, IL
Paducah Cooperative Ministry—Paducah, KY
Peoria Friendship House of Christian Service—Peoria, IL
Reading Berks Conference of Churches—Reading, PA
The Rhode Island State Council of Churches—Providence, RI
St. Paul Area Council of Churches—St. Paul, MN
San Fernando Valley Interfaith Council—Chatsworth, CA
Schenectady Inner City Ministry—Schenectady, NY
Staten Island Council of Churches—Staten Island, NY
Tarrant Area Community of Churches—Fort Worth, TX
Toledo Ecumenical Area Ministries—Toledo, OH
Troy Area United Ministries—Troy, NY
United Churches of Lycoming County—Williamsport, PA
United Ministries—Greenville, SC
United Religious Community of St. Joseph County—South Bend, IN

Hunger/Food Programs

Allegheny Valley Association of Churches—Natrona Heights, PA
Arkansas Interfaith Conference—Scott, AR
Asheville-Buncombe Community Christian Ministry (ABCCM)—Asheville, NC
The Associated Churches of Fort Wayne & Allen County, Inc.—Fort Wayne, IN
Associated Ministries of Tacoma-Pierce County—Tacoma, WA
Associated Ministries of Thurston County—Olympia, WA
Association of Christian Churches—Sioux Falls, SD
Attleboro Area Council of Churches, Inc.—Attleboro, MA
Bergen County Council of Churches—Bergenfield, NJ
Brooklyn Council of Churches—Brooklyn, NY
Broome County Council of Churches, Inc.—Binghamton, NY
California Council of Churches/California Church Impact—Sacramento, CA
Capital Area Council of Churches, Inc.—Albany, NY
Center City Churches—Hartford, CT
Christian Churches United of the Tri-County Area—Harrisburg, PA
Christian Community Action~—New Haven, CT
Church Council of Greater Seattle—Seattle, WA
The Church Federation of Greater Indianapolis, Inc.—Indianapolis, IN
Churches United of the Quad City Area—Rock Island, IL
Community Ministry of Montgomery County—Rockville, MD
Concerned Ecumenical Ministry to the Upper West Side—Buffalo, NY
Corpus Christi Metro Ministries—Corpus Christi, TX
Council of Churches of Chemung County, Inc.—Elmira, NY
Council of Churches of Greater Bridgeport, Inc.—Bridgeport, CT
Council of Churches of Greater Springfield—Springfield, MA
Council of Churches of the Ozarks—Springfield, MO
The Council of Churches of Santa Clara County—San Jose, CA
Council of Churches and Synagogues of Southwestern Connecticut—Stamford, CT
Des Moines Area Religious Council—Des Moines, IA
East End Cooperative Ministry—Pittsburgh, PA
Eastern Area Community Ministries—Louisville, KY
Ecclesia—Trenton, NJ
Ecumenical Conference of Greater Altoona—Altoona, PA
The Ecumenical Council of Pasadena Area Churches—Pasadena, CA
Ecumenical Ministries of Oregon—Portland, OR
Evanston Ecumenical Action Council—Evanston, IL
Fern Creek/Highview United Ministries—Louisvlle, KY
Genesee County Churches United, Inc.—Batavia, NY
Genesee-Orleans Ministry of Concern—Albion, NY
Grand Rapids Area Center for Ecumenism (GRACE)—Grand Rapids, MI
Greater Bethlehem Area Council of Churches—Bethlehem, PA
Greater Chicago Broadcast Ministries—Chicago, IL
Greater Dallas Community of Churches—Dallas, TX

Greater Minneapolis Council of Churches—Minneapolis, MN
Greater New Orleans Federation of Churches—New Orleans, LA
Greater Waterbury Interfaith Ministries, Inc.—Waterbury, CT
Greensboro Urban Ministry—Greensboro, NC
Hanover Area Council of Churches—Hanover, PA
In One Accord—Battle Creek, MI
Inter-Church Ministries of Erie County—Erie, PA
Interchurch Ministries of Nebraska—Lincoln, NE
Interfaith Community Council, Inc.—New Albany, IN
Interfaith Community Services—St. Joseph, MO
Interfaith Conference of Greater Milwaukee—Milwaukee, WI
Inter-Faith Council of Santa Fe, New Mexico—Santa Fe, NM
Inter-Faith Ministries-Wichita—Wichita, KS
Interfaith Mission Service—Huntsville, AL
The Joint Religious Legislative Coalition—Minneapolis, MN
Kansas Ecumenical Ministries—Topeka, KS
Kentuckiana Interfaith Community—Louisville, KY
Lancaster County Council of Churches—Lancaster, PA
Lebanon County Christian Ministries—Lebanon, PA
Lehigh County Conference of Churches—Allentown, PA
Lincoln Interfaith Council—Lincoln, NE
The Long Island Council of Churches—Hempstead, NY
Madison Urban Ministry—Madison, WI
The Metropolitan Christian Council: Detroit-Windsor—Detroit, MI
Minnesota Council of Churches—Minneapolis, MN
Network of Religious Communities—Buffalo, NY
New Britain Area Conference of Churches (NEWBRACC)—New Britain, CT
New York State Community of Churches, Inc.—Albany, NY
Northern Kentucky Interfaith Commission, Inc.—Newport, KY
Northside Common Ministries—Pittsburgh, PA
Northside Inter-Church Agency (NICA)—Fort Worth, TX
Northwest Harvest/E. M. M.—Seattle, WA
Oak Park-River Forest Community of Congregations—Oak Park, IL
Ohio Council of Churches—Columbus, OH
Paducah Cooperative Ministry—Paducah, KY
Peoria Friendship House of Christian Service—Peoria, IL
Queens Federation of Churches—Richmond Hill, NY
The Rhode Island State Council of Churches—Providence, RI
St. Paul Area Council of Churches—St. Paul, MN
San Fernando Valley Interfaith Council—Chatsworth, CA
Schenectady Inner City Ministry—Schenectady, NY
South Coast Ecumenical Council—Long Beach, CA
South East Associated Ministries (SEAM)—Louisville, KY
South Hills Interfaith Ministries—Library, PA
South Louisville Community Ministries—Louisville, KY
Southeast Ecumenical Ministry—Rochester, NY
Southside Area Ministries, Inc. (SAM)—Fort Worth, TX
Spokane Council of Ecumenical Ministries—Spokane, WA
Staten Island Council of Churches—Staten Island, NY
Toledo Ecumenical Area Ministries—Toledo, OH
Troy Area United Ministries—Troy, NY
United Churches of Lycoming County—Williamsport, PA
United Ministries—Greenville, SC
United Religious Community of St. Joseph County—South Bend, IN
Vermont Ecumenical Council and Bible Society—Burlington, VT
Washington Association of Churches—Seattle, WA
West Central Neighborhood Ministry, Inc.—Fort Wayne, IN
West Side Ecumenical Ministry—Cleveland, OH
West Virginia Council of Churches—Charleston, WV
Wilkinsburg Community Ministry—Pittsburgh, PA
York County Council of Churches—York, PA

Immigration Issues

Association of Religious Communities—Danbury, CT
Christian Council of Metropolitan Atlanta—Atlanta, GA
Community Ministries of Rockville—Rockville, MD
Concerned Ecumenical Ministry to the Upper West Side—Buffalo, NY
Eastern Area Community Ministries—Louisville, KY
Ecumenical Ministries of Oregon—Portland, OR
Greater Chicago Broadcast Ministries—Chicago, IL
The Joint Religious Legislative Coalition—Minneapolis, MN
Lincoln Interfaith Council—Lincoln, NE

The Long Island Council of Churches—Hempstead, NY
Minnesota Council of Churches—Minneapolis, MN
Mississippi Religious Leadership Conference—Jackson, MS
Network of Religious Communities—Buffalo, NY
New York State Community of Churches, Inc.—Albany, NY
Northside Inter-Church Agency (NICA)—Fort Worth, TX
Ohio Council of Churches—Columbus, OH
The Pennsylvania Council of Churches—Harrisburg, PA
Peoria Friendship House of Christian Service—Peoria, IL
The Rhode Island State Council of Churches—Providence, RI
San Fernando Valley Interfaith Council—Chatsworth, CA
South Coast Ecumenical Council—Long Beach, CA
Southside Area Ministries, Inc. (SAM)—Fort Worth, TX
York County Council of Churches—York, PA

Interfaith Dialogue/Relationships

Akron Area Association of Churches—Akron, OH
Arkansas Interfaith Conference—Scott, AR
The Associated Churches of Fort Wayne & Allen County, Inc.—Fort Wayne, IN
Associated Ministries of Tacoma-Pierce County—Tacoma, WA
Associated Ministries of Thurston County—Olympia, WA
Association of Christian Churches—Sioux Falls, SD
Association of Religious Communities—Danbury, CT
Attleboro Area Council of Churches, Inc.—Attleboro, MA
Austin Metropolitan Ministries—Austin, TX
Bergen County Council of Churches—Bergenfield, NJ
Berrien County Association of Churches—Benton Harbor, MI
Brooklyn Council of Churches—Brooklyn, NY
Broome County Council of Churches, Inc.—Binghamton, NY
Capital Area Council of Churches, Inc.—Albany, NY
Christian Churches United of the Tri-County Area—Harrisburg, PA
Christian Conference of Connecticut—Hartford, CT
The Christian Council of Delaware and Maryland's Eastern Shore—Baltimore, MD
Christian Council of Metropolitan Atlanta—Atlanta, GA
Church Council of Greater Seattle—Seattle, WA
The Church Federation of Greater Indianapolis, Inc.—Indianapolis, IN
Churches United of the Quad City Area—Rock Island, IL
Community Ministries of Rockville—Rockville, MD
Community Ministry of Montgomery County—Rockville, MD
Concerned Ecumenical Ministry to the Upper West Side—Buffalo, NY
Cooperative Metropolitan Ministries—Newton, MA
Council of Churches of Chemung County, Inc.—Elmira, NY
Council of Churches of the City of New York—New York, NY
Council of Churches of Greater Springfield—Springfield, MA
The Council of Churches of Santa Clara County—San Jose, CA
Council of Churches and Synagogues of Southwestern Connecticut—Stamford, CT
Des Moines Area Religious Council—Des Moines, IA
Dutchess Interfaith Council, Inc.—Poughkeepsie, NY
East End Cooperative Ministry—Pittsburgh, PA
Eastern Area Community Ministries—Louisville, KY
Ecclesia—Trenton, NJ
Ecumenical Conference of Greater Altoona—Altoona, PA
The Ecumenical Council of Pasadena Area Churches—Pasadena, CA
Ecumenical Ministries of Oregon—Portland, OR
Evanston Ecumenical Action Council—Evanston, IL
Florida Council of Churches—Orlando, FL
Georgia Christian Council—Macon, GA
Grand Rapids Area Center for Ecumenism (GRACE)—Grand Rapids, MI
Graymoor Ecumenical & Interreligious Institute—New York, NY
Greater Bethlehem Area Council of Churches—Bethlehem, PA
Greater Chicago Broadcast Ministries—Chicago, IL
Greater Dayton Christian Connections—Dayton, OH
Greater Flint Council of Churches—Flint, MI
Greater New Orleans Federation of Churches—New Orleans, LA
Greater Rochester Community of Churches—Rochester, NY
Greater Waterbury Interfaith Ministries, Inc.—Waterbury, CT
Greensboro Urban Ministry—Greensboro, NC
In One Accord—Battle Creek, MI
Inter-Church Council of Greater New Bedford—New Bedford, MA

Inter-Church Ministries of Erie County—Erie, PA
Interchurch Ministries of Nebraska—Lincoln, NE
Interfaith Community Council, Inc.—New Albany, IN
Interfaith Community Services—St. Joseph, MO
Interfaith Conference of Greater Milwaukee—Milwaukee, WI
InterFaith Conference of Metropolitan Washington—Washington, DC
Interfaith Council of Contra Costa County—Walnut Creek, CA
Inter-Faith Council of Santa Fe, New Mexico—Santa Fe, NM
Inter-Faith Ministries-Wichita—Wichita, KS
Interfaith Mission Service—Huntsville, AL
Interfaith Service Bureau—Sacramento, CA
InterReligious Council of Central New York—Syracuse, NY
Kentuckiana Interfaith Community—Louisville, KY
Lancaster County Council of Churches—Lancaster, PA
Lehigh County Conference of Churches—Allentown, PA
Lincoln Interfaith Council—Lincoln, NE
The Long Island Council of Churches—Hempstead, NY
Louisiana Interchurch Conference—Baton Rouge, LA
Mahoning Valley Association of Churches—Youngstown, OH
Maine Council of Churches—Portland, ME
Marin Interfaith Council—Novato, CA
Massachusetts Council of Churches—Boston, MA
Metropolitan Christian Council of Philadelphia—Philadelphia, PA
Metropolitan Interfaith Council on Affordable Housing (MICAH)—Minneapolis, MN
Michigan Ecumenical Forum—Lansing, MI
Minnesota Council of Churches—Minneapolis, MN
Mississippi Religious Leadership Conference—Jackson, MS
Montana Association of Churches—Billings, MT
Network of Religious Communities—Buffalo, NY
New Britain Area Conference of Churches (NEWBRACC)—New Britain, CT
New Hampshire Council of Churches—Concord, NH
New Mexico Conference of Churches—Albuquerque, NM
New York State Community of Churches, Inc.—Albany, NY
North Carolina Council of Churches—Raleigh, NC
Northern California Interreligious Conference—Oakland, CA
Northern Kentucky Interfaith Commission, Inc.—Newport, KY
Northside Common Ministries—Pittsburgh, PA
Northwest Interfaith Movement—Philadelphia, PA
Oak Park-River Forest Community of Congregations—Oak Park, IL
Ohio Council of Churches—Columbus, OH
Oklahoma Conference of Churches—Oklahoma City, OK
Pennsylvania Conference on Interchurch Cooperation—Harrisburg, PA
Peoria Friendship House of Christian Service—Peoria, IL
Reading Berks Conference of Churches—Reading, PA
The Rhode Island State Council of Churches—Providence, RI
St. Paul Area Council of Churches—St. Paul, MN
San Fernando Valley Interfaith Council—Chatsworth, CA
South Carolina Christian Action Council, Inc.—Columbia, SC
South Coast Ecumenical Council—Long Beach, CA
South Hills Interfaith Ministries—Library, PA
Southern California Ecumenical Council—Pasadena, CA
Spokane Council of Ecumenical Ministries—Spokane, WA
Staten Island Council of Churches—Staten Island, NY
Texas Conference of Churches—Austin, TX
Toledo Ecumenical Area Ministries—Toledo, OH
Tulsa Metropolitan Ministry—Tulsa, OK
United Religious Community of St. Joseph County—South Bend, IN
Vermont Ecumenical Council and Bible Society—Burlington, VT
Virginia Council of Churches, Inc.—Richmond, VA
Washington Association of Churches—Seattle, WA
West Side Ecumenical Ministry—Cleveland, OH
West Virginia Council of Churches—Charleston, WV
Wisconsin Council of Churches—Sun Prairie, WI
York County Council of Churches—York, PA

Prison Chaplaincy

Asheville-Buncombe Community Christian Ministry (ABCCM)—Asheville, NC
The Associated Churches of Fort Wayne & Allen County, Inc.—Fort Wayne, IN
Association of Christian Churches—Sioux Falls, SD
Bergen County Council of Churches—Bergenfield, NJ

Broome County Council of Churches, Inc.—Binghamton, NY
Capital Area Council of Churches, Inc.—Albany, NY
Christian Associates of Southwest Pennsylvania—Pittsburgh, PA
Christian Churches United of the Tri-County Area—Harrisburg, PA
Christian Conference of Connecticut—Hartford, CT
Christians United in Beaver County—Beaver, PA
Church Council of Greater Seattle—Seattle, WA
The Church Federation of Greater Indianapolis, Inc.—Indianapolis, IN
Churches United of the Quad City Area—Rock Island, IL
Council of Christian Communions of Greater Cincinnati—Cincinnati, OH
Council of Churches of the City of New York—New York, NY
Council of Churches of Greater Springfield—Springfield, MA
Ecclesia—Trenton, NJ
Ecumenical Ministries—Fulton, MO
Genesee County Churches United, Inc.—Batavia, NY
Greater Bethlehem Area Council of Churches—Bethlehem, PA
Greater Chicago Broadcast Ministries—Chicago, IL
Greater Minneapolis Council of Churches—Minneapolis, MN
The Greater Wheeling Council of Churches—Wheeling, WV
Inter-Church Ministries of Erie County—Erie, PA
Interfaith Council of Contra Costa County—Walnut Creek, CA
InterReligious Council of Central New York—Syracuse, NY
Lehigh County Conference of Churches—Allentown, PA
The Long Island Council of Churches—Hempstead, NY
Madison Urban Ministry—Madison, WI
Minnesota Council of Churches—Minneapolis, MN
Montana Association of Churches—Billings, MT
Muskegon County Cooperating Churches—Muskegon, MI
Network of Religious Communities—Buffalo, NY
New Hampshire Council of Churches—Concord, NH
North Dakota Conference of Churches—Bismarck, ND
Northern Kentucky Interfaith Commission, Inc.—Newport, KY
Ohio Council of Churches—Columbus, OH
Reading Berks Conference of Churches—Reading, PA
The Rhode Island State Council of Churches—Providence, RI
St. Paul Area Council of Churches—St. Paul, MN
United Churches of Lycoming County—Williamsport, PA
Vermont Ecumenical Council and Bible Society—Burlington, VT
West Virginia Council of Churches—Charleston, WV
Wisconsin Council of Churches—Sun Prairie, WI
York County Council of Churches—York, PA

Public Education Advocacy

Akron Area Association of Churches—Akron, OH
Arkansas Interfaith Conference—Scott, AR
The Associated Churches of Fort Wayne & Allen County, Inc.—Fort Wayne, IN
Association of Religious Communities—Danbury, CT
Bergen County Council of Churches—Bergenfield, NJ
Berrien County Association of Churches—Benton Harbor, MI
California Council of Churches/California Church Impact—Sacramento, CA
The Capitol Region Conference of Churches—Hartford, CT
Church Council of Greater Seattle—Seattle, WA
The Church Federation of Greater Indianapolis, Inc.—Indianapolis, IN
Community Ministries of Rockville—Rockville, MD
Community Ministry of Montgomery County—Rockville, MD
Council of Churches of the City of New York—New York, NY
The Council of Churches of Santa Clara County—San Jose, CA
East End Cooperative Ministry—Pittsburgh, PA
Ecclesia—Trenton, NJ
Ecumenical Ministries—Fulton, MO
Ecumenical Ministries of Iowa (EMI)—Des Moines, IA
Evanston Ecumenical Action Council—Evanston, IL
Grand Rapids Area Center for Ecumenism (GRACE)—Grand Rapids, MI
Greater Bethlehem Area Council of Churches—Bethlehem, PA
Greater Chicago Broadcast Ministries—Chicago, IL
Greater Fairmont Council of Churches—Fairmont, WV
Greater Waterbury Interfaith Ministries, Inc.—Waterbury, CT
The Greater Wheeling Council of Churches—Wheeling, WV

Inter-Church Council of Greater New Bedford —New Bedford, MA
Interchurch Ministries of Nebraska—Lincoln, NE
Interfaith Conference of Greater Milwaukee—Milwaukee, WI
Kansas Ecumenical Ministries—Topeka, KS
Lincoln Interfaith Council—Lincoln, NE
The Long Island Council of Churches—Hempstead, NY
Madison Urban Ministry—Madison, WI
Marin Interfaith Council—Novato, CA
Massachusetts Council of Churches—Boston, MA
Metropolitan Christian Council of Philadelphia—Philadelphia, PA
Metropolitan Interfaith Council on Affordable Housing (MICAH)—Minneapolis, MN
Michigan Ecumenical Forum—Lansing, MI
Minnesota Council of Churches—Minneapolis, MN
Network of Religious Communities—Buffalo, NY
New Hampshire Council of Churches—Concord, NH
New York State Community of Churches, Inc. —Albany, NY
North Carolina Council of Churches—Raleigh, NC
Northern California Interreligious Conference —Oakland, CA
Northside Common Ministries—Pittsburgh, PA
Ohio Council of Churches—Columbus, OH
The Pennsylvania Council of Churches—Harrisburg, PA
Peoria Friendship House of Christian Service —Peoria, IL
The Rhode Island State Council of Churches—Providence, RI
South Carolina Christian Action Council, Inc.—Columbia, SC
Spokane Council of Ecumenical Ministries—Spokane, WA
Tarrant Area Community of Churches—Fort Worth, TX
Toledo Ecumenical Area Ministries—Toledo, OH
United Churches of Lycoming County—Williamsport, PA

Refugee Assistance Programs

Association of Religious Communities—Danbury, CT
Austin Metropolitan Ministries—Austin, TX
Christian Council of Metropolitan Atlanta—Atlanta, GA
Churches United of the Quad City Area—Rock Island, IL
Eastern Area Community Ministries—Louisville, KY
Ecumenical Ministries of Oregon—Portland, OR
Interfaith Service Bureau—Sacramento, CA
InterReligious Council of Central New York—Syracuse, NY
The Joint Religious Legislative Coalition—Minneapolis, MN
Lincoln Interfaith Council—Lincoln, NE
The Long Island Council of Churches—Hempstead, NY
Minnesota Council of Churches—Minneapolis, MN
Mississippi Religious Leadership Conference —Jackson, MS
Network of Religious Communities—Buffalo, NY
Northside Inter-Church Agency (NICA)—Fort Worth, TX
The Rhode Island State Council of Churches—Providence, RI
Southside Area Ministries, Inc. (SAM)—Fort Worth, TX
United Religious Community of St. Joseph County—South Bend, IN
Virginia Council of Churches, Inc.—Richmond, VA
Washington Association of Churches—Seattle, WA

Rural Issues

Alaska Christian Conference—Fairbanks, AK
Asheville-Buncombe Community Christian Ministry (ABCCM)—Asheville, NC
Association of Christian Churches—Sioux Falls, SD
Ecumenical Ministries of Iowa (EMI)—Des Moines, IA
Ecumenical Ministries of Oregon—Portland, OR
Georgia Christian Council—Macon, GA
Interchurch Ministries of Nebraska—Lincoln, NE
Interfaith Conference of Greater Milwaukee—Milwaukee, WI
The Joint Religious Legislative Coalition—Minneapolis, MN
Kansas Ecumenical Ministries—Topeka, KS
Kentucky Council of Churches—Lexington, KY
Lincoln Interfaith Council—Lincoln, NE
Louisiana Interchurch Conference—Baton Rouge, LA
Madison Urban Ministry—Madison, WI
Minnesota Council of Churches—Minneapolis, MN
Mississippi Religious Leadership Conference —Jackson, MS
Montana Association of Churches—Billings, MT
New York State Community of Churches, Inc. —Albany, NY
North Carolina Council of Churches—Raleigh, NC
North Dakota Conference of Churches—Bismarck, ND

Ohio Council of Churches—Columbus, OH
Oklahoma Conference of Churches—Oklahoma City, OK
The Pennsylvania Council of Churches—Harrisburg, PA
Reading Berks Conference of Churches—Reading, PA
The Rhode Island State Council of Churches—Providence, RI
Rural Migrant Ministry—Poughkeepsie, NY
United Churches of Lycoming County—Williamsport, PA
Virginia Council of Churches, Inc.—Richmond, VA
West Virginia Council of Churches—Charleston, WV
Wisconsin Council of Churches—Sun Prairie, WI

Senior Citizen Programs

Allegheny Valley Association of Churches—Natrona Heights, PA
Asheville-Buncombe Community Christian Ministry (ABCCM)—Asheville, NC
The Associated Churches of Fort Wayne & Allen County, Inc.—Fort Wayne, IN
Association of Religious Communities—Danbury, CT
Attleboro Area Council of Churches, Inc.—Attleboro, MA
Austin Metropolitan Ministries—Austin, TX
Bergen County Council of Churches—Bergenfield, NJ
Broome County Council of Churches, Inc.—Binghamton, NY
Capital Area Council of Churches, Inc.—Albany, NY
The Capitol Region Conference of Churches—Hartford, CT
Center for Community Concerns—Racine, WI
Christians United in Beaver County—Beaver, PA
Church Council of Greater Seattle—Seattle, WA
Community Ministries of Rockville—Rockville, MD
Concerned Ecumenical Ministry to the Upper West Side—Buffalo, NY
Council of Churches of the Ozarks—Springfield, MO
Council of Churches and Synagogues of Southwestern Connecticut—Stamford, CT
Eastern Area Community Ministries—Louisville, KY
Fern Creek/Highview United Ministries—Louisvlle, KY
Georgia Christian Council—Macon, GA
Greater Bethlehem Area Council of Churches—Bethlehem, PA
Greater Chicago Broadcast Ministries—Chicago, IL
Greater Minneapolis Council of Churches—Minneapolis, MN
Inter-Church Council of Greater New Bedford—New Bedford, MA
Inter-Church Ministries of Erie County—Erie, PA
Interfaith Community Council, Inc.—New Albany, IN
Interfaith Community Services—St. Joseph, MO
Interfaith Council of Contra Costa County—Walnut Creek, CA
InterReligious Council of Central New York—Syracuse, NY
The Joint Religious Legislative Coalition—Minneapolis, MN
Lincoln Interfaith Council—Lincoln, NE
Louisiana Interchurch Conference—Baton Rouge, LA
Michigan Ecumenical Forum—Lansing, MI
Northside Inter-Church Agency (NICA)—Fort Worth, TX
Northwest Interfaith Movement—Philadelphia, PA
Oak Park-River Forest Community of Congregations—Oak Park, IL
Oklahoma Conference of Churches—Oklahoma City, OK
Paducah Cooperative Ministry—Paducah, KY
Peoria Friendship House of Christian Service—Peoria, IL
The Rhode Island State Council of Churches—Providence, RI
San Fernando Valley Interfaith Council—Chatsworth, CA
South Hills Interfaith Ministries—Library, PA
South Louisville Community Ministries—Louisville, KY
Southeast Ecumenical Ministry—Rochester, NY
Southside Area Ministries, Inc. (SAM)—Fort Worth, TX
Tarrant Area Community of Churches—Fort Worth, TX
Toledo Ecumenical Area Ministries—Toledo, OH
United Churches of Lycoming County—Williamsport, PA
Washington Association of Churches—Seattle, WA
West Central Neighborhood Ministry, Inc.—Fort Wayne, IN
West Side Ecumenical Ministry—Cleveland, OH

Substance Abuse Programs

Asheville-Buncombe Community Christian Ministry (ABCCM)—Asheville, NC
Austin Metropolitan Ministries—Austin, TX
Bergen County Council of Churches—Bergenfield, NJ
Christian Conference of Connecticut—Hartford, CT
Community Ministries of Rockville—Rockville, MD

Corpus Christi Metro Ministries—Corpus Christi, TX
Council of Churches of the Ozarks—Springfield, MO
East End Cooperative Ministry—Pittsburgh, PA
Eastern Area Community Ministries—Louisville, KY
Ecumenical Ministries of Oregon—Portland, OR
Evanston Ecumenical Action Council—Evanston, IL
Graymoor Ecumenical & Interreligious Institute—New York, NY
Greater Chicago Broadcast Ministries—Chicago, IL
Greensboro Urban Ministry—Greensboro, NC
The Joint Religious Legislative Coalition—Minneapolis, MN
Lincoln Interfaith Council—Lincoln, NE
Metropolitan Ecumenical Ministry Community Development Corp.—Newark, NJ
New Hampshire Council of Churches—Concord, NH
New York State Community of Churches, Inc.—Albany, NY
Northside Common Ministries—Pittsburgh, PA
The Rhode Island State Council of Churches—Providence, RI
Staten Island Council of Churches—Staten Island, NY
Toledo Ecumenical Area Ministries—Toledo, OH
United Churches of Lycoming County—Williamsport, PA
United Religious Community of St. Joseph County—South Bend, IN

Theology and Worship Programs

Akron Area Association of Churches—Akron, OH
The Associated Churches of Fort Wayne & Allen County, Inc.—Fort Wayne, IN
Associated Ministries of Tacoma-Pierce County—Tacoma, WA
Association of Christian Churches—Sioux Falls, SD
Attleboro Area Council of Churches, Inc.—Attleboro, MA
Bergen County Council of Churches—Bergenfield, NJ
Berrien County Association of Churches—Benton Harbor, MI
Broome County Council of Churches, Inc.—Binghamton, NY
Capital Area Council of Churches, Inc.—Albany, NY
Christian Council of Metropolitan Atlanta—Atlanta, GA
Church Council of Greater Seattle—Seattle, WA
The Church Federation of Greater Indianapolis, Inc.—Indianapolis, IN
Churches United of the Quad City Area—Rock Island, IL
Council of Churches of Greater Springfield—Springfield, MA
The Council of Churches of Santa Clara County—San Jose, CA
Council of Churches and Synagogues of Southwestern Connecticut—Stamford, CT
Ecclesia—Trenton, NJ
Ecumenical Conference of Greater Altoona—Altoona, PA
The Ecumenical Council of Pasadena Area Churches—Pasadena, CA
Ecumenical Ministries—Fulton, MO
Ecumenical Ministries of Iowa (EMI)—Des Moines, IA
Ecumenical Ministries of Oregon—Portland, OR
Georgia Christian Council—Macon, GA
Grand Rapids Area Center for Ecumenism (GRACE)—Grand Rapids, MI
Greater Chicago Broadcast Ministries—Chicago, IL
Greater Dayton Christian Connections—Dayton, OH
Greater Fairmont Council of Churches—Fairmont, WV
Greater New Orleans Federation of Churches—New Orleans, LA
Greater Rochester Community of Churches—Rochester, NY
The Greater Wheeling Council of Churches—Wheeling, WV
Greensboro Urban Ministry—Greensboro, NC
Illinois Conference of Churches—Springfield, IL
In One Accord—Battle Creek, MI
Indiana Partners for Christian Unity and Mission—Indianapolis, IN
Inter-Church Council of Greater New Bedford—New Bedford, MA
Inter-Church Ministries of Erie County—Erie, PA
Interchurch Ministries of Nebraska—Lincoln, NE
Interfaith Mission Service—Huntsville, AL
Kansas Ecumenical Ministries—Topeka, KS
Kentucky Council of Churches—Lexington, KY
Lehigh County Conference of Churches—Allentown, PA
Lincoln Interfaith Council—Lincoln, NE
Marin Interfaith Council—Novato, CA
Massachusetts Council of Churches—Boston, MA
Metropolitan Christian Council of Philadelphia—Philadelphia, PA
The Metropolitan Christian Council: Detroit-Windsor—Detroit, MI
Michigan Ecumenical Forum—Lansing, MI

Montana Association of Churches—Billings, MT
Muskegon County Cooperating Churches—Muskegon, MI
Network of Religious Communities—Buffalo, NY
New Britain Area Conference of Churches (NEWBRACC)—New Britain, CT
North Carolina Council of Churches—Raleigh, NC
Northern Kentucky Interfaith Commission, Inc.—Newport, KY
Northside Common Ministries—Pittsburgh, PA
Northside Inter-Church Agency (NICA)—Fort Worth, TX
Oak Park-River Forest Community of Congregations—Oak Park, IL
Ohio Council of Churches—Columbus, OH
Oklahoma Conference of Churches—Oklahoma City, OK
The Pennsylvania Council of Churches—Harrisburg, PA
The Rhode Island State Council of Churches—Providence, RI
Schenectady Inner City Ministry—Schenectady, NY
South Coast Ecumenical Council—Long Beach, CA
South East Associated Ministries (SEAM)—Louisville, KY
South Louisville Community Ministries—Louisville, KY
Southern California Ecumenical Council—Pasadena, CA
Spokane Council of Ecumenical Ministries—Spokane, WA
Staten Island Council of Churches—Staten Island, NY
Tarrant Area Community of Churches—Fort Worth, TX
Texas Conference of Churches—Austin, TX
Toledo Ecumenical Area Ministries—Toledo, OH
Vermont Ecumenical Council and Bible Society—Burlington, VT
Virginia Council of Churches, Inc.—Richmond, VA
Washington Association of Churches—Seattle, WA
West Virginia Council of Churches—Charleston, WV
Wisconsin Council of Churches—Sun Prairie, WI
Worcester County Ecumenical Council—Worcester, MA

Women's Issues

Asheville-Buncombe Community Christian Ministry (ABCCM)—Asheville, NC
The Associated Churches of Fort Wayne & Allen County, Inc.—Fort Wayne, IN
Bergen County Council of Churches—Bergenfield, NJ
Berrien County Association of Churches—Benton Harbor, MI
Center for the Prevention of Sexual and Domestic Violence—Seattle, WA
Christian Council of Metropolitan Atlanta—Atlanta, GA
Church Council of Greater Seattle—Seattle, WA
Community Ministries of Rockville—Rockville, MD
Concerned Ecumenical Ministry to the Upper West Side—Buffalo, NY
Council of Churches of the City of New York—New York, NY
The Council of Churches of Santa Clara County—San Jose, CA
East End Cooperative Ministry—Pittsburgh, PA
Ecclesia—Trenton, NJ
The Ecumenical Council of Pasadena Area Churches—Pasadena, CA
Georgia Christian Council—Macon, GA
Greater Chicago Broadcast Ministries—Chicago, IL
Greater Minneapolis Council of Churches—Minneapolis, MN
Inter-Church Council of Greater New Bedford—New Bedford, MA
Interchurch Ministries of Nebraska—Lincoln, NE
The Joint Religious Legislative Coalition—Minneapolis, MN
Lincoln Interfaith Council—Lincoln, NE
The Long Island Council of Churches—Hempstead, NY
Metropolitan Christian Council of Philadelphia—Philadelphia, PA
Network of Religious Communities—Buffalo, NY
New Mexico Conference of Churches—Albuquerque, NM
New York State Community of Churches, Inc.—Albany, NY
North Carolina Council of Churches—Raleigh, NC
Oklahoma Conference of Churches—Oklahoma City, OK
Peoria Friendship House of Christian Service—Peoria, IL
The Rhode Island State Council of Churches—Providence, RI
South Coast Ecumenical Council—Long Beach, CA
South Hills Interfaith Ministries—Library, PA
Spokane Council of Ecumenical Ministries—Spokane, WA
United Ministries—Greenville, SC
Virginia Council of Churches, Inc.—Richmond, VA
Washington Association of Churches—Seattle, WA

West Central Neighborhood Ministry, Inc.—Fort Wayne, IN
Wisconsin Council of Churches—Sun Prairie, WI

Youth Activities

Arkansas Interfaith Conference—Scott, AR
Asheville-Buncombe Community Christian Ministry (ABCCM)—Asheville, NC
The Associated Churches of Fort Wayne & Allen County, Inc.—Fort Wayne, IN
Association of Christian Churches—Sioux Falls, SD
Attleboro Area Council of Churches, Inc.—Attleboro, MA
Austin Metropolitan Ministries—Austin, TX
Bergen County Council of Churches—Bergenfield, NJ
Brooklyn Council of Churches—Brooklyn, NY
Broome County Council of Churches, Inc.—Binghamton, NY
Center City Churches—Hartford, CT
Christian Council of Metropolitan Atlanta—Atlanta, GA
Church Council of Greater Seattle—Seattle, WA
The Church Federation of Greater Indianapolis, Inc.—Indianapolis, IN
Concerned Ecumenical Ministry to the Upper West Side—Buffalo, NY
Council of Churches of Greater Bridgeport, Inc.—Bridgeport, CT
The Council of Churches of Santa Clara County—San Jose, CA
East End Cooperative Ministry—Pittsburgh, PA
Eastern Area Community Ministries—Louisville, KY
Ecclesia—Trenton, NJ
Ecumenical Ministries—Fulton, MO
Evanston Ecumenical Action Council—Evanston, IL
Fern Creek/Highview United Ministries—Louisvlle, KY
Genesee-Orleans Ministry of Concern—Albion, NY
Greater Bethlehem Area Council of Churches—Bethlehem, PA
Greater Chicago Broadcast Ministries—Chicago, IL
Greater Fairmont Council of Churches—Fairmont, WV
Greater Minneapolis Council of Churches—Minneapolis, MN
Inter-Church Council of Greater New Bedford—New Bedford, MA
Interfaith Community Council, Inc.—New Albany, IN
Interfaith Community Services—St. Joseph, MO
Lehigh County Conference of Churches—Allentown, PA
Lincoln Interfaith Council—Lincoln, NE
The Long Island Council of Churches—Hempstead, NY
Metropolitan Ecumenical Ministry Community Development Corp.—Newark, NJ
Network of Religious Communities—Buffalo, NY
New Britain Area Conference of Churches (NEWBRACC)—New Britain, CT
Northside Common Ministries—Pittsburgh, PA
Northside Inter-Church Agency (NICA)—Fort Worth, TX
Oak Park-River Forest Community of Congregations—Oak Park, IL
Peoria Friendship House of Christian Service—Peoria, IL
Reading Berks Conference of Churches—Reading, PA
The Rhode Island State Council of Churches—Providence, RI
Rural Migrant Ministry—Poughkeepsie, NY
St. Paul Area Council of Churches—St. Paul, MN
Schenectady Inner City Ministry—Schenectady, NY
South Coast Ecumenical Council—Long Beach, CA
South East Associated Ministries (SEAM)—Louisville, KY
South Hills Interfaith Ministries—Library, PA
South Louisville Community Ministries—Louisville, KY
Southside Area Ministries, Inc. (SAM)—Fort Worth, TX
Spokane Council of Ecumenical Ministries—Spokane, WA
Toledo Ecumenical Area Ministries—Toledo, OH
United Churches of Lycoming County—Williamsport, PA
West Central Neighborhood Ministry, Inc.—Fort Wayne, IN
West Side Ecumenical Ministry—Cleveland, OH
West Virginia Council of Churches—Charleston, WV

8. Canadian Regional and Local Ecumenical Bodies

Most of the Organizations listed below are councils of churches in which churches participate officially, whether at the parish or judicatory level. They operate at the city, metropolitan area, or county level. Parish clusters within urban areas are not included.

Canadian local ecumenical bodies operate without paid staff, with the exception of a few which have part-time staff. In most cases the name and address of the president or chairperson is listed. As these offices change from year to year, some of this information may be out of date by the time the *Yearbook of American and Canadian Churches* is published.

ALBERTA

Calgary Council of Churches

c/o Anna Tremblay, Ecumenical & Inter-religious Affairs, 120 17th Ave., Calgary, AB T2S 2T2, (403)218-5521

Calgary Inter-Faith Community Association

P.O. Box 93, Stn. M, Calgary, AB T2P 2G9, (403)262-5111

BRITISH COLUMBIA

Canadian Ecumenical Action

Co-ordinator, 1410 West 12th Ave., Vancouver, BC V6H 1M8

Greater Victoria Council of Churches

c/o Rev. Edwin Taylor, St. Alban's Church, 1468 Ryan St. at Balmont, Victoria, BC V8R 2X1

Vancouver Council of Churches

Murray Moerman, 700 Kingsway, Vancouver, BC V5V 3C1 Tel. (604)420-0761

MANITOBA

Association of Christian Churches in Manitoba

The Rev. Ted Chell, President, 484 Maryland St., Winnipeg, Manitoba R3G 1M5 Tel. (204)774-3143 or (204)775-3536

NEW BRUNSWICK

Atlantic Ecumenical Council of Churches

Rev. Rufus Onyewuchi, 170 Daniel Ave., Saint John, NB E2K 4S7, (506) 652-8732

First Miramichi Inter-Church Council

Pres., Ellen Robinson, Doaktown, NB E0C 1G0

Moncton Area Council of Churches

Rev. Donald Routledge, 135 Mount Royal Blvd., Moncton, NB E1E 2V5, (506) 382-7725

NEWFOUNDLAND

St. John's Area Council Of Churches

Rev. Canon Ralph Billard, 31 Hazelwood Cres., St. John's, NF, A1E 6B3, (709)579-0536

NOVA SCOTIA

Amherst and Area Council of Churches

Mrs. Jean Miller, President, R.R.#3 1065 HWY 204, Amherst, NS B4H 3Y1 Tel. (902)667-8107

Atlantic Ecumenical Council of Churches

Pres., Rev. John E. Boyd, Box 637, 90 Victoria St., Amherst, NS B4H 4B4

Bridgewater Inter-Church Council

Pres., Wilson Jones, 30 Parkdale Ave., Bridgewater, NS B4V 1L8

Cornwallis District Inter-Church Council

Pres., Mr. Tom Regan, Centreville, R.R. #2, Kings County, NS BOT 1JO

Halifax-Dartmouth Council of Churches

Mrs. Betty Short, 3 Virginia Avenue, Dartmouth, NS B2W 2Z4

Industrial Cape Breton Council of Churches

Rev. Karen Ralph, 24 Huron Ave., Sydney Mines, NS B1S 1V2

Kentville Council of Churches
Rev. Canon S.J.P. Davies, 325-325 Main St., Kentville, NS B4N 1C5

Lunenburg Queens BA Association
Mrs. Nilda Chute, 56 Hillside Dr., R.R. #4, Bridgewater, NS B4V 2W3

Mahone Bay Interchurch Council
Patricia Joudrey, R.R. #1., Blockhouse, NS B0J 1E0

Pictou Council of Churches
Rev. D. J. Murphy, Sec., P.O. Box 70, Pictou, NS B0K 1H0

Queens County Association of Churches
Mr. Donald Burns, Box 537, Liverpool, NS B0T 1K6

ONTARIO

Burlington Inter-Church Council
Mr. Fred Townsend, 425 Breckenwood, Burlington, ON L7L 2J6

Christian Leadership Council of Downtown Toronto
Ken Bhagan, Chair, 40 Homewood Ave, #509, Toronto, ON M4Y 2K2

Ecumenical Committee
Rev. William B. Kidd, 76 Eastern Ave., Sault Ste. Marie, ON P6A 4R2

Glengarry-Prescott-Russell Christian Council
Pres., Rev. G. Labrosse, St. Eugene's, Prescott, ON K0B 1P0

Hamilton & District Christian Churches Association
The Rev. Dr. John Johnston, 147 Chedoke Avenue, Hamilton, ON L8P 4P2 Tel. (905) 529-6896, (905)528-2730, Fax (905)521-2539

Ignace Council of Churches
Box 5, 205 Pine St., St. Ignace, ON P0T 1H0

Inter Church Council of Burlington
Michael Bittle, Box 62120 Burlington Mall R.P.O., Burlington, ON L7R 4K2 Tel. (905) 526-1523 Fax (509)526-9056
Email: mbittle@istar.ca
Website: http://home.istar.cal/mbittle/eo_schl.htm

Kitchener-Waterloo Council of Churches
Rev. Clarence Hauser, CR, 53 Allen St. E., Waterloo, ON N2J 1J3

London Inter-City Faith Team
David Carouthers, Chair, c/o United Church, 711 Colbourne St., London, ON N6A 3Z4

Massey Inter-Church Council
The Rev. Hope Jackson, Box 238, Massey, ON P0P 1P0 Tel. (705)865-2630

Ottawa Christian Council of the Capital Area
1247 Kilborn Ave., Ottawa, ON K1H 6K9

St. Catharines & Dist. Clergy Fellowship
Rev. Victor Munro, 663 Vince St., St. Catharines, ON L2M 3V8

Spadina-Bloor Interchurch Council
Rev. Frances Combes, Chair, c/o Bathurst St. United Church, 427 Bloor St. W, Toronto, ON M5S 1X7

Stratford & District Council of Churches
Rev. Ted Heinze, Chair, 202 Erie St., Stratford, ON N5A 2M8

Thorold Inter-Faith Council
1 Dunn St., St. Catharines, ON L2T 1P3

Thunder Bay Council of Churches
Rev. Richard Darling, 1800 Moodie St. E., Thunder Bay, ON P7E 4Z2

PRINCE EDWARD ISLAND

Atlantic Ecumenical Council
The Rev. Arthur Pendergast, Secretary, Immaculate Conception Church, St. Louis, PEI C0B 1Z0 Tel. (902)963-2202 or (902)822-2622

Summerside Christian Council
Ms. A. Kathleen Miller, P.O. Box 1551, Summerside, PEI C1N 4K4

QUEBEC

Canadian Centre for Ecumenism/ Centre d'oecuménisme
Fr. Emmanuel Lapierre, 2065 Sherbrooke Street West, Montreal, QC H3H 1G6 Tel. (514)937-9176 Fax (514)937-2684

Christian Direction
The Rev. Glen Smith, #3602-465 St. Antoine St. W., Montreal, QC H2Z 1J1

The Ecumenical Group
c/o Mrs. C. Haten, 1185 Ste. Foy, St. Bruno, QC J3V 3C3

Hemmingford Ecumenical Committee

c/o Catherine Priest, Box 300, Hemmingford, QC J0L 1H0

Montréal Council of Churches

The Rev. Ralph Watson, 4995 Coronation Avenue, Montréal, QC H4V 2E1 Tel. (514)484-7196

Montreal Association for the Blind Foundation

The Rev. Dr. John A. Simms, 7000 Sherbrooke St. W., Montreal, QC H4B 1R3 Tel. (514)489-8201

SASKATCHEWAN

Humboldt Clergy Council

Fr. Leo Hinz, OSB, Box 1989, Humboldt, SK S0K 2A0

Melville Association of Churches

Attn., Catherine Gaw, Box 878, Melville, SK S0A 2P0

Regina Council of Churches

The Rev. Bud Harper, 5 Robinson Crescent, Regina, SK S4R 3R1 Tel. (306)545-3375

Saskatoon Centre for Ecumenism

Nicholas Jesson, 1006 Broadway, Saskatoon, SK S7N 1B9 Tel. (306)553-1633 Fax (306)242-8916

Email: sce@sfn.saskatoon.sk.ca

Saskatoon Council of Churches

Dr. Colin Clay, 812 Colony St., Saskatoon, SK S7H 0S1

9. Theological Seminaries and Bible Colleges in the United States

The following list includes theological seminaries and departments in colleges and universities in which ministerial training is given. Many denominations have additional programs. The lists of Religious Bodies in the United States (Directory 3) should be consulted for the address of denominational headquarters.

Inclusion in or exclusion from this list implies no judgment about the quality or accreditation of any institution. Those schools that are members of the Association of Theological Schools are marked with an asterisk (*). Additional information about enrollment in ATS member schools can be found in the "Trends in Seminary Enrollment" section of chapter III.

Each of the listings include: the institution name, denominational sponsor when appropriate, location, the president or dean of the institution, telephone and fax numbers, and email and website addresses when available.

Abilene Christian University (Churches of Christ), Royce Money, Ph.D., President, ACU Box 29100, Abilene, TX 79699-9100 Tel. (915)674-2412, Fax (915)674-2958
Email: moneyr@acu.edu
Website: www.acu.edu

Alaska Bible College (Nondenominational), Steven J. Hostetter, President, P.O. Box 289, Glennallen, AK 99588 Tel. (907)822-3201, Fax (907)822-5027
Email: info@akbible.edu
Website: www.akbible.edu

Alliance Theological Seminary* (The Christian and Missionary Alliance), David L. Rambo, President, 350 N. Highland Ave., Nyack, NY 10960-1416 Tel. (914)353-2020, Fax (914) 358-2651

American Baptist College (National Baptist Convention U.S.A., Inc.), Dr. Forrest E. Harris, President, 1800 Baptist World Center Dr., Nashville, TN 37207 Tel. (615)228-7877, Fax (615)226-7855
Email: harrisfe@abcnash.edu

American Baptist Seminary of the West* (American Baptist Churches in the U .S.A.), Dr. Keith A. Russell, President, 2606 Dwight Way, Berkeley, CA 94704-3029 Tel. (510)841-1905, Fax (510)841-2446
Email: krussell@absw.edu
Website: www.absw.edu

Anderson University School of Theology* (Church of God (Anderson, Ind.)), David Sebastian, President, Anderson University, Anderson, IN 46012-3495 Tel. (765)641-4032, Fax (765)641-3005

Andover Newton Theological School* (American Baptist Churches in the U.S.A.; United Church of Christ), Benjamin Griffin, President, 210 Herrick Rd., Newton Centre, MA 02459 Tel. (617)964-1100, Fax (617)965-9756
Email: admissions@ants.edu
Website: www.ants.edu

Appalachian Bible College (Nondenominational), Daniel L. Anderson, President, P.O. Box ABC, Bradley, WV 25818 Tel. (304) 877-6428 or (800)678-9222, Fax (304)877-5082
Email: abc@appbibco.edu
Website: www.abc.edu

Aquinas Institute of Theology* (The Roman Catholic Church), Charles E. Bouchard, President, 3642 Lindell Blvd., St. Louis, MO 63108 Tel. (314)977-3882, Fax (314)977-7225
Email: aquinas@slu.edu
Website: www.ai.edu

Arizona College of the Bible (Interdenominational), Douglas K. Winn, President, 2045 W. Northern Ave., Phoenix, AZ 85021-5197 Tel. (602)995-2670, Fax (602)864-8183

Arlington Baptist College (Baptist), David Bryant, President, 3001 W. Division, Arlington, TX 76012-3425 Tel. (817)461-8741, Fax (817)274-1138

Asbury Theological Seminary* (Interdenominational), Maxie D. Dunnam, President, 204 N. Lexington Ave., Wilmore, KY 40390-1199 Tel. 859-858-3581, Fax 859-858-2248
Website: www.asburyseminary.edu

Ashland Theological Seminary* (Brethren Church (Ashland, Ohio)), Frederick J. Finks, President, 910 Center St., Ashland, OH 44805 Tel. (419)289-5161, Fax (419)289-5969

Assemblies of God Theological Seminary* (Assemblies of God), Byron D. Klaus, President, 1435 North Glenstone Avenue, Springfield, MO 65802-2131 Tel. (417)268-1000, Fax (417)268-1001
Email: agts@agseminary.edu
Website: www.agts.edu

Associated Mennonite Biblical Seminary* (Mennonite Church; General Conference Mennonite Church), J. Nelson Kraybill, President, 3003 Benham Ave., Elkhart, IN 46517-1999 Tel. (219)295-3726, Fax (219) 295-0092

Email: nkraybill@ambs.edu
Website: www.ambs.edu

Athenaeum of Ohio* (The Roman Catholic Church), Robert J. Mooney, President, 6616 Beechmont Ave., Cincinnati, OH 45230-2091 Tel. (513)231-2223, Fax (513)231-3254

Atlanta Christian College (Christian Churches and Churches of Christ), R. Edwin Groover, President, 2605 Ben Hill Rd., East Point, GA 30344 Tel. (404)761-8861, Fax (404)669-2024
Email: admissions@acc.edu
Website: www.acc.edu

Austin Presbyterian Theological Seminary* (Presbyterian Church (U.S.A.)), Robert M. Shelton, President, 100 E. 27th St., Austin, TX 78705-5797 Tel. (512)472-6736, Fax (512) 479-0738
Website: www.austinseminary.edu

Azusa Pacific University* (Interdenominational), Jon R. Wallace, Acting President, 901 E. Alosta, P.O. Box 7000, Azusa, CA 91702 Tel. (626)969-3434, Fax (626)969-7180
Website: www.apu.edu

Bangor Theological Seminary* (United Church of Christ), William C. Imes, President, 300 Union St., Bangor, ME 04401 Tel. (207)942-6781, Fax (207)942-4914
Email: jwiebe@bts.edu
Website: www.bts.edu

Baptist Bible College (Baptist Bible Fellowship International), Leland Kennedy, President, 628 E. Kearney, Springfield, MO 65803 Tel. (417)268-6060, Fax (417)268-6694

Baptist Bible College and Seminary (Baptist), Jim Jeffery, President, 538 Venard Rd., Clarks Summit, PA 18411 Tel. (570)586-2400, Fax (570)586-1753
Email: bbc@bbc.edu
Website: www.bbc.edu

Baptist Missionary Association Theological Seminary (Baptist Missionary Association of America), Charley Holmes, President, 1530 E. Pine St., Jacksonville, TX 75766 Tel. (903) 586-2501, Fax (903)586-0378
Email: bmaisem@flash.net-
Website: www.geocities.com/Athens/Acropolis/3386

Baptist Theological Seminary at Richmond* (Cooperative Baptist Fellowship), Thomas H. Graves, President, 3400 Brook Rd., Richmond, VA 23227 Tel. (804)355-8135, Fax (804)355-8182
Email: btsr@btsr.edu
Website: www.btsr.edu

Barclay College (Interdenominational), Maurice G. Chandler, President, 607 N Kingman, Haviland, KS 67059 Tel. 620-862-5252, Fax 620-862-5403
Email: barclaycollege@havilandtalco.com

Bay Ridge Christian College (Church of God (Anderson, Ind.)), Dr. Verda Beach, President, P.O. Box 726, Kendleton, TX 77451 Tel. 979-532-3982, Fax 979-532-4352

Beeson Divinity School of Samford University* (Interdenominational), Timothy George, Dean, President, 800 Lakeshore Dr., Birmingham, AL 35229-2252 Tel. (205)726-2991, Fax (205)726-2003
Email: tfgeorge@samford.edu
Website: http://beeson.samford.edu

Bethany College (Assemblies of God), Tom Duncan, President, 800 Bethany Dr., Scotts Valley, CA 95066 Tel. (408)438-3800, Fax (408)438-4517

Bethany Lutheran Theological Seminary (Evangelical Lutheran Synod), G. R. Schmeling, President, 6 Browns Ct., Mankato, MN 56001 Tel. (507)344-7354, Fax (507)344-7426
Email: gschmeli@blc.edu
Website: www.blts.edu

Bethany Theological Seminary* (Church of the Brethren), Eugene F. Roop, President, 615 National Rd. W., Richmond, IN 47374 Tel. (765)983-1800, Fax (765)983-1840
Email: roopge@bethanyseminary.edu
Website: www.brethren.org/bethany

Bethel Seminary* (Baptist General Conference), George K. Brushaber, President, 3949 Bethel Dr., St. Paul, MN 55112 Tel. (651)638-6230, Fax (651)638-6008
Email: webmaster@bethel.edu
Website: www.bethel.edu

Bethel Seminary of the East* (Conservative Baptist Association of America), Philip J. Baur, President, 1605 N. Limekiln Pike, Dresher, PA 19025 Tel. (215)641-4801, Fax (215)641-4804

Beulah Heights Bible College (The International Pentecostal Church of Christ), Samuel R. Chand, President, 892 Berne St. SE, Atlanta, GA 30316 Tel. (404)627-2681, Fax (404)627-0702
Email: b.h.b.c@beulah.org
Website: www.beulah.org

Bible Church of Christ Theological Institute (Nondenominational), Roy Bryant; Sr., President, 1358 Morris Ave., Bronx, NY 10456-1402 Tel. (718)588-2284, Fax (718) 92-5597
Website: www.thebiblechurchofchrist.org

Biblical Theological Seminary* (Interdenominational), David G. Dunbar, President, 200 N. Main St., Hatfield, PA 19440 Tel. (215)368-5000, Fax (215)368-7002
Email: president@biblical.edu
Website: www.biblical.edu

Boise Bible College (Christian Churches and Churches of Christ), Dr. Charles A. Crane, President, 8695 Marigold St., Boise, ID 83714 Tel. (208)376-7731, Fax (208)376-7743
Email: boisebible@boisebible.edu
Website: www.boisebible.edu

Boston University (School of Theology)* (The United Methodist Church), Dr. Robert C. Neville, Dean, 745 Commonwealth Ave., Boston, MA 02215 Tel. (617)353-3050, Fax (617)353-3061
Website: www.bu.edu

Brite Divinity School, Texas Christian University* (Christian Church (Disciples of Christ)), Leo G. Perdue, President, TCU Box 298130, Ft. Worth, TX 76129 Tel. (817)921-7575, Fax (817)921-7305
Email: L.Perdue@tcu.edu
Website: www.brite.tcu.edu/brite/

Calvary Bible College and Theological Seminary (Independent Fundamental Churches of America), James L. Anderson, President, 15800 Calvary Rd., Kansas City, MO 64147-1341 Tel. (800)326-3960, Fax (816)331-4474

Calvin Theological Seminary* (Christian Reformed Church in North America), President Cornelius Plantinga, Jr., President, 3233 Burton St. S.E., Grand Rapids, MI 49546-4387 Tel. (616)957-6036, Fax (616) 957-8621
Email: kprg@calvin.edu
Website: www.calvin.edu/seminary

Candler School of Theology, Emory University* (The United Methodist Church), Russell E. Richey, Dean, 500 Kilgo Circle N.E., Emory Univ., Atlanta, GA 30322 Tel. (404)727-6324, Fax (404)727-3182
Email: candler@emory.edu
Website: www.emory.edu/candler

Catholic Theological Union at Chicago* (The Roman Catholic Church), Donald Senior, C.P., President, 5401 S. Cornell Ave., Chicago, IL 60615-5698 Tel. 773-324-8000, Fax 773-324-8490
Website: www.ctu.edu

Catholic University of America* (The Roman Catholic Church), Rev. Stephen Harper, STD., Dean, 113 Caldwell Hall, Cardinal Sta., Washington, DC 20064 Tel. (202)319-5683, Fax (202)319-4967
Email: cua-deansrs@cua.edu
Website: www.cua.edu/www/srs/

Central Baptist College (Baptist Missionary Association of Arkansas), Charles Attebery, President, 1501 College Ave., Conway, AR 72032 Tel. (501)329-6872, Fax (501)329-2941
Email: Cattebery@cbc.edu
Website: www.cbc.edu

Central Baptist Theological Seminary* (Baptist), Thomas E. Clifton, President, 741 N. 31st St., Kansas City, KS 66102-3964 Tel. (913)371-5313, Fax (913)371-8110
Email: central@cbts.edu
Website: www.cbts.edu

Central Baptist Theological Seminary in Indiana (National Baptist Convention U.S.A., Inc.), F. Benjamin Davis, President, 1535 Dr. A. J. Brown Ave. N., Indianapolis, IN 46202 Tel. (317)636-6622
Email: henriettabrown@webtv.net

Central Bible College (Assemblies of God), M. Wayne Benson, President, 3000 N. Grant Ave., Springfield, MO 65803 Tel. (417)833-2551, Fax (417)833-5141
Email: info@cbcag.edu
Website: www.cbcag.edu

Central Christian College of the Bible (Christian Churches and Churches of Christ), Russell N. James III, President, 911 E. Urbandale Dr., Moberly, MO 65270-1997 Tel. (660)263-3900, Fax (660)263-3936
Email: develop@cccb.edu
Website: www.cccb.edu

Central Indian Bible College (Assemblies of God), Robert Koscak, President, P.O. Box 550, Mobridge, SD 57601 Tel. (605)845-7801, Fax (605)845-7744

Chicago Theological Seminary* (United Church of Christ), Susan Brooks Thistlethwaite, President, 5757 South University Ave., Chicago, IL 60637-1507 Tel. (773)752-5757, Fax (773)752-5925
Email: sthistle@chgosem.edu
Website: www.chgosem.edu

Christ the King Seminary* (The Roman Catholic Church), Richard W. Siepka, President, 711 Knox Rd., P.O. Box 607, East Aurora, NY 14052-0607 Tel. (716)652-8900, Fax (716)652-8903
Email: rsiepka@cks.edu

Christ the Savior Seminary (The American Carpatho-Russian Orthodox Greek Catholic Church), Nicholas Smisko, President, 225 Chandler Ave., Johnstown, PA 15906 Tel. (814)539-8086, Fax (814)536-4699
Email: mrosco2@excite.com

Christian Theological Seminary* (Christian Church (Disciples of Christ)), Dr. Edward L. Wheeler, President, 1000 W. 42nd St., Indianapolis, IN 46208 Tel. (317)931-2305, Fax (317)923-1961
Email: ewheeler@cts.edu
Website: www.cts.edu

Church Divinity School of the Pacific* (Episcopal Church), Donn F. Morgan, President, 2451 Ridge Rd., Berkeley, CA 94709 Tel. (510)204-0700, Fax (510)644-0712
Email: rateaver@cdsp.edu

Church of God Theological Seminary* (Church of God (Cleveland, Tenn.)), Cecil B. Knight, President, P.O. Box 3330, Cleveland, TN 37320-3330 Tel. (423)478-1131, Fax (423) 478-7711
Email: cogseminary@wingnet.com
Website: www.wingnet.net/~cogseminary

Cincinnati Bible College and Seminary (Christian Churches and Churches of Christ), David A. Grubbs, President, 2700 Glenway Ave., Cincinnati, OH 45204-3200 Tel. (513) 244-8100 Fax (513)244-8140
Email: info@cincybible.edu
Website: www.cincybible.edu

Circleville Bible College (Churches of Christ in Christian Union), John Conley, President, P.O. Box 458, Circleville, OH 43113 Tel. (614)474-8896, Fax (614)477-7755
Email: cbc@biblecollege.edu
Website: www.biblecollege.edu

Claremont School of Theology* (The United Methodist Church), Philip A. Amerson, President, 1325 N. College Ave., Claremont, CA 91711-3199 Tel. (800)626-7821, Fax (909)626-7062
Email: admissions@cst.edu
Website: www.cst.edu

Clear Creek Baptist Bible College (Southern Baptist Convention), President Bill Whittaker, President, 300 Clear Creek Rd., Pineville, KY 40977 Tel. (606)337-3196, Fax (606)337-2372
Email: ccbbc@ccbbc.edu
Website: www.ccbbc.edu

Colegio Biblico Pentecostal de Puerto Rico (Church of God (Cleveland, Tenn.)), Luz M. Rivera, President, P.O. Box 901, Saint Just, PR 00978 Tel. (787)761-0640, Fax (787)748-9228

Colgate Rochester-Crozer Divinity School* (American Baptist Churches in the USA), G. Thomas Halbrooks, President, 1100 S. Goodman St., Rochester, NY 14620 Tel. (716)271-1320, Fax (716)271-8013
Website: www.crcds.edu

Colorado Christian University (Nondenominational), Larry R. Donnithorne, President, 180 S. Garrison St., Lakewood, CO 80226 Tel. (303)202-0100, Fax (303)274-7560
Website: www.ccu.edu

Columbia International University* (Multi-denominational), George W. Murray, President, P.O. Box 3122, Columbia, SC 29230-3122 Tel. (803)754-4100, Fax (803) 786-4209

Columbia Theological Seminary* (Presbyterian Church (U.S.A.)), Laura S. Mendenhall, President, 701 Columbia Dr., P.O. Box 520, Decatur, GA 30031 Tel. (404) 378-8821, Fax (404)377-9696
Website: www.ctsnet.edu

Concordia Seminary* (The Lutheran Church-Missouri Synod), John F. Johnson, President, 801 De Mun Ave., St. Louis, MO 63105 Tel. (314)505-7000, Fax (314)505-7001

Concordia Theological Seminary* (The Lutheran Church-Missouri Synod), Dean O. Wenthe, President, 6600 N. Clinton St., Ft. Wayne, IN 46825-4996 Tel. (219)452-2100, Fax (219)452-2121
Email: sem_relations@ctsfw.edu
Website: www.ctsfw.edu

Covenant Theological Seminary* (Prebyterian Church in America), Bryan Chapell, President, 12330 Conway Rd., St. Louis, MO 63141-8697 Tel. (314)434-4044, Fax (314)434-4819
Email: admissions@covenantseminary.edu
Website: www.covenantseminary.edu

Cranmer Seminary (The Episcopal Orthodox Church; The Anglican Orthodox Church; The Anglican Rite Synod in the Americas; The Orthodox Anglican Communion), The Most Rev. Scott E. McLaughlin, D.D., Ph.D., President, 901 English Rd., High Point, NC 27262 Tel. 336-885-6032, Fax 336-885-6021
Email: seminaryinfo@orthodoxanglican.net
Website: http://cranmerseminary.orthodoxanglican.net

Criswell Center for Biblical Studies (Southern Baptist Convention), , President, 4010 Gaston Ave., Dallas, TX 75246 Tel. (214)821-5433, Fax (214)818-1320

Crown College (The Christian and Missionary Alliance), Gary M. Benedict, President, 6425 County Rd. 30, St. Bonifacius, MN 55375-9001 Tel. (952)446-4100, Fax (952)446-4149
Email: crown@crown.edu
Website: www.crown.edu

Cummins Theological Seminary (Reformed Episcopal Church), James C. West, President, 705 S. Main St., Summerville, SC 29483 Tel. (843)873-3451, Fax (843)875-6200
Email: jcw121@aol.com

Dallas Christian College (Christian Churches and Churches of Christ), Dr. John Derry, President, 2700 Christian Pkwy, Dallas, TX 75234 Tel. (972)241-3371, Fax (972)241-8021
Email: dcc@dallas.edu
Website: www.dallas.edu

Dallas Theological Seminary* (Interdenominational), Dr. Mark L. Bailey, President, 3909 Swiss Ave., Dallas, TX 75204 Tel. (214)824-3094, Fax (214)841-3625
Website: www.dts.edu

Denver Seminary* (Conservative Baptist Association of America), Clyde B. McDowell, President, President, Box 10,000, Denver, CO 80250-0100 Tel. (303)761-2482, Fax (303) 761-8060
Email: info@densem.edu
Website: www.gospelcom.net/densem/

The Disciples Divinity House of the University of Chicago* (Christian Church (Disciples of Christ)), Dr. Kristine A. Culp, Dean, 1156 E. 57th St., Chicago, IL 60637-1536 Tel. (773)643-4411, Fax (773)643-4413
Email: ddh.uchicago.admin@attglobal.net
Website: ddh.uchicago.edu

Dominican House of Studies* (The Roman Catholic Church), Thomas McCreesh, O.P., President, 487 Michigan Ave. N.E., Washington, DC 20017-1585 Tel. (202)529-5300, Fax (202)636-4460
Email: opassistant@aol.com
Website: www.dhs.edu

Dominican School of Philosophy and Theology* (The Roman Catholic Church), Gregory Rocca, President, 2401 Ridge Rd., Berkeley, CA 94709 Tel. (510)849-2030, Fax (510)849-1372

Dominican Study Center of Bayamon Central University (The Roman Catholic Church), P. Felix Struik, O.P., President, Apartado Postal 1968, Bayamon, PR 00960-1968 Tel. (787) 787-1826, Fax (787)798-2712

Drew University (Theological School)* (The United Methodist Church), Maxine C. Beach, President, 36 Madison Ave., Madison, NJ 07940-4010 Tel. (973)408-3258, Fax (973) 408-3534
Website: www.drew.edu

Duke University (Divinity School)* (The United Methodist Church), Dean L. Gregory Jones, Dean, Box 90968, Durham, NC 27708-0968 Tel. (919)660-3400, Fax (919)660-3473
Email: info@div.duke.edu
Website: divinity.duke.edu

Earlham School of Religion* (Interdenominational-Friends), Jay W. Marshall, Dean, 228 College Ave., Richmond, IN 47374 Tel. (800)432-1377, Fax (765)983-1688
Email: woodna@earlham.edu
Website: www.esr.earlham.edu/esr

Eastern Baptist Theological Seminary* (American Baptist Churches in the U.S.A.), R. Scott Rodin, President, 6 Lancaster Ave., Wynnewood, PA 19096 Tel. (800)220-3287, Fax (610)649-3834
Website: www.ebts.edu

Eastern Mennonite Seminary* (Mennonite Church), Joseph L. Lapp, President, Eastern Mennonite Seminary, Harrisonburg, VA 22802 Tel. (540)432-4260, Fax (540)432-4444
Email: info@emu.edu
Website: www.emu.edu/seminary

Eden Theological Seminary* (United Church of Christ), President David M. Greenhaw, President, 475 E. Lockwood Ave., St. Louis, MO 63119-3192 Tel. (314)961-3627, Fax (314)918-2626
Website: www.eden.edu

Emmanuel School of Religion* (Christian Churches and Churches of Christ), C. Robert Wetzel, President, One Walker Dr., Johnson City, TN 37601-9438 Tel. (423)926-1186, Fax (423)926-6198
Email: wetzelr@esr.edu
Website: www.esr.edu

Emmaus Bible College (Christian Brethren (also known as Plymouth Brethren)), Kenneth Alan Daughters, President, 2570 Asbury Rd., Dubuque, IA 52001 Tel. (563)588-8000, Fax (563)588-1216
Email: info@emmaus1.edu
Website: www.emmaus.edu

Episcopal Divinity School* (Episcopal Church), The Rt. Rev. Steven Charleston, President and Dean, 99 Brattle St., Cambridge, MA 02138-3494 Tel. (617)868-3450, Fax (617)864-5385
Email: fphillips@episdivschool.org
Website: www.episdivschool.org

Episcopal Theological Seminary of the Southwest* (Episcopal Church), Durstan R. McDonald, Dean, P.O. Box 2247, Austin, TX 78768-2247 Tel. (512)472-4133, Fax (512) 472-3098
Website: www.etss.edu

Erskine Theological Seminary* (Associate Reformed Presbyterian Church (General Synod)), John L. Carson, President, Drawer 668, Due West, SC 29639 Tel. (864)379-8885, Fax (864)379-2171
Email: carson@erskine.edu
Website: www.erskine.edu/seminary/

Eugene Bible College (Open Bible Standard Churches, Inc.), Robert L. Whitlow, President, 2155 Bailey Hill Rd., Eugene, OR 97405 Tel. (503)485-1780, Fax (503)343-5801

Evangelical School of Theology* (The Evangelical Congregational Church), Kirby N. Keller, President, 121 S. College St., Myerstown, PA 17067 Tel. (717)866-5775, Fax (717)866-4667
Website: www.evangelical.edu

Faith Baptist Bible College and Theological Seminary (General Association of Regular Baptist Churches), Richard W. Houg, President, 1900 N.W. 4th St., Ankeny, IA 50021-2152 Tel. (515)964-0601, Fax (515) 964-1638
Website: www.faith.edu

Faith Evangelical Lutheran Seminary (Conservative Lutheran Association), R. H. Redal, President, 3504 N. Pearl St., Tacoma, WA 98407 Tel. (206)752-2020, Fax (206)759-1790
Email: fsinfo@faithseminary.edu
Website: www.faithseminary.edu

Florida Christian College (Christian Churches and Churches of Christ), A. Wayne Lowen,

President, 1011 Bill Beck Blvd., Kissimmee, FL 34744 Tel. (407)847-8966, Fax (407)847-3925
Email: fcc@fcc.edu
Website: www.fcc.edu

Franciscan School of Theology (The Roman Catholic Church), William M. Cieslak, President, 1712 Euclid Ave., Berkeley, CA 94709 Tel. (510)848-5232, Fax (510)549-9466

Free Will Baptist Bible College (National Association of Free Will Baptists), Tom Malone, President, 3606 West End Ave., Nashville, TN 37205 Tel. (615)383-1340, Fax (615)269-6028
Email: president@fwbbc.edu
Website: www.fwbcc.edu

Fuller Theological Seminary* (Interdenominational), Richard J. Mouw, President, 135 N. Oakland Ave., Pasadena, CA 91182 Tel. (626)584-5200, Fax (626)584-5644
Email: lguernse@fuller.edu
Website: www.fuller.edu

Garrett-Evangelical Theological Seminary* (The United Methodist Church), Ted A. Campbell, President, 2121 Sheridan Rd., Evanston, IL 60201-3298 Tel. (847)866-3900, Fax (847)866-3957
Email: seminary@nwu.edu
Website: www.garrett.northwestern.edu

The General Theological Seminary* (Episcopal Church), Ward B. Ewing, President, 175 Ninth Ave., New York, NY 10011-4977 Tel. (212) 243-5150, Fax (212)727-3907
Website: www.gts.edu

George Fox Evangelical Seminary (Interdenominational), Ed Stevens, President, 12753 S.W. 68th Ave., Portland, OR 97223 Tel. (503)554-6101, Fax (503)598-4338
Email: seminary@georgefox.edu
Website: www.georgefox.edu/seminary

George Mercer Jr. Memorial School of Theology (Episcopal Church), -vacant-, President, 65 Fourth St., Garden City, NY 11530 Tel. (516)248-4800, Fax (516)248-4883

God's Bible School and College (Nondenominational), Michael Avery, President, 1810 Young St., Cincinnati, OH 45210 Tel. (513) 721-7944, Fax (513)721-3971
Email: GBS.po@juno.com
Website: www.gbs.edu

Golden Gate Baptist Theological Seminary* (Southern Baptist Convention), William O. Crews, President, 201 Seminary Dr., Mill Valley, CA 94941-3197 Tel. (415)380-1300, Fax (415)380-1302
Email: seminary@ggbts.edu
Website: www.ggbts.edu/index.html

Gonzaga University* (The Roman Catholic Church), Fr. Robert Spitzer, S.J., President, 502 E. Boone Ave., Spokane, WA 99258-0001 Tel. (509)328-4220, Fax (509)323-5718
Email: large@gonzaga.edu

Gordon-Conwell Theological Seminary* (Interdenominational), Walter C. Kaiser, Jr., President, 130 Essex St., South Hamilton, MA 01982 Tel. (978)468-7111, Fax (978)468-6691
Email: -info@gcts.edu
Website: www.gordonconwell.edu

Grace Bible College (Grace Gospel Fellowship), Bruce Kemper, President, P.O. Box 910, Grand Rapids, MI 49509 Tel. (616) 538-2330, Fax (616)538-0599
Email: gbc@gbcol.edu
Website: www.gbcol.edu

Grace Theological Seminary (Fellowship of Grace Brethren Churches), Ronald E. Manahan, President, 200 Seminary Dr., Winona Lake, IN 46590-1294 Tel. (219)372-5100, Fax (219)372-5139
Website: www.grace.edu

Grace University (Independent), Dr. James Eckman, President, 1311 South 9th St., Omaha, NE 68108 Tel. (402)449-2809, Fax (402)341-9587

Great Lakes Christian College (Christian Churches and Churches of Christ), Larry Carter, President, 6211 W. Willow Hwy., Lansing, MI 48917 Tel. (517)321-0242, Fax (517)321-5902

Greenville College (Free Methodist Church of North America), President Robert E. Smith, President, 315 E. College Ave., P.O. Box 159, Greenville, IL 62246 Tel. (618)664-2800, Fax (618)664-1748
Email: rsmith@Greenville.edu
Website: www.greenville.edu

Harding University Graduate School of Religion (Churches of Christ), Evertt W. Huffard, Executive Director, 1000 Cherry Rd., Memphis, TN 38117 Tel. (901)761-1352, Fax (901)761-1358

Hartford Seminary* (Interdenominational), Heidi Hadsell, President, 77 Sherman St., Hartford, CT 06105-2260 Tel. (860)509-9502, Fax (860)509-9509
Email: info@hartsem.edu
Website: www.hartsem.edu

Harvard Divinity School* (Nondenominational), J. Pryan Hehir, Chair of the Executive Committee, President, 45 Francis Ave., Cambridge, MA 02138 Tel. (617)495-5761, Fax (617)495-9489
Website: www.hds.harvard.edu

Hebrew Union College- Jewish Institute of Religion, NY (Jewish), Sheldon Zimmerman,

President, 1 W. 4th St., New York, NY 10012 Tel. (212)674-5300, Fax (212)533-0129

Hebrew Union College-Jewish Institute of Religion (Jewish), Rabbi David Ellenson, President, 3077 University Ave., Los Angeles, CA 90007 Tel. (213)749-3424, Fax (213)747-6128
Website: www.huc.edu

Hobe Sound Bible College (Nondenominational), P. Daniel Stetler, President, P.O. Box 1065, Hobe Sound, FL 33475 Tel. (407)546-5534, Fax (407)545-1421

Holy Cross Greek Orthodox School of Theology* (Greek Orthodox Archdiocese of America), Rev. Nicholas C. Triantafilou, President, 50 Goddard Ave., Brookline, MA 02445-7495 Tel. (617)731-3500, Fax (617) 850-1460
Email: admissions@hchc.edu
Website: www.hchc.edu

Holy Trinity Orthodox Seminary (The Russian Orthodox Church Outside of Russia), Archbishop Laurus Skurla, President, P.O. Box 36, Jordanville, NY 13361 Tel. (315)858-0945, Fax (315)858-0945
Email: seminary@telenet.net

Hood Theological Seminary* (African Methodist Episcopal Zion Church), Albert J.D. Aymer, President, 800 W. Thomas St., Salisbury, NC 28144 Tel. 704-216-6113, Fax 704-216-6844

Hope International University (Christian Churches and Churches of Christ), President E. LeRoy Lawson, President, 2500 E. Nutwood Ave., Fullerton, CA 92831 Tel. (714) 879-3901, Fax (714)526-0231
Email: ellawson@hiu.edu
Website: www.hiu.edu

Houston Graduate School of Theology* (Friends), Dr. David Robinson, President, 1311 Holman, Ste. 200, Houston, TX 77004-3833 Tel. (713)942-9505 Fax (713)942-9506
Email: hgst@hgst.edu
Website: www.hgst.edu

Howard University School of Divinity* (Nondenominational), Clarence G. Newsome, President, 1400 Shepherd St. N.E., Washington, DC 20017 Tel. (202)806-0500, Fax (202)806-0711

Huntington College, Graduate School of Christian Ministries (Church of the United Brethren in Christ), G. Blair Dowden, President, 2303 College Ave., Huntington, IN 46750 Tel. (219)356-6000, Fax (219)358-3700
Email: gscm@huntington.edu
Website: www.huntington.edu/academics/gscm

Iliff School of Theology* (The United Methodist Church), David Maldonado, Jr., President, 2201 S. University Blvd., Denver, CO 80210-4798 Tel. (303)744-1287, Fax (303) 777-0164
Website: www.iliff.edu

Immaculate Conception Seminary School of Theology* (The Roman Catholic Church), Robert F. Coleman, President, 400 S. Orange Ave., South Orange, NJ 07079 Tel. (201)761-9575, Fax (201)761-9577
Email: theology@shu.edu
Website: www.shu.edu

Indiana Wesleyan University (The Wesleyan Church), James Barnes, President, 4201 S. Washington, Marion, IN 46953-4999 Tel. (765)674-6901, Fax (765)677-2499
Email: jbarnes@indwes.edu
Website: www.indwes.edu

Interdenominational Theological Center* (Interdenominational), Dr. Robert M. Franklin, President, 700 Martin Luther King, Jr. Dr. S.W., Atlanta, GA 30314-4143 Tel. (404)527-7770, Fax (404)527-0901
Email: info@itc.edu
Website: www.itc.edu

International School of Theology* (non-denominational), Donald A. Weaver, President, 7623 East Avenue, Fontana, CA 92336 Tel. 909-770-4000, Fax 909-770-4001
Website: www.leaderu.com/isot

Jesuit School of Theology at Berkeley* (The Roman Catholic Church), T. Howland Sanks, President, 1735 LeRoy Ave., Berkeley, CA 94709 Tel. (510)841-8804, Fax (510)841-8536

Jewish Theological Seminary of America (Jewish), Ismar Schorsch, President, 3080 Broadway, New York, NY 10027-4649 Tel. (212)678-8000, Fax (212)678-8947
Email: webmaster@jtsa.edu
Website: www.jtsa.edu

John Wesley College (Interdenominational), Brian C. Donley, President, 2314 N. Centennial St., High Point, NC 27265 Tel. (336)889-2262, Fax (336)889-2261
Email: admissions@johnwesley.edu
Website: www.johnwesley.edu

Johnson Bible College (Christian Churches and Churches of Christ), David L. Eubanks, President, 7900 Johnson Dr., Knoxville, TN 37998 Tel. (865)573-4517, Fax (865)251-2336
Email: jbc@jbc.edu
Website: www.jbc.edu

Kansas City College and Bible School (Church of God (Holiness)), Gayle Woods, President, 7401 Metcalf Ave., Overland Park, KS 66204 Tel. (913)722-0272, Fax (913)722-2135

Kenrick-Glennon Seminary* (The Roman Catholic Church), Rev. Msgr. Dennis Delaney, President, 5200 Glennon Dr., St. Louis, MO 63119 Tel. (314)792-6100, Fax (314)792-6500

Kentucky Christian College (Christian Churches and Churches of Christ), Keith P. Keeran, President, 100 Academic Parkway, Grayson, KY 41143 Tel. (606)474-3000, Fax (606)474-3155
Email: knights@email.kcc.edu
Website: www.kcc.edu

Kentucky Mountain Bible College (Interdenominational), Philip Speas, President, Box 10, Vancleve, KY 41385 Tel. (606)666-5000, Fax (606)666-7744

La Sierra University (Seventh-day Adventist Church), Lawrence T. Geraty, President, 4700 Pierce St., Riverside, CA 92515-8247 Tel. (909)785-2000, Fax (909)785-2901
Email: pr@lasierra.edu
Website: www.lasierra.edu

Lancaster Bible College (Nondenominational), Gilbert A. Peterson, President, 901 Eden Rd., Lancaster, PA 17601 Tel. (717)569-7071, Fax (717)560-8213
Website: www.lbc.edu

Lancaster Theological Sem. of the United Church of Christ* (United Church of Christ), Peter Schmiechen, President, 555 W. James St., Lancaster, PA 17603-2897 Tel. (717)393-0654, Fax (717)393-0423
Email: dean@lts.org
Website: www.lts.org

Lexington Theological Seminary,* (Christian Church (Disciples of Christ)), Harold R. Watkins, Interim President, 631 S. Limestone St., Lexington, KY 40508 Tel. (859)252-0361, Fax (859)281-6042
Website: www.lextheo.edu

Liberty Baptist Theological Seminary (Independent Baptist), A. Pierre Guillermin, President, 1971 University Blvd., Lynchburg, VA 24502-2269 Tel. (804)582-2000, Fax (804) 582-2304

L.I.F.E. Bible College (International Church of the Foursquare Gospel), Dick Scott, President, 1100 Covina Blvd., San Dimas, CA 91773 Tel. (909)599-5433, Fax (909)599-6690

Lincoln Christian College and Seminary* (Christian Churches and Churches of Christ), Keith H. Ray, President, 100 Campus View Dr., Lincoln, IL 62656 Tel. (217)732-3168, Fax (217)732-5914
Email: sbaker@lccs.edu
Website: www.lccs.edu

Logos Evangelical Seminary* (Evangelical Formosan Church), Felix Liu, President, 9358 Telstar Ave., El Monte, CA 91731 Tel. (626) 571-5110, Fax (626)571-5119
Email: logos@les.edu
Website: www.les.edu

Louisville Presbyterian Theological Seminary* (Presbyterian Church (U.S.A.)), John M. Mulder, President, 1044 Alta Vista Rd., Louisville, KY 40205 Tel. (502)895-3411, Fax (502)895-1096
Website: www.lpts.edu

Loyola Univiversity Chicago Institute of Pastoral Studies* (The Roman Catholic Church), Mary Elsbernd, OSF, STD, Director, 6525 North Sheridan Rd., Chicago, IL 60626 Tel. (773)508-2320, Fax (773)508-2319
Website: www.luc.edu/depts/ips

Luther Seminary* (Evangelical Lutheran Church in America), David L. Tiede, President, 2481 Como Ave., St. Paul, MN 55108 Tel. (651)641-3456, Fax (651)523-1609
Email: mthompso@luthersem.edu
Website: www.luthersem.edu/

Lutheran Bible Institute in California* (Intersynodical Lutheran), Benjamin Johnson, President, 5321 University Dr., Ste. H, Irvine, CA 92612-2938 Tel. (949)262-9222, Fax (949) 262-0283
Email: LBIC@aol.com

Lutheran Brethren Seminary (Church of the Lutheran Brethren of America), Dean Eugene L. Boe, Ph.D., President, 815 W. Vernon, Fergus Falls, MN 56537 Tel. (218)739-3375, Fax (218)739-1259
Email: lbs@clba.org
Website: www.lbs.edu

Lutheran School of Theology at Chicago* (Evangelical Lutheran Church in America), James Kenneth Echols, President, 1100 E. 55th St., Chicago, IL 60615-5199 Tel. (773) 256-0700, Fax (773)256-0782
Website: www.lstc.edu

Lutheran Theological Seminary at Gettysburg* (Evangelical Lutheran Church in America), The Rev. Michael L. Cooper-White, President, 61 Seminary Ridge, Gettysburg, PA 17325-1795 Tel. (717)334-6286, Fax (717) 334-3469
Email: info@ltsg.edu
Website: www.ltsg.edu

Lutheran Theological Seminary at Philadelphia* (Evangelical Lutheran Church in America), Robert G. Hughes, President, 7301 Germantown Ave., Philadelphia, PA 19119 Tel. (215)248-4616, Fax (215)248-4577
Email: mtairy@ltsp.edu
Website: www.ltsp.edu

Lutheran Theological Southern Seminary* (Evangelical Lutheran Church in America), H. Frederick Reisz, President, 4201 North Main St., Columbia, SC 29203 Tel. (803)786-5150, Fax (803)786-6499
Email: Freisz@ltss.edu
Website: www.ltss.edu

Magnolia Bible College (Churches of Christ), Les Ferguson, Sr., President, P.O. Box 1109, Kosciusko, MS 39090 Tel. (662)289-2896, Fax (601)288-1850
Email: mbcpres@bellsouth.net
Website: www.magnolia.edu

Manhattan Christian College (Christian Churches and Churches of Christ), Kenneth Cable, President, 1415 Anderson Ave., Manhattan, KS 66502 Tel. (785)539-3571, Fax (785)539-0832
Website: www.mccks.edu

McCormick Theological Seminary* (Presbyterian Church (U.S.A.)), Cynthia M. Campbell, President, 5555 S. Woodlawn Ave., Chicago, IL 60637 Tel. (773)947-6300, Fax (773) 288-2612
Email: ccampbell@mccormick.edu
Website: www.mccormick.edu

Meadville-Lombard Theological School* (Unitarian Universalist Association), William R. Murry, President, 5701 S. Woodlawn Ave., Chicago, IL 60637 Tel. (773)256-3000, Fax (773) 753-1323
Email: bmurry@meadville.edu
Website: www.meadville.edu

Memphis Theological Seminary of the Cumberland Presbyterian Church* (Cumberland Presbyterian Church), Larry A. Blakeburn, President, 168 E. Parkway S at Union, Memphis, TN 38104-4395 Tel. (901) 458-8232, Fax (901)452-4051
Email: lblakeburn@mtscampus.edu
Website: www.mtscampus.edu

Mennonite Brethren Biblical Seminary* (General Conference of Mennonite Brethren Churches), President Henry J. Schmidt, President, 4824 E. Butler Ave. (at Chestnut Ave.), Fresno, CA 93727-5097 Tel. (559)251-8628, Fax (559)251-7212
Email: mbseminary@aol.com
Website: www.fresno.edu/MBSeminary

Methodist Theological School in Ohio* (The United Methodist Church), President Norman E. Dewire, President, 3081 Columbus Pike, P.O. Box 8004, Delaware, OH 43015-8004 Tel. (740)363-1146, Fax (740)362-3135
Email: pres@mtso.edu
Website: www.mtso.edu

Mid-America Bible College (The Church of God), Dr. John D. Fozard, President, 3500 S.W. 119th St., Oklahoma City, OK 73170 Tel. (405)691-3800, Fax (405)692-3165
Email: mbcinfo@mabc.edu
Website: www.mabc.edu

Midwestern Baptist Theological Seminary* (Southern Baptist Convention), Dr. R. Philip Roberts, President, 5001 N. Oak Trafficway, Kansas City, MO 64118-4697 Tel. (816)414-3700, Fax (816)414-3799
Website: www.mbts.edu

Minnesota Bible College (Christian Churches and Churches of Christ), Robert W. Cash, President, 920 Mayowood Rd. S.W., Rochester, MN 55902 Tel. (507)288-4563, Fax (507)288-9046
Email: academic@mnbc.edu
Website: www.mnbc.edu

Moody Bible Institute (Interdenominational), Joseph M. Stowell, President, 820 N. La Salle Blvd., Chicago, IL 60610 Tel. (312)329-4000, Fax (312)329-4109
Website: www.moody.edu

Moravian Theological Seminary* (Moravian Church in America (Unitas Fratrum)), Ervin J. Rokke, President, 1200 Main St., Bethlehem, PA 18018 Tel. (610)861-1516, Fax (610)861-1569
Email: seminary@moravian.edu
Website: www.moravianseminary.edu

Moreau Seminary (Congregation of Holy Cross) (The Roman Catholic Church), Rev. Wilson Miscanible, C.S.C., President, Moreau Seminary, Notre Dame, IN 46556 Tel. (219) 631-7735, Fax (219)631-9233

Morehouse School of Religion (Interdenominational Baptist), William T. Perkins, President, 645 Beckwith St. S.W., Atlanta, GA 30314 Tel. (404)527-7777, Fax (404)681-1005

Mount Angel Seminary* (The Roman Catholic Church), Rev. Nathan Fodrow, Administrator, St. Benedict, OR 97373 Tel. (503)845-3951, Fax (503)845-3126
Website: www.mtangel.edu

Mt. St. Mary's Seminary* (The Roman Catholic Church), Very Rev. Kevin C. Rhoades, Rector, 16300 Old Emmitsburg Rd., Emmitsburg, MD 21727-7797 Tel. (301)447-5295, Fax (301)447-5636
Email: rhoades@msmary.edu
Website: www.msmary.edu

Mt. St. Mary's Seminary of the West* (The Roman Catholic Church), Gerald R. Haemmerle, President, 6616 Beechmont Ave., Cincinnati, OH 45230 Tel. (513)231-2223, Fax (513)231-3254
Email: jhaemmer@mtsm.org
Website: mtsm.org

Multnomah Bible College and Biblical Seminary* (Interdenominational), Dr. Daniel R. Lockwood, President, 8435 N.E. Glisan St., Portland, OR 97220 Tel. (503)255-0332, Fax (503)254-1268
Website: www.multnomah.edu

Mundelein Seminary of the Univ. of St. Mary-of-the-Lake* (The Roman Catholic Church), John Canary, Rector-President, 1000 E. Maple, Mundelein, IL 60060-1174 Tel. (847) 566-6401, Fax (847)566-7330
Email: syopusml@usml.edu
Website: www.vocations.org

Nashotah House (Theological Seminary)* (Episcopal Church), Robert S. Munday, President, 2777 Mission Rd., Nashotah, WI 53058-9793 Tel. (262)646-6500, Fax (262) 646-6504
Email: nashotah@nashotah.edu
Website: www.nashotah.edu

Nazarene Bible College (Church of the Nazarene), Hiram Sanders, President, 1111 Academy Park Loop, Colorado Springs, CO 80910-3717 Tel. (719)884-5000, Fax (719) 884-5199
Email: info@nbc.edu
Website: www.nbc.edu

Nazarene Theological Seminary* (Church of the Nazarene), Ron Benefiel, President, 1700 E. Meyer Blvd., Kansas City, MO 64131 Tel. (816)333-6254, Fax (816)333-6271
Email: rbenefiel@nts.edu
Website: www.nts.edu

Nebraska Christian College (Christian Churches and Churches of Christ), Richard D. Milliken, President, 1800 Syracuse Ave., Norfolk, NE 68701-2458 Tel. (402)379-5000, Fax (402) 391-5100
Email: info@nechristian.edu
Website: www.nechristian.edu

New Brunswick Theological Seminary* (Reformed Church in America), President Norman J. Kansfield, President, 17 Seminary Pl., New Brunswick, NJ 08901-1107 Tel. (732)247-5241, Fax (732)249-5412
Email: prf@nbts.edu
Website: www.nbts.edu

New Orleans Baptist Theological Seminary* (Southern Baptist Convention), Charles S. Kelley, President, 3939 Gentilly Blvd., New Orleans, LA 70126 Tel. (504)282-4455, Fax (504)286-3623
Email: nobts@nobts.edu
Website: www.nobts.edu

N.Y. City Full Gospel Theological Seminary (Full Gospel Assembly), Frank A. Garofalo, President, 6902 11th Ave., Brooklyn, NY 11228 Tel. (908)302-9553, Fax (908)302-9553

New York Theological Seminary* (Non-Denominational), Dr. Ileana Rodriguez-Garcia, Acting Pres., 5 W. 29th St., 9th Fl., New York, NY 10001 Tel. (212)532-4012, Fax (212)684-0757
Website: www.nyts.edu

North American Baptist Seminary* (North American Baptist Conference), G. Michael Hagan, President, 1525 S. Grange Ave., Sioux Falls, SD 57105-1526 Tel. (605)336-6588, Fax (605)335-9090
Email: admission@nabs.edu or nabs@nabs.edu
Website: www.nabs.edu

North Central Bible College (Assemblies of God), Gordon L. Anderson, President, 910 Elliot Ave. S., Minneapolis, MN 55404 Tel. (612)332-3491, Fax (612)343-4778

North Park Theological Seminary* (The Evangelical Covenant Church), John E. Phelan, President and Dean, President, 3225 W. Foster Ave., Chicago, IL 60625 Tel. (773) 244-6214, Fax (773)244-6244
Email: jphelan@northpark.edu
Website: www.northpark.edu/cs

Northern Baptist Theological Seminary* (American Baptist Churches in the U.S.A.), Charles W. Moore, President, 660 E. Butterfield Rd., Lombard, IL 60148-5698 Tel. (630)620-2100, Fax (630)620-2194
Email: chapman@seminary.edu
Website: www.seminary.edu

Northwest College (Assemblies of God), Don H. Argue, Ed.D., President, 5520 108th Ave. N.E., P.O. Box 579, Kirkland, WA 98083-0579 Tel. (425)822-8266, Fax (425)827-0148
Email: mail@ncag.edu
Website: www.nwcollege.edu

Notre Dame Seminary* (The Roman Catholic Church), Most Rev. Gregory M. Aymond, D.D., President, 2901 S. Carrollton Ave., New Orleans, LA 70118-4391 Tel. (504)866-7426, Fax (504)866-3119

Oak Hills Christian College (Interdenominational), Dr. Thomas J. Bower, President, 1600 Oak Hills Rd. S.W., Bemidji, MN 56601 Tel. (218)751-8670, Fax (218)751-8825

Oblate School of Theology* (The Roman Catholic Church), J. William Morell, President, 285 Oblate Dr., San Antonio, TX 78216-6693 Tel. (210)341-1366, Fax (210) 341-4519

Oral Roberts University School of Theology and Missions* (Interdenominational), Dr. Thomson K. Mathew, Dean, 7777 S. Lewis Ave., Tulsa, OK 74171 Tel. (918)495-6096, Fax (918)495-6259
Email: jcoper@oru.edu
Website: www.oru.edu

Ozark Christian College (Christian Churches and Churches of Christ), President Dr. Kenneth D. Idleman, President, 1111 N. Main St., Joplin, MO 64801 Tel. (417)624-2518, Fax (417)624-0090
Email: pres@occ.edu

Pacific Lutheran Theological Seminary* (Evangelical Lutheran Church in America), President Timothy F. Lull, President, 2770 Marin Ave., Berkeley, CA 94708-1597 Tel. (510)524-5264, Fax (510)524-2408
Email: president@plts.edu
Website: www.plts.edu

Pacific School of Religion* (Interdenominational), William McKinney, President, 1798 Scenic Ave., Berkeley, CA 94709 Tel. (510) 848-0528, Fax (510)845-8948
Email: comm@psr.edu
Website: www.psr.edu

Payne Theological Seminary* (African Methodist Episcopal Church), Obery M. Hendricks, Jr., Ph.D., President, P.O. Box 474, 1230 Wilberforce-Clifton Rd., Wilberforce, OH 45384-0474 Tel. (937)376-2946, Fax (937)376-3330
Email: dbalsbau@payne.edu
Website: www.payne-seminary.org

Pepperdine University (Churches of Christ), Andrew K. Benton, Chair of Religion Division, Religion Division, Malibu, CA 90263-4352 Tel. (310)506-4352, Fax (310) 317-7271
Email: rick.marrs@pepperdine.edu
Website: http://arachnid.pepperdine.edu/religion div/home.htm

Perkins School of Theology (Southern Methodist University)* (The United Methodist Church), Robin W. Lovin, Dean, Kirby Hall, Dallas, TX 75275-0133 Tel. (214) 768-2293, Fax (214)768-4245
Email: theology@mail.smu.edu
Website: www.smu.edu/theology

Philadelphia Biblical University (Nondenominational), W. Sherrill Babb, President, 200 Manor Ave., Langhorne, PA 19047-2990 Tel. (215)752-5800, Fax (215)702-4341
Email: president@pbu.edu
Website: www.pbu.edu

Phillips Theological Seminary* (Christian Church (Disciples of Christ)), William Tabbernee, President, 4242 S. Sheridan Rd., Tulsa, OK 74145 Tel. (918)610-8303, Fax (918)610-8404
Email: ptspres@fullnet.net
Website: www.ptsem.org

Piedmont Baptist College (Baptist (Independent)), Howard L. Wilburn, President, 716 Franklin St., Winston-Salem, NC 27101 Tel. (336)725-8344, Fax (336)725-5522
Email: admissions@pbc.edu
Website: www.pbc.edu

Pittsburgh Theological Seminary* (Presbyterian Church (U.S.A.)), Carnegie Samuel Calian, President, 616 N. Highland Ave., Pittsburgh, PA 15206 Tel. (412)362-5610, Fax (412)363-3260
Email: calian@pts.edu
Website: www.pts.edu

Point Loma Nazarene College (Church of the Nazarene), Bob Brower, President, 3900 Lomaland Dr., San Diego, CA 92106 Tel. (619)849-2200, Fax (619)849-7007
Website: www.ptloma.edu

Pontifical College Josephinum* (The Roman Catholic Church), Brian R. Moore, Acting President, President, 7625 N. High St., Columbus, OH 43235 Tel. (614)885-5585, Fax (614)885-2307
Website: www.pcj.edu

Pope John XXIII National Seminary* (The Roman Catholic Church), Francis D. Kelly, President, 558 South Ave., Weston, MA 02193 Tel. (617)899-5500, Fax (617)899-9057

Practical Bible College (Independent Baptist), Dale E. Linebaugh, President, Box 601, Bible School Park, NY 13737 Tel. (607)729-1581, Fax (607)729-2962
Email: pbc@lakenet.org
Website: www.lakenet.org/~pbc

Princeton Theological Seminary* (Presbyterian Church (U.S.A.)), Thomas W. Gillespie, President, P.O. Box 821, Princeton, NJ 08542-0803 Tel. (609)921-8300, Fax (609) 924-2973
Email: comm-pub@ptsem.edu
Website: www.ptsem.edu

Protestant Episcopal Theological Seminary in Virginia* (Episcopal Church), Martha J. Horne, Dean, 3737 Seminary Rd., Alexandria, VA 22304 Tel. (703)370-6600, Fax (703)751-0214
Email: mhorne@vts.edu
Website: www.vts.edu

Puget Sound Christian College (Christian Churches and Churches of Christ), R. Allan Dunbar, President, 410 Fourth Ave. N., Edmonds, WA 98020-3171 Tel. (425)775-8686, Fax (425)775-8688
Email: president@pscc.edu
Website: www.pscc.edu

Rabbi Isaac Elchanan Theological Seminary (Jewish), Dr. Norman Lamm, President, 2540 Amsterdam Ave., New York, NY 10033 Tel. (212)960-5344, Fax (212)960-0061
Website: www.yu.edu/riets/

Reconstructionist Rabbinical College (Jewish), David A. Teutsch, President, Church Rd. and Greenwood Ave., Wyncote, PA 19095 Tel. (215)576-0800, Fax (215)576-6143
Email: rrcinfo@rrc.edu

Reformed Bible College (Interdenominational), Nicholas Kroeze, President, 3333 East Beltline N.E., Grand Rapids, MI 49525-9749 Tel. (616)222-3000, Fax (616)988-3608
Email: administration@reformed.edu
Website: www.reformed.edu

Reformed Episcopal Seminary (Reformed Episcopal Church), Wayne A. Headman, President, 826 Second Ave., Blue Bell, PA 19422-1257 Tel. (610)292-9852, Fax (610) 292-9853
Email: info@ptsorec.edu
Website: www.ptsofrec.edu

Reformed Presbyterian Theological Seminary* (Reformed Presbyterian Church of North America), Jerry F. O*Neill, President, 7418 Penn Ave., Pittsburgh, PA 15208-2594 Tel. (412)731-8690, Fax (412)731-4834
Email: rpseminary@aol.com
Website: www.rpts.edu

Reformed Theological Seminary* (Non-denominational), -vacant, President, 5422 Clinton Blvd., Jackson, MS 39209-3099 Tel. (601)923-1600, Fax (601)923-1654
Email: rts.jackson@rts.edu
Website: www.rts.edu

Regent University School of Divinity* (Interdenominational), Dr. Pat Robertson, President, 1000 Regent University Dr., Virginia Beach, VA 23464-9801 Tel. (757) 226-4401, Fax (757)226-4597
Email: divschool@regent.edu
Website: www.regent.edu

Roanoke Bible College (Christian Churches and Churches of Christ), William A. Griffin, President, 714 N. Poindexter St, Elizabeth City, NC 27909-4054 Tel. (252) 334-2090 or (252) 334-2070, Fax (252)334-2071
Email: wag@roanokebible.edu
Website: www.roanokebible.edu

Sacred Heart Major Seminary* (The Roman Catholic Church), The Most Reverend Allen H. Vigneron, President, 2701 Chicago Blvd., Detroit, MI 48206 Tel. (313)883-8500, Fax (313)868-6440

Sacred Heart School of Theology* (The Roman Catholic Church), James D. Brackin, S.C.J., President-Rector, P.O. Box 429, Hales Corners, WI 53130-0429 Tel. (414)425-8300, Fax (414)529-6999
Email: shst@msn.com
Website: www.shst.edu

Saint Bernard's Institute* (The Roman Catholic Church), Patricia A. Schoelles, President, 1100 S. Goodman St., Rochester, NY 14620 Tel. (716)271-3657, Fax (716)271-2045
Email: pschoelles@sbi.edu

St. Charles Borromeo Seminary* (The Roman Catholic Church), Rev. Msgr. Michael F. Burbidge, Ed.D., Rector, 100 East Wynnewood Rd., Wynnewood, PA 19096-3001 Tel. (610)667-3394, Fax (610)667-7635

St. Francis Seminary* (The Roman Catholic Church), Very Rev. Andrew L. Nelson, President, 3257 S. Lake Dr., St. Francis, WI 53235 Tel. (414)747-6400, Fax (414)747-6442
Email: anelson1@sfs.edu
Website: www.sfs.edu

St. John's Seminary* (The Roman Catholic Church), Timothy Moran, President, 127 Lake St., Brighton, MA 02135 Tel. (617)254-2610, Fax (617)787-2336

St. John's Seminary College* (The Roman Catholic Church), Rev. Kenneth Rudnick, S.J., President, 5118 Seminary Rd., Camarillo, CA 93012-2599 Tel. (805)482-2755, Fax (805) 987-5097

St. John's University, School of Theology Seminary* (The Roman Catholic Church), William J. Cahoy, Dean, Box 7288, Collegeville, MN 56321-7288 Tel. (320)363-2100, Fax (320)363-3145
Website: www.csbsju.sot

St. Joseph's Seminary* (The Roman Catholic Church), Edwin F. O*Brien, President, 201 Seminary Ave., (Dunwoodie) Yonkers, NY 10704 Tel. (914)968-6200, Fax (914)968-7912

St. Louis Christian College (Christian Churches and Churches of Christ), Kenneth L. Beck, President, 1360 Grandview Dr., Florissant, MO 63033 Tel. (314)837-6777, Fax (314)837-8291
Email: questions@slcc4ministry.edu
Website: www.slcc4ministry.edu

St. Mary Seminary and Graduate School of Theology* (The Roman Catholic Church), Donald B. Cozzens, President, 28700 Euclid Ave., Wickliffe, OH 44092 Tel. (216)943-7600, Fax (216)943-7577

St. Mary's Seminary* (The Roman Catholic Church), Rev. Msgr. Chester L. Borski, Rector, 9845 Memorial Dr., Houston, TX 77024-3498 Tel. (713)686-4345, Fax (713) 681-7550

St. Mary's Seminary and University* (The Roman Catholic Church), Robert F. Leavitt, President, 5400 Roland Ave., Baltimore, MD 21210 Tel. (410)864-4000, Fax (410)864-4278
Website: www.stmarys.edu

St. Meinrad School of Theology* (The Roman Catholic Church), Mark O'Keefe, President, St. Meinrad, IN 47577 Tel. (812)357-6611, Fax (812)357-6964

St. Patrick's Seminary* (The Roman Catholic Church), Gerald D. Coleman, President, 320 Middlefield Rd., Menlo Park, CA 94025 Tel. (415)325-5621, Fax (415)322-0997

Saint Paul School of Theology* (The United Methodist Church), Lovett H. Weems, Jr., President, 5123 Truman Rd., Kansas City, MO 64127-2499 Tel. (816)483-9600, Fax (816) 483-9605
Email: spst@spst.edu
Website: www.spst.edu

St. Paul Seminary School of Divinity* (The Roman Catholic Church), Phillip J. Rask, President, 2260 Summit Ave., St. Paul, MN 55105 Tel. (612)962-5050, Fax (612)962-5790

St. Tikhon's Orthodox Theological Seminary* (The Orthodox Church in America),

Archbishop Herman, Rector, Box 130, St. Tikhon's Rd., South Canaan, PA 18459-0121 Tel. (570)937-4411, Fax (570)937-3100
Email: stots@stots.edu (Admin.)
stotsfac@stots.edu (Faculty)
library@stots.edu (Library)
Website: www.stots.edu and
www.oca.org/OCA/pim/oca-stostots.html

St. Vincent de Paul Regional Seminary* (The Roman Catholic Church), Pablo A. Navarro, President, 10701 S. Military Trail, Boynton Beach, FL 33436-4899 Tel. (561)732-4424, Fax (561)737-2205

St. Vincent Seminary* (The Roman Catholic Church), Very Rev. Kurt Belsole, O.S.B., President, 300 Fraser Purchase Rd., Latrobe, PA 15650-2690 Tel. (724)537-4592, Fax (724) 532-5052

St. Vladimir's Orthodox Theological Seminary* (The Orthodox Church in America), His Beatitude Metropolitan Theodosius, Dean, 575 Scarsdale Rd., Crestwood, NY 10707-1699 Tel. (914)961-8313, Fax (914)961-4507
Email: info@svots.edu
Website: www.svots.edu

San Francisco Theological Seminary* (Presbyterian Church (U.S.A.)), , President, 2 Kensington Rd., San Anselmo, CA 94960 Tel. (415)258-6500, Fax (415)258-1608
Email: sftsinfo@sfts.edu
Website: www.sfts.edu

San Jose Christian College (Christian Churches and Churches of Christ), Bryce L. Jessup, President, 790 S. 12th St., P.O. Box 1090, San Jose, CA 95108 Tel. (408)293-9058, Fax (408) 293-7352
Email: admissions@sjchristian.edu
Website: www.sjchristian.edu

Savonarola Theological Seminary (Polish National Catholic Church of America), Most Rev. John F. Swantek, Rector, 1031 Cedar Ave., Scranton, PA 18505 Tel. (570)343-0100

Seabury-Western Theological Seminary* (Episcopal Church), James B. Lemler, Dean, 2122 Sheridan Rd., Evanston, IL 60201-2976 Tel. (847)328-9300, Fax (847)328-9624
Email: seabury.admissions@seabury.edu
Website: www.swts.seabury.edu

Seattle University School of Theology and Ministry* (The Roman Catholic Church and 10 Mainline Protestant Denominations and Associations), Rev. Patrick Howell, S.J., Interim Dean, 900 Broadway, Seattle, WA 98122 Tel. (206)296-5330, Fax (206)296-5329
Email: millerdi@seattleu.edu
Website: www.seattleu.edu

Seminario Evangelico de Puerto Rico* (Interdenominational), Samuel Pagán, President, 776 Ponce de Le¢n Ave., San Juan, PR 00925 Tel. (787)763-6700, Fax (787)751-0847
Email: drspagan@icepr.com or jvaldes@tld.net
Website: netministries.org/see/charmin/CM01399

Seminary of the Immaculate Conception* (The Roman Catholic Church), Msgr. Francis J. Schneider, J.C.D., President, 440 West Neck Rd., Huntington, NY 11743 Tel. (516)423-0483, Fax (516)423-2346

Seventh-day Adventist Theological Seminary* (Seventh-day Adventist Church), John K. McVay, Dean, Andrews University, Berrien Springs, MI 49104-1500 Tel. (616)471-3537, Fax (616)471-6202
Email: seminary@andrews.edu
Website: www.andrews.edu/sem

Seventh Day Baptist School of Ministry (Seventh Day Baptist General Conference), Gabriel Bejjani, Dean of School of Ministry, 3120 Kennedy Rd., P.O. Box 1678, Janesville, WI 53547 Tel. (608)752-5055, Fax (608)752-7711
Email: sdbgen@inwave.com

Shaw Divinity School (Baptist), James T. Roberson, Dean, 118 East South St., Raleigh, NC 27601 Tel. 919-546-8571, Fax 919-546-8569

Simpson College (The Christian and Missionary Alliance), James M. Grant, President, 2211 College View Dr., Redding, CA 96003 Tel. (916)224-5600, Fax (916)224-5608

Southeastern Baptist College (Baptist Missionary Association of America), Jentry W. Bond, President, 4229 Highway 15N, Laurel, MS 39440 Tel. (601)426-6346, Fax (601)426-6346

Southeastern Baptist Theological Seminary* (Southern Baptist Convention), President Paige Patterson, President, 150-A North White Street, P.O. Box 1889, Wake Forest, NC 27588-1889 Tel. (919)556-3101
Website: www.sebts.edu

Southeastern Bible College (Interdenominational), John D. Talley, President, 3001 Highway 280 E., Birmingham, AL 35243 Tel. (205)969-0880, Fax (205)970-9207
Email: 102064.406@compuserve.com
Website: www.sebc.edu

Southeastern College of the Assemblies of God (Assemblies of God), Mark Rutland, President, 1000 Longfellow Blvd., Lakeland, FL 33801 Tel. (863)667-5000, Fax (863)667-5200
Email: info@secollege.edu
Website: www.secollege.edu

Southern Baptist Theological Seminary* (Southern Baptist Convention), R. Albert Mohler, Jr., President, 2825 Lexington Rd.,

Louisville, KY 40280 Tel. (502)897-4121, Fax (502)899-1770
Email: presoffice@sbts.edu
Website: www.sbts.edu

Southern Christian University (Churches of Christ), President Dr. Rex A. Turner, Jr., President, 1200 Taylor Rd., Montgomery, AL 36117-3553 Tel. (334)387-3877, Fax (334) 387-3878
Email: southernchristian@southernchristian.edu
Website: www.southernchristian.edu

Southern Wesleyan University (The Wesleyan Church), President David J. Spittal, President, 907 Wesleyan Dr., P.O. Box 1020, Central, SC 29630-1020 Tel. (864)644-5000, Fax (864) 644-5900
Email: dspittal@swu.edu
Website: www.swu.edu

Southwestern Assemblies of God University (Assemblies of God), Delmer R. Guynes, President, 1200 Sycamore St., Waxahachie, TX 75165 Tel. (972)937-4010, Fax (972)923-0488

Southwestern Baptist Theological Seminary* (Southern Baptist Convention), Kenneth S. Hemphill, President, P.O. Box 22000, Fort Worth, TX 76122 Tel. (817)923-1921, Fax (817) 923-0610
Website: www.swbts.edu

Southwestern College (Conservative Baptist Association of America), Brent D. Garrison, President, 2625 E. Cactus Rd., Phoenix, AZ 85032 Tel. (602)992-6101, Fax (602)404-2159

SS. Cyril and Methodius Seminary* (The Roman Catholic Church), Francis B. Koper, Rector, 3535 Indian Trail, Orchard Lake, MI 48324-1623 Tel. (248)683-0311, Fax (248) 738-6735
Email: 103244.3555@compuserve.com OR deansoff@sscms.edu
Website: www.metronet.lib.mi.us/aml.html (Library)
www.sscms.edu/deansoff (Seminary)

Starr King School for the Ministry* (Unitarian Universalist Association), Rebecca Parker, President, 2441 LeConte Ave., Berkeley, CA 94709 Tel. (510)845-6232, Fax (510)845-6273

Swedenborgian House of Studies at the Pacific School of Religion (The Swedenborgian Church), Dr. James F. Lawrence, Dean, 1798 Scenic Ave., Berkeley, CA 94709 Tel. (510) 849-8228, Fax (510)849-8296
Email: jlawrence@shs.psr.edu

Talbot School of Theology* (Nondenominational), Dennis H. Dirks, Dean, 13800 Biola Ave., La Mirada, CA 90639-0001 Tel. (562) 903-4816, Fax (562)903-4759
Website: www.talbot.edu

Temple Baptist Seminary (Independent Baptist), Barkev Trachian, President, 1815 Union Ave., Chattanooga, TN 37404 Tel. (423)493-4221, Fax (423)493-4471

Theological School of the Protestant Reformed Churches (Protestant Reformed Churches in America), Russell J. Dykstra, President, 4949 Ivanrest Ave., Grandville, MI 49418 Tel. (616)531-1490, Fax (616)531-3033
Email: dykstra@prca.org

Toccoa Falls College (The Christian and Missionary Alliance), Donald O. Young, President, P.O. Box 800777, Toccoa Falls, GA 30598 Tel. (706)886-6831, Fax (706)282-6005
Email: president@toccoafalls.edu
Website: www.toccoafalls.edu

Trevecca Nazarene University (Church of the Nazarene), Millard Reed, President, 333 Murfreesboro Rd., Nashville, TN 37210-2877 Tel. (615)248-1200, Fax (615)248-7728
Website: www.trevecca.edu

Trinity Bible College (Assemblies of God), Howard Young, President, 50 S. 6th Ave., Ellendale, ND 58436 Tel. (701)349-3621, Fax (701)349-5443

Trinity College of Florida (Nondenominational), Paul L. Alford, President, 2430 Welbilt Blvd., New Port Richey, FL 34655-4401 Tel. (727) 376-6911, Fax (727)376-0781
Email: admin@trinitycollege.edu
Website: www.trinitycollege.edu

Trinity Episcopal School for Ministry* (Episcopal Church), The Very Rev. Peter C. Moore, Dean and President, President, 311 Eleventh St., Ambridge, PA 15003 Tel. (724) 266-3838, Fax (724)266-4617
Email: maxinemoore@tesm.edu
Website: www.episcopalian.org

Trinity International University* (The Evangelical Free Church of America), Gregory L. Waybright, President, 2065 Half Day Rd., Deerfield, IL 60015 Tel. (847)945-8800, Fax (847)317-8090
Email: tedsadm@tiu.edu
Website: www.tiu.edu

Trinity Lutheran College (Interdenominational-Lutheran), John M. Stamm, President, 4221 - 228th Ave. S.E., Issaquah, WA 98029-9299 Tel. (425)392-0400, Fax (425)392-0404
Email: info@tlc.edu
Website: www.tlc.edu

Trinity Lutheran Seminary* (Evangelical Lutheran Church in America), Mark R. Ramseth, President, 2199 E. Main St., Columbus, OH 43209-2334 Tel. (614)235-4136, Fax (614)238-0263
Email: webmaster@trinity.capital.edu
Website: www.trinity.capital.edu

Union Theological Seminary* (Interdenominational), Joseph C. Hough, Jr., President, 3041 Broadway, New York, NY 10027 Tel. (212)662-7100, Fax (212) 280-1416

Union Theological Seminary and Presbyterian School of Christian Education (Union-PSCE)* (Presbyterian Church (U.S.A.)), Louis B. Weeks, President, 3401 Brook Rd., Richmond, VA 23227 Tel. (804) 355-0671, Fax (804)355-3919
Website: www.union-psce.edu

United Theological Seminary* (The United Methodist Church), Rev. Dr. G. Edwin Zeiders, President, 1810 Harvard Blvd., Dayton, OH 45406-4599 Tel. (937)278-5817, Fax (937)278-1218
Email: utscom@united.edu
Website: www.united.edu

United Theological Seminary of the Twin Cities* (United Church of Christ), Wilson Yates, President, 3000 Fifth St. N.W., New Brighton, MN 55112 Tel. (651)633-4311, Fax (651)633-4315
Email: general@unitedseminary-mn.org
Website: www.unitedseminary-mn.org

University of Chicago (Divinity School)* (Interdenominational), Richard Rosengarten, Dean, 1025 E. 58th St., Chicago, IL 60637 Tel. (773)702-8221, Fax (773)702-6048
Website: www2.uchicago.edu/divinity

University of Dubuque Theological Seminary* (Presbyterian Church (U.S.A.)), Jeffrey Bullock, President, 2000 University Ave., Dubuque, IA 52001 Tel. (319)589-3223, Fax (319)589-3682

University of Notre Dame, Dept. of Theology* (The Roman Catholic Church), John C. Cavadini, Department Chair, President, Notre Dame, , IN 46556 Tel. (219)631-7811, Fax (219) 631-4291

University of St. Thomas School of Theology (The Roman Catholic Church), Louis T. Brusatti, President, 9845 Memorial Dr., Houston, TX 77024 Tel. (713)686-4345, Fax (713)683-8673

University of the South School of Theology* (Episcopal Church), Guy Fitch Lytle, Dean, President, 335 Tennessee Ave., Sewanee, TN 37383-0001 Tel. (931)598-1288, Fax (931) 598-1412
Email: glytle@seraph1.sewanee.edu
Website: www.sewanee.edu

Valley Forge Christian College (Assemblies of God), Earl Baldwin, President, 1401 Charlestown Rd., Phoenixville, PA 19460 Tel. (610)935-0450, Fax (610)935-9353

Vanderbilt University Divinity School* (Interdenominational), Joseph Hudnut-Brewer, Dean, Nashville, TN 37240 Tel. (615) 322-2776, Fax (615)343-9957
Email: HoughJC@CTRVax.Vanderbilt.edu
Website: www.vanderbilt.edu

Vennard College (Interdenominational), W. Edward Rickman, President, Box 29, University Park, IA 52595 Tel. (641)673-8391, Fax (641)673-8365
Email: vennard@vennard.edu
Website: www.vennard.edu

Virginia Union University (School of Theology)* (American Baptist Churches in the USA, National Baptist Convention, USA, Inc., Progressive National Baptist Convention, Inc., Lott Carey), John W. Kinney, Dean, President, 1500 N. Lombardy St., Richmond, VA 23220 Tel. (804)257-5715, Fax (804)342-3911

Walla Walla College (School of Theology) (Seventh-day Adventist Church), Ernest Bursey, Dean, President, 204 S. College Ave., College Place, WA 99324-1198 Tel. (509)527-2194, Fax (509)527-2253
Email: burser@wwc.edu
Website: www.wwc.edu

Wartburg Theological Seminary* (Evangelical Lutheran Church in America), Duane H. Larson, President, 333 Wartburg Pl., PO Box 5004, Dubuque, LA 52004-5004 Tel. (563) 589-0200, Fax (563)589-0333
Email: mailbox@wartburgseminary.edu
Website: www.wartburgseminary.edu

Washington Bible College-Capital Bible Seminary (Nondenominational), Homer Heater, President, 6511 Princess Garden Pkwy., Lanham, MD 20706 Tel. (301)552-1400, Fax (301)552-2775

Washington Theological Consortium (Nondenominational), John W. Crossin, Executive Director, 487 Michigan Ave. N.E., Washington, DC 20017 Tel. (202)832-2675, Fax (202)526-0818
Email: wtconsort@aol.com
Website: www.washtheocon.org

Washington Theological Union* (The Roman Catholic Church), Daniel McLellan, O.F.M., President, 6896 Laurel St. N.W., Washington, DC 20012 Tel. (202)726-8800, Fax (202)726-1716
Email: mclellan@wtu.edu
Website: www.wtu.edu

Wesley Biblical Seminary* (Interdenominational), Robert R. Lawrence, President, P.O. Box 9938, Jackson, MS 39286-0938 Tel. (601) 957-1314, Fax (601)957-1314

Wesley Theological Seminary* (The United Methodist Church), G. Douglass Lewis, President, 4500 Massachusetts Ave. N.W.,

Washington, DC 20016-5690 Tel. (800)882-4987, Fax (202)885-8600
Email: admissions@wesleysem.edu
Website: www.WesleySem.edu

Western Seminary (Conservative Baptist Association of America), Bert E. Downs, President, 5511 S.E. Hawthorne Blvd., Portland, OR 97215 Tel. (503)517-1800, Fax (503)517-1801
Website: westernseminary.edu

Western Theological Seminary* (Reformed Church in America), Dennis N. Voskuil, President, 101 E. 13th St., Holland, MI 49423 Tel. (616)392-8555, Fax (616)392-7717
Website: www.westernsem.org

Westminster Theological Seminary* (Nondenominational), Samuel T. Logan, President, Chestnut Hill, P.O. Box 27009, Philadelphia, PA 19118 Tel. (215)887-5511, Fax (215)887-3459
Email: slogan@wts.edu
Website: www.wts.edu

Westminster Theological Seminary in California* (Nondenominational), W. Robert Godfrey, President, 1725 Bear Valley Pkwy, Escondido, CA 92027-4128 Tel. (760)480-8474, Fax (760)480-0252
Website: www.wtscal.edu

Weston Jesuit School of Theology* (Roman Catholic), Robert Manning, President, 3 Phillips Pl., Cambridge, MA 02138 Tel. (617) 492-1960, Fax (617)492-5833
Email: Admissionsinfo@wjst.edu

William Tyndale College (Interdenominational), Jerry D. Bringard, Acting President, 35700 W. Twelve Mile Rd., Farmington Hills, MI 48331 Tel. (248)553-7200, Fax (248)553-5963
Website: www.williamtyndale.edu

Winebrenner Theological Seminary* (Churches of God, General Conference), David E. Draper, President, 701 E. Melrose Ave., P.O. Box 478, Findlay, OH 45839 Tel. (419)422-4824, Fax (419)422-3999
Email: wts@winebrenner.edu
Website: www.winebrenner.edu

Wisconsin Lutheran Seminary (Wisconsin Evangelical Lutheran Synod), David J. Valleskey, President, 11831 N. Seminary Dr., 65W, Mequon, WI 53092 Tel. (262)242-8100, Fax (262)242-8110
Website: www.wls.wels.net

Yale University Divinity School*, Richard J. Wood, President, 409 Prospect St., New Haven, CT 06511 Tel. (203)432-5303, Fax (203)432-5356
Email: ydsadmsn@yale.edu
Website: www.yale.edu/divinity

10. Theological Seminaries and Bible Colleges in Canada

The following list includes theological seminaries and departments in colleges and universities in which ministerial training is provided. Many denominations have additional programs. Consult Directory 4, "Religious Bodies in Canada" for headquarters information for these denominations. The list has been developed from direct correspondence with the institutions. Inclusion in or exclusion from this list implies no judgment about the quality or accreditation of any institution. Those schools that are members of the Association of Theological Schools are marked with an asterisk (*). Each of the listings include: the institution name, denominational sponsor when appropriate, location, the president or dean, telephone and fax numbers when known and email and website addresses when available.

Acadia Divinity University* (United Baptist Convention of the Atlantic Provinces), Lee M. McDonald, Principal, Acadia University, Wolfville, NS B0P 1X0 Tel. (902)585-2210, Fax (902)542-7527
Email: adcinfo@acadiau.ca
Website: ace.acadiau.ca/divcol

Alberta Bible College (Christian Churches and Churches of Christ in Canada), Ronald A. Fraser, President, 635 Northmount Dr. N.W., Calgary, AB T2K 3J6 Tel. (403)282-2994, Fax (403)282-3084
Email: abbible@cadvision.com
Website: www.abc-ca.org

Associated Canadian Theological Schools of Trinity Western University* (Baptist General Conference of Canada, Evangelical Free Church of Canada, The Fellowship of Evangelical Baptist Churches in Canada, Christian and Missionary Alliance, Canadian Conference of Mennonite Brethren Churches), Dr. Phil Zylla, Executive Directro, 7600 Glover Rd., Langley, BC V2Y 1Y1 Tel. (604) 513-2044, Fax (604)513-2045
Email: acts@twu.ca
Website: www.acts.twu.ca

Atlantic School of Theology* (Interdenominational), Gordon MacDermid, President, 640 Francklyn St., Halifax, NS B3H 3B5 Tel. (902)423-6801, Fax (902)492-4048

Baptist Leadership Training School(Canadian Baptist Ministries), Hugh Fraser, President, 4330 16th St. S.W., Calgary, AB T2T 4H9 Tel. (403)243-3770, Fax (403)287-1930
Email: blts@imag.net
Website: www.yet.ca

Bethany Bible College-Canada (The Wesleyan Church), Dr. David S. Medders, President, 26 Western St., Sussex, NB E4E 1E6 Tel. (506) 432-4400, Fax (506)432-4425
Email: meddersd@bethany-ca.edu
Website: www.bethany-ca.edu

Bethany Bible Institute (Canadian Conference of Mennonite Brethren Churches of SK; Canadian Conference of Mennonite Brethren Churches of AB; Evangelical Mennonite Mission Conference of SK), Rick Schellenberg, President, Box 160, Hepburn, SK S0K 1Z0 Tel. (306)947-2175, Fax (306) 947-4229
Email: bethany_bbi@qlo.com
Website: www.bethany.sk.ca

Briercrest Biblical Seminary* (Interdenominational), , President, Enrollment Services, Briercrest Family of Schools 510 College Dr., Caronport, SK S0H 0S0 Tel. (800)667-5199, Fax (306)756-3366
Email: chartenburg@briercrest.ca or pwilder@briercrest.ca
Website: www.briercrest.ca

Briercrest Family of Schools (Bible College & Seminary)* (Transdenominational), Dr. Paul Magnus, President, Enrollment Services, Briercrest Family of Schools 510 College Dr., Caronport, SK S0H 0S0 Tel. (800)667-5199, Fax (306)756-3366
Email: enrollment@briercrest.ca
Website: www.briercrest.ca

Canadian Bible College (Christian and Missionary Alliance in Canada), Dr. George Durance, President, 4400-4th Ave., Regina, SK S4T 0H8 Tel. (306)545-1515, Fax (306) 545-0210
Email: gdurance@cbccts.ca
Website: www.cbccts.ca

Canadian Lutheran Bible Institute (Lutheran), Pastor Harold Rust, President, 4837 52A St., Camrose, AB T4V 1W5 Tel. (780)672-4454, Fax (780)672-4455
Email: clbi@clbi.edu
Website: www.clbi.edu

Canadian Mennonite Bible College at Canadian Mennonite University (Mennonite Brethren Churches MC Canada Churches), Gerald Gerbrandt, President, 500 Shaftesbury Blvd, Winniped, Manitoba R3P 2N2 Tel. (204) 487-3300, Fax (204)487-3858
Email: reception@cmu.ca
Website: www,cmu.ca

Canadian Nazarene University College (Church of the Nazarene Canada), Riley Coulter, President, 610, 833 4th Ave. SW, Calgary, AB T2P 3T5 Tel. (403)571-2550, Fax (403)571-2556
Email: cncoff@nuc.edu
Website: www.nuc.edu

Canadian Theological Seminary* (Christian and Missionary Alliance in Canada), Dr. George Durance, President, 4400-4th Ave., Regina, SK S4T 0H8 Tel. (306)545-1515, Fax (306)545-0210
Email: gdurance@cbccts.ca
Website: www.cbccts.ca

Central Pentecostal College, University of Saskatchewan (The Pentecostal Assemblies of Canada), D. Munk, President, 1303 Jackson Ave., Saskatoon, SK S7H 2M9 Tel. (306)374-6655, Fax (306)373-6968
Email: admissions@cpc-paoc.edu
Website: www.cpc-paoc.edu

Centre for Christian Studies (The Anglican Church of Canada, The United Church of Canada), Caryn Douglas, Principal, 60 Maryland, Winnipeg, MB R3G 1K7 Tel. (204) 783-4490, Fax (204)786-3012
Email: centre@escape.ca
Website: www.escape.ca/~centre

College Biblique Québec (The Pentecostal Assemblies of Canada), William Raccah, President, 740 Lebourgneuf, Ste. 100, Ancienne Lorette, QC G2J 1E2 Tel. (418)622-7552, Fax (418)622-1470

Colläge Dominicain de Philosophie et de Théologie (The Roman Catholic Church in Canada), Michel Gourgues, President, 96 Avenue Empress, Ottawa, ON K1R 7G3 Tel. (613)233-5696, Fax (613)233-6064

College of Emmanuel and St. Chad (The Anglican Church of Canada), Dr. Walter Deller, President, 1337 College Dr., Saskatoon, SK S7N 0W6 Tel. (306)975-3753, Fax (306)934-2683
Email: walter.deller@usask.ca

Columbia Bible College (Mennonite), Ron Penner, Merv Boschman, Interim Presidential Team, 2940 Clearbrook Rd., Abbotsford, BC V2T 2Z8 Tel. (604)853-3358, Fax (604)853-3063
Email: info@columbiabc.edu
Website: www.columbiabc.edu

Concord College at Canadian Mennonite University (Mennonite Brethren Churches, Mennonite Church Canada), John H. Unger, President, 500 Shaftesbury Blvd., Winnipeg, MB R3P 2N2 Tel. (204)487-3300, Fax (204) 487-3858
Email: reception@cmu.ca
Website: www.cmu.ca

Concordia Lutheran Seminary* (Lutheran Church-Canada), Arthur D. Bacon, President, 7040 Ada Blvd., Edmonton, AB T5B 4E3 Tel. (780)474-1468, Fax (780)479-3067
Email: info@concordiasem.ab.ca

Concordia Lutheran Theological Seminary* (Lutheran Church-Canada), Jonathan Grothe, President, 470 Glenridge Ave., St. Catharines, ON L2T 4C3 Tel. (905)688-2362, Fax (905) 688-9744
Email: concordia@brocku.ca

Covenant Bible College (The Evangelical Covenant Church of Canada), , President
Campuses: CANADA, 630 Westchester Rd., Strathmore, AB T1P 1H8 Fax (403) 934-6220
Email: office@covenantbiblecollege.ab.ca
Website: www.covenantbiblecollege.ab.ca
COLORADO: 675 Southwood Ln., Windsor, CO 80550 Tel. (970) 686-6977, Fax (970)686-6977
Email:cbc@covbibcolorado.edu

Edmonton Baptist Seminary* (North American Baptist Conference), Dr. Marvin Dewey, President, 11525-23 Ave., Edmonton, AB T6J 4T3 Tel. (780)431-5200, Fax (780)436-9416
Email: marv.dewey@nabcebs.ab.ca
Website: www.nabcebs.ab.ca

Emmanuel Bible College (The Evangelical Missionary Church of Canada), Thomas E. Dow, President, 100 Fergus Ave., Kitchener, ON N2A 2H2 Tel. (519)894-8900, Fax (519) 894-5331
Email: dmin@ebcollege.on.ca
Website: www.ebcollege.on.ca

Emmanuel College* (The United Church of Canada), S. Peter Wyatt, Principal, 75 Queens Park Crescent, Toronto, ON M5S 1K7 Tel. (416)585-4539, Fax (416)585-4516
Email: ec.office@utoronto.ca
Website: vicu.utoronto.ca

Faculté De Théologie Évangélique (Union d'Églises Baptistes Françaises au Canada), Amar Djaballah, President, 2285 Avenue Papineau, Montréal, QC H2K 4J5 Tel. (514) 526-2003, Fax (514)526-6887

Faith Alive Bible College (Nondenominational), David Pierce, President, 637 University Dr., Saskatoon, SK S7N 0H8 Tel. (306)652-2230, Fax (306)665-1125
Email: faithalive@dlcwest.com

Full Gospel Bible Institute (Apostolic Church of Pentecost of Canada Inc.), Rev. Lauren E. Miller, President, Box 579, Eston, SK S0L 1A0 Tel. (306)962-3621, Fax (306)962-3810
Email: fgbi.eston@sk.sympatico.ca
Website: fgbi.sk.ca

Gardner College, A Centre for Christian Studies (Church of God (Anderson, Ind.)), John Alan Howard, President, 4704 55th St., Camrose,

AB T4V 2B6 Tel. (780)672-0171, Fax (780) 672-6888
Email: gardnerc@cable-lynx.net
Website: cable-lynx/~gardnerc

Grand Seminaire de Montréal* (The Roman Catholic Church in Canada), Marcel Demers, p.s.s., President, 2065 Sherbrooke Ouest, Montréal, QC H3H 1G6 Tel. (514)935-1169, Fax (514)935-5497
Email: Information Generale, info@gsdm.qc.ca or Bibliotheque: biblio@gsdm.qc.ca
Website: www.gsdm.qc.ca

Great Lakes Bible College (Churches of Christ in Canada), Mr. Arthur Ford, President, 62 Hickory St. W., Waterloo, ON N2L 3J4 Tel. (519)884-4310, Fax (519)884-4412
Email: learn@glbc.on.ca
Website: www.glbc.on.ca

Heritage College and Seminary* (The Fellowship of Evangelical Baptist Churches in Canada), Marvin Brubacher, President, 175 Holiday Inn Dr., Cambridge, ON N3C 3T2 Tel. (519)651-2869 or 800-465-1961, Fax (519)651-2870
Email: recruitment@heritage-theo.edu
Website: www.heritage-theo.edu

Huron University College* (The Anglican Church of Canada), Dr. David Bevan, Principal, 1349 Western Rd., London, ON N6G 1H3 Tel. (519)438-7224, Fax (519)438-3938
Email: huron@uwo.ca
Website: www.huronuc.on.ca

Institut Biblique Beree (The Pentecostal Assemblies of Canada), André L. Gagnon, President, 1711 Henri-Bourassa Est, Montréal, QC H2C 1J5 Tel. (514)385-4238, Fax (514) 385-4238

Ecole de Theologie Evangelique de Montreal (Canadian Conference of Mennonite Brethren Churches), Eric Wingender, President, 1775, boul Édouard-Laurin, Ville Saint-Laurent, QC H4L 2B9 Tel. (514)331-0878, Fax (514)331-0879
Email: iblinstitute@proxyma.net

Institute for Christian Studies (Nondenominational), Harry Fernhout, President, 229 College St., Suite 200, Toronto, ON M5T 1R4 Tel. (416)979-2331 or 1 (888)326-5347, Fax (416)979-2332
Email: email@icscanada.edu
Website: www.icscanada.edu

International Bible College (Church of God (Cleveland, Tenn.)), Cheryl Busse, President, 401 Trinity La., Moose Jaw, SK S6H 0E3 Tel. (306)692-4041, Fax (306)692-7968

Joint Board of Theological Colleges* (Interdenominational), Dr. John Simons, President, 3473 University St., Montréal, QC H3A 2A8 Tel. (514)849-8511, Fax (514)849-4113
Email: dio@colba.net
Website: www.mcgill.ca/religion/jbtc.htm

Key-Way-Tin Bible Institute (Nondenominational), Dir. Dave Petkau, President, Box 540, Lac La Biche, AB T0A 2C0 Tel. (780) 623-4565, Fax (780)623-1788
Email: kbi@telusplanet.net

Knox College* (The Presbyterian Church in Canada), J. Dorcas Gordon, Principal, 59 St. George St., Toronto, ON M5S 2E6 Tel. (416)978-4500, Fax (416)971-2133
Email: knox.college@utoronto.ca
Website: www.utoronto.ca/knox

Living Faith Bible College (Fellowship of Christian Assembies (Canada)), Cliff A. Stalwick, President, Box 100, Caroline, AB T0M 0M0 Tel. (403)722-2225, Fax (403)722-2459
Email: office@lfbc.net
Website: www.lfbc.net

Lutheran Theological Seminary* (Evangelical Lutheran Church in Canada), Faith Rohrbough, President, 114 Seminary Crescent, Saskatoon, SK S7N 0X3 Tel. (306) 966-7850, Fax (306)966-7852
Email: lutheran.seminary@usask.ca
Website: www.usask.ca/stu/luther

Maritime Christian College (Christian Churches and Churches of Christ in Canada), Fred C. Osborne, President, 503 University Ave., Charlottetown, PE C1A 7Z4 Tel. (902) 628-8887, Fax (902)892-3959
Email: registrar@maritimechristiancollege.pe.ca
Website: www.maritimechristiancollege.pe.ca

Master's College and Seminary (The Pentecostal Assemblies of Canada), Evon G. Horton, President, 780 Argyle St., Peterborough, ON K9H 5T2 Tel. (705)748-9111, Fax (705)748-3931
Email: info@mcs.edu
Website: www.mcs.edu

McGill University Faculty of Religious Studies* (Interdenominational), Donna R. Runnalls, President, 3520 University St., Montréal, QC H3A 2A7 Tel. (514)398-4121, Fax (514)398-6665

McMaster Divinity College* (Baptist), , Principal/Dean, McMaster Divinity College , Hamilton, ON L8S 4K1 Tel. (905)525-9140 Ext 24401, Fax (905)577-4782
Email: divinity@mcmaster.ca
Website: www.mcmaster.ca/divinity

Menno Simons College at Canadian Mennonite University (Mennonite Brethren Churches

MC Canada Churches), Dean Peachey, President, 500 Shaftesbury Blvd, Winnipeg, Manitoba R3P 2N2 Tel. (204)487-3300, Fax (204)487-3858
Email: reception@cmu.ca
Website: www.cmu.ca

Millar College of the Bible (Interdenominational), A. Brian Atmore, President, Box 25, Pambrun, SK S0N 1W0 Tel. (306)582-2033, Fax (306)582-2027

Montreal Diocesan Theological College* (The Anglican Church of Canada), The Rev. Dr. Jon Simons, Principal, 3473 University St., Montreal, QC H3A 2A8 Tel. (514)849-3004, Fax (514)849-4113
Email: diocoll@netrover.com
Website: www.montreal.anglican.org/mdtc

Mount Carmel Bible School (Christian Brethren (also known as Plymouth Brethren)), Gordon King, President, 4725 106 Ave., Edmonton, AB T6A 1E7 Tel. (780)465-3015 Toll-free 1(800) 561-6443, Fax (780)466-2485
Email: mail@mountcarmel.net

National Native Bible College (Elim Fellowship of Evangelical Churches and Ministers), Donovan Jacobs, College Director, Box 478, Deseronto, ON K0K 1X0 Tel. (613)396-2311, Fax (613)396-2314

Newman Theological College* (The Roman Catholic Church in Canada), Dr. Christophe Potworowski, President, 15611 St. Albert Trail, Edmonton, AB T6V 1H3 Tel. (780)447-2993, Fax (780)447-2685
Email: ntc.webmaster@newman.edu
Website: www.newman.edu

Nipawin Bible Institute (Interdenominational), Mark Leppington, President, Box 1986, Nipawin, SK S0E 1E0 Tel. (306)862-5095, Fax (306)862-3651
Email: info@nipawinbibleinstitute.ca
Website: www.nipawinbibleinstitute.sk.ca

Northwest Baptist Theological College and Seminary (The Fellowship of Evangelical Baptist Churches in Canada), Dr. Larry Perkins, Interim President, 7600 Glover Rd., Langley, BC V2Y 1Y1 Tel. (604)888-7592, Fax (604)513-8511
Email: nbs@twu.ca
Website: www.nbseminary.com

Northwest Bible College (The Pentecostal Assemblies of Canada), G. Johnson, President, 11617-106 Ave., Edmonton, AB T5H 0S1 Tel. (780)452-0808, Fax (780)452-5803
Email: info@nwbc.ab.ca
Website: www.nwbc.ab.ca

Ontario Christian Seminary (Christian Churches and Churches of Christ in Canada), James R. Cormode, President, P.O. Box 324, Stn. D 260 High Park Ave., Toronto, ON M6P 3J9 Tel. (416)769-7115, Fax (416)769-7047

Pacific Life Bible College (Foursquare), Rob Buzza, President, 15100 66 A Ave., Surrey, BC V3S 2A6 Tel. (604)597-9082, Fax (604)597-9090
Email: paclife@pacificlife.edu
Website: www.pacificlife.edu

Parole de Vie Bethel/Word of Life Bethel (Nondenominational), Ken Beach, President, 1175 Chemin Woodward, Lennoxville, QC J1M 2A2 Tel. (819)823-8435, Fax (819)823-2468
Email: quebec@canada.wol.org
Website: www.wol.org

Peace River Bible Institute (Interdenominational), Reuben Kvill, President, Box 99, Sexsmith, AB T0H 3C0 Tel. (780)568-3962, Fax (780)568-4431
Email: prbi@prbi.edu
Website: www.prbi.edu

Prairie Graduate School* (Interdenominational), Rick Down, President, 2540 5 Ave. NW, Calgary, AB T2N 0T5 Tel. (403)777-0150, Fax (403)270-2336
Email: prairie@pbi.ab.ca
Website: www.pbi.ab.ca

The Presbyterian College, Montreal* (Presbyterian Church in Canada), John Vissers, Principal, 3495 University St., Montreal, QC H3A 2A8 Tel. (514)288-5256, Fax (514)288-8072

Providence College and Theological Seminary* (Interdenominational), August H. Konkel, President, General Delivery, Otterburne, MB R0A 1G0 Tel. (204)433-7488, Fax (204)433-7158
Email: info@providence.mb.ca
Website: www.providence.mb.ca

Queens College* (The Anglican Church of Canada), Boyd Morgan, President, 210 Prince Phillip Dr., St. Johns, NF A1B 3R6 Tel. (709)753-0116, Fax (709)753-1214
Email: queens@mun.ca
Website: www.mun.ca/queens

Queen's Theological College* (The United Church of Canada), M Jean Stairs, President, Queen's Theological College , Kingston, ON K7L 3N6 Tel. (613)533-2110, Fax (613)533-6879
Email: theology@post.queensu.ca
Website: www.queensu.ca/theology

Reformed Episcopal Theological College (Reformed Episcopal Church of Canada), Rt. Rev. Michael Fedechko, President, 320 Armstrong St., Box 2532, New Liskeard, ON P0J 1P0 Tel. (705)647-4565, Fax (705)647-4565
Email: fed@nt.net
Website: forministry.com/REC-Canada

Regent College* (Interdenominational), Roc Wilson, PhD, President, 5800 University Blvd., Vancouver, BC V6T 2E4 Tel. (800)663-8664 or (604)224-3245, Fax (604)224-3097
Email: administration@regent-college.edu
Website: www.regent-college.edu

Regis College* (The Roman Catholic Church in Canada), John Allan Loftus, S.J, President, 15 St. Mary St., Toronto, ON M4Y 2R5 Tel. (416)922-5474, Fax (416)922-2898
Email: regis.registrar@utoronto.ca
Website: www.utoronto.ca/regis

Rocky Mountain College, Centre for Biblical Studies (The Evangelical Missionary Church of Canada), Gordon Dirks, President, 4039 Brentwood Rd. NW, Calgary, AB T2L 1L1 Tel. (403)284-5100, Fax (403)220-9567
Email: admissions@rockymc.edu
Website: www.rockymc.edu

St. Andrew's Theological College* (The United Church of Canada), Dr. Christopher Lind, President, 1121 College Dr., Saskatoon, SK S7N 0W3 Tel. (306)966-8970, Fax (306)966-8981
Website: www.usask.ca/stu/standrews

St. Augustine's Seminary of Toronto* (The Roman Catholic Church in Canada), John A. Boissonneau, President, 2661 Kingston Rd., Scarborough, ON M1M 1M3 Tel. (416)261-7207, Fax (416)261-2529
Website: www. canxsys.com/staugust.htm

St. John's College, Univ. of Manitoba, Faculty of Theology (The Anglican Church of Canada), B. Hudson McLean, President, 92 Dysart Rd., Winnipeg, MB R3T 2M5 Tel. (204)474-6852, Fax (204)261-1215

Saint Paul University, Faculty of Theology (The Roman Catholic Church), David B. Perrin, Ph.D., Dean, 223 Main St., Ottawa, ON K1S 1C4 Tel. (613)236-1393 x. 2246, Fax (613)751-4016
Email: fquesnal@ustpaul.uottawa.ca
Website: www.ustpaul.ca

St. Peter's Seminary* (The Roman Catholic Church in Canada), Thomas C. Collins, President, 1040 Waterloo St., London, ON N6A 3Y1 Tel. (519)432-1824, Fax (519)432-0964

St. Stephen's College, Grad. & Continuing Theological Education* (The United Church of Canada), Dr. Christopher Lind, President, 8810 112th St., Edmonton, AB T6G 2J6 Tel. (780)439-7311, Fax (780)433-8875
Email: westema@ualberta.ca
Website: www.ualberta.ca/st.stephens

Salvation Army College for Officer Training (The Salvation Army in Canada), Wayne N. Pritchett, Principal, 2130 Bayview Ave., North York, ON M4N 3K6 Tel. (416)481-6131, Fax (416)481-6810; (416)481-2895 (Library)

The Salvation Army William and Catherine Booth College (The Salvation Army in Canada), Dr. Jonathan S. Raymond, President, 447 Webb Pl., Winnipeg, MB R3B 2P2 Tel. (204)947-6701, Fax (204)942-3856
Email: wcbc@sallynet.org
Website: www.wcbc-sa.edu

Steinbach Bible College (Mennonite), Abe Bergen, President, Box 1420, Steinbach, MB R0A 2A0 Tel. (204)326-6451, Fax (204)326-6908
Email: info@sbcollege.mb.ca
Website: www.sbcollege.mb.ca

Taylor College of Education (Church Army Canada), Rev. Capt. David Edwards, Principal, 230 Hawthorne Ave Ext, Saint John, NB E2K 3S9 Tel. 506-693-8975, Fax 506-657-8217
Email: edwa@nbnet.ca

Theological College of the Canadian Reformed Churches (Canadian and American Reformed Churches), N. H. Gootjes, President, 110 West 27th St., Hamilton, ON L9C 5A1 Tel. (416) 575-3688, Fax (416)575-0799

Toronto Baptist Seminary and Bible College (Nondenominational), Andrew M. Fountain, Principal, 130 Gerrard St., E., Toronto, ON M5A 3T4 Tel. (416)925-3263, Fax (416)925-8305
Email: tbs@tbs.edu
Website: www.tbs.edu

Toronto School of Theology* (Interdenominational), W. David Neelands, Director, 47 Queens Park Crescent E., Toronto, ON M5S 2C3 Tel. (416)978-4039, Fax (416)978-7821
Email: registrar.tst@utoronto.ca
Website: www.tst.edu

Trinity College, Faculty of Divinity* (The Anglican Church of Canada), Brian Ruttan, Acting Dean, 6 Hoskin Ave., Toronto, ON M5S 1H8 Tel. (416)978-2133, Fax (416)978-4949
Email: divinity@trinity.utoronto.ca
Website: www.trinity.utoronto.ca/divinity

Tyndale College & Seminary* (Trans-denominational), Dr. Brian C. Stiller, President, 25 Ballyconnor Ct., Toronto, ON M2M 4B3 Tel. (416)226-6380, Fax (416)226-6746
Email: info@tyndale.ca
Website: www.tyndale.ca

United Theological College/Le Séminaire Uni* (The United Church of Canada), Rev. Philip Joudrey, President, 3521 rue Université, Montréal, QC H3A 2A9 Tel. (514)849-2042, Fax (514)849-8634
Email: admin@utc.ca
Website: www.utc.ca

Université Laval, Faculté de théologie et de sciences religieuses (The Roman Catholic Church in Canada), Marc Pelchat, President, CitÇ Universitaire, Ste-Foy, QC G1K 7P4 Tel. (418)656-2131, Fax (418)656-3273
Email: ftsr@ftsr.ulaval.ca
Website: www.ftsr.ulaval.ca

Université de Montréal, Faculté de théologie (The Roman Catholic Church in Canada), Jean-Marc Charron, President, C. P. 6128 Succ. Centre Ville, Montréal, QC H3C 3J7 Tel. (514)343-7160, Fax (514)343-5738
Email: theologie@ere.umontreal.ca
Website: www.theo.umontreal.ca

Université de Sherbrooke, Faculté de theologié, d'éthique et de philosophie (The Roman Catholic Church in Canada), Jean-Franáois Malherbe, President, 1111, rue Saint-Charles Ouest, Tourquest - Bureau 310, Longueuil, QC J4K 5G4 Tel. 450-670-7157, Fax 450-670-1959
Email: jf.malherbe@sympatico.ca
Website: www.usherb.ca/longueuil

University of St. Michael's College, Faculty of Theology* (The Roman Catholic Church in Canada), Dr. Anne Anderson, CSJ, Dean of Theology, 81 St. Mary St., Toronto, ON M5S 1J4 Tel. (416)926-7140, Fax (416)926-7294
Website: www.utoronto.ca/stmikes/index.html

The University of Winnipeg, Faculty of Theology* (Multi-denominational and the United Church of Canada), Gordon MacDermid, Dean of Faculty of Theology, Dean, 515 Portage Ave., Winnipeg, MB R3B 2E9 Tel. (204)786-9390, Fax (204)772-2584
Email: theology@uwinnipeg.ca
Website: www.uwinnipeg.ca/academic/theology

Vancouver School of Theology* (Interdenominational), Dr. Kenneth G. MacQueen, President, 6000 Iona Dr., Vancouver, BC V6T 1L4 Tel. (604)822-9031, Fax (604)822-9212
Email: vstinfo@vst.edu
Website: www.vst.edu

Waterloo Lutheran Seminary* (Evangelical Lutheran Church in Canada), Richard C. Crossman, President, 75 University Ave. W., Waterloo, ON N2L 3C5 Tel. (519)884-1970, Fax (519)725-2434
Email: seminary@wlu.ca
Website: www.wlu.ca/~wwwsem/

Western Christian College (Churches of Christ in Canada), John McMillan, President, Box 5000, 220 Whitmore Ave. W., Dauphin, MB R7N 2V5 Tel. (204)638-8801, Fax (204)638-7054
Email: president@westernchristian.ca
Website: www.westernchristian.ca

Western Pentecostal Bible College (The Pentecostal Assemblies of Canada), James G. Richards, President, Box 1700, Abbotsford, BC V2S 7E7 Tel. (604)853-7491, Fax (604) 853-8951
Email: wpbcr@uniserve.com
Website: www.wpbc.edu

Wycliffe College* (The Anglican Church of Canada), Rev. Dr. George R. Sumner, Jr., President, 5 Hoskin Ave., Toronto, ON M5S 1H7 Tel. (416)946-3535, Fax (416)946-3545
Email: wycliffe.college@utoronto.ca
Website: www.chass.utoronto.ca/wycliffe

11. Religious Periodicals in the United States

This list focuses on publications of the organizations listed in Directory 3, "Religious Bodies in the United States," however there are also some independent publications listed. The list does not include all publications prepared by religious bodies, and not all the publications listed here are necessarily the official publication of a particular church. Regional publications and newsletters are not included. A more extensive list of religious periodicals published in the United States can be found in *Gale Directory of Publications and Broadcast Media*, (Gale Research, Inc., P.O. Box 33477, Detroit MI 48232-5477).

Each entry in this directory contains: the title of the periodical, frequency of publication, religious affiliation, editor's name, address, telephone and fax number and e-mail and website addresses when available. The frequency of publication, which appears in parenthesis after the name of the publication is represented by a "W." for weekly; "M." for monthly; "Q." for quarterly.

US PERIODICALS

21st Century Christian, (M.) Churches of Christ, M. Norvel Young and Prentice A. Meador, Jr., Box 40304, Nashville, TN 37204 Tel. (800)331-5991, Fax (615)385-5915

The A.M.E. Christian Recorder, (bi-W.) African Methodist Episcopal Church, Ricky Spain, 1134 - 11th St NW, Suite 202 Washington, DC 20001 Tel. 202-216-4294, Fax 202-216-4293
Email: rspain5737@aol.com
Website: www.amecnet.org

A.M.E. Church Review, (Q.) African Methodist Episcopal Church, Paulette Coleman, PhD., 500 Eighth Ave., S., Ste.211, Nashville, TN 37203-4181 Tel. (615)256-7020, Fax (615) 256-7092
Email: AMERVW@aol.com

Action, (10-Y.) Churches of Christ, Dr. R. H. Tex Williams, P.O. Box 2169, Cedar Park, TX 78630-2169 Tel. (512)345-819, Fax (512) 345-6634
Email: wbschool@bga.com
Website: www.wbschool.org

Adra Today, (Q.) Seventh-day Adventist Church, Beth Schaefer, 12501 Old Columbia Pike, Silver Spring, MD 20904-6600 Tel. (301)680-6355, Fax (301)680-6370
Email: 74617.2105@compuserve.com
Website: www.adra.org

Adult Lessons Quarterly, (Q.) Nondenominational, Braille and cassette tape only, Darcy Quigley, John Milton Society for the Blind, 475 Riverside Dr., Rm. 455 New York, NY 10115-0455 Tel. (212)870-3335, Fax (212) 870-3229
Email: order@jmsblind.org
Website: www.jmsblind.org

The Adult Quarterly, (Q.) Associate Reformed Presbyterian Church (General Synod), Mr. W. H. F. Kuykendall PhD., P.O. Box 575, Due West, SC 29639 Tel. (864)379-2284
Email: wkuykend@erskine.edu

Advent Christian News, (M.) Advent Christian Church, Rev. Keith D. Wheaton, P.O. Box 23152, Charlotte, NC 28227 Tel. (704)545-6161, Fax (704)573-0712
Email: Mayerpub@aol.com

The Advent Christian Witness, (M.) Advent Christian Church, Rev. Keith D. Wheaton, P.O. Box 23152, Charlotte, NC 28227 Tel. (704)545-6161, Fax (704)573-0712
Email: Mayerpub@aol.com

Adventist Review, (W.) Seventh-day Adventist Church, W. G. Johnsson, 12501 Old Columbia Pike, Silver Spring, MD 20904-6600 Tel. (301)680-6560, Fax (301)680-6638
Email: 74617,15.compuserve.com
Website: www.adventistreview.com

The Advocate, (10-Y.) Episcopal, Kay Collier-Slone, Ph.D., PO Box 610, Lexington, KY 40588-0610 Tel. (606)252-6527, Fax (606) 231-9077
Email: diolex@aol.com

Again Magazine, (Q.) The Antiochian Orthodox Christian Archdiocese of North America, R. Thomas Zell, P.O. Box 76, Ben Lomond, CA 95005-0076 Tel. (831)336-5118, Fax (831) 336-8882
Email: marketing@conciliarpress.com
Website: www.conciliarpress.com

Agenda, (10-Y.) Church of the Brethren, Howard Royer and Walt Wiltschek, 1451 Dundee Ave., Elgin, IL 60120-1676 Tel. (847) 742-5100
Email: hroyer_gb@brethren.org or wwiltschek_gb@brethren.org
Website: www.brethren.org

AIM Magazine, (bi-M.) Free Will Baptists, National Association of, Ida Lewis, Home Missions Office, P.O. Box 5002 Antioch, TN 37011-5002 Tel. (615)731-6812, Fax (615) 731-7655
Email: ida@nafwb.org

Alive Now, (6-Y.) The United Methodist Church, Melissa Tidwell, Interim Editor, P.O. Box 34004, Nashville, TN 37203-0004 Tel. (615) 340-7218
Email: alivenow@upperroom.org
Website: www..alivenow,org

The Allegheny Wesleyan Methodist, (M.) The Allegheny Wesleyan Methodist Connection (Original Allegheny Conference), Michael Marshall, P.O. Box 357, Salem, OH 44460 Tel. (330)337-9376, Fax (330)337-9700
Email: awmc@juno.com

Alliance Life, (M.) The Christian and Missionary Alliance, Stephen P. Adams, P.O. Box 35000, Colorado Springs, CO 80935 Tel. (719)599-5999, Fax (719)599-8234
Email: alife@cmalliance.org
Website: www.alliancelife.org

American Baptist In Mission, (6-Y.) American Baptist Churches in the USA, Richard W. Schramm, P.O. Box 851, Valley Forge, PA 19482-0851 Tel. (610)768-2077, Fax (610) 768-2320
Email: richard.schramm@abc-usa.org
Website: www.abc-usa.org

American Baptist Quarterly, (Q.) American Baptist Churches in the USA, Dr. Robert E. Johnson, P.O. Box 851, Valley Forge, PA 19482-0851 Tel. (610)768-2269, Fax (610) 768-2266
Email: dbvanbro@abc-usa.org
Website: www.abc-usa/abhs

American Bible Society Record, (6-Y.) Nondenominational, Peter Feuerherd, 1865 Broadway, New York, NY 10023-7505 Tel. (212)408-1502, Fax (212)408-1456
Email: absrecord@americanbible.org
Website: www.americanbible.org

El Aposento Alto, (6-Y.) The United Methodist Church, Carmen Gaud, P.O. Box 340004, Nashville, TN 37203-0004 Tel. (615)340-7253, Fax (615)340-7267
Email: ElAposentoAlto@upperroom.org
Website: www.upperroom.org

The Armenian Church, (M.) Diocese of the Armenian Church of America, Michael A. Zeytoonian, 630 Second Avenue, New York, NY 10016 Tel. (212)686-0710, Fax (212)779-3558

The Associate Reformed Presbyterian, (M.) Associate Reformed Presbyterian Church (General Synod), Mr. Ben Johnston, One Cleveland St., Greenville, SC 29601 Tel. (864)232-8297, Fax (864)271-3729
Email: arpmaged@arpsynod.org
Website: www.arpsynod.org

Attack, A Magazine for Christian Men, (Q.) National Association for Free Will Baptists, James E. Vallance, P.O. Box 5002, Antioch, TN 37011-5002 Tel. (615)731-4950, Fax (615) 731-0771

The Banner of Truth, (M.) Netherlands Reformed Congregations, J. den Hoed, 824 18th Ave. S., Rock Valley, IA 51247 Tel. (712) 476-2442

The Banner, (24-Y.) Christian Reformed Church in North America, John A. Suk, 2850 Kalamazoo Ave., S.E., Grand Rapids, MI 49560 Tel. (616)224-0732, Fax (616)224-0834
Email: editorial@thebanner.org
Website: www.thebanner.org

The Baptist Bible Tribune, (M.) Baptist Bible Fellowship International, Mike Randall, P.O. Box 309, Springfield, MO 65801-0309 Tel. (417)831-3996, Fax (417)831-1470
Email: editors@tribune.org
Website: www.tribune.org

Baptist Bulletin, (M.) General Association of Regular Baptist Churches, David M. Gower, 1300 N. Meacham Rd., Schaumburg, IL 60173-4806 Tel. (847)843-1600, Fax (847) 843-3757
Email: baptistbulletin@garbc.org
Website: www.garbc.org

Baptist History and Heritage, (3-Y.) Baptist History and Heritage Society, Merrill M. Hawkins, Jr., Carson-Newman College, P.O. Box 71919 Jefferson City, TN 37760 Tel. (865)471-3246, Fax (865)471-3502
Email: mhawkins@cn.edu
Website: www.baptisthistory.org

Baptist Peacemaker, (Q.) Baptist, Katie Cook, 4800 Wedgewood Dr., Charlotte, NC 28210 Tel. (704)521-6051, Fax (704)521-6053
Email: bpfna@bpfna.org
Website: www.bpfna.org

The Baptist Preacher, (Bi-M.) Baptist Bible Fellowship International, Mike Randall, P.O. Box 309 HSJ, Springfield, MO 65801 Tel. (417)831-3996, Fax (417)831-1470
Email: editors@tribune.org
Website: www.tribune.org

Baptist Progress, (Q.) Progresive National Baptist Convention, Inc., Archie Logan, 601 50th St. NE, Washington, DC 20019 Tel. (202) 396-0558, Fax (202)398-4998

Baptist Witness, (M.) Primitive Baptists, Lasserre Bradley, Jr., Box 17037, Cincinnati, OH 45217 Tel. (513)821-7289, Fax (513)821-7303
Email: bbh45217@aol.com
Website: www.BaptistBibleHour.org

The Bible Advocate, (10-Y.) The Church of God (Seventh Day), Denver, Colo., Calvin Burrell, PO Box 33677, Denver, CO 80233 Tel. (303)452-7973, Fax (303)452-0657
Email: bibleadvocate@cog7.org
Website: www.cog7.org/BA

US PERIODICALS

The Brethren Evangelist, (M.) Brethren Church (Ashland, Ohio), Rev. Richard C. Winfield, 524 College Ave., Ashland, OH 44805 Tel. (419)289-1708, Fax (419)281-0450
Email: brethren@brethrenchurch.org

Brethren Journal, (10-Y.) Unity of Brethren, Rev. Milton Maly, 6703 FM 2502, Brenham, TX 77833-9803 Tel. (409)830-8762

The Bridegroom's Messenger, (bi-M.) The International Pentecostal Church of Christ, Janice Boyce, 121 W. Hunters Trail, Elizabeth City, NC 27909 Tel. (919)338-3003, Fax (919) 338-3003

Builder, (M.) Mennonite Church USA and Canada, David R. Hiebert, 616 Walnut Ave., Scottdale, PA 15683 Tel. (724)887-8500, Fax (707)897-3788
Email: Hiebert@mph.org
Website: www.mph.org/builder/

The Burning Bush, (Q.) The Metropolitan Church Association, Inc. (Wesleyan), Rev. Gary Bowell, The Metropolitan Church Assoc., 415 Broad St., #2 Lake Geneva, WI 53147 Tel. (262)248-6786

The Calvary Messenger, (M.) Beachy Amish Mennonite Churches, David Sommers, Rt. 2, Box 187-A, Abbeville, SC 29620 Tel. (814) 662-2483

Campus Life, (9-Y.) Nondenominational, Christopher Lutes, 465 Gunderson Dr., Carol Stream, IL 60188 Tel. (630)260-6200, Fax (630)260-0114
Email: clmag@campuslife.net
Website: www.campuslife.net

Capsule, (M.) General Association of General Baptists, Jack Eberhardt, 100 Stinson Dr., Poplar Bluff, MO 63901 Tel. (573)785-7746, Fax (573)785-0564

Caring, (4-Y.) Assemblies of God, Owen Wilkie, Gospel Publishing House, 1445 N. Boonville Ave. Springfield, MO 65802 Tel. (417)862-2781, Fax (417)862-4832
Email: benevolences@ag.org
Website: www.benevolences.ag.org

Cathedral Age, (Q.) Interdenominational, Craig W. Stapert, Mass & Wisconsin Ave. NW, Washington, DC 20016-5098 Tel. (202)537-5681, Fax (202)364-6600
Email: cathedral_age@cathedral.org
Website: www.cathedral.org/cathedral

Catholic Chronicle, (bi-W.) The Roman Catholic Church, Patricia Lynn Morrison, PO Box 1866, Toledo, OH 43603-1866 Tel. (419)885-6397, Fax (419)885-6398
Email: catholicchronicle@earthlink.net

Catholic Digest, (M.) The Roman Catholic Church, Richard Reece, 2115 Summit Avenue, St. Paul, MN 55105-1081 Tel. (612)962-6725, Fax (612)962-6755
Email: Cdigest@stthomas.edu
Website: www.CatholicDigest.or

Catholic Herald, (W.) The Roman Catholic Church, Ethel M. Gintoft, 3501 S. Lake Dr., St. Francis, WI 53235-0913 Tel. (414)769-3468
Email: chn@execpc.com
Website: www.execpc.com/~chn

Catholic Light, (bi-W.) The Roman Catholic Church, William R. Genello, 300 Wyoming Ave., Scranton, PA 18503 Tel. (570)207-2229, Fax (570)207-2271
Email: billgenello@worldnet.att.net
Website: www.dioceseofscranton.org

The Catholic New World, (W.) The Roman Catholic Church, Thomas H. Sheridan, 1144 W. Jackson Blvd., Chicago, IL 60607 Tel. (312)243-1300, Fax (312)243-1526
Email: Neworld201@aol.com
Website: catholicnewworld.com

The Catholic Peace Voice, (Q.) The Roman Catholic Church, Dave Robinson, 532 W. 8th Street, Erie, PA 16502 Tel. (814)453-4955, Fax (814)452-4784

The Catholic Review, (W.) The Roman Catholic Church, Daniel L. Medinger, P.O. Box 777, Baltimore, MD 21203 Tel. (410)547-5380, Fax (410)385-0113
Email: mail@catholicreview.org
Website: www.catholicreview.org

Catholic Standard and Times, (W.) The Roman Catholic Church, Rev Paul S. Quinter, 222 N. 17th St., Philadelphia, PA 19103 Tel. (215) 587-3660, Fax (215)587-3979

The Catholic Transcript, (W.) The Roman Catholic Church, Christopher M. Tiano, 467 Bloomfield Ave, Bloomfield, CT 06002 Tel. (203)527-1175, Fax (203)947-6397

Catholic Universe Bulletin, (bi-W.) The Roman Catholic Church, Dennis Sadowski, 1027 Superior Ave., N.E., Cleveland, OH 44114-2556 Tel. (216)696-6525, Fax (216)696-6519

Catholic Worker, (7-Y.) The Roman Catholic Church, Brian Harte, 36 E. First St., New York, NY 10003 Tel. (212)777-9617

Cela Biedrs, (10-Y.) The Latvian Evangelical Lutheran Church in America, Rev. Indra Skuja-Grisle, 601-850 Cambridge St., Winnipeg, MB R3M 3W8 Tel. (204)452-3844

Celebration: An Ecumenical Worship Resource, (M.) Interdenominational, Patrick Marrin, P.O. Box 419493, Kansas City, MO 64141-6493 Tel. (816)531-0538, Fax (816) 968-2280
Email: patmarrin@aol.com
Website: www.ncrpub.com

The Challenge, (Q.) The Bible Church of Christ, Inc., A.M. Jones, 1358 Morris Ave., Bronx, NY 10456 Tel. (718)588-2284, Fax (718)992-5597 Website: www.thebiblechurchofchrist.org

Charisma, (M.) Nondenominational, J. Lee Grady, 600 Rinehart Rd., Lake Mary, FL 32746 Tel. (407)333-0600, Fax (407)333-7133 Email: grady@strang.com Website: www.charismamag.com

The Children's Friend, (Q.) Seventh-day Adventist Church, Gaylena Gibson, P.O. Box 6097, Lincoln, NE 68506 Tel. (402)488-0981, Fax (402)488-7582 Email: editorial@christianrecord.org Website: www.ChristianRecord.org

Christadelphian Advocate, (M.) Christadelphians, Edward W. Farrar, 4 Mountain Park Ave., Hamilton, ON L9A 1A2 Tel. (905)383-1817, Fax (905)383-2705

Christadelphian Tidings, (M.) Christadelphians, Donald H. Styles, 42076 Hartford Dr., Canton, MI 48187 Tel. (313)844-2426, Fax (313)844-8304

Christadelphian Watchman, (M.) Christadelphians, George Booker, 2500 Berwyn Cir., Austin, TX 78745 Tel. (512)447-8882

The Christian Baptist, (M.) Primitive Baptists, Elder S. T. Tolley, P.O. Box 68, Atwood, TN 38220 Tel. (901)662-7417 Email: cbl@aeneas.net

Christian Bible Teacher, (M.) Churches of Christ, Bob Connel, bobconnel@aol.com, Box 1060, Abilene, TX 79604 Tel. (915)677-6262, Fax (915)677-1511 Email: publications@qpabilene.com Website: www.qpabilene.com

The Christian Century, (26-Y.) Nondenominational, John Buchanan, 104 South Michigan Ave., Chicago, IL 60603 Tel. (312)263-7510, Fax (312)263-7540 Email: main@christiancentury.org Website: www.christiancentury.org

The Christian Chronicle, (M.) Churches of Christ, Bailey McBride, Box 11000, Oklahoma City, OK 73136-1100 Tel. (405) 425-5070, Fax (405)425-5076

The Christian Community, (8-Y.) International Council of Community Churches, Rev. Michael E. Livingston, 21116 Washington Pkwy., Frankfort, IL 60423 Tel. (815)464-5690, Fax (815)464-5692 Email: ICCC60423@aol.com

Christian Education Counselor, (bi-M.) Assemblies of God, Sylvia Lee, Sunday School Promotion and Training, 1445 Boonville Ave., Springfield, MO 65802-1894 Tel. (417)862-2781, Fax (417)862-0503 Email: salee@publish.ag.org Website: www.we-build-people.org/cec

The Christian Endeavor World, (Q.) Nondenominational, David G. Jackson, P.O. Box 820, 3575 Valley Rd. Liberty Corner, NJ 07938-0820 Tel. (908)604-9440, Fax (908) 604-6075

The Christian Index, (M.) Christian Methodist Episcopal Church, Dr. Kenneth E. Jones, P.O. Box 431, Fairfield, AL 35064 Tel. (205)929-1640, Fax (205)791-1910 Email: goodoc@aol.com Website: www.c-m-e.org

Christian Leader, (M.) U.S. Conference of Mennonite Brethren Churches, Carmen Andres, Box 220, Hillsboro, KS 67063 Tel. (316)947-5543, Fax (316)947-3266 Email: chleader@southwind.net

Christian Living, (8-Y.) Mennonite Church, Sarah Kehrberg, 616 Walnut Ave., Scottdale, PA 15683 Tel. (724)887-8500, Fax (724)887-3111 Email: cl@mph.org Website: www.mph.org/cl/

Christian Monthly, (M.) Apostolic Lutheran Church of America, Linda Mattson, P.O. Box 2126, Battle Ground, WA 98604 Tel. (360) 687-6493, Fax 360-687-6493 Email: christianm@apostolic-lutheran.org Website: www.Apostolic-Lutheran.org

Christian Outlook, (M.) Pentecostal Assemblies of the World, Inc., Johnna E. Hampton, 3939 Meadows Dr., Indianapolis, IN 46205 Tel. (317)547-9541, Fax (317)543-0512

The Christian Reader, (bi-M.) Nondenominational, Bonne Steffer, 465 Gunderson Dr., Carol Stream, IL 60188 Tel. (630)260-6200, Fax (630)260-0114

Christian Record, (Q.) Seventh-day Adventist Church, Gaylena Gibson, P.O. Box 6097, Lincoln, NE 68506 Tel. (402)488-0981, Fax (402)488-7582 Email: editorial@christianrecord.org Website: www.ChristianRecord.org

The Christian Science Journal, (M.) Church of Christ, Scientist, William E. Moody, One Norway St., Boston, MA 02115 Tel. (617)450-2000, Fax (617)450-2707 Email: moodyw@csps.com Website: www.csjournal.com

The Christian Science Monitor, (d&W) Church of Christ, Scientist, David T. Cook, One Norway St., Boston, MA 02115 Tel. (617) 450-2000, Fax (617)450-7575 Website: www.csmonitor.com

Christian Science Quarterly Weekly Bible Lessons, (Q.) Church of Christ, Scientist, Carol Humphry, Circulation Marketing Manager, One Norway St., C-40, Boston, MA 02115 Tel. (617)450-2000, Fax (617)450-7575

Email: service@csps.com
Website: www.biblelesson.com

Christian Science Sentinel, (W.) Church of Christ, Scientist, William E. Moody, One Norway St., Boston, MA 02115-3112 Tel. (617)450-2000, Fax (617)450-2707
Email: moodyw@csps.com
Website: www.cssentinel.com

Christian Social Action, (bi-M.) The United Methodist Church, vacant, 100 Maryland Ave. NE, Washington, DC 20002 Tel. (202)488-5621, Fax (202)488-1617
Website: www.umc-gbcs.org

Christian Standard, (W.) Christian Churches and Churches of Christ, Sam E. Stone, 8121 Hamilton Ave., Cincinnati, OH 45231 Tel. (513)931-4050, Fax (513)931-0950
Email: christianstd@standardpub.com
Website: www.standardpub.com

Christian Woman, (bi-M.) Churches of Christ, Sandra Humphrey, Box 150, Nashville, TN 37202 Tel. (615)254-8781, Fax (615)254-7411

Christianity & The Arts, (Q.) Nondenominational, Marci Whitney-Schenck, P.O. Box 118088, Chicago, IL 60611, Tel. (312)642-8606 Fax (312)266-7719
Email: chrnarts@aol.com

The Church Advocate, (Q.) Churches of God, General Conference, Rachel L. Foreman, P.O. Box 926, 700 E. Melrose Ave. Findlay, OH 45839 Tel. (419)424-1961, Fax (419)424-3433
Email: communications@cggc.org
Website: www.cggc.org

Church of God Evangel, (M.) Church of God (Cleveland, Tenn.), Bill George, P.O. Box 2250, Cleveland, TN 37320 Tel. (423)478-7592, Fax (423)478-7616
Email: bill_george@pathwaypress.org
Website: www.pathwaypress.org

Church of God Missions, (bi-M.) Church of God (Anderson, Ind.), J. David Reames, Box 2337, Anderson, IN 46018-2337 Tel. (765)648-2128, Fax (765)642-4279
Email: mbchogvp@aol.com

Church of God Progress Journal, (bi-M.) Church of God General Conference (Oregon, Ill. & Morrow, GA), David Krogh, Box 100,000, Morrow, GA 30260 Tel. (404)362-0052, Fax (404)362-9307
Email: info@abc-coggc.org
Website: www.abc-coggc.org

The Church Herald, (11-Y.) Reformed Church in America, Christina Van Eyl, 4500 60th St., SE, Grand Rapids, MI 49512 Tel. (616)698-7071, Fax (616)698-6606
Email: cvaneyl@rca.org

Church History: Studies in Christianity and Culture, (Q.) Scholarly, Elizabeth A. Clark, Grant Wacker, Hans J. Hillerbrand, and Richard P. Heitzenrater, The Divinity School, Duke University, Box 90975 Durham, NC 27708-0975 Tel. (919)660-3470, Fax (919) 660-3473
Email: church-history@duke.edu
Website: www.churchhistory.org

The Church Messenger, (bi-M.) , James S. Dutko, 280 Clinton St., Binghamton, NY 13905

Church School Herald, (Q.) African Methodist Episcopal Zion Church, Ms. Mary A. Love, P.O. Box 26769, Charlotte, NC 28221-6769 Tel. (704)599-4630 ext. 324, Fax (704)688-2548

Church & Society Magazine, (bi-M.) Presbyterian Church (U.S.A.), Kathy Lancaster, 100 Witherspoon St., Louisville, KY 40202-1396 Tel. (502)569-5810, Fax (502) 569-8116
Email: kathyl@ctr.pcusa.org
Website: horeb.pcusa.org/churchsociety

The Churchman's Human Quest, Non-denominational, Edna Ruth Johnson, 1074 23rd Ave. N., St. Petersburg, FL 33704 Tel. (813)894-0097

Churchwoman, (Q.) Interdenominational, Annie Songco, Editor/Publication Chief, 475 Riverside Dr., New York, NY 10115 Tel. (212)870-2347, Fax (212)870-2338
Email: cwu@churchwomen.org
Website: www.churchwomen.org

Circuit Rider, (6-Y.) The United Methodist Church, Jill S. Reddig, 201 Eighth Ave. S., Nashville, TN 37202 Tel. (615)749-6538, Fax (615)749-6061
Email: jreddig@umpublishing.org
Website: www.umph.org

Clarion Herald, (bi-W.) The Roman Catholic Church, Peter P. Finney, Jr., P. O. Box 53247, 1000 Howard Ave. Suite 400 New Orleans, LA 70153 Tel. (504)596-3035, Fax (504)596-3020

The Clergy Journal, (10-Y.) Nondenominational, Sharilyn A. Figueroa, Managing Editor & Clyde J. Steckel, Executive Editor, 6160 Carmen Avenue E, Inver Grove Heights, MN 55076-4422 Tel. (800) 328-0200, Fax (651)457-4617
Email: fig@logostaff.com
Website: www.joinhands.com

Club Connection, (Q.) Assemblies of God, Debby Seler, 1445 Boonville Ave., Springfield, MO 65802-1894 Tel. (417)862-2781, Fax (417) 862-0503
Email: clubconnection@ag.org
Website: www.missionettes.ag.org

CoLaborer, (bi-M.) National Association of Free Will Baptists, Sarah Fletcher, Women Nationally Active for Christ, P.O. Box 5002 Antioch, TN 37011-5002 Tel. (615)731-6812, Fax (615)731-0771
Email: wnac@nafwb.org

Collegiate Quarterly, (Q.) Seventh-day Adventist Church, Gary B. Swanson, 12501 Old Columbia Pike, Silver Spring, MD 20904 Tel. (301)680-6160, Fax (301)680-6155

Columbia, (M.) The Roman Catholic Church, Tim S. Hickey, One Columbus Plaza, New Haven, CT 06510 Tel. (203)772-2130, Fax (203)777-0114
Email: thickey@kofc-supreme.com
Website: www.kofc.org

The Commission, (10-Y.) International Mission Board, Southern Baptist Convention, Bill Bangham, Editor-in-chief, Box 6767, Richmond, VA 23230-0767 Tel. (804)219-1253, Fax (804)219-1410
Email: commission@imb.org
Website: www.imb.org/commission

Common Lot, (4-Y.) United Church of Christ, Martha J. Hunter, 700 Prospect Ave., Cleveland, OH 44115 Tel. (216)736-2150, Fax (216)736-2156

Commonweal, (bi-W.) The Roman Catholic Church, Margaret O'Brien Steinfels, 475 Riverside Drive, Rm 405, New York, NY 10115 Tel. (212)662-4200, Fax (212)662-4183
Email: commonweal@msn.com
Website: www.commonwealmagazine.org

Communique, (M.) National Baptist Convention of America, Inc., Robert Jeffrey, 1320 Pierre Avenue, Shreveport, LA 71103 Tel. (318)221-3701, Fax (318)222-7512

The Congregationalist, (5-Y.) National Association Congregational Christian Churches, Joseph B. Polhemus, 1105 Briarwood Rd., Mansfield, OH 44907 Tel. (419)756-5526, Fax (419)756-5526
Email: jbpedit@aol.com
Website: www.congregationalist.org

Conqueror, (bi-M.) United Pentecostal Church International, John F. Sills, 8855 Dunn Rd., Hazelwood, MO 63042 Tel. (314)837-7300, Fax (314)837-4503
Email: GYouth8855@aol.com

Contact, (M.) National Association of Free Will Baptists, Jack Williams, P.O. Box 5002, Antioch, TN 37011-5002 Tel. (615)731-6812, Fax (615)731-0771

Context, (22-Y.) Nondenominational, Martin Marty, 205 W. Monroe St., Chicago, IL 60606-5013 Tel. (312)236-7782, Fax (312)236-8207
Email: editors@uscatholic.org
Website: www.contextonline.org

Cornerstone Connections, (Q.) Seventh-day Adventist Church, Gary B. Swanson, 12501 Old Columbia Pike, Silver Spring, MD 20904 Tel. (301)680-6160, Fax (301)680-6155

Courage in the Struggle for Justice and Peace, (Q.) United Church of Christ, Sandy Sorensen, 110 Maryland Ave., Ste. 207, NE, Washington, DC 20002 Tel. (202)543-1517, Fax (202)543-5994

The Covenant Companion, (M.) Evangelical Covenant Church, Jane K. Swanson-Nystrom, 5101 N. Francisco Ave., Chicago, IL 60625 Tel. (773)906-3326, Fax (773)784-4366
Email: communication@covchurch.org
Website: www.covchurch.org/cov/companion

Covenant Home Altar, (Q.) Evangelical Covenant Church, Donald L. Meyer, 5101 N. Francisco Ave., Chicago, IL 60625 Tel. (773) 784-3000, Fax (773)784-4366
Email: covcom@compuserve.com

Covenant Quarterly, (Q.) Evangelical Covenant Church, Wayne C. Weld, 3225 W. Foster Ave., Chicago, IL 60625-4895 Tel. (773)244-6230, Fax (773)244-6244
Email: wweld@northpark.edu

The Covenanter Witness, (11-Y.) Reformed Presbyterian Church of North America, Drew Gordon and Lynne Gordon, 7408 Penn Ave., Pittsburgh, PA 15208 Tel. (412)241-0436, Fax (412)731-8861
Email: cwmailbag@aol.com
Website: www.psalms4u.com

Credinta—The Faith, (Q.) The Romanian Orthodox Church in America, V. Rev. Archim. Dr. Vasile Vasilac, 45-03 48th Ave., Woodside, Queens, NY 11377 Tel. (313)893-8390

Credo, (M.) The Antiochian Orthodox Christian Archdiocese of North, Charles Dinkler, P.O. Box 84, Stanton, NJ 08885-0084 Tel. (908) 236-7890

The Criterion, (W.) The Roman Catholic Church, John F. Fink, P. O. Box 1717, 1400 N. Meridian Indianapolis, IN 46206 Tel. (317) 236-1570

Cross Walk, (W.) Church of the Nazarene, Jim Hampton, Word Action Publishing, 6401 The Paseo, Kansas City, MO 64131 Tel. (816)333-7000, Fax (816)333-4315
Email: crosswalk@nazarene.org
Website: www.nazarene.org

The Cumberland Flag, (M.) Cumberland Presbyterian Church in America, Rev. Robert Stanley Wood, 226 Church St., Huntsville, AL 35801 Tel. (205)536-7481, Fax (205)536-7482

The Cumberland Presbyterian, (11-Y.) Cumberland Presbyterian Church in America, Patricia P. Richards, Box 155, Lincoln, IL 62656 Tel. (217)732-2813, Fax (217)732-2813
Email: ppr@cumberland.org
Website: www.cumberland.org/cpmag/

Currents in Theology and Mission, (6-Y.) Evangelical Lutheran Church in America, Ralph W. Klein, 1100 E. 55th St., Chicago, IL 60615 Tel. (773)256-0695, Fax (773)256-0782
Email: currents@lstc.edu
Website: www.lstc.edu/pub_peo/pub/currents.html

Decision, (11-Y.) Nondenominational, Kersten Beckstrom, 1300 Harmon Pl., Minneapolis, MN 55403 Tel. (612)338-0500, Fax (612)335-1299
Email: decision@bgea.org
Website: www.decisionmag.org

The Disciple, (10-Y.) Christian Church (Disciples of Christ), Patricia R. Case, 6219 N Guilford, Suite B Indianapolis, IN 46220 Tel. (317)253-1600, Fax (317)253-1460
Email: thedisciple@cbp21.org
Website: www.thedisciple.com

Discovery, (Q.) Nondenominational, Braille Only, for Youth, Darcy Quigley, John Milton Society for the Blind, 475 Riverside Drive, Rm 455 New York, NY 10115-0455 Tel. (212)870-3335, Fax (212)870-3229
Email: order@jmsblind.org
Website: www.jmsblind.org

Ecu-Link, (Q.) Interdenominational, Sarah Vilankulu, 475 Riverside Drive, Rm 850, New York, NY 10115-0050 Tel. (212)870-2227, Fax (212)870-2030
Email: sarah@ncccusa.org

Ecumenical Trends, (M.) Nondenominational, Kevin McMorrow, SA, Graymoor Ecumenical & Interreligious Institute, PO Box 300 Garrison, NY 10524 Tel. (845)424-3671 ext. 3323, Fax (845)424-2163
Email: kmcmorrow@atonementfriars.org
Website: www.atonementfriars.org

Eleventh Hour Messenger, (bi-M.) Wesleyan Holiness Association of Churches, John Brewer, 11411 N US Hwy 27, Fountain City, IN 47341-9757 Tel. (317)584-3199

Elim Herald, (Q.) Elim Fellowship, Bernard J. Evans, 1703 Dalton Road, P.O. Box 57A Lima, NY 14485 Tel. (716)582-2790, Fax (716)624-1229
Email: 75551.743@compuserve.com

EMC Today, (Q.) Evangelical Mennonite Church, Ronald J. Habegger, 1420 Kerrway Ct., Fort Wayne, IN 46805 Tel. (219)423-3649, Fax (219)420-1905
Email: emc@emctoday.com
Website: www.emctoday.com

Emphasis on Faith and Living, (bi-M.) The Missionary Church, Rev. Robert Ransom, PO Box 9127, Ft. Wayne, IN 46899 Tel. (219)747-2027, Fax (219)747-5331
Email: emphasisfandl@aol.com
Website: www.mcusa.org

Enrichment: A Journal for Pentecostal Ministry, (Q.) Assemblies of God, Gary Allen; Rick Knoth, Managing Editor, 1445 N. Boonville Ave., Springfield, MO 65802 Tel. (417)862-2781, Fax (417)862-0416
Email: gallen@ag.org
Website: www.enrichmentjournal.ag.org

The Ensign, (M.) The Church of Jesus Christ Latter-day Saints, Brian K. Kelly, Managing Editor, 50 E North Temple Street, 24th Fl, Salt Lake City, UT 84150 Tel. (801)240-2950, Fax (801)240-5732

Epiphany Journal, (Q.) Interdenominational, Nun Macaria, 1516 N. Delaware, Indianapolis, IN 46202 Tel. (317)926-7468

Episcopal Life, (M.) The Episcopal Church, Jerrold Hames, 815 Second Ave., New York, NY 10017-4503 Tel. (800)334-7626, Fax (212) 949-8059
Email: jhames@episcopalchurch.org
Website: www.episcopal-life.org

The Evangel, (6-Y.) American Association of Lutheran Churches, The, Rev. Charles D. Eidum, 801 W. 106th St, Suite 203 Minneapolis, MN 55420-5603 Tel. (952)884-7784, Fax (952)884-7894
Email: aa2aalc@aol.com
Website: www.taalc.com

The Evangel, (Q.) The Evangelical Church Alliance, Derick Miller, 205 W. Broadway, Bradley, IL 60915 Tel. (815)937-0720, Fax (815)937-0001
Email: eca@keynet.net
Website: www.keynet.net/~eca

The Evangelical Advocate, (M.) Churches of Christ in Christian Union, Ralph Hux, P.O. Box 30, Circleville, OH 43113 Tel. (740)474-8856, Fax (740)477-7766
Email: cccudoc@bright.net
Website: www.bright.net/~cccudoc

Evangelical Beacon, (7-Y.) The Evangelical Free Church of America, Ms. Carol Madison, 901 East 78th St., Minneapolis, MN 55420-1300 Tel. (612)854-1300, Fax (612)853-8488

Evangelical Challenge, (Q.) The Evangelical Church, John F. Sills, 7733 West River Road, Minneapolis, MN 55444 Tel. (763)561-0886, Fax (763)561-0774
Email: jsditzel@juno.com

Evangelism USA, (Bi-M.) International Pentecostal Holiness Church, Dr. Ronald W. Carpenter, Sr., P.O. Box 12609, Oklahoma City, OK 73157 Tel. (405)787-7110, Fax (405)789-3957
Email: rwcsr@aol.com
Website: www.iphc.org/evusa/ev

The Evangelist, (W.) The Roman Catholic Church, James Breig, 40 N. Main Ave., Albany, NY 12203 Tel. (518)453-6688, Fax (518)453-8448
Email: evannews@global2000.net
Website: www.evangelist.org

Explorations, (4-Y.) Nondenominational, Irvin J. Borowsky, 321 Chestnut Street, 4th Floor, Philadelphia, PA 19106-2779 Tel. (215)925-2800, Fax (215)925-3800
Email: aii@interfaith-scholars.org

Extension, (M.) The Roman Catholic Church, Bradley Collins, 150 S. Wacker Drive, 20th Floor Chicago, IL 60606 Tel. (312)236-7240, Fax (312)236-5276
Email: magazine@catholic-extension.org
Website: www.catholic-extension.org

Faith & Fellowship, (M.) Church of the Lutheran Brethren of America, Brent Juliot, P.O. Box 655, Fergus Falls, MN 56538 Tel. (218)736-7357, Fax (218)736-2200
Email: ffpress@clba.org
Website: www.faithandfellowship.org

Faith-Life, (bi-M.) Lutheran, Pastor Marcus Albrecht, 2107 N. Alexander St., Appleton, WI 54911 Tel. (920)733-1839, Fax (920)733-4834
Email: malbrecht@milwpc.com

Faith and Truth, (M.) Pentecostal Fire-Baptized Holiness Church, Edgar Vollratlt, 593 Harris-Lord Rd., Commerce, GA 30529 Tel. (706) 335-5796

Fellowship, (6-Y.) Interfaith, Richard Deats, P.O. Box 271, Nyack, NY 10960-0271 Tel. (845)358-4601, Fax (845)358-1179
Email: fellowship@forusa.org
Website: www.forusa.org/~

Fellowship Focus, (bi-M.) Fellowship of Evangelical Bible Churches, Robert L. Frey, 5800 S. 14th St., Omaha, NE 68107 Tel. (402) 731-4780, Fax (402)731-1173
Email: febcoma@aol.com
Website: members.aol.com/febcoma

Fellowship News, (M.) Bible Fellowship Church, Carol Snyder, 3000 Fellowship Drive, Whitehall, PA 18052-3343 Tel. (717)337-3408, Fax (215)536-2120
Email: ccsnyder@supernet.com
Website: www.bfc.org

Fellowship Tidings, (Q.) Full Gospel Fellowship of Churches and Ministers International, Cindy Mattox, Paula Boyer, 1000 N. Beltline Road, Irving, TX 75061 Tel. 214-492-1254, Fax 214-492-1736
Email: FGFCMI@aol.com
Website: www.fgfcmi.org

Firm Foundation, (M.) Churches of Christ, H. A. Dobbs, P.O. Box 690192, Houston, TX 77269-0192 Tel. (713)469-3102, Fax (713) 469-7115
Email: HAD@onramp.net

First Things: A Monthly Journal of Religion & Public Life, (10-Y.) Interdenominational, Richard J. Neuhaus, 156 Fifth Ave., Ste. 400, New York, NY 10010 Tel. (212)627-1985, Fax (212)627-2184
Email: ft@firstthings.com
Website: www.firstthings.com

The Flaming Sword, (M.) Bible Holiness Church, Susan Davolt, 10th St. & College Ave., Independence, KS 67301 Tel. (316)331-2580, Fax (316)331-2580

For the Poor, (bi-M.) Primitive Baptists, W. H. Cayce, PO Box 38, Thornton, AR 71766 Tel. (501)352-3694

Foresee, (bi-M.) Conservative Congregational Christian Conference, William V. Nygren, 7582 Currell Blvd., #108, St. Paul, MN 55125 Tel. (651)739-1474, Fax (651)739-0750
Email: dmjohnson@ccccusa.org
Website: www.ccccusa.org

Forum Letter, (M.) Independent, Intra-Lutheran (companion publication to the quarterly, Lutheran Forum), Pastor Russell E. Saltzman, Ruskin Heights Lutheran Church, 10801 Ruskin Way Kansas City, MO 64134 Tel. (816)761-6815, Fax (816)761-6523
Email: Saltzman@Integritynetwork.net
Website: www.alpb.org

Forward, (Q.) United Pentecostal Church International, Rev. J. L. Hall, 8855 Dunn Rd., Hazelwood, MO 63042 Tel. (314)837-7300, Fax (314)837-4503

Forward in Christ-Northwestern Lutheran, (M.) Wisconsin Evangelical Lutheran Synod, Gary Baumler, 2929 N. Mayfair Rd., Milwaukee, WI 53222 Tel. (414)256-3210, Fax (414)256-3899
Email: fic@sab.wels.net
Website: www.wels.net

Foursquare World Advance, (6-Y.) International Church of the Foursquare Gospel, Dr. Ron Williams, PO Box 26902, 1910 W. Sunset Blvd., Ste 200 Los Angeles, CA 90026-0176 Tel. (213)989-4220, Fax (213) 989-4544
Email: ron@foursquare.org
Website: www.foursquare.org

Free Methodist World Mission People, (4-Y.) Free Methodist Church of North America, Paula Innes, Magazine Editor, P.O. Box 535002, Indianapolis, IN 46253-5002 Tel. (317)244-3660, Fax (317)241-1248
Email: fmcPeople@aol.com
Website: www.fmcna.org/fmwm

Free Will Baptist Bible College Bulletin, (6-Y.) National Association of Free Will Baptists, Bert Tippett, 3606 West End Ave., Nashville, TN 37205 Tel. (615)383-1340,Fax (615)269-6028
Email: bert@fwbbc.edu
Website: www.fwbbc.edu

Free Will Baptist Gem, (M.) National Association of Free Will Baptists, Nathan Ruble, P.O. Box 991, Lebanon, MO 65536 Tel. (417)532-6537

The Free Will Baptist, (M.) Original Free Will Baptist Church, Tracy A McCoy, P.O. Box 159, 811 N. Lee Street Ayden, NC 28513 Tel. (919)746-6128, Fax (919)746-9248

Friend Magazine, (M.) The Church of Jesus Christ of Latter-day Saints, Vivian Paulsen, 50 E South Temple Street, 24th Fl, Salt Lake City, UT 84150 Tel. (801)240-2210, Fax (801)240-2270

Friends Bulletin, (10-Y.) Religious Society of Friends, Anthony Manousos, 5238 Andalucia Court, Whittier, CA 90601 Tel. (562)699-5670, Fax (562)692-2472
Email: friendsbul@aol.com
Website: www.quaker.org/fb and www.quaker.org/western

Friends Journal, (M.) Friends General Conference, Susan Corson-Finnerty, 1216 Arch St., 2A Philadelphia, PA 19107-2835 Tel. (215) 563-8629, Fax (215)568-1377
Email: info@friendsjournal.org
Website: www.friendsjournal.org

The Friends Voice, (4-Y.) Evangelical Friends International—North America Region, Becky Towne, 2748 E. Pikes Peak Ave, Colorado Springs, CO 80909 Tel. (719)632-5721, Fax (719)636-2194
Email: mcrcs@codenet.net
Website: evangelical-friends.org

Front Line, (4-Y.) Conservative Baptist Association of America, Al Russell, P.O. Box 58, Long Prairie, MN 56347 Tel. (320)732-8072
Email: chaplruss@aol.com
Website: www.cbchaplains.net

Full Gospel Ministries Outreach Report, (Q.) Full Gospel Assemblies International, Simeon Strauser, P.O. Box 1230, Coatsville, PA 19320 Tel. (610)857-2357, Fax (610)857-3109

The Gem, (W.) Churches of God, General Conference, Rachel Foreman, P.O. Box 926, Findlay, OH 45839 Tel. (419)424-1961, Fax (419)424-3433
Email: communications@cggc.org
Website: www.cggc.org

General Baptist Messenger, (M.) General Association of General Baptists, Samuel S. Ramdial, 400 Stinson Dr., Poplar Bluff, MO 63901 Tel. (573)686-9051, Fax (573)686-5198

The Gleaner, (M.) Baptist Missionary Association of America, F. Donald Collins, P.O. Box 193920, Little Rock, AR 72219-3920 Tel. (501)455-4977, Fax (501)455-3636
Email: BMAAM@aol.com

Global Partners, (Q.) Baptist Bible Fellowship International, Loran McAlister, P.O. Box 191, Springfield, MO 65801 Tel. (417)862-5001, Fax (417)865-0794

God's Field, (bi-W.) Polish National Catholic Church of America, Very Rev. William Chromey (English) and Rt. Rev. Casimir Grotnik (Polish), 1006 Pittston Ave., Scranton, PA 18505 Tel. (570)346-9131, Fax (570)346-2188

Gospel Advocate, (M.) Churches of Christ, Neil W. Anderson, Box 150, Nashville, TN 37202 Tel. (615)254-8781, Fax (615)254-7411
Email: info@gospeladvocate.com
Website: www.gospeladvocate.com

The Gospel Herald, (M.) Church of God, Mountain Assembly, Inc., Bob Vance, P.O. Box 157, Jellico, TN 37762 Tel. (423)784-8260, Fax (423)784-3258
Email: cgmahdq@jellico.com
Website: www.cgmahdq.org

The Gospel Light, (Q.) The Bible Church of Christ, Inc., Carol Crenshaw, 1358 Morris Ave., Bronx, NY 10456 Tel. (718)588-2284, Fax (718)992-5597
Website: www.thebiblechurchofchrist.org

The Gospel Messenger, (M.) Congregational Holiness Church, Inc., Cullen L. Hicks, Congregational Holiness Church, 3888 Fayetteville Highway Griffin, GA 30223 Tel. (770-228-4833, Fax (770-228-1177
Email: CHChurch@bellsouth.net
Website: www.CHChurch.com

The Gospel News, (M.) The Church of Jesus Christ (Bickertonites), Donald Ross, 201 Royalbrooke Dr., Venetia, PA 15367 Tel. (412) 348-6828, Fax (412)348-0919

The Gospel Truth, (Bi M.) Church of the Living God, C.W.F.F., W.E. Crumes, 430 Forest Avenue, Cincinnati, OH 45229 Tel. (513)569-5660, Fax (513)569-5661
Email: cwff430@aol.com

Grow Magazine, (4-Y.) Church of the Nazarene, Neil B. Wiseman, 6401 The Paseo, Kansas City, MO 64131 Tel. (816)333-7000, Fax (816)361-5202

Guide, (W.) Seventh-day Adventist Church, Randy Fishell, 55 W. Oak Ridge Dr., Hagerstown, MD 21740 Tel. (301)393-4038, Fax (301)393-4055
Email: guide@rhpa.org
Website: www.guidemagazine.org

The Handmaiden, (Q.) The Antiochian Orthodox Christian Archdiocese of North America, Virginia Nieuwsma, P.O. Box 76, Ben Lomond, CA 95005-0076 Tel. (831)336-5118, Fax (831)336-8882
Email: czell@conciliarpress.com

The Happy Harvester, (M.) Church of God of Prophecy, Diane Pace, P.O. Box 2910, Cleveland, TN 37320-2910 Tel. (423)559-5435, Fax (423)559-5444
Email: JoDiPace@wingnet.net

HeartBeat, (M.) The Evangelical Church, John F. Sills, 7733 West River Road, Minneapolis, MN 55444 Tel. (763)561-8404, Fax (763)561-2899
Email: jsditzel@juno.com

Heartbeat, (bi-M.) National Association of Free Will Baptists, Don Robirds, Foreign Missions Office, P.O. Box 5002 Antioch, TN 37011-5002 Tel. (615)731-6812, Fax (615)731-5345
Email: Heartbeat@NAFWB.org

Helping Hand, (bi-M.) International Pentecostal Holiness Church, Mrs. Doris Moore, P.O. Box 12609, Oklahoma City, OK 73157 Tel. (405) 787-7110, Fax (405)789-3957

Herald, (M.) Community of Christ, Linda L. Booth, 1001 W Walnut, Independence, MO 64050 Tel. (816)833-1000, Fax (816)521-3043

The Herald of Christian Science, (M.) Church of Christ, Scientist, Mary M. Trammell, The Christian Science Publishing Society, One Norway St. Boston, MA 02115 Tel. (617)450-2000, Fax (617)450-2707
Email: trammellm@csps.com
Website: www.csherald.com

Heritage, (Q.) Assemblies of God, Wayne E. Warner, 1445 Boonville Ave., Springfield, MO 65802 Tel. (417)862-1447, Fax (417)862-6203
Email: wwarner@ag.org
Website: www.agheritage@ag.org

High Adventure, (Q.) Assemblies of God, Jerry Parks, Gospel Publishing House, 1445 N. Boonville Ave. Springfield, MO 65802-1894 Tel. (417)862-2781, Fax (417)831-8230
Email: rangers@ag.org
Website: www.royalrangers.org

Higher Way, (bi-M.) Apostolic Faith Mission of Portland, Oregon, Darrel D. Lee, 6615 S.E. 52nd Ave., Portland, OR 97206 Tel. (503)777-1741, Fax (503)777-1743
Email: kbarrett@apostolicfaith.org
Website: www.apostolicfaith.org

Holiness Digest, (Q.) Nondenominational, Marlin Hotle, 263 Buffalo Road, Clinton, TN 37716 Tel. (423)457-5978, Fax (423)463-7280

Holiness Today, (M.) Church of the Nazarene, R. Franklin Cook, 6401 The Paseo, Kansas City, MO 64131 Tel. (816)333-7000, Fax (816) 333-1748
Email: HolinessToday@nazarene.org
Website: www.nazarene.org

The Holiness Union, (M.) United Holy Church of America, Inc., Bishop John Lewis, 13102 Morningside La., Silver Spring, MD 20904 Tel. (215)724-1346, Fax (215)748-1480

Homiletic and Pastoral Review, (M.) The Roman Catholic Church, Kenneth Baker, 50 S Franklin Tpk, PO Box 297 Ramsey, NJ 07446 Tel. (201)236-9336

Horizons, (7-Y.) Presbyterian Church (U.S.A.), Susan Jacobson David, Presbyterian Women, 100 Witherspoon St. Louisville, KY 40202-1396 Tel. (502)569-5368, Fax (502)569-8085
Email: susand@ctr.pcusa.org
Website: www.pcusa.org/horizons

Horizons, (M.) Christian Churches and Churches of Christ, Reggie Hundley, Box 13111, Knoxville, TN 37920-0111 Tel. (800) 655-8524, Fax (865)573-5950
Email: msa@missionservices.org
Website: www.missionservices.org

Insight, (W.) Seventh-day Adventist Church, Lori Peckham, 55 W. Oak Ridge Dr., Hagerstown, MD 21740 Tel. (301)393-4038, Fax (301)393-4055
Email: insight@rhpa.org
Website: www.insightmagazine.org

Insight, (Q.) Advent Christian Church, Dawn Rutan, P.O. Box 23152, Charlotte, NC 28227 Tel. (704)545-6161, Fax (704)573-0712
Email: ACPub@adventchristian.org
Website: www.adventchristian.org

Interlit, (6-Y.) Nondenominational magazine on Christian publishing worldwide, Kim A. Pettit, 4050 Lee Vance View Drive, Colorado Springs, CO 80918 Tel. (719)536-0100, Fax (719)536-3266
Email: ccmintl@ccmi.org
Website: www.ccmi.org

International Bulletin of Missionary Research, (Q.) Nondenominational, Jonathan J. Bonk, 490 Prospect St., New Haven, CT 06511-2196 Tel. (203)624-6672, Fax (203) 865-2857
Email: ibmr@OMSC.org
Website: www.omsc.org

Interpretation, (Q.) Presbyterian Church (U.S.A.), John T. Carroll and William P. Brown, 3401 Brook Rd., Richmond, VA 23227 Tel. (804) 278-4296, Fax (804)278-4208
Email: email@interpretation.org
Website: www.interpretation.org

el Interprete, (6-Y.) The United Methodist Church, Martha E. Rovira Raber, P.O. Box 320, Nashville, TN 37202-0320 Tel. (615)742-5115, Fax (615)742-5460
Email: elinterprete@umcom.umc.org
Website: www.interpretermagazine.org

Interpreter, (8-Y.) The United Methodist Church, M. Garlinda Burton, P.O. Box 320, Nashville, TN 37202-0320 Tel. (615)742-5107, Fax (615)742-5460
Email: gburton@umcom.umc.org
Website: www.interpretermagazine.org

IssacharFile, (M.) International Pentacostal Holiness Church, Shirley Spencer, P.O. Box 12609, Oklahoma City, OK 73157 Tel. (405) 787-7110, Fax (405)789-3957

John Milton Magazine, (Q.) Nondenominational, Large Print, Darcy Quigley, John Milton Society for the Blind, 475 Riverside Drive, Rm 455 New York, NY 10115-0455 Tel. (212)870-3335, Fax (212)870-3229

Email: order@jmsblind.org
Website: www.jmsblind.org

John Three Sixteen, (Q.) Bible Holiness Church, Mary Cunningham, 10th St. & College Ave., Independence, KS 67301 Tel. (316)331-2580, Fax (316)331-2580

Journal of the American Academy of Religion, (Q.) Nondenominational, Glenn Yocum, Whittier College, PO Box 634 Whittier, CA 90608-0634 Tel. (562)907-4200, Fax (562) 907-4910
Email: gyocum@whittier.edu
Website: www.aarweb.org

Journal of Adventist Education, (5-Y.) Seventh-day Adventist Church, Beverly Rumble, 12501 Old Columbia Pike, Silver Spring, MD 20904-6600 Tel. (301)680-5075, Fax (301) 622-9627
Email: 74617.1231@compuserve.com

Journal of Christian Education, (Q.) African Methodist Episcopal Church, Kenneth H. Hill, 500 Eighth Ave., S., Nashville, TN 37203 Tel. (615)242-1420, Fax (615)726-1866
Email: ameced@edge.net
Website: www.ameced.com

Journal of Ecumenical Studies, (Q.) Interdenominational, Leonard Swidler, Temple Univ. (022-38), 1114 West Berks St.- Anderson 511 Philadelphia, PA 19122-6090 Tel. (215) 204-7714, Fax (215)204-4569
Email: nkrody@astro.temple.edu

The Journal of Pastoral Care, (Q.) Nondenominational, Orlo Strunk Jr., 1068 Harbor Dr., SW, Calabash, NC 28467 Tel. (910)579-5084, Fax (910)579-5084
Email: jpcp@jpcp.org
Website: www.jpcp.org

Journal of Presbyterian History: Studies in Reformed History and Culture, (Q.) Presbyterian Church (U.S.A.), James H. Moorhead; Frederick J. Heuser, Jr., 425 Lombard St., Philadelphia, PA 19147 Tel. (215)627-1852, Fax (215)627-0509
Email: refdesk@history.pcusa.org
Website: www.history.pcusa.org

Journal From the Radical Reformation, (Q.) Church of God General Conference (Morrow, GA, Kent Ross and Anthony Buzzard, Sr. Editors, Box 100,000, Morrow, GA 30260-7000 Tel. (404)362-0052, Fax (404)362-9307
Email: kenthross@cs.com
Website: www.abc-coggc.org

Journal of Theology, (4-Y.) Church of the Lutheran Confession, Prof. Paul Schaller, Immanuel Lutheran College, 501 Grover Rd. Eau Claire, WI 54701-7199 Tel. (715)832-9936, Fax (715)836-6634
Email: schallers@usa.net
Website: www.primenet.com/~clcpub/clc/clc.html

The Joyful Noiseletter, (10-Y.) Interdenominational, Cal Samra, P.O. Box 895, Portage, MI 49081-0895 Tel. (616)324-0990, Fax (616) 324-3984
Email: joyfulnz@aol.com
Website: www._joyful_noiseletter.com

Judaism, (Q.) Jewish, Murray Baumgarten, 15 E. 84th St., New York, NY 10028 Tel. (212) 879-4500, Fax (212)249-3672
Email: judaism@cats.ucsc.edu

Keeping in Touch, (M.) Universal Fellowship of Metropolitan Community Churches, Ravi Verma, 8704 Santa Monica Blvd, 2nd Fl., West Hollywood, CA 90069-4548 Tel. (310) 360-8640, Fax (310)360-8680
Email: UFMCCHQ@aol.com
Website: www.ufmcc.com

Kindred Minds, (Q.) Sovereign Grace Baptists, Larry Scouten, P.O. Box 10, Wellsburg, NY 14894 Tel. (607)734-6985

The Lantern, (bi-M.) National Baptist Convention of America, Inc., Robert Jeffrey, 1320 Pierre Avenue, Shreveport, LA 71103 Tel. (318)221-3701, Fax (318)222-7512

Leadership: A Practical Journal for Church Leaders, (Q.) Nondenominational, Marshall Shelley, 465 Gundersen Dr., Carol Stream, IL 60188 Tel. (630)260-6200, Fax (630)260-0114
Email: LeaderJeditor@leadershipjournal.net
Website: www.Leadershipjournal.net

Liahona, (varies by language) The Church of Jesus Christ of Latter-day Saints (44 language editions), Marvin K. Gardner, 50 East North Temple St., Salt Lake City, UT 84150-3223 Tel. (801)240-2490, Fax (801)240-4225
Email: CUR-Liahona-IMag@ldschurch.org
Website: www.lds.org

Liberty, (bi-M.) Seventh-day Adventist Church, Clifford R. Goldstein, 12501 Old Columbia Pike, Silver Spring, MD 20904 Tel. (301)680-6691, Fax (301)680-6695

Lifeglow, (Q.) Seventh-day Adventist Church, Large Print, Gaylena Gibson, P.O. Box 6097, Lincoln, NE 68506 Tel. (402)488-0981, Fax (402)488-7582
Email: editorial@christianrecord.org
Website: www.christianrecord.org

Light and Life Magazine, (Bi-M.) Free Methodist Church, Douglas M. Newton, P.O. Box 535002, Indianapolis, IN 46253-5002 Tel. (317)244-3660
Email: llmeditor@fmcna.org
Website: www.freemethodistchurch.org

Liguorian, (10-Y.) The Roman Catholic Church, Allan J. Weinert, C.SS.R., 1 Liguori Dr., Liguori, MO 63057 Tel. (636)464-2500, Fax (636)464-8449
Email: aweinert@liguori.org
Website: www.liguori.org

Listen, (M.) Seventh-day Adventist Church, Lincoln E. Steed, 55 W. Oak Ridge Dr., Haggerstown, MD 21740 Tel. (301)791-7000, Fax (301)790-9734

Living Orthodoxy, (bi-M.) The Russian Orthodox Church Outside of Russia, Fr. Gregory Williams, 1180 Orthodox Way, Liberty, TN 37095 Tel. (615)536-5239, Fax (615)536-5945
Email: info@kronstadt.org
Website: www.kronstadt.org

The Long Island Catholic, (W.) The Roman Catholic Church, Elizabeth O'Connor, P. O. Box 9000, 200 W Centennial Ave Suite 201 Roosevelt, NY 11575 Tel. (516)594-1000, Fax (516)594-1092

The Lookout, (W.) Christian Churches and Churches of Christ, Shawn McMullen, 8121 Hamilton Ave., Cincinnati, OH 45231 Tel. (513)931-4050, Fax (513)931-0950
Email: lookout@standardpub.com
Website: www.standardpub.com

The Lutheran, (M.) Evangelical Lutheran Church in America, Rev. David L. Miller, 8765 W. Higgins Rd., Chicago, IL 60631-4183 Tel. (773)380-2540, Fax (773)380-2751
Email: lutheran@elca.org
Website: www.thelutheran.org

The Lutheran Ambassador, (16-Y.) The Association of Free Lutheran Congregations, Craig Johnson, 86286 Pine Grove Rd., Eugene, OR 97402 Tel. (541)687-8643, Fax (541)683-8496
Email: cjohnson@efn.org

The Lutheran Educator, (Q.) Wisconsin Evangelical Lutheran Synod, Prof. John R. Isch, Martin Luther College, 1995 Luther Ct. New Ulm, MN 56073 Tel. (507)354-8221, Fax (507)354-8225
Email: lutheraneducator@mlc-wels.edu

Lutheran Forum, (Q.) Interdenominational Lutheran, Ronald B. Bagnall, 207 Hillcrest Ave., Trenton, NJ 8618 Tel. (856)696-0417

The Lutheran Layman, (M.) The Lutheran Church—Missouri Synod, Gerald Perschbacher, 660 Mason Ridge Center Dr, St. Louis, MO 63141-8557 Tel. (314)951-4100, Fax (314)951-4295

Lutheran Parent, (bi-M.) Wisconsin Evangelical Lutheran Synod, Kenneth J. Kremer, 1250 N. 113th Street, Milwaukee, WI 53226-3284 Tel. (414)475-6600, Fax (414) 475-7684

Lutheran Parent's Wellspring, (bi-M.) Wisconsin Evangelical Lutheran Synod, Kenneth J. Kremer, 1250 N. 113th Street, Milwaukee, WI 53226-3284 Tel. (414)475-6600, Fax (414)475-7684

Lutheran Partners, (6-Y.) Evangelical Lutheran Church in America, Carl E. Linder, 8765 W. Higgins Rd., Chicago, IL 60631-4195 Tel. (773)380-2875, Fax (773)380-2829
Email: lutheran_partners@ecunet.org or lpartmag@elca.org
Website: www.elca.org/dm/lp

Lutheran Sentinel, (M.) Evangelical Lutheran Synod, Theodore Gullixson, 105 Indian Ave., Forest City, IA 50436 Tel. (641)585-1683
Email: elsentinel@wctatel.net

The Lutheran Spokesman, (M.) Church of the Lutheran Confession, Rev. Paul Fleischer, 710 4th Ave., SW, Sleepy Eye, MN 56085 Tel. (507)794-7793, Fax (507)794-7793
Email: pgflei@prairie.lakes.com
Website: www.clclutheran.org/library/spokesman_arch/current.html

Lutheran Synod Quarterly, (Q.) Evangelical Lutheran Synod, G.R. Schmeling, Bethany Lutheran Theological Seminary, 6 Browns Ct. Mankato, MN 56001 Tel. (507)344-7855, Fax (507)344-7426
Email: elsynod@blc.edu
Website: www.blts.edu

The Lutheran Witness, (M.) The Lutheran Church—Missouri Synod, Rev. David Mahsman, 1333 S. Kirkwood Road, St. Louis, MO 63122-7295 Tel. (314)965-9000, Fax (314)965-3396
Email: lutheran.witness@lcms.org

Lutheran Woman Today, (10-Y.) Evangelical Lutheran Church in America, Nancy Goldberger, 8765 W. Higgins Rd., Chicago, IL 60631-4101 Tel. (773)380-2743, Fax (773) 380-2419
Email: lwt@elca.org
Website: www.elca.org/wo/lwthome.html

Lyceum Spotlight, (10-Y.) National Spiritualist Association of Churches, Rev. Cosie Allen, 1418 Hall St., Grand Rapids, MI 49506 Tel. (616)241-2761, Fax (616)241-4703
Email: cosie@grgig.net

Magyar Egyhaz—Magyar Church, (Q.) Hungarian Reformed Church in America, Stephen Szabo, 464 Forest Ave., Paramus, NJ 7652 Tel. (201)262-2338, Fax (845)359-5771

Mar Thoma Messenger, (Q) Mar Thoma Syrian Church of India, Abraham Mattackal, 2320 S. Merrick Ave, Merrick, NY 11566 Tel. (516)377-3311, Fax (516)377-3322
Email: marthoma@aol.com

Maranatha, (Q.) Advent Christian Church, Dawn Rutan, P.O. Box 23152, Charlotte, NC 28227 Tel. (704)545-6161, Fax (704)573-0712
Email: acpub@adventchristian.org
Website: www.adventchristian.org

Marriage Partnership, (Q.) Nondenominational, Ron R. Lee, 465 Gundersen Dr.,

Carol Stream, IL 60188 Tel. (630)260-6200, Fax (630)260-0114
Email: Mpedit@aol.com
Website: www.christianity.net/

Maryknoll, (11-Y.) The Roman Catholic Church, Joseph R. Veneroso, P.O. Box 308, Maryknoll, NY 10545-0308 Tel. (914)941-7590, Fax (914)945-0670
Email: maryknollmag@igc.apc.org

Mature Years, (Q.) The United Methodist Church, Marvin W. Cropsey, 201 Eighth Ave. S, Nashville, TN 37202 Tel. (615)749-6292, Fax (615)749-6512
Email: matureyears@umpublishing.org

Mennonite Historical Bulletin, (Q.) Mennonite Church USA, John E. Sharp, 1700 South Main St., Goshen, IN 46526 Tel. (219)535-7477, Fax (219)535-7756
Email: archives@goshen.edu
Website: www.Goshen.edu/mcarchives

Mennonite Quarterly Review, (Q.) Mennonite Church, John D. Roth, 1700 S. Main St., Goshen, IN 46526 Tel. (219)535-7433, Fax (219)535-7438
Email: MQR@goshen.edu
Website: www.goshen.edu/mgr

The Mennonite, (48-Y.) Mennonite Church USA, Everett Thomas, 1700 S. Main St., Goshen, IN 46526 Tel. (219)535-6052, Fax (219)535-6050
Email: TheMennonite@mph.org
Website: www.themennonite.org

Message, (bi-M.) Seventh-day Adventist Church, Dr. Ron C. Smith, 55 West Oak Ridge Dr., Hagerstown, MD 21740 Tel. (301)393-4099, Fax (301)393-4103
Email: message@rhpa.org
Website: MESSAGEMAGAZINE.org

Message of the Open Bible, (bi-M.) Open Bible Standard Churches, Inc., Andrea Johnson, 2020 Bell Ave., Des Moines, IA 50315-1096 Tel. (515)288-6761, Fax (515)288-2510
Email: message@openbible.org
Website: www.openbible.org

Messenger, (11-Y.) Church of the Brethren, Fletcher Farrar, 1451 Dundee Ave., Elgin, IL 60120 Tel. (847)742-5100, Fax (847)742-1407
Email: wmcfadden_gb@brethren.org

Messenger of Truth, (bi-W.) Church of God in Christ (Mennonite), Gladwin Koehn, P.O. Box 230, Moundridge, KS 67107 Tel. (316)345-2532, Fax (316)345-2582

The Messenger, (M.) The (Original) Church of God, Inc., Wayne Jolley and William Dale, PO Box 3086, Chattanooga, TN 37404-0086, Tel. (800)827-9234

The Messenger, (M.) The Swedenborgian Church, Patte LeVan, PO Box 985, Julian, CA 92036 Tel. (760)765-2915, Fax (760)765-0218
Email: messenger@jinet.com

The Messenger, (M.) Pentecostal Free Will Baptist Church, Inc., George Thomas, P.O. Box 1568, Dunn, NC 28335 Tel. (910)892-4161, Fax (910)892-6876

Methodist History, (Q.) The United Methodist Church, Charles Yrigoyen Jr., P.O. Box 127, Madison, NJ 07940 Tel. (973)408-3189, Fax (973)408-3909
Email: cyrigoyen@gcah.org
Website: www.gcah.org

Mid-Stream: The Ecumenical Movement Today, (Q.) Christian Church (Disciples of Christ), Robert K. Welsh, P.O. Box 1986, Indianapolis, IN 46206-1986 Tel. (317)713-2586, Fax (317)713-2588
Email: rwelsh@ccu.disciples.org
Website: www.disciples.org/ccu

Ministry, (M.) Seventh-day Adventist Church, Willmore D. Eva, 12501 Old Columbia Pike, Silver Spring, MD 20904 Tel. (301)680-6510, Fax (301)680-6502
Email: 74532.2425@compuserve.com

Mission Herald, (bi-M.) National Baptist Convention, U.S.A., Inc., William J. Harvey, 701 S. 19th Street, Philadelphia, PA 19146 Tel. (215)735-9853, Fax (215)735-1721

Mission, Adult, and Youth Children's Editions, (Q.) Seventh-day Adventist Church, Charlotte Ishkanian, 12501 Old Columbia Pike, Silver Spring, MD 20904 Tel. (301)680-6167, Fax (301)680-6155
Email: 74532.2435@compuserve.com

The Missionary Magazine, (9-Y.) , Bertha O. Fordham, 800 Risley Ave., Pleasantville, NJ 08232-4250

The Missionary Messenger, (M.) Christian Methodist Episcopal Church, Doris F. Boyd, 213 Viking Dr., W., Cordova, TN 38108-7263 Tel. (901)757-1103, Fax (901)751-2104
Email: dboyd@pschem.com

The Missionary Messenger, (6-Y.) Cumberland Presbyterian Church, Carol Penn, 1978 Union Ave., Memphis, TN 38104 Tel. (901)276-4572, Fax (901)276-4578
Email: messenger@cumberland.org

Missionary Seer, (M.) African Methodist Episcopal Zion Church, Rev. Kermit J. DeGraffenreidt, 475 Riverside Dr., Rm. 1935, New York, NY 10115 Tel. (212)870-2952, Fax (212)870-2808

The Missionary Signal, (bi-M.) Churches of God, General Conference, Rachel Foreman, P.O. Box 926, Findlay, OH 45839 Tel. (419)424-1961, Fax (419)424-3433

Email: communications@cggc.org
Website: cggc.org

MissionsUSA, (bi-M.) Southern Baptist Convention, Wayne Grinstead, 4200 North Point Pkwy., Alphretta, GA 30202-4174 Tel. (770)410-6251, Fax (770)410-6006

Monday Morning, (21-Y.) Presbyterian Church (U.S.A.), Houston Hodges, 100 Witherspoon St., Louisville, KY 40202 Tel. (502)569-5502, Fax (502)569-8073
Email: H2@pcusa.org

Moody Magazine, (6-Y.) Nondenominational, Bruce Anderson, 820 N. LaSalle Blvd., Chicago, IL 60610 Tel. (312)329-2164, Fax (312)329-2149
Email: moodyltrs@moody.edu
Website: www.moody.edu/moodyma

The Moravian, (10-Y.) Moravian Church in America (Unitas Fratrum), Deanna L. Hollenbach, 1021 Center St., P.O. Box 1245, Bethlehem, PA 18016 Tel. (610)867-0593, Fax (610)866-9223
Email: pubs@mcnp.org
Website: www.moravian.org

The Mother Church, (M.) Western Diocese of the Armenian Church of North America, Rev. Fr. Sipan Mekhsian, 3325 N. Glenoaks Blvd., Burbank, CA 91504 Tel. (818)558-7474, Fax (818)558-6333
Email: armenianchwd@earthlink.net
Website: www.armenianchurchwd.com

My Soul Sings: A Magazine of Inspirational/ Gospel Music, (Q.) Nondenominational, Irene C. Franklin, President and Publisher, P.O. Box 16181, St. Louis, MO 63105 Tel. (888)862-0179, Fax (888)862-0179
Email: Irene@postnet.com
Website: www.mysoulsings.com

NAE Washington Insight, (M.) Interdenominational, Rev. Richard Cizik, 450 E. Gundersen Dr., Carol Stream, IL 60188 Tel. (630)665-0500, Fax (630)665-8575
Email: oga@nae.net
Website: www.nae.net

National Baptist Union Review, (M.) Nondenominational, Willie Paul, 6717 Centennial Blvd., Nashville, TN 37209-1000 Tel. (615)350-8000, Fax (615)350-9018

National Catholic Reporter, (44-Y.) The Roman Catholic Church, Tom Roberts, P.O. Box 419281, Kansas City, MO 64141 Tel. (816)531-0538, Fax (816)968-2280
Email: editor@natcath.org
Website: www.natcath.org

The National Christian Reporter, (W.) Nondenominational, Cynthia B. Astle, P.O. Box 660275, Dallas, TX 75266-0275 Tel. (214)630-6495, Fax (214)630-0079
Email: cbastle@umr.org

The National Spiritualist Summit, (M.) National Spiritualist Association of Churches, Rev. Sandra Pfortmiller, 3521 W. Topeka Dr., Glendale, AZ 85308-2325 Tel. (623)581-6686, Fax (623)581-5544
Email: G2s2pfort@aol.com

New Church Life, (M.) General Church of the New Jerusalem, Rev. Donald L. Rose, Box 277, Bryn Athyn, PA 19009 Tel. (215)947-6225 ext. 209, Fax (215)938-1871
Email: DonRocBACS-GC.org
Website: www.newchurch.org

The New Era, (M.) The Church of Jesus Christ of Latter-day Saints, Larry Hiller, 50 E. North Temple St., Salt Lake City, UT 84150 Tel. (801)240-2951, Fax (801)240-2270
Email: rmromney@chq.byu.edu

New Horizons in the Orthodox Presbyterian Church, (11-Y.) The Orthodox Presbyterian Church, Larry E. Wilson, 607 N. Easton Rd., Bldg. E, P.O. Box P Willow Grove, PA 19090-0920 Tel. (215)830-0900, Fax (215)830-0350
Email: wilson.l@opc.org
Website: www.opc.org/

New Oxford Review, (11-Y.) The Roman Catholic Church, Dale Vree, 1069 Kains Ave., Berkeley, CA 94706 Tel. (510)526-5374, Fax (510)526-3492
Website: www.newoxfordreview.org

New World Outlook, (bi-M.) Mission Magazine of The United Methodist Church, Christie R. House, 475 Riverside Dr., Rm. 1476, New York, NY 10115 Tel. (212)870-3765, Fax (212) 870-3654
Email: NWO@gbgm-umc.org
Website: gbgm-umc.org/nwo/

The News, (Q.) The Anglican Orthodox Church, The Rev. Roger Jessup, Anglican Orthodox Church, P.O. Box 128 Statesville, NC 28687-0128 Tel. (704)873-8365, Fax (704)873-5359
Email: aocusa@energyunited.net

Newscope, (W.) The United Methodist Church, Erik Alsgaard, P.O. Box 801, Nashville, TN 37202 Tel. (615)749-6320, Fax (615)749-6061
Email: ealsgaard@umpublishing.org
Website: www.umph.org

The North American Catholic, (M.) North American Old Roman Catholic Church, Theodore J. Remalt, 4154 W. Berteau Ave, Chicago, IL 60641 Tel. (312)685-0461, Fax (312)485-0461
Email: chapelhall@aol.com

The North American Challenge, (M.) Home Missions Division of The United Pentecostal Church International, Joseph Fiorino, 8855 Dunn Rd., Hazelwood, MO 63042-2299 Tel. (314)837-7300, Fax (314)837-5632

NRB Magazine, (10-Y.) Nondenominational, Christine Pryor, National Religious

Broadcasters, 7839 Ashton Ave Manassas, VA 20109-2883 Tel. (703)330-7000, Fax (703) 330-6996
Email: cpryor@nrb.org
Website: www.nrb.org

Nuestra Parroquia, (M.) The Roman Catholic Church, Carmen Aguinaco, 205 W. Monroe St., Chicago, IL 60606-5013 Tel. (312)236-7782, Fax (312)236-8207
Email: USCath@aol.com

On Course, (Q.) Assemblies of God, Melinda Booze, 1445 Boonville Ave., Springfield, MO 65802-1894 Tel. (417)862-2781, Fax (417) 866-1146
Email: oncourse@ag.org
Website: oncourse.ag.org

On the Line, (M.) Mennonite Church, Mary C. Meyer, 616 Walnut Ave., Scottdale, PA 15683 Tel. (724)887-8500, Fax (724-887-3111
Email: otl@mph.org
Website: www.mph.org/otl

Open Hands, (Q.) Interdenominational, Chris Glaser, 3801 N. Keeler Ave., Chicago, IL 60641-3007 Tel. (773)736-5526, Fax (773) 736-5475
Email: openhands@rcp.org
Website: www.rcp.org/openhands/index.html

Orthodox America, (8-Y.) The Russian Orthodox Church Outside of Russia, Mary Mansur, P.O. Box 383, Richfield Springs, NY 13439-0383 Tel. (315)858-1518
Email: niko@telenet.net
Website: www.roca.org/oa

The Orthodox Church, (M.) The Orthodox Church in America, Leonid Kishkovsky, P.O. Box 675, Syosset, NY 11791 Tel. (516)922-0550, Fax (516)922-0954
Email: info@oca.org

Orthodox Family, (Q.) The Russian Orthodox Church Outside of Russia, George Johnson and Deborah Johnson, P.O. Box 45, Beltsville, MD 20705 Tel. (301)890-3552
Email: 1lew@cais.com
Website: www.roca.org/orthodox

Orthodox Life, (bi-M.) The Russian Orthodox Church Outside of Russia, Fr. Luke, Holy Trinity Monastery, P.O Box 36 Jordanville, NY 13361-0036 Tel. (315)858-0940, Fax (315) 858-0505
Email: 72204.1465@compuserve.com

The Orthodox Observer, (M.) Greek Orthodox Archdiocese of America, Stavros H. Papagermanos, 8 E. 79th St., New York, NY 10021 Tel. (212)570-3555, Fax (212)774-0239
Email: observer@goarch.org
Website: www.observer.goarch.org

Orthodox Russia (English translation of Pravoslavnaya Rus), (24-Y.) The Russian Orthodox Church Outside of Russia, Archbishop Laurus, Holy Trinity Monastery, P.O. Box 36 Jordanville, NY 13361-0036 Tel. (315)858-0940, Fax (315)858-0505
Email: orthrus@telenet.net

Orthodox Voices, (4-Y.) The Russian Orthodox Church Outside of Russia, Thomas Webb and Ellen Webb, P.O. Box 23644, Lexington, KY 40523 Tel. (606)271-3877

The Other Side, (bi-M.) Interdenominational, Dee Dee Risher and Douglas Davidson, 300 W. Apsley St., Philadelphia, PA 19144-4221 Tel. (215)849-2178, Fax (215)849-3755
Email: editors@theotherside.org
Website: www.theotherside.org

Our Daily Bread, (M.) The Swedenborgian Church, Lee Woofenden, P.O. Box 396, Bridgewater, MA 02324 Tel. (508)946-1767, Fax (508)946-1757
Email: odb@swedenborg.org
Website: www.swedenborg.org/odb/odb.html

Our Little Friend, (W.) Seventh-day Adventist Church, Aileen Andres Sox, P.O. Box 5353, Nampa, ID 83653-5353 Tel. (208)465-2500, Fax (208)465-2531
Email: ailsox@pacificpress.com
Website: www.pacificpress.com

Our Sunday Visitor, (W.) The Roman Catholic Church, Gerald Corson, 200 Noll Plaza, Huntington, IN 46750 Tel. (219)356-8400, Fax (219)356-8472
Email: oursunvis@osv.com
Website: www.osv.com

Outreach, (10-Y.) Armenian Apostolic Church of America, Iris Papazian, 138 E. 39th St., New York, NY 10016 Tel. (212)689-7810, Fax (212)689-7168

Pastoral Life, (M.) The Roman Catholic Church, Matthew Roehrig, Box 595, Canfield, OH 44406-0595 Tel. (330)533-5503, Fax (330) 553-1076
Email: paultheapostle@msn.com
Website: www.albahouse.org

The Path of Orthodoxy (Serbian), (M.) Serbian Orthodox Church in the U.S.A. and Canada, V. Rev. Nedeljko Lunich, 300 Striker Ave., Joliet, IL 60436 Tel. (815)741-1023, Fax (815)741-1023
Email: nedlunich@home.com

Pentecostal Evangel, (W.) Assemblies of God, Hal Donaldson, Gospel Publishing House, 1445 N. Boonville Ave. Springfield, MO 65802-1894 Tel. (417)862-2781, Fax (417) 862-0416
Email: pe@ag.org
Website: www.pe.ag.org

Pentecostal Evangel, Missions World Edition, (M.) Assemblies of God, Hal Donaldson, Editor in Chief, Gospel Publishing House,

1445 Boonville Ave. Springfield, MO 65802 Tel. (417)862-2781, Fax (417)862-0085
Email: pe@ag.org
Website: www.pe.ag.org

The Pentecostal Herald, (M.) United Pentecostal Church International, Rev. J. L. Hall, 8855 Dunn Rd., Hazelwood, MO 63042 Tel. (314)837-7300, Fax (314)837-4503

Pentecostal Leader, (Q.) The International Pentecostal Church of Christ, Clyde M. Hughes, P.O. Box 439, London, OH 43140 Tel. (740)852-4722, Fax (740)852-0348
Email: hqipcc@aol.com

The Pentecostal Messenger, (M.) Pentecostal Church of God (Joplin, MO), John Mallinak, P.O. Box 850, Joplin, MO 64802 Tel. (417) 624-7050, Fax (417)624-7102
Email: johnm@pcg.org
Website: www.pcg.org

The People's Mouthpiece, (Q.) Apostolic Overcoming Holy Church of God, Inc., Bishop Franklin McNeil, THB, D.D., 1120 North 24th St., Birmingham, AL 35234 Tel. (205)324-2202
Email: bishopmcneil@hotmail.com
Website: www.ricetempleaoh.homestead.com

Perspectives, (10-Y.) Reformed Church in America, , PO Box 1196, Holland, MI 49422-1196 Tel. (616)698-7071
Email: perspectives_@hotmail.com

Perspectives on Science and Christian Faith, (Q.) Nondenominational, Roman J. Miller, 4956 Singers Glen Rd., Harrisonburg, VA 22802 Tel. (540)432-4412, Fax (540)432-4488
Email: millerrj@rica.net
Website: asa.calvin.edu

The Pillar Monthly, (12-Y.) , Donald J. Wolfram and Mark Tomlin, PO Box 9045, Zarephath, NJ 08890 Tel. (908)356-0561

The Pilot, (W.) The Roman Catholic Church, Monsignor Peter V. Conley, 141 Tremont st, Boston, MA 02111-1200 Tel. (617)482-4316, Fax (617)482-5647
Email: editorial@bostonpilot.org
Website: www.rcab.org

Pockets, (11-Y.) The United Methodist Church, Janet R. Knight, P.O. Box 34004, Nashville, TN 37203 Tel. (615)340-7333, Fax (615)340-7267
Email: pockets@upperroom.org
Website: www.upperroom.org/pockets

Polka, (Q.) Polish National Catholic Church of America, Cecelia Lallo, 1127 Frieda St., Dickson City, PA 18519-1304 Tel. (570)489-4364, Fax (570)346-2188

Pravoslavnaya Rus (Russian), (24-Y.) The Russian Orthodox Church Outside of Russia, Archbishop Laurus, Holy Trinity Monastery, P.O. Box 36 Jordanville, NY 13361-0036 Tel. (315)858-0940, Fax (315)858-0505
Email: orthrus@telenet.net

Pravoslavnaya Zhisn (Monthly Supplement to Pravoslavnaya Rus), (M.) The Russian Orthodox Church Outside of Russia, Archbishop Laurus, Holy Trinity Monastery, P.O. Box 36 Jordanville, NY 13361-0036 Tel. (315)858-0940, Fax (315)858-0505
Email: Orthrus@telenet.net

Praying, (bi-M.) Spirituality for Everyday Living, Rich Heffern, P.O. Box 419335, 115 E. Armour Blvd. Kansas City, MO 64141 Tel. (816)968-2258, Fax (816)968-2280

Preacher's Magazine, (bi-M.) Church of the Nazarene, Randal Denney, 6401 Paseo Blvd, Kansas City, MO 64131-1213

Presbyterian News Service "The News", (32-Y.) Presbyterian Church (U.S.A.), Jerry L. VanMarter, 100 Witherspoon St., Rm. 5418 Louisville, KY 40202 Tel. (502)569-5493, Fax (502)569-8073
Email: jerryv@ctr.pcusa.org

Presbyterian Outlook, (43-Y.) , Robert H. Bullock Jr., Box 85623, Richmond, VA 23285-5623 Tel. (804)359-8442, Fax (804)353-6369
Email: outlook.parti@pcusa.org
Website: www.pres-outlook.com

Presbyterians Today, (10-Y.) Presbyterian Church (U.S.A.), Eva Stimson, 100 Witherspoon St., Louisville, KY 40202-1396 Tel. (502)569-5637, Fax (502)569-8632
Email: today@pcusa.org
Website: www.pcusa.org/today

Preserving Christian Homes, (6-Y.) United Pentecostal Church International, Todd Gaddy, 8855 Dunn Rd., Hazelwood, MO 63042 Tel. (314)837-7300, Fax (314)837-4503
Email: youth@upci.org
Website: www.pentecostalyouth.org

Primary Treasure, (W.) Seventh-day Adventist Church, Aileen Andres Sox, P.O. Box 5353, Nampa, ID 83653-5353 Tel. (208)465-2500, Fax (208)465-2531
Email: ailsox@pacificpress.com
Website: www.pacificpress.com

The Primitive Baptist, (bi-M.) Primitive Baptists, W. H. Cayce, PO Box 38, Thornton, AR 71766 Tel. (501)352-3694

Priority, (M.) The Missionary Church, Rev. Robert Ransom, P.O. Box 9127, Ft. Wayne, IN 46899 Tel. (219)747-2027, Fax (219)747-5331
Email: mcdenomusa@aol.com
Website: mcusa.org

Providence Visitor, (W.) The Roman Catholic Church, Michael Brown, 184 Broad St., Providence, RI 02903 Tel. (401)272-1010, Fax (401)421-8418
Email: 102344.3235@compuserve.com

Purpose, (W.) Mennonite Church USA, James E. Horsch, 616 Walnut Ave., Scottdale, PA 15683 Tel. (724)887-8500, Fax (724)887-3111

Email: horsch@mph.org
Website: www.mph.org

Pursuit, (Q.) The Evangelical Free Church of America, Carol Madison, 901 East 78th St., Minneapolis, MN 55420-1300 Tel. (612)853-1763, Fax (612)853-8488

Qala min M'Dinkha (Voice from the East), (Q.) Apostolic Catholic Assyrian Church of the East, North A, Shlemon Hesequial, Diocesan Offices, 7201 N. Ashland Chicago, IL 60626 Tel. (773)465-4777, Fax (773)465-0776

Quaker Life, (10-Y.) Friends United Meeting, Patricia Edwards-Konic, 101 Quaker Hill Dr., Richmond, IN 47374-1980 Tel. (765)962-7573, Fax (765)966-1293
Email: QuakerLife@fum.org
Website: www.fum.org

Quarterly Review, (Q.) The United Methodist Church, Hendrik R. Pieterse, Box 340007, Nashville, TN 37203-0007 Tel. (615)340-7334, Fax (615)340-7048
Email: hpieterse@gbhem.org
Website: www.quarterlyreview.org

Quarterly Review, A.M.E. Zion, (Q.) African Methodist Episcopal Zion Church, Rev. James D. Armstrong, P.O. Box 33247, Charlotte, NC 28233 Tel. (704)599-4630, Fax (704)688-2544

Reflections, (bi-M.) United Pentecostal Church International, Melissa Anderson, PO Box 3, Collinsville, OK 74021 Tel. (918)371-2659, Fax (918)371-6320
Email: manderson@tums.org

Reformation Today, (bi-M.) Sovereign Grace Baptists, Erroll Hulse, c-o Tom Lutz, 3743 Nichol Ave. Anderson, IN 46011-3008 Tel. (317)644-0994, Fax (317)644-0994

Reformed Herald, (M.) Reformed Church in the United States, David Dawn, 3309 E 31st ST, Sioux Falls, SC 57103-4407

Reformed Worship, (Q.) Christian Reformed Chuch in North America, Emily R. Brink, 2850 Kalamazoo Ave. SE, Grand Rapids, MI 49560-0001 Tel. (616)224-0785, Fax (616) 224-0834
Email: info@reformedworship.org
Website: www.reformedworship.org

Rejoice!, (Q.) Mennonite & Mennonite Brethren Church, Philip Wiebe, 1218 Franklin St. NW, Salem, OR 97304 Tel. (503)585-4458, Fax (503)585-4458

Rejoice!, (Q.) Mennonite Church, Byron Rempel-Burkholder, 600 Shaftesbury Blvd., Winnipeg, MB R3P 0M4 Tel. (204)888-6781, Fax (204)831-5675
Email: byronrb@gcmc.org

Report From The Capital, (24-yr) Baptist Joint Committee, Larry Chesser, 200 Maryland Ave. NE, Washington, DC 20002-5797 Tel. (202) 544-4226, Fax (202)544-2094
Email: lchesser@bjcpa.org
Website: www.bjcpa.org

Reporter, (M.) The Lutheran Church—Missouri Synod, David Mahsman, 1333 S. Kirkwood Rd., St. Louis, MO 63122-7295 Tel. (314)965-9000, Fax (314)965-3396
Email: REPORTER@lcms.org
Website: www.lcms.org

The Rescue Herald, (3-Y.) American Rescue Workers, Rev. Col. Robert N. Coles, National Field Office, 1209 Hamilton Blvd. Hagerstown, MD 21742 Tel. (301)797-0061, Fax (301)797-1480
Email: chiefcoles@aol.com
Website: www.arwus.com

Response, (M.) The United Methodist Church, Dana Jones, 475 Riverside Dr., Room 1356, New York, NY 10115 Tel. (212)870-3755, Fax (212)870-3940

The Restitution Herald, (bi-M.) Church of God General Conference (Oregon, Ill. & Morrow, Jeffery Fletcher, Box 100,000, Morrow, GA 30260-7000 Tel. (504)543-0290, Fax (404) 362-9307

Restoration Herald, (M.) Christian Churches and Churches of Christ, H. Lee Mason, 5664 Cheviot Rd., Cincinnati, OH 45247-7071 Tel. (513)385-0461, Fax (513)385-0660
Email: thecra@aol.com
Website: www.thecra.org

Restoration Quarterly, (Q.) Churches of Christ, James W. Thompson, Box 28227, Abilene, TX 79699-8227 Tel. (915)674-3781, Fax (915) 674-3776
Email: rq@bible.acu.edu
Website: www.rq.acu.edu

Restoration Witness, (bi-M.) Community of Christ, Richard A. Brown, Herald Publishing House, P.O. Box 390 Independence, MO 64051-0390 Tel. (816)521-3043, Fax (816) 521-3043
Email: rbrown@cofchrist.org
Website: www.cofchrist.org

Review for Religious, (bi-M.) The Roman Catholic Church, David L. Fleming, S.J., 3601 Lindell Blvd., St. Louis, MO 63108 Tel. (314)977-7363, Fax (314)977-7362
Email: review@slu.edu

Review of Religious Research, (4-Y.) Non-denominational, Dr. Darren E. Sherkat & Dr. Christopher Ellison, Co-editors, Sociology Department, University of Texas-Austin Austin, TX 78712 Tel. (512)471-1122, Fax (512)471-1748
Email: cellison@jeeves.la.utexas.edu

Rocky Mountain Christian, (M.) Churches of Christ, Ron L. Carter, P.O. Box 26620,

Colorado Springs, CO 80936 Tel. (719)598-4197, Fax (719)528-1549
Email: 76102.2461@compuserve.com

Sabbath Recorder, (M.) Seventh Day Baptist General Conference, USA and Canada, Rev. Kevin J. Butler, 3120 Kennedy Rd., P.O. Box 1678 Janesville, WI 53547 Tel. (608)752-5055, Fax (608)752-7711
Email: sdbmedia@charter.net
Website: www.seventhdaybaptist.org

Sabbath School Leadership, (M.) Seventh-day Adventist Church, Faith Crumbly, Review and Herald Publishing Assoc., 55 W. Oak Ridge Dr. Hagerstown, MD 21740 Tel. (301)393-4090, Fax (301)393-4055
Email: sabbathschoolleadership@rhpa.org
Website: www.rhpa.org

Saint Anthony Messenger, (M.) The Roman Catholic Church, Jack Wintz, O.F.M., St. Anthony Messenger Editorial, Dept., 28 W. Liberty St. Cincinnati, OH 45210 Tel. (513)241-5616, Fax (513)241-0399
Email: StAnthony@AmericanCatholic.org
Website: www.americancatholic.org

Saint Willibrord Journal, (Q.) Christ Catholic Church, The Rev. MonsignorCharles E. Harrison, P.O. Box 271751, Houston, TX 77277-1751 Tel. (713)515-8206, Fax (713) 622-5311
Website: www.christcatholic.org

SBC Life, (10-Y.) Southern Baptist Convention, Bill Merrell, 901 Commerce St., Nashville, TN 37203 Tel. (615)244-2355, Fax (615)782-8684
Email: jrevell@sbc.net
Website: sbc.net

The Schwenkfeldian, (Q.) The Schwenkfelder Church, Andrew C. Anders, 105 Seminary Street, Pennsburg, PA 18073 Tel. (215)244-2355

SCROLL—Computer Resources for Church and Family, (6-Y.) Nondenominational, Marshall N. Surratt, 304C Crossfield Drive, P.O. Box 603 Versailles, KY 40383-0603 Tel. (606)873-0550, Fax (606)879-0121
Email: scroll@deerhaven.com
Website: wwww.deerhaven.com/

Searching Together, (Q.) Sovereign Grace Believers, Jon Zens, Box 548, St. Croix Falls, WI 54024 Tel. (651)465-6516, Fax (651)465-5101
Email: jon@searchingtogether.org
Website: www.searchingtogether.org

The Secret Place, (Q.) American Baptist Churches USA, Kathleen Hayes, Senior Editor, P.O. Box 851, Valley Forge, PA 19482-0851 Tel. (610)768-2240, Fax (610)768-2441

Seeds for the Parish, (bi-M.) Evangelical Lutheran Church in America, Kate Elliott, 8765 W. Higgins Rd., Chicago, IL 60631-4101 Tel. (773)380-2949, Fax (773)380-1465
Email: kelliott@elca.org

Shiloh's Messenger of Wisdom, (M.) Israelite House of David, William Robertson, P.O. Box 1067, Benton Harbor, MI 49023

The Shining Light, (bi-M.) Church of God (Anderson, Ind), Wilfred Jordan, Box 1235, Anderson, IN 46015 Tel. (317)644-1593

Signs of the Times, (M.) Seventh-day Adventist Church, Marvin Moore, P.O. Box 5353, Nampa, ID 83653-5353 Tel. (208)465-2577 Fax (208)465-2531

The Silver Lining, (M.) Apostolic Christian Churches of America, Bruce Leman, R.R. 2, Box 50 Roanoke, IL 61561-9625 Tel. (309) 923-7777, Fax (309)923-7359

Social Questions Bulletin, (bi-M.) The United Methodist Church, Rev. Kathryn J. Johnson, 212 East Capitol St., NE, Washington, DC 20003 Tel. (202)546-8806, Fax (202)546-6811
Email: mfsa@olg.com
Website: www.olg.com/mfsa

Sojourners, (6-Y.) Nondenominational, Jim Wallis, 2401 15th St. NW, Washington, DC 20009 Tel. (202)328-8842, Fax (202)328-8757
Email: sojourners@sojourners.com
Website: www.sojo.net

Solia - The Herald, (M.) The Romanian Orthodox Episcopate of America, Rev. Protodeacon David Oancea, P.O. Box 185, Grass Lake, MI 49240-0185 Tel. (517)522-3656, Fax (517) 522-5907
Email: roeasolia@aol.com
Website: www.roea.org

Sound of Grace, (Q.) Soverign Grace Believers, 5317 Wye Creek Dr, Frederick, MD 21703-6938

The Southern Methodist, (bi-M.) Southern Methodist Church, Thomas M. Owens, Sr., P.O. Box 39, Orangeburg, SC 29116-0039 Tel. (803)534-9853, Fax (803)535-3881
Email: foundry@bellsouth.net

Spectrum, (bi-M.) Conservative Baptist Association of America (CBAmerica), Dr. Dennis L. Gorton, 1501 W. Mineral Ave., Suite B Littleton, CO 80120 Tel. (720)283-3030, Fax (720)283-3333
Email: CBA@CBAmerica.org
Website: www.CBAmerica.org

Spirit, (Q.) Volunteers of America, Arthur Smith and Denis N. Baker, 1809 Carrollton Ave, New Orleans, LA 70118-2829 Tel. (504)897-1731

The Spiritual Sword, (Q.) Churches of Christ, Alan E. Highers, 1511 Getwell Rd., Memphis, TN 38111 Tel. (901)743-0464, Fax (901)743-2197
Email: getwellcc@aol.com
Website: www.getwellchurchofchrist.org

The Standard Bearer, (21-Y.) Protestant Reformed Churches in America, David J. Engelsma, 4949 Ivanrest Ave., Grandville, MI 49418 Tel. (616)531-1490, Fax (616)531-3033 Email: engelsma@prca.org

The Standard, (M.) Baptist General Conference, Gary D. Marsh, 2002 S. Arlington Heights Rd., Arlington Heights, IL 60005 Tel. (847)228-0200, Fax (847)228-5376
Email: gmarsh@baptistgeneral.org
Website: www.bgcworld.org

Star of Zion, (bi-W.) African Methodist Episcopal Zion Church, Mr. Mike Lisby, P.O. Box 26770, Charlotte, NC 28221-6770 Tel. (704)599-4630 ext.318, Fax (704)688-2546
Email: editor@thestarofzion.org
Website: www.thestarofzion.org

Stewardship USA, (Q.) Nondenominational, Raymond Barnett Knudsen II, 4818 Quarton Rd., Bloomfield Hills, MI 48302 Tel. (248) 737-0895, Fax (248)737-0895

Story Friends, (M.) Mennonite Church, Rose Mary Stutzman, 616 Walnut Ave., Scottdale, PA 15683 Tel. (724)887-8500, Fax (724)887-3111
Email: rstutz@mph.org
Website: www.mph.org

The Student, (M.) Seventh-day Adventist Church, Jerry Stevens, P.O. Box 6097, Lincoln, NE 68506 Tel. (402)488-0981, Fax (402)488-7582
Email: CRSnet@compuserve.com
Website: www.ChristianRecord.org

Sunday, (Q.) Interdenominational, Timothy A. Norton, 2930 Flowers Rd., S., Atlanta, GA 30341-5532 Tel. (770)936-5376, Fax (770) 936-5385
Email: tnelson@ldausa.org
Website: www.sundayonline.org

The Tablet, (W.) The Roman Catholic Church, Ed Wilkinson, 653 Hicks St., Brooklyn, NY 11231 Tel. (718)858-3838, Fax (718)858-2112

Theology Digest, (Q.) The Roman Catholic Church, 3634 Lindell Blvd., St. Louis, MO 63108-3395 Tel. (314)977-3410

Theology Today, (Q.) Nondenominational, Patrick D. Miller, Ellen T. Cherry, P.O. Box 29, Princeton, NJ 08542 Tel. (609)497-7714, Fax (609)497-7870
Email: theology.today@ptsem.edu
Website: theologytoday.ptsem.edu

These Days, (bi-M.) Interdenominational, Kay Snodgrass, 100 Witherspoon St., Louisville, KY 40202-1396 Tel. (502)569-5080, Fax (502) 569-5113
Website: www.pcusa.org/ppc/

The Tidings, (W.) The Roman Catholic Church, Tod M. Tamberg, 3424 Wilshire Blvd., Los Angeles, CA 90010 Tel. (213)637-7360, Fax (213)637-6360
Website: www.the-tidings.com

Timbrel: The Publication of Mennonite Women, (6-Y.) Mennonite Church and General Conference Mennonite Church, Cathleen Hockman-Wert, 828 Washington St., Apt. 3B Huntingdon, PA 16652 Tel. (814)641-5259
Email: timbrel@vicon.net

Today's Christian Woman, (6-Y.) Nondenominational, Jane Johnson Struck, 465 Gundersen Dr., Carol Stream, IL 60188 Tel. (630)260-6200 Fax (630)260-0114
Email: TCWedit@christiantoday.com
Website: www.christianity.net/

Tomorrow Magazine, (Q.) American Baptist Churches in the USA, Sara E. Hopkins, 475 Riverside Dr., Room 1700, New York, NY 10115-0049 Tel. (800)986-6222, Fax (800) 986-6782

The Tover of St. Cassian, (2-Y.) Apostolic Episcopal Church- Province of the East, Rt. Rev. Francis C. Spataro DD, Order of Corporate Reunion- US Council/Society of St. Cassian, 80-46 234th Street Jamaica, NY 11427 Tel. (718)740-4134
Email: vilatte@aol.com
Website: vgusa.InJesus.com

Truth, (Q.) Grace Gospel Fellowship, Phil Cereghino, 2125 Martindale SW, Grand Rapids, MI 49509 Tel. (616)247-1999, Fax (616)241-2542
Email: ggfinc@aol.com
Website: www.ggfusa.org

Truth Magazine, (bi-W.) Churches of Christ, Mike Willis, Box 9670, Bowling Green, KY 42102 Tel. (800)428-0121
Website: truthmagazine.com

U.S. Catholic, (M.) The Roman Catholic Church, Rev. Mark J. Brummel, 205 W. Monroe St., Chicago, IL 60606 Tel. (312)236-7782, Fax (312)236-8207
Email: editors@uscatholic.org
Website: www.uscatholic.org

Ubique, (Q.) The Liberal Catholic Church—Province of the United States, Rev. James Voirol, 40 Krotona Rd, Ojai, CA 93023
Email: jvoirol@aol.com
Website: www.thelcc.org

Ukrainian Orthodox Herald, () Ukrainian Orthodox Church in America (Ecumenical Patriarch, Rev. Dr. Anthony Ugolnik, P.O. Box 774, Allentown, PA 18105

United Church News, (10-Y.) United Church of Christ, W. Evan Golder, 700 Prospect Ave., Cleveland, OH 44115 Tel. (216)736-2218, Fax (216)736-2223
Email: goldere@ucc.org
Website: www.ucc.org

UMR Communications, Inc., () Independent, Protestant organization which publishes: The United Methodist Reporter (w); The United Methodist Reporter (bi-w); The National Christian Reporter (w); Good Works Online (daily Internet); Reporter Interactive (daily Internet), Cynthia B. Astle, P.O. Box 660275, Dallas, TX 75266-0275 Tel. (214)630-6495, Fax (214)630-0079
Email: umr4news@umr.org
Website: www.umr.org

The Upper Room, (6-Y.) The United Methodist Church, Janice Grana, P.O. Box 189, Nashville, TN 37202 Tel. (615)340-7200, Fax (615)340-7006

Vibrant Life, (bi-M.) Seventh-day Adventist Church, Larry Becker, 55 W. Oak Ridge Dr., Hagerstown, MD 21740 Tel. (301)393-4019, Fax (301)393-4055
Email: vibrantlife@rhpa.org
Website: www.vibrantlife.com

Victory (Youth Magazine), (Q.) Church of God of Prophecy, David Bryan, P.O. Box 2910, Cleveland, TN 37320-2910 Tel. (423)559-5321, Fax (423)559-5461
Email: david@cogop.org
Website: www.cogop.org

The Vindicator, (M.) Old German Baptist Brethren Church, Steven L. Bayer, 6952 N. Montgomery Co. Line Rd., Englewood, OH 45322-9748 Tel. (937)884-7531, Fax (937) 884-7531

Visitor, (6-Y.) Brethren in Christ Church, Ronald C. Ross, P.O. Box 166, Nappanee, IN 46550 Tel. (219)773-3164, Fax (219)773-5934

Vista, (bi-M.) Christian Church of North America, General Council, Eric Towse, 1294 Rutledge Rd., Transfer, PA 16154 Tel. (412) 962-3501, Fax (412)962-1766
Email: ccna@nauticom.net
Website: www.ccna.org

Voice!, (Q.) General Association of General Baptists, Rev. Ron Byrd, 100 Stinson Dr., Poplar Bluff, MO 63901 Tel. (573)785-7746, Fax (573)785-0564
Email: gbnm@pbmo.net
Website: www.generalbaptist.com

The Voice, (6-Y.) IFCA International, Inc., Les Lofquist, P.O. Box 810, Grandville, MI 49468-0810 Tel. (616)531-1840, Fax (616) 531-1814
Email: Voice@ifca.org

The Voice, (Q.) The Bible Church of Christ, Inc., Montrose Bushrod, 1358 Morris Ave., Bronx, NY 10456 Tel. (718)588-2284, Fax (718)992-5597
Website: www.thebiblechurchofchrist.org

The War Cry, (bi-W.) The Salvation Army, Marlene Chase, 615 Slaters Lane, Alexandria, VA 22313 Tel. (703)684-5500, Fax (703)684-5539
Email: warcry@usn.salvationarmy.org
Website: publications.salvationarmyusa.org

Weavings: A Journal of the Christian Spiritual Life, (6-Y.) The United Methodist Church, John S. Mogabgab, P.O. Box 189, Nashville, TN 37202 Tel. (615)340-7254, Fax (615)340-7267
Email: weavings@upperroom.org
Website: www.upperroom.org

The Wesleyan Advocate, (11-Y.) The Wesleyan Church, Norman G. Wilson, P.O. Box 50434, Indianapolis, ID 46250-0434 Tel. (317)570-5204, Fax (317)570-5260
Email: wilsonn@wesleyan.org
Website: www.wesleyan.org

Wesleyan Woman, (Q.) The Wesleyan Church, Martha Blackburn, P.O. Box 50434, Indianapolis, IN 46250 Tel. (317)570-5164, Fax (317)570-5254
Email: ww@wesleyan.org
Website: www.wesleyan.org/women/

Wesleyan World, (Q.) The Wesleyan Church, Wayne Derr, P.O. Box 50434, Indianapolis, IN 46250 Tel. (317)570-5172, Fax (317)570-5256
Email: wwm@wesleyan.org
Website: www.wesleyan.org

The White Wing Messenger, (bi-W.) Church of God of Prophecy, Virginia E. Chatham, P.O. Box 3000, Cleveland, TN 37320-3000 Tel. (423)559-5413, Fax (423)559-5444
Email: jenny@wingnet.net
Website: www.cogop.org

Whole Truth, (M.) The Church of God in Christ, Larry Britton, P.O. Box 2017, Memphis, TN 38101 Tel. (901)578-3841, Fax (901)57-6807

Wineskins, (bi-M.) Churches of Christ, Mike Cope and Rubel Shelly, Box 41028, Nashville, TN 37024-1028 Tel. (615)373-5004, Fax (615) 373-5006
Email: wineskinsmagazine@msn.com
Website: www.wineskins.org

The Winner, (9-Y.) Nondenominational, Lincoln Sterd, The Health Connection, P.O. Box 859 Hagerstown, MD 21741 Tel. (301) 790-9735, Fax (301)790-9734

Wisconsin Lutheran Quarterly, (Q.) Wisconsin Evangelical Lutheran Synod, John F. Brug, 11831 N. Seminary Dr., Mequon, WI 53092 Tel. (262)242-8139, Fax (262)242-8110
Email: brugj@wls.wels.net
Website: www.wls.wels.net

With: The Magazine for Radical Christian Youth, (6-Y.) Interdenominational, Carol Duerksen, P.O. Box 347, Newton, KS 67114 Tel. (316)283-5100, Fax (316)283-0454
Email: deliag@gcmc.org
Website: withonline.org

The Witness, (10-Y.) Nondenominational, Julie A. Wortman, 7000 Michigan Ave., Detroit, MI 48210 Tel. (313)841-1967, Fax (313)841-1956
Email: office@thewitness.org
Website: www.thewitness.org

Woman to Woman, (M.) General Association of General Baptists, Stephana Deckard, 100 Stinson Dr., Poplar Bluff, MO 63901 Tel. (573)785-7746, Fax (573)785-0564
Email: gbwmin@semo.net

The Woman's Pulpit, (Q.) Nondenominational, LaVonne Althouse, 5227 Castor Ave., Philadelphia, PA 19124-1742 Tel. (215)743-4528

Woman's Touch, (bi-M.) Assemblies of God, Lillian Sparks, 1445 N. Boonville Ave., Springfield, MO 65802-1894 Tel. (417)862-2781, Fax (417)862-0503
Email: womanstouch@ag.org
Website: www.ag.org/womanstouch

Women's Missionary Magazine, (9-Y.) African Methodist Episcopal Church, Dr. Bettye J. Allen, 17129 Bennett Dr, South Holland, IL 60473 Tel. (708)339-5997, Fax (708)339-5987
Email: bettye1901@aol.com

Word and Work, (11-Y.) Churches of Christ, Alex V. Wilson, 2518 Portland Ave., Louisville, KY 40212 Tel. (502)897-2831

The Word, (10-Y.) The Antiochian Orthodox Christian Archdiocese of North America, V. Rev. John Abdalah, 1777 Quigg Dr., Pittsburgh, PA 15241-2071 Tel. (412)681-2988, Fax (412)831-5554
Email: frjpa@aol.com
Website: www.antiochian.org

The Worker, (Q.) Progressive National Baptist Convention, Inc., Mattie A Robinson, 601 50th St. NE, Washington, DC 20019 Tel. (202)398-5343, Fax (202)398-4998
Email: info@pnbc.org
Website: www.pnbc.org

World Harvest Today, (Q.) United Pentecostal Church International, J. S. Leaman, 8855 Dunn Rd., Hazelwood, MO 63042 Tel. (314) 837-7300, Fax (314)837-2387

World Parish: International Organ of the World Methodist Council, (s-M.) Interdenominational Methodist (Christian World Communion of Methodist and WMC-Related Churches), George Freeman, P.O. Box 518, Lake Junaluska, NC 28745 Tel. (828) 456-9432, Fax (828)456-9433
Email: wmc6@juno.com

World Vision, (bi-M.) Open Bible Standard Churches, Inc., Paul V. Canfield, 2020 Bell Ave., Des Moines, IA 50315-1096 Tel. (515) 288-6761, Fax (515)288-2510
Email: missions@openbible.org
Website: www.openbible.org

World Vision Today, (Q.) Nondenominational, Terry Madison, PO Box 9716, Federal Way, WA 98063-9716 Tel. (253)815-1000, Fax (253) 815-3445
Email: wvtoday@worldvision.org

World Vision Today, (bi-M.) Nondenominational, , P.O. Box 9716, Federal Way, WA 98063-9716 Tel. (253)815-2237, Fax (253) 815-3445
Email: wvtoday@worldvision.org

Worldorama, (M.) Pentecostal Holiness Church, International, Donald Duncan, P.O. Box 12609, Oklahoma City, OK 73157 Tel. (405)787-7110, Fax (405)787-7729
Email: jds@iphc.org

Worship, (6-Y.) The Roman Catholic Church, R. Kevin Seasoltz, St. John's Abbey, Collegeville, MN 56321 Tel. (320)363-3883, Fax (320)363-3145
Email: kseasoltz@csbsju.edu
Website: www.sja.org/worship

Worship Arts, (6-Y.) Nondenominational, David A Wiltse, P.O. Box 6247, Grand Rapids, MI 49516-6247 Tel. (616)459-4503, Fax (616) 459-1051
Email: graphics@iserv.net

www.eccenter.com, (M.) The Evangelical Congregational Church, , 100 W. Park Ave, Myerstown, PA 17067
Email: eccenter@eccenter.com
Website: www.eccenter.com

Young & Alive, (Q.) Seventh-day Adventist Church, Braille and Large Print, Gaylena Gibson, P.O. Box 6097, Lincoln, NE 68506 Tel. (402)488-0981, Fax (402)488-7582
Email: editorial@christianrecord.org
Website: www.christianrecord.org

Youth Ministry Accent, (Q.) Seventh-day Adventist Church, David S.F. Wong, 12501 Old Columbia Pike, Silver Spring, MD 20904-6600 Tel. (301)680-6180, Fax (301)680-6155
Email: 74532.1426@compuserve.com

Zion's Advocate, (M.) Church of Christ, Mike McGhee, P.O. Box 472, Independence, MO 64051-0472 Tel. (816)796-6255

12. Religious Periodicals in Canada

The religious periodicals below constitute a basic core of important journals and periodicals circulated in Canada. The list does not include all publications prepared by religious bodies, and not all the publications listed here are necessarily the official publication of a particular church. Each entry gives: the title of the periodical, frequency of publication, religious affiliation, editor's name, address, telephone and fax number and email and website addresses when available. The frequency of publication, which appears in parenthesis after the name of the publication, is represented by a "W." for weekly; "M." for monthly; "Q." for quarterly.

Again, (Q.) The Antiochian Orthodox Christian Archdiocese of North America, R. Thomas Zell, Conciliar Press, P.O. Box 76 Ben Lomond, CA 95005-0076 Tel. (800)967-7377, Fax (831)336-8882
Email: conciliar@got.net
Website: www.conciliarpress.com

Anglican Journal, (10-Y.) The Anglican Church of Canada, Vianney (Sam) Carriere, 600 Jarvis St., Toronto, ON M4Y 2J6 Tel. (416)924-9199 x. 306, Fax (416)921-4452
Email: editor@national.anglican.ca
Website: www.anglicanjournal.com

The Anglican, (10-Y.) The Anglican Church of Canada, Stuart Mann, 135 Adelaide St. E., Toronto, ON M5C 1L8 Tel. (416)363-6021, Fax (416)363-7678

Armenian Evangelical Church Newsletter, (Q.) Armenian Evangelical Church, Yessayi Sarmazian, 2600 14th Avenue, Markham, ON L3R 3X1 Tel. (905)305-8144, Fax (905)305-8125
Email: aectoronto@yahoo.com

Aujourd'hui Credo, (10-Y.) The United Church of Canada, David Fines, 1332 Victoria, Greenfield Park, QC J4V 1L8 Tel. (450)446-7733, Fax (450)466-2664
Email: copermit@sympatico.ca
Website: www.egliseunie.org

The Banner, (bi-W.) Christian Reformed Church in North America, John A. Suk, 2850 Kalamazoo Ave. SE, Grand Rapids, MI 49560 Tel. (616)224-0732, Fax (616)224-0834
Email: editorial@thebanner.org
Website: www.thebanner.org

The Baptist Horizon, (M.) Canadian Convention of Southern Baptists, Nancy McGough, P.O. Box 300, Cochrane, AB T0L 0W0 Tel. (403)932-5688, Fax (403)932-4937
Email: office@ccsb.ca

B.C. Fellowship Baptist, (Q.) The Fellowship of Evangelical Baptist Churches in BC and Yukon, Bruce Christensen, #201-26620-56th Ave, Langley, BC V4W 3X5 Tel. (604)607-1192, Fax (604)607-1193
Email: fellowship@tellus.net

BGC Conference Corner, (4-Y.) Baptist General Conference of Canada, Abe Funk, 4306 97th St. NW, Edmonton, AB T6E 5R9 Tel. (780)438-9127, Fax (780)435-2478
Email: bgcc@bgc.ca
Website: www.bgc.ca

Blackboard Bulletin, (10-Y.) Old Order Amish Church, , Old Order Amish Church, Rt. 4 Aylmer, ON N5H 2R3

Die Botschaft, (W.) Old Order Amish Church, James Weaver, Brookshire Publishing, Inc., 200 Hazel St. Lancaster, PA 17603 Tel. (717)392-1321, Fax (717)392-2078

The Budget, (W.) Old Order Amish Church, George R. Smith, P.O. Box 249, Sugarcreek, OH 44681 Tel. (330)852-4634, Fax (330)852-4421

Cahiers de Spiritualite Ignatienne, (Q.) The Roman Catholic Church in Canada, Rene Champagne, Centre de Spiritualite Manrese, 2370 Rue Nicolas-Pinel Ste-Foy, QC G1V 4L6 Tel. (418)653-6353, Fax (418)653-1208

Canada Lutheran, (10-Y.) Evangelical Lutheran Church in Canada, Kenn Ward, 302-393 Portage Avenue, Winnipeg, MB R3B 3H6 Tel. (204)984-9150, Fax (204)984-9185
Email: canaluth@elcic.ca
Website: www.elcic.ca/clweb

Canada Update, (Q.) The Church of God of Prophecy in Canada, Adrian L. Varlack, P. O. Box 457, Brampton, ON L6V 2L4 Tel. (905)843-2379, Fax (905)843-3990

Canadian Adventist Messenger, (12-Y.) Seventh-day Adventist Church in Canada, Carolyn Willis, 1148 King St. E., Oshawa, ON L1H 1H8 Tel. (905)433-0011, Fax (905)433-0982
Email: cwillis@sdacc.org
Website: www.sdacc.org

The Canadian Baptist, (10-Y.) Baptist Convention of Ontario and Quebec, Larry Matthews, 195 The West Mall, Ste.414, Etobicoke, ON M9C 5K1 Tel. (416)622-8600, Fax (416)622-0780
Email: thecb@baptist.ca

Canadian Disciple, (4-Y.) Christian Church (Disciples of Christ) in Canada, Stanley Litke, 255 Midvalley Dr. SE, Calgary, AB T2X 1K8 Tel. (403)256-3280, Fax (403)254-6178
Email: litkes@cia.com

The Canadian Friend, (bi-M.) Canadian Yearly Meeting of the Religious Society of Friends, Anne Marie Zilliacus, 218 Third Ave., Ottawa, ON K1S 2K3 Tel. (613)567-8628, Fax (613) 567-1078
Email: zilli@cyberus.ca

The Canadian Lutheran, (9-Y.) Lutheran Church —Canada, Ian Adnams, 3074 Portage Ave., Winnipeg, MB R3K 0Y2 Tel. (204)895-3433 ext.24, Fax (204)897-4319
Email: communications@lutheranchurch.ca
Website: www.lutheranchurch.ca

Canadian Mennonite, (bi-W.) Mennonite Church Canada, Ron Rempel, Suite C5, 490 Dutton Dr. Waterloo, ON N2L 6H7 Tel. (519)884-3810, Fax (519)884-3331
Email: editor@canadianmennonite.org
Website: www.canadianmennonite.org

Canadian Orthodox Messenger, (Q.) Orthodox Church in America (Canada Section), Nun Sophia (Zion), P.O. Box 179, Spencerville, ON K0E 1X0 Tel. (613)925-064, Fax (613) 925-1521
Email: sophia@recorder.ca

The **Catalyst**, (6-Y.) Nondenominational, Murray MacAdam, Citizens for Public Justice, 229 College St. #311 Toronto, ON M5T 1R4 Tel. (416)979-2443, Fax (416)979-2458
Email: cpj@web.ca
Website: www.cpj.ca

Catherine, (10-Y.) The Salvation Army in Canada, Doreen Sturge, 2 Overlea Blvd., Toronto, ON M4H 1P4 Tel. (416)422-6113, Fax (416)422-6120

The Catholic Register, (W.) The Roman Catholic Church in Canada, Joseph Sinasac, 1155 Yonge St., Ste. 401, Toronto, ON M4Y 1W2 Tel. (416)934-3410, Fax (416)934-3409
Email: editor@catholicregister.org
Website: www.catholicregister.org

The Catholic Times (Montreal), (10-Y.) The Roman Catholic Church in Canada, Eric Durocher, 2005 St. Marc St., Montreal, QC H3H 2G8 Tel. (514)937-2301, Fax (514)937-3051

Channels, (3-Y) Presbyterian Church in Canada, Calvin Brown, Renewal Fellowship, 3819 Bloor St W Etobicoke, ON M9B 1K7 Tel. (416)233-6581, Fax (416)233-1743
Email: canoebill@sympatico.ca
Website: www.presbycan.ca/rfpc

Chinese Herald, (Q.) Canadian Conference of Mennonite Brethren Churches, Keynes Kan, 2622 St. Johns St., Port Moody, BC V3H 2B6 Tel. (604)939-8281, Fax (604)939-8201

The Christian Contender, (M.) Mennonite Church (Canada), James Baer, Box 584, McBride, BC V0J 2E0 Tel. (604)569-3302, Fax (604)569-0020

Christian Courier, (bi-W.) Nondenominational, Harry der Nederlanden, 261 Martindale Rd., Unit 4, St. Catharines, ON L2W 1A1 Tel. (905)682-8311, Fax (905)682-8313
Email: cceditor@aol.com

Church of God Beacon, (Q.) Church of God (Cleveland, Tenn.), Canute Blake, P.O. Box 2036, Brampton Commercial Service Center, Brampton, ON L6T 3T0 Tel. (905)793-2213, Fax (905)793-2213

Clarion-The Canadian Reformed Magazine, (bi-W.) Canadian and American Reformed Churches, J. Visscher, One Beghin Ave. Winnipeg, MB R2J 3X5 Tel. (204)663-9000 Fax (204)663-9202
Email: clarion@premier.mb.ca
Website: premier.mb.ca/clarion.html

CLBI-Cross Roads, (Q.) Lutheran, Jeremy Osterwalder, 4837-52A St., Camrose, AB T4V 1W5 Tel. (780)672-4454, Fax (780)672-4455
Email: clbipbad@cable-lynx.net
Website: www.clbi.edu

College News & Updates, (6-Y.) Church of God (Anderson, Ind.), John Alan Howard, 4707 56th St, Camrose, AB T4V 2C4 Tel. (780)672-0171, Fax (780)672-2465
Email: garnderc@cable-lynx.net
Website: cable-lynx/~gardnerc

The Communicator, (3-Y.) The Roman Catholic Church in Canada, P. Giroux, P.O Box 142, Tantallon, NS B0J 3J0 Tel. (902) 826-7236, Fax (902)826-7236

Companion Magazine, (10-Y.) The Roman Catholic Church in Canada, Friar Philip Kelly OFM Con., Conventual Franciscan Centre, 695 Coxwell Ave., Suite 600 Toronto, ON M4C 5R6 Tel. (416)690-5611, Fax (416)690-3320
Email: companion@franciscan.on.ca
Website: www.franciscan.on.ca

Connexions, (4-Y.) Interdenominational, Ulli Diemer, P.O. Box 158, Stn. D, Toronto, ON M6P 3J8 Tel. (416)537-3949
Email: connexions@sources.com
Website: www.connexions.org

The Covenant Messenger, (5-Y.) The Evangelical Covenant Church of Canada, , 279 Pembina Hwy., Winnipeg, MB R3T 2H5 Tel. (204)269-3437, Fax (204)269-3584
Email: messengr@escape.ca

Crux, (Q.) Nondenominational, Donald Lewis Regent College, 5800 University Blvd Vancouver, BC V6T 2E4 Tel. (604)224-3245 Fax (604)224-3097

Diakonia-A Magazine of Office-Bearers, (4-Y.) Canadian and American Reformed Churches, J. Visscher, Brookside Publishing 3911 Mt. Lehman Rd. Abbotsford, BC V4X 2M9 Tel. (604)856-4127, Fax (604)856-6724

The Diary, (M.) Old Order Amish Church, Don Carpenter, P.O. Box 98, Gordonville, PA 17529 Tel. (717)529-3938, Fax (717)529-3292

Discover the Bible, (W.) The Roman Catholic Church in Canada, Guy Lajoie, P.O. Box 2400, London, ON N6A 4G3 Tel. (519)439-7211, Fax (519)439-0207

Ecumenism-Oecumenisme, (Q.) Interdenominational, , 2065 Sherbrooke St. W, Montreal, QC H3H 1G6 Tel. (514)937-9176, Fax (514) 937-4986
Email: ccocce@total.net
Website: www.total.net/~ccocce

The Edge (Christian Youth Magazine), (10-Y.) The Salvation Army in Canada, Captain Brenda Smith, 2 Overlea Blvd., Toronto, ON M4H 1P4 Tel. (416)422-6114, Fax (416)422-6120
Email: edge@sallynet.org
Website: www.salvationarmy.ca

Eesti Kirik, (Q.) The Estonian Evangelical Lutheran Church, Rev. U. Petersoo, 383 Jarvis St., Toronto, ON M5B 2C7 Tel. (416)925-5465, Fax (416)925-5688

L'Eglise Canadienne, (11-Y.) The Roman Catholic Church in Canada, Madame Rolande Parrot, C.P. 990, Ville Mont-Royal, QC H3P 3M8 Tel. (514)278-3020 x. 228, Fax (514) 278-3030
Email: cmilette@novalis-inc.com
Website: www.novalis.ca

EMMC Recorder, (M.) Evangelical Mennonite Mission Conference, Jack Heppner, Box 52059 Niakwa P.O., Winnipeg, MB R2M 5P9 Tel. (204)253-7929, Fax (204)256-7384
Email: emmc@mb.sympatico.ca
Website: www.sbcollege.mb.ca/emmc/

En Avant!, (24-Y.) The Salvation Army in Canada, Marie-Michäle Roy, 2050 Rue Stanley, bureau 400, Montreal, QB H3A 3G3 Tel. (514)288-2848, Fax (514)849-7600
Email: foivie@sallynet.org

The Ensign, (M.) The Church of Jesus Christ of Latter-day Saints, Brian K. Kelly, Managing Editor, 50 E. North Temple St., 24th Floor Salt Lake City, UT 84150 Tel. (801)240-2950, Fax (801)240-5732
Email: toddjm@ldschurch.org

Esprit, (Q.) Evangelical Lutheran Church in Canada (Evangelical Lutheran Women), Gayle Johannesson, 302-393 Portage Avenue, Winnipeg, MB R3B 3H6 Tel. (204)984-9160, Fax (204)984-9162
Email: esprit@elcic.ca
Website: www.elw.ca

Evangel-The Good News of Jesus Christ, (4-Y.) Canadian and American Reformed Churches, D. Moes, 21804 52nd Ave., Langley, BC V2Y 1L3 Tel. (604)576-2124, Fax (604)576-2101
Email: canrc@uniserve.com or visscher@direct.ca

The Evangelical Baptist, (5-Y.) The Fellowship of Evangelical Baptist Churches in Canada, Terry D. Cuthbert, 679 Southgate Dr., Guelph, ON N1G 4S2 Tel. (519)821-4830, Fax (519) 821-9829
Email: president@fellowship.ca
Website: www.fellowship.ca

Faith and Fellowship, (M.) Church of the Lutheran Brethren, Brent Juliot, P.O. Box 655, Fergus Falls, MN 56538 Tel. (218)736-7357, Fax (218)736-2200
Email: ffpress@clba.org
Website: www.clba.org/ffmag.htm

Faith & Friends, (M.) The Salvation Army in Canada, Geoff Moulton, 2 Overlea Blvd., Toronto, ON M4H 1P4 Tel. (416)422-6110, Fax (416)422-6120
Email: faithandfriends@sallynet.org
Website: faithandfriends.sallynet.org

Faith Today, (bi-M.) Evangelical Fellowship of Canada (a cooperative organization), Gail Reid, M.I.P. Box 3745, Markham, ON L3R 0Y4 Tel. (905)479-5885, Fax (905)479-4742
Email: ft@efc-canada.com
Website: www.faithtoday.ca

Family Life, (11-Y.) Old Order Amish Church, Joseph Stoll and David Luthy, Old Order Amish Church, Rt. 4 Aylmer, ON N5H 2R3

Family Life Network News, (3-Y) Canadian Conference of Mennonite Brethren Churches, Dorothy Siebert, 225 Riverton Ave., Winnipeg, MB R2L 0N1 Tel. (204)667-9576, Fax (204)669-6079
Email: info@fln.ca
Website: www.fln.ca

Fellowship Magazine, (4-Y.) The United Church of Canada, Gail Reid, Box 237, Barrie, ON L4M 4T3 Tel. (705)737-0114 or (800)678-2607, Fax (705)726-7160
Email: felmag@planeteer.com
Website: wwwebcity.com/fellowshipmug

Foi & Vie, (M.) The Salvation Army in Canada, Marie-Michele Roy, 2050 rue Stanley, Bureau 400 Montreal, QC H3A 3G3 Tel. (514)288-2848, Fax (514)288-4657
Email: foivie@sallynet.org
Website: enavant@sallynet.org

The Free Methodist Herald, (bi-M.) Free Methodist Church in Canada, Donna Elford, 3719-44 St. SW, Calgary, AB T3E 3S1 Tel. (403)246-6838, Fax (403)686-3787
Email: fmccan@inforamp.net

Glad Tidings, (6-Y.) Presbyterian Church in Canada, L. June Stevenson, Women's

Missionary Society, 50 Wynford Dr. North York, ON M3C 1J7 Tel. (800)619-7301, Fax (416)441-2825
Email: jstevenson@presbyterian.ca
Website: www.presbyterian.ca

Global Village Voice, (Q.) The Roman Catholic Church in Canada, Jack J. Panozzo, 420-10 Saint Mary St., Toronto, ON M4Y 1P9 Tel. (416)922-1592, Fax (416)922-0957

Good Tidings, (10-Y.) The Pentecostal Assemblies of Newfoundland, Rev. A.Earl Batstone, 57 Thorburn Rd., P.O. Box 8895, Sta. A, St. John's, NF A1B 3T2 Tel. (709)753-6314, Fax (709)753-4945
Email: paon@paon.nf.ca
Website: www.paon.nf.ca

The **Gospel Contact**, (4-Y.) Church of God (Anderson, Ind.), Editorial Committee, 4717 56th St., Camrose, AB T4V 2C4 Tel. (780)672-0772, Fax (780)672-6888
Email: wcdncog@cable-lynx.net
Website: www.chog.ca

Gospel Herald, (M.) Churches of Christ in Canada, Wayne Turner and Eugene C. Perry, 4904 King St., Beamsville, ON L0R 1B6 Tel. (905)563-7503, Fax (905)563-7503
Email: points@gospelherald.org OR editorial@gospelherald.org
Website: www.gospelherald.org

The Gospel Standard, (M.) Nondenominational, Perry F. Rockwood, Box 1660, Halifax, NS B3J 3A1 Tel. (902)423-5540

Gospel Tidings, (M.) Independent Holiness Church, R. E. Votary, 1564 John Quinn Rd., Greely, ON K4P 1J9 Tel. (613)821-2237, Fax (613)821-4663
Email: rvotary@hotmail.com
Website: www.holiness.ca

The Grape Vine, (12-Y.) Reformed Episcopal Church in Canada, Lynne Ellis, 626 Blanshard Street, Victoria, BC V8W 3G6 Tel. (250)383-8915, Fax (250)383-8916
Email: cool@islandnet.com
Website: www.churchofourlord.org

Hallelujah!, (bi-M.) The Bible Holiness Movement, Wesley H. Wakefield, Box 223, Postal Stn. A, Vancouver, BC V6C 2M3 Tel. (250)492-3376

Handmaiden, (Q.) The Antiochian Orthodox Christian Archdiocese of North America, Virginia Nieuwsma and Carla Zell, Conciliar Press, P.O. Box 76 Ben Lomond, CA 95005-0076 Tel. (800)967-7377, Fax (831)336-8882
Email: czell@conciliarpress.com
Website: conciliarpress.com

Herold der Wahrheit, (M.) Old Order Amish Church, Cephas Kauffman, 1829 110th St., Kalona, IA 52247

Horizons, (bi-M.) The Salvation Army in Canada, Frederich Ash, 2 Overlea Blvd., Toronto, ON M4H 1P4 Tel. (416)425-6118, Fax (416)422-6120
Email: horizons@sallynet.org

IdeaBank, (Q.) Canadian Conference of Mennonite Brethren Churches, Sharon Johnson, Christian Ed. Office, 3-169 Riverton Ave. Winnipeg, MB R2L 2E5 Tel. (204)669-6575, Fax (204)654-1865
Email: cem@mbconf.ca
Website: www.mbconf.ca

InfoMission, (10-Y.) Canadian Baptist Ministries, Donna Lee Pancorvo, 7185 Millcreek Dr., Mississauga, ON L5N 5R4 Tel. (905)821-3533, Fax (905)826-3441
Email: dlpancorvo@cbmin.org
Website: www.cbmin.org

Insight-Insound-In Touch, (6-Y. (Insight); 6-Y. (In Sound); 4-Y. (In Touch)) Interdenominational. Insight (large print newspaper); In Sound (audio magazine); In Touch (braille newspaper), Rebekah Chevalier, Graham Down, John Milton Society for the Blind in Canada, 40 St. Clair Ave. E., Ste. 202 Toronto, ON M4T 1M9 Tel. (416)960-3953, Fax (416)960-3570
Email: jmscan@netcom.ca

Intercom, (bi-M.) The Fellowship of Evangelical Baptist Churches in Canada, Terry D. Cuthbert, 679 Southgate Dr., Guelph, ON N1G 4S2 Tel. (519)821-4830, Fax (519)821-9829
Email: president@fellowship.ca
Website: www.fellowship.ca

ISKRA, (20-Y.) Union of Spiritual Communities of Christ (Orthodox Doukhobors in Canada), Dmitri E. (Jim) Popoff, Box 760, Grand Forks, BC V0H 1H0 Tel. (604)442-8252, Fax (604) 442-3433
Email: iskra@sunshinecable.com

Istocnik, (4-Y.) Serbian Orthodox Church in the U.S.A. and Canada, Diocese of Canada, Very Rev. VasilijeTomic, 7470 McNiven Rd., RR 3, Campbellville, ON L0P 1B0 Tel. (905)878-0043, Fax (905)878-1909
Email: vladika@istocnik.com
Website: www.istocnik.com

Le Lien, (11-Y.) Canadian Conference of Mennonite Brethren Churches, Annie Brosseau, 1775 Edouard-Laurin, St. Laurent, QC H4L 2B9 Tel. (514)331-0878, Fax (514) 331-0879
Email: LeLien@total.net
Website: www.mbconf.ca/comm/lelien

Liturgie, Foi et Culture (Bulletin Natl. de Liturgie), (4-Y.) The Roman Catholic Church in Canada, Service des Editions de la CECC, Office national de liturgie, 3530 rue Adam Montreal, QC H1W 1Y8 Tel. (514)522-4930, Fax (514)522-1557

Email: onl@videotron.ca
Website: www.cccb.ca

Mandate, (4-Y.) The United Church of Canada, Rebekah Chevalier, Div. of Communication, 3250 Bloor St W., Ste. 300 Etobicoke, ON M8X 2Y4 Tel. (416)231-5931, Fax (416)231-3103
Email: rchevali@uccan.org
Website: www.uccan.org/mandate

The Mantle, (M.) Independent Assemblies of God International (Canada), Philip Rassmussen, P.O. Box 2130, Laguna Hills, CA 92654-9901 Tel. (514)522-4930, Fax (514) 522-1557

Marketplace, The- A Magazine for Christians in Business, (bi-M.) Interdenominational Mennonite, Wally Kroeker, 302-280 Smith St., Winnipeg, MB R3C 1K2 Tel. (204)956-6430, Fax (204)942-4001
Website: www.meda.org

Mennonite Brethren Herald, (bi-W.) Canadian Conference of Mennonite Brethren Churches, Jim Coggins, 3-169 Riverton Ave., Winnipeg, MB R2L 2E5 Tel. (204)669-6575, Fax (204) 654-1865
Email: mbherald@mbconf.ca
Website: www.mbherald.com

Mennonite Historian, (Q.) Canadian Conference of Mennonite Brethren Churches, Mennonite Church Canada, Abe Dueck and Alf Redekopp, Ctr. for Menn. Brethren Studies, 169 Riverton Ave. Winnipeg, MB R2L 2E5 Tel. (204)669-6575, Fax (204)654-1865
Email: adueck@mbconf.ca
Website: mbconf.ca/mbstudies/

Die Mennonitische Post, (bi-M.) Interdenominational Mennonite, Abe Warkentin, Box 1120, 383 Main St. Steinbach, MB R0A 2A0 Tel. (204)326-6790, Fax (204)326-6302

Mennonitische Rundschau, (M.) Canadian Conference of Mennonite Brethren Churches, Brigitte Penner; Marianne Dulder, 3-169 Riverton Ave., Winnipeg, MB R2L 2E5 Tel. (204)669-6575, Fax (204)654-1865
Email: MR@mbconf.ca
Website: www.mbconf.ca

Messenger (of the Sacred Heart), (M.) The Roman Catholic Church in Canada, F. J. Power, Apostleship of Prayer, 661 Greenwood Ave. Toronto, ON M4J 4B3 Tel. (416)466-1195

Messenger of Truth, (bi-W.) Church of God in Christ (Mennonite), Gladwin Koehn, P.O. Box 230, Moundridge, KS 67107 Tel. (620)345-2532, Fax (620)345-2582

The Messenger, (22-Y.) The Evangelical Mennonite Conference, Terry Smith, Editor; Becky Buhler, Assistant Editor, Box 1268, Steinbach, MB R0A 2A0 Tel. (204)326-6401, Fax (204)326-1613
Email: emcmessenger@mts.net
Website: www.emconf.ca

The Messenger, (Q.) The Reformed Episcopal Church of Canada, Rt. Rev. Michael Fedechko, 320 Armstrong St., New Liskeard, ON P0J 1P0 Tel. (705)647-4565, Fax (705) 647-4565
Email: fed@nt.net

The Messenger, (bi-M.) Church of God (Anderson, Ind.), Rev. Sieg Pudel, 39 Tanager Square, Brampton, ON L6Z 1X1 Tel. (416)431-9800
Email: smhope@interlog.com

Missions Today, (bi-M.) Roman Catholic, Patricia McKinnon, Society for the Propagation of the Faith, 3329 Danforth Ave. Scarborough, ON M1L 4T3 Tel. (416)699-7077 or 800-897-8865, Fax (416)699-9019
Email: missions@eda.net
Website: www.eda.net/~missions

The Monitor, (M.) The Roman Catholic Church in Canada, Larry Dohey, P.O. Box 986, St. John's, NF A1C 5M3 Tel. (709)739-6553, Fax (709)739-6458
Email: 1dohey@seascape.com
Website: www.delweb.com/rcec/monitor.htm

Multiply, (4-Y.) Presbyterian Church in America (Canadian Section), Fred Marsh, 1700 N Brown, Suite 101 Lawrenceville, GA 30043-8143 Tel. (678)825-1200, Fax (404)982-9108
Email: mna@pcanet.org
Website: www.pcanet.org/mna

NABtoday, (6-Y.) North American Baptist Conference, Marilyn Schaer, 1 S. 210 Summit Ave., Oakbrook Terrace, IL 60181 Tel. (630)495-2000, Fax (630)495-3301
Email: NABtoday@nabconf.org
Website: NABConference.org

National Bulletin on Liturgy, (4-Y.) The Roman Catholic Church in Canada, Margaret Bick, 90 Parent Ave., Ottawa, ON K1N 7B1 Tel. (613)241-9461 x. 276, Fax (613)241-8117
Email: liturgy@cccb.ca
Website: www.cccb.ca

The New Freeman, (W.) The Roman Catholic Church in Canada, Bill Donovan, One Bayard Dr., Saint John, NB E2L 3L5 Tel. (506)653-6806, Fax (506)653-6818

News of Québec, Christian Brethren (also known as Plymouth Brethren), Richard E. Strout, P.O. Box 1054, Sherbrooke, QC J1H 5L3 Tel. (819)820-1693, Fax (819)821-9287

Orthodox Way, (M.) Greek Orthodox Metropolis of Toronto (Canada), Orthodox Way Committee, 86 Overlea Blvd., 4th Floor

Toronto, ON M4H 1C6 Tel. (416)429-5757, Fax (416)429-4588
Website: www.gocanada.org

Passport, (3-Y.) Interdenominational, Lois Penner, Briercrest Family of Schools, 510 College Dr. Caronport, SK S0H 0S0 Tel. (306) 756-3200, Fax (306)756-3366
Email: info@briercrest.ca
Website: www.briercrest.ca

PMC-The Practice of Ministry in Canada, (4-5-Y.) Interdenominational, Jim Taylor, 10162 Newene Rd., Winfield, BC V4V 1R2 Tel. (604)766-2778, Fax (604)766-2736
Email: jimt@silk.net
Website: www.interword.com/pmc

Pourastan, (bi-M.) Armenian Holy Apostolic Church - Canadian Diocese, N. Ouzounian, 615 Stuart Ave., Outremont, QC H2V 3H2 Tel. (514)279-3066, Fax (514)276-9960
Email: ararat@videotron.ca
Website: www.sourpkrikor.org

Prairie Messenger, (W.) The Roman Catholic Church in Canada, Andrew M. Britz, O.S.B., Box 190, Muenster, SK S0K 2Y0 Tel. (306)682-1772, Fax (306)682-5285
Email: pm.editor@stpeters.sk.ca
Website: www.stpeters.sk.ca/prairie_messenger

The Presbyterian Message, (10-Y.) Presbyterian Church in Canada, Janice Carter, Kouchibouguac, NB E0A 2A0 Tel. (506)876-4379
Email: mjcarter@nb.sympatico.ca

Presbyterian Record, (11-Y.) The Presbyterian Church in Canada, John Congram, 50 Wynford Dr., Toronto, ON M3C 1J7 Tel. (416) 441-1111, Fax (416)441-2825
Email: pcrecord@presbyterian.ca
Website: www.presbyterian.ca/record

Presence, (8-Y.) The Roman Catholic Church in Canada, Jean-Claude Breton, Presence Magazine Inc., 2715 Chemin de la Cote St. Catherine Montreal, QC H3T 1B6 Tel. (514) 739-9797, Fax (514)739-1664
Email: presence@presencemag.qc.ca
Website: www.dominicains.ca

The Pulse, (4-Y.) Evangelical Free Church of Canada, Rev. Terry Kaufman, Editor-in-Chief; Tracy Morris, M, Box 850, LCDI, Langley, BC V3A 8S6 Tel. (604)888-8668, Fax (604) 888-3108
Email: efcc@twu.ca
Website: www.twu.ca/efcc

Quaker Concern, (Q.) Canadian Yearly Meeting of the Religious Society of Friends, Jane Orion Smith, 60 Lowther Ave., Toronto, ON M5R 1C7 Tel. (416)920-5213, Fax (416)920-5214
Email: cfsc@web.ca
Website: www.web.net/~cfsc

Reformed Perspective: A Magazine for the Christian Family, (M.) Canadian and American Reformed Churches, Jon Dykstra, 13820-106 A Avenue, Edmonton, AB T5N 1C9 Tel. (780)452-3978
Email: editor@reformedperspective.ca
Website: www.reformedperspective.ca

Relations, (8-Y.) The Roman Catholic Church in Canada, Jean Belleferrille, 25 Jarry Ouest, Montreal, QC H2P 1S6 Tel. (514)387-2541, Fax (514)387-0206
Email: relations@cjf.qc.ca

RESCUE, (bi-M.) Association of Gospel Rescue Missions, Philip Rydman, 1045 Swift, N. Kansas City, MO 64116 Tel. (816)471-8020, Fax (816)471-3718
Email: iugm@iugm.org
Website: www.iugm.org

Revival Fellowship News, (Q.) Interdenominational, Harold Lutzer, Canadian Revival Fellowship, Box 584 Regina, SK S4P 3A3 Tel. (306)522-3685, Fax (306)522-3686
Email: crf@dlewest.com
Website: www.revivalfellowship.com

Rupert's Land News, (10-Y.) The Anglican Church of Canada, J. D. Caird, M.A. Jackson, Anglican Centre, 935 Nesbitt Bay Winnipeg, MB R3J 3R1 Tel. (204)453-6130 or (204)284-2097, Fax (204)452-3915

Saints Herald, (M.) Community of Christ, Linda Booth, The Herald Publishing House, P.O. Box 1770 Independence, MO 64055-0770 Tel. (816)252-5010, Fax (816)252-3976
Email: comdiv@rlds.org
Website: www.rlds.org

Scarboro Missions, (9-Y.) The Roman Catholic Church in Canada, G. Curry, S.F.M., 2685 Kingston Rd., Scarborough, ON M1M 1M4 Tel. (416)261-7135 or 800-260-4815 (In Canada), Fax (416)261-0820
Email: sfmmag@scarboromissions.ca
Website: www.web.net/~sfms

Servant Magazine, (4-Y.) Interdenominational, Phil Callaway, Prairie Bible Institute, Box 4000 Three Hills, AB T0M 2N0 Tel. (403)443-5511, Fax (403)443-5540
Website: www.pbi.ab.ca

The Shantyman, (bi-M.) Nondenominational, Kevin R. James, Editor in Chief; Phil Hood, Managing Editor, 2476 Argentia Rd., Ste. 213, Mississauga, ON L5N 6M1 Tel. (905)821-6310. Fax (905)821-6311
Email: shanty@pathcom.com
Website: www.shantymen.org

Sister Triangle, (Q.) Churches of Christ, Marilyn Muller, P.O. 948, Dauphin, MB R7N 3J5 Tel. (204)638-9812, Fax (204)638-6231
Email: dmmuller@mb.sympatico.ca

Solia - The Herald, (M.) The Romanian Orthodox Episcopate of America (Jackson, MI), Rev. Protodeacon David Oancea, P.O. Box 185, Grass Lake, MI 49240-0185 Tel. (517)522-3656, Fax (517)522-5907
Email: ROEASOLIA@aol.com
Website: www.roea.org

SR- Studies in Religion- Sciences religieuses, (Q.) Nondenominational, Willi Braun, University of Alberta, 347 Arts Bldg Edmonton, AB T6H 2E6 Tel. (780)492-2879
Email: willi.braun@ualberta.ca

St. Luke Magazine, (M.) Christ Catholic Church International, Donald W. Mullan, 5165 Palmer Ave., Niagara Falls, ON L2E 6S8 Tel. (905)354-2329, Fax (905)354-9934
Email: dmullan1@home.com
Website: members.home.net/dmullan1

Testimony, (M.) The Pentecostal Assemblies of Canada, Richard P. Hiebert, 2450 Milltower Ct., Mississauga, ON L5N 5Z6 Tel. (905)542-7400, Fax (905)542-7313
Email: testimony@PAOC.org

Topic, (10-Y) The Anglican Church of Canada, Neale Adams, 580-401 W. Georgia St., Vancouver, BC V6B 5A1 Tel. (604)684-6306 ext. 23, Fax (604)684-7017
Email: nadams@vancouver.anglican.ca
Website: www.vancouver.anglican.ca

United Church Observer, (M.) The United Church of Canada, Muriel Duncan, 478 Huron St., Toronto, ON M5R 2R3 Tel. (416)960-8500, Fax (416)960-8477
Email: general@ucobserver.org
Website: www.ucobserver.org

La Vie Chretienne (French), (M.) Presbyterian Church in Canada, Jean Porret, PO Box 272, Suzz. Rosemont, Montreal, QC H1X 3B8 Tel. (514)737-4168

La Vie des Communautes religieuses, (5-Y.) The Roman Catholic Church in Canada, Religious Communities (Consortium), 251 St-Jean-Baptiste, Nicolet, QC J3T 1X9 Tel. (819)293-8736, Fax (819)293-2419
Email: vicar@concepta.com

Vie Liturgique, (8-Y.) The Roman Catholic Church in Canada, Novalis, 6255 Rue Hutchison, Bureau 103 Montreal, QC H2V 4C7 Tel. (800)668-2547, Fax (514)278-3030
Email: info@novalis-inc.com
Website: www.novalis.ca

VIP Communique, Foursquare Gospel Church of Canada, Timothy Peterson, 8459-160th St., Ste. 100, Surrey, BC V3S 3T9 Tel. (604)543-8414, Fax (604)543-8417
Email: fgcc@canada.com

Visnyk-The Herald, (2-M) Ukrainian Orthodox Church of Canada, Rt. Rev. Fr. William Makarenko, 9 St. John's Ave., Winnipeg, MB R2W 1G8 Tel. (204)586-3093, Fax (204)582-5241
Email: visnky@uocc.ca
Website: www.uocc.ca

Voce Evangelica-Evangel Voice, (Q.) The Italian Pentecostal Church of Canada, Rev. Daniel Costanza, 140 Woodbridge Ave., Suite 400 Woodbridge, ON L4L 4K9 Tel. (905)850-1578, Fax (905)850-1578
Email: bethel@idirect.com
Website: www.the-ipcc.org

The War Cry, (M.) The Salvation Army in Canada, Sharon Stinka, 2 Overlea Blvd., Toronto, ON M4H 1P4 Tel. (416)425-2111, Fax (416)422-6120
Email: warcry@sallynet.org
Website: sallynet.org

Word Alive, (Q.) Nondenominational, Dwayne Janke, Wycliffe Bible Translators of Canada Inc., 4316 10 St. NE Calgary, AB T2E 6K3 Tel. (403)250-5411, Fax (403)250-2623
Email: dwayne_janke@wycliffe.ca
Website: www.wycliffe.ca

The Word, (10-Y.) The Antiochian Orthodox Christian Archdiocese of North America, John P. Abdalah, 1777 Quigg Dr., Pittsburgh, PA 15241-2071 Tel. (412)831-7388, Fax (412) 831-5554
Email: wordmag@aol.com
Website: antiochian.org

UU World- The Magazine of the Unitarian Universalist Association, (bi-M.) Unitarian Universalist, Tom Stites, 25 Beacon St., Boston, MA 02108 Tel. (617)742-2100, Fax (617)742-7025
Email: world@uua.org
Website: www.uua.org

Young Companion, (11-Y.) Old Order Amish Church, Joseph Stoll and Christian Stoll, Old Order Amish Church, Rt. 4 Aylmer, ON N5H 2R3

13. Church Archives and Historical Records Collections

American and Canadian history is interwoven with the social and cultural experience of religious life and thought. Most repositories of primary research materials in North America will include some documentation on religion and church communities. This directory is not intended to replace standard bibliographic guides to those resources. The intent is to give a new researcher entry to major archival holdings of religious collections and to programs of national scope. In the interest of space, no attempt has been made to list the specific contents of the archives or to include the numerous specialized research libraries of North America. The repositories listed herein are able to re-direct inquirers to significant regional and local church archives, and specialized collections such as those of religious orders, educational and charitable organizations, and personal papers. This directory has been thoroughly re-edited to include updated entries and contact information.

Repositories marked with an asterisk (*) are designated by their denomination as the official archives. The reference departments at these archives will assist researchers in locating primary material of geographic or subject focus.

UNITED STATES

Adventist

Adventist Heritage Center, James White Library, Andrews University, Berrien Springs, MI 49104, Curator: Jim Ford, Tel. (616)471-3274, Fax (616)471-6166, Email: ahc@ andrews.edu, Website: http://www.andrews.edu/library/collections/departments/ahc.html

Large collection of Seventh-day Adventist material.

Aurora University, Charles B. Phillips Library, 347 S. Gladstone, Aurora, IL 60506, Volunteer Curator: David T. Arthur, Tel. (630)844-5437, Fax (630)844-3848, Email: jhuggins@aurora.edu

Advental archival materials on the Millerite/Early Adventist movement (1830-1860); also denominational archives relating to Advent Christian Church, Life and Advent Union, and to a lesser extent, Evangelical Adventists and Age-to-Come Adventists.

Department of Archives and Special Collections Ellen G. White Estate Branch Office, Loma Linda University Library, Loma Linda, CA 92350, Chairman/Director: Elder Merlin D. Burt, Tel. (909)558-4942, Fax (909)558-0381, Email: whiteestate@llu.edu, Website: http://www llu.edu/llu/library/heritage

Photographs, sound and video recordings, personal papers, and library pertaining to the Seventh-day Adventist Church.

Ellen G. White Estate, Inc., 12501 Old Columbia Pike, Silver Spring, MD 20904, Archivist: Tim Poirier, Tel. (301)680-6540, Fax (301)680-6559, Website: http://www.whiteestate.org

Records include letters and manuscripts (1840s to 1915), pamphlets and publications, and the White papers.

*General Conference of Seventh-day Adventists: Archives and Statistics, 12501 Old Columbia Pike, Silver Spring, MD 20904-6600, Director: Bert Haloviak, Tel. (301)680-5022, Fax (301)680-5038, Email: HaloviakB@GCAdventist.org, Website: http://www.adventist.org/ast

Repository of the records created at the world administrative center of the Seventh-day Adventist Church and includes the period from the 1860s to the present.

Assemblies of God

*Flower Pentecostal Heritage Center, 1445 Boonville Ave., Springfield, MO 65802, Director: Wayne Warner, Tel. (417)862-1447 ext. 4400, Fax (417)862-6203, Email: archives@ag.org, Website: http://www.agheritage.org

Official repository for materials related to the Assemblies of God, as well as materials related to the early Pentecostal movement in general.

Baptist

*American Baptist Archives Center, P.O. Box 851, Valley Forge, PA 19482-0851, Archivist: Betty Layton, Tel. (610)768-2374, Fax (610)768-2266, Website: http://www.abc-usa.org/abhs

Repository for the non-current records of the national boards and administrative organizations of American Baptist Churches in the USA. Collections include mission files, publications, correspondence, official minutes and annual reports.

American Baptist-Samuel Colgate Historical Library, 1106 S Goodman St., Rochester, NY 14620-2532, Director: Stuart W. Campbell, Tel. (716)473-1740, Fax (716)473-1740 [Call first], Website: http://www.crds.edu/abhs/default.htm

Manuscript holdings include collections of

Baptist ministers, missionaries, and scholars, and some records of Baptist churches, associations, and national and international bodies.

Andover Newton Theological School, Franklin Trask Library, 169 Herrick Rd., Newton Centre, MA 02459, Associate Director for Special Collections: Diana Yount, Tel. (617)964-1100 ext. 252, Fax (617)965-9756, Email: dyount@ants.edu, Website: http://www.ants.edu

The collections document Baptist, Congregational and United Church history, including personal papers relating to national denominational work and foreign missions, with emphasis on New England Church history.

Primitive Baptist Library of Carthage, Illinois, 416 Main St., Carthage, IL 62321, Director of Library: Elder Robert Webb, Tel. (217)357-3723, Fax (217)357-3723, Email: bwebb9@juno.com, Website: http://www.carthage.lib il.us/community/churches/primbap/pbl.html

Collects the records of congregations and associations.

*Seventh-day Baptist Historical Society, 3120 Kennedy Rd., P.O. Box 1678, Janesville, WI 53547, Historian: Don A. Sanford, Tel. (608) 752-5055, Fax (608)752-7711, Email: sdbhist@inwave.com, Website: http://www.seventhday baptist.org

Serves as a depository for records of Seventh-day Baptists, Sabbath and Sabbath-keeping Baptists since the mid-seventeenth century.

*Southern Baptists Historical Library & Archives, 901 Commerce St., Suite 400, Nashville, TN 37203-3630, Director and Archivist: Bill Sumners, Tel. (615)244-0344, Fax (615)782-4821, Email: bill@sbhla.org, Website: http://www.sbhla.org

Central depository of the Southern Baptist Convention. Materials include official records of denominational agencies; personal papers of denominational leaders; records of related Baptist organizations; and annual proceedings of national and regional bodies.

Brethren in Christ

*Brethren in Christ Historical Library and Archives, One College Avenue, P.O. Box 3002, Grantham, PA 17027, Director: Dori I. Steckbeck, Tel. (717)691-6048, Fax (717)691-6042, Email: archives@messiah.edu

Records of general church boards and agencies, regional conferences, congregations and organizations; also includes library, manuscripts, and oral history collection.

Church of the Brethren

*Brethren Historical Library and Archives, 1451 Dundee Ave., Elgin IL 60120, Librarian/Archivist: Kenneth M. Shaffer, Jr., Tel. (847) 742-5100, Fax (847)742-6103, Email: kshaffer_gb@brethren.org, Website: http://www.brethren.org/genbd/bhla

Archival materials dating from 1800-present relating to the cultural, socio-economic, theological, genealogical, and institutional history of the Church of the Brethren.

Churches of Christ

Center for Restoration Studies, Abilene Christian University, 760 Library Court, P.O. Box 29208, Abilene, TX 79699, Archivist: Erma Jean Loveland, Tel. (915)674-2538, Fax (915) 674-2202, Email: lovelande@acu.edu, Website: http://www.bible.acu.edu/crs

Archival materials connected with the Stone-Campbell Movement. The chief focus is on the Church of Christ in the twentieth century.

Emmanuel School of Religion Library, One Walker Drive, Johnson City, TN 37601-9438, Director: Thomas E. Stokes, Tel. (423)926-1186, Fax (423)926-6198, Email: library@esr.edu, Website: http://www.esr.edu

Materials related to the Stone-Campbell/Restoration Movement tradition. Collection includes items from the Christian Church and Churches of Christ, the a cappella Churches of Christ, and the Christian Church (Disciples of Christ).

Churches of God, General Conference

*Winebrenner Theological Seminary, 701 East Melrose Ave., Findlay, OH 45804, Director of Library Services: Margaret Hirschy, Tel. (419) 422-4824, Fax (419)422-3999, Email: wts@winebrenner.edu, Website: http://www. winebrenner.edu

Archival materials of the Churches of God, General Conference including local conference journals.

Disciples of Christ

Christian Theological Seminary Library, 1000 W. 42nd St., P.O. Box 88267, Indianapolis, IN 46208, Archives Manager: Don Haymes, Tel. (317)931-2368, Fax (317)931-2363, Email: don.haymes@cts.edu, Website: http://www.cts.edu

Archival materials dealing with the Disciples of Christ and related movements.

*Disciples of Christ Historical Society, 1101 19th Ave. South, Nashville, TN 37212, Director of Library and Archives: Sara Harwell, Tel. (615)327-1444, Fax (615)327-1445, Email: dishistsoc@aol.com, Website: http://www.users.aol.com/dishistsoc.index.html

Collects documents of the Stone-Campbell Movement.

Episcopal

*Archives of the Episcopal Church, P.O. Box 2247, Austin, TX 78768-2247, Director: Mark J. Duffy, Tel. (512)472-6816, Fax (512)480-0437, Email: Research@EpiscopalArchives. org, Website: http://www.EpiscopalArchives.org

Repository for the official records of the

national Church, its corporate bodies and affiliated agencies, personal papers, and some diocesan archives. Contact the Archives for reference to diocesan and parochial church records.

Evangelical Congregational Church

*Archives of the Evangelical Congregational Church, Evangelical School of Theology, Rostad Library, 121 S. College St., Myerstown, PA 17067, Archivist: Terry M. Heisey, Tel. (717)866-5775, Fax (717)866-4667, Email: theisey@evangelical.edu, Website: http://www.evangelical.edu

Repository of records of the administrative units of the denomination, affiliated organizations, and closed churches. Also collected are records of local congregations and materials related to the United Evangelical Church and the Evangelical Association.

Evangelical and Reformed

*Evangelical and Reformed Historical Society, Lancaster Theological Seminary, 555 W. James St., Lancaster, PA 17603, Archivist: Richard R. Berg, Tel. (717)290-8704, Fax (717)393-4254, Email: ehrs@lts.org, Website: http://www.lts.org/erhs/erhs.htm

Manuscripts and transcriptions of early German Reformed Church (U.S.) 1725-1863; Reformed Church in the United States 1863-1934, and Evangelical and Reformed Church 1934-1957 records of coetus, synods, and classes, pastoral records, and personal papers.

Friends

*Historical Library of Swarthmore, Swarthmore College, 500 College Ave., Swarthmore, PA 19081-1399, Acting Curator: Christopher Densmore, Tel. (610)328-8496, Email: friends@swarthmore.edu, Website: http://www swarthmore. edu/library/friends

Official depository for the records of the Philadelphia, Baltimore, and New York Yearly Meetings. Comprehensive collection of originals and copies of other Quaker meeting archives.

Special Collections/Quaker Collection, Haverford College, 370 Lancaster Ave., Haverford, PA 19041-1392, Quaker Bibliographer: Emma Jones Lapsansky, Tel. (610)896-1161, Fax (610)896-1102, Email: elapsans@haverford.edu, Website: http://www. haverford.edu/library/special

Repository for material relating to the Society of Friends (Quakers), especially to the segment known from 1827 to the mid-20th century as "Orthodox" in the Delaware Valley.

Interdenominational

American Bible Society Library and Archives, 1865 Broadway, New York, NY 10023-9980, Director: Mary F. Cordato, Tel. (212) 408-1258, Fax (212)408-1526, Email: mcordato@americanbible.org, Website: http://www.americanbible.org

Core of collections includes founders' documents, minutes, and correspondence related to the worldwide mission of the ABS.

Billy Graham Center Archives, Wheaton College, 500 College Ave., Wheaton, IL 60187-5593, Director of Archives: Robert Shuster, Tel. (630) 752-5910, Fax (630)752-5916, Email: bgcarc @wheaton.edu, Website: http://www.wheaton.edu/bgc/archives.archhp1.html

Graduate Theological Union Archives, 2400 Ridge Road, Berkeley, CA 94709, Archivist: Lucinda Glenn Rand, Tel. (510)649-2507, Fax (510)649-2508, Email: LGlenn@gtu.edu, Website: http://www.gtu.edu/library/archives.html

Holy Spirit Research Center, Oral Roberts University (LRC 5E 02), 7777 S. Lewis Ave., Tulsa OK 74171, Director: Mark E. Roberts, Tel. (918)495-6898, Fax (918)495-6662, Email: hsrc@oru.edu, Website: http://www.oru.edu/university/library/holyspirit

Pentecostal and Charismatic records, with emphasis on divine healing.

National Council of Churches of Christ Archives, Department of History and Records Management Services, Presbyterian Church (USA), 425 Lombard St., Philadelphia, PA 19147-1516, Manager: Margery N. Sly, Tel. (215)627-1852, Fax (215)627-0509, Email: preshist@shrsys.hslc.org, Website: http://www.libertynet.org/pacscl/phs/

Schomburg Center for Research in Black Culture, 515 Malcolm X Blvd., New York, NY 10037, Manuscripts, Archives, and Rare Books Division, Curator: Diana Lachatanere, Tel. (212)491-2224, Fax (212)491-6067, Email: scmarbref@nypl.org, Website: http://www.schomburgcenter.org

Union Theological Seminary, Burke Library, 3041 Broadway, New York, NY 10027, Archivist and Head of Special Collections: Claire McCurdy, Tel. (212)280-1502, Fax (212)280-1456, Email: awt@uts.columbia.edu, Website: http://www.uts.columbia.edu

University of Chicago, Regenstein Library, 1100 E 57th St., Chicago, IL 60537-1502, Bibliographer for Humanities: Curtis Bochanyin, Tel. (773)702-8442, Email: boc7@midway.uchicago.edu, Website: http://www.lib.uchicago.edu/e/su/rel/

Yale Divinity School Library, 409 Prospect St., New Haven, CT 06511, Research Services Librarian: Martha Smalley, Tel. (203)432-6374, Fax (203) 432-3906, Email: divinity.library@yale.edu, Website: http://www.Library.yale.edu/div

Jewish

American Jewish Historical Society (2 locations): Center for Jewish History, 15 W. 16th St., New York, NY 10011, Director: Michael

Feldberg, Tel. (212)294-6162, Fax (212)294-6161, Email: ajhs@ajhs.org, Website: http://www.ajhs.org

Friedman Memorial Library, 2 Thornton Rd., Waltham, MA 02453, Director: Michael Feldberg, Tel. (781)891-8110, Fax (781)899-9208, Email: mfeldberg@ajhs.cjh.org, Website: http://www.ajhs.org

Archival repositories of the Jewish people in America, including significant religious contributions to American life.

Jacob Rader Marcus Center of the American Jewish Archives, 3101 Clifton Ave., Cincinnati, OH 45220, Chief Archivist: Kevin Proffitt, Tel. (513)221-1875, Fax (513)221-7812, Email: aja@cn.huc.edu, Website: http://www.huc.edu/aja

Materials documenting the Jewish experience in the Western Hemisphere with emphasis on the Reform movement. Included in the collection are congregational and organizational records, personal papers of rabbis and secular leaders, and genealogical materials.

Latter-day Saints

*Archives, Church of Jesus Christ of Latter-day Saints, 50 E. North Temple, Salt Lake City, UT 84150-3800, Director: Steven R. Sorensen, Tel. (801)240-2273, Fax (801)240-6134

Repository of official records of church departments, missions, congregations, and associated organizations. Includes personal papers of church leaders and members.

Family History Library, 35 North West Temple, Salt Lake City, UT 84150-3400, Tel. (801) 240-2331, Fax (801)240-5551, Email: fhl@ldschurch.org

Primarily microfilmed vital, church, probate, land, census, and military records including local church registers.

Lutheran

*Archives of the Evangelical Lutheran Church in America, 8765 West Higgins Rd., Chicago, IL 60631-4198, Chief Archivist: Elisabeth Wittman, Tel. (847)690-9410, Fax (847)690-9502, Email: archives@elca.org, Website: http://www.elca.org/os/archives/intro.html

Official repository for the churchwide offices of the ELCA and its predecessors. For further information on synod and regional archives, contact the Chicago archives or check the ELCA World Wide Web site. For ELCA college and seminary archives, contact those institutions directly, or consult the ELCA Archives.

*Concordia Historical Institute, Dept. of Archives and History, Lutheran Church-Missouri Synod, 801 De Mun Ave., St. Louis, MO 63105-3199, Director: Daniel Preus, Tel. (314)505-7900, Fax (314)505-7901, Email: chi@chi.lcms.org, Website: http://chi.lcms.org

Official repository of The Lutheran Church-Missouri Synod. Collects synodical and congregational records, personal papers and records of Lutheran agencies.

Lutheran History Center of the West, 1712 Greentree Dr., Concord, CA 94521-1028, Editor: Duane A. Peterson, Tel. (925)825-2109, Email: duanep@astound.net

Mennonite

*Archives of the Mennonite Church, 1700 South Main, Goshen, IN 46526, Directory: John E. Sharp, Tel. (219)535-7477, Fax (219)535-7293, Email: johnes@goshen.edu, Website: http://www.goshen.edu/mcarchives

Repository of the official organizational records of the Mennonite Church and personal papers of leaders and members.

*Center for Mennonite Brethren Studies, 1717 S. Chestnut, Fresno, CA 93702, Archivist: Kevin Enns-Rempel, Tel. (559)453-2225, Fax (559) 453-2124, Email: kennsrem@fresno.edu, Website: http://www.fresno.edu/affiliation/cmbs

Official repository for the General Conference of Mennonite Brethren churches.

*Mennonite Library and Archives, Bethel College, 300 East 27th Street, North Newton, KS 67117-0531, Archivist: John Thiesen, Tel. (316)284-5304, Fax (316)284-5843, Email: mla@bethelks.edu, Website: http://www.bethelks.edu/services/mla

An official repository for the General Conference Mennonite Church and several other organizations related to the General Conference.

Methodist

B. L. Fisher Library, Asbury Theological Seminary, 204 N. Lexington Ave., Wilmore, KY 40390, Archivist and Special Collections Librarian: Bill Kostlevy, Tel. (859)858-2235, Fax (859)858-2350, Email: bill_kostlevy@asburyseminary.edu, Website: http://www.asburyseminary.edu

Documents the Holiness Movement and evangelical currents in the United Methodist Church. Holdings include records of related associations, camp meetings, personal papers, and periodicals.

Center for Evangelical United Brethren Heritage, United Theological Seminary, 1810 Harvard Blvd., Dayton, OH 45406-4599, Director: James D. Nelson, Tel. (937)278-5817 ext. 214, Fax (937)275-5701, Email: jnelson@united.edu, Website: http://www.united.edu/eubcenter

Documents predecessor and cognate church bodies of the United Methodist Church including the Evangelical Association, United Brethren in Christ, United Evangelical, Evangelical, Evangelical United Brethren, Evangelical Congregational, and Evangelical of North America.

*General Commission on Archives and History, The United Methodist Church, P.O. Box 127,

Madison, NJ 07940, Archivist/Records Administrator: L. Dale Patterson, Tel. (973) 408-3189, Fax (973)408-3909, Email: gcah@gcah.org, Website: http://www.gcah.org

Collects administrative and episcopal records, and personal papers of missionaries and leaders. Holds limited genealogical information on ordained ministers. Will direct researchers to local and regional collections of congregational records and information on United Methodism and its predecessors.

*Heritage Hall at Livingstone College, 701 W. Monroe St., Salisbury, NC 28144, Director: Phyllis H. Galloway, Tel. (704)638-5664

Records of the African Methodist Episcopal Zion Church

*Office of the Historiographer of the African Methodist Episcopal Church, P.O. Box 301, Williamstown, MA 02167, Historiographer: Dennis C. Dickerson, Tel. (413)597-2484, Fax (413) 597-3673, Email: dennis.c.dickerson@williams.edu

General and annual conference minutes; reports of various departments such as missions and publications; and congregational histories and other local materials. The materials are housed in the office of the historiographer and other designated locations.

Moravian

Moravian Archives, Southern Province, Drawer L, Winston-Salem, NC 27108, Archivist: C. Daniel Crews, Tel. (336)722-1742, Fax (336) 725-4514, Email: nblum@mcsp.org, Website: http://www.moravianarchives.org

Repository of the records of the Moravian Church, Southern Province, its congregations, and its members.

The Moravian Archives, 41 W. Locust St., Bethlehem, PA 18018-2757, Archivist: Vernon H. Nelson, Tel. (610)866-3255, Fax (610)866-9210

Records of the Northern Province of the Moravian Church in America, including affiliated provinces in the Eastern West Indies, Nicaragua, Honduras, Labrador, and Alaska.

Nazarene

*Nazarene Archives, Church of the Nazarene, 6401 The Paseo, Kansas City, MO 64131, Archives Manager: Stan Ingersol, Tel. (816) 333-7000 ext. 2437, Fax (816)361-4983, Email: singersol@nazarene.org, Website: http://www.nazarene.org/hoo/archives.html

Focus is on general and district materials, including those of leaders, agencies, and study commissions. The Archives also collects materials on congregations, church-related colleges and seminaries world-wide, and social ministries.

Pentecostal

David du Plessis Archives, Fuller Theological Seminary, 135 North Oakland, Pasadena, CA 91182, Archivist: Roger Robins, Tel. (626) 584-5311, Fax (626)584-5644, Email: archive@fuller.edu, Website: http://www.fuller.edu/archive

Collects material related to the Pentecostal and Charismatic movements; also includes material related to Charles Fuller and the Old Fashioned Revival Hour broadcast, Fuller Theological Seminary, and neo-evangelicalism.

*Hal Bernard Dixon Jr. Pentecostal Research Center, 260 11th St. NE, Cleveland, TN 37311, Director: David G. Roebuck, Tel. (423) 614-8576, Fax (423)614-8555, Email: dixon_research@leeuniversity.edu, Website: http://www.leeuniversity.edu/library/dixon

Official repository of the Church of God (Cleveland, TN). Also collects other Pentecostal and Charismatic materials.

*International Pentecostal Holiness Church Archives and Research Center, P.O. Box 12609, Oklahoma City, OK 73157, Director: Harold D. Hunter, Tel. (405)787-7110, Fax (405)789-3957, Email: archives@iphc.org, Website: http://www.pctii.org/arc/archives.html

Official repository for records and publications produced by the international headquarters, conferences, and influential leaders.

United Pentecostal Church International Historical Center, 8855 Dunn Rd., Hazelwood, MO 63042, Chair, Historical Committee: J. L. Hall, Tel. (314)837-7300, Fax (314)837-4503, Email: main@upci.org, Website: http://www.upci.org

Collects a variety of Pentecostal archives, primarily the United Pentecostal (Oneness) Branch.

Polish National Catholic

*Polish National Catholic Church Commission on History and Archives, 1031 Cedar Ave., Scranton, PA 18505, Chair: Joseph Wieczerzak, Tel. (717)343-0100

Documents pertaining to the Church's national office, parishes, Prime Bishop, leaders, and organizations.

Presbyterian

*Historical Foundation of the Cumberland Presbyterian Church and the Cumberland Presbyterian Church in America, 1978 Union Ave., Memphis, TN 38104, Archivist: Susan Knight Gore, Tel. (901)276-8602, Fax (901) 272-3913, Email: skg@cumberland.org, Website: http://www.cumberland.org/hfcpc

*Presbyterian Historical Society, Presbyterian Church (USA) (2 offices): Headquarters, 425 Lombard St., Philadelphia, PA 19147-1516, Deputy Director: Margery N. Sly, Tel. (215) 627-1852, Fax (215)627-0509, Email: refdesk@history.pcusa.org, Website: http://www. history.pcusa.org

Southern Regional Office, P.O. Box 849, Montreat, NC 28757, Tel. (828)669-7061, Fax (828)669-5369, Email: pcusadoh@montreat.edu

Collects the official records of the Church's national offices and agencies, synods, presbyteries, and some congregations. The Society also houses records of the Church's predecessor denominations, personal papers of prominent Presbyterians, and records of ecumenical organizations. In addition, the Southern Regional Office in Montreat, NC holds local and regional records for the fourteen southern states.

*Presbyterian Church in America Historical Center, 12330 Conway Rd., St. Louis, MO 63141, Director: Wayne Sparkman, Tel. (314) 469-9077, Email: wsparkman@pcanet.org, Website: http://www.pcanet.org/history

Center serves as the official archive of the Presbyterian Church in America. The Center also holds the records of four other Presbyterian denominations and the manuscript collections of some fifty individuals connected with these church bodies.

Princeton Theological Seminary Libraries, Library Place and Mercer Street, P.O. Box 111, Princeton, NJ 08542-0803, Librarian for Archives and Special Collections: William O. Harris, Tel. (609)497-7950, Fax (609)497-1826, Email: william.harris@ptsem.edu, Website: http://www.ptsem.edu/grow/library/index.htm

Documents the history of American Presbyterianism, with an extensive collection of alumni biographies, congregational histories, and missionary reports.

Reformed

*Heritage Hall, Calvin College, 3201 Burton St. S.E., Grand Rapids, MI 49546, Curator of Archives: Richard H. Harms, Tel. (616) 957-6313, Fax (616)957-6470, Email: rharms@calvin.edu, Website: http://www.calvin.edu/hh

Repository of the official records of the Christian Reformed Church in North America, including classes, congregations, and denominational agencies and committees.

*Reformed Church Archives, 21 Seminary Place, New Brunswick, NJ 08901-1159, Archivist: Russell Gasero, Tel. (732)246-1779, Fax (732) 249-5412, Email: rgasero@rca.org, Website: http://www.rca.org

Official repository for denominational records including congregations, classes, synods, missions, and national offices.

Roman Catholic

Catholic University of America (Mullen Library), 5 Mullen, Washington, DC 20064, Archivist: Timothy Meagher, Tel. (202)319-5065, Fax (202)319-6554, Email: meagher@cua.edu

Marquette University, Department of Special Collections and Archives, P.O. Box 3141, Milwaukee, WI 93201-3141, Department Head: Charles Elston, Tel. (414)288-7256, Fax (414)288-6709, Email: charles.elston@marquette.edu, Website: http://www.marquette.edu/library/collections/archives/index.html

Collection strengths are in the areas of Catholic social action, American missions and missionaries, and other work with Native Americans and African Americans.

U.S. Catholic Documentary Heritage Project, For holdings information on various dioceses and religious orders, see: http://www.uschs.com

University of Notre Dame Archives, 607 Hesburgh Library, Notre Dame, IN 46556, Curator of Manuscripts: William Kevin Cawley, Tel. (219)631-6448, Fax (219)631-7980, Email: archives.1@nd.edu, Website: http://www.nd.edu/~archives

Papers of bishops and prominent Catholics and records of Catholic organizations. Includes parish histories, but few parish records.

Salvation Army

*Salvation Army Archives and Research Center, 615 Slaters Lane, Alexandria, VA 22313, Archivist: Susan Mitchem, Tel. (703)684-5500, Fax (703)299-5552, Email: archives@usa.salvationarmy.org, Website: http://www.salvationarmy.org

Holds the documents of Salvation Army history, personalities, and events in the United States from 1880.

Swedenborgian

*Bryn Athyn College of the New Church, Swedenborg Library, 2875 College Drive, P.O. Box 740, Bryn Athyn, PA 19009-0740, Director: Carroll C. Odhner, Tel. (215)938-2547, Fax (215)938-2637, Email: ccodhner@newchurch.edu, Website: http://www.newchurch. edu/college/facilities/swedlib.html

Unitarian Universalist Association

*Andover-Harvard Theological Library, Harvard Divinity School, 45 Francis Ave., Cambridge, MA 02138, Curator: Frances O'Donnell, Tel. (617)496-5153, Fax (617)496-4111, Email: frances_odonnell@harvard.edu, Website: http://www.hds.harvard.edu/library/bms/index.html

Institutional archives of the Unitarian Universalist Association including the Unitarian Universalist Service Committee; also houses records of many congregations; personal papers of ministers and other individuals.

Unitarian and Universalist

Meadville/Lombard Theological School Library, 5701 S. Woodlawn Ave., Chicago, IL 60637,

Director: Neil W. Gerdes, Tel. (773)256-3000 ext. 225, Fax (773)256-3008, Email: ngerdes@meadville.edu, Website: http://www.meadville.edu

Repository for materials relating to Unitarian Universalism in particular and liberal religion in general. Includes personal papers of several noted UU ministers, and church records from many UU churches in the Midwestern USA.

United Church of Christ

Andover Newton Theological School, Franklin Trask Library, 169 Herrick Rd., Newton Centre, MA 02459, Associate Director for Special Collections: Diana Yount, Tel. (617) 964-1100 ext. 252, Fax (617)965-9756, Email: dyount@ants.edu, Website: http://www.ants.edu

Collections document Baptists, Congregational, and UCC history. Some personal papers relating to national denominational work and foreign missionary activity; majority of collections relate to New England history.

Archives of the Evangelical Synod of North America, Eden Theological Seminary, Luhr Library, 475 E. Lockwood Ave., Webster Groves, MO 63119-3192, Archivist: Clifton W. Kerr, Tel. (314)918-2515, Email: ckerr@eden.edu

Archival records include organization records, personal papers and immigration records.

Congregational Library, 14 Beacon St., Boston, MA 02108, Archivist: Jessica Steytler, Tel. (617)523-0470, Fax (617)523-0491, Email: jsteytler@14beacon.org, Website: http://www.14beacon.org

Documentation on the Congregational, Congregational Christian, Christian, and United Church of Christ throughout the world, including local church records, associations, charitable organizations, and papers of clergy, missionaries and others.

Elon University Library, P.O. Box 187, Elon, NC 27244, Archivist/Technical Services Librarian: Connie L. Keller, Tel. (336)278-6578, Fax (336)278-6638, Email: keller@elon.edu

Collection of membership records and other archival material on the predecessor churches of the UCC: Christian Church and the Southern Conference of the Christian Church; also maintains records of churches that no longer exist.

*United Church of Christ Archives, 700 Prospect Ave., Cleveland, OH 44115, Archivist: Ng. George Hing, Tel. (216)736-3285, Fax (216) 736-2120, Email: hingg@ucc.org

Records created in the national setting of the Church since its founding in 1957, including the General Synod, Executive Council, officers, instrumentalities, and bodies created by and/or related to the General Synod.

Standard Guides to Church Archives

Edmund L. Binsfield, "Church Archives in the United States and Canada: A Bibliography," in *American Archivist*, v. 21, no. 3 (July 1958) pp. 311-332, 219 entries.

Nelson R. Burr, "Sources for the Study of American Church History in the Library of Congress," 1953. 13 pp. Reprinted from *Church History*, v. XXII, no. 3 (Sept. 1953).

Canadian Archival Resources on the Internet: University of Saskatchewan Archives, Web Site maintained by Cheryl Avery and Steve Billington at http://www.usask.ca/archives/menu.html

Donald L. DeWitt, "Articles Describing Archives and Manuscript Collections in the United States: An Annotated Bibliography," in *Bibliographies and Indexes in Library and Information Science*, no. 11 (1997).

Andrea Hinding, ed. *Women's History Sources: A Guide to Archives and Manuscript Collections in the U.S.* (New York, Bowker, 1979) 2 vols.

Kay Kirkham, *A Survey of American Church Records, for the Period Before the Civil War, East of the Mississippi River* (Salt Lake City, 1959-60) 2 vols. Includes the depositories and bibliographies.

Martha Lund Smalley, "Archives and Manuscript Collections in Theological Libraries," in *The American Theological Library Association*, ed. by M. Graham (1996) pp. 122-130.

Evangeline Thomas, *Women's Religious History Sources: A Guide to Repositories in the United States* (New York, Bowker, 1983).

U.S. National Historical Publications and Records Commission, *Directory of Archives and Manuscript Repositories in the United States* (Washington, DC, 1988).

U.S. Library of Congress, Washington, DC, *The National Union Catalog of Manuscript Collections*, serially published from 1959 to 1993 (1959-1993). Contains many entries for collections of church archives. Researchers may consult the cumulative paper indexes or use the NUCMC home page to access the RLIN database of archives and manuscripts collections at http:/lcweb.loc.gov/coll/nucmc/nucmc.html

CANADA

Anglican

*General Synod Archives, 600 Jarvis St. Toronto, ON M4Y 2J6, Archivist: Terry Thompson, Tel. (416)924-9199 ext. 279, Fax (416)968-7983, Email: archives@national.anglican.ca, Website: http://www.anglican.ca

Collects the permanent records of the General Synod, its committees, and its employees. The Archives has a national scope, and provides referral services on local Church records.

Baptist

*Atlantic Baptist Historical Collection of the Acadia University Archives, Vaughan Memorial Library, Wolfville, NS BOP 1XO, Archivist: Patricia Townsend, Tel. (902)585-1412, Fax (902)585-1748, Email: patricia.townsend@acadiau.ca, Website: http://www.acadiau.ca/vaughan/archives

Records of associations and churches of the United Baptist Convention of the Atlantic Provinces; also personal papers of pastors and missionaries.

Canadian Baptist Archives, McMaster Divinity College, Hamilton, ON L8S 4K1, Director: Kenneth R. Morgan, Tel. (905) 525-9140 ext. 23511, Fax (905) 577-4782, Email: morgankr@mcmaster.ca, Website: http://www.mcmaster.ca/divinity/archives.html

Friends

Canadian Yearly Meeting Archives, Pickering College, 16945 Bayview Ave., New Market, ON L3Y 4X2, Yearly Meeting Archivist: Jane Zavitz-Bond, Tel. (905)895-1700, Fax (905) 895-9076

Holds the extant records for Quakers in Canada beginning with Adolphus in 1798 to the present, including the records of the Canadian Friends Service Committee.

Interdenominational

Canadian Council of Churches Archives, on deposit in National Archives of Canada, 395 Wellington, Ottawa, ON K1A 0N3, Tel. Research Services Division: (613)992-3884; Genealogical assistance: (613) 996-7458, Fax (613)995-6274, Email: reference@archives.ca, Website: http://www.archives.ca

National Archives of Canada, 395 Wellington, Ottawa, ON K1A 0N3, Director: Ian E. Wilson, Tel. Research Services Division: (613)992-3884; Genealogical assistance: (613)996-7458, Fax (613) 995-6274, Email: reference@archives.ca, Website: http://www.archives.ca

Records of interdenominational and ecumenical organizations, missionary societies, denominational churches, parish registers, and papers of prominent clergy.

Jewish

Canadian Jewish Congress National Archives, 1590 Avenue Docteur Penfield, Montreal, QC H3G 1C5, Director of Archives: Janice Rosen, Tel. (514)931-7531 ext. 2, Fax (514)931-0548, Email: archives@cjc.ca, Website: http://www.cjc.ca/archives.html

Collects documentation on all aspects of social, political, and cultural history of the Jewish presence in Quebec and Canada.

Lutheran

*Archives of the Evangelical Lutheran Church in Canada, 302-393 Portage Ave., Winnipeg, MB R3B 3H6, National Secretary/Archivist: Robert H. Granke, Tel. (204)984-9150, Fax (204)984-9185, Email: rhgranke@elcic.ca, Website: http://www.elcic.ca

Official repository for the ELCIC and its predecessor bodies, the Evangelical Lutheran Church of Canada and the Evangelical Lutheran Church of America-Canada Section.

Lutheran Historical Institute, 7100 Ada Blvd., Edmonton, AB T5B 4E4, Archivist: Karen Baron, Tel. (403)474-8156, Fax (403)477-9829, Email: abclcc@connect.ab.ca

Mennonite

*Centre for Mennonite Brethren Studies, 1-169 Riverton Ave., Winnipeg, MB R2L 2E5, Director: Abe Dueck, Tel. (204)669-6575, Fax (204)654-1865, Email: adueck@mbconf.ca, Website: http://www.mbconf.ca/mbstudies/indes.html

Institutional records of the boards and agencies of the Mennonite Brethren Church in Canada with some holdings pertaining to other parts of North America; also personal papers of leaders.

*Mennonite Heritage Centre, 600 Shaftesbury Blvd., Winnipeg, MB R3P OM4, Director: Alf Redekopp, Tel. (204)888-6781, Fax (204)831-5675, Email: aredekopp@mennonitechurch.ca, Website: http://www.mennonitechurch.ca/heritage/mhc.html

Institutional records and personal papers of leaders within the Mennonite Community. Holdings include the records of the Conference and related agencies.

Pentecostal

*Pentecostal Assemblies of Canada, 2450 Milltower Court, Mississauga, ON L5N 5Z6, Director of Archives: James D. Craig, Tel. (905)542-7400, Fax (905)542-7313, Email: archives@paoc.org, Website: http://www.paoc.org

Repository of archival records created by the Pentecostal Assemblies of Canada.

Presbyterian

*Presbyterian Church in Canada Archives and Records, 50 Wynford Dr., North York, ON M3C 1J7, Archivist/Records Administrator: Kim M. Arnold, Tel. (416)441-1111 ext. 310, Fax (416)441-2825, Email: karnold@presbyterian.ca, Website: http://www.presbyterian.ca

Records of the Presbyterian Church in Canada, its officials, ministers, congregations and organizations.

Roman Catholic

Research Centre for the Religious History of Canada, St. Paul University, 223 Main St.,

Ottawa, ON K1S 1C4, Director: Pierre Hurtubise, Tel. (613)236-1393 ext. 2270, Fax (613)782-3001, Email: crh-rc-rhc@ustpaul.uottowa.ca, Website: http://www.ustpaul.ca

Holds 900 linear feet of documents, mainly records on deposit from other institutions; and also guides to many Canadian Catholic archives.

Salvation Army

George Scott Railton Heritage Centre, 2130 Bayview Ave., Toronto, ON M4N 3K6, Director: Ira Barrow, Tel. (416)481-4441, Fax (416)481-6096, Email: Ira.Barrow@sallynet.org

Records include publications; also financial, personnel, social welfare, and immigration records.

United Church of Canada

*United Church of Canada Central Archives, Victoria University, 73 Queens Park Crescent, Toronto, ON M5S 1K7, Chief Archivist: Sharon Larade, Tel. (416)585-4563, Email: uccvu.archives@utoronto.ca, Website: http://www.vicu.utoronto.ca/archives/archives.htm

Records of the United Church and its antecedent denominations and local and regional records of the Church in Ontario. Call or view the web page for information on other regional archives.

III

STATISTICAL SECTION

Guide to Statistical Tables

Since there are no questions regarding religion in the United States Census, the *Yearbook of American & Canadian Churches* is as near an "official" record of denominational statistics as is available.

Because the data represent the most complete annual compilation of church statistics, there is a temptation to expect more than is reasonable. These tables provide the answers to very simple and straightforward questions. Officials in church bodies were asked: "How many members does your organization have?" "How many clergy?" and "How much money does your organization spend?" Each respondent interprets the questions according to the policies of the organization.

Caution should, therefore, be exercised when comparing statistics across denominational lines, comparing statistics from one year to another and adding together statistics from different denominations.

Some particular methodological issues and therefore cautions in interpretation include the following considerations:

1. Definitions of membership, clergy, and other important characteristics differ from religious body to religious body. In this section, full or confirmed membership refers to those with full communicant status. Inclusive membership refers to those who are full communicants or confirmed members plus other members baptized, non-confirmed or non-communicant. Each church determines the age at which a young person is considered a member. Churches also vary in their approaches to statistics. For some, very careful counts are made of members. Other groups only make estimates.

2. Each year the data are collected with the same questions. While most denominations have consistent reporting practices from one year to the next, any change in practices is not noted in the tables. Church mergers and splits can also influence the statistics when they are compared over a number of years. Churches have different reporting schedules and some do not report on a regular basis.

3. The two problems listed above make adding figures from different denominations problematic. However, an additional complication is that individuals who attend two different churches may be included more than once. For example, a person who attends the Church of God in Christ Wednesday evening and an AME service on Sunday morning will likely be included in both counts.

Table 1. Membership Statistics in Canada

Religious Body	Year Reporting	Number of Churches Reporting	Full Communicant or Confirmed Members	Inclusive Membership	Number of Pastors Serving Parishes	Total Number of Clergy	Number of Sunday or Sabbath Schools	Total Enrollment
The Anglican Church of Canada	1997	2,346	717,708	717,708	1,546	3,320	1,698	64,317
Antiochian Orthodox Christian Archdiocese of North America	1996	215	350,000	350,000	400	445	200	
Apostolic Christian Church (Nazarene)	1985	14		830	49	49		
The Apostolic Church in Canada	1999	17	1,200	1,600	17	21	17	350
Apostolic Church of Pentecost of Canada, Inc.	2000	143	24,000	24,000	311	445		
Armenian Holy Apostolic Church—Canadian Diocese	2000	15	85,000	85,000	10	47	5	424
Associated Gospel Churches	2000	139	10,293	10,293	129	260		
Association of Regular Baptist Churches (Canada)	1994	12			8	11		
Baptist Convention of Ontario and Quebec	1999	373	43,541	58,507	278	546		
Baptist General Conference of Canada	1999	92		7,045	95	143		4,079
Baptist Union of Western Canada	2000	155	20,427	20,427	279	530		
The Bible Holiness Movement	2000	19	623	954	16	18	20	
Brethren in Christ Church, Canadian Conference	1998	40	3,387	3,387	19	43		1,673

Table 1. Membership Statistics in Canada *(continued)*

Religious Body	Year Reporting	Number of Churches Reporting	Full Communicant or Confirmed Members	Inclusive Membership	Number of Pastors Serving Parishes	Total Number of Clergy	Number of Sunday or Sabbath Schools	Total Enrollment
Canadian and American Reformed Churches	2000	49	8,808	15,429	45	64		
Canadian Baptist Ministries	1996	1,133	129,055	129,055				
Canadian Conference of Mennonite Brethren Churches	2000	234	34,288	34,288				
Canadian Convention of Southern Baptists	1999	152	9,626	9,626	120	131	133	7,620
Canadian District of the Moravian Church in America, Northern Province	2000	9	1,196	1,818	8	11	9	500
Canadian Evangelical Christian Churches	2000	50	10,000	10,000	40	100	40	3,500
Canadian Yearly Meeting of the Religious Society of Friends	1995	22	1,125	1,893			30	
Christian Brethren (also known as Plymouth Brethren)	1999	600		50,000		250	550	
Christian Church (Disciples of Christ) in Canada	2000	27	1,604	2,732	28	38	23	418
Christian and Missionary Alliance in Canada	2000	418	37,588	112,207	980	1,196	377	41,813
Christian Reformed Church in North America	2000	242	50,304	82,572	204	318		
Church of God (Anderson, Ind.)	1998	47	3,777	3,777	64	97	43	1,994

Table 1. Membership Statistics in Canada *(continued)*

Religious Body	Year Reporting	Number of Churches Reporting	Full Communicant or Confirmed Members	Inclusive Membership	Number of Pastors Serving Parishes	Total Number of Clergy	Number of Sunday or Sabbath Schools	Total Enrollment
Church of God (Cleveland, Tenn.)	1999	130	10,914	10,914	106	128	120	9,376
Church of God in Christ (Mennonite)	2000	48	4,258	4,258	157	175	48	
Church of God of Prophecy in Canada	1995	40	3,107	3,107	98	100	37	
The Church of Jesus Christ of Latter-day Saints in Canada	2000		157,000					
Church of the Lutheran Brethren	1999	10	383	587	10	11	10	513
Church of the Nazarene in Canada	2000	165	12,189	12,199	130	326	147	16,075
Churches of Christ in Canada	1997	140	8,000	8,000				
Congregational Christian Churches in Canada	2000	100		7,500	153	235		
The Coptic Orthodox Church in Canada	2000		45,000		32	32		
The Estonian Evangelical Lutheran Church	1997	11	5,089	5,089	10	13	3	106
The Evangelical Covenant Church of Canada	1997	22	1,290	1,290	15	25	21	1,763
Evangelical Free Church of Canada	2000	151	7,690	7,690		147	144	
Evangelical Lutheran Church in Canada	1999	631	138,857	193,915	406	856	389	15,257
The Evangelical Mennonite Conference	1999	53	7,000	7,000		220		

Table 1. Membership Statistics in Canada *(continued)*

Religious Body	Year Reporting	Number of Churches Reporting	Full Communicant or Confirmed Members	Inclusive Membership	Number of Pastors Serving Parishes	Total Number of Clergy	Number of Sunday or Sabbath Schools	Total Enrollment
Evanglical Mennonite Mission Conference	1997	44	4,633	4,633	75	201		
The Evangelical Missionary Church of of Canada	1993	145	9,923	12,217	172	367	125	7,475
The Fellowship of Evangelical Baptist Churches in Canada	1995	506	72,288					
Foursquare Gospel Church of Canada	1996	54	3,063	3,063	66	103		1,258
Free Methodist Church in Canada	2000	136	6,930	6,930	123	238		
Free Will Baptists	1998	10	347		3	4	8	
Greek Orthodox Metropolis of Toronto (Canada)	1997	76	350,000	350,000	58	71	76	
Independent Assemblies of God International (Canada)	2000	310			458	701		
Independent Holiness Church	1994	5		150	4	10	4	118
Jehovah's Witnesses	1998	1,383	113,136	184,787				
Lutheran Church—Canada	2000	324	58,932	79,909	231	378	284	10,993
Mennonite Church (Canada)	2000	223	35,995	35,995	665			14,577
North American Baptist Conference	2000	124	17,486	17,486	135	208	124	

Table 1. Membership Statistics in Canada *(continued)*

Religious Body	Year Reporting	Number of Churches Reporting	Full Communicant or Confirmed Members	Inclusive Membership	Number of Pastors Serving Parishes	Total Number of Clergy	Number of Sunday or Sabbath Schools	Total Enrollment
The Old Catholic Church of Canada	2000	4	30	100	4	5	0	0
Old Order Amish Church	1999	24						
Open Bible Faith Fellowship of Canada	2000	90	3,000	10,000	152	220	90	4,600
Orthodox Church in America (Canada Section)	1993	606	1,000,000	1,000,000	740		502	
Patriarchal Parishes of the Russian Orthodox Church in Canada	2000	24	1,200	1,200	5	6	4	116
The Pentecostal Assemblies of Canada	1995	1,100		218,782	1,758	1,758	753	65,928
Pentecostal Assemblies of Newfoundland	1997	140	14,715	29,361	189	301	121	10,272
Presbyterian Church in America (Canadian Section)	1997	16	701	1,140	20	27		457
Presbyterian Church in Canada	2000	992	134,213	200,811		1,259		27,774
Reformed Church in Canada	2000	41	3,875	6,267	28	74		
The Reformed Episcopal Church of Canada	2001	10	350	470	9	12	3	15
Reinland Mennonite Church	1995	6	877	1,816	10	13	5	347
Reorganized Church of Jesus Christ of Latter Day Saints	1995	75	11,264	11,264	1,020	1,020		

Table 1. Membership Statistics in Canada *(continued)*

Religious Body	Year Reporting	Number of Churches Reporting	Full Communicant or Confirmed Members	Inclusive Membership	Number of Pastors Serving Parishes	Total Number of Clergy	Number of Sunday or Sabbath Schools	Total Enrollment
The Roman Catholic Church in Canada	1997	5,716	12,498,605	12,498,605		10,760		
The Romanian Orthodox Episcopate of America (Jackson, MI)	2000	22	900	1,400	13	16	12	
The Salvation Army in Canada	1998	376	27,920	80,180	638	1,959	346	
Serbian Orthodox Church in the U.S.A. and Canada, Diocese of Canada	1998	23	6,000	230,000	24	27	14	1,876
Seventh-day Adventist Church in Canada	2000	327	49,632	49,632	157	267	365	29,224
Syrian Orthodox Church of Antioch	1995	5	2,500	2,500	3	4		
Ukranian Orthodox Church of Canada	1988	258		120,000	75	91		
Union d'Églises Baptistes Françaises au Canada	1999	27	1,264	1,294	32	39	27	760
United Baptist Convention of the Atlantic Provinces	2000	555	62,276	62,276	266	497	323	
United Brethren Church in Canada	1992	9	835	835	5	12	9	447
The United Church of Canada	1999	3,764	668,579	1,589,886	1,949	4,160	2,989	76,751
United Pentecostal Church in Canada	1997	199				340		

Table 1. Membership Statistics in Canada *(continued)*

Religious Body	Year Reporting	Number of Churches Reporting	Full Communicant or Confirmed Members	Inclusive Membership	Number of Pastors Serving Parishes	Total Number of Clergy	Number of Sunday or Sabbath Schools	Total Enrollment
Universal Fellowship of Metropolitan Community Churches	1992	12	50	1,500	8	9	1	36
The Wesleyan Church of Canada	1999	75	5,698	5,992	121	188	75	3,336
TOTALS		**25,900**	**17,111,514**	**18,815,178**	**14,979**	**35,696**	**10,324**	**426,138**

Table 2. Membership Statistics in the United States

Religious Body	Year Reporting	Number of Churches Reporting	Full Communicant or Confirmed Members	Inclusive Membership	Number of Pastors Serving Parishes	Total Number of Clergy	Number of Sunday or Sabbath Schools	Total Enrollment
Advent Christian Church	2000	303	16,862	26,264	290	425	298	15,098
African Methodist Episcopal Church*	2000	6,200	2,500,000	2,500,000		8,000	8,000	
African Methodist Episcopal Zion Church*	2000	3,218	1,080,256	1,296,662	3,231	3,537	1,729	72,618
Albanian Orthodox Diocese of America	2000	2	2,203	2,203	0	2	2	56
Allegheny Wesleyan Methodist Connection (Original Allegheny Conference)	2000	115	1,734	1,864	85	185	116	5,721
The Alliance of Baptists in the U.S.A.*	2000	130	64,105	64,105	280			
The American Association of Lutheran Churches	1999	101	14,095	18,252	91	141	83	3,612
The American Baptist Association	1998	1,760		275,000	1,740	1,760		
American Baptist Churches in the USA*	2000	5,756	1,436,909	1,436,909	4,714	8,922		165,432
The American Carpatho-Russian Orthodox Greek Catholic Church	2000	80	13,480	13,480	90	108	76	
American Catholic Church	1997	100		25,000	80	100		
American Rescue Workers	1999	15	2,500	2,500	35	35	8	285
Antiochian Orthodox Christian Archdiocese of North America*	2000	227	70,000	70,000	300	367	208	18,800
Apostolic Christian Church (Nazarene)	1993	63	3,723	3,723	217	234	55	

Table 2. Membership Statistics in the United States *(continued)*

Religious Body	Year Reporting	Number of Churches Reporting	Full Communicant or Confirmed Members	Inclusive Membership	Number of Pastors Serving Parishes	Total Number of Clergy	Number of Sunday or Sabbath Schools	Total Enrollment
Apostolic Christian Churches of America	2000	86	12,900	12,900	297	381	85	6,900
Apostolic Episcopal Church	2001	250	14,000	14,000	300	315	50	1,150
Apostolic Faith Mission Church of God	2000	18	8,291	10,661	36	45	18	3,904
Apostolic Faith Mission of Portland, Oregon	1994	54	4,500	4,500	60	85	54	
Apostolic Lutheran Church of America	2000	58			61	73		
Apostolic Orthodox Catholic Church	2000	21		1,400	20	26	15	
Apostolic Overcoming Holy Church of God, Inc.	2000							
Armenian Apostolic Church of America	2000	36	360,000	360,000	36	46	25	1,675
Armenian Apostolic Church, Diocese of America*	1991	72	14,000	414,000	49	70		
Assemblies of God	2000	12,084	1,506,834	2,577,560	18,304	32,310	11,360	1,360,732
Associate Reformed Presbyterian Church (General Synod)	2000	255	25,641	41,500	221	357	203	
The Association of Free Lutheran Congregations	2000	245	28,060	36,400	145	222		
Baptist Bible Fellowship International	2000	4,500	1,200,000	1,200,000		7,500	4,500	
Baptist General Conference	2001		143,200	143,200				
Baptist Missionary Association of America	1999	1,334	234,732	234,732	1,525	3,055	1,300	88,921

Table 2. Membership Statistics in the United States *(continued)*

Religious Body	Year Reporting	Number of Churches Reporting	Full Communicant or Confirmed Members	Inclusive Membership	Number of Pastors Serving Parishes	Total Number of Clergy	Number of Sunday or Sabbath Schools	Total Enrollment
Beachy Amish Mennonite Churches	2000	153	9,205	9,205	435	453		
Berean Fundamental Church	2000	51	8,000	8,000				
The Bible Church of Christ, Inc.	1993	6	4,150	6,850	11	52	6	
Bible Fellowship Church	2000	57	7,258	7,258	56	113	57	5,126
Brethren in Christ Church	2000	229	20,587	20,587	152	342		12,800
Brethren Church (Ashland, Ohio)	2000	119	13,096	13,096	79	171	107	
The Catholic Church	2000	19,544	63,683,030	63,683,030		46,075		
Christ Catholic Church	2000	7	1,213	1,240	7	8	2	20
Christ Community Church (Evangelical-Protestant)	2000	3	1,027	1,690	5	9	1	369
Christian Brethren (also known as Plymouth Brethren)	2000	1,125		95,000		530	1,010	
Christian Church (Disciples of Christ) in the United States and Canada*	2000	3,781	527,363	820,286	3,305	7,022	3,527	211,609
Christian Church of North America, General Council	1999	96	7,200	7,200	100	157	96	
Christian Churches and Churches of Christ	1988	5,579		1,071,616	5,525			
The Christian Congregation, Inc.	2000	1,439	119,391	119,391	1,437	1,438	1,295	39,100
Christian Methodist Episcopal Church*	1999	3,069	784,114	784,114	2,058	2,378	2,103	
The Christian and Missionary Alliance	2000	1,959	185,133	364,949	1,731	2,613		120,490

Table 2. Membership Statistics in the United States *(continued)*

Religious Body	Year Reporting	Number of Churches Reporting	Full Communicant or Confirmed Members	Inclusive Membership	Number of Pastors Serving Parishes	Total Number of Clergy	Number of Sunday or Sabbath Schools	Total Enrollment
Christian Reformed Church in North America	1999	739	135,994	196,604	675	1,240		
Church of the Brethren*	2000	1,071	135,978	135,879	843	1,915	798	39,897
The Church of Christ (Holiness) U.S.A.	2000	163	10,475	10,475	191	224	153	7,689
Church of Christ, Scientist	1998	2,200						
Church of God (Anderson, Indiana)	1998	2,353	234,311	234,311	3,034	5,468		115,946
The Church of God in Christ	1991	15,300	5,499,875	5,499,875	28,988	33,593		
Church of God in Christ, Mennonite	2000	106	12,479	12,479	439	439	106	
Church of God (Cleveland, Tennessee)	2000	6,426	895,536	895,536	4,578	9,649	5,247	363,831
Church of God by Faith, Inc.	2000	149	25,000	35,000	182	268		
Church of God General Conference (Oregon, IL and Morrow, GA)	2000	89	4,037	5,248	65	80	73	2,227
The Church of God, Mountain Assembly, Inc.	1994	118	6,140	6,140				
Church of God of Prophecy	2000	1,865	72,899	72,899				68,746
The Church of God (Seventh Day), Denver, Colorado	2000	200	8,998	8,998	95	130		
The Church of Illumination	1996	4		1,200		16	1	216
The Church of Jesus Christ (Bickertonites)	1989	63		2,707	183	262		
The Church of Jesus Christ of Latter-day Saints	2000	11,562	4,679,110	5,208,827	34,686	38,964	11,562	4,064,625

Table 2. Membership Statistics in the United States *(continued)*

Religious Body	Year Reporting	Number of Churches Reporting	Full Communicant or Confirmed Members	Inclusive Membership	Number of Pastors Serving Parishes	Total Number of Clergy	Number of Sunday or Sabbath Schools	Total Enrollment
Church of the Living God (Motto: Christian Workers for Fellowship)	1985	170		4,200	170			
Church of the Lutheran Brethren of America	2000	115	8,229	13,920	136	230	105	9,182
Church of the Lutheran Confession	2000	75	6,527	8,671	60	90	67	1,163
Church of the Nazarene	2000	5,070	633,264	636,564	4,504	9,898	4,798	794,443
Church of Our Lord Jesus Christ of the Apostolic Faith, Inc.	1999	500						
Church of the United Brethren in Christ	1997	228	23,585	23,585	315	449	228	12,837
Churches of Christ	1999	15,000	1,500,000	1,500,000	14,500	16,350	12,500	1,600,000
Churches of Christ in Christian Union	2000	216	10,104	10,104	208	601		10,050
Churches of God, General Conference	2000	342	32,380	32,380	264	454	342	15,033
Community of Christ	1999	1,236	137,038	137,065		20,370		
Congregational Holiness Church	1993	190		2,468			190	
Conservative Baptist Association of America (CBAmerica)	1998	1,200	200,000	200,000				
Conservative Congregational Christian Conference	1999	242	40,414	40,414	273	545	223	13,263
Conservative Lutheran Association	2000	5	845	1,262	8	25	4	142
Coptic Orthodox Church*	2000	100	250,000	300,000	140	145	100	5,500

Table 2. Membership Statistics in the United States *(continued)*

Religious Body	Year Reporting	Number of Churches Reporting	Full Communicant or Confirmed Members	Inclusive Membership	Number of Pastors Serving Parishes	Total Number of Clergy	Number of Sunday or Sabbath Schools	Total Enrollment
Cumberland Presbyterian Church	2000	779	86,519	86,519	540	857	685	37,041
Cumberland Presbyterian Church in America	1996	152	15,142	15,142	141	156	152	9,465
Elim Fellowship	2000	98			650	850		
Episcopal Church*	1999	7,359	1,814,380	2,300,461	7,741	14,428	6,128	303,199
The Estonian Evangelical Lutheran Church	1997	21	3,508	3,508	10	12		
The Evangelical Church	2000	133	12,475	12,475	164	255	125	8,000
The Evangelical Congregational Church	2000	145	21,939	21,939	163	234	136	
The Evangelical Covenant Church	2000	800	101,003	101,003	679	1,259	725	88,780
The Evangelical Free Church of America	1995	1,224	124,499	242,619	1,936	2,436		
Evangelical Friends International—North American Region	2000	284	36,814	36,814				
Evangelical Lutheran Church in America*	2000	10,816	3,810,785	5,125,919	9,496	17,651	8,796	917,368
Evangelical Lutheran Synod	2000	138	16,569	21,729	108	178	128	3,209
Evanglical Mennonite Church	2001	34	5,278	5,278	35	73	34	4,633

Table 2. Membership Statistics in the United States *(continued)*

Religious Body	Year Reporting	Number of Churches Reporting	Full Communicant or Confirmed Members	Inclusive Membership	Number of Pastors Serving Parishes	Total Number of Clergy	Number of Sunday or Sabbath Schools	Total Enrollment
Evangelical Methodist Church	1997	123	8,615	8,615	105	215	120	6,547
Evangelical Presbyterian Church	2000	189	61,187	64,939	270	439	163	33,367
Fellowship of Evangelical Bible Churches	2000	17	2,150	2,150	13	37	17	578
Fellowship of Fundamental Bible Churches	1999	22	1,125	1,125	29	46	22	1,036
Fellowship of Grace Brethren Churches	1997	260	30,371	30,371		564		
Free Methodist Church of North America	2000	971	62,453			1,871	860	87,784
Friends General Conference	2000	650	34,577	34,577	0	0	400	
Friends United Meeting*	2000	487	34,863	34,863	289	289	409	
Full Gospel Assemblies International	2000	17	1,342	1,342		241		
Full Gospel Fellowship of Churches and Ministers International	2000	896	325,000	325,000	2,070	2,424	896	364,000
Fundamental Methodist Church, Inc.	1993	12	682	787	17	22	12	454
General Association of General Baptists	2000	587	55,549	55,549	868	1,033	587	21,415
General Association of Regular Baptist Churches	1999	1,398	92,129	92,129				

Table 2. Membership Statistics in the United States *(continued)*

Religious Body	Year Reporting	Number of Churches Reporting	Full Communicant or Confirmed Members	Inclusive Membership	Number of Pastors Serving Parishes	Total Number of Clergy	Number of Sunday or Sabbath Schools	Total Enrollment
General Church of the New Jerusalem	2000	33	3,115	5,791	28	63		
General Conference of Mennonite Brethren Churches	1996	368	50,915	82,130	590			34,668
Grace Gospel Fellowship	1992	128		60,000	160	196	128	
Greek Orthodox Archdiocese of America*	2000	508		1,500,000	893	893	500	
The Holy Eastern Orthodox Catholic and Apostolic Church in North America, Inc.	2000	18	4,072	4,072	11	16		
Hungarian Reformed Church in America*	1998	27		6,000	27	30		
Hutterian Brethren	2000	444	36,800	43,000	600	600		
IFCA International, Inc.	1999	659	61,655	61,655			659	57,768
International Church of the Foursquare Gospel	2000	1,793	242,616	277,616	5,644	8,044		52,265
International Council of Community Churches*	2000	217	200,263	200,263	249	352		
The International Pentecostal Church of Christ	2000	71	2,184	5,408	65	161	61	5,408
International Pentecostal Holiness Church	2000	1,868	197,972	197,972	1,625	2,553		96,013
Jehovah's Witnesses	2000	11,636	998,166	998,166				
Korean Presbyterian Church in America, General Assembly of the*	2000	310	35,802	50,221	450	568		

Table 2. Membership Statistics in the United States *(continued)*

Religious Body	Year Reporting	Number of Churches Reporting	Full Communicant or Confirmed Members	Inclusive Membership	Number of Pastors Serving Parishes	Total Number of Clergy	Number of Sunday or Sabbath Schools	Total Enrollment
The Latvian Evangelical Lutheran Church in America	2000	71	12,990	14,528	44	68	20	
The Liberal Catholic Church—Province of the United States of America	2000	23	6,500	6,500	59	59		
The Lutheran Church—Missouri Synod (LCMS)	2000	6,150	1,934,057	2,554,088	5,196	8,257	5,658	505,690
Mar Thoma Syrian Church of India*	2000	68	32,000	32,000	42	47	55	4,000
Mennonite Church USA	2000	1,063	120,381	120,381			1,041	58,103
The Missionary Church	2000	368	29,948	49,765	617	908	184	23,163
Moravian Church in America (Northern Province)*	2000	93	20,281	25,872	89	176	92	6,523
National Association of Congregational Christian Churches	2000	430	65,569	65,569	530	707		
National Association of Free Will Baptists	2000	2,472	199,134	199,134	2,472	4,229	2,472	131,709
National Baptist Convention of America, Inc.*	2000		3,500,000	3,500,000				
National Missionary Baptist Convention of America*	1992			2,500,000				

Table 2. Membership Statistics in the United States *(continued)*

Religious Body	Year Reporting	Number of Churches Reporting	Full Communicant or Confirmed Members	Inclusive Membership	Number of Pastors Serving Parishes	Total Number of Clergy	Number of Sunday or Sabbath Schools	Total Enrollment
National Organization of the New Apostolic Church of North America	2000	380	36,438	36,438	1,890	1,890	317	2,634
National Spiritualist Association of Churches	1999	136	3,000	3,000	87	87	46	1,221
Netherlands Reformed Congregations	2000	25	4,437	9,320	8	9		
North American Baptist Conference	2000	270	47,097	47,097	305	440	270	
Old German Baptist Brethren	2000	54	6,084	6,084	257	257		
Old Order Amish Church	1993	898	80,820	80,820	3,592	3,617	55	
Open Bible Standard Churches, Inc.	1999	357	35,700	35,700	477	1,061		
The Orthodox Church in America*	2000	721	1,000,000	1,000,000	760	830	493	
The Orthodox Presbyterian Church	2000	216	17,914	26,008	406	406	381	12,538
Patriarchal Parishes of the Russian Orthodox Church in the U.S.A.*	2000	32	20,000		45	48		
Pentecostal Assemblies of the World, Inc.	1998	1,750	1,500,000	1,500,000	4,500	4,500		
Pentecostal Church of God	2000	1,212	46,800	102,000		1,788		
Pentecostal Fire-Baptized Holiness Church	1996	27	223	223		28	25	400

Table 2. Membership Statistics in the United States *(continued)*

Religious Body	Year Reporting	Number of Churches Members	Full Communicant or Confirmed	Inclusive Membership Parishes	Number of Pastors Serving	Total Number of Clergy	Number of Sunday or Sabbath Schools	Total Enrollment
The Pentecostal Free Will Baptist Church, Inc.	1998	150	28,000	28,000	175	280	160	
Polish National Catholic Church of America*	1960	162						
Presbyterian Church in America	2000	1,458	247,010	306,156		2,980	1,215	119,166
Presbyterian Church (U.S.A.)*	2000	11,178	2,525,330	3,485,332	8,891	21,065	9,332	1,084,347
Primitive Advent Christian Church	1993	10	345	345	11	11	10	292
Primitive Methodist Church in the U.S.A.	1999	77	4,607	6,031	70	112	77	3,197
Progressive National Baptist Convention, Inc.*	1995	2,000	2,500,000	2,500,000				
Protestant Reformed Churches in America	2000	28	3,770	6,713	25	39	23	
Reformed Church in America*	2000	898	177,281	289,392	773	1,877		
Reformed Church in the United States	1998	40	3,201	4,257	34	42	37	869
Reformed Episcopal Church	1998	125	6,400	6,400	150	185		
Reformed Mennonite Church	2000	10		300		19		
Reformed Presbyterian Church of North America	1997	86	4,363	6,105	70	137	78	3,373
Religious Society of Friends (Conservative)	1994	1,200		104,000				

Table 2. Membership Statistics in the United States *(continued)*

Religious Body	Year Reporting	Number of Churches Reporting	Full Communicant or Confirmed Members	Inclusive Membership	Number of Pastors Serving Parishes	Total Number of Clergy	Number of Sunday or Sabbath Schools	Total Enrollment
The Romanian Orthodox Episcopate of America	1990	56	6,606	25,000	37	81	30	1,800
The Russian Orthodox Church Outside of Russia	1994	177			319	319		
The Salvation Army	1999	1,410	124,922	472,871	3,072	5,415	1,410	108,139
The Schwenkfelder Church	1995	5	2,524	2,524	8	9	5	701
Separate Baptists in Christ	1992	100	8,000	8,000	95	140	100	
Serbian Orthodox Church in the U.S.A. and Canada*	1986	68		67,000	60	62		
Seventh-day Adventist Church	2000	4,486	880,921	880,921	2,484	5,249	4,836	514,143
Seventh Day Baptist General Conference, USA and Canada	1995	80	4,800		46	74		
Southern Baptist Convention	2000	41,588	15,960,308	15,960,308	77,810	101,446	39,440	816,415
Southern Methodist Church	1999	117	7,686	7,686	82	114	115	3,987
Sovereign Grace Believers	2000	350	4,000	4,000	450	450	350	
The Swedenborgian Church*	2000	44	2,104	2,104	28	44		
Syrian (Syriac) Orthodox Church of Antioch*	1999	22	32,500	32,500	18	23	17	1,380

Table 2. Membership Statistics in the United States *(continued)*

Religious Body	Year Reporting	Number of Churches Reporting	Full Communicant or Confirmed Members	Inclusive Membership	Number of Pastors Serving Parishes	Total Number of Clergy	Number of Sunday or Sabbath Schools	Total Enrollment
The Syro-Russian Orthodox Catholic Church, Romano Byzantine	2000	100	25,000	27,000	80	115	30	1,250
True Orthodox Church of Greece (Synod of Metropolitan Cyprian), American Exarchate	1993	9	1,095	1,095	18	19		
Unitarian Universalist Association of Congregations	2000	1,051		220,000			1,050	61,482
United Christian Church	2000	10	334	334	8	13	9	448
United Church of Christ*	2000	5,923	1,377,320	1,377,320	4,202	10,263	3,122	331,537
The United Methodist Church*	2000	35,469	8,340,954	8,340,954	24,991	44,118	32,795	3,590,824
United Pentecostal Church International	1995	3,790			7,903			
United Zion Church	1998	13	883	883	13	23	11	818
Unity of the Brethren	1998	27	2,548	3,218	25	39	24	1,442
Universal Fellowship of Metropolitan Community Churches	1998	300		44,000	324	372		
The Wesleyan Church	2000	1,602	114,084	123,181	1,974	3,181	1,602	390,445
Wisconsin Evangelical Lutheran Synod	2000	1,241	316,386	721,665	1,245	1,781		43,138
Totals		**319,365**	**138,171,179**	**152,134,407**	**334,178**	**559,642**	**201,616**	**19,217,380**

*National Council of Churches of Christ in the U.S.A. member communion

Table 3. Membership Statistics for the National Council of the Churches of Christ in the U.S.A.

Religious Body	Year Reporting	Number of Churches Reporting	Inclusive Membership	Number of Pastors Serving Parishes
Advent Christian Church	2000	303	26,264	290
African Methodist Episcopal Church	2000	6,200	2,500,000	
African Methodist Episcopal Zion Church	2000	3,218	1,296,662	3,231
The Alliance of Baptists in the U.S.A.	2000	130	64,105	280
American Baptist Churches in the U.S.A.	2000	5,756	1,436,909	4,714
The Antiochian Orthodox Christian Archdiocese of North America	2000	227	70,000	300
Armenian Apostolic Church, Diocese of America	1991	72	414,000	49
Christian Church (Disciples of Christ) in the United States and Canada	2000	3,781	820,286	3,305
Christian Methodist Episcopal Church	1999	3,069	784,114	2,058
Church of the Brethren	2000	1,071	135,879	843
Coptic Orthodox Church	2000	100	300,000	140
Episcopal Church	1999	7,359	2,300,461	7,741
Evangelical Lutheran Church in America	2000	10,816	5,125,919	9,496
Friends United Meeting	2000	487	34,863	289
General Assembly of the Korean Presbyterian Church in America	2000	310	50,221	450
Greek Orthodox Archdiocese of America	2000	508	1,500,000	893
Hungarian Reformed Church in America	1998	27	6,000	27
International Council of Community Churches	2000	217	200,263	249
Malankara Orthodox Syrian Church, Diocese of America				

Table 3. Membership Statistics for the National Council of the Churches of Christ in the U.S.A. *(continued)*

Religious Body	Year Reporting	Number of Churches Reporting	Inclusive Membership	Number of Pastors Serving Parishes
Mar Thoma Syrian Church of India	2000	68	32,000	42
Moravian Church in America (Northern Province)	2000	93	25,872	89
National Baptist Convention of America, Inc.	2000		3,500,000	
National Baptist Convention, U.S.A., Inc.				
National Missionary Baptist Convention of America	1992		2,500,000	
The Orthodox Church in America	2000	721	1,000,000	760
Patriarchal Parishes of the Russian Orthodox Church in the U.S.A.	2000	32		45
Philadelphia Yearly Meeting of the Religious Society of Friends	2000		11,000	105
Polish National Catholic Church of America	1960	162		
Presbyterian Church (U.S.A.)	2000	11,178	3,485,332	8,891
Progressive National Baptist Convention, Inc.	1995	2,000	2,500,000	
Reformed Church in America	2000	898	289,392	773
Serbian Orthodox Church in the U.S.A. and Canada	1986	68	67,000	60
The Swedenborgian Church	2000	44	2,104	28
Syrian (Syriac) Orthodox Church of Antioch	1999	22	32,500	18
United Church of Christ	2000	5,923	1,377,320	4,202
The United Methodist Church	2000	35,469	8,340,954	24,991

STATISTICAL SECTION

Table 4. Selected Statistics of Chu

				TOTAL CONTRIBUTIONS		
Religious Body	Year	Full or Confirmed Members	Inclusive Members	Total Contributions	Per Capita Full or Confirmed Members	Per In Me
The Antiochian Orthodox Christian Archdiocese of North America	1996	350,000	350,000	$3,475,000	$9.93	$
The Apostolic Church in Canada	1999	1,200	1,600	$1,184,700	$987.25	$7
Armenian Holy Apostolic Church—Canadian Diocese	2000	85,000	85,000	$855,000	$10.06	$
Baptist Union of Western Canada	1999	20,427	20,427	$5,107,654	$250.04	$2
The Bible Holiness Movement	1999	623	954	$256,834	$412.25	$2
Brethren in Christ Church, Canadian Conference	1998	3,387	3,387	$5,283,709	$1,560.00	$1,
Canadian District of the Moravian Church in America, Northern Province	2000	1,196	1,818	$1,305,011	$1,091.15	$7
Christian Church (Disciples of Christ) in Canada	2000	1,604	2,732	$1,540,358	$960.32	$5
Church of God (Anderson Ind.)	1998	3,777	3,777	$630,769	$167.00	$1
Church of God (Cleveland, Tenn.)	1999	10,914	10,914	$3,950,557	$361.97	$3
Church of the Lutheran Brethren	1999	383	587	$595,181	$1,554.00	$1,
Church of the Nazarene in Canada	2000	12,189	12,199	$9,454,655	$775.67	$7
The Evangelical Covenant Church of Canada	1997	1,290	1,290	$7,690,321	$5,961.49	$5,
Evangelical Lutheran Church in Canada	1999	138,857	193,915	$59,407,907	$427.84	$3
Foursquare Gospel Church of Canada	1996	3,063	3,063	$4,376,923	$1,428.97	$1,
Lutheran Church—Canada	2000	58,932	79,909	$37,200,000	$631.24	$4
North American Baptist Conference	2000	17,486	17,486	$30,994,685	$1,772.54	$1,
Pentecostal Assemblies of Newfoundland	1997	14,715	29,361	$3,143,197	$213.60	$1
Presbyterian Church in America (Canadian Section)	1997	701	1,140	$1,708,607	$2,437.39	$1,
Presbyterian Church in Canada	1997	134,683	200,738	$85,326,113	$633.53	$4
Reformed Church in Canada	2000	3,875	6,627	$4,661,667	$1,203.01	$7
The Reformed Episcopal Church of Canada	2001	350	470	$370,160	$1,057.60	$7
Seventh-day Adventist in Canada	2000	49,632	49,632	$45,400,979	$914.75	$9
Union d'Eglises Baptistes Françaises au Canada	1999	1,264	1,294	$1,106,209	$875.17	$8
The United Church of Canada	1999	668,549	1,589,886	$301,471,981	$450.93	$1
The Wesleyan Church of Canada	1997	5,698	5,992	$10,193,278	$1,788.92	$1,

nances—Canadian Churches

NGREGATIONAL FINANCES			BENEVOLENCES			
otal egational ibutions	Per Capita Full or Confirmed Members	Per Capita Inclusive Members	Total Benevolences	Per Capita Full or Confirmed Members	Per Capita Inclusive Members	Benevolences as a Percentage of Total Giving
85,000	$3.96	$3.96	$2,090,000	$5.97	$5.97	60%
69,200	$891.00	$668.25	$115,500	$96.25	$72.19	10%
0,000	$5.06	$5.06	$425,000	$5.00	$5.00	50%
2,511	$27.54	$27.54	$4,545,143	$222.51	$222.51	89%
1,685	$50.86	$33.21	$225,149	$361.39	$236.01	88%
97,458	$1,357.38	$1,357.38	$686,251	$202.61	$202.61	13%
04,988	$1,007.52	$662.81	$100,023	$83.63	$55.02	8%
12,802	$880.80	$517.13	$1,275.56	$79.52	$46.69	8%
5,698	$70.35	$70.35	$365,071	$96.66	$96.66	58%
69,948	$336.26	$336.26	$280,609	$25.71	$25.71	7%
0,140	$1,201.41	$783.88	$135,041	$352.59	$230.05	23%
26,764	$633.91	$633.39	$1,727,891	$141.76	$141.64	18%
96,979	$1,625.57	$1,625.57	$5,593,342	$4,335.92	$4,335.92	73%
05,651	$373.81	$267.67	$7,502,256	$54.03	$38.69	13%
48,451	$1,387.02	$1,387.02	$128,472	$41.94	$41.94	3%
400,000	$549.79	$405.46	$4,800,000	$81.45	$60.07	13%
110,764	$1,493.24	$1,493.24	$4,993,921	$285.60	$285.60	16%
35,046	$124.71	$62.50	$1,308,151	$88.90	$44.55	42%
86,362	$2,120.35	$1,303.83	$222,245	$317.04	$194.95	13%
507,501	$545.78	$366.19	$11,818,612	$87.75	$58.88	14%
39,918	$1,016.75	$628.68	$721,749	$186.26	$115.17	15%
1,700	$347.71	$258.94	$248,460	$709.89	$528.63	67%
990,837	$302.04	$302.04	$30,410,142	$612.71	$612.71	67%
50,000	$593.35	$579.60	$356,209	$281.81	$275.28	32%
096,100	$384.56	$161.71	$44,375,881	$66.38	$27.91	15%
55,161	$1,536.53	$1,461.14	$1,438,117	$252.39	$240.01	14%

Table 5. Selected Statistics of Chu

Religious Body	Year	Full or Confirmed Members	Inclusive Members	TOTAL CONTRIBUTION Total Contributions	Per Capita Full or Confirmed Members	Per Inc Me
African Methodist Episcopal Zion Church*	2000	1,080,256	1,296,662	$99,237,535	$91.86	$7
Albanian Orthodox Diocese of America	1996	2,203	2,203	$171,900	$78.03	$7
Allegheny Wesleyan Methodist Connection (Original Allegheny Conference)	2000	1,734	1,864	$5,275,226	$3,042.23	$2,8
American Baptist Churches in the U.S.A.*	2000	1,436,909	1,436,909	$398,660,887	$277.44	$2
Apostolic Faith Mission Church of God	2000	8,291	10,661	$969,000	$116.87	$9
Associate Reformed Presbyterian Church (General Synod)	2000	25,641	41,500	$40,952,973	$1,597.17	$9
Baptist Missionary Association of America	1998	234,732	234,732	$70,087,434	$298.58	$2
Bible Fellowship Church	2000	7,258	7,258	$12,963,005	$1,786.03	$1,7
Brethren in Christ Church	2000	20,587	20,587	$30,852,143	$1,498.62	$1,4
Christ Community Church (Evangelical-Protestant)	2000	1,027	1,690	$1,107,628	$1,078.51	$6
Christian Church (Disciples of Christ) in the United States and Canada*	2000	527,363	820,286	$482,691,744	$915.29	$5
The Christian and Missionary Alliance	2000	185,133	364,949	$323,275,281	$1,746.18	$8
Christian Reformed Church in North America	2000	135,994	196,604	$291,100,000	$2,140.54	$1,4
Church of the Brethren*	2000	135,978	135,879	$84,329,261	$620.17	$6
The Church of Christ (Holiness) U.S.A.	2000	10,475	10,475	$9,550,000	$911.69	$9
Church of God (Anderson, Ind.)	1997	234,311	234,311	$223,492,670	$953.83	$9
Church of God General Conference (Oregon, IL and Morrow, GA.)	2000	4,037	5,248	$3,842,273	$951.76	$7
Church of the Lutheran Brethren of America	2000	8,229	13,920	$12,284,566	$1,492.84	$8
Church of the Lutheran Confession	2000	6,527	8,671	$5,394,097	$826.43	$6
Church of the Nazarene	2000	633,264	636,564	$638,992,208	$1,009.05	$1,0
Church of the United Brethren in Christ	1997	23,585	23,585	$27,184,899	$1,152.64	$1,1
Churches of Christ	1997	1,500,000	1,500,000	$1,445,000,000	$963.33	$9
Churches of God, General Conference	2000	32,380	32,380	$25,573,777	$789.80	$7
Community of Christ	1997	137,038	137,065	$39,691,085	$223.96	$2
Conservative Congregational Christian Conference	1999	40,414	40,414	$37,096,674	$917.92	$9
Cumberland Presbyterian Church	2000	86,519	86,519	$46,744,751	$540.28	$5

ances—United States Churches

STATISTICAL SECTION

NGREGATIONAL FINANCES			BENEVOLENCES			
tal egation butions	Per Capita Full or Confirmed Members	Per Capita Inclusive Members	Total Benevolences	Per Capita Full or Confirmed Members	Per Capita Inclusive Members	Benevolences as a Percentage
56,232	$88.84	$74.01	$3,271,303	$3.03	$2.52	3%
,600	$74.72	$74.72	$7,300	$3.31	$3.31	4%
8,221	$2,409.59	$2,241.53	$1,097,005	$632.64	$588.52	21%
25,688	$234.62	$234.62	$61,535,199	$42.82	$42.82	15%
,000	$47.04	$36.58	$579,000	$69.83	$54.31	60%
30,852	$1,235.55	$763.39	$9,272,121	$361.61	$223.42	23%
81,427	$244.88	$244.88	$12,606,007	$53.70	$53.70	18%
42,940	$1,425.04	$1,425.04	$2,620,065	$360.99	$360.99	20%
8,637	$1,221.58	$1,221.58	$5,703,506	$277.04	$277.04	18%
4,628	$880.85	$535.28	$203,000	$197.66	$120.12	18%
65,354	$822.90	$529.04	$48,726,390	$92.40	$59.40	10%
03,697	$1,531.89	$777.11	$39,671,584	$214.29	$108.70	12%
00,000	$1,650.81	$1,141.89	$66,600,000	$489.73	$338.75	23%
85,361	$494.83	$495.19	$17,043,900	$125.34	$125.34	20%
6,063	$869.31	$869.31	$443,937	$42.38	$42.38	5%
38,623	$829.83	$829.83	$29,054,047	$124.00	$124.00	13%
2,160	$800.63	$615.88	$610,113	$151.13	$116.26	16%
63,380	$1,259.37	$744.50	$1,921,186	$233.47	$138.02	16%
25,633	$708.69	$533.46	$768,464	$117.74	$88.62	14%
708,125	$815.94	$811.71	$122,284,083	$193.10	$192.10	19%
70,417	$1,007.86	$1,007.86	$3,414,482	$144.77	$144.77	13%
,000,000	$942.67	$942.67	$31,000,000	$20.67	$20.67	2%
78,740	$650.98	$650.98	$4,495,037	$138.82	$138.82	18%
21,761	$116.19	$116.16	$14,769,324	$107.78	$107.75	48%
65,218	$771.15	$771.15	$5,931,456	$146.77	$146.77	16%
33,829	$456.94	$456.94	$6,591,617	$76.19	$76.19	14%

Table 5. Selected Statistics of Chu

				TOTAL CONTRIBUTIONS		
Religious Body	Year	Full or Confirmed Members	Inclusive Members	Total Contributions	Per Capita Full or Confirmed Members	Per Inc Me
Cumberland Presbyterian Church in America	1996	15,142	15,142	$40,408,524	$2,668.64	$2,
Episcopal Church*	1999	1,857,186	2,311,398	$2,146,835,718	$1,155.96	$9
The Evangelical Church	2000	12,475	12,475	$15,632,985	$2,153.15	$2,
The Evangelical Congregational Church	2000	21,939	21,939	$19,642,117	$895.31	$8
The Evangelical Covenant Church	2000	101,003	101,003	$184,599,003	$1,827.66	$1,
Evangelical Lutheran Church in America	2000	3,810,785	5,125,919	$2,298,427,601	$603.41	$4
Evangelical Lutheran Synod	2000	16,569	21,729	$11,859,530	$715.77	$5
Evangelical Mennonite Church	2001	5,278	5,278	$12,899,752	$2,444.06	$2,
Fellowship of Evangelical Bible Churches	2000	2,150	2,150	$1,762,675	$819.85	$8
Free Methodist Church of North America	2000	62,453	62,453	$112,284,044	$1,797.90	$1,
General Conference of Mennonite Brethren Churches	1996	50,915	82,130	$65,851,481	$1,293.36	$8
The Latvian Evangelical Lutheran Church in America	2000	12,990	14,528	$3,217,000	$247.65	$2
The Lutheran Church—Missouri Synod (LCMS)	2000	1,934,057	2,554,088	$1,229,244,829	$635.58	$4
Mennonite Church USA	2000	120,381	120,381	$130,664,814	$1,085.43	$1,
The Missionary Church	2000	29,948	49,765	$60,803,450	$2,030.30	$1,
Moravian Church in America (Northern Province)*	2000	20,281	25,872	$14,337,156	$706.93	$5
North American Baptist Conference	2000	47,097	47,097	$64,711,783	$1,374.01	$1,
Open Bible Standard Churches	1999	35,700	35,700	$4,416,377	123.71	$1
The Orthodox Presbyterian Church	2000	17,914	26,008	$34,098,799	$1,903.47	$1,
Presbyterian Church (U.S.A.)*	2000	2,525,330	3,485,332	$2,915,880,334	$1,154.65	$8
Primitive Methodist Church in the U.S.A.	1999	4,607	6,031	$4,733,757	$1,027.51	$7
Reformed Church in America*	2000	177,281	289,392	$263,776,862	$1,487.90	$9
Reformed Church in the United States	1998	3,201	4,257	$3,657,850	$1,142.72	$8
Reformed Presbyterian Church of North America	1997	4,363	6,105	$6,446,899	$1,477.63	$1,
Seventh-day Adventist Church	2000	880,921	880,921	$991,562,883	$1,125.60	$1,
Southern Baptist Convention	2000	15,960,308	15,960,308	$8,437,177,940	$528.64	$5
United Church of Christ*	2000	1,377,320	1,377,320	$823,517,120	$597.91	$5
The United Methodist Church*	2000	8,340,954	8,340,954	$4,761,148,280	$570.82	$5
Unity of the Brethren	1998	2,548	3,218	$165,184	$64.83	$5

nances—United States Churches (*continued*)

NGREGATIONAL FINANCES			BENEVOLENCES			
otal regation ributions	Per Capita Full or Confirmed Members	Per Capita Inclusive Members	Total Benevolences	Per Capita Full or Confirmed Members	Per Capita Inclusive Members	Benevolences as a Percentage
921,064	$2,306.24	2,306.24	$5,487,460	$362.40	$362.40	14%
4,535,013	$1,014.73	$815.32	$262,300,705	$141.24	$113.48	12%
84,502	$1,024.82	$1,024.81	$2,848,483	$228.34	$228.34	18%
656,789	$804.95	$804.95	$1,982,328	$90.36	$90.36	10%
361,490	$1,597.59	$1,597.59	$23,237,513	$230.07	$230.07	13%
7,208,285	$542.46	$403.29	$231,219,316	$60.67	$45.11	10%
910,109	$658.47	$502.10	$949,421	$57.30	$43.69	8%
563,872	$2,001.49	$2,001.49	$2,335,880	$442.57	$442.57	18%
346,953	$626.49	$626.49	$415,722	$193.36	$193.36	24%
853,770	$1,582.85	$1,582.85	$13,430,274	$215.05	$215.05	12%
832,814	$998.39	$618.93	$15,018,667	$294.98	$182.86	23%
553,000	$196.54	$175.73	$644,000	$49.58	$44.33	20%
1,690,594	$569.63	$431.34	$127,554,235	$65.95	$49.94	10%
843,112	$796.16	$796.16	$34,821,702	$289.26	$289.26	27%
460,687	$1,851.90	$1,114.45	$5,342,763	$178.40	$107.36	9%
391,991	$660.32	$517.62	$945,165	$46.60	$36.53	7%
866,431	$1,164.97	$1,164.97	$9,845,352	$209.04	$209.04	15%
624,156	$45.49	$45.49	$2,792,221	$78.21	$78.21	63%
120,325	$1,569.74	$1,081.22	$5,978,474	$333.73	$229.87	18%
7,278,130	$996.81	$722.25	$398,602,204	$157.84	$114.37	14%
072,620	$884.01	$675.28	$661,137	$143.51	$109.62	14%
,555,821	$1,277.95	$782.87	$37,221,041	$209.96	$128.62	14%
008,116	$939.74	$706.63	$649,734	$202.98	$152.63	18%
792,856	$1,327.72	$948.87	$654,043	$149.91	$107.13	10%
,562,375	$359.35	$359.35	$675,000,508	$766.24	$766.24	68%
7,410,662	$429.65	$429.65	$1,579,767,278	$98.98	$98.98	19%
,991,925	$540.90	$540.90	$78,525,195	$57.01	$57.01	10%
54,328,165	$462.10	$462.10	$906,820,115	$108.72	$108.72	19%
51,465	$20.20	$15.99	$113,719	$44.63	$35.34	69%

Table 5. Selected Statistics of Chu

				TOTAL CONTRIBUTIONS		
Religious Body	Year	Full or Confirmed Members	Inclusive Members	Total Contributions	Per Capita Full or Confirmed Members	Per In Me
Universal Fellowship of Metropolitan Community Churches	1998		44,000	$1,570,860		$
The Wesleyan Church	2000	114,084	123,181	$232,848,597	$2,041.03	$1,
Wisconsin Evangelical Lutheran Synod	1999	316,386	721,665	$223,183,803	$705.42	$3

*National Council of the Churches of Christ in the U.S.A. member communion

Summary Statitis

				TOTAL CONTRIBUTIONS		
Nation	Number Reporting	Full or Confirmed Members	Inclusive Members	Total Contributions	Per Capita Full or Confirmed Members	Per Incl Mer
United States	65	44,401,451	49,178,675	$29,464,889,024	$663.60	$59
Canada	28	31,925,671	34,116,123	$20,207,164,577	$632.94	$59

nances—United States Churches *(continued)*

ONGREGATIONAL FINANCES			BENEVOLENCES			
Total gregation tributions	Per Capita Full or Confirmed Members	Per Capita Inclusive Members	Total Benevolences	Per Capita Full or Confirmed Members	Per Capita Inclusive Members	Benevolences as a Percentage
,415,000		$32.16	$155,860		$3.54	10%
4,711,754	$1,794.39	$1,661.88	$28,136,843	$246.63	$228.42	12%
8,509,021	$564.21	$247.36	$44,674,782	$141.20	$61.91	20%

ˆ Church Finances

ONGREGATIONAL FINANCES			BENEVOLENCES			
Total gregational ıtributions	Per Capita Full or Confirmed Members	Per Capita Inclusive Members	Total Belevolences	Per Capita Full or Confirmed Members	Per Capita Inclusive Members	Benevolences as a Percentage of Total Contributions
ı75,897,453	$551.24	$497.69	$4,988,352,266	$112.35	$101.43	17%
268,238,206	$509.57	$476.85	$3,939,906,371	$123.38	$115.46	19%

Trends in Seminary Enrollment

Data Provided by The Association of Theological Schools (ATS) in the United States and Canada

Table 1: ATS total student enrollment figures include the number of individuals enrolled in degree progr well as persons enrolled in non-degree programs of study. Growth in total enrollment is a function c increased enrollment in the seminaries and the increased number of member schools in the Association. Th count enrollment in all member schools increased by 7,091 students, an increase of 10.8% from fall 1996 2000. Over the same five years, the full-time equivalent (FTE) enrollment increased by 10.3%.

Table 1 Number of Member Schools from 1988 to 2000

Year	Number of Schools	Total Enrollment	Canada Head Count	Canada FTE	United States Head Count	United States FTE	By Membership Accredited	By Membership Non-Accr
1988	207	55,746	3,995	2,679	51,751	34,827	51,683	4,063
1989	205	56,178	4,142	2,668	52,036	35,013	52,949	3,229
1990	211	59,003	4,053	2,636	54,950	37,590	54,052	4,951
1991	211	59,897	4,648	2,631	55,249	36,456	55,028	4,869
1992	220	63,484	4,897	2,999	58,587	39,554	57,784	5,700
1993	219	63,429	5,040	3,150	58,389	39,506	57,823	5,606
1994	226	65,089	5,241	3,212	59,848	40,293	60,490	4,599
1995	224	64,480	5,203	3,267	59,277	39,834	59,813	4,667
1996	233	65,637	5,568	3,304	60,069	40,111	60,527	5,110
1997	229	65,361	5,544	3,225	59,817	40,022	61,498	3,863
1998	237	68,875	5,847	3,683	63,028	40,994	64,412	4,463
1999	237	70,432	6,010	3,224	64,422	41,528	65,674	4,758
2000	243	72,728	5,868	3,251	68,860	44,627	69,850	2,878

Table 2: ATS computes enrollment both by the total number of individual students (Head Count) and the alent of full-time students (FTE). If all students were enrolled full-time, the Head Count number and the fu equivalency number would be the same. The FTE is calculated by dividing the total number of credits re for the degree by the number of semesters prescribed for degree duration to determine the average academi The total of credit hours taken by all students in a given degree program in a semester is then divided by th age academic load. During the last five years, full-time equivalent enrollment as a percentage of head count ment has generally decreased, indicating an increasing number of part-time students. The enrollment fig 2000 run counter to this trend.

Table 2 Head Count and FTE for all Member Schools 1988 to 2000

Year	Head Count	% Change	FTE	% Change	FTE % of Head C
1988	55,746	-0.04	37,506	-2.15	67.3%
1989	56,178	0.77	37,681	0.47	67.1%
1990	59,003	5.03	40,226	6.75	68.2%
1991	59,897	1.52	39,087	-2.83	65.3%
1992	63,484	5.99	42,553	8.87	67.0%
1993	63,429	0.09	42,656	0.24	67.2%
1994	65,089	2.62	43,505	1.99	66.8%
1995	64,480	-0.94	43,101	-0.93	66.8%
1996	65,637	1.79	43,414	0.73	66.1%
1997	65,361	-0.42	43,247	-0.38	66.2%
1998	68,875	5.38	44,678	3.31	64.9%
1999	70,432	2.17	44,845	0.68	63.7%
2000	72,728	3.26	47,876	6.76	65.8%

ble 3: ATS member schools offer a variety of degree programs, as reflected in Table 3. Table 3 displays enroll- by categories of degree programs. The Master of Divinity (M.Div.) degree is the normative degree to pre- persons for ordained ministry and for pastoral and religious leadership responsibilities in congregations. The v. experienced the largest increase in the *number* of students enrolled from fall 1996 to fall 2000, an increase 3%. In the same five-year period, the greatest increases by *percentage* in student head count enrollment were Master of Arts in a variety of specialized ministry areas (+39.43%) within the Basic Ministerial Leadership -M.Div.) category. This is followed by an increase (in the same degree category of 19.81% in the Master of ral Studies degree program.

e 3 Head Count Enrollment by Degree Categories 1988–2000
gories based on accrediting standards—adopted in 1996)

ar	Basic Ministerial Leadership (M.Div.)	Basic Ministerial Leadership (Non-M.Div.)	General Theological Studies	Advanced Ministerial Leadership	Advanced Theological Research	Others
88	26,581	5,131	5,423	6,511	4,203	7,897
89	25,954	5,080	5,485	7,004	4,186	8,469
90	25,615	5,284	6,144	7,417	5,046	9,497
91	25,710	5,805	6,105	7,598	5,044	9,635
92	26,956	5,812	6,872	7,961	5,036	10,847
93	27,264	6,536	7,131	8,302	5,157	9,039
94	27,240	6,891	7,229	7,841	5,330	10,558
95	27,497	6,964	7,211	8,233	5,302	9,273
96	28,035	7,474	7,157	8,315	5,499	9,157
97	28,283	7,463	7,048	8,195	5,391	8,981
98	29,263	8,066	7,601	8,641	5,712	9,591
99	29,842	8,361	7,862	8,743	5,396	10,228
00	30,427	9,098	8,436	8,758	5,692	10,317

ble 4: In fall 2000, women constituted 34.91% of the total enrollment in all ATS schools and 30.87% of the count enrollment in the M.Div. degree program. When ATS first began gathering enrollment data by gender 72, women represented 10.2% of the enrollment. Only once in the past 25 years has the number of women ents decreased from one year to the next, that being in 1993, with a 0.65% decrease.

e 4 Women Student Head Count Enrollment 1988–2000

Year	Number of Students	% Annual Increase	% of Total Enrollment
1988	16,326	0.00	29.29%
1989	16,525	1.20	29.42%
1990	17,498	5.56	29.66%
1991	18,188	3.79	30.37%
1992	19,856	8.40	31.28%
1993	19,727	-0.65	31.10%
1994	20,564	4.07	31.59%
1995	20,795	1.12	32.25%
1996	21,523	3.50	32.76%
1997	21,652	0.60	33.10%
1998	23,176	7.04	33.65%
1999	24,057	3.73	34.16%
2000	25,391	5.55	34.91%

Tables 5, 6, 7: Enrollment of North American racial/ethnic minority students in ATS schools has grown from of total head count enrollment in 1977 to 20.75% in 2000. Over the past five years (1996 to 2000), the numb African American students increased by 29.03%; Hispanic students by 50.42%; and Pacific/Asian American stu by 11.38%. Tables 5, 6, and 7 show the number of African American, Hispanic, and Pacific/Asian American stu enrolled by year.

Table 5 African American Student Head Count Enrollment 1988 to 2000

Year	Number of Students	% Annual Increase	% of Total Enrollment
1988	3,660	8.72	6.57%
1989	3,925	6.75	6.99%
1990	4,265	7.97	7.23%
1991	4,658	8.44	7.78%
1992	5,558	16.19	8.75%
1993	5,223	-6.41	8.23%
1994	5,526	5.48	8.49%
1995	5,698	3.11	8.84%
1996	5,550	-2.60	8.45%
1997	5,802	4.54	8.87%
1998	6,328	9.07	9.19%
1999	6,854	8.31	9.73%
2000	7,161	4.48	9.85%

Table 6 Hispanic Student Head Count Enrollment 1988–2000

Year	Number of Students	% Annual Increase	% of Total Enrollment
1988	1,415	1.13	2.54%
1989	1,485	4.71	2.64%
1990	1,912	22.33	3.24%
1991	1,626	-17.59	2.71%
1992	1,689	3.73	2.66%
1993	1,790	5.64	2.82%
1994	1,799	0.50	2.76%
1995	1,817	1.00	2.82%
1996	1,785	-1.76	2.72%
1997	1,915	7.28	2.93%
1998	2,176	13.58	3.16%
1999	2,256	3.72	3.10%
2000	2,685	19.02	3.69%

Table 7 Pacific/Asian American Student Head Count Enrollment 1988–2000

Year	Number of Students	% Annual Increase	% of Total Enrollment
1988	1,963	13.75	3.52%
1989	2,062	4.80	3.67%
1990	2,437	15.39	4.13%
1991	2,649	8.00	4.42%
1992	3,142	15.69	4.95%
1993	3,631	13.47	5.72%
1994	3,876	6.32	5.95%
1995	4,245	9.52	6.58%
1996	4,492	5.82	6.84%
1997	4,545	1.18	6.95%
1998	4,992	8.95	7.25%
1999	4,932	-1.20	6.78%
2000	5,003	1.44	6.88%

IV

A CALENDAR FOR CHURCH USE

2002–2005

This Calendar presents for a four-year period the major days of religious observances for Christians, Jews, Baha'is, and Muslims; and, within the Christian community, major dates observed by Roman Catholic, Eastern and Oriental Orthodox, Episcopal, and Lutheran churches. Within each of these communions many other days of observance, such as saints' days, exist, but only those regarded as major are listed. Dates of interest to many Protestant communions are also included.

In the Orthodox dates, immovable observances are listed in accordance with the Gregorian calendar. Movable dates (those depending on the date of Easter) often will differ from Western days, since the date of Easter (Pascha) in the Orthodox communions does not always correlate with the date for Easter of the Western churches. For Orthodox churches that use the old Julian calendar, observances are held thirteen days later than listed here.

For Jews and Muslims, who follow differing lunar calendars, the dates of major observances are translated into Gregorian dates. Since the actual beginning of a new month in the Islamic calendar is determined by the appearance of the new moon, the corresponding dates given here on the Gregorian calendar may vary slightly. Following the lunar calendar, Muslim dates fall roughly eleven days earlier each year on the Gregorian calendar.

(Note: "RC" stands for Roman Catholic, "O" for Orthodox, "E" for Episcopal, "L" for Lutheran, "ECU" for Ecumenical, "M" for Muslim).

Event	**2002**	**2003**	**2004**	**2005**
New Year's Day (RC-Solemnity of Mary; O-Circumcision of Jesus Christ; E-Feast of Holy Name; L-Naming of Jesus)	Jan 01	Jan 01	Jan 01	Jan 01
Epiphany (Christian)	Jan 06	Jan 05	Jan 04	Jan 05
Armenian Christmas (O)	Jan 06	Jan 06	Jan 06	Jan 06
Feast Day of St. John the Baptist (Armenian O)	Jan 13	Jan 13	Jan 13	Jan 13
First Sunday After Epiphany (Feast of the Baptism of Our Lord) (Christian)	Jan 13	Jan 12	Jan 11	Jan 09
Week of Prayer for Christian Unity (ECU)	Jan 18	Jan 18	Jan 18	Jan 18
Theophany (Oriental O)	Jan 19	Jan 19	Jan 19	Jan 19
Ecumenical Sunday (ECU)	Jan 20	Jan 19	Jan 18	Jan 16
Week of Prayer for Christian Unity, Canada (ECU)	Jan 21	Jan 20	Jan 19	Jan 17
Tu B'Shevat (Jewish)	Jan 28	Jan 18	Feb 07	Jan 25
Presentation of Jesus in the Temple (Candlemas; Purification of the Virgin Mary; O—The Meeting of Our Lord and Savior Jesus Christ) (Christian)	Feb 02	Feb 02	Feb 02	Feb 02
Ash Wednesday (Western Churches)	Feb 13	Mar 05	Feb 25	Feb 02
Brotherhood Week (Interfaith)	Feb 17	Feb 16	Feb 15	Feb 20
Waqf al Arafah (Eve of Eid al-Adha) (Muslim)	Feb 21	Feb 10	Jan 31	Jan 19
Eid al-Adha (Festival of Sacrifice at time of Pilgrimage to Mecca) (Muslim)	Feb 23	Feb 12	Feb 02	Jan 21
Purim (Jewish)	Feb 26	Mar 18	Mar 07	Mar 25
World Day of Prayer (ECU)	Mar 01	Mar 07	Mar 05	Mar 04
Baha'i Fasting Season begins (19 days) (Baha'i)	Mar 02	Mar 02	Mar 02	Mar 02
Muharram Begins (First Day of the Month of Muharram; Muslim New Year) (Muslim)	Mar 15	Mar 05	Feb 22	Feb 10
Great Lent (First Day of Lent) (O)	Mar 18	Mar 10	Mar 01	Mar 14

Event	2002	2003	2004	2005
Joseph, Husband of Mary (RC, E, L)	Mar 19	Mar 19	Mar 19	Mar 19
Feast of Naw-Ruz (Baha'i New Year) (Baha'i)	Mar 21	Mar 21	Mar 21	Mar 21
Holy Week (Western Churches)	Mar 22	Apr 14	Apr 04	Mar 20
Ashura' (Martyrdom of Imam Hussein) (Muslim [Shi'a])	Mar 24	Mar 14	Mar 02	Feb 19
The Annunciation (Christian)	Mar 25	Mar 25	Mar 25	Mar 25
Holy Thursday (Western Churches)	Mar 28	Apr 17	Apr 08	Mar 24
Passover (Pesach) (8 days) (Jewish)	Mar 28	Apr 17	Apr 06	Apr 24
Good Friday (Friday of the Passion of Our Lord) (Western Churches)	Mar 29	Apr 18	Apr 09	Mar 25
Easter (Western Churches)	Mar 31	Apr 20	Apr 11	Mar 27
Yom Hashoah (Jewish)	Apr 09	Apr 29	Apr 18	May 06
Yom Haatzmaut (Jewish)	Apr 17	May 07	Apr 26	May 12
Feast of Ridvan (Declaration of Baha'u'llah) (12 days) (Baha'i)	Apr 21	Apr 21	Apr 21	Apr 21
Palm Sunday (O)	Apr 28	Apr 20	Apr 04	Apr 24
Holy Week (O)	Apr 28	Apr 20	Apr 04	Apr 24
Lag B'Omer (Jewish)	Apr 30	May 20	May 09	May 27
National Day of Prayer (ECU)	May 02	May 01	May 06	May 05
Holy Thursday (O)	May 02	Apr 24	Apr 08	Apr 28
May Fellowship Day (ECU)	May 03	May 02	May 07	May 06
Holy Friday (Good Friday; Burial of Jesus Christ) (O)	May 03	Apr 25	Apr 09	Apr 29
Pascha (Orthodox Easter) (O)	May 05	Apr 27	Apr 11	May 01
Ascension Thursday (Western Churches)	May 09	May 29	May 20	Apr 28
Rural Life Sunday (ECU)	May 12	May 11	May 09	May 08
Shavuout (Pentecost) (2 days) (Jewish)	May 17	Jun 06	May 26	Jun 13
Declaration of the Bab (Baha'i)	May 23	May 23	May 23	May 23
Pentecost (Whitsunday) (Western Churches)	May 19	Jun 08	May 30	May 15
Declaration of the Bab (Baha'i)	May 23	May 23	May 23	May 23
Mawlid an-Nabi (Anniversary of the Prophet Muhammed's Birthday) (Muslim)	May 24	May 14	Jul 02	Apr 21
Holy Trinity (RC, E, L)	May 26	Jun 15	Jun 06	May 22
Ascension of Baha'u'llah (Baha'i)	May 29	May 29	May 29	May 29
Visitation of the Blessed Virgin Mary (RC, E, L)	May 31	May 31	May 31	May 31
Corpus Christi (RC)	Jun 02	Jun 22	Jun 13	May 29
Sacred Heart of Jesus (RC)	Jun 07	Jun 27	Jun 18	Jun 10
Martyrdom of the Bab (Baha'i)	Jun 09	Jun 09	Jun 09	Jun 09
Ascension Day (O)	Jun 13	Jun 05	May 20	Jun 02
Pentecost (O)	Jun 23	Jun 15	May 30	Jun 19
Nativity of St. John the Baptist (RC, E, L)	Jun 24	Jun 24	Jun 24	Jun 24
Saint Peter and Saint Paul, Apostles of Christ (O)	Jun 29	Jun 29	Jun 29	Jun 29
Feast Day of the Twelve Apostles of Christ (O)	Jun 30	Jun 30	Jun 30	Jun 30
Tisha B'Av (Jewish)	Jul 18	Aug 07	Jul 27	Aug 14
Transfiguration of the Lord (RC, O, E)	Aug 06	Aug 06	Aug 06	Aug 06
Assumption of the Blessed Virgin Mary (E-Feast of the Blessed Virgin Mary; O-Falling Asleep) (Domition of the Blessed Virgin) (RC, O, E)	Aug 15	Aug 15	Aug 15	Aug 15
Rosh Hashanah (New Year) (2 days) (Jewish)	Sep 07	Sep 27	Sep 16	Oct 04
The Birth of the Blessed Virgin (RC,O)	Sep 08	Sep 08	Sep 08	Sep 08
Holy Cross Day (RC-Triumph of the Cross); (O-Adoration of the Holy Cross) (Christian)	Sep 14	Sep 14	Sep 14	Sep 14
Yom Kippur (Day of Atonement) (Jewish)	Sep 16	Oct 06	Sep 25	Oct 13
Sukkot (Tabernacles) (7 days) (Jewish)	Sep 21	Oct 11	Sep 30	Oct 18
Sh'mini Atzeret (Solemn Assembly (Jewish)	Sep 28	Oct 18	Oct 07	Oct 25
Simchat Torah (Rejoicing of the Law) (Jewish)	Sep 29	Oct 19	Oct 08	Oct 26
Michaelmas (St. Michael and All Angels) (Christian)	Sep 29	Sep 29	Sep 29	Sep 29
Laylat al Miraj (Ascent of the Prophet) (Muslim)	Oct 04	Sep 24	Sep 12	Sep 01
World Communion Sunday (ECU)	Oct 06	Oct 05	Oct 03	Oct 02
Laity Sunday (ECU)	Oct 13	Oct 12	Oct 10	Oct 09

Event	2002	2003	2004	2005
Thanksgiving Day (Canada) (National)	Oct 14	Oct 13	Oct 11	Oct 10
Birth of the Bab (Baha'i)	Oct 20	Oct 20	Oct 20	Oct 20
Laylat al Bara'a (Muslim)	Oct 22	Oct 12	Sep 30	Sep 19
Reformation Sunday (L)	Oct 27	Oct 26	Oct 31	Oct 30
Reformation Day (L)	Oct 31	Oct 31	Oct 31	Oct. 31
All Saints Day (RC, E, L)	Nov 01	Nov 01	Nov 01	Nov 01
Ramadan Begins (First day of the month of Ramadan) (Muslim)	Nov 06	Oct 27	Oct 15	Oct 04
World Community Day (ECU)	Nov 07	Nov 06	Nov 04	Nov 03
Birth of Baha'u'llah (Baha'i)	Nov 12	Nov 12	Nov 12	Nov 12
Bible Sunday (ECU)	Nov 17	Nov 16	Nov 21	Nov 20
National Bible Week (ECU)	Nov 17	Nov 16	Nov 21	Nov 20
Thanksgiving Sunday (U.S.) (Christian)	Nov 17	Nov 16	Nov 21	Nov 20
Presentation of the Blessed Virgin Mary in the Temple (Presentation of the Theotokos) (O)	Nov 21	Nov 21	Nov 21	Nov 21
Thanksgiving Day (U.S.) (National)	Nov 22	Nov 28	Nov 27	Nov 25
Last Sunday After Pentecost (L-Feast of Christ the King) (RC, L)	Nov 24	Nov 23	Nov 21	Nov 20
The Day of the Covenant (Baha'i)	Nov 26	Nov 26	Nov 26	Nov 26
Ascension of 'Abdu'l-Baha (Baha'i)	Nov 28	Nov 28	Nov 28	Nov 28
Thanksgiving Day (U.S.) (National)	Nov 28	Nov 27	Nov 25	Nov 24
Hanukkah (Chanukah, Festival of Lights) (8 days) (Jewish)	Nov 30	Dec 20	Dec 08	Dec 25
Feast Day of St. Andrew the Apostle (RC, O, E, L)	Nov 30	Nov 30	Nov 30	Nov 30
First Sunday of Advent (Advent Sunday) (Christian)	Dec 01	Nov 30	Nov 28	Nov 27
Laylat al Qadr (Night of Destiny, Revelation of the Holy Qur'an) (Muslim)	Dec 02	Nov 22	Nov 10	Oct 30
Eid al- Fitr (Festival of the End of Ramadan; First day of the month of Shawwal) (Muslim)	Dec 06	Nov 26	Nov 14	Nov 03
Immaculate Conception of the Blessed Virgin May (RC)	Dec 08	Dec 08	Dec 08	Dec 08
Fourth Sunday of Advent (Christmas Sunday) (Christian)	Dec 22	Dec 21	Dec 19	Dec 18
Christmas (Christian Except Armenian)	Dec 25	Dec 25	Dec 25	Dec 25

V
INDEXES
Organizations

INDEX

INDEX

INDEX

INDEX

INDEX

Individuals

INDEX

INDEX

INDEX

INDEX

INDEX

INDEX

INDEX

INDEX

INDEX

INDEX

INDEX

INDEX

INDEX

INDEX

INDEX

INDEX

INDEX

INDEX

INDEX

INDEX

INDEX

INDEX

INDEX

3. Gellman, *Good Neighbor Diplomacy*, 191–93; R. A. Humphreys, *Latin America and the Second World War*, 2 vols. (London: University of London Athlone Press, 1982), 2, chap. 6; Randall Bennett Woods, *The Roosevelt Foreign-Policy Establishment and the "Good Neighbor": The United States and Argentina, 1941–1945* (Lawrence: Regents Press of Kansas, 1979), chaps. 1–3.

4. Gellman, *Good Neighbor Diplomacy*, 196–97.

5. Gellman, *Good Neighbor Diplomacy*, chap. 14; Gaddis Smith, *The Last Years of the Monroe Doctrine, 1945–1993* (New York: Hill and Wang, 1994), 44.

6. Stephen G. Rabe, "The Elusive Conference: United States Economic Relations with Latin America, 1945–1952," *Diplomatic History* 2 (Summer 1978): 279; Humphreys, *Latin America*, 2, chap. 8.

7. Humphreys, *Latin America*, 215, chap. 2.

8. Rabe, "Elusive Conference," 281–82.

9. Humphreys, *Latin America*, 216–17, chap. 2.

10. Smith, *Last Years*, 43, 48–49, 55; Humphreys, *Latin America*, 220–21, chap. 2.

11. Walter LaFeber, *America, Russia, and the Cold War, 1945–1992*, 7th ed. (New York: McGraw-Hill, 1993), chap. 1; Howard Jones and Randall B. Woods, "Origins of the Cold War in Europe and the New East: Recent Historiography and the National Security Imperative," in *America in the World: The Historiography of American Foreign Relations since 1941*, ed. Michael J. Hogan (New York: Cambridge University Press, 1995), chap. 9.

12. Smith, *Last Years*, 56.

13. Thomas G. Paterson and Dennis Merrill, eds., *Major Problems in American Foreign Relations*, 2 vols., 4th ed. (Lexington, MA: D. C. Heath, 1995), 259–61, chap. 2.

14. Smith, *Last Years*, 56.

15. Roger R. Trask, "The Impact of the Cold War on United States-Latin American Relations, 1945–1949," *Diplomatic History* 1 (Summer 1977): 277.

16. Trask, "The Impact of the Cold War," 274; Trask, "Spruille Braden versus George Messersmith: World War II, the Cold War, and Argentine Policy, 1945–1947," *Journal of Inter-American Studies and World Affairs* 26 (February 1984): 69–95; Jesse H. Stiller, *George S. Messersmith: Diplomat of Democracy* (Chapel Hill: University of North Carolina Press, 1987), chap. 7.

17. Trask, "Impact of the Cold War," 277–79; Smith, *Last Years*, 58–59.

18. Trask, "Impact of the Cold War," 277–78; Rabe, "Elusive Conference," 285.

19. Smith, *Last Years*, 62.

20. Trask, "Impact of the Cold War," 279–80.

21. Stephen J. Randall, *Colombia and the United States: Hegemony and Interdependence* (Athens: University of Georgia Press, 1992), 192–94; Trask, "Impact of the Cold War," 281–82. See also Herbert Braun, *The Assassination of Gaitán: Public Life and Urban Violence in Colombia.* (Madison: University of Wisconsin Press, 1986).

22. Trask, "Impact of the Cold War," 281–82.

23. O. Carlos Stoetzer, *The Organization of American States*, 2d ed. (Westport, CT: Praeger, 1993), 35.

24. Leslie Bethell and Ian Roxborough, "Latin America between the Second World War and the Cold War: Some Reflections on the 1945–8 Conjuncture," *Journal of Latin American Studies* 20 (May 1988): 167–89.

25. Leslie Bethell and Ian Roxborough, eds., *Latin America between the Second World War and the Cold War: Crisis and Containment, 1944–1948* (New York: Cambridge University Press, 1994), 1–2.

26. Bethell and Roxborough, eds., *Latin America*, 1–7, 10–20, 22–23, 26–28.

27. LaFeber, *America, Russia, and the Cold War*, 96.

28. Smith, *Last Years*, 66; LaFeber, *America, Russia, and the Cold War*, 96–97; Ernest R. May, ed., *American Cold War Strategy: Interpreting NSC 68* (Boston: St. Martin's Press, 1993).

29. Smith, *Last Years*, 61, 67–68.

30. Roger R. Trask, "George F. Kennan's Report on Latin America (1950)," *Diplomatic History* 2 (Summer 1978): 307–11.

31. Smith, *Last Years*, 69–71.

32. Bruce Cummings, *The Origins of the Korean War*, 2 vols. (Princeton: Princeton University Press, 1981, 1990) states a revisionist case. Burton I. Kaufman, *The Korean War: Challenges in Crisis, Credibility, and Command* (New York: Alfred A. Knopf, 1986); and William W. Stueck, *The Korean War: An International History* (Princeton: Princeton University Press, 1995), take more traditional approaches.

33. Stueck, *Korean War*, 194.

34. Gordon Connell-Smith, *The United States and Latin America: An Historical Analysis of Inter-American Relations* (New York: John Wiley & Sons, 1974).

35. Randall, *Colombia and the United States*, 199. See also Bradley Coleman, *Colombia and the United States: The Making of an Inter-American Alliance, 1939-1960* (Kent, OH: The Kent State University Press), 2008.

36. Stueck, *Korean War*, 198.

37. Connell-Smith, *United States and Latin America*, 207.

38. Connell-Smith, *United States and Latin America*, 207; Edwin Lieuwen, *Arms and Politics in Latin America*, rev. ed. (New York: Frederick A. Praeger, 1961), 198–202.

39. LaFeber, *America, Russia, and the Cold War*, 136.

40. Stephen G. Rabe, *Eisenhower and Latin America: The Foreign Policy of Anticommunism* (Chapel Hill: University of North Carolina Press, 1988), 6.

41. Stephen G. Rabe, *Eisenhower and Latin America*, 1–5, 26; Mary S. McAulliffe, "Commentary: Eisenhower, the President," *Journal of American History* 68 (December 1981): 625–32; Fred I. Greenstein, *The Hidden-Hand Presidency: Eisenhower as Leader* (New York: Basic Books, 1982); Mark T. Gilderhus, "An Emerging Synthesis? U.S.-Latin American Relations since 1945," in Hogan, *America in the World*, 445–50. See also Stephen Kinzer, *The Brothers: John Foster Dulles, Allen Dulles, and Their Secret World War* (New York: Times Books), 2013.

42. Rabe, *Eisenhower and Latin America*, 26–29; H. W. Brands, Jr., "Milton Eisenhower and the Coming Revolution in Latin America," in Brands, *Cold Warriors: Eisenhower's Generation and American Foreign Policy* (New York: Columbia University Press, 1988); Milton S. Eisenhower, *The Wine Is Bitter: The United States and Latin America* (Garden City, NY: Doubleday, 1963), chap. 2.

43. Rabe, *Eisenhower and Latin America*, 29–30.

44. Robert J. McMahon, "Eisenhower and Third World Nationalism: A Critique of the Revisionists," *Political Science Review* 101 (Fall 1986): 457.

45. Rabe, *Eisenhower and Latin America*, 30–36; Chester J. Pach, Jr., *Arming the Free World: The Origins of the United States Military Assistance Program, 1945–1950* (Chapel Hill: University of North Carolina Press, 1991), chap. 2; Lieuwen, *Arms and Politics*, chaps. 8–9.

46. Gilderhus, "An Emerging Synthesis?" 444; Bryce Wood, *The Dismantling of the Good Neighbor Policy* (Austin: University of Texas Press, 1985), chap. 9; Richard H. Immerman, *The CIA in Guatemala: The Foreign Policy of Intervention* (Austin: University of Texas Press, 1982); Piero Gleijeses, *Shattered Hope: The Guatemalan Revolution and the United States, 1944–1954* (Princeton: Princeton University Press, 1991).

47. Kenneth J. Grieb, *Guatemalan Caudillo: The Regime of Jorge Ubico, Guatemala, 1931–1944* (Athens: Ohio University Press, 1979), 18, 21.

48. Rabe, *Eisenhower and Latin America*, 43–47.

49. Smith, *Last Years*, 75–78.

50. Stephen E. Ambrose and Richard H. Immerman, *Ike's Spies: Eisenhower and the Espionage Establishment* (Garden City, NY: Doubleday, 1981); John Prados, *Presidents' Secret Wars: CIA and Pentagon Covert Operations since World War II* (New York: William Morrow, 1986); Rhodri Jeffreys-Jones, *The CIA and American Democracy* (New Haven: Yale University Press, 1989); Charles D. Ameringer, *U.S. Foreign Intelligence: The Secret Side of American History* (Lexington, MA: D. C. Heath, 1990).

51. Smith, *Last Years*, 70, 78; Wood, *Dismantling of the Good Neighbor Policy*; Immerman, *CIA in Guatemala*; Gleijeses, *Shattered Hope*.

52. Rabe, *Eisenhower and Latin America*, 49–56.

53. Smith, *Last Years*, 82–86; Rabe, *Eisenhower and Latin America*, 56.

54. Rabe, *Eisenhower and Latin America*, 64; Burton I. Kaufman, *Trade and Aid: Eisenhower's Foreign Economic Policy, 1953–1961* (Baltimore: Johns Hopkins University Press, 1982).

55. Rabe, *Eisenhower and Latin America*, 64–75.

56. Victor Bulmer-Thomas, *The Economic History of Latin America since Independence* (New York: Cambridge University Press, 1994), chaps. 8–9.

57. Rabe, *Eisenhower and Latin America*, 75–77. For consideration of an anomaly, see Kenneth Lehman, "Revolutions and Attributions: Making Sense of Eisenhower Administration Policies in Bolivia and Guatemala," *Diplomatic History* 21 (Spring 1997): 185–213.

58. Rabe, *Eisenhower and Latin America*, 86, 89–90, 92, 102, chap. 6; Richard M. Nixon, *Six Crises* (Garden City, NY: Doubleday, 1962), chap. 4.

59. Rabe, *Eisenhower and Latin America*, 114.

60. Tad Szulc, *Twilight of the Tyrants* (New York: W. W. Holt, 1959); Rabe, *Eisenhower and Latin America*, 107.

61. Rabe, *Eisenhower and Latin America*, 96–97, 110–14.

The twenty images that follow reflect both a long, sometimes contentious U.S.–Latin American relationship and the cultural uniqueness of the region. Most of the images were made recently by David LaFevor.

Chapter Five

Castro, Cuba, and Containment, 1959–1979

After 1959, the Cuban Revolution became the focal point of U.S. policy toward Latin America. Fidel Castro's triumph challenged the traditional relationship while espousing radical alternatives, thereby establishing an unacceptable precedent from Washington's perspective. Successive administrations responded with efforts to contain Castro's influence or to destroy it. Perceived as a communist vanguard in the Western Hemisphere, the new regime in Cuba provoked fears of Soviet encroachments in the Caribbean. It also provided an opportunity for asserting the utility of noncommunist models of economic development for the rest of Latin America and a justification for subsequent acts of intervention by the United States in the Dominican Republic, Chile, Central America, and elsewhere. During the ensuing decades, stalwart opposition to radical regimes became the hallmark of U.S. policy toward Latin America and the justification for supporting right-wing military dictatorships.

UNDER IKE

The rebel forces making up the 26th of July Movement took control of Havana, the capital city, on January 1, 1959. This victory marked the end of a three-year guerrilla struggle against Fulgencio Batista, the Cuban strongman who had dominated the island by one means or another since the 1930s. In 1952, Batista returned as the head of state, following a military coup d'état against president Carlos Prío Socarrás. Castro, the son of a Spanish immigrant and sugar planter, assumed the role of political activist and agitator as a young man. While earning a law degree at the University of Havana, he embraced the martyr of Cuban independence, José Martí, as his national hero. Martí's anti-imperialist ideas would form the intellectual justification for much of Castro's subsequent confrontation with the United States. On July 26, 1953, in defiance of Batista, he led a group of students in a failed attack on the Moncada army barracks in the southeastern city of Santiago. For his crime, he received a fifteen-year jail sentence but served only two, when Batista proclaimed an amnesty in 1955.

Castro and his brother Raúl then fled to Mexico City, where they planned an uprising against Batista for early December 1956. Following a harrowing, week-long voyage aboard an overcrowded, undersupplied, and unreliable vessel called *Granma,* eighty-one bedraggled, seasick invaders clambered ashore in a mangrove swamp at the southeastern end of the island, only to meet with disaster. Batista's waiting forces killed most of the insurrectionists within a few days. No more than twenty survivors, including Fidel, Raúl, and Ernesto "Che" Guevara, an Argentine expatriate who had witnessed U.S. covert intervention in Guatemala, withdrew into the mountains, the Sierra Maestra. From secret base camps, they attracted new recruits, mounted occasional attacks, and gradually extended the rebellion into the more populated regions. By the end of 1958, even though no clear idea of Castro's intentions had emerged, most of the Cuban people had turned against Batista.[1]

During the insurgency, Castro assumed an eclectic, nondoctrinaire stance. In one statement, the "History Will Absolve Me" speech, delivered at the end of his trial in 1953, he invoked José Martí's nationalism as the basis for reform and change. This lengthy self-defense drew on political philosophers ranging from Thomas Aquinas to John Locke. Among other things, he supported the principle of equality before the law, the restoration of constitutional rights, the distribution of land to landless farmers, the adoption of profit sharing for workers, the confiscation of illicit wealth stolen by public officials, and the nationalization of the electric and telephone companies.[2] His indictment of the Batista regime focused on domestic developmental issues, accusations of state-directed torture of political dissidents, and labeled the president a "criminal and a thief."[3] He gave another example of his eclecticism in a dramatic interview with Herbert Matthews, a *New York Times* correspondent, at a backcountry base in February 1957. On this occasion, Castro placed greater emphasis on reform than on radical change. He had not yet given final form to his programs. At this juncture, moreover, he lacked any particular attachment to Marxist-Leninist ideology, or to the Soviet Union. Indeed, the Cuban Communist Party—one of the largest in Latin America, with 17,000 members—regarded him as a putschist: an adventurer and potential suicidalist engaged in premature revolutionary action.[4]

Nevertheless, Castro's charismatic leadership capitalized on high levels of Cuban discontent, and the 26th of July Movement became the most visible of several armed insurrectionary groups. Under Batista, corruption, dissolu-

This print appeared in the satirical magazine *Puck* in January 1899, shortly after the Spanish-American War (1898) whereby the United States took control of Cuba, Puerto Rico, and the Philippines. Here, Uncle Sam is represented as a stern teacher instructing the "new" students: "Now children," says Uncle Sam, "you've got to learn these lessons whether you want to or not!" Published in *Puck*. (January 1899, New York).

This photograph of a Cuban farmer, or guajiro, was taken at the town of Ceiba Mocha, founded for Afro-descended Spanish subjects displaced by imperial rivalries over what is now the state of Florida. To this day, many in Latin America rely on animal power for labor and transportation. David LaFevor, 2014.

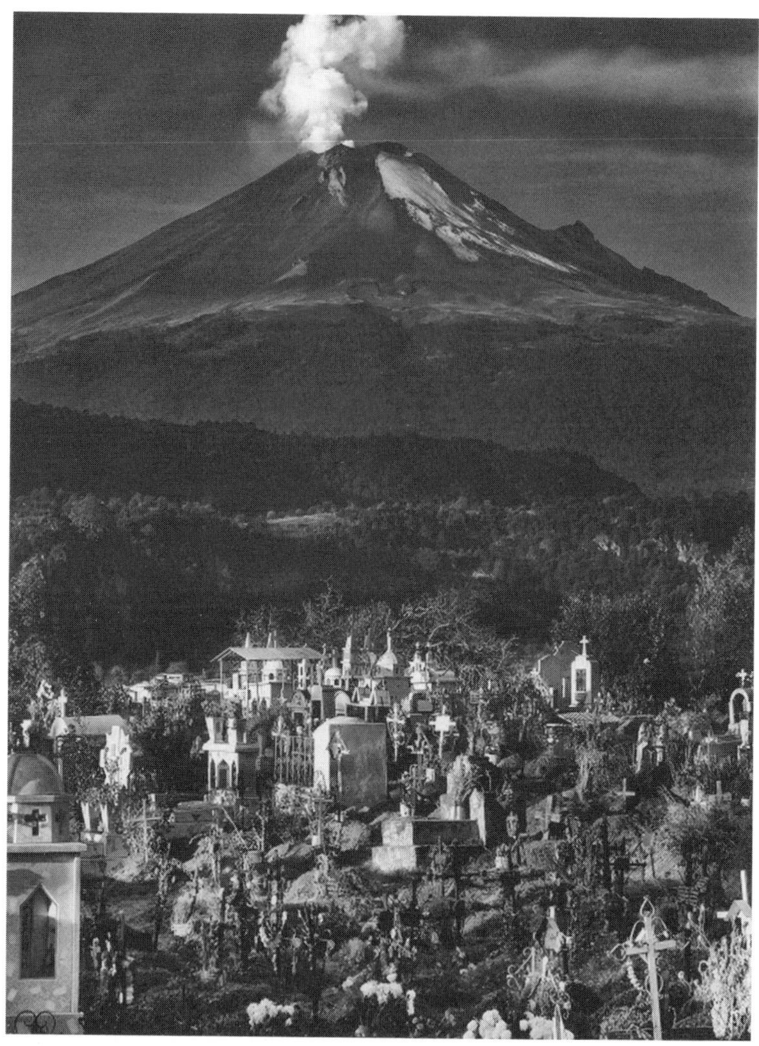

"El Popo," or Popocatépetl, is an active volcano and was a sacred site for pre-Columbian peoples such as the Nahua (Aztecs). Rights to exploit the land around the volcano (for tourism, sulfur, and ice mining) were sold to a New York–based company for $300,000 in 1904 during the rule of Porfirio Díaz (1872–1911), a period when U.S. investment in Mexico was strongly encouraged. David LaFevor, 2012.

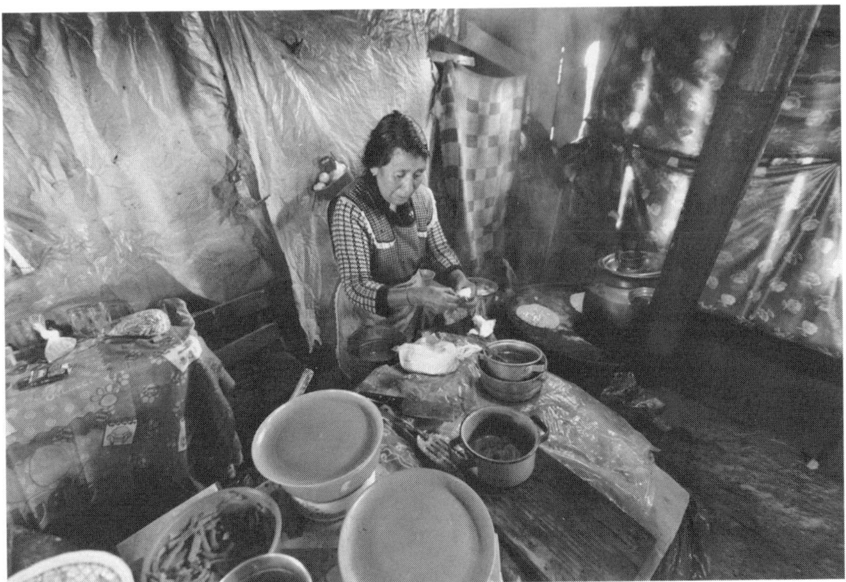

An indigenous woman prepares food at her roadside lunch stand. Many Latin Americans survive as entrepreneurs in the informal economy. While these types of livelihoods have a long tradition in the region, they pose challenges for taxation and "official" planning and are generally the first businesses to go bust when neoliberal economic reforms take hold. David LaFevor, 2012.

This scene is from the annual Festival del Caribe (Caribbean Festival) in Santiago de Cuba celebrating the peoples and cultures of the Caribbean. The religious procession combines Catholic and Santeria traditions; the festivity concludes with the traditional "Quema del Diablo"—a symbolic, ritualistic burning of the Devil. David LaFevor, 2008.

This print represents the Mexican Revolution (1910–1920) as a dangerous, unpredictable "mad dog." Uncle Sam stands poised to shoot the dog with a pistol labeled "Intervention" while European powers look on, helplessly, behind the wall of the [1823] Monroe Doctrine. "Mad Dog" by Udo Keppler. Published in *Puck* (August 1913, New York).

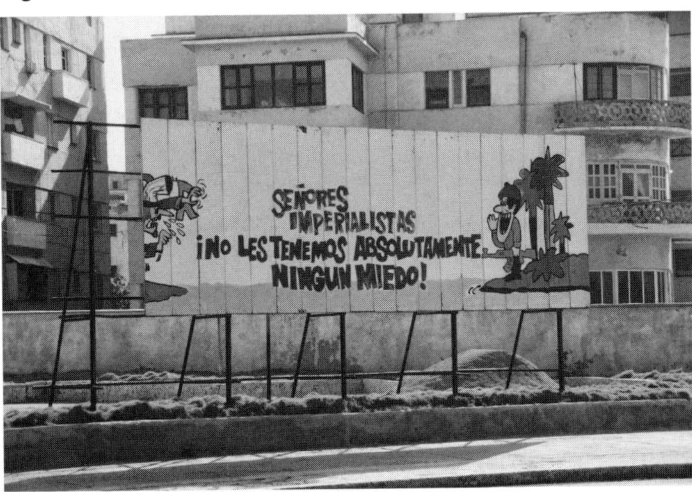

This Cuban billboard (2008) reflects the Castro government's defiant attitude toward U.S. political, economic, and cultural influences. The caption reads "Señores imperialistas: ¡No les tenemos absolutamente ningún miedo!" ("Gentlemen Capitalists: We are absolutely unafraid of you!") David LaFevor, 2008.

Taken at the General Assembly meeting of the United Nations in New York City, this photo shows new allies Fidel Castro and Nikita Khrushchev. The Cuban-Soviet relationship deeply influenced U.S.–Latin American relations during a thirty-year period through the collapse of the Soviet Union in 1989. Herman Miller, 1960. Archived at the Library of Congress in Washington, DC.

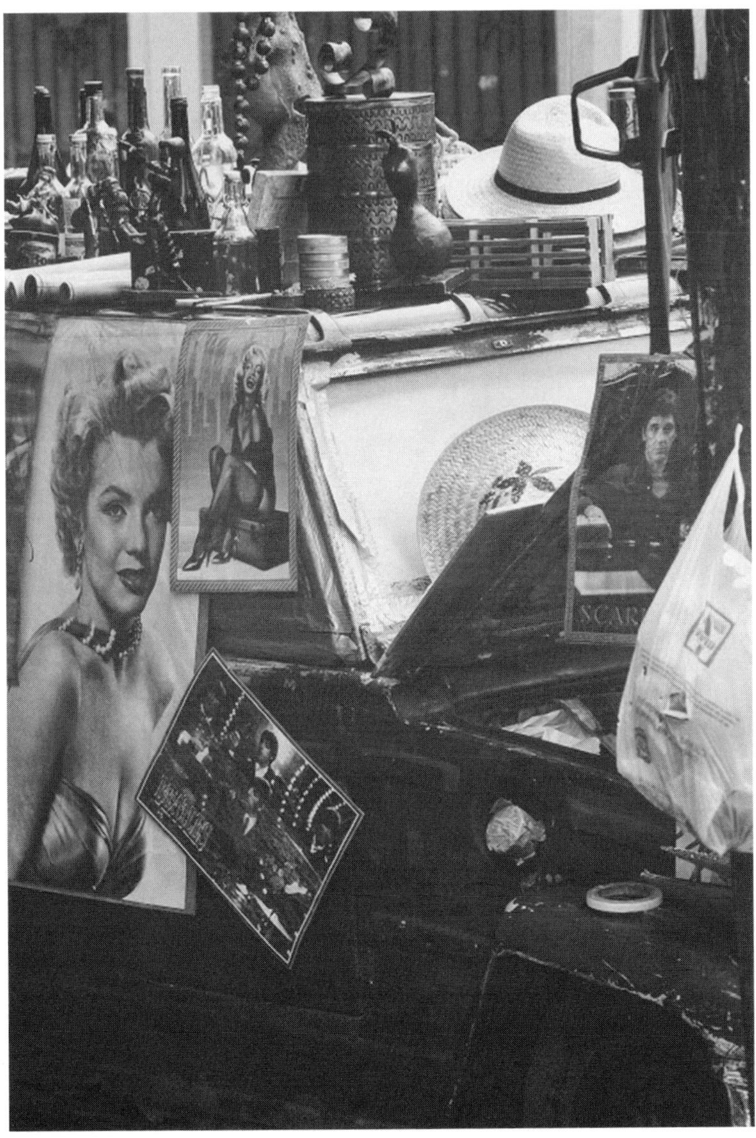

A street vendor in Mexico sells iconic images from the American film industry. For much of the twentieth century, many Latin Americans received their "American" education through U.S. films, and film stars like Marilyn Monroe and *Scarface*'s Al Pacino. New technology—the Internet—has created new opportunities and challenges in promoting transcontinental cultural contact and education. David LaFevor, 2007.

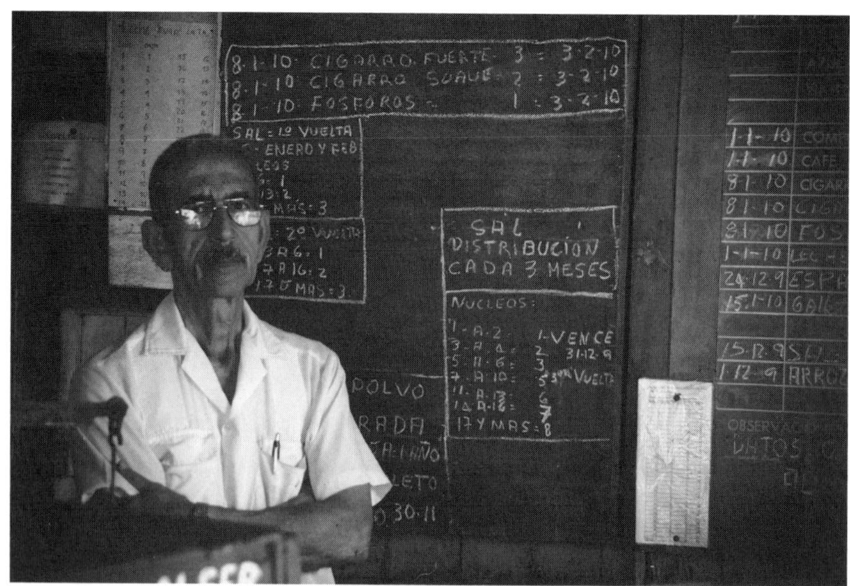

This neighborhood store in Havana sells heavily subsidized staple goods (Sal distribución cada tres meses): Salt distributed every three months. During the "Special Period" after the fall of the Soviet Union (1990–present), severe austerity became the norm for most Cubans—a reality clearly reflected in the resigned expression of the shopkeeper. David LaFevor, 2008.

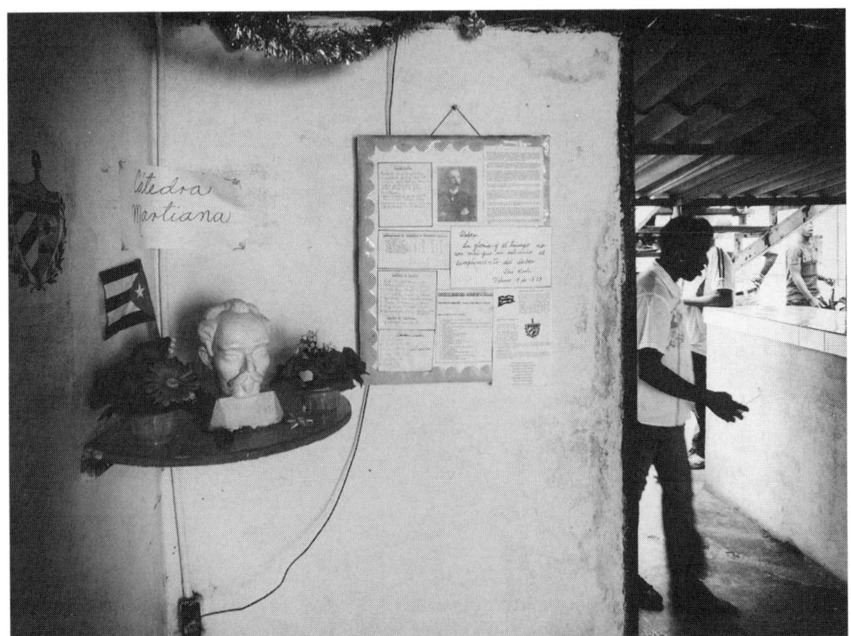

Athletes who enter this boxing gym in Old Havana must pass by a shrine to Cuban national hero, independence leader, and anti-imperialist, José Martí. Martí was killed in 1895 while fighting to liberate the island from Spanish domination. The juxtaposition of an imported cultural form (boxing) with a pan–Latin American hero (Martí) reflects the complexity of the U.S.-Latin American relationship. David LaFevor, 2008.

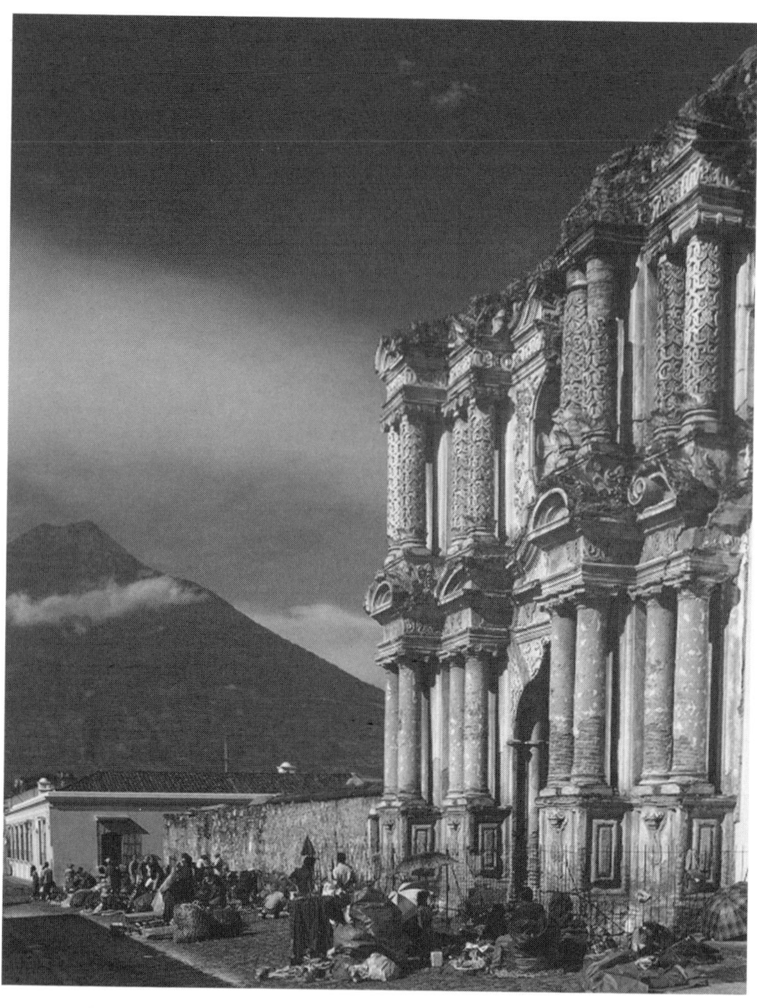

This scene of an informal indigenous market is situated in front of the ruins of a Catholic Church destroyed by the 1773 earthquake that leveled the city of Santiago de los Caballeros de Guatemala (today, Antigua). The sharp contrast between natural and built environment is reflected in this photograph, which also shows the resiliency of people who occupy that space. David LaFevor, 2009.

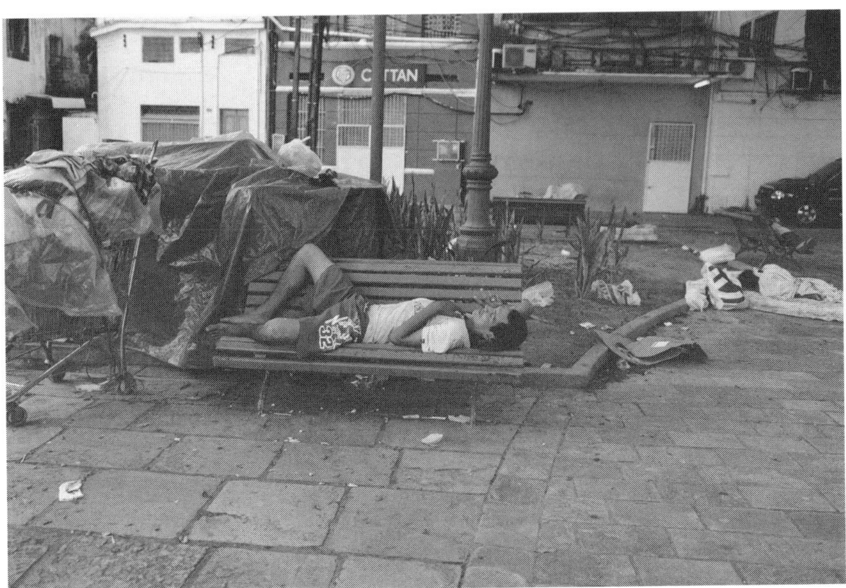

Latin America is the most urbanized region in the world. Rapid urbanization has created impressive concentrations of wealth amidst sprawling zones of poverty and despair. The cities, such as this scene from Medellín, Colombia's second largest urban area, reflect the greatest contrasts between the wealth and poverty that characterize the region. David LaFevor, 2010.

Migration from Mexico and Central America to the United States has added to the complexity of the U.S.-Latin American relationship. This sign, at a bus stop in Mexico City, displays the cover of a popular Mexican news magazine, *Cambio*, and suggests Mexican discontent with draconian anti-immigration laws passed in various U.S. states. It reads, "Arizona: Mexico Sends Greetings." David LaFevor, 2012.

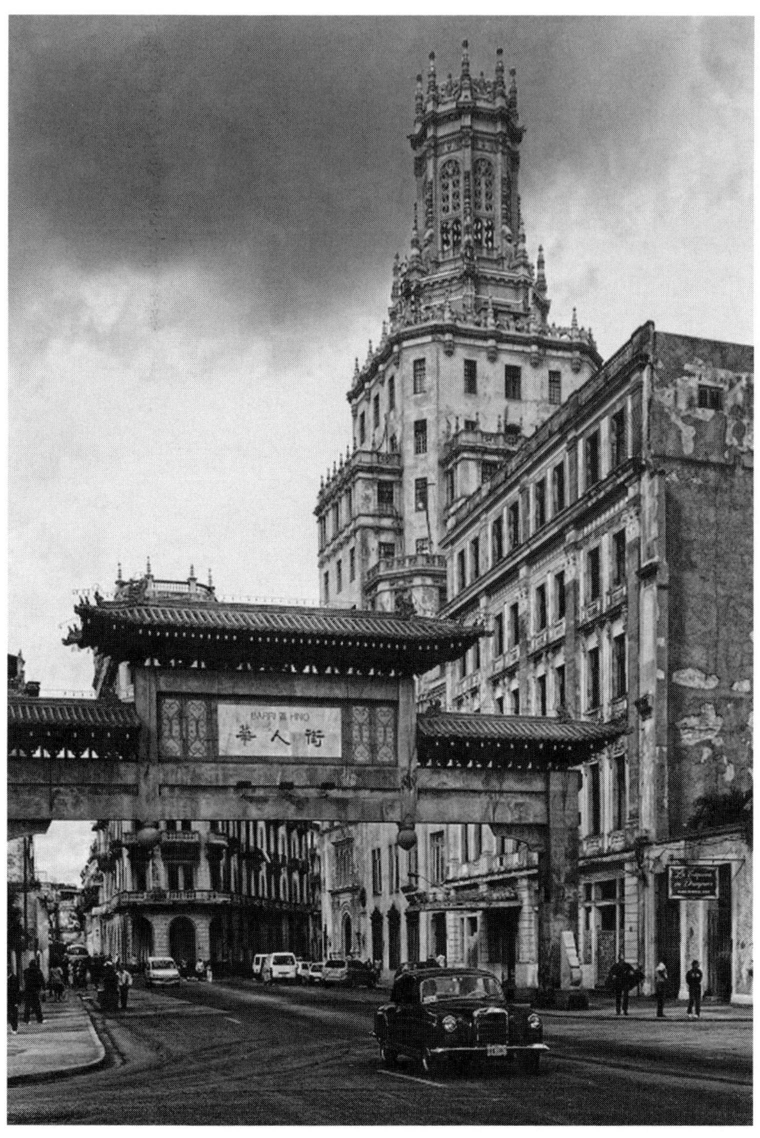

Havana's historic Chinatown represents a long history of migration to Latin America. In addition to African, European, and indigenous peoples, Middle Eastern and Asian immigrants have played important roles in the formation of national identities in the region. The building that dominates the background is the former Cuban headquarters of International Telephone and Telegraph, IT&T. David LaFevor, 2008.

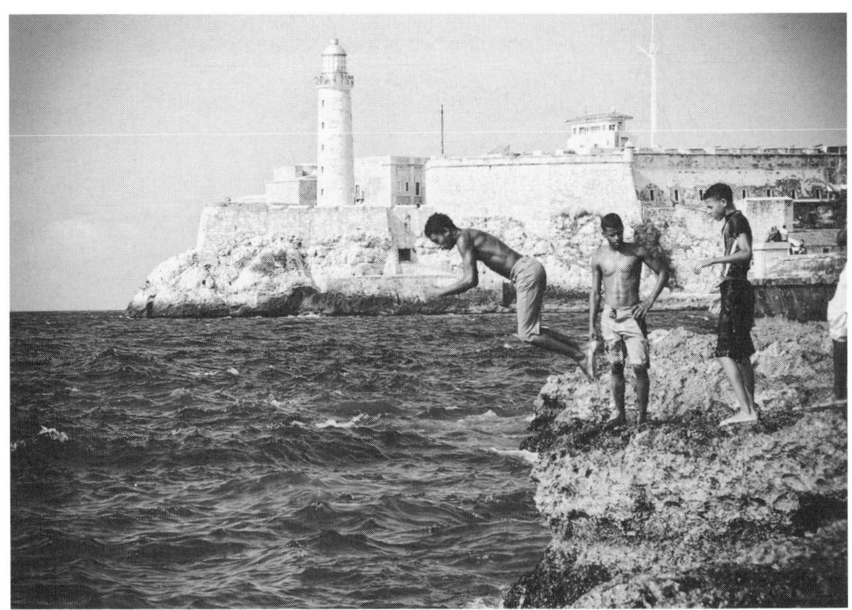

Havana youth dive into the ocean in front of the iconic sixteenth-century Spanish fort, El Morro. The majority of the 11.5 million Cubans have been born since the 1959 Revolution, and they will be responsible for helping shape the changing relationship with the United States. David LaFevor, 2006.

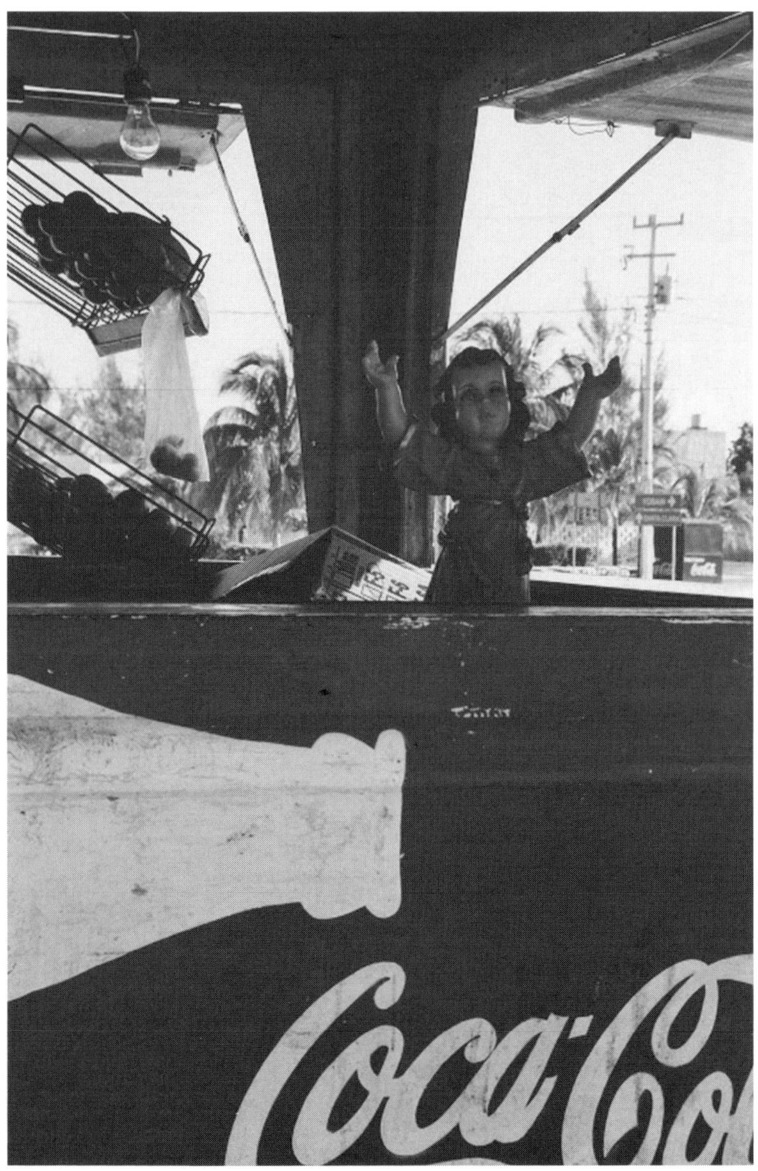

A food stand in a popular tourist area of Mexico is sponsored by Coca-Cola. The popular Latin American image of the boy Jesus—the Divino Niño Jesús—provides a curious juxtaposition between Latin American religious devotion and American capitalist penetration. David LaFevor, 2006.

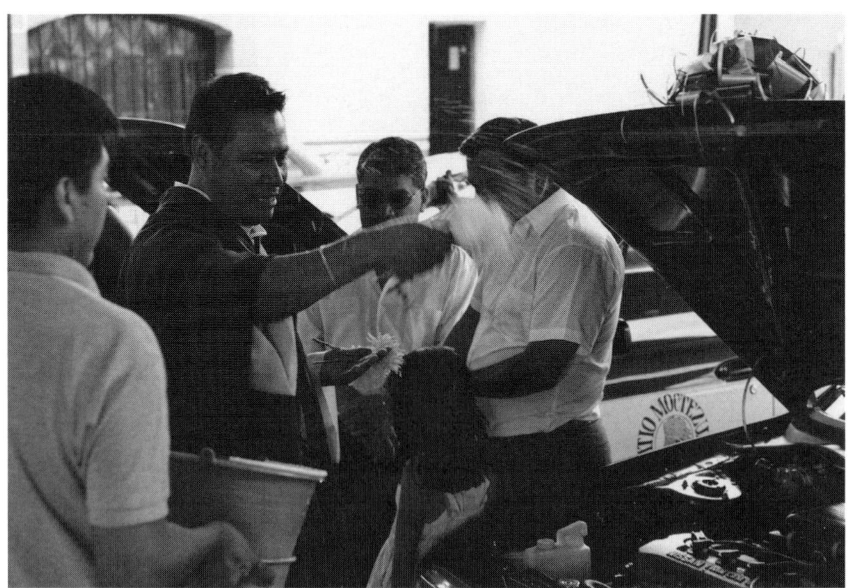

A Catholic priest sprinkles holy water on taxi drivers and the engines of their cars during the "Day of the Taxi Driver" in Mexico. Catholicism continues to dominate religious practice in Mexico, though challenges from Protestant denominations—many from the United States—continue throughout Latin America. David LaFevor, 2016.

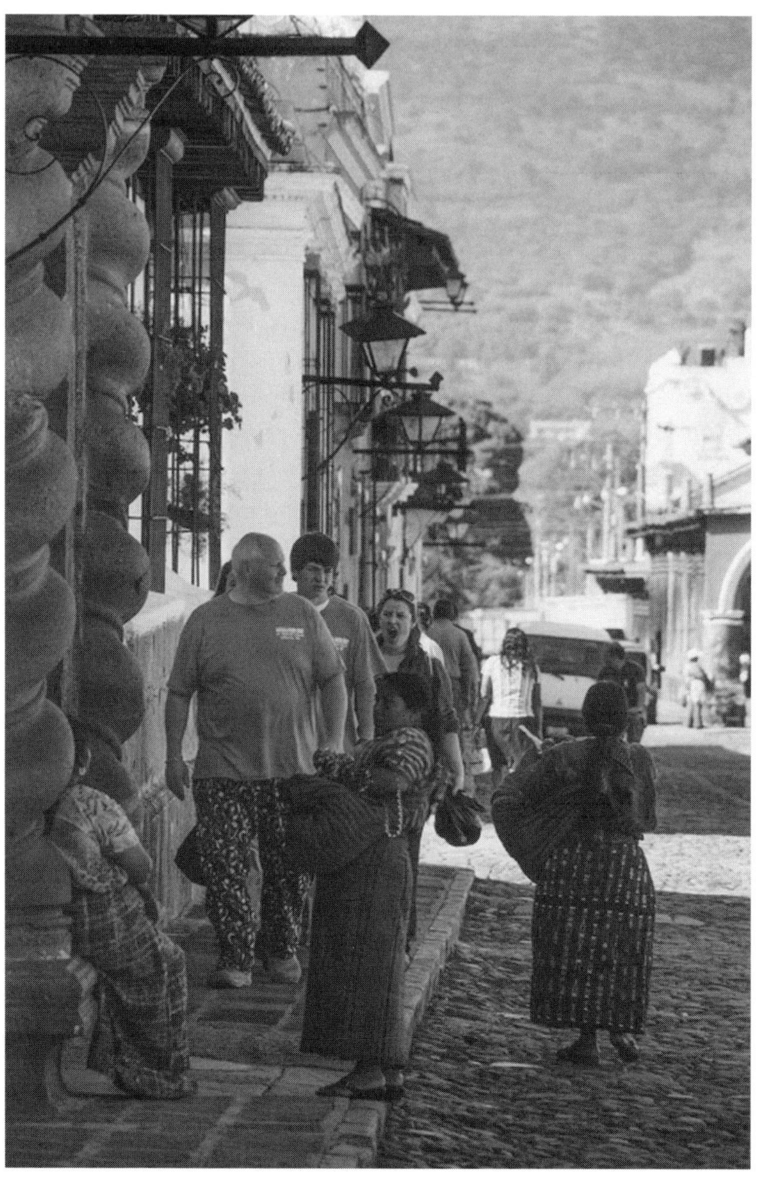

Americans from St. Richard's Catholic Church in Gibsonia, Pennsylvania, walk the historic streets of Antigua, Guatemala. David LaFevor, 2010.

The recent rapprochement between Cuba and the United States has had wide-ranging consequences. This graffiti, photographed in Havana in June 2016, shows José Martí, Cuban national hero, supporting faster, freer Internet service on the island. U.S.-based Google Inc. has offered to subsidize Internet service on the island. To date, Cuba has the most restricted and expensive access to online information in the Western Hemisphere. David LaFevor, 2016.

tion, and greed for tourist dollars had exacerbated the decades-long image of Havana as a wide-open purveyor of alcohol, narcotics, saloons, brothels, and casinos, promising satisfaction for all manner of tastes. These activities meant big profits for U.S. mobsters, such as Meyer Lansky and Santo Trafficante, who collaborated with Cuban criminals, but the disparities of opportunity, privilege, power, and wealth rankled other Cubans. Per capita annual income averaged $400—not so bad by Caribbean standards, but very low in comparison with the United States. In the preceding fifty years, many Cubans had come to associate well-being with U.S. levels of consumption, but by the late 1950s, these aspirations were increasingly frustrated.[5] As an example, the seasonal sugar harvest required a large labor force but, once completed, left rural workers without jobs for the rest of the year. Similarly, slums and sweatshops had a pervasive presence in the towns, where the burdens of hardship and exploitation fell most heavily on Cubans of African descent. These poorest among the poor also endured the effects of racial discrimination and segregation. For discontented persons among the middle classes, the primary characteristics of a corrupted Cuban political system appeared in various forms of repression, tyranny, depravity, brutality, and inefficiency. Energized by Castro's revolt, large segments of Cuban society coalesced against Batista, hoping for change.

As conceived by many Cubans, the traditional U.S. role in their country accentuated their problems. An object of admiration and envy for its wealth and power, the United States also seemed responsible for Cuban failures. According to this view, U.S. political and economic dominance over the years had slowed the island's maturation by perpetuating conditions of monoculture and dependency. Cuba relied too much on sugar sales in the U.S. market; Cuban buyers purchased too many finished goods from U.S. sellers, creating an unfavorable balance of trade. Other indicators underscored the magnitude of economic presence. Direct U.S. investment in Cuba, calculated at $900 million at the time, ranked as the second largest in Latin America. U.S. companies controlled 40 percent of Cuba's sugar production, 36 of the 161 sugar mills, 2 of the 3 oil refineries, 90 percent of the public utilities, and 50 percent of the mines and railroads. For such reasons, many Cubans looked upon their island as an economic appendage of the United States.[6]

Until the mid-1950s, U.S. policy under Eisenhower had supported and sustained Batista for reasons of security and order. Regarded officially as "a good thing from the standpoint of the U.S.," the Batista regime obtained $16 million in military aid during this period, much like other Caribbean dictatorships that, according to this view, propagated stability. But then the administration shifted its ground, seeking to create at least an appearance of evenhandedness. Subsequently, diplomats were urged to avoid unduly partisan displays in Batista's favor. In 1957, the administration sent a new ambassador, Earl E. T. Smith, a Wall Street financier and a faithful Republican, who had no diplomatic experience and no knowledge of Spanish. Upon his arrival in Havana, he supported Batista, mistrusted Castro, and soon found himself in a difficult bind.

Smith invested scant faith in the reliability of the rebel movement and hoped for an honest presidential election in November 1958 to resolve the problem of the presidential succession. But Batista's manipulations got in the way: The dictator tried to rig the outcome in favor of his preferred candidate, Dr. Andrés Rivero Agüero. Reacting against this ploy, the Eisenhower administration somewhat unrealistically hoped to find a replacement for Batista who could head off Castro while simultaneously maintaining order and the appearance of procedural regularity. The Spanish phrase *Batistianismo sin Batista* affirmed the goal, calling for the preservation of the regime's essential features but without the dictator. To pursue this purpose, the administration sent an emissary, William Pawley, a former ambassador to Brazil and Peru. He urged the dictator to resign in favor of a military junta. But Batista refused, pending a variety of assurances, terms, and conditions. Bowing to necessity, the Eisenhower administration then cut him loose, serving notice on December 17, 1958, that Batista no longer enjoyed the official support of the U.S. government.

Unsure what to expect, U.S. officials also had doubts about the intentions and capabilities of Castro and the 26th of July Movement. At the time, U.S. leaders could find no convincing evidence of communist contaminations, but could the insurrectionists exercise control over Cuba? Would they respect U.S. interests? On December 31, 1958, Batista fled from the island, taking refuge initially in the Dominican Republic, under Rafael Trujillo's protection. When Castro took over on January 1, 1959, the United States promptly extended diplomatic recognition and, as an indication of goodwill, also recalled Ambassador Smith, now regarded in Cuba as an undesirable presence. His replacement, Philip Bonsal, a career Foreign Service officer and former ambassador to Bolivia, expressed a more nuanced attitude toward change in Latin America. Indeed, he appraised Cuba's future optimistically, looking upon Batista's fall as evidence of progress toward democracy and justice.

Such expectations diminished quickly in January and February 1959, when Castro allowed the Communist Party to operate legally in Cuba, ousted political moderates from positions of authority, disallowed electoral proceedings for a period of two years, and declared himself the prime minister of the country. He also inaugurated a series of public trials and executions for war crimes; through these means, he eliminated some five hundred former high-level Batista supporters. Nevertheless, when Castro came to the United States in April 1959 for an eleven-day tour arranged by the American Society of News Editors, he retained some measure of credibility, projecting in Stephen G. Rabe's phrase "a sincere, progressive image."[7] Speaking frankly, Castro explained why conditions in Cuba required improvements and corrections. He included agrarian reform among his aims. He admitted that his plans might cause disagreements with the United States but disclaimed any intention of instituting a communist regime.

During his stay, Castro spent three hours with vice president Richard M. Nixon as a stand-in for Eisenhower, who refused an audience because of the political trials and executions. Nixon later reported in his memoirs, *Six Crises,* that all along he had favored a policy of getting tough with Castro. At the time, however, he displayed some sympathy and understanding, despite his suspicions of the new Cuban leader's presumed socialist tendencies. Nixon refrained from branding Castro a communist, expressed appreciation for those "indefinable qualities which make him a leader of men," and anticipated that he would function as "a great factor in the development of Cuba and very possibly in Latin American affairs generally." Nixon wanted "to orient him in the right direction"—in favor of the United States.[8]

Castro nevertheless pursued his own course and soon offended U.S. officials. His critical understanding of Cuban-U.S. relations and his demands for respect of Cuban sovereignty angered and confused the Eisenhower administration.[9] Upon his return home, he promulgated an agrarian reform law that provided for the expropriation of agrarian properties, including his father's, larger than a thousand acres and also for compensation in the form of Cuban bonds. The values would depend on the declarations property owners had made for tax purposes in 1958. Caught in a trap of their own making, sugar growers who had submitted low estimates to justify low taxes had to endure the consequences. To make matters worse, Castro disallowed foreign ownership of agricultural properties and named Antonio Núñez Jiménez, a Cuban communist, as the administrator in charge of the expropriation.

Growing numbers of disenchanted Cubans deserted the island, often seeking safe haven in Miami, Florida, while denouncing Castro as a communist. During the ensuing months, exile groups organized an anti-Castro opposition. Among other things, they flew missions out of Florida to drop propaganda leaflets over Cuba and set fire to sugarcane fields. Castro charged U.S. authorities with responsibility for such actions and warned Cubans of an impending invasion to restore Batista to power. In September 1959, in a speech before the United Nations, he denounced U.S. imperialism as the fundamental cause of Cuba's plight. In February 1960, he signed a commercial agreement with the Soviet Union. It provided for the annual purchase of a million tons of Cuban sugar during the next five years and for a credit of $100 million to finance the purchase of Soviet equipment and machines. This important initiative signaled Castro's determination to weaken Cuba's dependence on the United States and his willingness to move his country toward the Soviet Bloc.[10]

Various accounts of Castro's behavior have stimulated an ongoing debate. Critics have insisted that Castro always possessed communist preferences and revealed them at last by embracing the Soviet Union. Apologists have castigated the United States, holding that Eisenhower's inflexibility drove Castro into a reliance upon the Soviets. Neither view is correct. For Castro as a young man, the Cuban patriot José Martí exercised more ideological authority than Marx, Lenin, or Stalin. Martí's writings upheld as absolute the principles of human equality and national sovereignty. Castro thought the Cuban Revolution should adhere to the same ideals. These meant the abolition of inequality based on the distinctions of race and class and also the elimination of U.S. power and privilege. After all, in the 1890s, Martí had warned of the danger of exchanging one form of subservience to Spain for another to the United States. Castro's critique of race relations in the United States and his subsequent embrace of Black nationalism further antagonized this relationship and increased his regime's legitimacy for many developing nations that identified the Civil Rights Movement as a key symbol of American hypocrisy.

At least in its initial stages, then, Castro's attempts to obtain a Soviet counterweight against the U.S. had practical purposes and effects, less connected with the requirements of Marxist-Leninist ideology than with tactical considerations and a considered realignment of Cuban allegiances.[11] Anti-Castro sentiments within the Eisenhower administration grew stronger as the year 1959 advanced. Taking the lead was Christian Herter, the former undersecretary who became secretary of state when Dulles died of cancer. He advised Eisenhower on November 5 that U.S. policies should "encourage within Cuba and elsewhere in Latin America opposition to the extremist, anti-American course of the Castro regime." Convinced that Cuban "policies and attitudes" ran counter to "minimum United States security requirements," he reported high levels of communist infiltration into the government, apparently with Castro's sanction. If "emulated by other Latin American countries," Herter warned, such practices would have "serious adverse effects on Free World support of our leadership." Moreover, he cautioned, the nationalization of property posed a danger to the U.S. business interests and menaced the principles of free trade and investment all over Latin America. Herter wanted a set of policies to bring about either "a reformed Castro regime or a successor to it." At the same time, he advised against stirring up nationalistic responses by arousing Latin American fears of U.S. intervention. The problem was how to accomplish such contradictory aims.

The CIA spymaster, Allen Dulles, was among the first to suggest Castro's ouster. On January 13, 1960, he expressed his view that "over the long run" the United States could not "tolerate the Castro regime in Cuba" and might have to use covert action to precipitate his downfall. About the same time,

Eisenhower boiled over in a rage in which he characterized Castro as a "mad man" who was "going wild and harming the whole American structure"; Ike imagined various responses, including a naval blockade of Cuba and a build-up of U.S. forces at Guantánamo Bay. Later, he cooled down; nevertheless, a hard-line view had won him over.

On March 17, 1960, the president indicated his approval of a course of possible action suggested by a CIA task force and the NSC. It recalled the Guatemala operation, in 1954, and bore the title "A Program of Covert Action against the Castro Regime." The recommendations consisted of four parts: first, the creation of "a responsible and unified Cuban opposition to the Castro regime located outside of Cuba"; second, the instigation of "a powerful propaganda offensive" against Castro inside Cuba; third, the establishment of a "covert action and intelligence organization within Cuba"; and fourth, "the development of a paramilitary force outside of Cuba for future guerrilla action." Ike later placed a benign construction on such preparations by drawing a distinction between a "program" or general approach and a "plan" entailing specific acts. He also denied any connection with or responsibility for the subsequent Bay of Pigs invasion, in 1961. In Stephen G. Rabe's view, his explanations allow for some believability, since the March 1960 decision "was not an irrevocable commitment to invade Cuba." At the same time, it "ended any possibility of a rapprochement between the Eisenhower administration and Castro." The United States no longer would tolerate mischief from the Cuban upstart. The decision to pursue regime change, based on the short-term success of similar actions in Guatemala, would further antagonize the tenuous relationship with Cuba.

Other undertakings in 1960 had the intention of curbing Castro's appeal in the rest of Latin America. Leaders in the Eisenhower administration now understood more clearly some of the connections between the wretchedness of social and economic conditions for the poor and the causes of violence and revolution. To alleviate the misery, they accepted the necessity of using higher levels of economic aid and assistance as a means of promoting growth and diverting the growing international appeal of Castro's policies. In the course of a trip to Argentina, Brazil, Chile, and Uruguay in February 1960, Eisenhower had something of an epiphany when he encountered placards among the crowds along the way reading, "We Like Ike; We Like Fidel Too." Such displays underscored the extent to which Castro functioned as a symbol of hope and change in Latin America. In July, the president announced the creation of a new program for Latin America. Mainly the brainchild of Milton Eisenhower, the Social Progress Trust Fund called for $500 million in U.S. loans. Aimed at health, education, housing, and land reform, the project operated through the Inter-American Development Bank, an agency created in 1959 for this purpose. Though small in scope compared with the Marshall Plan, the undertaking established a point of departure for the subsequent Alliance for Progress under Kennedy.[12]

Meanwhile, the administration proceeded with plans to employ covert operations against Castro. Drawing upon the Guatemala experience and relying on some of the same men—such as Allen Dulles, Richard Bissell, and E. Howard Hunt—the leaders of the CIA prepared for the training of a guerrilla force in Guatemala. They also sought to sabotage Castro's regime, to isolate Castro economically and diplomatically, and to assassinate him. According to the November 1975 report of the U.S. Senate Select Committee, chaired by senator Frank Church of Idaho, findings based on "concrete evidence" indicated no less than eight plots to assassinate Castro between 1960 and 1965, some of which never advanced beyond "the stage of planning and preparation." The plots involved the enlistment of gangsters and underworld characters such as John Rosselli, Morna Salvatore "Sam" Giancana, and Santo Trafficante as prospective executioners, using "poison pills, poison pens, deadly bacterial powders, and other devices which strain the imagination." One especially exotic scheme, really slapstick, called for the use of thallium salt, a depilatory: Sprinkle the stuff into Castro's shoes and make his body hair fall out. Bald and beardless, according to the plan, he could not hold the political loyalties of macho-minded Cubans.[13]

In 1960, leaders in the Eisenhower administration imposed additional penalties. They prohibited U.S. refineries in Cuba from processing Soviet crude oil, slashed the Cuban sugar quota in the United States by 700,000 tons, and imposed trade restrictions under which only food and medicine could enter Cuba. Caught up in an escalating sequence of moves and countermoves, Castro retaliated by expropriating U.S. properties in Cuba, including sugar mills, petroleum refineries, public utilities, tire plants, and banks. These actions bolstered Castro's domestic legitimacy and narrowed the possibility of a diplomatic solution to the growing crisis.[14] By the end of October 1960, these measures had wiped out the direct investments of the United States in his country. Eisenhower then broke diplomatic relations with Castro's government on January 3, 1961, as one of his final presidential acts.[15] The unsolved Cuban problem, a kind of diplomatic tiger trap, awaited the untested new administration of president John F. Kennedy.

UNDER JFK

Young, vibrant, handsome, rich, and a former Massachusetts congressman and senator, Kennedy won the presidential election by a close margin in November 1960. During the campaign, few fundamental differences in foreign relations separated the two candidates. Both Kennedy and Nixon endorsed the Containment policy, Nixon defending the Eisenhower record,

Kennedy subjecting it to hyperbolic attacks. Among other things, Kennedy claimed that the United States had fallen behind the Soviet Union in the Cold War competition, specifically alleging a "missile gap," a drop in U.S. prestige in the Third World, and a significant setback when Cuba went over to the communist side. This indulgence in political tit for tat recalled Republican charges that Democrats had lost Eastern Europe and China to the Reds. As the historian Thomas G. Paterson notes, "Apparently unaware that President Dwight D. Eisenhower had initiated a clandestine CIA program to train Cuban exiles for an invasion of the island, candidate Kennedy bluntly called for just such a project."[16] The similarity of policy across parties illustrated a remarkable consistency of United States' perception that the Cuban Revolution represented a central threat to American dominance in the region and its global position in the context of the Cold War.

Kennedy's appeal mobilized support among members of a younger generation. Many of his top aides and advisers had served in the Second World War, as had Kennedy himself. They looked upon themselves as "the best and the brightest" and regarded the Eisenhower administration, in contrast, as worn out and sclerotic. Through the exercise of youth, energy, and imagination, they proposed to get the country moving again, for example, by winning victories in the Cold War. For them, the omnipresent communist menace recalled the lessons of Munich in 1938. Appeasement could never stop totalitarian dictators from aggression, only vigilance and strength.[17]

The Kennedy administration embraced the Containment policy as a global necessity, especially in response to recent Soviet pronouncements. Two weeks before Kennedy's inauguration on January 20, 1961, Soviet premier Nikita Khrushchev had delivered a speech in which he prophesied an ultimate victory for his side as a consequence of communist support for "wars of national liberation." This appeal for the hearts and minds of men, consistent with Soviet-style anti-imperialism, focused on Latin America, Asia, and Africa. Specifically, Khrushchev called for alliances between communists and nationalists in the Third World. By working together, serious radicals presumably could engage in a joint struggle in favor of self-determination and in opposition to the adverse legacies of Western imperialism.

For Kennedy, Soviet initiatives required vigorous responses. Consequently, he inaugurated a military buildup marked by a 15 percent increase in the defense budget to enhance both nuclear deterrence and conventional capabilities. Specifically, he wanted more intercontinental ballistic missiles to close the alleged missile gap, a larger number of combat-ready infantry and armored divisions to expand war-fighting abilities on the ground, and a new emphasis on counterinsurgency techniques. The last called for the development and utilization of special forces capable of employing guerrilla-style tactics against potential insurgents in the Third World. He also displayed a readiness to build upon Eisenhower's policies by instituting larger-scale programs of economic aid and assistance.[18]

Once established in office, the Kennedy administration disclosed ambitious plans. One called for a means to undercut Castro through the promotion of economic growth and modernization in Latin America. Called the Alliance for Progress, this approach followed up on earlier Eisenhower initiatives and entertained grandiose expectations. The White House first announced them at a ceremony on March 13, 1961, before 250 guests, including an assembly of Latin American diplomats. The proposal called for "a vast cooperative effort, unparalleled in magnitude and nobility of purpose, to satisfy the basic needs of the Latin American people for homes, work and land, health and schools—*techo, trabajo y tierra, salud y escuela.*"Among other things, Kennedy sought the eradication of illiteracy, hunger, and disease. These ideas, consciously or not, paralleled many of the successful early initiatives of the Cuban Revolution. Designating the 1960s as "the Decade of Development," JFK promised an allocation of $500 million to begin a process of long-term economic planning and integration, scientific and technical cooperation, and an expansion of cultural relations. He also called for political and social reforms to accompany material progress. Democracy, constitutional order, and a reduction of class distinctions were the goals, including the elimination of military despots, antiquated tax laws, and feudalistic systems of land tenure. Kennedy's vision affirmed the attainability of freedom and progress within the context of democratic capitalism, a preferred and viable alternative to the Castro example.

Even higher expectations appeared in August 1961 at an inter-American conference held in a Uruguayan resort town, Punta del Este. Speaking for the Kennedy administration but without specific authorization, secretary of the treasury C. Douglas Dillon pledged ongoing U.S. support in the amount of $20 billion over the next ten years. The funds supposedly would come from public and private sources, including international lending agencies, charitable foundations, and U.S. investors. Supplemented by an additional $80 billion from Latin American sources, this expanded level of investment would generate an anticipated economic growth rate of 2.5 percent a year, about twice that of the 1950s. For good measure, Dillon also predicted the elimination of illiteracy among Latin American children by 1970.[19]

Such ambitious aims always exceeded capabilities and never achieved the mark. Under presidents John F. Kennedy and Lyndon B. Johnson, the United States made good on a large part of its share by contributing $18 billion in various forms of public and private investment. Nevertheless, the programs floundered, falling far short of transforming Latin America into the image envisioned by the U.S. planners. A variety of things went wrong. In aggregate, Latin American economies grew slowly during the 1960s, at about 1.5 percent a year. Consequently, already high unemployment increased from 18 to 25 million, while agricultural production went into decline and population growth increased. In crucial areas, such as health care and education, the hope of extending life expectancy and reducing illiteracy defied fulfillment. And too frequently, the mechanisms for maintaining democratic and constitutional order broke down. In most countries, the traditional ruling elites remained very much in charge, typically in cooperation with martial leaders. During the Kennedy years, military officers ousted popularly elected presidents in six countries.[20]

Ultimately, as Jerome Levinson and Juan de Onís have observed, the Alliance for Progress "lost its way." Most historians accept this appraisal but differ over the reasons. Some scholars emphasize Latin American obstacles such as the accumulation of deep-seated inequities over long expanses of time and the traditional elites' entrenched resistance to change. Other scholars attribute the shortcomings to false expectations and faulty execution on the part of U.S. officials. Rabe shows that the interaction of both sets of causes contributed to the creation of formidable barriers.[21]

First, the Kennedy administration embraced inflated expectations. As Rabe explains, the leaders "undoubtedly overestimated their ability to foster change" and "underestimated the daunting nature of Latin America's socioeconomic problems." For example, Teodoro Moscoso, a high-level administrator, typified "naïve optimism," in 1962, when he proclaimed "within a decade the direction and results of centuries of Latin American history are to be changed." This sort of statement verged on hubris and, in some countries, collided with debilitating realities: 90 percent illiteracy rates, life expectancy of thirty-five years, and 11 percent infant mortality. These daunting figures applied especially to peoples of Amerindian and African descent, at a time when similar socioeconomic inequities in the United States received increased attention from international observers.

Next, U.S. projections neglected the effects of a population explosion. With an annual growth rate of 3 percent, Latin America's population of 195 million was expanding faster than the economy. (It was cruelly ironic that a reduction in the infant mortality rate would have offset economic gains.) The problem was complicated by religious convictions and cultural mores in favor of large families. Out of expediency, the Kennedy administration sidestepped these issues, in part because of unwillingness to offend Roman Catholic opinion. Secretary Dillon dismissed the matter, affirming his belief that "in Latin America the question of population control is not as serious as it may be in other areas of the world because there are substantial resources, substantial land, substantial availability for a growing, expanding population." According to this view, supply, not demand, would prevail in the end.

Finally, U.S. officials invested too much faith in Latin American receptivity to reform and change. Latin American nationalists could draw on clear historical examples of United States self-interested resistance to change across the region. Optimistic assessments presumed the readiness of the elites to accommodate the emerging "middle sectors." U.S. planners counted upon these mainly urban groups, defined as democratic, capitalist, and modern, to exercise a moderating influence and to behave in conformance with the precepts of established social-scientific theory and the United States' long-standing self-perception as benevolent instructor in modernity.[22] As Louis Pérez has illustrated, the U.S. relied upon a paternalistic interpretation of Cuba's population to justify sustained imperialism. According to the views of, for example, Walt Rostow, a presidential adviser and the author of *The Stages of Economic Growth: A Non-Communist Manifesto* (1960), the advent of middle-class reform movements in Latin America meant that democratic capitalism could serve as the best means for moving into the future without the costs of a social revolution.

The sources of such anticipations included misleading historical parallels and assumptions. The Marshall Plan served officials as a kind of model but led to an insufficient appreciation of important distinctions. The processes of economic development in Latin America in the 1960s differed in context from those of economic recovery in Europe in the 1940s, and responded to dissimilar incentives, stimuli, and techniques. What succeeded in Europe would not necessarily apply in Latin America. Thomas Mann, a State Department official who mistrusted the whole effort, later attributed its failure to an "illusion of omnipotence" among leaders in the Kennedy administration. Since the Marshall Plan had such good effects in Europe, they reasoned erroneously, "it's going to work in Latin America."

Still another misperception developed from a particular reading of U.S. history. According to this view, enlightened programs of reform and change undertaken by elites at propitious times could ward off revolutionary threats by accommodating political antagonisms and class differences. For Kennedy officials, historical experiences during the Progressive era and the New Deal confirmed the point and implied a kind of universal, at least hemispheric, applicability. In contrast, Latin American elites derived other premises from their own history. To them, reform appeared not so much as a way to head off revolution but rather as a first step toward bringing it about; therefore, tinkering with the system was a high-risk option with the potential to weaken traditional conceptions of order and constraint, to unleash pent-up furies and frustrations, and to create situations with unpredictable consequences. Clearly, this interpretation served to justify draconian repression of dissent and resistance to change, of any sort.

Following established patterns, most Latin American military organizations functioned to support their notion of stability. During the Kennedy years, army officers seized power in six countries: Argentina, Ecuador, Guatemala, Honduras, Peru, and the Dominican Republic. In response, U.S. officials tried uncertainly to balance ideas of constitutional order against concerns over Castro and communism. Consequently, perceptions of the internal communist threat and assessments of the prevailing attitudes toward Cuba influenced administration leaders who determined the policies of diplomatic recognition. Staunchly anticommunist regimes usually obtained it. As explained by assistant secretary of state Edwin M. Martin, in October 1963, the U.S. government preferred constitutional democracy as a framework for economic development but understood the limitations, because "in most of Latin America there is so little experience with the benefits of political legitimacy." As Martin remarked, the United States lacked the ability to create "effective democracy" by keeping "a man in office . . . when his own people are not willing to fight to defend him."

Support for military organizations appeared prominently in Kennedy's efforts to achieve internal security and counterinsurgency. As seen from Washington, "Communist subversion and indirect attack" had become "the principal threat." Administration leaders particularly worried about guerrilla wars, possibly instigated by Fidel Castro in conjunction with "wars of national liberation." As a counter, the Kennedy administration provided $77 million a year in military aid, a 50 percent increase. The emphasis fell on training programs to enhance techniques of riot control, psychological warfare, and counter-guerrilla operations. For the enthusiasts within the administration, such efforts were legitimate means of strengthening national security and, more dubiously, democratic institutions. Critics pointed out that the military officers responsible for the political overthrows usually had received training and assistance from the United States. Though unwilling to say so in public, the Kennedy administration used military aid to preserve access to and influence with the military establishments regarded as the arbiters of Latin American political life.[23] This decision to increase collusion with Latin American armed forces would contribute, over the next three decades, to numerous civil wars and the deaths of hundreds of thousands of people across the region.

The Cuban policy yielded two portentous episodes during the Kennedy presidency. The Bay of Pigs invasion in 1961, a fiasco, by most accounts, that humiliated administration leaders and signified a damaging setback. Holding larger implications, the Cuban missile crisis in 1962 produced a confrontation between the two great powers, the United States and the Soviet Union, and conjured a nightmarish prospect of nuclear war. In each instance, an incapacity to distinguish between Cuban nationalism and Soviet communism deepened the problem.

The Kennedy plan for a clandestine move against Castro took shape during the early part of the new administration. The president-elect, only forty-three years old, learned of the proposed covert action soon after his victory during the course of CIA briefings from Allen Dulles and Richard Bissell. Later, Kennedy consented to it but disallowed direct participation by

U.S. forces. The earliest versions called for an invasion by Cuban exiles near Trinidad, a city near the south Cuban coast and the Escambray Mountains. Subsequently, the site shifted to the Bay of Pigs, a location about forty miles west of Trinidad along the Zapata Peninsula, where the CIA planners hoped to achieve a surprise. Isolated, remote, and removed from the mountains by eighty miles of swamp, the operation's architects anticipated only light opposition and not much need for air cover.

Misgivings within the administration were not strong enough to head off the ensuing debacle. The Joint Chiefs of Staff reacted against the stifling secrecy, wondered about the invaders' fighting proficiency, and warned of insufficient intelligence, both about the terrain and about Cuban political attitudes. Would the people really rise in revolt against Castro? Dean Rusk, Kennedy's taciturn Secretary of State, reportedly questioned such assumptions in private but withheld a full articulation of his views. Other skeptics included J. William Fulbright, an Arkansas senator and the chair of the Senate Foreign Relations Committee; Chester Bowles, Undersecretary of State; Arthur Schlesinger, Jr., a historian working as a White House adviser; and Dean Acheson, the former Secretary of State, who thought the military imbalance favored Castro. Characterizing the idea as potentially "disastrous," Acheson correctly anticipated that some 1,500 Cubans could not cope with Castro's forces, numbering some 225,000 regular troops and militia.[24]

The Kennedy administration nevertheless accepted the risks, only to experience what the historian Trumbull Higgins called "the perfect failure." The calamity at the Bay of Pigs resulted from an underestimation of Castro's forces, defective planning, bureaucratic malfunctions, poor leadership, and a measure of hubris. As defense secretary Robert McNamara remembered, "We were hysterical about Castro at the time of the Bay of Pigs and thereafter."[25] According to most authorities, the untried Kennedy administration disregarded an assortment of dangers and warnings. Perhaps unduly awed by the experts and equally unwilling to show doubt or weakness, administration officials unwisely accepted, at face value, the CIA's exaggerated enthusiasm. As eager advocates for success, Dulles and Bissell lost the capacity for dispassionate appraisal; secretary of defense Robert McNamara and national security adviser McGeorge Bundy succumbed to the prevailing views and conveyed to the president a false impression of full confidence. Perhaps intimidated by Eisenhower's reputation as "the greatest military man in America," the hero under whom the plan initially took shape, Kennedy—untested, inexperienced, and in this instance vulnerable—became the victim of "a situation where insufficient bureaucratic safeguards existed, and the excessive security only compounded the problem." The president and his advisers accepted the likelihood of a safe landing and a successful move into the Escambrays—through swamp, eighty miles away—while Dulles and Bissell held to a notion that Kennedy would not allow the invasion to fail.[26]

Viewed in retrospect, the Bay of Pigs invasion appears as a sure failure. By trusting to good luck—his "Midas touch," as enthusiasts described it—Kennedy magnified the invaders' capabilities, exaggerated the likelihood of a Cuban uprising, and failed to calculate Castro's abilities to take countermeasures. The brigade of Cuban exiles lost the element of surprise, on April 15, 1961, when a bomber force of eight old B-26s, under exile command, launched an airstrike. It not only destroyed much of Castro's air force but also triggered a military alert. Castro dispersed his remaining planes and rounded up nearly 100,000 suspects in the anti-Castro underground. Then Kennedy, seeking to avoid direct U.S. involvement, canceled another air attack scheduled in support of the invasion on the morning of April 17. By so doing, according to critics such as Samuel Flagg Bemis, he sacrificed all chance of success. More likely, the cancellation of the airstrike made no difference; the invasion would have failed anyway. Castro's ground and air forces moved in fast, pinned down the invaders on the beach, killed about two hundred, and captured the rest.

The rapid defeat of the invading exile force at the Bay of Pigs, according to historian Luis Martínez-Fernández, was "Kennedy's low point [and] Castro's high point." The U.S.-backed force of around 1,400 was repelled by Cuban army and militia estimated at 50,000–60,000. Foreign minister Raúl Roa denounced U.S. aggression on the floor of the United Nations, while Adlai Stevenson, Ambassador to the United Nations, denied U.S. involvement. Khrushchev wrote to Kennedy that the Soviet Union would provide "all necessary assistance" to defeat the armed invasion of Cuba. This existential threat to the revolution justified increased militarization of Cuban society, further imprisonment of suspected dissidents, and likely destroyed any possibility of a diplomatic resolution. Over a year later, most of the invaders taken prisoner were exchanged for $53 million worth of food and medicine; Castro had built on military victory with a public relations triumph.[27] The day after the invasion failed, Castro announced publicly for the first time that the revolution was "socialist."

Thoroughly shaken, Kennedy wondered out loud how he could have been stupid enough to go ahead. At the same time, he retained his anti-Castro commitments. During the following year, the United States persisted in punishing Cuba by tightening the economic blockade, arranging for Cuba's eviction from the Organization of American States, intensifying the propaganda campaign, and conspiring against Castro's life. In addition, Operation Mongoose, another CIA enterprise, encouraged anti-Castro exiles to engage in hit-and-run attacks against Cuban economic targets. Other plans under Operation Mongoose were declassified in 1997. They include Operation Northwoods, which called for fake attacks against various U.S. targets designed to "cause a helpful wave of national indignation," and provoke war with Cuba.[28] From Castro's standpoint, the likelihood of an outright U.S. invasion appeared very high in the early 1960s, and encouraged him to obtain Soviet military assistance as a safeguard for his regime.

The consequence, a Big-Power confrontation in October 1962, ranked as one of the most dangerous periods of the Cold War. Moreover, the missile crisis originated not in Soviet aggression but in the high levels of tension in relations between the United States and Cuba. As Thomas G. Paterson explains, if there had been "no exile expedition, no destructive covert activities, and no economic and diplomatic boycott"—in other words, "no concerted United States vendetta to quash the Cuban Revolution"—then "there would not have been an October missile crisis." Indeed, "Nikita Khrushchev would never have had the opportunity to begin his dangerous missile game." U.S. policy makers knew of Cuban fears. A CIA report in September 1962 concluded that "the main purpose of the present military build-up in Cuba is to strengthen the Communist regime there against what the Cubans and Soviets conceive to be a danger that the U.S. may attempt, by one means or another, to overthrow it." The U.S. threat against Cuba linked Castro and Khrushchev together in a mutual endeavor. Each calculated a vital interest in the installation of medium- and intermediate-range rockets. For Castro, such weapons were a way to discourage a U.S. invasion. For Khrushchev, they underscored Soviet deterrence capability in defense of a new ally.[29]

In an important book, entitled *Inside the Kremlin's Cold War: From Stalin to Khrushchev,* the Russian scholars Vladislav Zubok and Constantine Pleshakov provide illuminating insights. According to them, Khrushchev mixed hard-boiled realpolitik with romantic, revolutionary zeal. He had initially regarded Castro and his followers "as anything but Marxists" and "discounted their chances of success." Later, he experienced a change of heart, "embraced" the Cuban Revolution, and acquired an emotional commitment to it. Indeed, he looked upon "the young Cubans as heroes who had revived the promise of the Russian Revolution" and admired them for daring "to do it under the very nose of the most powerful imperialist country on earth." During an encounter in New York City, in September 1960, Khrushchev hugged and kissed Castro. According to Zubok and Pleshakov, Khrushchev allowed himself "to get carried away" and subsequently gambled dangerously on Operation *Anadyr,* the Soviet code name for deploying missiles in Cuba.[30] This emotional attachment to Cuba mirrored the sense of betrayal that underpinned U.S. policy toward the revolution.

Zubok and Pleshakov downplay the impact of strategic calculations on Khrushchev's thinking and emphasize instead a commitment in defense of the Cuban Revolution. Khrushchev regarded the nuclear balance as an "important" but "not crucial" consideration in the conduct of Soviet international relations. More significantly, they argue, Khrushchev became "fervently dedicated" to Cuba, seeking to preserve the revolution against a possible U.S. invasion. For him, this aim became a means of upholding "the victorious march of communism around the globe and Soviet hegemony in the Communist camp." To obtain maximum deterrent effect, the Soviets decided early in the summer of 1962 to supply medium-range (MRBM) and intermediate-range (IRBM) ballistic missiles. With surface-to-surface ranges of 1,020 and 2,200 nautical miles, respectively, these missiles could hit targets in the United States. Forty-two MRBMs arrived in Cuba; the IRBMs never made it.

U.S. officials received "hard" evidence of the missile sites in Cuba from photographs taken by a U-2 spy plane, on October 14, 1962. When informed of Soviet actions on the 16th, Kennedy, who had cautioned Khrushchev against placing "offensive" missiles in Cuba, snapped, "He can't do that to me!" The president immediately convened a meeting of top advisers. He particularly wanted to know whether the missiles carried nuclear warheads and had the capacity of firing them. As a tentative answer in each instance, intelligence appraisals said probably not but warned that they might have operational capability in a short while. These discussions centered on possible military responses—specifically, whether to use an airstrike or an invasion as the most expeditious method of eliminating the threat. In either case, Soviet technicians and soldiers would most likely die.

In a second meeting on the same day, diplomatic considerations became more prominent. Secretary of State Rusk favored "a direct message to Castro" instead of an air attack. Sharply divided, participants such as general Maxwell Taylor, Secretary of Defense McNamara, and Secretary of the Treasury Dillon contemplated the effects on "the strategic balance." Did the missiles in Cuba provide Moscow with an advantage or at least the appearance thereof? The advisers also wondered whether Khrushchev's move had any bearing on Berlin, a city divided by the Cold War, or perhaps on Turkey, where the United States had based Jupiter missiles with targets in the Soviet Union.[31]

During the next several days an advisory group called the Executive Committee, or Ex Comm, met in exhausting, secret sessions under high pressure. The participants included national security adviser McGeorge Bundy, secretary of state Dean Rusk, secretary of defense Robert McNamara, attorney general Robert Kennedy, vice president Lyndon Johnson, CIA director John McCone, secretary of the treasury C. Douglas Dillon, chief presidential counsel Theodore Sorensen, undersecretary of state George Ball, deputy undersecretary of state U. Alexis Johnson, chairman of the joint chiefs Maxwell Taylor, assistant secretary of state for Latin America Edwin M. Martin, former ambassador to the USSR Llewellyn Thompson, deputy secretary of defense Roswell Gilpatric, and assistant secretary of defense Paul Nitze. Sometimes, UN ambassador Adlai Stevenson and former secretary of state Dean Acheson also joined in.[32]

The exchanges occasioned heated disagreements. As General Taylor later summarized them, the policy options, boiled down, consisted of three choices: “talk them out,” “squeeze them out,” or “shoot them out.” The majority finally settled on a middle course: a quarantine, a semantic evasion meaning but not saying naval blockade; an actual blockade under international law could not exist, except in time of war. McNamara functioned as an advocate in opposition to Taylor, McCone, and Acheson, all of whom favored an airstrike. Robert Kennedy, the president’s brother, also recommended against risky military responses, warning of a Pearl Harbor effect, in reverse, possibly leading to an atomic war.

President Kennedy, meanwhile, arrived at two decisions. First, he ordered the deployment of U.S. warships around Cuba to prevent the arrival of more missiles and to display his resolve. If subsequently challenged, he could move on to more drastic measures. Second, he chose to announce his action by means of a television address. By going public instead of relying on diplomatic channels, Kennedy presumably intended to rally opinion in the United States and to convey his seriousness of purpose to the Soviets. Unlike secret diplomacy, this gambit allowed for almost no space to maneuver. Once having stated his position to the nation, the president could not easily back down.

The president’s address on the evening of October 22 placed the responsibility for the crisis squarely on Soviet leaders. Kennedy reviewed the special relationship of the United States with other Western Hemisphere nations, recalled the lessons of Munich and the Second World War, and defined as imperative the need to resist manifestations of totalitarian aggression. He also called upon the Soviets to reverse their “deliberately provocative” behavior by dismantling their “strategic” missiles in Cuba. The quarantine constituted an “initial” step. Unless the Soviets acquiesced, other measures—unspecified—could follow. Moreover, the president warned, a missile launched from Cuba would precipitate instant retaliation against the Soviet Union. Over the facilities of the U.S. Information Agency, his words went around the world in thirty-seven languages, including Spanish. For the Cubans, Kennedy emphasized that Castro and his minions had become “puppets” of an “international conspiracy” led by the Soviet Union.

As Paterson describes the ensuing events, the missile crisis now became “an international war of nerves.” More than sixty U.S. naval vessels assumed the responsibility of patrolling Cuban waters; the Strategic Air Command went on nuclear alert, meaning that B-52 bombers with atomic weapons stood ready; military forces in the southeastern United States prepared for a possible invasion. U.S. diplomats, accordingly, informed the NATO allies of these steps; the OAS voted to endorse the Kennedy policy; and the United Nations Security Council embarked upon a debate. The Soviets, meanwhile, neither mobilized their forces nor tested the quarantine. Instead, their vessels turned around and went back home, leaving U.S. officials to wonder, what next? If the Soviets stalled on the removal of the missiles from Cuba, a military strike still could occur. Without investing too much faith in the effort, Kennedy also allowed Brazilian diplomats to act as intermediaries, urging Castro to sever ties with the Soviets.[33]

A means of resolution then appeared from an unlikely source. On the afternoon of October 26, a Soviet embassy officer, Aleksandr Fomin—actually the KGB chief in Washington—arranged for a meeting with John Scali, an ABC news correspondent, in the course of which he presented a proposal for transmission to the State Department. According to its terms, a straight-across deal, the Soviet Union would take out the missiles if the United States would promise not to invade Cuba. In response, Rusk sent an indication of interest. Meanwhile, a letter from Khrushchev arrived for Kennedy, conveying the same offer and a reminder that this trouble had come about because of the threatening U.S. attitude toward Cuba.

A crisis atmosphere resumed on the following day, the 27th, when a second letter from Khrushchev amplified the stakes. Possibly influenced by hard-line pressure at home, he now offered to remove the Soviet missiles in Cuba if the Americans similarly agreed to remove theirs in Turkey. This stipulation made a larger strategic connection explicit for the first time. In anger and frustration, President Kennedy spelled out the dilemma: "We are now in a position of risking war in Cuba . . . over missiles in Turkey which are of little military value." Indeed, he already had considered the possibility of phasing them out but was unwilling to appear to be caving in before nuclear blackmail; he wanted to accept no such public obligation while confronted with Soviet pressure.

The difficulty deepened during the afternoon when a surface-to-air missile (SAM) shot down a U-2 plane over Cuba. Regarding the event as a dangerous escalation, Robert McNamara expressed his concern that "invasion had become almost inevitable." But President Kennedy resisted the temptation, still seeking a peaceful resolution. Following his brother Robert's advice, the president took a gamble by accepting the terms not in Khrushchev's second letter but in the first. He also sent Robert Kennedy to confer with the Soviet ambassador, Anatoly Dobrynin; Kennedy would say, in effect, that if the Soviets had not begun to take out the missiles within forty-eight hours, then "we would remove them." At the same time, he offered a concession. When Dobrynin inquired about the Jupiter missiles in Turkey, Robert Kennedy promised to get rid of them but emphasized the need for secrecy; if word leaked out, the United States would not feel bound by the offer.

Thoroughly panicked at this point by the consequences of his own rash acts, Khrushchev refrained from seeking advantage, accepted the settlement as outlined, and concluded the crisis short of the nuclear brink. An unwritten agreement called for the elimination of the MRBMs, under UN supervision, and a U.S. pledge against launching an invasion. In this way, each Great

Power could claim the fulfillment of one of its goals. Later, in April 1963, the removal of Jupiter missiles in Turkey completed the remaining obligation. Castro, meanwhile, brooded and fussed. Unconsulted by his Soviet ally during the final stages, he felt betrayed and demeaned.[34]

Kennedy's handling of the missile crisis has elicited divergent assessments. Enthusiastic administration memoirists depicted his performance as a model, indeed, a masterpiece of crisis management that effectively combined toughness and restraint. In this view, the president, characteristically cool under pressure, acted rationally, retained control, and skillfully manipulated rewards and punishments. His strong stand, moderated by appropriate concessions at propitious times, allowed for a peaceful denouement at acceptable cost.[35] Consequently, he emerged as a kind of victor, his defense of the Western Hemisphere and the Monroe Doctrine supposedly vindicated.

Less laudatory appraisals portray the outcome as "a near miss." Thomas G. Paterson's account, for example, raises questions about "a mythology of grandeur," contending that "illusion" and "embellishment" have "obscured" important facets. As John Kenneth Galbraith observed, "We were in luck, but success in a lottery is no argument for lotteries." Paterson emphasizes the uncertainties and contingencies. What if Cuban exile groups had conducted raids or tried to kill Castro? What if Soviet vessels had challenged the blockade or merely blundered across the line? What if naval vessels or submarines had started shooting out of fear or miscalculation? What if caution and prudence had lapsed among the top leaders? Any one of these possibilities could have escalated the crisis and resulted in deeper difficulties. The tension and stress among the Ex Comm members approached the intolerable, depriving them of sleep and clearheadedness. Presumably, similar processes took place in the Kremlin. Whether Kennedy could have de-escalated the crisis sooner by accepting a diplomatic option remains a source of sharp contention.[36]

In the aftermath of the Cuban Missile Crisis, the leaders in Washington and Moscow installed a teletype hotline to place them in ready communication. The war scare in 1962 also encouraged the two Great Powers to accept the Limited Test Ban Treaty on July 25, 1963. A partial effort, disallowing nuclear explosions in the atmosphere but permitting them underground, it had only a small effect on the arms race. Indeed, the Soviets emerged from the Cuban encounter with their nuclear inferiority exposed and a strong determination to catch up. They also maintained large-scale subsidies for the Cuban economy. Still in power, Castro elicited animosity from his Cuban enemies. For them, the Cuban Revolution still constituted a source of communist contagion in the Western Hemisphere. It remained the defining issue in the New World.

UNDER LBJ

President John F. Kennedy died on November 22, 1963, in Dallas, Texas, the victim of an assassin. His successor, vice president Lyndon B. Johnson, a Texan, had served in the Congress since 1938, first in the House of Representatives and later in the Senate, where he was the Democratic majority leader during Eisenhower's second term. A sure-handed consensus builder and deal maker, Johnson practiced domestic politics as the art of constructing working majorities but lacked any equivalent experience, or expertise, in foreign relations. This shortcoming, a kind of tragic flaw, destroyed his administration after his reelection, in 1964, and later drove him out of office. Under Johnson, the escalation of the Vietnam War became the nation's preoccupation, transforming a small-scale insurgency in a far-off place into a large-scale conflict that engaged 535,000 U.S. troops.

Among the ramifications of Kennedy's death were changes in priority and perception. Latin Americans regarded President Kennedy with special appreciation. They liked his reputation for eloquence and idealism, his beautiful, Spanish-speaking wife, Jacqueline, and his advocacy of the Alliance for Progress. His death touched them emotionally. Johnson, in contrast, appeared more provincial and less sympathetic. Although he claimed on occasion to understand Mexicans on the basis of his dealings with them as a young man in Texas, he never persuaded Latin Americans that he knew or cared very much about them or their countries.[37]

Typical of his generation, Johnson embraced the lessons of Munich and the Second World War as crucial guides. For him, the communist menace recalled the Nazi threat and required constant vigilance. Collective security, alliance systems, and military supremacy ranked high as international priorities. The prospect of "wars of national liberation" in third-world regions still caused some worry. When political opposition forced the Soviet leader Nikita Khrushchev into retirement in 1964, his successors, Leonid Brezhnev and Alexei Kosygin, inspired no more confidence in the Johnson administration. To counter Soviet activity in other countries, Johnson proposed, in a literal-minded sort of way, to uphold the containment principle wherever necessary. He also sought legitimation by claiming continuities of policy and purpose with the Kennedy administration and retained foreign policy advisers, such as William and McGeorge Bundy, Walt Rostow, Robert McNamara, and Dean Rusk. One of the best books on Lyndon Johnson, Paul Conkin's *Big Daddy from the Pedernales,* provides an insightful account.[38]

As a tribute to President Kennedy, Johnson pledged an ongoing commitment to the Alliance for Progress at his first White House ceremony, on November 27, 1963, where his audience included the Latin American ambassadors. Johnson's priorities centered on political stability and economic growth rather than on democracy and reform. To an extent, this emphasis showed the influence of Thomas Mann, appointed by Johnson as Undersecretary of State for Latin American affairs. Another Texan, a career Foreign Service officer, and a former ambassador to Mexico, Mann possessed a reputation for hard-boiled practicality. He regarded the Cuban Revolution with special aversion, describing it as a "cancer" that could be remedied only by heavy doses of free enterprise and private investment. In taking over the coordination of Latin American policy, Mann encountered a variety of bureaucratic obstacles. As Joseph S. Tulchin explains, no matter what the investment of time and energy, the Johnson administration engaged primarily in improvisational responses. Tulchin characterizes them as "spasmodic reactions" to "an overpowering fear that instability would lead to 'another Cuba' in the hemisphere." Unwilling to tolerate any such outcome, Johnson assumed a defensive stance toward Castro at a time when the Vietnam War functioned as a powerful diversion.[39]

Johnson encountered his first difficulties with Latin America over the Panama Canal. A source of contention since the Hay–Bunau-Varilla Treaty of 1903, U.S. sovereign rights in the Canal Zone affronted Panamanian nationalists for many reasons. They objected to the imperialist implications, the division of their country into two parts, and other manifestations of inequality, such as racial discrimination and low wages. As rectification, they wanted to assert Panamanian sovereignty over the Canal Zone and to share more fully in the management and the profits. An episode on Panamanian Independence Day, November 3, 1959, suggested the magnitude of tension. A volatile circumstance turned ugly when student demonstrators, carrying Panamanian flags, marched into the Canal Zone, and ensuing encounters with police and military forces precipitated riots lasting several days. President Eisenhower, while professing puzzlement, attributed the responsibility to "extremists."[40]

Panamanian officials then invited diplomatic discussions as a means of resolving the difficulties and hoped to do so on their terms. In 1962, president Roberto Chiari asked for the negotiation of a new treaty. In response, the Kennedy administration stalled, claiming a need for feasibility studies of alternate canal routes, and then permitted a modest concession: It allowed Panamanians to fly their flag at sixteen designated points in the Canal Zone. Seeking in this way to circumvent theoretical debates over the "formalisms of sovereignty," the United States also tried to uphold its prerogatives for reasons of military defense. But the issue would not go away.

In January 1964, a series of confrontations between Panamanian nationals and Canal Zone authorities over flag-flying privileges led to more violence, killing over twenty people. As an indication of the seriousness, U.S. officials, anticipating a showdown with "left wing agitators," evacuated the embassy staff and destroyed classified documents and code machines. Meanwhile, President Chiari suspended diplomatic relations, pending a response to his demand for the negotiation of a new treaty. When Johnson would not budge under pressure, Chiari broke diplomatic relations.

The Johnson administration ruled out large concessions. As White House adviser McGeorge Bundy explained, expediency permitted flexibility but not "retreat." He would stand strong "on gut issues," especially those concerned with the perpetual-rights clause and "our own ultimate responsibility for the security and effectiveness of the Canal." Senator Mike Mansfield of Montana, the president's friend, warned against any misunderstanding and emphasized the historical context. The Panama difficulty, he explained, "comes mainly from the inside." In his words, "Don't credit Castro for the problems; they existed before Castro and will continue to exist as long as the canal is there."

Meanwhile, presidential politics in each country constricted opportunities for an early resolution. For Johnson, seeking election in 1964, any concessions on Panama could serve Republican opponents as a campaign issue. Taking an unbending stance, he urged his counterpart, the Panamanian presidential candidate, Marco Robles, to appreciate the practicalities: Since economic advantages had more importance to his country than abstract notions of sovereignty, he should focus on questions of aid and assistance, profit sharing, and the like, all of which depended upon a cooperative attitude on other issues.

The election victories of Johnson and Robles subsequently allowed for diplomatic engagement. The drafts of three treaties at the end of June 1967 produced an uneven compromise, favoring the northern neighbor. Under its terms, the United States could expand the Panama Canal or build a new one. In either case the right to defend the neutrality and security of the existing canal resided with the United States. Meanwhile, Panama obtained sovereignty over the Canal Zone, but in a limited way. U.S. control of canal operations and military bases continued under extended leases. Regarded by Panamanian nationalists as unacceptable, these provisions became divisive issues provoking protest and turmoil. Consequently, treaty ratification became impossible in Panama, allowing for no settlement during the next decade.

Leaders in the Johnson administration struggled to bring coherence and focus to Latin American policy. On March 18, 1964, undersecretary Thomas Mann announced a statement of purpose and intent. Known as the Mann Doctrine, this formulation displayed insistent apprehension over possibilities of communist subversion. To defend against it, Mann favored stability and growth over democratic reform. As Tulchin explains, the latter issue, never completely absent as "a policy objective in the region," became less conspicuous in comparison with the administration's other concerns over Communist sedition.[41]

The implications of the Mann Doctrine acquired special significance in relations with Brazil. During the Cold War, the "unwritten alliance" with the United States experienced severe strains, in the Brazilian view, because of unfulfilled promises. During the Second World War, Brazilian leaders had supported the United States in the struggle against the Axis powers, anticipating a reward consisting of economic aid and assistance. But for Brazilians, satisfactory programs never developed, and the absence of a payoff, a Marshall Plan for Latin America, caused distress and disenchantment. Another contentious point concerned the means of economic development. In the U.S. view, Brazil demonstrated too much susceptibility to nationalistic formulas based on state planning and intervention and too little appreciation for proven capitalist methods—free enterprise and private investment. In the late 1950s, president Juscelino Kubitschek had produced particular irritation among U.S. officials by pressing for the adoption of "Operation Pan America," an ambitious but vague proposal involving large-scale U.S. aid, multilateral endeavors, and anticommunism. President Eisenhower reportedly had trouble concealing his personal dislike of Kubitschek.[42]

Brazilian foreign policy then moved in new directions by affirming more independence from the United States. Kubitschek broke loose from traditional Cold War constraints with initiatives seeking broader international connections. In the United Nations, his government supported disarmament programs and third-world interests; it also invited more extensive diplomatic and economic relations with the communist world. In the Western Hemisphere, Brazil still functioned as a mediator between the United States and the rest of Latin America but "with an unusual twist." Abandoning traditional efforts "to soften Latin American hostility to U.S. proposals," Kubitschek's government functioned as "the advocate" of Latin America, attempting thereby to bring U.S. positions into line with Brazilian inclinations.

These tendencies persisted under Kubitschek's successor. In the election of 1960, Brazilians voted for Jânio Quadros, a former state governor of São Paulo. This choice worried U.S. leaders, who perceived Quadros as a political deviant, insufficiently tough on communists. He favored a more neutral stance in the Cold War, supported Castro's right to maintain his regime, urged the promotion of economic growth by nationalist methods, and promised to lead Brazil toward its destiny as a Great Power. The era of the unwritten alliance was over. In 1961, a kind of transposition took place, whereby the two countries switched roles, the United States now acting as the ardent suitor. Seeking to have its way, the United States later resorted to covert actions that aided conspiratorial antigovernment groups and facilitated a coup d'état, on March 31, 1964. The result was a military dictatorship.

The Kennedy administration tried to court Quadros in conjunction with the Alliance for Progress but obtained ambivalent responses. Quadros wanted loans and assistance to cope with inflation and balance-of-payments problems but condemned intervention, including the Bay of Pigs invasion. At the same time, he opened discussions of trade-and-aid issues with West Germany and Eastern bloc nations, though without much success. Meanwhile, the Kennedy administration suppressed its exasperation while negotiating a $500-million aid-and-assistance package, hoping for good effects but worried about mass poverty and discontent in Brazil's northeastern regions, viewed as potentially "the next Cuba."

Confusion mounted on August 25, 1961, when Quadros suddenly and without explanation resigned his position as president. In a risky political gamble, he may have wanted the Congress and the army to insist upon his reinstatement and to lure him back by bestowing upon him special powers. If so, he lost his bet; instead, his act confirmed impressions of him as mercurial, impulsive, and unreliable. To make matters worse, his presumed successor, vice president João Goulart, seemed to share such traits, causing a coalition of congressional and military factions to stipulate the terms under which he could take office. In an extraordinary arrangement, they imposed strict controls on presidential prerogatives, resulting for a short while in the creation of a Brazilian parliamentary system. Taken unaware, U.S. leaders regarded Goulart as dangerous and demagogic but had no say in the succession crisis.

For U.S. leaders, Brazil under Goulart became recalcitrant and troublesome. For example, in January 1962, at a foreign ministers meeting in Punta del Este, Uruguay, the Brazilian delegation resisted U.S. efforts to expel Cuba from the Organization of American States. A few weeks later, Goulart's brother-in-law, Leonel Brizola, the state governor of Rio Grande do Sul, expropriated a subsidiary of the International Telephone and Telegraph Company. Though actually the culmination of a dispute going back to the early 1950s, this act appeared to be part of a coordinated campaign against property rights in Brazil, and Kennedy officials feared there was worse to come. With Brazil suffering high inflation, low productivity, food shortages, rural unrest, and urban tension, Goulart seemed maladroit and indecisive. He could neither command congressional majorities nor articulate a viable course of action. Meanwhile, a process of political polarization dividing the country at the extremes suggested the possibility of civil war. The Kennedy administration, always on guard, reviewed the applicability of counterinsurgency plans and sent colonel Vernon Walters as a military attaché and troubleshooter. A talented linguist, Walters had served with the U.S. Army as a liaison with Brazilian forces in Italy during the Second World War and retained connections with high-ranking members of the officer corps. He now assumed a responsibility for cultivating and consolidating ties with military officials.

Relations deteriorated further in 1963. A plebiscite in January reestablished a presidential system, but Goulart made no headway against the economic crisis. In his view, the fault resided with the Kennedy administration's reluctance to supply him with unconditional, large-scale, long-term aid and assistance. As mounting chaos in many places took the form of local protests, strikes, military mutinies, and outbreaks of rural violence, Goulart contemplated the declaration of a state of siege. U.S. ambassador Lincoln Gordon was similarly alarmed. In August 1963, he saw signs of "substantial imminent danger" of a communist takeover in Brazil.

Following the assassination of President Kennedy in November 1963, the troubles deepened. According to W. Michael Weis, "a majority of Brazilians" anticipated either a communist revolution or a presidential coup. To salvage his position, Goulart tried ineffectively to win over the Johnson administration and to rally popular support, especially among the political left. By so doing, he further alienated the political right, resulting in the military coup of March 31, 1964. As Weis explains, "virtually no one" was willing "to risk anything" to save him. The takeover was quick and easy.

Elated U.S. officials applauded the outcome. The Johnson administration had considered the possibilities of direct action but preferred indirect means. On March 16, Johnson, Rusk, Mann, and other top officials endorsed stability as the main priority, thereby affirming the central premise of the Mann Doctrine. Two days later, Lincoln Gordon met in Washington with Rusk, Mann, McNamara, and CIA director John McCone to discuss policy options, including intervention, in the event of a coup d'état or a civil war. Meanwhile, conspiratorial efforts in Brazil, probably with U.S. encouragement, coalesced around general Humberto Castelo Branco, the army chief of staff. By March 27, the U.S. Embassy in Brazil had prepared contingency plans to assist the Brazilian military with arms and supplies, a decision that may have functioned as a green light. Preparing also for more extreme measures, the Johnson administration assembled a U.S. carrier task force. Code-named "Brother Sam," this operation got under way on March 31. Fortunately for U.S. leaders, Goulart's ouster that day nullified any need for it to proceed. An endorsement of the interim government's legitimacy quickly followed. On April 1, U.S. officials authorized emergency aid and also characterized the change as constitutional, thereby avoiding the question of diplomatic recognition. Johnson sent "warmest wishes" to the new leaders, commending them for resolving the Brazilian crisis "within a framework of constitutional democracy and without civil strife."[43]

Such euphemistic words served the U.S. interest in order and sustained the Brazilian army in the creation of a dictatorship. On April 9, 1964, the Supreme Revolutionary Command issued the first of a series of "Institutional Acts," the effects of which were to consolidate military control and suspend constitutional privileges. They also allowed for the declaration of a state of siege and the denial of citizenship rights to persons regarded as threats to national security. This latter provision soon took effect against three former presidents (Kubitschek, Quadros, and Goulart), two members of the Supreme

Court, six state governors, fifty-five congressmen, and three hundred other political figures. On April 11, under careful military supervision, the Brazilian Congress elected general Castelo Branco as president. He became the first of five military dictators to rule Brazil through 1985. They functioned as the conservators of internal security and national development, operating under the auspices of political authoritarianism and market capitalism.[44]

Another such experience became a defining episode for the Johnson administration, during the U.S. military intervention in the Dominican Republic in 1965. As Tulchin explains, "crisis management" in the Western Hemisphere became a short-term substitute for the articulation of long-term goals and objectives, coupled with the suppression of perceived communist threats. Without a crisis to manage, regional specialists had difficulty getting Johnson to pay much attention at all. The Dominican crisis revealed some of the pitfalls of improvisation.

The Dominican Republic, a former protectorate, had experienced U.S. interventions before. In 1905, president Theodore Roosevelt took control of the customs offices to ward off the possibility of European intrusions. As justified by the Roosevelt corollary to the Monroe Doctrine, the president chose to exercise an international police power to ensure civilized behavior. Later, U.S. Marines occupied the country from 1916 until 1924. When they withdrew, a police constabulary, established by U.S. authorities, served as a base for an aspiring dictator, Rafael Leónidas Trujillo Molina. For three decades after he took power in 1930, Trujillo and his family ruled the Dominican Republic as a fiefdom, growing ostentatiously rich over the years. Posing much of the time as a champion of anticommunism, Trujillo operated with U.S. tolerance if not outright support. Yet by the late 1950s, embarrassment over his heavy-handed excesses and murderous ways encouraged the Eisenhower administration to initiate an anti-Trujillo operation. This policy persisted under President Kennedy who demonstrated his unhappiness with Trujillo while courting Latin American reformers. Trujillo's enemies in the Dominican Republic gunned him down on May 31, 1961—possibly with CIA assistance: Tulchin asserts that "the story of CIA involvement in the assassination . . . told in many versions . . . is no longer disputed."[45]

The ensuing crises over political succession then produced an intervention. Following the dictator's death, the United States used various means, including diplomatic influence and the deployment of warships off the coast, to prevent Trujillo's sons and brothers from retaining power. Meanwhile, the Dominican military exercised authority until a presidential election took place in December 1962—the first free exercise of voting rights in thirty years, possibly ever. The victor, Juan Bosch, a prominent reformer and social democrat, identified his political program with the goals and aspirations of the Alliance for Progress but could not contain fractious disputes over land and labor reform and military prerogatives. Conservative opponents among the propertied elites and the military officers undermined his regime. Moreover, because his shows of radicalism appeared to leaders in the Kennedy administration as evidence of a pro-Castro proclivity, they accepted without much complaint his ouster by Dominican military contingents in September 1963.

From exile, Bosch placed the blame for his downfall on the United States and urged support from his loyalists. Subsequently, as Tulchin notes, "jealousies among the military leaders and the absence of any strong civilian alternatives to Bosch made the transition back to civilian rule very complicated."[46] Nevertheless, preparations proceeded for a new election, but before it took place, a military contingent loyal to Bosch attempted a seizure of power, on April 24, 1965, seeking to put him back in office. During the next few days, civil war threatened as a consequence of the struggle between pro- and anti-Bosch elements in the Dominican military.

The Johnson administration, in what critics regard as an overreaction, allowed the requirements of crisis management to override the nonintervention provisions of the OAS charter. On April 28, seeking to protect the rights and interests of U.S. citizens, Johnson ordered five hundred U.S. Marines into the capital city, Santo Domingo. Subsequent reports, probably overstated, indicated high levels of violence and atrocities with a strong likelihood of communist involvement. Unwilling to permit another Cuba, Johnson then authorized a full-scale military intervention with twenty-three thousand troops, intending to keep Bosch out of office, to eliminate the chances of a communist takeover, and to "avoid another situation like that in Vietnam." Throughout, according to Tulchin, "Johnson exaggerated the danger to U.S. lives" and used the threat of communist subversion mainly as a "gambit" to arouse public support. His main concern was to prevent another Castro, but he lost interest when Bosch faded as a threat. Disgusted by what he saw as the "venality" of Dominican politicians and "the corruption and deceit of the military leaders," Johnson arranged for an OAS "cover," calling upon a multinational peacekeeping force, from Nicaragua, Honduras, El Salvador, Costa Rica, and Brazil, to enforce the ensuing cease-fire agreements.[47]

Through a difficult sequence of failed efforts and diplomatic breakdowns, U.S. officials subsequently obtained the means of safeguarding order and authority. To facilitate the process, as sardonically noted by the historian Robert Freeman Smith, many of the factional leaders in the Dominican military accepted overseas jobs. An agreement signed on August 31, 1965, called the Act of Dominican Reconciliation, provided for an interim government until elections could take place in 1966. The winner, Dr. Joaquín Balaguer, a politician with Trujillista antecedents, served two consecutive terms, represented elite interests under a democratic facade, and became a fixture in Dominican politics for the next twenty-five years. For U.S. officials, the Dominican intervention as an exercise in crisis management constituted an acceptable outcome, admittedly costly but nevertheless a pointed demonstration of administrative resolve against radical threats. As suggested by the Kennan corollary years earlier, it showed a readiness to act in support of anticommunist stability within the U.S. sphere of influence, no matter what the effects on the OAS charter. To Johnson's growing legion of critics, in contrast, it seemed an unhappy regression to the imperialist practices of Theodore Roosevelt and Woodrow Wilson, part of a larger pattern exemplified by the Vietnam War.[48]

After the Dominican crisis, U.S. policy toward Latin America concentrated on "damage control," that is, "trying to salvage something from the ashes of the dream." Thomas Mann left the government early in 1967. Johnson became even more absorbed with Vietnam. When on occasion he showed concern for Western Hemisphere issues, he focused on "specific, uncontroversial development projects, such as roads." Improvements in physical infrastructure became "his mantra in conversations with visitors from Latin America." Though Cuba remained an obsessional subject, the Alliance for Progress became a lost cause for administration leaders. They blamed the failure on Latin Americans, whom they regarded as self-centered, irresponsible, and unwilling to engage in "constructive cooperation" with the United States to safeguard the hemisphere against internal and external threats.

Latin Americans likewise became disenchanted with the United States. A mounting sense of alienation disposed many of them against U.S. definitions of multilateral endeavor and hemispheric security.[49] For them, the Cold War fixation entailed neglect and subordination; indeed, it perpetuated ongoing patterns of exploitation and underdevelopment. To counter them, Latin Americans recast the issues on a North-South basis, highlighting the asymmetries between "modern" and "modernizing" nations and the alleged responsibility of the former for conditions of poverty and destitution among the latter. In the versions called "dependency theory," this formulation contrasted starkly with the East-West emphasis, that is, the tendency to understand most international issues as a function of U.S.-Soviet relations.

Dependency theory adapted Marxist analysis to account for the prevalence of poverty and inequality. Among other things, it posited the existence of a world capitalist system by which the very structure of economic relationships enabled the metropolitan centers—London in the nineteenth century and New York in the twentieth—to maintain ascendancy by expropriating the wealth of peripheral regions in the Third World. According to this critique, the terms of exchange operated as a form of neo-imperialism, assuring economic subservience by discriminating against those countries that produced cheap primary materials and favoring those that turned out more expensive "finished goods." Moreover, a central part of this analysis asserted that the system operated in such a way as to perpetuate underdevelopment and dependency in large portions of the world, keeping them subordinate, unless the victimized regions could find viable ways of breaking loose through the adoption of more equitable, conceivably noncapitalist alternatives. In whatever form, the North-South perspective established different categories for understanding the plight of third-world nations in a world dominated by the East-West considerations of the Cold War.[50]

UNDER NIXON AND KISSINGER

The Johnson administration's self-destruction over Vietnam opened the way for a Republican restoration in January 1969. Richard M. Nixon, the new president, had served Eisenhower as vice president during the 1950s, and failed in his run for the presidency against Kennedy in 1960. As the Republican candidate in 1968, he unveiled a "new" Nixon, supposedly more mellow and less partisan. Claiming foreign relations as his expertise, he promised peace with honor in Vietnam. His partner, national security adviser and later secretary of state Henry A. Kissinger, shared the president's proclivities. A professor of political science from Harvard University, previously a minor player in the national security establishment, and a German Jew whose family had fled from Hitler in the 1930s, Kissinger brought with him to the White House an attraction for European frames of reference. Conceptions of realpolitik in his usage allowed for limited notice of Latin America.

As conservative geopoliticians, Nixon and Kissinger regarded order and equilibrium among the Great Powers as essential requirements. As political realists, they disliked utopian designs, eschewed idealistic and moralistic abstractions, and favored stability as the road toward peace and predictability in a dangerous world. Their statecraft, seeking détente, or a relaxation of tension, centered on relations with the Soviet Union, Western Europe, Japan, and the People's Republic of China. Premised on the possibility of achieving some measure of consensus and cooperation, this strategy anticipated the concentration of power among the Great Powers and provided incentives for accepting the essential parts of the international status quo. Once created, a community of common interest might result in the containment of communist expansion by subtle means and the enlistment of Soviet and Chinese assistance in the termination of the Vietnam War.[51]

In peripheral regions such as Latin America, the intricacies of Nixon-Kissinger diplomacy, with its balancing and calibration of Great-Power interests, suggested a perception of second-class status. When confronted with such matters, Kissinger sometimes showed impatience. In June 1969, for example, the Chilean foreign minister, Gabriel Valdés, criticized U.S. policy for disregarding economic development in Latin America. Kissinger disparaged his concerns: "Nothing important can come from the South. History has never been produced in the South. The axis of history starts in Moscow, goes to Bonn, crosses over to Washington, and then goes to Tokyo. What happens in the South has no importance." When Valdés responded by suggesting that Kissinger knew nothing of Latin America, the so-called Doctor of Diplomacy replied, "No, and I don't care."[52] On another occasion, Kissinger dismissed Chile on geopolitical grounds, describing the country as "a dagger aimed at the heart of Antarctica."[53] Subsequently, in writing their memoirs, neither Kissinger nor Nixon displayed much interest in Latin American affairs. For them, Latin America functioned primarily as an annoyance when North-South issues intruded upon the more significant patterns of East-West relations.

For such reasons, Cuba remained a source of irritation, following the missile crisis. Perceived as a Soviet stand-in, Fidel Castro espoused a brand of revolutionary romanticism, supposedly a threat to the stable countries of Latin America. Often out-of-sync with more cautious Soviet renditions of Marxist doctrine and practice, Castro's long, emotional speeches presented a radical call for heroic struggles against daunting odds. His rhetoric anticipated the advent of revolution throughout the Third World, igniting many Vietnams and precipitating a collapse of world capitalism by means of violent overthrow. Yet the extent to which Castro supported his words with acts is subject to debate. On at least one occasion, in Bolivia, his proposed strategy for exporting the revolution failed dramatically in actual application.

Headed by Ernesto "Che" Guevara, an Argentine revolutionary associated with Castro since Mexico City days, the Cuban expedition into Bolivia late in 1966 obtained a base in the southwestern part of the country, in the Andean foothills. Modeling his efforts on Castro's experience in the Sierra Maestra, Guevara expected to set off uprisings among the rural poor with subsequent domino effects into Peru, Paraguay, and adjacent regions. But false hopes and defective plans caused setbacks in an inhospitable environment. Uncooperative and hostile, the native peoples spoke a dialect of Guaraní, not the Quechua that Guevara had anticipated, and received the revolutionary message with incomprehension. Guevara could not adapt. Forlorn and isolated, the Cuban revolutionaries experienced a sequence of breakdowns culminating in disaster: In October 1967, Guevara was captured by contingents of the Bolivian army and executed before a firing squad soon thereafter. As the historian Robert Quirk explains, his memory then passed from history into myth. After death, his reputation for heroism as a guerrilla fighter, however much embellished, became part of radical iconography around the world.[54]

Allegations of Cuban support for third-world revolution distressed Richard Nixon. His friend Bebe Rebozo, an anti-Castro Cuban, reinforced his suspicions. Kissinger once suggested that Nixon had "a neuralgic problem" on the subject. Cubans reciprocated in kind. They looked upon the new president, an old enemy, as a fascist. To underscore the point, Cuban propaganda employed a distinctive spelling of his name, replacing the "x" in Nixon with a swastika.[55]

Trouble developed in August 1970, when photographic reconnaissance over Cuba discovered an installation under construction, in the harbor at Cienfuegos. To some intelligence analysts, the images looked like a Soviet base for nuclear submarines. Kissinger accepted this appraisal. With Sherlockian powers of deduction, he observed soccer fields in the picture and warned of possible war, explaining, "Cubans play *baseball.* Russians play *soccer.*" His inference, though partly wrong—Cubans do play soccer—correctly identified a Soviet submarine facility. In September, Kissinger told Nixon that such a base could mark "a quantum leap in the strategic capability of the Soviet Union against the United States."[56] With no need to return home for service and maintenance, Soviet submarines with nuclear weapons could multiply in number off the Atlantic coast.

Back in the limelight as an East-West issue, Cuban malfeasance aroused Kissinger's indignation. Viewed as a violation of bans on offensive weapons during the missile crisis, Soviet actions as Kissinger portrayed them could have produced another confrontation. But in these circumstances, Nixon for his own reasons chose another course. He wanted no political uproar over Cuba to place his administration on the defensive before the congressional elections in November 1970. Moreover, he attributed higher priority to questions of détente in relations with the Soviets. As described by his biographer, Stephen E. Ambrose, his display of "intelligent and admirable restraint" allowed for quiet diplomacy, enabling the Soviets to save face while accepting retreat. No threat of war developed. As before, Cubans had no say in the resolution.

Cuban revolutionary enthusiasms still nettled administration leaders and warded off suggestions for placing relations with Castro's government on a more regular basis. During Nixon's second term, discussions in the Organization of American States over the possibility of dropping economic and diplomatic sanctions against Cuba went nowhere. Opposition among anti-Castro exiles obstructed any such process, as did questions of compensation for U.S. losses to Cuban nationalization and Castro's leadership efforts in the Third World. Indeed, Castro ruined all hope of rapprochement in the mid-1970s when he sent Cuban troops into a complex civil war in Angola, a former Portuguese colony in Africa. Something of a public relations coup for the Cubans, the intervention highlighted Castro's claim to champion revolutionary nationalism in the Third World. Kissinger railed against Castro's audacity, viewing it as a consequence of Soviet manipulations.

The geopolitical propensities of the administration continued to arouse Latin American misgivings, and Kissinger sometimes responded to them. In October 1972, he attended a luncheon with Latin America delegates to the United Nations. As described by an aide, William J. Jorden, once "warmed by the evident good fellowship in the room," Kissinger waxed eloquent and promised the beginning of "a new dialogue" on hemispheric affairs. Though rhetorical in intent, Kissinger's statement engaged Latin American diplomats, who showed signs of taking it seriously. To an extent, this expectation formed a context for and perhaps moved the administration toward a softer line when a new round of discussions got under way with Panama over the canal and the 1903 treaty.

These issues ranked among the most conspicuous legacies of U.S. imperialism in the Western Hemisphere. For the Panamanian government, now dominated by the military strongman Omar Torrijos, the renegotiation of terms and provisions retained a vital importance but initially did not for President Nixon; during his first term, he avoided discussions of them. After his reelection he shifted ground. Perhaps in a gesture to mollify third-world opinion, his administration reopened the talks, with Ellsworth Bunker in charge. An experienced diplomat, Bunker encountered a complicated array of competing interests and objectives, including questions of sovereignty and the management and defense of the canal. Unsusceptible to easy resolution, the difficulties remained unsettled when Nixon resigned the presidency because of the Watergate scandal in August 1974. Subsequently, under president Gerald Ford, fundamental differences prevented further progress in part because leading Republicans such as Ronald Reagan, the former governor of California, vehemently opposed concessions to Panama.[57]

Another set of issues came about in relations with Chile during the presidency of Dr. Salvador Allende Gossens—a murky episode over which suspicions, allegations, and polemics have abounded. Allende's government fell from power in September 1973 during a military uprising in the course of which Allende died under mysterious circumstances, by either suicide or assassination. Critics attributed complicity to the United States for supposedly orchestrating a campaign against him.

Allende, a physician of bourgeois origins but with Marxist philosophical tastes, had unsuccessfully sought the presidency in 1958 and 1964 before his victory in 1970. As a Socialist party member, he denied communist affiliations but accepted communist support and campaigned on the need for radical changes. His priorities included the redistribution of land and wealth and the nationalization of basic enterprises, including banks, insurance companies, public utilities, and extractive industries. For an assortment of reasons, his presence in La Moneda, the Chilean executive mansion, disconcerted Nixon and Kissinger, who pressed for countermeasures.

Large-scale U.S. political involvements in Chile had accelerated in the 1960s. A tempestuous, multiparty democracy, inhabited by ten million people, Chile experienced economic distress during the postwar period because of high inflation, maldistribution of income, and heavy reliance on copper exports, especially those of the U.S.-owned corporations Anaconda and

Kennecott. The 1964 election of president Eduardo Frei Montalva, a reform-minded Christian Democrat supported by CIA funds, made Chile a centerpiece during the Alliance for Progress. An adherent of democratic capitalism, Frei favored land, labor, and tax reform and a larger share of the profits from the copper companies but failed to achieve his goals. Moreover, his independence in foreign relations offended Richard Nixon who viewed him as a creature of previous Democratic administrations. By 1970, Nixon was happy for Frei's term to end.[58]

To replace Frei, the presidential campaign of that year featured a three-way race. Allende, a Socialist, ran with communist support against Radomiro Tomic, a Christian Democrat, and Jorge Alessandri, a conservative former president. U.S. officials opposed Allende but had trouble choosing between the other two. Their apprehensions deepened when Allende won a plurality with 36 percent of the vote. Kissinger complained of standing by and letting Chile "go Communist due to the irresponsibility of its own people." He anticipated no more free elections if Allende took office. The geopolitical implications for South America and the effects on U.S. corporations also caused worry. For such reasons, Kissinger and Nixon considered various means of preventing Allende from becoming president. One possibility entailed political manipulation. Since under law the power of choice fell to the Chilean Congress when no candidate obtained a majority, deals among other parties might head him off. Another option was covert action, possibly leading to a military coup, but this route became impossible when resistance developed among military officers, some of whom took threats of civil war seriously. When anti-Allende conspirators botched an attempted kidnapping in October 1970 and shot to death general René Schneider, an opponent of military intervention, Chileans closed ranks in support of the constitution and inaugurated Salvador Allende as president in November.[59]

Allende subsequently challenged the status quo. He blamed economic woes on dependency and exploitation, supposedly the consequences of an alliance between foreign capitalists and domestic elites who looted resources and sent them overseas. To retain the wealth for Chile's benefit, he favored nationalization and expropriation. He also identified his positions with third-world radicals, such as the Vietcong, and underscored the point by establishing diplomatic ties with communist countries: Cuba, the German Democratic Republic, North Korea, North Vietnam, and the People's Republic of China. For him, the apparatus of hemispheric cooperation, including the Organization of American States, functioned as a tool of U.S. dominance. He regarded it as a "servant" of the United States in the Cold War, operating "against the interests of Latin America." Such expressions animated Allende's foreign policy. For Chileans to become free, they required liberation from U.S. hegemony, capitalist exploitation, and economic dependency.

For Allende and his supporters, U.S. corporations in Chile became powerful symbols of an assortment of ills. Anaconda and Kennecott, for example, controlled the country's most important resource, copper, which accounted for most of the state revenue and hard currency. Chileans with otherwise divergent political views agreed on a need to share more fully in the profits. Eduardo Frei had favored a strategy of buying into the companies with stock purchases; Allende wanted to take them over and, soon after assuming office, he introduced nationalization legislation. Under the prescribed proceedings, as subsequently enacted into law by the Chilean Congress, compensation was subject to special terms. If foreign companies had earned "excess profits," as calculated by the government, then the totals would shrink by that amount. For Anaconda and Kennecott, the calculations permitted no compensation at all, and the companies complained of confiscation. The U.S. State Department objected to Chilean deviations from "accepted standards of international law." As punishment, the Nixon administration arranged for restrictions on international credit through private U.S. banks, the Inter-American Development Bank, and the World Bank which reduced Allende's capacity to finance his economic programs. Significantly, no equivalent acts stopped military aid to the Chilean armed forces.[60]

A sequence of domestic crises later engulfed Chile. State-run enterprises functioned inefficiently and output declined. Consequently, inflation mounted as did worker discontent. A truckers' strike in October 1972 caused special embarrassment. Other difficulties developed over food shortages, urban protests, and rural violence. Nevertheless, the government retained power, until September 11, 1973, when the Chilean military executed a coup d'état. The circumstances of Allende's death during the fighting, around La Moneda, remain the subject of speculation and polemical debate.

The same is true of allegations of U.S. responsibility. According to critics, the Nixon administration engineered the drive against Allende for geopolitical and economic reasons. Allende's death, though probably unintended, nevertheless came about as a consequence of U.S. policies, especially its clandestine efforts to destabilize the regime, engender economic distress, and mobilize the opposition. By cutting off bank credit while allowing military aid, the Nixon administration sent unmistakable signals, in effect inviting a move by the military. Other accounts place the blame on Allende, who compounded the deleterious effects of economic coercion with chronic mismanagement. According to this view, his regime collapsed as a result of its own incompetency and failure. These divergent accounts test the capacity of scholars to tolerate high levels of ambiguity, uncertainty, and contradiction.[61]

Yet, by 2016, most of the mystery surrounding Allende's death and Pinochet's rise to power had been settled. The U.S. intervention in Chile after the election of Allende was widespread and sinister. There were covert payments and arms shipments to anti-Allende forces from the CIA. President Nixon ordered the CIA to "make the economy scream" —that is, create an environment in Chile whereby price inflation and scarcity would ensue. After Nixon's disgraceful departure from the White House, less than one year after President Allende's death, the United States Senate felt the need to reassert control over the rogue, runaway administration. Senator Frank Church of Idaho organized a long, public series of congressional investigations in 1975. The "U.S. Senate Select Committee to Study Governmental Operations with Respect to Intelligence Activities" (the Church Committee) issued a scathing, but dispassionate account of covert activities in Chile (Staff Report, "Covert Action in Chile 1963–1973"). Further U.S. complicity in the downfall and death of Allende was made public in 2003 when the American scholar Peter Kornbluh unveiled a cache of documents, through the National Security Archive, at George Washington University in Washington, DC; the documents were declassified in 1999 during the Clinton administration and published in book form as *The Pinochet File: A Declassified Dossier on Atrocity and Accountability.*

Following the military takeover in Chile on September 11, 1973, a junta under general Augusto Pinochet Ugarte instituted its authority by repressive means. Although estimates vary, as many as ten thousand Chileans suspected of pro-Marxist sympathies were killed during the ensuing roundup and crackdown. Later, many more spent hard time in prison, fled the country, turned up dead as victims of political murder, or simply disappeared. General Pinochet, sometimes compared in his methods with Spain's Francisco Franco, became the embodiment of order and an object of derisive, international criticism among human rights advocates. His government ruthlessly secured Chile for anticommunism and free enterprise. Under his purview, Anaconda and Kennecott obtained payments in cash and bonds for their mines and equipment, and the country again became receptive to infusions of foreign investment. Free-market economic doctrines associated with Adam Smith, Milton Friedman, and the "University of Chicago Boys" became the official guides. Subsequently, under Nixon and Ford, U.S. dealings with Chile became more satisfactory. Pinochet's government assured anticommunist stability and a friendly environment for foreign capital— while Chilean political dissidents paid for their opposition with their lives.[62]

UNDER CARTER

In 1976, a political outsider from Plains, Georgia, won the presidency for the Democrats. James Earl Carter, better known as Jimmy, came out of nowhere by capitalizing on public disenchantment with the Vietnam War and the Watergate scandal. The Nixon administration had accomplished an important goal late in January 1973 by disengaging U.S. forces from the fighting and calling the outcome “a peace with honor.” In May 1975, North Vietnamese forces won the war by sweeping into Saigon, the South Vietnamese capital, and taking control of the country. Meanwhile, Nixon’s presidency had collapsed under high crimes and misdemeanors. When he resigned in August 1974, vice president Gerald R. Ford became the president and effectively ended his chance for election in his own right by pardoning Nixon. U.S. voters wondered how to account for such disasters. The political effects made Carter a winner.

A 1946 U.S. Naval Academy graduate, Carter carried out his service obligation until 1953 when he returned home to Georgia for a career in agriculture, business, and politics. As governor in the early 1970s, he decided to run for the presidency. A devout Baptist, he aspired to make politics conform more closely with his personal standards. His insistence upon ethical integrity, an essential part of his message, later hamstrung him because political success at the national level required both obfuscation and deception. According to his critics, a puritanical streak and an absence of savoir faire reduced his political effectiveness. In a more favorable assessment, Gaddis Smith has characterized his term in office as a creative attempt to reconcile the imperatives of morality and reason with power.[63]

In foreign affairs, Carter possessed strong convictions but no experience. For Gaddis Smith, such traits recall “the ghost of Woodrow Wilson.” Nevertheless, Carter sought to enhance his understanding, in 1973, by accepting membership in the Trilateral Commission. This elite group, based in New York City, consisted of business, political, and academic leaders who defined the triangular relationship of the United States, Western Europe, and Japan as critical. However vague and unformed, Carter’s views during the campaign suggested his readiness to move away from the geopolitical formulations of Nixon and Kissinger. Espousing more principled approaches, he wanted to slow the arms race, diminish competition with the Soviets, and overcome outdated Cold War notions in East-West relations. At the same time, his absorption with questions of human rights disposed him more readily toward the Third World and North-South issues.

Once in office, Carter had trouble bringing focus to his policies, partly because of his choice of top advisers. Secretary of state Cyrus R. Vance, a Yale-trained lawyer and pillar of the foreign-policy establishment, operated in the traditions of Elihu Root, Charles Evans Hughes, Henry L. Stimson, and Dean Acheson by moving easily among power elites in the corporate world and the government. Also, the well-connected head of the National Security Council, Zbigniew Brzezinski, a Harvard-educated political scientist and Columbia professor, resembled other university-based social scientists and policy makers, such as McGeorge Bundy, Walt and Eugene Rostow, and Henry Kissinger. In the Carter administration, Vance and Brzezinski, both strong-willed and assertive, produced confusion for outside observers by giving divergent, sometimes contradictory signals. Vance, a proponent of accommodation with the Soviet Union, responded with sympathy to North-South problems. Brzezinski, more inclined toward Cold War orthodoxies, accepted East-West definitions of international relations as the dominant reality.

For the Carter administration, Latin America presented an opportunity to open "a new, happier era of relations." The defense of human rights became an organizing theme. As Gaddis Smith notes, new presidents often engage in "a ritual" of proclaiming a "more sensitive and understanding approach," but in Carter's case the promise assumed some measure of actuality. During the campaign, he vowed to move away from responding with "an attitude of paternalism or punishment or retribution" if Latin Americans did not "yield to our persuasion." This statement implied an aversion to any more invasions or interventions or exercises in destabilization. Vance and Brzezinski shared Carter's view. Early on, Brzezinski noted that in the United States the Monroe Doctrine might appear as "a selfless . . . contribution to hemispheric security," but "to most of our neighbors to the south it was an expression of presumptuous U.S. paternalism." As Gaddis Smith observes, administration speakers never used the term "Monroe Doctrine" in public.

Carter took something of a personal interest in Latin America. He knew some Spanish and, with his wife, Rosalynn, traveled in Mexico and Brazil. He saw the region as an appropriate place to apply what Smith calls his "philosophy of repentance and reform," that is, "admitting past mistakes" and "making the region a showcase for human-rights policy." Moreover, at least in the beginning, he perceived Soviet involvement in the Western Hemisphere as insufficiently large or purposeful to warrant much concern. His priorities included negotiations with Panama, to resolve the status of the Canal Zone, and efforts to engage with Castro's Cuba. Ironically, it was his much criticized reaction to a Latin American issue, the Nicaraguan revolution in 1979, that helped establish his reputation for incompetency in foreign affairs. This perception, as much as anything, made him a one-term president.

Stalled for a dozen years, negotiations over the status of the canal assumed a top priority. Carter wanted a success, hoping to obtain "a positive impact throughout Latin America" and "an auspicious beginning for a new era." But domestic politics got in the way. Conservatives, represented by the former actor Ronald Reagan, then California governor, strongly opposed concessions. For them, a compromise on this matter signified a loss of will, steadfastness, and national greatness. As a candidate for the Republican nomination in 1976, Reagan had made the canal a central issue. His applause line affirmed an unbending position: "We bought it, we paid for it, it's ours and we're going to keep it." For Carter to prevail, a new treaty would have to reconcile an assortment of rival demands and expectations.

Under general Omar Torrijos, a shrewd leader, the Panamanian government had kept the canal issue in the international spotlight. Consequently, in 1974, secretary of state Henry Kissinger and Panamanian foreign minister Juan Antonio Tack agreed to a set of principles. They called for the eventual abrogation of the 1903 treaty and the negotiation of new terms, providing for a fixed termination of the date and a more generous distribution of revenues for Panama. In addition, Panama would assume full sovereignty over the Canal Zone and responsibility for operating the waterway, at some point in the future. At the same time, Panama would have to grant to the United States the right to protect the canal.[64]

The urgency appeared obvious. In 1976, a U.S. Commission on Latin America headed by Sol Linowitz, a Xerox Corporation executive, described the Panama problem as one of the most pressing in the region. The Carter administration went into quick action. Soon after the inauguration in early 1977, the leaders endorsed the Kissinger-Tack principles as the basis for diplomatic discussions. As a negotiator, Sol Linowitz teamed with Ellsworth Bunker, a veteran diplomat. U.S. ambassador William Jorden has described the ensuing processes in detail.

Three principal issues confronted the diplomats. How much money should go to Panama? How long should the United States retain authority over the canal? What words should describe U.S. rights, once Panama took control? Through patience and effort, the diplomats found solutions. Wisely, they drafted two treaties. The first set the termination date of U.S. control over the canal for December 31, 1999, and granted Panama joint responsibility in the interim; meanwhile, Panama would receive $10 million a year and additional sums out of operating revenues. The second defined U.S. rights to defend the canal thereafter. As described by Brzezinski, these accomplishments represented for Carter "the ideal fusion of morality and politics." They did "something good for peace," responded to "the passionate desires of a small nation," and helped "the long-range U.S. national interest."

Nevertheless, tough fights lay ahead. To put the treaties into effect, both Panamanian voters and two-thirds of the U.S. Senate had to register their approval. For political reasons, Torrijos had to claim the acquisition of full sovereignty and a permanent end to the threat of U.S. intervention. Similarly, Carter had to affirm an ongoing prerogative to safeguard access to the canal, in all circumstances. Such contradictions elicited intense debate. When senator Dennis DeConcini, a Democrat from Arizona, proposed an amendment authorizing all necessary measures, including the use of force, to keep the canal open, he nearly stalled the proceedings. Panama would not accept any such amendment. Happily for the Carter administration, DeConcini consented to place his affirmation of U.S. prerogatives in a reservation; as such, it required no Panamanian approval. Nevertheless, the terminology almost provoked General Torrijos into forsaking the effort. As it turned out, the treaties won acceptance by Panamanian voters and the U.S. Senate, where ratification took place in March and April 1978 by identical margins of 68 to 32. A shift of two votes would have resulted in a defeat. Torrijos later said that he would have destroyed the canal if the proceedings had gone the other way. Normally, Gaddis Smith notes, "a President grows stronger by winning a hard political fight." But Carter's narrow victory brought him no credit among the constituents of the conservative right. In fact, the treaties turned into liabilities when Ronald Reagan, the most likely Republican challenger in 1980, assailed them as signs of weakness. According to Reagan, the Carter administration had given away the Panama Canal, thereby running a risk of making "this nation Number Two."

A second risky endeavor for President Carter concerned clear overtures to Fidel Castro, seeking a return of normal diplomatic relations. As Cyrus Vance explained to Carter in October 1976, "The time has come to move away from our past policy of isolation." As reasons, he claimed that "our boycott has proved ineffective, and there has been a decline of Cuba's export of revolution in the region." Moreover, he suggested, Castro might reciprocate with greater restraint in Africa. Though ambivalent during the campaign, Carter subsequently removed restrictions on travel to Cuba and authorized "interest sections" in third-world embassies to facilitate quasi-official communications. Castro responded with caution, indicating that he welcomed better relations and might release some American prisoners from Cuban jails.

Nevertheless, there were insuperable problems. Officials in the Carter administration objected to the presence of Cuban troops already in Angola, and to a parallel move into Ethiopia, early in 1978. In the U.S. view, these acts in unstable African regions served Soviet interests, not legitimate Cuban concerns. Other difficulties arose with reports of Soviet misbehavior in Cuba. In 1978, Carter's critics alleged the arrival of twenty-three Soviet MiG fighter-bombers, presumably in violation of earlier agreements, and, in 1979, a combat brigade. Though unsubstantiated and probably overdrawn, such suspicions effectively ruined all hopes for a Cuban rapprochement during the Carter presidency.

Finally, the Carter administration's advocacy of human rights pertained most directly to the ABC countries. Historically different from the smaller and weaker nations of Central America and the Caribbean, Argentina, Brazil, and Chile on occasion had displayed more capacity to resist pressures from Washington. During the Carter years, they had all operated under authoritarian military rulers who lacked much sensitivity to human rights. In fact, murderous campaigns against political dissidents had resulted in outrageous violations. Moreover, each regime responded with fierce resentment to criticism from the Carter administration. As Brzezinski noted, the United States consequently ran the risk "of having bad relations simultaneously" with all three.[65]

In Argentina, a military junta under army chief of staff Jorge Rafael Videla took over on March 24, 1976. Seeking order after a period of instability, inflation, and despair, the government cracked down on dissent, waging "a dirty war" at home, with scant recognition of traditional political or civil rights. Armed gangs, ostensibly operating with official sanction, attacked suspected subversives. They often vanished without a trace, becoming known as *desaparecidos*; probably as many as ten thousand were killed. The ensuing mix of authoritarian politics and free-market economics constituted an intriguing contradiction.[66]

Such violations ran counter to Carter's human rights policy. To ignore them would render the policy meaningless. Soon after taking office, Secretary of State Vance in February 1977 expressed disapproval by announcing a $17 million dollar reduction in foreign aid. Argentine officials responded with denunciations of U.S. interference in their internal affairs. Meanwhile, human rights champions in the U.S. Congress also demanded cuts in military aid. The Carter administration agreed and arranged to block Argentine loans through the Inter-American Development Bank and the Export-Import Bank and to impose trade penalties. How to measure the consequences is a problem. In all likelihood, the sanctions had more impact on U.S. companies doing business in Argentina than on the government. Still, President Videla promised, in March 1978, to restore civilian government in another year or so—a promise he did not keep—and he also released some political prisoners. "On balance," Gaddis Smith explains, "the application of human-rights principles" in relations with Argentina was a mixed thing, a combination of sticks and carrots, favoring the former. As Smith also suggests, it was "not pure, but it was good." In response, the junta may have adjusted its practices somewhat.

In relations with Brazil, defined as the most developed country in the Third World, the era of the "unwritten alliance" had long since passed away. For the most, part the military authoritarians in control since the mid-1960s had pursued their own course, more or less independent of the United States, unless they found it advantageous to do otherwise. Carter had offended them during the campaign by characterizing their regime as "a military dictatorship" that was in many instances "highly repressive to political prisoners." Consequently, early in 1977, when the State Department issued a report on Brazilian human rights violations, president Ernesto Geisel simply canceled a 25-year-standing military assistance agreement. In this way, he rejected the aid before the Carter administration could deny it.

Another issue in Brazilian relations concerned nuclear proliferation. In 1967, Brazil refused the Treaty of Tlatelolco, banning nuclear weapons from Latin America. Then, in June 1975, Brazil struck a deal with West German suppliers to increase nuclear-generating capability and to acquire the means for reprocessing uranium for weapons production. Distressed by the implications, U.S. officials objected, and the Ford administration tried without much success to mitigate the effects. Upon assuming the presidency, Carter authorized a protest to chancellor Helmut Schmidt of West Germany against sales of nuclear materials to Brazil, which outraged Brazilian leaders who claimed that this was an unwarranted and devious interference in their affairs. Seeking then to repair the damage, the Carter administration let up on the pressure over human rights and nuclear issues and, instead, commended Brazil for moving toward a more open political system. For symbolic reasons, the administration also arranged for a series of official visits to Brazil, in 1977 and 1978, by Cyrus Vance, Rosalynn Carter, and the president himself. Despite such shows, the United States could not persuade Brazil to participate in the grain embargo against the Soviet Union after the invasion of Afghanistan in 1979.

Relations with Chile also soured during the Carter years. The regime under General Pinochet was friendly toward U.S. corporations but not to Carter who, during the campaign, had attacked the Nixon administration's complicity in the overthrow of Salvador Allende. Though the worst excesses had ended by 1977, the State Department remained critical of human rights violations and cut back aid. Pinochet in turn aroused U.S. anger by refusing to extradite three Chileans accused of murdering a Pinochet opponent, Orlando Letelier, in Washington.[67] Poor relations persisted. The record of accomplishment for human rights advocacy remained mixed.

The Carter administration's effort to break loose from traditional Cold War constraints fell short of its aims. The Panama negotiations, despite treaties, entailed damaging political costs because of Republican attacks. The Cuban issue defied settlement, and attempts to uphold human rights in Argentina, Brazil, and Chile had ambivalent consequences. The defense of morality and reason in conjunction with power had side effects, sometimes unforeseen, that almost always precipitated complications in relations with countries defined as friendly. For the Carter administration, everything got worse during the disastrous year of 1979. A resurgence of Cold War tensions following the Soviet invasion of Afghanistan altered the international context and enhanced perceptions of Carter as a weak and ineffective president. The triumph of revolutionary movements in Nicaragua and Iran had similar effects, and Carter's critics eviscerated him. In 1980, Ronald Reagan and the Republicans promised to set things right.

NOTES

1. Robert E. Quirk, *Fidel Castro* (New York: W. W. Norton, 1993), chaps. 1–6; Morris H. Morley, *Imperial State and Revolution: The United States and Cuba, 1952–1986* (New York: Cambridge University Press, 1987), chap. 2.

2. Thomas G. Paterson, *Contesting Castro: The United States and the Triumph of the Cuban Revolution* (New York: Oxford University Press, 1994), 20.

3. Fidel Castro Ruz, *History Will Absolve Me* (Havana: Editorial de Ciencias Sociales, 1975).

4. Stephen G. Rabe, *Eisenhower and Latin America: The Foreign Policy of Anticommunism* (Chapel Hill: University of North Carolina Press, 1988), 118.

5. Louis Pérez, Jr., *On Becoming Cuban* (Chapel Hill: University of North Carolina Press, 1999).

6. Rabe, *Eisenhower and Latin America,* 120; Paterson, *Contesting Castro,* chaps. 1–4; Louis A. Pérez, Jr., *Cuba and the United States: Ties of Singular Intimacy* (Athens: University of Georgia Press, 1990), chaps. 8–9.

7. Rabe, *Eisenhower and Latin America,* 120–23.

8. Richard M. Nixon, *Six Crises* (Garden City, NY: Doubleday, 1962), 352; Rabe, *Eisenhower and Latin America,* 124.

9. Alejandro de la Fuente, *A Nation for All : Race, Inequality, and Politics in Twentieth-Century Cuba* (Chapel Hill: University of North Carolina Press, 2001), chaps. 5–7.

10. Rabe, *Eisenhower and Latin America,* 124–25.

11. Richard E. Welch, Jr., *Response to Revolution: The United States and the Cuban Revolution, 1959–1961* (Chapel Hill: University of North Carolina Press, 1985), 9–26; Pérez, *Cuba and the United States,* chap. 9; Paterson, *Contesting Castro,* chaps. 21–22.

12. Rabe, *Eisenhower and Latin America,* 127–33, 141, 149.

13. Rabe, *Eisenhower and Latin America,* 137; Thomas G. Paterson and Dennis Merrill, eds., *Major Problems in American Foreign Relations,* 2 vols., 4th ed. (Lexington, MA.: D. C. Heath, 1995), 462–67, chap. 2.

14. Luis Martínez-Fernández, *Revolutionary Cuba: A History* (Gainesville: University Press of Florida, 2014).

15. Rabe, *Eisenhower and Latin America,* 163–73.

16. Thomas G. Paterson, "Fixation with Cuba: The Bay of Pigs, Missile Crisis, and Covert War against Fidel Castro," in *Kennedy's Quest for Victory: American Foreign Policy, 1961–1963,* ed. Thomas G. Paterson (New York: Oxford University Press, 1989), 126.

17. Thomas G. Paterson, "John F. Kennedy's Quest for Victory and Global Crisis," in Paterson, *Kennedy's Quest,* 3–23.

18. James N. Giglio, *The Presidency of John F. Kennedy* (Lawrence: University Press of Kansas, 1991), 45–48.

19. Stephen G. Rabe, "Controlling Revolutions: Latin America, the Alliance for Progress, and Cold War Anti-Communism," in Paterson, *Kennedy's Quest,* 105–22.

20. Rabe, "Controlling Revolutions," 105; Edwin Lieuwen, *Generals vs. Presidents: Neomilitarism in Latin America* (New York: Frederick A. Praeger, 1964), 10–68.

21. Jerome Levinson and Juan de Onís, *The Alliance That Lost Its Way: A Critical Report on the Alliance for Progress* (Chicago: Quadrangle Books, 1970); Rabe, "Controlling Revolutions," 110–13.

22. Louis Pérez, *Cuba in the American Imagination: Metaphor and the Imperial Ethos* (Chapel Hill: The University of North Carolina Press, 2008).

23. Rabe, "Controlling Revolutions," 110–12, 115–19; Edwin McCammon Martin, *Kennedy and Latin America* (Lanham, MD: University Press of America, 1994), chap. 10.

24. Giglio, *Presidency of John F. Kennedy,* 52–55.

25. Thomas G. Paterson, ed., *Kennedy's Quest for Victory: American Foreign Policy, 1961-1963* (New York: Oxford University Press, 1989), 123.

26. Trumbull Higgins, *The Perfect Failure: Kennedy, Eisenhower, and the CIA at the Bay of Pigs* (New York: W. W. Norton, 1989); Giglio, *Presidency of John F. Kennedy,* 51, 55, 57.

27. Martínez-Fernández, *Revolutionary Cuba,* 76–80.

28. Martínez-Fernández, *Revolutionary Cuba*, 80–82.

29. Higgins, *Perfect Failure,* chaps. 7–8; Paterson, "Fixation with Cuba," 132, 136–41.

30. Vladislav Zubok and Constantine Pleshakov, *Inside the Kremlin's Cold War: From Stalin to Khrushchev* (Cambridge, MA: Harvard University Press, 1996), 206–7.

31. Zubok and Pleshakov, *Inside the Kremlin's Cold War,* 260; Paterson, "Fixation with Cuba," 142–43.

32. Giglio, *Presidency of John F. Kennedy,* 193; Michael R. Beschloss, *The Crisis Years: Kennedy and Khrushchev, 1960–1963* (New York: Edward Burlingame Books, 1991), 450.

33. Paterson, "Fixation with Cuba," 143–45.

34. Zubok and Pleshakov, *Inside the Kremlin's Cold War,* 262, 266–68; Paterson, "Fixation with Cuba," 145.

35. Roger Hilsman, *To Move a Nation: The Politics of Foreign Policy in the Administration of John F. Kennedy* (New York: Dell, 1964), chaps. 13–16; Arthur M. Schlesinger Jr., *A Thousand Days: John F. Kennedy in the White House* (Greenwich, CT: Fawcett, 1965), chap. 30; Theodore C. Sorensen, *Kennedy* (New York: Harper & Row, 1965), chap. 24.

36. Paterson, "Fixation with Cuba," 148–55; Richard J. Walton, *Cold War and Counter-Revolution: The Foreign Policy of John F. Kennedy* (Baltimore: Penguin Books, 1972), chap. 7.

37. Joseph S. Tulchin, "The Promise of Progress: U.S. Relations with Latin America during the Administration of Lyndon B. Johnson," in *Lyndon Johnson Confronts the World: American Foreign Policy, 1963–1968,* ed. Warren I. Cohen and Nancy Bernkopf Tucker (New York: Cambridge University Press, 1994), 211.

38. Paul K. Conkin, *Big Daddy from the Pedernales: Lyndon Baines Johnson* (Boston: Twayne, 1986), 176–200.

39. Tulchin, "Promise of Progress," 219–20, 227–28.

40. John H. Coatsworth, *Central America and the United States: The Clients and the Colossus* (New York: Twayne, 1994), 96; Michael L. Conniff, *Panama and the United States: The Forced Alliance* (Athens: University of Georgia Press, 1992), 116–25.

41. Tulchin, "Promise of Progress," 228–32; Coatsworth, *Central America and the United States,* 112, 14–16.

42. Gerald K. Haines, *The Americanization of Brazil: A Study of U.S. Cold War Diplomacy in the Third World, 1945–1954* (Wilmington, DE: Scholarly Resources, 1989), chaps. 4–8; Samuel L. Baily, *The United States and the Development of South America, 1945–1975* (New York: New Viewpoints, 1976), chap. 5; W. Michael Weis, *Cold Warriors and Coups d'Etat: Brazilian-American Relations, 1945–1964* (Albuquerque: University of New Mexico Press, 1993), 135; Elizabeth A. Cobbs, *The Rich Neighbor: Rockefeller and Kaiser in Brazil* (New Haven, CT: Yale University Press, 1992).

43. Weis, *Cold Warriors,* 134, 138–39, 141, 143–46, 149–57, 162, 166–67.

44. Weis, *Cold Warriors,* 166–68; William O. Walker III, "Mixing the Sweet with the Sour: Kennedy, Johnson, and Latin America," in *The Diplomacy of the Crucial Decade: American Foreign Relations during the 1960s,* ed. Diane B. Kunz (New York: Columbia University Press, 1994), 62.

45. Tulchin, "Promise of Progress," 233–35; Piero Gleijeses, *The Dominican Crisis: The 1965 Constitutionalist Revolt and American Intervention,* trans. Lawrence Lipson (Baltimore: Johns Hopkins University Press, 1978), chaps. 1–3; G. Pope Atkins and Larman C. Wilson, *The Dominican Republic and the United States: From Imperialism to Transnationalism* (Athens: University of Georgia Press, 1998), chaps. 4–5.

46. Tulchin, "Promise of Progress," 235.

47. Robert Freeman Smith, *The Caribbean World and the United States: Mixing Rum and Coca-Cola* (New York: Twayne, 1994), 49; Tulchin, "Promise of Progress," 236.

48. Tulchin, "Promise of Progress," 236–37; Atkins and Wilson, *Dominican Republic and the United States,* chaps. 6–8.

49. Tulchin, "Promise of Progress," 236–37, 241.

50. Introductions to dependency theory appear in Andre Gunder Frank, *Latin America: Underdevelopment or Revolution: Essays on the Development of Underdevelopment and the Immediate Enemy* (New York: Monthly Review Press, 1969); Ronald H. Chilcote and Joel C. Edelstein, eds., *Latin America: The Struggle with Dependency and Beyond* (New York: John Wiley & Sons, 1974); Chilcote and Edelstein, eds., *Latin America: Capitalist and Socialist Perspectives of Development and Underdevelopment* (Boulder, CO: Westview Press, 1986); and Fernando Henrique Cardoso and Enzo Faletto, *Dependency and Development in Latin America* (Berkeley: University of California Press, 1979). Robert A. Packenham, *The Dependency Movement: Scholarship and Politics in Development Studies* (Cambridge, MA: Harvard

University Press, 1992), presents a devastating criticism, seeking to disenroll dependency theory as a form of knowledge.

51. Robert D. Schulzinger, *Henry Kissinger: Doctor of Diplomacy* (New York: Columbia University Press, 1989).

52. Seymour M. Hersh, *The Price of Power: Kissinger in the White House* (New York: Summit Books, 1983), 263.

53. Paul E. Sigmund, *The United States and Democracy in Chile* (Baltimore: Johns Hopkins University Press, 1993), 91.

54. Quirk, *Fidel Castro,* 567–85; Jorge Domínguez, *To Make a World Safe for Revolution: Cuba's Foreign Policy* (Cambridge, MA: Harvard University Press, 1989), chap. 8.

55. Michael J. Francis, "United States Policy toward Latin America during the Kissinger Years," in *United States Policy in Latin America: A Quarter Century of Crisis and Challenge, 1961–1986,* ed. John D. Martz (Lincoln: University of Nebraska Press, 1988), 35.

56. Stephen E. Ambrose, *Nixon,* 3 vols. (New York: Simon and Schuster, 1989), 381, chap. 2.

57. Ambrose, *Nixon,* 382–83, chap. 2; Francis, "Kissinger Years," 39–42; Coniff, *Panama and the United States,* 128–34.

58. William F. Sater, *Chile and the United States: Empires in Conflict* (Athens: University of Georgia Press, 1990), 139–58.

59. Hersh, *Price of Power,* 265, 278; Sater, *Chile and the United States,* 167–71.

60. Sater, *Chile and the United States,* 167–71.

61. Sater, *Chile and the United States,* presents a balanced view. Hersh, *Price of Power,* and James D. Cockcroft, *Latin America: History, Politics, and U.S. Policy,* 2d ed. (Chicago: Nelson-Hall, 1996), chap. 17, are critical of the U.S. role. Mark Falcoff, *Modern Chile, 1970–1989* (New Brunswick, NJ: Transactions, 1989), holds Allende responsible for his own demise.

62. Sater, *Chile and the United States;* Sigmund, *United States and Democracy in Chile.*

63. Gaddis Smith, *Morality, Reason, and Power: American Diplomacy in the Carter Years* (New York: Hill and Wang, 1986), chap. 1.

64. G. Smith, *Morality, Reason, and Power,* 15, 40, 109–13.

65. G. Smith, *Morality, Reason, and Power,* 115, 117, 127; William J. Jorden, *Panama Odyssey* (Austin: University of Texas Press, 1984).

66. Joseph S. Tulchin, *Argentina and the United States: A Conflicted Relationship* (Boston: Twayne, 1990), 141–45.

67. G. Smith, *Morality, Reason, and Power,* 129–31.

Chapter Six

Cuba, the United States, and the World: From Mariel to Obama

The Cuban Revolution dominated U.S. policy toward Latin America during the Cold War and beyond. This relationship had a deep and complex history that created context for the events of 1959. For historian Louis Pérez, Jr., Cuba had been a proving ground for the broader extension of U.S. political, economic, and cultural influence since the nineteenth century:

> Cuba occupies a special place in the history of American imperialism. It has served as something of a laboratory for the development of the methods by which the United States has pursued the creation of a global empire. In the aggregate, the means used by the United States in Cuba constitute a microcosm of the American imperial experience: armed intervention and military occupation; nation building and constitution writing; capital penetration and cultural saturation; the installation of puppet regimes, the formation of clientele political classes, and the organization of proxy armies; the imposition of binding treaties; the establishment of a permanent military base; economic assistance—or not—and diplomatic recognition—or not—as circumstances warranted. And after 1959, trade sanctions, political isolation, covert operations, and economic embargo. All that is American imperialism has been practiced in Cuba.[1]

The election of Ronald Reagan signaled a return to antagonism in the bilateral relationship between the United States and Cuba. A decade later, the dismantling of Eastern European communism and the evaporation of Soviet subsidies worsened an already bleak economic situation, culminating in the worst material conditions in Cuba since the beginning of the revolution. The Cuban government responded, in survival mode, with austerity policies known as the Special Period. In the early 1990s, a flood of studies confidently proclaimed a deathwatch for the regime. Despite the threat of economic collapse, the elimination of Soviet security guarantees, and the escalation of the United States' economic embargo, the Castro government remained in power. It continued to demand respect for Cuban sovereignty as a precondition for any negotiations toward normalization with the United States.[2] The George H. W. Bush administration sustained the policies of its predecessor, while increasing pressure for its vision of democratic reforms through the Cuban Democracy Act of 1992 (popularly known as the Torricelli Act).

The Clinton years saw some tentative overtures and a brief return to Carter-era incremental steps toward normalization—steps that the Castro government viewed as continued attempts to undermine its sovereignty. Electoral politics in the United States combined with a series of international crises to preserve the political impasse. These events resulted in legislation that tightened and further codified the embargo—removing it from presidential purview and giving Congress control over the preconditions for negotiation. These policies could no longer be justified under the national security paradigms of the Cold War. By the 1990s, Cuba terminated significant military support to revolutionary and socialist regimes in Africa and Latin America. Accordingly, new laws were articulated in a moral language that positioned the United States as a defender of democracy and human rights. These notions of moral uplift were not new; they formed a fundamental base of United States policy toward Cuba since the Spanish-American War a century before.[3]

The reconfiguration of American foreign policy after September 11, 2001, led to heightened antagonism and mutually increased suspicion. The continued presence of Cuba on the State Department list of state sponsors of terrorism combined with portrayals of the Castro regime as an honorary member of the "Axis of Evil."[4] Despite this categorization, wars in Afghanistan and Iraq ensured that Cuban policy remained a vague concern, mostly in the hands of powerful anti-Castro domestic interests. The Cuban government, which initially did not object to the imprisonment of terror suspects at the Guantánamo Bay Naval Base, sympathized with the United States' experience of terrorism. According to this view, Cubans had been the victims of terrorist attacks launched from U.S. territory since the beginning of the revolution, often with the collusion of U.S. security forces.[5] Fidel Castro formally resigned his position as president in 2008, ceding power to his younger brother Raúl, but the fundamental actors and tenets of the government remained.

The election of Barack Obama in 2008 signaled a potential breakthrough, although during his first term little significant movement occurred in the relationship. His second term saw the most significant steps toward normalization since the Carter administration.[6] Though important aspects of the embargo still remained toward the end of his second term, such as the general travel ban and trade restrictions, the Obama White House removed Cuba from the State Department's list of sponsors of international terror and celebrated the reopening of the United States Embassy in Havana in 2015.[7] Despite issuing an executive order mandating the closure of the prison at Guantánamo Bay late in his second term, this campaign promise remained unfulfilled.[8] Important disputes, such as the status of fugitives from the United States residing in Cuba and the restitution for property seized by the revolutionary government, remain. A majority of U.S. respondents had been in favor of reestablishing diplomatic relations with Cuba for nearly every year that information is available (since 1974).[9] The inertia of U.S.-Cuban relations is the focal point of this chapter. The 2016 U.S. presidential election, which featured two outspokenly anti-Castro Cuban American candidates, promises to be decisive in the direction of this new opening.[10]

EL MARIEL AND CARTER

Movement toward improving relations between Havana and Washington stalled toward the end of Carter's term. In 1977, as noted in the previous chapter, the administration negotiated the opening of "interest sections" in Havana and Washington. Though these posts were officially hosted by third-country embassies (Switzerland for the United States and Czechoslovakia for Cuba), these reciprocal acts were the most substantial steps toward restoration of diplomatic relations since the closure of the United States embassy in Havana in 1961. Carter also diluted the travel ban and sanctioned direct flights between the United States and Cuba. The Cuban government responded by allowing Cuban Americans to visit the island and releasing nearly 3,000 political prisoners.[11] Diplomatic and back channel negotiations toward détente, however, fell victim to a series of external events that revived underlying Cold War alignments.

In November 1979, Iranian students invaded the U.S. Embassy in Tehran, taking fifty-two United States citizens hostage. A month later, the Soviet Union invaded Afghanistan. The Cuban government refused to condemn those actions in the United Nations. Despite leadership in the Non-Aligned Movement, an organization that included Afghanistan, Castro was unwilling to criticize the Soviet Union in public. Cuba also maintained its support for socialist governments and revolutionary movements in Nicaragua and Grenada, in addition to its large-scale combat operations in Angola and Ethiopia.[12] While the Cuban government argued that their domestic and foreign policies were not subject to negotiation, Washington was in no mood to accept these arguments of sovereignty. The scale of this military assistance was exceeded by Cuban civilian aid, including "construction workers, physicians, technicians, engineers, agronomists, and teachers . . . in nearly 40 countries on three continents."[13] Cuba's foreign policy, directed from Moscow or not, impeded the necessary Washington consensus for the normalization of relations.

Most historians of Cuba now reject the notion that Cuban troops, advisors, and "civilian internationalists" operated on Moscow's orders. Historian Piero Gleijeses, examining previously unavailable archives in Havana, has determined that the USSR was often frustrated by its lack of control over Cuban foreign policy.[14] This crucial detail—that Cuba pursued a largely independent internationalist strategy—was absent from the Carter administration's strategic vision.

Bureaucratic competition over the Cuba question, within Carter's cabinet, further complicated the formulation of coherent policy due to the dual position of the island as a national security risk and a diplomatic conundrum. National security adviser Zbigniew Brzezinski argued for an unyielding approach to Cuba as a Soviet client in clear accord with a realist Cold War approach. Secretary of state Cyrus Vance advocated a more flexible and conciliatory line that focused on bilateral relations and negotiation.[15] Amid this strategic confusion, it was a manufactured migrant crisis that derailed Carter's attempts to change the narrative.

In 1979, over 100,000 Cuban Americans visited Cuba. The Carter administration's loosening of prohibitions on family travel had the largely unintended consequence of showing Cubans the comparative material success of relatives living in the United States. These comparisons were aggravated by economic hardship linked to a dramatic fall in sugar prices and Cuban overborrowing of cheap petrodollars. The Cuban Adjustment Act of 1966 also gave anyone fleeing the island preferential immigration status as an automatic permanent resident, a policy that Cuban authorities consistently portrayed as a provocation and an inducement for risky and illegal attempts at flight.[16] Some Cubans, during 1979 and 1980, attempted to leave the island by seeking asylum in foreign embassies; multiple hijackings of boats and planes by Cubans who hoped to flee only worsened economic and political conditions. Castro labeled those wishing to leave as traitors to the nation and blamed the crisis on the United States for its unique policy toward Cuban migrants. In October 1978 and, again, in February 1980, armed Cubans stole boats and sailed to the United States. In the latter case, sixty-five hijackers forced the captain of a ship, at gunpoint, to take them to the Florida Keys; they were "walking the streets of Miami's Little Havana by that evening."[17] Media outlets portrayed these illegal actions as brave acts of resistance against tyranny. Ramón Sánchez-Parodi, then head of the Cuban Interests Section in Washington, DC, blamed the refusal of the United States government to accept more legal Cuban migrants for the events that followed.[18]

On April 1 of 1980, a driver crashed a bus through the gates of the Peruvian embassy in a suburb of Havana. The driver and his passengers were promptly granted political asylum by the Peruvian ambassador. In protest, the Cuban government removed its guards at the embassy. Shortly thereafter, over 10,000 Cubans poured into the few acres that constituted Peruvian territory in Cuba. This event proved an embarrassment to the Cuban government as international media published accounts of horrifying conditions that Cubans on the embassy grounds were willing to endure, while waiting to be processed as political refugees and transported from the country. In response, the Cuban government organized a march of nearly one million people in support of the revolution and against those seeking asylum.[19]

Amid a growing public relations disaster, Castro announced that those wishing to leave would be free to do so through the port of El Mariel, on the northwestern coast. Over the next five months, a makeshift flotilla from Florida, directed by Cuban Americans, evacuated over 125,000 individuals. Ill-prepared to manage this influx, the Carter administration scrambled to house and process the *marielitos*. Several complications in this improvisational process became domestic political liabilities and exposed divisions within the powerful Cuban exile community in Miami.

Seeing an opportunity to dispose of "undesirables," the Cuban government had encouraged "hundreds of prison inmates, mental patients, lazy individuals, homosexuals, individuals who refused to work, and religious dissenters" to join the throng headed for Florida.[20] The number of criminals was greatly embellished by U.S. media, but critical events, such as the rioting of Cubans relocated and detained in Arkansas, further damaged Carter's prospects for reelection. Bill Clinton, then governor of Arkansas, would later remember his acceptance of Mariel refugees as a prime factor in the only election he ever lost.[21]

The Mariel crisis highlighted the costs of mutual antagonism. Since the Cuban Adjustment Act of 1966, any Cuban who reached U.S. shores was allowed to remain. This unique status stood in contrast to regulations governing other would-be migrants, such as the Haitian "boat people," who also fled poverty and a repressive regime but enjoyed none of the privileges allotted to Cubans. When Carter ordered the Coast Guard to stem the flow he was criticized from the right by then candidate Ronald Reagan, who questioned the president's "humanitarianism in shutting that off."[22]

Carter's vacillating policy on Cuba ended with his failure to win reelection. Early in the Reagan administration, rumors of a full-scale U.S. invasion of Cuba prompted renewed military mobilization on the island.[23] Mikhail Gorbachev's reforms, known as *perestroika* and *glasnost*, strained the Soviet relationship with Cuba and threatened to destabilize the foundations of the regime's survival.

REAGAN RETURNS TO BIPOLARITY

The presidential election of 1980 featured more debate on Cuba than any election since 1960. Ronald Reagan regularly characterized Cuban foreign policy as a sort of "Soviet proxy" which created instability in Central America. Support for the Sandinistas in Nicaragua, the civil wars in El Salvador and Guatemala, and alliance with the island of Grenada were proof, for Reagan and secretary of state Alexander Haig, of Cuba's menace to Washington's hegemony in its sphere of influence. Reagan denied Cuban membership in the "civilized world."[24] Cuba was "a colony of the Soviet Union"; "owned lock stock and barrel"; a "virus"; and "a roving wolf . . . with hungry eyes and sharp teeth." Though Haig's tenure was brief, his solution to the Cuba problem was unambiguous: the United States should turn "that fucking island into a parking lot."[25] In 1982, the State Department included the island on its list of state sponsors of terror for its support of revolutionary, socialist, and national liberation movements, especially those in Central America. That same year, eager to reverse Carter's initiatives, Reagan reinstated the general travel ban (aside from those visiting relatives).

The Cuban government posed other threats. In November 1983, the head of the Drug Enforcement Administration asserted that Fidel Castro was involved in "distributing narcotics to the United States to raise money for subversive activities in Latin America."[26] While acknowledging that the administration did not have legally sustainable proof of these charges, Francis M. Mullen, Jr. reasoned, "but that doesn't mean it isn't happening." These allegations established Cuba as a dynamic security threat, both international terrorist and malefactor in the domestic drug war. The Cuban Interests Section's press officer, Angelo Pino, denied these accusations, citing the numerous Americans in Cuban jails for drug trafficking.[27]

Despite this rhetorical polarization, by the end of Reagan's second term the United States had reached agreements based on "mutual interests that could only be advanced by cooperation" on migration and southern Africa policy. From a Cuban perspective, the United States scapegoated them for all instability in Latin America. Accordingly, this erroneous simplification ignored U.S. support for right-wing military dictatorships and its role in the debt crisis that led to the "lost decade" of the 1980s in Latin America.[28] By the time George H. W. Bush entered office in 1989, the collapse of eastern European communism had begun to reinvigorate the goals of regime change and replaced those geared toward containment of Cuban influence that had dominated American policy since the Bay of Pigs.

The Cuban government took the Reagan administration's rhetoric seriously. It strengthened its military while advising allies, such as the Sandinistas in Nicaragua, to moderate their attitude toward negotiations with Washington. Cuban diplomats renewed talks with Wayne Smith, Chief of the U.S.

Interests Section, on multilateral solutions to the civil war in El Salvador. Cuban negotiators, while ostensibly willing to assist in a negotiated settlement, demanded that their Salvadoran allies be part of any negotiation. When Smith forwarded this conciliatory approach from Havana to Washington, he was told that the administration was not interested. Mexican president José López Portillo and his foreign minister Jorge Castañeda also sought to serve as intermediaries, but the administration's hard-line approach precluded any significant dialogue.

In September 1981, the administration announced plans to establish Radio Martí to broadcast anti-Castro propaganda from Florida. Smith, the most experienced Cuba expert at the State Department, advised against it. He reasoned that such broadcasts would be counterproductive and would have no effect other than to further polarize relations.[29] Even after meeting with Cuban vice minister of foreign affairs Ricardo Alarcón and forwarding his offers to mediate the conflict in El Salvador and support free elections, Smith's council was ignored.

In November, the highest-level meeting between Cuban and U.S. diplomats during the Reagan presidency took place in Mexico City; Alexander Haig and Cuban vice president Carlos Rodríguez sat for talks. Their negotiation followed a familiar script with Haig making demands and Rodríguez questioning Washington's right to demand anything of a sovereign country as a precondition for talks on normalization. Subsequent meetings in Havana, however, further emphasized Cuban willingness to negotiate their support of rebels in El Salvador and for the Sandinistas—this was the first instance since 1959 that Cuban diplomats accepted compromise with the United States in the formulation of foreign policy. These overtures were ignored as insincere, in secret debriefings, while senior White House officials claimed publicly that the Cubans had never made such overtures. Wayne Smith resigned in protest to what he considered clear mendacity.[30]

In October of 1983, the tiny Caribbean island of Grenada, producer of nutmeg, became the site of the Reagan administration's first direct military intervention in the Caribbean. Officials declared that U.S. involvement was a matter of national security: Cubans were helping to construct an airstrip that, the CIA advised, could be used to land Soviet military aircraft. The Grenadian government argued that the airstrip was only intended for tourism.[31] There were also a number of American medical students studying at a medical college and their safety was a concern to the Reagan administration.

Maurice Bishop's socialist government had taken power in a 1979 coup. By 1983, it had developed close ties with Nicaragua and Cuba and hosted approximately five hundred Cuban construction workers, under the direction of a British contractor. Alongside these workers were two-dozen military advisors and a host of teachers, doctors, and other technicians. Though the Carter administration had opposed Cuban involvement in Grenada, it had avoided military intervention. It responded with theatrical shows of force, such as naval maneuvers and the landing of nearly 2,000 marines, at the Guantánamo Naval Base.[32]

On October 25, U.S. Forces invaded Grenada, on the pretext of protecting United States' medical students from civil unrest, following Bishop's ouster by more radical elements of his government. Since security officials advised that Grenada was a beachhead for Cuban forces and a staging ground for Soviet expansion, this tiny island became an opportunity to put into action what Reagan intended when he signed National Security Decision Directive 75 earlier in the year. The United States would use military force to regain "credibility" in the face of Soviet aggression.[33]

The Cuban workers in Grenada were taken by surprise. Before the U.S. Interests Section in Havana could advise the Cuban government about the focus of the intervention, the construction workers acted to defend themselves. Though the workers were not the official targets, in the ensuing confusion and combat, twenty-four Cubans were killed and over fifty were wounded. The airport, which had been so central to the Reagan administration's justification for invasion, was subsequently completed with aid from the United States. In reaction to these events and to the jingoistic rhetoric from the Reagan administration, Fidel Castro responded in kind, labeling the leadership of the United States "Nazi-fascist barbarians" who were "blinded by their own stupidity" to commit a "monstrous crime" by invading Grenada.[34]

Reagan's national security decisions were guided by the assumption that any political movement in Central America and the Caribbean not denounced by the Cubans was directly in their employ and beholden to Moscow. While most administration officials with expertise on El Salvador, for example, argued that the resistance to the brutal oligarchic regime there was composed of a broad array of forces, from religious and student groups to the leftist FMLN (Farabundo Martí Liberation Front or Frente Farabundo Martí para la Liberación Nacional), Reagan and his ally in the Senate, archconservative Jesse Helms, confidently pronounced that there were only two sides in El Salvador: communist and anticommunist. Accordingly, Salvadoran guerillas were part of a "larger imperialistic plan" guided by Cuba to "impose a Marxist-Leninist dictatorship." Robert White, a former ambassador to El Salvador, labeled this reductionism that saw Cuban nefariousness as the root cause of social unrest as "towering nonsense . . . tactically and factually wrong."[35] As political scientist Lars Schoultz has demonstrated, of the thirteen members forming the National Bipartisan Commission on Central America, under Reagan and chaired by Henry Kissinger, none were specialists on Central America.[36]

Since the Mariel crisis of 1979–1980, the Reagan White House had strained to reach an agreement with Castro on the return of "excludables":

those Cubans with violent criminal records or who were otherwise undesirable. After negotiations stretched into the mid-1980s, Cuba agreed to the repatriation of 2,746 individuals, if they were returned incrementally, in groups of 100 per month. This rare cooperative venture lasted only five months, until the first propaganda transmissions from Radio Martí went live.

Despite this violation of international law, the U.S.-funded radio broadcasts, guided by the CIA and designed to destabilize the Cuban government, went back to 1960. Cuba had reciprocated with transmissions of its own, such as the short-lived Radio Free Dixie, a station run from Cuba by African American civil rights activist Robert F. Williams, who had advocated armed resistance to white supremacist violence in North Carolina.[37] Most of these stations, on both sides of the Florida straight, had disappeared by the mid-1970s. During the Reagan administration, a new coalition between civil society and policy makers planned to resurrect the problematic power of radio.

The Cuban American National Foundation (CANF), a staunchly anti-Castro lobbying group led by Jorge Mas Canosa, was founded in 1981 and immediately pursued a strategy that led to Cuban American "capture of United States policy toward Cuba."[38] At the end of the Cold War, it stepped into the policy vacuum created when Cuba no longer posed a national security threat. Luis Posada Carriles, a dissident Cuban exile who the Cuban government accuses of terrorism for his role in multiple anti-Castro bombings, has alleged that CANF funded his activities. One of CANF's other pet projects, Radio Martí, was shepherded through several failed attempts to gain legislative approval by Jesse Helms: "Radio Martí was as much a product of domestic politics as of foreign policy. The station was the top priority of the newly formed Cuban American National Foundation (CANF), a lobbying group of wealthy Miami exiles created to assure that no U.S. president would make concessions to Castro's Cuba."[39] It finally went on air in 1985. This action resulted in the rollback of the small progress that had been made in the area of immigration.

By the end of Reagan's second term, concern with Cuba was further curtailed due to the Iran-contra affair. Highly publicized trials of administration officials uncovered arms-for-hostage deals with Iran and the illegal arming of the anti-Sandinista contra forces fighting to overthrow the government in Nicaragua. In this context, administration officials transitioned from justifying Cuba policy in geostrategic and national security terms toward a moral and ethical justification for continued embargo and isolation. The unilateral embargo was unnecessary to contain the spread of communism in the hemisphere; the authoritarian one-party state became the new target of the then nearly thirty-year policy of isolation. Despite several failures to secure a denunciation of the regime for violation of human rights in the United Nations, the Reagan administration continuously compared the Castro government to those of Stalin and Hitler. With customary outrage, Castro pointed out what he viewed as hypocritical U.S. foreign policy: "This is amazing. When we see the excellent relations it has with the military government of Argentina, where thousands of people disappeared; the excellent relations with Pinochet who murdered and caused so many people to disappear; the excellent relations with South Africa, which oppresses twenty-million blacks—I am really amazed."[40] Few in Washington were still alarmed by Moscow's designs in Latin America, and the Cuban American community was positioning itself to create U.S. policy toward Cuba.[41] With fundamental changes in international relations on the horizon, the bilateral relationship between Cuba and the United States remained paralyzed.

GEORGE H. W. BUSH, CUBA, AND THE POLITICS OF INERTIA

The series of events that led to the end of communism in Eastern Europe and the collapse of the Council for Mutual Economic Assistance presented the Castro government with its most dire existential crisis to date. This trend continued in Latin America, where the Nicaraguan Sandinistas suffered electoral defeat in 1990. Most observers of Cuba predicted the rapid demise of the moribund regime.[42]

By the late 1980s, the Soviet bloc provided nearly 85 percent of Cuban trade and subsidized 90 percent of the island's energy needs. Between 1989 and 1992, the volume of crucial imports plummeted. Food production decreased in some sectors by 80 percent, and the economy, as a whole, shrank by over 40 percent.[43] These contractions were compounded by dramatic increases in world prices for subsistence imports such as wheat, chicken, milk, and petroleum; prices for Cuban exports such as nickel and sugar dropped by 25 percent.[44] As historian Louis Pérez, Jr. argues, "The rise of market economies in eastern Europe had calamitous consequences in Cuba."[45] The complex series of trade agreements with the Soviet bloc had underwritten the economic survival of the government, but it was not the decline of communism taking place in Eastern Europe alone that accounted for Cuba's economic crisis. The eighties had been a disastrous decade for the island's economy. Heavy borrowing of petrodollars had led to several defaults on loan payments, credit downgrades, and low sugar prices were aggravated by stifling production inefficiencies, obsolete infrastructure, and the continuing U.S. economic embargo. Cuba survived, in part, by selling highly subsidized, surplus Soviet oil on the international market. This measure alone could not provide the Castro government with enough exchangeable currency to service its growing debt. With the fall of the Soviet Union, even this tenuous source of revenue disappeared.

In the early 1990s, press accounts, along with Bush administration interpretations of events on the island, confidently predicted the downfall of Fidel

Castro.[46] Bumper stickers in Miami read "Christmas in Havana," to express the confidence among Cuban Americans that the government was in its final days.[47] President George H. W. Bush was certain: "Castro will not survive this . . . I'm not going to change American policy. We will not lighten up. We are going to stay with it."[48]

Fidel Castro drew one clear lesson from events in Eastern Europe: Any concessions toward market reforms would inexorably lead to the downfall of his government and the loss of Cuban sovereignty. *Perestroika* and *glasnost,* accordingly, were errors. The answer was to dig in further, call for belt-tightening amid growing material scarcity, and return to moral over material incentives for collective action. This policy was a rollback of nascent economic reforms, such as allowing farmers' markets, introduced in the late seventies and early eighties. This process came to be known as the "rectification of errors and negative tendencies."[49]

Both Castro and George H. W. Bush refused to amend the intransigent approach of the previous decade under Reagan. Washington, however, now accelerated its plans for regime change.[50] Every presidential administration since Eisenhower had spoken out against the dictatorial nature of the government in Cuba. The Bush administration, however, became the first to demand political transition as a precondition for any improvement in relations.[51] Avoiding substantial bilateral talks, Bush opted to put pressure on Mikhail Gorbachev to end the aid and trade infusion, which amounted to roughly five billion dollars per year. On multiple occasions, the U.S. president made this alteration of Soviet economic policy a precondition for desperately needed U.S. aid to the Soviet economy. Gorbachev and, later, Boris Yeltsin, courted this assistance. By 1992, virtually all aid to Cuba, from the former USSR and the eastern bloc, along with all remaining military personnel, evaporated. Cuba, echoing big power negotiations over the fate of the island over the last century, was not consulted, and learned of these policy changes via press releases of the meetings between secretary of state James Baker and Soviet/Russian leaders.

When the Castro government did not immediately collapse of its own weight and the continued economic embargo, CANF's leader, Jorge Mas Canosa, shepherded legislation to hasten "regime change." The Torricelli Bill was signed into law as the Cuban Democracy Act in 1992. Robert Torricelli, a U.S. Representative from New Jersey, had taken over as chair of the House Subcommittee on Western Hemisphere Affairs and had close ties with the anti-Castro CANF in a state with a high concentration of Cuban American voters. The law, introduced as an ideologically driven defense of "human rights and democratic values," was intended to make material scarcity even more unbearable for Cubans. This would, ostensibly, create a critical mass of discontent necessary to delegitimize the Cuban government and lead transition to a neoliberal regime, directed and supported by the United

States. The method proposed to reach this shift was to implement prohibitions against overseas subsidiaries of American companies doing business in Cuba. In 1975, Gerald Ford had allowed these subsidiaries to obtain licenses from the Treasury Department's Office of Foreign Assets Control (OFAC) to conduct business with Cuba. The reasoning was clear: strangling the Cuban economy was not worth the potential risk to other U.S. international relationships by imposition of extraterritorial laws that sought to dictate the trade policy of its allies. In the context of the Cold War, it had made little sense to try to bully sovereign nations to achieve policy goals against Cuba.

Since the revocation of Soviet subsidies, the volume of this trade had nearly doubled to roughly $705 million. Mr. Mas Canosa and CANF, along with their chief allies in the House and Senate, Representative Torricelli and Senators Helms (NC) and Graham (FL), now controlled this aspect of U.S. foreign policy. *The New York Times*, in a 1992 profile of Mas Canosa, accurately displayed the ambiguity of his effect on Cuban and Latin American policies for both parties. As Bill Clinton and George Bush courted his approval in pursuit of the Cuban American vote, he was "Statesman to some, bully to others."[52] Proponents of the law likened it to policies that brought about the fall of the apartheid regime in South Africa.[53] These views overlooked that Cuban forces had fought in Angola and supported Namibia *against* South Africa and that the embargo against the racialist government was a multilateral United Nations action—not a unilateral embargo like the one against Cuba. This type of reasoning was exemplar of the post–Cold War shift back to the U.S. role as a mediator of democracy for "lesser nations." Compromise and debate was now a legal impossibility. As one Cuban diplomat wrote, "if Reagan killed normalization, Bush and his allies were its grave diggers."[54]

The new law went beyond commercial relations and further restricted travel from the United States to Cuba. It authorized OFAC to level civil penalties of up to $50,000 for violations of the travel ban. The Cuban Democracy Act also allowed OFAC to sidestep the Justice Department—with its presumption of innocence—to facilitate penalizing those violating the travel ban. As Lars Schoultz demonstrates, this violation of Sixth Amendment rights also disregarded the right of U.S. citizens to travel, in exercise of their First Amendment rights as established by the Supreme Court in 1969.[55]

While the Cuban Democracy Act allowed the U.S. president some latitude on enforcement, it set preconditions on the nature of change in Cuba: "the law now stipulated what constituted a free and fair election, and Cuba's acceptance of that blueprint represented a nonnegotiable demand: the president was authorized to lift or waive the sanctions when—and only when—Cuba capitulated . . . [and] added the requirement that Cuba accept the prevailing U.S. blueprint of how an economy should be organized, stipulating that sanctions could not be waived unless Cuba 'is moving toward establishing a free market economic system.'"[56] The United States now expanded its self-designated power over Cuba into the realm of defining its future economic philosophy.

Though George H. W. Bush showed some reluctance to sign the Cuban Democracy Act, domestic politics in an election year prevailed. The strategic importance of Mas Canosa and the Cuban American vote overrode clear indications that U.S. allies would be ruffled by the extraterritorial stipulations that demanded U.S. jurisdiction over companies operating within their boundaries. While Bush wavered, his opponent, democrat Bill Clinton, was certain. If elected president, he would sign the act into law. On the campaign trail, he labeled Bush as too accommodating on Cuba. Fearing the loss of the Cuban American vote in the crucial state of Florida, Bush flew to Miami where he signed the Cuban Democracy Act, in front of Mas Canosa and his CANF associates, a week before the 1992 election.[57] Bush won Florida by a margin of 100,000 votes, down from the 500,000 that had given him easy victory in 1988. Despite losing in Florida, Bill Clinton became president and would have to wrestle with Cuba for the next eight years.

CLINTON, HELMS-BURTON, BROTHERS TO THE RESCUE, AND ELIÁN GONZÁLEZ

No longer a security threat, the government of Fidel Castro was thus characterized by Washington as a political relic, a sore loser unable to accept defeat, and a dictatorship that egregiously violated the human rights of its citizens. Clinton had made two trips to Miami's "Little Havana" to tout his "anti-Castro credentials." After a private meeting with Clinton, Jorge Mas Canosa outraged Republicans by announcing that any fear he may have had about Clinton's militancy against Castro had "dissipated."[58] The radical changes in international politics over the preceding decade had firmly ensconced Cuban policy as a domestic electoral issue.[59]

During his confirmation hearings, nominee for Secretary of State, Warren Christopher, was questioned by Jesse Helms about the new administration's intentions toward Cuba in general and the Cuban Democracy Act in particular. Christopher responded that the current course inherited from the Bush administration needed no revision. This view was seconded by Anthony Lake, the new national security advisor, who characterized Cuba as one of five "outlaw states" whose existence was an assault on the "basic values" of the family of nations.[60] This novel focus on domestic political and economic transformations in Cuba and the salience of CANF as a clearinghouse for the important Cuban American vote framed Clinton's policies. Pressure from CANF was successful in sinking nominations for important cabinet posts and in dominating any discussion of Cuba in Washington.

Despite CANF efforts, an unlikely coalition of Democrats including representative Charles Rangel (D-NY) and farm state agricultural interests, hoping to capture Cuban demand for staple food products, began to call for adjustments in the economic embargo. Perhaps fearing a shift in consensus on the draconian isolation of Cuba, terrorist groups like the Miami-based Alpha-66 pledged to attack any Cuban Americans who tried to visit the island. These threats were backed up with the firebombing of a company that directed charter flights to Havana and several bombings of tourist targets in Havana during the 1990s.

As economic conditions in Cuba deteriorated in the early- to mid-1990s, the government was forced to implement important changes in economic policy in order to ease the material scarcities that plagued daily life. Taking advantage of the flow of cash remittances from relatives in the United States, Cuba legalized the use of the U.S. dollar and allowed for some small-scale private businesses, such as family restaurants known as *paladares* and agricultural markets where farmers were permitted to sell surplus produce. The government also refocused long-term investment in tourism—creating joint ventures with European and Canadian companies to attract the sun and sand and curiosity-seekers, who brought hard currency to the island.

The most important legislative action during the Clinton years was the Helms-Burton Act. It was largely penned by wealthy Cuban American interests, such as Bacardí and the National Association of Sugar Mill Owners, and built upon the Cuban Democracy Act of 1992. The most controversial aspect of Helms-Burton was its extraterritoriality and its ex post facto–granting of some citizenship rights to Cuban Americans. Its authors sought to sanction and penalize any foreign investor or corporation that invested in Cuban property that had been expropriated by the revolutionary government. Amazingly, the bill called for protection of Cuban American property rights "whether or not the United States national qualified as a United States national at the time of the Cuban government action."[61] For U.S. legislators, the most troubling aspect of the law was its perceived aggression against third-country corporations. Not only did it potentially extend the jurisdiction of U.S. courts into the sovereign territory of several European allies, it threatened to deny U.S. entry visas to employees of any foreign corporation not abiding by the dictates of that law. Importantly, Helms-Burton also stipulated over a dozen preconditions for any negotiation toward normalization.

While this bill worked its way through Congress toward the end of 1995, Clinton announced a series of measures to loosen travel restrictions and to fund and encourage the fledgling civil society in Cuba. On February 24, 1996, the Cuban air force shot down two American civilian airplanes over Cuban airspace. The planes and pilots belonged to an organization called Brothers to the Rescue, a Cuban American group that had begun flights in the early 1990s over the Florida Strait to locate and rescue endangered migrants/

rafters. After the *balsero* crisis had subsided, the pilots shifted their focus, regularly violating Cuban airspace and dropping pro-democracy pamphlets over Havana. Between 1995 and 1996, the Cuban government lodged multiple formal complaints with the United States, making it clear that its patience for these acts of provocation would not last forever. On February 24, 1996, the Cuban Air Force made good on its threats, shooting down two planes and killing four U.S. citizens. Prompted by public outrage over this event, a clear violation of international law in response to intentionally provocative flights that were also a clear violation of international law, Clinton put aside his objections to Helms-Burton and gave his full backing to even the most controversial extraterritorial provisions. In signing the bill, the president also abandoned executive control over the embargo: For the first time, it was codified into federal law; it would now take congressional action to overturn it. Neither Clinton nor his advisors had clearly understood the ramifications of this surrender of executive control. Years later, Clinton remembered that the decision, made regretfully, was good election-year politics (1996), and it likely helped deliver Florida for the Democrats for the first time since 1976.[62] Since the Kennedy administration, the embargo had been maintained by executive order. As the polarization of the Cold War faded, Helms-Burton illustrated the shift from containment to regime change.

The final episode of Clinton-era Cuban policy played out around the fate of a seven-year-old Cuban boy who was rescued, by fishermen, floating on an inner tube in the Florida Strait. In November 1999, Elían González's mother and others drowned while attempting to escape Cuba to join relatives in Miami. González's father, who had not known of his ex-wife's plan, immediately sought to have his son returned to Cuba. U.S. Immigration and Naturalization Service had temporarily placed the boy with relatives in Miami. The Miami relatives were loathe to return the angelic Elián to communist Cuba. The father, Juan Miguel, a hard-working party loyalist and—by all accounts—loving father accused the relatives of kidnapping. The ensuing battle over repatriation worked its way through the courts. Media coverage revealed the intensity of anti-Castro sentiment among the powerful Cuban American community, as it fought to intercede in order to grant Elián asylum. The months-long saga also provided a national cause for the Cuban government. Even with material scarcities of the Special Period, thousands of shirts bearing the image of the boy's face and the slogan "Let's save Elián" were distributed at rallies in Cuba. When the U.S. Supreme Court refused to hear the case, INS agents stormed his relatives' Miami home, providing one of the most iconic photographs of the Cuban-U.S. relationship: Law enforcement officers, fully armed with riot gear, pulling a terrified child from a closet and out of the arms (literally) of the Miami relatives. Even though a majority of Americans were in favor of returning Elián to his father, CANF waged an all-out propaganda war against it.[63] The political costs of repatriation were high. Bill Clinton suggests in his memoir that the decision to reunite Elián with his father likely cost Al Gore the state of Florida and the presidency in 2000.[64] Though Clinton had eased some restrictions on people-to-people contact in an attempt to strengthen civil society, the weight of Helms-Burton further tipped the scales toward the continued isolation of Cuba.

GEORGE W. BUSH AND THE DEMAND FOR DEMOCRACY IN CUBA

The Cuban government's reaction to the election of George W. Bush and his two terms in office was unambiguous. For Sánchez-Parodi, Bush was "perhaps the most inept president the northern nation has ever had."[65]

Bush's tenuous victory in the 2000 presidential elections gave conservative Cuban Americans control of Cuba policy as a reward for support during the campaign. According to Lars Schoultz, these highly placed political operators within the State Department and on the National Security Council all had "deep ties to the anti-Castro world." Thinking ahead to the 2004 elections, it was clear that Bush would need a strong showing in Florida and was willing to deliver Cuba policy to the loudest Cuban American voices:

> The result of these calculations was obvious: after the 2000 election, Cuban Americans were handed U.S. policy toward Cuba in the same way that agricultural interests have traditionally received U.S. farm policy—not unchecked, of course, but allowed to go one step beyond the high-level lobbying access that Cuban immigrants had earned after two decades of generous campaign contributions and solid bloc voting . . . and while the political beliefs of the Cuban-American community were becoming increasingly diverse, such was not the case for the conservatives appointed by President Bush.[66]

Secretary of state Colin Powell made clear his disdain for Fidel Castro and his regime, but beyond ad hominem verbal attacks on the Cuban leader as "an aging starlet" and "a relic," there was little discussion of plans to actively precipitate the fall of the regime. Cuba was largely irrelevant as a foreign policy issue; it had become a domestic political focus. These conditions emerged when the United States was attacked on September 11, 2001.

In the post-9/11 context, the designation of Cuba as a sponsor of terrorism became increasingly unjustifiable. Even with an official policy of antagonism, U.S. agricultural interests were gaining momentum toward normalization of commercial relations by successful circumvention of the embargo on food sales to the island. Leaders representing the farm lobby, Republican and Democrat, argued that U.S. policy unfairly hindered the free market and trade with the largest island in the Caribbean. Combined with the Bush administration's pledge to allow food aid for Cuba in the aftermath of the devastating Hurricane Michelle in late 2001, these important shifts created a bipartisan pathway forward. In 2002, a number of Republican senators, along with former president Jimmy Carter, traveled to Cuba and came back with firsthand accounts of Cuba that encouraged greater dialogue. During his trip, Carter was allowed to address the Cuban public with no preconditions on the content of his remarks. He praised dissident Cubans while calling for an end to the embargo. In 1999, a group of aging Cuban musicians named the "Buena Vista Social Club" were introduced to the American public and received enormous acclaim for their music and the documentary portrayal of their lives. Despite this economic and cultural engagement, the politics of inertia continued to dominate the relationship.

Bush moved to reapply strict prohibitions on travel to Cuba. His administration, through the Office of Foreign Assets Control (OFAC), began stepping up fines for those thought to have traveled illegally to the island—reversing the lax and unfunded enforcement during the Clinton years. U.S. citizens were free to travel to almost any other country. Libertarians and Democrats joined to question this policy, which Jimmy Carter had called "an imposition on the human rights of American citizens." As the 2004 election approached, Bush unveiled the focal point of his Cuba policy in an attempt to hold on to the Cuban American vote: The Commission for Assistance to a Free Cuba.

The 2004 report, authored by the Council on Foreign Relations, reserved for the United States the right to define the nature of Cuba's future. The central tenets of the plan were for free elections (unless the results did not fit Washington's model), a neoliberal market economy, and the provision of U.S. subsidies. Far from novel, the presumption that the political and economic models approved by Washington were best for Cubans followed those patterns that began in the nineteenth century. These latest recommendations focused on further tightening the embargo and supporting Cuban dissident and civic social organizations on the island.

New restrictions on travel and remittances most directly affected Cuban Americans who could now visit the island once every three years (instead of yearly), could only bring forty-four pounds of luggage, and were limited to spending fifty dollars per day. The new policy also cut down on academic and person-to-person exchanges. The second strategy—to destabilize the government by supporting internal dissent—was funded by millions of dollars dedicated to strengthening Radio and TV Martí, and a range of other initiatives designed to foster discontent into organized resistance to the government. Though several of these initiatives built on Clinton-era policies, the Bush administration ramped up enforcement and funding for often highly questionable expenditures, ostensibly dedicated to hastening the transition.[67]

Under James Cason, the U.S. Cuban Interests Section became a node for distributing pro-democracy literature and thousands of shortwave radios to Cuban dissidents. It provided on-site Internet via a rooftop satellite connection, allowing a few Cubans to bypass stringent access restrictions. USAID focused on multiple projects designed to provide Cubans with information technologies that would allow them to access the Internet. In 2005, Cason's replacement, Michael Parmly, inaugurated a large electronic billboard across the entire side of the Interests Section. The sign criticized the Cuban government and reproduced pro-democracy quotations. Enraged, the Cuban government responded by raising 138 black flags, which blocked the billboard. The relationship between the United States and Cuba had been brought to its most sophomoric level.

In July of 2006, after emergency intestinal surgery, Fidel Castro handed power to his younger brother Raúl. Speculation on the elder Castro's imminent death ran wild as conservative Cuban Americans danced in the Miami streets.[68] Raúl Castro, in one of his first major speeches as president, called for dialogue with the United States. Even though many commentators again predicted the sure demise of the socialist regime, his words could have been cut and pasted from the 1960s, with an offer of negotiation "based on the principles of equality, reciprocity, noninterference, and mutual respect."[69] Bush's policies had been designed to hasten a transition to democracy in Cuba. Despite the millions of dollars spent and the provocative antics of the U.S. Interests Section, none of these major objectives were accomplished. Wars in Iraq and Afghanistan and the epochal global war on terror made Cuban policy a relatively unimportant curiosity. When Barack Obama was elected president in 2008, he carried the state of Florida. Despite criticizing the "failed policy with Cuba for the last fifty years," he promised to promote democracy there as the centerpiece of his approach.

BARACK OBAMA AND A RETURN TO THE TABLE

Obama's victory in Florida showed that the unyielding hard-line on Cuba was no longer necessary to win the state's twenty-seven electoral votes. Following the election, Cubans wore t-shirts that bore the U.S. president's image, portrayed in a laudatory light, on the streets of Havana—a public display of affection that would have been unthinkable during the previous eight years. Other Latin American governments bore high hopes that a changing stance toward Cuba would signal a renewed willingness to engage the rest of the region on the basis of equal sovereignty. At the U.S. Interests Section in Havana, the electronic billboard went dark. The administration lifted the more draconian travel restrictions on academic and cultural exchanges, and for those with family on the island. It opened negotiations on migration that had been suspended since 2004. Despite these overtures, Cuba remained on the State Department's list of state sponsors of terrorism, and the general travel ban continued. The administration still funded "semi-covert" democracy promotion, a holdover from the Bush years, to the tune of $20 million annually for both 2009 and 2010. Obama also continued several USAID programs designed to hasten a democratic transition. At the end of his first year in office, despite rhetoric to the contrary, Cuba policy was still more restrictive than it had been under Bill Clinton and Jimmy Carter.[70]

Secretary of state Hillary Clinton continued to call on Cuba to democratize, release political prisoners, and model its society more closely on blueprints from Washington. The Cuban government, unsurprisingly, critiqued these demands; Raúl Castro portrayed them as domestic political rewards for Cuban American support, and reminded anyone who would listen that the economic embargo remained in place. Washington continued to call for "Net Freedom" in Cuba, reasoning that social networking sites such as Twitter and Facebook constituted important public spaces and that the ability to access them was a modern form of free assembly rights. This conviction increased in 2011, with the series of events known as the Arab Spring. These pro-democracy movements in the Middle East and North Africa relied heavily on social media to organize protests and criticize governments. Dissident Cuban bloggers, such as Yoani Sánchez, were embraced by the Obama administration as the symbol of its vision for a new and critical generation of Cuban dissidents using the Internet to undermine the political monopoly on the media.

Amid these novel forces, the old relationship persisted. In December 2009, Alan Gross, a contractor funded by USAID to distribute communications technologies and set up clandestine Internet access, was arrested by Cuban agents on his fifth trip to the island. Likely prodded by the growing popularity and international clout of dissident bloggers, Raúl Castro cited Gross' actions as proof of the continued attempts by Washington to overthrow the Cuban government. The United States responded by demanding Gross' release before any further talks on normalization could continue. Following this well-established pattern of détente and rupture, this seemed like more of the same. Despite these forebodings, Obama's second term saw the most significant changes in U.S. policy since the beginning of the Cuban Revolution.

These events occurred in relatively rapid succession. After over a year of secret mediation brokered by Pope Francis I, the United States and Cuba announced plans for the restoration of diplomatic relations on December 17, 2014. These announcements were accompanied by a prisoner swap in which the Cuban government released Mr. Gross and a CIA officer in return for the three remaining Cubans convicted of espionage in the late 1990s. In May 2015, the State Department dropped Cuba from its list of state sponsors of terrorism, for the first time in over thirty years. After further negotiations, the U.S. Interests Section reopened in August 2015 as the U.S. Embassy, more than fifty-four years after its closure. In his speech at the flag-raising ceremony, secretary of state John Kerry remarked that both leaders, Obama and Castro, had agreed to "stop being the prisoners of history." While sounding this hopeful note, he also added that "the United States will always remain a champion of democratic principles and reforms," and further impugned the Cuban government to mold its society on principles held by "every other country in the Americas."

By early 2016, the Obama administration had reached the limit to what it could do without a congressional vote to repeal the Helms-Burton law, which had codified the embargo under Bill Clinton. Its stipulations prohibited lifting the economic embargo unless Cuba underwent domestic reforms and democratization. Mr. Obama's second term overtures also had unintended consequences. Due to the Cuban Adjustment Act of 1966, Cuban migrants received preferential treatment and were allowed permanent resident status if they reached U.S. soil. Prompted by movement toward normalization and the fear that they would no longer receive special treatment, thousands of migrants have left the island, taking circuitous and often dangerous paths to reach the United States. While thousands of migrants from other impoverished Latin American nations such as El Salvador, Guatemala, and Honduras were deported from the United States or turned away at the border, Cubans received asylum.[71] This policy, among several idiosyncrasies born of the U.S.-Cuban relationship, is unlikely to change in the near future.

As of this writing, the most important determining factor in the future of this diplomatic relationship which has so often served as a microcosm of U.S.-Latin American relations will be the outcome of the 2016 U.S. presidential elections. One of the Republican candidates, senator Ted Cruz of Texas, is vehemently anti-Castro and portrays the Cuban government as an evil pariah. He pledged to reverse many of Barack Obama's executive actions if successful in winning the election. Both candidates on the Democratic side, senator Bernie Sanders of Vermont and former secretary of state Hillary Clinton, have called for a continuation of diplomatic détente and an end to the economic embargo. They also agree on the need to close the Guantánamo Bay prison, an important stumbling block both in the bilateral relationship and in the perception of U.S. foreign policy in the broader world.

During March 21–23, Barack Obama became the first sitting American president to visit Cuba since 1928. At that time, President Coolidge had disembarked on an island still legally bound by the Platt amendment to truncated sovereignty under the dictatorship of Gerardo Machado. In 2016, Cuba remained under economic embargo and subject to the dictatorship of a one-party state. Appearing at a joint press conference with the eighty-four-year-old Raúl Castro, President Obama struck a conciliatory tone and looked to build on the openings initiated during his second term. He sought to defuse some of the volatile issues of previous negotiations while restating the standard U.S. critique of the regime: "Cuba's destiny will not be decided by the United States or any other country. . . . but the U.S. will continue to speak out on behalf of democracy and human rights."[72] Raúl Castro's remarks impugned what he labeled U.S. hypocrisy on this important issue: "We find it inconceivable that a government does not defend and secure the right to healthcare, equal pay and the rights of children. We oppose political double standards in the approach of human rights."

Though images of Barack Obama and Raúl Castro saturated the front pages of newspapers around the world, implying further reconciliation, the Cuban government continued to demand a return of Guantánamo Bay and a complete lifting of the U.S. economic embargo before full normalization. A few days after these events, Fidel Castro, who had not met with Obama during the visit, responded with a critique of the American's message that gives insight into the continuing impasse. His article, published in the Communist Party newspaper, the *Granma*, quoted Obama's message: "It is time, now, for us to leave the past behind." Castro bristled at Obama's dismissal of the role of history in the present and located Cuban dignity in the accomplishments of the past. Mr. Castro wrote, "all of us were at risk of a heart attack upon hearing these words from the President of the United States."[73] The history of the relationship remains as contested as its future.

NOTES

1. Louis A. Pérez, Jr., *Cuba in the American Imagination: Metaphor and the Imperial Ethos* (Chapel Hill: University of North Carolina Press, 2008), 1.
2. Ramón Sánchez-Parodi, *Cuba-USA: Diez tiempos de una relación* (México D.F.: Ocean Sur, 2011).
3. Louis A. Pérez, Jr., *Cuba in the American Imagination Metaphor and the Imperial Ethos* (Chapel Hill: Univ. of North Carolina Press, 2008).
4. J. R. Bolton, "Beyond the Axis of Evil: Additional Threats from Weapons of Mass Destruction," Heritage Lecture No. 743, May 6, 2002. Online. Available:http://www.heritage.org/research/lecture/beyond-the-axis-of-evil (accessed December 26, 2015); Nigel D. White, *The Cuban Embargo Under International Law: El Bloqueo* (New York: Routledge Press, 2015), 79.
5. Louis A. Pérez, Jr., *Cuba and the United States: Ties of Singular Intimacy* (Athens: University of Georgia Press, 1990), p. xiv; Keith Bolender, *Voices from the Other Side: An Oral History of Terrorism against Cuba* (London: Pluto, 2010).
6. Jeff Zeleny, "Obama, in Miami, Calls for Engaging With Cuba," *The New York Times,* May 24, 2008.
7. Jeff Rathke, "Rescission of Cuba as a State Sponsor of Terrorism," Department of State Press Release, May 29, 2015. Online. Available:http://www.state.gov/r/pa/prs/ps/2015/05/242986.htm (accessed December 27, 2015); John Kerry, "Remarks at Flag Raising Ceremony," Department of State, August 14, 2015. Online. Available: http://www.state.gov/secretary/remarks/2015/08/246121.htm (accessed December 27, 2015).
8. Mattathias Schwartz, "Is Obama Serious About Closing Guantánamo?" *The New Yorker*, January 22, 2016.

9. Gallup Poll, "Do you favor or oppose re-establishing U.S. diplomatic relations with Cuba?" Data available from 1975–2015. Online. Available:http://www.gallup.com/poll/1630/cuba.aspx (accessed January 4, 2016). No reliable statistics exist for Cuban opinions on the same question.

10. Lizette Alvarez and Manny Fernandez, "Marco Rubio and Ted Cruz Diverge in Approach to Their Hispanic Identity," *The New York Times*, December 16, 2015.

11. Marifeli Pérez-Stable, *The Cuban Revolution: Origins, Course and Legacy* (New York: Oxford University Press, 2012), 119–23.

12. Piero Gleijeses, *Conflicting Missions: Havana, Washington, and Africa, 1959–1976* (Chapel Hill: University of North Carolina Press, 2002).

13. Louis A. Pérez, Jr., *Cuba: Between Reform and Revolution*, 5th ed. (New York: Oxford University Press, 2015), 300.

14. Gleijeses, *Conflicting Missions*; Piero Gleijeses, *Visions of Freedom: Havana, Washington, Pretoria, and the Struggle for Southern Africa, 1976–1991* (Chapel Hill: University of North Carolina Press, 2016).

15. Lars Schoultz, *That Infernal Little Cuban Republic: The United States and the Cuban Revolution* (Chapel Hill: University of North Carolina Press, 2009), chap. 10.

16. "Illegal exits" were defined by the Cuban government as any flight without prior exit visa. Another type of illegal emigration that caused diplomatic friction was the hijacking of Cuban boats and airplanes to the United States. These sometimes involved killings and other violent crimes.

17. Schoultz, *That Infernal Little Cuban Republic*, 354.

18. See Sánchez-Parodi, *Cuba-USA.*

19. Luis Martínez-Fernández, *Revolutionary Cuba: A History* (Gainesville: University Press of Florida, 2014), 157–63.

20. Martínez-Fernández, *Revolutionary Cuba,* 160.

21. Schoultz, *That Infernal Little Cuban Republic,* 469.

22. Schoultz, *That Infernal Little Cuban Republic,* 359–60.

23. Pérez, Jr., *Cuba: Between Reform and Revolution,* 302.

24. Schoultz, *That Infernal Little Cuban Republic*, 362.

25. William M. LeoGrande and Peter Kornbluh, *Back Channel to Cuba: The Hidden History of Negotiations Between Washington and Havana* (Chapel Hill: University of North Carolina Press, 2014), 225.

26. Leslie Maitland Werner, "U.S. Officials Link Castro and Drugs," *The New York Times*, November 10, 1983.

27. Werner, "U.S. Officials Link Castro and Drugs."

28. Sánchez-Parodi, *Cuba-USA,* 197.

29. LeoGrande and Kornbluh, *Back Channel to Cuba,* 226–27.

30. LeoGrande and Kornbluh, *Back Channel to Cuba,* 226–27.

31. Schoultz, *That Infernal Little Cuban Republic,* 390–91.

32. Martínez-Fernández, *Revolutionary Cuba*, 150–51.

33. Schoultz, *That Infernal Little Cuban Republic,* 390–91.

34. Stephen Kinzer, "Castro Denounces Reagan in Speech," *New York Times,* January 3, 1984.

35. LeoGrande and Kornbluh, *Back Channel to Cuba,* 388–89.

36. Schoultz, *That Infernal Little Cuban Republic*, 389–90.

37. Timothy B. Tyson, *Radio Free Dixie: Robert F. Williams and the Roots of Black Power* (Chapel Hill: University of North Carolina Press, 1999), chap. 8.

38. Schoultz, *That Infernal Little Cuban Republic,* 402.

39. LeoGrande and Kornbluh, *Back Channel to Cuba,* 245.

40. Quoted in Schoultz, *That Infernal Little Cuban Republic*, 417.

41. Schoultz, *That Infernal Little Cuban Republic*, 418.

42. Andrés Oppenheimer, *Castro's Final Hour: An Eyewitness Account of the Disintegration of Castro's Cuba* (NY: Simon and Schuster, 1992).

43. Pérez, Jr., *Cuba: Between Reform and Revolution*, 304–05.

44. Schoultz, *That Infernal Little Cuban Republic,* 429.

45. Pérez, Jr., *Cuba: Between Reform and Revolution* 304.
46. Clifford Krauss, "The Last Stalinist," *New York Times*, February 10, 1991.
47. Susan Kaufman Purcell, "Cuba's Cloudy Future," *Foreign Affairs* 69, no. 3 (Summer 1990): 130–45.
48. United States, *Public Papers of the Presidents of the United States, George Bush: July 1 to December 31, 1991* (Washington, DC: U.S. G.P.O., 1992), 1495.
49. Susan Eckstein, "The Rectification of Errors or the Errors of the Rectification Process in Cuba," *Cuban Studies* 20 (1990): 67–85.
50. Schoultz, *That Infernal Little Cuban Republic,* 424–25.
51. LeoGrande and Kornbluh, *Back Channel to Cuba,* 266.
52. Larry Rohter, "A Rising Cuban-American Leader: Statesman to Some, Bully to Others," *The New York Times*, October 29, 1992.
53. United States, The Cuban Democracy Act of 1992, S. 2918: Hearing Before the Subcommittee on Western Hemisphere and Peace Corps Affairs of the Committee on Foreign Relations, United States Senate, One Hundred Second Congress, Second Session, August 5, 1992 (Washington: U.S. G.P.O., 1992), 62.
54. Sánchez-Parodi, *Cuba-USA*, 203.
55. Schoultz, *That Infernal Little Cuban Republic,* chap. 12.
56. Schoultz, *That Infernal Little Cuban Republic,* 451.
57. LeoGrande and Kornbluh, *Back Channel to Cuba,* 271.
58. Larry Rohter, "The 1992 Campaign: Florida; Clinton Sees Opportunity to Break G.O.P Grip on Cuban-Americans," *The New York Times*, October 31, 1992.
59. Jessica F. Gibbs, *US Policy Towards Cuba: Since the Cold War* (Milton Park, NY: Routledge, 2011), p. 27–55.
60. Schoultz, *That Infernal Little Cuban Republic,* chap. 13.
61. Schoultz, *That Infernal Little Cuban Republic,* 478.
62. Bill Clinton, *My Life, Volume II: The Presidential Years* (New York: Vintage Books, 2005), 310.
63. Lorena G. Barberia, "U.S. Immigration Policies Toward Cuba," in Jorge I. Domínguez, Rafael Hernández, and Lorena G. Barbeira, eds., *Debating U.S.-Cuban Relations: Shall We Play Ball?* (New York: Routledge, 2012), 180–201.
64. Schoultz, *That Infernal Little Cuban Republic,* 515.
65. Sánchez-Parodi, *Cuba-USA,* 215.
66. Sánchez-Parodi, *Cuba-USA,* 516.
67. Schoultz, *That Infernal Little Cuban Republic,* 546–47.
68. LeoGrande and Kornbluh, *Back Channel to Cuba,* 365.
69. LeoGrande and Kornbluh, *Back Channel to Cuba,* 366.
70. LeoGrande and Kornbluh, *Back Channel to Cuba,* 372.
71. Jonathan Blitzer, "The Cuban Migrant Crisis," *The New Yorker,* January 16, 2016.
72. Dan Roberts and Jonathan Watts, "Castro Demands Return of Guantánamo Bay During Historic Obama Visit," *The Guardian,* March 21, 2016.
73. Fidel Castro Ruz, "Brother Obama" *Granma,* March 28, 2016.

Chapter Seven

The Limits of Hegemony? 1979–c. 1990

Perceptions of failure in foreign relations ruined the Carter presidency in 1979 and 1980. A seeming incapacity to respond effectively to the Soviet invasion of Afghanistan created impressions of incompetence and impotence, and the overthrow of dictatorial but pro-U.S. regimes by revolutionary forces in Iran and Nicaragua reinforced the point. According to the distinction established by Jeane J. Kirkpatrick, the United States possessed a responsibility to support and sustain less-than-perfect *authoritarian* rulers as bulwarks against more insidious forms of *totalitarian* communism. Under Reagan in the 1980s, the United States sought to correct the failure to do so through the exercise of determination and strength.

CARTER'S LAST DAYS

In Latin America, Jimmy Carter's attempt to affirm a more valid combination of morality, reason, and power obtained a kind of vindication in the Panama Canal treaties. As Walter LaFeber notes, those agreements actually constituted a "diplomatic triumph" for the United States. By agreeing to give up control of the Canal Zone after a period of twenty-five years, the Carter administration successfully eliminated what had become a constant irritant in Latin American relations and, at the same time, John Coatsworth observes, secured from Panama an agreement to permit unilateral intervention "in perpetuity." Although the United States gave up military bases in Panama, it retained the right for its warships and commercial vessels to have top priority in case of an emergency.[1] Nevertheless, clamorous outrage among political rightists in the United States exacted a political cost. Chief among the critics, Ronald Reagan, a presidential aspirant in 1980, excoriated Carter for giving away the canal.[2]

Other conspicuous difficulties in Central America emanated to an extent from economic conditions. Unlike the 1960s, a time of booming exports for coffee and bananas, the 1970s saw trade contractions that caused instability and political polarization. The rise in oil prices during the shock of 1973 also hit Central America hard. The combined effects increased popular discontent "to levels unprecedented in Central American history." As Coatsworth explains, organizational efforts among workers and peasants seeking amelioration led to protests and demonstrations. In Costa Rica, Honduras, and Panama, conciliation on the part of political leaders headed off full-scale crises, but in Nicaragua, Guatemala, and El Salvador, the traditional elites responded with ruthless repression. The result was chronic violence and conflict that reached a peak late in the 1970s.

None of Carter's advisers, who had viewed Central America as a region in which to press for human rights, anticipated the actual extent of the turmoil. In El Salvador, widespread discontent over a fraudulent election in 1977 encouraged the government of general Carlos Humberto Romero to employ terror against the opposition, using government-sanctioned death squads. Such methods ignited a civil war. Similarly, rigged elections in Guatemala brought into power the military governments of general Kjell Laugerud in 1974 and general Romeo Lucas García in 1978. Each used armed force indiscriminately against a growing guerrilla movement in the countryside, wreaking havoc among rural people. Many of the 200,000 to 300,000 Guatemalans who lost their lives for political reasons after 1954 did so during the crackdown between 1977 and 1983.[3] In fact, one of the more nefarious periods in contemporary Latin American history is associated with the Efraín Ríos Montt administration in Guatemala. General Ríos Montt took power in a military coup in 1982 and remained in power until another coup removed him a year later. However, during his short tenure in office, the general and his supporters conducted a scorched earth campaign designed to eliminate all communists from Guatemala. The campaign was supported with military equipment from the United States and the approbation of President Reagan in Washington.

Guatemala's rich indigenous heritage was viewed as an obstacle to the Ríos Montt regime, and as many as 600 villages were destroyed by the military. These villages were viewed as safe havens for "subversives"; for orchestrating this brutal campaign, the general was convicted of genocide in a Guatemalan court in 2013. The conviction was overturned, however, by the Guatemalan constitutional court (Corte de Constitucionalidad). After his ouster, the war raged on for another thirteen years until peace accords were signed in 1996, ending a thirty-six year civil war that killed perhaps a quarter-million Guatemalans.

Two years after the accords were signed, in April 1998, the "Recovery of Historical Memory Project" (*Recuperación de la Memoria Histórica—*

REMHI) released its report titled "Guatemala: Nunca Más!"; two days later, Juan José Gerardi, the Catholic bishop who had served on the National Reconciliation Commission—a man respected for his deep, long-standing commitment to human rights—was bludgeoned to death in his garage. This crime seemed almost like magic—black magic—and the investigation of the murder was written up in an extraordinary book that is a sort of hybrid between murder-mystery and journalism, by Guatemalan writer Francisco Goldman, titled *The Art of Political Murder: Who Killed the Bishop?*

At the height of the Ríos Montt military campaign in Guatemala, a young indigenous woman named Rigoberta Menchú Tum published a book that would earn her worldwide fame and a Nobel Peace Prize in 1992. Ms. Menchú revealed her story, orally, to a French anthropologist, Elisabeth Burgos, and the book that emerged in 1983, *Me llamo Rigoberta Menchú y así me nació la conciencia*, shocked people in Europe and the United States for its clear, unsentimental account of the atrocities being committed in Guatemala, a place most people didn't even know existed. The book was translated to English in 1984 as *I, Rigoberta Menchú.*

In Nicaragua, by contrast, a broad-based revolutionary movement actually succeeded in taking power by ousting the right-wing regime of Anastasio Somoza. Named for Augusto César Sandino, the revolutionary hero assassinated in 1934, the Frente Sandinista de Liberación Nacional (FSLN), or Sandinista National Liberation Front, encompassed a range of political views affirmed through a collective leadership. The group asserted strong nationalism, Marxist convictions, and Christian religious fervor by embracing a form of liberation theology. This shift in Roman Catholic thinking weakened the traditional association between the church hierarchy and the conservative elites of Latin America. Based on Pope John XXIII's encyclicals of 1961 and 1963, liberation theology stressed the importance of human rights and decent living standards for all people. Without these, the pope warned, a deluge of violence and revolution could engulf the Christian world. At the Second Vatican Council (1963–1965), he encouraged studies of economic development through the use of the social sciences. One effect was to expose Roman Catholic clergy to dependency theory as a means of explaining the stagnation of Latin American economies and the gap between the rich and the poor.

At the Second General Conference of Latin American Bishops at Medellín, Colombia, in 1968, church officials went on record in support of social justice and condemned the prevalence of "institutionalized violence." This term referred to structural inequalities presumably built into political, economic, and social systems, the effects of which were poverty and powerlessness for millions of people. As a means of alleviating inequities, the bishops called upon poor people to assume greater responsibility for their own well-being by joining in positive action to ensure a fairer distribution of freedom, justice, and opportunity. Seeking to avoid the extremes of capitalism and communism, they hoped to locate a third and independent option. Just where it might reside, no one knew for sure.

To its detractors, liberation theology was seen as a Marxist takeover of the Roman Catholic Church. Pope John Paul II, elected to the papacy in 1978, was strongly against priests committing to political work and believed priests and bishops should stay out of temporal affairs and focus on spiritual questions related to the church's sacraments and institutional traditions. Karol Wojtyla witnessed the extremes of politics in his native Poland during the Second World War and, later, with the Soviet Union's domination; thus, his agenda was eminently conservative and he had little patience for politicized priests.

Wojtyla was able to undo much of the "liberationist" work of the late 1960s by removing or appointing bishops and cardinals who reflected his thinking. Cardinal Paolo Evaristo Arns, for example, in Brazil, a leading proponent of the poor and a supporter of liberation theology, saw his archdiocese reduced to the center city of São Paulo. Yet, Colombian Alfonso López Trujillo, a strict conservative cleric, was elevated to cardinal in 1983, under John Paul II, and became president of the Pontifical Council for the Family in Rome. There, he advocated hierarchical, conservative programs that stressed the traditional teachings of the Roman Catholic Church.

Priests motivated by the 1968 Medellín meeting lived throughout the Latin American region, and the leading proponents of this "new" theology and theoreticians were: Peruvian Gustavo Gutiérrez; Brazilians Dom Helder Câmara, Clodovis and Leonardo Boff; Chilean Manuel Larraín; and Panamanian Marcos McGrath. Not surprisingly, many of the important practitioners of liberation theology lived in Central America. Five priests, in fact, rose to prominence in the 1979 Sandinista government in Nicaragua; Fernando Cardenal became Minister of Education, Ernesto Cardenál—a well-known poet—was appointed Minister of Culture, and Miguel D'Escoto became the Foreign Minister in the new revolutionary government. These priests, and others, were committed to working with and helping the poor in a nation that had been ravaged by a single family—the Somozas—who collectively had lorded over that land since the 1930s. It is estimated that, at the time of his departure for Paraguay (where he was later killed), Anastasio Somoza and family controlled between 33 and 50 percent of the entire Nicaraguan economy.

Political activists in Central America and throughout Latin America found hope in the idea of working directly with poor people. As one means of doing so, priests and nuns in various localities established base communities from which to advance the interests of peasants and workers in a kind of grassroots operation. Though usually nonviolent in intent, such forms of engagement and agitation exposed priests, nuns, and other dissidents to retaliation, sometimes in the form of torture and murder. In El Salvador a vigilante group known as the White Warriors circulated pamphlets that exhorted: "Be a patriot! Kill a priest!" In response, some clerics subordinated commitment to nonviolence in favor of direct political action. Consequently, by the time the Third General Conference of Latin American Bishops met at Puebla, Mexico in 1979, many priests and nuns at the parish level had undergone a process of radicalization that marked a growing political distance between them and their more conservative superiors. At Puebla the bishops struggled with the difficulty of achieving social justice. They condemned both capitalist and communist systems for tending to abuse human beings; at the same time, they opposed the violence perpetrated by guerrilla forces and by government thugs. They also criticized the selfishness of multinational corporations, affirmed the irrelevancy for most Third World countries of Walt Rostow's "stages of economic growth" theories, and endorsed broad definitions of human rights for all peoples. Church leaders paid the price; according to one source, about 850 priests, nuns, and other officials in Latin America, during the 1970s, experienced intimidation, harassment, torture, or murder. As LaFeber remarks, the Roman Catholic Church had moved onto "the firing line."[4]

The advocates of change in Central America won a significant victory on July 19, 1979, when the FSLN took over the government in Nicaragua. Founded in 1961, the movement had been fighting the Somoza dictatorship for eighteen years. President Anastasio Somoza Debayle, son of the founder of the dynasty, had withstood Sandinista guerrilla actions in the 1960s and early 1970s, usually with the aid and assistance of the United States. But his power had waned significantly after the earthquake of December 23, 1972. In response to the devastation in the capital city, Managua, his government's display of corruption and incompetency alienated and offended even former loyalists in the business community and elsewhere. Consequently, as Coatsworth explains, "widespread popular discontent" developed among workers, peasants, and students who reacted to deteriorating wages and landlessness with demands for democracy and justice. Meanwhile, strong denunciations of Somoza's rule appeared in the newspaper *La Prensa* and among the intellectual and political leaders of the opposition.

As the country descended into civil war, the FSLN emerged as a major force among Somoza's enemies. The Sandinistas had tried unsuccessfully to coordinate a major military effort against Somoza in October 1977, but they benefited politically on January 10, 1978, when unknown assailants assassinated a journalist, Pedro Joaquín Chamorro, the anti-Somoza publisher of *La Prensa.* This event triggered a series of strikes lasting three weeks and further unsettled the nation's economy. In 1978 and 1979, the anti-Somoza agitation increased and the guerrilla movement escalated. To the surprise of many observers, Somoza's military force, the National Guard, could not ensure victory against the insurgents and Somoza, as a consequence, conceded defeat. On July 17, 1979, he fled to Paraguay. Coatsworth sums up the outcome with these words: "Support for the revolution was so widespread among all social classes and political organizations in the country that the survival of the Somoza regime, with or without Somoza at the helm, could not have been guaranteed without a foreign occupation."

When the Carter administration took office in January 1977, U.S. officials displayed a tendency to overestimate Somoza's staying power. For more than two years, Carter officials followed a consistent strategy seeking, simultaneously, Somoza's departure from office and a takeover by political moderates instead of the FSLM. Conceivably, free elections could do the trick, but Somoza's term would not end until 1981. U.S. officials therefore indulged in a double game; on the one hand, allowing the FSLN to put pressure on Somoza, and, on the other, looking for a more moderate alternative. They hoped to achieve a political transition in which the traditional political parties and the business community could play a major role. Meanwhile, Somoza attempted to save himself through obstruction and delay, seeking to prevent the emergence of a moderate alternative.

Neither strategy had the desired effect. For the United States, no workable means for locating a moderate alternative ever materialized, and Somoza was unable to save his regime. During the spring and summer of 1978, the intensification of the guerrilla war reinforced the view in the Carter administration that Somoza would have to go. The stabilization of the country presumably depended upon it, for a protracted struggle might produce such polarization that moderation could not exist. The efforts of the OAS to mediate a settlement met with failure, largely because of Somoza's resistance, and the idea of holding a national referendum, favored by other Latin Americans, also came to nothing. The United States, meanwhile, chose to wait until military setbacks forced Somoza into negotiations.

By the summer of 1979, the FSLN stood on the verge of a victory unless the United States intervened in some dramatic way to alter the outcome. U.S. leaders at this point wanted to encourage Somoza's resignation but hoped to avoid a full-scale defeat of the National Guard in order to retain some leverage for picking a successor. That aim eluded fulfillment. On June 17, 1979, the opposition established an interim government by creating a Council of National Reconstruction, a process in which the Carter administration had no say. The group consisted of Daniel Ortega, Sergio Ramírez, and Moisés Hassan—all representatives of the FSLN—plus Violeta Chamorro, the widow of the murdered newspaper editor, and Alfonso Robelo, a businessman. This fairly broad-based collectivity attracted support from all the anti-Somoza organizations in Nicaragua and U.S. ambassador Lawrence Pezzullo failed in his efforts to expand the presence of political moderates. Meanwhile, units of Somoza's National Guard disintegrated completely. On July 19, 1979, the Sandinistas announced a victory.[5]

Bitter recriminations quickly followed. When the Sandinistas endorsed Marxist principles and accepted aid and support from Cuba, Carter's critics in the United States rushed to the microphones. Ranking high among them, Jeane J. Kirkpatrick, a political scientist from Georgetown University, assailed Carter's shortcomings in the November 1979 issue of *Commentary*, a journal of neoconservative opinion. Her essay, "Dictatorships and Double Standards," argued that Carter's "lack of realism" rather than "deep historical forces" had accounted for recent disasters in foreign affairs, typified by the overthrow of Somoza and the Iranian Shah whom Kirkpatrick described as old friends of the United States. In her view, Carter had erred by failing to appreciate the distinction between authoritarian and totalitarian rulers. To be sure, corrupt authoritarian governments in Latin America, including the defunct regimes of Trujillo and Batista, had committed acts of oppression and thievery against their own people. But their leaders had affirmed friendship for the United States and respect for its interests; moreover, sometimes they had moved toward democracy. For such reasons, they deserved support from the United States. In contrast, totalitarians such as Hitler or Stalin deserved none because of the immensity of their crimes and atrocities; moreover, they had never moved toward democracy.[6]

Such theoretical formulations established no basis for predicting the collapse of the Soviet Union a decade later but did provide effective grounds for attacking Jimmy Carter. In the Nicaraguan case, Kirkpatrick criticized Carter for selling out a sympathetic and friendly authoritarian, whose ouster opened the way for a takeover by supposedly hostile totalitarians. Instead of undercutting Somoza with criticism and pressure, she asserted, the United States should have sustained him against his enemies. Ronald Reagan agreed with this assessment and later, as president, named Kirkpatrick U.S. ambassador to the United Nations. Subsequently, when Reagan left office and a team of ghostwriters assembled his autobiography under the title *An American Life,* the nuances of Kirkpatrick's analysis escaped them completely. In fact, they reversed the distinction by describing venal Latin American despots as totalitarians and absolute rulers in the Kremlin as authoritarians.[7]

The question of whether Carter ever possessed the means to preserve Somoza in power or to prevent a Sandinista victory has inspired a polemical debate. His critics have claimed that wiser policies could have altered the outcome: He should have followed precedents by accepting Somoza on his terms and defending him against his enemies; or he should have headed off a Sandinista victory by getting rid of Somoza earlier; or perhaps he should have stabilized the situation by intervening with U.S. troops.

Coatsworth finds no reason for thinking that any such proposals could have succeeded. Carter officials reduced their own room to maneuver by consistently overrating Somoza's ability to remain in power. Although they hoped for his resignation, they regarded the pressure on him primarily as a means of diverting political unrest into peaceful channels through reform. Moreover, they lacked the means to shut down the anti-Somoza opposition in Nicaragua or to muzzle shows of sympathy and support for the Sandinistas all around the world. Any attempt to displace the dictator at an earlier time, in favor of Nicaraguan moderates, surely would have failed because of Somoza's intransigence. Finally, a U.S. military intervention would have culminated in disaster. Because of Vietnam, no support for military action existed in the United States; critics everywhere in Latin America would have opposed it; and almost certainly an intervention would have transformed Nicaragua's civil struggle into a war against foreign occupation.

As one way to limit the damage, it seemed imperative to contain the trouble by preventing an expansion of revolutionary turmoil into Guatemala and El Salvador, where rising levels of discontent entailed the possibility of civil war. During the 1970s the military-dominated governments in Guatemala responded with repression and terror, paying scant heed to Carter's emphasis on human rights. In El Salvador, however, the administration located a more effective means of exercising influence by taking advantage of divisions, within the dominant military and political elites, and playing them off against one another.

Carter officials initially criticized the Salvadoran regime of Carlos Humberto Romero for abusing human rights, hoping to encourage a transition to democratic rule. In 1979, seeking to avoid another Nicaragua, they shifted their ground by placing more importance on maintaining the integrity of the Salvadoran armed forces. For them, this goal required the creation of a pro-U.S. government under civilian control but willing to work with the military in support of pacification. Within the Salvadoran military the officers debated whether to pursue the goal by means of conciliation or suppression. Divisions over this issue ran deep. Meanwhile, violence mounted in rural areas. Mainly the work of right-wing elements, it centered on peasants, agitators, dissidents, and other people suspected of political infractions.

On October 15, 1979, junior officers in favor of reform carried out a takeover. A ruling council, or junta, consisted of two military men and three civilians. They promised free elections, the rule of law, and other changes to improve the agrarian, banking, and tax systems. Subsequently, as the worst forms of repression lifted, discontented groups took advantage by engaging in strikes, demonstrations, and protests. Sometimes these acts were disruptive or violent, but according to Coatsworth, "the vast majority were relatively peaceful expressions of pent-up frustration over falling real wages, declining living conditions, the lack of basic public services, and the abusive treatment of the police and the military." Nevertheless, conservative military elements reacted with "a wave of brutal attacks on popular organizations, including death-squad kidnappings and executions." The junta's orders to stop such murderous outrages proved futile. Early in January 1980, the civilian members resigned their positions, claiming that the military's behavior had destroyed a historic opportunity for a peaceful and democratic solution in El Salvador. At the insistence of the United States, the army then asked the Salvadoran Christian Democratic party to represent the civilian sector in a new junta, but the party split over the issue of whether to cooperate with military officers. As an incentive in January 1980, the Carter administration restored programs of aid and assistance and tried to supervise the day-to-day activities of the Salvadoran government. Consequently, the middle-of-the-road Christian Democrats, now regarded as objects of political disdain by both extremes, became dependent on U.S. support to remain in power. Meanwhile, out-of-control security forces operating independently of the government's authority killed more than nine thousand people in 1980, most of them unarmed civilians.

The Christian Democrats cracked under the pressure and divided into factions. Only the most conservative, led by José Napoleón Duarte, agreed to remain in the government. The army instituted a state of siege and developed plans to relocate into strategic hamlets, or concentration camps, the peasant peoples suspected of aiding the guerrillas. On March 24, 1980, a death squad consisting of army officers assassinated Óscar Romero, the peace-promoting archbishop of El Salvador who had criticized the military. At the time of his murder, he was saying Mass. At his funeral, army contingents fired on the mourners, killing fifty and wounding six hundred.

Later that same year, in an event which galvanized the American public in the period after the election of Ronald Reagan but before he assumed office, four American churchwomen were brutally abducted, raped, and murdered in El Salvador. Sisters Ita Ford, Maura Clarke, Dorothy Kazel, and lay worker Jean Donovan died senselessly in El Salvador. They were motivated and energized by their work with the nation's poorest people and, for committing to such work, were labeled "subversives" and killed. The crime was a sort of precursor to the Reagan era which drew a black/white distinction in Central America between our allies, who were fighting communism and receiving U.S. military aid, and the rest of the people. As such, people died—violently—by the tens of thousands in Central America during the 1980s.

Against high levels of repression, the battered opposition parties fought to preserve political viability. On April 18, they founded the Democratic Revolutionary Front (FDR) as an umbrella organization. It became one of the largest political movements in the nation's history by including liberal and left-wing parties, trade unions, professionals, and Roman Catholic activists. More radical guerrilla groups formed a joint political-military structure called the Farabundo Martí National Liberation Front (FMLN—Frente Farabundo Martí para la Liberación Nacional), named for the communist martyr killed during the great massacre of thirty thousand peasants by the government of general Maximiliano Hernández Martínez in 1932. Subsequently, the

FDR and the FMLN, though distinct political groups, engaged in cooperative endeavors to advance common causes.

The election of Ronald Reagan in 1980 encouraged Salvadoran elites to anticipate the abandonment of human rights issues. More murder and mayhem followed in response to the FMLN's planned "final offensive." The rebels wanted this effort to coincide with Reagan's inauguration in January 1981, but failed to accomplish much, lacking the requisite firepower.

When Carter left office, his administration could claim the accomplishment of two of its goals in El Salvador. The Salvadoran army remained a functioning military force and a pro-U.S. government with a civilian front retained authority in the capital. But the costs of such "successes" were substantial, taking the form of a full-scale civil war. Tensions also abounded in relations with Nicaragua during the remainder of Carter's tenure. After the Sandinista victory, the administration tried to uphold proprieties by maintaining formal relations while encouraging moderates in the governing coalition. By making aid and loans available and avoiding shows of hostility, U.S. leaders hoped to sidestep a confrontation. They wanted no repeat of the experience with Castro's Cuba two decades earlier. Ultimately, they sought some sort of accommodation. In contrast, the Sandinistas intended to consolidate their political authority, to establish sufficient military capability to safeguard their regime, and to keep U.S. influence in Nicaragua at a minimum. While pursuing these goals the collective leadership, increasingly under FSLN control, shifted leftward and announced a postponement of elections until 1985. By the end of 1980, FSLN dominance in the Nicaraguan government was almost complete.

Relations deteriorated further during the acrimonious U.S. presidential campaign of 1980. The agreement with Nicaragua then in effect contained an important provision stipulated by Congress: It required a halt to U.S. aid and assistance if credible evidence showed signs of Sandinista support for guerrilla insurgencies in other countries. Suspicions centered on El Salvador. By January 1981, the U.S. government possessed what it described as proof of arms shipments and other forms of support for Salvadoran guerrillas.[8] But Carter officials refrained from cutting off the aid, leaving that decision for the new administration. Under Reagan, the goals and methods of U.S. foreign policy shifted significantly.

UNDER REAGAN

President Ronald Reagan, a former sportscaster, movie actor, and television announcer, lacked experience in and, according to critics, understanding of foreign relations. His two terms as governor of California in the 1960s provided a grounding in the operations of government, but as president he often displayed a flimsy grasp of the details and implications of public issues. On one occasion, he expressed the erroneous view that intercontinental ballistic missiles could return to base after launch. On another, he was astonished to learn that the U.S. Air Force lacked the means for shooting down incoming Soviet rockets.[9]

No intellectual, Reagan won the hearts of voters and enjoyed two landslide victories in 1980 and 1984 for other reasons. His amiability, his down-to-earth homespun manner, his apparent sincerity of purpose, and his self-deprecating humor all helped to deflect criticism. Representative Patricia Schroeder, a Democrat from Colorado, called the Reagan presidency "Teflon-coated": No matter how big the mess, nothing seemed to stick to it. As Reagan once remarked, "Being a good actor pays off."

Dubbed "the great communicator," Reagan espoused simple, presumably self-evident truths. For him the federal government was the problem, not the solution, and in foreign affairs the Soviet Union was the source of most wrongdoing in the world. To combat it, Reagan assigned to his administration a conscious mission to revive U.S. hegemony. To do so, he would have to shake the country free from the effects of "the Vietnam syndrome," a debilitation supposedly suffered by the Carter administration and manifested in diplomatic impotency. Reagan embarked upon a different course; he promised to rearm the United States and to act with boldness and initiative in defense of vital interests. To confront the "evil empire"—a reference to the movie *Star Wars,* typical of Reagan's style—he mounted the greatest military buildup in the history of the world. It cost over $2 trillion. To overcome "self-doubt," he wanted a "national reawakening" based on traditional religious, patriotic, and capitalist beliefs in God, country, and enterprise. Proclaiming his own election in 1980 a portentous event, he affirmed, "We've closed the door on a long, dark period of failure." Reagan's policies differed from Jimmy Carter's in many ways. The leaders in the new administration attached less importance to the defense of human rights and to North-South issues than to the East-West collision between the United States and the Soviet Union. For them, the Cold War assumed the highest priority, Moreover, they embraced the Kirkpatrick distinction, seeking to avoid Jimmy Carter's error by sustaining friendly authoritarians and opposing unfriendly totalitarians. In a phrase, they would allow no more Nicaraguas.

In public, administration leaders tried to present a solid phalanx of ideological unity, but behind the scenes they squabbled in fierce bureaucratic conflicts over questions of power, prerogative, and privilege. The president often seemed aloof and oblivious. His first secretary of state, general Alexander M. Haig, Jr., an aggressive professional soldier with a propensity for mixing metaphors and giving offense, conducted a sequence of feuds with officials around him. In a light moment, Reagan joked about it, saying, "Sometimes our right hand doesn't know what our far-right hand is doing."

In June 1982, Haig resigned his position, frustrated, he claimed, by the absence of centralized leadership. Indeed, he said the Reagan White House was "as mysterious as a ghost ship; you heard the creak of the rigging and the groan of the timbers and even glimpsed the crew on deck. But which one of the crew was at the helm?" Haig's successor, secretary of state George P. Shultz, carried on the tradition by dueling bureaucratically over various issues with secretary of defense Caspar W. Weinberger. Among other things, Shultz criticized Weinberger, a big military spender presiding over a massive buildup, for his hesitation to employ military force in support of foreign policy objectives. Nevertheless, as Thomas G. Paterson notes, "Unlike Haig, Shultz accepted his role as the president's servant and team player" and retained Reagan's favor.[10]

In Latin America, the Reagan administration disfavored those regimes defined as hostile to the United States because of reformist or revolutionary enthusiasms and tried to cultivate improved relations with military rulers. The preferred security doctrines attached special importance to Central America and the Caribbean. As UN ambassador Jeane J. Kirkpatrick explained, those regions have become "the most important place in the world for us," because the ability of the United States to wield global influence and to face down Soviet challenges depended on "not having to devote the lion's share of our attention and our resources to the defense of ourselves in our own hemisphere." Other officials spoke ominously of a "Moscow-Havana" axis threatening to spread revolution. Reagan warned specifically of enemy plans to choke off the U.S. "lifeline to the outside world" and to promote destabilization by encouraging tides of unassimilable immigrants into the country. He also described Nicaragua under the Sandinistas as a "Soviet ally in the American mainland." When in an imaginative leap he envisioned an advance guard of Sandinistas driving a convoy of armed pickup trucks to attack the border town of Harlingen, Texas, Garry Trudeau, a political philosopher and satirist, resorted to parody in his comic strip *Doonesbury*. Trudeau had a group of "good ole" Texas boys with big hats and hunting rifles going out to repel the invaders.[11]

The Reagan effort to revive U.S. hegemony introduced some significant changes. The president outlined the economic component in an address before the OAS on January 24, 1982. Called the Caribbean Basin Initiative, it invoked free market models as the best guarantee of economic growth. The program offered modest aid and lower tariffs on exports to the United States as rewards for those Caribbean countries willing to implement free market economic reforms, but to other Latin American countries featuring pro-U.S. military regimes the president offered no equivalent. Politically, he moved toward a tougher stance. In Nicaragua, U.S. leaders stood strong in opposition to the Sandinistas and eventually tried to overthrow them. In El Salvador, they called for strong U.S. support of the military in order to suppress the guerrillas.

Viewed in retrospect, Reagan's policies in Central America, despite herculean efforts, failed to achieve the primary goals. When Reagan left office early in 1989, deteriorating economic conditions around the Caribbean had produced decreases in trade and investment; the Sandinistas still held power in Nicaragua; and the FMLN still waged guerrilla war in El Salvador. According to observers such as John Coatsworth, the United States had lost some of its hegemonic capability to dominate the politics of the region. Yet, U.S. policies still exerted a huge impact on Central America. During the 1980s, a large-scale mobilization of the region's resources took place either for or against U.S. objectives. Estimated military expenditures increased from $140 million to $600 million, and the number of soldiers employed by Central American governments expanded from 48,000 to 207,000. In El Salvador, Guatemala, and Nicaragua, at least two hundred thousand people died as a consequence of political violence, and as many as two million became refugees or immigrants to other countries, sometimes the United States. As Coatsworth observes, "The carnage and dislocation had profound effects on Central American society, politics, and culture," effects that might persist well into the future.

The leaders in the new Reagan administration established El Salvador as a top priority. Fearing an insurgent victory, they asked for the Pentagon's assistance in preparing a strategy to defeat the guerrillas. U.S. leaders also boosted economic and military aid, mainly in the form of outright grants. From 1980 to 1984, the military share expanded from $5.9 million to $196.6 million. Such increases, favored by the administration, required congressional approval—a potential obstacle, since leaders in the House and the Senate had grown skittish over reports of human rights violations by the armed forces. Some of them probably wanted to bring about the defeat of the insurgents but also wanted the Salvadoran government to promote reform as a means of attracting popular support. Others preferred some kind of negotiated settlement. The Reagan administration initially responded with allegations of conspiracy, depicting the Salvadoran guerrillas as creatures of a plot engineered by the Soviets, Cubans, and Nicaraguans. To establish the point, the administration issued a White Paper on February 23, 1981, supposedly based on FMLN documents, but this move failed to win over the skeptics and doubters. The Congress later sanctioned an aid package for El Salvador but attached an important condition: Every six months the president would have to certify that the Salvadoran government was making progress in defense of human rights; otherwise, the aid would stop.

On July 16, 1981, Thomas Enders, the new assistant secretary of state for inter-American affairs, delivered a speech intended to reassure members of Congress. He promised U.S. support for human rights, democratic procedures, agrarian reform, and a negotiated end to the civil war. At the same time, administration leaders sought a military victory and wanted to provide the Salvadoran army with the means for winning the war. Military advisers encouraged the adoption of smaller-scale, more fluid tactics, in part because they would inflict less collateral damage on innocent civilians than large-scale, more indiscriminate operations.

To advance at least the appearance of political authenticity, the Reagan administration facilitated the election of a constituent assembly in 1982, even though the liberal-left parties associated with the FDR (Frente Democrático Revolucionario) refused to take part. The major players were the Christian Democrats, a party of the political center, and two new parties of the right, both pro-military: the Partido de Conciliación Nacional (PCN) and the Alianza Republicana Nacionalista (NRA). The new constitution completed in 1983 required a presidential election the following year. To head off right-wing candidates and to maintain congressional support, the leaders in the Reagan administration championed the candidacy of José Napoleón Duarte, a Christian Socialist. His reputation as an honorable politician with democratic commitments made the policy workable, and the Congress continued the flow of U.S. aid into El Salvador during Reagan's second term. Nevertheless, Duarte's mixed record as president included significant failures. He never succeeded in curbing the excesses of the Salvadoran military, in implementing programs of agrarian reform, or in negotiating a compromise settlement with the FDR-FMLN. Yet he did manage to pull off a significant accomplishment. Ironically, according to some observers, Duarte's tenure in office resulted in the creation of a complex, hybrid regime which, though certainly not a democracy in any conventional sense, established a set of political arrangements that had the effect of expanding the limits of political activity in the country. Meanwhile, the Salvadoran civil war turned into a stalemate between the army and the guerrillas. By the time President Reagan left office the number of deaths had passed seventy thousand.

In the parallel case of Nicaragua, U.S. policy under Reagan never strayed very far from the basic goal of overthrowing the Sandinista regime by supporting its enemies. At the same time, shifting domestic and international pressures required various forms of accommodation and subterfuge, some of which bordered on illegality. During Reagan's years in office, as Coatsworth explains, U.S. policy toward Nicaragua moved through four phases, in the course of which administration tactics shifted depending on circumstances. But the main objective remained the same: getting rid of the Sandinistas through limited forms of intervention.

During the first phase, from Reagan's inauguration on January 20, 1981, until early in December 1983, the administration increased the pressure, resulting in a steady escalation of tensions in relations with Nicaragua. More specifically, the leaders employed a variety of military measures against the

Sandinistas, including the organization and funding of a counterrevolutionary military group called the contras, an abbreviation of the Spanish *contrarevolucionarios*. Led by former military officers in Somoza's National Guard, they initially mounted raids into Nicaragua out of bases in Honduras and Costa Rica. During this phase, Reagan officials rejected Nicaraguan proposals for negotiations, spurned West European and Latin American calls for mediation, employed CIA agents to mine harbors and attack other targets in Nicaragua, sponsored large-scale and intimidating military exercises from outposts in Honduras, and asked the Pentagon to investigate the workability of direct military intervention. The administration also suspended the economic aid program initiated by President Carter, pressured the West Europeans to scale back their assistance, and reduced the Nicaraguan sugar quota in the United States by 90 percent. This phase ended late in 1983 when, as a political choice, the president decided to downplay the Nicaraguan issue in preparation for his bid for reelection.

In the second phase, extending until the presidential election on November 6, 1984, the administration shifted ground, making a show of seeking accommodation. The administration publicly accepted a congressional ban on aid to the contras but secretly attempted to circumvent it. They also claimed readiness to open negotiations with Nicaragua and to support mediation by the so-called Contadora Group, named for Panama's Contadora Island which was the location of a meeting between representatives of the governments of Colombia, Mexico, Panama, and Venezuela. Unexpectedly, the group's efforts nearly succeeded when the Nicaraguans surprised everyone by agreeing to sign a proposed peace agreement—but not one that the Reagan leadership really wanted. Hoisted by its own petard, the administration had a problem based on its own rhetoric, having created a false impression that mediation actually could bring about an acceptable agreement.

During the third phase, lasting until November 1986, Reagan's second administration escalated the conflict with Nicaragua. The leaders suspended negotiations, imposed a full economic embargo, refused to accept the jurisdiction of the International Court of Justice over Central American matters, and persuaded Congress to vote military aid to the contras for the first time. Other endeavors sought to isolate Nicaragua from international sources of aid and assistance—activities constituting a form of intervention but stopping short of outright military action. In any case, the latter became unfeasible after November 4, 1984, when the Republicans lost control of the Senate to the Democrats in the midterm elections. Two weeks later, troubles deepened for the Reagan administration because of the Iran-contra scandal.

During the fourth phase, from November 1986 until the inauguration of George H. W. Bush in January 1989, the Reagan administration displayed less and less capacity to exercise control of events in Central America. As a proposed means of working toward peace, the so-called Arias Plan generated a great deal of interest, despite administration opposition, by obtaining endorsements from the Contadora Group, other South American countries, and the Soviet bloc. The U.S. Congress also extended support, significantly, while rejecting appeals for more military aid to the contras. By January 1989, the peace process in full swing had isolated the contras politically and enabled the Nicaraguan government to begin planning for elections. Again, according to Coatsworth, "U.S. policy toward Nicaragua had virtually collapsed."[12]

The Reagan administration had opposed the Sandinistas from the beginning, arguing that, under them, Nicaragua would become a Marxist-Leninist bastion and an agency for extending Soviet influence—another Cuba in the New World. Academic specialists and journalists called the claim into question. Many doubted the relevance of communist models for Nicaragua. According to Coatsworth, the Sandinistas "never abandoned [their] public commitment to 'pluralist democracy' and a mixed economy," never carried out large-scale programs of nationalization, and never imposed "a single-party monopoly on political power." They, of course, did "consolidate their authority as the country's dominant political party, mobilize domestic support through a diverse array of mass organizations, create a new security apparatus impervious to U.S. influence, and seek closer relations, including economic and military aid, from a wide range of foreign governments"—among them, countries from the Soviet bloc. Nevertheless, Coatsworth speculates that the Sandinista regime, if left to its own devices, might have developed according to "a populist variant of the Mexican model," resulting in "a relatively open political system." Similarly, in economics, the regime probably would have embraced "a state-centered development model" in which investors and entrepreneurs would have had to accept high levels of supervision and regulation. At the same time, Nicaragua's dependence on trade would have functioned as a powerful incentive for assigning some autonomy to the private sector.[13]

Sandinista foreign policies favored nonalignment, admittedly with a tilt away from the United States. The leaders preferred caution both in dealings with the United States and in exporting the revolution to other countries. No doubt the regime extended some aid to the Salvadoran FMLN in 1980–1981, hoping, perhaps, to deflect the Reagan administration from concentrating too exclusively on Nicaragua. Sandinista leaders never made a secret of their sympathy for the Salvadoran rebels but hesitated to engage in large-scale efforts in their support.

The Reagan administration nevertheless accused the Sandinistas of totalitarian proclivities and shifted U.S. support away from political moderates, mainly businessmen and politicians, in favor of the more extreme right-wing contras. In the ensuing diplomatic tug-of-war, Sandinista leaders tried to show Washington their willingness to lift restrictions on civil liberties if, in return, Reagan officials would call off the contras. But administration leaders, though engaged in various forms of subterfuge for public relations purposes, remained committed to the ouster of the FSLN by military means.

During the contra war, the Sandinistas refrained from systematic repression of the opposition but not from periodic harassment. Their government compiled a mixed record: It censored the main opposition newspaper, *La Prensa,* and also radio broadcasts put on by the Roman Catholic Church, yet opposition parties ran candidates in the 1984 elections and also participated in writing the new constitution. Still, their wartime restrictions on civil liberties never resulted in the wholesale abuses so common in El Salvador, Guatemala, and, previously, in Somoza's Nicaragua.[14]

Soon after the Sandinistas took over, the contras initiated raids into Nicaragua from along the Honduran border. Such practices had the sanction of Honduran officials who wanted to contain the revolution in Nicaragua. The contras also won support from the Argentines, whose right-wing, military government, under general Leopoldo Galtieri, provided military training for them as a favor to the Reagan administration. This association, as it turned out, conveyed false impressions to Argentine leaders. Because of delusionary notions about the existence of intimate ties with the United States, the Argentine government, in 1982, indulged in the colossal miscalculation of allowing the armed forces to settle an old issue by challenging Great Britain for control of the Falkland Islands (Islas Malvinas). The Argentines premised this undertaking on a mistaken supposition that the United States would stand with them against Great Britain, in defense of the Monroe Doctrine. The magnitude of their error became evident in a short war, beginning in April 1982, in which Argentine military and naval forces took a drubbing. Contrary to their expectation, the United States provided neither assistance nor solace. On the bright side, the defeat discredited the Argentine generals and accelerated a process toward democratization, ending the "dirty war" against alleged radicals and subversives.[15]

Reagan officials had advised members of the Senate Intelligence Committee in March 1981 of their intentions to create a paramilitary force of five hundred men, supposedly for the purpose of stopping the flow of military supplies from Nicaragua to the guerrillas in El Salvador; they later committed nearly $20 million in support of the plan. The CIA assisted in the creation of the Nicaraguan Democratic Front to take political charge. The contra forces had expanded to about fifteen thousand by the late 1980s, mainly through the recruitment of peasant boys from remote regions. Fighting capabilities depended upon arms and supplies provided by the U.S. government, either directly or through intermediaries. Early on, the funding came from the CIA. In 1983, the U.S. Congress voted in favor of continuing it, but in the following year a series of damaging revelations undermined congressional resolve to support the administration. Reports indicated that CIA operatives had carried out terrorist attacks and mined Nicaraguan harbors; other sources of information attributed corruption, human rights abuses, and possibly drug trafficking to the contras.[16] Consequently, congressional support, especially among Democrats, became sporadic and unreliable.

From the administration's viewpoint, Congress was indulging in obstructionism. In December 1982, the so-called Boland Amendment, the first of two named for representative Edward P. Boland, a Massachusetts Democrat who chaired the House Select Committee on Intelligence, forbade any U.S. expenditure for the purpose of overthrowing the Sandinista government. The Reagan administration responded with evasion, claiming no intent to force out the Sandinistas but only to interdict the flow of military supplies into El Salvador. Congress reacted by imposing the same restriction a second time but without much effect. In 1984, it passed another Boland Amendment, this one flatly banning any aid by U.S. intelligence agencies to the contras. The Reagan administration then permitted an elaborate deception, under the conduct of colonel Oliver North, a Marine Corps officer on loan to the National Security Council. Taking the form of clandestine operations, North's illicit activities provided more than $50 million in arms and supplies to the contras between 1984 and 1986, and precipitated what came to be known as the Iran-contra scandal, a major episode during the second Reagan administration.

The funds came from various sources, including private donors and foreign countries—among them, Costa Rica, El Salvador, Guatemala, Honduras, Israel, Panama, Saudi Arabia, and Taiwan—and moved through complicated networks organized by North and other U.S. military and intelligence officials. The most blatant of these undertakings, the one tying Iran to the ensuing scandal, actually engaged the administration in violations of its own policy banning the sale of weapons to alleged terrorists. Under such terms, Iranian leaders—that is, the Islamic fundamentalists who had taken power in 1979 while denouncing the United States as "the great Satan"—did not qualify. But North's deal provided a loophole: They could buy antitank missiles and weapons parts if, in return, they provided assistance in seeking freedom for a group of U.S. hostages held by other alleged terrorists in Lebanon. The proceeds from the sales may have run as high $30 million. When the news broke during the fall of 1986 amid great public outrage, congressional support for the Reagan administration's policies in Central America collapsed.

Even with arms and supplies provided by these dubious methods, the contras lacked the capacity to throw the Sandinistas out of office. Successes on the battlefield eluded them in confrontations with the Nicaraguan Army. In addition, they never developed enough political credibility; too many of Somoza's former National Guard officers occupied positions of authority. Together, military incapacity and political weakness rendered the contra stand against the Sandinista revolution futile.

Meanwhile, the Reagan administration reiterated its willingness to accept a negotiated settlement but never seriously attempted one. In 1981, for example, assistant secretary of state Thomas Enders suggested the possibility of improving relations if the Sandinistas would sever ties with the Soviets, stop their aid to the FMLN in El Salvador, and scale back the size of their armed forces. The Sandinistas expressed some interest in the plan but had their own expectations. In particular, the Reagan administration would have to halt its aid to the contras. The proposed negotiations went nowhere. The same held true for another such attempt in 1984. No subsequent efforts took place. In a bitter characterization of the U.S. position, Nicaraguan foreign minister Miguel D'Escoto complained, "What President Reagan has said is: 'You drop dead or I will kill you.'"

Documents released during the Iran-contra investigations show that administration leaders understood the inherent limitations of the contra movement. Why then did the United States embark upon a course of action bound to fail? The body of literature suggests various interpretations. The journalist Roy Gutman points to bureaucratic politics. According to him, Reagan's uninvolved style of decision making invited competition among the policy makers and resulted in a failure to develop coherent diplomatic objectives. This circumstance supposedly favored hard-line contra supporters who exploited the president's deficiencies for their own purposes. Another line of explanation places the responsibility on domestic politics: The administration could not abandon the contras without alienating the right wing of the Republican party upon whose vote the leaders depended to sustain them. A third explanation places Nicaraguan policy within a larger context. Though possibly irrational in a narrow sense, William LeoGrande has argued, the pro-contra commitment made sense as part of "the longer term goal of breaking the back of the domestic political opposition to Reagan's aggressive use of military force to overthrow the government of Nicaragua." In other words, the long-term intent sought "to create the political support necessary for a direct U.S. military intervention." As Coatsworth remarks, Reagan officials never publicly proposed to employ U.S. military forces to overthrow the Sandinista government. On the other hand, they never ruled out the option. Indeed, by undertaking "Operation Urgent Fury" in October 1982, a military intervention against a government described as communist on the tiny Caribbean island of Grenada, the Reagan administration may have intended, among other things, to underscore the possible validity of similar measures elsewhere—for example, in Nicaragua.[17]

U.S. policies in Central America elicited a sequence of efforts by other countries to find political solutions. Early attempts by the Contadora Group—Colombia, Mexico, Panama, Venezuela—failed, but a subsequent effort in 1987 did succeed, once the Iran-contra scandal had sufficiently weakened faith in the administration's position. The Arias Plan—named for its main sponsor, president Óscar Arias of Costa Rica—won support from the Contadora Group, the other countries of Central America, and the speaker of the house Jim Wright, a Democrat from Texas. Wright played a vital role in extracting from the Reagan administration a commitment to abandon its efforts to overthrow the Sandinistas in exchange for specific Nicaraguan concessions.

Fundamentally, the agreement contained these provisions. The Nicaraguan government and the contras would initiate a process aimed at a cease-fire, after which the United States would terminate military aid to the contras; similarly, the Soviet bloc would cease arms shipments to the Sandinistas. Humanitarian aid, in contrast, could continue in each instance. To round out the arrangements, Nicaragua would move away from the state of emergency, restore civil liberties, create an electoral commission with representation for all parties, and make plans for a national election. Support from many sources helped to clinch the deal, especially from Argentina, Brazil, Peru, and Uruguay (the four new South American democracies), the West European countries, the Soviet bloc, the United Nations, and the Organization of American States. If the Reagan administration counted on Nicaraguan opposition to defeat the Arias Plan, as was probably the case, the Sandinistas served up another surprise by endorsing it, even though acceptance required negotiation with the hated contras and subjected Nicaraguan politics to external supervision. According to Coatsworth, "The Sandinista leaders took a calculated risk: they traded sovereignty for peace, with the expectation that internationally supervised elections would, in the end, confirm the FSLN in power." Economic necessity probably compelled it. The contra war, U.S. economic sanctions, and the Sandinistas' own miscalculations had placed their country in an economic depression. By the time Reagan left office in January 1989, the Nicaraguans had complied with the peace accord and set a date for national elections on February 25, 1990. They did so in the expectation of winning the contest and then repairing the damage already done to their ravaged economy.[18]

The Reagan administration focused on other nations in Latin America outside of Central America. Peru, for example, presented some pressing challenges to the United States and the world with the emergence, in 1980, of a long-simmering regional guerrilla movement called "Sendero Luminoso"—the Shining Path. The organization was founded in a remote, poor, southwest region of the nation, the state of Ayacucho, which means "corner of death" in the Quechua language. An important agricultural region and center of Spanish power during the colonial period, the city's thirty-three Roman Catholic churches reflect the power and influence of European culture in a remote corner of Latin America.

Peru has never successfully bridged the cultural, linguistic, and geographic divide that separates people in the countryside from those in the coastal cities, especially the powerful capital center at Lima. People living in the Andes have been culturally and economically marginalized, excluded from the economic gains brought from the nineteenth century guano boom, and later riches generated through mining, agriculture, and commercial fishing. An agrarian reform, imposed when a left-leaning military government took power in Lima in 1968, failed to resolve generational, endemic poverty in the country, especially in the remote highlands.

Ironically, 1968 is also the year professor Abimaél Guzmán founded the Sendero organization at the Universidad Nacional de San Cristobál de Huamanga in Ayacucho. An energetic, magnetic philosophy professor, Mr. Guzmán was influenced by Maoism and the Communist Party of Nepal. He adopted a sort of slow burn, popular war ideology that sought gradual control of the countryside followed by a surrounding and strangulation of the urban centers of power and government. Guzmán and his followers sought to return Peru to a pre-1532 platform, when the people of the Andes ruled themselves and the Europeans had not yet invaded. He sought a sort of Andean *pachacuti*, or total reordering of society. Peruvians living along the coast were cautiously optimistic in 1980 when democracy returned with the election of Fernando Belaúnde Terry, a stalwart of the political establishment—the man who had been overthrown in 1968—but discouraged by the 1980 pronouncements of a regional group from Ayacucho unwilling to play by the traditional political norms of engagement.

Peru scholar Cynthia McClintock offers a now-classic exploration of the rise of Sendero. In 1984, she explored the physical remoteness of the region from which Sendero emerged. Describing the economy there as "agricultural," she noted that Sendero swept out of a geographic zone, "ill-suited for agriculture . . . most of the terrain is arid, stony, precipitous and windswept."[19] From that place, no one could have imagined the origins of a conflict and counterinsurgency that lasted about two decades (1980–2000) and produced 70,000 deaths, 54 percent of them attributed to Sendero, the other half attributed to Peruvian security forces and extrajudicial killings.

If the 1980s in Peru is defined by Sendero and Guzmán, the 1990s was shaped by the presidency of Alberto Fujimori, a man who was elected in 1990 and ruled until 2000, when he fled to Japan and, via the fax machine, sent in his resignation. In April 1992, Fujimori overthrew his own government in an *autogolpe* but emerged as a popular figure after capturing Sendero's leader, Mr. Guzmán, later that same year. Fujimori was reelected to a second term in 1995. Widespread corruption charges and human rights abuses in the military campaign against the Shining Path led to his resignation from the presidency in 2000, after winning a third term that many considered unconstitutional.

The United States, with some initial hesitation, recognized the Fujimori regime after the 1992 coup. Military and economic aid flowed to Peru throughout the Fujimori years and now, much of the U.S. aid to Peru is part of the contemporary antinarcotics campaign. The Peruvian economy has grown recently due to the demand for minerals and other exports, but the cultural bifurcation that has long divided the nation continues unabated and is best described by a Peruvian writer, the Nobel laureate Mario Vargas Llosa.[20]

In Colombia, the late 1980s and early 1990s represented a terrible time of violence and serious challenges to state autonomy. A sort of mini–coup d'état occurred, in a nation accustomed to constitutional procedure and civilian government, in November 1985 when leftist insurgents stormed the Palace of Justice and, essentially, held the Supreme Court hostage. The Colombian military counter-stormed the palace, using a lightweight Brazilian tank, and took back the building, with a terrible death toll. Some people inside the building, including auxiliary magistrate judge Carlos Horacio Urán were removed from the building and later "disappeared" by government security forces.

At about the same time, a small-time thug from Medellín, Pablo Escobar, was determined to corner the market for the production, sale, and distribution of illegal narcotics, mainly cocaine. When Colombian minister of justice Rodrigo Lara Bonilla decided to investigate and prosecute money laundering operations, he was killed (in 1984) on Escobar's orders. Escobar also ordered the assassination of Luis Carlos Galán, a man seeking the Colombian presidency with zero tolerance policies for the nation's drug cartels. Mr. Galán was murdered during a campaign rally on the outskirts of Bogotá in August 1989.

When Escobar was finally killed in 1993 by an elite Colombian military unit, the drug exporting business did not end; it simply changed, becoming more decentralized and lower-key. There was money to be made in the production and distribution of narcotics—billions of U.S. dollars. Both the FARC (Revolutionary Armed Forces of Colombia), which began operations in 1964, and a relatively new group called the AUC (the United Self-defense Forces of Colombia) moved to cash in. The AUC, paramilitary forces formed in the 1980s, were hired by the large landholders who were tired of paying bribes to the leftist FARC. The FARC made money through extortion, kidnapping and "protecting" the illegal narcotics operations. By the late 1990s, as almost surreal massacres were perpetrated in Colombia with nearly zero accountably or prosecution and as the number of FARC insurgents grew to perhaps 30,000, Colombia seemed to be spinning out of control.

The United States took an active interest in the Colombian crisis at this time. Partly as a result of the strong personal friendship between then president Andrés Pastrana Arango (1998–2002) and Bill Clinton (1993–2001), a "Plan Colombia" was designed to halt the spread of the insurgency and seek peace through diplomacy. The United States Congress—in 2000—authorized a massive amount of military aid for Colombia, about 1.35 billion dollars, and Plan Colombia was born. The military aid continued (and, as of this writing in early 2016, amounts to about ten billion dollars in the past fifteen years), but the Pastrana peace initiative crashed and burned in 2002, paving the way for a new, hard-liner approach via the election of a maverick politician to the presidency of Colombia, Mr. Álvaro Uribe Vélez. He took the oath of office on August 8, 2002.

The challenges in Peru and Colombia during the past twenty-five years or so seem isolated to internal structural and local historical/geographic realities, yet, from 1989 to 1993, a sequence of astonishing events transformed the structure of international relations for the entire world: After more than forty years, the Cold War suddenly came to an end. To the surprise of most observers, the Soviet Union precipitated the process by allowing the East European nations to declare independence and then itself dissolved and disappeared as the various constituent states of the USSR affirmed their sovereign rights.[21]

For Latin Americans, these world events had at least three main consequences: First, the end of the Cold War reduced the levels of rivalry and competition among the Great Powers in the Western Hemisphere. The Soviet Union, a principal player, no longer existed, and others—mainly the West Europeans and (during the 1990s) the Japanese—shifted their attention toward the new states emerging from the former Soviet Union. For Latin Americans, not all of the implications were positive. For example, what if these changes diverted the international flow of capital away from the south toward the east, thereby enhancing Latin American dependence on the United States? In response, Latin Americans engaged in maneuvers to enlarge political and economic relations with West Europeans and the emerging East Asian markets—notably China—and to structure dealings with the United States to benefit themselves, notably through the negotiation of free trade agreements.

Second, the presumed security threat posed to the United States in the Western Hemisphere by the Soviet Union and its allies simply ceased to exist. This shift altered the debate in the United States over Central America, specifically by undermining a principal argument in favor of interventionist activities. Seeking to place this matter in a proper context, Coatsworth argues that no significant U.S. security interests ever had been at stake in Central America during the 1980s. Rather, the region had taken on importance for the Reagan administration largely as a function of maintaining U.S. credibility in the East-West struggle. Consequently, when the Cold War ended, Central America ceased to have as much importance.

Third, the Soviet collapse shuffled political priorities in Latin America. Notably, it set back and confused various radical and populist movements traditionally looked upon by the United States as hostile to its interests. At the same time, it also undermined the position of right-wing, pro-military, and anticommunist groups whose status derived at least in part from U.S. support. In other words, the end of the Cold War played down the incentive for the United States to become involved in local politics. It also strengthened a trend toward democratization, the long-term consequences of which might favor social reform.

The George H. W. Bush administration (1989–1992) responded to these new conditions with diverse policies, some of which suggested continuity and others change. Bush built on the Caribbean Basin Initiative of the Reagan era by adding, in 1990, a new Free Enterprise Initiative for the Americas. Its promises included increases in U.S. aid and the negotiation of free trade agreements as rewards, if Latin American countries complied with U.S. policy preferences in economic affairs. On similar grounds, President Bush also encouraged new agreements on debts, allowing Latin Americans to reduce debt service obligations if they would accept austerity programs. Since relations with Mexico also required attention after some deterioration during the Reagan years, in part because of Mexican opposition to U.S. policies in Central America, in 1993 the United States, Mexico, and Canada signed the North American Free Trade Agreement (NAFTA) for the purpose of obtaining closer political and economic ties among the three nations. These "trade" issues are taken up in greater detail in the next chapter.

As one of their top priorities, the leaders in the Bush administration wanted to eliminate Central America as a political issue and a cause of contention between the White House and Congress. Acting fast, they dealt with one trouble spot, Panama, by removing from power the head of state, general Manuel Antonio Noriega. Though once a CIA asset in the funneling of aid to the contras, he had become a liability as a notorious drug smuggler and a violator of human rights. In disregard of the OAS charter, U.S. military forces unilaterally invaded Panama on December 23, 1989, seized Noriega, and installed a new government. The former strongman ended up in a federal detention center in Miami where, in 1992, he was convicted on drug charges and sentenced to a long prison term. In explanation, Coatsworth argues that the Panama invasion "was not undertaken to defend traditional U.S. economic or security interests" but "in response to U.S. domestic political circumstances." Noriega's defiant involvement with drug smuggling threatened the Bush administration by jeopardizing its relations with Congress and its credibility in foreign affairs.

The Bush administration also responded favorably to the outcome of elections in Nicaragua. On February 25, 1990, Violeta Chamorro, widow of the murdered publisher of *La Prensa* and the candidate backed by a coalition of fourteen opposition parties, won a majority of the votes in an election supervised by international authorities. The defeat of president Daniel Ortega, the Sandinista nominee, came as a surprise to many observers and may have occurred in part because Nicaraguan voters anticipated a positive reaction from the United States, perhaps in the form of economic aid to help revive their sagging economy. Moreover, the intervention in Panama may have persuaded some Nicaraguans that their country might come next. Mr. Ortega, it should be noted, returned to the presidency in 2007 and remains president of Nicaragua as of this writing.

The conflict in El Salvador finally terminated on December 31, 1991, when the guerrillas and the government signed a peace agreement. According to its terms, the guerrillas had to lay down their arms. In return, the government would scale back the size of the armed forces, eliminate abuses by the military, and guarantee the exercise of political and human rights. In this case the George H. W. Bush administration, unlike its predecessor, came around to support the negotiation process as a viable means of solving the problem.[22]

As mentioned earlier, the Guatemalan war ended in 1996, but full peace, stability, and democracy has eluded the small Central American nation. In September 2015, the sitting Guatemalan president, Otto Pérez Molina resigned and was sent to jail, where he now awaits trial on charges of corruption and kickbacks. About 54 percent of the population lives in poverty. The indigenous population makes up approximately 40 percent of the Guatemalan population and 73 percent of that population lives in poverty.

For the rest of Latin America, the end of the Cold War entailed, at the very least, uncertainty about what new kind of international order might emerge from the wreckage of the old and how it would affect the conduct of relations with the United States and the rest of the world. In *Talons of the Eagle: Dynamics of U.S.-Latin American Relations* published in 1996, the political scientist Peter H. Smith provided some insight into a new "age of uncertainty." He identified three fundamental effects. First, the end of the Cold War produced a new "multipolarity" that contrasted markedly with the "bipolar dominance" of the United States and the Soviet Union and meant a more even distribution of power and capability among the nations of the world. Second, it encouraged a process of "democratization," that is, a "transition . . . from authoritarianism toward pluralism," whose effects appeared prominently in East European countries (the former East Germany, Poland, Hungary, and Czechoslovakia) and in Latin America, most notably in Argentina, Brazil, Chile, and Peru. Third, it reduced the blatant competition and hostility associated with the Cold War and offered the possibility of establishing new priorities for defining goals and allocating resources.[23]

Accounting for such momentous change immediately set off a polemical debate in which one side underscored the importance of indigenous causes within the Soviet Union and the other the significance of competitive pressures from the United States. The question of whether the Soviet Union collapsed primarily for internal or for external reasons will probably divide historians forever. According to Thomas G. Paterson, "The Cold War waned because the contest had undermined the power of its two main protagonists." The costs had exceeded the gains in a cyclical process experienced by other Great Powers since the fifteenth century. To maintain themselves, the superpowers required "the restoration of their economic well-being and the preservation of their diminishing global positions." Bringing an end to the Cold War became a matter of enlightened self-interest. To be sure, the Soviet Union took a far greater fall than the United States; nevertheless, "the implications of decline became unmistakable for both: The Cold War they made in the 1940s had to be unmade if the two nations were to remain prominent international superintendents."[24] In the process, the old Soviet Union ceased to exist.

How to measure the impact on U.S. relations with Latin America also poses many problems. According to some observers, the U.S. ability to exercise hegemony over Latin America declined gradually during the Cold War and dropped off even further after 1989. For example, the U.S. share of Latin American exports fell from 45 percent in 1958 to 34 percent in the late 1970s. The U.S. share of direct foreign investments went down—in Brazil's case, from over 50 percent in 1965 to 30 percent in 1979—as did weapons sales. All during the 1980s, Central American difficulties functioned as public relations disasters for the United States in the rest of Latin America. And, in 1982, the Reagan administration could not head off an unwanted war over the Falkland Islands. Such outcomes suggested a reduced capacity to dominate the region.[25] Still another argument in support of this claim depicts U.S. interventions in Latin America during the Cold War as manifestations of weakness. According to political scientist Abraham Lowenthal, for example, U.S. efforts to overthrow Salvador Allende in Chile were "anachronistic" since "U.S. preponderance in the Americas was already substantially diminished." Similarly, according to Paterson, U.S. interventions in the 1970s and 1980s "attested not to U.S. strength but to the loosening of its imperial net." This view implies that the survival of Castro's regime in Cuba shows the limits of U.S. hegemonic capability.[26]

In a contradictory assessment, Peter H. Smith argues that "this notion of declining hegemony rests on dubious assumptions," specifically, the erroneous notions that hegemony requires "near total control" over Latin America and that Latin American resistance became a bigger problem for the United States during the 1980s than it was before. Yet even in the 1950s, the refusal of most Latin American countries to send troops to Korea (Colombia did send in troops), the anti-Nixon riots in Caracas, and the Cuban Revolution all showed the limits of U.S. domination. Nevertheless, the United States, in his view, has exercised "a strong and continuous degree of hegemony over the Western Hemisphere from the 1950s to the 1990s." If "within this overall pattern, U.S. hegemony suffered a slight decline from the 1960s to the

1980s," it "climbed to an all-time high between the mid-1980s and mid-1990s." In other words, "the general trend has *always* been for the United States to exert a great degree of influence over Latin American countries," even though "the level of this influence revealed some oscillation (up, down, up) from the mid-1950s to the present time."

To substantiate the point, Smith presents an array of data concerning gross domestic product (GDP) and population size. As he argues, "The differences in demographic trajectories are startling." In 1950, the number of people in all the Latin American countries and in the United States was about the same, 150 million. By 1990, the population of Latin America had exceeded that of the United States by a margin of 436 million to 250 million. Yet, the U.S. economy consistently outproduced the economies of Latin America. The GDP of the United States was more than seven times as large as Latin America's in 1950, seven times as large in 1970, and five times as large in 1990. In 1950 the U.S. GDP was thirty times Argentina's, thirty-three times Brazil's, and thirty-seven times Mexico's; in 1990, it was fifty-eight times Argentina's, thirteen times Brazil's, and twenty-three times Mexico's. To underscore the implications, he claims, "Within the global arena, the United States lost a good deal of ground in relation to the other major powers between 1950 and 1990; within the Western Hemisphere, by contrast, the United States managed to retain its position of preponderance."

Smith draws similar conclusions from the data on trade. In spite of gains by the West Europeans and the Japanese, the United States in 1990 ranked as the largest single trading partner for every country in the region. As for investments, from 1990 to 1992 the United States put about $22 billion into Latin America—nearly twice the amount from Western Europe and Japan—suggesting that it "thus asserted and affirmed its hemispheric position of economic supremacy." Though the West Europeans and the Japanese improved their positions, "they did not begin to pose a political challenge to Washington's preeminence in the Americas."

Smith explains the circumstance by holding that "United States predominance resulted in large part from a systematic retreat by extrahemispheric rivals," resulting in "hegemony by default" because "outside powers withdrew from the Americas and directed their attention elsewhere." The West Europeans concentrated on Eastern Europe; the Russians disengaged to deal with matters at home; and the Japanese too had other priorities. Lacking much competition the United States retained its "supremacy," characterized by Smith as "uncontested " and "complete."

What importance should the United States as a Great Power attach to Latin America in the post–Cold War era? The answer in many ways holds more significance for the people of Latin America than for the United States. In purely economic terms, Latin America has declined in significance for the United States. Its share of total U.S. trade worldwide declined from 28–35 percent in 1950 to 12–14 percent in the mid-1970s, where it has remained for the most part ever since. By the 1990s, Mexico accounted for half of the U.S. trade in Latin America, establishing the southern neighbor as the third-ranked trading partner, behind Canada and Japan. Trade elsewhere in the region amounted to less and less for the United States, certainly in comparison with the 1950s.

Patterns of investment reflected a similar decline in relative importance. In 1950, Latin America accounted for over one-third of U.S. direct overseas investments. By 1970, Latin America absorbed about 16 percent and by 1990, less than 10 percent; Western Europe, Canada, and Asia had become much more significant. To be sure, the absolute value of U.S. investments in Latin America and the Caribbean regions ran toward $71.6 billion, a substantial sum. Yet in the global context, Latin America had less importance to the United States than previously. As Smith states, such trends in trade and investment "meant that in comparison with previous periods the United States would have *less* at stake in its dealings with Latin America—at a time when Latin America would have *more* at stake in the United States." Of course, the North American Free Trade Agreement, and FTA mania in general, would shift these numbers as Latin America, in fact, became very important and closely connected to the United States economy—especially after 1994. Notwithstanding NAFTA's many critics, the trade agreement did push a significant amount of FDI—foreign direct investment—to Mexico. In 2007, the United States invested, via FDI, 173 billion dollars in Latin America, and about 50 percent of this total went to one nation: Mexico. That 2007 FDI figure represented 22.7 percent of the world FDI in Latin America. Most of this investment moved into the natural resources or mining sector of Latin America, a sector which turns significant profit for investors and employs relatively few local workers.

U.S. FDI in Latin America fell to 159 billion dollars in 2014, reflecting the world economic downturn of 2007–2009. However, it is important to note that profits on Latin American foreign-owned capital stock rose from about $20 billion in 2002 to $100 billion twelve years later. These numbers suggest the efficacy and profitability of investment in Latin America; the push during the late 1980s and 1990s to secure unfettered access to Latin American markets and materials, through "free" trade agreements, seems to have produced the desired effects for investors and friends of investors.[27]

NOTES

1. Walter LaFeber, *The Panama Canal: The Crisis in Historical Perspective*, rev. ed. (New York: Oxford University Press, 1978), 161; John H. Coatsworth, *Central America and the United States: The Clients and the Colossus* (New York: Twayne, 1994), 134.

2. Gaddis Smith, *Morality, Reason, and Power: American Diplomacy in the Carter Years* (New York: Hill and Wang, 1986), 115.

3. Coatsworth, *Central America and the United States,* 132–33, 135–37.

4. Walter LaFeber, *Inevitable Revolutions: The United States in Central America* (New York: W. W. Norton, 1983), 219–26.

5. Coatsworth, *Central America and the United States,* 138–46; Thomas E. Leonard, *Central America and the United States: The Search for Stability* (Athens: University of Georgia Press, 1991), chap. 9.

6. Jeane J. Kirkpatrick, "Dictatorships and Double Standards," *Commentary* 68, no. 5 (November 1979): 34–45.

7. Ronald Reagan, *An American Life* (New York: Pocket Books, 1990), 239, 360, 471.

8. Coatsworth, *Central America and the United States,* 144–47, 151–59.

9. Michael J. Schaller, *Reckoning with Reagan: America and Its President in the 1980s* (New York: Oxford University Press, 1992), 122, 132; Thomas G. Paterson and J. Garry Clifford, *America Ascendant: U.S. Foreign Relations since 1939* (Lexington, MA: D. C. Heath, 1995), 260–64.

10. Paterson and Clifford, *America Ascendant,* 256–60.

11. Schaller, *Reckoning with Reagan,* 142, 149.

12. Coatsworth, *Central America and the United States,* 164–66, 170–71, 174–78.

13. Mark T. Gilderhus, "An Emerging Synthesis? U.S.-Latin American Relations since 1945," in *America in the World: The Historiography of American Foreign Relations since 1941*, ed. Michael J. Hogan (New York: Cambridge University Press, 1995), 456–58; Mark T. Berger, *Under Northern Eyes: Latin American Studies and U.S. Hegemony in the Americas, 1898–1990* (Bloomington: Indiana University Press, 1995), chaps. 4–5.

14. Coatsworth, *Central America and the United States,* 180–82.

15. Joseph S. Tulchin, *Argentina and the United States: A Conflicted Relationship* (Boston: Twayne, 1990), 154–58; Tulchin, "The Malvinas War of 1882: An Inevitable Conflict That Never Should Have Happened," *Latin American Research Review* 22, no. 3 (1987): 123–41.

16. See Greg Grandin, *Empire's Workshop: Latin America, The United States, and the Rise of the New Imperialism* (New York: Metropolitan Books, 2006), especially chap. 3.

17. Coatsworth, *Central America and the United States,* 181–87; Schaller, *Reckoning with Reagan,* chap. 6; Peter H. Smith, *Talons of the Eagle: Dynamics of U.S.-Latin American Relations* (New York: Oxford University Press, 1996), 176–80.

18. Coatsworth, *Central America and the United States,* 199–200, 202.

19. See Cynthia McClintock, "Why Peasants Rebel: The Case of Peru's Sendero Luminoso," *World Politics* 37, no. 1 (October 1984): 59.

20. See Mario Vargas Llosa, "Questions of Conquest: What Columbus Wrought, and What He Did Not," *Harper's Magazine* 281 (December 1990): 51. The piece is controversial, but compelling.

21. Michael J. Hogan, ed., *The End of the Cold War: Its Meaning and Implications* (New York: Cambridge University Press, 1992); Lars Schoultz, ed., *The United States and Latin America in the 1990s: Beyond the Cold War* (Chapel Hill: University of North Carolina Press, 1992).

22. Coatsworth, *Central America and the United States,* 207–8, 210, 214–16. Michael L. Conniff, *Panama and the United States: The Forced Alliance* (Athens: University of Georgia Press, 1992), chap. 9.

23. Smith, *Talons of the Eagle,* 218–19.

24. Robert J. McMahon, "Making Sense of American Foreign Policy during the Reagan Years," *Diplomatic History* 19, no. 2 (Spring 1995): 367–84; Thomas G. Paterson, *On Every Front: The Making and Unmaking if the Cold War,* rev. ed. (New York: W. W. Norton, 1992), 192–93; Paul Kennedy, *The Rise and Fall of the Great Powers: Economic Change and Military Conflict from 1500 to 2000* (New York: Random House, 1987, see chap. 8).

25. Smith, *Talons of the Eagle,* 223–24.

26. Abraham F. Lowenthal, *Partners in Conflict: The United States and Latin America* (Baltimore: Johns Hopkins University Press, 1987), 32; Paterson, *On Every Front,* 32.

27. See Shannon K. O'Neil, "Foreign Direct Investment in Latin America," June 4, 2015. Blogs, Council on Foreign Relations, Washington, DC. Online. Available: http://blogs.cfr.org/oneil/2015/06/04/foreign-direct-investment-in-latin-america/.

Chapter Eight

NAFTA to Now in Three Keys: Commerce, Conflict, and Culture

Writing about the past twenty years of U.S.-Latin America relations presents some clear challenges. We have decided to focus on three aspects of the relationship—commerce, conflict, and culture—as a way to organize and analyze a tumultuous, continuously evolving relationship between the United States and Latin America.

In terms of commerce, the most significant trade agreement in modern times was ratified in late 1993 and went into effect on January 1, 1994. Negotiations to secure the NAFTA (North American Free Trade Agreement) were brutal, but the treaty's passage represented a new spirit of collaboration and mutual respect among the three partner nations, Canada, Mexico, and the United States. Conflict between the United States and Central America diminished during the 1990s as Nicaraguans held free elections (in 1990) which brought Violeta Chamorro to power, ending the eleven-year rule of the Sandinista revolutionary government. Both El Salvador and Guatemala sought peace through negotiations during the 1990s, but new populist leaders emerged in resource-rich Venezuela, Ecuador, and Bolivia, challenging the United States' historic hegemony in South America. These "neopopulists" pushed an agenda that favored state controls and socialist rhetoric.

Other leaders who have opted for a middle way between market-driven capitalism, as advocated by the United States, and state-supported development include Michelle Bachelet in Chile (2006–2010 and 2014 to present); Luiz Inacio "Lula" da Silva in Brazil who took office in 2003 and ruled through 2010; the Kirchners in Argentina (Néstor, 2003–2007, and Cristina Fernández de Kirchner, 2007–2015); and José Mujíca in Uruguay, who served as president from 2010–2015. All of these leaders reacted against the strict application of a "Washington Consensus" free trade agenda, characterized by the push for massive privatization of state-supported industry, inflows of direct foreign investment, and free market advice from U.S. and European economists.

Conflict, then, between the United States and Latin America has neither taken the form of "gunboat" diplomacy of the past nor has the United States, since 1989, directly invaded Latin America. In December of that year, U.S. Marines entered Panama to remove strongman and former CIA employee Manuel Noriega. Mr. Noriega was convicted on narcotics trafficking charges. Ironically, the two Latin American nations most associated with the trade in illegal narcotics—Colombia and Mexico—have been reliable allies of the United States. Tensions, however, have mounted in recent years between the United States and Mexico, since the epicenter of drug violence has moved from the South American Andes to the border space between Mexico and its northern neighbor.

The cultural richness and diversity of the Latin American region forms a significant segment of U.S. mainstream culture. No longer is Latin American culture viewed as "exotic," as it was in the late 1920s and early 1930s when painter Diego Rivera opened a show of his monumental frescos at New York City's MoMA (Museum of Modern Art) in 1931; he was the first Mexican to exhibit in a one-man show there. Now, Latin American music features heavily on Billboard's Top 100; films from Mexico, Argentina, and Brazil win awards in the United States. Hispanic television markets in the United States consume *telenovelas* at an astonishing rate; Latin America has infused, and dramatically improved, American cuisine and, ironically, America's pastime—Major League Baseball. As of 2014, roughly 27 percent of all MLB players were "Latino."

COMMERCE—THE FREE TRADE FRENZY: WELCOME TO THE 1990S

If the 1980s is "the lost decade" in Latin America, the 1990s could certainly be called the decade of free market trade. The drive for a "Washington Consensus" economic development program which stressed free market–based development and wholesale sell-offs of state-run industries (utility grids, the petroleum sector, telephone systems, and airlines) was the prevailing and accepted economic dogma during the 1980s. With strong conservative laissez-faire leadership in Washington and Great Britain during the Reagan years and Margaret Thatcher's rule, the sanctity of the market could not be overstated.

Understanding the frenetic movement toward free, market-driven trade requires a brief review of the region's history, starting with the early 1970s. In Latin America, democracy was hardly in vogue, with military generals ruling Chile, Argentina, and Brazil; the Chilean economy came under the direction of the "Chicago Boys"—Chilean economists who had trained at the University of Chicago and advocated deregulation, privatization, and "supply-side" policies, which included lower tax rates for corporations.

In 1973, the price of oil spiked from about $3 a barrel to over $30, plunging the world into recession; interest rates floated upwards and loans, offered to Latin America by Western banks for development projects during the 1960s, became unmanageable as interest payments galloped out of control. The so-called "debt crisis" forced governments to cut government services and social programs to service growing debt. The extremes became almost surreal: in Bolivia, the inflation rate grew to about 11,000 percent in 1985 and, by the middle of the 1980s, about half of Mexico's working-age population was under- or unemployed. Debt rose to $400 billion in the region and, by the middle of the 1980s, GDP had fallen everywhere.[1]

Negotiations for NAFTA began during the George H. W. Bush administration (1989–1993), but the final agreement was signed during the first days of the Clinton administration. NAFTA promised increased prosperity for all in the Americas—at least in the three signatory nations—but a great, somewhat histrionic debate took shape in the United States over the admission of Mexico to a free trade agreement, penned and settled in 1987, between the United States and Canada. Could Mexico, a developing nation, with a lower wage structure and lower levels of education, become a viable partner in a massive trade pact where goods, services, and financial transactions (but, it's important to note, not people) would flow relatively freely between three nations? Texas billionaire Ross Perot didn't think so and, during a failed run for the U.S. presidency in 1992, he famously spoke of the "giant sucking sound" he heard in his future-tense imagination as well-paying, industrial, solidly "middle class" jobs migrated from what's now known as the "rust belt" (Indiana, Ohio, and Michigan) to the Rio Grande Valley. In the Valley, Mexican workers were earning about $9 a day, without benefits or union representation.

Perot's imagination proved portentous. NAFTA has resulted in wage stagnation and decline, especially for those in the United States without a college degree. A massive expansion in the maquiladora industry, just south of the U.S. border with Mexico, shows some of the limits of NAFTA. These foreign-owned (mostly American) assembly plants depend on a vast supply of cheap Mexican labor and help push up "export" numbers from U.S. factories as parts for automobiles and refrigerators, for example, are manufactured and shipped from the United States to the maquiladora factories. Then, a finished product is assembled in Mexico and shipped back over the border (duty free) for sale to U.S. consumers. The main winner in this scenario is clearly big business, which saves on labor costs while assuming relatively minor shipping costs. In 2012, industrial wages in Mexico were 18 percent of those paid in U.S. factories; trade, of course, has expanded dramatically across the three nations participating in the NAFTA agreement, totaling $918 billion in 2010.[2] Total trade between the three countries was $109 billion in 1994 and $622 billion six years later. The recent political discussion in the United States that focuses on income inequality is, in part, related to NAFTA policies. For example, it was reported in 2015 that the median U.S. income ($52,000 per year) has been falling over the past fifteen years in 81 percent of America's counties.[3] The ratio of pay between the CFO (chief financial officer) in America and the average worker is now 354:1, and the bottom 40 percent of households in America control 0.3 percent of the wealth in America. Clearly the bottom has fallen out from under America's middle class and Perot's warnings from nearly a quarter-century ago seem to have predicted the current political debate in the United States; as one party rails against international trade treaties, the other side has focused on income inequality and the declining middle class in America.

In Mexico, NAFTA, as many predicted, hurt the agrarian sector as more efficient, better-capitalized farmers in the north dumped wheat, corn, and other staples into Mexico. Mexican agricultural workers—44 percent of all Mexican nationals who cross into the United States (despite the fact that only 25 percent of the total Mexican labor force is connected to agriculture)—have been disproportionally affected by NAFTA. Mexican poverty rates for 2013 registered at about 46 percent of the national population.

On the day NAFTA was implemented, January 1, 1994, a new armed insurgency group appeared in the rural south of the nation, calling itself the Zapatistas; they took their name from revolutionary hero Emiliano Zapata to remind the world that his unwavering campaign—*tierra y libertad* (land and freedom for all)—had yet to materialize. With about 10 percent (or ten million) of the nation's citizens living in extreme poverty in 2012, it is clear that the NAFTA political cheerleaders and their corporate donors were, at best, willfully naïve in setting and relying on a (mostly) unfettered market to solve most socioeconomic problems in the Americas.

Exactly one year after NAFTA began operating, MERCOSUR (Mercado Común del Sur or Common Market of the South) went into effect, linking the economies of Argentina, Brazil, Paraguay, and Uruguay. Negotiations for this trade bloc began about a decade before the pact's implementation and emerged out of the capitals of Argentina and Brazil. Both nations threw off military dictatorships at about the same time (Argentina in 1983, Brazil two years later) and, in a spirit of South American collaboration not witnessed in decades, the presidents of the two powers decided to build on their size and industrial base by emphasizing regional trade while reducing tariff rates. Much to the chagrin of its neighbors, Chile decided to opt out of these negotiations and, instead, organized a bilateral trade treaty with the United States; that treaty went into effect in 2004.

MERCOSUR has been fraught with tensions: For example the nation of Paraguay was suspended for a brief time in 2012 and oil-rich Venezuela (under the contentious leadership of Hugo Chávez) became a member during that year. Political disputes between leaders of the member nations have led to questions about the future viability of a trade bloc that represents a total of $2.9 trillion in GDP, using data from 2012. MERCOSUR is the fourth largest trade bloc in the world, but alarming levels of economic inequity between the South American nations have generated the sort of suspicion and political intrigue that, in theory, trade agreements are designed to mollify.

One South American nation that sought to avoid these tensions was Chile. In 2003 Chile signed the FTA (free trade agreement) with the United States, which activated on January 1, 2004. Political intrigue surrounded the signing of this pact: When Chile refused to support the G. W. Bush administration's war in Iraq in 2003, the nation was briefly frozen out of free trade negotiations. The tensions, however real, did not derail the agreement.

Trade treaties extend back to the 1950s in Central America. Given the relative weak position of the Central American nations, individually, to compete in the world markets, and their close proximity to the United States market, trade pacts have been popular there. For example, in the early 1960s, an economic pact developed—known as the Central American Common Market—which was based on a nascent political unification, developed in 1951, referred to as the Organization of Central American States (ODECA, Organización de Estados Centroamericanos). This common market registered real gains during the 1960s as intraregional exports grew from 7 to 26 percent. But El Salvador, the most densely populated nation in Central America and the most industrialized, derived most of the benefits from this agreement, resulting in regional tensions. In fact, a short war between El Salvador and Honduras in 1969, known to outside pundits as "The Soccer War," left 3,000 dead and all but collapsed the Central American Common Market. National conflicts in Guatemala, El Salvador, and Nicaragua during this period certainly did not facilitate regional economic or political integration.

When NAFTA went into effect, trade patterns shifted toward the American north; in July 2005, some ten years after NAFTA had been implemented, a new regional trade treaty was ready for signature between the Central American nations (plus the Dominican Republic) and the United States. In a very close vote, 217–215, CAFTA-DR passed the U.S. House of Representatives and entered into effect in 2006. The original member nations were the United States, El Salvador, Guatemala, Honduras, and Nicaragua. The Dominican Republic joined in 2007 and Costa Rica joined two years later. This trade treaty, like NAFTA before it, generated strong debate within the United States. The labor bloc cooperated with the sugar industry to oppose it, but U.S. manufacturing interests—in their continuous search for markets and cheap labor—pushed mightily for this free trade agreement. During its first ten years of implementation, CAFTA-DR has registered an 86 percent increase (to $31.3 billion) in exports from the United States to the five Central American nations and the Dominican Republic.[4]

A free trade agreement with Colombia became a priority of the G. W. Bush administration. Given President Bush's strong friendship with President Álvaro Uribe Vélez (2002–2010), the agreement was negotiated in 2006 but not implemented until 2011, during the Obama administration. There was much opposition to this FTA. The Democratic Party in the United States, with strong union representation, opposed the treaty—unions traditionally oppose FTAs because they dissolve organizing capacity. Union leaders in the United States claim that about 5.2 million high-paying manufacturing jobs have been lost since the early 1990s as a consequence of FTAs. Given union strength in crucial midwestern battleground states (Ohio and Pennsylvania for example), candidate Obama clearly and compellingly campaigned against the FTA with Colombia. Quoted in the *Wall Street Journal* in April 2008, the Senator from Illinois said that he would oppose, as president, a FTA with Colombia, "because the violence against unions in Colombia would make a mockery of the very labor protections that we have insisted be included in these kinds of agreements."[5]

Mr. Obama was referring to a very real phenomenon in Colombia. Since the mid-1980s, union leaders there—people defending the rights of workers—have been the target of harassment, humiliation, and murder. As many as 3,000 union leaders have been killed there, and very few of the killers have been captured or prosecuted. In fact, Amnesty International reports a 95 percent impunity rate for murderers of union leaders in Colombia. Once elected to the presidency, however, Mr. Obama caved to business interests and signed a FTA with Colombia in 2011, which went into effect in 2012. The FTA has pushed up trade between the two nations. For example, in 2013, total exports to Colombia amounted to about $19 billion and imports totaled $22 billion. Those numbers represent net increases—from a decade earlier—of 395 percent and 239 percent, respectively.

Giddy with free trade expectations, capitalists from the Americas, after NAFTA's implementation, began planning for a FTAA—Free Trade Area of the Americas—a 34-nation free trade zone. In theory, this huge trading bloc would have extended from Canada to Tierra del Fuego, easing trade restrictions and tariffs along a massive North-South corridor. Cuba, of course, was excluded from the initial negotiations. But activists, social movements in Latin America, and president Hugo Chávez of Venezuela (who ruled from 1999 until his death in 2013) mobilized to defeat what Chávez called "a system of oppression." The FTAA did not meet its 2005 target date for implementation. The gigantic program, written to reflect the interests of the wealthy business class in the Americas with little input from workers, farmers, or the poor, collapsed under its own weight and from sustained, withering attacks from its opponents. At the Fourth Summit of the Americas, held in November 2005 at Mar del Plata, Argentina, there was a pseudo showdown between President Chávez and U.S. president George W. Bush over the FTAA. Chávez won. Massive street mobilizations against the FTAA were organized and supported by the charismatic Venezuelan populist leader; Chávez's opening remarks, before the summit even began, set the stage for what was to come. "I believe," he said, "we came here to bury the FTAA."

Commercial relations between the United States and Latin America have been critical to the health of the U.S. economy and the economies of Latin America. The negotiations during the 1980s leading to NAFTA, authorized by the U.S. Senate in 1993, have generated more trade, reduced barriers, and increased tax incentives; each one of these alterations tends to privilege large entities (agricultural and manufacturing) over smaller ones. Jobs have migrated to places where wages are low, labor unions weak, and workers disposable. Since NAFTA, manufacturing jobs have moved out of the industrial heartland of the United States; wages have remained flat while productivity has grown. In simple words, the market has conquered the people—throughout the Americas. The Zapatistas in Mexico, opposed to globalization, have warned repeatedly of the dangers of the market. In their Sixth Declaration of the Lacandón Jungle, issued in July 2005, they noted how "Globalization means that they no longer control the workers in one or several countries, but the capitalists are trying to dominate everything all over the world."[6] While this might sound somewhat paranoid to the modern reader, studying the breathtaking reach of the proposed FTAA forces some critical reflection on the ambitions of "the capitalists."

CONFLICT: APPARENT PEACE, BILATERAL TENSIONS

Conflict has defined the political, social, and economic relationship between the United States and Latin America. However, a focus on conflict fails to capture the concurrent search for stability and conflict resolution. The following section in this chapter, which focuses on culture, is designed to demonstrate some themes and time periods in recent U.S.-Latin American relations where collaboration has been the fundamental objective.

One specific place in the Caribbean which seems to be a clear case of nearly continuous conflict between the United States and Latin America is Haiti. In the early 1990s, at the beginning of Bill Clinton's presidency, Haiti seemed to be spiraling out of control; however, a long historic pattern of poverty and inequality suggests the limits of and challenges to the United States' Haiti policy. Also, the United States has been, far more often than not, rooting for the wrong team in Haitian history.

The Haiti conflict goes back to the earliest days of the nineteenth century when the nation broke free, via violent revolution, from its French masters. France was reluctant to lose its profitable Caribbean sugar operation—based on slave labor—but the Haitian fighters understood the "universalness" of the 1789 declaration: *liberté, egalité, fraternité* applied to all humans, everywhere, all the time.

The Haitian people, for daring and succeeding to overthrow the French, have suffered the scorn and, at times, outright hostility of Western democracies. French/Cuban writer Alejo Carpentier captures the difficulty of establishing democratic rule there in his classic 1949 novel *The Kingdom of this World.* Paul Farmer, the American physician and anthropologist, contextualized and problematized Haiti's historic struggles in his important 1999 work, *Infections and Inequalities.*

While the nineteenth century offered more of the same for the people of Haiti—poverty, a monocrop economy, few friends in the world, and seemingly insurmountable corruption and racism—the twentieth century brought little relief. The U.S. Marines invaded in 1915 and stuck around for about twenty years, and one family named Duvalier, adopting heavy-handed, antidemocratic tactics, ruled the island from the late 1950s through the overthrow of Jean-Claude "Baby Doc" Duvalier in 1986. In 1990, Jean-Bertrand Aristide, a Roman Catholic priest steeped in the theory and practice of liberation theology, was elected president of the nation. He was the first democratically elected president in the nation's history.

Aristide's rule ran into trouble with the Haitian military and elite; neither party was comfortable with his "liberationist" rhetoric. The president was removed from office in a coup staged by the military, which long considered his views, his speeches, and his very being subversive. A (new) reign of terror ensued in Haiti, and an early challenge of the newly installed Clinton administration (January 1993) was the restoration of the legitimate, democratically elected leader of Haiti. Aristide successfully lobbied in the United States; church leaders, the Congressional Black Caucus, and others rallied to his cause. Clinton threatened a massive military intervention to restore Aristide to power and, as the force advanced on the Caribbean nation, the Haitian military and civilian coup-makers negotiated. Aristide returned to power and finished out his term, leaving office in 1996.

But, generations of poverty, corruption, and neglect could not be resolved, or even diminished, with one presidential election and, as in prior historic periods, the international community—focusing mostly on "democratic" elections and processes—quickly lost interest in the Haiti dilemma. Aristide, reelected in 2000, was again removed from power, this time in early 2004.

During his time in office, President Aristide made some mistakes: For example, in 2003, he demanded France pay the equivalent of $21 billion

(U.S.) in restitutions—an amount he claimed was equal (in real terms) to the amount paid out by Haiti to France—in gold—at the end of the independence struggle in the early nineteenth century. Neither the French, nor the other powerful Western nations, were amused. Citing irregularities in the 2000 election, rebel groups began to move in Haiti; some of these paramilitary groups were essentially retooled Tonton Macoutes (terrorists) of the dark Duvalier days. They ravaged the countryside and the cities and forced the president's removal. Aristide claims he was "kidnapped" by the United States. Indeed, a U.S.-supplied and -piloted Boeing 757 jet carried Mr. Aristide out of Haiti to the Central African Republic.

Other areas of conflict in Latin America are related to the so-called "Pink Tide" that has washed over the region. The Pink Tide is a term used to describe the emergence of a new "wave" of leftist leaders in Latin America who differ dramatically from revolutionaries of previous eras. The three leaders generally associated with this movement of the "new left" are Venezuela's Hugo Chávez (1999–2013); Evo Morales of Bolivia, who has ruled there since 2006; and Rafael Correa of Ecuador. Dr. Correa (he holds a PhD degree in economics from the University of Illinois) was elected in 2006 and has ruled continuously since.

The leaders of the "new left" have held to some predictable policies and rhetorical flourishes. They have moved their nations away from the so-called "Washington Consensus" but they've kept their societies (unlike Mr. Fidel Castro in Cuba in the early 1960s) firmly in the fold of the capitalist market order. They have expropriated, or sought to control, certain key sectors of their nations' industries. In Venezuela and Ecuador, petroleum is a critically important creator of revenue for the national economy. In Bolivia, natural gas, coca leaf production, and tin are key economic components.

Mr. Hugo Chávez was a gifted orator, politician, and populist. He emerged out of the Venezuelan military and took the country, during his fourteen-year rule, in a path that diverged significantly from Washington's wishes and expectations. Chávez exerted significant control over the oil industry, after a strike by petroleum workers, and he used robust oil profits to help the poor. He waged a war of words against then sitting U.S. President, George W. Bush. In 2006 he called Mr. Bush "the Devil" from the podium of the United Nations in New York and on his television show, *Aló Presidente* (*Hello President*), he referred to Mr. Bush as "Mister Danger" and a "donkey."

The theatrical, verbal assaults belied the degree to which Chávez commandeered the Venezuelan economy: He resisted a devastating strike of oil executives and workers in 2003. The strike ended with thousands of workers losing their jobs and furthered Chávez's consolidation of the state run industry. The strike brought on a significant (but temporary) reversal of GDP in Venezuela during that period. Despite this, high international oil prices from

2000–2008, with recovery again after 2009, meant that tens of billions of dollars from the state-run oil company, PDVSA (Petróleos de Venezuela, S.A.), were directed toward the government's social programs (the Bolivarian Missions) which supported the construction and staffing of hospitals and significant subsidies on food and housing for the poor.

Veteran journalist Jon Lee Anderson wrote a searing critique of the Chávez regime in *The New Yorker*. He focused on Caracas's "Tower of David," an unfinished ziggurat rising from the city center, named for oil tycoon David Brillembourg. A sort of squatter community emerged there, with security guards controlling entryways, and an ex-con turned evangelical minister, Alexander Daza, commanding the operation. The unfinished building (construction began before Chávez assumed power) still stands as a clear symbol of the gap between Chávez's soaring rhetoric and the city's current reality. In March 2014, a year after Mr. Chávez's death, the 3,000 or so "residents" of the tower were removed by the government of Nicolás Maduro.[7]

With the price of oil faltering for the past twenty-two months and holding at just under $50 a barrel as of this writing (in August 2016), the future of the Venezuelan economy and the Bolivarian social mission is in jeopardy. However, according to the World Bank, overall poverty fell in the period from 1998 to 2013 and the nation's Gini coefficient, which measures absolute inequality, moved from 49 in 1998 to 39 in 2012. Zero on the coefficient represents perfect equality.

In Ecuador, similar metrics have been measured. President Rafael Correa, an economist by training, decided to focus more on social spending and less on debt reduction; he decreed that external debt financing could not exceed 3 percent of GDP and he has increased the education budget from 3 to 6 percent of GDP. Poverty has fallen, especially during the days of high oil prices on the international market. From 2006 to 2014, poverty rates dropped by about 15 percent.

Despite these positive developments in poverty reduction and the construction of social infrastructure, the response from Washington toward the new left has been tepid at best, and outright hostile at worst. For example, in 2002, a coup in Venezuela briefly toppled President Chávez; Mr. Chávez claimed the coup was cooked up in Washington and the relative speed with which the George W. Bush administration supported the coup-makers—against his legitimate, popularly elected government—certainly seemed suspicious. Immediately after the coup commenced and when it appeared that Chávez had been toppled, the United States recognized the coup leader, Mr. Pedro Carmona. A trio of U.S. policy makers—Elliot Abrams, Otto Reich, and John Negroponte—all with strong ties to the dark days of the 1980s Central American expeditions, actually "sanctioned" the coup, and hoped that it would succeed. The people of Venezuela quickly pulled away from the coup when Carmona and his U.S.-backed allies immediately began rolling back the Chávez reforms. Rallies erupted in the streets. Chávez returned.

In Honduras, the democratically elected president removed in a 2009 coup did not return to power. Manuel Zelaya, who was elected and assumed the presidency in January 2006, was ousted from power, ostensibly by the Supreme Court and the military. He had been ordered by the Court to desist from holding a constitutional referendum, viewed by many as an attempt to extend his time in power. Zelaya ignored the Court and the military moved in, in what has been derisively referred to as a *Golpe Profiláctico*—a coup to prevent what follows. He was forced from the presidential palace early in the morning of June 28, 2009, placed on a plane, flown to Costa Rica, and left at an airport there wearing his pajamas.

The Obama administration quickly, but gently, denounced the coup. Zelaya, since gaining power in 2006, had gravitated toward the centrifugal pull of Hugo Chávez and his Bolivarian Revolution. Zelaya's policies meant a rise in the minimum wage for Hondurans, free education for children, and a significant (about 10 percent) reduction in poverty during his brief tenure. None of this pleased the wealthy ruling elite in Honduras or the conservative elements in the Roman Catholic Church and, rather than fight for Zelaya's return to office—as was the Clinton strategy with Aristide and Haiti—American officials called for "new" elections. Those elections were held in late 2009 and Porfirio Lobo, a Conservative, became the new president of Honduras.

A clear, complex area of conflict between Latin America and the United States emerged in 2003 when the administration of George W. Bush took the United States and a small "coalition of the willing" to war in Iraq. That coalition did not include the powerful nations of France, Germany, Italy, Russia, or China. Nor did it include Latin America. In fact, the most influential nations—Mexico, Brazil, Argentina, and Chile—openly condemned the illegal invasion and the Bush-Fox alliance (Vicente Fox, the conservative president of Mexico) temporarily collapsed. President Chávez of Venezuela likened the war to fighting "terrorism with terrorism," and Costa Rica withdrew support after its constitutional court determined that the war was in violation of international law.

One nation in South America, Colombia, supported the war. Colombia at the time was ruled by the conservative Álvaro Uribe, who was a close ally of President Bush. Mr. Uribe's plan to eradicate the leftist insurgency there, the FARC (Fuerzas Armadas Revolucionarias de Colombia or Revolutionary Armed Forces of Colombia), was predicated upon receiving billions of dollars in mostly military aid from the United States. The Colombians, essentially, were held hostage by the Bush administration and their support was limited to rhetorical, government-to-government support. The Colombian government neither sent troops nor equipment for the 2003 U.S. war in the Middle East.

The United States Naval Base at Guantánamo, Cuba, has been a century-long source of tension but that tension intensified in 2002 when the base became a prison camp for detainees in the United States' seemingly interminable War on Terror. The Bush administration dumped "enemy combatants" from the Middle East at Guantánamo, claiming these individuals had no rights under international law. The U.S. Supreme Court disagreed: In a landmark 2006 decision, *Hamdan v. Rumsfeld*, the court declared that article 3 of the Geneva Conventions (which prohibits torture, indefinite detention, and insists on access to fair trials) applies to all people, everywhere, at all times. As of this writing in late August 2016, nine detainees have died in captivity and sixty-one remain at Guantánamo in a surreal legal limbo: The U.S. Congress will not authorize any funds for the transfer of these people to the U.S. mainland and, since evidence against some of the detainees was derived from torture, rulings from civilian courtroom procedures could never hold up.

Some Latin American governments have supplied relief for the nightmare scenario at Guantánamo, a prison that has cost U.S. taxpayers about $5 billion since 2002 and has seriously jeopardized U.S. leadership and authority in the world and region. José Mujica, sitting president of Uruguay from 2010–2014 offered to take in six prisoners from Guantánamo, and those individuals were transferred from Cuba to Uruguay on Sunday December 7, 2014. Mr. Mujica had a clear understanding of the plight of prisoners: he was detained for fourteen years—much of this time spent in solitary confinement—as a political prisoner for participating in Uruguay's Tupamaros guerrilla organization during the early 1970s.

Conflict has defined the relationship between the United States and Mexico; the collaboration and enthusiasm during the go-go days of NAFTA negotiation ended in 1995 with a major devaluation of the peso, and a Washington-arranged bailout.

The year 1994, sardonically referred to as "the year of living dangerously" by Mexican writer Carlos Fuentes, was marked by the implementation of NAFTA on January 1; the emergence (on the same day) of the Zapatista revolutionary movement in the south; the March murder of the hand-picked presidential candidate, Luis Donaldo Colosio; and the collapse of the Mexican peso in December. The devaluation in late 2004 triggered a $50-billion bailout. President Clinton pushed the international community to help Mexico and the funds flowed through the IMF (International Monetary Fund). The United States offered—essentially—a $20-billion credit line, of which $12.5 billion was used. Mexico paid back these funds to the United States within two years, two years ahead of schedule and with $500 million in interest payments. Though the relationship between the United States and Mexico has always been tense, this period was especially strange. Reflecting on the crises of 1994 and 1995 in his native Mexico, Mr. Fuentes wrote that "the only strange thing is that it didn't happen earlier."[8]

Drug smuggling through Mexico has become a serious source of tension between the United States and Mexico. With the collapse of cartels in Colombia in the early 1990s—first the Medellín cartel with the death of Pablo Escobar in 1993 and, shortly thereafter, the collapse of the Cali cartel—drug smuggling "ballooned" north and west, away from Colombia toward Central America and the west coast of Mexico. Though Mexico is not a producer of cocaine—that still happens in Colombia, Peru, and other places in the Andes and South American jungles—it is estimated that, by 2007, about 90 percent of all cocaine entering the U.S. market moved in through Mexico, with Central America serving as an important transshipment point.

Mexican cartels, not unlike the Colombian cartels of a decade earlier, moved the product and outmaneuvered, outgunned, and outspent the national government. When Mexican president Felipe Calderón (2006–2012) decided to fight the cartels, the cartels fought back, and blood flowed. The United States, during the waning days of the George W. Bush administration (2001–2009) announced the Mérida Initiative, a $1.3-billion security assistance package for Mexico. Mérida, in addition to providing weaponry to fight the cartels, was designed to help build the Mexican judicial system. The efficaciousness of that system has been repeatedly called into question, most recently in September 2014, when forty-three college students studying at a severely underfunded teachers college were kidnapped, murdered, and burned beyond identification. Mr. José Luis Abarca, the mayor of the town of Iguala, in the state of Guererro, is widely believed to have orchestrated the crime. He is accused of ordering the local police to capture the students, who were then turned over to a criminal gang; gang leaders—it has been reported—apparently mistook the students for a rival gang and executed them. The case produced widespread protest and dismay from Mexicans who have historically held a deep skepticism for their nation's leaders and institutions. The prison escapes of Mr. Joaquín "El Chapo" Guzmán Loera, only reinforced such skepticism. The billionaire leader of the Sinaloa cartel, "El Chapo," twice escaped from Mexican prisons, embarrassing Mexican and U.S. authorities. He was recaptured on January 8, 2016, and, the next day, *Rolling Stone* magazine published an "in-depth" interview between the cartel leader and the American actor Sean Penn. The piece, titled "El Chapo Speaks," was written after a clandestine meeting in Mexico between the actor and the *narcotraficante* somewhere in Mexico in October 2015. Mexican *telenovela* actress Kate del Castillo facilitated the meeting.

Prior to Mexico's emergence as a major transport route and supplier of cocaine to the U.S. market, most narco discussion focused on one South American nation: Colombia. In fact, at the end of his administration, president Bill Clinton pushed through Congress a "Plan Colombia" designed to save the Colombian nation. Colombia had seen increased criminal activity during the 1990s as the cartels dispersed and new actors, including paramilitary organizations, wreaked havoc. The leftist insurgency contributed to the chaos and, by the year 2000 when the plan was announced, as many as 25,000 men, women, and children were thought to form the Marxist-inspired insurgency known by its Spanish acronym, FARC. At that time, the FARC was generating between $300 and $500 million annually, through extortion, protection of the narcotics industry, and kidnapping. It was the largest and wealthiest insurgency group in the Americas. Plan Colombia, a $1.3-billion aid package to Colombia, breezed through the U.S. Congress, and was designed to fortify the Colombian army and judiciary.

As of this writing, about $10 billion (2000–2015) has flowed from the United States to Colombia in mostly military aid. The Colombian government of Juan Manuel Santos and the FARC leadership have agreed to a broad outline which became formalized in "Peace Accords." The signing of a peace agreement—which occurred on September 26, 2016—represents a critical turning point for Colombian society after a long, nearly four-year "Peace Process" in Havana that captivated the world and was energetically endorsed by—among others—Pope Francis I and Miss Universe (2015), Colombia's Paulina Vega. The peace process has been relatively concise, when compared to the conflict which has endured for decades in Colombia and has left—according to some estimates—over five million victims.[9] On March 30, 2016, the Colombian government announced that peace talks would begin with the ELN—the National Army of Liberation (Ejército de Liberación Nacional), a leftist insurgency inspired by the Cuban Revolution. The ELN probably counts on 1,500 armed combatants but even with such limited numbers, they have been effective at attacking the nation's infrastructure, especially oil pipelines. This round of peace talks is scheduled to begin in Ecuador and then move to Venezuela, Brazil, Chile, and Cuba.

A continuous area of contention between the United States and Latin America involves immigration. In 2014, 11.7 million undocumented persons lived in the United States (down from 12.8 million in 2007); and the majority (5.6 million) originate from one country, Mexico. However, the United States is hardly "drowning" in immigrants from the South: In November 2015, the Pew Research Center, a widely respected authority on immigration issues, reported that from 2009 to 2014 there was an aggregate 130,000-person outflow from the United States to Mexico; that is, about a million persons returned to Mexico during that period while "only" 870,000 arrived.[10] But much recent attention has focused on the plight of Central American arrivals to the United States—especially unaccompanied minors. This reality turned into a "crisis" in the summer of 2014 when, during a seven-month period, approximately 30,000 unaccompanied minors were detained at the U.S. border. Many factors contributed to this humanitarian crisis: First, the Central American civil wars of the 1970s–1990s helped destabilize the region. Recent trade policies/liberalization have not generated prosperity for the Central American people; in fact, some 60 percent of Hondurans live in poverty, according to 2014 statistics. Criminal gangs and drug smuggling networks have prospered throughout the region. The situation became so acute by 2014 that mothers in Honduras chose to send their children— alone, on a harrowing voyage through Central America and Mexico—to seek refugee status and relative safety in U.S. detention centers over the potential peril of gang and other violence in the towns and cities of Central America.

CULTURAL DIFFUSION IN THE AMERICAS

While violence and conflict capture the attention of the U.S. and Latin American media outlets, more subtle, stable, and ultimately more important forms of exchange between the United States and Latin America involve cultural contact and integration. Music, art, architecture, literature, film, sport, and cuisine all move from Latin America to the United States and vice versa. When American rapper and actor Tupac Amaru Shakur (né Lesane Parish Crooks) was killed in Las Vegas, Nevada, in 1996, most people had no idea that he was renamed as a three-year-old in honor of an eighteenth-century rebellion leader in the south of Peru. Tupac Amaru II, né José Gabriel Condorcanqui (1742–1781), led a major, widespread rebellion in Peru (and what is today Bolivia) to assert the rights of poor, indigenous peoples. He died a martyr and his message of struggle and revolution—and violence—traveled across place and time.

Now, with the Internet, culture throughout the Americas remains vital while access and diffusion has spread, allowing people in the United States to learn about music, film, and literature from Latin America without ever entering a concert hall, theater, or library. American cuisine has been enhanced and enriched through the incorporation of Latin food traditions. Americans are now consuming locally produced tacos in all major cities. Taco Bell—the fast food, corporate cliché of Mexico—is no longer the only source for "Mexican food"; in fact, a significant percent of Taco Bell's sales take place between the hours of 1:00 and 4:00 a.m. Many of these consumers have been working and need quick, easy-to-handle food that is eaten, generally, behind the wheel of a car.

Ceviche—which can't be consumed in a car—has become popular in the United States in recent years. This traditional coastal dish from Peru (and Ecuador) is made from raw seafood, *aji* (a burning spice made from the *rocoto* pepper found in Peru), cilantro, onions, salt, and lime. The seafood is essentially "cooked" in the lime juice, and Peruvians of all socioeconomic classes eat ceviche, normally at lunch time. But even in middle America, in the city of Louisville, a restaurant named "Seviche" (to help with pronunciation) opened ten years ago, which suggests that ceviche and other Latin staples are no longer confined to Miami, Los Angeles, or New York City. The chef in Louisville, Anthony Lamas, is himself a product of Latino fusion: His father is Puerto Rican and his mother hails from Mexico.

American cuisine has made its way to Latin America; an upscale hamburger franchise in Colombia called "La Hamburguesería" is popular with the upwardly mobile in Bogotá and the menu features hamburgers and French fries. TGI Friday's, McDonald's, and P. F. Chang's are frequented by middle-class patrons in Bogotá. In Mexico City, in the elite neighborhoods of Condesa and the Zona Rosa, "Burgers by Buba" recently opened and sells a cheeseburger for 78 pesos—about $5 U.S. at current exchange rates. While there is no authentic "American cuisine," many Latin Americans associate American cuisine with the hotdog and hamburger. Expanding on this idea, Carlos Fuentes wrote the chapter "Spoils" in his novel *The Crystal Frontier.* The chapter is a devastating critique of U.S. consumption patterns, the unimaginative nature of American fast food, and the resultant obesity epidemic in America. That book, published in Spanish in 1995 and released in an English language edition in 1997, is a fictitious, artistic interpretation of American cuisine, but the critique contains some uncomfortable kernels of truth.

As America becomes more Latin—it is estimated that by 2050, 30 percent of the U.S. population will be of Latin American origin—food offerings from Latin America will continue to emerge into the mainstream. We know that long ago "salsa" began outselling ketchup in American supermarkets and, today, youngsters on the West Coast eat more fresh fish tacos than Mrs. Paul's fish sticks—an American, frozen food staple from the generation of their grandparents.

Sports in the Americas has long been an area of academic interest; the journal *Studies in Latin American Popular Culture* has been disseminating research on cultural questions in Latin America, and the American historian Joseph L. Arbena focused on sport in Latin America during his long career at Clemson University.[11] Two sports—baseball and soccer—will constitute the focus of this section; one made in the USA and the other drifting north from Latin America but originating with British sailors during their extended stays in Latin America, especially Argentina, in the late nineteenth century.

Baseball, with its desegregation in the United States in 1947, has changed in terms of demographics. No longer an "all white" sport, Major League Baseball is now about 27 percent Hispanic; about 24 percent of players were born in Latin American counties. Major League Baseball now caters to Latin audiences in the United States by broadcasting games in Spanish, hosting exhibition matches abroad, and commercializing their players' roots. Much baseball talent originates in the pan-Caribbean region—Mexico, the Dominican Republic, Cuba, Puerto Rico, Colombia, and Venezuela. Some of these places, especially Mexico and Colombia, are "soccer-centric" societies, but soccer tends to dominate in the highland, capital areas (Mexico City and Bogotá are both interior, high altitude cities) and baseball is more popular in the coastal regions.

Soccer has spread in the USA and American youth are playing more soccer than baseball, a trend that continues to advance. With the recent emphasis on dangers from concussions, it seems logical that parents will steer their kids away from "American" football and toward *fútbol.*[12] Many "American" soccer players play in Latin American leagues, such as Mexico's "Liga MX," which provides lucrative contracts to players who—for financial reasons—forgo America's MLS—Major League Soccer. Statistics from 2014 show the MLS average salary of $213,000 U.S. is significantly lower than the Mexican Liga MX salary of $265,625.

Los Angeles, California, with its close geographic proximity to Mexico and Central America, is a soccer mecca in the United States and the soccer played there, along with youth development programs in Los Angeles, has impacted the USA writ large. For example, whereas American-born soccer coaches—up until recently—attempted to apply "football" logic to the game of soccer (that is, through emphasis on strength, power, and set plays at the expense of intuition, finesse, and technical ability), many contemporary coaches, with roots and training in Latin America, have revolutionized the game here in America. Latin players have transformed the game in Europe: both the Spanish and German soccer leagues are dominated by Latin American players and one team, Barcelona, fields the three best players in the world: Lionel Messi from Argentina, Luis Alberto Suárez from Uruguay, and Neymar da Silva Santos Júnior from Brazil. The focus on international stars, the outrageous sums paid to professional players,[13] belies a more sober reality in America: in any American city, there is most likely an adult soccer league populated by both Hispanic and non-Hispanic players. Soccer will continue to spread in America, probably at the expense of American football, and America's rich immigrant tradition is reflected, each day, on soccer pitches across the nation.

Film is a significant source of cross-cultural contact, and many Americans and Latin Americans learn by watching the movies, both fictional and reality-based. In fact, an entire generation of Americans viewed the Mexican Revolution not through Carlos Fuentes's dense, stream-of-consciousness novel *The Death of Artemio Cruz* (1962), but through an American-made film—*Viva Zapata!*—directed by Elia Kazan in 1952. The film starred Marlon Brando, with screenplay by John Steinbeck; Brando played Emiliano Zapata, the film's hero and martyr. *Viva Zapata!* attempts to explain the mayhem, intrigue, and outside agitation that defined the 1910 revolution—a revolution that churned for more than a decade.

Ten years prior to *Viva Zapata!* Orson Welles was sent to Brazil on a goodwill tour through the "Office of the Coordinator of Inter-American Affairs," a federal agency set up by president Franklin D. Roosevelt in 1940. Tensions quickly developed between Welles and his American backers (RKO Radio Pictures) and the film was never completed; however, one segment of the film was discovered in UCLA's archives, cleaned up, and released in 1993 as the documentary *It's All True*. The final part of the documentary shows a section of Welles's work in Brazil, called "Four Men on a Raft," filmed in Brazil in 1942. Welles told the story of the *jangadeiros*—the four fishermen who traveled more than 1,600 miles, in 1941, from the northeast city of Fortaleza to Rio de Janeiro on a creaky raft to dramatize their daily struggles and seemingly inescapable poverty. During the filming in Rio, that is, during the reenactment of the actual voyage, the leader of the group, Manoel Olimpio Meira (nicknamed Jacaré—Alligator), drowned when the raft capsized. Welles was devastated by this accident, but remained determined to finish the film. Sadly, the studio executives in New York worried more about Jacaré's politics (he was a communist) than the sacrifice he made for the film. RKO pulled the plug on the project.

In the seventy years or so since the Welles/RKO dustup in Rio, much has changed in terms of cinematic integration in the Americas. Alfonso Cuarón was the first Mexican to win an Academy Award as best director for his film *Gravity*. The film took a total of seven awards in 2014. But the "Mexican invasion" began earlier with director Alejandro González Iñárritu, who shocked audiences with his powerful, realistic film depicting chaos, violence, urban poverty, and the search for redemption in Mexico City. That film, *Amores Perros* (2000), translated as *Love's a Bitch,* garnered immediate worldwide recognition for the young Mexican director. His 2003 film, *21 Grams,* starred Sean Penn and was shot in Memphis, Tennessee; the director—before making the film—described the broad outline of the movie to Lynn Hirschberg, a writer for the *New York Times Magazine*: "it's a movie about guilt and forgiveness," said the director. "In America, that would be considered an art film. Here, it's the way we live."[14] Mr. González Iñárritu won back-to-back Oscars in the category of "Best Director" for *Birdman* (2015) and *The Revenant* (2016).

American directors and artists have made significant contributions to understanding and cross-cultural collaboration between the United States and Latin America. In 1997, American John Sayles wrote and directed the astonishing film, *Men with Guns*, based on the 1992 book *The Long Night of the White Chickens* by Guatemalan American writer Francisco Goldman. The film is a stark, seemingly surreal look at the endemic violence that has plagued Latin America—especially Central America—though the film never identifies a specific location. Sayles, clearly, was commenting on the brutality of the 36-year Guatemalan civil war, 1960–1996, but suggested that the root causes of the violence were universal to the region: endemic poverty, gross economic inequality, historic racism, societal indifference, and men with guns. American folk musician Ry Cooder traveled to Cuba in 1997 to work on an album with traditional Cuban musicians. He "discovered" a tremendously talented but nearly unknown group of musicians who once played at the Buena Vista Social Club—a private social club shuttered once the revolution, with its discourse of popular, plural, and public, took hold in 1959. Cooder convinced the German director Wim Wenders to film the studio sessions, and the documentary film *Buena Vista Social Club* was released in 1999. The once-ignored, nearly anonymous Cuban musicians became instant international celebrities.

In 2006, American director Tommy Lee Jones weighed in on a politically sensitive topic in the United States: Immigration as it pertains to the U.S. border with Mexico. Mr. Jones made a powerful film in 2006 titled *The Three Burials of Melquiades Estrada.* Filmed in west Texas, the beauty and extension of the physical landscape becomes an actual character; the film deals with friendship, loyalty, and sacrifice and portrays the U.S. Border Patrol in a light that could be characterized as dim.

During the past twenty-five years, some films from Latin America have had a major impact on United States culture. In 1992, *Like Water for Chocolate* was released, based on the same-titled novel (1989) by Mexican writer Laura Esquivel. The film was widely seen in the United States and blended the intrigue of Mexican cooking and traditional recipes with the violence of the Mexican revolution. The "narration" of the revolution, from the perspective of a female protagonist and an American border physician, Dr. Brown, is presented in an optimistic, positive light. *Fresa y Chocolate* (*Strawberry and Chocolate*) was made in Cuba in 1993 by veteran filmmaker Tomás Gutiérrez Alea. The film proved controversial because it dealt openly with censorship and treatment of gay people in Cuba. Cuban watchers saw the film as a watershed moment, an *abertura*—a slight opening up of the repressive, controlling Castro regime.

In 2002, the Brazilian film *Cidade de Deus* or *City of God* was released, based on the 1997 book of the same name by Paulo Lins. The film was unusual for its unsentimental look at life and violence in the Brazilian *favela*—specifically, a marginalized segment of Rio de Janeiro named Cidade de Deus. The actors who starred in the movie were people who lived in this neighborhood and the film's dire conclusion suggested that the quest for power, money, guns, drugs, and authority is both endemic and patrilineal. Two years later, *Motorcycle Diaries* was released, based on the 1952 transcontinental voyage of Ernesto "Che" Guevara who traveled with his friend Alberto Granado. This film represented a truly trans-American collaboration:

American filmmaker Robert Redford was one of the backers (as co-producer), Mexican actor Gael García Bernal played the Argentine folk hero/revolutionary (Che Guevara), and the movie was directed by Brazilian filmmaker Walter Salles.

Literary currents and traditions have moved along the same pathways as film. The conclusion of the First World War had a profound effect on literary production and dissemination. In Latin America, a new *indigenismo* emerged; this was a post-war focus on pre-Columbian peoples, traditions, and languages. No longer would culture be defined solely by the Parisian avant-garde. Writers and painters presented themes drawn from their own Latin American experiences and realities. Some would write in indigenous languages, as was the case with Peru's José María Arguedas, who published in Spanish and Quechua. In the United States, the 1920s represented one of the richest periods in modern American literary history. Ernest Hemingway, F. Scott Fitzgerald, Eugene O'Neill, John Dos Passos, Langston Hughes, and Gertrude Stein were all prominent during this period and they wrote some of the most significant, enduring works of the twentieth century. One writer, though, William Faulkner, would reverberate in the American south and South America like no other writer in American history. Faulkner, who created a county called Yoknapatawpha, situated most of his novels in this place somewhere in Mississippi. Likewise, Gabriel García Márquez created "Macondo," a fictitious place on the Colombian Caribbean coast, to set his 1967 novel *One Hundred Years of Solitude.* The Colombian writer has acknowledged the southerner's influence: In his 1982 acceptance speech before the Nobel Committee, Mr. García Márquez referred to William Faulkner as *mi maestro*—my teacher, my master.

Many other Latin American writers of the so-called "boom"—the explosive power of Latin American literature as it emerged into the world (read English language) market during the 1960s—were influenced by Faulkner. But the clearest expression of Faulknerian magic and madness is found in the work of Mexicans Juan Rulfo and Carlos Fuentes, Argentines Jorge Luis Borges and Julio Cortázar, Chilean José Donoso and Mr. García Márquez of Colombia. In 2007, three years before winning the Nobel prize in literature, Peruvian Mario Vargas Llosa reflected on his debt to Faulkner: "Faulkner, for me, was a revelation: he taught me things—lessons really—about the handling of space and time that I've never abandoned."[15]

During the past twenty years or so, a number of important writers have explored, in their work, their Latin heritage. Many of these writers were born in the United States and their success suggests the strength of Latin American themes in writing and culture. New York–born, Dominican American Julia Alvarez published a searing historical novel about the Trujillo dictatorship in the Dominican Republic titled *In the Time of the Butterflies.* American-born writers, both of Mexican descent, Ana Castillo and Sandra

Cisneros have introduced Latin American themes into the American literary mainstream: Castillo, a poet and essayist, published, in 1996, an important collection on the Virgin of Guadalupe titled *Goddess of the Americas/La Diosa de las Américas: Writings on the Virgin of Guadalupe*. Colombian American Sergio de la Pava, who works as a public defense attorney in New York City, stunned the literary establishment with his massive novel *A Naked Singularity*, which is a scathing fictitious study of the inequities in our contemporary criminal justice system. Junot Díaz and Horacio Castellanos Moya are also both influential writers living in the United States; Mr. Díaz won the Pulitzer Prize for his novel—*The Brief and Wondrous Life of Oscar Wao*—about the Dominican immigrant experience in the United States. He teaches writing at the Massachusetts Institute of Technology. Mr. Castellanos Moya, who lives in exile from Central America (he was born in Honduras and grew up in El Salvador), teaches at the University of Iowa and has addressed the violence of his native region with a novella appropriately titled *Senselessness*.

Trade agreements of the past quarter century—negotiated by business executives and politicians—suggest a high degree of consensus between the Latin American region and the United States. Trade policy has been the subject of much recent scrutiny and criticism, generating a sociopolitical backlash known euphemistically as the "Pink Tide"—politicians elected in Latin America seeking to gradually disengage from the Washington Consensus with its sanctimonious, self-serving prescriptions. Conflict has taken the form of trade disagreements, characterized by an inability to see the strength and durability of Latin American nationalism in historical context. Also, Washington's facile definition of democracy as "elections only" has tended to occlude rather than promote hemispheric integration. What ultimately has integrated north and south in recent years has been the persistent, creative march of cultural patterns and traditions; culture has deeply influenced both hemispheres and will continue to flourish and encourage integration in the immediate and distant future.

NOTES

1. See Michael J. LaRosa and Germán R. Mejía, *An Atlas and Survey of Latin American History* (New York: M. E. Sharpe, 2007), p. 138.

2. See Julián Aguilar, "Twenty Years Later, NAFTA Remains a Source of Tension," *The New York Times*, December 7, 2012. See also, Mark Stevenson, "At 20 Years, NAFTA Didn't Close Mexico Wage Gap," *Associated Press,* December 31, 2013.

3. Larry Schwartz, "35 Soul-Crushing Facts about American Income Inequality," *Salon,* July 15, 2015.

4. See Dominican Republic-Central America-United States Free Trade Agreement (CAFTA-DR). Online. Available: http://2016.export.gov/FTA/cafta-dr/.

5. Susan Davis, "Obama Vows Opposition to Colombia Trade Deal," *Wall Street Journal*, April 2, 2008.

6. This, and the majority of the Zapatista Declarations, are written by "Subcomandante Marcos," né Rafael Sebastian Guillen Vincente (July 2005).

7. See two articles by Jon Lee Anderson in *The New Yorker*: "Slumlord: What has Hugo Chávez Wrought in Venezuela?" (January 28, 2013), and "Emptying Out the Tower of David" (July 24, 2014).

8. Carlos Fuentes, *A New Time for Mexico* (New York: Farrar, Straus & Giroux, 1996), p. 81.

9. "5.5 millones de víctimas y contando," *Semana*, Junio 3–10, 2013, Edición Especial, no. 1622.

10. Julia Preston, "More Mexican Immigrants Leaving U.S. Than Entering, Report Finds," *New York Times*, November 19, 2015.

11. Professor Arbena died in 2013.

12. Concussions can present in soccer; generally this occurs when two players try to "head" the ball and unintentionally crash into one another.

13. In 2014, Mr. Messi signed a contract for 50 million dollars in salary, per year, with Barcelona FC.

14. Lynn Hirschberg, "A New Mexican: Alejandro González Iñárritu," *New York Times Magazine* (March 18, 2001).

15. Robert Boyers and Gene Bell-Villada, "Exhilaration and Completeness: An Interview with Mario Vargas Llosa," *Salmagundi* 155–156 (2007).

Conclusion

This book, *The Third Century,* covers a period from 1889 to 2016, a 127-year time of engagement, between the United States and Latin America. So much has occurred during those years that it seems almost futile to try and tie things up in a single "conclusion." The relationship has evolved and the "players" have changed, significantly. By 1889, Brazil had been a republic for less than a year; Cuba and Puerto Rico were still under Spanish domination; and Mexico was dominated by dictator Porfirio Díaz, whose rule on behalf of the well-educated and wealthy led, inexorably, toward revolution. In 1889, Latin America was among the most rural regions in the world; today it is the most urban.

No longer can the United States force its will upon the people or governments of Latin America. The days when a U.S. president essentially "creates" a Latin American nation (Teddy Roosevelt and Panama, 1903) are in the distant past, and recent U.S. administrations—from Clinton, to Bush, to Obama—have sought a more conciliatory, collaborative relationship with Latin America. We've learned that collaboration can generate profit: For example, the North American Free Trade Agreement of 1994—which pushed profits to better-educated persons, professionals, investors, and the wealthy in the United States, Mexico, and Canada—has been at the center of political debate, especially in the United States. Questions of income inequality tied to trade agreements, and growing inequality in general, have animated young people and those who understand a basic tenant of the modern capitalist economy: U.S. workers are expensive and thanks to advances in technology and transportation networks, less expensive workers can be found abroad and excluded from the profit taking that has pushed levels of income inequality to frightening proportions. In our interlinked "global" economy, downward pressure on wages in one place affects the wage structure everywhere. As such, statistics produced in 2015 by the Center for Equitable Growth show how the bottom 90 percent of U.S. income earners (averaging $33,000 a year) made nine times less in income than the top 10 percent, who made (on average) about $296,000. These, and similar statistics, have grabbed the attention of the American people, who have been looking for scapegoats and finding them in obscure, complex trade deals (like NAFTA); some sectors of the American electorate seem to be supporting jingoistic rhetoric and wall building, and many are angry at politics as usual—politics that have ignored the plight of the poor, the working poor, and the lower middle class in America.

While trade creates some political conflict and economic prosperity—a prosperity that distributes unevenly in our modern capitalist, free trade–focused economy—real political, economic, and societal tensions remain between the United States and its hemispheric neighbors. Neopopulist, independent-minded leaders in Latin American have been greeted recently with disapprobation from Washington elites and politicians. In recent years, Ecuador, Bolivia, Venezuela, and Nicaragua have elected leaders who have tried to steer their societies out of the U.S. orbit, away, essentially, from the "Washington Consensus" which advocates free trade and privatization of key sectors of the economy, and favors the cold calculus of the economists over the passions of the people. Sometimes, though, the passions reflect physical hunger. As such, in oil-rich Venezuela, people turned to a charismatic military leader, Hugo Chávez, who ruled from 1999 until his death in 2013; he cut poverty dramatically by offering state subsidies to the poor and pushing oil profits to the people. None of this pleased Washington or advocates of the free market. His death from cancer, the uninspired leadership of his successor, and a collapse in the global price of oil has generated serious tensions in Venezuela, and Washington—for the most part—has been relegated to the sidelines, in a sort of gloomy, sometimes sadistic, voyeurism.

The United States' relationship with Mexico has always been difficult. The issues hark back to the mid-nineteenth century when a U.S.-led war relieved Mexico of 51 percent of its territory. Since then, mutual mistrust and suspicion have defined a relationship that, at times, seems cordial, but never is quite right. When Felipe Calderón was elected president in 2006 he decided to challenge the authority of the entrenched Mexican drug cartels and provoked, essentially, a war that has left 80,000 dead as of this writing. The United States, in 2008, funded the "Mérida Initiative," designed to support judicial and police reform in Mexico in an attempt to quell the violence. The United States also contributed technical assistance and weapons to the Mexican government. The complexity of sharing a 2,000-mile border is clearly reflected by the fact that many of the illegal weapons used in the killings in Mexico originate in the United States, in addition to the dollars that finance the operations and much of the market that consumes the illegal products: cocaine, heroin, and methamphetamines.

In Central America, social chaos and political uncertainty prevail, particularly in Honduras, Guatemala, El Salvador, and Nicaragua—nations that received an essentially unhealthy dose of U.S. advice and arms shipments, especially during the 1980s. As transshipment points for illegal narcotics originating in South America, the Central American nations have witnessed a disproportionate impact from the scourge of drugs, and the resultant fast money and violence. The leadership has been uninspired at best, inept/corrupt at worst. For example, the sitting president of Guatemala, Otto Pérez Molina, was stripped of his power by Congress in early September 2015 and taken into custody shortly thereafter; the charges against him involve corruption via skimming tax revenues from imports. At this point, it is unclear how the Central American nations can create social peace for their people, but U.S. policy during the past thirty-five years or so has not been particularly helpful in advancing the peace of those places.

In June 2015, New York real estate tycoon Donald Trump announced that he was campaigning to become President of the United States; he used the opportunity to let loose a verbal assault against the people of Mexico, referring to them as "rapists and murderers." Most people in the United States viewed his candidacy as a quirky affair that could hardly endure. Ten months later, as we prepare to submit this manuscript for final editing, the Trump candidacy has surpassed all expectations, and one of his major policy priorities involves building a wall between the United States and Mexico. Mr. Trump has assured the world that Mexico will pay for this wall, but has not indicated how he plans to manage the payment plan. At least two former Presidents of Mexico have expressed exasperation at Trump's talk: Felipe Calderón, in February 2016, called Trump "completely crazy"; Vicente Fox, the same month, showed less restraint when he declared, on live television with journalist Jorge Ramos, "I am not going to pay for that fucking wall."

Of course, there is plenty of good news upon which to conclude this text: First, the détente with Cuba has been a surprising and exciting development that many Latin American watchers assumed would never happen. The return to normal diplomatic relations between the two nations and the bridging of barriers between U.S. and Cuban culture is a long-awaited development, and we believe this diplomatic/political initiative will have long-lasting, positive economic and cultural implications for the peoples of both places. Yet, even amid this optimism, the gravity of the past pulls heavily on the paths toward normalization. Cuba remains exceptional—migrants from the island still receive privileged access to U.S. residency over other Latin Americans fleeing violence, including some societies (such as Honduras) with the highest murder rates in the world. An enduring irony is that much of this violence is created by U.S. consumers' demand for narcotics, but since the violence isn't narrowly defined as "political" it does not generally meet the mark of warranting asylum.

A strange and strained area of U.S.-Latin American relations involves the continued U.S. occupation of Guantánamo Bay in eastern Cuba. Despite campaign promises from Barack Obama to close the prison there, as of 2016 it remains open, an impasse driven by U.S. domestic politics and the all-encompassing War on Terror. Despite rhetoric of openness and adherence to international laws and respect for sovereignty from U.S. diplomats, the Guantánamo question continues to cast a long shadow on the present and into the future of American relations with rest of the hemisphere.

Culture continues to draw together the United States and Latin America. Latin American culture is—in some segments of the United States—part of everyday life. The Hispanic presence in the United States is about 18.5 percent of the nation's total and, by 2050, 30 percent of all people living in the United States will be of Latin American descent. This demographic reality frightens some but energizes others, and the energized tend to be young people who eagerly embrace the challenges and possibilities represented by the integration of Latin culture in the United States. We hope to see more financing for student exchange programs to and from Latin America; both authors of *The Third Century* have benefited from extended study in Latin America—LaFevor in Cuba, Mexico, and Brazil; LaRosa in Colombia. While much can be absorbed through texts, much more of Latin America is engaged through a difficult to articulate *perception* of the place. Nuanced understanding of Latin America comes through direct engagement, by listening, smelling, seeing, and imagining the place, its past and potential.

Two topics of concern, not focal points in this book, are the environment and the movement of peoples across borders—immigration. The environment affects all peoples, all over the world, and the poor play an especially central role as they cannot afford to insulate themselves from unclean water, impure air, and over-farmed, nutrient-depleted land. Environmental education seems like the purview of elite liberal arts college curricula, but it is in everyone's best interest to learn what we are doing to the planet, and how our actions affect future political decisions and social conditions. One of the most discouraging environmental sites in North America is located at the border between the United States and Mexico; the region has grown demographically since the passage of NAFTA in 1994. Water scarcity, soil erosion, and—thanks to the rush to build maquiladora assembly plants—foul air make living in this semiarid location unpleasant and hazardous for the millions of people forced to reside in that space.[1]

Immigration from Latin American nations to the United States continues to pose a challenge and some politicians have used the issue as a "wedge" to gain political support. The stronger U.S. economy will continue to attract migrants from poorer nations, especially nations that are relatively easy to access over land, that is, the nations of Central America and Mexico. Only the U.S. Congress can help regularize the immigration status of the eleven million people in the United States without proper documentation (the majority hail from one nation, Mexico). But, a preponderance of undocumented (read, "inexpensive") labor is beneficial to wide sectors of U.S. commerce. For example, American corporations are loath to pay union ("expensive") wages, American citizens are uninterested in picking strawberries, and much work performed in the United States is on a "cash" basis (that is, unrecorded for tax purposes—translation—fraudulent). We should all stop blaming the victims in this scenario—the poor people who arrive here hoping to work and earn money. Many local and national organizations have stepped in to fill the leadership gap where politicians have failed us: One of the best organizations is located in Tennessee—TIRRC, the Tennessee Immigrant and Refugee Rights Coalition—which advocates to protect the rights and aspirations of poor immigrants and refugees who arrive to the state. TIRRC offers outreach programs, helps educate the public at large, and commits to legislative work. Their excellent work was acknowledged when President Obama selected Nashville, Tennessee, to deliver a major address on immigration in December 2014.

There was a time—during the first century and certainly during segments of the second century of Latin America's independence—when it looked like Latin America would be forever at the mercy of a more powerful nation to the north. But in *The Third Century,* the strength, the originality, and the dynamism of Latin America's development—culturally, politically, economically, and socially—while certainly uneven, is undeniably ascendant. Thirty-five years ago, while accepting the Nobel Prize in Literature, Colombian author Gabriel García Márquez forecast a new era for the region: "Latin America neither wants," he declared, "nor has any reason to be a pawn without a will of its own."[2]

NOTES

1. For an expansive (1,307-page) discursive discussion, see William T. Vollmann, *Imperial* (New York: Viking, 2009). For a more formal, scholarly treatment, see Matthew C. LaFevor, "Environmental Concerns Facing the U.S. and Mexico: An International Perspective" in Michael J. LaRosa and Frank O. Mora, *Neighborly Adversaries: Readings in U.S.-Latin American Relations*, 3rd ed. (Lanham, MD: Rowman & Littlefield Publishers, Inc., 2015), chapter 22.

2. See Gabriel García Márquez, "The Solitude of Latin America" (speech before the Swedish Academy, Stockholm, Sweden, upon receipt of the Nobel Prize in Literature, December 8, 1982).

Selected Bibliography

Adams, Frederick C. *Economic Diplomacy: The Export-Import Bank and American Foreign Relations, 1934–1939.* Columbia: University of Missouri Press, 1976.

Albert, Bill. *South America and the First World War: The Impact of the War on Brazil, Argentina, Peru, and Chile.* New York: Cambridge University Press, 1988.

Ambrose, Stephen E. *Nixon.* 3 vols. New York: Simon and Schuster, 1987–1992.

Ambrose, Stephen E., and Richard Immerman. *Ike's Spies: Eisenhower and the Espionage Establishment.* Garden City, NY: Doubleday, 1981.

Ameringer, Charles D. *U.S. Foreign Intelligence: The Secret Side of American History.* Lexington, MA: D. C. Heath, 1990.

Atkins, G. Pope, and Larman C. Wilson. *The Dominican Republic and the United States: From Imperialism to Transnationalism.* Athens: University of Georgia Press, 1998.

Bailey, Thomas A. *A Diplomatic History of the American People.* 9th ed. Englewood Cliffs, NJ: Prentice-Hall, 1974.

Baily, Samuel L. *The United States and the Development of South America, 1945–1975.* New York: New Viewpoints, 1976.

Bastert, Russell H. "A New Approach to the Origins of Blaine's Pan American Policy." *Hispanic American Historical Review* 39 (May 1959): 375–412.

Beezley, William H., and Colin M. MacLachlan. *El Gran Pueblo: A History of Greater Mexico.* 2 vols. Englewood Cliffs, NJ: Prentice-Hall, 1994.

Beisner, Robert L. *Twelve Against Empire: The Anti-Imperialists, 1898–1900.* 1968. Reprint, New York: McGraw-Hill, 1971.

———. *From the Old Diplomacy to the New, 1865–1900.* 2nd ed. Arlington Heights, IL: Harlan Davidson, 1986.

Bemis, Samuel Flagg. *The Latin-American Policy of the United States: An Historical Interpretation.* 1943. Reprint, New York: W. W. Norton, 1967.

Berger, Mark T. *Under Northern Eyes: Latin American Studies and U.S. Hegemony in the Americas, 1898–1990.* Bloomington: Indiana University Press, 1995.

Beschloss, Michael R. *The Crisis Years: Kennedy and Khrushchev, 1960–1963.* New York: Edward Burlingame Books, 1991.

Bethell, Leslie, and Ian Roxborough. "Latin America between the Second World War and the Cold War: Some Reflections on the 1945–8 Conjuncture." *Journal of Latin American Studies* 20 (May 1988): 167–189.

———, eds. *Latin America between the Second World War and the Cold War: Crisis and Containment, 1944–1948.* New York: Cambridge University Press, 1994.

Blight, James G., Bruce J. Allyn, and David A. Welch. *Cuba on the Brink: Castro, the Missile Crisis, and the Soviet Collapse.* New York: Pantheon Books, 1993.

Boeker, Paul H., ed. *Henry L. Stimson's American Policy in Nicaragua: The Lasting Legacy.* New York: Markus Wiener, 1991.

Bornet, Vaughn Davis. *The Presidency of Lyndon B. Johnson.* Lawrence: University Press of Kansas, 1983.

Bouvier, Virginia, ed. *The Globalization of U.S.-Latin American Relations: Democracy, Intervention, and Human Rights.* Westport, CT: Praeger, 2002.

Brands, H. W., Jr. *Cold Warriors: Eisenhower's Generation and American Foreign Policy.* New York: Columbia University Press, 1988.

Braun, Herbert. *Our Guerrillas, Our Sidewalks: A Journey into the Violence of Colombia.* 2nd ed. Lanham, MD: Rowman & Littlefield Publishers, Inc., 2003.

Brewer, Stewart. *Borders and Bridges: A History of U.S.-Latin American Relations.* Westport, CT: Praeger Security International, 2006.

Bulmer-Thomas, Victor. *The Economic History of Latin America since Independence.* New York: Cambridge University Press, 1994.

Burns, E. Bradford. *The Unwritten Alliance: Rio-Branco and Brazilian-American Relations.* New York: Columbia University Press, 1966.

———. *At War in Nicaragua: The Reagan Doctrine and the Politics of Nostalgia.* New York: Harper & Row, 1987.

Calder, Bruce J. *The Impact of Intervention: The Dominican Republic during the U.S. Occupation of 1916–1924.* Austin: University of Texas Press, 1984.

Calhoun, Frederick S. *Uses of Force and Wilsonian Foreign Policy.* Kent, OH: Kent State University Press, 1993.

Calvert, Peter, and Susan Calvert. *Latin America in the Twentieth Century.* New York: St. Martin's Press, 1990.

Campbell, Charles S. *The Transformation of American Foreign Relations, 1865–1900.* New York: Harper & Row, 1976.

Cannon, Lou. *President Reagan: A Role of a Lifetime.* New York: Simon and Schuster, 1991.

Cardoso, Fernando Henrique, and Enzo Faletto. *Dependency and Development in Latin America.* Berkeley: University of California Press, 1979.

Carothers, Thomas. *In the Name of Democracy: U.S. Policy toward Latin America during the Reagan Years.* Berkeley: University of California Press, 1991.

Casey, Clifford B. "The Creation and Development of the Pan American Union." *Hispanic American Historical Review* 13 (November 1933): 437–56.

Castañeda, Jorge. *Mañana Forever? Mexico and the Mexicans.* New York: Vintage, 2012.

Chilcote, Ronald H., and Joel C. Edelstein, eds. *Latin America: The Struggle with Dependency and Beyond.* New York: John Wiley & Sons, 1974.

———. *Latin America: Capitalist and Socialist Perspectives of Development and Underdevelopment.* Boulder, CO: Westview Press, 1986.

Churchill, Lindsey Blake. *Becoming the Tupamaros: Solidarity and Transnational Revolutionaries in Uruguay and the United States.* Nashville: Vanderbilt University Press, 2014.

Clark, Paul Coe, Jr. *The United States and Somoza, 1933–1956: A Revisionist Look.* Westport, CT: Praeger, 1992.

Coatsworth, John H. *Central America and the United States: The Clients and the Colossus.* New York: Twayne, 1994.

Cobbs, Elizabeth A. *The Rich Neighbor Policy: Rockefeller and Kaiser in Brazil.* New Haven, CT: Yale University Press, 1992.

Cockcroft, James D. *Latin America: History, Politics, and U.S. Policy.* 2nd ed. Chicago: Nelson-Hall Publishers, 1996.

Cohen, Warren I. *Empire without Tears: American Foreign Relations, 1921–1933.* Philadelphia: Temple University Press, 1987.

Cohen, Warren I., and Nancy Bernkopf Tucker, eds. *Lyndon Johnson Confronts the World: American Foreign Policy, 1963–1968.* New York: Cambridge University Press, 1994.

Collin, Richard H. *Theodore Roosevelt, Culture, Diplomacy, and Expansion: A New View of American Imperialism.* Baton Rouge: Louisiana State University Press, 1985.

———. *Theodore Roosevelt's Caribbean: The Panama Canal, the Monroe Doctrine, and the Latin American Context.* Baton Rouge: Louisiana State University Press, 1990.

Combs, Jerald A. *American Diplomatic History: Two Centuries of Changing Interpretations.* Berkeley: University of California Press, 1983.

Conkin, Paul K. *Big Daddy from the Pedernales: Lyndon Baines Johnson.* Boston: Twayne, 1986.

Connell-Smith, Gordon. *The Inter-American System.* New York: Oxford University Press, 1966.

———. *The United States and Latin America: An Historical Analysis of Inter-American Relations.* New York: John Wiley & Sons, 1974.

Conniff, Michael L. *Panama and the United States: The Forced Alliance.* Athens: University of Georgia Press, 1992.

Cottam, Martha L. *Images and Intervention: U.S. Policies in Latin America.* Pittsburgh: University of Pittsburgh Press, 1994.

Crandall, Russell. *The United States and Latin America after the Cold War.* Cambridge, MA: Cambridge University Press, 2008.

Cummings, Bruce. *The Origins of the Korean War.* 2 vols. Princeton: Princeton University Press, 1981, 1990.

Dallek, Robert. *Franklin D. Roosevelt and American Foreign Policy, 1932–1945.* New York: Oxford University Press, 1979.

Davis, Harold Eugene, John J. Finian, and F. Taylor Peck. *Latin American Diplomatic History: An Introduction.* Baton Rouge: Louisiana State University Press, 1977.

DeConde, Alexander. *Herbert Hoover's Latin-American Policy.* Palo Alto: Stanford University Press, 1951.

Delpar, Helen. *The Enormous Vogue of Things Mexican: Cultural Relations between the United States and Mexico, 1920–1935.* Tuscaloosa: University of Alabama Press, 1992.

Didion, Joan. *Salvador.* New York: Simon and Schuster, 1983.

Divine, Robert A. *Roosevelt and World War II.* Baltimore: Johns Hopkins University Press, 1969.

Dobson, John. *Reticent Expansionism: The Foreign Policy of William McKinley.* Pittsburgh: Duquesne University Press, 1988.

Domínguez, Jorge I. *To Make a World Safe for Revolution: Cuba's Foreign Policy.* Cambridge, MA: Harvard University Press, 1989.

Domínguez, Jorge I., and Rafael Fernández de Castro, eds. *Contemporary U.S.-Latin American Relations: Cooperation or Conflict in the 21st Century?* New York: Routledge, 2010.

Dosal, Paul J. *Doing Business with the Dictators: A Political History of United Fruit in Guatemala, 1899–1944.* Wilmington, DE: Scholarly Resources, 1993.

Dozer, Donald Marquand. *Are We Good Neighbors? Three Decades of Inter-American Relations, 1930–1960.* Gainesville: University Press of Florida, 1961.

Drake, Paul W. *The Money Doctor in the Andes: The Kemmerer Missions, 1923–1933.* Durham, NC: Duke University Press, 1989.

———, ed. *Money Doctors, Foreign Debts, and Economic Reforms in Latin America from the 1890s to the Present.* Wilmington, DE: Scholarly Resources, 1994.

Eisenhower, Milton S. *The Wine Is Bitter: The United States and Latin America.* Garden City, NY: Doubleday, 1963.

Ekirk, Arthur A. *Ideologies and Utopias: The Impact of the New Deal on American Thought.* Chicago: Quadrangle Books, 1969.

Ellis, L. Ethan. *Republican Foreign Policy, 1921–1933.* New Brunswick, NJ: Rutgers University Press, 1968.

Espinosa, J. Manuel. *Inter-American Beginnings of U.S. Cultural Diplomacy, 1936–1948.* Washington, DC: U.S. Department of State, 1976.

Ewell, Judith. *Venezuela and the United States: From Monroe's Hemisphere to Petroleum's Empire.* Athens: University of Georgia Press, 1996.

Falcoff, Mark. *Modern Chile, 1970–1989.* New Brunswick, NJ: Transactions, 1989.

Fausold, Martin L. *The Presidency of Herbert Hoover.* Lawrence: University Press of Kansas, 1985.

Field, James A., Jr. "American Imperialism: The Worst Chapter in Almost Any Book." *American Historical Review* 83 (June 1978): 644–83.

Fifer, J. Valerie. *United States Perceptions of Latin America, 1850–1930: A "New West" South of Capricorn?* New York: Manchester University Press, 1991.

Fox, Frank W. *J. Reuben Clark: The Public Years.* Provo, UT: Brigham Young University Press, 1980.

Frank, Andre Gunder. *Latin America: Underdevelopment or Revolution: Essays on the Development of Underdevelopment and the Immediate Enemy.* New York: Monthly Review Press, 1969.

Freidel, Frank. *The Splendid Little War.* New York: Dell, 1958.

Friedman, Max Paul. *Nazis and Good Neighbors: The United States Campaign against the Germans of Latin America in World War II.* Cambridge, MA: Cambridge University Press, 2003.

Fry, Joseph A. "William McKinley and the Coming of the Spanish-American War: A Study of the Besmirching and Redemption of an Historical Image." *Diplomatic History* 3 (Winter 1979): 77–98.

Fuentes, Carlos. *A New Time for Mexico.* New York: Farrar, Straus & Giroux, 1996.

Gantenbein, James W., ed. *The Evolution of Our Latin-American Policy: A Documentary Record.* New York: Octagon Books, 1971.

Gardner, Lloyd C. *Economic Aspects of New Deal Diplomacy.* Madison: University of Wisconsin Press, 1964.

Garrard-Burnett, Virginia, Mark Atwood Lawrence, and Julio Moreno, eds. *Beyond the Eagle's Shadow: New Histories of Latin America's Cold War.* Albuquerque: University of New Mexico Press, 2013.

Garthoff, Raymond L. *Reflections on the Cuban Missile Crisis.* Washington, DC: Brookings Institution, 1987.

Gelfand, Lawrence E. *The Inquiry: American Preparations for Peace, 1917–1919.* New Haven: Yale University Press, 1963.

Gellman, Irwin F. *Good Neighbor Diplomacy: United States Policies in Latin America, 1933–1945.* Baltimore: Johns Hopkins University Press, 1979.

———. *Secret Affairs: Franklin Roosevelt, Cordell Hull, and Sumner Welles.* Baltimore: Johns Hopkins University Press, 1995.

Giglio, James N. *The Presidency of John F. Kennedy.* Lawrence: University Press of Kansas, 1991.

Gilderhus, Mark T. "Carranza and the Decision to Revolt, 1913: A Problem in Historical Interpretation." *Americas* 33 (October 1976): 298–310.

———. *Diplomacy and Revolution: U.S.-Mexican Relations under Wilson and Carranza.* Tucson: University of Arizona Press, 1977.

———. *Pan American Visions: Woodrow Wilson in the Western Hemisphere, 1913–1921.* Tucson: University of Arizona Press, 1986.

———. "An Emerging Synthesis? U.S.-Latin American Relations since 1945." In *America in the World: The Historiography of American Foreign Relations since 1941,* edited by Michael J. Hogan, 424–61. New York: Cambridge University Press, 1995.

———. *History and Historians: A Historiographical Introduction.* 3rd ed. Englewood Cliffs, NJ: Prentice-Hall, 1996.

———. "Founding Father: Samuel Flagg Bemis and the Study of U.S.-Latin American Relations." *Diplomatic History* 21 (Winter 1997): 1–14.

Glade, William. "Latin America and the International Economy, 1870–1914." In *The Cambridge History of Latin America,* vol. 4, *c. 1870–1930,* edited by Leslie Bethell, 1–56. New York: Cambridge University Press, 1986.

Gleijeses, Piero. *The Dominican Crisis: The 1965 Constitutionalist Revolt and American Intervention.* Translated by Lawrence Lipson. Baltimore: Johns Hopkins University Press, 1978.

———. *Shattered Hope: The Guatemalan Revolution and the United States, 1944–1954.* Princeton: Princeton University Press, 1991.

———. *Conflicting Missions: Havana, Washington, and Africa, 1959–1976.* Chapel Hill: University of North Carolina Press, 2002.

Goldberg, Joyce S. *The "Baltimore" Affair.* Lincoln: University of Nebraska Press, 1986.

Goldman, Francisco. *The Long Night of White Chickens.* New York: Grove Press, 1992.

Gould, Lewis L. *The Presidency of William McKinley.* Lawrence: Regents Press of Kansas, 1980.

———. *The Spanish-American War and President McKinley.* Lawrence: University Press of Kansas, 1982.

———. *The Presidency of Theodore Roosevelt.* Lawrence: University Press of Kansas, 1991.

Grandin, Greg. *The Last Colonial Massacre: Latin America in the Cold War*. Chicago: University of Chicago Press, 2004.

———. *Empire's Workshop: Latin America, the United States, and the Rise of the New Imperialism*. New York: Metropolitan Books, 2006.

———. *Fordlandia: The Rise and Fall of Henry Ford's Forgotten Jungle City*. New York: Metropolitan Books, 2009.

Green, David. *The Containment of Latin America: A History of the Myths and Realities of the Good Neighbor Policy.* Chicago: Quadrangle Books, 1971.

Green, James Naylor. *We Cannot Remain Silent: Opposition to the Brazilian Military Dictatorship in the United States*. Durham, NC: Duke University Press, 2010.

Greene, John Robert. *The Presidency of Gerald R. Ford.* Lawrence: University Press of Kansas, 1995.

Greenstein, Fred I. *The Hidden-Hand Presidency: Eisenhower as Leader.* New York: Basic Books, 1982.

Grieb, Kenneth J. *The United States and Huerta.* Lincoln: University of Nebraska Press, 1969.

———. *Guatemalan Caudillo: The Regime of Jorge Ubico, Guatemala, 1931–1944.* Athens: Ohio University Press, 1979.

Guillermoprieto, Alma. *Looking for History: Dispatches from Latin America.* New York: Vintage, 2001.

Haines, Gerald K. "Under the Eagle's Wing: The Franklin Roosevelt Administration Forges an American Hemisphere." *Diplomatic History* 1, no. 4 (Fall 1977): 377–88.

———. *The Americanization of Brazil: A Study of U.S. Cold War Diplomacy in the Third World, 1945–1954.* Wilmington, DE: Scholarly Resources, 1989.

Hale, Charles A. "Political and Social Ideas in Latin America, 1870–1930." In *The Cambridge History of Latin America,* vol. 4, *c. 1870–1930,* edited by Leslie Bethell, 367–442. New York: Cambridge University Press, 1986.

Hall, Linda B. *Oil, Banks, and Politics: The United States and Postrevolutionary Mexico, 1917–1924.* Austin: University of Texas Press, 1995.

Hall, Linda B., and Don M. Coerver. *Revolution on the Border: The United States and Mexico, 1910–1920.* Albuquerque: University of New Mexico Press, 1988.

Harrison, Lawrence E. *The Pan-American Dream: Do Latin America's Cultural Values Discourage True Partnership with the United States and Canada?* Boulder, CO: Westview Press, 1997.

Hart, John M. *Revolutionary Mexico: The Coming and Process of the Mexican Revolution.* Berkeley: University of California Press, 1987.

———. *Empire and Revolution: The Americans in Mexico since the Civil War*. Berkeley: University of California Press, 2002.

Hartlyn, Jonathan, Lars Schoultz, and Augusto Varas, eds. *The United States and Latin America in the 1990s: Beyond the Cold War.* Chapel Hill: University of North Carolina Press, 1992.

Healy, David. *Drive to Hegemony: The United States in the Caribbean, 1889–1917.* Madison: University of Wisconsin Press, 1988.

Heinrichs, Waldo H. *Threshold of War: Franklin* D. *Roosevelt and American Entry into World War II.* New York: Oxford University Press, 1988.

Hernández, José M. *Cuba and the United States: Intervention and Militarism, 1868–1933.* Austin: University of Texas Press, 1993.

Hersh, Seymour M. *The Price of Power: Kissinger in the White House.* New York: Summit Books, 1983.

Higgins, Trumbull. *The Perfect Failure: Kennedy, Eisenhower, and the CIA at the Bay of Pigs.* New York: W. W. Norton, 1989.

Hilsman, Roger. *To Move a Nation: The Politics of Foreign Policy in the Administration of John F. Kennedy.* New York: Dell, 1964.

Hilton, Stanley E. *Brazil and the Great Powers, 1930–1939: The Politics of Trade Rivalry.* Austin: University of Texas Press, 1975.

———. *Hitler's Secret War in South America, 1939–1945: German Military Espionage and Allied Counterespionage in Brazil.* Baton Rouge: Louisiana State University Press, 1981.

Hofstadter, Richard. *The American Political Tradition and the Men Who Made It.* New York: Alfred A. Knopf, 1948.

———. *The Paranoid Style in American Politics and Other Essays.* New York: Vintage Books, 1967.

Hogan, Michael J., ed. *The End of the Cold War: Its Meaning and Implications.* New York: Cambridge University Press, 1992.

Hogan, Michael J., and Thomas G. Paterson, eds. *Explaining the History of American Foreign Relations.* New York: Cambridge University Press, 1991.

Holden, Robert H., and Eric Zolov. *Latin America and the United States: A Documentary History.* 2nd ed. New York: Oxford University Press, 2010.

Humphreys, R. A. *Latin America and the Second World War.* 2 vols. London: University of London Athlone Press, 1982.

Immerman, Richard H. *The CIA in Guatemala: The Foreign Policy of Intervention.* Austin: University of Texas Press, 1982.

Jeffreys-Jones, Rhodri. *The CIA and American Democracy.* New Haven: Yale University Press, 1989.

Johnson, John J. *Latin America in Caricature.* Austin: University of Texas Press, 1980.

———. *A Hemisphere Apart: The Foundations of United States Policy toward Latin America.* Baltimore: Johns Hopkins University Press, 1990.

Jones, Howard, and Randall B. Woods. "Origins of the Cold War in Europe and the New East: Recent Historiography and the National Security Imperative." In *America in the World: The Historiography of American Foreign Relations since 1941,* edited by Michael J. Hogan, 234–69. New York: Cambridge University Press, 1995.

Joseph, Gilbert M., Catherine C. LeGrand, and Ricardo D. Salvatore, eds. *Close Encounters of Empire: Writing the Cultural History of United States-Latin American Relations.* Durham: Duke University Press, 1998.

Kagan, Robert. *A Twilight Struggle: American Power and Nicaragua, 1977–1990.* New York: Free Press, 1996.

Karnes, Thomas L. "Hiram Bingham and His Obsolete Shibboleth." *Diplomatic History* 3 (Winter 1979): 39–57.

Katz, Friedrich. *The Secret War in Mexico: Europe, the United States, and the Mexican Revolution.* Chicago: University of Chicago Press, 1981.

———. "Mexico: Restored Republic and Porfiriato, 1867–1910." In *The Cambridge History of Latin America,* vol. 5, *c. 1870–1930,* edited by Leslie Bethell, 3–78. New York: Cambridge University Press, 1988.

Kaufman, Burton. *Expansion and Efficiency: Foreign Trade Organization in the Wilson Administration.* Westport, CT: Greenwood Press, 1974.

———. *Trade and Aid: Eisenhower's Foreign Economic Policy, 1953–1961.* Baltimore: Johns Hopkins University Press, 1982.

———. *The Korean War: Challenges in Crisis, Credibility, and Command.* New York: Alfred A. Knopf, 1986.

———. *The Presidency of James Earl Carter, Jr.* Lawrence: University Press of Kansas, 1993.

Kennedy, Paul. *The Rise and Fall of the Great Powers: Economic Change and Military Conflict from 1500 to 2000.* New York: Random House, 1987.

Kenworthy, Eldon. *America/Américas: Myth in the Making of U.S. Policy toward Latin America.* University Park: Pennsylvania State University Press, 1995.

Kiernan, V. G. *America: The New Imperialism, from White Settlement to World Hegemony.* London: Zed Press, 1978.

Kimball, Warren F. *The Juggler: Franklin Roosevelt as Wartime Statesman.* Princeton: Princeton University Press, 1991.

Kinzer, Stephen, *The Brothers: John Foster Dulles, Allen Dulles, and Their Secret World War.* New York: Times Books, 2013.

Kirkpatrick, Jeane J. "Dictatorships and Double Standards." *Commentary* 68, no. 5 (November 1979): 34–45.

Knight, Alan. *The Mexican Revolution.* 2 vols. New York: Cambridge University Press, 1986.

Kornbluh, Peter. *The Pinochet File: A Declassified Dossier on Atrocity and Accountability.* New York: The New Press, 2013.

Krenn, Michael L. *United States Policy toward Economic Nationalism in Latin America, 1917–1929.* Wilmington, DE: Scholarly Resources, 1990.

———. *The Chains of Interdependence: U.S. Policy toward Central America, 1945–1954.* New York: M. E. Sharpe, 1996.

Kryzanek, Michael J. *U.S.-Latin American Relations.* New York: Praeger, 1985.

———. *U.S.-Latin American Relations*. 4th ed. New York: Praeger, 2008.

Kyvig, David F., ed. *Reagan and the World.* New York: Praeger, 1990.

Lael, Richard L. *Arrogant Diplomacy: U.S. Policy toward Colombia, 1903–1922.* Wilmington, DE: Scholarly Resources, 1987.

LaFeber, Walter. *The New Empire: An Interpretation of American Expansion, 1860–1898.* Ithaca, NY: Cornell University Press, 1963.

———. *The Panama Canal: The Crisis in Historical Perspective.* Rev. ed. New York: Oxford University Press, 1979.

———. *Inevitable Revolutions: The United States in Central America.* New York: W. W. Norton, 1983.

———. *The American Age: United States Foreign Policy at Home and Abroad Since 1750.* New York: W. W. Norton, 1989.

———. *America, Russia, and the Cold War, 1945–1992.* 7th ed. New York: McGraw-Hill, 1993.

———. *The American Search for Opportunity, 1865–1913.* Vol. 2 in *The Cambridge History of American Foreign Relations.* New York: Cambridge University Press, 1993.

Langley, Lester D. *The Banana Wars: An Inner History of American Empire, 1900–1934.* Lexington: University Press of Kentucky, 1983.

———. *America and the Americas: The United States in the Western Hemisphere.* Athens: University of Georgia Press, 1989.

———. *Mexico and the United States: The Fragile Relationship.* Boston: Twayne, 1991.

Langley, Lester D., and Thomas D. Schoonover. *The Banana Men: American Mercenaries and Entrepreneurs in Central America, 1880–1930.* Lexington: University Press of Kentucky, 1995.

LaRosa, Michael J., and Germán Mejía. *Colombia: A Concise Contemporary History*. Updated ed. Lanham, MD: Rowman & Littlefield Publishers, Inc., 2013.

LaRosa, Michael J., and Frank Mora, eds. *Neighborly Adversaries: Readings in U.S.-Latin American Relations*. 3rd ed. Lanham, MD: Rowman & Littlefield Publishers, Inc., 2015.

Lazo, Dimitri D. "Lansing, Wilson, and the Jenkins Incident." *Diplomatic History* 22 (Spring 1998): 177–98.

Leffler, Melvyn P. "Expansionist Impulses and Domestic Constraints, 1921–32." In *Economics and World Power: An Assessment of American Diplomacy since 1789,* edited by William H. Becker and Samuel F. Wells, Jr. New York: Columbia University Press, 1984.

Lehman, Kenneth. "Revolutions and Attributions: Making Sense of Eisenhower Administration Policies in Bolivia and Guatemala." *Diplomatic History* 21 (Spring 1997): 185–213.

Leonard, Thomas E. *Central America and the United States: The Search for Stability.* Athens: University of Georgia Press, 1991.

Leuchtenburg, William E. *Franklin D. Roosevelt and the New Deal.* New York: Harper & Row, 1963.

———. *The FDR Years: On Roosevelt and His Legacy.* New York: Columbia University Press, 1995.

Levin, N. Gordon, Jr. *Woodrow Wilson and World Politics: America's Response to War and Revolution.* New York: Oxford University Press, 1968.

Levinson, Jerome, and Juan de Onís. *The Alliance That Lost Its Way: A Critical Report on the Alliance for Progress.* Chicago: Quadrangle Books, 1970.

Lieuwen, Edwin. *Arms and Politics in Latin America.* Rev. ed. New York: Frederick A. Praeger, 1961.

———. *Generals vs. Presidents: Neomilitarism in Latin America.* New York: Frederick A. Praeger, 1964.

Linder, Andrew M., and Daniel N. Hawkins. "Globalization, Culture Wars, and Attitudes toward Soccer in America: An Empirical Assessment of How Soccer Explains the World." *The Sociological Quarterly* 53, no. 1 (Winter 2012).

Livingstone, Grace. *America's Backyard: The United States and Latin America from the Monroe Doctrine to the War on Terror.* London: Zed, 2009.

Long, Tom. *Latin America Confronts the United States: Asymmetry and Influence.* New York: Cambridge University Press, 2015.

Longley, Kyle. *The Sparrow and the Hawk: Costa Rica and the United States during the Rise of José Figueres.* Tuscaloosa: University of Alabama Press, 1997.

Loveman, Brian. *No Higher Law: American Foreign Policy and the Western Hemisphere since 1776.* Chapel Hill: University of North Carolina, 2010.

Lowenthal, Abraham F. "United States Policy toward Latin America: 'Liberal,' 'Radical,' and 'Bureaucratic' Perspectives." *Latin American Research Review* 8 (Fall 1973): 3–25.

———. *Partners in Conflict: The United States and Latin America.* Baltimore: Johns Hopkins University Press, 1987.

———, ed. *Exporting Democracy: The United States and Latin America.* Baltimore: Johns Hopkins University Press, 1991.

Lowenthal, Abraham F., Theodore J. Piccone, and Laurence Whitehead, eds. *Shifting the Balance: Obama and the Americas.* Washington, DC: Brookings Institution, 2011.

Macaulay, Neil. *The Sandino Affair.* Chicago: Quadrangle Books, 1971.

Major, John. *Prize Possession: The United States and the Panama Canal, 1903–1979.* New York: Cambridge University Press, 1993.

Marks, Frederick W., III. *Velvet on Iron: The Diplomacy of Theodore Roosevelt.* Lincoln: University of Nebraska Press, 1979.

Martin, Edwin McCammon. *Kennedy and Latin America.* Lanham, MD: University Press of America, 1994.

Martin, Gerald. "The Literature, Music, and Art of Latin America, 1870–1930." In *The Cambridge History of Latin America,* vol. 4, *c. 1870–1930,* edited by Leslie Bethell, 443–526. New York: Cambridge University Press, 1986.

Martz, John D., ed. *United States Policy in Latin America: A Quarter Century of Crisis and Challenge, 1961–1986.* Lincoln: University of Nebraska Press, 1988.

May, Ernest R. *The World War and American Isolation, 1914–1917.* Cambridge, MA: Harvard University Press, 1959.

———, ed. *American Cold War Strategy: Interpreting NSC 68.* Boston: Bedford Books of St. Martin's Press, 1993.

McAulliffe, Mary S. "Commentary: Eisenhower, the President." *Journal of American History* 68 (December 1981): 625–32.

McBeth, B. S. *Juan Vicente Gómez and the Oil Companies in Venezuela, 1908–1935.* New York: Cambridge University Press, 1983.

McCann, Frank D. *The Brazilian-American Alliance, 1937–1945.* Princeton: Princeton University Press, 1974.

———. "Brazil, the United States, and World War II: A Commentary." *Diplomatic History* 3 (Winter 1979): 59–76.

McCormick, Thomas J. *China Market: America's Quest for Informal Empire, 1893–1901.* Chicago: Quadrangle Books, 1967.

McCullough, David G. *The Path between the Seas: The Creation of the Panama Canal, 1870–1914.* New York: Simon and Schuster, 1977.

McGann, Thomas F. *Argentina, the United States, and the Inter-American System, 1889–1914.* Cambridge, MA: Harvard University Press, 1961.

McMahon, Robert J. "Eisenhower and Third World Nationalism: A Critique of the Revisionists." *Political Science Review* 101 (Fall 1986): 453–73.

———. "Making Sense of American Foreign Relations during the Reagan Years." *Diplomatic History* 19 (Spring 1995): 367–84.

McPherson, Alan L. *Intimate Ties, Bitter Struggles: The United States and Latin America since 1945*. Washington, DC: Potomac, 2006.

———. *The Invaded: How Latin Americans and Their Allies Fought and Ended U.S. Occupations*. Oxford: Oxford University Press, 2014.

Mecham, J. Lloyd. *The United States and Inter-American Security, 1889–1960.* Austin: University of Texas Press, 1961.

Meyer, Lorenzo. *Mexico and the United States in the Oil Controversy, 1917–1942.* Translated by Muriel Vasconcellos. Austin: University of Texas Press, 1977.

Meyer, Michael C. *Huerta: A Political Portrait.* Lincoln: University of Nebraska Press, 1972.

Moreno, Julio. *Yankee Don't Go Home! Mexican Nationalism, American Business Culture, and the Shaping of Modern Mexico, 1920–1950*. Chapel Hill: University of North Carolina Press, 2003.

Morgan, H. Wayne. *America's Road to Empire: The War with Spain and Overseas Expansion.* New York: John Wiley & Sons, 1965.

Morley, Morris H. *Imperial State and Revolution: The United States and Cuba, 1952–1986.* New York: Cambridge University Press, 1987.

———. *Washington, Somoza, and the Sandinistas: State and Regime in United States Policy toward Nicaragua, 1969–1981.* New York: Cambridge University Press, 1994.

Morris, Edmund. *The Rise of Theodore Roosevelt.* New York: Coward, McCann & Geoghegan, 1979.

———. *Theodore Rex.* New York: Random House, 2001.

———. *Colonel Roosevelt.* New York: Random House, 2010.

Munro, Dana G. *Intervention and Dollar Diplomacy in the Caribbean, 1900–1921.* Princeton: Princeton University Press, 1964.

Newton, Robert C. *The "Nazi Menace" in Argentina, 1931–1945.* Palo Alto: Stanford University Press, 1992.

Niblo, Stephen R. *War, Diplomacy, and Development: The United States and Mexico, 1938–1954.* Wilmington, DE: Scholarly Resources, 1995.

Niess, Frank. *A Hemisphere to Itself: A History of U.S.-Latin American Relations.* Translated by Harry Drost. London: Zed Books, 1990.

Nixon, Richard M. *Six Crises.* Garden City, NY: Doubleday, 1962.

O'Brien, Thomas F. *Making the Americas: The United States and Latin America from the Age of Revolutions to the Era of Globalization*. Albuquerque: University of New Mexico, 2007.

Offner, John L. *An Unwanted War: The Diplomacy of the United States and Spain over Cuba, 1895–1898.* Chapel Hill: University of North Carolina Press, 1992.

Pach, Chester J., Jr. *Arming the Free World: The Origins of the United States Military Assistance Program, 1945–1950.* Chapel Hill: University of North Carolina Press. 1991.

Pach, Chester J., Jr., and Elmo Richardson. *The Presidency of Dwight D. Eisenhower.* Rev. ed. Lawrence: University Press of Kansas, 1991.

Packenham, Robert A. *Liberal America and the Third World: Political Development Ideas in Foreign Aid and Social Science.* Princeton: Princeton University Press, 1973.

———. *The Dependency Movement: Scholarship and Politics in Development Studies.* Cambridge, MA: Harvard University Press, 1992.

Park, James William. *Latin American Underdevelopment: A History of Perspectives in the United States, 1870–1965.* Baton Rouge: Louisiana State University Press, 1995.

Parrini, Carl. *Heir to Empire: United States Economic Diplomacy, 1916–1923.* Pittsburgh: University of Pittsburgh Press, 1969.

Pastor, Robert A. *Exiting the Whirlpool: U.S. Foreign Policy toward Latin America and the Caribbean*. 2nd ed. Boulder, CO: Westview Press, 2001.

———. *Not Condemned to Repetition: The United States and Nicaragua*. Boulder, CO: Westview Press, 2002.

Paterson, Thomas G. "Fixation with Cuba: The Bay of Pigs, Missile Crisis, and Covert War against Fidel Castro." In *Kennedy's Quest for Victory: American Foreign Policy, 1961–1963,* edited by Thomas G. Paterson, 123–77. New York: Oxford University Press, 1989.

———. *On Every Front: The Making and Unmaking of the Cold War.* Rev. ed. New York: W. W. Norton, 1992.

———. *Contesting Castro: The United States and the Triumph of the Cuban Revolution.* New York: Oxford University Press, 1994.

Paterson, Thomas G., and J. Garry Clifford. *America Ascendant: U.S. Foreign Relations since 1939.* Lexington, MA: D. C. Heath, 1995.

Paterson, Thomas G., J. Garry Clifford, and Kenneth J. Hagan. *American Foreign Relations: A History.* 2 vols. 4th ed. Lexington, MA: D. C. Heath, 1995.

Paterson, Thomas G., and Dennis Merrill, eds. *Major Problems in American Foreign Relations.* 2 vols. 4th ed. Lexington, MA: D. C. Heath, 1995.

Pérez, Louis A., Jr. *Cuba and the United States: Ties of Singular Intimacy.* Athens: University of Georgia Press, 1990.

———. *On Becoming Cuban: Identity, Nationality, and Culture.* Chapel Hill: University of North Carolina Press, 1999.

———. *Cuba in the American Imagination: Metaphor and the Imperial Ethos.* Chapel Hill: University of North Carolina Press, 2008.

Perkins, Bradford. *The Great Rapprochement: England and the United States, 1895–1914.* New York: Atheneum, 1968.

Philip, George. *Oil and Politics in Latin America: Nationalist Movements and State Companies.* New York: Cambridge University Press, 1982.

Pike, Frederick B. *The United States and Latin America: Myths and Stereotypes of Civilization and Nature.* Austin: University of Texas Press, 1992.

———. *FDR's Good Neighbor Policy: Sixty Years of Generally Gentle Chaos.* Austin: University of Texas Press, 1995.

Pletcher, David M. *The Awkward Years: American Foreign Relations under Garfield and Arthur.* Columbia: University of Missouri Press, 1962.

———. *The Diplomacy of Trade and Investment: American Economic Expansion in the Hemisphere, 1865–1900.* Columbia: University of Missouri Press, 1998.

Plummer, Brenda Gayle. *Haiti and the Great Powers, 1902–1915.* Baton Rouge: Louisiana State University Press, 1988.

———. *Haiti and the United States: The Psychological Moment.* Athens: University of Georgia Press, 1992.

Poitras, Guy. *The Ordeal of Hegemony: The United States and Latin America.* Boulder, CO: Westview Press, 1990.

Prados, John. *Presidents' Secret Wars: CIA and Pentagon Covert Operations since World War II.* New York: William Morrow, 1986.

Quirk, Robert E. *Fidel Castro.* New York: W. W. Norton, 1993.

Raat, W. Dirk. *Mexico and the United States: Ambivalent Vistas.* Athens: University of Georgia Press, 1992.

Rabe, Stephen G. "The Elusive Conference: United States Economic Relations with Latin America, 1945–1952." *Diplomatic History* 2 (Summer 1978): 279–94.

———. *The Road to OPEC: United States Relations with Venezuela, 1919–1976.* Austin: University of Texas Press, 1982.

———. *Eisenhower and Latin America: The Foreign Policy of Anticommunism.* Chapel Hill: University of North Carolina Press, 1988.

———. "Controlling Revolutions: Latin America, the Alliance for Progress, and Cold War Anti-Communism." In *Kennedy's Quest for Victory: American Foreign Policy, 1961–1963,* edited by Thomas G. Paterson, 105–22. New York: Oxford University Press, 1989.

———. *The Killing Zone: The United States Wages Cold War in Latin America.* 2nd ed. New York: Oxford University Press, 2016.

Randall, Stephen J. *Colombia and the United States: Hegemony and Interdependence.* Athens: University of Georgia Press, 1992.

Reagan, Ronald. *An American Life.* New York: Pocket Books, 1990.

Reid, Michael. *Forgotten Continent: The Battle for Latin America's Soul.* New Haven: Yale University Press, 2007.

Richmond, Douglas W. *Venustiano Carranza's Nationalist Struggle, 1893–1920.* Lincoln: University of Nebraska Press, 1983.

Rock, David, ed. *Latin America in the 1940s: War and Postwar Transitions.* Berkeley: University of California Press, 1994.

Rosen, Fred, ed. *Empire and Dissent: The United States and Latin America.* Durham: Duke University Press, 2008.

Rosenberg, Emily. *Spreading the American Dream: American Economic and Cultural Expansion, 1890–1945.* New York: Hill and Wang, 1982.

Rout, Leslie B., Jr., and John F. Bratzel. *The Shadow War: German Espionage and United States Counterespionage in Latin America during World War II.* Frederick, MD: University Publications of America, 1986.

Ruíz, Ramón Eduardo. *The Great Rebellion: Mexico, 1905–1924.* New York: W. W. Norton, 1980.

Sadlier, Darlene J. *Americans All: Good Neighbor Cultural Diplomacy in World War II.* Austin: University of Texas Press, 2012.

Safford, Jeffrey J. *Wilsonian Maritime Diplomacy, 1913–1921.* New Brunswick, NJ: Rutgers University Press, 1978.

Sater, William. *Chile and the United States: Empires in Conflict.* Athens: University of Georgia Press, 1990.

Schaller, Michael. *Reckoning with Reagan: America and Its President in the 1980s.* New York: Oxford University Press, 1992.

Schlesinger, Arthur, Jr. *A Thousand Days: John F. Kennedy in the White House.* Greenwich, CT: Fawcett, 1965.

Schlesinger, Stephen C., and Stephen Kinzer. *Bitter Fruit: The Story of the American Coup in Guatemala.* Cambridge, MA: Harvard University, David Rockefeller Center for Latin American Studies, 2005.

Schmidt, Hans. *The United States Occupation of Haiti, 1915–1934.* New Brunswick, NJ: Rutgers University Press, 1971.

Scholes, Walter V., and Marie V. Scholes *The Foreign Policies of the Taft Administration.* Columbia: University of Missouri Press, 1970.

Schoultz, Lars. *Beneath the United States: A History of U.S. Policy toward Latin America.* Cambridge, MA: Harvard University Press, 1998.

———. *That Infernal Little Cuban Republic: The United States and the Cuban Revolution.* Chapel Hill: University of North Carolina Press, 2009.

Schuler, Friedrich E. *Mexico between Hitler and Roosevelt: Mexican Foreign Relations in the Age of Lázaro Cárdenas, 1934–1940.* Albuquerque: University of New Mexico Press, 1998.

Schulzinger, Robert D. *Henry Kissinger: Doctor of Diplomacy.* New York: Columbia University Press, 1989.

Shurbutt, T. Ray, ed. *United States-Latin American Relations, 1800–1850.* Tuscaloosa: University of Alabama Press, 1991.

Sigmund, Paul E. *The United States and Democracy in Chile.* Baltimore: Johns Hopkins University Press, 1993.

Smith, Daniel M. *Aftermath of War: Bainbridge Colby and Wilsonian Diplomacy, 1920–1921.* Philadelphia: American Philosophical Society, 1970.

Smith, Gaddis. "The Two Worlds of Samuel Flagg Bemis." *Diplomatic History* 9, no. 4 (Fall 1985): 295–302.

———. *Morality, Reason, and Power: American Diplomacy in the Carter Years.* New York: Hill and Wang, 1986.

———. *The Last Years of the Monroe Doctrine, 1945–1993.* New York: Hill and Wang, 1994.

Smith, Joseph. *Unequal Giants: Diplomatic Relations between the United States and Brazil, 1889–1930.* Pittsburgh: University of Pittsburgh Press, 1991.

———. *The United States and Latin America: A History of American Diplomacy, 1776–2000.* 2nd ed. London: Routledge, 2010.

Smith, Peter H. *Talons of the Eagle: Dynamics of U.S.-Latin American Relations.* New York: Oxford University Press, 1996.

Smith, Peter H., and Thomas E. Skidmore. *Modern Latin America.* 2nd ed. New York: Oxford University Press, 1992.

———. *Talons of the Eagle: Dynamics of U.S.-Latin American Relations*. 4th ed. Oxford: Oxford University Press, 2012.

Smith, Robert Freeman. *The United States and Revolutionary Nationalism in Mexico, 1916–1932.* Chicago: University of Chicago Press, 1972.

———. "The Good Neighbor Policy: The Liberal Paradox in United States Relations with Latin America." In *Watershed of Empire: Essays on New Deal Foreign Policy,* edited by Leonard P. Liggio and James Martin, 65–94. Colorado Springs: Ralph Myles, 1976.

———. "Latin America, the United States, and the European Powers, 1830–1930." In *The Cambridge History of Latin America,* vol. 4, *c. 1870–1930,* edited by Leslie Bethell, 83–120. New York: Cambridge University Press, 1986.

———. "U. S. Policy-Making for Latin America under Truman." *Continuity: A Journal of History* 16 (Fall 1992): 87–111.

———. *The Caribbean World and the United States: Mixing Rum and Coca-Cola.* New York: Twayne, 1994.

Socolofsky, Homer E., and Allan B. Spetter. *The Presidency of Benjamin Harrison.* Lawrence: University Press of Kansas, 1987.

Sorenson, Theodore C. *Kennedy.* New York: Harper & Row, 1965.

Spector, Ronald H. *Professors of War: The Naval War College and the Development of the Naval Profession.* Newport, RI: Naval War College Press, 1977.

Steward, Dick. *Trade and Hemisphere: The Good Neighbor Policy and Reciprocal Trade.* Columbia: University of Missouri Press, 1975.

Stiller, Jesse H. *George S. Messersmith: Diplomat of Democracy.* Chapel Hill: University of North Carolina Press, 1987.

Stoetzer, O. Carlos. *The Organization of American States.* 2nd ed. Westport, CT: Praeger, 1993.

Stuart, Graham H., and James L. Tigner. *Latin America and the United States.* Englewood Cliffs, NJ: Prentice-Hall, 1975.

Stueck, William W. *The Korean War: An International History.* Princeton: Princeton University Press, 1995.

Szulc, Tad. *Twilight of the Tyrants.* New York: W. W. Holt, 1959.

Thorp, Rosemary. "Latin America and the International Economy from the First World War to the World Depression." In *The Cambridge History of Latin America,* vol. 4, *c. 1870–1930,* edited by Leslie Bethell, 57–82. New York: Cambridge University Press, 1986.

———, ed. *Latin America in the 1930s: The Role of the Periphery in World Crisis.* New York: St. Martin's Press, 1984.

Trani, Eugene P., and David L. Wilson. *The Presidency of Warren G. Harding.* Lawrence: Regents Press of Kansas, 1977.

Trask, David F. *The War with Spain in 1898.* New York: Macmillan, 1981.

Trask, Roger R. "The Impact of the Cold War on United States-Latin American Relations, 1945–1949." *Diplomatic History* 1 (Summer 1977): 271–84.

———. "George F. Kennan's Report on Latin America (1950)." *Diplomatic History* 2 (Summer 1978): 307–11.

———. "Spruille Braden versus George Messersmith: World War II, the Cold War, and Argentine Policy, *1945–1947."Journal of Inter-American Studies and World Affairs* 26 (February 1984): 69–95.

Truett, Samuel, and Elliott Young. *Continental Crossroads: Remapping U.S.-Mexico Borderlands History.* Durham: Duke University Press, 2004.

Tulchin, Joseph. *Argentina and the United States: A Conflicted Relationship.* Boston: Twayne, 1990.

Walker, William O., III. "Mixing the Sweet with the Sour: Kennedy, Johnson, and Latin America." In *The Diplomacy of the Crucial Decade: American Foreign Relations during the 1960s,* edited by Diane B. Kunz, 42–79·New York: Columbia University Press, 1994.

Walton, Richard J. *Cold War and Counter-Revolution: The Foreign Policy of John F. Kennedy.* Baltimore: Penguin Books, 1972.

Weeks, Gregory Bart. *U.S. and Latin American Relations*. 2nd ed. New York: Pearson Longman, 2008.

Weis, W. Michael. *Cold Warriors and Coups d'Etat: Brazilian-American Relations, 1945–1964.* Albuquerque: University of New Mexico Press, 1993.

Welch, Richard E., Jr. *Response to Revolution: The United States and the Cuban Revolution, 1959–1961.* Chapel Hill: University of North Caroline Press, 1985.

———. *The Presidencies of Grover Cleveland.* Lawrence: University Press of Kansas, 1988.

Weld, Kirsten. *Paper Cadavers: The Archives of Dictatorship in Guatemala*. Durham: Duke University Press, 2014.

Whitaker, Arthur P. *The Western Hemisphere Idea: Its Rise and Decline.* Ithaca, NY: Cornell University Press, 1954.

Wilgus, A. Curtis. "James G. Blaine and the Pan American Movement." *Hispanic American Historical Review* 5 (November 1922): 662–708.

Williams, Mark Eric. *Understanding U.S.-Latin American Relations: Theory and History*. New York: Routledge, 2012.

Williams, William Appleman. *The Tragedy of American Diplomacy.* Rev. ed. New York: Delta, 1962.

Wilson, Joan Hoff. *American Business and Foreign Policy, 1920–1933.* Lexington: University Press of Kentucky, 1971.

———. *Herbert Hoover: Forgotten Progressive.* Boston: Little, Brown, 1975.

Wood, Bryce. *The Making of the Good Neighbor Policy.* New York: Columbia University Press, 1961.

———. *The United States and Latin American Wars, 1932–1942.* New York: Columbia University Press, 1966.

———. *The Dismantling of the Good Neighbor Policy.* Austin: University of Texas Press, 1985.

Woods, Randall Bennett. *The Roosevelt Foreign-Policy Establishment and the "Good Neighbor": The United States and Argentina, 1941–1945.* Lawrence: Regents Press of Kansas, 1979.

Wright, Thomas C. *Latin America in the Era of the Cuban Revolution.* New York: Praeger, 1991.

Zubok, Vladislav, and Constantine Pleshakov. *Inside the Kremlin's Cold War: From Stalin to Khrushchev.* Cambridge, MA: Harvard University Press, 1996.

Index

About the Authors

Mark T. Gilderhus was a specialist in U.S. military and diplomatic history and a former president of the Society for Historians of American Foreign Relations. After teaching at Colorado State University for twenty-nine years, he became Lyndon Baines Johnson Chair at Texas Christian University in Fort Worth. He wrote several books, including *History and Historians: A Historiographical Introduction* (1996) and *Diplomacy and Revolution: U.S.-Mexican Relations under Wilson and Carranza* (1977). He earned degrees from Gustavus Adolphus College and the University of Nebraska. Professor Gilderhus died in 2015.

David C. LaFevor is assistant professor of history at University of Texas, Arlington. He earned a BA degree in Latin American studies from Rhodes College and a PhD in history from Vanderbilt University.

Michael J. LaRosa is associate professor of history at Rhodes College. He holds a BA degree in international relations from George Washington University and a PhD in history from the University of Miami.